General Editors: David Anderson, QC
Barrister at Brick Court Chambers and
Visiting Professor of Law at King's College London.
Piet Eeckhout, Professor of Law at King's College London,
and Director of the College's Institute of European Law.

EU JUSTICE AND HOME AFFAIRS LAW

Third Edition

OXFORD EU LAW LIBRARY

The aim of this series is to publish important and original studies of the various branches of EC and EU Law. Each work provides a clear, concise, and original critical exposition of the law in its social, economic, and political context, at a level which will interest the advanced student, the practitioner, the academic, and government and Community officials. Formerly the Oxford European Community Law Library Series.

Other Titles in the Library

EU External Relations Law
Second edition
Piet Eeckhout

The European Union and its
Court of Justice
Second edition
Anthony Arnull

The General Principles of EU Law
Second edition
Takis Tridimas

EU Company Law
Vanessa Edwards

EU Anti-Discrimination Law
Fifth edition
Joanna Goyder and Albertina
Albons-Llorens

EU Agriculture Law
Second edition
J.A. Usher

Intellectual Property Rights in EU Law
Vol 1: Free Movement and
Competition Law
David T. Keeling

EU Customs Law
Second edition
Timothy Lyons, QC

EC Employment Law
Third edition
Catherine Barnard

Directives in EU Law
Second edition
Sacha Prechal

The Law of Money and Financial
Services in the EU
Second edition
J.A. Usher

Workers, Establishment, and Services
in the European Union
Robin C.A. White

EU Justice and Home Affairs Law

Third Edition

STEVE PEERS

Professor of Law
University of Essex

OXFORD
UNIVERSITY PRESS

OXFORD

UNIVERSITY PRESS

Great Clarendon Street, Oxford, OX2 6DP,
United Kingdom

Oxford University Press is a department of the University of Oxford.
It furthers the University's objective of excellence in research, scholarship,
and education by publishing worldwide. Oxford is a registered trade mark of
Oxford University Press in the UK and in certain other countries

British Library Cataloguing in Publication Data
Data available

Library of Congress Cataloging in Publication Data
Data available

ISBN 978–0–19–960490–6
ISBN 978–0–19–965997–5 (pbk.)

Printed in Great Britain by
CPI Group (UK) Ltd, Croydon, CR0 4YY.

Links to third party websites are provided by Oxford in good faith and
for information only. Oxford disclaims any responsibility for the materials
contained in any third party website referenced in this work.

To my mother Heather Bell, my father-in-law
Ajit Kumar Chatterjee, my wife Pamela, and my children Kiran,
Isabella, Serena, and Sophia, with much love and
thanks for your support.

Series Editors' Foreword

There was a time, a quarter of a century ago, when the removal of national frontiers within the European Union (EU) could be viewed principally in terms of its liberating effect on the flow of the means of production between Member States. That is the case no longer. Changes designed to facilitate the free movement of economically active Member State nationals have also facilitated the free movement of immigrants and asylum seekers, criminals, terrorists, and abductors of children. The common external tariff that governs trade in goods needs a human equivalent, necessarily more complex: a common external frontier, complete with common policies on asylum, immigration, and external border controls. National security and criminal justice, long viewed as the heartland of Member State competence, must be harmonized to the extent necessary to ensure mutual recognition of systems, and meaningful cooperation between police and criminal courts across the Union. Judicial cooperation in civil matters must be enhanced, with particular reference to the resolution of family disputes with a cross-border dimension.

That such developments are required by the logic of the single market does not render them in any way uncontroversial: for as so often, the devil is in the detail. To a greater extent than any other area of Union competence, the measures proposed are liable to impinge upon individual liberty and civil rights. It is remarkable, then, that when cooperation in the field of justice and home affairs first appeared on the EU agenda in the Maastricht Treaty of 1992, the Member States should have placed this most sensitive policy area in the intergovernmental third pillar, remote from the influence both of the European Parliament and of the courts. The Amsterdam Treaty of 1997 moved some of it into the first pillar. It was the Lisbon Treaty, however, which merged the pillars and largely completed the transition from intergovernmental consensus to qualified majority voting, co-decision and judicial control. This was, perhaps, the most significant of all the Lisbon reforms.

The third edition of this standard work is well timed to take account of the new framework, both as it appears on paper and as it is starting to be applied in practice. The author has shirked none of the complexities: the Justice and Home Affairs (JHA) acquis, the transitional provisions, and the convoluted arrangements made to accommodate the United Kingdom, Ireland, and Denmark are all spelled out reliably and in a manner that practitioners will find helpful. But nor does he lose sight of the big picture. Every chapter contains a valuable section on human rights, and a short but often trenchant conclusion that commands respect because of the thoroughness of the analysis that precedes it.

The potential of rules in this area to conflict with civil liberties is obvious, and often remarked upon. A more insidious threat is posed by their sheer complexity, which seems calculated to promote lawyerly confusion, media indifference, and public incomprehension. By demystifying this difficult subject and presenting it with rigour and clarity, the author has performed a rare service. We commend his work to all who have an interest in the human aspects of European integration.

David Anderson
Piet Eeckhout
October 2010

Preface to the third edition

Nine years have passed since the terrorist attacks of September 11, 2001, and the development of EU Justice and Home Affairs (JHA) Law now encompasses not just a response to those attacks, but a counter-reaction to that response, in large part prompted by civil liberties concerns.

More generally, the tension in this field between the objectives of ensuring security and controlling migration, on the one hand, and the protection of human rights and civil liberties, on the other, is ongoing and will continue.

The time was ripe for a third edition of this book, most obviously in order to explain and examine the major institutional changes that the Treaty of Lisbon has made to this area of EU law, but also to analyse and assess the many significant legislative and case law developments since the second edition was completed in July 2006.

As before, the book begins with an overview of the main themes of EU Justice and Home Affairs Law and then examines the institutional framework, followed by chapters on each of the substantive areas of law. The chapters have been restructured and reordered where necessary in order to match the structure of the JHA Articles of the Treaty on the Functioning of the European Union, as amended by the Treaty of Lisbon. As in previous editions, the focus is on the primary sources of EU JHA law, rather than the secondary literature.

I have provided more in-depth treatment of selected areas of law where there has been case law already or which are likely to prove important in practice, for instance the Borders Code, the visa code, the family reunion Directive, the 'Blue Card' Directive, the Returns Directive, the European Arrest Warrant, suspects' rights, victims' rights, and cross–border double jeopardy rules.

I am, as before, indebted to Tony Bunyan and Statewatch for continued advice and assistance.

I have endeavoured to state the law as of September 11, 2010.

Steve Peers
September 11, 2010

Preface to the Paperback edition

In the period between the completion of this third edition (September 2010) and May 2012, there were a number of significant legislative and judicial developments in the field of EU Justice and Home Affairs (JHA) law.

In the area of border controls, there have been major changes to the rules governing Frontex, the EU border control agency.[1] Furthermore, the EU has established an agency to manage its JHA information systems (the Visa Information System, the Schengen Information System and Eurodac).[2] The border traffic Regulation has been amended to extend its scope to the entire Russian region of Kaliningrad,[3] and the Schengen rules on travel documents have been amended.[4] The Commission has proposed amendments to the borders code Regulation which would, *inter alia*, permit the collective re-imposition of internal border controls if a State is failing to control its part of the common external border.[5] It has also proposed other sundry changes to the borders code,[6] as well as legislation to establish 'Eurosur', an integrated borders management system.[7] The Court of Justice was asked to give a number of further judgments on the interpretation of the borders code Regulation,[8] as well as (for the first time) the border traffic Regulation.[9]

As for visas (chapter 4), the EU has amended its visa list legislation to waive visa requirements for Albania, Bosnia-Herzegovina, and Taiwan.[10] There has also been a minor amendment to the visa code.[11] Further proposed amendments to the visa list would, *inter alia*, provide for the re-imposition of visa controls on some countries as an emergency safeguard.[12] A visa facilitation treaty with Georgia entered into force,[13] and the Court of Justice was asked for the first time to interpret the visa code Regulation.[14]

---

[1] Reg 1168/2011, [2011] OJ L 304/1.   [2] Reg 1077/2011, [2011] OJ L 286/1.
[3] Reg 1342/2011 [2011] OJ L 347/41.   [4] [2011] OJ L 287/9.
[5] COM (2011) 560, 16 Sep 2011. See the parallel revised proposal for a Regulation on the Schengen evaluation process (COM (2010) 624, 16 Nov 2010, as amended: COM (2011) 559, 16 Sep 2011).
[6] COM (2011) 118, 10 Mar 2011.   [7] COM (2011) 873, 12 Dec 2011.
[8] Case C-430/10 *Gaydarov*, judgment of 17 Nov 2011. See also Cases C-355/10 *EP v Council* (opinion of 17 April 2012), C-606/10 *Association Nationale d'Assistance aux Frontières pour les Etrangers* (opinion of 29 Nov 2011), C-23/12 *Zakaria*, and C-88/12 *Jaoo*, all pending.
[9] Case C-254/11 *Shomodi*, pending.
[10] Regs 1091/2010 ([2010] OJ L 329/1) and 1211/2010 ([2010] OJ L 339/6).
[11] Reg 154/2012, [2012] OJ L 58/3.   [12] COM (2011) 290, 24 May 2011.
[13] [2011] OJ L 52/33.
[14] Case C-83/12 PPU *Vo*, judgment of 10 April 2012, not yet reported. See also Cases C-39/12 *Dang* and C-84/12 *Koushkaki*, pending. The Court has also been asked to rule on the validity of many Member States' imposition of visas on Turkish visitors: Case C-221/11 *Demirkan*, pending.

Next, in the area of asylum (chapter 5), the EU has adopted a recast version of the qualification Directive – a keystone in the development of the second phase of the Common European Asylum System.[15] The legislation amending the Refugee Fund as regards resettlement has also been adopted.[16] In the meantime, the Commission has revised its proposals for second-phase Directives on reception conditions and asylum procedures, in order to facilitate their adoption.[17]

In this field, both the Court of Justice and the European Court of Human Rights gave important judgments ruling that the Dublin regime on responsibility for asylum seekers had to be suspended where there was a sufficient risk of a serious breach of human rights in the Member State with responsibility.[18] The Court also gave rulings on other aspects of the Dublin rules,[19] the qualification Directive,[20] and (for the first time) the asylum procedures Directive.[21] It has also been asked to rule for the first time on the Directive on reception conditions.[22]

On the issue of legal migration (chapter 6), the abolition of unanimous voting has led to the adoption of a number of legislative measures, namely the revised rules on social security for third-country nationals,[23] the Directive extending the long-term residents' Directive to refugees and beneficiaries of subsidiary protection,[24] and the single permit Directive.[25] The Court of Justice has given its first rulings on interpretation of the long-term residents' Directive,[26] as well as the Regulation on social security for third-country nationals.[27] It has also been asked to rule on the interpretation of the students' Directive for the first time.[28] The Court has also addressed a number of issues concerning third-country national family members of EU citizens,[29] as well as the position of third-country nationals pursuant to the EU's association agreements.[30]

---

[15] Directive 2011/95, [2011] OJ L 337/9.   [16] [2012] OJ L 92/1.

[17] COM (2011) 319 and 320, 1 June 2011.

[18] Respectively Joined Cases C-411/10 NS and C-493/10 M.E and others, judgment of 21 Dec 2011 and MSS v Belgium and Greece, judgment of 21 Jan 2011 (neither yet reported).

[19] Case C-620/10 Kastrati, judgment of 3 May 2012 (not yet reported). See also Cases: C-4/11 Puid, C-245/11 K, C-528/11 Halaf, C-648/11 MA, and C-666/11 M and others (all pending).

[20] Joined Cases C-57/09 and C-101/09 B and D, judgment of 9 Nov 2010 (not yet reported). See also Cases: C-71/11 Y and C-99/11 Z (opinion of 19 April 2012), C-277/11 MM (opinion of 26 April 2012), C-364/11 El Kott, C-141/12 YS, and C-199/12 X (all pending).

[21] Case C-69/10 Samba Diouf, judgment of 28 July 2011 (not yet reported). See also Case C-175/11 H.I.D., pending.

[22] Case C-179/11 CIMADE and GISTI, pending.   [23] Reg 1231/2010, [2010] OJ L 344/1.

[24] Directive 2011/51, [2011] OJ L 132/1.   [25] Directive 2011/98, [2011] OJ L 343/1.

[26] Cases C-571/10 Kamberaj, judgment of 24 April 2012 and C-508/10 Commission v Netherlands, judgment of 26 April 2012 (neither yet reported). See also Case C-502/10 Singh, pending.

[27] Case C-247/09 Xhymshiti, judgment of 18 Nov 2010 (not yet reported).

[28] Case C-15/11 Sommer (opinion 1 March 2012), pending.

[29] See in particular Cases C-34/09 Zambrano, judgment of 1 March 2011, C-434/09 McCarthy, judgment of 5 May 2011, and C-256/11 Dereci, judgment of 15 Nov 2011 (none yet reported).

[30] See in particular Cases: C-300/09 and C-301/09 Toprak and Oguz, judgment of 9 Dec 2010; C-383/08 Bozkurt, judgment of 22 Dec 2010; C-485/07 Akdas, judgment of 26 May 2011; C-484/07

On the issue of irregular migration (chapter 7), the EU adopted amendments to the legislation concerning immigration liaison officers,[31] and readmission treaties with Pakistan and Georgia entered into force.[32] For its part, the Court of Justice clarified a number of key issues concerning the relationship between the Returns Directive and national criminal law as regards detention.[33]

As for civil cooperation (chapter 8), the EU adopted the Rome III Regulation 1259/2010 on choice of law in divorce proceedings.[34] The Commission also proposed major amendments to Regulation 44/2001 on civil and commercial jurisdiction,[35] as well as new legislation on the choice of law and jurisdiction on matrimonial property and on registered partnerships,[36] the civil law enforcement of protection orders,[37] and account preservation orders.[38] As regards external relations in this field, the Council concluded the Hague Convention on maintenance obligations[39] and the Protocol to the 1974 Athens Convention 1974 on the carriage of passengers and luggage by sea, on behalf of the EU.[40] The Commission also proposed that the Council approve the accession of a number of third countries to the Hague Child Abduction Convention.[41] On the judicial front, the number of cases referred to the Court of Justice increased in 2010 and 2011. The Court continued to rule on a number of issues concerning the Brussels Regulation,[42] but also ruled on issues concerning the Brussels II Regulation,[43] the insolvency Regulation,[44] Regulation on

---

Pehlivan, judgment of 16 June 2011; C-186/10 *Oguz*, judgment of 21 July 2011; C-187/10 *Unal*, judgment of 29 Sep 2011; C-256/11 *Dereci* (ibid); C-371/08 *Ziebell*, judgment of 8 Dec 2011; and C-7/10 and 9/10 *Kahveci*, judgment of 29 March 2012 (none yet reported).

[31] Reg 493/2011, [2011] OJ L 141/13.

[32] Respectively [2010] OJ L 287/50 and [2011] OJ L 52/45.

[33] Cases C-61/11 PPU *El Dridl Hassen*, judgment of 28 April 2011 and C-329/11 *Achughbabian*, judgment of 6 Dec 2011 (neither yet reported). See also Cases: C-430/11 *Sagor*, C-522/11 *Mbaye*, C-534/11 *Arslan*, C-51/12 to 54/12 *Zhu and others*, and C-73/12 to 75/12 *Ettaghi and others* (all pending).

[34] Reg 1259/2010, [2010] OJ L 343/10.   [35] COM (2010) 748, 14 Dec 2010.

[36] COM (2011) 126 and 127, 16 Mar 2011.   [37] COM (2011) 276, 18 May 2011.

[38] COM (2011) 445, 25 July 2011.   [39] [2011] OJ L 192/39.

[40] [2012] OJ L 8/1 and 13.

[41] COM (2011) 904, 908, 909. 911, 912, 915, 916 and 917, 21 Dec 2011.

[42] Cases: C-585/08 *Pammer*, judgment of 7 Dec 2010; C-144/09 *Hotel Alpenhof*, judgment of 7 Dec 2010; C-144/10 *Berliner Verkehrsbetriebe*, judgment of 12 May 2011; C-87/10 *Electrosteel*, judgment of 9 June 2011; C-139/10 *Prism Investments*, judgment of 13 Oct 2011; C-406/09 *RealChemie*, judgment of 18 Oct 2011; C-509/09 *eDate Advertising*, judgment of 25 Oct 2011; C-161/10 *Martinez*, judgment of 25 Oct 2011; C-327/10 *Lindner*, judgment of 17 Nov 2011; C-145/10 *Painer*, judgment of 1 Dec 2011; C-292/10 *G*, judgment of 15 Mar 2012; C-213/10 *F-Tex*, judgment of 19 April 2012; and C-523/10 *Wintersteiger*, judgment of 19 April 2012 (none yet reported).

[43] Cases: C-400/10 PPU *McB*, judgment of 5 Oct 2010; C-296/10 *Purrucker II*, judgment of 9 Nov 2010; C-497/10 PPU *Mercredi*, judgment of 22 Dec 2010; C-491/10 PPU *Aguirre Zarraga*, judgment of 22 Dec 2010; and C-92/12 PPU *Health and Safety Executive*, judgment of 26 April 2012 (none yet reported).

[44] Cases: C-396/09 *Interedil*, judgment of 20 Oct 2011; C-112/10 *Zaza Retail*, judgment of 17 Nov 2011; and C-191/10 *Rastelli Davide and C*, judgment of 15 Dec 2011 (none yet reported).

transmission of evidence,[45] the Rome Convention,[46] and (for the first time) the Rome II Regulation.[47]

As regards criminal procedure (chapter 9), the EU has adopted a Directive on a European protection order,[48] as well as two Directives concerning suspects' rights – on interpretation and translation and the right to information in criminal proceedings.[49] The Commission has also proposed Directives concerning crime victims' rights,[50] suspects' rights of access to lawyer and communication rights,[51] and the freezing and confiscation of criminal proceeds.[52] In this field, the Court of Justice gave a number of further judgments concerning the Framework Decision on the European Arrest Warrant[53] and the Framework Decision on crime victims' rights.[54] Also, the first cases on the Framework Decision on the recognition of financial penalties were referred from national courts.[55]

In the area of substantive criminal law (chapter 10), the EU institutions adopted Directives on trafficking in persons and the sexual exploitation of children,[56] and the Commission proposed Directives on attacks on information systems and financial market abuse.[57]

Finally, as regards police cooperation (chapter 12), the EU has adopted legislation on the exchange of information on traffic offences,[58] and the Commission has proposed a Directive on passenger name records.[59] The Council has also concluded new treaties with Australia and the USA on the exchange of such records.[60]

Steve Peers

4 May 2012

---

[45] Case C-283/09 *Werynski,* judgment of 17 Feb 2011 (not yet reported).

[46] Cases C-29/10 *Koelzsch,* judgment of 15 March 2011, and C-384/10 *Voogsgeerd,* judgment of 15 Dec 2011 (neither yet reported).

[47] Case C-412/10 *Homawoo,* judgment of 17 Nov 2011 (not yet reported).

[48] Directive 2011/99, [2011] OJ L 338/2.

[49] Respectively Directive 2010/64 ([2010] OJ L 280/1) and Directive 2012/13 ([2012] OJ L 142/1).   [50] COM (2011) 275, 18 May 2011.

[51] COM (2011) 326, 8 June 2011.   [52] COM (2012) 85, 12 March 2012.

[53] Cases: C-306/09 *I.B.,* judgment of 21 Oct 2010 and C-261/09 *Mantello,* judgment of 16 Nov 2010 (neither yet reported). See also Cases C-42/11 *Lopes da Silva Jorge* (opinion of 20 Mar 2012), C-396/11 *Radu,* and C-399/11 *Melloni,* all pending.

[54] Cases: C-205/09 *Eredics,* judgment of 21 Oct 2010; C-483/09 *Gueye* and C-1/10 *Salmeron Sanchez,* judgment of 15 Sep 2011, and C-507/10 *X,* judgment of Dec 2011 (none yet reported). See also Case C-79/11 *Giovanardi,* pending.

[55] See Cases C-27/11 *Vinkov* and C-60/12 *Balasz,* both pending.

[56] Respectively Directive 2011/36 ([2011] OJ L 101/1) and Directive 2011/92 ([2011] OJ L 335/1).

[57] Respectively COM (2010) 517, 30 Sep 2010 and COM (2011) 654, 20 Oct 2011.

[58] Directive 2011/82 ([2011] OJ L 288/1), which has been challenged on 'legal base' grounds: Case C-43/12 *Commission v EP and Council,* pending.

[59] COM (2011) 32, 2 Feb 2011.

[60] COM (2011) 280 and 281, 19 May 2011 (Australia) and COM (2011) 805 and 807, 23 Nov 2011 (USA).

Contents

Chapter 9: Criminal Law: Mutual Recognition and Criminal Procedure

Table of Abbreviations

ACP	Africa, Caribbean, and Pacific
ADS	Approved Destination System
All ER	All England Reports
ATV	Airport Transit Visa
BYIL	British Yearbook of International Law
CA	Court of Appeal
CATS	Article Thirty-Six Committee [French acronym]
CCI	Common Consular Instructions
CEAS	Common European Asylum System
CETS	Council of Europe Treaty Series
CIREA	Centre for Information, Discussion, and Exchange on Asylum [French acronym]
CIREFI	Centre for Information, Discussion, and Exchange on the Crossing of Borders and Immigration [French acronym]
CIS	Customs Information System
CFI	Court of First Instance
CFR	Common Frame of Reference
CFSP	Common Foreign and Security Policy
CMLR	Common Market Law Reports
CMLRev	Common Market Law Review
Coreper	Committee of Permanent Representatives [French acronym]
COSI	Committee on Internal Security [French acronym]
CUP	Cambridge University Press
CYELS	Cambridge Yearbook of European Legal Studies
DCFR	Draft Common Frame of Reference
DNA	Deoxyribonucleic acid
EASO	European Asylum Support Office
EAW	European Arrest Warrant
EC	European Community
ECR	European Court Reports

ECHR	European Convention on Human Rights
ECRE	European Council on Refugees and Exiles
ECRIS	European Criminal Records Information System
ECSC	European Coal and Steel Community
ECtHR	European Court of Human Rights
EDPS	European Data Protection Supervisor
EDU	Europol Drugs Unit
EEA	European Economic Area
EEC	European Economic Community
EEW	European Evidence Warrant
EFARev	European Foreign Affairs Review
EIO	European Investigation Order
EIPA	European Institute of Public Administration
EJLR	European Journal of Law Reform
EJML	European Journal of Migration and Law
EJN	European Judicial Network
ELJ	European Law Journal
ELRev	European Law Review
EP	European Parliament
EPC	European Political Cooperation
EPL	European Public Law
EPO	European Protection Order
EPP	European Public Prosecutor
EPRIS	European Police Records Index System
ERTA	European Road Transport Agreement
ETS	European Treaty Series
EU	European Union
FIU	Financial intelligence unit
FYROM	Former Yugoslav Republic of Macedonia
GATS	General Agreement on Trade in Services
HL	House of Lords
HRQ	Human Rights Quarterly
IANLJournal	Immigration, Asylum and Nationality Law Journal
IJCCLCJ	International Journal of Crime, Criminal Law and Criminal Justice

ICCPR	International Covenant on Civil and Political Rights
ICLQ	International and Comparative Law Quarterly
ID	Identity
IIA	Inter-Institutional Agreement
IJRL	International Journal of Refugee Law
ILM	International Legal Materials
ILO	Immigration Liaison Officer
ILO	International Labour Organization
ILPA	Immigration Law Practitioners' Association
JHA	Justice and Home Affairs
JSWFL	Journal of Social Welfare and Family Law
LIEI	Legal Issues of European [Economic] Integration
LTV	Limited Territorial Validity
MEP	Member of the European Parliament
NGO	Non-Governmental Organisation
OECD	Organization for Economic Cooperation and Development
OJ	Official Journal [of the European Union]
OLAF	European Anti-Fraud Office [French acronym]
OUP	Oxford University Press
PCA	Partnership and Cooperation Agreement
PIF	Protection of Financial Interests
PNR	Passenger Name Records
PPU	Urgent Preliminary Ruling Procedure [French acronym]
QB	Queen's Bench
QMV	Qualified majority vote
RABIT	Rapid Border Action Teams
RPS	Regulatory Procedure with Scrutiny
RSQ	Refugee Studies Quarterly
SAA	Stabilization and Association Agreement
Sch/Com-ex	Schengen Executive Committee
SCIFA	Strategic Committee on Immigration, Frontiers, and Asylum
SEA	Single European Act
SIS	Schengen Information System
SIS II	Second generation Schengen Information System
TEU	Treaty on European Union

TFEU	Treaty on the Functioning of the European Union
UCLAF	Task Force for the Coordination of Crime Prevention
UK	United Kingdom
UKNCCL	United Kingdom National Committee for Comparative Law
UN	United Nations
UNHCR	United Nations High Commission for Refugees
US	United States of America
VAT	Value Added Tax
VIP	Very Important Person
VIS	Visa Information System
WLR	Weekly Law Reports
WTO	World Trade Organization
YEL	Yearbook of European Law

Table of Cases

European Civil Service Tribunal

European Court of Human Rights

Judgments

Table of Legislation

Recommendations

Recommendations

Council of Europe

Council of Europe Recommendations

Hague Conventions

OECD

Table of Proposed Legislation

EU MEASURES

Joint Actions

Framework Decisions

1

Introduction

Immigration, asylum, policing, and criminal law are among the topics of greatest public concern. Given the sensitivity of such issues, and the initial perception that they were 'internal' issues with limited relevance, it was not surprising that they were among the last topics to be addressed in the European integration project. But due to a combination of increasing economic integration in Europe and increased public anxiety about migration and security issues in particular following the terrorist attacks of September 11, 2001, Justice and Home Affairs (JHA) matters have moved up the EU's agenda.

This book sets out and analyses both the institutional arrangements for JHA cooperation and the substantive law which has been adopted (and to some extent, which is under discussion) in various JHA fields. These fields are united by a series of four common and closely connected themes which are discussed in each chapter.

First and foremost, a central issue in EU Justice and Home Affairs law is the balance between protection of human rights and civil liberties on the one hand and the State interests in public order, security, or migration control on the other. This balance has become particularly difficult to maintain since September 11, 2001. Although human rights issues arise in all areas of EU law, both the rights to be secured and the public interests to be protected are particularly fundamental in the area of JHA law. Therefore the relationship between EU JHA law and human rights obligations is analysed throughout this book, in order to assess whether the EU is striking the right balance between the protection of rights and the interests of security and control.[1]

A second theme, now largely of historical importance following the entry into force of the Treaty of Lisbon, is the complex and often controversial interaction and overlap between the supranational European Community legal order and the intergovernmental legal order of the EU's 'third pillar' (as those legal orders were known before the Treaty of Lisbon came into force). This interaction and overlap still applies to the issues addressed in this book, because of the distinct institutional rules which applied to these areas in the past, and which were in force when much of the relevant legislation was adopted. Furthermore, to some extent, the 'third pillar' rules limiting the jurisdiction of the Court of Justice and the legal

---

[1] See s 3 of chs 2–12.

effect of the relevant measures will continue to apply for a transitional period after the Treaty of Lisbon has entered into force. Furthermore, this theme is linked to the first, because a lack of adequate judicial and parliamentary accountability and control has led to an increased risk that the EU JHA measures adopted in the past did not ensure sufficient standards of human rights protection, and because the maintenance of unanimous voting by Member States before most JHA measures could be approved arguably contributed to the lowering of standards in JHA legislation. So the relationship between EU JHA law and other (non-JHA) EU law rules, in particular concerning the free movement of persons, is analysed throughout this book, in order to define the borderline between the two and to compare the relevant substantive law.[2]

The third theme is the continued dispute over the scope of the powers granted to the EU in the areas of JHA law, because the issues in question are considered to be central to the sovereignty of each State, and because there has often been a great reluctance to amend the details of particular national laws. This theme is connected with the other two, because Member States are in some cases reluc- tant to change their laws because they wish to maintain a particular approach to human rights protection, and because the prior requirement for unanimous voting in most JHA areas (before the entry into force of the Treaty of Lisbon) allowed any one Member State to insist on the narrowest interpretation of EC or EU competence. Therefore the extent of EU competence is analysed throughout this book, in order to suggest a coherent interpretation of the scope of that com- petence in light of the text and context of the Treaties.[3]

Finally, the fourth theme is the convoluted territorial scope of EU JHA law, which has several elements. First of all, the underlying objections of some Member States to any EU obligations in certain areas of JHA law resulted in the creation of a complex series of 'opt-outs' for the UK, Ireland, and Denmark. Secondly, with the 2004 and 2007 enlargement of the EU, there was a lengthy delay before some areas of JHA law applied to the new Member States (and some of those new Member States are still not covered by all EU JHA rules). A similar delay will apply to any future enlargements. Thirdly, Norway, Iceland, Switzerland, and Liechtenstein are very closely associated with parts of EU JHA law, but not at all associated with the other parts of that law. Therefore, the territorial scope of EU and EC JHA measures is explained throughout this book, so that readers can, if they wish, determine which rules apply to a particular State (or States).[4]

The entry into force of the Treaty of Amsterdam in 1999 created hopes that EU decision-making on JHA matters would be more open, that judicial control in this area would be improved, and that the substantive EU measures to be adopted would strike an acceptable balance between the protection of human rights and civil liberties and the interests of migration control and ensuring

---

[2] See s 4 of chs 2–12.   [3] See s 2.3 of chs 2–12.   [4] See s 2.4 of chs 2–12.

public security. Unfortunately, in practice, taken as a whole, there were widespread doubts about the adequacy of the substantive standards adopted by the EU from 1999–2009 in many areas of JHA law, and the democratic and judicial controls over the adoption, interpretation, and legality of EC and EU acts were by and large clearly deficient. Therefore there was a continued imbalance in both the substantive and institutional JHA law of the EU, favouring prosecutorial and repressive values and principles over other values and principles long established in European societies, and in particular over the human rights which the European Union claims to respect.

However, the entry into force of the Treaty of Lisbon has brought the possibility of fundamental change in this area, in light of the improved rules on decision-making, judicial accountability, and human rights protection set out in the Treaty. It is too early to tell for certain what impact this Treaty will actually have, but its possibilities and the application of the Treaty in practice in the first nine months following its entry into force are fully discussed throughout this book.

2

Institutional Framework

2.1. Introduction

The central theme in the institutional development of EU Justice and Home Affairs (JHA) law has been the debate as to whether the law in this area should be adopted and applied on an 'intergovernmental' basis, reserving essentially all power to the national governments of the Member States, or instead on the basis of the supranational 'Community method', which gives much of the power instead to the more integration-minded EU institutions (the Commission, the European Parliament, and the EU's Court of Justice). Before the Treaty of Lisbon, the EU framework for the adoption of JHA measures largely took an intergovernmental approach, allowing national executives to agree on measures without the usual level of control exercised by national parliaments and national courts, and without sufficient controls exercised by the European Parliament or the EU courts by way of a substitute. The key reason for establishing an intergovernmental system was (some) Member States' view that these issues are so central to their sovereignty that the supranational Community method should not be applied. The intergovernmental approach impacted on the content of policy: unsurprisingly, the national ministries took this opportunity to focus on law enforcement and migration control objectives, arguably at the expense of a more balanced approach. But measures in this area also raise acute issues concerning human rights protection, legitimacy, and accountability, simply due to their subject matter, and the practical effectiveness of an intergovernmental approach was also questioned.

Time will tell whether the entry into force of the Treaty of Lisbon has enabled the EU to address a number of these concerns, given the changes resulting from that Treaty: the simplification and normalization of the framework for decision-making and the jurisdiction of the EU courts; the single legal framework for legal instruments, their legal effects, and the adoption of implementing and delegated measures; the strengthening of the position of the European Parliament (EP) and (more tenuously) national parliaments; the enhanced rules on openness and transparency of the EU institutions and bodies; and the increased level of human rights protection in relation to the EU's Charter of Fundamental Rights and planned EU accession to the European Convention on Human Rights (ECHR). It is notable, however, that as with prior Treaty amendments in this field, the trade-off for the greater application of the traditional 'Community method' to JHA law was the greater capacity for those Member States (the UK, Ireland, and Denmark) which were reluctant to see this method applied to JHA law to stand aside and not participate fully in the EU's policies.

Because of continuing disputes between Member States on JHA institutional issues and the resulting renegotiations of the basic legal framework concerning JHA as set out in the Treaties establishing the EU, the institutional framework for EU JHA law is historically complex, in particular due to its use of different rules over time regarding decision-making, jurisdiction of the EU courts, legal instruments and their legal effect, and territorial scope. This chapter examines first of all the historical development of the institutional framework in this area, while fully examining the interpretation of the current rules as set out in the Treaty of Lisbon. It next looks at issues of EC and EU competence, the rules concerning the non-participation of some Member States from aspects of JHA cooperation, and the inclusion of some non-Member States (Norway, Iceland, Switzerland, Liechtenstein) in aspects of those rules. The chapter then provides an overview of: the rules concerning human rights protection in EU law; the division and overlap between the rules concerning JHA cooperation and other areas of EU law; the use of the EU budget to fund JHA cooperation; and the external relations aspects of JHA cooperation. Each of Chapters 3–12 then follows the same structure, examining ten particular topics from the same perspective, as well as analysing in detail (except for less detail as regards civil law) the particular EU measures in each field. This chapter also provides a specific overview of the issues of transparency and legitimacy in EU JHA law.

2.2. Overview of the institutional framework

The European Communities were originally established in the form of three treaties: the Treaty establishing the European Coal and Steel Community (ECSC), in force in 1952, later joined by the Treaties establishing the European Economic Community (EEC) and the European Atomic Energy Community (Euratom), both in force in 1958. The ECSC Treaty expired in 2002, and the EEC Treaty (later renamed the European Community, or EC Treaty) has been the subject of five substantial amendments.

First of all, the Single European Act (SEA), which entered into force on 1 July 1987, focused on the completion of the internal market by the end of 1992. Secondly, the Treaty on European Union (TEU), or Maastricht Treaty, which entered into force 1 November 1993, focused on the creation of economic and monetary union and set up special legal frameworks for the adoption of rules concerning a Common Foreign and Security Policy (CFSP) and JHA in the new Treaty on European Union,[1] which stood alongside (but also amended) the three Community treaties.[2] Because of the different rules governing the adoption of measures concerning economic integration in the Community treaties, as compared to the rules concerning the CFSP and JHA, it was often suggested that the TEU created a sort of 'Greek temple' structure with 'three pillars', which comprised in turn the Community treaties (first pillar), CFSP (second pillar), and JHA (third pillar). This temple structure was held together by common core rules in the TEU concerning the foundations of the Union on the one hand,[3] and the final provisions of the TEU (addressing issues such as accession to the EU and amendment of the Treaties) on the other.[4]

Thirdly, the Treaty of Amsterdam, which entered into force 1 May 1999,[5] transferred part of the third pillar (dealing with immigration, asylum, and civil law) to the EC Treaty, subject to specific rules which differed considerably, at least initially, from the normal rules which applied to the first pillar. This Treaty also significantly amended the rules applicable to the issues which remained in the TEU's 'third pillar', namely police and criminal law cooperation. Alongside these changes, this Treaty also integrated the substantive rules (the 'Schengen *acquis*') which had been developed by a core group of Member States outside the EU and EC legal framework, due to the absence of consensus among all Member States over whether all internal border checks between Member States should be abolished, into the EC and EU legal order.[6] The Schengen *acquis* comprised the 1985 Schengen Agreement to abolish border checks between Member States, the 1990 Convention implementing the Schengen Agreement ('Schengen Convention'), and the measures implementing the Schengen Convention.[7]

Next, the Treaty of Nice, which entered into force 1 February 2003, made modest changes to issues relating to JHA cooperation, as it mainly focused on other amendments to the Treaties which were believed to be necessary to prepare the EU for substantial enlargement, which took place subsequently in 2004 and 2007.

Finally, the Treaty of Lisbon, which entered into force on 1 December 2009, transferred the remaining third pillar to the first pillar and made a number of changes to all aspects of JHA cooperation.[8] The European Community and the European Union, previously legally distinct entities, were merged into a single

---

[1] Respectively Arts J–J.11 TEU and K–K.9 TEU, as originally introduced by the Maastricht Treaty.

[2] Arts G, H, and I of the TEU, as originally introduced by the Maastricht Treaty, amended the three Community treaties.

[3] Arts A–F TEU, as originally introduced by the Maastricht Treaty.

[4] Arts L–S TEU, as originally introduced by the Maastricht Treaty.

[5] See further 2.2.2 below.

[6] On the process of integrating the Schengen *acquis* into the EC and EU legal order, see 2.2.2.3 below.

[7] For the text of the Schengen *acquis*, see [2000] OJ L 239.   [8] See 2.2.3 below.

entity called the European Union. As a consequence, the EC Treaty was renamed the Treaty on the Functioning of the European Union (TFEU), and the TEU was revised considerably, so that it now contains the basic rules on the institutional foundations of the Union along with (as before) the detailed rules (as amended) on the Union's Common Foreign and Security Policy.

Since the Articles of the TEU have been amended significantly twice, this book refers throughout to the Maastricht Treaty version as the 'original TEU', the Treaty of Amsterdam version as the 'previous TEU', and the Treaty of Lisbon version as the 'revised TEU'.

Although the Treaty of Lisbon transformed the institutional framework applicable to JHA issues, it is still necessary to examine the previous institutional frameworks briefly, because many pre-Lisbon measures still remain in force, and the legal effect of those measures has been preserved pursuant to transitional rules set out in the Treaty of Lisbon.[9]

There were four key distinctions between the Community method and the intergovernmental system for adoption of EU law. The first distinction was the role of the EU's political institutions. Within the first pillar, the Commission, made up of persons appointed by the Council or the European Council (see below) and approved by the directly elected European Parliament, had a monopoly over proposals for measures in the vast majority of cases. The Council, made up of ministers from Member States, acted to adopt measures by a qualified majority vote (QMV) in a sizable majority of cases. Although the job of implementing Community legislation was in principle left to the Member States, there are cases where implementing powers were conferred on the Commission, or, in exceptional cases, upon the Council.[10] Also, the European Parliament had a substantial role in the adoption of legislation, in particular by means of the so-called 'co-decision' procedure, which gave it an equal role with the Council in the procedure for agreeing a large proportion of legislation.[11] However, in the 'intergovernmental' process, the Commission had no power of initiative or at least had to share its monopoly with Member States. The Council almost invariably had to vote unanimously, giving each Member State's representative a veto. The EP was at best consulted.

Secondly, there were distinctions as regards the EU's Court of Justice. Within EC law, the Court had extensive jurisdiction, particularly over: actions to enforce EC law, where the Commission sued the Member States for a declaration that they have breached their EC obligations;[12] references for

---

[9] On those rules, see 2.2.3.3 below.

[10] See Art 202 EC (now Art 291 TFEU after the Treaty of Lisbon). See further 2.2.2.1 below.

[11] The rules of the co-decision procedure were set out in Art 251 EC (now the ordinary legislative procedure, as set out in Art 294 TFEU, after the Treaty of Lisbon).

[12] Art 226 EC; see also Art 227 EC (Member States suing Member States) and Art 228 EC (power to impose fines and penalties if Member States disobey an Art 226 ruling). See now Arts

a preliminary ruling on the interpretation or validity of EC law, which could be sent by any national court or tribunal;[13] and annulment actions against acts of the EC institutions.[14] There was also a special procedure applicable in advance of the EC's conclusion of an international treaty, to determine whether conclusion of that treaty would be compatible with EC law.[15] In contrast, the third pillar provided for special rules which significantly restricted the Court's jurisdiction.

Thirdly, there were distinctions as regards the legal instruments used. EC law applies via means of Directives, Regulations, and Decisions.[16] In contrast, EU third pillar law used different instruments, although those instruments changed with the adoption of the Treaty of Amsterdam.[17]

Finally, there was a distinction as regard the effect of the law. EC law measures had 'direct effect', meaning that they are applicable in national courts and could be directly invoked as part of national law if they were clear, precise, and unconditional (although Directives did not have direct effect against private parties). National law also had to be interpreted to be consistent with Directives 'as far as possible'. Furthermore, there were detailed rules on the remedies which had to be adopted to give effect to EC law, including, in certain conditions, a right of damages against a Member State which breached EC law. Finally, EC law was supreme over Member States' national law, requiring that conflicting national provisions be set aside. As we shall see, these principles did not fully apply to third pillar measures.

In either the first or the third pillar, the EU institutions could only act where the relevant Treaties conferred a power upon them. Each 'legal base' conferring power set out the limits of the relevant power and the applicable decision-making procedure.

With the entry into force of the Treaty of Lisbon, the previous 'first pillar' rules apply to all policing and criminal law measures adopted afterwards, as well as to all measures in the areas previously subject to the rules of 'Community law' (ie the 'first pillar'). Since this Treaty also provides that the Community has been subsumed by the Union, this book refers in most cases to 'EU' legislation and policy, except in special cases where it is necessary to distinguish between the Community and the Union for historical purposes.

258–260 TFEU after the Treaty of Lisbon, which has also amended these provisions to some extent.

[13] Art 234 EC, now Art 267 TFEU after the Treaty of Lisbon.

[14] Art 230 EC. See also Art 232 EC (actions for failure to act) and Art 235 EC (actions for damages against the EC institutions). These provisions are respectively now Arts 263, 265, and 268 TFEU after the Treaty of Lisbon.

[15] Art 300 EC (now Art 218(11) TFEU after the Treaty of Lisbon).

[16] See Art 249 EC (now Art 288 TFEU after the Treaty of Lisbon).   [17] See 2.2.2.2 below.

2.2.1. Framework prior to the Treaty of Amsterdam

2.2.1.1. Framework prior to the Maastricht Treaty

Informal cooperation on JHA matters began in the 1960s and 1970s, when various drafts of a Convention addressing fraud against the EEC budget were considered, although not agreed.[18] Member States also signed Conventions as far back as 1968 on the mutual recognition of companies and on the jurisdiction over and recognition of civil and commercial judgments, followed by a Convention in 1980 on choice of law in contractual disputes.[19] Such Conventions were partly foreseen by Article 220 EEC (later Article 293 EC, and then repealed by the Treaty of Lisbon), which called upon the Member States, 'insofar as is necessary', to negotiate treaties between themselves on certain specified matters which were likely to assist the Communities' initial objective of market integration.

Prior to the Maastricht Treaty, the formal role of the EC institutions in JHA cooperation was nil. All negotiations were treated as discussions between the Member States, and any resulting acts were classified as public international law, not EC law. All agreements had to be reached unanimously. The Commission was an observer in these talks and the EP was occasionally asked for its opinion. Nor was there any role for the EC institutions in the 1985 Schengen Agreement or the 1990 Schengen Convention. As for the EU's Court of Justice, there was no interest in giving it jurisdiction to interpret intergovernmental measures, except for those dealing with civil cooperation.[20]

Furthermore, only a limited range of instruments were used during this 'informal' intergovernmental period. The only hard-law instruments adopted were Conventions, which are a standard form of international treaty. Although ten such Conventions were agreed before 1993 (excluding the Schengen Conventions, as they were not in principle agreed among all Member States), mostly within the framework of 'European Political Cooperation' (EPC), the original system for EU foreign policy cooperation, only the Rome and Dublin Conventions (dealing respectively with conflict of law in contractual disputes and allocation of responsibility over asylum applications) were ever ratified.[21] Also the Brussels Convention on jurisdiction over and recognition of civil and commercial judgments, linked to the EEC Treaty by Article 220 EEC, was ratified.[22] Otherwise there was occasional use of 'soft-law' Resolutions and Recommendations of interior ministers of the Member States.

Finally, the legal effect of the various measures adopted was up to national law to determine. So those Member States taking a 'dualist' view of the effect of public international law required changes to their national law before a Convention could take effect in their domestic legal order, and those taking a

---

[18] For further detail, see p 9 of the first edition of this book.   [19] See further ch 8.
[20] See 2.2.1.2 below.   [21] See chs 8 and 5 respectively; on the other Conventions see ch 9.
[22] See ch 8.

'monist' view of public international law saw each Convention as an essential part of their legal system. Since the soft-law measures were not binding, their effect in practice depended upon how many Member States wished to implement them.

2.2.1.2. Framework in the Maastricht Treaty

The intergovernmental approach was entrenched by the Maastricht Treaty, which effectively established a 'formal intergovernmental' system for JHA cooperation. While some Member States wished substantial amounts of this cooperation to take place within the framework of the supranational EC Treaty, other Member States wanted no application of the EC method whatsoever to JHA issues. In a compromise agreement, certain aspects of visa policy were included within the EC Treaty, but all other measures remained subject to the intergovernmental system established by the Maastricht Treaty.

As noted above, the Maastricht Treaty consisted of a single Treaty—the Treaty on European Union—ostensibly governing all aspects of integration among the EC's Member States, but this Treaty contained three separate approaches to integration, commonly referred to as 'pillars'.[23] The rules governing the bulk of JHA cooperation constituted the 'third pillar'. By way of exception, two provisions inserted into the EC Treaty addressed specific issues related to visas (the adoption of a visa blacklist, and a common visa format).[24]

The specific provisions of the original version of the third pillar rules began with the original Article K TEU, which formally established JHA cooperation as part of the European Union process. Article K.1 then listed nine items which the Member States regarded as matters of 'common interest', '[f]or the purposes of achieving the objectives of the Union, in particular for the free movement of persons, and without prejudice to the powers of the European Community': asylum policy; rules on crossing of external borders; immigration policy; combating drug addiction; combating international fraud; civil judicial cooperation; criminal judicial cooperation; customs cooperation; and police cooperation.

Next, the original Article K.2 stated that JHA cooperation had to be 'dealt with in compliance with' the European Convention on Human Rights (ECHR), the 1951 Geneva Convention on the status of refugees and Member States' standards of protection for persons persecuted on political grounds, and asserted that the EU Treaty could not affect 'the exercise of the responsibilities incumbent

---

[23] On the 'pillar structure', see R McMahon, 'Maastricht's Third Pillar: load-bearing or purely decorative?' (1995) LIEI 1: 51; P Muller-Graff, 'The legal bases of the Third Pillar and its position in the framework of the Union Treaty' (1994) 29 CMLRev 493; D Curtin, 'The Constitutional structure of the Union: A Europe of bits and pieces' (1993) 30 CMLRev 17; and E Denza, *The Intergovernmental Pillars of the European Union* (OUP, 2002), ch 1.

[24] Arts 100c and 100d EC, subsequently repealed by the Treaty of Amsterdam.

upon Member States with regard to the maintenance of law and order and the safeguarding of internal security'.

The original Article K.3(2) TEU provided that the Council, not the Member States, was to adopt JHA measures, except for Conventions, which the Council was to draw up and recommend to Member States for adoption in accordance with each Member State's constitutional requirements. The Council had to adopt measures unanimously, except for procedural questions, measures implementing Joint Actions (see below), and measures implementing Conventions, which had to be adopted by a two-thirds vote of Member States unless the relevant Convention provided otherwise.

The Commission had a *shared* power along with the Member States to make proposals in the first six areas of common interest, but only the Member States could make proposals in the other three (criminal judicial cooperation; customs cooperation; and police cooperation). The original Article K.6 TEU gave the EP only limited rights, in particular the right to be 'regularly inform[ed]' of discussions and 'consult[ed]' by the Member State holding the rotating Council Presidency on the 'principal aspects' of discussions.

Besides Conventions, the original Article K.3(2)(a) allowed the Council to adopt 'joint positions'; the original Article K.3(2)(b) allowed for the adoption of 'joint actions' where the Union's objectives could be better achieved by such action than by the Member States acting alone; and Article K.5 referred to 'common positions', which Member States were to defend 'within international organizations and at international conferences'.

In practice, ten Conventions were agreed during the Maastricht period,[25] along with five Protocols on the Court of Justice[26] and four other Protocols.[27] Two Conventions concerned civil law, and both were replaced by Community acts before Member States began ratifying them.[28] The remaining eight concerned criminal law, customs, and policing.

Five of these eight Conventions have entered into force, although two of those five Conventions were then subsequently replaced by measures adopted during the 'Amsterdam era' of the third pillar (between 1999 and 2009).[29]

---

[25] The Conventions on Europol, the Customs Information System fraud ([1995] OJ C 316/1 33, and 48); service of documents ([1997] OJ C 261/1); parental responsibility ([1998] OJ C 221/1); customs cooperation ([1998] OJ C 24/1); driving disqualification ([1998] OJ C 216/1); corruption ([1997] OJ C 195/1); consented extradition ([1995] OJ C 78/1); and disputed extradition ([1996] OJ C 313/11).

[26] Protocols to the Europol, the Customs Information System, fraud, service of documents, and parental responsibility Conventions (respectively [1996] OJ C 299/1, [1997] OJ C 151/15, [1997] OJ C 151/1, [1997] OJ C 261/18, and [1998] OJ C 221/19).

[27] Protocol on Europol privileges and immunities ([1997] OJ C 221/1), First Protocol to fraud Convention ([1996] OJ C 313/1); Second Protocol to fraud Convention ([1997] OJ C 221/12); and Protocol to Customs Information System Convention ([1999] OJ C 91/1).

[28] These were the Conventions on service of documents and parental responsibility. See 8.2.2.2 below.   [29] On this replacement process, see 2.2.2.2 below.

The first Convention to come into force was the Europol Convention on 1 October 1998, followed shortly by the Protocols to that Convention on jurisdiction for the Court of Justice (29 December 1998) and on immunities of Europol staff (1 July 1999), at which point Europol began operations.[30] The Convention and its Protocols were subsequently replaced by another third pillar act, adopted under the legal framework established by the Treaty of Amsterdam, as from 1 January 2010.[31] Secondly, the Convention on fraud against the EC budget entered into force on 17 October 2002, along with the first substantive Protocol to that Convention and the Protocol conferring jurisdiction on the Court of Justice. The Second Protocol to the Convention then came into force on 19 May 2009. Some of the newer Member States have not yet ratified the Convention and its Protocols.[32] Thirdly, the Convention on corruption came into force on 29 September 2005, following its ratification by the last of the first fifteen Member States on 30 June 2005. All except two of the newer Member States have ratified it.[33]

Fourthly, the Customs Information System (CIS) Convention, and the Protocol to this Convention on Court of Justice jurisdiction, entered into force on Christmas Day 2005; every Member State has ratified the Convention (although Malta has not ratified the Protocol on the Court of Justice). Previously, pursuant to an Agreement on provisional application of the Convention, the Convention had provisionally applied to eight of the first fifteen Member States from 1 November 2000, and to a further six of the first fifteen Member States subsequently, so the CIS system became operational in March 2003.[34] A later Protocol to this Convention, adopted in 1999, came into force on 14 April 2008; it also applies to all Member States.[35] However, like the Europol Convention, the CIS Convention and the 1999 Protocol have been replaced by a Decision adopted in 2009.[36] Finally, the Naples II Convention on customs cooperation came into force on 25 June 2009, and has been ratified by all Member States.

Of the three criminal, customs, and policing Conventions that have not entered into force, all are subject to possible early application, permitting Member States which have ratified a Convention to declare that the Convention is applicable in the interim to relations with those other Member

---

[30] [1999] OJ C 185/1. The Convention and Protocols also entered into force for all of the Member States which joined the EU in 2004 and 2007. Further Protocols to the Convention were also adopted after the entry into force of the Treaty of Amsterdam: [2000] OJ C 358/1, [2002] OJ C 312/2, and [2004] OJ C 2/1.   [31] [2009] OJ L 121/37.

[32] See Appendix I.   [33] The exceptions were the Czech Republic and Malta.

[34] [1995] OJ C 316/58. For details of the CIS in practice, see 12.6.1.2 below.

[35] A further Protocol was agreed after the entry into force of the Treaty of Amsterdam: [2003] OJ C 139/1.

[36] [2009] OJ L 323/20, replacing the Convention and its substantive Protocols from 27 May 2011 (Art 36).

States which had also ratified it and made the same declaration. Taking the earliest Conventions first, fourteen of the first fifteen Member States and several of the new Member States have ratified the 1995 and 1996 extradition Conventions, and many of these Member States apply the Conventions in advance of ratification.[37] However, these two Conventions have been replaced by the Framework Decision on the European arrest warrant with effect from 1 January 2004, except for certain derogations allowing for the possible continued application of the Conventions in specified cases.[38] Finally, the driving disqualification Convention has only been ratified by a small number of Member States, although some of those states apply it in advance of its entry into force.[39]

In most cases, the Council adopted an explanatory report on interpretation of Conventions and Protocols, but the interpretation advocated by such reports is only persuasive, not mandatory.[40] It should be kept in mind that the Conventions did not apply automatically to the ten Member States that joined the EU in 2004 as from 1 May 2004. Instead, the newer Member States had to accede to the Conventions;[41] the ratification position has been set out above. On the other hand, the Conventions applied to Romania and Bulgaria pursuant to Council Decisions adopted following their accession to the EU.[42]

Thirty-nine Joint Actions were adopted during the Maastricht period. They largely concerned criminal law and policing, with a few (ten) addressing asylum funding or aspects of visas or immigration law. None concerned civil cooperation. Only sixteen are still in force,[43] and one of those will be repealed as from late 2010.[44] Twelve Joint Actions are no longer in force because they had lapsed once the funding programmes they established came to an end or were replaced,[45] and two others lapsed once Europol began operations.[46] The two Joint Actions regarding a uniform residence permit and airport transit visas were replaced by EC Regulations;[47] three other Joint Actions were replaced by Framework

---

[37] For ratification and application details, see Appendix I.

[38] [2002] OJ L 190/1. See 9.5.2 below.

[39] For ratification and application details, see Appendix I.

[40] For instance, see Case 157/80 *Rinkau* [1980] ECR 1391 on the explanatory report to the Brussels Convention. The Court of Justice has taken into account the explanatory report to a third pillar Convention in one case: Case C-388/08 PPU *Leymann and Pustovarov* [2008] ECR I-8993, para 74. No reports were drawn up for the Europol and CIS Conventions or their Protocols, or the Court of Justice Protocol to the fraud Convention. For a list of these explanatory reports, see Appendix I.   [41] See further 2.2.5.3 below.

[42] Ibid.   [43] For the list of Joint Actions still in force, see Appendix II.

[44] Joint Action on racism and xenophobia ([1996] OJ L 185/5), repealed by Art 11 of the Framework Decision on racism and xenophobia ([2008] OJ L 328/55) as from 28 Nov 2010.

[45] See 2.6 below. Technically, one of these twelve (establishing the 'Sherlock' programme) did not lapse as such, but rather was repealed by the Joint Action establishing the 'Odysseus' programme (see 2.6 below).   [46] See 12.8 below.

[47] See further 4.7 and 6.9 below.

Decisions;[48] three were replaced by Decisions;[49] and the unpublished Joint Action on the 'Balkan Drug Route' is assumed to have lapsed.[50] Of the sixteen remaining Joint Actions, one has been amended by a Framework Decision.[51]

Joint Positions fell into desuetude, with only two ever adopted.[52] A further three were apparently adopted, but it was not clear whether these were instead 'Common Positions' as provided for by Article K.5.[53] The Council also adopted a number of Decisions and many soft-law Resolutions, Conclusions, and Recommendations during the Maastricht period.

What was the legal effect of these measures? As noted above, Conventions were an established instrument of public international law, so there was no doubt that they were binding on each Member State at international level once ratified. But in the absence of any indication that the EU Treaty aimed (at the time) to create a supranational legal system like the Community's, it was presumably still left up to each Member State to determine the legal effect of a Convention in its national law.

There was ongoing controversy over the legal effect of Joint Actions, with thirteen of the first fifteen Member States backing the Council legal service's view that all Joint Actions were 'obligatory in law and that the extent of the obligation on the Member States depends on the content and the terms of each Joint Action', and two (the UK and Portugal) arguing that Joint Actions 'were not automatically...legally binding...the whole question of whether [a Joint Action] was legally binding depended on its actual text'.[54] The Council legal service invited the Court of Justice to settle this point in a legal action brought by the Commission to annul a Joint Action, but the ECJ implicitly (and rightly) followed its Advocate General's advice that the issue was irrelevant to the case

[48] The Joint Actions on trafficking in persons and sexual exploitation, private corruption, and organized crime (respectively [1997] OJ L 63/2, [1998] OJ L 358/2, and [1998] OJ L 351/1); for the replacement Framework Decisions, see [2002] OJ L 203/1, [2004] OJ L 13/44, [2003] OJ L 192/54, and [2008] OJ L 300/42. On these measures, see 10.5.1.2 below.

[49] The Decisions on liaison officers ([2003] OJ L 67/27; see 12.6.3 below), synthetic drugs ([2005] OJ L 127/32; see 10.5.1.2 below), and the European Judicial Network ([2008] OJ L 348/130; see 9.9 below), replacing Joint Actions on the same topics (respectively [1996] OJ L 268/2, [1997] OJ L 167/1, and [1998] OJ L 191/4).

[50] This Joint Action was unpublished; see the press release of the Fisheries Council, 19–20 Dec 1996.

[51] The Joint Action on money laundering ([1998] OJ L 333/1), as amended by Art 5 of the Framework Decision on money laundering ([2001] OJ L 182/1). See 9.6.2 and 9.7.4 below.

[52] Joint Position on the definition of 'refugee' ([1996] OJ L 63/2) and on joint training of airline staff and joint assistance in non-EU airports ([1996] OJ L 281/1). These measures have not been repealed.

[53] [1997] OJ L 279/1; [1997] OJ L 320/1; and [1999] OJ L 87/1. The first two concerned planned OECD and Council of Europe Conventions on corruption, and the third concerned a planned UN Convention on organized crime. They have never been repealed, but are obsolete as the treaties in question have now been drawn up.

[54] Outcome of proceedings of K.4 Committee of 7 Apr 1995 (Council doc 6684/95, 4 May 1995).

before it.[55] In practice, most Joint Actions appeared to use mandatory language, although not necessarily in every clause. As for Joint Positions, it is not clear what legal effect they had; the Joint Position on the definition of 'refugee' stated expressly that it would 'not bind the legislative authorities or affect decisions of the judicial authorities of the Member States'.[56] The Council appeared to believe that Common Positions could bind Member States.[57]

In any event, the legal effect of these third pillar measures will change if they are amended after the entry into force of the Treaty of Lisbon, pursuant to the transitional rules established by that Treaty. Similarly, the Maastricht rules on the jurisdiction of the Court of Justice over third pillar measures remain relevant until 1 December 2014, the end of the transitional period established by the Treaty of Lisbon as regards this issue, after which the general rules on the Court's jurisdiction will apply.[58]

During the Maastricht era, the Court had no *mandatory* jurisdiction over third pillar matters.[59] However, Article K.3(2)(c) EU provided that the Court *could* be given jurisdiction to interpret or settle disputes concerning Conventions, 'in accordance with such arrangements' as each Convention might (or might not) lay down. There was no provision for jurisdiction of the Court over any other third pillar measures. In practice, there were fierce disputes between the Member States on the role of the Court of Justice in third pillar Conventions not long after the Maastricht Treaty entered into force. Eventually this issue was settled by agreement in 1996 on standard rules to be used for criminal law and policing Conventions, beginning with the Europol, CIS, and fraud Conventions.[60] Three further Conventions on criminal and customs cooperation (concerning corruption, driving disqualifications, and customs operations) also ultimately contained a role for the Court in receiving preliminary rulings concerning each Convention.[61] On the other hand, the Court was not given jurisdiction to interpret the two extradition Conventions (which have not entered into force), although it nonetheless touched on their interpretation in the context of cases concerning the Framework Decision on the European Arrest Warrant, which replaced them for most purposes.[62] The Protocol to the Europol Convention concerning the privileges and immunities of Europol staff also precluded any

---

[55] Case C-170/96 *Commission v Council* [1998] ECR I-2763.   [56] See n 52 above.

[57] For instance, see the text of the Common Position on the UN organized crime Convention (n 53 above).   [58] See 2.2.3.3 below.

[59] For further details of the Court's jurisdiction during this period, see the first edition of this book, pp 27–9, and S Peers, 'Who's Judging the Watchmen?' The Judicial System of the Area of Freedom, Security and Justice' (2000) 18 YEL 337 at 343–50.

[60] See Protocols to these Conventions (n 26 above). The Court of Justice Protocol to the fraud Convention also applies to the substantive Protocols to that Convention (n 27 above).

[61] See n 35 above.

[62] Cases C-296/08 *Santesteban Goicoechea* [2008] ECR I-6307 and *Leymann and Pustovarov* (n 40 above). On the substance of these cases, see 9.5.2 below.

role for the Court of Justice, although this restriction became moot following the replacement of this Protocol, along with the main Europol Convention, by a third pillar Decision as from the start of 2010.[63] In the particular case of the CIS Convention, a further Protocol was agreed after the entry into force of the Treaty of Amsterdam;[64] this Protocol is presumably subject, for the transitional period set out in the Treaty of Lisbon, to the standard rules on the Court's jurisdiction over third pillar measures set out in that Treaty, until it is replaced also by a third pillar Decision with effect from 27 May 2011.[65]

In each case, the Court can settle disputes between Member States on the interpretation or application of the Convention, if a dispute has not been settled within the Council after six months. Also, the Court has varying forms of jurisdiction over disputes between the Commission and the Member States on the interpretation or application of the Conventions. As for references from national courts, there was an agreement to disagree. Member States can either provide for no jurisdiction at all for the Court of Justice, or permit only final courts to refer questions, or permit all courts or tribunals to refer questions. They can also compel their final court(s) to refer a question. It seems logical that where measures have been adopted to implement a Convention, the Court also has jurisdiction to interpret those measures. This is confirmed by the case law on Europol staff disputes, interpreting Europol's staff Regulations, which were adopted pursuant to the previous Europol Convention.[66] In the view of the Commission, the rules on the Court's jurisdiction of Conventions adopted before the entry into force of the Treaty of Amsterdam were replaced automatically by the Treaty of Amsterdam rules regarding the Court's jurisdiction,[67] but this interpretation should be rejected in the absence of any express wording to this effect, given that Conventions are independent treaties.

Two civil law Conventions agreed during the Maastricht period provided for *sui generis* jurisdiction for the Court of Justice.[68] However, these two Conventions were replaced before they ever entered into force by EC Regulations agreed shortly after the entry into force of the Treaty of Amsterdam,[69] and so their rules on the Court's jurisdiction are not further considered here as they were ultimately irrelevant. However, two earlier civil cooperation Conventions which did enter

---

[63] See n 31 above.   [64] See n 35 above. On this Protocol, see 2.2.2.2 below.

[65] See n 36 above.

[66] For instance, see Cases T-143/03 *Smit* [2005] ECR II-171 and T-258/03 *Mausolf* [2005] ECR II-189.

[67] See the Commission communication on application of the PFI Convention (COM (2008) 77, 14 Feb 2008) and the attached staff working paper (SEC (2008) 188, 14 Feb 2008, p 16).

[68] The Conventions and Protocols on the service of documents and matrimonial matters (nn 25 and 26 above).

[69] Regs 1347/2000 on jurisdiction over, and enforcement of, matrimonial and custody judgments ([2000] OJ L 160/19) and 1348/2000 on service of documents ([2000] OJ L 160/37). See further ch 8.

into force were subject to special rules on the jurisdiction of the Court of Justice, pursuant to separate Protocols: the Brussels Convention on civil jurisdiction and recognition of civil and commercial judgments and the Rome Convention on conflict of laws in contract.[70] These Conventions have both now been replaced by EC Regulations,[71] entailing eventually the application of the usual rules on the Court of Justice's jurisdiction (after the entry into force of the Treaty of Lisbon). However, it should be noted that the Brussels Convention still applies to litigation commenced before the replacement Regulation applied,[72] and the Rome Convention still applies to contracts concluded before the replacement Regulation applied,[73] as well as to Denmark.[74] In practice, over a hundred cases on the Brussels Convention were referred to the Court of Justice from national courts since the relevant Protocol to that Convention entered into force on 1 September 1975, and two cases have been referred to the Court of Justice regarding the Rome Convention.[75]

Finally, as for the Court's jurisdiction over pre-Amsterdam third pillar measures in practice, to date the only cases to reach the EU courts have concerned staff disputes against Europol.[76]

2.2.2. Treaty of Amsterdam

During negotiation of the Treaty of Amsterdam,[77] amendments to the JHA provisions of the TEU became a key issue, in particular on the grounds that: the objectives of JHA cooperation were not clear; the institutional roles were ill-defined and left in part for future negotiation; the legal effect of the new instruments was ambiguous; and aspects of the third pillar/first pillar borderline were controversial.

However, Member States were split on the issue of how decisively to introduce elements of the Community method to this area, and how much intergovernmentalism to retain. Also, the Member States participating in the Schengen

---

[70] See the consolidated texts of the Brussels Convention and Protocols ([1998] OJ C 27/1) and the Rome Convention and its Protocols ([2005] OJ C 334/1). The latter Convention and its Protocols have been extended to the Member States which joined the EU in 2004 and 2007: see [2005] OJ C 169/1 and [2007] OJ L 347/1.

[71] Regs 44/2001 ([2001] OJ L 12/1) and 593/2008 ([2008] OJ L 177/6).

[72] The date of application of Reg 44/2001 was 1 Mar 2002 (Art 76). The Brussels Convention was replaced as regards Denmark only later, by a treaty between Denmark and the EC that applied from 1 July 2007 ([2005] OJ L 299/61; [2006] OJ L 120/22). See further 2.2.5.2 below.

[73] Reg 593/2008 applied from 17 Dec 2009 (Art 28).

[74] Denmark is not covered by Reg 593/2008 due to its opt-out from EU civil law (see 2.2.5.2 below).

[75] Case C-133/08 *ICF* [2009] ECR I-9687 and C-29/10 *Koelzsch*, pending. The relevant Protocols concerning the Court's jurisdiction over the Rome Convention entered into force 1 Aug 2004, and Ireland opted out of them.   [76] See n 66 above.

[77] [1997] OJ C 340; in force 1 May 1999.

Convention wanted to integrate the Convention and its associated implementing measures (the Schengen *acquis*) into the EU legal system. However, the UK and Ireland were not participants in the Schengen rules, and one Schengen participant (Denmark) had reservations about the legal effect of integrating portions of the Schengen *acquis* into EC law, consistent with its previous objections to the transfer of any third pillar matters to the first pillar.[78] Furthermore, most Member States wished to confirm that the EC Treaty required the abolition of all internal border controls,[79] but the UK and Ireland still resisted this interpretation.

The result was a complex compromise, establishing two different forms of modified intergovernmentalism, establishing opt-outs for the UK, Ireland, and Denmark, and providing for specific rules for the integration of the Schengen *acquis* into the EU legal system. Most fundamentally, the framework for JHA was split up during this period between the rules governing the adoption of immigration, asylum, and civil law measures on the one hand, and the rules on the adoption of policing and criminal law measures, on the other. The former issues were transferred to the first pillar, where they were addressed by new rules inserted as Title IV of Part Three of the EC Treaty ('Title IV');[80] these new rules also included the visa issues which were previously the subject of Article 100c and 100d EC.[81] The latter issues were still addressed within the framework of the third pillar, but the relevant rules were comprehensively amended.[82] The Treaty of Nice subsequently made limited amendments to each set of rules.[83]

One particular feature of JHA cooperation since the Treaty of Amsterdam is the role played by the European Council, the formal name for the regular summit meetings of EU leaders, which became an official EU institution with the entry into force of the Treaty of Lisbon.[84] The European Council had long had a role approving specific JHA measures and action plans in certain JHA areas (such as an immigration and asylum plan approved by the Maastricht European Council in 1991). In 1998, the European Council became further involved in the detail, approving an action plan for implementing the new JHA provisions of the Treaty of Amsterdam.[85] Subsequently, in autumn 1999, the European Council held a special summit devoted to JHA issues in Tampere (a town in Finland), adopt-

---

[78] See 2.2.5.2 below.   [79] Art 7a EC, subsequently Art 14 EC, and now Art 26 TFEU.

[80] Arts 61–69 EC.

[81] Arts 100c and 100d EC were therefore repealed by the Treaty of Amsterdam.

[82] Previous Arts 29–42 TEU (previous Title VI of the TEU).

[83] [2001] OJ C 80; in force 1 Feb 2003. The Treaty added Art 67(5) EC to Title IV, as well as a Protocol relating to Art 66 EC. Within the third pillar, it amended Art 29 TEU, added a new Art 31(2) TEU, and revised the rules relating to enhanced cooperation (Arts 40, 40a, and 40b replaced Art 40 TEU).

[84] Art 15, revised TEU, and see also Art 68 TFEU, discussed further below (2.2.3.2). Before the Treaty of Lisbon, see the previous Art 4 TEU. It should be stressed that the European Council is a distinct body from the *Council*.

[85] [1999] OJ C 19. This became known as the 'Vienna' Action Plan, due to the location of the relevant European Council.

ing a further plan which largely set out broad political principles, in particular concerning asylum, migration, and criminal law (for instance, endorsing the principle of mutual recognition as the 'cornerstone' of EU criminal law measures), which are referred to further throughout Chapters 3–12 of this book. JHA issues played a greater or lesser role at a number of later summits, which included a special summit called in the wake of the terrorist attacks of September 11, 2001, a review of the implementation of the Tampere conclusions at the Laeken summit of December 2001, and a focus on immigration and asylum issues at the Seville summit of June 2002.

Following the end of the five-year transitional period set out in the Treaty of Amsterdam, it was considered that it was time to adopt a new policy plan, and so the 'Hague Programme', named after the location of the informal meeting of JHA ministers which agreed most of the text, was adopted by the European Council of November 2004.[86] Subsequently, the European Council of June 2005 took note of an action plan to implement the Hague Programme, which had been adopted by the JHA Council, on the basis of a draft by the Commission.[87]

In general, the role of the 'supranational' EU institutions (the Commission, the EP, and the EU courts) increased with the entry into force of the Treaty of Amsterdam and increased further in practice after that, as evidenced in particular by the Commission's decision to create a Directorate General for Justice and Home Affairs in 2000. Nevertheless, Member States still retained greater control over all aspects of JHA integration than they did over economic integration within the Community framework.

2.2.2.1. Immigration, asylum, and civil law

Although Community instruments (principally Directives and Regulations) were now used in this field, the decision-making rules in Title IV EC remained at first, from a political point of view, essentially intergovernmental, at least for an initial five-year transitional period, which ended on 1 May 2004 (coincidentally the same date as the enlargement of the EU from fifteen to twenty-five Member States).[88] During this transitional period, the Commission shared its usual right of initiative with any individual Member State. The Council still continued to act by unanimity, following consultation with the EP, except for the issues (visa list, visa format, emergency measures) which were already subject to QMV in the Council by the end of the Maastricht period. At the end of the transitional period, QMV in the Council and co-decision for the EP applied immediately to measures concerning the conditions and procedures for issuing visas, and the rules on a uniform visa, but any further change to decision-making in the Council and EP was subject to a further decision which the Council had to adopt unanimously.[89] Late in 2004, it was

---

[86] [2005] OJ C 53.   [87] [2005] OJ C 198/1.
[88] Art 67 EC, now repealed by the Treaty of Lisbon.   [89] See Art 67(2) EC.

agreed as part of the Hague Programme that the Council would adopt a decision changing the rules to apply QMV and co-decision to all Title IV matters except legal migration and family law, which remained subject to unanimity in Council and consultation of the EP, and visa lists and visa formats, which remained subject to QMV in Council with consultation of the EP.[90] This Decision took effect from 1 January 2005.[91]

In the meantime, the Treaty of Nice had amended the decision-making rules so that from its entry into force, civil law measures (except family law) were already subject to QMV and co-decision, and the decision-making rules on asylum matters (except for burden-sharing between Member States) would shift to QMV and co-decision as soon as the Council adopted EC measures 'defining the common rules and basic principles' on asylum issues.[92] The Treaty of Nice also added a Protocol to the EC Treaty which required the Council to act by QMV, consulting the EP, when adopting measures on administrative cooperation within the scope of Title IV.[93]

This remained the position until the entry into force of the Treaty of Lisbon, as the Commission's suggestions to extend QMV and co-decision to legal migration and to a specific aspect of family law (maintenance proceedings) were not accepted by the Council.[94]

As for implementing measures, Title IV was covered by the standard rule in Article 202 EC (as it was then) that the Commission should in principle have power to adopt measures implementing EC legislation at Community level, assisted by various committees of Member States' representatives ('comitology committees'), but in special circumstances the power to adopt implementing measures can be conferred upon the Council.[95] The case law of the Court of Justice made clear that basic rules could not be the subject of implementing measures, but must be set out following the full legislative process, and that implementing measures could not be ultra vires the powers delegated by the parent measure.[96] There was a basic decision of the Council setting out the types of committee which assist

---

[90] Emergency measures (Art 64(2) EC) remained subject to QMV in Council with no EP involvement.

[91] [2004] OJ L 396/45. For discussion, see S Peers, 'Transforming Decision-Making on EC Immigration and Asylum Law' (2005) 30 ELRev 283.

[92] Art 67(5). On the interpretation of this clause, see Case C-133/06 *EP v Council* [2008] ECR I-3189. The decision-making rules on asylum burden-sharing shifted separately to QMV and co-decision on 1 Jan 2005 (see ibid).   [93] Art 66 EC.

[94] See respectively COM (2006) 331, 28 June 2006 and COM (2005) 648, 15 Dec 2005.

[95] From a large literature, see M Andenas and V Turk, eds, *Delegated Legislation and the Role of Committees in the EU* (Kluwer, 2000); C Joerges and E Vos, eds, *EU Committees: Social Regulation, Law and Politics* (Hart, 1999); and K Lenaerts and Verhoeven, 'Towards a Legal Framework for Executive Rule-Making in the EU? The Contribution of the new Comitology Decision' (2000) 37 CMLRev 645.

[96] See particularly Case 25/70 *Koster* [1970] ECR 1161 and Case C-93/00 *EP v Council* [2001] ECR I-10119.

the Commission (advisory, regulatory, and management committees),[97] and the EC legislative process was rife with disputes about the form of committee to be established: sometimes these disputes reached the Court of Justice.[98]

In practice, in the area of civil law, implementing powers were conferred upon the Commission,[99] with only one exception: the Regulation on insolvency proceedings.[100] The question of implementing measures was more controversial in the area of immigration and asylum law, where the Council gave power to itself (and, in part, the individual Member States) to adopt measures amending two key provisions of the Schengen *acquis* which were integrated into EC law: the Common Consular Instructions for visa applications and the Common Manual concerning external borders.[101] The Council also gave itself the most important powers to adopt measures implementing the Regulation establishing Eurodac (the system for comparing asylum seekers' fingerprints).[102] However, otherwise the Council was willing to apply the normal rule and confer powers on the Commission, except as regards the decision to apply the temporary protection Directive and two common lists of countries which could be adopted to supplement the asylum procedures Directive.[103]

Some of these exceptions from the normal rule were challenged. Firstly, the Commission disputed the decision of the Council to confer power upon itself and the Member States to implement the Schengen visas and borders rules before the Court of Justice. Ultimately, the Commission lost this case, as the Court upheld the Council's decision, inter alia because in 2001 the issues had until recently been dealt with pursuant to the 'third pillar', the transitional period for Title IV decision-making was still in force in 2001, the subject matter being delegated was clearly circumscribed, and the Council had committed itself to review the delegation to itself by 2004.[104] Ultimately, when the Schengen measures were replaced by EU codes in 2006 and 2009, these special powers were replaced by

---

[97] See initially Decision 87/393 ([1987] OJ L 197/33), replaced by Decision 1999/468 ([1999] OJ L 184/33) as amended in 2006 ([2006] OJ L 200/11).

[98] Cases C-378/00 *Commission v EP and Council* [2003] ECR I-937; C-122/04 *Commission v EP and Council* [2006] ECR I-2001; C-443/05 P *Common Market Fertilizers v Commission* [2007] ECR I-7209; and C-14/06 and C-295/06 *Parliament v Commission* [2008] ECR I-1649.

[99] Arts 44 and 45, Reg 1347/2000 (n 69 above); Arts 17 and 18, Reg 1348/2000 (idem); Arts 74 and 75, Reg 44/2001 (n 71 above); Arts 11 and 12, Reg 290/2001 ([2001] OJ L 43/1); Arts 19 and 20, Reg 1206/2001 ([2001] OJ L 174/1); Arts 12 and 13, Reg 743/2002 ([2002] OJ L 115/1); Art 17, Dir 2003/8 ([2003] OJ L 26/41); Art 70, Reg 2201/2003 ([2003] OJ L 338/1); Art 32, Reg 805/2004 ([2004] OJ L 143/15); Art 11 of the 2007 civil law funding decision ([2007] OJ L 257/16); and Art 73, Reg 4/2009 ([2009] OJ L 7/1).

[100] Art 45 of Reg 1346/2000 ([2000] OJ L 160/1), which provides for the implementing measures to be adopted by the Council by QMV on the initiative of a Member State or the Commission.

[101] Regs 789 and 790/2001 ([2001] OJ L 116/2 and 5).

[102] Arts 22 and 23, Reg 2725/2000 ([2000] OJ L 316/1).

[103] Art 5, Dir 2001/55 ([2001] OJ L 212/12) and Arts 29 and 36(3), Dir 2005/85 ([2005] OJ L 326/13). On the substance, see 5.6 and 5.7 below.

[104] Case C-257/01 *Commission v Council* [2005] ECR I-345.

the normal rule that the power to adopt implementing measures is conferred upon the Commission.[105]

Secondly, the EP successfully challenged before the Court of Justice the validity of the special powers which the Council had awarded itself to adopt common lists implementing the asylum procedures Directive. The Court of Justice ruled in this case that EC law did not include a power to adopt secondary legislative acts (as distinct from implementing measures), which the Council had argued for.[106] Finally, the special rules on implementing the Eurodac Regulation would be dropped if proposed amendments to the Regulation are adopted.[107]

The basic rules governing comitology committees were amended in 2006 to establish a new 'regulatory procedure with scrutiny' (RPS), which gave the EP and the Council extra scrutiny powers where a measure adopted pursuant to the co-decision procedure 'provides for the adoption of measures of general scope designed to amend non-essential elements of that instrument, inter alia by deleting some of those elements or by supplementing the instrument by the addition of new non-essential elements'.[108] These new rules were applied to pre-existing Title IV legislation which was adopted or which *would* (by 2006) have been adopted by means of the co-decision process.[109] The rules were also applied to Title IV legislation adopted subsequently, up until the entry into force of the Treaty of Lisbon.[110] After that point, the RPS system was replaced by a new system of 'delegated acts', discussed further below,[111] although the provisions in pre-existing legislation providing for the RPS process are still applicable until they are amended. Pending proposals providing for the use of the RPS procedure will therefore also have to be amended before their adoption.[112]

In the event that Member States' representatives blocked a draft Commission implementing measure, special procedures applied as regards the possible adoption

---

[105] See Art 33 of the borders code, Reg 562/2006 ([2006] OJ L 105/1), and Art 52 of the visa code, Reg 810/2009 ([2009] OJ L 243/1).

[106] Case C-133/06, n 92 above. The Commission's proposal to amend the asylum procedures Directive would drop these provisions from the text (COM (2009) 554, 21 Oct 2009).

[107] COM (2008) 825, 3 Dec 2008, replaced by COM (2009) 342, 10 Sep 2009.

[108] [2006] OJ L 200/11.

[109] First of all, an amendment to this end was added to the Borders Code (n 105 above), which was one of the priority measures for application of the RPS rules (Reg 296/2008, [2008] OJ L 97/60; on the priority measures issue, see the statement in [2006] OJ C 255/1, point (e)). Next, an 'omnibus' measure, Reg 1103/2008 ([2008] OJ L 304/80), revised the 'Dublin II' Regulation (Reg 343/2003, [2003] OJ L 50/1) and three civil law measures (Regs 44/2001, 1206/2001, and 805/2004, nn 71 and 100 above) to the same end. A dispute over the adoption of a measure implementing the Borders Code is pending before the Court of Justice: Case C-355/10 *EP v Council*.

[110] As regards civil law, see: Reg 1896/2006 on orders for payment ([2006] OJ L 399/1, Art 31); Reg 862/2007 on small claims ([2007] OJ L 199/1, Arts 26 and 27); and Reg 1393/2007 on the service of documents ([2007] OJ L 324/79, Art 18), which replaced Reg 1348/2000 (n 69 above). As regards immigration and asylum law, see the visa code, Reg 810/2009 (n 105 above), Art 52(3).

[111] 2.2.3.1.

[112] See Art 40(3) of the proposed Regulation on responsibility for asylum applications (COM (2008) 820, 3 Dec 2008).

of an implementing measure by the Council instead. These special rules were invoked as regards JHA measures, first as regards the adoption of rules concerning tests related to the development of the second-generation Schengen Information System, and then as regards rules concerning the coordination of maritime surveillance by Frontex, the EU's border control agency.[113]

As for the Court of Justice, it was also subject to a distinct regime as compared to the rest of the first pillar (or 'EC law', as it was then). While the normal rules on the Court's jurisdiction as regards infringement actions and annulment actions were applicable to Title IV, its jurisdiction over references for a preliminary ruling from national courts were highly curtailed. Most importantly, the Court was only competent to receive references from the final courts of Member States, not from every court or tribunal.[114] Another special rule on the Court provided that it had no jurisdiction 'to rule on any measure or decision taken pursuant to Article 62(1) [concerning the abolition of internal border controls] relating to the maintenance of law and order and the safeguarding of internal security'.[115] Finally, the Treaty provided for the Council, the Commission, or a Member State to request an interpretation from the Court of either Title IV of the Treaty or the interpretation of any measure based on it.[116] In practice, the Court was never asked to interpret the exclusion relating to the abolition of border controls, or sent a request for interpretation pursuant to the final special rule.

Although the Treaty provided that the Council had to 'adapt' the rules relating to the Court's jurisdiction after the end of the initial five-year transition period in 2004, the Council failed to do so, even after the Commission proposed a Decision to this effect in 2006.[117] So the Court's jurisdiction over Title IV matters remained curtailed until the entry into force of the Treaty of Lisbon.

However, the Council was able to agree in December 2007 on the establishment of an emergency procedure to govern some JHA cases referred from national courts, known in practice as the 'PPU' procedure.[118] This special procedure was used particularly in child abduction cases and cases involving the legality of continued detention.[119]

---

[113] Council Reg 189/2008 ([2008] OJ L 57/1) and Decision 2010/252 ([2010] OJ L 111/20).

[114] Art 68(1) EC, derogating from Art 234 EC (now Art 267 TFEU). However, the wording of Art 68(1) did suggest that there was an obligation to send references in such cases ('shall').

[115] Art 68(2) EC.   [116] Art 68(3).

[117] See COM (2006) 346, 28 June 2006. This proposal has not been withdrawn, although it is now obsolete (see Annex 4 of COM (2009) 665, 2 Dec 2009).

[118] Amendments to the Court's Statute and Rules of Procedure, and related statement [2008] OJ L 24/42, 39, and 44. For discussion of this procedure in practice, see C Barnard, 'The PPU: Is it worth the candle? An early assessment' (2009) 34 ELRev 281.

[119] The Title IV cases concerned were Cases: C-195/08 *Rinau* [2008] ECR I-5271, on the rules in Reg 2201/2003 ([2003] OJ L 338/1) on child abduction; C-357/09 PPU *Kadzoev*, judgment of 30 Nov 2009, not yet reported (interpretation of the immigration detention rules in the Returns Directive—Dir 2008/115, [2008] OJ L 348/98); and C-403/09 PPU *Detiček*, 23 Dec 2009, not yet

In practice, despite the restrictions on the Court's jurisdiction regarding Title IV, final national courts sent an increasing number of references on EC civil law legislation, totalling fifty-three references by the time the Treaty of Lisbon entered into force.[120] On the other hand, there were significantly fewer references relating to immigration and asylum law, with a total of only eleven cases before the Treaty of Lisbon came into force.[121] It should also be noted that the Commission brought a number of infringement actions in this area, in particular to ensure that Member States implemented Title IV Directives,[122] and that a number of annulment actions were brought before the Court concerning inter-institutional disputes and questions relating to the UK's opt-out from Title IV measures.[123] Due to the overlap between the special rules on Title IV cases and the rules applying to the Court's non-JHA jurisdiction, there was a possibility of 'mixed jurisdiction', ie cases which arguably fell within the scope of both rules. This issue is considered further below.[124]

2.2.2.2. Policing and criminal law

As noted above, the rules governing the adoption of EU policing and criminal law in force before the Treaty of Lisbon retain more than historical interest after the entry into force of that Treaty, because of the transitional rules applicable to the legal effect of the measures adopted as well as the Court of Justice's jurisdiction over those measures.[125]

The basic rules on decision-making and legal instruments were set out in the previous Article 34 TEU. The Council still had to act unanimously when

reported, also concerning the child abduction rules in Reg 2201/2003. For the criminal law cases concerned, see 2.2.2.2 below.

[120] For details, see 8.2.2 below.

[121] Decided cases: C-241/05 *Bot* [2006] ECR I-9627 (Art 20 of Schengen Convention, on freedom to travel); C-19/08 *Petrosian* [2009] ECR I-495 (interpretation of 'Dublin II' Reg, Reg 343/2003, [2003] OJ L 50/1); C-465/07 *Elgafaji and Elgafaji* [2009] ECR I-921 (interpretation of Dir 2004/83 on refugee and subsidiary protection status, [2004] OJ L 304/12); C-139/08 *Kqiku* [2009] ECR I-2887 (transit legislation); C-261/08 *Zurita Garcia* and C-348/08 *Choque Cabrera*, judgment of 22 Oct 2009, not yet reported (interpretation of Borders Code and Schengen Convention); C-357/09 PPU *Kadzoev* (n 119 above); C-175/08 to C-179/08 *Abdulla and others*, judgment of 2 Mar 2010, not yet reported (Dir 2004/83); C-578/08 *Chakroun* (interpretation of Dir 2003/86 on family reunion, [2003] OJ L 251/12), judgment of 4 Mar 2010, not yet reported; and C-31/09 *Bolbol* (Dir 2004/83; judgment of 17 June 2010, not yet reported). Pending cases: C-57/09 and C-101/09 *B* and *D* (Dir 2004/83; opinion of 1 June 2010) and C-247/09 *Xhymshiti* (interpretation of Reg 859/2003 on social security for third-country nationals, [2003] OJ L 123/1).

[122] See chs 5–7 below.

[123] Cases: C-257/01 *Commission v Council* [2005] ECR I-345; C-540/03 *EP v Council* [2006] ECR I-5769; C-77/05 *UK v Council* [2007] ECR I-11459; C-137/05 *UK v Council* [2007] ECR I-11593; and C-133/06 *EP v Council* (n 92 above). See also Joined Cases C-317/04 and C-318/04 *EP v Council and Commission* [2006] ECR I-4721 and the challenge to a related third pillar Decision (Case C-482/08 *UK v Council*, pending, opinion of 24 June 2010).   [124] See 2.4.2.

[125] On the transitional rules, see 2.2.3.3 below.

adopting third pillar measures, but implementing measures had to be adopted by another form of vote (see below).

The Commission increased its power, gaining a shared initiative with the Member States for the items in the remaining third pillar. In practice, it was active in using this initiative, proposing many of the most important criminal law measures adopted by the Council.[126] As before, Member States holding the rotating Council Presidency were active in making proposals; in several cases, there were joint proposals from several Member States, particularly from several Member States holding the Council Presidency in succession.

As for the EP, Article 39 EU retained its Maastricht-era powers, but the Treaty of Amsterdam also added the right to be consulted by the Council before adopting most third pillar legal acts (with the exception of Common Positions—see below), within a time limit that the Council laid down, although this period had to be at least three months. However, as might be expected, the opinions of the EP had limited if any impact upon Council third pillar measures.

The Treaty required third pillar implementing measures to be adopted by the Council, by means of QMV for implementing Decisions and a two-thirds vote for implementing Conventions.[127] However, on several occasions the Council conferred implementing powers upon the Commission.[128] Was this legally possible? While in general conferring implementing powers upon the Commission appeared to be ruled out by the EU Treaty, it could be argued that where an EU measure regulated spending from the EC budget, the Commission had to be given the same powers of implementation as it generally enjoys regarding the implementation of spending measures, pursuant to Article 41(4) EU, which provided that if the Council spent EC budget money to implement a third pillar measure, the EC's budgetary procedure applied.[129] As regards measures implementing the Decision establishing the second-generation Schengen Information System (SIS II), it might exceptionally be argued that the Commission had to be (or at least could be) given powers to implement those third pillar measures which overlapped with parallel first pillar acts, for the sake of coherence and consistency.[130]

In practice, the use of Conventions was phased out after the Treaty of Amsterdam provisions entered into force. Only one new Convention was adopted, shortly

---

[126] See, for instance, the Framework Decisions on the European arrest warrant and on terrorism ([2002] OJ L 190/1 and [2002] OJ L 164/3; see 9.5.2 and 10.5.1.2 below).

[127] Art 34(2)(c) and (d), previous TEU.

[128] For example, see the Decisions on management of the project to establish a second-generation Schengen Information System (SIS II: [2001] OJ L 328/1), on implementation of the SIS II ([2007] OJ L 205/63), and on funding programmes (2.6 below).

[129] See also Art 268 EC, and by analogy, the general discussion below of the application of EC law principles to the third pillar.

[130] See the previous Art 3 EU. This argument is elaborated upon in S Peers, 'Salvation outside the Church: Judicial Protection in the Third Pillar after the *Pupino* and *SEGI* judgments' (2007) 44 CMLRev 883 at 906–908. See also the discussion of the Court's jurisdiction below.

after the Amsterdam provisions took effect,[131] along with five new Protocols to pre-existing Conventions.[132]

All of the six Conventions and Protocols adopted after the Treaty of Amsterdam entered into force, since that Treaty required that Conventions entered into force once at least half of the Member States had ratified them, with respect to the ratifying Member States, 'unless they provide otherwise'.[133] The 2000 Convention on mutual assistance and its Protocol needed eight of the first fifteen Member States to ratify them in order to enter into force,[134] and obtained the requisite number of ratifications in 2005, following which the Convention entered into force on 23 August 2005 and the Protocol entered into force on 6 October 2005.[135] However, several Member States have yet to ratify the Convention and/or the Protocol. Part of the mutual assistance Convention was implemented early by a Framework Decision; another Framework Decision will overlap with many of its provisions once it is implemented; and there is a proposal for a Directive in this area, which would, if adopted, largely replace the Convention and Protocol.[136]

The three Protocols amending the Europol Convention entered into force in spring 2007, after they were ratified by all Member States, but they were later repealed, along with the main Europol Convention, by a third pillar Decision, with effect from 1 January 2010.[137] Finally, the Protocol to the CIS Convention entered into force ninety days after eight of the first fifteen Member States ratified it,[138] which took place on 15 October 2007.[139] A few Member States have not yet, at the time of writing, ratified the Protocol.[140] This Protocol has also been repealed with effect from 27 May 2011, due to the replacement of the CIS Convention with a third pillar Decision.[141] It should be noted that the Court of Justice confirmed that the EU had the power to replace Conventions with Framework Decisions (and, by analogy, by Decisions as well).[142]

---

[131] Convention on mutual assistance on criminal matters ([2000] OJ C 197/1). See further 9.6.1 and 12.9 below.

[132] See three Protocols amending the Europol Convention ([2000] C 358/1, [2002] OJ C 312/1, and [2004] OJ C 2/1); the Protocol to EU Mutual Assistance Convention ([2001] OJ C 326/1); and the Protocol to the CIS Convention, regarding customs files ([2003] C 139/1).

[133] Art 34(2)(d), previous TEU.

[134] Art 27(3), 2000 Convention (n 131 above); Art 13(3), 2001 Protocol (n 132 above).

[135] For the ratification details, see Appendix I.

[136] See respectively: the Framework Decision on joint investigation teams ([2002] OJ L 162/1); the Framework Decision on the European evidence warrant ([2008] OJ L 350/72), which must be implemented by 19 Jan 2011 (Art 23(1)); and the proposed Directive establishing a European investigation order ([2010] OJ C 165/22). For details, see 12.9 and 9.6 below.

[137] The Decision establishing Europol, which repealed the three Protocols to the Europol Convention ([2009] OJ L 121/37).   [138] Art 2(3), CIS Protocol (n 132 above).

[139] Art 2(4), CIS Protocol (ibid).   [140] For the ratification details, see Appendix I.

[141] Art 35 of the Decision establishing the CIS ([2009] OJ L 323/20).

[142] See Case C-303/05 *Advocaten voor de Wereld* [2007] ECR I-3633.

With Conventions phased out, the Council became attracted instead to the instrument of Framework Decisions, in particular since they were binding upon Member States and applied by a certain date (generally two years at the latest) without the need for national treaty ratification procedures. In practice, the Council adopted a total of thirty-four Framework Decisions;[143] two more were agreed in principle but could not be adopted before the Treaty of Lisbon entered into force;[144] and active discussion on three others had to terminate when that Treaty entered into force.[145] Of the adopted Framework Decisions, two were annulled by the Court of Justice for encroaching upon EC competence,[146] but none were repealed before the entry into force of the Treaty of Lisbon, although there were two proposals under discussion at the time of the entry into force of that Treaty to replace existing Framework Decisions with new Framework Decisions.[147]

In particular, Framework Decisions were used for the harmonization of sub-stantive criminal law and for harmonization of both domestic criminal proce-dural law and for the adoption of rules on mutual recognition in criminal matters, with a few of them addressing police cooperation issues.

Decisions were frequently adopted during the 'Amsterdam era' of the third pillar, with the adoption of fifty-seven formal Decisions as provided for in the Treaty.[148] In practice, Decisions set up EU-wide bodies or networks or EU

---

[143] For a full list, see the Table of Legislation.

[144] Proposals for: a Framework Decision on the right to interpretation and translation in the framework of criminal proceedings (proposal in COM (2009) 338, 8 July 2009, agreed at the JHA Council of 23 Oct 2009; agreed text in Council doc 14792/2009, 23 Oct 2009); and a Framework Decision on trafficking in human beings (proposal in COM (2009) 136, 25 Mar 2009, largely agreed at the JHA Council of 23 Oct 2009; agreed text in Council doc 15011/09, 27 Oct 2009). After the Treaty of Lisbon entered into force, the first proposal was replaced both by an initia-tive of a group of Member States for a Directive ([2010] OJ C 69/1) and by a proposal from the Commission (COM (2010) 82, 9 Mar 2010) for a Directive, while the trafficking proposal was replaced by a new Commission proposal for a Directive (COM (2010) 95, 29 Mar 2010). The first proposal was agreed between the EP and Council in spring 2010 (Council doc 10984/10, 23 June 2010), and the trafficking proposal was agreed by the JHA Council in June 2010 (Council doc 10845/10, 10 June 2010).

[145] Proposals or initiatives for Framework Decisions on: passenger name records (COM (2007) 654, 6 Nov 2007); sexual exploitation and pornography (COM (2009) 135, 25 Mar 2009); and the transfer of criminal proceedings ([2009] OJ C 219/7). One of these proposals was subsequently replaced by a proposal for a Directive after the Treaty of Lisbon entered into force (sexual exploi-tation and pornography: COM (2010) 94, 29 Mar 2010). The Commission intends to propose a Directive on passenger name records in 2010: see the 2010 work programme (COM (2010) 135, 31 Mar 2010).

[146] These were the Framework Decisions on environmental crime and on shipping pollution (respectively [2003] OJ L 29/55 and [2005] OJ L 255/164), annulled respectively by Cases C-176/03 *Commission v Council* [2005] ECR I-7879 and C-440/05 *Commission v Council* [2007] ECR I-9097. Both measures were subsequently replaced by EC Directives: Dirs 2008/99 ([2008] OJ L 328/28) and 2009/123 ([2009] OJ L 280/52). See further 2.4.2 and 10.2.4 below.

[147] The proposals on trafficking in human beings and sexual exploitation and pornography (nn 144 and 145 above).

[148] For a full list, see the Table of Legislation.

funding programmes, or facilitate cross-border activity of national authorities.[149] In addition, the Council also adopted other types of Decisions, for instance to implement Conventions,[150] or to extend the scope of the Conventions on corruption and in order to sign or extend the scope of third pillar treaties.[151] At the time of entry into force of the Treaty of Lisbon, forty-three formal third pillar Decisions were still in force.[152] Thirteen Decisions had either been repealed and replaced by other measures, or had lapsed because they were concluded only for a limited period of time (because they related to funding programmes). Three more Decisions will be repealed once SIS II becomes operational,[153] and one Decision was the subject of a pending annulment action when the Treaty of Lisbon entered into force.[154]

Common Positions were used in several cases for their pre-Amsterdam purpose, to establish EU negotiating positions at international conferences.[155] This then entailed the application of Article 37 EU (since repealed by the Treaty of Lisbon), which specified that Member States had to 'defend' those Common Positions at 'international organisations and at international conferences in which they take part'. Article 37 was also used to coordinate positions without the adoption of a formal Common Position.[156] The Council also adopted Common Positions on other international matters, comprising one measure on the transfer of data to Interpol,[157] and a series of controversial Common Positions on anti-terrorism measures, which had a joint 'legal base' of the 'second pillar' and the

---

[149] For example, see the Decisions on Eurojust ([2002] OJ L 63/1), funding programmes (2.6 below), a network for protection of public figures ([2002] OJ L 333/1), and on the use of liaison officers ([2003] OJ L 76/27).

[150] On the measures implementing the Europol Convention, see 12.8 below.

[151] See respectively [2003] OJ L 226/27 (extending Convention to Gibraltar) and (for instance) [2003] OJ L 181/25 (treaty with USA) and [2009] OJ L 325/4 (extension in scope of agreement with USA).   [152] See Appendix II.

[153] Art 69 of the 2007 Decision establishing SIS II (n 128 above).

[154] The Decision on law enforcement access to the Visa Information System ([2008] OJ L 218/129), which was the subject of Case C-482/08 UK v Council, pending. The Advocate-General's opinion of 24 June 2010 supports the validity of the Decision.

[155] See the Common Positions on the proposed Council of Europe 'Cyber-crime' Convention ([1999] OJ L 142/1), on the proposed firearms Protocol to the UN Convention on organized crime ([2000] OJ L 37/1), and on the proposed UN Convention on corruption (Council docs 12837/2/01, 8897/4/02, and 12215/2/02, all dated 30 Oct 2003 (adopted 2001 and 2002), unpublished). The Council subsequently adopted a number of unpublished Common Positions setting out the EU position at conferences of parties to these Conventions. See Council docs: 15012/1/06 rev 1, 30 Nov 2006, concerning the corruption Convention, adopted by JHA Council, 4–5 Dec 2006; 11171/1/08, 22 Sep 2008, concerning the UN Convention against Transnational Organized Crime (UNTOC), adopted by the JHA Council, 25 Sep 2008; and 11452/2/09, 30 Sep 2009 adopted by the JHA Council on 23 Oct 2009, concerning the UN Convention against corruption. With the adoption of the relevant treaties, or following the relevant international meetings, these measures are all now redundant, although they have never been formally repealed.

[156] See 2.7 below.

[157] Common Position on transfer of data to Interpol ([2005] OJ L 27/61).

'third pillar'.[158] Only three of these Common Positions were still in force as of the entry into force of the Treaty of Lisbon.[159]

The legal effect of the types of third pillar instruments provided for in the Amsterdam version of the third pillar was, in two cases, expressly laid out.[160] Framework Decisions 'aim[ed] to approximat[e]...the laws and regulations of the Member States' and were 'binding on the Member States as to the result to be achieved but' left 'to the national authorities the choice of form and methods'. This second part of this definition was identical to the definition of Directives then set out in Article 249 EC (now Article 288 TFEU), except that it is also specified that Framework Decisions 'shall not entail direct effect'. Decisions could be adopted 'for any other purpose consistent with the objectives of [the third pillar]', excluding 'any approximation of the laws and regulations of the Member States'. These measures were also binding and did not entail direct effect. It should be emphasized that the previous EU Treaty third pillar rules apparently did not merely leave the legal effect of Decisions and Framework Decisions for each Member State to determine according to its rules on the effect of public international law within the domestic legal system, but rather appeared to harmonize the effect of those measures within national legal orders. In other words, even if a Member State is ordinarily 'monist', the rules appeared to preclude Framework Decisions and Decisions from having direct effect in its legal system. On the other hand, the rules were silent as to the legal effect of Conventions and Common Positions, although the Treaty specified that Common Positions shall 'define the approach of the Union to a particular matter'.

The Court of Justice has ruled on the legal effect of both Framework Decisions and Common Positions. The leading case on Framework Decisions is the 2005 judgment of the Court of Justice in *Pupino*, in which an Italian court asked the Court of Justice whether the Framework Decision on the rights of crime victims in criminal procedure had an 'indirect effect' equivalent to that of Directives.[161] The Court answered that it did, because of: the comparison between the definitions of EC Directives and EU Framework Decisions; the binding nature of Framework Decisions; the existence of the Court's jurisdiction (albeit less extensive than for EC law), which 'would be deprived of most of its useful effect if

---

[158] One concerns general policy in combatting terrorism ([2001] OJ L 344/90) and transposes relevant Security Council resolutions into EU law. The other concerns the application of specific measures to combat terrorism ([2001] OJ L 344/93), and has been implemented by further measures listing individuals and groups considered to be 'terrorist' by the Council and taking certain action against them. See further 12.4.5 and 2.2.3.2 below.

[159] The Common Positions on combating terrorism (ibid) and on the transfer of data to Interpol (n 157 above). On the 'legal base' for the subsequent amendments to the Common Position on the application of specific measures to combat terrorism, see 2.2.3.2 below.

[160] Art 34(2)(b) and 34(2)(c) EU.

[161] Case C-105/03 [2005] ECR I-5285. On the principle as it applies to Directives, see the case law beginning with Cases 14/83 *Von Colson and Kamann* [1984] ECR 1891 and Case C-105/89 *Marleasing* [1990] ECR I-4135.

individuals were not entitled to invoke framework decisions in order to obtain a conforming interpretation of national law before the courts of the Member States'; and the principle of loyalty to the Union as set out in Article 10 EC, which applied implicitly to the third pillar.[162]

However, the Court confirmed that, just like Directives, unimplemented Framework Decisions could not impose criminal liability upon individuals or aggravate such liability, for this would breach the principle of the legality of criminal law.[163] For those Framework Decisions that aim to harmonize substantive national criminal law,[164] this distinction is crucial. But the Court then ruled in *Pupino* that such a limitation did not apply to measures concerning criminal *procedure*: for such measures, national law must be interpreted in light of a Framework Decision unless that would entail a breach of the right to a fair trial.[165]

Subsequently, the Court elaborated on the nature of Framework Decisions as compared to other third pillar legal instruments in the *Advocaten voor de Wereld* judgment.[166] In this case, the Court ruled that the Framework Decision on the European Arrest Warrant took the correct legal form, given that this measure harmonized national laws as regards criminal law, and the Treaty did not confine the use of Framework Decisions to the issue of substantive criminal law. This measure could not have taken the form of a Decision, since Decisions cannot harmonize national law, or a Common Position, since such measures are limited to defining the Union's approach to a particular matter (see further below). It could have taken the form of a Convention, but since the Treaty did not establish any form of priority between third pillar instruments, the Council had a choice of whether to adopt a Framework Decision or a Convention, and could not be criticized for choosing to adopt a Framework Decision. Moreover, it was open to the Council to replace Conventions by means of Framework Decisions, as a more restrictive interpretation was not supported by the Treaty and would limit the effectiveness of the Council's power to adopt Framework Decisions.

As for Common Positions, the Court of Justice ruled on their legal effect in the case of *SEGI*,[167] which was an appeal from an order of the Court of First Instance which had rejected an action for damages from an organization which the EU had labelled as terrorist, by means of a Common Position. Since the organization was based inside the EU, the Union did not impose financial sanctions upon it, on

---

[162] Paras 31–43 of the judgment (ibid). Following the entry into force of the Treaty of Lisbon, the application of the loyalty principle to all areas of EU activity is explicit (Art 4(3), second and third sub-paragraphs, revised TEU).   [163] Paras 44 and 45 of the judgment (ibid).

[164] See 10.5 below.   [165] Paras 43–48, 58, and 59 of the judgment (n 161 above).

[166] Case C-303/05, n 142 above, paras 24–43.

[167] Cases C-354/04 P *Gestoras pro Amnistia* [2007] ECR I-1579 and C-355/04 P *SEGI* [2007] ECR I-1657.

the assumption that before the entry into force of the Treaty of Lisbon, it lacked competence to do this.[168] The Court of Justice ruled that:[169]

Article 34 EU provides that the Council may adopt acts varying in nature and scope . . . A common position requires the compliance of the Member States by virtue of the principle of the duty to cooperate in good faith, which means in particular that Member States are to take all appropriate measures, whether general or particular, to ensure fulfilment of their obligations under European Union law (see *Pupino*, paragraph 42).

Article 37 EU thus provides that the Member States are to defend the common positions '[w]ithin international organisations and at international conferences in which they take part'. However, a common position is not supposed to produce of itself legal effects in relation to third parties.

It can be presumed that Conventions, as an established instrument of public international law, are binding. *A contrario* reasoning from the Treaty provisions defining Framework Decisions and Decisions, and the Court's judgment in *Advocaten voor de Wereld*, suggests that Conventions could be used to approximate national laws *or* for any other purpose consistent with Title VI, or for a combination of these purposes.

Although the Court of Justice has not ruled directly on the legal status and effect of third pillar Decisions, it follows from the *Advocaten voor de Wereld* judgment that they could not be used to harmonize national law, but could (by analogy) replace previously adopted Conventions. In fact, the Council adopted Decisions to replace the Conventions establishing Europol and the Customs Information System, and their related Protocols.[170]

Other 'first pillar' principles applicable to the third pillar include the rule that provisions of legislation which do not refer to national law should be interpreted as having an autonomous Union-wide meaning,[171] the rule that statements by the EU institutions cannot normally be used to interpret binding acts,[172] and the principle that new procedural rules apply to procedures pending at the time when those new rules enter into force.[173]

The Court of Justice has not ruled on whether the principle of supremacy applies to the third pillar. The best view is that it does not, given the clear intention of the drafters of the Maastricht Treaty and the Treaty of Amsterdam to provide for a different legal system as compared to the Community legal order.[174]

---

[168] More precisely, the organization was only subject to Art 4 of the Common Position on the application of specific measures to combat terrorism (n 158 above). The competence to adopt financial sanctions against such alleged terrorists is now arguably conferred by Art 75 TFEU: see further 2.2.3.2 below.   [169] Para 52 of the *SEGI* judgment (n 167 above).

[170] [2009] OJ L 121/37 and [2009] OJ L 323/20.

[171] Case C-66/08 *Koslowski* [2008] ECR I-6041, paras 42–43. See also the opinion of 7 Sep 2010 in Case C-261/09 *Mantello*, pending.   [172] *SEGI* (n 167 above), paras 58–62.

[173] Case C-467/05 *Dell'Orto* [2007] ECR I-5557, paras 47–49.

[174] For this argument, see 'Salvation outside the Church' (n 130 above), at 919–920. However, see the argument in K Lenaerts and T Corthaut, 'Of Birds and Hedges: The Role of Primacy in

There is a stronger argument that the principles of damages liability for Member States for breaches of EU law, and of equal and effective remedies for breach of EC law, apply also to some degree to the third pillar, along with some principles relating to external competence.[175] Finally, in light of *Pupino*, it could be argued that Conventions confer direct effect (as the application of the principle to these measures has not been ruled out by the EU Treaty); the Court of Justice has not yet addressed this question either.[176]

As for the jurisdiction of the Court of Justice over the third pillar in the Amsterdam era,[177] the Court's role was expanded significantly as compared to the pre-Amsterdam rules. Article 46(b) of the previous TEU stated that the Court's first pillar jurisdiction only applied to the third pillar to the extent set out in Article 35 of the previous TEU. First of all, Article 35(1)–(4) of the previous TEU, along with Declaration 10 in the Final Act of the Treaty of Amsterdam, copied precisely the preliminary rulings jurisdiction which had already been awarded to the Court as regards several Conventions in 1996, and which was subsequently awarded in several other pre-Amsterdam Conventions:[178] an option for Member States to award the Court jurisdiction over references from national courts; a further option to limit that jurisdiction to final courts only; and a final option as to whether to require final national courts to send references to the Court. But the scope of this jurisdiction was expanded by the Treaty of Amsterdam to include not only jurisdiction over Conventions and measures implementing them, but also 'on the validity and interpretation of framework decisions and decisions, on the interpretation of conventions established under this Title and on the validity and interpretation of measures implementing them'. The extent of the Court's jurisdiction as regards third pillar treaties was unclear,[179] and its jurisdiction pursuant to the Protocol on the Schengen *acquis* is discussed below.[180]

Nineteen Member States opted in to the Court's post-Amsterdam third pillar jurisdiction over preliminary rulings: twelve of the first fifteen Member States (all except the UK, Denmark, and Ireland), plus seven of the twelve Member States joining the EU in 2004 and 2007 (all except Estonia, Poland, Slovakia, Bulgaria, and Malta).[181] All of these Member States except Spain permitted all national courts or tribunals to send questions. Eleven Member States reserved the right

---

Invoking Norms of EU Law' (2006) 31 ELRev 287 at 289–291. The opinion in *Koslowski* (n 171 above) argues for application of the supremacy principle to the third pillar (paras 113–126), but does not appear to suggest that the *consequences* of supremacy go any further than the principle of indirect effect. On the possible stronger legal effect of third pillar measures that give effect to human rights principles, see 2.3 below.

[175] On the damages liability and effective remedies principles, see 'Salvation outside the Church' (n 130 above), at 921–924. On external competence, see 2.7.2 below.

[176] On the other hand, it cannot be argued that Common Positions have direct effect, given that (according to the *SEGI* case) they cannot affect the legal position of third parties.

[177] See E Denza, *The Intergovernmental Pillars of the European Union* (OUP, 2002), ch 9, and 'Salvation outside the Church' (n 130 above), at 885–909.   [178] See 2.2.1.2 above.

[179] See 2.7.2 below.   [180] See 2.2.2.3 below.   [181] [2010] OJ L 56/14.

to require their final courts to refer (the exceptions are Greece, Cyprus, Latvia, Lithuania, Portugal, Finland, Sweden, and Hungary).

Next, Article 35(5) of the previous TEU set out another type of exclusion from jurisdiction: the Court of Justice could not 'review the validity or proportionality of operations carried out by the police or other law enforcement services of a Member State or the exercise of the responsibilities incumbent upon Member States with regard to the maintenance of law and order and the safeguarding of internal security'. This was expressly a restriction on the Court's ability to rule on certain acts committed by national authorities; it did not restrict the Court from ruling on the validity or interpretation of EU acts, and in any event, the final judgment in cases referred from national courts is given by the national courts.

Article 35(7) of the previous TEU, first sentence, followed the model of interstate dispute settlement already agreed for six pre-Amsterdam criminal, policing, or customs law Conventions, allowing Member States to sue each other after six months of attempting to reach a settlement in the Council. However, this provision widened the Court's dispute-settlement jurisdiction to cover all measures adopted under Article 34(2) of the previous TEU, namely Common Positions, Framework Decisions, Decisions, Conventions, and measures implementing Decisions and Conventions. The second sentence of Article 35(7) followed the model of Commission/Member State dispute settlement also seen (with more variety) in five pre-Amsterdam criminal and customs law Conventions. Here the Commission could only sue Member States where there was a dispute over a Convention; but it could do so as regards any Convention and for any provision of a Convention, whereas some of the pre-Amsterdam Conventions had either ruled out the power for the Commission to bring proceedings or limited that power to certain provisions. There was no reference to disputes over implementing measures, but it would be illogical to block the Commission from bringing disputes regarding implementing measures to the Court, given that it has such power over parent Conventions.

Finally, Article 35(6) of the previous TEU gave the Court the power of direct judicial review, a wholly new power compared to its pre-Amsterdam jurisdiction. It could rule on the legality of Framework Decisions or Decisions on grounds of 'lack of competence, infringement of an essential procedural requirement, infringement of this Treaty or any rule of law relating to its application, or misuse of powers'. These grounds were taken from Article 230 EC (now Article 263 TFEU). Only the Commission and Member States had the power to bring such cases; other persons, including the EP, did not. This power became redundant shortly after the entry into force of the Treaty of Lisbon, because proceedings for annulment had to be initiated within two months of the publication of the measure concerned.

In practice, when the Treaty of Lisbon entered into force the Court had ruled on: ten references for interpretation of some of the third pillar provisions of the

Schengen *acquis*;[182] three references for interpretation of the Framework Decision on crime victims' rights;[183] a reference on the validity of the Framework Decision on the European arrest warrant;[184] four references on the interpretation of the same Framework Decision;[185] a challenge against an act of Eurojust, the EU's prosecutors' agency;[186] and two annulment actions against Framework Decisions adopted by the Council.[187] Two of these cases were subject to the special JHA emergency ruling procedure, mentioned above.[188] No dispute settlement cases were brought.

Also, the Court of First Instance (as it then was) delivered several judgments concerning the EU's staff regulations and the integration of the 'Schengen Secretariat' into the EU Council Secretariat,[189] as well as the *SEGI* case on non-contractual liability for listing a group as a 'terrorist' organization,[190] which was appealed to the Court of Justice.[191] Moreover, the EU's Civil Service Tribunal has given a judgment in a case brought by a Eurojust staff member.[192]

The cases pending when the Treaty of Lisbon entered into force comprised four further references for interpretation of Framework Decisions and an annulment action against a Council Decision.[193]

---

[182] Cases: C-187/01 and C-385/01 *Gozutok and Brugge* [2003] ECR I-1345; C-469/03 *Miraglia* [2005] ECR I-2009; C-436/04 *Van Esbroek* [2006] ECR I-2333; C-467/04 *Gasparini* [2006] ECR I-9199; C-150/05 *Van Straaten* [2006] ECR I-9327; C-288/05 *Kretzinger* [2007] ECR I-6441; C-367/05 *Kraaijenbrink* [2007] ECR I-6619; C-297/07 *Bourquain* [2008] ECR I-9425; and C-491/07 *Turansky* [2008] ECR I-11039. All concerned the Schengen 'double jeopardy' rules. Two other cases on the same issue were withdrawn: C-491/03 *Hiebeler* and C-272/05 *Bowens*. On the judgments, see 11.8 below; on the Schengen *acquis*, see 2.2.2.3 below.

[183] *Pupino* (n 161 above); Case C-467/05 *Dell'Orto* [2007] ECR I-5557; and Case C-404/07 *Katz* [2008] ECR I-7607. On the substance of these cases, see 9.8.3 below.

[184] Case C-303/05 *Advocaten voor de Wereld* [2007] ECR I-3633; for the Framework Decision see n 126 above. On the substance see 9.5.2 below.

[185] Cases: C-66/08 *Koslowski* [2008] ECR I-6041; C-296/08 PPU *Santesteban Goicoechea* [2008] ECR I-6307; C-388/08 PPU *Leymann and Pustovarov* [2008] ECR I-8993; and C-123/08 *Wolzenburg* [2009] ECR I-9621. On the substance, see ibid.

[186] Case C-160/03 *Spain v Eurojust* (on the language requirements of Eurojust staff) [2005] ECR I-2077.

[187] Case C-176/03 *Commission v Council* and C-440/05 *Commission v Council* (both n 146 above). On the substance of these cases, see 2.4.2 and 10.2.4 below.

[188] *Santesteban Goicoechea* and *Leymann and Pustovarov*, n 185 above.

[189] Case T-107/99 R *Garcia de Retortillo v Council* [1999] ECR II-1939 (interim measures; the main action was later withdrawn); Joined Cases T-164/99 *Leroy v Council*, T-37/00 *Chevalier-Delanoue v Council*, and T-38/00 *Joaquim Matos v Council* [2001] ECR II-1819; Case T-166/99 *Andres de Dios v Council* [2001] ECR II-1857. On the integration of the Schengen *acquis* into EU law, see further 2.2.2.3 below.

[190] Order of the Court of First Instance in Case T-338/02 *SEGI and others* [2004] ECR II-1647.

[191] See n 167 above.   [192] Case F-61/06 *Sapara v Eurojust*, judgment of 10 July 2008.

[193] Cases (all pending): C-205/09 *Eredics* (opinion of 1 July 2010) and C-403/09 *Gueye*, both on interpretation of the Framework Decision on standing of victims; C-261/09 *Mantello* (opinion of 7 Sep 2010) and C-306/09 *IB* (opinion of 6 July 2010), on interpretation of the Framework Decision on the European Arrest Warrant; and C-482/08 *UK v Council*, on the validity of the Decision giving law enforcement bodies access to the Visa Information System (opinion of 24 June 2010).

The Court's third pillar judgments to date have answered some important questions, but raised certain others. In the *Pupino* judgment, the Court stated that 'the system under Article 234 EC is capable of being applied to Article 35 EU, subject to the conditions laid down in Article 35'.[194] It followed that the usual rules on admissibility of references,[195] the definition of a 'court or tribunal' which can send references,[196] and the control of the national court over the questions sent, all apply.[197] In the *Commission v Council* cases, the underlying principles governing annulment actions under Article 230 EC (now Article 263 TFEU) were applied.[198]

But did the Court have any third pillar jurisdiction *besides* that conferred upon it by Article 35 of the EU Treaty? In the *SEGI* judgment,[199] the Court of Justice stated that it had 'only' the third pillar jurisdiction provided for in Article 35, and that it had 'no jurisdiction...whatsoever' regarding damages actions against the EU institutions in third pillar matters. More broadly, 'as regards the Union, the treaties have established a system of legal remedies in which, by virtue of Article 35 EU, the jurisdiction of the Court is less extensive under Title VI of the Treaty on European Union than it is under the EC Treaty'. However, since the EU was 'founded on the principle of the rule of law', national courts had an obligation to ensure effective judicial protection regarding drawing up and compensation for losses resulting from third pillar acts. In the case of Common Positions, their limited legal effect (see above) explained the limited jurisdiction of the Court of Justice over them, although the Court retained jurisdiction (on a reference from a national court) to decide whether measures were correctly adopted as Common Positions, rather than in the form of another type of third pillar act, if they in fact had legal effects against third parties.

Despite this judgment, it seems that the Court's ordinary EC law jurisdiction applied where aspects of third pillar cooperation were subject to EC Treaty rules, which at least comprised the provisions of the EC Treaty referred to in the previous Article 41 TEU,[200] and could include at least some other EC rules not referred

---

[194] Para 28 of the judgment (n 160 above). The point has been reiterated in: *Santesteban Goicoechea*, para 36; *Dell'Orto*, para 34; *Katz*, para 29; *van Straaten*, para 31; and *Gasparini*, para 41 (nn 182–185 above).

[195] See paras 29 and 30 of the judgment, ibid. The point has been reiterated in: *Katz*, paras 31–34; *Gasparini*, paras 42–46; *Advocaten voor de Wereld*, paras 19–22; *Van Straaten*, paras 32–39; and *Dell'Orto*, paras 37–46 (nn 182–185 above).

[196] See para 22 of *Pupino*, and also *Santesteban Goicoechea*, paras 39–41, and *Dell'Orto*, para 35 (nn 183 and 185 above).

[197] See *Santesteban Goicoechea*, paras 45–46, and *Katz*, paras 37–38 (nn 183 and 185 above).

[198] See n 146 above.   [199] See n 167 above.

[200] This includes jurisdiction relating to EU spending measures (see by analogy Case T-231/04 *Greece v Commission* [2007] ECR II-63, which concerned foreign policy spending) and access to documents (Case T-174/95 *Svenska Journalistforbundet* [1998] ECR II-2289; see further 2.5 below).

to there.[201] The Court also confirmed that it had jurisdiction to interpret the previous Title VI of the EU Treaty itself, as distinct from acts adopted pursuant to it, at least where the validity of a third pillar act was challenged in light of the provisions of the previous Title VI.[202] Moreover, in practice, the Court was willing to interpret Title VI of the EU Treaty, as well as Title I of that Treaty (where it also lacked jurisdiction, except regarding the prior Articles 6(2) and 7 EU) on several occasions in order to give an answer to questions before it.[203]

Finally, as with the special rules applicable during this period to immigration, asylum, and civil law cases, the special regime applicable to the Court's jurisdiction in this area potentially overlapped with other jurisdictional rules, creating a possibility of 'mixed jurisdiction' in some cases. This issue is discussed further below.[204]

2.2.2.3. Integrating the Schengen *acquis*[205]

Article K.7 of the Maastricht version of the EU Treaty, later repealed by the Treaty of Amsterdam, expressly permitted Member States to engage in bilateral or multilateral action as long as this did not 'conflict with, or impede' third pillar cooperation.[206] This was particularly relevant to the development of the Schengen *acquis*, in the form of the 1985 Agreement, the 1990 Convention, and the measures implementing the Convention.

The 1990 Convention came into force on 1 September 1993 in seven Member States (France, Germany, the Benelux States, Spain, and Portugal), but was not applied until 26 March 1995. Accession treaties were signed with Italy, then Greece, then Austria, then in December 1996 with Sweden, Denmark, and Finland. The latter accession was accompanied by an 'association agreement' with Norway and Iceland, because the Nordic EU Member States were not willing to abolish the border-free agreement that they shared with the non-EU Nordic states. The accession treaties with Italy and Austria entered gradually into force between 1996 and March 1998; but by the entry into force of the Treaty

---

[201] This includes jurisdiction relating to staff cases (see *Spain v Eurojust*, n 186 above, and the Schengen Secretariat staff cases, n 189 above). Also, infringement proceedings concerning EU free movement law could touch upon third pillar issues (see C-503/03 *Commission v Spain* [2006] ECR I-1097) and annulment actions against first pillar measures could argue that those measures should have been based on the third pillar (see, for instance, Cases C-317/04 and C-318/04 *EP v Council and Commission* [2006] ECR I-4721 and C-301/06 *Ireland v Council and EP* [2009] ECR I-593). See generally the discussion in 2.4.2 below and 'Salvation outside the Church' (n 130 above), at 902–908.

[202] *Advocaten voor de Wereld* (n 142 above), para 18.

[203] See, for instance: *Gozutok and Brugge*, para 36, *Miraglia*, para 34, *Gasparini*, para 36, and *Van Esbroek*, para 29, interpreting Art 2 and/or Title VI of the previous TEU (all n 182 above); *Pupino* (n 161 above), interpreting Arts 1, 34, and 35 of the previous TEU; and *Spain v Eurojust* (n 186 above) and various other cases (n 194 above), interpreting Art 35 EU. In the Schengen Secretariat cases (n 189 above), and in Case C-503/03 *Commission v Spain* (n 201 above), the Court also interpreted the Protocol on the Schengen *acquis*.   [204] See 2.4.2.

[205] On the relationship between the Schengen *acquis* and EU law, see 2.4.2 below.

[206] See also the parallel Art 100c(7) EC, which was also repealed by the Treaty of Amsterdam.

of Amsterdam, the accession treaty with Greece was only partly in force and the Scandinavian accession was still at least a year away.[207]

The ongoing 'widening' and 'deepening' of the Schengen rules, alongside developments in the EU, resulted in an increasing cross-over between Schengen and JHA cooperation.[208] In order to reconcile the overlap between the two processes, the Treaty of Amsterdam integrated the Schengen *acquis* into the framework of the EC and EU Treaties. This was accomplished by means of a Protocol on the Schengen *acquis*, attached to the EC and EU Treaties ('the Schengen Protocol'). This Protocol has subsequently been amended by the Treaty of Lisbon, partly to update it because the Schengen *acquis* has already been integrated into the EC and EU legal orders.[209]

According to the Annex to this Protocol, the Schengen *acquis* consisted of the 1985 Schengen Agreement; the 1990 Convention implementing that Agreement; the measures implementing the Convention adopted by its Executive Committee; and the acts of the other organs established by the Convention pursuant to implementing powers conferred by the Executive Committee.[210]

The core of the Protocol was initially the application of the Schengen *acquis*, from the date of entry into force of the Treaty of Amsterdam (1 May 1999) to the thirteen participating Member States, within the framework of the EU.[211] Following the entry into force of the Treaty of Lisbon, the core of the Protocol is now the application of the Schengen *acquis* to twenty-five Member States (again, all except the UK and Ireland).[212]

The Protocol initially gave the Council the power, with a unanimous vote of all Member States, to 'determine, in conformity with the relevant provisions of the Treaties', the legal basis for each of the provisions or decisions which constitute the Schengen *acquis*.[213] Such a determination was necessary because the Schengen *acquis* included measures falling within the scope of the third pillar, Title VI EU (as amended by the Treaty of Amsterdam), Title IV EC (ie the rules on immigration), and even other parts of the EC Treaty. After that determination, the EU's Court of Justice had the jurisdiction over the *acquis* that it otherwise would have under 'the relevant applicable provisions of the Treaties', but it had no jurisdiction on 'measures or decisions relating to the maintenance of law and order and the

---

[207] See annual report of the Schengen Central Group for 1997 (Sch/C (98) 60, 22 June 1998).

[208] See particularly s 2 of chs 3, 4, 7, 9, and 12.

[209] The Treaty of Lisbon also made amendments to the Schengen Protocol relating to the specific position of the UK, Ireland, and Denmark. On these amendments, see 2.2.5.1 and 2.2.5.2 below. All references in this subsection are to the Schengen Protocol, unless otherwise indicated.

[210] The Annex was repealed by the Treaty of Lisbon.   [211] Original Arts 1 and 2(1).

[212] Revised Arts 1 and 2, which are 'without prejudice' to the specific rules regarding the phased application of the Schengen *acquis* to new Member States in the 2003 and 2005 Acts of Accession (on which, see 2.2.5.3 below).

[213] Previous Art 2(1), second sub-paragraph. This provision was repealed when Art 2 was amended by the Treaty of Lisbon, presumably because the power was now spent.

safeguarding of internal security'.[214] This appeared to be a wider exception to the Court's jurisdiction than provided for in Article 68 EC or the previous Article 35(5) TEU.[215] With the amendments to the Court's JHA jurisdiction following the entry into force of the Treaty of Lisbon,[216] the provision relating to the EC Treaty is no longer relevant, while the restriction relating to the third pillar is presumably still valid as regards those provisions of the *acquis* allocated to the third pillar, pursuant to the transitional rules on the Court's jurisdiction.[217]

To the extent that the Council had failed to allocate the *acquis*, the Protocol established a 'default' position: the entirety of the measures in the Schengen *acquis* would have been regarded as third pillar acts for as long as the Council had been unable to agree upon their allocation.[218] Also, the Protocol gave the Council the power, with the unanimous vote of the participating Schengen States, to 'take any measure necessary for the implementation of' the integration of the Schengen *acquis* into the EU legal order.[219]

Within three weeks of the entry into force of the Treaty of Amsterdam, the Council used the latter power to adopt a Decision determining which provisions of the Schengen *acquis* needed to be allocated to the EC or EU Treaties.[220] This Decision specified that certain parts of the *acquis* did not need to be allocated because, for example, they were redundant, had been overtaken by EC law (such as most of the firearms provisions of Schengen), or had been overtaken by Conventions concluded among all the Member States (such as the asylum provisions of Schengen, which had been overtaken by the Dublin Convention). The Decision also required the Council to publish all of the Schengen *acquis* which were being allocated to the EC and EU Treaties, except for those parts of the *acquis* which the Schengen Executive Committee had decided to keep secret.[221] Simultaneously, the Council adopted a Decision allocating those provisions of the *acquis* to legal bases in the EC or EU Treaties, with the exception of the provisions relating to the Schengen Information System (SIS).[222] As a result, the SIS provisions of the *acquis* had to be regarded as based on the third pillar. The failure to allocate these provisions was due to disagreement over whether to

---

[214] Previous Art 2(1), third sub-paragraph, also repealed by the Treaty of Lisbon amendments to Art 2.   [215] See discussion in 'Watchmen' (n 59 above), at 409–412.

[216] See 2.2.3.1 below. This presumably explains why this provision of the Schengen Protocol was repealed by the Treaty of Lisbon.   [217] On those transitional rules, see 2.2.3.3 below.

[218] Previous Art 2(1), fourth sub-paragraph, also repealed by the Treaty of Lisbon amendments to Art 2.

[219] Previous Art 2(1), second sub-paragraph, also repealed by the Treaty of Lisbon amendments to Art 2.

[220] Decision 1999/435 ([1999] OJ L 176/1). This Decision was later corrected by Decision 2000/645 ([2000] OJ L 272/24), which corrected Schengen Executive Committee Decision SCH/Com-ex (94) 15 rev.

[221] The *acquis* was finally published over a year later ([2000] OJ L 239). On the secret provisions of the *acquis*, including later declassification of some provisions, see further 2.5 below.

[222] Decision 1999/436 ([1999] OJ L 176/17).

allocate some of them to an EC Treaty legal base (because of the use of the SIS for immigration control) along with an EU Treaty legal base (because of the use of the SIS for police investigations and in relation to criminal proceedings), and if so, to what extent.[223]

Now that the powers to allocate the *acquis* have been repealed from the Schengen Protocol, along with the default rule, arguably this default allocation remains fixed, until the Schengen *acquis* relating to the SIS is fully replaced by subsequent acts, which it will be once the planned second generation Schengen Information System (SIS II) is operational.[224] On the other hand, in the meantime, a number of measures which amend the Schengen *acquis* relating to the SIS were adopted under EC or EU Treaty legal bases before the entry into force of the Treaty of Lisbon, and some of these measures were amended in turn in June 2010, after the entry into force of that Treaty.[225] As a consequence, it can be argued that the SIS rules as a whole have already been de facto allocated to the correct legal bases; if this is correct, the immigration-related measures of the SIS are therefore already subject to the Court's normal jurisdictional rules as from the entry into force of the Treaty of Lisbon (or alternatively, from the point when those rules were amended in June 2010), and similarly the SIS provisions relating to the third pillar are subject to the Court's normal jurisdiction after the adoption of the post-Lisbon measures. In the alternative, the Court of Justice has its normal jurisdiction at least as regards the measures which have amended the original SIS rules concerning immigration, and as regards the post-Lisbon amendment to the original SIS rules concerning policing and criminal law.[226]

Next, the Council had the power to decide on when the Schengen provisions would be fully extended to the Schengen states which were not yet fully participating in the Schengen rules at the time of the entry into force of the Treaty of Amsterdam.[227] This power was used in 1999 to extend the Schengen rules fully to Greece as from March 2000,[228] and again in 2000 to extend the Schengen rules fully to Denmark, Sweden, and Finland as from March 2001.[229] At that point,

---

[223] On the 'legal bases' for the allocation of the SIS *acquis*, see further 2.4.2 below.

[224] In accordance with the transitional rules on the legal effect of third pillar measures adopted before the entry into force of the Treaty of Lisbon and the Court of Justice's jurisdiction over those measures (see 2.2.3.3 below), this interpretation would mean that the original SIS provisions which have not been amended remain subject to the old third pillar rules governing the Court's jurisdiction and the legal effect of those provisions, until those are further amended after the entry into force of the Treaty of Lisbon or replaced once SIS II becomes operational.

[225] On the substance of those measures, see 12.6.2.1 below.

[226] Again, see the discussion of the transitional rules (2.2.3.3 below).

[227] Previous Art 2(2). The Council had to act with the unanimous vote of the Schengen States.

[228] Decision 1999/848 ([1999] OJ L 327/58); see Declaration, [1999] OJ C 369/1.

[229] Decision 2000/777 ([2000] OJ L 309/24); see Declaration, [2000] OJ L 309/28. Note that distinct rules apply to Denmark: see 2.2.5.2 below.

this power was spent,[230] and this provision was duly repealed by the Treaty of Lisbon.[231]

As for the staff of the Schengen Secretariat, the Protocol provided for the Council to adopt arrangements for their integration into the Council's staff.[232] The Council's decision to this end was unsuccessfully challenged.[233]

The Council also decided to adopt further measures concerning the management and financing of contracts relating to the SIS,[234] and providing a Secretariat for the Schengen data supervisory authority.[235] The latter Decision was later repealed when a joint secretariat for different third pillar data supervisory authorities was established.[236]

The Protocol also set out specific rules for measures, adopted after the entry into force of the Treaty of Amsterdam, which 'build upon' the Schengen *acquis*. Such measures shall be 'subject to the relevant provisions of the treaties'.[237] So after that point all Schengen-related measures have had to be regarded as 'regular' parts of EC law (until the Treaty of Lisbon entered into force) or EU law, with no special rules applying as regards their legal base (and therefore no special rules relating to decision-making or the Court of Justice, other than those rules applicable to any JHA measures adopted in the same area). However, there are still differences between measures building upon the Schengen *acquis* and other measures to be adopted under the EC or EU Treaties, as regards the territorial scope of the measures.[238]

In practice, nearly all EU measures concerning visas, border controls, and irregular immigration adopted or proposed since 1 May 1999 have built upon the Schengen *acquis*.[239] So have a handful of measures concerning legal migration,[240]

---

[230] On the separate issue of the extension of the Schengen *acquis* to the Member States that joined the EU later, see 2.2.5.3 below; on the later extension of the *acquis* to Switzerland and Liechtenstein, see 2.2.5.4 below.   [231] It does not appear in the amended version of Art 2.

[232] Previous Art 7; this was the only provision of the Protocol which provided for the Council to act by QMV. This article was repealed by the Treaty of Lisbon, presumably because this power was now spent.   [233] [1999] OJ L 119; on the case law, see n 189 above.

[234] One set of Decisions was applicable from 1999–2003 (Council Decisions 1999/322 and 1999/323, [1999] OJ L 123/49 and 51, repealed as of 27 Nov 2003 by Council Decisions 2003/835 and 2003/836, [2003] OJ L 318/22 and 23), while the other has been applicable since 1999 and 2000 (Council Decisions 1999/870 and 2000/265, [1999] OJ L 337/41 and [2000] OJ L 85/12; the latter has been amended by Decisions 2000/664/EC ([2000] OJ L 278/24), 2003/171 ([2003] OJ L 69/25), 2007/155 ([2007] OJ L 68/5), 2008/319 ([2008] OJ L 109/30), 2008/670 ([2008] OJ L 220/19), and 2009/915 ([2009] OJ L 323/9)). See also Decision 2007/149 ([2007] OJ L 66/19) and the amendments to the relevant Decision of the Schengen Executive Committee ([2000] OJ L 239/444) in [2007] OJ L 179/50, [2008] OJ L 113/21, and [2010] OJ L 14/9.

[235] Decision 1999/438 ([1999] OJ L 176/34).

[236] Decision 2000/641 ([2000] OJ L 271/1), which replaced Decision 1999/438 as from 1 Sep 2001 (Art 6, Decision 2000/641). On third pillar data protection, see further 12.3 and 12.6 below.

[237] Art 5(1), first sub-paragraph, which was *not* amended by the Treaty of Lisbon. This applied despite any failure to allocate the original *acquis* (see Art 5(2), repealed by the Treaty of Lisbon). Despite the repeal of Art 5(2), the general rule in the first sub-paragraph of Art 5(1) would still prevent the adoption of any measure relating to the SIS (ie the only parts of the *acquis* which were not allocated to a Treaty base) from being adopted using the 'wrong' legal base.

[238] See 2.2.5 below.   [239] See 2.5 of chs 3, 4, and 7.   [240] See 6.2.5.

and certain measures concerning criminal procedure and policing.[241] The result is that a substantial proportion of the Schengen Convention and a large number of the secondary Schengen measures integrated into the EU and EC legal orders in 1999 have been or would be amended, repealed, or supplemented by EC or EU acts.[242]

The Court of Justice has ruled on the provisions of the Schengen *acquis* on a number of occasions, in relation to the double jeopardy rules;[243] the adoption of subsequent implementing measures;[244] the integration of the Schengen Secretariat staff into the Council;[245] the operation of the SIS;[246] the freedom to travel rules;[247] the rules on external borders;[248] and on the scope of the rules concerning the British opt-in to the Schengen *acquis*.[249] A case concerning SIS contracts was settled.[250]

The Court has not yet determined the legal effect of the Schengen measures, or any provision of them,[251] although it has ruled on the relationship between the Schengen *acquis* and EU free movement law.[252] Also, the Court has ruled that the integration of the Schengen *acquis* into the EC and EU legal order means that the *acquis* can no longer be interpreted according to the normal rules of public international law, but rather interpreted taking the EU framework into account.[253] On the other hand, the historical context of the pre-existence of the Schengen *acquis* was one factor justifying the Council's decision to apply unusual rules concerning the adoption of visas and borders implementing measures,[254] and the Court of First Instance (as it then was) also justified the adoption of unusual measures concerning the hiring of Council staff in light of the Schengen Protocol.[255] With respect, there appears to be a fundamental inconsistency in the case law as to whether the Schengen *acquis* should be subject to special treatment or not.

2.2.3. Treaty of Lisbon

2.2.3.1. Overview

The institutional framework governing EU JHA law again changed significantly with the entry into force of the Treaty of Lisbon on 1 December 2009.[256] First of

[241] See s 2.5 of chs 9 and 12.   [242] For details, see Appendix II.   [243] See 11.8 below.
[244] Case C-257/01 *Commission v Council* [2005] ECR I-345.   [245] See n 189 above.
[246] Case C-503/03 *Commission v Spain* [2006] ECR I-1097.
[247] Case C-241/05 *Bot* [2006] ECR I-9627. See 4.9 below.
[248] Joined Cases C-261/08 *Zurita Garcia* and C-348/08 *Choque Cabrera*, judgment of 22 Oct 2009, not yet reported. See 3.6.1 below.
[249] Cases C-77/05 *UK v Council* [2007] ECR I-11459 and C-137/05 *UK v Council* [2007] ECR I-11593. See also C-482/08 *UK v Council*, pending (opinion of 24 June 2010). See 2.2.5.1.3 below.
[250] Case T-447/04 R *Cap Gemini* [2005] ECR II-257.
[251] See also, as regards external competence and the Schengen *acquis*, 2.7 below.
[252] Case C-503/03 *Commission v Spain* (n 201 above); see further 2.4.2 below.
[253] See *Gozutok and Brugge* (n 182 above). In particular, the double jeopardy rules aim to prevent multiple prosecutions as a consequence of exercise of free movement rights (see generally 11.8 below).
[254] Case C-257/01 (n 244 above); see further 2.2.2.1 above.   [255] See n 189 above.
[256] [2007] OJ C 306.

all, the basic rules governing JHA cooperation were 'reunited' in one Title (Title V of Part Three) of the EC Treaty, which was in turn renamed the Treaty on the Functioning of the European Union (TFEU), because pursuant to the Treaty of Lisbon, the EU replaced and succeeded the European Community.[257] In effect, the previous 'third pillar' was transferred into what was formerly known as the Community legal order, and the TEU no longer contains any detailed provisions on JHA matters. However, the TEU still specifies that the development of JHA law as a whole remains an objective of the EU:[258]

The Union shall offer its citizens an area of freedom, security and justice without internal frontiers, in which the free movement of persons is ensured in conjunction with appropriate measures with respect to external border controls, asylum, immigration and the prevention and combating of crime.

The previous third pillar has, for now, a form of legal 'afterlife', in the form of transitional rules relating to the jurisdiction of the Court of Justice over third pillar measures adopted before the entry into force of the Treaty of Lisbon ('pre-existing measures') and the legal effect of those measures.[259] Although the Treaty of Lisbon contains most of the provisions of the rejected Constitutional Treaty,[260] it is not identical to that Treaty, in particular as regards the opt-outs applicable to JHA law.

Title V contains in turn general provisions;[261] rules on immigration and asylum;[262] an Article on civil law;[263] five Articles on criminal law;[264] and three articles on policing.[265] Because of the abolition of the third pillar, 'Community' legal instruments (Directives and Regulations) have had to be used to regulate policing and criminal law since the entry into force of the Treaty of Lisbon. It follows that the principles of direct effect and supremacy of 'Community' instruments apply to measures in this field adopted after that date as well.

As for decision-making rules, the Treaty of Lisbon extended QMV in the Council and co-decision with the EP (now known as the 'ordinary legislative

---

[257] Art 1, third paragraph, revised TEU.

[258] Art 3(2), revised TEU. This provision is identical to the prior Art 2, fourth indent TEU, except for the added words 'without internal frontiers' and the replacement of the obligation to 'maintain and develop' the area of freedom, security, and justice with the obligation to 'offer' it. But note that the 'objectives' clause of the EC Treaty (as it then was) has been deleted by the Treaty of Lisbon, including Art 3(1)(d) EC, which had defined the objectives of the Community. This clause had been relevant in some cases concerning the interpretation of the powers of the EC; see, for instance, Case C-170/96 *Commission v Council* [1998] ECR I-2763. Equally, the Court of Justice had referred to the prior Art 2, fourth indent TEU in some criminal law judgments: see 2.2.2.2 above.

[259] See 2.2.3.3 below.

[260] [2004] OJ C 310. On the JHA provisions of the Constitutional Treaty, see the second edition of this book, pp 85–90.   [261] Ch 1 of Title V (Arts 67–76 TFEU), discussed in 2.2.3.2 below.

[262] Ch 2 of Title V (Arts 77–80 TFEU), discussed in chs 3–7 below.

[263] Ch 3 of Title V (Art 81 TFEU), discussed in ch 8 below.

[264] Ch 4 of Title V (Arts 82–86 TFEU), discussed in chs 9–11 below.

[265] Ch 5 of Title V (Arts 87–89 TFEU), discussed in ch 12 below.

procedure')[266] to legal migration and to most criminal law and policing issues.[267] However, unanimity in the Council was retained for some sensitive issues of criminal law and policing, family law, and the adoption of measures relating to passports and similar documents.[268] In most of these cases, the EP is only consulted, but it has a new power of consent in some cases.[269] These cases of decision-making are examples of 'special legislative procedures' that differ from the ordinary procedure.[270] Legislative proposals that were pending when the Treaty of Lisbon entered into force were subject to the revised decision-making procedures immediately as regards immigration, asylum, and civil law, but proposals relating to policing and criminal law lapsed due to the change in legal basis,[271] and had to be proposed again.[272]

Unanimity in the Council (or European Council) also applies to possible extensions of competence, or changes to decision-making rules.[273] The revised TEU also provides for a general power to alter decision-making rules (known as a *'passerelle'*), which applies to Title V as well as most of the rest of the Treaties. This permits a decision, without Treaty amendment, to move from unanimity to QMV or from a special legislative procedure to the ordinary legislative procedure.[274] Finally, Title V provides for two different variations of decision-making rules—a special rule (widely known as the 'emergency brake') relating to some areas of criminal law, if a Member State considers that a proposal 'would affect fundamental aspects of its criminal justice system',[275] and a special rule (referred to in this book as the 'pseudo-veto') relating to some cases where unanimity applies in the Council.[276] In either case, a 'fast track' to 'enhanced cooperation',

[266] The details of this procedure are set out in Art 294 TFEU, which does not differ in substance from the previous Art 251 EC.　　　　　　　　　　　　　　[267] See s 2.3 of chs 6 and 9–12.

[268] Arts 86(1) (European Public Prosecutor), 87(3) (police operations), 89 (cross-border police operations), 81(3) (family law), and 77(3) (passports) TFEU.

[269] The EP has the power of consent as regards legislation concerning the European Public Prosecutor (Art 86(1) TFEU).

[270] On this concept, see Art 289(2) TFEU.　　　　[271] See COM (2009) 665, 3 Dec 2009.

[272] See particularly 9.2.3, 10.2.3, and 12.2.3 below, as well as the treaties discussed in 2.7.2 below.

[273] This applies to any decision to extend criminal law competence (Arts 82(1)(d) and 83(1), third sub-paragraph TFEU), to alter decision-making rules relating to family law (Art 81(3), second sub-paragraph TFEU), or to extend the powers of the European Public Prosecutor (Art 86(4) TFEU). The latter measure would be adopted by the European Council, rather than the Council. The EP has the power of consent except as regards Art 81(3) TFEU, where it need only be consulted.

[274] Art 48(7), revised TEU. The *passerelle* procedure requires the unanimous support of the Member States and the consent of the EP, plus involvement by national parliaments. This procedure only applies to acts of the *Council*, so cannot apply to Art 86(4) TFEU, which provides for action by the European Council. There are several specific provisions in the Treaties which are not subject to this procedure (Art 353 TFEU), but none of these exemptions concern JHA matters. It should also be noted that in the context of enhanced cooperation, the Member States participating in that cooperation can agree that the decision-making rules will change *for them*: see Art 333 TFEU and further 2.2.5.5 below.　　　　　　　　　　　　　　[275] Arts 82(3) and 83(3) TFEU.

[276] These cases are Arts 86 (European Public Prosecutor) and 87(3) (operational police cooperation) TFEU.

ie authorization of some Member States to proceed without the others, is provided for.[277]

Next, as regards policing and criminal law, there is no longer any right for individual Member States to submit initiatives for legislation, but it is still open to a group of one-quarter of the Member States (meaning, at present, at least seven Member States) to submit a joint initiative.[278]

JHA law is also subject to the general changes which the Treaty of Lisbon made to EU law as regards legislative and non-legislative acts. The 'ordinary' and 'special' legislative procedures (as described above) are subject to particular rules concerning openness, transparency, and scrutiny by national parliaments.[279] The Treaty also now provides for the adoption of 'delegated' acts implementing legislative measures, as follows:[280]

A legislative act may delegate to the Commission the power to adopt non-legislative acts of general application to supplement or amend certain non-essential elements of the legislative act.

The objectives, content, scope and duration of the delegation of power shall be explicitly defined in the legislative acts. The essential elements of an area shall be reserved for the legislative act and accordingly shall not be the subject of a delegation of power.

The legislation in question must explicitly lay down the conditions for such delegations of power, which 'may' be either the revocation of the delegated power by the EP or the Council, and/or a power for the EP or the Council to block the entry into force of the delegated act by objecting to it within a specified period.[281] The conditions for the application of the delegated powers rule are very similar to those which previously applied to the 'regulatory procedure with scrutiny' (RPS), a special rule which gave the EP and the Council powers of scrutiny over the Commission's adoption of measures 'implementing' EC legislation adopted by means of the co-decision procedure (as it was then known) before the entry into force of the Treaty of Lisbon.[282] However, the *control process* is different, and the delegated powers provision applies to *all* EU legislation, not just legislation adopted by the ordinary legislative procedure (as it is now called). Due to the abolition of the previous third pillar, this also means that this provision will also apply to policing and criminal law measures adopted after the entry into force of the Treaty of Lisbon, although measures implementing pre-existing third pillar acts continue to be subject to the previous rules on implementing third pillar measures for as long as the relevant transitional rules are applicable.[283] There will not be any general rules on the use of the delegated acts procedure, but rather

---

[277] On the enhanced cooperation rules following the entry into force of the Treaty of Lisbon, see 2.2.5.5 below.   [278] Art 76 TFEU, discussed further below (see 2.2.3.2).
[279] See further 2.5 below.   [280] Art 290(1) TFEU.   [281] Art 290(2) TFEU.
[282] See further 2.2.2.1 above.
[283] On the substance of the previous rules, see 2.2.2.2 above; on the transitional rules, see 2.2.3.3 below.

specific provisions in each legislative act which provides for the procedure.[284] So far, no JHA legislation which provides for the adoption of delegated acts has been adopted or proposed; it remains to be seen if and when the measures adopted before the Treaty of Lisbon which provide for RPS (including the relevant JHA measures) will be amended to provide for the delegated acts procedure instead.

There is still provision for the adoption of implementing measures in other cases,[285] and the general legal framework governing the adoption of implementing measures will likely be replaced shortly after the entry into force of the Treaty of Lisbon.[286] The new general rules will replace the rules which previously governed the adoption of implementing measures (including as regards JHA measures), except for the prior rules concerning the use of the RPS procedure for measures adopted before the entry into force of the Treaty. Again, measures implementing pre-existing third pillar acts will continue to be subject to the previous rules on implementing third pillar measures for as long as the relevant transitional rules are applicable.[287]

Moving on to the jurisdiction of the Court of Justice over JHA matters, the restrictions previously imposed relating to immigration, asylum, and civil law on the one hand (the former Title IV EC), and the former third pillar on the other (the former third pillar), were both removed,[288] save for an exception which relates only to policing and criminal law (leaving aside the transitional rules for pre-existing third pillar measures).[289] This exception is the retention of the previous exception, as set out in the former Article 35(5) TEU,[290] relating to jurisdiction over 'the validity or proportionality of operations carried out by the police or other law-enforcement services of a Member State or the exercise of the responsibilities incumbent upon Member States with regard to the maintenance of law and order and the safeguarding of internal security'.[291]

The special 'urgency' procedure for certain JHA cases before the Court of Justice, first created in 2008, remains in force.[292] In addition, the Treaty of Lisbon

---

[284] See the Commission communication on the use of the procedure (COM (2009) 673, 9 Dec 2009).

[285] Art 291 TFEU, which amended the prior Art 202 EC. Again, on the previous rules, see 2.2.2.1 above.

[286] The Commission proposed new general rules shortly after the entry into force of the Treaty of Lisbon: COM (2010) 83, 9 Mar 2010.

[287] On the substance of the previous rules, see 2.2.2.2 above; on the transitional rules, see 2.2.3.3 below.

[288] For the basic rules on the Court's jurisdiction and functioning after the Treaty of Lisbon, see Art 19, revised TEU, and Arts 251–281 TFEU.

[289] On these transitional rules, see 2.2.3.3 below.   [290] See 2.2.2.2 above.

[291] Art 276 TFEU. Because the wording of this exception has not been amended, any future jurisprudence concerning the interpretation of the former Art 35(5) TEU must apply to Art 276 TFEU and vice versa. For interpretation of the previous clause, see 2.2.2.2 above. While, as noted above, there are no cases to date touching upon the interpretation of the former Art 35(5) TEU, it is possible that the Court will be asked to interpret this provision pursuant to its transitional jurisdiction over pre-existing third pillar measures (see 2.2.3.3 below).   [292] See 2.2.2 above.

added a new paragraph to Article 267 TFEU (former Article 234 EC), concerning preliminary rulings from national courts to the Court of Justice, which provides that:

If such a question [for a preliminary ruling] is raised in a case pending before a court or tribunal of a Member State with regard to a person in custody, the Court of Justice of the European Union shall act with the minimum of delay.

This new provision, which presumably applies also to the Court's transitional jurisdiction over pre-existing third pillar measures, has already been applied twice after the entry into force of the Treaty, as regards persons held in detention in connection with EU anti-terrorist sanctions laws and the irregular crossing of internal borders; the Court has also given an emergency ruling in a child abduction case.[293] It does not create a separate new procedure by itself, but rather requires the Court to invoke the procedures (the urgent JHA procedure or the more general accelerated procedures) already set out in the Court's Statute and Rules of Procedure.

In practice, the Court of Justice received a number of JHA references from national courts in the first few months after the Treaty of Lisbon entered into force,[294] but it was too early to tell whether the Court of Justice's case load in this area would increase significantly or not. If it does increase significantly at some point, then there will have to be consideration of measures to address the overload on the EU judicial system, which could take the form of general changes to that system and/or specific changes relating to JHA cases.[295] But it is certainly too early to consider such changes yet, at least on JHA grounds alone.

The transfer of the third pillar to the first pillar also means that the 'Community' rules on external relations are applicable to policing and criminal law matters, in place of the rules on external relations which were applicable to the former third pillar.[296] It should also be noted that the Treaty of Lisbon widened the scope of the JHA opt-out rules applicable to the UK, Ireland, and Denmark, and furthermore made significant changes to those rules. These developments are considered further below.[297]

---

[293] Cases (none yet reported): C-550/09 *E and F*, judgment of 29 June 2010; C-188/10 and C-189/10 *Melki and Abdeli*, judgment of 22 June 2010; and C-211/10 PPU *Povse*, judgment of 1 July 2010. A further child abduction case is pending: Case C-400/10 PPU *McB*.

[294] On immigration and asylum law: Case C-69/10 *Diouf*, pending and *Melki and Abdeli,* ibid; on civil law: Cases C-509/09 *eDate Advertising*, C-87/10 *Electrosteel*, C-112/10 *Zaza Retail*, C-139/10 *Prism Investments*, C-144/10 *Berliner Verkehrsbetriebe*, C-145/10 *Painer*, C-161/10 *Martinez*, C-191/10 *Rastelli Davide and C*, C-213/10 *F-Tex, Povse* (ibid), C-296/10 *Purrucker II*, C-315/10 *Companhia Siderúrgica Nacional*, C-327/10 *Lindner*, and *McB* (ibid) all pending; on criminal law: Cases C-1/10 *Salmeron Sanchez* and C-264/10 *Kita*, all pending (except *Melki and Abdeli* and *Povse*); and on both asylum law and criminal law: Case C-105/10 PPU *Gataev and Gataeva*, withdrawn. See also the annulment action in Case C-355/10 *EP v Council*, pending.

[295] See S Peers, 'The Future of the EU Judicial System and EC Immigration and Asylum Law' (2005) 7 EJML 263.

[296] See further 2.7.2 below. On the substance of the treaties which have been agreed or are being negotiated in this area, see 9.10 and 12.11 below.   [297] See 2.2.5 below.

Certain amendments were also made to the Protocol integrating the Schengen *acquis* into the EU legal order.[298]

Finally, a number of the more general amendments to the Treaties made by the Treaty of Lisbon have a particular impact on EU JHA law. The amendments relating to the legitimacy and accountability of the EU are discussed further separately,[299] as are the general amendments relating to the competence of the EU.[300] The integration of the previous 'third pillar' into the EC Treaty (now the TFEU) means also that various general and final provisions of the TFEU apply to policing and criminal law. This could be relevant as regards provisions having general application,[301] data protection,[302] non-discrimination on grounds of nationality,[303] statistics,[304] EU liability,[305] dispute settlement,[306] national security exceptions,[307] pre-existing treaties with third states,[308] the EU's 'residual powers',[309] and the territorial scope of EU law.[310] The JHA provisions of the Treaties are covered (as they were before) by the provision on Treaty

---

[298] For details, see 2.2.2.3 above.   [299] See 2.5 below.   [300] See 2.2.4 below.

[301] Arts 8–13 TFEU, requiring all EU policies to take account of (respectively) sex equality, social concerns, non-discrimination, the environment, consumer protection, and the welfare of animals.

[302] Art 16 TFEU. See further 12.2.3 below.

[303] Art 18 TFEU (former Art 12 EC). It should be noted, however, that the previous Art 12 EC already applied to third pillar cooperation: see Case C-123/08 *Wolzenburg* [2009] ECR I-9621 and Case C-524/06 Huber [2008] ECR I-9705, and the discussion in 9.4 below.

[304] Art 338 TFEU (former Art 285 EC). On crime statistics, see 10.7 below.

[305] Art 340 TFEU (former Art 288 EC), which the Court of Justice has jurisdiction pursuant to Art 268 TFEU (former Art 235 EC). As discussed above (2.2.2.2), the Court of Justice confirmed that it had no jurisdiction 'whatsoever' over this issue as regards the prior third pillar: Case C-355/04 P *SEGI* [2007] ECR I-1657.

[306] Art 344 TFEU (former Art 292 EC), which reserves exclusive jurisdiction for disputes between Member States concerning EU law upon the Court of Justice, to the extent that it has jurisdiction over the matter concerned: see Case C-459/03 *Commission v Ireland* [2006] ECR I-4635. Until 1 Dec 2014, the special rule in the prior Art 35(7) TEU will apply to disputes concerning prior third pillar measures (see the transitional rules discussed in 2.2.3.3 below).

[307] Arts 346–348 TFEU (former Arts 296–298 EC). There is no reason to doubt that the jurisprudence on the interpretation of the previous Arts 296–298 EC continues to apply after the entry into force of the Treaty of Lisbon to Arts 346–348 TFEU, given the lack of substantive amendment to these provisions. On that case law, see the cases on the borderline between foreign policy and other areas of EU law, discussed in 3.2.4 below.

[308] Art 351 TFEU (former Art 307 EC). See further 2.7 below.

[309] Art 352 TFEU (former Art 308 EC), which provides for the adoption of measures by means of unanimity in the Council and consent of the EP '[i]f action by the Union should prove necessary, within the framework of the policies defined in the Treaties, to attain one of the objectives set out in the Treaties, and the Treaties have not provided the necessary powers'. The predecessor clause did not apply to the previous third pillar: see by analogy, Joined Cases C-402/05 P and C-415/05 P *Kadi and Al Barakaat* [2008] ECR I-6351, paras 194–205, and the discussion of Art 75 TFEU below (2.2.3.2).

[310] Art 52 TEU and Art 355 TFEU. Although the previous TEU did not define its territorial scope, some third pillar measures had specific provisions on the subject: see, for instance, Art 8 of the Framework Decision on unauthorized entry and residence ([2002] OJ L 328/1), applying that measure to Gibraltar.

amendment, including new provisions on simplified Treaty amendment.[311] There is still an obligation to ensure consistency between the various policies of the Union,[312] and the provisions concerning the relationship between the EU and its Member States, including the division of power between them, could be particularly relevant to JHA cooperation.[313] So could the revised rules on the protection of human rights within the EU legal order.[314]

2.2.3.2. General provisions

The general provisions of Title V of Part Three of the TFEU concern in turn: general objectives (Article 67 TFEU); the role of the European Council (Article 68 TFEU); the role of national parliaments (Article 69 TFEU); evaluation of JHA policies (Article 70 TFEU); the creation of a standing committee on operational security (Article 71 TFEU); a general security restriction (Article 72 TFEU); coordination of national security agencies (Article 73 TFEU); competence to adopt measures concerning administrative cooperation (Article 74 TFEU); competence over anti-terrorism measures (Article 75 TFEU); and a rule reserving power for Member States to propose policing and criminal law initiatives collectively (Article 76 TFEU). These provisions will be considered in turn.

First of all, Article 67 TFEU sets out objectives for the entire JHA Title, replacing the two separate provisions previously set out in Article 61 EC and Article 29 of the prior TEU:[315]

1. The Union shall constitute an area of freedom, security and justice with respect for fundamental rights and the different legal systems and traditions of the Member States.
2. It shall ensure the absence of internal border controls for persons and shall frame a common policy on asylum, immigration and external border control, based on solidarity between Member States, which is fair towards third-country nationals. For the purpose of this Title, stateless persons shall be treated as third-country nationals.
3. The Union shall endeavour to ensure a high level of security through measures to prevent and combat crime, racism and xenophobia, and through measures for coordination and cooperation between police and judicial authorities and other competent authorities, as well as through the mutual recognition of

---

[311] The possible use of the *passerelle* clause (revised Art 48(7) TEU) has been discussed above, but it should also be noted that the Treaty of Lisbon created the possibility for a slightly simplified system for amending the Treaty provisions concerning EU internal policies (revised Art 48(6) TEU), which applies inter alia to Title V TFEU. See generally G Barrett, 'Creation's Final Laws: The Impact of the Treaty of Lisbon on the "Final Provisions" of Earlier Treaties' (2008) 27 YEL 3.

[312] Art 7 TFEU, replacing the prior Art 3 TEU.

[313] Arts 4 and 5 TEU. See respectively 2.2.3.2 and 2.5 below. On the general rules on EU competence (Arts 2–6 TFEU), see 2.2.4 below.   [314] Arts 6 and 7 TEU; see 2.3 below.

[315] It should be recalled that Art 3(2), revised TEU, sets out general JHA objectives as part of the EU's overall objectives: see 2.2.3.1 above.

judgments in criminal matters and, if necessary, through the approximation of criminal laws.

4. The Union shall facilitate access to justice, in particular through the principle of mutual recognition of judicial and extrajudicial decisions in civil matters.

The Court of Justice has stated that Article 67(2) is only addressed to the Union, so implicitly does not bind the Member States.[315a] Equally, the other paragraphs of Article 67 address the Union, not the Member States, so presumably must be interpreted the same way.

All of the principles set out in Article 67 could be relevant to the interpretation or even possibly the validity of JHA measures. The first paragraph places at the centre of JHA policy the twin obligation to respect both human rights and the divergences between national laws across the EU. While human rights obligations are referred to separately in the Treaty,[316] the repeated mention of this issue in the specific field of JHA should reinforce this obligation *a fortiori* in this field. The obligation to respect divergent national traditions could be regarded as a particular application of the principle of subsidiarity.[317]

The second to fourth paragraphs define in turn the concepts of 'freedom', 'security', and 'justice', although the word 'freedom' does not explicitly appear in paragraph 2. Article 67(2) is based on the prior Article 61(a) and (b) EC. As compared to the previous Article 61(a) EC, the revised provision does not use the words 'free movement' or make reference to Article 14 EC (now Article 26 TFEU) any longer. However, it should be noted that a link between JHA measures as a whole and the free movement of persons and the abolition of internal frontiers is still made by the revised Article 3(2) TEU. The Union's other immigration-related policies are no longer described partly as 'flanking' the abolition of internal border controls, and the objectives clause in the JHA Title refers expressly now to the principles of fairness (toward third-country nationals) and solidarity (as between Member States).

Furthermore, unlike the previous Article 61(a) and (b) EC, all aspects of the Union's policy are described as 'common', stateless persons are expressly defined as third-country nationals, and there are new references to fairness and solidarity. The first of these changes reflects the 'common' policy on visas, asylum, and immigration referred to in Articles 77–79 TFEU, and makes clear that all aspects of that policy must be considered common. Next, while Article 79(1) refers to 'fair treatment' of legally resident third-country nationals, Article 67(2) requires that *all* EU JHA policies relating to third-country nationals must be 'fair', applying that principle therefore to irregular migrants and to asylum, visas, and borders policies. This principle in part derives from the 'Tampere programme' on JHA

[315a] Joined Case C-188/10 and C-189/10 *Melki and Abdeli*, judgement of 22 June 2010, not yet updated, para 62.   [316] Art 6 TEU; see 2.3 below.
[317] On which, see 2.5 below.

policy objectives adopted in 1999 (see the discussion of Article 68 TFEU below). Finally, the principle of solidarity is referred to in more detail in Article 80 TFEU, and EU legislation already frequently defined third-country nationals as implicitly including stateless persons.[318]

The first part of the third paragraph (up to the words, 'prevent and combat crime') is similar to the prior Article 61(e) EC, and the remainder of the paragraph is a succinct version of the prior Article 29 TEU, with the addition of a specific reference to mutual recognition in criminal matters but without a reference to any specific crimes other than racism and xenophobia. However, mutual recognition in criminal matters is in any event referred to as the basis of EU criminal law in Article 82(1) TFEU.

The fourth paragraph is more specific than the prior Article 61(c) EC, referring now expressly to the principle of 'access to justice' and to specific principles applicable to civil law. However, it should be noted that those principles are set out again (in the same words) in Article 81(1) TFEU, and an express power to adopt measures on 'effective access to [civil] justice' is set out in Article 81(1)(e) TFEU.[319] Moreover, the reference to civil law is not exhaustive ('in particular'), and so the reference to 'access to justice' should also be understood as applying to criminal law (as regards legal aid, for instance) and to administrative proceedings relating to immigration and asylum law.

Article 68 TFEU sets out a special role for the European Council in this area:

The European Council shall define the strategic guidelines for legislative and operational planning within the area of freedom, security and justice.

This new provision largely reflects the role which the European Council (the EU institution made up of Member States' heads of state or government) was already playing as regards JHA law before the Treaty of Lisbon.[320] In particular, the European Council had already agreed multi-annual guidelines for JHA cooperation.[321] This provision has already been applied to adopt the 'Stockholm programme', the latest multi-year JHA action programme, in December 2009.[322] Although the European Council is not a legislative body,[323] such guidelines are certainly politically highly significant since they are taken into account by other EU institutions.[324] They might also be legally relevant when interpreting JHA legislation, and as noted above, some aspects of the original JHA guidelines

---

[318] See, for instance, Art 2(a) of Dir 2003/86 on family reunion ([2003] OJ L 251/12).

[319] See ch 8 below.

[320] On the composition and functioning of the European Council, see the revised Art 15 TEU.

[321] See the 'Tampere programme', adopted in 1999, as well as the Hague programme adopted in 2004 ([2005] OJ C 53/1).   [322] [2010] OJ C 115.

[323] Art 15(1), revised TEU.

[324] See the discussion of the implementation of the Tampere and Hague programmes in s 2.2 of chs 3–12, and the discussion substance of the Stockholm programme in s 2.3 of chs 3–12.

adopted by the European Council in Tampere in 1999 are reflected in the measures adopted subsequently. These guidelines are adopted by 'consensus' in the European Council, although the Treaty does not expressly define this concept.[325] There is no specific role in JHA matters for the President of the European Council.[326] Article 68 TFEU differs from the prior role of the European Council in that there is a specific reference to operational cooperation, but surely the European Council would not expect to play a major role in as regards, for instance, the planning of operations by the relevant EU agencies (Europol, Eurojust, and Frontex, the EU border agency), since EU leaders obviously lack the specialist knowledge for this, and their involvement could compromise the agencies' operations.

Article 69 refers to a specific rule for national parliaments as regards scrutiny of JHA legislation:

National Parliaments ensure that the proposals and legislative initiatives submitted under Chapters 4 and 5 comply with the principle of subsidiarity, in accordance with the arrangements laid down by the Protocol on the application of the principles of subsidiarity and proportionality.

It should be noted that this special role for national parliaments only relates to measures concerning policing and criminal law. Article 69 is considered further as part of the analysis of the legitimacy of EU JHA measures below.[327]

Next, Article 70 TFEU permits the Council to adopt evaluation measures:

Without prejudice to Articles 258, 259 and 260, the Council may, on a proposal from the Commission, adopt measures laying down the arrangements whereby Member States, in collaboration with the Commission, conduct objective and impartial evaluation of the implementation of the Union policies referred to in this Title by Member States' authorities, in particular in order to facilitate full application of the principle of mutual recognition. The European Parliament and national Parliaments shall be informed of the content and results of the evaluation.

These evaluation measures are non-legislative acts to be adopted by QMV in Council on a proposal from the Commission, with no involvement of the EP.[328] This is a new provision in the Treaties inserted by the Treaty of Lisbon, although in fact a number of previous measures had been adopted concerning evaluation issues prior to the Treaty of Lisbon.

In particular, a general system for evaluation was put in place, with one JHA issue selected in turn for each cycle of evaluation,[329] and there were also specific systems for evaluating candidate Member States, the application of the Schengen

---

[325] Art 15(4), revised TEU.   [326] Art 15(5), revised TEU.   [327] See 2.5 below.
[328] On the accountability of evaluation measures, see 2.5 below.
[329] Joint Action ([1997] OJ L 344/7). The issues selected have been mutual assistance, drug trafficking, the supply of information to Europol, the European arrest warrant, and financial crime.

acquis, and the implementation of commitments concerning terrorism.[330] A suggestion by the Commission for a more elaborate system of evaluating JHA policies did not attract sufficient interest in the Council.[331] As for ensuring the correct implementation of Framework Decisions in national law, Member States agreed on a largely standard approach to assessing Member States' implementation of Framework Decisions. All but one Framework Decision specified that Member States should forward information on their implementation of each measure to the Commission and Council by or soon after the implementation deadline. Subsequently, the Commission and Council draw up reports on national implementation, and the Council was supposed to assess that implementation by a specified date.[332] Applying this procedure, there have been a large number of Commission reports and Council conclusions; the Council altered its procedure in 2005 to hold a full debate among ministers concerning the Commission's assertions about non-implementation of the Framework Decision on the European Arrest Warrant.[333] However, the Council stopped drawing up conclusions on national implementation of Framework Decisions after this point. The Commission has also produced reports concerning the national application of the Decision establishing Eurojust, and of the Convention on fraud against the EU's financial interests.[334] However, there was no ongoing evaluation of the application of most Decisions or Conventions, or of the Schengen Information System, or the Schengen rules on policing, criminal law, or border control, visas, and irregular immigration.

The Stockholm programme calls for regular evaluation of EU JHA policies, starting with judicial cooperation in criminal matters but including asylum procedures. It also calls upon the Commission to make proposals to implement Article 70 TFEU.[335] The action plan on implementation of the Stockholm programme provides for a communication on evaluation of JHA policies in 2010 and proposals concerning evaluation of anti-corruption policy (2012) and criminal justice cooperation (2011).[336]

As compared to other Treaty provisions, it is clear that evaluation measures may not concern the *substance* of EU JHA policy, in the absence of any wording conferring such competence. The point is obviously important because otherwise the EP's participation in the legislative process as regards the substance of policy

---

[330] Joint Action ([2000] OJ L 191/8); Schengen Executive Committee Decision SCH/Com-ex (98) 26 def ([2000] OJ L 239/138); and Decision ([2002] OJ L 349/1). The Commission made two proposals to amend the Schengen evaluation mechanism before the entry into force of the Treaty of Lisbon: COM (2009) 102 and COM (2009) 105, both 4 Mar 2009. The latter proposal lapsed with the entry into force of the Treaty of Lisbon, and the other has not been agreed or adopted; it now has the legal base of Art 74 TFEU (see COM (2009) 665, 2 Dec 2009), on which see below.

[331] COM (2006) 332, 28 June 2006.

[332] The exception is the second Framework Decision on counterfeiting currency, which makes no reference to a report or assessment ([2001] OJ L 329/3).

[333] For more detail, see 9.5.2 below.   [334] See respectively 11.9 and 10.5 below.

[335] See n 322 above, point 1.2.5.   [336] COM (2010) 171, 20 Apr 2010.

would be circumvented entirely, as would the role of national parliaments.[337] Similarly, any rules on the evaluation of specific legislative measures should be included within the relevant legislation.

Article 71 TFEU, another new Treaty provision, provides for the creation of a standing committee on internal security:

> A standing committee shall be set up within the Council in order to ensure that operational cooperation on internal security is promoted and strengthened within the Union. Without prejudice to Article 240, it shall facilitate coordination of the action of Member States' competent authorities. Representatives of the Union bodies, offices and agencies concerned may be involved in the proceedings of this committee. The European Parliament and national Parliaments shall be kept informed of the proceedings.

This committee (known as 'COSI', based on the French acronym) was established by the Council shortly after the date of entry into force of the Treaty of Lisbon.[338] The Decision establishing COSI makes clear that the committee does not have the competence to adopt legislative measures, and does not conduct operations,[339] but rather 'shall facilitate, promote and strengthen coordination of operational actions of the authorities of the Member States competent in the field of internal security', and 'shall also evaluate the general direction and efficiency of operational cooperation; it shall identify possible shortcomings or failures and adopt appropriate concrete recommendations to address them'.[340] It includes representatives from JHA agencies involved in operations.[341] As a Council committee it is subject to the rules on access to documents.[342]

There is no longer any reference, following the entry into force of the Treaty of Lisbon, to the previous committees which assisted the Council's discussions as regards the legislative (and to some extent the operational) aspects of the previous third pillar.[343] However, the Council (or, more precisely, Coreper)[344] has chosen to retain the committee that previously assisted its work as regards the legislative aspects of policing and criminal law, along with the 'Strategic Committee on Immigration, Frontiers and Asylum' and a number of other JHA working parties.[345]

---

[337] On the latter point, see 2.5 below.

[338] [2010] OJ L 52/50. The Council established the Committee as a procedural matter, pursuant to Art 240(3) TFEU, which meant that the Decision was adopted by a simple majority with no opt-out procedures possible. There was no role for the EP or the Commission.

[339] Art 4, COSI Decision.   [340] Arts 2 and 3(2), COSI Decision.

[341] Art 5, COSI Decision.   [342] See 2.5 below.

[343] These were the Art K.4 Committee before the Treaty of Amsterdam, and the Art 36 Committee after the Treaty of Amsterdam, named after the relevant Treaty articles.

[344] See Art 19 of the Council's rules of procedure ([2009] OJ L 325/35).

[345] See Council docs 16070/09, 16 Nov 2009 and 17653/09, 16 Dec 2009. The Art 36 Committee is now called the 'Coordinating Committee in the area of police and judicial cooperation in criminal matters', but still uses its prior French acronym ('CATS'; see Council doc 17611/09, 15 Dec 2009).

The next question is the extent of national competence as regards internal security. This issue arises most obviously in respect of Article 72 TFEU, which provides that '[t]his Title shall not affect the exercise of the responsibilities incumbent upon Member States with regard to the maintenance of law and order and the safeguarding of internal security'. In fact, this provision copies the wording of the previous Articles 64(1) EC and 33 TEU. But this issue also arises as regards Article 73 TFEU, which had no equivalent in the previous versions of the Treaties, and which provides that:

It shall be open to Member States to organise between themselves and under their responsibility such forms of cooperation and coordination as they deem appropriate between the competent departments of their administrations responsible for safeguarding national security.

Furthermore, the revised Article 4(2) TEU provides that:

The Union shall respect the equality of Member States before the Treaties as well as their national identities, inherent in their fundamental structures, political and constitutional, inclusive of regional and local self-government.
    It shall respect their essential State functions, including ensuring the territorial integrity of the State, maintaining law and order and safeguarding national security. In particular, national security remains the sole responsibility of each Member State.

Only the requirement to respect Member States' 'national identities' previously appeared expressly in the Treaties,[346] and the Court of Justice has only briefly touched upon the interpretation of this provision.[347] This may, however, be due to the exclusion of the Court's jurisdiction as regards this provision,[348] a restriction which was lifted by the Treaty of Lisbon. Furthermore, Articles 346–348 TFEU (previously Articles 296–298 EC) provide for specified exceptions relating to the arms trade and national security; those provisions were not substantively amended by the Treaty of Lisbon, and (as noted above) have applied to policing and criminal law matters as well after that Treaty entered into force.

    To what extent do these provisions reserve competence to Member States? First, Article 72 TFEU should be interpreted the same way as the previous Treaty Articles with identical wording. Although these Articles have not yet been interpreted by the Court of Justice, the best interpretation is that they confirmed that the use of coercive measures in order to enforce measures adopted pursuant to the JHA provisions of the Treaties is left to the Member States' authorities, in particular as regards arrest, detention, and the use of force. EU agencies are therefore limited to supporting actions of national authorities, except (and only)

---

[346] Previous Art 6(3) TEU.
[347] Case C-473/93 *Commission v Luxembourg* [1996] ECR I-3207.
[348] See the previous Art 46 TEU, and more generally 2.2.2.2 above.

to the extent that the Treaty confers express powers to act on such agencies.[349] This interpretation is also consistent with the limitation on the Court's jurisdiction pursuant to Article 276 TFEU.[350]

In particular, the express restriction upon Europol taking 'coercive measures' set out in Article 88 TFEU should be understood as a specific application of this general rule. However, Article 72 TFEU should not be understood to preclude the adoption of measures pursuant to Article 86 TFEU which confer upon the European Public Prosecutor those powers which the Treaty expressly provides for, or such further judicial or prosecutorial powers as would be clearly necessary to carry out the Prosecutor's functions. Fundamentally, this exclusion should not be seen as a restriction on the *subject matter* which the EU is competent to address, but rather as a rule regarding the division of powers between the EU and the Member States as regards the *execution* of operational measures necessary to implement EU rules. Where the drafters of the Treaty of Lisbon wished to restrict the Union's competence regarding specific JHA issues, they have done so expressly,[351] and so further specific restrictions on competence over specific subject matter cannot be inferred from a general rule like Article 72.

Next, to what extent does Article 73 TFEU limit the EU's competence? This Article does not as such exclude the EU from competence to adopt measures concerning cooperation regarding national security. This is particularly obvious when comparing it to the Treaty Article which quite clearly reserves 'competence' to Member States, such as Article 79(5) TFEU. Following the model of Article 79(5), if the drafters of Article 73 had wished to reserve national competence over security services unambiguously, Article 73 could simply have provided that, '[t]his Title shall not affect the competence of Member States to organise between themselves . . .'. In any event, Article 73 does not impact upon the ability of the EU to regulate security services *to the extent that they participate in law enforcement*. If the EU were precluded from regulating such matters, this would restrict the effectiveness of the EU to regulate law enforcement issues, given the involvement of security agencies in law enforcement, and so such an exclusion would surely have to be provided for expressly. Furthermore, this interpretation would significantly undermine the accountability of EU action in this area.

As for the adoption of EU measures regulating internal security cooperation per se, Article 73 leaves it 'open' to Member States to cooperate on this matter, but does not expressly rule out the adoption of EU measures on this issue. Nor does such cooperation fall outside the scope of the EU's JHA objectives of ensuring a 'high level of security' by means of measures concerning police, judicial, 'and *other* competent authorities'.[352]

---

[349] See more specifically 3.2.4, 11.2.4, and 12.2.4 below.
[350] On Art 276 TFEU, see further 2.2.2.2 above. [351] See Art 79(5) TFEU.
[352] See Art 67(3) TFEU, discussed further above.

Nevertheless, EU competence over the regulation of internal security agencies appears to be ruled out by one of the TEU's general clauses on the relationship between the EU and the Member States. As we have seen above, Article 4(2) TEU states that a 'particular' rule regarding the EU's respect for 'essential state functions' is that 'national security remains the sole responsibility of each Member State'. It is hard to see how an EU power to regulate such matters could be exercised without encroaching upon this 'sole responsibility'. Having said that, the general rule in Article 4(2) TEU should not be understood, any more than the specific rule in Article 73 TFEU, to exempt security agencies entirely from the scope of EU law when they exercise law enforcement functions, as distinct from functions relating to national security.

Finally, how should the broader requirement in Article 4(2) TEU of 'respect' for essential state functions, 'including...maintaining law and order and safeguarding national security', be interpreted? Since the reference to 'maintaining law and order' is identical to Article 72 TFEU in this respect, this part of Article 4(2) adds no further limitation to the EU's powers.[353] As for the reference to 'safeguarding national security', it is only relevant to the extent that *national* security is at issue, rather than *internal* security. But even to the extent of the overlap between the two provisions, the obligation to *respect* State functions as regards national security as set out in Article 4(2) TEU is less far-reaching than the requirement not to *affect* internal security responsibilities as set out in Article 72 TFEU. It must therefore be concluded that the general rule in the first sentence of Article 4(2) TEU does not lay down any additional restriction on EU action besides those spelt out in Article 72 TFEU as regards responsibilities for law and order and internal security, and in the second sentence of Article 4(2) TEU as regards the sole responsibility for national security.

Next, Article 74 TFEU provides for a power to adopt measures concerning administrative cooperation:

The Council shall adopt measures to ensure administrative cooperation between the relevant departments of the Member States in the areas covered by this Title, as well as between those departments and the Commission. It shall act on a Commission proposal, subject to Article 76, and after consulting the European Parliament.

This power previously existed before the Treaty of Lisbon as regards immigration, asylum, and civil law (see the prior Article 66 TEC), but was expanded by that Treaty to cover policing and criminal law as well, subject to the possibility that one-quarter of Member States are able to propose a measure in this area in

---

[353] It might be objected that where a Treaty rule is repeated, there must be some additional legal meaning accorded to the second appearance of the rule. However, the drafters of the Treaty of Lisbon were apparently quite content to repeat several provisions of the Treaty purely for the sake of emphasis—as evidenced by Arts 4(1) TEU and the second sentence of Art 5(2) TEU, for instance.

those fields.[354] These measures are adopted by a QMV in the Council after consultation of the EP, and are not legislative. Because of the different decision-making procedure, it is important to distinguish this provision from the substantive legal bases in Title V which provide either for the ordinary legislative procedure or unanimous voting in the Council. Given the limited wording of Article 74 and the express provisions conferring competence as regards substantive law, Article 74 cannot be the legal base for any measure affecting substantive JHA law, for instance concerning border checks; the substance or procedure relating to applications for visas, asylum, or residence permits; the rules relating to civil jurisdiction or civil procedure; the mutual recognition of criminal law decisions; or the exchange of information between law enforcement authorities. Instead, the Article is a legal base for measures concerning issues such as exchanges of personnel or exchanges of general information (as distinct from the exchange of information on specific individuals for law enforcement or immigration control purposes).[355]

Next, Article 75 TFEU provides for the adoption of legislation on anti-terrorist sanctions. This is a new provision inserted by the Treaty of Lisbon, so the background first of all needs to be explained.[356] Before the entry into force of the Treaty of Lisbon, the EU adopted measures freezing the assets and income of persons and groups who were believed to be terrorists but whose alleged activities were primarily outside the EU. One category of such groups and persons were those who were allegedly linked to al-Qaeda and the Taliban, and the EU established a legal framework by means of which it simply copied the lists of such persons and groups designated by a committee of the United Nations Security Council.[357] The second category (subject to separate legislation) consisted of those persons and groups which the EU institutions believed to be terrorists, but who were listed as terrorists on the basis that a 'competent authority' was investigating or prosecuting them for terrorist offences (the 'autonomous' list).[358]

In both cases, the legal bases for the adoption of the relevant measures were Articles 60, 301, and 308 of the previous EC Treaty. Article 301 provided for the adoption of economic sanctions against third countries by QMV in Council after a Commission proposal, with no involvement of the EP, following the adoption of a foreign policy measure pursuant to Title V of the previous TEU. Article 60 of the previous EC Treaty applied the same procedure as regards financial sanctions

---

[354] Art 76 TFEU, discussed further below. This rules out the prospect of a Member States' initiative concerning administrative cooperation across the whole of Title V.

[355] See further 2.4 of chs 3–12.

[356] On the substance of EU anti-terrorist sanctions legislation and the litigation concerning its application, see 12.4.5 below.

[357] Reg 881/2002, [2002] OJ L 139/9, as amended by Reg 561/2003, [2003] OJ L 82/1.

[358] Reg 2580/2001, [2001] OJ L 344/79, which applied alongside a foreign policy measure (Common Position 2001/931, [2001] OJ L 344/93).

against third countries.[359] Finally, Article 308 of the previous EC Treaty was used as an additional legal base so that the EU sanctions measures could be extended to persons and groups not connected with a third state's government; this provision was subject to unanimous voting in the Council and consultation of the EP, with no requirement of a prior foreign policy measure. No EU sanctions measures were adopted against persons or groups who were believed to be terrorists but whose activity was mainly *internal* to the EU, because it was believed (correctly or not) that the EC and EU had no power to adopt sanctions in that case. Following the entry into force of the Treaty of Lisbon, the correctness of that view is now moot. However, the EU nevertheless designated some such groups and persons as 'terrorists' on its autonomous list, for the (sole) purpose of cooperating as regards 'enquiries and proceedings' in respect of such persons within the scope of the third pillar (as it then was).[360] The legal bases used for these measures were upheld by the Court of Justice, which ruled that Articles 60 and 301 EC could be used as regards the material scope of sanctions against al-Qaeda, but not as regards the personal scope of such sanctions, because those Treaty articles only provided competence to adopt sanctions measures as regards entire countries or 'the rulers of such a country and also individuals and entities associated with or controlled, directly or indirectly, by them'. Article 308 EC gave the EC the power to extend the scope of those sanctions to persons not connected to a governing regime, because the failure to adopt uniform rules in this regard could impact upon the operation of the common market (which was at the time a requirement for the use of Article 308).[361]

The Treaty of Lisbon replaced Articles 60 and 301 EC with Article 215 TFEU, which applies to both economic and financial sanctions (without any special rule relating to national financial sanctions) and also now permits the EU to apply such sanctions 'against natural or legal persons and groups or non-State entities'. The decision-making process remains the same as before, with the addition of a requirement that the EU's High Representative for foreign policy jointly propose the measure concerned.[362] Article 215 also requires the adoption of 'legal safeguards' relating to sanctions measures; measures based on this Article are not legislative acts.

But the Treaty of Lisbon also added Article 75 TFEU, which provides that:

Where necessary to achieve the objectives set out in Article 67, as regards preventing and combating terrorism and related activities, the European Parliament and the Council, acting by means of regulations in accordance with the ordinary legislative procedure, shall

---

[359] Art 60(2) EC set out a specific rule relating to financial sanctions by Member States, but there was no equivalent rule in the prior Art 301 EC.

[360] See Art 4 of Common Position 2001/931 (n 358 above). The application of this provision was at issue in Case C-355/04 P *SEGI* [2007] ECR I-1657.

[361] Joined Cases C-402/05 P and C-415/05 P *Kadi and Al Barakaat* [2008] ECR I-6351, paras 163–178, 211–216, and 222–236.   [362] On this position, see Art 18, revised TEU.

define a framework for administrative measures with regard to capital movements and payments, such as the freezing of funds, financial assets or economic gains belonging to, or owned or held by, natural or legal persons, groups or non-State entities.

The Council, on a proposal from the Commission, shall adopt measures to implement the framework referred to in the first paragraph.

The acts referred to in this Article shall include necessary provisions on legal safeguards.

As compared to Article 215 TFEU, the basic measures to be adopted pursuant to Article 75 TFEU are legislative acts which must be adopted by the use of the ordinary legislative procedure, with no requirement of the adoption of a prior foreign policy act or for a joint proposal by the High Representative. There is also an opt-out from Article 75 measures for the UK and Denmark (but not Ireland), although the UK intends to opt in to such measures.[363] No opt-out applies to Article 215 TFEU.

Which of these provisions applies to the adoption of anti-terrorist measures? Unsurprisingly the EP argues that Article 75 applies,[364] but the Council and Commission argue that Article 215 applies. Shortly after the entry into force of the Treaty of Lisbon, the Council adopted a measure amending the basic framework for sanctions against al-Qeada and the Taliban on the basis of Article 215 TFEU,[365] and the EP has challenged this before the Court of Justice, primarily on the basis that this measure has the wrong 'legal base'.[366] The best view on this issue is that Article 75 is a *lex specialis* as regards anti-terrorist sanctions, and applies instead of Article 215 TFEU in the absence of any exclusion from or limitation of the scope of the JHA provision. Sanctions against any alleged terrorists contribute to the objectives set out in Article 67 TFEU (as Article 75 requires), given that Article 67 does not limit itself to actions carried out on EU Member States' territories and that the TEU provides that the protection of the EU's external objectives also takes place by means of the external aspects of the EU's internal policies.[367] Since all anti-terrorist measures are linked to some extent to Resolutions of the United Nations Security Council, the Council's approach would mean that Article 75 is deprived of all meaning. Article 215 could still be used as the legal base for the adoption of sanctions measures *not* concerning terrorism.

In the alternative, Articles 75 and 215 should be the joint legal base for the adoption of anti-terrorist measures. While there are differences between these two legal bases, in that Article 215 requires a joint proposal from the High Representative and the prior adoption of a foreign policy measure, the latter point was equally true as regards the joint use of Articles 60, 301, and 308 EC

---

[363] See 2.2.5.1 and 2.2.5.2 below.

[364] Use of Art 75 also entails scrutiny powers for national parliaments (see 2.5 below), whereas Art 215 does not.   [365] Reg 1265/2009, [2009] OJ L 346/42.

[366] Case C-130/10 *EP v Council*, pending.   [367] Art 21, revised TEU.

before the entry into force of the Treaty of Lisbon; nevertheless, the Court of Justice did not object to it in the *Kadi* judgment. Nor did the Court object in that judgment to the combined use of a legal base requiring consultation of the EP and a legal base giving the EP no role, so there is no reason to object to a combined legal base requiring the ordinary legislative procedure and the non-consultation of the EP.[368] The difference in the legal bases as regards the role (and non-role) of the High Representative is surely analogous, and no more problematic than, the difference as regards the role (and non-role) of the EP.[369]

However, since Articles 75 and 215 only apply to *sanctions*, they cannot be used merely to list alleged terrorists or terrorist groups for the mere purpose of enhancing judicial and police cooperation. The correct legal bases for that process after the Treaty of Lisbon are Articles 82 and 87 TFEU.[370] The Council has already made a legal error on this point, when it updated the list of external terrorist groups and persons who were subject to both sanctions and enhanced judicial and police cooperation after the entry into force of the Treaty of Lisbon, by means of the foreign policy powers conferred by Article 29, revised TEU.[371]

Finally, Article 76 TFEU provides for a continued possibility for Member States to propose measures concerning policing and criminal law:

The acts referred to in Chapters 4 and 5, together with the measures referred to in Article 74 which ensure administrative cooperation in the areas covered by these Chapters, shall be adopted:

(a) on a proposal from the Commission, or
(b) on the initiative of a quarter of the Member States.

This retains a power enjoyed (and often exercised) by Member States before the Treaty of Lisbon.[372] However, as compared to the prior third pillar, Member States cannot propose measures individually, but can make initiatives only if (at least) one-quarter of Member States propose them. So far, there have been three such initiatives.[373] The question arises whether Member States can withdraw or amend such initiatives, either collectively or individually. The TFEU provides that the *Commission* can always amend its proposals, and that Member

---

[368] Note that the Court of Justice has accepted joint legal bases which combine consultation of the EP with its pre-Lisbon co-decision rights: see for instance, Case C-166/07 *EP v Council* [2009] ECR I-7135.

[369] In fact, it is less problematic than the combination of unanimity and QMV in the Council, which the Court accepted without comment in both *EP v Council* (ibid) and *Kadi*.

[370] On the scope of Art 87 generally, see 12.2.4 below.

[371] Decision 2009/1004, [2009] OJ L 346/58.

[372] See the prior Art 34 TEU, discussed in 2.2.2.2 above.

[373] These are initiatives for Directives on: the right to interpretation and translation in the framework of criminal proceedings ([2010] OJ C 69/1); a European protection order ([2010] OJ C 69/5); and a European investigation order ([2010] OJ C 165/22). Note that the Commission issued a competing proposal on the first subject: COM (2010) 82, 9 Mar 2010.

States must normally vote unanimously to amend *Commission* proposals.[374] The absence of a reference to Member State initiatives suggests that these rules do *not* apply to such initiatives. In other cases, the TFEU sets out special rules for Member State initiatives.[375] However, although Member States cannot withdraw or amend their initiatives, there is nothing in the Treaty to prevent (a) Member State(s) voting against initiatives that it (or they) have made, or, where relevant, pulling an 'emergency brake' concerning those initiatives.[376] While it might seem odd that a Member State would vote against its own initiative, it is conceivable that a Member State might change its mind due to a change of government or in reaction to public discussion of the proposal, or because the proposal has been amended during the decision-making process and the Member State in question disagrees with such changes.

2.2.3.3. Transitional rules[377]

The transitional rules in the Treaty of Lisbon relating to the abolition of the former third pillar appear in a special transitional Protocol, which governs a number of issues concerning the transition from the previous rules in the Treaties to the new rules introduced by the Treaty of Lisbon. There are three different issues relating to the former third pillar addressed by the Protocol: the jurisdiction of the Court of Justice over third pillar measures adopted before the entry into force of the Treaty of Lisbon ('pre-existing third pillar measures') for a five-year transitional period (ending 1 December 2014); the legal effect of those same measures (*not* subject to a transitional period); and the possibility of the UK to opt out of those measures at the end of the five-year transitional period.[378] The first two issues are considered here, while the third issue is considered further below, along with the other opt-outs for the UK on JHA matters.[379] As noted above, there are no transitional restrictions on the full extension of the Court of Justice's jurisdiction as regards immigration, asylum, and civil law.[380]

First of all, the transitional provision on the Court of Justice states that the powers of the EU institutions, namely the role of the Commission in infringement actions and the jurisdiction of the Court of Justice, remains the same for pre-existing third pillar measures as before the Treaty of Lisbon for the five-year

---

[374] Art 293 TFEU. It is assumed in practice, at least by the Commission, that the former rule gives full discretion to the Commission to *withdraw* its proposals.

[375] See Arts 294(15) and 238(2) and (3)(b) TFEU, as regards the ordinary legislative procedure and Council voting rules respectively.

[376] Equally, there is nothing to stop (a) Member State(s) which proposed an initiative bringing an action to annul it after its adoption.

[377] For more detailed analysis of this issue, see S Peers, 'Finally "Fit for Purpose?" The Treaty of Lisbon and the End of the Third Pillar Legal Order' (2008) 27 YEL 47.

[378] A complete list of binding pre-existing third pillar acts which were in force at the date of entry into force of the Treaty of Lisbon, as well as subsequent amendments and proposed amendments to those acts, appears in Appendix II.   [379] See 2.2.5.1.4.

[380] See 2.2.3.1.

transitional period, including where a Member State accepted the jurisdiction of the Court of Justice over references for a preliminary ruling pursuant to the previous rules.[381] Presumably this refers not only to the rules on the Court's jurisdiction applicable to measures adopted between 1999 and 2009, but also to the jurisdictional rules applicable to measures adopted before 1999 (limited jurisdiction for Conventions, no jurisdiction for other acts), to the extent that the pre-Amsterdam measures are still in force.[382] It should be recalled that the pre-existing third pillar measures include the *immigration* provisions of the SIS, except to the extent that they have been amended since 1999, until SIS II becomes operational.

What does this mean in practice? As noted above,[383] for the third pillar measures adopted between 1999 and 2009: nineteen Member States accepted the Court's jurisdiction for preliminary rulings; no infringement actions were possible; there were special rules on the Court's jurisdiction as regards dispute settlement between Member States and between Member States and the Commission; and there were special rules on annulment actions (which were moot by early 2010 due to the time limit on bringing annulment actions).[384] So the limitation on the Court's jurisdiction is particularly relevant as regards those Member States that did not opt in to the Court's jurisdiction as regards preliminary rulings, and as regards the exclusion of the Commission's ability to bring infringement proceedings. Although one interpretation of the transitional protocol would suggest that Member States which did not opt in to the Court's preliminary rulings jurisdiction as regards pre-existing third pillar measures before the entry into force of the Treaty of Lisbon could not then do so during the transitional period, the better interpretation is that they are still able to do so, as this would facilitate the underlying purpose of the Protocol of providing for a smooth transition to the new jurisdictional rules set out in the Treaty of Lisbon.[385]

The transitional protocol contains an important qualification upon the continued limitations upon the Court's jurisdiction. Once a pre-existing third pillar act is amended, the Court's new jurisdiction will apply as regards those Member States for which the amended act is applicable.[386] This takes account of the possible

---

[381] Art 10(1), transitional protocol. All references in this subsection are to the transitional protocol, unless otherwise indicated. On the substance of the previous rules on the Court's jurisdiction, see 2.2.2.2 above.

[382] On the substance of the pre-Amsterdam rules on the Court's jurisdiction, see 2.2.1 above.

[383] See 2.2.2.2.

[384] It should be noted that the validity of a third pillar act can still be challenged through the national courts without any time limit, by means of a reference pursuant to the previous Art 35(1) TEU or (after the end of the transitional period) Art 267 TFEU.

[385] In any event, the relevant wording of Art 10(1)—'including where they have been accepted under Article 35(2) of the said Treaty on European Union'—does not unambiguously require that the relevant jurisdiction must 'have been accepted' before the entry into force of the Treaty of Lisbon. See also, by analogy, Case C-296/08 *Santesteban Goicoechea* [2008] ECR I-6307.

[386] Art 10(2).

restriction in territorial scope of the amended act, pursuant to the special opt-out rules applying to the UK, Ireland, and Denmark, the general rules on enhanced cooperation, and the special voting rules applicable to aspects of EU policing and criminal law, which could lead to a 'fast-track' application of the enhanced cooperation rules.[387] In any event, whether a pre-existing third pillar act is amended during the transitional period or not, the Court's normal jurisdiction will apply to all those acts at the end of the transitional period.[388]

As for the special rules on the legal effect of pre-existing third pillar measures, the transitional protocol provides that the legal effect of acts adopted on the basis of the TEU before the Treaty of Lisbon entered into force 'shall be preserved until those acts are repealed, annulled or amended in implementation of the Treaties'; this also applies to 'agreements concluded between Member States on the basis of' the TEU.[389] The latter provision covers third pillar Conventions. There is no time limit on the application of this provision, which at the very least preserves the lack of direct effect of pre-existing Framework Decisions and Decisions, and also preserves other restrictions which arguably exist as regards the legal effect of pre-existing third pillar measures as compared to other EU law.[390]

Obviously, much rests on the amendment of pre-existing third pillar acts, particularly within the five-year transitional period applicable to the jurisdiction of the Court of Justice.[391] The Final Act of the Treaty of Lisbon contains a declaration specifically addressing this issue:

The Conference invites the European Parliament, the Council and the Commission, within their respective powers, to seek to adopt, in appropriate cases and as far as possible within the five-year period referred to in Article 10(3) of the Protocol on transitional provisions, legal acts amending or replacing the acts referred to in Article 10(1) of that Protocol.

The Stockholm programme also makes specific reference to the transformation of pre-existing third pillar acts, stating that the Action Plan to implement the programme 'should include a proposal for a timetable for the transformation of instruments with a new legal basis'.[392] However, the Commission's Action Plan does not contain a specific timetable to this end, although implicitly a significant number of pre-existing measures would be replaced or amended within the transitional period.[393]

In practice, in the first nine months after the Treaty of Lisbon entered into force, the Commission tabled two proposals which would repeal prior third pillar

---

[387] See respectively 2.2.5.1, 2.2.5.2, 2.2.5.5, and 2.2.3.4, all below.   [388] Art 10(3).

[389] Art 9. This provision also applies to pre-existing CFSP acts, but they are not considered further here.   [390] On the legal effect of pre-existing third pillar measures, see 2.2.2.2 above.

[391] The amendment of pre-existing third pillar acts within the transitional period also has an impact on the scope of the UK's option to disapply all pre-existing acts at the end of that period: see 2.2.5.1.4 below.   [392] [2010] OJ C 115, point 1.2.10.

[393] COM (2010) 171, 20 Apr 2010.

acts (one of which was already agreed),[394] and one proposal which would amend a prior third pillar act (this proposal was subsequently adopted).[395] A group of Member States tabled an initiative to repeal a prior third pillar act and 'replace' the corresponding provisions of several others.[396]

A crucial question as regards the transitional protocol is the definition of an 'amendment' to a pre-existing third pillar act.[397] There is no de minimis rule, so it would seem that even a minor amendment to a pre-existing third pillar act would trigger the application of the new rules on the Court's jurisdiction and the legal effect to all the measure concerned. It makes sense that where there are measures implementing a parent act, only an amendment to the parent act would trigger the new rules concerned, which would then apply to the entirety of the parent act and all implementing measures as an *ensemble*, because the implementing measures depend on the parent act for their validity. In order to give the protocol its full effect, the new rules on legal effect and Court jurisdiction should apply to a pre-existing third pillar measure as soon as an amending act enters into force, rather than the date of applicability or the deadline for Member States to apply the amending act. For the same reasons, the provisions of the Schengen *acquis* allocated to the previous third pillar should be treated as a single act for the purposes of the protocol; but these provisions must be severed from the provisions of that *acquis* which were allocated to the EC legal order in 1999 (ie immigration measures), since the latter provisions are outside the scope of the transitional protocol.

2.2.3.4. Special decision-making rules

As noted above, in order to assuage some Member States' concerns about the loss of sovereignty in vital areas relating to criminal law and policing, the JHA provisions in the Treaty of Lisbon contain two special decision-making rules, one known as the 'emergency brake' and the other referred to in this book as the 'pseudo-veto'. The emergency brake applies to decisions regarding domestic

---

[394] These were proposals for Directives on sexual offences regarding children (COM (2010) 94, 29 Mar 2010) and trafficking in persons (COM (2010) 95, 29 Mar 2010), which would replace the Framework Decisions on the same subjects (respectively [2004] OJ L 13/44 and [2002] OJ L 203/1). The Council agreed on the trafficking proposal in June 2010, but, at the time of writing, still has to agree the text with the EP (Council doc 10845/10, 10 June 2010).

[395] This was a proposal for a Regulation (COM (2010) 15, 29 Jan 2010), amending the previous Decision on migration from the first-generation to the second-generation SIS as regards policing and criminal law ([2008] OJ L 299/43). The Regulation was adopted as Reg 542/2010, [2010] OJ L 155/23.

[396] Initiative for a Directive establishing a European investigation order ([2010] OJ C 165/22), which would repeal the Framework Decision establishing the European Evidence Warrant ([2008] OJ L 350/72) and replace the corresponding provisions of the EU Convention on Mutual Assistance ([2000] OJ C 197/1), its Protocol ([2001] OJ C 326/1), and the Schengen Convention ([2000] OJ L 239).

[397] This question is also relevant as regards the opt-outs of the UK, Ireland, and possibly in future Denmark from JHA matters, since special rules apply if they opt out of an amendment of an act which they are already bound by. See 2.2.5.1 and 2.2.5.2 below.

criminal procedure and substantive criminal law,[398] while the pseudo-veto applies to decisions regarding the European Public Prosecutor and operational police cooperation (except for measures building upon the Schengen *acquis*).[399] In each case it will be necessary to distinguish between the legal bases which are subject to these special rules, and those legal bases which are not.[400] Both of these special procedures could lead to a discussion of a draft proposal or initiative at the level of the European Council (the EU leaders) and in both cases, one possible outcome is a 'fast-track' approval for a group of Member States to adopt the relevant measure without the participation of other Member States (the concept of 'enhanced cooperation'), circumventing the substantive or procedural requirements which would normally apply before enhanced cooperation could be authorized.[401]

But there are differences between the two procedures, which will therefore be considered in turn. In particular, a veto is distinct from an emergency brake because there are no limitations of the grounds on which a Member State could exercise a veto, whereas an emergency brake can only be pulled on specified grounds; and even if a emergency brake could be challenged or overridden, a veto cannot. Moreover, the pseudo-veto would trigger enhanced cooperation in a *positive* way—ie a group of Member States *wanting* the adoption of a proposal would refer the issue to the European Council—whereas the emergency brake would trigger enhanced cooperation in a *negative* way, because it would be invoked by a single Member State objecting to a measure. Also, the Member States invoking the pseudo-veto process would have comparative 'safety in numbers'.

In either case, it should be recalled that as few as seven Member States could make a criminal law or policing proposal pursuant to the Treaty of Lisbon provisions, so in such a case those Member States would only have to find two more allies to ensure the adoption of the measure by means of enhanced cooperation.[402]

2.2.3.4.1. The emergency brake[403]

The Treaty rule which provides for this procedure as regards criminal law proposals or initiatives reads as follows:

Where a member of the Council considers that a draft directive as referred to in [the relevant provision] would affect fundamental aspects of its criminal justice system, it may

---

[398] Arts 82(3) and 83(3) TFEU, referring to Arts 82(2) and 83(1) and (2) TFEU. However, where the adoption of 'Community criminal law' measures pursuant to Art 83(2) TFEU requires unanimous voting (for instance, as regards tax or racism), the emergency brake procedure would implicitly not apply, since it can only be used to suspend the ordinary legislative procedure (Art 83(3) TFEU), which always entails QMV.   [399] Arts 86 and 87(3) TFEU.

[400] Notably Arts 82(1) (cross-border mutual recognition measures), 85 (Eurojust), 87(2) (other forms of police cooperation), 88 (Europol), and 89 (cross-border police operations). See further 9.2.4, 10.2.4, 11.2.4, and 12.2.4 below.   [401] For the details of those rules, see 2.2.5.5 below.

[402] See Art 76 TFEU, discussed in 2.2.3.2 above.

[403] This discussion is adapted from S Peers, 'EU Criminal Law and the Treaty of Lisbon' (2008) 33 ELRev 507 at 522–529.

request that the draft directive be referred to the European Council. In that case, the ordinary legislative procedure shall be suspended. After discussion, and in case of a consensus, the European Council shall, within four months of this suspension, refer the draft back to the Council, which shall terminate the suspension of the ordinary legislative procedure.

Within the same timeframe, in case of disagreement, and if at least nine Member States wish to establish enhanced cooperation on the basis of the draft directive concerned, they shall notify the European Parliament, the Council and the Commission accordingly. In such a case, the authorisation to proceed with enhanced cooperation referred to in Article 20(2) of the Treaty on European Union and Article 329(1) of this Treaty shall be deemed to be granted and the provisions on enhanced cooperation shall apply.

The following analysis sets out in turn: a comparison between the emergency brake rules and the rules on enhanced cooperation; an examination of the grounds for invoking the emergency brake, including the question of whether a decision to pull the brake is judicially reviewable; an analysis of the procedure in the European Council; and an assessment of the overall political context of the emergency brake. The relationship between the emergency brake and the British and Irish opt-outs is considered further below.[404]

First of all, the fast-track route to enhanced cooperation which would apply if the emergency brake were pulled would circumvent the usual requirements of a proposal from the Commission, the consent of the EP, and the support of a qualified majority of *all* Member States before enhanced cooperation is applied.[405] After enhanced cooperation is authorized, only the representatives of the participating Member States could vote on the legislation in the Council;[406] but in the EP, *all* MEPs would have a vote. It should also be pointed out that a Member State which did not originally participate in the adoption of the legislation could participate later if it were able to comply with the relevant conditions.[407] On the other hand, Member States joining the EU in future would not be obliged to participate in the relevant measure.[408]

The practical importance of circumventing the requirement for an approval of the enhanced cooperation by a qualified majority of *all* members of the Council can be demonstrated by the difficulties in adopting the Commission's original proposal on suspects' rights within the previous legal framework, where there was no fast-track route to enhanced cooperation.[409] Several Member States objected to the adoption of this proposal, preventing its adoption due to the previous requirement of unanimity for third pillar measures, but a qualified majority of Member States was in favour of the *proposal*. However, when the German Council Presidency in 2007 held an indicative vote as to whether there was enough support to authorize enhanced cooperation as regards this measure,

---

[404] See 2.5.5.1.   [405] Art 329(1) TFEU.   [406] Art 330 TFEU.

[407] Art 331(1) TFEU. This also applies to the UK and Ireland, if they decide to opt out of the legislation: see 2.2.5.1 below.   [408] Revised Art 20(4) TEU.

[409] COM (2004) 328, 28 Apr 2004. On the substance of this issue, see 9.8.2 below.

there was *not* a qualified majority in favour of *authorizing enhanced cooperation*. It can be seen that the Treaty of Lisbon rules, by removing the requirement of QMV approval by all Member States (along with other requirements), would therefore in principle make enhanced cooperation more likely. In fact, it is possible that the mere existence of the emergency brake process will encourage Member States (and the Commission and EP) to authorize enhanced cooperation more readily (as regards criminal law) pursuant to the normal authorization rules, thereby avoiding the high-profile drama of a referral of draft legislation to the European Council.[410]

Some important *substantive* conditions being circumvented would be the requirements not to 'undermine the internal market', not to 'constitute a barrier to or a discrimination in trade between Member States', and not to 'distort competition between them'.[411] This could be particularly relevant where some Member States do not participate in measures adopted pursuant to the 'Community criminal law competence' in Article 83(2) TFEU,[412] or in measures which are otherwise likely to have a significant impact on private industry (such as legislation concerning money laundering or relating to bank account information). The Final Act of the Treaty of Lisbon includes a declaration concerning the possible use of a special rule regarding distortion of competition in the event that this happens.[413]

Emergency brakes can be found elsewhere in the Treaties,[414] although such brakes have never in fact been used to date. They are always linked to QMV. The criminal law emergency brakes are distinct in that they are the only emergency brakes which could trigger a fast-track authorization of enhanced cooperation.

The second issue is the grounds for pulling an emergency brake, including the question of the extent to which a Member State's power to pull the emergency brake would be reviewable. The decision to pull the emergency brake should not be directly reviewable as such before the EU courts, since it would be a step in the decision-making process, rather than a final legal act.[415] But if a Member State's attempt to pull the emergency brake were overruled by other Member

---

[410] There is nothing in the Treaty to suggest that *only* the fast-track process, rather than the normal procedure, can be used to authorize enhanced cooperation as regards criminal law.

[411] Art 326 TFEU.   [412] On this competence, see further 10.4.1.2 below.

[413] Declaration 26, referring to Art 116 TFEU. It is arguable, however, that this Declaration only applies to opt-outs, rather than enhanced cooperation, since it refers to cases where a Member State 'opts not to participate' in a measure. Then again, if Member States which do not participate in a measure due to an opt-out are sanctioned, but those Member States which have not participated in the same measure due to enhanced cooperation are *not* sanctioned, this would breach the principle of equality of Member States, as set out in the revised Art 4(2) TEU.

[414] The current provisions relate to foreign policy (Art 31(2), revised TEU) and social security coordination (Art 48 TFEU). The Treaty of Amsterdam initially provided for emergency brakes as regards authorization for enhanced cooperation (Arts 11(2) TEC and previous Art 40(2) TEU), but the Treaty of Nice abolished them.

[415] See K Lenaerts, D Arts, and I Maselis, *Procedural Law of the European Union* (2nd edn, Thomson, 2006), 215–16.

States in the Council, the dissenting Member State could argue before the Court of Justice that it should have been allowed to pull the brake. Equally, if a Member State is allowed to pull the emergency brake and another Member State or the Commission argues that this should not have been allowed, there could be an annulment action before the Court of Justice raising this issue. In either case, the criteria for the use of the emergency brake would be justiciable.[416]

In considering the reviewability of an emergency brake, it will be necessary to strike a balance between the absolute right of a Member State to block a measure and the prospect that the majority of Member States might override one Member State's legitimate concerns about the integrity of its criminal justice system. So a Member State which wished to pull an emergency brake relating to criminal law would have to substantiate its argument that a draft measure would affect fundamental aspects of its criminal justice system. To do this, the dissenting Member State would have to demonstrate four things: its objections relate to a current draft proposal or initiative, not to a previous draft, or a hypothetical future draft; its concerns relate to its *criminal justice* system, not to another issue (such as world trade talks or the impact of the Second World War); the effect of the draft proposal or initiative on its criminal justice system, in order to prove that its national laws or principles would be required to change in some way; and why the relevant national rule is considered *fundamental*. In the latter two cases, any doubt would have to be resolved in favour of the Member State concerned, since that Member State is obviously the best judge (as it were) of its own criminal justice system, even if other Member States which have (or had) a similar or identical rule in their national legal system do not (or did not) consider that rule to be fundamental.

Implicitly it would be illegal for a *supporter* of the proposed legislation to use the emergency brake falsely, in order to trigger a fast-track authorization of enhanced cooperation, for the simple reason that such a Member State would not in fact have any genuine concerns about the impact of the proposal upon the fundamental aspects of its criminal justice system. Put another way, it has been pointed out by way of analogy that 'the abuse of emergency facilities is a crime in many Member States'.[417]

The third question is how the dispute settlement process in the European Council would work. The Treaty clearly specif that a 'request' to the European Council will suspend the ordinary legislative procedure, presumably even 'stopping the clock' on the deadlines that apply to the second or third reading.[418] Although the Treaty only refers to a resumption of the legislative process, in the

---

[416] The EP could not bring a legal challenge on this point, as it would have jointly adopted the legislation with the Council.

[417] S Carrera and F Geyer, *The Reform Treaty and Justice and Home Affairs: Implications for the Common Area of Freedom, Security and Justice* (CEPS Policy Brief No. 141, Aug 2007), 9.

[418] See Art 294 TFEU.

event of 'consensus', or a fast-track to enhanced cooperation; in the event of a 'disagreement',[419] it is also possible that there would be a 'disagreement' without nine Member States in favour of enhanced cooperation, in which case the discussions on the draft proposal or initiative would be suspended indefinitely.

As for the EP, even though it would not be involved in the decision-making by the European Council, and would lose its normal veto power over authorization of enhanced cooperation, it would still retain its normal decision-making powers pursuant to the ordinary legislative procedure when it came to adopt the subsequent legislation, whether there was a deal among all Member States or whether the fast-track enhanced cooperation had been authorized.

Of course, if enough Member States really dislike a particular proposal, they could always try to assemble a blocking minority rather than use the emergency brake.[420] If the emergency brake were not pulled, this would preclude access to fast-track authorization of enhanced cooperation—and even access to enhanced cooperation under the ordinary procedure for authorizing it, as long as the Member States which constitute the blocking minority are also willing to block the authorization of enhanced cooperation by the Council in that case. This might lead the Member States in favour of the proposal to consider mechanisms to adopt it outside the EU legal framework.

As regards the political context of the emergency brake, given the high-profile awkwardness of pulling the brake, it is possible that in practice the mere threat of pulling it, or even the clear indication that pulling it might be contemplated, would be sufficient to induce a majority in Council to offer sufficient concessions to the dissenting Member State. Even before the Treaty of Lisbon entered into force, there was some EU legislation which deferred to the constitutional or fundamental criminal justice rules of Member States.[421] In light of this, it might be expected that an emergency brake would actually be pulled only when the two sides in a dispute held intractably opposed and irreconcilable positions of principle, and/or when a Member State's relationship with the EU had generally broken down.

Finally, it seems likely that the existence of the emergency brake will reduce the likelihood that Member States will litigate against controversial criminal law legislation before the Court of Justice. Where Member States are able to

---

[419] Although a 'consensus' is not defined in the Treaty (see Art 15(4), revised TEU), presumably in this context at least it is implicitly defined by reference to a 'disagreement', and must therefore mean the consent of all Member States. It appears the UK, Ireland, and Denmark could also participate in the discussions in the European Council even if they have opted out of the original proposal, because the Protocol on their opt-out from JHA measures only refers to non-participation in discussions within the *Council* (Art 1, Title V Protocol; Art 1, Danish Protocol; and Art 1, Annex to Danish Protocol).

[420] For the definition of a blocking minority, see Art 16(4) and (5), revised TEU, and Art 3 of the transitional protocol.

[421] Art 9e of the Eurojust Decision, as amended ([2009] OJ L 138/14).

protect their interests by means of a political process, they should have less need of recourse to the courts.

2.2.3.4.2. The 'pseudo-veto'

The Treaty rule which provides for this procedure reads as follows:[422]

> In the absence of unanimity in the Council, a group of at least nine Member States may request that the draft [regulation/measures] be referred to the European Council. In that case, the procedure in the Council shall be suspended. After discussion, and in case of a consensus, the European Council shall, within four months of this suspension, refer the draft back to the Council for adoption.
>
> Within the same timeframe, in case of disagreement, and if at least nine Member States wish to establish enhanced cooperation on the basis of the draft [regulation/measures] concerned, they shall notify the European Parliament, the Council and the Commission accordingly. In such a case, the authorisation to proceed with enhanced cooperation referred to in Article 20(2) of the Treaty on European Union and Article 329(1) of this Treaty shall be deemed to be granted and the provisions on enhanced cooperation shall apply.

It can be seen that this process is identical to the emergency brake rules, except that in this case the trigger for the process is the request by a group of Member States, rather than an objection by a single Member State, and the underlying decision-making process is different (unanimity in Council, rather than the ordinary legislative procedure). Much of the above analysis of the emergency brake is therefore equally applicable to the pseudo-veto process. But there are two distinct issues which call for further comment.

First of all, as with the enhanced cooperation procedure, the Treaty rules on the pseudo-veto procedure do not provide for the possibility of *failure* to adopt the proposal at all, in the event that it is blocked in the European Council and there are not enough Member States wishing to adopt it by means of enhanced cooperation. However, as regards the pseudo-veto, it is very likely that the nine Member States which refer the issue to the European Council would be willing to adopt that measure by such means, and would be taking that consideration into account when they refer the issue, so the prospect of failure would be unlikely. It should be noted, though, that the Treaty would not *require* that the same nine Member States who refer the issue to the European Council would then have to embark upon enhanced cooperation in the event of a continued disagreement.

Secondly, it should be noted that participants in the enhanced cooperation would be able to change the decision-making rules to shift unanimity to QMV and to shift a special legislative procedure to an ordinary legislative procedure.[423]

Although the two sets of special procedures are complex, overall they should generally be welcomed. The emergency brake procedure strikes a reasonable balance between the need to ensure the effectiveness and democratic legitimacy

---

[422] Arts 86(1) and 87(3) TFEU.   [423] Art 333 TFEU; see further 2.2.5.5 below.

of EU policy on the one hand, by extending QMV and the role of the EP, and ensuring on the other hand that Member States can, if necessary, protect the fundamental elements of their criminal justice system. As for the pseudo-veto procedure, it also strikes a fair balance between the legitimate interests of Member States in protecting their sovereignty by means of a veto in the sensitive areas of police operations and the creation of a European Public Prosecutor and the desirability of facilitating enhanced cooperation within the EU framework for those Member States which are particularly committed to certain proposals. While these special procedures, if ever used, would fragment EU law to some extent, the alternative to this would not be no fragmentation at all—rather it would be fragmentation *outside* the EU framework, where the problems of legitimacy are even more acute than those which exist within the EU legal system.[424]

2.2.4. Competence issues

Historically, at least before the Treaty of Lisbon entered into force, the most intractable issue concerning the EC's or EU's competence over JHA matters has been the distinction between the various forms of JHA competence and the non-JHA competence of the Community. This issue is further dealt with below.[425] The remaining issues have concerned the scope and intensity of EC or EU competence over various JHA matters, and (where there are distinctions in decision-making rules) the distinctions between different JHA powers. Recurring issues in particular included the intensity of EC competence over asylum law, the scope of EC competence over access to employment by third-country nationals, the distinction between legal and irregular migration, the extent of any 'cross-border' requirement for the EC or EU to adopt criminal or civil law measures, and the intensity of EU powers over criminal procedure. These issues remain relevant even though the Treaty of Lisbon has entered into force, in the event that the validity of measures adopted prior to the entry into force of that Treaty are challenged.

In fact, many of these issues remain relevant even after the entry into force of the Treaty of Lisbon, in particular the cross-border requirements for criminal law in connection with the broader criminal procedure powers, as well as the newer question of the relationship between EU's criminal law and civil law powers. These issues are addressed in detail in various chapters of this book.[426] So far, there is no litigation concerning any of these issues, but the application of majority voting to most areas of JHA law obviously raises the prospect that outvoted Member States will raise competence issues in the Court of Justice, for

---

[424] See 2.5 below.   [425] See 2.4.   [426] See s 2.4 of chs 3–12.

those disgruntled Member States that do not have an opt-out or were not able to use an 'emergency brake' in the area in question.

It should be noted that the Treaty of Lisbon has introduced into the Treaties general horizontal rules concerning EU competence. JHA matters are described as a 'shared competence' between the EU and its Member States.[427] The Treaties define this concept as follows:[428]

When the Treaties confer on the Union a competence shared with the Member States in a specific area, the Union and the Member States may legislate and adopt legally binding acts in that area. The Member States shall exercise their competence to the extent that the Union has not exercised its competence. The Member States shall again exercise their competence to the extent that the Union has decided to cease exercising its competence.

It follows from the second sentence that in areas of shared competence, the EU could in principle 'occupy the field' by fully harmonizing the issue concerned.[429] However, Article 2(6) TFEU also points out that the precise 'scope' of the competence concerned is set out in the specific Treaty provisions related to each area, and in Title V of the TFEU, it is expressly stated that EU rules relating to substantive criminal law and domestic criminal procedure set 'minimum' standards only.[430] Furthermore, competence related to certain aspects of economic migration is ruled out,[431] and harmonization of national law is ruled out as regards measures concerning integration of third-country nationals and crime prevention.[432] There are also horizontal reserves of national competence in the general provisions of the JHA Title and in the TEU, discussed in detail above.[433] On the other hand, the EU has the power to 'frame a common policy on asylum, immigration and external border control',[434] which in principle suggests that the Union should be more ambitious as regards harmonization of such areas, without *requiring* the EU to harmonize the law in these areas fully.[435] But the reference to a common policy in these specific areas does not mean *a contrario* that full harmonization of the law is *excluded* in other areas (in particular, civil law, mutual recognition measures in

---

[427] Art 4(2)(j) TFEU.   [428] Art 2(2) TFEU.

[429] On the question of external competence, see Art 3(2) TFEU and the discussion in 2.7 below.   [430] Arts 82(2), 83(1), and (2) TFEU.

[431] Art 79(5) TFEU. See also Art 77(4), as regards Member States' competence to determine borders.

[432] Art 79(3) and 84 TFEU. The EU instead is limited to providing incentives, promoting, and supporting *Member States'* actions in these areas. See Art 2(5) TFEU. Oddly, these areas of activity are not listed in Art 6 TFEU, which appears prima facie to be an exhaustive list of areas where the EU can only 'support, coordinate or supplement' Member States' action.

[433] Arts 72 and 73 TFEU and Art 4(2), revised TEU, discussed in 2.2.3.2 above.

[434] Art 67(2) TFEU. See further Arts 77(2)(a), 78(1), and (2)(a)–(d), and 79(1) TFEU.

[435] Although the Treaty states that the Union 'shall' adopt 'uniform' and 'common' measures in these areas, this must be reconciled with the express allocation of JHA matters to the shared competence of the EU and the Member States.

criminal law, and policing law), since the possibility of full harmonization in areas of shared competence still applies to those parts of Title V as well.

Finally, it should be noted that the exercise of the EU's JHA competences is subject to the principles of subsidiarity and proportionality, which are discussed further elsewhere in this chapter.[436]

2.2.5. Territorial scope

Distinctions in the territorial scope of JHA measures have to some extent been created outside the EU legal framework, most prominently as regards the development of the Schengen *acquis* from 1985 onward, and also as regards the negotiation of a later treaty largely concerning police cooperation, the 'Prum Convention', among a group of Member States in 2005.[437]

Since the Treaty of Lisbon abolished the third pillar and applied normal EU rules on decision-making, legal instruments, and judicial control to all JHA matters, the question of the territorial scope of JHA measures remains the only issue that clearly differentiates JHA issues from most of the rest of EU law. The complexity of this issue results from the reluctance of several 'old' Member States to participate fully in EU integration in this area for various reasons, the unwillingness of all 'old' Member States to apply the full Schengen *acquis* immediately to new Member States, and the interest among several non-Member States in adopting the relevant EU measures.[438] The following overview addresses in turn issues specific to: the UK and Ireland; Denmark; the Member States which joined the EU in 2004 and 2007; and finally Norway, Iceland, Switzerland, and Liechtenstein. Finally, it examines the general rules in the Treaties concerning 'enhanced cooperation', which in principle allow for the adoption of measures across most areas of EU law, including JHA law, without the full participation of all Member States. These latter rules also apply whenever the UK or Ireland (and possibly in future Denmark) wish to opt in to a JHA measure that they initially opted out of.

It should also be recalled that the discretion to opt in (or out) of the Court of Justice's jurisdiction over preliminary rulings as regards third pillar measures, which still applies for a five-year transitional period as regards third pillar acts adopted before the Treaty of Lisbon entered into force, results in a different territorial scope of that jurisdiction (as distinct from a different territorial scope of

---

[436] See Art 5, revised TEU, and 2.5 below.

[437] On Schengen integration, see 2.2.2.3 above. For the text of the Prum Convention, see Council doc 10900/05, 7 July 2005. On its integration into the EU legal framework, see 12.6.2, 12.6.3, and 12.9 below.

[438] On the general issues regarding the integration of the Schengen *acquis* into the EU legal order, see 2.2.2.3 above.

third pillar *acts*).[439] Also, it should be recalled that even though an opt-out means that the representatives of the UK, Ireland, or Denmark respectively do not participate in the Council as regards the relevant measure, the MEPs from those states nevertheless vote on the relevant measures during the EP's proceedings; the Commissioners and Court of Justice judges from those Member States also play their normal role.

2.2.5.1. United Kingdom and Ireland

The UK and Ireland are both covered by a specific protocol on border controls, a specific protocol on the possibility of opting in to any Title IV measure, and to specific rules as regards the Schengen *acquis*. Since the Treaty of Lisbon, the UK alone also has an option to opt out of all third pillar measures adopted before the entry into force of the Treaty of Lisbon, with effect from the end of a five-year transitional period in 2014. These various opt-outs will be considered in turn.

2.2.5.1.1 Border controls

A Protocol attached to the Treaties by the Treaty of Amsterdam entitles the UK and Ireland to maintain the 'Common Travel Area' in force between them and to check individuals coming from other Member States, no matter what other Member States do and no matter what interpretation the Court of Justice may give to Article 14 EC (now Article 26 TFEU) or to anything else. This Protocol also specifically exempts the UK and Ireland from any EC (now EU) legislation requiring the abolition of border controls, thus overlapping with their general exemption from Title IV of the EC Treaty (now Title V TFEU). The Treaty of Lisbon made no substantive amendments to this Protocol; the interpretation of the Protocol is discussed further in Chapter 3.[440]

2.2.5.1.2. Title V TFEU

The UK and Ireland were granted an opt-out from all of the JHA issues transferred to Title IV of the EC Treaty (immigration, asylum, and civil law) under another Protocol attached to the EC Treaty by the Treaty of Amsterdam. This Protocol was extended in scope by the Treaty of Lisbon to cover all JHA measures within the scope of Title V TFEU,[441] so now including policing and criminal law, except that Ireland has no opt-out as regards anti-terrorist sanctions.[442] The Treaty of Lisbon also made changes to the Protocol as regards the procedure for

---

[439] See 2.2.3.3 above.   [440] See 3.2.5 below.

[441] The Treaty of Lisbon gave this Protocol a new name: the 'Protocol on the position of the United Kingdom and Ireland in respect of the area of freedom, security and justice'. This book refers to it more simply as the 'Title V Protocol' throughout. All references in this subsection are to this Protocol, unless otherwise indicated.

[442] Art 9, as inserted by the Treaty of Lisbon. The UK made a unilateral declaration to the Treaty of Lisbon asserting that it 'intends to exercise its right' to opt in to such measures (Declaration 65 in the Final Act).

opting out of measures which amend acts which the UK and Ireland are already bound by (see discussion below). It has become evident from the case law of the Court of Justice that this Protocol does not apply to measures which build upon the Schengen *acquis*, which are governed by different rules on participation by the UK and Ireland.[443]

Ireland (but not the UK) also has an option to denounce the Protocol altogether, which it has not invoked.[444] An Irish Declaration to the Final Act of the Treaty of Lisbon referred to its 'firm intention to exercise its right...to take part in the adoption of [JHA] measures...to the maximum extent it deems possible', stated that 'Ireland will, in particular, participate to the maximum possible extent in measures in the field of police cooperation', and in the context of the possibility of relinquishing the opt-out, announced that Ireland 'intends to review the operation of these arrangements within three years of the entry into force of the Treaty of Lisbon' (so by 1 December 2012).[445]

While the default position pursuant to the Title V Protocol is that the UK and Ireland opt-out of each individual JHA proposal,[446] the UK and Ireland can instead choose to 'opt-in' to each measure. To do this, they must tell the Council within a period of three months of receiving an initial proposal for a JHA act that they wish to take part in it. If one or both of these Member States opts in to a proposal, the Council then tries to agree the proposal with their participation. However, the Protocol provides that if it is not possible to obtain the agreement with the participation of the UK and Ireland after 'a reasonable period of time', the Council may go ahead and adopt the measure without them.[447] The UK and Ireland may then join in later under the general conditions applying to enhanced cooperation in the Treaties;[448] alternatively, if they decide to opt out in the first place, they can opt in after the proposal is adopted, by the same method.

In practice,[449] the UK and Irish governments have opted into: almost all civil cooperation measures; most or all of the *first-phase* measures establishing the Common European Asylum System, but only a few of the second-phase measures; a number of measures on irregular migration; but again only a few measures on visas, border controls, or legal migration. In the first few months after the

---

[443] Cases C-77/05 *UK v Council* [2007] ECR I-11459 and C-137/05 *UK v Council* [2007] ECR I-11593. See 2.2.5.1.3 below.

[444] Art 8 (not amended by the Treaty of Lisbon).

[445] Declaration 56 in the Final Act of the Treaty of Lisbon.

[446] Arts 1 and 2. The Treaty of Lisbon amended these articles only to update the cross-reference to the Council voting rules which apply in the event of an opt-out (now Art 238(3) TFEU).

[447] Art 3. The Treaty of Lisbon amended this article to (again) update the cross-reference to the Council voting rules which apply in the event of an opt-out (see ibid) and to provide for a special provision relating to JHA evaluations for the UK and Ireland (Art 70 TFEU, discussed in 2.2.3.2 above).

[448] Art 4. The Treaty of Lisbon amended this article to update the cross-reference to the general enhanced cooperation rules. On the substance of those rules, see 2.2.5.5 below.

[449] For further detail, see s 2.5 of chs 3–12.

Treaty of Lisbon, they opted in to most initial proposals for legislation concerning criminal law and policing and criminal law treaties. The approach of the two governments has been largely, but not entirely, consistent. There have been no cases where the Council went ahead and adopted JHA measures without either Member State's participation even though they had opted in to discussions, but in June 2010, the Spanish Council Presidency threatened that it would exclude the UK from participation in the proposed Directive establishing a European protection order (despite the UK's opt-in to discussions), because the UK was opposing the proposal, and terminating the UK's participation in negotiations would mean that there were no longer enough votes against the proposal to form a blocking minority in the Council.[450] This raises the question as to how much time has to pass before the UK's or Ireland's participation in discussions on a proposal can be terminated on the grounds that a 'reasonable period of time' has passed during which one or both Member States have blocked the proposal, or participated in a blocking minority.

Furthermore, there were three cases where the UK attempted to opt in to a proposal, but was rebuffed; each of these decisions was challenged by the UK before the Court of Justice. While the UK lost the first two of those challenges on the grounds that the measures concerned fell instead within the scope of the rules in the Schengen Protocol, at the time of writing the third challenge is still pending.[451]

There have been three occasions when Ireland initially did not participate in a proposal, but then opted in after its adoption,[452] and two other occasions when the UK did the same,[453] in each case pursuant to the enhanced cooperation rules which applied before the entry into force of the Treaty of Lisbon.[454] It should be noted that in the latter two cases, the UK opted out of the proposal, but nevertheless indicated an intention to opt in if the final text of the legislation

---

[450] See the press release of the JHA Council, 3–4 June 2010. The UK and the other dissenting Member States were objecting to this proposal due to (well-founded) concerns about its legal base: see 9.2.4 below. On the substance of the proposal, see 9.7.6 below; for the text, see [2010] OJ C 69/5.

[451] Cases C-77/05 and C-137/05 *UK v Council* (n 443 above) and C-482/08 *UK v Council*, pending. An Advocate-General's opinion of 24 June 2010 recommends dismissing the UK's challenge in the latter case.

[452] Dir 2001/55 on temporary protection ([2001] OJ L 212/12), Reg 1030/2002 ([2002] OJ L 157/1), and the Decision establishing a Migration Network ([2008] OJ L 131/7). The Commission approved Irish participation by means of Decisions, respectively: [2003] OJ L 251/23; Decision C(2007)4589/F of 11 Oct 2007 (not published in the OJ); and [2009] OJ L 138/53. See also the Commission opinions on Irish participation in: SEC (2003) 907, 6 Aug 2003; COM (2007) 506, 7 Sep 2007; and [2009] OJ C 1/1.

[453] Regs 593/2008 on conflict of law in contract (Rome I Reg) and 4/2009 on maintenance (respectively [2008] OJ L 177/6 and [2009] OJ L 7/1). The Commission approved UK participation by means of Decisions ([2009] OJ L 10/22 and [2009] OJ L 149/73). See also the Commission opinions on UK participation in COM (2008) 730, 7 Nov 2008 and COM (2009) 181, 21 Apr 2009.

[454] Art 11a EC, which has been replaced by Art 331(1) TFEU; see further 2.2.5.5 below.

satisfied particular concerns which the UK had about the proposal, and participated actively (albeit informally) in the negotiations to that end. On those two
occasions, this tactic (which is not as such provided for expressly in the Title V
Protocol) was successful.

With the application of QMV to most areas of JHA,[455] it is clear that, in the
absence of any contrary provisions in the Title V Protocol, a British or Irish opt-in
to a proposal will entail the possibility that those Member States could be outvoted
and therefore required to apply a proposal which they disagree with.[456] If one or
both Member States form part of a blocking minority in the Council, either the
Council could offer sufficient concessions to the other dissenting Member States
and then adopt the legislation *with* British and/or Irish participation, or it could
adopt the legislation without one or both of those Member States if, after a 'reasonable period of time', their opposition is partly or wholly blocking the adoption
of the proposal.[457] This may have resulted already in a greater reluctance by these
States to opt in to JHA proposals, with further reluctance in future following the
extension of QMV to more areas of JHA law pursuant to the Treaty of Lisbon.

A significant new provision in the Title V Protocol introduced by the Treaty
of Lisbon concerns the position of the UK and Ireland when a proposal is made
to amend a measure which they are already bound by.[458] This rule provides as
follows:

1. The provisions of this Protocol apply for the United Kingdom and Ireland also to
measures proposed or adopted pursuant to Title V of Part Three of the Treaty on the
Functioning of the European Union amending an existing measure by which they are
bound.

2. However, in cases where the Council, acting on a proposal from the Commission,
determines that the non-participation of the United Kingdom or Ireland in the amended
version of an existing measure makes the application of that measure inoperable for other
Member States or the Union, it may urge them to make a notification under Article 3
or 4. For the purposes of Article 3, a further period of two months starts to run as from
the date of such determination by the Council.

If at the expiry of that period of two months from the Council's determination the
United Kingdom or Ireland has not made a notification under Article 3 or Article 4, the
existing measure shall no longer be binding upon or applicable to it, unless the Member
State concerned has made a notification under Article 4 before the entry into force of the
amending measure. This shall take effect from the date of entry into force of the amending
measure or of expiry of the period of two months, whichever is the later.

For the purpose of this paragraph, the Council shall, after a full discussion of the matter,
act by a qualified majority of its members representing the Member States participating

---

[455] See 2.2.2.1 and 2.2.3.1 above.

[456] On this issue, see further the report of the EU Select Committee of the House of Lords on the
'Rome II' proposal (8th Report, 2003–04), paras 80–81.

[457] See the example of the European protection order proposal, discussed above.

[458] Art 4a, as inserted by the Treaty of Lisbon.

or having participated in the adoption of the amending measure. A qualified majority of the Council shall be defined in accordance with Article 238(3)(a) of the Treaty on the Functioning of the European Union.

3. The Council, acting by a qualified majority on a proposal from the Commission, may determine that the United Kingdom or Ireland shall bear the direct financial consequences, if any, necessarily and unavoidably incurred as a result of the cessation of its participation in the existing measure.

4. This Article shall be without prejudice to Article 4.

It can be seen that in principle the Protocol applies as usual to such cases.[459] However, it is possible for the Council, acting by QMV on a Commission proposal,[460] to determine that the non-participation of the UK or Ireland in the proposed amended measure makes the application of the existing measure 'inoperable' for other Member States or the EU, to urge the UK or Ireland to notify its intention to opt in to the proposal while under discussion or after its adoption.[461] If the UK or Ireland fail to do so, the existing measure ceases to apply to them.[462] The Council, acting by QMV, may also impose financial sanctions on the UK or Ireland subject to certain conditions.[463] However, it is always open to the UK or Ireland to opt in to the original act and its amending measure after the latter is adopted.[464] These provisions have not yet been applied in practice, although the UK and Ireland have opted out of several measures which would amend asylum legislation in which they already participate.[465]

The key question as regards these provisions is the definition of when the non-participation of the UK or Ireland in a measure should be considered to render that measure 'inoperable' as regards other Member States or the Union, for only in that case could the UK or Ireland be excluded from the existing measure or subjected to sanctions. Given that the EU has been able to tolerate prolonged periods when different versions of the same measure apply to most Member States on the one hand, and to Denmark or associated States on the other hand, the best interpretation of this rule is that it only applies where the non-participation of the UK or Ireland would make it genuinely and objectively *impossible* for the measure to apply in different forms in the UK or Ireland on the one hand and the other Member States on the other hand. It is not sufficient that it is *more difficult* to apply the two different sets of rules. Also, it should be noted that the high threshold is an

---

[459] Art 4a(1). The following analysis of these new rules draws upon S Peers, 'In a World of Their Own? Justice and Home Affairs Opt-outs and the Treaty of Lisbon' (2008–09) 10 CYELS 383.

[460] The Council acts only with the votes of the participating Member States: Art 4a(2), third sub-paragraph. For the applicable voting rules, see Art 238(3) TFEU. There is no role for the EP.

[461] Art 4a(2), first sub-paragraph.   [462] Art 4a(2), second sub-paragraph.

[463] Art 4a(3). Note that in this case, the UK and Ireland will participate in the vote. Again there is no role for the EP.

[464] Art 4a(4). Read literally, the UK or Ireland could opt in to either the original act or the act amending it, but this would undercut the purpose of Art 4a(2) and so is presumably ruled out (see by analogy Cases C-77/05 and C-137/05, n 443 above).

[465] For details of the measures concerned, see 5.2.5 below.

entirely objective test, applying not only if the UK or Ireland are reluctant to be excluded from the relevant pre-existing measure but also if those Member States are enthusiastic about the prospect of releasing themselves from their pre-existing obligations. The separate question of whether the UK and Ireland remain bound by a measure which they originally participated in, but which is repealed by a later measure which they did *not* participate in, is considered further below.[466]

The Protocol also specifies that non-participation in JHA measures exempts the UK and Ireland from the costs related to those specific measures,[467] and provides that the UK and Ireland are not bound by the general rules on data protection that may be adopted pursuant to Article 16 TFEU to the extent that they are not bound by the underlying policing or criminal law measure to which those general rules relate.[468]

The forced termination of participation in prior EU measures will presumably have the impact (as regards criminal law in particular) that any Council of Europe Conventions which had been disapplied in relations between Member States by the prior EU measures would then re-apply in relations between the UK and/or Ireland, on the one hand, and the other Member States, on the other, since the legal basis for disapplying those measures as between those States would no longer be in force.[469] It is even possible that *earlier* EU measures which had been repealed or disapplied as between those States by the prior EU act which no longer applied would also come back into application.[470]

2.2.5.1.3. Schengen Protocol

The Protocol on the Schengen *acquis* (the 'Schengen Protocol') gave the UK and Ireland the possibility of applying to participate in only part of the Schengen *acquis*, subject to a decision in favour by the Council, acting with the unanimous approval of the Schengen States.[471] The Council accepted the UK's application for partial participation in Schengen in 2000, and the parallel Irish application in 2002,[472] although the partial participation of these Member States in the Schengen rules only took effect (for the UK) or will take effect (for Ireland)

---

[466] See 2.2.5.1.5.

[467] Art 5, Title V Protocol. The Treaty of Lisbon amended this Art to provide that the Council could decide, acting with the unanimity of all Member States, to charge these costs to the UK or Ireland nonetheless. Obviously the latter Member States are unlikely to agree to this.

[468] Art 6a, Title V Protocol, inserted by the Treaty of Lisbon. See more generally 12.2.4 and 12.2.5 below.

[469] For example, the Council of Europe Convention on extradition and its Protocols would re-apply between those States if the Framework Decision on the European Arrest Warrant were disapplied between them.

[470] For example, the Schengen Convention provisions on extradition would arguably apply if the EAW Framework Decision were disapplied, and the Dublin Convention would arguably apply if the Dublin II Reg were disapplied.

[471] Art 4, Schengen Protocol. This provision has not been amended by the Treaty of Lisbon.

[472] Decisions 2000/365/EC ([2000] OJ L 131/43) and 2002/192/EC ([2002] OJ L 64/20).

when the Council approved or later approves it separately.[473] Both Member States participate (or will participate) in almost all of the criminal law and policing provisions of Schengen,[474] as well as the provisions on control of irregular migration.[475] However, they do not, or will not, participate in any of the rules relating to visas, border controls, or freedom to travel. Following this distinction, they will participate in the SIS to the extent that it applies to policing and judicial cooperation, but not as it applies to immigration. The Decision on UK participation sets out a more limited list of Schengen rules that will apply to Gibraltar, and provides that the UK may request the partial participation of the Channel Islands and Isle of Man in some Schengen rules (subject to unanimous approval of the Schengen States).[476]

Both Decisions initially also purported to require UK and Irish participation in measures building on the Schengen *acquis* which were adopted after the integration of the Schengen *acquis* into the EC and EU legal order. This applies to certain measures concerning the SIS,[477] to three other adopted measures (for Ireland),[478] and to all proposals and initiatives which build upon those portions of the Schengen *acquis* which the UK and Ireland participate in (each State 'shall be deemed irrevocably' to have notified its intention to 'take part in' such measures).[479]

As regards measures building on the Schengen *acquis* which the UK and Ireland are not purportedly obliged to opt into, the Schengen Protocol states that '[p]roposals and initiatives to build upon the Schengen *acquis* shall be subject to the relevant provisions of the Treaties'.[480] The UK and Ireland took the view that the Title IV Protocol (as it then was) therefore applied if they wished to opt in to such measures—ie they did not need the Council's approval to opt in. Conversely, the Council and Commission took the view that the UK and Ireland could *not* opt in to Title IV proposals where these measures built upon those provisions of the *acquis* which the UK and Ireland had *not* opted into. This dispute was ultimately settled by the Court of Justice, when the UK challenged its exclusion from the EU legislation on security features for EU passports and the creation of Frontex,

---

[473] See Art 6 of Decision 2000/365/EC and Art 4 of Decision 2002/192/EC (both ibid). The Council decided that the UK can participate in the Schengen *acquis* which it has opted into, except as regards the SIS (which will be subject to a later decision), from 1 Jan 2005 ([2004] OJ L 395/70), but no such decision has yet been adopted as regards Ireland.

[474] Art 1 of each Decision. The exceptions are cross-border hot pursuit by police (for the UK) and cross-border police hot pursuit and surveillance (for Ireland).

[475] Arts 26 and 27 of the Convention; see further 7.5.1 and 7.5.3 below.

[476] Art 5, Decision on UK participation.

[477] Art 5(1), Decision on Irish participation; Art 7(1), Decision on UK participation.

[478] Art 2(2), Decision on Irish participation.

[479] Art 6(2), Decision on Irish participation; Art 8(2), Decision on UK participation. On the date of application of measures building on the Schengen *acquis*, see Art 6(3) and 8(3) of the respective Decisions. On the practical application of these provisions, see s 2.5 of chs 3–7.

[480] Art 5(1), Schengen Protocol, not amended by the Treaty of Lisbon.

the EU borders agency.[481] A further case is pending on the question of whether access to the Visa Information System by UK law enforcement officials can be restricted.[482]

In the Court's view, the Commission and Council were correct: in order to preserve the 'effectiveness' of the rules on the UK and Ireland's participation in the Schengen *acquis*, there was a necessary link between the question of their participation in the original *acquis* and their participation in measures building upon it. Moreover, the Court adopted in these cases a broad interpretation of measures building upon the *acquis*, ruling that both measures *built* upon the *acquis* even though they did not actually *amend* it, because they were sufficiently linked to the control of external borders.[483]

The Treaty of Lisbon did not amend the provisions of the Schengen Protocol dealing with this issue, so presumably the Court's prior case law continues to apply. On the other hand, the Treaty of Lisbon *did* amend the rules governing the position if the UK and Ireland wish to opt out of a measure building upon a provision of the *acquis* which they are already bound by.[484] These rules now provide that the UK and Ireland can opt out of a proposal measure which builds on the parts of the Schengen *acquis* in which they already participate, if they notify the Council of their position within three months. In that case, the UK and Ireland will not be bound by the proposal, but the procedure to adopt it will be suspended until that notification is withdrawn (ie the UK or Ireland decides that it wishes to opt in after all) or until the end of a separate procedure to remove the UK or Ireland from their participation in aspects of the Schengen *acquis,* 'to the extent considered necessary by the Council' by a QMV on a Commission proposal. The Council shall 'seek to retain the widest possible measure of participation of the Member State concerned without seriously affecting the practical operability of the various parts of the Schengen *acquis*, while respecting their coherence', and must 'act within four months of the Commission proposal'.

If the Council has not acted within that period, any Member State 'may' refer the matter to the European Council, which must then, at its next meeting, acting by QMV on a Commission proposal, take a decision pursuant to the same criteria which apply to the Council. If *that* process fails, the decision-making procedure concerning the original proposal resumes, but in the event that the proposed measure is adopted, then the *Commission* must decide to terminate the UK or Ireland's participation in the Schengen *acquis* by the time that measure is

---

[481] Cases C-77/05 *UK v Council* and C-137/05 *UK v Council* (n 443 above).

[482] Case C-482/08 *UK v Council*, pending (opinion of 24 June 2010).

[483] For criticism of the approach ultimately adopted by the Court, see the second edition of this book, at pp 58–59.

[484] Art 5(2)–(5), Schengen Protocol. The previous Art 5(2) of the Protocol was repealed by the Treaty of Lisbon.

adopted, applying the same criteria, unless the UK and Ireland decide to opt in to the proposal after all.

It can be seen that these rules have effectively replaced the previous purported obligation to opt in to any measure building upon those provisions of the *acquis* which the UK and Ireland already participate in. These rules also apply to the policing and criminal law provisions of the Schengen *acquis*, which the UK and Ireland currently participate in widely. Unlike the revised provisions of the Title V Protocol, the process of excluding the UK and Ireland from the underlying measures is intended to be automatic, with the Council, the European Council, and the Commission called upon in turn to adopt the measure necessary to terminate part of the UK's or Ireland's participation in the Schengen *acquis*.[485]

2.2.5.1.4. Pre-existing third pillar measures

The fourth and final JHA opt-out applies, unlike the others, to the UK alone, not also to Ireland. It was inserted into the Treaties for the first time by the Treaty of Lisbon, and appears in the transitional Protocol which governs various aspects of the transition between the previous Treaty rules and the rules in the Treaty of Lisbon. This Protocol was already considered above as regards its rules on the legal effect of third pillar measures adopted before the entry into force of the Treaty of Lisbon ('pre-existing third pillar measures'), as well as the Court of Justice's jurisdiction over such acts,[486] but it also contains a special rule permitting the UK to opt-out of the application of all pre-existing third pillar measures which have not been amended at the end of the five-year transitional period applying to the Court's jurisdiction—so by 1 December 2014. There is no possibility for the UK to invoke such an opt-out before or after that date.[487]

In order to invoke this opt-out, the UK would have to notify the Council '[a]t the latest' six months before the end of the transitional period (so by 1 June 2014) that it objects to the powers of the EU institutions (ie the Court of Justice and the Commission, as regards infringement proceedings) becoming applicable to those measures. This would trigger the non-application of the acts concerned. Such an opt-out would not apply to any post-Lisbon policing and criminal law acts, or to any pre-existing third pillar measures which had been amended after the entry into force of the Treaty of Lisbon, in which the UK participates.

As a consequence, the Council, by QMV on a Commission proposal without UK participation, 'shall determine the necessary consequential and transitional arrangements'.[488] Also, the Council, acting by QMV on a Commission proposal *with* UK participation, 'may also adopt a decision determining that the United

---

[485] For a detailed discussion of these provisions, see Peers, n 459 above.
[486] See 2.2.3.3 above.   [487] Art 10(4), first sub-paragraph, transitional protocol.
[488] Art 10(4), second sub-paragraph, transitional protocol.

Kingdom shall bear the direct financial consequences, if any, necessarily and unavoidably incurred' by its ceased participation.[489]

However, the UK may 'at any time afterwards' notify the Council that it wishes to participate in pre-existing third pillar measures which it has opted out of.[490] Presumably the word 'afterwards' refers to a time after the *initial notification* of the opt-out, so it would be possible for the UK to opt back in to some pre-existing third pillar measures already during the six-month time period before the opt-out takes effect. In that case, the UK would in effect only be opting out of *part* of its pre-existing third pillar commitments. But as the wording of this provision makes clear ('at any time'), the UK could wait until any future date to embark upon this volte-face. Implicitly, it would be possible for the UK to opt back in to such measures in stages. The Protocol explicitly confirms that if the UK does opt back in to any measures, the jurisdiction of the Court of Justice and the Commission's powers over infringement actions will be applicable.

If the UK did wish to opt back in to participate in pre-existing third pillar measures it had opted out of, the relevant provisions of the Title V Protocol and the Schengen Protocol would apply, with the addition of a requirement that the EU institutions and the UK 'shall seek to re-establish the widest possible measure of participation of the United Kingdom in the *acquis* of the Union in the area of freedom, security and justice without seriously affecting the practical operability of the various parts thereof, while respecting their coherence'.

Time will tell whether this option appeals to the UK in 2014. In any case, this opt-out will only be relevant to the extent that pre-existing third pillar measures have not been amended in the meantime.

2.2.5.1.5. Opt-out by repeal?

The final issue as regards the JHA opt-outs of the UK and Ireland (which is potentially also relevant to Denmark) is the question of what happens when the UK or Ireland are bound by an existing JHA measure, but when that measure is repealed (not simply amended) by a later measure in which those Member States do *not* participate. Can it be argued that since the original JHA measure has been rescinded as regards most Member States, its repeal is also effective to those Member States which did not participate in its repeal? This has already happened in the case of the original measure establishing the EU's visa list,[491] and it might happen as regards much of the EU's first-phase asylum legislation.[492]

---

[489] Art 10(4), third sub-paragraph, transitional protocol.

[490] Art 10(5), transitional protocol.   [491] Reg 539/2001, [2001] OJ L 81/1.

[492] The UK and Ireland participated in the first-phase legislation concerning asylum procedures and the 'qualification' of refugees and persons needing subsidiary protection, and the UK participated in the first-phase legislation on reception conditions for asylum seekers, but they have opted out of the proposals which would repeal those measures. For more detail, see 5.2.5 below.

There is no express provision of the relevant Protocols addressing this issue. However, it is strongly arguable that in this scenario, the measure concerned would *not* be repealed as regards the UK or Ireland, and would therefore also continue to bind the other Member States as regards their relations with the UK and Ireland. The drafters of the Treaty of Lisbon specifically considered the issue of the termination of the participation of the UK and Ireland in JHA measures in which they already participate, and provided for two routes for the EU institutions to terminate the participation of those Member States in existing JHA measures, and one route for the UK to terminate its participation in some JHA measures unilaterally. Moreover, since the termination of participation of a Member State in an EU measure in which it already participates is a profound departure from the priniciple of the uniform application of EU law, any possibility of terminating that participation must be expressly and unambiguously provided for. It will still remain open for the EU institutions to terminate the UK or Ireland's participation in a pre-existing measure which has been repealed pursuant to the specific provisions of the revised Schengen and Title V Protocols, or for the UK to terminate its participation in pre-existing third pillar measures as from 1 December 2014, as discussed above, where the relevant conditions are met. But there is no additional unwritten rule allowing the UK or Ireland to end their participation in existing measures which have been repealed.

In one case, the Council has agreed to repeal an existing JHA measure only as regards the Member States which participate in the measure repealing it, leaving the existing measure in force as regards the UK.[493] If the interpretation above is correct, this is not the exercise of an option for the participating Member States, but merely a confirmation of their obligation, given that they presumably do not wish to terminate the UK's participation in the prior legislation on the grounds that the application of two different regimes is 'inoperable'. The Commission appears to accept this interpretation.[493a] It might be argued that it is not practical to leave one measure in force in only one or two Member States. But in fact the measure concerned will still be in force *as between* the UK or Ireland and *all of the other Member States*, since the latter can only repeal their obligations *to each other* when repealing the existing measure, unless they validly invoke the special rules in the Title V or the Schengen Protocol to terminate the UK's or Ireland's participation in the prior measure. Those special rules were designed precisely to deal with the practical issues that might result from the non-participation of the UK and Ireland in a JHA measure, in light of their previous participation in a measure.

---

[493] See the Council first-reading position on the proposed Reg on social security for third-country nationals (Council doc 11160/10, 26 July 2010). This measure must still be agreed with the EP before adoption.

[493a] 'Given that the United Kingdom will not take part in this proposal but will continue to apply [the prior Regulation], *it is not possible to repeal the latter completely*.' (COM (2010) 448, 2 Sep 2010, emphasis added).

In the event that the following analysis is not correct, it should be noted as regards criminal law measures that any Council of Europe treaties which had been disapplied by the EU measures being repealed would then re-apply as between the UK, Ireland, and the other Member States following the repeal of the EU measure.[494]

2.2.5.2. Denmark

The non-participation of Denmark in JHA matters did *not* begin, as is often thought, when a Decision of the Heads of State and Government (known as the Edinburgh Decision) was adopted in 1992 to attempt to persuade Danish voters to support the Maastricht Treaty.[495] In fact, Section D of this Decision stated unambiguously and without exception that 'Denmark will participate fully in cooperation on justice and home affairs on the basis of the provisions of Title VI of the Treaty on European Union' (referring to the original third pillar, which was the basis for most JHA cooperation at the time of the Maastricht Treaty). Denmark did not object to JHA cooperation in principle, but rather to the idea that JHA cooperation should take place within the framework of supranational EC law (as it then was). This view was to have a substantial effect on the position of Denmark as regards JHA cooperation in the Treaty of Amsterdam, and subsequently the Treaty of Lisbon.

In order to exempt Denmark from JHA matters that were transferred to EC law by means of the Treaty of Amsterdam, a general 'Protocol on the position on Denmark' (the 'Danish Protocol') governed Denmark's status as regards measures concerning, inter alia, immigration, asylum, and civil law (the former Title IV EC),[496] while the Schengen Protocol originally set out special rules for Denmark as regards the integration of that *acquis* into the EU legal order.[497] However, following the Treaty of Lisbon, all of the special rules relating to Denmark as regards the Schengen *acquis* appear in the Danish Protocol.

According to the Danish Protocol in its original form, Denmark was exempted from *almost* all Title IV EC measures,[498] except for measures determining a list of third countries whose nationals require visas to cross the external borders of the Member States, or of measures determining a common visa format,[499] as both of these issues were already within EC competence prior to the Treaty of

---

[494] See 2.2.5.1.2 above, *mutatis mutandis*.   [495] [1992] OJ C 348/1.

[496] The Danish Protocol also contains an opt-out relating to defence (originally Art 6 of the Protocol, renumbered Art 5 and amended by the Treaty of Lisbon), which is not further considered here. All further references in this subsection are to the Danish Protocol unless otherwise indicated.

[497] Art 3, Schengen Protocol: see discussion below. The Treaty of Lisbon amended this Art to refer instead to the Danish Protocol as regards Danish participation in acts building upon the Schengen *acquis*.   [498] Arts 1–3.

[499] Art 4, which was subsequently renumbered Art 6 (but not amended) by the Treaty of Lisbon.

Amsterdam.[500] In conjunction with the termination of the third pillar by the Treaty of Lisbon, the Protocol was enlarged in scope by that Treaty to exempt Denmark from policing and criminal law measures adopted after the entry into force of that Treaty.[501] Third pillar acts adopted *before* the entry into force of the Treaty of Lisbon 'which are amended shall continue to be binding upon and applicable to Denmark unchanged'.[502]

There are special rules relating to Denmark's continued connection with the Schengen *acquis*. First of all, the Schengen Protocol originally provided that those provisions of the *acquis* that were allocated to Title IV of the EC Treaty following the Treaty of Amsterdam (ie immigration provisions of the Schengen *acquis*) still continued to have the effect of public international law, rather than EC law, in Denmark.[503] However, this rule was deleted by the Treaty of Lisbon. As for measures which build upon the Schengen *acquis* and also fall within the scope of Title V TFEU, Denmark has six months to decide whether to apply each such measure within its national law.[504] If it does so, this decision creates 'an obligation under international law' between Denmark and the other Member States participating in the measure. If Denmark fails to apply such a measure, the other Schengen States and Denmark 'will consider appropriate measures to be taken'.[505] In practice, Denmark has consistently opted into all such measures building upon the Schengen *acquis*.[506]

Otherwise, unlike the UK or Ireland, Denmark does not have the ability to opt in to specific JHA measures, either when they are initially adopted or at a later date. If Denmark wishes to change this position, initially, the Protocol only gave Denmark the possibility of denouncing 'all or part' of the Danish Protocol, in which case it has to immediately apply all measures adopted in the relevant field without any need for the Commission or Council to approve its intention to apply those measures.[507] The Treaty of Lisbon now gives Denmark a further option: it may decide to replace the rules concerning its JHA opt-out with a

---

[500] On the interpretation of this clause in practice, see 4.2.5 below.

[501] Arts 1–3. The Treaty of Lisbon amended Arts 1 and 2 to this end, and updated the cross-reference to the Council voting rules which apply when Denmark does not participate in measures (see Art 238(3) TFEU). It also added a new Art 2a concerning data protection, which is equivalent to a clause inserted into the Title V Protocol for the UK and Ireland (see 2.2.5.1.2 above).

[502] Art 2, final sentence. Presumably the word 'amended' means amendments which are adopted after the Treaty of Lisbon entered into force, and also has the same meaning as it does in the Title V Protocol relating to the UK and Ireland (2.2.5.1 above) and in the transitional Protocol to the Treaty of Lisbon (2.2.3.3 above).   [503] Previous Art 3, Schengen Protocol.

[504] Art 5(1), renumbered Art 4(1) and amended by the Treaty of Lisbon as regards its scope, to refer to all JHA measures which build on the Schengen *acquis*, not just measures within the scope of the previous Title IV EC.

[505] Art 5(2), renumbered Art 4(2) and amended by the Treaty of Lisbon to refer also to Denmark's participation in any such decision. There is no indication of the voting rule applicable or what the 'appropriate measures' might entail.   [506] See s 2.5 of chs 3–4 and 6–7.

[507] Art 7, not amended by the Treaty of Lisbon.

different set of rules, which is almost identical to the Title V opt-outs for the UK and Ireland.[508] The only differences between the two opt-out rules are that first, if Denmark chooses this option, the previous Schengen *acquis* and prior acts building upon the Schengen *acquis* will apply fully to Denmark as EU law, rather than international law, six months after the Danish decision takes effect.[509] Second, there is no special rule on evaluations relating to Denmark.[510] Also, the Annex to the Danish Protocol differs from the Protocol concerning the UK, Ireland, and Schengen in that Denmark must make a decision on whether to apply measures building upon the Schengen *acquis* six months after their adoption; if it does not, the participating Member States and Denmark 'will consider appropriate measures to be taken'.[511] Furthermore, once Denmark opts in to a measure building on the Schengen *acquis*, it must opt in to any future measures that build upon that act to the extent that those future measures also build upon the Schengen *acquis*.[512] In practice, Denmark has not yet notified the other Member States that it wishes to apply the new opt-out rules. If it does so, obviously the new Danish rules should be interpreted consistently with the UK and Irish opt-out rules, *mutatis mutandis*.

In any event, there is a declaration to the Treaty of Lisbon concerning the adoption of acts which are partly applicable to Denmark and partly not applicable to that country, because they have a 'legal base' partly regarding JHA, pursuant to the Danish Protocol. In that case, 'Denmark declares that it will not use its voting right to prevent the adoption of the provisions which are not applicable to Denmark'.[513]

One peculiarity of the Danish position is that in the absence of a possibility for Denmark to opt in to Title IV measures (now extended to all JHA measures), the EC (as it then was) and Denmark were nevertheless willing in certain cases to negotiate international treaties regarding Danish participation. These treaties concern participation in measures concerning responsibility for asylum applications, civil and commercial jurisdiction, and service of documents, which Denmark had applied or agreed to before the adoption of Community acts on these subjects. The treaties require Denmark to apply the Community acts, with minor amendments to the civil jurisdiction rules (but not to the other two measures); moreover the relevant jurisdiction of the Court of Justice is applicable to Denmark, and has therefore been expanded pursuant

---

[508] Art 8(1), inserted by the Treaty of Lisbon, referring to an Annex inserted by the Treaty of Lisbon. This option is expressly 'without prejudice' to the possibility that Denmark can invoke Art 7 of the Protocol in order to relinquish any form of JHA opt-out entirely.

[509] Art 8(2), inserted by the Treaty of Lisbon.

[510] Compare Art 3 of the Title V Protocol to Art 3 of the Annex to the Danish Protocol.

[511] Art 6(1) of the Annex.

[512] Art 6(2) of the Annex. Presumably the concept of 'building upon' such an act has the same meaning as 'building upon' the Schengen *acquis* (see 2.2.5.1.3 above).

[513] Declaration 48 in the Final Act.

to the Treaty of Lisbon.[514] Denmark may refuse to apply subsequent measures amending or implementing the EC acts, but in such cases, the relevant treaty will be terminated.

2.2.5.3. Accession States

The Schengen Protocol specifies that all future Member States were to be bound by the entire Schengen *acquis*.[515] This was implemented first of all by the 2003 Accession Treaty,[516] which specifies that the ten new Member States which joined the EU pursuant to that Treaty applied as from the date of accession (1 May 2004) the measures in the *acquis* as integrated into the EC and EU Treaties 'and acts building on it or otherwise related to it', as referred to in Article 3(1) of the Act of Accession and listed in Annex 1 to the Act, along with other such measures adopted between agreement of the Accession Treaty and the date of accession. However, there was a delay in applying the remaining provisions of the Schengen *acquis* (or measures building upon it).[517] Those measures were *binding* on the new Member States as from 1 May 2004, but did not *apply* until a unanimous Council decision by the representatives of the Member States fully applying the Schengen *acquis* at that time and the Member State(s) seeking to participate fully. The UK and Ireland participated in that decision to the extent that they had opted in to the *acquis*. The Act of Accession further provides that the agreements associating Norway and Iceland with the Schengen rules, as referred to in the Schengen Protocol, were binding on the new Member States as from the date of their accession to the EU.[518]

More precisely, the provisions of the Schengen *acquis* and the measures building upon it which applied as from 1 May 2004 in the new Member States are the rules on: external border controls (except for checks in the SIS); certain aspects of visas (particularly the visa list and visa format); irregular migration; policing (other than hot pursuit and surveillance); criminal law cooperation (except for references to the SIS); drugs; firearms; and data protection (to the extent that the other Schengen rules apply).

Conversely, the rules on abolition of internal border controls; other aspects of the common visa policy; freedom to travel; cross-border hot pursuit and surveillance by police officers; and the SIS did not apply in practice until the later Council decision. As for Schengen-related measures adopted after agreement on the Accession Treaty, and subsequently adopted after accession, each measure

---

[514] For the text of the treaties, see [2006] OJ L 66/38 (asylum responsibility); [2005] OJ L 299/61 (jurisdiction rules); and [2005] OJ L 300/53 (service of documents). The asylum treaty entered into force on 1 Apr 2006 ([2006] OJ L 96/9), and the civil law treaties entered into force on 1 July 2007.   [515] Art 8, Schengen Protocol, renumbered Art 7 by the Treaty of Lisbon.
[516] [2003] OJ L 236/33 (Act of Accession).   [517] Art 3(2), Act of Accession, ibid.
[518] Art 3(3), Act of Accession.

indicated whether it applied immediately or after a delay to the new Member States.

The Act of Accession also provided that the new Member States had to accede to JHA conventions or instruments 'which are inseparable from the attainment of the objectives of' the EU Treaty,[519] whether those measures were opened for signature by the old Member States or drawn up by the Council in accordance with Title VI of the EU Treaty (ie the old third pillar); the new Member States also had to take the administrative and other measures necessary to facilitate JHA cooperation. Similarly, the new Member States had to accede to Conventions drawn up on the basis of Article 293 EC (since repealed by the Treaty of Lisbon) and those inseparable from the objectives of the EC Treaty.[520] They also had to accede to treaties established on the basis of Article 38 EU (external third pillar treaties).[521] In practice, the new Member States quickly ratified a significant number of Conventions and Protocols, although this ratification process is not yet complete.[522]

Next, the Act of Accession provided that until the end of 2006, there were transitional funds to assist with the application of EU law including, inter alia, assistance to implement JHA obligations,[523] along with a specific facility to assist new Member States with external land borders to apply their Schengen obligations, by funding buildings, equipment, and training.[524]

A specific JHA safeguard is set out in the Act, providing that for three years after the date of accession (so up until 1 May 2007), the Commission could have taken 'appropriate measures' if there had been insufficient application of a measure concerning mutual recognition in civil law or criminal law by a new Member State.[525] In practice, this safeguard clause was not applied. Also, a Protocol relating to the UK's military base on the island of Cyprus contains specific rules on border control.[526] Finally, Annex II to the Act of Accession contains a list of technical amendments to existing measures made necessary by accession.[527] Point 18 of this Annex lists amendments to JHA civil law measures; the Common Consular Instructions (concerning Schengen visa applications); the Border Manual (for use by external border guards); and the EC's visa list Regulation.

Ultimately nine of the ten Member States to join the EU in 2004 participated in the full Schengen system as from December 2007, and from March 2008 as regards air borders.[528] Only Cyprus was left out of the extension of the Schengen zone, because of the practical difficulties controlling the borders as long as the

---

[519] Art 3(4), Act of Accession.   [520] Art 5(2), Act of Accession.
[521] For details on these treaties, see 2.7.2 below.
[522] For ratification details, see Appendix I.   [523] Art 34, Act of Accession.
[524] Art 35, Act of Accession.   [525] Art 39, Act of Accession.
[526] Protocol 3 to the Act of Accession.
[527] See Art 20 of the Act of Accession, which gives effect to Annex II.
[528] [2007] OJ L 323/34.

country is divided. However, Cyprus has expressed an intention of applying the provisions of the Schengen *acquis* relating to visas; the Council has not yet acted on this request.[529] Specific issues relating to northern Cyprus have also arisen as regards the territorial scope of the EU's civil law legislation.[530]

The model set out in the 2003 Treaty of Accession was largely copied in the 2005 Treaty of Accession with Romania and Bulgaria, in force from 1 January 2007, except that this time most JHA Conventions applied to the new Member States from a date decided by the Council, acting unanimously.[531] Again the special JHA safeguard was not applied within its three-year period of applicability.[532]

2.2.5.4. Norway, Iceland, Switzerland, and Liechtenstein

As noted above, Norway and Iceland are in a distinct position as non-EU States whose participation in the Schengen rules was necessary if Sweden, Denmark, and Finland were to be able to participate in Schengen, because none of these States wished to relinquish the existing Nordic Passport Union. In fact, Norway and Iceland had already agreed to an association agreement with the Schengen States before the Treaty of Amsterdam was signed.[533] The Schengen Protocol therefore provided for conclusion of a replacement association agreement with Norway and Iceland, as well as for a separate agreement with those States concerning UK and Irish participation in the Schengen rules.[534] These treaties were agreed in 1999,[535] and the Schengen area was extended to Norway and Iceland in March 2001, at the same time it was extended to Nordic EU Member States.[536]

The Schengen association treaty requires Norway and Iceland to apply the Schengen *acquis*, including EC measures related to the *acquis*, as it existed in spring 1999. A Mixed Committee established by the treaty is a forum for discussions about implementation of the *acquis* and concerning measures building upon it.[537] If Norway or Iceland do not accept a measure building

---

[529] See 4.2.5 below.

[530] Case C-420/07 *Apostolides* [2009] ECR I-3571; see further 8.2.5 below.

[531] Art 3 and Annex I to Act of Accession ([2005] OJ L 157/203). In practice, the Council extended the application of all relevant Conventions to Romania and Bulgaria by the end of 2007: [2007] OJ L 200/47 (Europol); [2007] OJ L 307/20 (CIS); [2008] OJ L 9/23 (anti-fraud Convention); [2007] OJ L 304/34 (corruption); [2008] OJ L 9/21 (Naples II); [2007] OJ L 307/18 (mutual assistance); [2007] OJ L 307/22 (driving disqualification); and [2007] OJ L 347/1 (Rome Convention).

[532] Art 38 of the Act of Accession (ibid). There were regular reports from the Commission on the application by Romania and Bulgaria of, inter alia, standards regarding judicial reform. The most recent reports are in COM (2010) 112 and 113, 23 Mar 2010.

[533] Council doc 11780/97, 28 Oct 1997.

[534] Art 6, Schengen Protocol. The Treaty of Lisbon made a minor amendment to this Art, to delete a reference to the pre–Amsterdam association treaty with Norway and Iceland (ibid).

[535] See respectively [1999] OJ L 176/35 and [2000] OJ L 15/1; both treaties entered into force on 26 June 2000 ([2000] OJ L 149/36). See also a Decision on implementation of the first treaty (Decision 1999/437/EC, [1999] OJ L 176/31).   [536] Decision 2000/777 ([2000] OJ L 309/24).

[537] Arts 2–5 of the treaty; and see Decision 1/99 of the Mixed Committee, adopting its rules of procedure ([1999] OJ C 211/9). These rules were later amended by Decision 1/2004 ([2004] OJ C 308/1).

upon the *acquis*, the treaty is terminated regarding them, although the Mixed Committee may decide to retain it in force.[538] The parties must keep the judgments of the Court of Justice, and of Norwegian and Icelandic courts, under close review.[539] If a 'substantial difference' develops in judicial interpretation or national application of the agreement, and the Mixed Committee cannot agree a measure to ensure uniform interpretation or application of the treaty, or if a dispute relating to the agreement otherwise develops, then the Mixed Committee has a fixed period to settle the dispute, otherwise the agreement is terminated.[540]

It is striking that this treaty, in accordance with the Schengen Protocol, was negotiated by the Council, not the Commission, which normally negotiates treaties on behalf of the EC. Moreover, although the treaty was concluded by the Council, it is not clear whether the treaty also binds the EU as such, although the treaty does state that it creates obligations for the Community and its Member States.[541] It is not clear whether the Court of Justice has jurisdiction to interpret the agreement as far as the Community, the Union, or both is concerned, although in one judgment the Court's jurisdiction as regards the third pillar provisions of the treaty was assumed.[542]

In practice, the treaty has entailed Norwegian and Icelandic acceptance of most measures concerning visas, border control, and irregular migration, and certain measures concerning policing and criminal law.[543] Also, Norway and Iceland agreed a similar treaty on asylum responsibility, paralleling the EU Member States' Dublin Convention, which entered into force in March 2001 at the same time that their Schengen association agreement was applied.[544] Furthermore, those States ultimately agreed to further treaties associating them with the EU's mutual assistance Convention and Protocol;[545] the surrender of fugitives (a version of the EU's European arrest warrant);[546] the 'Prum Decision' relating to police cooperation;[547] the borders agency (Frontex);[548] the EU's borders funds

---

[538] Art 8 of the treaty.   [539] Art 9 of the treaty.   [540] Arts 10 and 11 of the treaty.

[541] Arts 8(3) and 15(4) of the treaty. On the issue of EU legal personality, see 2.7 below.

[542] Case C-436/04 *Van Esbroek* [2006] ECR I-2333.

[543] See s 2.5 of chs 3–4, 6–7, and 9–12 below.   [544] [2001] OJ L 93/38. See 5.2.5 below.

[545] [2004] OJ L 26/1. The treaty has not yet entered into force. The Commission proposed its conclusion after the entry into force of the Treaty of Lisbon (COM (2009) 704, 17 Dec 2009). See further 9.2.5 below.

[546] [2006] OJ L 292/1. The treaty has not yet entered into force. The Commission proposed its conclusion after the entry into force of the Treaty of Lisbon (COM (2009) 705, 17 Dec 2009). See further 9.2.5 below.

[547] [2009] OJ L 353/1. The treaty has been signed and applies provisionally, but has not yet entered into force (the EU concluded the treaty in July 2010, but the associated states have not ratified it yet). See further 12.2.5 below.

[548] [2007] OJ L 188/19. The treaty has not yet entered into force, but is being applied provisionally.

legislation;[549] and participation in comitology committees connected to the Schengen *acquis*.[550]

As for Switzerland, it agreed a treaty associating itself with the Schengen *acquis* in 2004, along with a parallel treaty on its application of the EU's asylum responsibility rules; these treaties entered into force on 1 March 2008,[551] and were applied as from 12 December 2008 (29 March 2009 as regards Schengen air borders).[552] These two agreements are essentially identical to the Schengen and asylum responsibility agreements with Norway and Iceland, except that: the Schengen treaty is expressly with the Community and Union (and creates obligations for the EC, the EU, and Member States); Liechtenstein may accede to either treaty; there is an obligation to negotiate parallel treaties with Denmark (as regards matters within the scope of the former Title IV of the EC Treaty),[553] Norway, and Iceland; Switzerland is not obliged to apply a particular rule relating to mutual criminal assistance; and the Schengen and asylum responsibility treaties are linked (denunciation of one will terminate the application of the other one).[554] A Protocol concerning accession of Liechtenstein to these treaties was agreed in 2006, but is not yet in force.[555] Also, Switzerland and Liechtenstein have agreed a treaty with the EC concerning their relationship with Frontex (paralleling the agreement with Norway and Iceland on this subject),[556] and are also parties to the treaties concerning association with the Borders Funds and comitology committees.[557] However, unlike Norway and Iceland, Switzerland and Liechtenstein have not agreed any further treaties relating to mutual assistance, the surrender procedure, or the Prum Decision on police cooperation with the EU.

---

[549] [2010] OJ L 169/22. The treaty has been signed, but is not yet in force.

[550] COM (2009) 605 and 606, 30 Oct 2009. The Council has agreed to sign this treaty, but it has not yet entered into force.

[551] [2008] OJ L 53/13 and 52. On the date of entry into force, see [2008] OJ L 53/18.

[552] [2008] OJ L 327/15 (Decision on full extension of Schengen *acquis*). For the rules of procedure of the Mixed Committee, see [2004] OJ C 308/2.

[553] As regards asylum responsibility, the EC (now EU) also had to be party to this parallel treaty alongside Switzerland and Liechtenstein. This treaty is in force as between the EU and Switzerland ([2009] OJ L 191/6).

[554] Arts 7(5) 13, 15, 16, and 18 of the Schengen treaty and Arts 11 and 14–16 of the asylum responsibility treaty. On the specific legislation which Switzerland applies, see s 2.5 of chs 3–7 and 9–12.

[555] COM (2006) 752–754, 1 and 4 Dec 2006. The Protocols were signed in 2008 ([2008] OJ L 83/3 and 5 as regards the Schengen Protocols; the signature relating to the Protocol on asylum responsibility was not published). Following the entry into force of the Treaty of Lisbon, the Protocol will be approved in the form of two revised Council decisions: see Council doc 6077/10, 26 Apr 2010. See also the amendment to the EU/Switzerland (Schengen) Mixed Committee rules of procedure ([2008] OJ L 83/37).

[556] COM (2009) 255, 4 June 2009. The treaty entered into force between the EU and Switzerland on 1 Aug 2010, but has not yet entered into force between the EU and Liechtenstein.

[557] [2010] OJ L 169/22 and COM (2009) 605 and 606 (nn 549 and 550 above).

2.2.5.5. General rules on enhanced cooperation

General provisions on 'enhanced cooperation', ie the process of some Member States participating in EU measures without some other Member States, were first introduced in the Treaty of Amsterdam, and these provisions were amended by the Treaty of Nice.[558] These rules were never in fact used, except in the context of the UK and Ireland opting in to immigration, asylum, and civil law measures after those measures had already been adopted.[559] However, it is striking to note that there were two attempts to use these provisions in the JHA area: as regards a proposal on criminal suspects' rights, where enhanced cooperation failed because there were insufficient votes in the Council to support authorization of enhanced cooperation when the issue was raised informally;[560] and as regards the 'Rome III' proposal for choice of law on divorce, because the Commission did not respond, before the Treaty of Lisbon entered into force, to a group of Member States which requested authorization for enhanced cooperation.[561]

The Treaty of Lisbon subsequently amended the enhanced cooperation rules again, inter alia, in order to merge the separate rules governing the former first and third pillars.[562] The basic rule is that a group of Member States may establish enhanced cooperation among themselves, within the context of the EU's non-exclusive competences, by 'applying the relevant provisions of the Treaties'.[563] In other words, once enhanced cooperation has been approved, the normal rules on competence and decision-making (for example, unanimity as regards family law measures) will apply. Enhanced cooperation is authorized by the Council 'as a last resort, when it has established that the objectives of such cooperation cannot be attained within a reasonable period by the Union as a whole', and at least nine Member States must participate.[564] Furthermore, enhanced cooperation must: 'aim to further the objectives of the Union, protect its interests and reinforce its integration process'; 'comply with the Treaties and Union law'; not 'undermine' the internal market or 'distort' competition, etc; and 'respect the competences, rights and obligations of those Member States which do not participate in it'. But in return, the non-participants 'shall not impede its implementation by the participating Member States'.[565] The Treaties are silent on the question of enhanced cooperation *outside* the EU legal framework, but of course there are prior examples of this taking place (the Schengen and Prum Conventions). It should follow

---

[558] See Arts 11 and 11a EC and Arts 43-45, previous TEU. There were specific rules for the third pillar in the prior Arts 40, 40a, and 40b TEU.   [559] See 2.2.5.1 above.

[560] See 2.2.3.4.1 above.   [561] On the substance of the Rome III proposal, see 8.6 below.

[562] Art 20, revised TEU and Arts 326–334 TFEU. There remain some distinct rules for foreign policy enhanced cooperation, which are not considered further here (Arts 328(2), 329(2), and 331(2) TFEU).

[563] Art 20(1), revised TEU, first sub-paragraph. All JHA matters are shared competences, and so are therefore non-exclusive: see Art 4(2)(j) TFEU and the discussion in 2.2.4 above.

[564] Art 20(2), revised TEU.

[565] Art 20(1), revised TEU, second sub-paragraph, and Arts 326 and 327 TFEU.

from the division of competences between the EU and the Member States that enhanced cooperation outside the EU legal framework is permissible as regards all issues outside the scope of the EU's exclusive competences (ie all JHA matters), provided that the participating Member States comply with the relevant EU law.

Member States that wish to establish enhanced cooperation must address a request to the Commission, which 'may' then make a proposal for enhanced cooperation. If the Commission does not make a proposal, it must tell the requesting Member States why.[566] If the Commission proposes authorization of enhanced cooperation, it must then be approved by the Council (by QMV) and consent of the EP to go ahead.[567] This process is distinct from the process of adopting the substantive proposal concerned—which could entail the application of the ordinary legislative procedure or a special legislative procedure such as unanimity in Council with the consultation of the EP (ie as regards family law). A crucial point is that *all* Member States, whether they wish to participate in the substantive measure or have a relevant opt-out, participate in the vote to authorize enhanced cooperation.[568] As already noted, a pre-Lisbon proposal to authorize enhanced cooperation as regards criminal procedure failed due to a lack of support from enough Member States; but it should be recalled that the Treaty of Lisbon provides for 'fast-track' authorization of enhanced cooperation in a number of areas of criminal law and policing in the event that a Member State pulls an 'emergency brake' or issues a veto.[569] This would mean that all of the substantive and procedural rules for authorization would be circumvented, including the requirement for Council authorization, although the EP could in practice still use its legislative powers over the *substance* of most of the legislation concerned to block its subsequent adoption.

All Member States can participate in discussions on enhanced cooperation measures, but only those Member States which participate in the measure in question can vote.[570] Any acts adopted within the framework of enhanced cooperation only bind the participating Member States, and new Member States joining the EU after the adoption of those acts are not obliged to apply them.[571]

If Member States which did not participate in an enhanced cooperation measure originally wish to join in later, the Treaty provides that enhanced cooperation

---

[566] Art 329(1) TFEU, first sub-paragraph. There is no time-limit set for the Commission's decision as to whether to propose enhanced cooperation or not.

[567] Art 329(1) TFEU, second sub-paragraph.

[568] See the distinction implicit in Art 20(2) and (3), revised TEU; and also *a contrario* the references to the voting rule in Art 330 TEU (as distinct from Art 329 TFEU) in Art 331(1) and 333(1) TFEU.							[569] See 2.2.3.4 above.

[570] Art 20(3), revised TEU and Art 330 TFEU, which refers to the rule recalculating Council voting weights to take account of non-participation of some Member States in adoption of measures, which is also applicable in the case of British, Danish, and Irish opt-outs (Art 238(3) TFEU).

[571] Art 20(4), revised TEU.

must 'be open at any time to all Member States'.[572] In particular, Member States joining enhanced cooperation after it is established must comply with the conditions of participation and any acts already adopted. The Commission and the participating Member States must 'promote participation by as many Member States as possible'.[573] A Member State wishing to join in must notify the Council and Commission. The Commission 'shall...confirm the participation of the Member State confirmed' within four months of this notification, and shall adopt 'any transitional measures necessary' to this end.[574] If the Commission rejects the application on the ground that the Member State concerned does not satisfy the conditions for participation, it shall indicate what further 'arrangements' must be adopted in order to fulfil those conditions, and set a deadline to re-examine the request. If the Commission at that point still rejects the application, the Member State concerned may appeal to the Council, which will decide on its participation by means of the vote of the participating Member States.[575]

Finally, the participants in enhanced cooperation can decide, acting unanimously, to change the decision-making rules governing the adoption of the substantive measures concerned from unanimity into QMV, or from a special legislative procedure into an ordinary legislative procedure. Unlike the general *passerelle* clause in the Treaties,[576] there is no requirement for consent of the EP or control by national parliaments. In the JHA area, this provision would permit a shift to QMV and/or the ordinary legislative procedure as regards passports etc, family law, the European Public Prosecutor, operational police cooperation, or decisions to extend EU criminal law competence.

Following the entry into force of the Treaty of Lisbon, the Commission formally proposed for the first time the use of the enhanced cooperation provisions, as regards the Rome III proposal for choice of law in divorce.[577] In this case, the Council had already determined that there was no prospect of agreement within a reasonable time by the EU as a whole, so this was a case where enhanced cooperation was a 'last resort'.[578] In the Commission's view, the subject matter concerned is a distinct 'area' of law for the purposes of the authorization of enhanced cooperation, and the proposal meets the applicable substantive criteria for authorization of enhanced cooperation. In July 2010, the Council authorized this enhanced cooperation.[579] More broadly, time will tell whether enhanced cooperation is used more frequently in JHA matters, in light of the past history of the Schengen and Prum Conventions and the comparative ease of showing that enhanced cooperation in this area will not undermine the internal market or distort competition.

---

[572] Art 20(1), revised TEU, second sub-paragraph.   [573] Art 328 TFEU.
[574] Art 331(1) TFEU, first and second sub-paragraphs.
[575] Art 331(1) TFEU, third sub-paragraph.   [576] Art 48(7), revised TEU.
[577] COM (2010) 104, 24 Mar 2010. The substantive proposal for the Rome III Reg appears in COM (2010) 105, 24 Mar 2010. On the substance, see further 8.6 below.
[578] See JHA Council press release, 5–6 June 2008.   [579] [2010] OJ L 189/12.

2.3. Human rights[580]

The issue of whether EU JHA measures are consistent with human rights obligations and principles is a key theme of this book. In section 3 of Chapters 3–12, the relevant human rights obligations are set out, and subsequently the compatibility of EU measures with those obligations is assessed in detail. But in order to lay the foundations for this analysis, it is necessary to set out the current framework for the protection of human rights in the EU legal order. This analysis examines in turn the overall legal framework, followed by the issues of the sources of EU human rights protection, the scope of EU human rights protection, the derogations and limitations upon human rights within the EU legal order, and the legal effect of EU human rights rules.

Since the entry into force of the Treaty of Lisbon, the basic legal framework on this issue is established by Article 6 TEU, as follows:

1. The Union recognises the rights, freedoms and principles set out in the Charter of Fundamental Rights of the European Union of 7 December 2000, as adapted at Strasbourg, on 12 December 2007, which shall have the same legal value as the Treaties.

The provisions of the Charter shall not extend in any way the competences of the Union as defined in the Treaties.

The rights, freedoms and principles in the Charter shall be interpreted in accordance with the general provisions in Title VII of the Charter governing its interpretation and application and with due regard to the explanations referred to in the Charter, that set out the sources of those provisions.

2. The Union shall accede to the European Convention for the Protection of Human Rights and Fundamental Freedoms. Such accession shall not affect the Union's competences as defined in the Treaties.

3. Fundamental rights, as guaranteed by the European Convention for the Protection of Human Rights and Fundamental Freedoms and as they result from the constitutional traditions common to the Member States, shall constitute general principles of the Union's law.

There are therefore three basic sources of human rights protection in the EU legal order (the Charter, the ECHR, and the general principles of EU law), although these three basic sources overlap considerably. These three basic sources will be examined in turn.

The first of the three basic sources to be established was the general principles of EU law. Although the initial EEC Treaty made no reference to human rights, the Court of Justice asserted from the late 1960s that the general principles of EC law (as they then were) included human rights protection. The sources of these

---

[580] From a huge literature on human rights as general principles of EU law, see B de Witte, 'Past and Future Role of the European Court of Justice in the Protection of Human Rights', in P Alston, ed, *The EU and Human Rights* (OUP, 1999), 859, and T Tridimas, *The General Principles of EU Law* (2nd edn, OUP, 2006), with further references.

human rights principles, according to the Court, were the national constitutions and international treaties upon which Member States have collaborated, with particular attention paid to the European Convention of Human Rights. This position was ultimately reaffirmed by the Treaties, in Article F(2) of the initial TEU, renumbered Article 6(2) by the Treaty of Amsterdam, which was in effect identical to the current wording of Article 6(3) TEU after the entry into force of the Treaty of Lisbon.

The TEU makes specific reference to the ECHR as a source of the general principles of EU law, confirming the long-standing case law of the Court of Justice which gives the ECHR a particular pre-eminence as a source of the general principles,[581] including the jurisprudence of the European Court of Human Rights and the (now-defunct) European Commission of Human Rights.[582] The Court of Justice has even stated that it 'must take account' of the judgments of the Strasbourg Court.[583] While many of the rights set out in the ECHR or its protocols have been recognized by the Court of Justice as forming part of the general principles of EU law, in particular the rights to private and family life; property; freedom of expression and association; the legality and non-retroactivity of criminal law; and to a fair trial; the Court of Justice has not had an opportunity to confirm that all the rights set out in the ECHR are protected as part of the EU general principles. But it is hard to imagine that the Court of Justice will deny that the EU general principles encompass, inter alia, the right to life, the freedom from torture or other inhuman or degrading treatment, and the limits upon arbitrary detention set out in the ECHR. Also, at least in one case, the protection conferred by the EU general principles is clearly wider in scope that that conferred by the ECHR: the right to a fair trial applies to any right set out in EU law, not just to trials in respect of civil obligations or criminal charges (as set out in Article 6 ECHR).[584] But on the other hand, it is not clear whether the rights set out in the Fourth and Seventh Protocols to the ECHR can all be regarded as recognized by the general principles of EU law, because not all Member States have ratified those Protocols. Then again, the rights in these Protocols are set out explicitly or implicitly in the ICCPR, which all Member States *have* ratified, and some of these rights have already been recognized by the Court of Justice as part of the general principles of EU law, and/or are set out in the EU's Charter of Fundamental Rights.[585]

---

[581] Case law beginning with Case 222/84 *Johnston* [1986] ECR 1651.

[582] See S Peers, 'The European Court of Justice and the European Court of Human Rights: Comparative Approaches', in E Orucu, ed, *Judicial Comparativism in Human Rights Cases* (UKNCCL, 2003), 107.

[583] See cases discussed in ibid and subsequently Case C-105/03 *Pupino* [2005] ECR I-5285.

[584] Compare the Court of Justice judgment in Case C-327/02 *Panayotova* [2004] ECR I-11055 (para 27) to the ECHR judgment in *Maaouia* v *France* (Reports 2000-X); see further 6.3.4 below.

[585] See s 3 of chs 3–5, 7, 9, and 11.

As for national constitutional traditions as a source of the EU general principles, the Court of Justice has recognized the right to carry on a business or profession and the right to human dignity.[586] EU law also recognizes a free-standing
general principle of equality, which applies across the scope of EU law.[587] It may
similarly be argued that the right to asylum must be recognized as a general principle, due to its recognition in several national constitutions.

Although there was no reference in Article 6(2) (and now Article 6(3)) TEU
to human rights treaties other than the ECHR, the Court of Justice nevertheless
still refers to such treaties occasionally. In particular, the Court refers occasionally
to the International Covenant for Civil and Political Rights (ICCPR) as a source
of the general principles, although it took a dismissive view of the impact of the
opinions of the Human Rights Committee set up to monitor the implementation
and application of the Covenant.[588] The Court has also referred to the Convention
on the Rights of the Child.[589] Moreover, Article 78 TFEU (previously Article
63 EC) expressly requires EC asylum policy to be 'in accordance with' the 1951
UN Geneva Convention on refugee status and 'other relevant treaties'. This suggests that the Geneva Convention and the other relevant treaties (the ECHR and
ICCPR again, plus the UN Convention against Torture) should be considered
to be sources of the general principles of EU law and/or that any breach of these
measures in the asylum field would be a violation of the Treaties.[590] The Court
of Justice has indeed confirmed that EU asylum legislation must be interpreted
'while respecting' the Geneva Convention and the other relevant treaties.[591]

The second basic source of human rights in EU law is the EU Charter of
Fundamental Rights, which was originally drawn up by a special 'Convention' in
2000.[592] Initially, the Court of Justice was reluctant to refer to the Charter, until
a landmark judgment in 2006, in which the Court ruled:[593]

The Charter was solemnly proclaimed by the Parliament, the Council and the
Commission in Nice on 7 December 2000. While the Charter is not a legally binding

---

[586] See respectively Joined Cases C-184/02 and C-223/02 *Spain and Finland v EP and Council*
[2004] ECR I-7789 and C-36/02 *Omega* [2004] ECR I-9609.

[587] For example, see Case C-144/04 *Mangold* [2005] ECR I-9981.

[588] Case C-249/96 *Grant* [1998] ECR I-621 and Case C-540/03 *EP v Council* [2006] ECR
I-5769. On the Court of Justice's references to international human rights treaties other than
the ECHR, see further A Rosas, 'The European Union and International Human Rights
Instruments', in V Kronenberger, ed, *The EU and the International Legal Order: Discord or
Harmony?* (Asser Press, 2001). For the argument that this dismissive approach must be overturned or distinguished, see S Peers, 'Human Rights, Asylum and European Community Law'
(2005) 24 RSQ 2:24.

[589] *EP v Council* (ibid) and Case C-244/06 *Dynamic Medien* [2008] ECR I-505.

[590] On the status of the Geneva Convention and associated 'soft law' within EU law, see Peers,
n 588 above.

[591] Judgments of 2 Mar 2010 in Joined Cases C-175/08, 176/08, 178/08, and 179/08 *Abdulla and
others*, and of 17 June 2010 in Case C-31/09 *Bolbol*, neither yet reported.

[592] [2000] OJ C 364.   [593] *EP v Council* (n 588 above), para 38.

instrument, the Community legislature did, however, acknowledge its importance by stating, in the second recital in the preamble to the Directive, that the Directive observes the principles recognised not only by Article 8 of the ECHR but also in the Charter. Furthermore, the principal aim of the Charter, as is apparent from its preamble, is to reaffirm 'rights as they result, in particular, from the constitutional traditions and international obligations common to the Member States, the Treaty on European Union, the Community Treaties, the [ECHR], the Social Charters adopted by the Community and by the Council of Europe and the case-law of the Court...and of the European Court of Human Rights'.

It can be seen that in this judgment, the Court confirms that the Charter was not legally binding, and had the 'principal' aim 'to reaffirm' rights which derive from the sources of the general principles of EU law. In a series of subsequent judgments before the Treaty of Lisbon entered into force, the Court of Justice referred to the Charter as having a subsidiary role 'reaffirming' the general principles.[594] This line of case law established, in effect, a 'Batman and Robin' approach to the protection of human rights in the EU legal order, with the general principles continuing to play the lead role in human rights protection and the Charter performing the role of sidekick—the 'Boy Wonder' of EU human rights law. The Court gave no further explanation of any role the Charter might have beyond its 'primary' role of 'reaffirming' existing rights, leaving open the question of whether the Charter might recognize further rights, or whether the Charter was different from the general principles as regards its scope or limitations on the rights. But obviously these questions had limited relevance anyway as long as the Charter was not legally binding.

However, the legal status of the Charter was transformed with the entry into force of the Treaty of Lisbon, which, as we have seen above, specifies that the Charter has the 'same legal value as the Treaties' (Article 6(1) TEU).[595] The Charter was subsequently amended in parallel with the signature of the Treaty, but continues to exist as a separate legal document.[596] It should be noted that the 2007 amendments did not alter the substantive rights recognized by the Charter, but rather the 'general' provisions concerning, inter alia, its scope and

---

[594] See in particular Cases: C-432/05 *Unibet* [2007] ECR I-2271, para 37; C-303/05 *Advocaten voor de Wereld* [2007] ECR I-3633, para 46; C-438/05 *Viking Line* [2007] ECR I-10779, para 44; C-341/05 *Laval* [2007] ECR I-11767, para 91; C-450/06 *Varec* [2008] ECR I-581, para 48; *Dynamic Medien* (n 589 above), para 41; C-402/05 P and C-415/05 P *Kadi and Al Barakaat International Foundation v Council and Commission* [2008] ECR I-6351, para 335; C-47/07 P *Masdar (UK) v Commission* [2008] ECR I-9761, para 50; C-385/07 P *Der Grüne Punkt—Duales System Deutschland GmbH v Commission* [2009] ECR I-6155, para 179; and C-12/08 *Mono Car Styling* [2009] ECR I-6653, para 47. But see the stronger reference in Case C-275/06 *Promusicae* [2008] ECR I-271, para 64.

[595] The revised text of the Charter (and the explanations concerning the Charter) is at [2007] OJ C 303.

[596] There is no specified procedure to amend the Charter again. But since Art 6(1), revised TEU, refers to the legal effect of the Charter *as adopted in 2000 and amended in 2007*, any further amendments to the Charter could *not* have the same legal value as the Treaties unless Art 6(1) TEU were amended to refer to them.

interpretation.[597] The explanations related to the Charter were also amended at the same time. It should be recalled that the revised Article 6(1) TEU places particular stress on the general provisions (emphasizing that the Charter does not extend the EU's competences) and on the explanations of the Charter.[598]

Since the entry into force of the Treaty of Lisbon, the early case law of the Court of Justice shows a tendency to refer to the Charter in practice as the sole or main source of human rights rules in the EU legal order, with more limited references to the general principles of EU law than before.[599] But the Court has not yet articulated the rationale for this different approach. Nor has the Court touched on the fundamental question of whether the rights in the Charter can be considered entirely identical, greater than, or lesser than those in the general principles,[600] or whether the general principles still retain the dynamic quality (ie to evolve by case law, rather than by formal amendment) which the Charter apparently lacks.

As for the sources of the rights in the Charter, as the Court of Justice pointed out (see above) the main sources are national constitutions, the ECHR, the EC/EU treaties, and other international treaties. While the general provisions of the Charter address the relationship between the Charter and some of these sources,[601] the Court of Justice has not yet addressed this issue. Indeed the Court has not yet referred to the general provisions of the Charter or the explanations relating to the Charter. It should be noted that while the Charter includes most of the rights which appear in the ECHR and its Protocols, certain rights listed in the Fourth and Seventh Protocols to the ECHR are not mentioned in the Charter.[602] In that case, at the very least Member States remain bound by their

---

[597] Arts 1–50 of the Charter set out the substantive rights, while Arts 51–54 are the general provisions (Chapter VII).

[598] Both these specific points appear in the general provisions: Arts 51(2) and 52(7) of the Charter. The explanations to the Charter can be found in [2007] OJ C 303/17.

[599] See Cases: C-323/08 *Mayor*, judgment of 10 Dec 2009; *Abdulla* (n 591 above); C-578/08 *Chakroun*, judgment of 4 Mar 2010; C-403/09 PPU *Detiček*, judgment of 23 Dec 2009; C-555/07 *Kucukdeveci*, judgment of 19 Jan 2010; C-570/07 and C-571/07 *Blanco Perez*, judgment of 1 June 2010; C-31/09 *Bolbol*, judgment of 17 June 2010; C-188/10 and C-189/10 PPU *Melki and Abdeli*, judgment of 22 June 2010; C-407/08 P *Knauf Gips*, judgment of 1 July 2010; C-211/10 PPU *Povse*, judgment of 1 July 2010; and C-271/08 *Commission v Germany*, judgment of 15 July 2010 (none yet reported). In *Abdulla*, *Chakroun*, *Kucukdeveci*, *Melki and Abdeli*, *Knauf Gips*, and *Commission v Germany*, the Court expressly referred to the wording of the revised Art 6(1) TEU. But see the more traditional approach in Joined Cases C-317/08 to C-320/08 *Alassini*, judgment of 18 Mar 2010, not yet reported; and note that in *Kucukdeveci*, the judgment mainly stressed the general principles, not the Charter. See further the discussion of the legal effect of these measures below.

[600] Note that Protocol 30 to the Treaties, which concerns the position of Poland, the UK, and (in future) the Czech Republic as regards the Charter, states that 'the Charter reaffirms the rights, freedoms and principles recognised in the Union and makes those rights more visible, but *does not create new* rights or principles' (sixth recital in the preamble). However, this Protocol also states that it 'is without prejudice to the application of the Charter to other Member States' (eleventh recital in the preamble).   [601] Art 52(2)–(4); see also Art 53 of the Charter.

[602] See n 585 above.

international commitments, and it is furthermore arguable that such rights must be recognized as part of the general principles of EU law, even though they are not referred to in the Charter.

Next, the third basic source of human rights protection in EU law is the ECHR itself. As we have seen, Article 6(2) TEU requires the EU to accede to the Convention. This provision of the Treaty was inserted by the Treaty of Lisbon; prior to that Treaty, despite the pre-eminent position of the ECHR and the case law of the Convention organs as a source of the human rights principles of EU law, the Court of Justice ruled that the EC (as it then was) lacked the competence to accede to the ECHR.[603] The question of accession to the ECHR by the EU (as then distinct from the EC) was not considered during this period.

Although the EC was not able to accede to the Convention, the Convention organs nevertheless declared themselves competent to exercise a form of 'indirect' review of acts of the EC bodies, to the extent that Member States implemented such acts. The extent of this jurisdiction was clarified in the *Bosphorus Airways* judgment of the Strasbourg Court.[604] According to this judgment, where Member States lack discretion over whether to implement EC rules, they are subject to only limited review by the Convention organs; otherwise there is no limit on the review by those organs. Furthermore, the limited review is only justified as long as the EC 'is considered to protect fundamental rights, as regards both the substantive guarantees offered and the mechanisms controlling their observance, in a manner which can be considered at least equivalent to that for which the Convention provides'. The Strasbourg Court makes it clear that 'equivalent' means 'comparable', not 'identical', but that any finding of equivalence 'could not be final and would be susceptible to review in the light of any relevant change in fundamental rights' protection'.[605]

The presumption of compliance could be rebutted if there were a manifest case of non-compliance with ECHR standards, but it seems from *Bosphorus Airways* that in practice the presumption extended to the EC (now the EU) will be well-nigh irrebuttable,[606] due to the extent of human rights protected afforded by the EU legal order, in particular because of the substantive protection for ECHR rights guaranteed by that legal order and by the level of effective procedural protection for individuals offered by the EU judicial system in most cases. However, the Strasbourg Court did not comment on whether the level of procedural protection then applying to immigration and asylum cases, or policing and criminal law cases, was sufficient. It is arguable that it was not under the EU judicial system

---

[603] *Opinion 2/94* [1996] ECR I-1759.

[604] *Bosphorus Airways v Ireland*, judgment of 30 June 2005 (Reports of Judgments and Decisions 2005-VI). [605] Para 155 of the judgment.

[606] Indeed, see the subsequent decisions in *Cooperative des Agriculteurs de Mayenne and Cooperative Laitière Maine-Anjou v France* (10 Oct 2006) and *Cooperatieve Producentenorganisatie van de Nederlandse Kokkelvisserij ua v Netherlands* (20 Jan 2009), neither yet reported, in which the presumption was not rebutted.

prior to the entry into force of the Treaty of Lisbon,[607] but that since that Treaty entered into force the procedural protection is sufficient as regards EU immigration, asylum, and civil law, and as regards any policing and criminal law measures adopted or amended after the entry into force of the Treaty of Lisbon. The system is still insufficient as regards policing and criminal law measures adopted before the entry into force of that Treaty, at least as regards those Member States which have not opted into the Court's jurisdiction, as long as the transitional restrictions on the Court's jurisdiction are applicable.[608] For now then, the EU measures concerned do not benefit from any presumption of compliance with the ECHR, and there is no restriction on the 'indirect review' by the Strasbourg Court of EU acts in this area.[609]

On the ECHR side, the ECHR provides for EU accession (as from the entry into force of the Fourteenth Protocol to the Convention, on 1 June 2010),[610] but this is dependent upon the negotiation of some form of accession treaty. On the EU side, the process of EU accession to the ECHR requires a negotiating mandate from the Council to the Commission, successful negotiations by the Commission, and then signature and conclusion of the accession treaty by the Council. The Council needs to act unanimously throughout the process, and the accession treaty will also require the consent of the EP and ratification by each Member State's national parliament before it enters into force.[611]

There are also substantive limits on EU accession set out in a special Protocol to the Treaties, which requires that the accession treaty 'shall make provision for preserving the specific characteristics of the Union and Union law, in particular' as regards: 'the specific arrangements for the Union's possible participation in' ECHR control bodies, and 'mechanisms necessary to ensure that proceedings by non-Member States and individual applications are correctly addressed to Member States and/or the Union as appropriate'.[612] Furthermore, the agreement concerned 'shall ensure that' EU accession to the ECHR 'shall not affect the competences of the Union or the powers of its institutions' and that nothing in that treaty 'affects the situation of Member States' as regards the ECHR, 'in particular' as regards Member States' position regarding Protocols to the ECHR,[613] derogations from the ECHR made by Member States pursuant to Article 15 ECHR, and reservations to the ECHR made by Member States.[614] Finally, the Protocol provides that the accession treaty shall not affect Article 344 TFEU (formerly

---

[607] See the critique in 2.5 below.

[608] On the transitional rules concerning the Court's jurisdiction, see 2.2.3.3 above.

[609] See previously the admissibility decision in *TI v UK*, discussed in 5.3.1 below.

[610] See Art 59 ECHR, as revised by the Fourteenth Protocol.

[611] See Art 218(6)(a)(ii) and (8) TFEU. It is likely that the treaty will also need to be ratified by the other contracting parties to the ECHR.   [612] Art 1, Protocol 8.

[613] Implicitly the question arises as to which substantive ECHR Protocols the EU will ratify. All Member States have ratified Protocols 1 and 6, whereas only some have ratified Protocols 4, 7, 12, and 13.   [614] Art 2, Protocol 8.

Article 292 EC), which awards exclusive jurisdiction to the Court of Justice to settle disputes between Member States as regards EU law.[615]

In practice, the Stockholm programme setting out a JHA agenda from 2010–14 states that starting the process of EU accession to the ECHR is a matter of 'urgency',[616] and the Commission requested a negotiation mandate from the Council in March 2010; the Council approved this mandate in June 2010.[617] It remains to be seen how the final accession treaty will address the specific issues raised in the relevant Protocol on this issue. In any event, it should follow that after the EU's accession to the ECHR, the particular doctrine of limited review of EU action set out in the *Bosphorus Airways* judgment will cease to apply, since it was designed to address the specific issues arising from the EU's status as a *non-contracting* party to the ECHR.

Moving on to the *scope* of the EU human rights rules, first of all, the general principles of EU law apply when assessing the interpretation and validity of EU measures, along with Member States' implementation of those acts and Member States' derogations from EU law.[618] On the other hand, the general principles of EU law do not apply unless an issue is linked to EU law: for example, the Court had no jurisdiction to rule on the human rights aspects of the family reunion of Turkish workers pursuant to the EU–Turkey Association agreement, because that agreement does not address the initial admission of workers' family members.[619] But the scope of EU law is of course subject to change; such a case now falls within the scope of the general principles of EU law, following the adoption of the EU's family reunion Directive.[620]

The issue of the scope of the Charter is addressed in Article 51 concerning the Charter's 'field of application', as amended in 2007, which reads:

1. The provisions of this Charter are addressed to the institutions, bodies, offices and agencies of the Union with due regard for the principle of subsidiarity and to the Member States only when they are implementing Union law. They shall therefore respect the rights, observe the principles and promote the application thereof in accordance with their respective powers and respecting the limits of the powers of the Union as conferred on it in the Treaties.

---

[615] Art 3, Protocol 8. Since the Treaty of Lisbon, this provision also applies to policing and criminal law. For the application of this clause, see Case C-459/03 *Commission v Ireland* [2006] ECR I-4635.   [616] [2010] OJ C 115, point 2.1.

[617] See JHA Council press release, 3–4 June 2010.

[618] See particularly Case 5/88 *Wachauf* [1989] ECR 2609 (national implementation) and Case C-260/89 *ERT* [1991] ECR I-2925 (derogations). As regards Member States' derogations from EU JHA law, see *EP v Council*, n 588 above.

[619] Case 12/86 *Demirel* [1987] ECR 3719. As regards criminal law, see Cases C-299/95 *Kremzow* [1997] ECR I-2629 and C-328/04 *Vajnai* [2005] ECR I-8577. See also Cases: C-287/08 *Savia* [2008] ECR I-136*; C-535/08 *Pignataro* [2009] ECR I-50*; C-302/06 *Kowalsky* [2007] ECR I-11*; and C-333/09 *Noel* (order of 27 Nov 2009, unreported).

[620] On the substance of that Directive, see 6.6 below.

2. The Charter does not extend the field of application of Union law beyond the powers of the Union or establish any new power or task for the Union, or modify powers and tasks as defined in the Treaties.

To this end, the Court of Justice has dismissed cases in which the Charter was invoked for lack of a link with EU law, both implicitly and explicitly.[621] In practice, the Court's case law has taken a similar approach as regards the limits on the scope of the Charter and of the general principles, although the Court has not yet expressly addressed the question of whether or not the limitations on the scope of the two sources of rights can be regarded as identical.

As for accession to the ECHR, the relevant Treaty Article and Protocol do not expressly address the question of the scope of the EU's accession to the ECHR, although it is clearly assumed that Member States will remain parties to the ECHR alongside the EU. The precise scope of the EU's accession to the ECHR therefore remains to be determined, either by the accession treaty itself or the case law of the Court of Justice.[622]

Next, the question of limitations on rights, as regards the general principles of law, has been addressed by the Court of Justice, ruling that 'restrictions may be imposed on the exercise of [human] rights, in particular in the context of a common organisation of the markets, provided that those restrictions in fact correspond to objectives of general interest pursued by the Community and do not constitute, with regard to the aim pursued, a disproportionate and intolerable interference, impairing the very substance of those rights'. The Court often also states that 'fundamental rights are not absolute rights but must be considered in relation to their social function'.[623] However, in some cases, the Court instead follows the limitations rules set out in the ECHR, including the relevant jurisprudence.[624]

As for the Charter, it contains a general rule on limitations of rights (Article 52(1)), which reads as follows:

Any limitation on the exercise of the rights and freedoms recognised by this Charter must be provided for by law and respect the essence of those rights and freedoms. Subject to the principle of proportionality, limitations may be made only if they are necessary and genuinely meet objectives of general interest recognised by the Union or the need to protect the rights and freedoms of others.

---

[621] For implicit dismissals of a sufficient link with EU law to invoke the Charter, see *Vajnai*, n 619 above and Case C-361/07 *Polier* [2008] ECR I-6*. For explicit dismissals of a sufficient link, see Case C-217/08 *Mariano* [2009] ECR I-35*, para 29, which refers expressly to Art 51(2) of the Charter, and Case C-323/08 *Mayor*, judgment of 10 Dec 2009, not yet reported, paras 58–59.

[622] See the case law relating to the conclusion of mixed agreements and the Court's jurisdiction over them, discussed in 2.7 below.

[623] Joined Cases C-20/00 and C-64/00 *Booker Aquaculture* [2003] ECR I-7411, para 68, quoting established case law.   [624] See Peers, n 582 above.

However, the Charter also contains other provisions referring to consistency of interpretation with the rights set out already in the Treaties, the ECHR, and national constitutional rules, which should be understood as cross-references to the different rules on limitations of rights set out in those particular sources.[625] As for the ECHR, there are specific rules on limitations upon and derogations from the relevant rights expressly set out in the Convention, which the EU will obviously be bound by once it accedes to it.

Finally, as for the legal effect of the relevant measures, the practical impact of the general principles of EU law is that an act adopted by an EU body could be considered invalid, or interpreted in light of, the relevant human rights principle. This applies equally to national law, and the Court of Justice has in particular ruled that even in cases concerning the application of Directives between private parties, where Directives normally do not have direct effect, the principle of supremacy means that national law which infringes the rights in the Directive which give effect to the principle of equality must be set aside.[626] The precise scope of these judgments is not clear, as regards other general principles; the Court might even rule that *any* provisions of Directives have this effect, even if there is no link to any human rights principles. It could also be argued by analogy that third pillar measures adopted before the Treaty of Lisbon have the same legal effect, at least where human rights are concerned.[627]

As for the Charter, Article 52(5) states that the Charter provisions which recognize *principles* 'shall be judicially cognisable only in the interpretation of' acts by EU bodies and Member State acts implementing these, 'and in the ruling on their legality'. This suggests *a contrario* that Charter provisions which recognize *rights* have a stronger legal impact, in particular direct effect and supremacy. However, Protocol 30 to the Treaties states that within the UK and Poland, the Charter 'does not extend the ability of the Court of Justice' or national courts to rule that national laws 'are inconsistent with the fundamental rights, freedoms and principles that it reaffirms'; '[i]n particular', nothing in Title IV of the Charter (setting out social rights) 'creates justiciable rights applicable to' those countries 'except in so far as' each of those countries 'has provided for such rights in its national law'. This Protocol will in future be extended to the Czech Republic.[628]

---

[625] Art 52(2)–(4); see also Art 53. Furthermore, Art 52(6) states that '[f]ull account shall be taken of national laws and practices' referred to in the Charter; see the approach taken by the Court in *Laval* and *Viking Line* (n 594 above) as regards limitations on the right to strike, and the discussion of Protocol 30 below. For an analysis of the issue of limitations of rights under the general principles of law and the Charter, see S Peers, 'Taking Rights Away? Derogations and Limitations' in S Peers and A Ward, eds, *The EU Charter of Rights: Politics, Law and Policy* (Hart, 2004), 141. Note that the Court has already referred to Art 52(1) and 52(6) in (respectively) *Knauf Gips* and *Commission v Germany* (n 599 above).

[626] See the judgments in *Mangold* and particularly *Kucukdeveci* (nn 587 and 599 above).

[627] On the general rules on the legal effect of those measures, see 2.2.2.2 above.

[628] See Annex I to the conclusions of the Oct 2010 European Council meeting.

The Protocol also states that '[t]o the extent that a provision of the Charter refers to national laws and practices, it shall only apply to' those countries 'to the extent that the rights or principles that it contains are recognised in the law or practices of' those countries.

Protocol 30 does not in any way limit the legal effect of the general principles, or of the ECHR once the EU accedes to it (see below).[629] So the Protocol is only relevant to the extent that the Charter in some way *adds value* to the general principles, either because it recognizes *additional rights* as compared to the general principles, is *wider in scope* than the general principles, or allows for *fewer limitations* of rights than pursuant to the general principles. If the Charter adds no value or is of lesser value than the general principles, then the Protocol is irrelevant because the general principles will in any event apply. It remains to be seen whether the case law of the Court of Justice clarifies these issues, but it is notable that in one of the first cases after the Charter gained enhanced legal effect with the entry into force of the Treaty of Lisbon, the Court of Justice relied largely on the *general principles*, rather than the Charter, to conclude that national law which breached the equality provisions of an EU Directive had to be set aside. So it seems prima facie clear that the general principles have the precise legal effect which Protocol 30 seeks to preclude, in two (and soon three) Member States, as regards the Charter.

As for the ECHR, once the EU accedes to it, it should be noted that many international treaties concluded by the EU are subject to the principles of direct effect and supremacy. The ECHR should easily meet the relevant criteria developed by the Court of Justice to this end.[630]

As regards JHA issues in particular, where acute and complex human rights issues are legion, the role of the Court of Justice in interpreting and ruling on the validity of EU acts in light of human rights, and ruling on national implementation and derogation from EU law, has already been significant,[631] and will likely grow in importance in light of the extension of the Court's jurisdiction over JHA matters pursuant to the Treaty of Lisbon.

Finally, while this section has focused on judicial mechanisms for protecting human rights in the EU, there are also non-judicial mechanisms. The Commission has a procedure for checking the compatibility of its legislative proposals with the Charter.[632] Article 7 TEU, inserted into the EU Treaty by the Treaty of Amsterdam, provides for the Council to adopt sanctions, including suspension of the rights of the Member State concerned, against a Member State which

---

[629] The Protocol expressly states that it 'is without prejudice to other obligations devolving upon Poland and the [UK] under the TEU, the TFEU, "and Union law generally"' (twelfth recital in the preamble; see also the seventh recital).   [630] See further 2.7 below.

[631] See in particular *EP v Council* (n 588 above), *Chakroun* (n 599 above), *Abdulla* (n 591 above), and *Advocaten voor de Wereld* (n 594 above).

[632] COM (2005) 172, 27 Apr 2005 and COM (2009) 205, 29 Apr 2009.

commits a 'serious and persistent breach' of the values of the EU, as defined in the revised Article 2 TEU, which asserts that:

The Union is founded on the values of respect for human dignity, freedom, democracy, equality, the rule of law and respect for human rights, including the rights of persons belonging to minorities. These values are common to the Member States in a society in which pluralism, non-discrimination, tolerance, justice, solidarity and equality between women and men prevail.

To this end, Article 7 TEU provides for a special decision-making procedure, with limited jurisdiction for the Court of Justice.[633] Article 7 was amended by the Treaty of Nice, to provide for a 'yellow card' to warn a Member State which might commit a serious and persistent breach. None of the provisions of Article 7 have been used.[634] However, it should be noted that the Treaty of Lisbon broadened the grounds on which a Member State can be sanctioned, as previously Article 7 referred to a breach of the principles of human rights, democracy, and the rule of law.[635] These values (as revised by the Treaty of Lisbon) are also conditions for membership of the EU, according to Article 49 TEU.

Despite the lack of use of the sanctions procedure, the enshrinement of basic principles (now values) as the cornerstone of the EU legal system has a broader constitutional significance, as is clear from the Court of Justice ruling in *Kadi*, which established human rights protection as a core rule of EU law, prevailing over other primary rules set out in the Treaties as well as primordial international obligations of Member States. The subsequent entrenchment in the Treaties of the key 'values' of the Union has already affected the case law of the Court of Justice as regards substantive JHA matters: the Court has ruled that the 'assessment of the extent of the risk [of persecution as defined by the Geneva Convention on refugee status] must, in all cases, be carried out with vigilance and care, since what are at issue are issues relating to the integrity of the person and to individual liberties, issues which relate to the *fundamental values* of the Union'.[636]

Finally, in 2007 the EU created an Agency for Fundamental Rights, established in Vienna, which has the role of collecting data, carrying out studies, and formulating opinions and conclusions.[637] Its effectiveness to date might be questioned, given that it does not have any powers of investigation or dispute settlement, and can only express its opinion on proposed legislation if requested.

---

[633] See Art 269 TFEU.

[634] See B De Witte and G Toggenburg, 'Human Rights and Membership of the European Union', in Peers and Ward (eds) (n 625 above) and the Commission Communication on the application of Art 7 (COM (2003) 606, 15 Oct 2003).   [635] Previous Art 6(1) TEU.

[636] Para 90 of the *Abdulla* judgment, n 591 above (emphasis added).

[637] Reg 168/2007, [2007] OJ L 53/1; see also the multi-annual framework for the Agency's activities ([2008] OJ L 63/14). On the Agency's role in JHA matters, see S Peers, 'Civil and Political Rights: the Role of an EU Human Rights Agency', in P Alston and O De Schutter, eds, *Monitoring Fundamental Rights in the EU: The Contribution of the Fundamental Rights Agency* (Hart, 2005). See also the decision on funding human rights policies ([2007] OJ L 110/33).

In order to establish the Agency as an effective actor in EU human rights protection, it should be given the right to express its opinion on any draft EU measure (without being requested) and any national implementation of EU measures, and should moreover issue guidance as regards national implementation of EU measures. While the Agency's role was limited, before the entry into force of the Treaty of Lisbon, to Community matters only, the effect of merging the EC and the EU means that since that Treaty entered into force, the Agency has competence to address policing and criminal law matters as well.

2.4. Relationship with other EU law

It is obviously important in practice to distinguish between JHA rules (in their various forms) and the rules governing other areas of EU law ('non-JHA law'), because the latter, but not the former, usually entails full application of the law to all Member States.[638] Before the Treaty of Lisbon, there were also distinctions between JHA law and non-JHA law regarding the full jurisdiction of the Court of Justice, the legal effect of the legislation concerned, and the relevant decision-making rules; the rules on legal effect and jurisdiction still remain relevant during the transitional periods established by the Treaty of Lisbon. The following examines in turn the relationship of JHA law with non-JHA law during the 'Maastricht era', the 'Amsterdam era', and then following the entry into force of the Treaty of Lisbon. This is a horizontal overview; further more specific points are discussed in the remaining chapters of this book, including the broader relationship between JHA law and non-JHA law, particularly as regards EU free movement law and association agreements.[639]

2.4.1. Competence issues, 1993–1999

A number of provisions of the original version of the EU Treaty addressed the relationship between the first and third pillars. First and foremost, Article M of the EU Treaty stated that nothing in the second or third pillars could affect the EC Treaty, and Article K.1 stated that the third pillar was without prejudice to the EC's powers. Furthermore, Article K.8(1) EU expressly made twenty-two clauses of the EC Treaty applicable to the third pillar; these were the articles dealing with the essential structure of the Council, Commission, and EP, as well as the rules on the EC's official languages. Article K.8(2) provided that administrative expenses related to the third pillar were to be charged to the EC budget, while operational expenses could be charged to that budget if the Council agreed

---

[638] For the detailed rules governing the territorial scope of JHA measures, see 2.2.5 above.
[639] See s 2.4 in each of chs 3–12.

following a unanimous vote of the Member States.[640] Otherwise, spending would be charged to the Member States on a scale to be determined.

Two JHA issues in fact fell within the EC's powers. The Maastricht Treaty inserted a new Article 100c into the EC Treaty, providing for the Council to adopt measures on a common visa format and on a common list of countries whose nationals would need visas to enter the EU. Article 100c included the 'standard' institutional rules of EC law: monopoly of initiative by the Commission, consultation of the EP, and QMV in the Council.[641]

Furthermore, Article K.9 of the original EU Treaty provided for a simplified system for potentially transferring the first six aspects of JHA cooperation to the first pillar. This would have required a unanimous vote of the Council and ratification by the Member States in accordance with their constitutional rules. However, Article K.9 was never applied in practice. So the scope of the JHA provisions remained unamended until the Treaty of Amsterdam entered into force. In the meantime, the Council, the EP, the Commission, and various Member States took different views on the first/third pillar borderline. The first relevant dispute concerned the validity of an EC development policy treaty with India. Portugal challenged the Council's conclusion of this treaty on the grounds, inter alia, that the provisions it contained on drug addiction had a 'legal base' in the third pillar, not the first.[642] However, Portugal lost on the merits because the Court of Justice ruled that drugs cooperation as provided for in the treaty with India fell within the scope of the EC's development policy powers.

There were particularly intractable disputes over competence over visas and internal border controls. Ultimately, the Commission decided to sue the Council when the latter adopted a third pillar Joint Action setting out a list of countries whose nationals would have to carry airport transit visas,[643] although the Commission believed that this issue fell within the scope of EC powers to adopt a list of countries whose nationals would have to carry a visa to cross the EC Member States' external borders.[644] Although the UK challenged the admissibility of the action, on the grounds that the Court of Justice had no jurisdiction over Joint Actions, the Court of Justice ruled that Article L EU (subsequently Article 46 EU), defining the Court's jurisdiction over the EU Treaty) gave it jurisdiction to interpret Article M EU (later Article 47 EU), which, as noted above, provided that nothing in the EU Treaty amended the EC Treaty except those provisions expressly amending the latter. Therefore it was 'the task of the Court to ensure that acts which, according to the Council, fall within Article K.3(2) of the [TEU] do not encroach upon the powers conferred by' the EC Treaty 'upon

---

[640] In that case, EC rules relating to the budget were applicable: see Art 199 EC (later Art 268 EC). On funding of JHA measures, see 2.6 below.

[641] However, there was a transition period: before 1 Jan 1996, voting on the visa list had to be unanimous.   [642] Case C-268/94 *Portugal v Council* [1996] ECR I-6177.

[643] [1996] OJ L 63/8.   [644] Case C-170/96 *Commission v Council* [1998] ECR I-2763.

the Community'. It thus had jurisdiction to rule whether the measure 'should have been adopted' pursuant to Article 100c EC (the 'legal base' for adoption of visa list measures), rather than the third pillar. Implicitly, the Court also rejected the Danish argument that the scope of the 'pillars' was movable at the will of the EU/EC institutions,[645] and declined to analyse the issue by comparing the EU's third pillar powers with the EC's powers pursuant to Article 100c EC. Rather, the Court looked only at the scope of Article 100c EC and determined, by interpreting the Joint Action, whether it fell within the scope of that EC's power. So the Court did not offer a view on the powers conferred upon the Union at that time by the third pillar.[646]

Subsequently, the EU's Court of First Instance (CFI) expressly concluded that the Council's access to documents rules covered third pillar documents, and that the EU courts had jurisdiction to consider disputes concerning access to third pillar documents.[647] A parallel dispute arose over the competence of the EU's Ombudsman to hear disputes over the application of the Council's access to documents rules to third pillar documents. In March 1997, after Tony Bunyan, editor of Statewatch Bulletin, had complained to the Ombudsman about the Council's application of the Council rules to third pillar documents, the Council voted 9–6 to reject the Ombudsman's competence to examine the Council's administration of its rules as far as third pillar documents were concerned. But the Ombudsman maintained his position, and in June 1997 the Council reversed itself and maintained that it would consider the complaint as far as it related to the application of the Decision, not the substance of the documents.[648]

In one case, the EC and EU adopted parallel measures in the first and third pillar: a Convention concerning the third pillar aspects of the Customs Information System and a Regulation concerning the first pillar aspects.[649]

2.4.2. Treaty of Amsterdam

During the 'Amsterdam era' (1 May 1999 to 1 December 2009), the dividing line between JHA measures and non-JHA measures remained important. Previously, there had been a single division between matters governed by EC law and matters governed by the third pillar. But for over ten years there were three categories of law: non-JHA measures; the provisions of the EC Treaty addressing asylum,

---

[645] See para 9 of the Advocate General's Opinion, where this interpretation was explicitly rejected.

[646] To the same effect, see the earlier judgment in Case C-392/95 *EP v Council* [1997] ECR I-3213, particularly the Opinion of the Advocate General.

[647] Case T-174/95 *Svenska Journalistforbundet* [1998] ECR II-2289. See further s 2.5 below.

[648] See *Statewatch Bulletin*, Jan/Feb 1997 and May/June 1997.

[649] See further 12.6.1.2 below.

immigration, and civil law; and the revised third pillar provisions. Additionally, the Schengen *acquis* was integrated into all three of these compartments, raising a number of further legal issues.

First of all, as regards the distinction between the first and third pillars, in several cases (as before), parallel first and third pillar measures were adopted.[650] Nevertheless, there were still disputes about the scope of EC powers over criminal law and policing-related issues. These arguments culminated in two judgments of the Court of Justice supporting the Commission's view that the EC, not the EU, had power during this period to adopt legislation concerning the enforcement of environmental law, or law relating to the environment, by means of imposing criminal liability.[651] The approach of the Court to the first/third pillar dividing line in these judgments was to apply the previous Article 47 TEU (which provided that the TEU did not affect the Community treaties) to assess whether the subject matter of the contested third pillar Framework Decisions fell within the scope of the first pillar. Since it did, there was implicitly no need to assess whether the Framework Decisions could have fallen within the scope of the third pillar. Therefore, once a measure fell within the scope of a first pillar power, Article 47 EU automatically precluded the application of any third pillar competence, without any need to compare the first and third pillar competence or any possibility that a third pillar *lex specialis* might prevail over a more general first pillar power. It was not necessary for the EC to have exercised its competence previously; the mere *existence* of such a competence was enough.

This approach was also applied to the first/third pillar dividing line as regards policing issues, where the Court ruled that measures solely regulating law enforcement bodies' *use* of data supplied by the private sector fell outside the scope of the first pillar (and so implicitly within the scope of the third pillar),[652] but measures solely regulating the private sector's *supply* of that data to the law enforcement authorities fell within the scope of Community law (as it was then).[653]

Also, Court judgments on the dividing line between the first pillar and the second pillar (foreign policy) were surely relevant by analogy to the first/third pillar dividing line. On this point, the Court ruled that where an issue fell within the scope of both the EC's development policy powers and the EU's foreign policy powers, as where EU funding was offered to assist developing

---

[650] For examples, see 12.6.1.1 below regarding the SIS and 7.5.3 below regarding facilitation of irregular migration.

[651] Cases C-176/03 *Commission v Council* [2005] ECR I-7879 and C-440/05 *Commission v Council* [2007] ECR I-9097. This led to the adoption of EC legislation providing for criminal penalties: Dirs 2008/99 ([2008] OJ L 328/28), 2009/123 ([2009] OJ L 280/52), and 2009/52 ([2009] OJ L 168/24). See also the Commission communication on this issue (COM (2005) 583, 23 Nov 2005), and the detailed comments in 10.4 below.

[652] Joined Cases C-317/04 and C-318/04 *EP v Council and Commission* [2006] ECR I-4721.

[653] Case C-301/06 *Ireland v Council and EP* [2009] ECR I-593.

states to destroy small arms, Article 47 EU required that the issue be addressed solely on the basis of the Community's powers, even though development policy was a shared parallel power (ie the Member States had the power to adopt their own development policy measures outside the EC legal order, even acting collectively).[654] Although the EP successfully challenged a Commission decision applying the EU's development policy legislation to fund Philippine anti-terrorist measures, this was because the legislation concerned did not extend in scope to such measures, not because the EC lacked the competence to address them.[655] Furthermore, the Court of Justice ruled that the previous Article 308 EC, which gave residual powers to the EC to act to achieve its objectives when no more specific clause did so, could not apply as regards foreign policy objectives. More broadly:[656]

...the coexistence of the Union and the Community as integrated but separate legal orders, and the constitutional architecture of the pillars, as intended by the framers of the Treaties now in force...constitute considerations of an institutional kind militating against any extension of the bridge to articles of the EC Treaty other than those with which it explicitly creates a link.

There were also disputes concerning the precise dividing line between Title IV of the EC Treaty and the non-JHA EC Treaty,[657] although the Court of Justice confirmed that issues concerning the admission of third-country national family members of EU citizens to the territory of the EU fell within the scope of EU free movement law (not Title IV), whenever the EU citizen sponsor of the family member concerned was exercising free movement rights.[658] It should also be emphasized that many aspects of non-JHA Community law overlapped with the subject matter of various JHA powers, in particular EU free movement law (as regards third-country national family members of EU citizens, posted third-country national workers, and private security services); EU association agreements; and the enforcement of EU law.[659]

As for the Schengen *acquis*, the original Schengen Convention and the Protocol on the Schengen *acquis* both stated expressly, before the Treaty of Lisbon, that EC and EU law took priority over the *acquis* in the event of a conflict.[660] This position was confirmed and clarified in the 2006 judgment in *Commission v Spain*, which concerned the conflict between the Schengen

---

[654] Case C-91/05 *Commission v Council* [2008] ECR I-3651.

[655] Case C-403/05 *EP v Commission* [2007] ECR I-9045. There is now EU development policy legislation addressing such issues: Reg 1717/2006, [2006] OJ L 317/1.

[656] Joined Cases C-402/05 P and C-415/05 P *Kadi and Al Barakaat* [2008] ECR I-6351, para 202. [657] See s 4 of chs 3–7.

[658] Case C-127/08 *Metock* [2008] ECR I-6241. [659] See s 4 of chs 3–12.

[660] Art 134 of the 1990 Convention ([2000] OJ L 239), and the preamble and (more ambiguously) Art 1 of the Protocol. On the position after the Treaty of Lisbon, see 2.4.3 below.

rules on automatic refusal of visas and entry at the external border for persons listed on the SIS, and the provisions of EU free movement law, which require an individual assessment of the extent of the threat posed by third-country national family members of EU citizens, and set a higher threshold for refusing entry than the SIS sets out for listing persons to be refused entry.[661] The Court of Justice rejected the Spanish argument that, following the integration of the Schengen *acquis* into the EC and EU legal order, the provisions of the *acquis* 'cannot be contrary to Community law'.[662] Instead, the Court referred to the relevant provisions of the 1990 Convention and the Schengen Protocol,[663] and ruled that 'the compliance of an administrative practice with the provisions of the [Convention] may justify the conduct of the competent national authorities only in so far as the application of the relevant provisions is compatible with the Community rules governing freedom of movement for persons'.[664] Although, in the Court's view, the automatic nature of the Schengen blacklist was a necessary aspect of Schengen integration, the application of the Schengen rules in individual cases still had to be examined for conformity with EU free movement law. The Court did not address the question of the relationship between measures building on the *acquis* and other EU law, although it should be noted that most of these measures expressly give precedence to and/or do not affect other EU law.[665]

As for the allocation of the Schengen *acquis*, as noted above,[666] the provisions on the SIS were not allocated, and so fell by default into the third pillar. But subsequent measures concerning the management of the SIS II project, the update of the Sirene manual, the amendment of the SIS rules, and the migration from SIS to SIS II entailed the adoption of parallel first and third pillar measures, including also a measure within the scope of the EC's transport powers.[667] The legislation establishing SIS II followed the same approach. Given the application of the SIS to external border controls and the issue of visas in particular, this approach was surely correct.[668]

---

[661] Case C-503/03 *Commission v Spain* [2006] ECR I-1097. For more on the substance and implications of the judgment, see 3.4.1, 4.4.1, 6.4.1, and 7.4.1 below.

[662] Para 30 of the judgment, ibid.

[663] The previous Art 134 of the Convention gave priority to EU law before the entry into force of the Treaty of Amsterdam, while the third recital in the preamble to the Protocol gave priority to EU law afterward. It seemed that Art 1 of the Protocol also played a role (paras 33 and 34 of the judgment). [664] Para 35 of the judgment, ibid.

[665] See, for instance, Art 3 of the borders code (Reg 562/2006, [2006] OJ L 105/1) and Art 1(2) of the visa code (Reg 810/2009, [2009] OJ L 243/1), and the more detailed comments in 3.4.1, 4.4.1, and 7.4.1 below. [666] See 2.2.2.3.

[667] See 12.6.1.1 below.

[668] On the process of integrating the Schengen *acquis*, see D Thym, 'Schengen Law: A Challenge for Legal Accountability in the European Union' (2002) 8 ELJ 218 and S Peers, '*Caveat Emptor?* Integrating the Schengen *Acquis* into the European Union Legal Order' (2000) 2 CYELS 87.

The overlap between the various areas of EU policy subject to different rules on decision-making, jurisdiction, legal effect, and territorial scope was reflected in the case law of the Court of Justice. In five judgments, two different JHA regimes overlapped, as the Court confirmed its interpretation of the Brussels Convention by comparison with the Title IV Regulation later replacing that Convention (or another civil law Regulation);[669] similarly, one annulment action challenged a Commission decision applicable to both the third pillar and first pillar aspects of the SIS.[670] In other cases, Title IV issues arose in the context of non-JHA EU law, when the Court mentioned the EU's visa list Regulations and family reunion Directive when ruling on issues of EU free movement law.[671] Also, in several other cases, Advocates General of the Court suggested an interpretation of Title IV or adopted, or proposed measures based on Title IV in the context of cases concerning non-JHA EU law,[672] although some of these cases were not referred from final courts or were referred from Member States which had partly opted out of Title IV measures. Conversely, there have been cases where non-JHA EU law overlapped with JHA measures.[673] There were also cases where third pillar issues overlapped with non-JHA issues.[674]

---

[669] Cases C-167/00 *Henkel* [2002] ECR I-8111, para 49; C-111/01 *Gantner Electronics* [2003] ECR I-4207, para 28; C-104/03 *St Paul Dairy Industries* [2005] ECR I-3481, para 23; C-112/03 *Société financière et industrielle du Peloux* [2005] ECR I-3707, para 41; and C-292/05 *Lechoritou* [2007] ECR I-1519, para 45. Also, the opinions in several other cases interpreted the Convention in light of Title IV civil law legislation: Cases C-256/00 *Besix* [2002] ECR I-1699; C-334/00 *Fonderie Officine Meccaniche Tacconi* [2002] ECR I-7357; C-271/00 *Baten* [2002] ECR I-10489; C-437/00 *Pugliese* [2003] ECR I-3573; C-18/02 *DFDS Torline* [2004] ECR I-1417; C-159/02 *Turner* [2004] ECR I-3565; C-281/02 *Owusu* [2005] ECR I-1383; C-3/05 *Verdoliva* [2006] ECR I-1579; and C-539/03 *Roche Netherlands* [2006] ECR I-6535.

[670] See interim measures ruling in Case T-447/04 R *Cap Gemini* [2005] ECR II-257; the case was later withdrawn.

[671] Cases C-459/99 *MRAX* [2002] ECR I-6591 and C-157/03 *Commission v Spain* [2005] ECR I-2911 (visa list), and C-127/08 *Metock* [2008] ECR I-6241 (family reunion). See also the Opinion in Case C-257/99 *Barkoci and Malik* [2001] ECR I-6557, which interprets an association agreement in light of the EU's 1999 visa list Regulation.

[672] Opinions in Cases C-416/96 *El-Yassini* [1999] ECR I-1209; C-387/97 *Wijsenbeek* [1999] ECR I-3207; C-70/99 *Commission v Portugal* [2001] ECR I-4845; C-109/01 *Akrich* [2003] ECR I-9607; C-467/02 *Cetinkaya* [2004] ECR I-10895; C-1/05 *Jia* [2007] ECR I-1; C-325/05 *Derin* [2007] ECR I-6495; C-16/05 *Tum and Dari* [2007] ECR I-7415; and C-337/07 *Altun* [2008] ECR I-10323. See earlier references to pre-Amsterdam JHA measures in the Opinions in *Barkoci and Malik* (ibid) and Case C-235/99 *Kondova* [2001] ECR I-6427. In Case C-237/02 *Panayatova* [2004] ECR I-11055, the Advocate General asserted in a non-JHA case that in principle he had jurisdiction to interpret the Schengen *acquis*.

[673] See the cases listed in 8.4 below, concerning the relevance of 'normal' EU rules to Brussels Convention cases, and Case C-276/06 *El-Youssfi* [2007] ECR I-2851. See also Case C-137/09 *Josemans* (opinion of 15 July 2010), pending.

[674] Cases: C-503/03 *Commission v Spain* [2006] ECR I-1097; C-467/04 *Gasparini* [2006] ECR I-9199; and C-123/08 *Wolzenburg* [2009] ECR I-9621.

The Court of Justice gave two rulings more specifically addressing the relationship between JHA measures and non-JHA rules, both concerning the EU's association agreement with Turkey. In *Payir*, the Court ruled that a Directive concerning third-country national students was 'not relevant' to the interpretation of the EU–Turkey rules as regards the status of students, because that Directive specifically permitted the EU and/or its Member States to agree treaties with third States establishing more favourable rules.[675] In *Soysal*, there was a direct conflict between the EU visa list Regulation, which required visas to be imposed on Turkish nationals, and the 'standstill' rule in the EU–Turkey rules relating to service providers, which specified that the EU and its Member States could not make the provision of services in the EU by Turkish service providers more difficult than it was for them when those rules entered into force for the Member State concerned. The Court of Justice simply ruled that the priority of international agreements over EU secondary legislation meant that the latter had to be interpreted consistently with the former—overlooking the direct conflict between the two sources of law, which could not be solved by means of consistent interpretation.[676]

These 'overlap' cases raise questions about the Court over-reaching (or under-reaching) its jurisdiction as regards the relevant judicial regimes which apply, and also about the appropriateness of interpreting a general EU rule applicable to all Member States in light of a rule applicable to only some Member States. The latter point has also arisen in cases concerning free movement of capital, which some Advocates General have argued should be interpreted in light of monetary union.[677]

What approach should be taken to these issues, which remain relevant after the entry into force of the Treaty of Lisbon due to its transitional rules on the Court of Justice's jurisdiction and due to the continued differences in the territorial scope of JHA measures?[678] In *Soysal*, where the question of the Court's jurisdiction was explicitly raised because a lower court had referred questions on the EU–Turkey agreement which also mentioned a Title IV measure, the Court of Justice simply stated that the questions concerned solely concerned the EU–Turkey agreement—which, with great respect, was just not true.[679] Leaving aside this ostrich-like approach to the issue, first of all, in a genuine case of 'mixed jurisdiction', where the issues to be decided are interconnected and fall within the scope of more than one judicial regime, it is arguable that a 'most favourable

---

[675] Case C-294/06 [2008] ECR I-203, paras 47–48.

[676] Case C-228/06 [2009] ECR I-1031, paras 53–59.

[677] See, for instance the Opinion in Case C-446/04 *Test Claimants in the FII Group Litigation* [2006] ECR I-11753, para 121, which moreover concerns a Member State not participating in monetary union (the UK).   [678] See respectively 2.2.3.3 and 2.2.5 above.

[679] Paras 38–42 of the judgment, n 676 above. See the wording of the national court's questions in para 37 of the judgment.

jurisdiction' rule applies to ensure that the Court of Justice is not prevented from dealing with cases which it would normally have the competence to address.[680]

Next, the different rules on the Court's jurisdiction should not prevent the Court considering ancillary matters outside its jurisdiction where this is necessary to give judgment in a case which falls within its jurisdiction. Otherwise the Court would be precluded from fully taking account of the relevant legal context when giving a ruling on cases which it has jurisdiction over. So the Advocate General was right to suggest in *Panayatova* that, if necessary to interpret the Europe Agreements, the Court could analyse the Schengen *acquis* on visas, even on a reference from a lower national court; and the Court necessarily had to consider the operation of the SIS when ruling in an infringement action concerning EU free movement law. But the Court must take care that the main focus of its judgment in such cases remains the issue over which it has jurisdiction, and that the matters outside its jurisdiction are genuinely relevant to the matters within it. On the latter point, with respect, the Opinion in *Akrich* was wrong to suggest that EU free movement law should be (re-)interpreted in light of the existence of Title IV and Title IV legislation, given that Title IV and Title IV measures did not address the question at issue in that case; and the Opinion in *Kondova* was wrong to suggest that the Europe Agreements should be interpreted in light of unconnected soft law adopted at a later date, without the participation of the other parties to the relevant agreements, considering also the primacy of the EU's international agreements over binding EU legislation—never mind third pillar soft law.

As for the differences in territorial scope of measures, there can be no objection to the Court of Justice interpreting general rules in light of specific rules applicable to some Member States only, as long as this does not have the effect of imposing the specific rules upon Member States which would otherwise not be covered by them. So it is unobjectionable for the Court to consider the EU's visa list legislation in the context of a judgment on EU free movement law, as long as the UK and Ireland are not thereby bound by the EC visa list. On the other hand, the Opinion in *Akrich* went too far in interpreting EU free movement law in light of Title IV EC and Title IV measures which were not binding on the UK (in addition to their irrelevance to the facts at hand).[681] In such cases, the Court must make clear when its interpretation of a general EU measure in light of a specific measure is relevant to all Member States. For example, the Court wisely made clear that the ban on discriminatory taxes on airline flights applies

---

[680] S Peers, 'Who's Judging the Watchmen?' The Judicial System of the Area of Freedom, Security and Justice' (2000) 18 YEL 337 at 397–399. This approach could easily have been applied in the *Soysal* case.

[681] With great respect, the Opinion also suffers from several factual errors and breached the procedural rights of the parties to the national proceeding by basing its reasoning on issues not raised by or before the national court, or before the Court of Justice.

to *all* Member States due to its infringement of the free movement of services, and avoided leaving the impression that this rule only applied to Schengen States. And in the *Payir* case, the Court was right to point out simply that the Title IV legislation left it open for Member States and the EU to agree treaties that were more favourable to students.

2.4.3. Treaty of Lisbon

As noted already, the relationship between EU JHA and non-JHA law is less critical after the entry into force of the Treaty of Lisbon, since most of the institutional distinctions have been removed; but the distinction still remains relevant as regards the transitional rules for ex-third pillar matters (as regards legal effect and the Court of Justice's jurisdiction) and as regards the territorial scope of JHA measures as compared to most non-JHA measures. The approach to 'mixed jurisdiction' issues advocated above should apply *mutatis mutandis*, although it should be noted that once criminal law and policing measures are adopted after the entry into force of the Treaty of Lisbon, there will be for the first time mixed jurisdiction within the same subject matter, which makes it more likely that there will be cases where issues falling with the scope of different judicial regimes are interconnected.

As for the Schengen *acquis*, the amendments to the Schengen Protocol made by the Treaty of Lisbon include the deletion of the clause in the preamble to that Protocol which unambiguously stated that EU law took priority over the Schengen *acquis*. The issue of the relationship between that *acquis* (and measures building upon it) and other EU law is therefore governed since the Treaty of Lisbon by a more general provision in that Protocol, which states that Schengen cooperation 'shall be conducted within the institutional and legal framework of the European Union and with respect for the relevant provisions of the Treaties'.[682]

There is already one case pending regarding the distinction between the JHA and non-JHA 'legal bases' after the Treaty of Lisbon.[683] Issues might also arise as regards the relationship between the non-JHA provision concerning data protection rules (Article 16 TFEU), and specific JHA legislation which addresses data protection issues.[684] It should be borne in mind that Article 47 of the previous TEU, which as interpreted by the Court of Justice, gave a strong priority to the first pillar over the second and third pillars, has been repealed by the Treaty of Lisbon.[685]

---

[682] Art 1 of the Schengen Protocol, as amended by the Treaty of Lisbon.

[683] Case C-130/10 *EP v Council*, regarding the scope of Art 75 TFEU (anti-terrorist sanctions) as compared to Art 215 TFEU (foreign policy sanctions), discussed in 2.2.3.2 above.

[684] See 12.2.4 below.

[685] See instead Art 40 of the revised TEU, which takes a more balanced approach to the distinction between foreign policy and other EU policies. There is no replacement clause concerning the distinction between policing and criminal law and other EU policies.

2.5. Legitimacy and accountability

An ongoing concern regarding the development of EU JHA law has been the legitimacy and accountability of the EU's activities in these areas of great public concern, considering the close link of these issues to national sovereignty, the political sensitivity of the subject, and the perceived remoteness and lack of transparency of the EU. These concerns have applied *a fortiori* to the development of JHA law outside the EU framework (most notably the Schengen and Prum Conventions).

The legitimacy of EU measures should be considered from the perspective of two different aspects of legitimacy: the democratic legitimacy and legal legitimacy (or more broadly, the rule of law) of adopted measures. The accountability of those measures should be evaluated in light of the effectiveness of any measures to hold persons responsible for implementing EU measures in practice to account. Legitimacy and accountability are intrinsic elements of human rights standards, which require limits on rights to be prescribed by law and confer procedural rights on individuals to challenge restrictions on rights imposed by state authorities. Finally, it should also be kept in mind that given the extent of state powers of control and coercion involved, immigration, asylum, criminal law, and policing measures have traditionally (unlike foreign policy) been subject to extensive control by national parliaments and national courts.

The Treaty of Lisbon made an attempt to address these issues as regards the democratic and judicial accountability of EU action, by means of significantly increasing the powers of the European Parliament over legislation and treaty-making in this area, along with the application of the standard rules on the jurisdiction of the Court of Justice (except as regards the transitional period relating to pre-existing third pillar acts).[686] More general attempts to address the legitimacy issue include the enhancement of human rights protection within the EU legal order,[687] the clarification of EU competences,[688] and the development of rules on the powers of national parliaments and the level of openness and transparency within the EU. These latter developments are considered further in this section.

First of all, openness and transparency assists public participation in, debate of, and awareness of activities of the public authorities, and contributes to the accountability of those who apply the policies in practice. Initially, the level of transparency during the Maastricht era (1993–99) was wholly inadequate, in particular as regards non-publication of many adopted measures and the negotiation of those measures; this applied in particular to the Schengen integration process (which was then separate from the EU process as a whole).[689] There

---

[686] See generally 2.2.3 above and (as regards treaties) 2.7 below.   [687] See 2.3 above.
[688] See 2.4 above, and s 2.3 and 2.4 of chs 3–12 as regards specific areas of JHA law.
[689] For further detail, see the second edition of this book, at pp 19–20.

was some improvement in access to documents after an NGO, Statewatch, brought successful complaints to the EU Ombudsman against the Council's practices of, inter alia, destroying copies of meeting agendas, not maintaining a register of documents, and refusing many requests for access to documents on dubious grounds.[690] As a result of these complaints, the Council began to conserve agendas and make more documents available, and established a register of documents on the Internet, which soon included access to the full text of many documents. Also, a 1998 judgment of the CFI (as it then was) confirmed that the Council's general access to document rules applied to 'third pillar' matters and that the EU Courts had jurisdiction over the Council's application of the rules to JHA documents.[691] A series of Court judgments ruled against the Council's interpretation of the access to document rules as regards JHA documents: in *Carvel*, the Council was wrongly automatically refusing requests for access to documents relating to Council proceedings without considering the balance between the applicant's rights and the Council's interests; in *Svenska*, the Council had wrongly applied the 'public security' exception to the rules on access, in particular to deny access to a document concerning Europol's office furniture requirements; in *Kuijer I*, the Council's reasons for denying a number of asylum documents relating to conditions in the countries of origin of asylum seekers on 'international relations' grounds were too sweeping; and in *Kuijer II*, the Council had misapplied the 'international relations' exception relating to the same documents, in particular by failing to consider the impact of releasing each document on the EU's relationship with each particular third State.[692]

Next, the Treaty of Amsterdam inserted into Article 1 of the previous EU Treaty a requirement that the EU act 'as openly as possible', and a new Article 255 into the EC Treaty that required the EU institutions to adopt legislation covering access to documents of the EP, Council, and Commission. A Regulation on this subject was duly adopted in 2001.[693] Among other things, the Regulation retains exceptions for 'public security', 'international relations', and institutional decision-making, but it does extend the scope of the EU rules to include documents submitted from outside the institutions. In practice, the interpretation of the Regulation by the Court of Justice has been mostly encouraging, with the Court limiting Member States' veto on the release of documents which they

---

[690] See text of complaints in *The Statewatch Case* (Statewatch publication).

[691] Case T-174/95 *Svenska Journalistforbundet* [1998] ECR II-2289. See earlier Case T-194/94 *Carvel and Guardian Newspapers* [1995] ECR II-2765, where it was simply assumed that the rules applied to third pillar documents. The Council's initial access rules appeared in [1993] OJ L 340/43.

[692] *Svenska* and *Carvel* (ibid), and Cases T-188/98 *Kuijer I* [2000] ECR I-1959 and T-211/00 *Kuijer II* [2002] ECR I-485.

[693] Reg 1049/2001 ([2001] OJ L 145/43). For detailed comments, see S Peers, 'The New Regulation on Access to Documents: A Critical Analysis' (2001–2002) 21 YEL 385, with further references.

'authored', and giving a strong priority to the requirement to release access to documents as regards the EU's legislative activity.[694]

However, the Court has given a wide scope of application to the 'public security' exception, with the effect that the rules on public access to documents do not benefit persons whose income and assets are frozen because they are considered to be 'terrorists'.[695] However, the EU Courts have nonetheless developed specific procedural protections for such persons when ruling on more direct challenges to the EU's anti-terrorist legislation.[696]

The Treaty of Lisbon gave a wider scope to the basic Treaty rule on access to documents, and required all Council and EP meetings to be held in public insofar as they concern legislative discussions.[697] However, the legislation on access to documents has not yet been amended, and a proposal to amend those rules released before the entry into force of the Treaty of Lisbon would have made no positive improvement as regards any aspect of transparency, and would even have lowered standards as regards some important issues.[698] In practice, the Council now releases most draft texts under discussion, but only upon request (resulting in a delay of several weeks before release) and usually with the names of Member States taking particular positions blacked out; these restrictions still hinder public knowledge of Council discussions. A limited number of texts are made available in connection with open meetings—sometimes after the meeting has taken place. The Council could also do more to hold discussions on non-legislative measures in public.[699]

As for the Commission, the main Commission register of documents is simply superficial, since it only lists documents which will be made public imminently anyway and only makes those documents available on the register after their official release; and the Commission's specialized comitology register is far from complete, as many JHA documents are not present.[700]

A particular transparency issue concerns the Schengen *acquis*, which included two Schengen Executive Committee Decisions on confidentiality, which designated certain Schengen acts as classified.[701] These measures were amended several times to declassify certain measures, and then repealed entirely, as classification of such documents is now determined entirely by the Council's security rules.[702]

As for the democratic legitimacy of EU JHA measures, joint control by the EP, via means of the ordinary legislative procedure, applies now to almost all JHA

---

[694] Respectively Case C-64/05 P *Sweden v Commission* [2007] ECR I-11389 and Joined Cases C-39/05 P and C-52/05 P *Sweden and Turco v Council* [2008] ECR I-4723.

[695] Case C-266/05 P *Sison* [2007] ECR I-1233 .   [696] See 12.4.5 below.

[697] Art 15 TFEU, which has replaced the prior Art 255 EC.

[698] COM (2008) 229, 30 Apr 2008. See the article-by-article commentary, online at: <http://www.statewatch.org/foi/sw-analysis-docs-june-2008.pdf>.

[699] See Art 8 of the Council's rules of procedure (current version in [2009] OJ L 325/35).

[700] The registers are at: <http://ec.europa.eu/transparency/regdoc/registre.cfm?CL=en>.

[701] [2000] OJ L 239/127 and 139.   [702] [2004] OJ L 5/78.

measures. So if the EP is considered to be a sufficiently legitimate institution—and its legitimacy is an issue beyond the scope of this book—then the application of the ordinary legislative procedure now secures the democratic legitimacy of JHA measures in these areas (except for those matters subject to a special legislative procedure, if the EP is only consulted). But the ordinary legislative procedure is subject to significant defects in transparency, because it is largely subject to ad hoc negotiations between EP and Council staff which are not subject to any formal rules or any effective transparency.[703]

Democratic legitimacy can also be assured by giving national parliaments sufficient control over acts of the EU. Full national parliamentary control could only be ensured if every act had to be ratified by each national parliament, but this would obviously impose a high cost on efficiency, as evidenced by the lengthy delays before ratification of JHA Conventions (even though Conventions did not in fact require a full parliamentary approval process in the legal systems of all Member States).[704] An alternative solution, reconciling the objectives of both efficiency and democracy, would have been to provide for a reasonable fixed period for national parliaments to object to a text; an objection within would require a full ratification procedure to be followed, while an absence of objection would entail the immediate entry into force of the measure (with a further period allowed for adaptation of national legislation, if necessary).[705]

Instead, the Treaty of Amsterdam and the Treaty of Lisbon replaced national parliamentary control over Conventions with the adoption of secondary EU law, clearly fully binding on all Member States' organs but without a requirement of national parliamentary involvement besides the modest rules in the Protocols on national parliaments and subsidiarity (as amended by the Treaty of Lisbon), which provide for a very short period of national parliamentary scrutiny and no adequate means of blocking proposed measures entirely.[706] It still remains open for Member States individually to provide for some additional degree of national parliamentary scrutiny or control of executive decision-making in the JHA framework, but the degree of national parliamentary involvement is highly divergent and it is doubtful whether many national parliaments, or the general public, are fully satisfied with their degree of involvement, given the traditionally pre-eminent role which national parliaments play in the adoption of legislation as regards justice and home affairs. At least the existence of 'emergency brakes' and vetoes in key

---

[703] The Joint Declaration on the co-decision procedure ([2007] OJ C 145/5) does not regulate these informal negotiations sufficiently. There is no information at all on *whether* informal negotiations are underway, never mind any information on the texts under discussion. See the detailed suggestions for reform in the Statewatch analysis, 'Proposals for Greater Openness, Transparency and Democracy in the EU', online at: <http://www.statewatch.org/analyses/proposals-for-greater-openness-peers-08.pdf>.   [704] See 2.2.2.2 above.

[705] See the procedure set out in Art 48(7), revised TEU, as regards changes to EU decision-making.   [706] See also Art 69 TFEU. For reform proposals, see n 703 above.

areas of criminal law and policing should ensure that the concerns of the public and national parliaments will be addressed in some cases.

A further problem stems from the pre-eminent role of the European Council in setting out the overall agenda for JHA matters. The European Council now applies the Council's rules on access to documents,[707] but has not established for any system of public input; nor is it collectively accountable to national parliaments, the European Parliament, or anyone else. It is doubtful whether the individual accountability of Presidents and Prime Ministers to each individual national parliament (or national public) can make up for this,[708] since the European Council is a separate body making collective policy decisions.

Conversely, one positive development since the entry into force of the Treaty of Amsterdam is the increased role of the Commission issuing Green Papers and similar documents on JHA matters and holding wide public consultations before proposing legislation, allowing for a degree of public input into the early stages of the decision-making process. Previously, this was unknown, as the Council had no experience or interest in arranging for public consultation or input when developing JHA policy, and individual Council Presidencies could not claim any collective legitimacy outside their own Member State. Indeed, where groups of Member States exercise the right of initiative as set out in Article 76 TFEU, these forms of public consultation are still unknown.[709]

As for the rule of law, the intrinsic lack of legal clarity due to the complexity of the institutional framework of JHA law has been an issue in itself, as has the unjustified restriction of the jurisdiction of the Court of Justice. These criticisms have largely been answered by the entry into force of the Treaty of Lisbon, but the framework remains unacceptably confusing as regards transitional rules and the rules on opt-outs. The EU's secondary JHA measures remain highly complex, particularly where they are connected to the Schengen *acquis*, and much more should be done to consolidate the measures concerned, considering the impact of the legislation on individuals and the need to ensure it is usable by practitioners.

As for accountability, the key issue is the scrutiny of the implementation of JHA measures at EU level (by the Council, Commission, or an EU agency) or at national level. The Treaty of Lisbon includes specific provisions on scrutiny of evaluation measures, of the Committee on internal security, and on Europol and Eurojust,[710] but it remains to be seen how these provisions are implemented. In the absence of their implementation, it is difficult for the public to assess the practical impact of many key JHA measures, in particular to consider whether they are justified in light of their cost and their effect upon human rights.

As for implementing and delegated measures adopted by the Commission, the procedures for controlling the Commission's exercise of its implementing

---

[707] Art 10(2) of the European Council's Rules of Procedure ([2009] OJ L 315/51).
[708] See Art 10(2), revised TEU.
[709] On Member States' right of initiative more generally, see 2.2.3.2 above.
[710] Arts 70, 71, 85, and 88 TFEU.

powers have often been criticized for their opaque nature and lack of sufficient democratic scrutiny:[711] the lack of transparency has been commented on above. It is too early to tell whether there will be greater transparency and accountability as regards the Commission's adoption of delegated acts. Finally, it is important in the area of JHA matters to have effective systems of accountability for the EU's agencies, in particular Europol, Eurojust, and the EU Borders Agency: this issue is examined in more depth in separate chapters.[712]

2.6. EU funding

Since the advent of formalized JHA cooperation in the Maastricht Treaty, JHA funding has come to take up an increased amount of the EC budget (now the EU budget). In general, the budget is set annually by joint agreement of the EP and Council,[713] but the annual budgets are themselves agreed within the framework of a 'multi-annual financial framework', which was, until the entry into force of the Treaty of Lisbon, set out in the form of Inter-Institutional Agreements (IIAs) negotiated between the Commission, Council, and EP, but which is now to be set out in the form of legislative acts.[714] Recent IIAs have governed spending for the period 1993–99, 2000–06, and now 2007–13.[715] Community (now Union) revenue is provided for in a series of 'own resources' decisions, adopted pursuant to Article 311 TFEU (previously Article 269 EC). All expenses must in principle be governed by EC (now EU) legislation adopted in accordance with the relevant provisions of the Treaties, although the Commission has a limited capacity to establish pilot or preparatory programmes.[716]

The EU Treaty, in the Maastricht period, initially provided that operational spending on JHA matters was left to be agreed between Member States, with the EC budget playing a role *only* if all Member States agreed.[717] Subsequently, the Treaty of Amsterdam brought spending on immigration, asylum, and civil law automatically within the EC budget framework as a consequence of the transfer of those issues to the first pillar. Spending on the remaining third pillar issues of police and criminal law cooperation was subject to the EC budget *unless* all Member States agreed otherwise.[718] With the entry into force of the Treaty of Lisbon, there is no longer any scope to charge JHA spending outside the EU budget.

---

[711] See literature cited in 2.2.2.1 above.   [712] See 3.10.1, 11.9, and 12.8 below.

[713] On the annual budget process, see Art 314 TFEU (previously Art 272 EC).

[714] Art 312 TFEU.   [715] [2006] OJ C 139/1.

[716] See Case C-106/96 *UK v Commission* [1998] ECR I-2729, and Art 49 of the Financial Regulation (Reg 1605/2002, [2002] OJ L 248/1, as amended by Regs 1995/2006, [2006] OJ L 390/1 and 1525/2007, [2007] OJ L 343/9). See now the proposed recast Reg (COM (2010) 260, 28 May 2010).   [717] Original Art K.8(2) EU.

[718] Previous Art 41(3) EU.

During the Maastricht period, the Council initially adopted a Joint Action on JHA funding in 1995,[719] which was implemented by further Council Decisions as regards spending in 1995 and 1996.[720] Subsequently, the EU adopted Joint Actions on specific issues: a series of short-term asylum funding measures;[721] the 'Sherlock' programme on identity documents,[722] subsumed into the broader 'Odysseus' programme, which ran until 2002;[723] the 'Grotius' programme on incentives and exchanges for legal practitioners, established initially from 1996 until 2000;[724] the 'STOP' programme on combating sexual exploitation, also initially applicable from 1996–2000;[725] the 'Oisin' programme on support for law enforcement, applicable from 1997–2000;[726] and the 'Falcone' programme on combating international organized crime, applicable from 1998–2002.[727] On the other hand, the Europol Convention required that Europol be funded from Member States' budgets,[728] although this changed from 2010, when a new Decision replaced the Europol Convention (see further below).

The JHA funding programmes were provided for in the EC's annual budgets during this period. For example, the 1998 budget provided for €11.8 million for the named JHA funding programmes (including the planned Odysseus and Falcone progammes) and the ad hoc refugee programmes.[729] The 1999 budget provided for €21.9 million for the JHA funding programmes and a European refugee fund, while referring to possible additional funding for Eurodac and Europol.[730]

The Treaty of Amsterdam entered into force shortly before the application of the EU's new financial framework for 2000–06. During this period, the prior ad hoc measures on asylum funding were replaced by the European Refugee Fund, initially adopted for the years 2000–04,[731] then for 2005–10.[732] The Odysseus programme was replaced by the 'Argo' programme, which supported national spending on asylum, immigration, visas, and borders.[733] In the sphere of civil law, the Community first extended the Grotius programme for a further year (2001) as regards civil law,[734] and then adopted a funding programme covering 2002–06.[735] As for the third pillar, the Grotius, Oisin, and STOP programmes were extended for 2001–02, joined at the time by a fourth

---

[719] [1995] OJ L 238/1.   [720] [1995] OJ L 238/2 and [1996] OJ L 268/1.

[721] [1997] OJ L 205/3 and 5; [1998] OJ L 138/6 and 8; and [1999] OJ L 114/2.

[722] [1996] OJ L 287/7.   [723] [1998] OJ L 99/2.   [724] [1996] OJ L 287/3.

[725] [1996] OJ L 322/7.   [726] [1997] OJ L 7/5.   [727] [1998] OJ L 99/8.

[728] Art 35, Europol Convention ([1995] OJ C 316/1).   [729] [1998] OJ L 44/1.

[730] [1999] OJ L 39/1.

[731] [2000] OJ L 252/12. The reference amount for spending was €216 million over five years.

[732] [2004] OJ L 381/52. The reference amount for spending is €114 million over the first two years, with the remaining funding to be decided later.

[733] [2002] OJ L 161/11. The reference amount for spending was €25 million over five years. The Decision was later amended ([2004] OJ L 371/48).

[734] Reg 290/2001 ([2001] OJ L 43/1). The reference amount for spending was €650,000 for the year.   [735] Reg 743/2002 ([2002] OJ L 115/1). There is no reference amount for spending.

programme concerning crime prevention (Hippocrates).[736] They were then replaced by a general third pillar funding programme, 'AGIS', running from 2003–07.[737]

The EC budget was also used to fund operational measures, in particular Eurodac, the development of the second version of the Schengen Information System (SIS II), and the Visa Information System.[738] The third pillar aspects of SIS II funding had to be charged to the EC budget, as the necessary unanimity for charging the Member States' budgets did not exist.[739] As for EU agencies, the prosecutors' agency, Eurojust, was from the outset funded by the EC budget,[740] while the European Police College was initially funded by Member States;[741] however, the College is now funded from the EC budget since an overhaul of its institutional framework in 2005.[742] As a Community agency, the External Borders Agency (Frontex) had to be funded by the EC budget.[743]

The annual EU budgets have kept pace with developments. Each annual budget includes as JHA spending several issues falling outside the scope of the EU/EC's JHA powers strictly speaking, but which fall within the competence of the Commission's Directorate General for Justice, Liberty, and Security (ie Justice and Home Affairs). To this end, the 2000 JHA budget included: the 'Daphne' programme on combating domestic violence, a preparatory action concerning anti-discrimination measures, the EC's anti-racism and anti-drugs agencies, and action against harmful or illegal Internet content.[744] The budget also included funding for a preparatory action against drug trafficking. JHA funding commitments now amounted to €52 million, with further possible funding to be added.

The 2001 JHA budget jumped up again to €91.6 million,[745] including a pilot programme concerning child exploitation and committed funding for Eurodac. The 2002 JHA budget then topped the €100 million mark, allocating €103.5 million and for the first time committing funds for development of SIS II; supporting the European migration network (a preparatory programme) and for human rights research and evaluation (a pilot programme); and referring to possible funding for Eurojust.[746] The 2003 budget for the first time committed specific funds for Eurojust and for a pilot programme on the integration of third-country nationals, inter alia raising JHA spending to €122.7 million.[747]

---

[736] [2001] OJ L 186/1, 4, 7, and 11. The reference amounts for spending were respectively €4, 8, 4, and 2 million over the two years.

[737] [2002] OJ L 203/5. The reference amount for spending is €65 million over the five years.

[738] See respectively Reg 2725/2000 ([2000] OJ L 316/1); Reg 2424/2001 and third pillar Decision ([2001] L 328/1 and 4; and [2004] OJ L 213/5).

[739] See JHA Council conclusions, 28/29 May 2001.

[740] [2002] OJ L 63/1; see amendment to the financial rules in [2003] OJ L 245/44.

[741] [2000] OJ L 336/1.   [742] [2005] OJ L 256/63.

[743] Reg 2007/2004 ([2004] OJ L 349/1).   [744] [2000] OJ L 40.

[745] [2001] OJ L 56.   [746] [2002] OJ L 29.   [747] [2003] OJ L 54.

The 2004 budget saw a further jump to €161.7 million, with reference made to spending to assist application of the Schengen rules in the new Member States and for Lithuania to regulate movement from the Russian enclave of Kaliningrad, a huge increase in funding for the ARGO programme; the creation of pilot programmes for judicial exchange and support for victims of terrorism; a preparatory programme to support civil society in the new Member States; funding related to the development of crime statistics; a huge increase in funding for SIS II development; and reference to funding for the Visa Information System.[748] The 2005 budget, following adjustments for enlargement and the integration of the Schengen fund for new Member States, entailed a whopping increase in JHA spending to €570.6 million, with reference now made to a subsidy for the European Borders Agency, funding for a preparatory action on a 'European Return Fund', and commitments relating to the Visa Information System for the first time.[749] The 2006 budget increased spending to €590 million, providing for a specific subsidy for the European Police College and setting aside funds for EU crisis management.[750]

Implementing the new financial framework, the EU institutions agreed during 2007 on a number of new programmes, to run until 2013: a new Borders Fund, Integration Fund, and Return Fund;[751] a revised Refugee Fund;[752] a revised civil justice programme;[753] programmes focused on criminal justice and law enforcement;[754] and programmes outside the scope of JHA law as such, concerning human rights protection, domestic violence, and anti-terrorist crisis management.[755]

The 2007 budget duly integrated these new programmes, raising the spending on EU JHA programmes to €612 million, and introducing also a preparatory action for migration management.[756] The 2008 budget provided for a large increase in spending to €713 million for JHA programmes, including a huge increase in spending on the EU's border agency, Frontex (from €21 million to €68 million), and new pilot or preparatory programmes on children's rights; an alert system for missing children; and the development of European contract law.[757] The 2009 budget provided for an even bigger increase in JHA spending, to the level of €923 million, including a huge increase in the budget for the EU borders fund; significant increases for the other ongoing funding programmes, a new measure concerning harmonization of national law on violence against women and children.[758] Finally, the 2010 budget drove EU JHA spending above

---

[748] [2004] OJ L 53.   [749] [2005] OJ L 60.   [750] [2006] OJ L 78.
[751] [2007] OJ L 144/22, [2007] OJ L 168/18, and [2007] OJ L 144/45. See 3.11, 6.10, and 7.8 below.   [752] [2007] OJ L 144/1. See 5.10.2 below.
[753] [2007] OJ L 257/16. See 8.8 below.
[754] [2007] OJ L 58/7 and 13. See 9.9 and 12.10 below.
[755] [2007] OJ L 110/33, [2007] L 173/19, and [2007] L 58/1. See 2.3 above and 12.10 below.
[756] [2007] OJ L 77.   [757] [2008] OJ L 71.   [758] [2009] OJ L 69.

€1 billion, up to €1,060 million,[759] including new budget entries on Schengen evaluation and the European Asylum Support Office, and (most significantly) the full integration of Europol funding into the EU budget.

The EU financial framework for 2007–13 provides for an annual 15 per cent increase in JHA spending, from €600 million in 2007 to €1,390 million in 2013.[760] But this will still be a small proportion of the overall EU budget, and although the JHA budget is set to double, this could be compared to the ten-fold increase in JHA spending from 2000–06. A modest increase in JHA spending will also result from the planned accession of Croatia.[761]

The increase in JHA funding from the EU budget has entailed a growing role in JHA policy for the Commission, which implements EU funding programmes and other EU expenditure, and for the EP, which had (until the entry into force of the Treaty of Lisbon) a greater role in the annual budget process than it had adopting JHA legislation (except for measures adopted by co-decision). In particular, the EP often pushes for the indicative spending for various programmes to be altered and for the creation of pilot or preparatory programmes dealing with subjects which it considers to be political priorities.

2.7. External relations[762]

2.7.1. General rules on EU external relations

Before the Treaty of Lisbon entered into force, distinct rules applied to the external relations aspects of the former third pillar. Presumably these rules are still relevant to the third pillar treaties adopted during this period, and so they are considered further below.[763] On the other hand, since the entry into force of the Treaty of Amsterdam, external relations as regards immigration, asylum, and civil law were governed by Community law principles on external relations—now the general EU rules on external relations. Since the Treaty of Lisbon, external relations concerning policing and criminal law are governed by the same rules.

The general EU external relations rules provide that the Union, which has legal personality enabling it to become party to treaties,[764] can enjoy external relations competence either expressly, by a provision such as Article 207 TFEU (ex-Article 133 EC), which grants express power for the EU to adopt treaties concerning trade policy, or implicitly, 'where the Treaties so provide or where the conclusion

---

[759] [2010] OJ L 64.   [760] Annex I to the 2006 IIA (n 715 above).

[761] See COM (2009) 595, 29 Oct 2009.

[762] See generally B Martenczuk and S van Thiel (eds), *Justice, Liberty, Security: New Challenges for EU External Relations* (VUBPress, 2008).

[763] See 2.7.2.

[764] Art 47, revised TEU. Before the Treaty of Lisbon, the EC had legal personality (Art 210 EC), but the EU's legal personality was open to dispute (see 2.7.2 below).

of an agreement is necessary in order to achieve, within the framework of the Union's policies, one of the objectives referred to in the Treaties, or is provided for in a legally binding Union act or is likely to affect common rules or alter their scope' (ie as a corollary of the exercise of its internal powers).[765] Title V of the TFEU is governed by the implied powers principle, except as regards readmission treaties, where there has been an express external power since the Treaty of Lisbon came into force.[766]

Another question is the intensity of EU external relations power: it becomes *exclusive*, leaving no competence for Member States, when EU powers over an issue are inherently exclusive,[767] or also where its powers are in principle shared but 'when [a treaty's] conclusion is provided for in a legislative act of the Union or is necessary to enable the Union to exercise its internal competence, or in so far as its conclusion may affect common rules or alter their scope',[768] in particular where the EU has fully harmonized the issue internally.[769] This principle is relevant for JHA matters, which are in principle issues of shared competence,[770] but where in many respects the EU is either obliged to establish a 'common' policy or 'uniform' rules,[771] or in any event is not precluded from fully harmonizing the relevant area.[772] For example, the EU has exclusive external power over visa waiver treaties, due to the full harmonization of the visa list issue by internal EC (now EU) law.[773] On the other hand, where the EU can only set minimum standards as regards internal rules, external competence is necessarily shared between the EU and its Member States.[774] It should also be noted that a Protocol and several declarations attempt to clarify the issue of external competence as regards several aspects of JHA issues; these are considered elsewhere in this book.[775]

However, even where the EU has exclusive competence, it may still empower the Member States to adopt legally binding acts, including treaties.[776] In the JHA sphere, the EU has authorized the Member States to sign treaties within the EC's (now the EU's) exclusive competence relating to civil law, subject to a specific control procedure.[777] Arguably the legislation establishing another specific proce-

---

[765] Art 216(1) TFEU.   [766] Art 79(3) TFEU. On readmission treaties, see further 7.9.1 below.

[767] See the list of exclusive EU powers in Art 3(1) TFEU.   [768] Art 3(2) TFEU.

[769] The possibility of full harmonization in areas of shared competence is implicitly provided for in the definition of shared competence in Art 2(2) TFEU.   [770] See Art 4(2)(j) TFEU.

[771] Arts 77(2)(a), 78(1), 78(2) and 2(a)–(d), and 79(1) TFEU.

[772] The only JHA provisions which restrain the EU to adopt 'minimum' rules only are Arts 82(2) and 83(1) and (2) TFEU.

[773] By way of exception, Member States retain competence over issues such as waivers for transport or diplomatic staff, where the EC legislation does not fully harmonize the law: see 4.5 below.

[774] For instance, see Arts 82(2) and 83 TFEU. On the underlying competence issues, see 2.2.4 above.

[775] See 3.12 (Protocol on external borders), 6.2.4 (declaration on immigration competence), and 8.9, 9.10, 10.8, 11.12, and 12.11 below (declaration as regards civil law, criminal law, and policing external competence).

[776] See the definition of exclusive EU competence in Art 2(1) TFEU.

[777] Regs 662/2009 and 664/2009 ([2009] OJ L 200/25 and 46). See further 8.9 below.

dure authorizing Member States to sign treaties on local border traffic is another example of such delegation of powers.[778]

Otherwise, where the EU has only partially harmonized a field falling within the shared competence of the EU and its Member States, the EU's external competence is in principle shared with the Member States, and treaties within the field of shared competence are often 'mixed agreements', containing provisions falling with the scope of both EU and Member State power,[779] and which must therefore be ratified by both the EU and the Member States, thereby giving Member States a de facto veto over the negotiation of the agreement. However, it is striking that in the field of immigration, asylum, and civil law (and, following the entry into force of the Treaty of Lisbon, policing and criminal law), Member States have not insisted to date on their participation, alongside the Community (now the EU), in treaties which they believe fall within the scope of shared competence.[780] In any case, even as regards areas of shared competence or in which there are already mixed agreements, Member States have some obligations to the Community (now the EU) in relation to treaty-making or other aspects of external competence, due to the 'loyalty' principle set out in Article 4(3) of the revised TEU (previously Article 10 EC).[781]

There is some protection for Member States' treaties in Article 351 TFEU (formerly Article 307 EC), which provides that Member States are entitled to retain in force pre-existing treaties which they ratified before their membership of the EC (now EU), but those treaties must ultimately be amended or denounced if they conflict with internal EC (now EU) obligations.[782]

The process for negotiating and concluding EU treaties starts with a Commission proposal for a mandate to negotiate.[783] This must be approved by the Council, and then the Commission begins negotiations on the EU's behalf. When negotiations conclude, the Commission initials the completed text, and then proposes it to the Council for signature and ratification (called 'conclusion'

---

[778] Reg 1931/2006 ([2006] OJ L 405/1). See further 3.8 below.

[779] For a full analysis of these principles with detailed references, see P Eeckhout, *External Relations of the European Union: Legal and Constitutional Foundations* (OUP, 2004), chs 3 and 4.

[780] See in particular, as regards readmission treaties, 7.9.1 below.

[781] See particularly Cases C-266/03 *Commission v Luxembourg* [2005] ECR I-4805; C-433/03 *Commission v Germany* [2005] ECR I-6905; and C-459/03 *Commission v Ireland* [2006] ECR I-4635; as well as the judgment of 20 Apr 2010 in Case C-246/07 *Commission v Sweden*, not yet reported. There are also obligations deriving from the 'loyalty' principle in the context of *exclusive* external competence: see Case C-45/07 *Commission v Greece* [2009] ECR I-701.

[782] See Cases C-62/98 *Commission v Portugal* [2000] ECR I-5171; C-84/98 *Commission v Portugal* [2000] ECR I-5215; C-475/98 *Commission v Austria* [2002] ECR I-9797; C-203/03 *Commission v Austria* [2005] ECR I-935; C-205/06 *Commission v Austria* [2009] ECR I-1301; C-249/06 *Commission v Sweden* [2009] ECR I-1335; and C-118/07 *Commission v Finland*, judgment of 19 Nov 2009, not yet reported. See generally J Klabbers, *Treaty Conflict and the European Union* (Cambridge University Press, 2009).

[783] On the EU's treaty conclusion procedure, see Art 218 TFEU (ex-Art 300 EC) and Eeckhout (n 779 above), ch 6.

by the Union). Throughout the procedure, the Council follows the same voting rule as applies to the adoption of internal EU legislation concerning the same subject matter. So, for instance, most Title V treaties are now subject to QMV in the Council, following the general application of QMV to most JHA issues starting between 2003 and 2005 (as regards immigration, asylum, and civil law), and most remaining issues from December 2009, with the entry into force of the Treaty of Lisbon.[784] The EP must consent to all treaties inter alia concerning issues which are subject to the ordinary legislative procedure or the consent procedure as regards internal legislation;[785] this applies to most JHA matters.[786] It is possible, where EU involvement in particular treaty negotiations or ratification is impracticable, for the Council to authorize the Member States to act on the Union's behalf.[787]

Treaties concluded by the EC (now the EU) are binding on the Community (now the Union) institutions and the EU's Member States,[788] and take precedence over secondary EC (now EU) law; but the Treaties and the general principles of EC (now EU) law take precedence over treaties concluded by the Community (now the Union).[789]

To date, the EC (now the EU) has negotiated or concluded a considerable number of treaties within the scope of Title V.[790] There is also an important external relations aspect to several Title V subjects, leaving aside the formal adoption of treaties.[791] It has been assumed in practice that the allocation of parts of the Schengen *acquis* to the EC Treaty gave the EC competence over such measures in the normal way; in particular, the EC (jointly with the EU) negotiated a treaty with Switzerland on association with the Schengen *acquis*, as well as a Protocol to that Treaty as regards Liechtenstein.[792] An earlier treaty with Norway and Iceland apparently also binds the Community, although it was negotiated according to a *sui generis* procedure set out in the Schengen Protocol.[793]

The Court of Justice has jurisdiction to interpret and to rule on the legal effect of treaties concluded by the EC (now the EU), and measures implementing them, on preliminary rulings from national courts, and to enforce such treaties via infringement proceedings; it can also rule that the conclusion or termination of a treaty is invalid (as a matter of internal EU law) pursuant to an annulment action or an indirect challenge to validity through the

---

[784] See 2.2.2 and 2.2.3 above.   [785] Art 218(6)(a) TFEU.

[786] The only exceptions relate to for example passports, family law, 'Community criminal law' where the underlying subject matter is subject to unanimous voting (eg tax issues), and operational police cooperation (Arts 77(3), 81(3), 83(2), 87(3), and 89 TFEU).

[787] See the examples of civil law treaties, referred to in 8.9 below.

[788] Art 216(2) TFEU (ex-Art 300(7) EC).   [789] See Eeckhout (n 779 above), ch 9.

[790] See 3.12, 4.11, 7.9, 8.9, 9.10, and 12.11 below; and s 2.5 of each of chs 3–9 and 12.

[791] See 5.11 and 7.9 below.   [792] See 2.2.5.4 above.   [793] See ibid.

national courts.[794] The Court also has a special jurisdiction as regards external relations, to give an opinion on whether a planned treaty would conflict with the Treaties, including the division of competence between the EU and its Member States.[795] Only one case concerning a JHA treaty has reached the Court of Justice, a special proceeding concerning the extent of EC competence over a civil law treaty, the Lugano Convention; here the Court found that the EC was exclusively competent to conclude this Convention, as regards both the rules for jurisdiction and the rules on recognition of judgments.[796]

It should be reiterated that, where not all Member States participate in particular internal EC (now EU) legislation, the non-participating Member States are not bound by the EC's (now EU's) external competence in the relevant field; this principle is obviously practically important to JHA issues. In fact, the EC took the unusual step of negotiating treaties with one of its Member States (Denmark), in order to associate that State with certain civil law and asylum legislation despite its opt-out from the relevant internal rules.[797]

A particular issue could arise if the EU wishes to negotiate further treaties concerning data protection as regards policing and criminal law with third states after the entry into force of the Treaty of Lisbon, given the existence of a specific power in the revised TEU concerning data protection within the scope of the CFSP.[798] However, this competence would be limited to matters concerning the common foreign and security policy of the EU, and could not 'affect the application of the procedures and the extent of the powers of the institutions laid down by the Treaties' as regards any other competences (including any JHA competences).[799]

2.7.2. External relations and the former third pillar

First of all, during the 'Maastricht era',[800] procedures were drawn up for applying Article K.5 EU, which required the defence of EU common positions at international conferences. Usually Member States' positions were coordinated informally, with only three formal Common Positions on the defence of an EU

---

[794] This jurisdiction extends to mixed agreements, at least as regards those provisions that fall within EU competence or are linked to EU legislation, and treaties concluded by the EU can have 'direct effect', under conditions similar to EU legislation, depending on the nature and purpose of the treaty. See in detail Eeckhout (n 779 above), ch 8.

[795] Art 218(11) TFEU (ex-Art 300(6) EC).   [796] *Opinion 1/2003* [2006] ECR I-1145.

[797] See 2.2.5.2 above.

[798] Art 39, revised TEU. The external competence related to this provision would flow from Art 37 TEU.

[799] Art 40 revised TEU, which is within the jurisdiction of the Court of Justice pursuant to Art 275 TFEU.

[800] For more on external relations and JHA during this period, see the first edition of this book, pp 33–34.

position at international conferences drawn up during this period.[801] There was also a developed programme of links with non-EU countries. In particular, the EU's enlargement was prepared for by a Joint Action concerning evaluation of applicant States' adoption of the EU third pillar *acquis*.[802]

After the Treaty of Amsterdam entered into force, external relations within the scope of the third pillar were subject to Articles 37 and 38 EU. Article 37 provided for the coordination of EU action in international conferences and the defence of relevant Common Positions in conferences. As noted above, it resulted in the adoption of common positions on several occasions.[803] Member States also coordinated their positions on certain proposed treaties without the adoption of formal Common Positions, for example when the Council of Europe's anti-terrorism Convention was under negotiation. This resulted in the adoption of 'disconnection' clauses in treaties, allowing for the continued existence of separate third pillar measures applicable to the EU Member States; this was a pre-existing Community practice which was extended to the third pillar.[804]

The adoption of treaties within the scope of the third pillar was subject to Article 38 EU, now repealed by the Treaty of Lisbon. This provided that Article 24 EU (which concerned CFSP international treaties) applied to the third pillar; this Article was also repealed by the Treaty of Lisbon.[805] Article 24 EU, as amended by the Treaty of Nice, stated that the Council Presidency, rather than the Commission, negotiated third pillar treaties on a mandate from the Council, and proposed them to the Council for conclusion. A special rule (Article 24(5) EU) provided that:

No agreement shall be binding on a Member State whose representative in the Council states that it has to comply with the requirements of its own constitutional procedure; the other members of the Council may agree that the agreement shall nevertheless apply provisionally.

In practice, the first treaty within the scope of the third pillar was the treaty associating Norway and Iceland with the Schengen *acquis*, negotiated in accordance with the *sui generis* rules applicable to that issue set out in the Schengen Protocol. The EU also negotiated third pillar treaties with Norway and Iceland and the United States regarding mutual assistance and extradition; with Japan regarding mutual assistance; with the USA and Australia as regards passenger name data;

---

[801] [1997] OJ L 279, [1997] OJ L 320, and [1997] OJ L 87/1, on the OECD and Council of Europe corruption Conventions and the UN Convention on organized crime.

[802] [1998] OJ L 191/8.   [803] See 2.2.2.2 above.

[804] See Art 26(3) of the Council of Europe Convention on prevention of terrorism (CETS 196); Art 40(3) of the Council of Europe Convention on trafficking in persons (CETS 197); Art 52(4) of the Council of Europe Convention on money laundering (CETS 198); and Art 43(3) of the Council of Europe Convention on child protection (CETS 201).

[805] While Art 37, revised TEU, confers express power to conclude CFSP treaties, the detailed rules on negotiation of those treaties are now set out along with the general EU treaty-making rules in Art 218 TFEU, which includes some special rules on CFSP treaties.

with Norway and Iceland as regards association with the 'Prum Decision' rules on police cooperation; and (alongside the Community) with Switzerland and Liechtenstein as regards association with the Schengen *acquis*.[806] Member States repeatedly invoked their constitutional rules as regards the conclusion of third pillar agreements, thereby delaying their entry into force considerably.[807]

As a consequence, by the time of the entry into force of the Treaty of Lisbon, only the Schengen association treaties with Norway, Iceland, and Switzerland (but not the Protocol regarding Liechtenstein), along with the mutual assistance and extradition treaties with the USA, were in force. Presumably, since (as a matter of EU law) new procedural rules apply immediately to ongoing procedures which have not been completed at the time when those new procedural rules enter into force, those treaties which had not been concluded when the Treaty of Lisbon entered into force have to be concluded in accordance with the general rules on EU external relations, as described above. While this means that Member States will no longer be able to invoke their constitutional procedures before the relevant treaties can be ratified, it might instead be argued that some or all of these treaties could or must be subject to the full participation of the Member States as parties alongside the Union in the form of 'mixed agreements', depending on whether or not those agreements fall within the EU's exclusive competence and if not, whether Member States insist upon becoming parties alongside the EU (see the discussion above).

In practice, shortly after the Treaty of Lisbon entered into force, the Commission proposed the conclusion of seven of the eight EU policing and criminal law treaties which had been signed, but not ratified, before the Treaty of Lisbon entered into force.[808] The EP voted down one such treaty,[809] but the others were still under consideration at time of writing. The Commission has also negotiated and proposed the conclusion of a new treaty in this area, to replace the treaty which the EP refused to consent to; the EP approved the second treaty.[810]

It is not clear whether the Court of Justice has, during the five-year transitional period when its jurisdiction over pre-existing third pillar acts is limited, even its third pillar jurisdiction over these treaties, although the Court assumed that it had jurisdiction over the third pillar provisions of the Schengen association

---

[806] On the third pillar treaties, see 2.2.5.4 above and 9.2.5, 9.10, 12.2.5, and 12.11 below.

[807] On the Prum treaty decision, see Council doc 5554/1/09, 15 Sep 2009. On the mutual assistance and surrender treaties with Norway and Iceland, see Council docs 7988/07, 2 Apr 2007 and 7097/1/07, 19 Mar 2007. On the PNR treaty with Australia, see Council doc 10439/2/08, 25 June 2008. On the PNR treaty with the USA, see Council doc 5311/1/09, 19 Mar 2009. On the Schengen association agreement with Liechtenstein, see Council doc 12428/1/08, 16 Sep 2008. On the Schengen association agreement with Switzerland, see previously Council doc 14207/07, 23 Oct 2007.

[808] COM (2009) 701–707, 17 Dec 2009. The exception was the association agreement with Liechtenstein (n 807 above), presumably because the Commission had already proposed its conclusion before the Treaty of Lisbon entered into force.   [809] See 12.11 below.

[810] See ibid.

agreement with Norway and Iceland.[811] By analogy with the Court's jurisdiction over Community treaties,[812] and in light of the Court's flexible approach to its third pillar jurisdiction,[813] it is arguable that its normal third pillar jurisdiction does apply. After the transitional period expires on 1 December 2014, of course the Court's normal general jurisdiction will apply to those treaties.

Even though, as noted above, the EU Treaty did not expressly confer legal personality upon the Union until the entry into force of the Treaty of Lisbon, the pre-existing third pillar treaties all appear to be concluded with the Union, as a distinct entity with its own international legal personality, rather than with its Member States, thus apparently assuming that the Union had an implied legal personality during this period. A more controversial question is whether the Community rules (now the general EU rules) concerning external competence, including Article 351 TFEU (ex-Article 307 EC), or at least a variant of those principles, applied to the previous third pillar, including presumably the provisions of the Schengen *acquis* allocated to the third pillar. This question must be raised in particular in light of the Court of Justice ruling that the 'loyalty' principle of EC law (as it then was) implicitly applied to the previous third pillar,[814] given the relevance of that principle for EC external relations law, as noted above. If the EC rules were applicable, the impact would be that Member States were already restrained as regards their treaty-making concerning criminal law and policing due to the adoption of third pillar acts, even before the entry into force of the Treaty of Lisbon,[815] and therefore continue to be restrained as regards pre-existing third pillar acts even before those acts are amended. While the Commission cannot challenge Member States' actions to this end by means of infringement actions in relation to pre-existing third pillar acts during the five-year limitation period on the Court of Justice's jurisdiction, it is possible to invoke the special external relations jurisdiction of the Court of Justice if the question concerns competence to conclude a treaty after the Treaty of Lisbon entered into force.

Even if the EC external relations rules (as they then were) did not apply to the third pillar before the entry into force of the Treaty of Lisbon, at the very least, the rules of international law concerning conflicts among treaties presumably applied. Moreover, if Article 351 TFEU in particular only began to apply to Member States as regards policing and criminal law as from the entry into force of the Treaty of Lisbon, the question arises whether it only protects Member States' treaties in this area which were concluded before they joined the EU, or whether

---

[811] Case C-436/04 *Van Esbroek* [2006] ECR I-2333.   [812] See 2.7.1 above.

[813] See 2.2.2.2 above.

[814] See C-105/03 *Pupino* [2005] ECR I-5285 and discussion in 2.2.2.2 above.

[815] Although the legal effect of pre-existing third pillar measures has been preserved until they are annulled, repealed, or amended (Art 9 of the transitional protocol; see 2.2.3.3 above), this begs the question as to what the legal effect of these measures was as regards external competence.

it protects all treaties concluded up until the entry into force of the Treaty of Lisbon, because that is the first point that Article 351 TFEU became applicable to this area of law.

2.8. Conclusions

In light of the issues addressed by JHA measures, JHA cooperation at EU level should be subject to parliamentary and judicial control, and effective human rights protection, at least equivalent to the principles established by the best national traditions in this area. Until the Treaty of Lisbon, it was clearly not. The institutional framework for JHA law was unduly complex; insufficiently open and transparent; lacked sufficient democratic and legal legitimacy and accountability; raised serious human rights concerns; has a convoluted relationship with other areas of EU law; and in some areas provided for insufficient financial control. The Treaty of Lisbon has addressed most of these problems sufficiently in theory, although it remains to be seen how well the revised rules work in practice. In any event, there has consistently been a fundamental trade-off as regards the institutional framework of JHA law between applying the 'normal' institutional rules of EU law and allowing ever-wider and more complex opt-outs for the UK, Ireland, and Denmark.

3

Border Controls

3.1. Introduction

The abolition of internal border controls on persons is at the very heart of the European integration project. But the necessary corollary of this abolition, the shifting of controls to the external borders of the Member States, has become equally symbolic as a signal to the outside world that the EU Member States have a collective border which they aim (using the medium of the European Union) to defend and strengthen. As a consequence of the creation of a collective external border, the EU has become involved in the issues of identity, control, and security that are enmeshed with the concept of a border.

Yet in light of the individual rights and interests affected by border controls, such as the human right to seek asylum, to visit family members, and procedural rights related to borders, along with the effects of globalization, the issue of border control has become a pivotal battleground between, on the one hand, States' desire to retain discretion over control of their borders as a key aspect of their sovereignty, and on the other hand, the need to ensure effective protection of rights and liberties.

A further complication in this field is that two Member States—the UK and Ireland—maintained for some time that the abolition of internal border controls was not part of the European integration process at all, leading to two divergent processes of integration first outside, and then inside, the EU legal framework.

The dispute over border controls initially led to disputes over EC competence, the boundaries between the first and third pillars, the substantive rules which the Union should adopt and the territorial scope of Union measures. It also led to a massive experiment in 'black market' European integration in the form of the Schengen process, which the Treaty of Amsterdam later absorbed awkwardly into the 'official' EU legal system, while those aspects of integration that the UK could agree to during the Maastricht period led in large part to the expansion of 'official' EU JHA cooperation. Within Schengen, the core act of negative legal integration (abolition of internal border controls) led to considerable positive legal integration, particularly the strengthening of external barriers.

This chapter, like the others in this book, begins with a historical overview of the substance and institutional framework of the subject, including issues of legal competence and the territorial scope of the rules, followed by an analysis of the relevant rules of human rights law and other areas of EU law (ie non-JHA law). Then it examines in detail the Schengen and EC/EU rules applying to the abolition of internal border controls and the strengthening of external border controls, then the specific issues of the Schengen Information System, local border traffic, biometric passports, and operational cooperation on border controls, examining also the issues of administrative cooperation and external relations in this field.

The issues addressed in this chapter have close links with the issues discussed in other chapters, particularly Chapter 4 concerning visas and freedom to travel, which deals with issues intrinsically linked to border control matters but which forms a distinct chapter due to the separate details of visa rules. This chapter is also closely linked to Chapter 7, concerning irregular migration. Border controls are obviously aimed at preventing irregular or undesired entry into the territory of the Member States or intercepting irregular entry at the border. It follows that the definition of irregular migration is significantly influenced by the rules relating to external borders (where persons enter irregularly, or violate the conditions attached to the authorization to enter). More particularly, the creation of the Schengen Information System to list all persons who should be denied a visa or entry into the Member States' territories also, in practice, resulted in that system holding information for a wide array of criminal law and policing purposes, along with other immigration and asylum purposes. Furthermore, the EU's border agency has powers relating to expulsion, the network of immigration liaison officers established pursuant to EU powers over irregular migration assist border control in practice, and transfer of passenger data from carriers facilitates both control of irregular migration and external border control.

There are also important links between border control and asylum law (the subject of Chapter 5), in particular because one of the principal effects of border controls is to prevent asylum seekers (whether their claim for asylum would likely be well-founded or not) from reaching the territory of the EU's Member States. More particularly, the EU's rules on responsibility for asylum applications in some cases assign responsibility for dealing with a claim based on the irregular or authorized entry of an asylum seeker at an external border, resulting in a close link between the responsibility rules and the EU's border policies. Finally, border controls are linked to longer-term migration (the subject of Chapter 6) as well, in particular to the questions of whether longer-term migration can be authorized for persons who have only entered on a short-term basis without their return to their home country first, and to the denial or withdrawal of a residence permit or a long-stay visa due to inclusion of a person's name on the list of persons to be denied entry. This chapter (rather than Chapter 6) addresses certain other issues concerning long-stay visas that are indissolubly linked to the issue of external border control.

3.2. Institutional framework and overview

3.2.1. Framework prior to the Treaty of Amsterdam[1]

3.2.1.1. EEC Member States' cooperation pre-Maastricht

The Single European Act (SEA), agreed late in 1985 and in force 1 July 1987, inserted an Article 8a into the EEC Treaty (as it then was), requiring the Community (as it then was) 'to adopt measures with the aim of progressively establishing the internal market over a period ending on 31 December 1992' by using certain specific legal bases in the EEC Treaty (without prejudice to any of the others). Article 8a then defined the entity that had to be created: '[t]he internal market shall comprise an area without internal frontiers in which the free movement of goods, services, persons and capital is ensured in accordance with the provisions of this Treaty'.

Member States agreed that border controls on all goods, capitals, and services had to be abolished by the end of 1992, but the UK in particular took the view that border controls on persons need only be abolished as regards nationals of EEC Member States, because they were arguably the only, and certainly the principal, beneficiaries of the free movement of persons.[2] But in practice it was not possible to choose between checking no persons crossing an internal border and checking non-EEC nationals only. The only practical choice was between checking *no one* and checking *everyone*, since it was not possible to know whether a person was a national of an EEC Member State without checking them. The UK argued that two Declarations attached to the SEA bolstered its view.[3]

Moreover, the abolition of internal border checks would necessarily mean that there had to be some harmonization of national law as regards external borders, immigration, and asylum, as otherwise with the abolition of internal borders; it would not be practical for Member States to retain completely distinct policies on these issues. In that case, it could be arguable that the EEC had competence to adopt measures on such issues using either Article 100 EEC (later Article 94 EC, and now Article 115 TFEU), giving the EC power to adopt measures harmonizing national law regarding the common market or Article 235 EEC (later Article 308 EC, and now Article 352 TFEU), giving the EC 'residual' power to

---

[1] For a more detailed overview, see E Guild, *European Community Law from a Migrant's Perspective* (Kluwer, 2001), chs 7 and 8, and C Gortazar, 'Abolishing Border Controls: Individual Rights and Common Control of EU External Borders' in E Guild and C Harlow, eds, *Implementing Amsterdam* (Hart, 2001), 121.

[2] The UK has 'internal borders' with Member States other than Ireland, because the concept of 'internal borders' includes borders crossed by air, ferry, or tunnel.

[3] For more on the legal debate during this period, see C Timmermans, 'Free Movement of Persons and the Division of Powers Between the Community and its Member States: Why do it the Intergovernmental Way?' in H Schermers et al, eds, *Free Movement of Persons in Europe: Legal Problems and Experiences* (Martinus Nijhoff, 1993), 352.

adopt measures where no specific power was conferred by the rest of the Treaty. However, those articles provided for unanimous voting of Member States in the Council, so this left the UK in a position to veto any proposal for EEC legislation which would have abolished internal border checks on persons. It was not possible to use Article 100a EC (later Article 95 EC, and now Art 114 TFEU), which permits qualified majority voting (QMV) in the Council to adopt measures harmonizing national law relating to the internal market, because Article 100a(2) excluded measures 'relating to the free movement of persons' from the scope of Article 100a.[4] Furthermore, the UK again pointed to the two relevant Declarations to the SEA on this issue, which also appeared to bolster its view that the EEC lacked competence on this matter. So although the Commission had announced in its well-known White Paper on completion of the internal market that it would propose EEC immigration and asylum laws in the late 1980s,[5] it never did so.

The Commission was this reticent because it could see which way the wind was blowing. There was no prospect that EEC legislation on this issue would be adopted, and in the meantime a number of Member States had begun the Schengen process (discussed further below) and all had begun to adopt intergovernmental measures in this area. For example, all Member States had agreed to adopt the Schengen asylum responsibility rules in the form of the Dublin Convention.[6] So the Commission supported such measures as an interim solution, hoping that the time would one day come when Member States could agree to address these issues using Community law.

Some aspects of the treatment of third-country nationals definitely or arguably fell within the scope of Community law even prior to the adoption of the SEA.[7] While Article 52 EEC on freedom of establishment only referred to EEC nationals, Article 48 EEC on free movement of workers referred to 'workers of the Member States' and Article 59 EEC expressly gave the Council competence to extend the EEC rules on free movement of services to 'nationals of a third country who are established and provide services within the Community'.[8] But there was great opposition to the notion that Article 48 EEC could be used to further free movement of non-EEC nationals and the Commission did not present a proposal to extend services rights to third-country nationals until 1999.[9] The Commission did win a modest victory when the Court of Justice held that the Commission could adopt a Decision (even prior to the SEA) requiring Member States to supply information on their policies regarding third-country nationals under Article 118 EEC (later Article 140 EC and now Article 156 TFEU) to the extent that such policies affected the EEC employment situation.[10] This particularly applied to

---

[4] Art 114(2) TFEU still contains the same exclusion.   [5] See White Paper (COM (85) 310).
[6] See 5.8.1 below.   [7] On the current competence issues, see 3.2.4 below.
[8] Now respectively Arts 45, 49, and 56 TFEU.   [9] See further 6.4.4 below.
[10] Joined Cases 281-283, 285, and 287/85 *Germany and others v Commission* [1987] ECR 3203.

national policies on working conditions and access to employment of third-country nationals. However, this did not give the EC competence to adopt legislation concerning these issues under the social policy provisions of the Treaty, which were then quite limited. Eventually it became clearer that certain aspects of immigration law as regards association agreements and other aspects of the free movement of services fell within the scope of Community law even before the entry into force of the Treaty of Amsterdam,[11] but the majority of developments remained intergovernmental, including Resolutions of the Council and the Member States.[12]

3.2.1.2. Schengen integration

Outside the Community legal system, a group of Member States agreed first the 1985 Schengen Agreement and then the 1990 Convention implementing the Schengen Agreement (the 'Schengen Convention').[13] The former Agreement provided for the principle of abolishing internal border checks among its signatories and set out a detailed list of measures to be agreed in order to implement this objective. The latter Convention in turn set out detailed rules on abolishing internal border checks; strengthening external border controls; harmonizing visa policy; and regulating movement of third-country nationals between its signatories;[14] in parallel with further rules restricting irregular immigration;[15] allocating responsibility for asylum requests;[16] addressing criminal judicial cooperation and police cooperation issues;[17] and creating a database (the Schengen Information System (SIS)).[18] The underlying logic of the Schengen rules was that there must be extensive 'compensatory' measures, including a common visa policy and a transfer of checks to the external borders of the signatories, in order to ensure that internal border checks could be abolished without a corresponding loss of security.

Although the UK and several other Member States would not accept the Schengen Convention's centrepiece obligation to abolish internal border controls, they could accept certain aspects of the Schengen rules, in particular the idea of strengthened border controls without the corresponding internal freedoms.[19] Therefore, they negotiated an External Frontiers Convention, largely

---

[11] See further 6.4 below.

[12] Resolutions on simplified control at internal borders for nationals of Member States ([1984] OJ C 159/1) and on standard signs at the internal and external borders ([1986] OJ C 303/1).

[13] [2000] OJ L 239/13 and 19. On the initial Convention, see J Schutte, 'Schengen: Its Meaning for the Free Movement of Persons in Europe' (1991) 28 CMLRev 549; D O'Keeffe, 'The Schengen Convention: A Suitable Model for European Integration?' (1991) 11 YEL 185; and J Donner, 'Abolition of Border Controls', in Free Movement of Persons in Europe (n 3 above), 5.

[14] Arts 1–25. See 3.5, 3.6, 4.5, 4.6, 4.7, and 4.9 below.

[15] Arts 26–27. See 7.5.1 and 7.5.3 below.   [16] Arts 28–38. See 5.8.1 below.

[17] Arts 39–91. See generally ch 9 and 12.6 and 12.9 below.

[18] Arts 92–119. On the application of the SIS for border control purposes, see 3.7 below. On the SIS generally, see 12.6.1.1 below.

[19] They could also accept some other provisions: see further chs 5, 6, 7, 9, 11, and 12.

based on the relevant provisions of the Schengen Convention, and nearly agreed this Convention in 1991 except only for the territorial scope, as Spain and the UK could not agree on whether the Convention would apply to Gibraltar.

3.2.1.3 Maastricht-era framework and overview

The negotiators of the TEU compromised on the issue of whether the EC was competent to address issues relating to visas and border controls, and did not settle the question of whether Article 8a EEC (which was renumbered Article 7a EC by the Maastricht Treaty) required the abolition of border checks on all persons. A new provision (Article 100c) was inserted into the EC Treaty (as it was then renamed), giving the Community certain powers relating to visas.[20] However, a number of other related issues were expressly part of the third pillar powers of the EU and listed in the original Article K.1 EU: asylum policy; rules on the crossing of external borders and related controls; and policy on immigration and third-country nationals, particularly 'conditions of entry and movement', 'conditions of residence...including family reunion and access to employment', and 'combatting unauthorized immigration, residence and work'. However, there was no explicit mention of internal borders in the third pillar provisions (although the reference to the 'movement' of third-country nationals could arguably have covered internal borders issues), and it will be recalled that the third pillar was without prejudice to and could not encroach upon Community law.[21] So the issue of whether the EC had competence over internal borders issues was still open.

Indeed, the Commission proposed three Directives on border controls issues in 1995,[22] following a legal challenge which the European Parliament (EP) brought against it for 'failure to act' because it had not proposed any measure to abolish border checks by the end of 1992.[23] As a result of the Commission's proposals, the EP's case was subsequently pulled. However, since the Commission's two key proposals were based on Article 100 EC,[24] and therefore still subject to unanimous voting requirements as discussed above, there was no prospect of the Council adopting them due to the UK's opposition.[25]

---

[20] For details, see 4.2.2 below.   [21] See 2.4 above.

[22] COM (95) 348, 347, and 346, 12 July 1995 ([1995] OJ C 289/16, C 306/5, and C 307/18), which concerned respectively the abolition of internal border controls, freedom to travel for third-country nationals within the EU for up to six months, and consequential amendments to EC free movement legislation. Amended versions of the former two proposals were presented in spring 1997 (COM (97) 102, 20 Mar 1997; [1997] OJ C 140/21). See S Peers, 'Border in Channel: Continent cut off' (1998) 19 JSWFL 108.

[23] Case C-445/93 *EP v Commission*. On the Court of Justice's jurisdiction over EU institutions' 'failure to act', see Art 265 TFEU.

[24] The proposal concerning consequential amendments to free movement legislation was based on Arts 49, 54(2), and 63(2) EC (now Arts 46, 50, and 59 TFEU).

[25] Indeed, following the entry into force of the Treaty of Amsterdam, the proposals were later officially withdrawn (COM (2001) 763, 21 Dec 2001).

The EU's third pillar powers were also used to adopt a Recommendation on provision of forgery detection equipment at frontiers and a Joint Position on joint training of airline staff and joint assistance in third-country airports.[26] A number of other proposed EU measures, including a revived proposal for an external frontiers Convention, failed due to fundamental disputes about the scope of EC or EU powers, the desirability of extensive EU action, and the application of the proposed Frontiers Convention to Gibraltar.[27]

In the meantime, the Schengen Convention came into effect from March 1995. Its territorial scope was regularly expanded thereafter,[28] and a large number of measures implementing the Convention, many of which concern border controls, were adopted by the Executive Committee which it set up.[29] In practice, EC or EU measures on border controls adopted or discussed up to the entry into force of the Treaty of Amsterdam were clearly strongly influenced by developments among the Schengen States.

3.2.2. Treaty of Amsterdam

3.2.2.1. Institutional framework

The Treaty of Amsterdam renumbered Article 7a EC on the creation of the internal market EC as Article 14 EC, but did not otherwise amend that Article. Within Title IV of the EC Treaty, the special Title added by the Treaty of Amsterdam addressing immigration, asylum, and civil law, Article 61(a) EC specified that '[i]n order to establish progressively an area of freedom, security and justice, the Council shall adopt' within five years of the entry into force of that Treaty (so by 1 May 2004) 'measures aimed at ensuring the free movement of persons in accordance with Article 14, in conjunction with directly related flanking measures with respect to external border controls, asylum and immigration, in accordance with the provisions of Article 62(2) and (3) and Article 63(1)(a) and (2)(a), and measures to prevent and combat crime in accordance with the provisions of Article 31(e) of the Treaty on European Union'.[30] As regards border controls, the means of accomplishing this were set out in Article 62 EC, which required the Council to adopt the following within this five-year period:

1. measures with a view to ensuring, in compliance with Article 14, the absence of any controls on persons, be they citizens of the Union or nationals of third countries, when crossing internal borders;

---

[26] See respectively [1998] OJ C 189/19 and [1996] L 281/1.

[27] For more detail of the proposed measures, see the first edition of this book, 71–75. For the proposed Convention, see COM (93) 684, 10 Dec 1994 ([1994] OJ C 11/15).

[28] For details, see 2.2.2.3 above.

[29] On some of these implementing measures, see 3.5, 3.6, and 4.7.1 below.

[30] On the criminal law measures adopted, see ch 10 below.

2. measures on the crossing of the external borders of the Member States which shall establish:

  (a) standards and procedures to be followed by Member States in carrying out checks on persons at such borders . . .[31]

The structure of these provisions closely followed the structure of Articles 1–25 of the Schengen Convention,[32] and furthermore closely paralleled EC or EU measures that had previously been proposed or adopted. The wording of Article 62(1) definitively settled the argument as to whether third-country nationals were covered by the abolition of internal border controls. However, the Court of Justice confirmed that the Treaty provisions merely conferred power on the EC institutions to adopt measures, and did not in themselves have the objective of granting rights to third-country nationals or obligations for Member States.[33]

Moreover, Article 64(1) EC provided that Title IV 'shall not affect the exercise of the responsibilities incumbent upon Member States with regard to the maintenance of law and order and the safeguarding of internal security'. Again, there was a relevant Declaration in the final Act of the Treaty of Amsterdam: '[t]he Conference agrees that Member States may take into account foreign policy considerations when exercising their responsibilities under Article [64(1)] of the [EC] Treaty'. Article 64(2) provided for an amended version of the 'emergency' power previously provided for in Article 100c EC, which was no longer concerned solely with visas:

In the event of one or more Member States being confronted with an emergency situation characterised by a sudden inflow of nationals of third countries and without prejudice to paragraph 1, the Council may, acting by qualified majority on a proposal from the Commission, adopt provisional measures of a duration not exceeding six months for the benefit of the Member States concerned.

There was also a power to adopt measures on administrative cooperation between the Member States, or between the Member States and the Commission (Article 66 EC), which also applied to border control issues.[34]

As for decision-making,[35] Article 67(1) EC provided that the EC's border control powers were subject to unanimous voting in the Council, consultation of the EP, and shared initiative of the Commission and the Member States up until 1 May 2004. However, the powers over emergency measures in Article 64

---

[31] Art 62(2)(b) and (3) concerned visas and freedom to travel; see further 4.2.2 below.

[32] See 3.2.1.2 above.

[33] See Joined Cases C-261/08 *Zurita Garcia* and C-348/08 *Choque Cabrera*, judgment of 22 Oct 2009, not yet reported, para 43.

[34] On administrative cooperation and EU funding in this area, see 3.11 below.

[35] For an overview of all the decision-making rules applicable to Title IV EC, see 2.2.2.1 above.

were subject from the outset to QMV in the Council and the sole initiative of the Commission, but with no role for the EP.

From 1 May 2004, according to Article 67(2) EC, the Commission gained the sole right of initiative on all borders matters. The same provision obliged the Council to change decision-making rules as regards some aspects of Title IV, and it duly amended the rules concerning both internal border controls so that it acted by QMV and co-decision on these issues as from 1 January 2005.[36] Furthermore, a Protocol attached to the EC Treaty by the Treaty of Nice automatically changed the decision-making procedure applicable to Article 66 EC to QMV in Council with consultation of the EP from 1 May 2004.

In addition to the new provisions of the main EC Treaty concerning visas and border controls, the Treaty of Amsterdam added a Protocol to the EC Treaty, concerning external EC competence over external border control treaties.[37]

Finally, it should be recalled that in the area of visas and borders, the Court of Justice was subject during the 'Amsterdam era' not only to restrictions on receiving references from lower national courts (as in the rest of Title IV EC), but also to a restriction on its jurisdiction as regards measures based on Article 62(1) EC.[38] Due to the general restriction on its jurisdiction, despite the extensive Schengen *acquis* which formed part of the EC legal order since 1 May 1999, the Court received only two references in this area from national courts during this period.[39]

3.2.2.2. Overview of practice

The entry into force of the Treaty of Amsterdam immediately entailed the integration of the Schengen *acquis* in this area into the EC legal order by means of the Protocol on the Schengen *acquis* and the Council Decisions defining and allocating the *acquis*,[40] with the exception of the immigration provisions of the Schengen Information System, which remained in the third pillar provisionally in the absence of any agreement within the Council on which 'legal base' to allocate these provisions to.[41] At a stroke, the EC legal order contained an extensive set of rules concerning the abolition of internal border controls and the strengthening of external border controls.

Given the extent of this *acquis*, there was little immediate interest in further development of it. The issue of border controls was only briefly canvassed in the conclusions of the Tampere European Council of October 1999:

...The European Council calls for closer co-operation and mutual technical assistance between the Member States' border control services, such as exchange programmes and

---

[36] [2004] OJ L 396/45. See further ibid.   [37] See 3.12 below.

[38] On the Court's role during this period, see further 2.2.2.1 above.

[39] Joined Cases C-261/08 *Zurita Garcia* and C-348/08 *Choque Cabrera*, judgment of 22 Oct 2009, not yet reported. On the substance of these cases, see 3.6.1 below.

[40] On the process on integrating the Schengen *acquis* generally, see 2.2.2.3 above. For details of the borders provisions of the *acquis* integrated into EC law, see 3.5 and 3.6 below.

[41] See further 2.2.2.3 above.

technology transfer, especially on maritime borders, and for the rapid inclusion of the applicant States in this co-operation.

There were no developments in this area until 2002, apart from a Regulation of April 2001, unsuccessfully contested by the Commission, conferring power upon the Council to amend key secondary Schengen borders rules,[42] which was applied several times subsequently.[43] From the end of 2001, the Council began to develop plans for an 'integrated border management system', culminating in a Council Action Plan on control of external borders, adopted in June 2002.[44] In the same month, the Seville European Council set a number of objectives for enhancing administrative cooperation between Member States and carrying out joint border control operations. Two other action plans adopted in 2002, both concerning irregular migration, also have some relevance to border controls.[45] Subsequently, the 2004 Hague programme and its related implementation plan called for a number of detailed measures concerning border controls.[46]

To realize these objectives, a number of important legislative measures were adopted beginning in 2003, in particular concerning: the creation of an EU borders agency, known as 'Frontex' (amended in 2007); the stamping of travel documents at external borders; a harmonized border traffic regime; rules on passport security; a code comprising (and revising) all existing EU and Schengen rules on external (and internal) borders, known as the 'Schengen Borders Code'; and legislation to establish the new version of the Schengen Information System (SIS II).[47] Also, a Directive on transmission of passenger data by carriers was adopted in 2004, in part by using the EC's powers over external border control.[48] The Commission carried out a first review of the three Action Plans of 2002 in 2003,[49] and subsequently produced three 'annual' reports on the application of the Action Plans, in 2004, 2006, and 2009.[50] A 2006 communication on policy priorities as regards irregular immigration set out in part a future agenda relating to border controls;[51] this was followed up

---

[42] The Commission disputed the Council's decision to confer implementing powers on itself, but the Court of Justice rejected its challenge (Case C-257/01 *Commission v Council* [2005] ECR I-345). For more on this issue, see 2.2.2.1 above.

[43] On the implementing measures, see 5.6 below.

[44] Council doc 10019/02, 14 June 2002. See earlier Commission Communication (COM (2002) 233, 7 May 2002).

[45] Action Plans on illegal immigration and trafficking in human beings ([2002] OJ C 142/23) and on return (Council doc 14673/02, 25 Nov 2002). On the implementation of these plans, see ch 7 below.   [46] [2005] OJ C 53/1 and [2005] OJ C 198/1.

[47] On the details of these measures, see 3.5–3.10 below.

[48] The Directive was also adopted by use of the EC's powers over irregular migration, and so is discussed separately in 7.5.2 below.   [49] COM (2003) 323, 3 June 2003.

[50] SEC (2004) 1349, 25 Oct 2004; SEC (2006) 1010, 19 July 2006; and SEC (2009) 320, 8 Mar 2009.   [51] COM (2006) 402, 19 July 2006.

by three communications relating to the future development of border control policy in 2008.[52]

A fundamental development during the Amsterdam period was the continued extension of the Schengen free movement area, first (fully) to Greece in 1999, then to Nordic Member States (and associates Norway and Iceland) in 2001, then to nine newer Member States in 2007, and then to Switzerland in 2008.[53]

In the related area of administrative cooperation and Community funding, the Council inter alia established a funding programme which became focused in practice on border control projects, and was followed by a dedicated Borders Fund in 2007.[54] The special emergency powers conferred by Article 64 EC were never used. Finally, the EC's implied external relations powers over borders were used to agree treaties associating non-Member States with the relevant Schengen *acquis* and with the EU's borders agency.[55]

3.2.3. Treaty of Lisbon

The entry into force of the Treaty of Lisbon on 1 December 2009 amended the legal powers of the EC (now the EU) in this area, and also extended the normal jurisdiction of the Court of Justice to this field, in particular permitting all national courts and tribunals to send questions on EU immigration and asylum law to the Court of Justice.

The EC Treaty was renamed the Treaty on the Functioning of the European Union (TFEU) and the provisions relevant to border controls, now found in Article 77 TFEU, read as follows:

1. The Union shall develop a policy with a view to:
    (a) ensuring the absence of any controls on persons, whatever their nationality, when crossing internal borders;
    (b) carrying out checks on persons and efficient monitoring of the crossing of external borders;
    (c) the gradual introduction of an integrated management system for external borders.
2. For the purposes of paragraph 1, the European Parliament and the Council, acting in accordance with the ordinary legislative procedure, shall adopt measures concerning:
    . . .
    (b) the checks to which persons crossing external borders are subject;
    . . .

---

[52] COM (2008) 67, 68, and 69, 13 Feb 2008, concerning respectively the future development of Frontex, the development of a European surveillance system (Eurosur), and the plans for an entry-exit system. See further 5.10 and 5.6.2 below.   [53] See 3.2.5 below.
[54] See 3.11 below.   [55] See 3.2.5 and 3.10 below.

(d) any measure necessary for the gradual establishment of an integrated management system for external borders;

(e) the absence of any controls on persons, whatever their nationality, when crossing internal borders.

3. If action by the Union should prove necessary to facilitate the exercise of the right referred to in Article 20(2)(a), and if the Treaties have not provided the necessary powers, the Council, acting in accordance with a special legislative procedure, may adopt provisions concerning passports, identity cards, residence permits or any other such document. The Council shall act unanimously after consulting the European Parliament.

4. This Article shall not affect the competence of the Member States concerning the geographical demarcation of their borders, in accordance with international law.

Comparing the revised article to the previous text, the provision relating to internal borders no longer refers to Article 14 EC (now Article 26 TFEU), but is otherwise substantively unchanged.[56] As regards external borders, the Treaty no longer refers to 'standards' and 'procedures', but rather to 'efficient monitoring' of external border crossing. However, it is difficult to see what difference this slightly different wording makes.

A more substantial change is the addition of the objective of introducing gradually 'an integrated management system for external borders', along with an accompanying legal base. The full implications of this apparently new competence are considered further below,[57] but it should be noted that this new provision is subject, like the previous (and now revised) powers on border controls, to QMV and the co-decision procedure, now renamed the 'ordinary legislative procedure'.[58]

An even more significant change is the addition of a new express power relating to the adoption of measures concerning 'passports, identity cards, residence permits or any other such document', which are 'necessary to facilitate the exercise of the right referred to in Article 20(2)(a)' TFEU: the right in question is the right of EU citizens 'to move and reside freely within the territory of the Member States'. This compares to the equivalent provision in the citizenship Title of the Treaty before this amendment, which had provided that the power to adopt legislation facilitating EU citizens' free movement rights, which was subject to QMV and co-decision (as from the entry into force of the Treaty of Nice) 'shall not apply to provisions on passports, identity cards, residence permits or any other such document or to provisions on social security or social protection'.[59] While this provision apparently ruled out EC powers to adopt measures on these issues entirely, the TFEU now provides for these powers for the EU, subject to unanimous voting in the Council and consultation of the EP (known now as a

---

[56] While the reference to non-Union nationals is slightly different, the revised Treaty provisions make clear that stateless persons are to be regarded as third-country nationals (Art 67(2) TFEU).

[57] See 3.2.4 below.   [58] See Arts 289(1) and 294 TFEU.   [59] Previous Art 18(3) EC.

form of 'special legislative procedure').[60] In fact, this is the only special legislative procedure now provided for in the immigration and asylum part of the Treaty. It is necessary therefore not only to define the scope of these new powers, but also to distinguish them from the EU's powers relating to border control—an issue discussed further below.[61]

The new paragraph 4 reserves certain powers regarding the definition of their borders to Member States. It should be noted, however, that some EC legislation adopted before the entry into force of the Lisbon Treaty already provided for the same reservation of competence.[62]

As for the general provisions of the JHA Title of the revised Treaty,[63] Article 67(2) TFEU now provides that the EU 'shall ensure the absence of internal border controls for persons and shall frame a common policy on asylum, immigration and external border control, based on solidarity between Member States, which is fair towards third-country nationals'. There are still separate references to 'free movement' and the abolition of internal frontiers within the definition of JHA policy set out in the revised Article 3(2) TEU.[64]

The other general provisions of the revised Title V of the TFEU include the European Council's power to adopt general guidelines relating to 'legislative and operational planning' (Article 68 TFEU), which could be relevant to border control operations as well as legislation. The new express provision relating to evaluation of JHA policies will obviously be relevant to the process of evaluating Schengen states' application of the Schengen *acquis* ('Schengen evaluations').[65] Next, the standing committee on operational security has a role in border security.[66] It remains to be seen whether the committee will add any value to the operations of Frontex and/or Member States' authorities.

There is a general security restriction in Article 72 TFEU which simply repeats the previous Article 64(1) EC.[67] On the other hand, the previous Article 64(2) EC, concerning emergency measures, has been replaced by a provision relating only to asylum matters, so it no longer has any potential direct relevance to border control issues, although it is arguable that it has an indirect relevance (in the sense that the article may be used to adopt measures relating to border control in order to satisfy an objective relating to asylum).[68] Finally, the power to adopt

---

[60] On the concept of a 'special legislative procedure', see Art 289(2) TFEU. It should be noted that while Art 77(3) TFEU does not mention the previously excluded power to adopt social security and social protection measures to facilitate EU citizens' free movement rights, there is now a power in the citizenship Title to adopt legislation on such issues, subject again to unanimity in Council and consultation of the EP (Art 21(3) TFEU). The real difference between the provisions on such as, passports and social security/social protection is that the former, but not the latter, is subject to potential opt-outs by the UK, Ireland, and Denmark (on which see 3.2.5 below).   [61] See 3.2.4 below.

[62] For instance, see the visa list legislation: Art 6 of Reg 539/2001 ([2001] OJ L 81/1).

[63] See further 2.2.3.2 above.   [64] See further ibid.   [65] Art 70 TFEU.

[66] Art 71 TFEU; see the Decision establishing this body ([2010] OJ L 52/50).

[67] On interpretation of this provision, see 3.2.4 below.

[68] Art 78(3) TFEU. On the interpretation of this provision, see 5.2.4 below.

measures concerning cooperation between administrations remains in the Treaty, unchanged as regards borders (or other immigration-related) measures, and still subject to QMV in Council but consultation of the EP.[69] The protocol relating to external competence as regards external borders also remains unchanged,[70] although changes relating to the opt-outs for the UK, Ireland, and Denmark from JHA policies could be relevant for borders matters.[71]

As for the implementation of these provisions to date, legislation proposed before the entry into force of the Treaty of Lisbon concerning amendments to the Schengen evaluation mechanism;[72] the creation of a new agency to operate the second-generation Schengen Information System (SIS II);[73] the regulation of long-term visas;[74] and the implementation of SIS II[75] were still under discussion when that Treaty entered into force. The legislation on long-term visas and the implementation of SIS II was adopted early in 2010,[76] but the other proposals remained under discussion as this book went to press. Also, shortly after the Treaty of Lisbon entered into force, the Commission proposed further amendments to the rules governing Frontex, the EU border agency.[77] This proposal was also still under discussion when this book went to press.

Future plans involve in particular legislative proposals (in 2011) for the development of an entry-exit system to keep precise track of the persons entering and leaving the Schengen area, alongside the development of a registered traveller programme and corresponding amendments to the Schengen Borders Code, and a communication on the possible development of a system for electronic travel authorization for non-visa nationals (ie third-country nationals living outside the EU who do not require a visa to enter it).[78] The Stockholm programme also calls for: a further extension of the full Schengen area to those Member States which do not yet participate in it (Cyprus, Romania, and Bulgaria);[79] a debate on the 'the feasibility of the creation of a European system of border guards'; the continued development of Eurosur, the border surveillance system; and the coordination of different types of border checks.[80]

Finally, the Treaty of Lisbon had limited immediate impact on the number of cases reaching the Court of Justice in this area, since there was only one reference

---

[69] Art 74 TFEU, replacing Art 66 EC. The measures concerned are not legislative acts.

[70] See 3.12 below.   [71] See 3.2.5 below.

[72] COM (2009) 102, 4 Mar 2009. On the issue of Schengen evaluation, and JHA evaluation in general, see 2.2.3.2 above.

[73] COM (2009) 293, 24 June 2009; revised after the Treaty of Lisbon entered into force: COM (2010) 93, 19 Mar 2010. See 12.6.1 below.   [74] COM (2009) 91, 27 Feb 2009.

[75] COM (2009) 508, 29 Sep 2009.

[76] Regs 265/2010, [2010] OJ L 85/1, and 541/2010 ([2010] OJ L 155/19). For the border controls aspect of the former Regulation, see 3.6.1 below.   [77] COM (2010) 61, 24 Feb 2010.

[78] See Commission 2010 work programme (COM (2010) 135, 31 Mar 2010), Annexes II and III.

[79] See 3.2.5 below.

[80] [2010] OJ C 115, s 5.1. This part of the Stockholm programme largely reflects the relevant part of the prior Immigration and Asylum pact (Council doc 13440/08, 24 Sep 2008, Part III).

to the Court on border control issues in the first few months after the Treaty
entered into force.[81]

3.2.4. Competence issues

To some extent, the argument over the existence and extent of EC competence
over borders issues is now purely historic. But even following the entry into force
of the Treaty of Amsterdam, and now the Treaty of Lisbon, there are some issues
concerning the division of competence between the borders powers in Title V of
the TFEU and the rest of that Treaty, concerning the division of powers within
Title V itself, and concerning the extent of competence conferred by these provisions.[82] The first of these three issues is addressed further below,[83] while the other
two are addressed in turn in the rest of this subsection.

The arguments concerning the distinctions between 'legal bases' are practically relevant because of the different rules pursuant to different legal bases
as regards decision-making and the participation of Member States (where the
comparison is between Title V and the rest of the TFEU). As regards legal bases,
the Court of Justice has held: that the choice of the legal basis for a Community
(now Union) measure must rest on objective factors amenable to judicial review,
which include in particular the aim and the content of the measure; that in principle measures which pursue more than one purpose or component should be
based on only one legal basis, corresponding to the main purpose or component;
that exceptionally, where there is more than one purpose or component that is
inextricably linked, the institution must adopt the measure using multiple legal
bases; but that multiple legal bases are not possible if the various decision-making
procedures are incompatible with each other.[84] Such incompatibility exists where
the Council is obliged to vote unanimously throughout a procedure designed to
give more power to the EP, throughout which it would normally vote by QMV;
in that case, a 'tie-break' rule requires use of the procedure most favourable to
the EP.[85] But incompatibility does not exist where the Council votes entirely

---

[81] Joined Cases C-188/10 and C-189/10 *Melki and Abdeli*, judgment of 22 June 2010, not yet
reported. See 3.5 below. The EP has also brought an annulment action against a measure implementing the Schengen Borders Code: Case C-355/10, *EP v Council*, pending.

[82] There are also issues regarding the EU's external competence; these are considered in 3.12
below.   [83] See 3.4 below.

[84] See particularly Case C-300/89 *Commission v Council* [1991] ECR I-2867; Case C-211/01
Commission v Council [2003] ECR I-8913; Joined Cases C-164/97 and C-165/97 *Parliament v Council*
[1999] ECR I-1139; and Case C-338/01 *Commission v Council* [2004] ECR I-4829.

[85] Case C-300/89, ibid. It should be noted, however, that two recent judgments of the Court
are inconsistent with this line of case law: Cases C-402/05 P and C-415/05 P *Kadi and Al-Barakaat*
[2008] ECR I-6351 and C-166/07 *EP v Council* [2009] ECR I-7135. In both cases the Court accepts
without explanation the combination of legal bases involving unanimous voting on the one hand
and QMV on the other.

by QMV while simultaneously involving the EP both through the co-decision procedure and consultation.[86]

As regards borders measures, originally all measures were subject to unanimity in Council and consultation of the EP. Following the changes to decision-making rules that entered into force on 1 May 2004 and 1 January 2005,[87] there was a different distinction between two categories of decision-making applicable to this area: measures subject to QMV and co-decision (rules on internal and external border controls) and measures subject to QMV and consultation of the EP (administrative cooperation). This essential distinction remains after the entry into force of the Treaty of Lisbon, which adds a further distinction between measures relating to such as, passports (subject to unanimous voting and consultation of the EP) and the other two types of decision-making.

It is therefore necessary first of all to define the distinction between Articles 74 and 77 TFEU, in particular in relation to borders issues. This issue is relevant, for instance, to any decision-making concerning the databases (such as the SIS), for it will determine whether the legislation is subject to any effective parliamentary control.[88] The logical distinction between Articles 74 and 77 is that any measures which concern checks on individuals at the border, including the collection of or processing of personal data to those ends, clearly fall within the scope of the former article, as such measures fall within the scope of its core subject matter. Therefore, Article 74 must govern cooperation between administrations where the subject matter does not relate to regulating the movement of persons across borders in concrete situations, governing instead issues such as exchanges of personnel or of general information. On the other hand, the exchange of information on individuals for specific purposes related to (for instance) border checks concerns the substantive law relating to border checks, and so falls within the scope of Article 77.[89]

A complex question relating to the EU's various border control powers has been posed by the addition of Article 77(3) TFEU, concerning passports and similar documents.[90] It is obviously necessary to distinguish this provision from the general external borders powers because, as noted above, it is subject to unanimity in Council and consultation of the EP, rather than the ordinary legislative procedure (ex-co-decision). Furthermore, surely the passports legal base, and measures adopted pursuant to it, have to be interpreted in light of EU citizenship,

---

[86] Case C-491/01 *BAT* [2002] ECR I-11453, paras 101–111; see also Case C-178/03 *Commission v EP and Council* [2006] ECR I-107 and particularly Case C-155/07 *EP v Council* [2008] ECR I-8103.   [87] See 3.2.2.1 above.

[88] The EP would ensure effective control to the extent that it has co-decision powers, while national parliaments could in principle exercise effective scrutiny over the provision concerning passports and similar documents, due to the unanimity requirement. Use of Art 74 would deny a significant role to parliaments at either level.   [89] On Art 74 generally, see 2.2.3.2 above.

[90] See also 3.2.5 below, on the territorial scope of measures to be adopted pursuant to this legal base.

not in light of the objectives of the borders powers or the general objectives of Title V of the Treaty.

In order to interpret the scope of the new provision, it should be recalled, first of all, that the previous Article 18(3) EC, which was part of the Treaty Article concerning the free movement rights of EU citizens, ruled out the adoption of measures on such issues.[91] The Council nonetheless adopted in 2004 a Regulation on security features in passports issued by Member States, on the basis of the EC's external borders powers, on the grounds that such rules help to facilitate checks at external borders.[92] However, the common format of the EU passport has traditionally been set out in Resolutions of Member States, on the assumption that the EC lacked the competence to regulate such matters.[93] At first sight, this assumption was clearly correct in light of the previous Article 18(3) EC, for (by analogy with the case law relating to public health) the Community should not be able to circumvent restrictions on its competence set out in one legal base by employing another legal base instead.[94]

On the same grounds, it was doubtful whether the previous external borders legal base in fact provided competence for the EC to adopt the passport security Regulation, as passports are not merely used at the external borders of the Member States, but also at EC internal borders (to the extent that passport checks are still carried out), to prove identity within Member States, and to cross the borders of non-Member States. Indeed, one purpose of the passport security Regulation was to continue to ensure visa-free entry for the nationals of most Member States into the US. However, the Court of Justice's judgment on the validity of the passport security Regulation implicitly endorsed the use of the EC's external borders powers as a valid legal base for this measure.[95]

The position after the Treaty of Lisbon came into force is that the Union has express competence to regulate not just passports, but also identity cards, residence permits, and similar documents. But this is subject to two provisos: such measures must be necessary for facilitating EU citizens' rights to 'move and reside freely'; and this power can only be applied if other provisions of the Treaty 'have not provided the necessary powers'. Taking the second proviso first, it is arguable that the general external borders legal base can still be used to adopt measures relating to passport *security*, because such measures will ensure more

---

[91] See 3.2.3 above.

[92] On the substance of the Regulation (which was subsequently amended in 2009), see 3.9 below.   [93] See further 3.4.1 below.

[94] For an elaboration of the following arguments concerning the passport security Reg, see the second edition of this book, 108–109, with further references. See in particular Case C-376/98 *Germany v EP and Council* (tobacco advertising) [2000] ECR I-8419.

[95] Case C-137/05 *UK v Council* [2007] ECR I-11593, paras 58–66, concerning Reg 2252/2004 ([2004] OJ L 385/1). On the implications of this judgment, see 3.2.5 below. However, there is nothing in the Court's judgment that addresses the *human rights* arguments against the validity of this Regulation. See by analogy 12.3 below.

effective checks at the external borders by reducing the risk of document fraud.[96] The objection that the use of the external borders legal base is circumventing an express prohibition elsewhere in the Treaty is obviously no longer valid. As for identity cards, at first sight the external borders legal base cannot be used, since identity cards cannot be used for crossing external borders, unless they are considered to be travel documents or documents authorizing the person concerned to cross the border.[97] Next, as for residence permits or similar documents, the question is moot for EU citizens since they do not require such documents to cross the external borders.[98] The issue is not moot, however, for third-country national family members of EU citizens, since a 'residence card' (which could be considered an 'other such document') will simplify border checks for them.[99]

As for the proviso relating to facilitation of free movement rights, an EU citizen crossing the border between a Schengen State and a non-Schengen State is simultaneously crossing an internal border (from a free movement perspective) and a Schengen border (from the perspective of Title V), and passports and identity cards can be used to cross such a border.[100] The same is true of citizens' family members' residence cards.[101] Therefore the two provisos relating to the use of the new power would overlap. Also, passports and identity cards can be used by EU citizens to exercise the right to reside in another Member State,[102] as can passports for third-country national family members.[103] But since EU citizens do not need residence permits to cross the internal borders or to reside in Member States, there is no link to facilitation of free movement rights there.

The best resolution of these conflicts is to accept that the EU's external borders competence is a valid legal base for the adoption of measures concerning the *security features* of EU citizens' passports, identity cards held by EU citizens, and residence cards held by EU citizens' family members, since such measures relate to checks at external borders, at least where such borders are also internal borders between Schengen and non-Schengen Member States. Moreover, the harmonization of such security features would not as such facilitate EU citizens' right to move and reside freely. On the other hand, harmonization of the format of such documents facilitates free movement of EU citizens and their family members

---

[96] See Art 7 of the Schengen Borders Code (Reg 562/2006, [2006] OJ L 105/1), discussed in 3.6.1 below. It follows that a Resolution of Member States concerning passport security, adopted in 2000, could be adopted on the basis of the external borders powers ([2000] OJ C 310/1). Indeed, this measure fell within the scope of those powers even before the entry into force of the Treaty of Lisbon, in light of the Court's judgment in *UK v Council*.

[97] See Art 5 of the Borders Code (ibid), which moreover only sets out entry conditions for third-country nationals.   [98] Ibid.

[99] See Art 10(2) of the Borders Code.

[100] Arts 4 and 5, Directive 2004/38 on EU citizens' movement rights ([2004] OJ L 158/77). It should also be noted that the preamble to the 1981 Resolution on a uniform passport format ([1981] OJ C 241/1) asserted that the uniform passport 'is likely to facilitate the movement of nationals of the Member States'.   [101] Art 5(2), Dir 2004/38.

[102] Art 6(1), Dir 2004/38.   [103] Art 6(2), Dir 2004/38.

(the latter free movement constituting a corollary of the former), because a common format ensures the immediate recognition of such documents by border guards when crossing internal EU borders—not just when entering and exiting the Schengen area, but also when entering and exiting non-Schengen EU Member States as well.

Also, it should be pointed out that the 'passports' legal base does not confer power on the EU to regulate the issue of identity cards, residence permits or any other such documents to *third-country nationals*, other than the family members of EU citizens, because the issue of such documents to such persons is unconnected with the free movement of EU citizens. So is the issue of passports to such persons, but of course in any event the issue of passports to third-country nationals (even those who are family members of EU citizens) is a matter for their countries of nationality, not Member States or the EU. The external borders power is still a valid legal base regarding the issue of travel documents by Member States to third-country nationals, where there is a link to external border crossing but no link to facilitation of free movement.[104]

It is clear, though, that neither legal base has conferred competence upon the EU to require Member States to introduce identity cards or to harmonize national law on the *internal* use (ie within a Member State's national territory) of such cards. Such matters are not sufficiently connected to the crossing of external borders *or* the facilitation of EU citizens' free movement rights, considering that identity cards are only an *optional* method of proving nationality when crossing internal borders.

To what extent could either legal base govern the creation of databases and the exchange of information concerning such documents? Extrapolating from the previous analysis, the external borders power would be a sufficient legal basis for the adoption of such measures to the extent that storing, exchanging, and accessing such data was linked to checks at the Member States' external borders. The applicable data protection rules would, however, have to be adopted on the basis of Article 16 TFEU, although these general rules could be supplemented by specific rules set out in the external borders legislation.[105] But the 'passports' legal base does not confer power to establish or regulate such databases, or exchange of information, since the development of such policies would not facilitate EU citizens' rights to move and reside freely.

The next question is the extent of the EU's powers over borders. As for measures adopted during the Treaty of Amsterdam period, the Council correctly allocated the Schengen *acquis* concerning the regulation of border guards to the first pillar, not the third, since the measures concerned regulated border control, as distinct from other forms of law enforcement. For the same reasons, the EU border agency was rightly a creation of EC legislation, not a third pillar measure.

---

[104] See Art 1 of Reg 2252/2004 (n 95 above).   [105] See further 12.2.4 below.

An interesting issue relating to both the borders and visas powers of the EU is their relationship with the foreign policy provisions of Title V of the TEU, where a number of measures have been adopted requiring Member States to refuse entry and transit to certain third-country nationals, in pursuit of foreign policy objectives, both before and after the entry into force of the Treaty of Lisbon.[106] These measures apply to all Member States, quite apart from the different decision-making procedures, jurisdictional rules, and legal effect involved.[107] It is submitted that the correct legal base for such measures is Title V TFEU, *not* the foreign policy provisions of Title V TEU. Although such measures have foreign policy objectives, their *content* is the regulation of entry of persons into the EU. There is extensive case law making it clear that measures fall within the scope of the EU's common commercial policy even if they have foreign policy objectives,[108] or other objectives besides commercial policy objectives,[109] if their essential *content* is the regulation of international trade.[110] Moreover, there were declarations to the Treaty of Amsterdam (set out above) accepting that the EC's visa powers and Article 64(1) EC (now Article 72 TFEU) are to be exercised with regard to foreign policy considerations. Furthermore, secondary EC (now EU) measures (and previously the Schengen *acquis*) refer to foreign policy issues,[111] although this is not decisive for interpretation of the Treaty.[112] It should be noted that, following the entry into force of the Treaty of Lisbon, the persons concerned now have the power to bring annulment actions against the relevant foreign policy measures.[113]

Next, what is the extent of the EU's competence to harmonize the law on borders? Logically, the powers conferred by Article 77 TFEU to harmonize rules on border checks must be extensive, given the obligation to abolish internal border checks; the corollary freedom to travel (which is moreover subject to

---

[106] For example, before the Treaty of Lisbon, see the Common Position banning the entry of persons whom the Council considers to be obstructing the work of the International Criminal Tribunal for the former Yugoslavia ([2004] OJ L 94/65). After the Treaty of Lisbon, see the amendment to the list of Burmese nationals banned from entry ([2009] OJ L 338/90).

[107] See Title V TEU, as revised by the Treaty of Lisbon.

[108] Cases C-83/94 and C-70/94 *Werner and Leifer* [1995] ECR I-3189 and Case C-124/95 *Centrocom* [1997] ECR I-81. See also the judgments concerning defence equipment and EU customs law: Cases C-284/05 *Commission v Finland*; C-294/05 *Commission v Sweden*; C-372/05 *Commission v Germany*; C-387/05 *Commission v Italy*; C-409/05 *Commission v Greece*; C-461/05 *Commission v Denmark*; C-239/06 *Commission v Italy* (all judgments of 15 Dec 2009, not yet reported); and C-38/06 *Commission v Portugal* (judgment of 4 Mar 2010, not yet reported).

[109] *Opinion 1/78* [1979] ECR 2871 and Case 45/86 *Commission v Council* (GSP) [1987] ECR 1493.

[110] On the analogy between the common commercial policy and Title IV (now Title V) powers, see S Peers, 'EU Borders and Globalisation', in E Guild, P Minderhoud, and K Groenendijk (eds), *In Search of Europe's Borders* (Kluwer, 2003), 45.

[111] See, for instance, Art 5(1)(e) of the Schengen Borders Code (n 96 above) and Art 21(3)(d) of the visa code (Reg 810/2009, [2009] OJ L 243/1). [112] See *Opinion 1/94* [1994] ECR I-5273.

[113] Art 275 TFEU.

a 'uniform application');[114] the earlier Treaty reference to a 'uniform' visa (and now to a 'common policy on visas'); and comparison with the structure of the EC Treaty rules governing free movement of goods.[115] The Court of Justice's ruling in *Wijsenbeek*, emphasizing the link between the abolition of border controls pursuant to the previous Article 14 EC and the harmonization of the relevant law,[116] also bolsters this interpretation. Although that judgment concerned the legal position prior to the entry into force of the Treaty of Amsterdam, the subsequent Treaty amendments have maintained the link with the internal market (or more specifically, the free movement of persons, following the Treaty of Lisbon amendments) as the primary factor for interpreting the EU's borders powers, even though it is not the sole factor, as it was for the EC's visa list powers when the Court first ruled on their scope.[117]

Finally, does Article 72 TFEU, which refers to Member States' responsibilities as regards law, order, and security, limit the EU's competence? Since the Court of Justice has always interpreted derogations from the EC Treaty restrictively, and long ago rejected the idea that all immigration issues must be considered matters of public order,[118] the better view is that Article 72 simply confirms that implementation of measures adopted pursuant to Title V of Part Three of the TFEU is left to the Member States' authorities, particularly as regards coercive measures. This is consistent with the specific limits placed upon EU police and criminal law bodies. The EU's borders control agency must therefore continue to be limited to supporting actions of national authorities.[119]

Finally, the revised Treaty, as noted above, contains now a power to adopt measures related to an 'integrated management system' for the external borders. A definition of this concept can be found in JHA Council conclusions adopted in December 2006, which specify that there are five 'dimensions' to the concept:

- Border control (checks and surveillance) as defined in the Schengen Borders Code, including relevant risk analysis and crime intelligence.
- Detection and investigation of cross border crime in coordination with all competent law enforcement authorities.
- The four-tier access control model (measures in third countries, cooperation with neighbouring countries, border control, control measures within the area of free movement, including return).

---

[114] See Case C-241/05 *Bot* [2006] ECR I-9627, para 41.

[115] On the competence issues, see S Peers, 'EU Immigration and Asylum Law: Internal Market Model or Human Rights Model?', in T Tridimas and P Nebbia, eds, *EU Law for the Twenty-First Century: Rethinking the New Legal Order, Vol 1* (Hart, 2004), 345 at 356. For a detailed comparison of the various rules on free movement and their external elements, see S Peers, 'EU Borders and Globalisation' (n 110 above).   [116] See discussion in 3.4.1 below.

[117] Case C-170/96 *Commission v Council* [1998] ECR I-2763.

[118] See Joined Cases 281–283, 285, and 287/85 *Germany and others v Commission* [1987] ECR 3203.   [119] On the Agency, see 3.10.1 below. On Arts 72 and 73 generally, see 2.2.3.2 above.

- Inter-agency cooperation for border management (border guards, customs, police, national security, and other relevant authorities) and international cooperation.
- Coordination and coherence of the activities of Member States and Institutions and other bodies of the Community and the Union.

While it may be tempting to adopt the definition in these Council conclusions in order to define the scope of the powers conferred by the new legal base, this approach should be rejected. The basic problem with that analysis is that the TFEU contains specific legal bases relating to criminal law, policing, expulsion, and customs cooperation, as well as specific provisions on internal security,[120] which are subject to some extent to different rules as regards decision-making; the scope of EU competence; participation by Member States and non-Member States; and even (as regards operational police actions) the jurisdiction of the Court of Justice.[121] In the absence of anything in the Treaty to indicate such an all-encompassing notion of 'integrated border management', these various Treaty provisions should each be regarded as a *lex specialis*.

It is submitted therefore that while the Council may wish to develop a broad concept of integrated border management for political purposes, from a legal point of view the correct approach to interpreting the legal base concerning this issue is much narrower. However, it cannot be interpreted so narrowly as to add nothing to the powers relating to external border checks, considering that the Treaty drafters took the decision to add a new power for the Union on this issue. The best interpretation is therefore that the legal base should instead be understood to cover the regulation of the *link* between external border control and the activities regulated pursuant to other provisions of the Treaty. But in light of the variations in the different legal bases as regards opt-outs, the association of non-Member States, competence, and decision-making, a dividing line has to be drawn, for example, between the regulation of the movement of goods at the external borders per se (subject to the customs cooperation powers) and the regulation of the synergy between the different borders administrations (subject to the 'integrated management' powers).[122]

3.2.5. Territorial scope[123]

The small number of EU and EC measures in this area agreed before the Treaty of Amsterdam are applicable to all Member States.[124] But most law in this area

---

[120] See generally 2.2.3.1 above.   [121] Art 276 TFEU: see 2.2.2.2 above.

[122] The customs cooperation powers (formerly Art 135 EC), as amended by the Treaty of Lisbon, are now set out in the internal market provisions of the TFEU (Art 33). See further 12.4.1 below.

[123] For a general overview of the rules on the territorial scope of all JHA measures, see 2.2.5 above.   [124] See 3.2.1.3 above.

derives from the Schengen *acquis* or was adopted after the Treaty of Amsterdam, and therefore is subject to the complex opt-out rules set out in the Treaty of Amsterdam, as amended by the Treaty of Lisbon, which were agreed in order to settle the question of whether to abolish internal border checks between all Member States. To avoid convoluted repetitions of the territorial scope of the relevant rules, this chapter refers throughout to the position of 'Member States', on the understanding that most of the rules discussed are not applicable to all Member States, and are moreover applicable to some non-Member States. Readers who are concerned to know precisely which States are covered by which rules should refer to the following overview.

First of all, the position of the UK and Ireland as regards border controls is affected by no fewer than three Protocols attached to the EC Treaty (and now to the TEU and the TFEU) by the Treaty of Amsterdam: the Protocols concerning internal border controls, Schengen, and Title IV. The second and third of these Protocols were substantively amended by the Treaty of Lisbon, which also made purely technical amendments to the first Protocol.

The first of these Protocols, as amended by the Treaty of Lisbon, specifies that notwithstanding any Treaty Article or measure, or judgment of the Court of Justice, the UK 'shall be entitled... to exercise... such controls on persons seeking to enter' the UK across an EU internal border 'as it may consider necessary' to check that they do have the right to enter pursuant to the European Economic Area (EEA) agreement and other treaties,[125] and 'of determining whether or not to grant other persons permission to enter the United Kingdom'. In particular, '[n]othing in Articles 26 and 77' of the TFEU, or any other Treaty or secondary measure, 'shall prejudice the right of the United Kingdom to adopt or exercise any such controls'.[126] The UK and Ireland are entitled to maintain arrangements between themselves on simplified border crossing, and as long as they do, then Ireland is equally entitled to maintain checks on its internal borders with other Member States.[127] The other Member States are accordingly authorized to maintain controls on their internal borders with the UK and Ireland.[128]

It is clear from the wording of this Protocol that the UK and Ireland cannot in any circumstances be forced to drop their internal border controls with other Member States. However, the Protocol does not give those Member States full discretion to determine the *consequences* of irregular crossing of their internal borders. In particular, in light of the *Wijsenbeek* judgment, those Member States are limited in the extent and type of penalties they can apply to EU citizens who cross the border without authorization.[129] The scope of the discretion conferred by the Protocol is also limited to checks at the internal borders; it does not give

---

[125] On the EEA agreement, see 3.4.2 below.   [126] Art 1 of the Protocol.
[127] Art 2 of the Protocol.   [128] Art 3 of the Protocol.   [129] See 3.4.1 below.

any power to refuse entry to persons who have the right to enter pursuant to EU free movement law or certain other measures.[130]

Secondly, as for the Schengen Protocol,[131] the UK and Ireland have not as such opted in to any part of the Schengen *acquis* (as integrated into the EC legal order in 1999) in the area of border controls. However, this begs the question as to whether the Protocol applies to measures 'building on the Schengen acquis' adopted after May 1999, and the consequences if it does (see below).

Finally, the Title IV Protocol (now the Title V Protocol) has been invoked a few times as regards measures in this area,[132] with both Member States opting in to the passenger data Directive,[133] the UK (but not Ireland) opting in to the ARGO programme,[134] and the UK (but again, not Ireland) seeking to opt in to the Regulations on the EU border agency and the security features of EU passports.[135] The latter attempts by the UK to opt in were rebuffed by the Council, resulting in unsuccessful challenges by the UK to the Council's decisions before the Court of Justice, which held that before the UK could opt in to those measures, it had to opt in to the underlying measures set out in the original Schengen *acquis*, pursuant to the rules in the Schengen Protocol.[136] As argued previously, the Court's interpretation of the relevant Protocols is incorrect.[137] Be that as it may, the consequence of the judgments is that the UK and Ireland cannot opt in to any EU legislation relating to external or internal borders, as long as they do not opt in to any of the underlying rules regulating those issues (in particular, the Schengen Borders Code). It should be noted that the Treaty of Lisbon did not alter the legal position on this point.

Next, the position of Denmark as regards border controls was governed, before the entry into force of the Treaty of Lisbon, by both the Schengen Protocol and the Protocol on Denmark; both Protocols were subsequently amended by the Treaty of Lisbon.[138] The former Protocol provided originally that Denmark was bound by those provisions of the Schengen *acquis* allocated to the former Title IV EC, but only as public international law; the Treaty of Lisbon has repealed this provision.[139] The latter Protocol provides (both before and after the Treaty of Lisbon) that as regards all Title IV EC (now Title V TFEU) measures building on the Schengen *acquis*, Denmark can decide within six months of their adoption

---

[130] See 3.4.1 and 3.4.2 below.

[131] For detailed discussion of this Protocol, see 2.2.5.1.3 above.

[132] For detailed discussion of this Protocol, see 2.2.5.1.2 above.

[133] This Directive is discussed in 7.5.2 below.   [134] See 3.11 below.

[135] See 3.9 below.

[136] Cases C-77/05 *UK v Council* [2007] ECR I-11459 and C-137/05 *UK v Council* [2007] ECR I-11593. See also by analogy Case C-482/08 *UK v Council*, pending (opinion of 24 June 2010), as regards an attempt of the UK to opt in fully to a measure governing law enforcement access to the Visa Information System.   [137] See the second edition of this book, at 58–59.

[138] On the Danish position generally, see 2.2.5.2 above.

[139] Previous Art 3, Schengen Protocol. See now Art 2, Schengen Protocol, which refers to the Protocol on Denmark for the legal position of Denmark as regards the Schengen *acquis*.

whether to apply them in its national law, in which case those measures bind Denmark and the other participating Member States as a matter of public international law.[140] Denmark has consistently applied this option to measures concerning border controls (and visas),[141] although it was not able to use this power as regards two issues discussed in this chapter (the ARGO programme and international treaties),[142] as these measures did not build upon the Schengen *acquis*.

Thirdly, the Member States joining the EU in 2004 and 2007 (the 'newer Member States') were subject upon accession to only part of the Schengen *acquis* and measures building upon it in this area.[143] In particular, the rules on external border controls (except for checks in the SIS) applied immediately. Also, the ARGO programme also applied immediately upon accession, as it did not build upon the Schengen *acquis*.[144] Conversely, the abolition of internal border controls would not apply until the entire Schengen *acquis* (and subsequent measures building on it) was fully applied to the newer Member States. As for measures adopted following the agreement on the Treaty of Accession, each measure indicates whether it applied immediately to the newer Member States or only after the extension of the Schengen *acquis* to those States.[145] Moreover, the 2003 Accession Treaty made a number of technical amendments to secondary measures to refer to the rules in the newer Member States,[146] and special legislation was adopted to regulate transit via the newer Member States in the interim period before the Schengen *acquis* applied to them fully.[147]

The extension of the Schengen area to the newer Member States was delayed when it proved impossible to implement a new version of the Schengen Information System (SIS II) when initially planned, due to the delays in proposing and negotiating the legislation and to operational problems.[148] This issue was eventually tackled by adopting a proposal from Portugal for the development of

---

[140] Current Art 4, Protocol on Denmark; see, before the entry into force of the Treaty of Lisbon, the former Art 5 of that Protocol.

[141] Council docs 14241/01, 24 Nov 2001; 9963/02, 20 June 2002; 14807/03, 14 Nov 2003; 14822/03, 14 Nov 2003; 14588/03, 14 Nov 2003; 5096/04, 9 Jan 2004; 12195/04, 10 Sep 2004; 12111/04, 7 Sep 2004; 12907/04, 29 Sep 2004; 10087/05, 14 Jun 2005; 5420/06, 17 Jan 2006; 12637/06, 14 Sep 2006; 7613/07, 16 Mar 2007; 8557/07, 18 Apr 2007; 11252/07, 26 June 2007; 13122/07, 20 Sep 2007; 12641/08, 5 Sep 2008; 8071/09, 26 Mar 2009; 12772/09, 28 Aug 2009; 14109/09, 6 Oct 2009; and 8339/10, 8 Apr 2010.   [142] See 3.11 and 3.12 below respectively.

[143] On the position of the newer Member States, see Art 3 of the 2003 Treaty of Accession and Annex I to that Treaty ([2003] OJ L 236), along with Art 4 of the 2005 Treaty of Accession and Annex II to that Treaty ([2005] OJ L 157/203). For a general discussion of the issue, see 2.2.5.3 above.   [144] On the substance, see 3.11 below.

[145] See, for instance, the Schengen Borders Code (Reg 562/2006, [2006] OJ L 105/1), which applied fully to all (Schengen) Member States immediately, except for the rules on internal border control abolition and the SIS, which did not (or will not) apply to newer Member States until the Schengen rules were (or will be) fully extended to them. On the substance of the Borders Code, see 3.6.1 below.

[146] Annex II, part 18, to the 2003 Accession Treaty ([2003] OJ L 236). There were no such amendments in the 2005 Accession Treaty ([2005] OJ L 157).   [147] See 4.2.5 below.

[148] See the 9th report of the House of Lords EU Select Committee (2006–07), para 23.

an 'SIS One4All', which extended the existing SIS to the new Member States (a solution which had previously been thought to be technically impossible). The JHA Council agreed upon this proposal in December 2006, setting a new date for the enlargement of the Schengen zone between end-2007 and March 2008, and accepting the resulting delay in the development of SIS II.[149] The 'SIS One4All' proposal was then implemented successfully, and the Schengen area was duly fully extended to nine new Member States (all except Cyprus, Romania, and Bulgaria) as from 21 December 2007, and as from 30 March 2008 as regards air borders.[150]

Fourthly, as for the position of non-Member States,[151] the Schengen and EU rules discussed in this Chapter are all fully applicable to Norway and Iceland as from March 2001 (or subsequently, for measures adopted later), following the Schengen association agreement with those States,[152] except for the ARGO programme, which did not build on the Schengen *acquis*.[153] Also, these States have agreed further treaties with the EU which set out specific arrangements for involvement in the EU borders agency and the Borders Fund,[154] along with their participation in committees which assist the Commission when it adopts implementing measures, in addition to those States' participation in the relevant Regulations.[155]

As for Switzerland, the Schengen association agreement signed with that country in 2004 entered into force on 1 March 2008,[156] and the Schengen *acquis* was then extended fully to Switzerland on 12 December 2008, except for the application of the *acquis* to air borders, which took place on 29 March 2009.[157] Switzerland has also agreed a treaty with the EU as regards its participation in the EU's border agency,[158] and also will participate along with Norway and Iceland in the treaties concerning the EU's border fund and participation in relevant Commission committees.[159]

---

[149] See the conclusions of the JHA Council of 2–3 Dec 2006 on these various issues.

[150] [2007] OJ L 323/34. The *acquis* regarding the SIS in fact applied to these new Member States from 1 Sep 2007, except that before the full application of the Schengen rules to the new Member States, those States were not able to enter alerts banning entry to third-country nationals into the SIS and were not obliged to act on such alerts ([2007] OJ L 179/46). Romania and Bulgaria now have limited use of the SIS, as a precursor to full participation in Schengen from 2011: [2010] OJ L 166/17.   [151] See further 2.2.5.4 above.

[152] [1999] OJ L 176/35.   [153] On the substance, see 3.11 below.   [154] See 3.11 below.

[155] Respectively [2007] OJ L 188/19; [2010] OJ L 169/22; and COM (2009) 605 and 606, 30 Oct 2009. The first treaty was signed in Feb 2007, but is not in force yet. The second treaty was signed in Mar 2010, but is not yet in force either. The Council agreed to sign the third treaty in July 2010.

[156] [2008] OJ L 53/18. For the treaty, see [2008] OJ L 53/52. On the parallel treaty on asylum applications, see 5.2.5 below.

[157] [2008] OJ L 327/15. The SIS had previously been extended first to Switzerland, subject to certain restrictions until the full extension of the Schengen *acquis* to that country ([2008] OJ L 149/74; see n 150 above on the equivalent restrictions for new Member States).

[158] COM (2009) 255, 4 June 2009. The treaty entered into force on 1 Aug 2010.

[159] On those treaties, see n 155 above.

The rules discussed in this chapter will also apply to Liechtenstein, pursuant to the relevant Protocol to the Schengen association agreement with Switzerland, once that Protocol is ratified and enters into force.[160] At that time, the EU–Swiss treaty on association with the EU borders agency will also apply to Liechtenstein, as will the treaties concerning the EU's border fund and participation in relevant Commission committees.[161] Again, for Switzerland and Liechtenstein, special legislation was adopted to regulate transit via those States in the interim period before the Schengen *acquis* applied to them fully.[162]

Finally, as regards the EU's power after the Treaty of Lisbon to regulate issues relating to passports and similar documents, it should be noted that any measures adopted on the basis of this power will not build upon the Schengen *acquis*, because of their link to the free movement of all EU citizens.[163] This means that if these measures apply to associated States, this would take place, if at all, on the basis of association agreements. For the UK, Ireland, and Denmark, the general Title V opt-out rules, rather than the Schengen rules, will apply.

3.3. Human rights

3.3.1. International human rights law

The starting point for any analysis of the application of human rights rules to migration issues is that as a general rule, there is no human right for anyone to enter or stay in a foreign country. However, human rights rules do entail a right to enter or stay in particular circumstances, although the precise scope of those circumstances is open to some dispute. To date, human rights rules have had more impact in practice on preventing the expulsion of persons who have a claim for asylum or some other need for international protection, or who have been resident for long periods.[164] The impact of human rights rules on entry is less clear. However, there are cases in which there is a right of entry for family reunion,[165] and arguably there is a right of entry in order to make a claim for international protection, since Article 33 of the Geneva Convention on refugee status (the *non-refoulement* clause) and Article 3 of the European Convention of Human Rights (ECHR) and other relevant ECHR Articles are applicable to persons who reach Member States' borders and make claims for protection.[166] Since the latter

---

[160] COM (2006) 752, 1 Dec 2006, signed in Feb 2008 ([2008] OJ L 83/3 and 5).

[161] See nn 158 and 155 above.   [162] See 4.2.5 below.

[163] In light of the Court of Justice's judgments in the *UK v Council* cases (n 136 above), it is hard to imagine a measure which falls within the scope of the external borders legal base but which does not build upon the Schengen *acquis*.   [164] See 5.3 and 6.3 below respectively.

[165] See 6.3.1 below.

[166] For detailed comments and further references, see ch 14 of S Peers and N Rogers, *EU Immigration and Asylum Law: Text and Commentary* (1st edn, Martinus Nijhoff, 2006).

category of entrants does not usually make a prior formal application for entry which can be examined by the host State's authorities and often attempts to cross the border irregularly, the rules governing entry control at the borders can be particularly important to their practical ability to enter and make a claim for protection. Also, Article 31 of the Geneva Convention exempts refugees who enter or stay without authorization from penalties, under certain circumstances.[167]

In which cases can persons claim the right to short-term entry? First of all, examining the rights set out in the ECHR, given their pre-eminence as a source of the general principles of EU law, their important role in connection with the EU Charter of Rights, and the EU's obligation to accede to the ECHR,[168] it is arguable that the 'right to respect for family life and private life' set out in Article 8 ECHR entails the right to short-term visits to family members, as broadly defined in light of the relationships between adult children and their parents and between adult siblings.[169] This principle could even apply to visits to friends, which would fall within the scope of 'private life'. To date, there is no judgment of the European Court of Human Rights (ECtHR) to confirm whether such an argument would be successful or not.[170]

The rights to freedom of religion, expression, and association in Articles 9–11 ECHR could equally serve as a basis for a right for short-term admission, in order (for example) to participate in a religious event, to express a political, artistic, or other opinion, or to join with a group of like-minded protesters demonstrating at a particular event. In the case of *Piermont* the Human Rights Court ruled that an expulsion of a person along with the ban on re-entry into the territory, and a refusal of entry into another territory, merely for expressing her political opinions, violated the right to freedom of expression guaranteed by Article 10 ECHR.[171] The Court has subsequently confirmed the obvious implication that in some cases at least, there must be a right to initial entry (or re-entry) to a person at least for the purpose of expressing an opinion and for the purposes of freedom of religion (Article 9 ECHR);[172] this principle must logically also apply (given the similar wording of Articles 9–11 ECHR) to the freedom of association. In each case, of course, an interference with the right could still be justified on grounds of for example, public order, if prescribed by law and necessary and proportionate in a democratic society.[173]

---

[167] See 7.3.2 below for details.   [168] See 2.3 above.

[169] As regards admission and stay for long periods, Art 8 appears to apply to a narrower scope of family members (see 6.3.1 below), but such restrictions of scope should not be applicable to family *visits*, which constitute a normal part of family life as enjoyed by adults and which in principle do not entail immigration to the host State.

[170] See, however, the admissibility decision in *Bartik v Russia* (16 Sep 2004, unreported), which fails to consider the argument made ibid.   [171] *Piermont v France* (A-314).

[172] See *Nolan and K v Russia*, 12 Feb 2009; *Perry v Latvia*, 8 Nov 2007; and *Cox v Turkey*, 20 May 2010. See also, by analogy, *Women on Waves v Portugal*, 3 Feb 2009.

[173] In *Piermont*, the invocation of Art 10(2) failed because the opinions in question were non-violent, were spoken at a peaceful demonstration, and did not result in any disorder. In *Nolan*, the

However, Article 16 ECHR provides that nothing in Articles 10, 11, or 14 of the Convention (Article 14 concerns non-discrimination) can prevent States 'from imposing restrictions on the political activity' of foreigners. The judgment in *Piermont* reasoned that Article 16 was not applicable since the applicant was both the national of another EU Member State and a Member of the European Parliament, leaving open the question of whether the subsequent creation of EU citizenship might afford even greater protection. Even the judges dissenting from the majority judgment accepted that '[a]ccount must be taken of the increased internationalisation of politics in modern circumstances', entailing limits on the application of Article 16; in their view, Article 16 merely accorded more discretion (but not absolute discretion) to a State when restricting foreigners' political expression than when restricting its own nationals' expression. In any event, Article 16 is not applicable to the freedom of religion pursuant to Article 9, or to the expression of *non*-political opinion. Moreover, the dissenting judges did not question the underlying principle that Article 10 entails rights in relation to immigration law. It should be emphasized that the applicant had *not* been exercising a free movement right under EU free movement law when she expressed her opinion, as the dispute concerned French territories where there is no right of free movement under EU law; so it follows that Article 10 curtails States' immigration law powers even in the absence of a free movement right.

Several other provisions of the Convention are relevant. Article 5 provides that a person can be deprived of liberty following a 'lawful arrest or detention...to prevent his [or her] effecting an unauthorized entry into the country', subject to obligations to inform that person about the grounds for detention, to permit judicial review, and to compensate persons in case of breaches of that Article.[174] Article 6 gives a right to a fair trial to 'everyone' to determine 'civil rights or obligations' or 'any criminal charge', but the Human Rights Court has held that this Article is not applicable to cases concerning immigration or asylum.[175] However, if an immigration or asylum case falls within the scope of another right protected by the Convention, there are in-built procedural protections connected with those rights.[176] Similarly, Articles 13 (the right to an effective remedy) and 14 (the right to non-discrimination) only apply where one of the ECHR rights has been violated. It should also be kept in mind that the right to respect for private

---

Art 9(2) ECHR defence failed because there was no evidence offered to prove the alleged risk to 'national security' of the person concerned; moreover, Art 9(2) ECHR does not list 'national security' as a possible ground to justify interference with the freedom of religion. In *Perry*, the national rules were not 'prescribed by law'. In *Cox*, the restrictions were disproportionate because although the applicant's opinions were controversial, she did not support violence.

[174] These provisions of Art 5 ECHR apply equally to expulsion, and so are considered in 7.3.2 below.

[175] *Maaouia v France* (Reports 2000-X). However, a State may be obliged to admit a person to take part in civil proceedings: see Commission decision in *Mangov v Greece* (18 Feb 1993, unreported).

[176] See the discussion in 6.3.3 below, and in particular the judgment in *Nolan* (n 172 above).

life set out in Article 8 also comprises a right to protection of personal data, which is increasingly relevant as regards border controls.[177]

As for the Protocols to the ECHR, the ECHR organs have held that the right to property set out in the First Protocol does not entail a right to permanent residence for foreigners in order to enjoy access to their property, leaving open the argument that there is a right to short-term entry to that end.[178]

Next, the Fourth Protocol contains a number of important rights, although it has not been ratified by two Member States.[179] Article 2(1) of the Protocol states that '[e]veryone lawfully within the territory of a State shall, within that territory, have the right to liberty of movement and freedom to choose his [or her] residence'. Article 2(2) of that Protocol provides that '[e]veryone shall be free to leave any country, including his [or her] own'. However, States may set limitations on these rights similar to the limits they may place on Articles 8–11 ECHR, and they may set broader 'public interest' restrictions on the first of these rights.[180] Also, Article 3 of the Protocol gives nationals the right to enter the territory of their own State, and freedom from expulsion from their own State; this provision is considered in Chapter 7.[181]

The jurisprudence on Article 2 of the Fourth Protocol makes clear that Article 2(1) only applies to those lawfully within the country; it does not apply to persons following their expulsion or if they have not been legally admitted to the territory.[182] However, it appears clear from the *Piermont* judgment and the wording of Article 2(1) that both visitors and residents fall within the scope of the right.[183]

As for Article 2(2) of the Fourth Protocol, the Human Rights Court has held that in principle it prohibits States from seizing an individual's passport, unless this can be justified by significant grounds of public order, for example.[184] Equally

---

[177] On the relevant ECtHR case law, see further 12.3.1 below; on EU data protection legislation, see 3.4.3 below. There is also a specific Convention of the Council of Europe concerning protection of personal data (ETS 108), which has been ratified by all Member States.

[178] Decision in *Ilic v Croatia* (Reports 2000-X).   [179] Greece and the UK.

[180] Art 2(3) and (4), Fourth Protocol.

[181] Also, the provisions prohibiting the collective expulsion of foreigners (Art 4, Fourth Protocol), and the procedural rights against expulsion for individual foreigners (Art 1, Seventh Protocol) are considered further in 7.3 below.

[182] *Piermont v France* (n 171 above). In the subsequent judgment of *Tatishvili v Russia* (22 Feb 2007), the Court found that a citizen of the former USSR fell within the scope of Art 2 of Protocol 4 in Russia, since at the relevant time such persons did not need a residence permit in Russia. In *Bolat v Russia* (2006 ECHR-XI), a violation of Art 2(1) was found as regards a foreigner, but in this case the Human Rights Court implicitly assumed that the person concerned was 'lawfully within' Russia for the purpose of Art 2.

[183] On other forms of restrictions on free movement, see, for example, the judgments in *Raimondo v Italy* (Series A-281); *Labita v Italy* (Reports 2000-IV); *Denizci and others v Cyprus* (Reports 2001-V); *Luordo v Italy* (Reports 2003-IX); *Antonenkov and others v Ukraine* (22 Nov 2005); and *Timishev v Russia* (12 Dec 2005).

[184] *Baumann v France* (Reports 2001-V); *Napijalo v Croatia* (13 Nov 2003); *Földes and Földesné Hajlik v Hungary* (31 Oct 2006).

a refusal to issue a travel document in the first place breaches Article 2(2),[185] as does a ban on travel outside the country.[186] Moreover, the Court has found that a withdrawal of a passport and a denial of exit from a territory can in certain circumstances violate Article 8 of the Convention, thus applying equivalent obligations to States which have not ratified the Fourth Protocol.[187] It laid particular stress on the cross-border family and economic links which many individuals enjoy in the modern world.

Despite the non-ratification of the Fourth Protocol by some Member States, it should be noted that the rights set out in Article 2 of that Protocol are enshrined in nearly identical terms in Article 12(1)–(3) of the International Covenant on Civil and Political Rights (ICCPR), which all Member States have ratified.[188]

3.3.2. Application to EU law

To what extent do the most relevant rights set out in international human rights law form part of the general principles of EU law? The Court of Justice has not yet ruled on whether the rights set out in Article 2 of the Fourth ECHR Protocol are protected as part of the general principles of EU law, but it has referred to certain provisions of EU free movement law as specific manifestations of the provisions of Article 2,[189] and it does recognize the principles set out in Article 3 of the Fourth Protocol that states cannot expel and must admit their own nationals.[190] So it seems probable that the rights set out in Article 2 of the Fourth Protocol also form part of the general principles of EU law. In fact, several provisions of EU immigration and asylum legislation specifically set out the right to free movement within a Member State,[191] and EU law might also be relevant for determining

---

[185] *Bartik v Russia* (21 Dec 2006). In this case the objective of protecting 'state secrets' was a legitimate ground for restriction pursuant to Art 2(3) of the Protocol, but nonetheless the restriction was disproportionate in all the circumstances.

[186] *Riener v Bulgaria* (23 May 2006). In this case the objective of ensuring payment of tax was a legitimate ground for restriction pursuant to Art 2(3) of the Protocol, but again the restriction was disproportionate in all the circumstances. See also *AE v Poland* (31 Mar 2009) and *Bessenyei v Hungary* (21 Oct 2008).　　　　　　　　　　　　　　[187] *Iletmis v Turkey* (Reports 2005-XII).

[188] On the implications of this, see 2.3 above. On the interpretation of the ICCPR provisions, see S Joseph, J Schultz, and M Castan, *The International Covenant on Civil and Political Rights: Cases, Materials and Commentary* (2nd edn, OUP, 2004), 348–364.

[189] Case 36/75 *Rutili* [1975] ECR 1219, para 28. See subsequently Case C-100/01 *Olazabal* [2002] ECR I-10981, where the Court failed to consider the human rights context.

[190] See 7.3.4 below.

[191] Art 7 of Dir 2003/9 on reception conditions for asylum seekers ([2003] OJ L 31/18) sets out permitted restrictions; Arts 11(1)(f) and 21(1) of Dir 2003/109 on long-term residents ([2003] OJ L 16/44) requires equal treatment with nationals, as does Art 14(1)(h) Dir 2009/50, the 'Blue Card' Directive on highly-skilled migration ([2009] OJ L 155/17); and Art 32 of Dir 2004/83 on refugee and subsidiary protection status ([2004] OJ L 304/12) requires equal treatment with third-country nationals. However, Dirs 2001/55 on temporary protection ([2001] OJ L 212/12); 2003/86 on family reunion ([2003] OJ L 251/12); 2004/81 on victims of trafficking ([2004] OJ L 261/19); 2004/114

whether a person is 'lawfully' within a Member State's territory. Moreover, it is arguable that within the scope of EU law, the relevant ECHR principles do not only apply within each individual Member State, but also have a *cross-border dimension*.

On the other hand, it is striking that the rights set out in Article 2 of the Fourth Protocol to the ECHR are not set out in the EU's Charter of Fundamental Rights. The Charter recognizes instead that EU citizens have the right to move and reside freely across the EU, while third-country nationals may be granted that right.[192] However, the wording of Article 6 of the revised TEU clearly indicates that the general principles and the Charter constitute separate sources of human rights protection in EU law. So despite the high degree of overlap between these two sources, it is entirely possible that one will be wider in scope than the other. In that case, the rights concerned are still protected pursuant to the general principles, even if the Charter does not refer to those rights. In any case, Member States will nonetheless have to uphold their obligations under international human rights treaties which they have ratified.[193] It remains to be seen whether the EU itself will ratify the Fourth Protocol, pursuant to the decision to begin negotiations for its accession to the ECHR.[194]

As for Article 6 of the ECHR, even though the ECHR does not confer procedural rights in general relating to refusal of entry at the border, it should be recalled that rights to procedural protection (a fair trial and effective remedies) are recognized as forming part of the general principles of EU law and the EU Charter (which also draw upon national constitutional principles as a source of law), and that such rights have a *wider scope* within EU law than they do under the ECHR.[195] Arguably, therefore, there is a right to a fair trial and effective remedies in relation to refusals of entry at the border; but at the very least, such rights should be recognized as regards visits to family members and, since the general principles of EU law and the Charter recognize the right to carry on a business,[196] short-term admission for business visits. The general principles and the Charter also recognize the rights to freedom of religion, expression, and association.[197]

Finally, it should be noted that the EU's border control legislation makes express provision for human rights in several respects. The Schengen Borders Code provides that the obligation to impose penalties for unauthorized crossing of external borders is 'without prejudice to' Member States' international

---

on students and others ([2004] OJ L 375/12); and 2005/71 on researchers ([2005] L 289/15) make no express reference to the right. Neither does EU visas or borders legislation.

[192] Art 45 of the Charter ([2007] OJ C 303).   [193] See generally 2.3 above.

[194] Press release of the JHA Council, 3–4 June 2010. The content of the decision to begin negotiations is not known.   [195] See 6.3.4 below.

[196] As regards the general principles, see, for example, Joined Cases C-184/02 and C-223/02 *Spain and Finland v Council and EP* [2004] ECR I-7789, paras 51 and 52. As for the Charter, see Art 16.

[197] See Arts 10–12 of the Charter and Case C-112/00 *Schmidberger* [2003] ECR I-5659.

protection obligations,[198] and furthermore the obligation to refuse entry to persons who do not meet the criteria for entry is 'without prejudice to the application of special provisions concerning the right of asylum and to international protection'.[199] The Borders Code also sets out procedural rights in the event of refusal of entry.[200] There are also data protection safeguards in the current rules governing the SIS, and the legislation governing the second-generation System sets out both data protection safeguards and procedural rights.[201]

3.4. The impact of other EU law

The debate over the extent to which 'other' (ie non-JHA) EU law applies to borders issues is not yet over.[202] Despite the powers now conferred by Article 77 TFEU (formerly Article 62 EC) regarding border controls and the special institutional rules applicable to them, other EU law rules still have an important impact on these issues, particularly in the area of free movement law, but association agreements and data protection law are also relevant. In case of any conflict between EC law (as it then was) and the initial Schengen *acquis* as integrated into the EC legal order in 1999, it should be kept in mind that EC law prevailed, according to the original version of the Schengen Protocol.[203] In the event of conflict between measures building on the *acquis* and EU free movement law; association agreements; the EU's general principles of law; or the EU Charter of Fundamental Rights (since the Treaty of Lisbon); the latter four sources of law are hierarchically superior to secondary EU law measures.[204] In any case, most measures building upon the Schengen *acquis* provide in some form expressly for priority for EU free movement law or human rights law.[205]

3.4.1. Free movement law

The starting point for any discussion of the effect of free movement law in this area is Article 14 EC (now Article 26 TFEU), concerning the abolition of internal border checks. The legal effect of Article 14 as regards checks on persons was

---

[198] Art 4(3) of Reg 562/2006 ([2006] OJ L 105/1). For more on the Code, see 3.6.1 below.

[199] Art 13(1) of the Regulation, ibid.   [200] Art 13(2) and (3) and Annex V of the Code.

[201] See further 3.7 and 12.6.1.1 below.

[202] The question of the application of EC law to borders issues *prior* to the Treaty of Amsterdam is considered in 3.2.1 above.   [203] See 2.2.2.3 above.

[204] See further 2.4.2 above.

[205] On the priority of human rights law, see 3.3.2 above; on the priority of EU free movement law, see 3.4.1 below.

finally clarified by the *Wijsenbeek* judgment of the Court of Justice in 1999.[206] Late
in 1993, after the entry into force of the original TEU but before the application
of the Schengen Convention, a Dutch MEP returning to the Netherlands had
refused to present his documents to Dutch border guards, and had faced a criminal conviction imposing a small fine (or a day's imprisonment) as a result. The
Court of Justice ruled that at the relevant time, Article 14 (then Article 7a) EC
(now Article 26 TFEU) did not have the automatic effect of abolishing internal
border checks between Member States. Such abolition could only result from
the harmonization of national law on visas, external border checks, asylum, and
immigration. It was not clear whether this harmonization of national law could
be attained at the time by Schengen or third pillar measures, or only by means
of Community legislation,[207] although given the subsequent development of EC
(now EU) rules, the point is now moot.

Similarly, the right of EU citizens to 'move and reside freely' within the
EU pursuant to Article 18 EC (Article 8a EC at the time of the dispute; now
Article 21 TFEU) did not preclude Member States from checking whether persons were indeed citizens of the Union who could benefit from that right. As for
the punishment imposed by the authorities, the Court reiterated the established
principle of free movement law that '[i]n the absence of Community rules governing the matter, the Member States remain competent to impose penalties
for breach of' obligations related to control of the movement and residence of
persons, 'provided that the penalties applicable are comparable to those which
apply to similar national infringements. However, Member States may not lay
down a penalty so disproportionate as to create an obstacle to the free movement
of persons, such as a term of imprisonment.' The Court then expressly stated that
'[t]he same considerations apply as regards breach of the obligation to present an
identity card or a passport upon entry into the territory of a Member State'.[208]
There is no reason to doubt that the Court's ruling on the issue of limited penalties for breach of such obligations applies fully to the UK, Ireland, Denmark, and
the new Member States, despite their particular positions as regards the abolition
of internal borders.[209]

The Court's judgment in *Wijsenbeek* did not rule on the legal effects of the
Declarations to the Single European Act, on whether the EU institutions were
subject to an obligation imposed by Article 14 EC (now Article 26 TFEU), on
whether that Article also applies to third-country nationals, on the effect of the
Treaty of Amsterdam (or, obviously, the later Treaty of Lisbon), or on the effect
of the Schengen *acquis*. These issues were all addressed in the Opinion of the
Advocate General, who concluded: that the declarations to the SEA could not

---

[206] Case C-378/97 *Wijsenbeek* [1999] ECR I-6207.
[207] Paras 40 and 43 of the judgment suggest the former interpretation, while para 42 suggests the
latter. See also discussion of the Advocate General's Opinion, below.
[208] On these established principles, see further below in this section.   [209] See 3.2.5 above.

affect the interpretation of the Treaty;[210] that Article 14 EC obliged the EC institutions to act in order to abolish internal border checks;[211] that the personal scope
of that Article necessarily included third-country nationals;[212] that the direct
effect of that Article was impossible before the EC gained the relevant powers
to act in the Treaty of Amsterdam; that the five-year deadline set by that Treaty
superseded the end-1992 deadline set by the previous Article 14 EC;[213] and that
the validity of national measures restricting EU citizens' right to 'move and reside
freely' should be assessed by national courts in light of the Schengen rules as they
applied before the entry into force of the Treaty of Amsterdam.[214]

　　This judgment left much to be decided in future, particularly regarding the
relationship between Article 14 EC (as it then was) and the Schengen rules abolishing internal border checks and harmonizing the other issues referred to by
the Court, which were integrated into EC law (as it then was) by the Treaty
of Amsterdam. Moreover, the Court did not address the question of whether
Article 14 EC (as it then was) contained binding obligations for *EC institutions*, as
distinct from directly effective rights. What can be discerned from the *Wijsenbeek*
judgment is that the Court has expressly recognized that the negative legal integration resulting from the abolition of internal border controls was subject to
the adoption of considerable positive legal integration measures. There was an
obligation to accompany free movement with security measures; but conversely
it should not be forgotten that those security measures are subsidiary, according
to the logic of the Court's analysis, to the abolition of internal borders provided
for in the previous Article 14 EC.

　　Although, due to the limitations on the jurisdiction of the Court of Justice in
this area, it has not been able to examine any further issues concerning the previous Article 14 EC, the Court has been able to build up a considerable jurisprudence on the previous Article 18 EC (now Articles 26 and 21 TFEU). However,
none of that jurisprudence, aside from the *Wijsenbeek* judgment, concerns border
controls.[215] The Treaty has conferred powers to implement Article 18 EC (now

---

[210] See paras 48–56 of the Opinion.　　[211] See paras 37–42 of the Opinion.

[212] Para 59 of the Opinion.　　[213] See paras 63–73 of the Opinion.

[214] See paras 108–114 of the Opinion.

[215] See particularly Cases C–85/96 *Martinez Sala* [1998] ECR I-2691 (delivered before the
Wijsenbeek judgment); C–184/99 *Grzelczyk* [2001] ECR I-6193; C–224/98 *D'Hoop* [2002] ECR
I-6191; C–413/99 *Baumbast and R* [2002] ECR I-7091; C–148/02 *Avello* [2003] ECR I-11613;
C–138/02 *Collins* [2004] ECR I-2703; C–482/01 and C–493/01 *Orfanopolous and Olivieri* [2004]
ECR I-5257; C–224/02 *Pusa* [2004] ECR I-5763; C–456/02 *Trojani* [2004] ECR I-7572; C–200/02
Chen and Zhu [2004] ECR I-9925; C–209/03 *Bidar* [2005] ECR I-2119; C–403/03 *Schempp* [2005]
ECR I-6421; C–258/04 *Ionnidis* [2005] ECR I-8275; C–408/03 *Commission v Belgium* [2006] ECR
I-2647; C–406/04 *De Cuyper* [2006] ECR I-6947; C–192/05 *Tas-Hagen and Tas* [2006] ECR I-10451;
C–300/04 *Eman and Sevinger* [2006] ECR I-8055; C–76/05 *Schwarz and Gootjes-Schwarz* [2007] ECR
I-6849; C–318/05 *Commission v Germany* [2007] ECR I-6957; C–11/06 and 12/06 *Morgan* [2007]
ECR I-9161; C–499/06 *Nerkowska* [2008] ECR I-3993; C–33/07 *Jipa* [2008] ECR I-5157; C–127/08
Metock [2008] ECR I-6241; C–353/06 *Grunkin and Paul* [2008] ECR I-7639; C–158/07 *Förster* [2008]
ECR I-8507; C–221/07 *Zablocka-Weyhermüller* [2008] ECR I-9029; C–524/06 *Huber* [2008] ECR

Article 21 TFEU) by further legislation, but originally those powers did 'not apply to provisions on passports, identity cards, residence permits or any other such document'.[216] Of course, the position on this issue changed with the Treaty of Lisbon.[217] Instead, before the entry into force of that Treaty, Member States adopted a series of Resolutions on a uniform passport format for EU citizens,[218] and the Council tried to circumvent the limitations on EC power to adopt passport legislation by adopting passport measures pursuant to the EC's external border control powers.[219] The Council also adopted conclusions on identity cards.[220]

Even though Articles 26 and 21 TFEU (and the predecessor Articles of the EC Treaty) so far have not had much effect on the issue of border controls, there are other relevant provisions of EC (now EU) free movement law which have frequently been the subject of judgments of the Court of Justice. These rules are set out in the free movement articles of the EC Treaty (now the TFEU) and secondary legislation, which was amended and consolidated in 2004 (see below). Prior to this point, Directive 68/360 set out the immigration law rules applicable to EU citizens who worked in another Member State and to their family members (regardless of nationality).[221] These rules also applied to EU citizens who moved for other reasons (along with their family members).[222] As regards exit,[223] this legislation provided that Member States had to allow EU citizens and their family the right to leave the territory to enter another Member State, 'on production of a valid identity card or passport', and could not demand exit visas or any equivalent document from their citizens. Member States had to issue such documents to their nationals 'in accordance with their laws': arguably this had to be read in light of their human rights obligations to issue passports to their citizens.[224] As for entry, Member States had to allow entry merely 'on production of a valid identity card or passport'.[225]

Interpreting these rules, the Court of Justice ruled that a policy of imposing an entry clearance stamp in an EU citizen's passport upon entry is an equivalent

---

I-9705; C-544/07 *Rüffler* [2009] ECR I-3389; C-22/08 and C-23/08 *Vatsouras and Koupatantze* [2009] ECR I-4585; C-103/08 *Gottwald* [2009] ECR I-9117; and C-135/08 *Rottman*, judgment of 2 Mar 2010, not yet reported.

[216] Previous Art 18(3) EC.   [217] See Art 77(3) TFEU, discussed in 3.2.3 and 3.2.4 above.

[218] [1981] OJ C 241/1; [1982] OJ C 179/1; [1986] OJ C 185/1; [1995] OJ C 200/1; [2000] OJ C 310/1; and [2004] OJ C 245/1.

[219] Reg 2252/2004 ([2004] OJ L 385/1). On EC competence to adopt this Regulation, see 3.2.4 above; on the substance, see 3.9 below.   [220] See 3.9 below.

[221] [1968] OJ Spec Ed L 257/13, p 485. On the definition of 'family members', see 6.4.1 below.

[222] Dir 73/148 ([1973] OJ L 172/14) (self-employed persons and service providers and recipients). Art 2(2) of each of Dirs 90/364 ([1990] OJ L 180/26), 90/365 ([1990] OJ L 180/28), and 93/96 ([1993] OJ L 317/59) extended the relevant provisions of Dir 68/360 to other groups of EU citizens.

[223] Art 2 of Dirs 68/360 and 73/148.

[224] See 3.3.1 above.   [225] Art 3 of Dirs 68/360 and 73/148.

measure to requiring a visa, and was therefore banned.[226] It was not permissible for border guards to ask EU citizens questions about the intended purpose of their visit, or their financial means.[227] On the other hand, the Court ruled that unsystematic and sporadic checks on EU citizens, on occasion at the border, to see if they are carrying the correct permits, did not violate EC (now EU) law if similar checks are carried out on that State's own nationals, unless those checks were 'carried out in a systematic, arbitrary or unnecessarily restrictive manner'.[228] As for third-country national family members of EU citizens, the Court ruled that they could be turned back at the border if they lacked an identity card or passport, or (if necessary) a visa, but not if they were able to prove their identity and conjugal ties and if there is no evidence that they were a risk to public policy, public security, or public health.[229] Third-country national family members were covered by the legislation setting out substantive limits to Member States' power to expel or deny entry to citizens of other EU Member States on grounds of public policy, public security, and public health, as well as procedural protection for those affected.[230]

The consolidated and amended rules applying to most aspects of free movement of EU citizens and their family members are now set out in Directive 2004/38, which Member States had to apply by 30 April 2006 (the 'EU citizens' Directive').[231] The rules on border controls in this Directive are the same as the previous rules,[232] except that the right of entry and exit is 'without prejudice to the provisions on travel documents applicable to national border controls', passports of third-country national family members cannot be stamped if they present the aforementioned residence card, and EU citizens and family members without the required documents must be given the chance to obtain them or corroborate their identity before being turned back.

The 2004 Directive does not incorporate most of the prior relevant case law, except as regards the possibility to corroborate identity at the border.[233] However, presumably the prior case law continues to apply in the absence of any indication to the contrary, since the intention of the Directive is to 'simplify and strengthen' EU citizens' free movement right, which 'should, if it is to be exercised under objective conditions of freedom and dignity, be also

---

[226] Case 157/79 *Pieck* [1980] ECR 2171.

[227] Case C-68/89 *Commission v Netherlands* [1991] ECR I-2637.

[228] Case 321/87 *Commission v Belgium* [1989] ECR I-997, para 15.

[229] Case C-459/99 *MRAX* [2002] ECR I-6591, paras 53–62. On the further implications of this judgment, see 4.4.1 and 7.4.1 below.

[230] Dir 64/221 ([1964] OJ Spec Ed L 850/64, p 117. Art 1(2) of the Directive expressly extended its scope to family members.

[231] [2004] OJ L 229/35. For further implications of this Directive, see 4.4.1, 6.4.1, and 7.4.1 below.   [232] Arts 4 and 5 of the Directive (ibid).

[233] The Commission report on the application of the Dir stated that six Member States did not apply this provision (Art 5(4)) at all, and three of them applied it incorrectly (COM (2008) 840, 10 Dec 2008).

granted to their family members, irrespective of nationality'.[234] The only possible apparent reduction in standards in this area is the reference to national rules on travel documents. On the other hand, there are two improvements on the existing rules and case law: the ban on stamping passports of some third-country national family members, and the possibility of obtaining the necessary travel documents before being turned back. However, it is likely that the latter rule could have been derived from interpretation of the previous legislation.

In its most important judgment on the EU citizens' Directive to date, the Court of Justice has confirmed that third-country national family members of EU citizens who have moved within the Community have a right of entry in order to stay on the territory of the host Member State with that EU citizen— even if those family members are entering directly from a non-Member State, and thereby crossing the EU's external border.[235] This judgment also confirms that the competence to address the issue of the entry across the external borders of the family members of EU citizens who have moved within the EU derives from EU free movement law, not the competences set out in Title IV of the EC Treaty, as it then was. There is no reason to doubt that this judgment is still good law following the entry into force of the Treaty of Lisbon.

Although there is no case law directly on this point, it is clear that EU citizens' right to move and reside freely encompasses also the right to visit another Member State to exercise human rights, such as the freedom of expression and of association or assembly.[236] In such cases, free movement law and human rights law will both support the legal position of the EU citizen.[237]

The relationship between EU free movement rules and the criteria for including a person on the SIS list of persons to be banned entry into the entire EU has been a matter of some controversy. On this point, the Commission took the view that in light of the Court of Justice's case law, a third-country national family member of an EU citizen cannot be listed in the SIS unless he or she is 'an actual, genuine and serious threat to public policy and public security in each Schengen State'.[238] The Court of Justice has upheld this interpretation,[239] ruling

---

[234] Recitals 3 and 5 in the preamble to Dir 2004/38. This interpretation has been confirmed by the *Metock* judgment (n 215 above).

[235] *Metock*, ibid. For more on *Metock*, see 4.4.1, 5.4.1, 6.4.1, and 7.4.1 below.

[236] This can be derived from the broad scope of the freedom to receive services (see, for instance, Cases 186/87 *Cowan* [1989] ECR 195 and C-274/96 *Bickel and Franz* [1998] ECR I-7637), and by analogy from the political rights of EU citizens set out in Art 19 EC (now Art 22 TFEU).

[237] This would be analogous to the link between free movement law and the right to family life, which has been confirmed in a number of cases: see 6.3.4 below.

[238] See Commission Communication on the derogations from EC free movement law (COM (1999) 372, 19 July 1999), p 19. See also the Declaration of the Schengen Executive Committee on this issue (SCH/Com-ex (96) decl 5, [2000] OJ L 239/458).

[239] Case C-503/03 *Commission v Spain* [2006] ECR I-1097. For further discussion, see 2.4.2 above (as regards the general issue of the relationship between Schengen rules and Community law).

that the Spanish government wrongly refused a visa and entry at the border to family members of EU citizens solely because their names were listed in the SIS by another Member State, without first using the mechanisms established (the Sirene system) to ensure that such persons actually were a sufficiently serious threat to a requirement of public policy affecting one of the fundamental interests of society—a far higher threshold than established by the Convention.[240] The legislation establishing the second-generation Schengen Information System (SIS II) now provides expressly that a SIS II alert can only be issued in conformity with the EU citizens' Directive, and also requires use of the Sirene manual in accordance with the Court's judgment.[241] Equally, the Schengen Borders Code provides expressly for the primacy of EU free movement law.[242]

Next, the right of EU companies to send their third-country national employees to other Member States, as part of the corporate provision of services,[243] has implications for border controls. It must follow from the Court's case law that the employees have a right of entry to another Member State, otherwise their employers' right to provide services would be entirely nugatory.[244]

3.4.2. Association agreements

The European Economic Area (EEA) agreement with Norway, Iceland, and Liechtenstein,[245] and a further agreement with Switzerland on free movement of persons,[246] extend EC (now EU) free movement law to these third States. The EU citizens' Directive applies as between EU Member States and EEA States,[247] while a distinct set of free movement rules, similar to the EU's previous legislation on free movement of persons, applies as between the EU and Switzerland.[248] To that extent, the rules concerning borders applicable to EU citizens and their family

---

[240] Art 96 of the Convention; on the substance of these rules, see 3.7.1 below.

[241] Art 25, Reg 1987/2006 ([2006] OJ L 381/4). On SIS II and border controls, see 3.7.2 below.

[242] Art 3(a), Reg 562/2006 ([2006] OJ L 105/1). See also the definition of beneficiaries of free movement in Art 2(5) of the Code, and the specific rules in Arts 7(2) and 10(2). On the substance of these provisions, see 3.6.1 below.

[243] Cases: C-43/93 *Van der Elst* [1994] ECR I-3803; C-445/03 *Commission v Luxembourg* [2004] ECR I-10191; C-244/04 *Commission v Germany* [2006] ECR I-885; C-168/04 *Commission v Austria* [2006] ECR I-9041; and C-219/08 *Commission v Belgium* [2009] ECR I-9213. For more on posted third-country national workers, see 4.4.1, 6.4.4, and 7.4.1 below.

[244] In the *Commission v Austria* judgment (ibid), the Court confirmed that a refusal to issue an entry permit to a worker who had entered without prior authorization and lacked a required visa was a breach of Art 49 EC (now Art 56 TFEU). This suggests strongly that there is an underlying right of entry for such workers.   [245] [1994] OJ L 1/1.

[246] [2002] OJ L 114/6.

[247] Pursuant to EEA Joint Committee Decision 158/2007 ([2008] OJ L 124/20), Directive 2004/38 applied to EEA States as from 4 Dec 2007 (Art 4).

[248] See Annex I to the EC–Swiss treaty (n 246 above).

members are equally applicable to citizens of the EEA States and Switzerland and their family members.

However, the situation resulting from other association agreements is more complex. The Court of Justice has confirmed that the initial admission of Turkish workers and their family members, pursuant to the Association Agreement with Turkey,[249] is a matter for Member States,[250] although such admission has since become subject in part also to the EU's internal law.[251] But it has also ruled that once such persons have acquired rights pursuant to the EU–Turkey association agreement and its implementing rules, they have a right to *return* to the Member State where they acquired those rights.[252] As for Turkish service providers and self-employed Turks, there is a directly effective standstill on national rules which make the provision of services or the exercise of establishment more restrictive.[253] The Court of Justice has confirmed that this standstill applies to rules on entry control.[254] So it follows that national rules on entry control for Turkish persons providing (or possibly also receiving) services or exercising establishment cannot become any more stringent than they were at the date when the relevant Protocol entered into force for the Member State concerned.[255] This equally applies to *EU* rules concerning border control.[256]

As for the freedom of establishment under the Europe Agreements with ten Central and East European States that have now joined the EU, the Court of Justice ruled that Member States could impose prior entry clearance requirements before nationals of the EU's associate members could enter and take up their right to establish themselves.[257] Presumably the same principles will govern the provisions on establishment in the Stabilization and Association Agreements (SAAs) with Western Balkan countries, once they are applied.[258]

---

[249] [1977] OJ L 261/60.   [250] See 6.4.3 below.

[251] See the legislation on the admission of third-country nationals, and family reunion for third-country nationals (6.5 and 6.6 below).

[252] See Cases C-351/95 *Kadiman* [1997] ECR I-2133, C-329/97 *Ergat* [2000] ECR I-1487, and C-188/00 *Kurz* [2002] ECR I-10691.

[253] Case C-37/98 *Savas* [2000] ECR I-2927 (self-employed persons); Joined Cases C-317/01 and C-369/01 *Abatay and others* [2003] ECR I-12301 (services).

[254] See Case C-16/05 *Tum and Dari* [2007] ECR I-7415. See also 4.4.2 below, as regards visas.

[255] For the first nine Member States, this date was 1 Jan 1973. However, for other Member States, the relevant date is not clear, because no Protocols extending the EU–Turkey agreements to other Member States have yet entered into force.

[256] By analogy with the case law applying the standstill to visas: Case C-228/06 *Soysal* [2009] ECR I-1031. See further the discussion in 4.4.2 below.

[257] See judgments in cases C-63/99 *Gloszczuk* [2001] ECR I-6369; C-235/99 *Kondova* [2001] ECR I-6427; C-257/99 *Barkoci and Malik* [2001] ECR I-6557; and C-268/99 *Jany* [2001] ECR I-8615. For further discussion, see 6.4.3 and 7.4.2 below.

[258] [2004] OJ L 84 (Former Yugoslav Republic of Macedonia (FYROM)); [2005] OJ L 26 (Croatia); [2009] OJ L 107 (Albania); and [2010] OJ L 108 (Montenegro). SAAs have also been signed with Bosnia-Herzegovina (COM (2008) 182, 8 Apr 2008), and Serbia (COM (2007) 743, 20 Nov 2007), but these two SAAs are not yet in force. No SAA can be agreed with Kosovo until all

3.4.3. Other issues

In practice, it has been assumed that EU data protection legislation[259] applies to the area of immigration and asylum law, including border controls.[260] Is this assumption correct? Although the EU data protection Directive excludes from its scope matters dealt with by Title VI EU (ie the former third pillar) and matters relating to public security and related issues, the first exclusion ceased to apply in respect of immigration-related issues as from 1 May 1999, with the entry into force of the Treaty of Amsterdam, because the relevant issues no longer fell inside the scope of the third pillar. By way of exception, the rules governing the Schengen Information System remained within the scope of the third pillar, because of a failure to allocate them to a legal base.[261] But even the SIS is covered by rules comparable to the EU's data protection legislation, because such rules form part of the general principles of EU law, which was applicable to the former third pillar.[262] In any event, several Community measures (as they then were) amended the original SIS rules, and it has been assumed that the data protection Directive is applicable in that context.[263]

As for the exclusions related to security matters, it should be recalled that as far back as 1987, the Court of Justice ruled that the entire issue of migration could not simply be subsumed within the concept of public order.[264] Furthermore, the

Member States have recognized its claim to independence. The SAA with FYROM provides that a decision will be made five years after entry into force of the agreement 'whether' to extend the establishment rules to self-employed persons (Art 48(4), FYROM SAA), while the other SAAs state that after four or five years, the 'modalities' of extending the establishment rules to self-employed persons will be adopted (Art 49(4), Croatia SAA; Art 50(4), Albania SAA; Art 53(4), Montenegro SAA; Art 51(3), Bosnia SAA; and Art 53(4), Serbia SAA). No decisions on this issue have been adopted or proposed.

[259] Dir 95/46 ([1995] OJ L 281/31) applies to Member States' processing of data, while Reg 45/2001 ([2001] OJ L 8/1) applies to EU bodies' processing of data. For more on EU data protection law, see 12.3.2 below.

[260] The Regulation establishing Frontex, the EU border control agency, refers to Reg 45/2001 (recital 19 in the preamble to Reg 2007/2004, [2004] OJ L 349/1), while the subsequent amendment concerning (inter alia) rapid reaction teams refers to Dir 95/46 (recital 19 in the preamble to Reg 863/2007, [2007] OJ L 199/30). The Regulation setting out security features for EU passports (Reg 2252/2004, [2004] OJ L 385/1) refers to Dir 95/46 in recital 8 in the preamble. The SIS II Reg (Reg 1987/2006, [2006] OJ L 381/4) states that Dir 95/46 is applicable, but is supplemented and clarified by the Regulation (recital 15 in the preamble; see also Arts 40, 42(1), and 44; recital 16 in the preamble and Arts 45(1) and 47 refer to Regulation 45/2001). The Directive also applies to a measure implementing the SIS II Reg (the Sirene manual: see [2008] OJ L 123, points 1.4.10(e) and 2.13.1).

[261] On this issue, see 2.2.2.3 above.   [262] See 12.3.2 below.

[263] The Commission Decision establishing the Sirene manual as regards the current SIS ([2006] OJ L 317/41) refers several times to Dir 95/46 (points 1.4.9, 2.9.2, 2.9.6.2, and 2.11.4 of the manual). The power to adopt this Decision was conferred by a Community act (Reg 378/2004, [2004] OJ L 64/5).

[264] Joined Cases 281-283, 285, and 287/85 *Germany and others v Commission* [1987] ECR 3203.

case law on the EC legislation has made clear that it applies regardless of whether or not there is a direct link to the exchange of personal data between Member States, and that it applies to the public sector.[265] It must be concluded that the practice of the EU institutions is correct as regards the applicability of the EU data protection legislation to Title IV issues.[266] This means that any data protection issues which arise must be interpreted in accordance with the case law of the European Court of Human Rights regarding the protection of personal data pursuant to Article 8 ECHR.[267]

Finally, does the ban on discrimination on the basis of nationality set out in Article 12 EC (now Article 18 TFEU) apply to third-country nationals?[268] The Court of Justice appeared to limit the application of Article 12 to citizens of EEC Member States in its *Khalil and Addou* judgment, but that judgment was explicitly confined to the legal position as it stood in 1971.[269] Subsequently, the Court has ruled out the application of Article 12 EC (now Article 18 TFEU) to third-country nationals generally;[270] there is no reason to doubt that this case is still good law after the entry into force of the Treaty of Lisbon. However, an Advocate General has argued that Article 12 EC (now Article 18 TFEU) applies to third-country national family members of EU citizens,[271] and this approach was later confirmed by the EU citizens' Directive.[272] Furthermore, three of the EU's association agreements contain their own non-discrimination rule.[273] Also, even though Article 18 TFEU does not apply to third-country nationals generally, the general principle of equality which forms part of EU law arguably does.[274]

---

[265] See Joined Cases C-465/00, C-138/01, and C-139/01 *Osterreichischer Rundfunk* [2003] ECR I-4989 and Case C-101/01 *Lindqvist* [2003] ECR I-12971.

[266] See also C-524/06 *Huber* [2008] ECR I-9705, which confirms the applicability of Dir 95/46 to EC free movement law, as well as the substantive analysis in that judgment.

[267] Paras 68–72 of the judgment in *Osterreichischer Rundfunk* (n 265 above). On that case law, see further 12.3.1 below.

[268] For a more detailed analysis of this issue, see E Guild and S Peers, 'Out of the Ghetto? The Personal Scope of EU Law' in S Peers and N Rogers, *EU Immigration and Asylum Law: Text and Commentary* (1st edn, Martinus Nijhoff, 2006).

[269] Joined Cases C-95/99–C-98/99 and C-180/99 *Khalil and Addou* [2001] ECR I-7413. On the further implications of this judgment, see 5.4.2 and 6.4.2 below.

[270] Joined Cases C-22/08 and C-23/08 *Vatsouras and Koupatantze*, judgment of 4 June 2009, not yet reported.

[271] Opinion in *MRAX* (Case C-459/99 [2002] ECR I-6591), para 59.

[272] Art 24(1) of Dir 2004/38 ([2004] OJ L 229/35).

[273] Art 4 of the EEA treaty ([1994] OJ L 1/1); Art 2 of the EU–Swiss treaty on free movement of persons ([2002] OJ L 114/6); and Art 9 of the EU–Turkey association agreement ([1977] OJ L 261/60). For more on these treaties, see 6.4.3 below.

[274] See E Guild and S Peers, n 268 above. Note that the equivalent provision of the EU Charter (Art 21(2) must be interpreted consistently with Art 18 TFEU, according to the explanatory memorandum to the Charter ([2007] OJ C 303).

3.5. Internal border controls

The EU rules on the abolition of internal border controls, including a power to reintroduce those controls, were initially set out, as mentioned above, in the Schengen Convention.[275] This provision of the Convention was also implemented by three Decisions adopted by the Schengen Executive Committee, which concerned the issues of: obstacles to traffic flows;[276] bringing the Convention into force;[277] and procedures for reintroducing border checks.[278] The relevant provision of the Schengen Convention and the three Executive Committee Decisions were then integrated into the legal order of the EC (as it then was) with the entry into force of the Treaty of Amsterdam; all were attributed the legal base of Article 62(1) EC (now Article 77(2)(e) TFEU).[279]

Research on the application of the Schengen Convention in two Member States indicated that following the abolition of internal controls, the size and powers of 'internal' border guard forces were increased considerably.[280] Also, the power to reintroduce controls was frequently invoked, in particular in the context of planned large-scale demonstrations at EU summit meetings.[281] The Council even adopted measures on this issue, which in particular provided for the exchange of information on alleged troublemakers, with the aim of lessening the effect of re-imposed internal border controls by means of targeted policing.[282]

As from 13 October 2006, the basic rules regulating the abolition of internal border controls derive from the Regulation establishing the Schengen Borders Code, which also sets out common rules on external border control.[283] The Code replaced the relevant provision of the Schengen Convention and two of the three Executive Committee Decisions.[284]

---

[275] Art 2 of the Convention ([2000] OJ L 239/1).

[276] SCH/Com-ex (94) 1 rev 2 ([2000] OJ L 239/157).

[277] SCH/Com-ex (94) 29 rev 2 ([2000] OJ L 239/130).

[278] SCH/Com-ex (95) 20 rev 2 ([2000] OJ L 239/133).

[279] Decision 1999/436 ([1999] OJ L 176/17). However, this Council Decision stated that Art 2(2) and (3) of the Convention were without prejudice to Art 64(1) EC (now Art 72 TFEU), which sets out Member States' responsibilities as regards law, order, and security. On the interpretation of this provision, see 3.2.4 above. Furthermore, Art 2(4) of the Convention was not allocated any legal base, because it was believed to be obsolete (see Decision 1999/435, [1999] OJ L 176/1).

[280] See K Groenendijk, 'New Borders Behind Old Ones: Post Schengen Controls Behind the Internal Borders—Inside the Netherlands and Germany' in E Guild, P Minderhoud, and K Groenendijk, eds, *In Search of Europe's Borders* (Kluwer, 2003) 131.

[281] See K Groenendijk, 'Reinstatement of Controls at the Internal Borders of Europe: Why and Against Whom?' (2004) 10 ELJ 150, and generally the second edition of this book, at 133.

[282] See: JHA Council conclusions (JHA Council press release, July 2001); a security handbook for police use at such events (Council doc 12637/3/02, 12 Nov 2002); and a Resolution on security at European Councils ([2004] OJ C 116/18). See further 12.7 below.

[283] Reg 562/2006 ([2006] OJ L 105/1), Art 40. On the external borders provisions, see 3.6.1 below. All references in the rest of this section are to the Borders Code Reg, unless otherwise indicated.

[284] Art 39(1) and 2(b) of the Code. The Decision which was not repealed was SCH/Com-ex (94) 29 rev 2 (n 277 above), setting out rules concerning the initial application of the Convention. It

Title III of the Code concerns internal border controls,[285] and Chapter I of this Title concerns the abolition of such controls.[286] The first provision repeats the basic rule at the core of the previous Schengen Convention, that 'internal borders can be crossed at any point without any checks on persons being carried out'.[287] Despite this basic rule, four types of checks are still permitted:[288] the exercise of police powers, where there is no 'effect equivalent to border checks'; security checks at ports and airports (if such checks also apply to movement within a Member State); the possibility to impose an obligation to hold or carry documents; and the registration requirement set out in the freedom to travel provisions of the Schengen Convention.[289]

The 'police powers' exception sets out four cases 'in particular' where the exercise of police powers shall not be considered equivalent to border checks:[290] the checks do not have border control as an objective; they are based on general police information and experience and aim 'in particular' at combating 'cross-border crime'; they are devised and executed differently from systematic checks at the external borders; and they do not entail spot-checks. It is not clear if these provisions are alternative or cumulative, although in any event the list is non-exhaustive (as is the second item on the list). Furthermore, there is no notification or transparency requirement which would assist in an assessment of whether the rules are being applied correctly. It could possibly be argued, however, that the concept of a police check with an 'effect equivalent to border checks' could be interpreted as broadly as a measure having an equivalent effect to a quantitative restriction on the free movement of goods.[291]

One key question is whether police checks would infringe the Code if they are carried out at or near the borders for the purposes of migration control. It is striking that there is no direct reference to this issue in this provision of the Code. In light of this, and since any checks carried out at or near borders for the main purpose or with the main effect of migration control must surely be considered as having the prohibited objective of border control (and perhaps also an effect equivalent to an internal border check), it must follow that such checks would violate the Code.

Finally, it should be noted that these police checks are not covered by the ban on discriminatory conduct set out elsewhere in the Borders Code, which only applies to checks at the external borders;[292] but surely it can be argued that a police check within the scope of this internal borders provision which is mainly aimed

---

has not subsequently been amended or repealed, although points 3 and 4 of this Decision are now clearly obsolete.

[285] Arts 20–31.   [286] Arts 20–22.   [287] Art 20.

[288] Art 21. Member States must notify the national provisions relating to the third and fourth exceptions to the Commission: Art 37. For these notifications, see: <http://ec.europa.eu/justice_home/doc_centre/freetravel/rights/doc_freetravel_rights_en.htm#notifications>.

[289] Art 22 of the Convention, which has not been amended or repealed; see 4.9 below.

[290] Art 21(a).   [291] See Art 28 EC (now Art 34 TFEU).   [292] Art 6(2).

at non-white people falls nonetheless within the scope of the principle of equality, which is protected as a general principle of EU law.

Next, Member States are obliged to remove road-traffic obstacles at the internal borders, including any unjustified special speed limits, but nonetheless they must be 'prepared to provide for facilities' to reintroduce internal border checks if necessary.[293]

Chapter II of Title III of the Borders Code concerns the reintroduction of internal border controls by a Member State.[294] The basic rule is that a Member State can 'exceptionally' reintroduce border controls for up to thirty days, or for a longer period if the duration of the relevant event is foreseeable, in the 'event of a serious threat to public policy or to internal security'; but the 'scope and duration' of the reintroduced checks 'shall not exceed what is strictly necessary to respond to the reintroduced checks'.[295] The reintroduction of controls may be continued for further renewable periods of up to thirty days, 'taking into account any new elements'.[296] Compared to the previous Schengen Convention rules,[297] the threshold for reintroduction of checks is higher, the time period is more precisely specified and the necessity rule is stricter.

The basic rule is supplemented by more specific rules, depending on whether the reintroduction of border checks is foreseeable or urgent. First of all, where the reintroduction of controls is foreseeable,[298] Member States must inform the Commission and other Member States 'as soon as possible' of its plans to reintroduce controls, and provide information 'as soon as available' on the reasons for and the scope of the reintroduction of controls, the authorized crossing points, the date and duration of the introduction, and (if relevant) the measures to be taken by other Member States. The Commission may issue an opinion on the planned reintroduction, and there shall be consultation on the planned controls between the Member States and the Commission in order to discuss the proportionality of the controls and possibly also 'mutual cooperation between the Member States'. These rules were a change from the previous procedures as regards the role of the Commission (which had no role at all previously), the date of the consultations (at least fifteen days before the reintroduction of controls), and the requirement to discuss the proportionality of the planned controls.[299]

Secondly, in the event that 'urgent action' is required, Member States may reintroduce controls without prior notification, provided that the relevant information is sent to the Commission and other Member States later.[300] As for

---

[293] Art 22. This clause took over the gist of Schengen Executive Committee Decision 94(1) (n 276 above), which was repealed.   [294] Arts 23–31.

[295] Art 23(1).   [296] Art 23(2).

[297] Art 2(2) of the Convention, repealed by the Borders Code.   [298] Art 24.

[299] Compare to point 1 of SCH/Com-ex (95) 20 (n 278 above), which has been repealed by the Code.

[300] Art 25. There is no change from the previous rules (point 2 of SCH/Com-ex (95) 20, ibid).

the procedure for prolonging controls, it simply requires the application of the procedure for reintroducing controls.[301]

Finally, Title III of the Code contains provisions on: informing the EP of decisions on reintroduced controls (and reporting to the EP following the third consecutive extension of reintroduced controls); clarifying that the external borders rules will apply when internal border checks are reintroduced; requiring a report when internal border controls are lifted, outlining the operation of the internal checks and their effectiveness; requiring information to the public about reintroduced controls unless there are overriding security reasons to the contrary; and requiring the EU institutions and other Member States to respect the confidentiality of information submitted by a Member State at its request.[302] Also, the Commission was obliged to report on the application of Title III of the Code by October 2009;[303] the report was to 'pay particular attention to any difficulties arising from the reintroduction of border control at internal borders' and '[where appropriate]...present proposals aimed at resolving such difficulties'. The Commission has not yet issued this report.

Of course, it should be recalled when considering the issue of internal border controls that until the entry into force of the Treaty of Lisbon, according to the prior Article 68(2) EC, the Court of Justice did not have 'jurisdiction to rule on any measure or decision taken pursuant to Article 62(1) [which conferred powers to adopt measures concerning internal borders] relating to the maintenance of law and order and the safeguarding of internal security'. This in effect prevented the Court of Justice from ruling on the validity of the reintroduction of internal border controls by any Member State. After this limit on its jurisdiction has been lifted, it was not long before the Court of Justice was asked to interpret the rules on internal border controls.[304] In the *Melki and Abdeli* judgment, it criticized the French practice for police controls behind the internal borders, in particular because the national law in question 'contains neither further details nor limitations on the power thus conferred—in particular in relation to the intensity and frequency of the controls which may be carried out on that legal basis—for the purposes of preventing the practical application of that power, by the competent authorities, from leading to controls with an effect equivalent to border checks'. To comply with the limitations in the Borders Code, national law 'granting a power to police authorities to carry out identity checks—a power which, first, is restricted to the border area of the Member State with other Member States and, second, does not depend upon the behaviour of the person checked or on specific circumstances giving rise to a risk of breach of public order—must provide the

---

[301] Art 26. Again, there is no change from the previous rules (point 3 of SCH/Com-ex (95) 20).

[302] Arts 27–31. Most of these provisions are new as compared to the previous rules.

[303] Art 38.

[304] Joined Cases C-188/10 and C-189/10 *Melki and Abdeli*, judgment of 22 June 2010, not yet reported.

necessary framework for the power granted to those authorities in order, inter alia, to guide the discretion which those authorities enjoy in the practical application of that power. That framework must guarantee that the practical exercise of that power, consisting in carrying out identity controls, cannot have an effect equivalent to border checks'.

In practice, it appears that border controls were reintroduced about seventeen times from the application date of the Borders Code until June 2010.[305] The large majority of cases concerned some form of political meeting (for instance, NATO and G8 summits, and the Copenhagen conference on climate change). Many of the reports on these reintroductions of controls are not available, but there are some available reports.[306]

Since many of the required reports on the reintroduction of border controls in individual cases are not available, and since the Commission has not produced its report on the internal borders rules, it is difficult to ascertain whether the Borders Code has had any impact on this issue. It is striking, however, that controls were apparently reintroduced more frequently in 2009 and 2010 than in previous years. One might surmise that the older Member States feel less secure since the enlargement of the Schengen zone.

3.6. External border controls: basic rules

Like the rules on the abolition of internal border controls, the basic rules on harmonized external border controls were initially set out in the Schengen Convention,[307] along with measures adopted by the Schengen Executive Committee, particularly a Common Manual for use by border control authorities,[308] along with two other Decisions of the Schengen Executive Committee.[309]

---

[305] Council docs: 13837/06, 11 Oct 2006; 15332/06, 15 Nov 2006; 6084/07, 7 Feb 2007; 10172/08, 30 May 2008; 13603/08, 1 Oct 2008; 7725/09, 18 Mar 2009; 7501/09, 20 Mar 2009; 11380/09, 25 June 2009; 13613/09, 24 Oct 2009; 13913/09, 1 Oct 2009; 13979/09, 2 Oct 2009; 16280/09, 20 Nov 2009; 16911/09, 1 Dec 2009; 7899/10, 23 Mar 2010; 8580/10, 15 Apr 2010; 9190/10, 21 Apr 2010; and 8584/10, add 1, 27 May 2010.

[306] For instance, see the report by Austria regarding reintroduction of controls during the 2008 European football championships (Council doc 15185/08, 5 Nov 2008).

[307] Arts 3–8 of the Convention ([2000] OJ L 239/1). On the provisions of the Schengen *acquis* regarding internal borders, see 3.5 above. For more detail on the measures concerning external border controls in force before the adoption of the Schengen Borders Code, see the second edition of this book, at 135–139.

[308] The Manual (as consolidated in Schengen Executive Committee Decision Sch/Com-ex (99) 13) was initially classified, but was subsequently mostly declassified (see Decisions in [2000] OJ L 303/29 and [2002] OJ L 123/49). It was published in [2002] OJ C 313/97.

[309] These were Sch/Com-ex (94) 17 on introducing the Schengen system and Sch/Com-ex (98) 1 on the activities of a task force ([2000] OJ L 239/168 and 191).

Following the integration of the Schengen *acquis* into the EC and EU legal order, in accordance with the Treaty of Amsterdam,[310] these measures were supplemented by EC acts, in particular a Decision concerning border signs and a Regulation on the stamping of documents.[311] Furthermore, the Council adopted in 2001 a Regulation which conferred upon itself (and Member States) the power to amend the Common Manual.[312] A challenge to this measure by the Commission before the Court of Justice (on the grounds that the Council had not adequately explained why it conferred those implementing powers upon itself, whereas the normal rule is to confer them on the Commission) was unsuccessful.[313] This Regulation was used to amend the Common Manual on several occasions, in particular to add a standard form for refusing entry and the border.[314] The Manual was also amended on several other occasions: by the EU's borders legislation,[315] by legislative acts concerning visas,[316] as well as incidentally when the Council amended the basic rules governing the procedure for visa applications (the Common Consular Instructions).[317]

In 2006, the various measures setting out the basic rules governing external border controls were all integrated and amended in the form of the Regulation establishing the Schengen Borders Code. The next major development in this area will be the development of an entry-exit system, ie a system which stores precise information on the movements of each third-country national across the external borders. These two issues will be considered in turn. Of course, these measures should be seen in the broader context of the other measures discussed

---

[310] Arts 2–8 of the Convention and Schengen Executive Committee Decisions Sch/Com-ex (94) 17 and Sch/Com-ex (98) 1 were allocated to Art 62(2)(a) EC (now Art 77(2)(b) TFEU), except for Art 7 of the Convention, which was allocated to Art 66 EC (now Art 74 TFEU), and Art 4 of the Convention, which was not allocated at all due to obsolescence. The Common Manual was allocated to Art 62 and 63 EC (now Arts 77–79 TFEU). See the Council Decisions on the definition and allocation of the *acquis* (1999/435 and 1999/436, [1999] OJ L 176/1 and 17).

[311] See respectively [2004] OJ L 261/119 and Reg 2133/2004, [2004] OJ L 369/5. The Regulation inter alia inserted two new provisions into the Schengen Convention (Arts 6a and 6b) and amended Art 6(2)(e) of the Convention, while the Decision inter alia amended Sch/Com-ex (94) 17 (n 309 above). [312] Reg 790/2001, [2001] OJ L 116/5.

[313] Case C-257/01 *Commission v Council* [2005] ECR I-345.

[314] The first two amendments ([2002] OJ L 123/47 and [2002] OJ L 187/50) made 'housekeeping' changes; the third amendment increased checks on minors ([2004] OJ L 157/36); and the fourth amendment introduced a common form to be used when refusing entry at the border ([2004] OJ L 261/36). [315] Art 3 of Reg 2133/2004 (n 311 above).

[316] Art 7(2) of Reg 539/2001 ([2001] OJ L 81/3); Art 2 of Reg 334/2002 ([2002] OJ L 53/7); Art 5(2) and (3) of Reg 415/2003 ([2003] OJ L 64/1); and Art 11(2) of Reg 693/2003 ([2003] OJ L 99/8). On the substance of these measures, see 4.5–4.7 below.

[317] Art 1(2), (4), and (5) of Decision 2001/329 ([2001] OJ L 116/32); Art 3 of Decision 2001/420 ([2001] OJ L 150/47); Art 2 of Decision 2002/44 ([2002] OJ L 20/5); the Decision on fees for considering visa applications ([2003] OJ L 152/82); Decisions 2003/585 and 2003/586 on transit visa requirements ([2003] OJ L 198/13 and 15); Art 2 of Decision 2004/17 on travel medical insurance requirements ([2004] OJ L 5/79); and the June 2006 Decision on visa fees ([2006] OJ L 175/77). On the substance of these measures, see 4.7.1 below.

in this chapter, concerning passport security, the Schengen Information System, and the EU's border agency, Frontex.

3.6.1. Schengen Borders Code

The Schengen Borders Code,[318] which applied from 13 October 2006,[319] also integrated and amended all the previous rules concerning internal borders.[320] As regards external borders, the Code repealed the relevant provisions of the Schengen Convention; one Schengen Executive Committee Decision; the Common Manual (as amended by EC measures); and the legislation on border signs; the stamping of documents; and the power to amend the Common Manual.[321] Subsequently, the Code has been amended on four occasions.[322] The Commission plans further amendments, pursuant inter alia to planned legislation on an entry-exit system.[323]

The Code confers powers upon the Commission to adopt implementing measures as regards three of its eight attached Annexes; the Commission can also adopt implementing measures as regards border surveillance.[324] All these measures are subject to the 'regulatory procedure with scrutiny', which entails greater scrutiny power for the EP; this process will likely be replaced by the 'delegated acts' procedure introduced by the Treaty of Lisbon at some point.[325] To date, one implementing measure has been adopted, regarding maritime surveillance (see the discussion below).[326]

Certain decisions relating to external border crossing (such as the penalties for crossing at unauthorized points or times) have been left to the Member States'

---

[318] Reg 562/2006 ([2006] OJ L 105/1). All further references in this section are to the Borders Code Reg, unless otherwise indicated.   [319] Art 40.

[320] Arts 23–31 of the Code; see 3.5 above.

[321] Art 39. More precisely, Sch/Com-ex (94) 17 was repealed, but Sch/Com-ex (98) 1 remained in force (for both, see n 310 above). The latter Decision has not been amended or repealed. Some provisions relating to the abolition of internal border controls were also deleted: see 3.5 above. Also, the Code deleted Annex 7 to the Common Consular Instructions (on which, see 4.7.1 below).

[322] Firstly, Reg 296/2008 ([2008] OJ L 97/60) regarding 'comitology', amended Arts 12, 32, and 33. Secondly, Reg 81/2009, regarding the use of the Visa Information System at borders ([2009] OJ L 35/56), amended Art 7(3). Thirdly, Art 55 of the visa code (Reg 810/2009, [2009] OJ L 234/1), amended Annex V. Finally, Reg 265/2010 ([2010] OJ L 85/1) amended Arts 5(1)(b) and 5(4)(a). The Code has not been consolidated.

[323] See the Commission's 2010 work programme COM (2010) 135, 31 Mar 2010. On the entry-exit plans, see further 3.6.2 below.

[324] Arts 12(5), 32, and 33, as amended by Reg 296/2008 (n 322 above). The implementing powers concern Annexes III, IV, and VIII, which concern signs for separate lanes at border crossings, stamping of travel documents, and proof that the border has been crossed without travel documents being stamped.   [325] See 2.2.2.1 and 2.2.3.1 above.

[326] [2010] OJ L 111/20. The legality of this measure has been challenged, on the grounds that the Council exceeded its powers to implement the Regulation when adopting it: Case C-355/10 *EP v Council*, pending.

discretion, but there is nevertheless an obligation for Member States to inform the Commission of these decisions; the Commission must then inform the public.[327] The Commission has also drawn up a Recommendation containing practical information for border guards.[328]

Moving on to the content of the Schengen Borders Code, it comprises forty Articles in four Titles, with (as noted already) eight attached Annexes.[329] Title I sets out the purpose of the Regulation, along with rules on definitions and the scope of the Code.[330] It is specified that while the Regulation applies 'to any person crossing the internal or external borders of Member States', it is 'without prejudice to' the rights of persons enjoying EU free movement rights or to 'the rights of refugees and persons requesting international protection, in particular as regards non-refoulement'.[331] The first of these categories follows from the priority of EU free movement law over Schengen rules,[332] while the latter arguably follows from the general principles of EU law.[333] Moreover, the Code does not address the issue of rules on local border traffic, which was the subject of separate legislation adopted some months later.[334]

Title II of the Code, which contains three Chapters,[335] sets out the main rules concerning external borders. Chapter I comprises two Articles, which set out in turn the rules concerning crossing external borders and the conditions for entry at the external borders.[336] Borders must be crossed at official points during official hours,[337] and notice of opening hours must be provided. Derogations may be permitted for pleasure shipping or coastal fishing;[338] seamen under certain conditions; individuals or groups where there is a 'requirement of a special nature' (subject to certain conditions); or individuals or groups in an unforeseen emergency.[339] Penalties must be imposed by Member States for breach of the obligation to cross at official points; these penalties shall be 'effective, proportionate and dissuasive', and this obligation is 'without prejudice to . . . [Member States'] international protection obligations'.[340] These two express provisions respectively

---

[327] Arts 34 and 37; this information is also available online at: <http://ec.europa.eu/justice_home/doc_centre/freetravel/rights/doc_freetravel_rights_en.htm#notifications>.

[328] C(2006) 5186, reproduced in Council doc 15010/06, 9 Nov 2006, amended by C(2008) 2976, reproduced in Council doc 11253/08, 30 June 2008.

[329] Title III of the Code solely concerns the abolition of internal border controls, and was considered in 3.5 above. Title IV solely sets out final provisions, and is not considered separately.

[330] Arts 1–3.   [331] Art 3. The former group is defined in Art 2(5).

[332] See the former Art 134 of the Schengen Convention, which was not integrated within the EC legal framework (Decision 1999/435, n 310 above); the Schengen Protocol; and Case C–503/03 [2006] ECR I–1097. See also 3.4.1 above.

[333] Compare to the former Art 135 of the Schengen Convention, which was not integrated within the EC legal framework (see Decision 1999/435, ibid).

[334] Art 35; see Reg 1931/2006 ([2006] OJ L 405/1), discussed in 3.8 below.

[335] Arts 4–19.   [336] Arts 4 and 5.

[337] Member States must notify their border crossing points to the Commission (Art 34(1)(b)).

[338] For definitions of these concepts, see Art 2(17) and (18).   [339] Art 4(2).

[340] Art 4(3). Member States must notify these penalties to the Commission (Art 37).

reflect the underlying effective sanctions principles of EU law and the exemption of refugees from penalties for irregular entry as set out in Article 31 of the Geneva Convention on refugee status.[341] It should be noted that these provisions do not require Member States to criminalize irregular border crossing; more generally, EU law is silent on the criminal law aspects of irregular migration except for specific obligations to criminalize the smuggling, trafficking, and employment of irregular migrants, which do not require criminalization of the irregular migrants themselves.[342]

The key provision of the Schengen Borders Code sets out the conditions for entry for short-term stays (three months within a six-month period).[343] These conditions 'shall be the following':

(a) possession of valid documents necessary to cross the border;[344]

(b) possession of a visa if required by the EU visa list legislation,[345] although a residence permit or a long-stay visa is equivalent to a visa for this purpose;[346]

(c) justification of the purpose and conditions of the stay, and possession of sufficient means of subsistence;

(d) absence from the list of persons banned from entry set up within the Schengen Information System (SIS);[347] and

(e) absence of a 'threat to public policy, national security or the international relations' of *any* of the Member States, 'in particular' where there is no alert in Member States' national databases refusing entry on such grounds.

The final provision could be interpreted as a requirement to check *all* Member States' national databases, but surely this is not practical on grounds of technical difficulties and cost. A 'non-exhaustive' list of documents providing justification of the stay is set out in Annex I to the Code, which is a straightforward list of documents which can serve as evidence of travel for business, studies, tourism or private reasons, or for political, scientific, cultural, sports, religious, or other reasons.[348] The subsistence requirement 'shall be assessed in accordance with the duration and the purpose of the stay and by reference to average prices for board

---

[341] On the first point, see Case 68/88 *Commission v Greece* (*Greek maize*) [1989] ECR 2685. On the second point, see 7.3.2 below.   [342] See 7.5 below.

[343] Art 5.

[344] The relevant documents are listed in a Manual of travel documents, established by Schengen Executive Committee Decisions Sch/com-ex (98) 56 and (99) 14 ([2000] OJ L 239/207 and 298), since updated pursuant to Reg 789/2001 ([2001] OJ L 116/2).

[345] On the content of the visa list, see 4.5 below.

[346] Art 2(15) defines 'residence permit'. The exception for long-stay visas was added by Reg 265/2010 (n 322 above).

[347] See further the definition in Art 2(7), which refers to Art 96 of the Schengen Convention, which concerns the grounds for issuing 'alerts' in the SIS for persons to be refused entry (see 3.7.1 below). There is also an express requirement to check the SIS upon entry (Art 7 of the Code, discussed below).   [348] Art 5(2).

and lodging',[349] and Member States' reference amounts for subsistence are to be notified to the Commission.[350] The possession of sufficient subsistence 'may' be verified, 'for example', by 'the cash, travellers' cheques and credit cards in the third-country national's possession' as well as sponsorship declarations, where a Member State's law recognizes such declarations, and guarantees from hosts, as defined by national law.[351] Arguably, the words 'shall be the following' create an obligation to admit the person concerned if the relevant conditions are satisfied.

There are three exceptions to the rules concerning entry conditions:[352]

(a) persons with a residence permit, a long-stay visa, or a re-entry visa from a Member State who wish to cross the external borders in transit back to the State which issued the permit shall be admitted across the border, unless they are listed on the watch-list of the Member State they wish to cross, along with instructions to refuse entry or transit;

(b) persons who do not meet the visa requirement, but who satisfy the criteria for obtaining a visa at the border set out in EU visa legislation, may be authorized to enter if a visa is issued at the border pursuant to those rules;[353] and

(c) a person may be permitted to enter if a Member State 'considers it necessary' to derogate from the criteria for entry on humanitarian grounds, national interest, or international obligations; but in such a case the permission to enter should be limited to the territory of that Member State, and other Member States must be informed of such decisions, if the person concerned is listed on the SIS.[354]

The first exception is mandatory ('shall be authorized to enter'); the residence permits concerned must be notified to the Commission.[355] The inevitable consequence of these rules is that persons who do not meet the criteria for entry must be denied entry, unless they fall into one of the three special categories listed above. However, the obligation to refuse entry is 'without prejudice to the application of special provisions concerning the right of asylum and to international protection or the issue of long-stay visas'.[356] The special provisions on the right to asylum and international protection are not further defined, and it could be argued that this is

---

[349] Art 5(3), first sub-paragraph.   [350] Art 34(1)(c).

[351] Art 5(3), second sub-paragraph.

[352] Art 5(4), amended by Reg 265/2010 (n 322 above), which added a reference to long-stay visas. See previously Art 18 of the Schengen Convention (n 307 above), as amended by Regulation 1091/2001 ([2001] OJ L 150/4). See also the transit decisions discussed in 4.2.5 below.

[353] This initially referred to Reg 415/2003 (n 316 above), but this Regulation has now been replaced by Arts 35 and 36 of the visa code (n 322 above).

[354] cf the provisions for visas with 'limited territorial validity', set out in Art 25 of the visa code (ibid).   [355] Art 34(1)(a).

[356] Art 13(1).

a reference to national law; to a uniform EU concept which could be defined by the Court of Justice; to a minimum EU standard which could again be defined by the Court; or to the asylum procedures Directive.[357] As for the special provisions on long-stay visas, this should now be understood as a reference to the provisions of the Borders Code itself.[358]

Next, Chapter II of Title II of the Code concerns border checks and refusal of entry.[359] As regards the conduct of border checks, border guards must respect human dignity, act proportionately and not discriminate on any listed grounds while carrying out border checks.[360]

The Code then addresses the crucial issue of the checks that must be carried out at external borders on entry and on exit. In particular, the 'minimum checks' to be carried out on all persons at external borders must entail a 'rapid and straightforward verification' of the validity of the documents carried, including an examination for signs of counterfeiting or falsification, using technical devices and consulting databases on lost or stolen documents 'where appropriate'.[361] Presumably it cannot seriously be intended that the documentation of every single traveller will be fully checked in all possible databases.

The Code specifies that while such checks are the 'rule' for persons exercising EU free movement rights, it is possible for border guards to check databases on a 'nonsystematic basis' in order to determine that such persons 'do not represent a genuine, present and sufficiently serious threat to the internal security, public policy, international relations of the Member States or a threat to the public health'.[362] There is no cross-reference as regards these grounds to EU free movement law, and this proviso differs from EU free movement law because it refers to 'internal security' rather than 'public security' and also to 'international relations'.[363] However, it is specified that such checks 'shall not jeopardise' the right of entry set out in free movement legislation,[364] and further that checks on persons with free movement rights must be carried out 'in accordance with' EU free movement law.[365] Although these safeguards (and the general safeguard for free movement law set out in the Code),[366] in conjunction with the Treaty free movement rights, should be interpreted to prevent any restriction on free movement rights as a result of checking databases, it is possible in practice that a border guard might apply these conflicting provisions more restrictively. In particular, it

---

[357] However, it should be recalled that the Schengen associates and Denmark do not apply the procedures Directive. On the substance of the Directive, see 5.7 below.

[358] Art 5(4)(a), as amended by Reg 265/2010 (see n 352 above).   [359] Arts 6–13.

[360] Art 6.   [361] Art 7(2), first sub-paragraph.   [362] Art 7(2), second sub-paragraph.

[363] Moreover, compared to Art 28(2) of Dir 2004/38 on EU citizens' free movement rights ([2004] OJ L 229/35), there is no reference to 'personal conduct' or to threatening the 'fundamental interests of society'. But at least the definition of 'public health' is identical (Art 29(1) of the Directive and Art 2(19) of the Code). For more on the free movement rules, see 3.4.1 above.

[364] Art 7(2), third sub-paragraph.   [365] Art 7(6).   [366] Art 3(a).

is objectionable that the border checks provision of the Code does not fully reflect free movement rules and refers to more extensive grounds than free movement law provides for.

The Code then specifies the 'thorough checks' to be carried out on third-country nationals (other than those with EU free movement rights). On entry, such persons shall be checked as regards their documents, the purpose and period of stay including subsistence requirements, along with checks in national databases and the SIS.[367]

Furthermore, once the Visa Information System (VIS) becomes operational, third-country nationals shall also (if they hold a visa) be checked in the VIS on entry for the purposes of verification (a 'one-to-one' search), using fingerprints and the visa sticker number.[368] Due to doubts about the practicality of this obligation, particularly as regards land borders,[369] it will be subject to a derogation, concerning the checking of fingerprints, for a transitional period of three years, beginning three years after the VIS has started operations.[370] The Commission must evaluate the application of the derogation and report on its implementation to the EP and the Council within two years of the start of the derogation. Either the EP or the Council may then suggest that the Commission table a proposal to amend the legislation.[371]

As for the substance of the derogation, it will apply where intense traffic results in excessive delay at border crossing points, all resources have been exhausted as regards staff, facilities, and organization, and 'on the basis of an assessment there is no risk related to internal security and illegal immigration'.[372] The first two criteria match the criteria applicable to the decision to relax border controls in the Borders Code,[373] but the third criterion (risk assessment) does not. Also, as compared to the rules on the relaxation of border controls, a Member State will not have to show (as regards the derogation from the obligation to check fingerprints in the VIS) that there were 'exceptional and unforeseeable

---

[367] Art 7(3)(a).

[368] Art 7(3)(aa), as inserted by Reg 81/2009 (n 322 above). For the details of the VIS, see 4.8 below. It should be noted that the VIS Reg (Reg 767/2008, [2008] OJ L 218/60) does not lay down a requirement for border guards to use the VIS; only an amendment to the Schengen Borders Code could do that.

[369] The practical difficulties at land borders have been ameliorated, however, by the extension of visa waivers to Western Balkan states, and will be further ameliorated if there are in future visa waivers for ex-Soviet countries (see 4.5 below).

[370] Art 7(3)(ae), as inserted by Reg 81/2009 (n 322 above). Presumably the transitional period does not begin for three years because of the three-year delay, after the VIS begins operations, before the VIS Reg permits the use of fingerprints to search the VIS at all borders (Art 18(2) of the VIS Reg, n 368 above). Art 18(2) of the VIS Reg permits that date to be brought forward as regards air borders; the Borders Code does not make any special provision for this situation.

[371] Ibid. See also Art 50(5) of the VIS Reg (ibid), which provides for evaluation of the provisions regarding fingerprint searches in the VIS by external border guards, one year and three years after the VIS starts operations.   [372] Art 7(3)(ab), as inserted by Reg 81/2009 (n 322 above).

[373] Art 8(1), discussed further below.

circumstances', which 'shall be deemed to be those where unforeseeable events' lead to the intense traffic in question.[374] It follows that in principle, the decision to relax border controls and the derogation from full use of the VIS on entry will not always apply simultaneously, although in practice it is likely that this will often be the case.

If the derogation applies, the VIS must still be searched in all cases using the visa sticker, and in random cases using fingerprints as well.[375] The VIS will also have to be searched using visa sticker and fingerprints in 'all cases where there is doubt as to the identity of the holder of the visa and/or the authenticity of the visa'. Decisions to apply the derogation will have to be taken by the border guard in command at the border post or at a higher level, and notified immediately to the other Member States and to the Commission.[376] Member States must report annually on the use of the derogation to the Commission, including providing information on 'the number of third-country nationals who were checked in the VIS using the number of the visa sticker only and the length of the waiting time' which justified the derogation.[377]

A statement was adopted by the Council and Commission when the relevant Regulation amending the Borders Code was adopted, asserting that 'the Council and the Commission stress that the derogation... should not be applied for a total period of more than 5 days or 120 hours per year at any border crossing point'. Also, the statement provides that the 'evaluation carried out by the Commission... will consider the infrastructure of the border crossing points, including recent and planned developments, as well as any factor that may have an influence on passenger flows, and may contain suggestions for improvements accordingly'.[378] It should be recalled that according to the Court of Justice, 'such a declaration cannot be used for the purpose of interpreting a provision of secondary legislation where... no reference is made to the content of the declaration in the wording of the provision in question. The declaration therefore has no legal significance.'[379]

Neither the obligation nor the option to check the VIS at external borders will apply to third-country national family members of EU citizens, since they are not subject to the relevant provisions of the Borders Code.[380] The point is

[374] Art 8(1).

[375] It should also be noted that passports also still have to be stamped, even where border controls are relaxed: see Art 8(3), discussed below.

[376] Art 7(3)(ac) of the Borders Code, inserted by Reg 81/2009. Note that the border guard on command at the border post also decides on whether to relax border controls in the first place: Art 8(2), discussed below. However, as compared to the VIS derogation, the Borders Code does not require the notification of each decision to relax border controls.

[377] Art 7(3)(ad), inserted by Reg 81/2009. Note that Member States must also report annually on the relaxation of border checks generally (Art 8(4), discussed below).

[378] Council doc 15501/08 add 1, 20 Nov 2008.

[379] Case C-292/89 *Antonissen* [1991] ECR I-745, para 18.

[380] Art 7(2) and (3), along with the definitions in Art 2(5) and (6). See 3.4.1 above.

important, because information on the persons concerned will nevertheless be stored in the VIS.[381]

These amendments to the Code will be relevant to the future establishment of an entry–exit system.[382] But it must be noted that an entry–exit system cannot function as long as a derogation applies at entry, and in the absence of an obligation to enter information on visa holders at exit points as well (on which, see below). The potential difficulties in applying such a system would obviously be multiplied if it applies to non-visa nationals as well, as the Commission intends, although the Commission has suggested the parallel development of a 'trusted traveller' system in order to avoid bottlenecks.[383]

If the VIS begins operations in 2010 as planned, the derogations in the VIS Regulation and the Borders Code concerning the use of biometrics in the VIS upon entry will expire in 2016—which is after the time frame in which the Commission estimates that an entry–exit system could begin operations.[384] It should also be recalled that the initial three-year derogation from the use of fingerprint checks at external borders in the VIS Regulation will overlap with the rolling out of the VIS—so the impact of the use of the VIS at external borders will be limited for some time.[385]

Moving on to controls on exit, checks must include a check on the validity and genuineness of travel documents and 'whenever possible' a verification that the person is not a threat to 'public policy, internal security, or the international relations of any of the Member States'.[386] Exit checks *may* also involve verification of a visa, checks as to whether a person overstayed, and checks in the SIS or national databases[387]—although of course the *required* check 'wherever possible' on whether the person is a threat to for example, public policy would seem to entail a mandatory SIS check. Member States will also have an option, once the VIS becomes operational, to check persons on exit in the VIS for the purposes of verification.[388] Again, these provisions are linked to the future development of an entry–exit system.[389]

Furthermore, once the VIS becomes operational, Member States will have an option to search the VIS, presumably either on entry or exit, to check persons in the VIS for the purposes of *identification* (a 'one-to-many' search).[390]

---

[381] See 4.4.1 below.   [382] See 3.6.2 below.   [383] See ibid.

[384] COM (2008) 69, 13 Feb 2008.

[385] On the timeframe to roll-out the VIS, see 4.8 below. This point is also relevant to the practicalities of imposing VIS checks at land borders. It remains to be seen which non-Member States bordering the EU, if any, are still subject to a visa obligation by the time that the VIS is rolled out to these neighbouring regions.   [386] Art 7(3)(b).

[387] Art 7(3)(c).

[388] Art 7(3)(c)(i), as amended by Reg 81/2009 (n 322 above). There is no derogation permitted.

[389] See 3.6.2 below.

[390] Art 7(3)(d), inserted by Reg 81/2009 (ibid). There is no derogation permitted.

Thorough checks will take place, if possible, in a non-public area, at the request of the person concerned.[391] Persons must be given information about the purpose of the check and the procedures applicable, and may request the name or service number of the border guard(s) carrying out the check and the location and the date of crossing.[392] Both these provisions should contribute to the objective of ensuring fair treatment during border checks. Finally, the information which must be registered at the borders is listed in Annex II to the Code:[393] the names of the border guards; any relaxation of checks; the issuing of documents at the borders; persons apprehended and complaints; persons refused entry (grounds for refusal and nationalities); information on the security stamps used and the guards using them; complaints from persons subject to checks; police or judicial action; and particular occurrences. These amendments should make a useful contribution respectively to ensuring reasonable behaviour by border guards and to combating corruption or other criminal activity regarding falsified documents. It would be even more useful if this data were published.

Member States are obliged to provide for separate lanes at airports for EU and EEA citizens and their family members, on the one hand, and for all (other) third-country nationals, on the other hand. They have an option as to whether to provide for separate lanes at sea and land borders.[394]

As noted already, the Code provides for the possible relaxation of checks in limited circumstances, 'as a result of exceptional and unforeseen circumstances', which are 'deemed to be those where unforeseeable events lead to traffic of such intensity that the waiting time at the border crossing point becomes excessive, and all resources have been exhausted as regards staff, facilities and organisation'.[395] In that case, entry checks must take priority over exit checks, and there is anyway an obligation to stamp each travel document on entry and exit.[396] Member States must submit an annual report on the relaxation of border checks to the EP and Commission,[397] but there is no information available on these reports.

Next, travel documents (usually passports) must be stamped when all third-country nationals cross the border, both on entry and exit, regardless of whether the travellers are subject to a visa obligation or not.[398] There is an exemption for third-country national family members of EU citizens if they hold residence cards, in accordance with EU free movement law.[399] There are also express exemptions for heads of state and dignitaries, certain transport workers, and to nationals of Andorra, San Marino, and Monaco. The obligation might also '[e]xceptionally'

---

[391] Art 7(4).   [392] Art 7(5).   [393] See Art 7(7).

[394] Art 9, which took over the provisions of a 2004 Decision on this issue (n 311 above).

[395] Art 8(1). Arts 8, 10, and 11 took over the provisions of Reg 2133/2004 (ibid).

[396] Art 8(2) and (3) respectively; on stamping of documents, see below.   [397] Art 8(4).

[398] Art 10(1). The detailed arrangements for stamping are set out in Annex IV (Art 10(4)).

[399] Art 10(2), interpreted a contrario; see 3.4.1 above.

be waived where stamping a travel document 'might cause serious difficulties' for an individual; in such cases, a separate sheet has to be stamped to record entry and exit.[400]

If a travel document is not stamped on entry, Member States may presume that the person concerned does not fulfil the conditions for the duration of stay in the Member State concerned.[401] This presumption can be rebutted by the traveller,[402] but if he or she cannot rebut it, they may be expelled.[403] The Court of Justice has confirmed that there is only an option, rather than an obligation, to expel the person concerned in this case,[404] although arguably the position will be affected in future by the application of the Returns Directive.[405]

The Commission reported on the application of the provisions on stamping of documents and presumptions of irregular stay in 2009.[406] According to this report, there have been no problems applying the stamping obligations fully; in particular the obligations have not caused long waiting times at borders. Difficulties have arisen where a passport was full, where the stamping was confusing or illegible (due to stamping on top of a previous stamp), where children did not have a separate passport, and as regards whether the passport of a third-country national with a residence permit from a Schengen State should be stamped. In the latter case, the Commission takes the view that the passport need not be stamped, because a risk of exceeding the authorized period of short stay does not arise. While this is a sensible argument, never-theless there is no express exception to this end in the Code.[407] Equally the

---

[400] Art 10(3).   [401] Art 11(1).   [402] Art 11(2) and Annex VIII.   [403] Art 11(3).

[404] Joined Cases C-261/08 *Zurita Garcia* and C-348/08 *Choque Cabrera*, judgment of 22 Oct 2009, not yet reported. Although the Spanish text of the Code states that the person 'must' be expelled, the Court gave priority to the wording in all of the other language versions, which indicate that there is an option to expel. With respect, it is not clear from the facts of these cases whether or not there was a failure to stamp the documents of the persons concerned; the Court (and Advocate General) simply assumed that Art 11 of the Code was applicable. The judgment also interpreted Art 23 of the Convention, which will be replaced by the Returns Directive (Dir 2008/115 ([2008] OJ L 348/98) as from 24 Dec 2010 (Arts 20 and 21 of the Directive). On this Art, see 7.7 below.

[405] Dir 2008/115 (ibid); see 7.7.1 below. The Directive did not amend the Borders Code and there is no express provision in the Directive indicating how the prima facie mandatory expulsion set out in Art 6 of the Directive relates to the optional expulsion referred to in Art 11(3) of the Code. However, the Directive does specify that it is 'without prejudice' to 'more favourable provisions' in the 'the Community *acquis* relating to immigration and asylum' (Art 4(2) of the Directive). This must surely mean that the optional expulsion in the Code must take precedence over the mandatory expulsion in the Directive, where the two rules overlap. It should also be noted that Art 11(1) of the Code only provides for an option, not an obligation, to presume in the first place that the conditions for stay have been breached in the event that the documents in questions are not stamped. On the relationship between the Code and the Directive on this point, see also the opinion in *Zurita Garcia* (ibid), note 23, which, with respect, fails to take Art 4(2) of the Directive into account.

[406] COM (2009) 489, 21 Sep 2009, pursuant to Art 10(6).

[407] The same point could be made where the person concerned holds a long-stay visa, but the Commission does not mention this. The Commission's argument raises the question whether the list of exceptions from the stamping obligation set out in Art 10(2) and (3) is exhaustive or non-exhaustive. The text of the Code does not make this clear, although the exclusion of third-country

Commission does not see the need to create an exception to the stamping obligation for lorry drivers, who are the main group affected by stamps filling up a passport early, due to the risk of illegal immigration; it argues that an entry-exit system will eventually address their position.[408] The Commission does intend, on the other hand, to propose an express exception from the stamping obligation for railway workers who regularly travel in and out of the EU. Also, the Commission takes the view that a stamping obligation cannot be applied at internal borders, even where border checks are reinstated pursuant to the applicable provisions of the Code,[409] given that the re-introduction of those checks cannot alter the total length of authorized stay. This is again undoubtedly a sound argument, but not expressly set out in the wording of the Code.[410]

As for the presumption of illegality, most Member States do not collect statistics on the numbers of persons who are found on the territory or detected while exiting without an entry stamp, or who are able or not able to rebut any presumption of irregular stay, although in fact the Code does not require them to do so.[411] The Commission rightly points out that this information would obviously be useful in order to assess the effect of the provisions on stamping, but the fault here lies with the legislation, which failed to set out an obligation in this respect. Equally, most Member States have not informed the Commission about their practices on the presumption of illegal stay, although on this point the Code does set out an obligation.[412] It is not clear from the information supplied to the Commission whether or not Member States always presume that the absence of an entry stamp indicates an irregular stay. Ultimately, the Commission draws no conclusions about the rules in the Code on the presumption of an illegal stay, and does not mention the issue of the link between these rules and the Returns Directive (see the discussion above).

---

national family members of EU citizens with residence cards from the stamping obligation is not expressly set out—it follows from an *a contrario* reading of Art 10(2) along with Art 3(a). It might be possible to argue (although the Commission does not) that the stamping obligation does not apply to such persons because the Code only applies to persons admitted for a short stay in the first place (see Art 5(1)). But if that were the case, why does the Code contain references to persons with long-stay visas and residence permits in other provisions (Art 5(1)(b) and (4)(a), for instance)?

[408] See 3.6.2 below. Note, however, that an entry-exit system is not forecast to be operational until 2015, so this would not alleviate the position of the lorry drivers in the meantime. The Commission seems unwilling to consider any special solution for this category of persons (the creation of a special permit, a system of employers' liability, reciprocal agreements with states of origin on special travel documents, or the development of a *sui generis* entry-exit system for the meantime).

[409] See 3.5 above.

[410] Art 28 provides that '[w]here border control at internal borders is reintroduced, the relevant provisions of Title II shall apply *mutatis mutandis*'. It might be deduced that Art 10(1) is not a 'relevant provision' for this purpose, but it might be better to specify exactly what these 'relevant provisions' are in the interests of legal certainty.

[411] This is a distinct issue from the obligation to provide statistics on *refusal of entry* decisions (Art 13(5)).   [412] Art 11(2), final sub-paragraph.

Next, the Code contains basic rules on border surveillance; addressing the purposes of surveillance; the types of units to be used; the numbers of border guards to be used and their methods; and the requirement to survey sensitive areas in particular.[413] Further measures concerning surveillance may be adopted in accordance with a comitology procedure, involving participation of the EP.[414] An implementing measure relating to maritime border surveillance was adopted in 2010.[415] This Decision only concerns surveillance operations coordinated by Frontex, so is discussed further below.[416]

The Code then sets out rules concerning refusal of entry, which are obviously among its most important provisions. As noted above, the general rule is that persons who do not meet the criteria for admission must be denied entry, subject to certain exceptions;[417] more detailed rules on the procedure for refusing entry are set out in an Annex to the Code.[418] There are also procedural rights for persons denied entry. Entry may only be refused 'by a substantiated decision stating the precise reasons for the refusal', which is given by means of a standard form annexed to the Code. The decision must be taken by a legally empowered authority, must take effect immediately, and the decision form must be given to the person concerned, who 'shall acknowledge receipt'.[419]

Persons refused entry have 'the right to appeal'; the appeal 'shall be conducted in accordance with national law'. Member States must give the person concerned a written list of contact points who could provide information on persons who could represent him or her. But appeals 'shall not have suspensive effect'. If successful, an appeal must entail that the cancelled entry stamp is corrected; this is '[w]ithout prejudice to any compensation granted in accordance with national law'.[420] Unsurprisingly, the Code specifies that border guards must ensure that persons refused entry shall not enter the territory of the Member States.[421] Member States must collect statistics on the numbers refused entry; their nationality; the grounds for refusal of entry; and the type of border where entry was refused. This information must be transmitted annually to the Commission; which must publish it every two years.[422]

It is possible that these provisions will overlap with the scope of the Returns Directive, which gives Member States an option (but not an obligation) to exclude persons refused entry in accordance with the Borders Code from the scope of that Directive, which contains its own specific rules on procedural rights and related issues such as detention. Member States may also exclude from the scope of that Directive those persons 'who are apprehended

[413] Art 12(1)–(4).   [414] Art 12(5), as amended by Reg 296/2008 (n 322 above).
[415] See n 326 above.   [416] See 3.10.1.   [417] Art 13(1); see the discussion of Art 5 above.
[418] Art 13(6), referring to Annex V, Part A, since amended by Art 55 of the visa code (n 322 above). Point 3 of this Annex refers to the Schengen and EU rules on carrier sanctions (see 7.5.1 below).
[419] Art 13(2) and Annex V, Part B.   [420] Art 13(3).   [421] Art 13(4)
[422] Art 13(5). For more on this, see 3.11 below.

or intercepted by the competent authorities in connection with the irregular crossing by land, sea or air of the external border of a Member State and who have not subsequently obtained an authorisation or a right to stay in that Member State'.[423] If Member States take up these options, the former category of persons will at least benefit from the procedural rights set out in the Borders Code.[424] But more problematically, the latter category of persons will not benefit from any procedural rights whatsoever as a matter of EU law; this position is impossible to defend. Arguably this category of persons falls sufficiently within the scope of EU law to be covered by the general principles of EU law, and can therefore derive procedural rights in that connection. In any event, the Returns Directive requires that for both categories of persons, Member States must 'ensure that their treatment and level of protection are no less favourable than' the rules in that Directive regarding limitations on use of coercive measures; postponement of removal; emergency health care; the needs of vulnerable persons, and detention conditions; and must also 'respect the principle of non-refoulement'.[425]

Next, Chapter III of Title II concerns cooperation between national authorities, as well as staff and resources for border controls.[426] Member States must deploy 'appropriate staff and resources' in order to carry out border checks as provided for in Chapter II, 'to ensure an efficient, high and uniform level of control at their external borders'.[427] Checks must be carried out by border guards in conformity with national law; the guards must be sufficiently specialized and trained, and encouraged to learn relevant languages. Member States must ensure effective coordination of all relevant national services, and notify the Commission of the services responsible for border guard duties.[428]

As for cooperation between Member States, there is a general requirement of assistance and cooperation in accordance with other provisions of Code. They must also exchange relevant information. The code refers to the role of Frontex in coordinating border operations, as well as Member States' role as regards operational coordination, including the exchange of liaison officers, as long as this does not interfere with the work of the Agency. Member States must provide for training of border guards on border control and fundamental rights, taking account of the standards developed by the Agency.[429] Furthermore, there

---

[423] Art 2(2)(a) of Dir 2008/115 (n 404 above).

[424] Conversely, of course, if a Member State does not invoke the exclusion, persons refused entry at the border will benefit from the provisions in both the Returns Directive and the Borders Code. Presumably, in the event of overlap, the rule setting the highest standards will apply, pursuant to Art 4(2) of the Returns Directive.

[425] Art 4(4), Dir 2008/115 (n 404 above). The obligation to respect the principle of non-refoulement is not further defined (cf also Art 5 of the Directive), although note that in any event the Directive is subject to more favourable provisions in other EU immigration and asylum measures (Art 4(2)). See further 7.7.1 below.   [426] Arts 14–17.

[427] Art 14.   [428] Art 15; see Art 34(1)(d) on notification.   [429] Art 16.

is a special rule concerning joint control of the common land borders of those Member States not yet fully applying the Schengen rules. Until the Schengen *acquis* is fully applicable to them, those States can jointly control their borders, without prejudice to Member States' individual responsibility. To this end, Member States may conclude bilateral agreements, which they must inform the Commission of.[430]

Finally, Chapter IV of Title II of the Code sets out specific rules for border checks in certain cases, concerning respectively different types of borders and different categories of persons.[431] For instance, the rules on crossing by road in particular permit drivers usually to stay in their vehicles during checks; the rules for checking trains en route to or from third countries have been amended to allow for 'juxtaposed control' in third States; the rules on air travel contain entirely new provisions on private flights; and the rules on sea borders were amended in particular to strengthen the rules on control of cruise ships and pleasure boats and to tighten the definition of fishing vessels which will not generally be checked.

As for checks on particular categories of persons, there are six categories of persons subject to special treatment: heads of state; pilots and other aircraft crew; seamen; holders of diplomatic, official, or service passports and of documents issued by international organization; cross-border workers; and minors. For example, the special rules for Heads of State and their delegation exempt them entirely from border checks; holders of diplomatic, official, or service passports and documents issued by international organizations are exempt from subsistence requirements, must be given priority when crossing, and cannot be refused entry by border guards unless the guards first check with foreign ministries; cross-border workers need not be subject to a check every time they cross the border, if they are 'well known' to the border guards due to their 'frequent crossing' and they were not listed in the SIS when an initial check was carried out; and minors must be the subject of 'particular attention' from border guards, to ensure that accompanied minors are with persons entitled to exercise parental care and that unaccompanied minors are not leaving the territory against the wishes of the person with parental care of them.[432]

3.6.2. Entry-exit system

The next major step in the development of EU external border controls could be the creation of an 'entry-exit' system, which, as noted above, would keep

---

[430] Art 17; see Art 37 on notification.
[431] Arts 18–19. The detailed rules appear in Annexes VI and VII.
[432] See subsequently the action plan on unaccompanied minors (COM (2010) 213, 6 May 2010) and the Council conclusions on this issue (JHA Council press release, 3 June 2010), which refer to regular collection of data and risk assessments by Frontex on this issue.

track of the entry into and out of the Schengen zone of most categories of third-country nationals. Such a system was suggested by the Commission in a detailed communication in February 2008, which also addressed the related issues of a 'trusted traveller' programme and a system of electronic travel authorization.[433] The Commission is planning to propose legislation on an entry-exit and trusted traveller systems, and a communication on electronic travel authorization, in 2011.[434]

According to the 2008 Commission communication, the main purpose of the entry-exit system would be to identify third-country nationals who had 'overstayed' their period of permitted stay in the Union, whether or not they were subject to a visa obligation. Such persons are the biggest category of irregular migrants in the EU.[435] The system would record data on 'the time and place of entry, the length of stay authorised, and the transmission of automated alerts' to the authorities on overstayers, once they violate the rules in question and also when they leave the EU. In case of change of status (justified overstay, or a grant of residence), the information concerned would be updated. It would be necessary for the VIS to be fully operational before the entry-exit system was applied to visa nationals.[436] As for non-visa nationals, they would have to give their biometric data when they first entered the EU once the new system was applicable; the Commission admits that this 'could potentially complicate the management of passenger flows, especially at certain land border crossing points'.

These problems, according to the Commission, could be addressed by introducing, in conjunction with the new entry-exit system, a new category of 'trusted traveller' for certain third-country nationals (again available to both visa nationals and non-visa nationals), based on a pre-screening process offered on a voluntary basis. These persons would be exempt from some of the conditions of entry at the border (regarding the purpose of stay, means of subsistence, and absence of threat to public order), and would also be admitted through automated border gates, which would register their identity and travel history as well as check their biometrics (fingerprints and photographs) against their travel document or database. The automated gates could also be used by EU citizens, nationals of EEA States, Swiss nationals, and family members of such persons, provided that they held biometric passports, with the proviso that in accordance with free movement law, their movement would not be recorded.

The 'common vetting criteria' for this status for third-country nationals could be, 'as a minimum . . . a reliable travel history (the person should not have exceeded

---

[433] Communication on the next steps in border management (COM (2008) 69, 13 Feb 2008).

[434] See the Commission's action plan for implementation of the Stockholm programme (COM (2010) 171, 20 Apr 2010).

[435] See the impact assessment attached to the Commission communication (SEC (2008) 153, 13 Feb 2008).   [436] On the VIS, see 4.8 below.

the authorised stay at previous visits to the EU), proof of sufficient means of subsistence, and holding a biometric passport', but '[f]urther criteria could be considered', and visa nationals could get registered traveller status on the basis of the criteria for obtaining multiple entry visas.[437] Applicants for this status would have to apply at consulates or common application centres. In the Commission's view, the entry-exit system and the accompanying trusted traveller programme could be applicable by 2015.

Finally, the possible electronic system of travel authorization would apply to non-visa nationals, 'who would be requested to make an electronic application supplying, in advance of travelling, data identifying the traveller and specifying the passport and travel details'. This data would be used to verify that the person concerned fulfilled the entry conditions 'before travelling to the EU, while using a lighter and simpler procedure compared to a visa'.

While waiting for the Commission's legislative proposal regarding an entry-exit system, the Council conducted a questionnaire to determine Member States' positions on the planned system,[438] and conducted a pilot project to register the number and categorization of all persons crossing the Schengen external borders during one week in September 2009.[439] There were 12.9 million entries or exits in a single week, comprising 9.3 million EU citizens and other persons with free movement rights, 2.1 million non-visa nationals, and 1.5 million visa nationals; 1.1 million people crossed at sea borders, 5.0 million at land borders, and 6.8 million at air borders.

3.6.3. Assessment

Taken as a whole, the Borders Code is clearly vastly better drafted than the texts it replaced, although it has several flaws. There are significant improvements as regards procedural rights, fair treatment, accountability, and transparency, but several provisions are unclear (as regards the use of databases on EU citizens, exit checks and the exercise of police powers) or ill-considered (the rules on exit controls, which are arguably impractical). The Code could more clearly have addressed the issue of whether there is a right to entry if the relevant conditions are satisfied, although it is arguable, as noted above, that a right to entry can be inferred from the wording of the entry conditions rules set out in the Code. While the additional provisions concerning asylum are welcome, the opportunity was missed to rethink the conditions for entry and to provide for detailed provisions ensuring that the right to asylum is respected at external borders; the latter

---

[437] On those criteria, see 4.7.2 below.

[438] Council docs 14334/08, 16 Oct 2008 and 15630/08, 1 Dec 2008. The questionnaire did not examine the parallel issue of developing a 'trusted traveller' system.

[439] Council doc 13267/09, 26 Sep 2009.

issue is complicated by the controversial and highly questionable provisions of the EU's asylum procedures Directive.[440]

The amendment to the Borders Code relating to the VIS may in particular prove to be impractical. It is striking that there was no impact assessment either of the proposal to amend the Code as regards VIS use or of the practical implications of this particular issue when the Commission assessed the impact of the original proposal for the VIS Regulation.[441] The derogation from use of the VIS upon entry set out in the Borders Code is drafted quite narrowly, and it may not prove feasible to spend time assessing the impact of granting a derogation when a quick decision has to be made to address traffic flows.[442] When the relevant derogations expire at the end of 2015, the rules on the full use of the VIS at borders may be more realistic, at least as regards land borders, if visa requirements are by then abolished for all Western Balkan states and perhaps at least some other neighbouring states. It is also possible that visa facilitation treaties might be amended to address this issue in future. Of course if an entry-exit system is by then operational and applies to all non-visa-nationals at the Commission intends, then the issue will present itself again—all the more so given that an entry-exit system would require non-EU citizens to be checked upon exit as well as entry.

As for the stamping of documents, the rules in the Code have proved practical according to the Commission's assertions, although it does not follow that the use of VIS at the borders, especially the extra time taken to obtain fingerprints, would still be feasible. It would be useful to know more about how presumption regarding irregular stay is actually applied.

This brings us to the planned entry-exit system. It should first of all be noted that in light of EU free movement law, it would not be legal to apply such a system to EU citizens and their family members, including citizens of non-Schengen States or Schengen associates. Also, there is little point in applying this system to non-visa nationals, given the relatively limited risk of overstay which they pose in practice as compared to the extra costs and complications that would result from applying the system to them. If nationals of a particular country not subject to visa obligations in fact have a high rate of overstaying, the obvious solution is simply to impose a visa obligation on nationals of that country, rather than impose an entry-exit system on all non-visa nationals. While an entry-exit system, if it

---

[440] See 5.7 below.

[441] See SEC (2004) 1628, 28 Dec 2004. This impact assessment simply states (at p 17) that 'time will be lost at entry and exit points by providing and checking biometric data', without assessing the feasibility of checking such data in all cases of entry. On the same page, the Commission estimates the 'very significant' financial costs of the VIS at EU level and for national visa authorities, but this does 'not include the costs for the border crossing points as these costs cannot be estimated at the present time'.

[442] The absolute obligation in the Borders Code to stamp the passports of third-country nationals, even when border controls are relaxed, will already slow down any attempt to clear a backlog at the border crossing.

works as planned, will identify overstayers effectively, it will not assist authorities to find them if they have disappeared. It is assumed that an entry-exit system will either be integrated into the VIS or applied seamlessly in parallel with it. The costs and complications of the development of a completely separate system do not bear thinking about. In any event, any system will have to be subject to robust data protection rules to avoid the effect of erroneous identification, and the penalties for overstay will have to be proportionate and take account of legitimate grounds for overstay such as *force majeure*, applications for international protection, and humanitarian reasons.

As for the other plans for future developments, an authorized traveller system would probably be essential if an entry-exit system is introduced, in order to ensure that delays at border crossings do not become intolerable. Again, such a system could not be used to store information on the movements of EU citizens, citizens of Schengen associates, and their family members. It will be essential to ensure that the rules for registration in this system are fair and transparent, and that data protection rights apply fully to the vetting process. On the other hand, the Commission has not yet made a very convincing case for the idea of developing a system of electronic travel authorization.

3.7. Schengen Information System[443]

The Schengen Information System (SIS) is a well-known and long-established element of the Schengen border control system, with the main purpose (in the immigration context) of making available to the relevant national officials a common list of names of persons who should not be allowed to enter the Schengen area. The current system has been amended and the EU also intends to establish a second-generation System (SIS II), which has been bedevilled by operational problems. The current SIS and future SIS II will be considered in turn.

3.7.1. Current Schengen Information System

The current SIS was initially established by Articles 92–119 (Title IV) of the 1990 Schengen Convention,[444] as applied from March 1995. Further rules are set out in various decisions of the Schengen Executive Committee,[445] including the Decision establishing the Sirene Manual, which governs subsequent exchanges of information following a 'hit' in the SIS.[446] Despite its dual application for immigration purposes on the one hand and criminal law and policing purposes on the

---

[443] On the general legal framework governing SIS and SIS II, see 12.6.1.1 below.
[444] [2000] OJ L 239.   [445] Ibid. For a list of these measures, see 12.6.1.1 below.
[446] [2003] OJ L 38.

other, the SIS remained almost entirely a 'third pillar' measure due to the failure to allocate the relevant provisions of the Schengen *acquis* to the EC Treaty in 1999, when the Treaty of Amsterdam integrated the *acquis* into the EC and EU legal order.[447] However, the Schengen Convention SIS rules were amended in 2004 and 2005 to provide for certain changes to the System pending the application of SIS II—the so-called 'SIS I+'.[448] Furthermore, the procedure for updating the Sirene Manual was set out in both first and third pillar legislation from 2004.[449]

Since the legal framework governing the SIS as regards immigration is now subject partly to measures allocated to the previous third pillar and partly to measures adopted within the framework of Community law (as it previously was), its legal position as a 'pure' (ex-)third pillar instrument is arguably now doubtful.[450] This point is relevant as regards both the legal effect of the SIS rules and the jurisdiction of the Court of Justice, for the transitional period of five years following the entry into force of the Treaty of Lisbon.

While the details of the SIS are considered elsewhere in this book, this chapter focuses upon the issue of the criteria for placing the name of a third-country national on the joint list of persons who should in principle be banned from entry to the Member States.[451] More precisely, the consequence of an 'alert' for denial of entry being placed in the SIS is that the person must in principle be refused entry at the external border or refused a visa,[452] although exceptionally on humanitarian or other grounds a person listed in the SIS can be permitted to enter or receive a visa for a single Member State only.[453]

The Convention provides that a name shall be entered into the list following 'decisions taken by the competent administrative authorities or courts' in accordance with national law.[454] Such decisions 'may be based on a threat to public policy or public security or to national security' posed by a third-country national's presence on national territory. This 'may arise in particular' where a person 'has been convicted of an offence carrying' a custodial sentence of at least one year, or where 'there are serious grounds for believing' that the person

---

[447] [1999] OJ L 176/17.

[448] These amendments can be found in Council Reg 871/2004 ([2004] OJ L 162/29) and a third-pillar Decision of 2005 ([2005] OJ L 68/44).

[449] The first pillar measure is Reg 378/2004 ([2004] OJ L 64/5); for the text of the updated Manual, following the application of this legislation, see the Commission Decisions in [2006] OJ L 317.   [450] See 2.2.2.3 above.

[451] See Art 96 of the Convention. Art 17(3)(g) of the Convention conferred power on the Executive Committee to define principles governing the drawing up of the common list, but this power was never used. Art 17(3)(g) has now been repealed by Art 56(1) of the visa code ([2009] OJ L 243/1).

[452] Arts 5(1)(d) and 15 of the Convention; the former Art has since been replaced by Art 5(1)(d) of the Schengen Borders Code (Reg 562/2006, [2006] OJ L 105/1) and the latter Art has now been replaced by Art 21(3)(c) of the visa code (Reg 810/2009, [2009] OJ L 234/1). See also Arts 18, 19(1), 20(1), and 25 of the Convention.

[453] Arts 5(2) and 16 of the Convention; the former Art has since been replaced by Art 5(4) of the Schengen Borders Code (ibid) and the latter Art has now been replaced by Art 25 of the visa code (ibid).   [454] Art 96(1) of the Convention.

'has committed serious criminal offences', including drugs offences as defined in the Convention, 'or in respect of whom there is clear evidence of an intention to commit such offences in the territory of a [Member State]'.[455] Furthermore, '[d]ecisions may also be based on the fact that the [person concerned] has been subject to measures involving deportation, refusal of entry or removal which have not been rescinded or suspended, including or accompanied by a prohibition on entry, or where applicable, a prohibition on residence, based on a failure to comply with national regulations on the entry or residence' of foreigners.[456] The Court of Justice has confirmed that the EU free movement rules take priority over the SIS rules.[457]

3.7.2. SIS II

The object of replacing the SIS with SIS II was initially twofold: to provide for more functions, including more categories of data (notably biometric data), and to permit the expansion of the SIS (and therefore the Schengen free movement zone) to include the new Member States. To this end, the Council adopted a Regulation in 2006 which will regulate the functioning of SIS II as regards immigration.[458] Parallel measures concern the use of SIS II by vehicle registration authorities[459] and a third pillar Decision concerning use of the system for policing and criminal law purposes.[460]

SIS II will be put into operation when the Council decides, inter alia, that the relevant technical requirements have been satisfied.[461] Due to repeated difficulties in satisfying these technical requirements, the start of operations of the new system has repeatedly been postponed; the latest deadline is the first quarter of 2013.[462] It remains to be seen whether the EU can keep to this schedule. In the meantime, the issue of enlargement of the Schengen area was addressed by means of a different technical solution, allowing newer Member States and Switzerland to participate in the existing SIS and therefore to join the Schengen area in 2007 and 2008, without waiting for SIS II to become operational.[463] When SIS II does become applicable, the previous provisions of the Schengen Convention concerning the SIS and the relevant Executive Committee Decisions, as well as the EC measures building upon this *acquis*, will be repealed or replaced.[464]

---

[455] Art 96(2) of the Convention.   [456] Art 96(3) of the Convention.

[457] Case C-503/03 *Commission v Spain* [2006] ECR I-1097; see 3.4.1 above.

[458] Reg 1987/2006 ([2006] OJ L 381/4). All references in this subsection are to this Regulation, except where otherwise noted.   [459] Reg 1985/2006 ([2006] OJ L 381/1).

[460] [2007] OJ L 205/63. See 12.6.1.1 for details.   [461] Art 55(2) and (3).

[462] See JHA Council press release, 3–4 June 2010.   [463] See 3.2.5 above.

[464] Arts 52 and 53.

The Commission has power to implement the SIS II Regulation by means of a 'comitology' committee which does not involve any extra control of the adoption of implementing measures by the EP.[465] It has already used this power on two occasions, to adopt a new version of the Sirene Manual governing action to be taken after a 'hit' in SIS II in 2008, and a security plan in 2010.[466] SIS II will be administered by a 'Management Authority', after an interim transitional period in which the Commission will nominally be designated as the manager of SIS II, but in practice will delegate this management to France and to Austria (where the backup site of the SIS II data will be located), who will nonetheless be held accountable for their management of the system in accordance with EU rules.[467] The Commission has proposed legislation to establish the relevant agency, which will also administer the VIS and Eurodac.[468]

As noted above, the SIS II Regulation provides for the inclusion of photographs and fingerprints in the system.[469] This biometric data will only be entered following a 'special quality check' in order to ensure data quality.[470] The specifics of this quality check will be established by the Commission pursuant to a 'comitology' procedure. Initially, biometric data will only be used to 'confirm the identity' of a person whose name has been found in the SIS following an alphanumeric search, likely meaning in practice that his or her name matches a name in the SIS.[471] But later biometrics will be used to 'identify' persons 'as soon as technically possible'.[472] This will entail a 'one to many' search (comparing one set of biometric data to much or all of the biometric data in the database). There will be no further vote before this important functionality is put into practice.

The biggest single issue, from the perspective of substantive immigration law, is the grounds for issuing an alert. On this point, the SIS II Regulation starts out by repeating the basic rule in the Schengen Convention (as set out above) that an alert is issued by a national body in accordance with national law, with the additional provisos that the decision must be taken 'on the basis of an individual assessment', and that '[a]ppeals against these decisions shall lie in accordance with national legislation'.[473]

Next, an alert 'shall' (not 'may') be issued where there is a threat to public policy or public security, or national security, which 'shall' (not 'may') be the case, 'in particular' in two cases: a conviction in a Member State for an offence carrying a deprivation of liberty for at least one year, or 'serious grounds' to believe that a person has committed a 'serious criminal offence' or 'clear indications' that the person intends to commit such offences.[474] This provision differs from the current rule in the Convention in that: the issue of an alert on these grounds is mandatory (although it is not clear how the issue of a mandatory alert is compatible

---

[465] Art 51. On the comitology process, see 2.2.2.1 and 2.2.3.1 above.
[466] [2008] OJ L 123 and [2010] OJ L 112/31.   [467] Art 15.   [468] See 12.6.1 below.
[469] Art 20(2).   [470] Art 22(a).   [471] Art 22(b).   [472] Art 22(c).   [473] Art 24(1).
[474] Art 24(2).

with the proportionality rule in the Regulation);[475] the threat could materialize in 'a Member State', rather than on national territory; a criminal conviction must have taken place in a Member State (although it should be recalled that the criteria remain non-exhaustive, so a Member State still has the option of issuing an alert on a person who was convicted of a crime in a non-Member State); and the current threshold of 'clear *evidence*' of an intention to commit offences has been lowered to the new 'clear *indications*' test. The SIS II Regulation retains the current option of issuing an alert following a breach of immigration law, using wording essentially identical to the current Convention.[476]

However, the general rules on issuing immigration alerts do not apply to a separate specific category of persons—individuals who have been barred from entry pursuant to an EU foreign policy measure.[477] Alerts relating to such persons 'shall' be entered into SIS II, and the rules concerning data which must be entered in respect of each alert, the obligation to carry out a specific assessment, and the requirement to permit appeals are not applicable.[478] However, this provision is '[w]ithout prejudice to' the second special category—third-country national family members of EU citizens. The SIS II Regulation confirms the case law of the Court of Justice relating to the current SIS rules as regards such persons, requiring conformity with the EU citizens' free movement Directive and providing for immediate use of the Sirene procedure after a 'hit' concerning such persons to contact the Member State issuing the alert to determine what action to be taken.[479]

The SIS II Regulation also requires the Commission to review the application of the basic rules on issuing alerts three years after SIS II starts operations, and then to 'make the necessary proposals to modify the provisions of this Article to achieve a greater level of harmonisation of the criteria for issuing alerts'.[480] However, this review clause has been superseded in the meantime by the adoption of the Returns Directive, which Member States must apply by 24 December 2010, well before the date for the review of the SIS II rules.[481] This Directive sets out specific rules relating to entry bans; an 'entry ban' is defined as an 'act prohibiting entry into and stay on the territory of the *Member States*',[482] not merely

---

[475] Art 21 reads: '[b]efore issuing an alert, Member States shall determine whether the case is adequate, relevant and important enough to warrant entry of the alert in SIS II'.

[476] Art 24(3).   [477] Art 24(4).

[478] Art 26. However, the proportionality rule in Art 21 is still applicable. Note that following the entry into force of the Treaty of Lisbon, challenges to the underlying travel bans can be brought pursuant to Art 275 TFEU. On the question of the correct 'legal base' for these travel bans, see 3.2.4 above and 4.2.4 below.

[479] Art 25. See Case C-503/03 *Commission v Spain* [2006] ECR I-1097 and 3.4.1 above.

[480] Art 24(5).

[481] Dir 2008/115 ([2008] OJ L 348/98), Art 20(1). SIS II will not be operational before the deadline to implement the Directive. For more on the Directive, see 7.7.1 below.

[482] Art 3(6), Dir 2008/115 (emphasis added); and see more clearly recital 14 in the preamble to the Directive.

an individual State. The link between these entry bans and the SIS II is recognized in the preamble to the Directive,[483] although there is not an express legal requirement to issue the entry bans as SIS II alerts; the Commission therefore stated when the Directive was adopted that the planned review of the SIS II rules would provide an 'opportunity to propose an obligation to register in the SIS entry bans issued under this Directive'.[484] Of course, in the meantime some or all Member States might well choose to register all entry bans issued pursuant to the Directive in the current SIS, and then the future SIS II, even in the absence of a legal obligation to do so. It should be recalled, though, that the Returns Directive binds those Member States which do not yet fully apply the Schengen *acquis*, whereas only full participants in Schengen use the SIS (or the future SIS II). The Directive's entry ban rules are themselves a topic for the Commission's first review of the implementation of the Directive, due in December 2013.[485]

As for the substance, the Returns Directive requires Member States to issue an entry ban in cases where a person has not been given a period for voluntary departure, or where an obligation to return has not been complied with,[486] although there is considerable discretion to waive this obligation.[487] In other cases, Member States *may* issue an entry ban.[488] There are also rules on the time period of entry bans,[489] and rules on procedural rights (the form of return ban decisions and the remedy against them) which are more specific than the rules in the SIS II Regulation,[490] although unlike the Regulation, the Directive does not explicitly require an individual assessment before an entry ban is issued.[491]

However, it must be pointed out that the Returns Directive is explicitly subject not only (like the SIS II Regulation, and the current SIS) to EU free movement law,[492] but also (*unlike* the SIS II Regulation, or the current SIS) to more favourable provisions in *other* EU immigration and asylum legislation.[493] More specifically, the entry ban rules in the Directive are expressly 'without prejudice'

---

[483] Recital 18 in the preamble, which provides that 'Member States should have rapid access to information on entry bans issued by other Member States. This information sharing should take place in accordance with [the SIS II Reg]'.

[484] Summary of Council acts for Dec 2008 (Council doc 7478/08, 11 Mar 2009).

[485] Art 19, Dir 2008/115.   [486] Art 11(1), first sub-paragraph, Dir 2008/115.

[487] Art 11(3), Dir 2008/115.   [488] Art 11(1), second sub-paragraph, Dir 2008/115.

[489] Art 11(2), Dir 2008/115.

[490] Arts 12 and 13, Dir 2008/115. Note that the legal aid rules in the Directive do not need to be applied by Member States until 24 Dec 2011 (Arts 13(4) and 20, Dir 2008/115).

[491] See, however, recital 6 in the preamble to the Directive, which states that, as a general principle of EU law, entry bans and other decisions under the Directive 'should be adopted on a case-by-case basis'. It can obviously be questioned whether the prima facie obligation to issue entry bans set out in Art 11(1) of the Directive is compatible with this general principle.

[492] Technically, the Directive does not apply to persons with free movement rights at all (Art 2(3), Dir 2008/115).

[493] Art 4(2), Dir 2008/115. The Directive is also subject to more favourable provisions of treaties concluded by the EC and/or the Member States (Art 4(1)), and by more favourable provisions of national law, provided they are 'compatible' with the Directive (Art 4(3)). It is not clear whether this provision gives Member States discretion to waive their obligations to issue entry bans above and

to EU asylum legislation.[494] So even if the Returns Directive is interpreted to mean that there is not a requirement to conduct an individual assessment before an entry ban is issued, the requirement in the SIS II Regulation to conduct an individual assessment before that ban is entered into the SIS must still apply.

Furthermore, to the extent that, following such an assessment, alerts are then issued in the SIS following entry ban decisions taken pursuant to the Returns Directive, the relevant EU immigration and asylum legislation must necessarily also take precedence *over the SIS II Regulation*, because the priority rule set out in the Directive would continue to govern those entry bans. The same will be true of immigration alerts issued in the current SIS, if they were issued pursuant to the entry ban rules in the Directive.[495] Where the Directive is not applicable, it is arguable even in the absence of a specific rule in the current SIS provisions or the SIS II Regulations giving priority to other EU immigration and asylum legislation, that legislation still takes precedence over the SIS and SIS II rules to the extent that it gives effect to human rights obligations.[496] Anyway, to the extent that a check in the SIS or the future SIS II leads to a refusal of entry, it should be recalled that this refusal is governed by the Borders Code, which does contain express derogations in relation to asylum.[497]

It should be also be noted that that the Returns Directive potentially has a narrower personal scope than the SIS II Regulation (or the current SIS), since Member States have the power to exclude from the scope of the Directive persons who are refused entry and persons intercepted in connection with irregular entry,[498] as well as persons who are subject to return as part of a criminal law sanction or because of a criminal conviction, or who are subject to extradition procedures.[499] To the extent that these exceptions are applied, the SIS II Regulation (or the current SIS rules) alone will govern any entry bans which are issued as alerts in SIS II (or the current SIS) in future. Conversely, if an entry ban issued pursuant to the Directive is not entered as an alert into SIS II (or the current SIS), given the absence of a legal obligation to do so, only the Directive is applicable.

The provisions of the SIS II Regulation relating to data protection include in particular a new right to information for persons who are the subject of an

---

beyond the discretion set out in Art 11(3) of the Directive. For a general discussion of such provisions in EU immigration and asylum law, see 5.2.4 below.

[494] Art 11(5) of the Directive, referring to Dir 2004/83 ([2004] OJ L 304/12), the 'qualification Directive'.

[495] As noted above, SIS II will not become operational before the deadline to apply the Returns Directive.

[496] On the hierarchical effect of human rights rules in the EU legal order, see 2.3 above. On Art 25 of the Schengen Convention in particular, see 4.9 below.

[497] Arts 3(b), 4(3), and 13(1) of the Code (Reg 562/2006, [2006] OJ L 105/1); see 3.6.1 above.

[498] Art 2(2)(a), Dir 2008/115; see further 3.6.1 above. Aspects of the Directive apply to such persons (Art 4(4) of the Directive), but this does not include the entry ban rules.

[499] Art 2(2)(b), Dir 2008/115. This exception would be relevant to many or all of the alerts issued pursuant to Art 24(2) of the SIS II Reg.

alert,[500] in accordance with the EU's data protection Directive,[501] and that the SIS II Regulation bans the transfer of SIS II immigration data to third countries and international organizations.[502] As regards the right to information, it should also be noted that both the borders code and the visa code require a person who is refused entry or refused a visa to know the reason why—and that reason might be that the person concerned is the subject of an alert in the SIS or the future SIS II.[503] It might be arguable that the right to appeal against the refusal or entry or a visa[504] also entails the right to challenge the underlying decision to issue the alert.

3.7.3. Assessment

The current SIS rules have been the subject of a great deal of commentary, much of it highly critical.[505] The main criticism of the rules concerns the extensive discretion for Member States as to whether to list a person on the SIS; the problematic nature of mutual recognition of another Member State's decisions in this field; the consequential effects on human rights for those who claim a need to enter a Member State in order to seek protection or on other human rights grounds; the lack of procedural rights and remedies where there is a need to challenge an SIS entry made by another Member State; the risk of discrimination on racial or ethnic origin as regards the application of the rules; and the limited data protection rights in relation to immigration alerts issued pursuant to the current SIS rules. The initial criticism of a lack of international judicial control has been addressed by giving the Court of Justice jurisdiction following the entry into force of the Treaty of Amsterdam, but that control has not been exercised in practice, except as regards family members of EU citizens.

To what extent would the SIS II Regulation, when it becomes applicable, address these concerns? First of all, as for the grounds for a SIS II listing, the obligation to provide for an individual assessment and appeals is very welcome, assuming that the wording of the Regulation is interpreted to mean that there

---

[500] See generally 12.6.4 below.

[501] Art 42(1), which refers to Arts 10 and 11 of the data protection Directive (Dir 95/46, [1995] OJ L 281/31).   [502] Art 39. This issue is not expressly addressed in the current SIS rules.

[503] Art 13(2) and Annex V, Part B of the borders code (n 497 above); Art 32(2) and Annex VI of the visa code (Reg 810/2009, [2009] OJ L 243/1). In the latter case (but not the former), the person concerned must be informed *which* Member State issued the alert.

[504] Art 13(3) of the borders code and Art 32(3) of the visa code (both ibid).

[505] For detailed analyses, see R Cholewinski, 'No Right of Entry: The Legal Regime on Crossing the EU External Border' in E Guild, P Minderhoud, and K Groenendijk, eds, *In Search of Europe's Borders* (Kluwer, 2003), 105 at 115–127; T Eicke, 'Paradise Lost? Exclusion and Expulsion from the EU' in idem, 147–168; R Cholewinski, *Borders and Discrimination in the European Union* (ILPA/MPG, 2002); J Steenbergen, 'Schengen and the Movement of Persons' in H Meijers, et al, *Schengen: Internationalisation of Central Chapters of the law on aliens, refugees, privacy, security and the police* (2nd edn, Stichting NJCM-Boekerij, 1992); P Boeles, 'Schengen and the Rule of Law' in idem; and Justice report, *The Schengen Information System: A Human Rights Audit* (Justice, 2000).

is a *right* to an appeal which is merely subject to more detailed regulation (as regards time limits and competent courts) by national law, rather than a discretion under national law to preclude a right to appeal altogether. It is submitted that the former interpretation is correct, in light of the general principles of EU law, which require an effective remedy for EU law rights, and that furthermore any national regulation of the right of appeal cannot render the right to appeal ineffective. It is unfortunate that the express clause giving priority to other EU immigration and asylum legislation was dropped, but as noted above, it is still arguable that such legislation takes priority over the SIS II legislation even in the absence of an express rule to that effect; and in any event the priority rules in the Returns Directive or the Borders Code may be applicable.

However, it is unfortunate that there was not some degree of greater harmonization of the grounds for issuing an alert, at the very least to provide that the rather vague grounds set out in the legislation are exhaustive grounds for issuing alerts. The Returns Directive has not subsequently ensured a sufficient degree of harmonization on this issue,[506] which should therefore be addressed in the near future in order to guarantee that alerts are only issued when they are genuinely objectively justified in light of the degree of criminality or seriousness of the breach of immigration law committed by a particular third-country national. There is also a fundamental problem in that there is no obligation to publish the national criteria for issuing alerts in the EU's Official Journal. Without that information it is clearly far more difficult for any person to know if the alert on him or her was correctly or lawfully added to SIS II, or for supervisory authorities to carry out their responsibilities to ensure correct application of the data protection rules more generally. A person refused entry at the border need not even be told which Member State issued a SIS (or future SIS II) alert on him or her. The resulting lack of foreseeability of the circumstances in which data will be collected and processed violates basic principles of data protection law.

In the case of persons subjected to a travel ban pursuant to EU sanction measures, the underlying problem is the inability to attack the 'pure' foreign policy acts of the EU directly in the EU courts, although, as noted above, the Treaty of Lisbon has remedied this problem.[507]

As for the use of biometric data, in certain cases it might have the positive effect of ensuring that individuals who are apparently listed in the SIS can 'clear their names', and certainly in many cases it will more quickly identify individuals who are genuinely the subject of an alert. But it remains to be seen in practice whether the risk of wrongful identification pointed to by data protection authorities in cases of 'one-to-many' searches has been sufficiently addressed.

Finally, since SIS immigration data was collected in the context of establishing joint border controls for the Schengen free movement zone, it would be

---

[506] See 7.7.1 below.   [507] Art 275 TFEU.

inappropriate, in light of the 'purpose limitation' principle of data protection law, to share that data with non-EU countries or bodies which do not participate in Schengen. Therefore the absolute ban on the transmission of that data outside the EU can only be welcomed.

3.8. Local border traffic

The original Schengen Convention provided for the Executive Committee to adopt standardized rules concerning exceptions for local border traffic,[508] but this power was never used before the integration of the Schengen *acquis* into the EU legal order. In turn, as noted above, the Schengen Borders Code provides for the adoption of separate specific rules on local border traffic.[509] Those rules on this issue were duly adopted in late 2006,[510] in parallel with amendments to the EU's visa list legislation which provided for visa exemptions for persons benefiting from the new border traffic rules.[511]

The border traffic Regulation principally establishes standardized rules for local border traffic, in particular by introducing a standard local border traffic permit.[512] Member States are authorized to agree treaties with neighbouring third countries that are in accordance with the rules of the Regulation.[513] The Regulation does not affect EU or national law concerning long-term stays, access to economic activities, or customs and tax matters.[514] A 'border area' means an area within 30 kilometres of the border, but this may stretch to 50 kilometres in order to include entire districts adjoining the border.[515] 'Local border traffic' is defined as a crossing for 'social, cultural or substantiated economic reasons, or for family reasons' by border residents,[516] who are defined as persons lawfully resident in the border area for more than one year, with a possibility of reducing this waiting period in 'exceptional' cases.[517]

Chapter II of the Regulation sets out the main features of an authorized local border traffic regime.[518] An external land border may be crossed by persons who hold a local border permit and possibly also travel documents (depending on agreements between Member States and non-Member States), who have been checked in the SIS, and who do not pose a threat to the public policy, public security, or public health of any Member State.[519] As compared to the normal rules for crossing borders,

---

[508] Art 3 of the Schengen Convention ([2000] OJ L 239).

[509] Art 35 of Reg 562/2006 ([2006] OJ L 105/1).

[510] Reg 1931/2006 ([2006] OJ L 405/1), which entered into force on 17 Jan 2007 (Art 21). All references in this section are to this Regulation, unless otherwise indicated.   [511] See 4.5 below.

[512] Art 1(1).

[513] Art 1(2). On the broader context of EU external relations law, see 3.12 below. See also the similar legislation conferring power on Member States to negotiate civil law treaties (8.9 below).

[514] Art 2.   [515] Art 3(2).   [516] Art 3(3).   [517] Art 3(6).   [518] Arts 4–6.

[519] Art 4.

there is no requirement to hold a visa (a relevant point, when the Regulation was first adopted, for all bordering non-Member States except Croatia, leaving aside Schengen associates and micro-states),[520] no requirement to show subsistence or the purpose of the visit, and no absolute requirement to hold a travel document.[521] Border residents may stay up to three months in a border area, depending on bilateral agreements; this does not derogate from the normal maximum of permitted short-term stays.[522] Although border residents are subject to entry and exit checks, their travel documents (when they require them) must not be stamped, by way of derogation from the normal rules.[523] It remains to be seen how the development of an entry-exit system would affect the local border traffic rules.[524]

Chapter III of the Regulation sets out the basic rules governing the special border traffic permit.[525] The permit is limited in validity to the border area of the issuing Member State.[526] It must bear a photograph of the holder and other basic information as specified in the Regulation.[527] There is no standard EU-wide format for the permit, but its security features and technical specifications must comply with the EU legislation establishing a standard format for residence permits.[528] Since the subsequent amendment of that EU legislation, this means that the permit will have to contain biometric information as from 2011 (photographs) and 2012 (fingerprints).[529]

A permit can only be issued if four conditions are met: possession of a valid travel document; proof of status as a border resident and of grounds to cross the external border frequently; a check in the SIS; and lack of any threat to the public policy, public security, or public health of any Member State.[530] The permits are valid for a period of between one and five years, and the fees charged cannot exceed those for issuing short-term visas: Member States may issue the permits free of charge.[531] The permits can be issued by national authorities or consulates, and Member States must keep a permanent record of them.[532] There

[520] Note that due to amendments to the EU visa list legislation adopted in 2009 and proposed in 2010, most citizens of Western Balkans States will be exempt from a visa requirement: see 4.5 below.

[521] Compare to the entry conditions in Art 5 of the Schengen Borders Code (n 509 above).

[522] Art 5.   [523] Art 6; cf Art 10 of the Schengen Borders Code (n 509 above).

[524] See 3.6.2 above.   [525] Arts 7–12.   [526] Art 7(2).   [527] Art 7(3).   [528] Art 8.

[529] Reg 1030/2002 ([2002] OJ L 157/1) was amended by Reg 380/2008 ([2008] OJ L 115/1) to provide for the introduction of biometric data (fingerprints and photographs) into residence permits. Biometric data must be integrated into the permits two years (as regards photographs) and three years (as regards fingerprints) from the adoption of the relevant implementing measures (Art 9 of Reg 1030/2002, as amended by Reg 380/2008). These measures were adopted in May 2009. See further 6.9 below.   [530] Art 9.

[531] Arts 10 and 11. Note that the visa code does not permit the issue of visas free of charge for persons in local border zones, so holding a local border traffic permit significantly simplifies the position (Art 16 of the visa code, Reg 810/2009, [2009] OJ L 243/1; see 4.7.2 below). Then again, most of the third countries in question are either now (or soon) on the EU visa whitelist (see 4.5 below), or have visa facilitation treaties with the EU, which reduce the fees for visa applications (see 4.11.2 below).   [532] Art 12.

are no other standardized conditions, so although the border traffic permit can be compared to a visa, the visa code (and previously the Common Consular Instructions) does not govern its issue, and the VIS will not apply. On the other hand, there are no express provisions conferring procedural rights on persons applying for or holding a border traffic permit, although it is arguable that implied rights exist nonetheless pursuant to the general principles of EU law.

Chapter IV of the Regulation concerns the implementation of the local border traffic regime.[533] The only means to introduce or maintain a local border traffic regime is by means of bilateral agreements between Member States and neighbouring third countries. Any new bilateral agreement must be compatible with the Regulation, and any existing agreements must be amended to conform to it.[534] In either case, Member States must allow the Commission to screen draft agreements, and make any amendments required by the Commission.[535] Presumably, if a Member State disagrees with a Commission decision, it can sue to annul that decision in the EU courts; conversely, the Commission could bring an infringement action against a Member State which does not comply with a Commission decision. The relevant bilateral agreements must contain provisions on the readmission of persons abusing the border traffic regime, in the event that the EU or the Member State concerned has not concluded a readmission agreement with the relevant country.[536] Since the entry into force of EU readmission agreements with most neighbouring third countries, this provision is only relevant as regards Belarus and Turkey.[537]

The bilateral agreements must confer reciprocal rights on EU citizens and legally resident third-country nationals living in the border areas of Member States. Also, bilateral agreements can 'exceptionally' liberalize the normal requirements to cross the borders only at authorized crossing points (on the condition that the Member States concerned still carry out surveillance and random checks along the borders, and ease the requirement that all third-country nationals must be subject to thorough checks at the external borders).[538]

Lastly, Chapter V of the Regulation sets out final provisions.[539] The Regulation does not affect the specific rules concerning Spanish enclaves in Morocco.[540] Member States must establish penalties for abuse of a permit, and report regularly to the Commission on cases of abuse.[541] Member States have to notify all bilateral agreements to the Commission, which must make them public.[542] The Schengen

---

[533] Arts 13–15.   [534] Art 13(1).   [535] Art 13(2).   [536] Art 13(3).

[537] On the EU's readmission agreements, see 7.9.1 below.

[538] Art 15; compare with Arts 4 and 7 of the Schengen Borders Code (n 509 above).

[539] Arts 16–21.   [540] Art 16.   [541] Art 17.

[542] Art 19. In practice, this information has not been made public, except in the context of the Commission's report on the application of the Regulation, on which see below.

Convention has been amended to refer to this Regulation, rather than national border traffic treaties.[543]

Also, the Commission had to report on the application of the Regulation by January 2009, possibly accompanied by legislative proposals.[544] This report was submitted in July 2009.[545] According to the Commission, a Hungary–Ukraine agreement entered into force in January 2008; a Poland–Ukraine treaty entered into force in July 2009; a Slovakia–Ukraine treaty applied from September 2008; and treaties were under discussion between Lithuania–Russia, Lithuania–Belarus, Latvia–Russia, Poland–Belarus, Bulgaria–Serbia, Bulgaria–FYROM, and Romania–Ukraine. One pre-existing agreement (Slovenia–Ukraine) was also examined. It should be noted that the report did not mention any local border traffic treaties agreed or under negotiation in respect of several external borders (for example, Greece–Albania, Greece–Turkey, Greece–FYROM, or Romania–Moldova).

As regards the possible derogations from the general rules on external border control, all of the treaties concerned were in some way stricter. Also, there had been ambiguities in interpreting the Regulation, in particular as regards the definition of the local border area and the imposition of a requirement to hold medical insurance. In the Commission's view, the former issue (ie Member States' desire to widen the relevant border zone) could be addressed by means of application of the EU's visa facilitation agreements.[546] Member States had not always accepted the Commission's demands to renegotiate agreements, although the Commission had not responded (as it could have done) by bringing infringement actions against those States.[547] The Commission concluded that in light of the limited experience with local border traffic treaties to date, it was too soon to propose changes to the legislation, but it would submit another report in the second half of 2010. However, the Commission did note that '[t]here were … no reports from the Member States that there was a wide misuse by owners of [local border traffic] permits or that the agreements raised some security risks for the Schengen area'.

The border traffic rules addressed the need to simplify border crossing for the many thousands of visa nationals who have been on the EU's external border following enlargement (until the visa waivers for the Western Balkan States began at the end of 2009), and whose economic, cultural, and personal links to the new Member States were sundered when visa obligations were applied to these neighbouring countries and the other EU visa rules were extended when

---

[543] Art 20, amending Art 136(3) of the Convention ([2000] OJ L 239). See further 3.12 below.
[544] Art 18.   [545] COM (2009) 383, 24 July 2009.
[546] On those agreements, see 4.11.2 below. Note that many of these agreements contain declarations regarding local border traffic issues.
[547] On the infringement procedure, see Art 226 EC (now Art 258 TFEU).

the full Schengen *acquis* applied to most new Member States. So the border traffic legislation in principle makes a useful contribution to enhancing both the EU's political relationship with its neighbours—who are expected to take on many obligations to assist the EU and who suffered substantial disadvantages following enlargement—and the daily life of many individual residents of border regions, including those EU citizens who benefit from maintaining economic, cultural, and personal links to the east.

3.9. Biometric passports

In December 2004, the Council adopted a Regulation harmonizing the security features of EU citizens' passports as regards the inclusion of biometric information (fingerprints and digital photographs).[548] This Regulation was subsequently amended in 2009,[549] partly in order to provide for exceptions from the obligation to include biometrics in passports. As noted above, the UK sued to annul the original 2004 Regulation because its attempt to opt in to the legislation was refused by the Council, but the UK's challenge was unsuccessful.[550] The Regulation is intended to be consistent with other measures requiring the insertion of photos and fingerprints into residence permits and visas, although ultimately it proved technically impossible to insert biometric information into visas.[551] It should be recalled that there are also Resolutions of Member States which have established other features of the design of a uniform format for EU passports.[552] While there are doubts about the Council's competence to adopt this Regulation, given the express exclusion (at the time) of power for the EC to adopt measures relating to passports, the correctness of the legal base has been implicitly endorsed by the Court of Justice.[553] It should also be recalled that the EU now has a power, conferred by the Treaty of Lisbon, to adopt measures related to passports and similar documents in order to facilitate EU citizens' free movement rights.[554]

The Regulation, largely prompted by American demands for the inclusion of high-security features in the passports of countries subject to the American visa waiver programme,[555] provides for mandatory inclusion of digital photographs and fingerprints in EU passports, in accordance with the technical standards set out in an Annex to the Regulation.[556] Passports must be issued as individual

---

[548] Reg 2252/2004, [2004] OJ L 385/1.

[549] Reg 444/2009, [2009] OJ L 144/1. The Regulation has not been consolidated.

[550] Case C-137/05 *UK v Council* [2007] ECR I-11593.

[551] See 4.6 and 6.9.1 below as regards Schengen visas and residence permits respectively.

[552] [1981] OJ C 241/1; [1982] OJ C 179/1; [1986] OJ C 185/1; [1995] OJ C 200/1; [2000] OJ C 310/1; and [2004] OJ C 245/1.   [553] Case C-137/05, n 550 above. See 3.2.4 above.

[554] Art 77(3) TFEU; see again 3.2.4 above.

[555] See the explanatory memorandum to the proposal (COM (2004) 116, 18 Feb 2004), p 3.

[556] Art 1(1) and (2).

documents,[557] and the Commission is due to report by 26 June 2012 on children travelling across the external borders in order to examine whether to adopt a common approach on the protection of children crossing the external borders.[558] Children under twelve years old are exempt from the fingerprinting obligation, although Member States which already fingerprinted children between six and twelve years old as of 26 June 2009 can continue to do so for a four-year period after that date.[559] The Commission must report by 26 June 2012 on whether to alter the age limit, based on an independent technical study of the accuracy of fingerprint data taken from children under twelve for 'identification and verification purposes' (ie checking the fingerprints on a one-to-one and one-to-many basis respectively).[560] Also, persons are exempt from the obligation if taking their fingerprints is physically impossible.[561]

The Regulation applies to passports and travel documents issued by Member States, but not to identity cards or to temporary passports or travel documents having a validity of under a year.[562] Biometric data must be collected by qualified national officials, who must act in accordance with international human rights law and ensure the dignity of the person concerned if the biometric information cannot be taken.[563] Further security standards can be adopted by the Commission, assisted by a 'comitology' committee of Member States' representatives.[564] There are basic data protection rules, and the Regulation specifies that checking the biometric information in the passport is without prejudice to the rules in the Schengen Borders Code concerning checks of EU citizens at the external borders.[565] Member States had to apply the Regulation eighteen months after the adoption of technical specifications as regards digital photographs, and thirty-six months after the adoption of technical specifications as regards fingerprints.[566] In practice, this obligation has applied as from 28 August 2007 as regards facial images, and 28 June 2009 as regards fingerprints.[567]

In the Commission's view, this is only a first step; that institution wishes to see the creation of '[a]t EU level, a centralised, biometrics-based, "EU passport

---

[557] Art 1(1), second sub-paragraph, as inserted by Reg 444/2009. This obligation must be implemented by 26 June 2012 (see final sub-paragraph of Art 6, as inserted by Reg 444/2009).

[558] Art 1(1), third sub-paragraph, as inserted by Reg 444/2009.

[559] Art 1(2a)(a), as inserted by Reg 444/2009.   [560] Art 5a, as inserted by Reg 444/2009.

[561] Art 1(2a)(b), as inserted by Reg 444/2009. There is a special rule if this impossibility is only temporary: see Art 1(2b), as inserted by Reg 444/2009.   [562] Art 1(3).

[563] Art 1a, as inserted by Reg 444/2009.

[564] Art 2, as amended by Reg 444/2009; see also Arts 3(1) and 5. For the English translations of two implementing measures, adopted by the Commission in 2005 and 2006, see: <http://ec.europa. eu/justice_home/doc_centre/freetravel/documents/doc_freetravel_documents_en.htm>.

[565] Art 4, as amended by Reg 444/2009, referring to Art 7(2) of the Borders Code (Reg 562/2006, [2006] OJ L 105/1); see 3.6.1 above. It should be noted that the passports Regulation does not amend the Borders Code, so there is no new legal requirement to check passports going beyond the rules in the Borders Code.   [566] Art 6, as amended by Reg 444/2009.

[567] See SEC (2009) 320, 9 Mar 2009, p 10.

register", which would contain the fingerprints of passport applicants' with the passport number 'and most probably some other, but limited, relevant data'.[568] However, the 2009 amendment to the Regulation states that the legislation is not a legal base regarding passport databases, which are 'strictly a matter of national law'.[569]

The Regulation was followed up by Council conclusions on the issue of national identity cards, adopted in December 2005.[570] While the conclusions are not legally binding, and do not require Member States either to adopt identity cards or to require biometric identifiers as part of the cards, they are likely to encourage this process. The conclusions state that the biometrics and security features of identity cards should be based on those applicable to passports, and set out guidelines for the process of issuing identity cards. A later Member States' resolution sets out agreed common technical standards for identity cards.[571] Again, it should be recalled that the EU now has a power, conferred by the Treaty of Lisbon, to adopt measures related to identity cards in order to facilitate EU citizens' free movement rights.[572]

3.10. Operational cooperation

Operational cooperation as regards border control within the EU has largely taken place within the context of the EU's border control agency, Frontex. But there have also been initiatives to establish a surveillance system for southern frontiers (Eurosur). These two issues will be examined in turn.

3.10.1. Frontex

A perceived need to adopt EU measures to ensure more effective operational cooperation as regards borders control was first addressed by the Council's 2002 Action Plan on external borders, which addressed the issues of coordination of operations and cooperation, risk analysis, joint use of personnel and equipment, legislation, and burden-sharing.[573] Initially, the implementation of the Plan was coordinated by the heads of border guards meeting within the framework of the Strategic Committee on Immigration, Frontiers, and Asylum (SCIFA), who were dubbed 'SCIFA+'. By June 2003, a number of joint operations had been held, the creation of ad hoc centres on sea, land, and air borders was underway,

---

[568] See points 2 and 8 of its explanatory memorandum (COM (2004) 116, 18 Feb 2004).

[569] Recital 8 in the preamble, Reg 444/2009. See also the discussion of competence issues in 3.2.4 above.   [570] JHA Council press release, 1–2 Dec 2005.

[571] JHA Council press release, 4–5 Dec 2006.

[572] Art 77(3) TFEU; see discussion in 3.2.4 above.

[573] Council doc 10019/02, 14 June 2002.

and projects on a common risk analysis and a core curriculum for border guards were under development.[574] But it was soon decided that joint operations and cooperation between Member States needed a stronger institutional structure, and the principle of creating a EU Borders Agency was approved by the October 2003 European Council. The Agency (known in practice as Frontex) was established by Regulation 2007/2004, adopted in autumn 2004;[575] the legality of the Regulation was subsequently upheld by the Court of Justice, dismissing a legal challenge by the UK, which had objected to its exclusion from participation in the adoption of the Frontex legislation.[576] The Council decided that the agency's seat was to be in Warsaw, and it started operations on 1 May 2005.[577]

The Frontex Regulation has been amended once, in 2007 (see below).[578] A separate proposal to amend the Regulation, dating from 2005, is blocked.[579] After a communication on the future of Frontex,[580] the Commission tabled a further proposal to amend the Frontex legislation in 2010, which is still under discussion.[581] It should also be noted that a measure implementing the Schengen Borders Code has established rules governing maritime surveillance operations coordinated by Frontex.[582] Frontex would also have a formal role in the EU's network of immigration liaison officers, according to separate proposed legislative amendments.[583]

The main tasks of Frontex are the coordination of operational cooperation between Member States; assistance with training; risk assessment; the follow-up to research on external borders; extra technical and operational assistance for Member States that need it; management of an inventory of Member States' equipment; and coordination of expulsion—an issue going beyond external border control.[584] However, the basic Regulation makes it clear that the powers of

---

[574] Council doc 10058/1/02, 11 June 2003. The creation of a network of immigration liaison officers was also linked to this process (see 7.5.5 below). For more on the development of the operational aspects of the border plan, see ch 7 of S Peers and N Rogers, *EU Immigration and Asylum Law: Text and Commentary* (1st edn, Martinus Nijhoff, 2006).

[575] [2004] OJ L 349/1. See the Frontex website at: <http://www.frontex.europa.eu/>.

[576] Case C-77/05 *UK v Council* [2007] ECR I-11459. See further 3.2.5 above.

[577] [2005] OJ L 114/15; see Art 34.

[578] Reg 863/2007, [2007] OJ L 199/30. The Frontex Reg has not been consolidated. All references in this subsection are to Reg 2007/2004, as amended, unless otherwise indicated. Note that as well as amending Reg 2007/2004, Reg 863/2007 contains distinct provisions of its own (Arts 1–11, Reg 863/2007).

[579] COM (2005) 190, 13 May 2005. The proposal concerns the procedure for reappointment of the Executive Director and Deputy Executive Director.

[580] COM (2008) 67, 13 Feb 2008. See also point 10 of the conclusions of the June 2008 European Council, the more detailed JHA Council conclusions on this issue (Council doc 9873/08, 23 May 2008), and the independent evaluation, online at: <http://www.frontex.europa.eu/specific_documents/other/>.   [581] COM (2010) 61, 24 Feb. 2010.

[582] [2010] OJ L 111/20. On the broader legal context, see 3.6.1 above. Note that the EP has brought an annulment action against this measure: Case C-355/10 *EP v Council*, pending.

[583] COM (2009) 322, 8 July 2009. See further 7.5.5 below.

[584] Art 2; and see further details in Arts 3–9.

Frontex are not exclusive; Member States can continue with bilateral cooperation between each other or cooperation with third States outside the framework of the Agency.[585] It is specified that executive acts by the Agency's staff on the territory of a Member State, or by the staff of one Member State on the territory of another, are subject to the national law of the host Member State; this obviously suggests that the Agency will carry out executive powers.[586] Nonetheless, the Regulation states that 'the responsibility for the control and the surveillance of external borders lies with the Member States'.[587]

The Regulation also provides for information exchange between Frontex, the Commission, and the Member States, although it is not clear whether this entails the collection or exchange of personal data.[588] However, the preamble refers to the EU rules on personal data protection applicable to EU institutions, bodies, or agencies,[589] so it appears that Frontex could indeed be involved in processing personal data.[590] Frontex may also exchange non-personal data with Europol, third countries, and international organizations.[591]

As for the status of Frontex,[592] it is an independent EU 'body' with legal personality. The Regulation also provides for the possibility of establishing specialized centres.[593] EU law rules on staff, privileges and immunities, liability, access to documents, fraud control, and budgets apply. Overall strategic control is in the hands of a Management Board, meeting three times a year and consisting of one member per Member State and two Commission representatives, although the Regulation gives each Member State a veto over operations conducted on or near its territory. However, the day-to-day management is in the hands of an Executive Director and Deputy Director, appointed by the Management Board on the basis of proposals from the Commission.

The 2007 amendments to the Frontex Regulation first of all established a mechanism to set up Rapid Border Action Teams (RABITs) in order to provide 'rapid operational assistance for a limited period to a Member State facing a situation of urgent and exceptional pressure', particularly a large number of illegal entrants.[594] The deployment of RABITs is now a specific task of Frontex.[595] Each team is composed of border guards nominated by Member States when an exceptional situation exists.[596] The Frontex Management Board, on a proposal from the Executive Director, decides by a two-thirds majority on the profile and overall numbers of border guards required for the team.[597] Member States then make the necessary guards available for deployment, 'unless they are faced

---

[585] Art 2(2).   [586] Art 10.   [587] Art 1(2).   [588] Art 11.
[589] On these rules, see further 3.4.3 above.   [590] Recital 19 in the preamble.
[591] Arts 13 and 14.   [592] Arts 15–32.
[593] See the study on this issue at: <http://www.frontex.europa.eu/specific_documents/other/>
[594] For the details of this mechanism, see Arts 3–11, Reg 863/2007, and Arts 8a–8h of the Frontex Reg, as inserted by Reg 863/2007.   [595] Art 2(1)(g), as inserted by Reg 863/2007.
[596] Art 4(1), Reg 863/2007; see also Art 8b(1) of the Frontex Reg, as inserted by Reg 863/2007.
[597] Art 4(2), Reg 863/2007.

with an exceptional situation substantially affecting the discharge of national tasks', although each Member State still decides which particular guards will be deployed and for how long.[598]

Secondly, the 2007 amendments regulate the tasks and powers of border guards who are on the territory of a different Member State in the context of 'joint operations and pilot projects' as defined in the original Frontex Regulation.[599] Both sets of amendments are 'without prejudice to the rights of refugees and persons requesting international protection, in particular as regards non-refoulement'.[600]

The 2010 Decision regulating maritime surveillance operations contains 'rules' on some issues and 'non-binding guidelines' on others. The 'rules' address such general issues as compliance with fundamental rights, non-refoulement of persons intercepted at sea, and assistance to persons with special needs, along with specific rules governing jurisdiction and powers to intercept vessels. The 'guidelines' concern issues relating to search and rescue operations and disembarkation of any persons rescued or intercepted, with 'priority' to be given to disembarkation in the country from which those persons departed.

As for the latest proposed amendments to the Frontex Regulation, they would, inter alia: insert references to human rights into the Regulation;[601] provide for powers to establish information systems, operate the EU's migration management mechanism (Iconet), and contribute to a border surveillance system;[602] revise the rules on pilot projects and joint operations, including the creation of Frontex Joint Support Teams;[603] allow Frontex to evaluate Member States' border control capacities;[604] strengthen the provisions on training, research, acquisition of equipment, and returns;[605] add new provisions on data protection and security;[606] and insert new rules concerning external relations, including the possibility of posting Frontex liaison officers to third countries as part of the EU network of information liaison officers.[607] For the future, the Commission intends to release a communication in 2014 'on the long term development of' the agency, 'including the feasibility of the creation of a European system of border guards'.

The Frontex website indicates that the agency has been conducting a growing number of joint or pilot operations (for example, fourteen in 2009). As for returns, the agency has taken an increased role, coordinating thirty-two operations in 2009 involving over 1,600 returnees. Frontex also has operational arrangements with a large number of third States and bodies. The EU institutions have almost

[598] Art 4(3), Reg 863/2007; see also Art 8b of the Frontex Reg, as inserted by Reg 863/2007.
[599] Art 1(2), Reg 863/2007, and Arts 10–10c of the Frontex Reg, as amended or inserted by Reg 863/2007.   [600] Art 2, Reg 863/2007.
[601] Proposed amendments to Arts 1(2) and 10(2), and new Arts 2(1a) and 33(2b).
[602] Proposed new Art 2(1)(h) and (i). On Iconet, see 7.8 below.
[603] Proposed amendment to Art 3 and new Arts 3a–3c.
[604] Proposed amendment to Art 4.   [605] Proposed amendments to Arts 5–7 and 9.
[606] Proposed new Arts 11a and 11b.
[607] Proposed amendments to Art 13 and 14. On the ILO network, see 7.5.5 below.

literally been 'pouring money' into Frontex, resulting in a 360% increase in funding from 2006–09.[608]

3.10.2. Other operational cooperation

In 2006, the Commission suggested the creation of a permanent 'Coastal
Patrol Network' for the southern maritime external borders and of a 'European
Surveillance System for Borders', or 'Eurosur'.[609] The latter suggestion has been
further developed, focusing on the southern maritime borders. A Commission
communication in 2008 suggested a three-phase approach,[610] with the first two
phases in parallel concerning the upgrading and extension of national border surveillance systems and the interlinking of national infrastructures in a communication network, as well as targeting research and development in order to improve
the performance of surveillance tools to develop their common application. The
third phase would then gather, analyse, and disseminate all the relevant data
between national authorities. Further detailed actions were then recommended.
This approach was supported by the JHA Council.[611]

According to a 2009 Commission report on the development of the Eurosur
system,[612] Member States had taken initial steps to set up national surveillance
systems and national coordination centres, draft guidelines for cooperation
between the national centres had been prepared, work on a technical infrastructure (including with third countries) was underway, and relevant research
projects were planned. As for the third phase, the Commission produced a communication on integrated maritime surveillance in 2009. A legislative proposal
establishing Eurosur is planned for 2011.[613]

3.10.3. Assessment

There is an ongoing fundamental question concerning the accountability of
EU operational action in this area, including the process for ensuring the legal
accountability for Frontex's actions before the EU courts. There is insufficient
information on the operations of Frontex and considerable concern about
some of the third States with which it has concluded informal (and invisible)

---

[608] See the 2009 annual report at: <http://www.frontex.europa.eu/gfx/frontex/files/general_
report/2009/general_report_2009_en.pdf>.

[609] COM (2006) 733, 30 Nov 2006. See earlier the Commission communication on migration
management (COM (2005) 621, 30 Nov 2005) and the Dec 2005 European Council conclusions,
Annex I.   [610] COM (2008) 68, 13 Feb 2008.

[611] See conclusions in the JHA Council press release, 5–6 June 2008.

[612] SEC (2009) 1265, 24 Sep 2009.

[613] Commission Action Plan on implementing the Stockholm programme (COM (2010) 171,
20 Apr 2010).

arrangements.[614] The rules on rescue and disembarkation should be binding and improved, making it clearer which State is responsible for disembarkation and consideration of asylum applications. The non-*refoulement* rule should be spelled out more clearly in these rules as well, for example ruling out removal to third States which do not apply sufficient standards as regards international protection. Finally, the idea of creating a European border force is simply not legally viable in light of the limits on the EU's competence to take direct coercive measures.[615]

3.11. Administrative cooperation and EU funding

During the Maastricht era, the Council first adopted a Joint Action establishing the 'Sherlock' programme, concerning cross-border cooperation between administrators checking identity documents.[616] This was later subsumed into a broader programme set up by a Joint Action establishing 'Odysseus', which funded cooperation on a wide variety of immigration, border control, and asylum issues, spending €12 million over four years.[617] By the time this programme expired, the Treaty of Amsterdam was in force, and so it was replaced from June 2002 by a Council Decision establishing a Community action programme called 'ARGO', which ran from 2002–06.[618] Over that period, €25 million was initially devoted to assistance to national administrations to assist with the correct application of EC law and to ensure that account was taken of Community rules. Subsequently, the budget was enlarged to €14 million for 2004, and the Decision was amended in 2004, to relax the original requirement that projects must involve more than one Member State.[619]

This programme was then replaced by the Decision establishing a European Borders Fund, which applies from 2007–13.[620] The objective of the fund is to contribute to the control and management of external borders and the uniform application of EU law, particularly the Borders Code,[621] and the amount of money to be spent is €1.32 billion over 2007–13.[622]

---

[614] The relevant part of the Frontex website is essentially content-free: <http://www.frontex.europa.eu/external_relations/>.   [615] See Art 72 TFEU, discussed in 2.2.3.2 and 3.2.4 above.

[616] [1996] OJ L 287/7. For an overview of EU funding of JHA matters, see 2.6 above.

[617] [1998] OJ L 99/2. For reports on the implementation of the programme, see: <http://ec.europa.eu/justice_home/funding/expired/odysseus/funding_odysseus_en.htm>.

[618] Decision 2002/463 ([2002] OJ L 161/11). For details of implementation of the programme, see: <http://ec.europa.eu/justice_home/funding/intro/funding_2004_2007_en.htm#argo>.

[619] [2004] OJ L 371/48.

[620] [2007] OJ L 144/22. See also the treaty with Schengen associates regarding this fund (see 3.2.5 above).   [621] Art 3(1) of the Decision (ibid).

[622] Art 13(1) of the Decision (ibid).

Furthermore, there is a secondary Schengen measure, which is still in force, concerning the exchange of statistical data as regards external borders.[623] This measure overlaps in part with the obligation to collect statistics pursuant to the Schengen Borders Code, concerning the numbers refused entry, the grounds for refusal, the nationality of the persons refused, and the type of border at which they were refused entry.[624] This obligation in turn overlaps entirely with the 2007 Regulation on immigration statistics, as regards statistics on persons refused entry at the border,[625] which replaced the previous informal collection of statistics (in this case, through CIREFI, the EU's clearing house on immigration control), which concerned the numbers refused and their nationalities only.[626] The statistics produced pursuant to the statistics Regulation are available for the years beginning in 2008,[627] while the statistics produced prior to that point are assessed by the Commission in its reports on EU policy in this area.[628] However, so far these statistics have not been effectively integrated into public analysis and discussion of the relevant issues.

3.12. External relations

As outlined elsewhere in this book,[629] the EC (now the EU) has implied external relations powers, in particular to conclude treaties, even in the absence of express external powers. The EU's external powers become exclusive if it has fully harmonized an issue in its internal law.

As regards external border controls, the EU's external competence is addressed by a special provision in the Treaties. This takes the form of Protocol to the EC Treaty (now the TFEU) attached originally by the Treaty of Amsterdam, concerning this issue. According to this Protocol, as amended by the Treaty of Lisbon,[630] Article 77(2)(b) TFEU (previously Article 62(2)(a) EC) is 'without prejudice to the competence of Member States to negotiate or conclude agreements with third countries as long as they respect Union law and other relevant international agreements'. This Protocol could be interpreted to mean either that the EU would fail to gain exclusive external power over this issue even if it fully harmonized the internal law, or merely that Member States retain external power as long as there is no internal legislation fully harmonizing the issue—in

---

[623] SCH/Com-ex (95) 21 ([2000] OJ L 239/176).

[624] Art 13(5) of the Code (Reg 562/2006, [2006] OJ L 105/1).

[625] Reg 862/2007 ([2007] OJ L 199/23), Art 5. See also Art 8(1)(c) of this Regulation, on possible further disaggregations.   [626] See 6.11 and 7.8 below.

[627] See: <http://appsso.eurostat.ec.europa.eu/nui/show.do?dataset=migr_eirfs&lang=en>.

[628] See the annexes to SEC (2006) 1010, 19 July 2006 and SEC (2009) 320, 8 Mar 2009.

[629] On EU external competence and the procedure for negotiating and concluding treaties in EU law, see 2.7 above.

[630] The Treaty of Lisbon did not make any substantive amendments to this Protocol.

other words, EU external power is not exclusive by *nature*, but can only become exclusive by *exercise*. Given the obligation to respect EU law as specified in the Protocol, the better interpretation is the latter one. This is confirmed by analogy by the interpretation of an Advocate General in a case concerning the non-exclusive aspects of the Common Commercial Policy (before the entry into force of the Treaty of Lisbon).[631]

However, it should be recalled that even where EU external powers are exclusive, the EU can always authorize the Member States to exercise some limited external powers anyway if it chooses.[632] In fact, there are already provisions of the Schengen *acquis* concerning Member States' competence to conclude external borders treaties.[633] Member States which wish to conduct negotiations on external borders with third States must inform the other signatories of the Schengen Convention in good time.[634] Moreover, Member States are banned from making agreements simplifying or abolishing border checks with third States, unless they have the consent of the other parties to the Schengen Convention; this is subject to the right of Member States to conclude treaties collectively.[635]

Following the integration of the Schengen *acquis* into the EC legal order, Member States' negotiation of any such treaties is also now governed by the principle of Community solidarity, which sets further implicit restrictions on Member States' exercise of their external competence in areas where the EC (now EU) has legislated.[636] But in any event, these provisions of the Schengen Convention need to be re-examined. They should either be repealed as obsolete in light of the Protocol attached to the TFEU, on the grounds that the Protocol regulates the issue sufficiently; or, if they are to be retained, they should be updated and integrated (for the sake of clarity) into the Schengen Borders Code. In particular, if Member States are to be permitted to conclude treaties simplifying or abolishing border checks, detailed substantive and procedural rules governing the exercise of this power (for instance, requiring the approval of the Commission) should be adopted, given the obvious impact of such treaties on the EU's external borders

---

[631] Opinion of 26 Mar 2009 in Case C-13/07 *Commission v Council*, withdrawn.

[632] Art 2(1) TFEU.

[633] Art 136 of the Schengen Convention ([2000] OJ L 239). This Art was allocated to Art 62(2)(b) EC, as it then was (Decision 1999/436, [1999] OJ L 176/17). Art 136(1) and (2) have not subsequently been repealed or amended by any EU measures, but Art 136(3) was amended by a Reg in 2006 (see below).

[634] Art 136(1) of the Convention. Art 1 of the Convention defines 'third states' as meaning any non-Contracting Parties to the Convention. Presumably, following the integration of the Schengen *acquis* into the EC legal order and the conclusion of Schengen association agreements by the EU, a 'third state' is now any country which is neither an EU Member State nor a Schengen associate.

[635] Art 136(2) of the Convention. Presumably, unless the Protocol on external competence as regards external borders is regarded as excluding EU external competence entirely (or as requiring all external borders agreements to be mixed), this should now be understood as a reference to the right of the EU to conclude such treaties.   [636] See 2.7.1 above.

regime.[637] The external borders Protocol is not a legal barrier to the adoption of such rules, because its reference to the obligation to respect EU law surely encompasses both the substantive EU law relating to external border controls as well as the possibility of adopting specific EU rules governing Member States' exercise of their external competence in this area.

In fact, an example of EU rules governing an aspect of Member States' competence over external border treaties is the specific issue of treaties on local border traffic. Initially, the Schengen Convention also contained a specific provision regarding Member States' power to conclude treaties on this issue.[638] Member States were allowed to conclude such treaties on condition that they complied with the rules on such agreements to be adopted by the Schengen Executive Committee pursuant to Article 3 of the Convention. But in fact, no such rules were agreed before the Schengen *acquis* was integrated into the EC legal order, and this provision of the Schengen Convention was later amended so that it now refers back to the Regulation which has established common rules to govern Member States' negotiation of local border traffic treaties.[639] This Regulation makes no reference to the external borders Protocol, but this is not problematic as for the reasons set out above, that Protocol does not preclude the adoption of EU rules which regulate Member States' exercise of their external competence as regards border controls.

As for the EU's exercise of its external competence in this area, as well as the various Schengen association agreements (which obviously concern other issues as well as border controls), the EU has negotiated or concluded several treaties solely or largely on the issue of border controls, dealing with the Schengen associates' further participation in Frontex, the EU's border funds programme, and the Commission's committees.[640]

In the longer term, in the interests of 'tidying up' the primary law of the EU, it would be desirable to repeal the Protocol on external competence as regards borders. If it is correct to interpret the Protocol as merely confirming that the EU's external competence on this issue is not a priori exclusive, but only exclusive by exercise, then the Protocol no longer serves any purpose, since this principle is now set out in the Treaty following the entry into force of the Treaty of Lisbon.[641] If, on the other hand, the Protocol must be interpreted as precluding the EU from obtaining exclusive external competence on this issue even if it has fully harmonized the internal law relating to border controls, then the Protocol needs to be repealed because this would be incompatible with the objective of establishing common rules at the external borders, given the obvious impact

---

[637] cf Reg 1931/2006 on border traffic treaties ([2006] OJ L 405/1); see 3.8 above.
[638] Art 136(3) of the Convention.   [639] Art 20 of Reg 1931/2006 (n 628 above).
[640] See 3.2.5 above.
[641] Art 2(2) TFEU; see 2.7.1 above.

which any unilateral treaty-making by individual Member States would have on the control of the common external border as a whole.

3.13. Conclusions

Estimates suggest that 14,000 would-be migrants lost their lives over a twenty-year period while attempting to gain entry to the EU.[642] Leaving aside the question of how much responsibility Member States and the EU have for these deaths, this death toll should remain foremost in the mind of EU policy-makers when developing policy in this area.

In general, the second generation of EU legislation on these matters is a clear improvement as compared to the less ambitious Schengen rules, which were in many respects fragmented and lacked coherence, legal certainty, and accountability. However, internal border controls have still been repeatedly reintroduced since the adoption of the Schengen Borders Code, and there is insufficient information to judge whether such measures are genuinely proportionate. While there have also been improvements in the rules relating to external borders, most notably the right to appeal against a refusal of entry, improved procedural rights in relation to SIS II, the exclusion of younger children from passport fingerprinting obligations, the development of local border traffic rules, and the adoption of human rights obligations in relation to Frontex operations; there is still a lack of clear rules on the relationship between asylum issues and this field and on the accountability of Member States' and Frontex's actions. The rules on entry bans in SIS II and the Returns Directive still lack precision and give Member States too much leeway for disproportionate penalization of persons who commit relatively minor breaches of immigration law. The plans to develop rules on an entry-exit system, together with a trusted traveller system, a system of electronic travel authorization and the use of the Visa Information System at the external borders, show signs of a disproportionate approach to these issues, and the most recent proposals to develop Frontex do not sufficiently improve its accountability and transparency, in particular as regards the development of Frontex information systems. Coupled with the development of the VIS and biometric passports and identity cards, there is a risk that the development and interlinking of various EU and national information systems and databases will constitute further steps toward the creation of a European surveillance society.

---

[642] See: <http://fortresseurope.blogspot.com/2006/02/immigrants-dead-at-frontiers-of-europe_16.html>.

4

Visas

4.1. Introduction

It was inherent in the process of abolishing internal border controls between (most) Member States and simultaneously constructing a collective external border that any persons who had been admitted for short-term stay or longer-term residence in one Member State would be entitled to the freedom to travel between Member States, once the prospect of checking their status at internal borders was removed. This, in turn, meant that Member States had to develop a common policy on short-term visas (authorizations for stay for a limited period), since a visa issued by one Member State would in effect allow travel to other Member States as well.

The initial source of rules on these issues was the 1990 Convention implementing the Schengen Agreement (the 'Schengen Convention'), providing for a uniform visa valid for the territory of all of the Schengen States (known in practice as a 'Schengen visa'). The rules on visas have since been developed much further by the European Community (now the EU), in particular to harmonize fully the list of third States whose nationals do and not require a visa, to adopt further rules governing visa applications, to establish a Visa Information System (a database of the information submitted by all visa applicants), and to develop an external policy in relation to visas.

The issues addressed in this chapter are inevitably inextricably linked with the issues of border control addressed in Chapter 3. Like the border control issues, they are also very closely linked with the issue of irregular migration, examined in detail in Chapter 7, since many irregular migrants have either entered the territory without a required visa, overstayed the period of authorization set out in the visa, or violated the conditions attached to the visa. Also, the freedom to travel within the EU for third-country nationals entails the possibility that some will violate the conditions for the exercise of that freedom, or travel without fulfilling them, and therefore be considered irregular.

Visa issues, like border control issues, are also linked to asylum issues (the subject of Chapter 5), since visa obligations also serve to prevent entry to the territory for asylum seekers, and the issue of a visa is also a ground for assigning responsibility among Member States for processing asylum applications. The latter link will be strengthened by the Visa Information System (VIS), once it becomes operational. There is also a link between visa policy and the regulation of long-term legal migration (the subject of Chapter 6), in particular the question of whether a person who is legally present on the basis of a short-term visa can make an application for a longer-term stay. Finally, there is a link between visa policy and policing, to the extent that the information in the VIS will also be available to law enforcement agencies.[1]

This chapter addresses in turn: the adoption of a common list of States whose nationals do or do not require visas to enter the EU; the development of a common visa format; the adoption of common rules for processing visa applications; the creation of the VIS; the rules governing freedom to travel between Member States (including related rules governing long-stay visas—ie visas for a stay longer than three months—and residence permits); and the EU's external visa policy.

4.2. Institutional framework and overview

4.2.1. Framework prior to the Treaty of Amsterdam[2]

Due to the legal and political difficulties which stood in the way of developing EEC-wide integration on visas issues prior to the Maastricht Treaty (the original Treaty on European Union, or TEU),[3] cooperation on those issues was first developed by a pioneer group of Member States within the framework of the 1985 Schengen Agreement and then the Schengen Convention.[4] The Convention contained detailed rules on short-term visa policy (Articles 9–17), supplemented by rules on freedom to travel (Articles 19–24).[5] These provisions of course formed part of an integrated whole, in particular in connection with the rules on abolishing internal border controls, harmonizing external border controls, and the establishment of the Schengen Information System (SIS).[6]

As for the EU as a whole, as part of the compromise in the original TEU on the issue of visas and border controls,[7] an Article 100c was inserted into the EC Treaty, giving the Community power to adopt 'a list of third countries whose nationals must be in possession of a visa when crossing the external borders of the Member States' and to 'adopt measures relating to a uniform format for visas'. The first power was subject to unanimous voting in the Council until 1 January 1996 and qualified majority voting (QMV) after that date, while the second power was subject to QMV from the outset. In both cases, the Council had to act on a proposal from the Commission, and consult the European Parliament (EP) before

---

[1] See 12.6.1.3 below.

[2] On this period, see in particular K Hailbronner, 'Visa Regulations and Third-Country Nationals in EC Law' (1994) 31 CMLRev 969–995.   [3] For details, see 3.2.1.1 above.

[4] For further details, see 3.2.1.2 above.

[5] Respectively Arts 9–17 and 19–24. See 4.5 to 4.9 below.   [6] See generally ch 3.

[7] See generally 3.2.1.3 above.

adopting the relevant measures; the Court of Justice had its normal EC law juris-diction (ie it could receive references for a preliminary ruling on the interpreta-tion or the validity of the legislation from all national court and tribunals). There was also a (never used) power in Article 100c EC to introduce a 'visa requirement for the nationals' of a country 'in an emergency situation' whose nationals were 'posing the threat of a sudden inflow...into the Community'. A corresponding amendment to Article 3 EC, which listed the activities of the Community, speci-fied that those activities included 'measures concerning the entry and movement of persons in the internal market as provided for in Article 100c'.[8]

The powers conferred by Article 100c EC were used to adopt a visa list Regulation and a visa format Regulation in 1995.[9] The visa list Regulation was annulled by the Court of Justice because the Council had failed to reconsult the EP despite the Council's legal obligation to do so, in the framework of the consul-tation procedure (as it was then), whenever the Council intends to adopt a meas-ure that differs essentially from the Commission's original proposal.[10] However, the Court preserved the legal effect of the Regulation until the Council adopted a replacement. Following reconsultation of the EP, the Council duly adopted a replacement Regulation in the spring of 1999, which was essentially the same text as it had adopted in 1995.[11]

As for other issues related to visas, the 'third pillar' powers of the EU as listed in Article K.1 of the original TEU included rules on the 'conditions of entry and movement' by third-country nationals (Article K.1(3)(c)); visas were not men-tioned specifically. The question therefore repeatedly arose as to what 'legal base' applied to the adoption of measures concerning visas. First of all, the Commission proposed legislation on third-country nationals' freedom to travel using the first pillar legal base of Article 100 EC (later Article 94 EC, now Article 115 TFEU). This was blocked by the UK's veto.[12]

Secondly, the Commission sued the Council in the Court of Justice regard-ing a particular dispute over the dividing line between the EC's first pillar visa powers and the EU's third pillar visa powers. After deleting provisions on airport transit visas (visas needed simply to change between planes in an airport) from the visa list Regulation in 1995, the Council then adopted in 1996 a third pillar 'Joint Action' comprising a list of ten non-EU states whose nationals would need airport transit visas in every Member State.[13] The Commission argued that the Joint Action should be annulled because its subject matter fell within the scope of the EC's powers as set out in Article 100c EC. This time the Council was successful,[14] as the Court ruled that persons in an airport transit zone had not yet crossed the *legal* (as distinct from the *physical*) external borders of the Member

---

[8] Art 3(d) EC.   [9] See respectively 4.5 and 4.6 below.
[10] Case C-392/95 *EP v Council* [1997] ECR I-3213.   [11] See 4.5 below.
[12] See 3.2.1.3 above.   [13] For the details, see 4.5 below.
[14] Case C-170/96 *Commission v Council* [1998] ECR I-2763.

States. The Court linked its interpretation of Article 100c EC to Article 3(d) EC, the 'Community activities' clause, and concluded that since persons within the airport transit zones could not be considered to be participating in the 'internal market' (as referred to in Article 3(d)), they had not crossed an external border for the purposes of Article 100c.

The EU's third pillar powers were also used to adopt: a Joint Action on school-children's visas; a Recommendation on consular cooperation; a list of honorary consuls who could issue uniform visas; and a Recommendation on the detection of false documents by visa authorities.[15]

In the meantime, as in the case of border controls, the application of the Schengen Convention from March 1995 was both preceded and followed by the adoption of a number of measures implementing that Convention relating to visas, adopted by the Executive Committee established by that Convention, which clearly influenced the development of EU and EC visa measures before the entry into force of the Treaty of Amsterdam.

4.2.2. Treaty of Amsterdam

4.2.2.1. Institutional framework

Like the issue of border controls,[16] the issues of visas and freedom to travel were addressed by EC powers conferred by Article 62 EC, as inserted by the Treaty of Amsterdam. The relevant provisions were Article 62(2)(b) and 62(3) EC, which required the Council to adopt:

(b) rules on visas for intended stays of no more than three months, including:
    (i) the list of third countries whose nationals must be in possession of visas when crossing the external borders and those whose nationals are exempt from that requirement;
    (ii) the procedures and conditions for issuing visas by Member States;
    (iii) a uniform format for visas;
    (iv) rules on a uniform visa;
(3) measures setting out the conditions under which nationals of third countries shall have the freedom to travel within the territory of the Member States during a period of no more than three months.

As noted in Chapter 3, the structure of Article 62 as a whole closely followed the structure of Articles 1–25 of the Schengen Convention,[17] and furthermore closely paralleled EC or EU measures that had previously been proposed or adopted. It is clear that the powers conferred by Article 62(3) were strictly limited to a

---

[15] Respectively: [1994] OJ L 327/1; [1996] OJ C 80/1; [1996] OJ C 274/58; and [1999] OJ C 140/1. On the first measure, see 4.9 below.   [16] See 3.2.2 above.
[17] Ibid.

three-month maximum, while the powers concerning visas were slightly more flexible ('intended stays' of a three-month maximum). There was also a relevant declaration (number 16) in the Final Act of the Treaty of Amsterdam, stating that '[t]he Conference agrees that foreign policy considerations of the Union and the Member States shall be taken into account in the application of Article [62(2)(b)] of the [EC] Treaty'. It should be noted that even 'uniform' visas are issued by Member States' authorities.

The EC's visa powers were also subject to the 'law and order' exception in Article 64(1) EC, the 'emergency powers' clause in Article 64(2) EC, and the power to adopt legislation on administrative cooperation in Article 66 EC.

As for decision-making, according to Article 67(1) EC, the powers concerning the procedures and conditions for issuing visas, rules on a uniform visa and the freedom to travel (Article 62(2)(ii) and (iv) and (3)) were subject to unanimous voting in the Council, consultation of the EP, and shared initiative of the Commission and the Member States up until 1 May 2004. However, Article 67(3) EC provided for a derogation: the powers concerning visa lists and visa formats were instead subject immediately upon entry into force of the Treaty of Amsterdam to QMV in the Council, consultation of the EP and the sole initiative of the Commission. The latter rule simply continued the position regarding the decision-making process applied to these powers under the Maastricht version of the EC Treaty.[18]

Article 67(2) EC provided that from 1 May 2004, the Commission gained the sole right of initiative on all visa issues, and Article 67(4) specified that at the same time, the powers over visa conditions, procedures, and rules automatically became subject to QMV in the Council and co-decision with the EP. Furthermore, Article 67(2) EC also obliged the Council, acting unanimously after consultation of the EP, to change some or all of the decision-making rules applying to the rest of Title IV after 1 May 2004, so that it used QMV and the co-decision procedure in further areas. Applying this power, the Council decided that the rules on freedom to travel would be adopted by QMV and co-decision as from 1 January 2005.[19] Finally, due to the relevant Protocol attached to the EC Treaty by the Treaty of Nice, measures based on Article 66 EC were subject to QMV and consultation of the EP as from 1 May 2004. So from this date, measures on administrative cooperation, the visa list, and visa formats were subject to QMV and consultation, whereas other visa measures were subject to QMV and co-decision. This gave rise to potential disputes between different legal bases, if those different legal bases involved different decision-making rules.[20]

---

[18] See 4.2.1 above.   [19] [2004] OJ L 396/45. See further 2.2.2.1 above.
[20] See 4.2.4 below.

As for the Court of Justice, in the area of visas, the Court of Justice was subject, as in the rest of the former Title IV EC, to restrictions on receiving references from lower national courts.[21] Due to the general restriction on its jurisdiction, despite the extensive Schengen *acquis* which formed part of the EC legal order since 1 May 1999, the Court received only four references in this area during this period from national courts, and two of these were inadmissible.[22] The admissible cases concerned the freedom to travel and transit rules.[23]

4.2.2.2. Overview of practice

As with the issue of border controls, the entry into force of the Treaty of Amsterdam immediately entailed the integration of the Schengen *acquis* in this area into the EC legal order by means of the Protocol on the Schengen *acquis* and the Council Decisions defining and allocating the *acquis*.[24] This meant that the EC legal order instantly contained an extensive set of rules concerning short-stay visas and freedom to travel for third-country nationals.

Because of this, there was little immediate interest in further development of the visa rules, although the Tampere European Council of October 1999 did call for:

... [a] common active policy on visas and false documents ... including closer co-operation between EU consulates in third countries and, where necessary, the establishment of common EU visa issuing offices.

However, the events of September 11, 2001 clearly changed the EU's priorities, with a perception that new visa measures could enhance the objectives of increased security and control, in particular the creation of a VIS, which would comprise a database of information on all Schengen visa applicants.[25]

The EC also moved swiftly after the entry into force of the Treaty of Amsterdam to complete fully harmonized lists of countries whose nationals need (or do not need) visas to enter the Member States by March 2001; this legislation was amended several times later. In April 2001, as in the area of external borders, the Council gave itself powers, unsuccessfully contested by the Commission,[26] to amend many key secondary Schengen visa rules, and it used these powers

---

[21] See further 2.2.2.1 above.

[22] Cases C-51/03 *Georgescu* [2004] ECR I-3203 and C-45/03 *Dem'Yanenko*, judgment of 18 Mar 2004 (unpublished). Also, the *MRAX* reference on EU free movement law touched on the interpretation of the first visa list Reg (see further 4.4.1 below), and the *Soysal* judgment concerning the EU–Turkey association agreement touched on the subsequent visa list Reg (see further 4.4.2 below). On the general issue of 'mixed jurisdiction' raised by these cases, see 2.4.2 above.

[23] Cases C-241/05 *Bot* [2006] ECR I-9627 and C-139/08 *Kqiku* [2009] ECR I-2887. On the substance, see respectively 4.9 and 4.2.5 below.

[24] On the process on integrating the Schengen *acquis* generally, see 2.2.2.3 above. For details of the visas and freedom to travel provisions of the *acquis* integrated into EC law, see 4.5, 4.6, 4.7, and 4.9 below.

[25] See the conclusions of the extraordinary JHA Council of 20 Sep 2001, point 26.

[26] Case C-257/01 *Commission v Council* [2005] ECR I-345.

subsequently to make a number of changes to these rules, aiming inter alia at further harmonization of visa policy. The Council amended the existing visa format Regulation, in particular to take account of security concerns. The special rules concerning the issue of visas at the border, in particular to seamen, were updated, and the Council adopted rules establishing special regimes for visas and border controls during the 2004 Summer Olympics and 2006 Winter Olympics; and as regards travel across EC territory (after enlargement) to and from Kaliningrad from the rest of Russia. The Council also adopted principles and initial legislation to establish the VIS in 2004, with plans for further legislation later.[27]

On the other hand, the Council was unable to agree any amendment to the Schengen rules relating to freedom to travel for third-country nationals, despite considering several proposals, although it did agree to extend this freedom to persons holding a long-stay visa, in certain circumstances.[28] The EC's implied external relations powers over visas (along with borders) were used to authorize Member States to sign a relevant treaty on the admission of seafarers on behalf of the EC, and to agree treaties associating Switzerland with the Schengen *acquis*, providing for special rules for Chinese tourists, and the first treaty facilitating the issue of visas for a non-EU country (Russia).[29]

The EC's activity as regards visas stepped up after the adoption of the Hague programme in 2004. This programme called for:[30] the eventual creation of common visa offices, starting with a proposal to establish common application centres (2005) and a broader review of the Schengen common consular instructions on visas (2006); the facilitation of visas to non-EU states prepared to assist the EU on readmission issues; and the development of the VIS. Implementing this programme, the EC adopted more detailed legislation to govern the operations of the VIS in 2008,[31] and amendments to the common consular instructions in 2009, inter alia concerning common visa application centres.[32] The EC also agreed a number of visa facilitation treaties with third States,[33] and amended the visa list legislation in 2006 and 2009, inter alia to exempt some non-Member States from visa requirements.[34] More fundamentally, in 2009 the EC overhauled the complex web of existing Schengen and Community rules governing the conditions for issuing visas, replacing them with a modernized visa code.[35] However, the EC was not able to agree on a fully fledged extension of the freedom to travel to long-stay visa holders, or proposed consolidations of the visa list and visa format legislation, before the Treaty of Lisbon entered into force.[36]

---

[27] See 4.8 below.   [28] See 4.9 below.

[29] See 4.2.5 and 4.11 below. The Chinese treaty also had a 'legal base' concerning irregular immigration.   [30] [2005] OJ C 53/1.

[31] See 4.8 below.   [32] See 4.7 below.   [33] See 4.11.2 below.

[34] See 4.5 below, and as regards connected visa waiver treaties, 4.11.1 below.

[35] Reg 810/2009, [2009] OJ L 243/1. See 4.7 below.

[36] See respectively: COM (2009) 91, 27 Feb 2009; COM (2008) 761, 28 Nov 2008; and COM (2008) 891, 29 Dec 2008.

4.2.3. Treaty of Lisbon

As with the area of external borders, the issue of visas has been subject to Article 77 of the Treaty on the Functioning of the European Union (TFEU), since the entry into force of the Treaty of Lisbon on 1 December 2009. The relevant provisions of the Treaty provide as follows:

1. The Union shall develop a policy with a view to:
    (a) ensuring the absence of any controls on persons, whatever their nationality, when crossing internal borders;
    (b) carrying out checks on persons and efficient monitoring of the crossing of external borders;
    (c) the gradual introduction of an integrated management system for external borders.
2. For the purposes of paragraph 1, the European Parliament and the Council, acting in accordance with the ordinary legislative procedure, shall adopt measures concerning:
    (a) the common policy on visas and other short-stay residence permits;
    ...
    (c) the conditions under which nationals of third countries shall have the freedom to travel within the Union for a short period
    ...
    (e) the absence of any controls on persons, whatever their nationality, when crossing internal borders.

Although the abolition of internal border controls and the control of external borders was examined in detail in Chapter 3,[37] it should of course be reiterated that these subjects remain closely linked to the issue of visas.

Comparing the previous version of the Treaty to the revised provisions, the power regarding a 'common policy on visas and other short-stay residence permits' is an *extension* of competence as compared to the previous competence concerning visas 'for an intended stay of no more than three months', as the Treaty provision has dropped the time limit on the competence and has added a new competence relating to 'other' forms of short-stay permit, which also form part of the 'common' policy. It is interesting to speculate whether, in practice, the EU might wish to offer to certain third countries, and/or to provide for the issue to certain categories of individuals, the issue of visas for more than three months or short-stay permits of a longer validity. Moreover, competence over visas is no longer broken down into four separate sub-areas. Another significant change is the extension of the co-decision process, now renamed the 'ordinary legislative procedure',[38] to cover the issues of visa lists and the visa format.

---

[37] See 3.2.3 above.   [38] See Arts 289(1) and 294 TFEU.

Next, the EU now has the power to regulate the freedom to travel of third-country nationals within the EU 'for a short period', rather than (under the previous Article 62(3) TEC) 'for a period of no more than three months'.[39]

The new provisions on visas and freedom to travel are also subject to the revised general provisions of the JHA Title of the revised Treaty,[40] including the more limited scope of the 'emergency powers' clause,[41] as well as the extended jurisdiction of the Court of Justice and the revised rules on opt-outs for the UK, Ireland, and Denmark.[42]

As for the impact of the Treaty of Lisbon, shortly after its entry into force the EU adopted a regulation which extended the freedom to travel for all long-stay visa holders.[43] The proposed consolidations of the visa list and visa format legislation have not yet been adopted, but are now subject to the ordinary legislative procedure.[44] So are the further proposals by the Commission to amend the visa list again, released after the entry into force of the Treaty.[45]

Looking toward future plans, the Stockholm programme called for ongoing reviews of the EU visa list, possible further visa facilitation negotiations, and continued application of the principle of visa reciprocity.[46] A more radical suggestion was for a move towards a new concept of issuing visas:

The European Council, with a view to creating the possibility of moving to a new stage in the development of the common visa policy, while taking account of Member States competences in this area, invites the Commission to present a study on the possibility of establishing a common European issuing mechanism for short term visas. The study could also examine to what degree an assessment of individual risk could supplement the presumption of risk associated with the applicant's nationality.

The EU's plans to develop an entry-exit system and a registered traveller system will have an impact on the visa issuing process also.[47]

Finally, as for the impact of the extended jurisdiction of the Court of Justice in this area, in the first few months after the entry into force of the Treaty of Lisbon, this had not yet resulted in any references to the Court of Justice regarding visa legislation.

4.2.4. Competence issues

As with the EC's powers concerning borders,[48] to some extent, the argument over the existence and extent of EC competence over visas is now purely historic. But

---

[39] On the competence issues arising from the previous wording, see 4.2.4 below.
[40] See further 2.2.5.2 and 3.2.3 above.   [41] See 5.2.3 and 5.2.4 below.
[42] See 4.2.5 below.
[43] Reg 265/2010, [2010] OJ L 85/1. For the substance of this measure as regards freedom to travel, see 4.9 below.   [44] COM (2008) 761, 28 Nov 2008 and COM (2008) 891, 19 Dec 2008.
[45] COM (2010) 256, 27 May 2010 and COM (2010) 358, 5 July 2010; see 4.5 below.
[46] [2010] OJ C 115, s 5.2.   [47] See 3.6.2 above.   [48] See 3.2.4 above.

even following the entry into force of the Treaty of Amsterdam, and now the Treaty of Lisbon, there are some issues concerning the division of competence between the visas powers of the EU in Title V of the TFEU (the JHA Title) and the rest of the Treaties, concerning the division of powers within Title V itself; and concerning the extent of competence conferred by these provisions.[49] The first of these three issues is addressed further below,[50] while the other two are addressed in turn in the rest of this subsection.

Regarding visas, the arguments concerning the distinctions between legal bases are practically relevant because of the different rules applied by different 'legal bases' as regards decision-making[51] and the different rules on the participation of Member States.[52]

Within the former Title IV EC, there was initially (from the entry into force of the Treaty of Amsterdam) only one distinction between two categories of visa powers: visa list and visa format powers on the one hand (subject to QMV in Council, a Commission monopoly on proposals, and applicable as EC law to Denmark) and all other rules on visas and freedom to travel (subject to unanimity in Council, with shared competence over proposals, and not applicable as EC law to Denmark). After the changes to decision-making rules dating from 2004 and 2005, there were, during the Amsterdam period, two sets of decision-making rules: measures subject to QMV and co-decision, but not applicable to Denmark as EC law (rules on a uniform visa, conditions for the issue of visas, and freedom to travel) and measures subject to QMV and consultation of the EP (visa lists, visa format, and administrative cooperation).[53] Following the entry into force of the Treaty of Lisbon, the only remaining distinction as regards decision-making in this area concerns cooperation between administrations pursuant to Article 74 TFEU (still subject to QMV and only consultation of the EP) and other measures concerning visas, based on Article 77 TFEU. However, as regards the participation of Member States, there is still a distinction for Denmark concerning legislation on visa lists and visa format (fully binding on Denmark as part of EU law) and other measures concerning visas and freedom to travel, unless Denmark decides to abrogate its opt-out on most JHA issues.[54]

The distinction between Articles 77 and 74 TFEU has already been examined in Chapter 3.[55] The argument there applies *mutatis mutandis* to the issue of visas, with the consequence that any measures regulating the consideration of visa applications or the conditions for freedom to travel fall within the scope of Article 77 (and the ordinary legislative procedure), rather than Article 74.

---

[49] On the EU's external competence, see 4.11 below.   [50] See 4.4 below.

[51] On the basic rules regarding the distinction between legal bases, see 3.2.4 above.

[52] See 4.2.5 below.

[53] The visa list and visa format rules were applicable as EC law to Denmark, whereas the administrative cooperation measures were not.   [54] See further 4.2.5 below.

[55] See 3.2.4 above. See also 2.2.3.2 above.

Next, the question which had arisen under the prior version of the Treaty as to which of the freedom to travel powers or the legal migration powers was the correct 'legal base' for legislation concerning the freedom to travel for persons with long-stay visas, along with an extended travel authorization for longer periods, is no longer relevant following the entry into force of the Treaty of Lisbon, since the two subjects are subject to identical decision-making procedures.[56] Also on this point, given the flexibility conferred by Article 77(2)(c) TFEU, the EU is now free to adopt a measure extending freedom to travel for more than three months. This issue is connected with a complex situation arising from the application of pre-existing treaties between Member States and third countries dealing with the issue.[57]

Similarly, following the entry into force of the Treaty of Lisbon, the question of whether the list of EC's visa powers was exhaustive or not became moot, given that Article 77 TFEU replaced the prior list of specific visa powers with a general power to adopt a 'common' short-term visa policy. Equally, for the same reasons, there are no longer any grounds to doubt the EU's competence to use its visa power to regulate the issue of airport transit visas.[58]

More broadly, what is the extent of the EU's competence to harmonize the law on visas? Logically, as with EU powers concerning borders, the powers conferred by Article 77 to harmonize rules on short-term visas must be extensive, given the connection with the core obligation to abolish internal border checks, the corollary freedom to travel, the Treaty reference to a 'common policy on visas', and comparison with the structure of the EC Treaty (now TFEU) rules governing free movement of goods.[59] Again by analogy with the rules relating to borders, the question of whether a ban on issuing visas on foreign policy grounds should have a foreign policy legal base, or a visas legal base, remains an outstanding issue even after the entry into force of the Treaty of Lisbon.[60]

Finally, on the question of the issue of visas to persons for the purpose of carrying out economic activities, it should be noted that the limitation of EU competence regarding the admission of third-country nationals from third countries coming to the EU seek work or self-employment, as set out in Article 79(5) TFEU, expressly only applies to that Article, and so cannot limit the EU's competence regarding visas for short-term economic migration. This distinction makes sense because persons admitted to the EU on the basis of short-term visas will obviously have less impact on the labour market than persons admitted to the labour market for a longer period.[61]

---

[56] It might be arguable that the distinction is still nonetheless relevant as regards Member States' (and non-Member States') participation in the relevant measures: see 4.2.5 below. On this dispute, see the second edition of this book, at 111–113.   [57] See 4.11.3 below.

[58] On these issues, see the second edition of this book, at 109–110.

[59] See further the analysis of the comparable issue regarding borders in 3.2.4 above.

[60] See further 3.2.4 above.   [61] See further 6.2.4 below.

4.2.5. Territorial scope[62]

The EC or EU measures relating to visas which were adopted before the entry into force of the Treaty of Amsterdam are (or were) applicable to all Member States. In practice, that means that the 1994 Joint Action on schoolchildren's freedom to travel is applicable to all Member States,[63] as was the 1996 Joint Action on airport transit visas,[64] which has subsequently been repealed by the EU's visa code.[65] Equally the 1995 Regulation on a visa list and the 1999 Regulation replacing it were applicable to all Member States, although the 1999 Regulation was subsequently repealed.[66] The repeal of the 1999 visa list Regulation and of the 1996 Joint Action on airport transit visas raise the question of whether the UK and Ireland, which did not participate in the measures repealing those acts, are still bound by those acts or not.[67] Also, the UK and Ireland are also bound by the original 1995 visa format Regulation; the UK opted in to the 2002 amendment to that Regulation, but Ireland did not. Neither the UK nor Ireland opted into the 2008 amendment to the Regulation.[68] This has created awkward questions as regards the Commission's proposal to consolidate the legislation.[69]

Following the integration of the Schengen *acquis* in this area into the EC legal order pursuant to the Treaty of Amsterdam, the UK and Ireland have not opted in to any measure of the 1999 *acquis* related to visas, and nor have they opted in to any measures adopted after that date, except for the UK's opt-in to the 2002 amendment to the visa format regulation. It follows from the Court of Justice judgments relating to the UK's attempts to opt in to border control measures that the UK or Ireland are prohibited from opting in to most or all EC (now EU) visa measures, as long as they have not opted in to the original Schengen *acquis* which those measures have built upon.[70] The precise application of these judgments to visa issues may be clarified by a pending case in which the UK is challenging its exclusion from police access to the information held in the VIS.[71]

Furthermore, it should be noted that the UK has consistently opted into the EU's readmission treaties, but not into the EU visa facilitation treaties agreed

---

[62] For a general overview of the rules on the territorial scope of all JHA measures, see 2.2.5 above.   [63] On the substance of this act, see 4.9 below.

[64] [1996] OJ L 63/8.   [65] Art 56(2)(c) of Reg 810/2009, [2009] OJ L 243/1.

[66] On the substance of these visa list measures, see 4.5 below.

[67] On this general issue, see 2.2.5.1.5 above.

[68] On the substance of these visa format measures, see 4.6 below.

[69] COM (2008) 891, 19 Dec 2008. See the 7th report of the House of Lords European Union Committee, 2008–09, online at: <http://www.publications.parliament.uk/pa/ld200809/ldselect/ldeucom/55/55.pdf>.

[70] Cases C-77/05 *UK v Council* [2007] ECR I-11459 and C-137/05 *UK v Council* [2007] ECR I-11593. See further 2.2.5.1.3 and 3.2.5 above.

[71] Case C-482/08 *UK v Council*, pending (opinion of 24 June 2010). On the substance of the relevant Decision, see 12.6.1.3 below.

in parallel to those treaties.[72] However, there is a declaration to each of the visa facilitation treaties encouraging side agreements with the UK and Ireland.

As for Denmark, it is bound as a matter of EU law by all measures concerning visa lists and a common visa format,[73] since it has accepted EC (now EU) competence in those areas since the original TEU first entered into force.[74] Otherwise, its position is governed (after the entry into force of the Treaty of Lisbon) by the Protocol on Denmark, which provides that Denmark can decide, as regards measures which build upon the Schengen *acquis*, which of them bind Denmark as a matter of international law.[75] Denmark has consistently opted for participation in visa measures on this basis.[76] The position is only different for measures which do not build upon the Schengen *acquis*, from which Denmark is excluded entirely. As regards visas, this only concerns the visa facilitation treaties concluded by the Community, and there is a declaration attached to each of these treaties urging Denmark and the third State concerned to negotiate a parallel treaty.[77]

There might be some question as to *which* measures bind Denmark as a matter of EU law, given the precise wording of the exceptions on this point.[78] This wording (referring to visa formats and the adoption of a list of countries whose nationals are subject to a visa requirement when crossing EU external borders) reflects the situation prior to the Treaty of Amsterdam, but the post-Amsterdam visa list power was worded slightly differently from the pre-Amsterdam power (in particular referring also to the adoption of a list of States whose nationals will *not* require visas), and the post-Lisbon power is worded differently again, referring broadly to a 'common policy on visas'. In practice it was assumed during the Amsterdam period (1999–2009) that Denmark is also fully covered by the post-Amsterdam legislation as part of EC law (as it then was), and presumably the same practice will apply following the entry into force of the Treaty of Lisbon.

Is this assumption correct? The former power to adopt a negative list did not expressly preclude the EC from fully harmonizing that list, and indeed the better interpretation is that full harmonization of the list was *required*.[79] The corollary

---

[72] See respectively 7.9.2 and 4.11.2 below.

[73] On these measures, see 4.5 and 4.6 below. On the position of Denmark generally, see 2.2.5.2 above.

[74] See 4.2.1 above. However, note that Denmark is not covered by Art 78(3) TFEU, which is the successor clause to the original 'emergency powers' provision in Art 100c EC.

[75] Art 4, revised Protocol on Denmark.   [76] For detailed references, see 3.2.5 above.

[77] On the substance of these treaties, see 4.11.2 below. Note that Denmark is fully covered by the EU's visa *waiver* treaties (see 4.11.1 below).

[78] See also the distinction between visa list and external borders measures made by the Court of Justice in Case C-139/08 *Kqiku* [2009] ECR I-2887.

[79] This follows from the link in the former Art 3(d) EC between the visa list and the internal market, from the obligation to harmonize visa matters implied by the previous Art 14 EC (now Art 26 TFEU, then Art 7a EEC), as established by the *Wijsenbeek* judgment (see 3.4.1 above), and from the application of the previous Art 14 to third-country nationals (as subsequently confirmed by the Treaty of Amsterdam).

of a fully harmonized negative list is obviously a fully harmonized positive list, so the revised visa list power (even following the Treaty of Lisbon, which has subsumed the visa list power into a general power to regulate visa policy) is therefore no different from the power which existed before the Treaty of Amsterdam. It should also be noted that Denmark has no opt-out from the general internal market clause (Article 26 TFEU), but in any event it appears that Article 26 by itself has limited legal effect.[80]

Thirdly, the Member States joining the EU in 2004 and 2007 (the 'newer Member States') were subject upon accession to only part of the Schengen *acquis* and measures building upon it in this area, namely the common visa list, the common visa format, and a small number of other provisions set out in the Schengen *acquis*.[81] Also, the visa format and visa list Regulations, as well as the Common Consular Instructions, were amended to add or remove technical references to newer Member States when they joined the EU.[82] The remaining visa rules, along with the rules on the freedom to travel, did not apply until the full extension of the Schengen *acquis* to nine of the newer Member States, as from December 2007.[83] There has been no such extension yet for Cyprus, Romania, and Bulgaria, which therefore remain bound so far only by the more limited set of EU visa measures referred to in the accession treaties, until the full extension of the Schengen *acquis* to these Member States.

However, a particular issue has arisen concerning the position of Cyprus, a non-Schengen Member State that cannot fully join Schengen for practical reasons until there is a political settlement in Cyprus, due to the de facto external border within Cyprus and the Cypriot government's lack of de facto control over northern Cyprus. Because Cyprus expressed an interest in participating in the VIS, the Council adopted a statement when adopting the VIS Regulation taking note of Cyprus' intention to participate in the VIS before its full participation in Schengen.[84] This will therefore entail two separate Council decisions setting two separate dates—one date 'for the implementation of the common visa policy by Cyprus including the VIS and other relevant parts of the Schengen acquis' and the other date for full implementation of Schengen. The Council declared that the first of these decisions will require readiness by Cyprus to apply the 'common visa policy . . . in particular its integration in' the SIS, and a verification following a Schengen evaluation procedure that Cyprus

---

[80] See 3.4.1 above.

[81] On the position of the newer Member States, see Art 3 of the 2003 Treaty of Accession and Annex I to that Treaty ([2003] OJ L 236), and Art 4 of the 2005 Treaty of Accession and Annex II to that Treaty ([2005] OJ L 157). For a general discussion of the issue, see 2.2.5.3 above.

[82] Annex II, part 18, to the 2003 Accession Treaty (ibid); Reg 1791/2006, [2006] OJ L 363/1, part 11.B (Romania and Bulgaria).

[83] For instance, see Reg 1295/2003 on visas for participants in the 2004 Olympic Games ([2003] OJ L 183/1, recital 17 in the preamble).

[84] See the summary of Council acts for June 2008 (Council doc 12750/08, 8–9 Sep 2008).

has met 'the necessary conditions' to apply these rules. No decision has yet been taken to this end.

Next, as regards non-Member States, all of the Schengen and subsequent EC (now EU) visa measures are all fully applicable to Norway and Iceland as from March 2001 (or following the subsequent adoption of the EU measures), pursuant to the Schengen association agreement with those States,[85] except for the EU's various visa treaties, which do not build on the Schengen *acquis*.[86] In each case though, the relevant treaty contains a declaration encouraging the potential conclusion of side agreements between the non-EU State and the EU's associates.

The EC (now EU) visa rules, except for the visa treaties, are similarly applicable to Switzerland, as from its application of the Schengen *acquis* in 2008/2009, and will be applicable to Liechtenstein once the Schengen rules are applicable there.[87] Again, there is an exception as regards the EU's visa treaties with third States, but the most recent treaties contain declarations on the conclusion of side agreements.[88]

Furthermore, in order to address the position of persons transiting through the newer Member States to the States fully applying Schengen rules, the EC adopted two transitional measures. First of all, as regards the ten Member States which joined the EU in 2004, the EC adopted a transitional Decision in 2006 which permitted (but did not require) those newer Member States to recognize as equivalent to their national visas, for the purpose of transit, Schengen visas, long-stay visas, and residence permits issued by the Member States fully applying the Schengen rules.[89] Newer Member States were also permitted to recognize the various 'national short-term visas, long-term visas and resident permits' issued by other newer Member States for the purpose of transit.[90] The transit could only last for a maximum of five days.[91] Eight out of the ten newer Member States applied this transitional Decision.[92] Following the enlargement of the Schengen zone at the end of 2007, this Decision now only applies to Cyprus.[93]

A similar Decision was adopted in June 2008, after Romania and Bulgaria had joined the EU in 2007.[94] These two Member States were given the same choice to recognize, for the purposes of transit, Schengen documents, documents issued by each other, and moreover documents issued by Cyprus: Cyprus in turn has the option to recognize documents issued by Romania and Bulgaria. All three States opted to apply this Decision.[95]

---

[85] See further 2.2.5.4 above.   [86] On the substance, see 4.11 below.

[87] See 2.2.5 above.

[88] See the visa waiver treaties with micro-States (see 4.11.1 below) and the EU–Georgia visa facilitation treaty (see 4.11.2 below).   [89] Art 2, 2006 Decision ([2006] OJ L 167/8).

[90] Art 3, 2006 Decision (ibid). The types of documents covered by this rule are listed in an Annex to the Decision.   [91] Art 4, 2006 Decision.

[92] [2006] OJ C 251/20. The exceptions were Estonia and Lithuania.

[93] Art 6, 2006 Decision.

[94] [2008] OJ L 161/30. Again, the national documents concerned are listed in an Annex to the Decision.   [95] [2008] OJ C 312/8.

A comparable approach was taken to the position of persons holding residence permits from Switzerland and Liechtenstein, before those States' full participation in the Schengen *acquis*. The EC adopted a separate transitional decision in 2006, which required full Schengen States to recognize residence permits issued by Switzerland and Liechtenstein as equivalent to a visa for the purposes of transit for a five-day period.[96] Member States which had joined the EU in 2004 had an option to apply this Decision, on condition that they also applied the transitional Decision relating to accession countries.[97] This Decision was then amended in 2008, to apply also to Romania and Bulgaria.[98] Since the extension of the Schengen zone to Switzerland at the end of 2008, the Decision applies only to residence permits issued by Liechtenstein.[99]

The Court of Justice was called upon to interpret the 2006 Decision relating to Switzerland and Liechtenstein, in the case of *Kqiku*.[100] In that case, a family holding passports issued by 'Serbia-Montenegro' (a country which has, of course, since split up) and residence permits from Switzerland, visited Germany for several days in the summer of 2006 without obtaining a visa, but they were not transiting via Germany to or from any non-Schengen state. The Court of Justice ruled that, according to its wording, the Decision applied only to situations of transit. This ruling obviously applies also to the 2008 amendment to this Decision, and also, by analogy, to the 2006 and 2008 Decisions relating to newer Member States, as regards Cyprus, Romania, and Bulgaria.

4.3. Human rights

The application of human rights principles to the EU's visa rules parallels the application of those principles to EU border control legislation, an issue already addressed in Chapter 3.[101]

It should be noted that the EU's visa legislation makes implied provision for human rights in several respects. The visa code provides that a fee for a visa application can be waived or reduced in individual cases for humanitarian reasons.[102] Also, the visa Code sets out procedural rights in the event of refusal of a visa application,[103] and there are parallel data protection safeguards in the legislation governing the VIS.[104] According to the visa code, Member States

---

[96] [2006] OJ L 167/8, Arts 1 and 3. The residence permits in question are listed in an Annex to the Decision.

[97] Art 3, 2006 Decision (ibid). Again, eight of ten of the newer Member States applied this Decision (see n 92 above).

[98] [2008] OJ L 162/27; the amended Decision has not been consolidated. Romania and Bulgaria both decided to apply this Decision (n 95 above).   [99] Art 5, 2006 Decision (n 96 above).

[100] Case C-139/08, n 78 above.   [101] See 3.3 above.

[102] Art 16(6) of Reg 810/2009 ([2009] OJ L 243/1). For more on the Code, see 4.7.2 below.

[103] Art 32(2) and (3) and Annex VI of the code.   [104] For detail, see 4.8 below.

may issue a visa even if the usual criteria for obtaining one are not met, inter alia for humanitarian reasons or because of international obligations.[105] This exception also applies where a person applies for a visa at the external borders,[106] thereby circumventing the rule that Member States can only issue visas at the border if, inter alia, there is certainty that the visa applicant will return to his or her country of origin or residence:[107] that criterion obviously cannot be applied to refugees.

However, there is no express power for Member States to *waive* a visa obligation altogether on humanitarian grounds, although there are certain special rules relating to refugees in the visa list legislation.[108] If a person does enter a Member State in breach of a visa obligation (or enters with a visa, but overstays the permitted period of stay) and is subsequently detected, it should be recalled that the Geneva Convention on Refugees provides that, subject to certain conditions, irregular entry by refugees cannot be penalized.[109]

4.4. The impact of other EU law

4.4.1. Free movement law

As set out in the previous chapter,[110] the principal source of rules concerning the issues of visas and border controls in the context of EU free movement law is the secondary legislation adopted to give effect to free movement rights. As regards visas, this legislation originally specified that Member States could not demand entry visas or an equivalent document, except for family members who were non-EU nationals. In that case, 'Member States [had to] afford to such persons every facility for obtaining any necessary visas'. These visas had to be free of charge.[111] The case law on these measures specified that in order to give the free movement Directives 'their full effect, a visa [where it is required] must be issued without delay and, as far as possible, on the place of entry into national territory'.[112]

These measures have now been replaced by Directive 2004/38 on the free movement of EU citizens, as from 30 April 2006 (the 'EU citizens'

---

[105] Art 25(1)(a) of the code.   [106] Art 35(4) and (5) of the code.
[107] Art 35(1) of the code.   [108] See 4.5 below.   [109] See 5.3 below.
[110] See 3.4.1 above.

[111] Art 9(2) of Dir 68/360 ([1968] OJ Spec Ed L 257/13, p 485) and Art 7(2) of Dir 73/148 ([1973] OJ L 172/14). Art 2(2) of each of Dirs 90/364 ([1990] OJ L 180/26), 90/365 ([1990] OJ L 180/28), and 93/96 ([1993] OJ L 317/59) extended the relevant provisions of Dir 68/360 to other groups of EU citizens.

[112] Case C-459/99 *MRAX* [2002] ECR I-6591, para 60. The Court referred to the visa list legislation (see 4.5 below) as regards the list of third countries whose nationals require visas. On the further implications of this judgment, see 7.4.1 below.

Directive').[113] This Directive incorporates the relevant provisions of the prior legislation, except that there is an explicit reference to the EU visa list legislation 'or, where appropriate...national law' as regards family members' visa requirements.[114] Third-country national family members are exempt from the visa requirement where they hold a residence card issued to third-country national family members of an EU citizen who resides in a different Member State, and visas must be issued 'as soon as possible and on the basis of an accelerated procedure'.[115]

As with the issue of border controls, Directive 2004/38 did not incorporate most of the prior relevant case law;[116] an exception is the express application of the EU's visa list legislation to determine which third-country national family members need a visa. On the other hand, there are two improvements on the previous rules and case law: the exemption of some third-country national family members from the visa requirement, and the obligation to issue visas 'as soon as possible and on the basis of an accelerated procedure'. However, it is arguable that the latter rule could have been derived from interpretation of the previous legislation. The former rule is largely relevant only for movement to and from Schengen states on the one hand to non-Schengen States on the other, and for movement between non-Schengen States, given that anyone resident in a Schengen state has the freedom to travel anyway to other Schengen states, if they have a residence permit or (as from April 2010) a long-stay visa.[117]

As for the case law on the EU citizens' Directive to date, the ruling in the *Metock* case that third-country national family members of EU citizens who have moved within the EU have a right of entry into the host Member State of the EU citizen, even when coming directly from non-EU States, has implications for the application of the EU's visa rules in such cases.[118] Also, this judgment confirms implicitly that the competence to address the issue of visas as regards the family members of EU citizens who have moved within the EU derived from EC free movement law (as it was then), not the competences set out in Title IV of the EC Treaty. There is no reason to think this legal position changed as a result of the Treaty of Lisbon.

---

[113] [2004] OJ L 229/35. For further implications of this Directive, see 3.4.1 above and 6.4.1, and 7.4.1 below.

[114] Presumably only the UK and Ireland apply national law, as they are the only Member States not bound to apply the EU visa list (see 4.2.5 above).   [115] Art 5(2) of the Dir (n 113 above).

[116] The case law on the previous legislation continues to be valid, however: see C-127/08 *Metock* [2008] ECR I-6241.   [117] See 4.9 below.

[118] See n 116 above. Read in conjunction with *MRAX* (n 112 above), the failure to get a visa or the overstay of a visa in such cases can only be subject to limited sanctions, and a prior breach of visa rules can be 'cured' by becoming a family member of an EU citizen who has moved within the EU. For more on *Metock*, see 3.4.1 above and 5.4.2, 6.4.1, and 7.4.1 below.

A Commission report on the application of Directive 2004/38 stated that only seven Member States set out legislative rules, as required by the Directive, to provide for accelerated access to a visa for third-country national family members of EU citizens who require one; two Member States comply with this obligation in practice.[119] Some (unnamed) Member States require those family members to comply with the entire visa process normally applicable to third-country nationals. Five Member States fail to exempt holders of residence cards from the visa obligation, and three Member States wrongly linked the right of residence for third-country national family members to the duration of their entry visa. Subsequently, the Commission's 2009 guidance on the implementation of the Directive argues for a four-week maximum for a response to a visa application from a third-country national family member of an EU citizen.[120] This clearly cannot be considered an 'accelerated' decision, given that the normal time for making a decision on a visa application for any third-country national is fifteen days;[121] the Commission has also forgotten about the case law which requires visas to be issued at the border to such family members.[122] However, the Commission is correct to point out that Member States cannot insist on documents other than a travel document and evidence of a family link in order to consider visa applications from such persons.

The Court of Justice has also confirmed the supremacy of EC (now EU) free movement law over the rules governing the SIS as regards the consideration of visa applications,[123] and the legislation establishing the second-generation Schengen Information System (SIS II) expressly confirms the application of the same free movement rules in future.[124] Equally, the visa code is expressly 'without prejudice' to EU free movement law.[125] On the other hand, it is striking that the Regulation establishing the VIS does not include any express special rule for the position of EU citizens' third-country national family members.[126] However, it must be presumed that in the event of any conflict, the EU free movement rules will take precedence over this Regulation as a higher rule of law, because the underlying substantive rules on visas are expressly subject to EU free movement law pursuant to the visa code. It should not be forgotten that many third-country national family members of EU citizens are exempt from

---

[119] COM (2008) 840, 10 Dec 2008.   [120] COM (2009) 313, 2 July 2009.

[121] See Art 23 of the EU visa code (Reg 810/2009, [2009] OJ L 243/1). This can be extended to thirty days in individual cases and to sixty days in exceptional cases.

[122] *MRAX* (n 112 above).

[123] Case C-503/03 *Commission v Spain* [2006] ECR I-1097. See further 2.4.2 above, as regards the general issue of the relationship between Schengen rules and EU free movement law.

[124] Art 24(1), Reg 1987/2006 ([2006] OJ L 381/4). On SIS II and border controls, see 3.7.2 above.

[125] Art 1(2), Reg 810/2009 ([2009] OJ L 243/1). See also the specific rules in Arts 3(5)(d) and 24(2)(a), and Art 4 of Annex XI. On the substance of the Code, see 4.7.2 below.

[126] Reg 767/2008 ([2008] OJ L 218/60).

visa requirements pursuant to the EU citizens' Directive, as discussed above. For those subject to the visa requirement, the amount of data which will be collected on them according to the VIS Regulation is legally dubious in light of the Court of Justice's judgment in *Huber*, which confirms that the personal data of EU citizens (and implicitly their family members) who move within the EU can only be kept in central databases if this is necessary pursuant to EU free movement legislation.[127]

Next, the right of EU companies to send their third-country national employees to other Member States, as part of the corporate provision of services,[128] has implications for visas. In particular, the Court of Justice has ruled that a prior check in connection with a visa procedure breaches Article 49 EC (now Article 56 TFEU) in this context, because a prior declaration would be sufficient.[129] The Court has also ruled that an automatic expulsion and refusal to regularize the position of a posted worker who does not possess the required visa is a breach of Article 49 EC (now Article 56 TFEU).[130] It should follow by implication from the Court's case law that posted workers should not be subject to a visa requirement at all, or at the very least (by analogy with the family members of EU citizens) the visas must be issued automatically at the border, free of charge, following an accelerated procedure, and the failure to obtain a visa can only be punished by proportionate penalties (ie no expulsion or imprisonment) which would not impinge upon the basic right to provide services.[131]

4.4.2. Association agreements

EU free movement law applies essentially to Norway, Iceland, Liechtenstein, and Switzerland, so the rules on visas applicable to EU citizens and their family members are largely applicable to these non-Member States.[132]

---

[127] Case C-524/06 *Huber* [2008] ECR I-9705.

[128] Cases C-43/93 *Van der Elst* [1994] ECR I-3803; C-445/03 *Commission v Luxembourg* [2004] ECR I-10191; C-244/04 *Commission v Germany* [2006] ECR I-885; C-168/04 *Commission v Austria* ([2006] ECR I-9041); and C-219/08 *Commission v Belgium* [2009] ECR I-9213. The Opinions in the *Commission v Germany* (para 16) and *Commission v Austria* (paras 112–114) cases also comment briefly on the relationship between the Schengen freedom to travel rules (see 4.9 below) and the free movement of services, but it is clear that the exemption from a visa requirement that follows from the freedom to travel rules is not a complete answer to the breach of Art 49 EC (now Art 56 TFEU), because of the posting of workers from non-Schengen States and postings for periods of more than three months. For more on posted third-country national workers, see 3.4.1 above and 6.4.4, and 7.4.1 below.   [129] *Commission v Germany* (ibid).

[130] *Commission v Austria* (n 128 above).

[131] Note that visa requirements might apply not just to nationals of States on the EU's visa list (or the UK or Irish national lists), but also to nationals of States on the visa-free list, because Member States may require visas for such persons if they pursue economic activities (see 4.5 below).

[132] See 3.4.2 above. However, as regards Switzerland, there is no visa exemption for third-country national family members with a residence card (Art 1 of Annex I to the EU-Swiss agreement on free

Next, under an Additional Protocol to the EU's association agreement with Turkey,[133] there is a directly effective standstill on national rules which make the provision of services or the exercise of establishment more restrictive.[134] The Court of Justice has confirmed that this standstill applies to rules on the imposition of visas.[135] So no new visa requirements can be imposed on Turkish persons providing services or exercising establishment following the date when the relevant Protocol entered into force for the Member State concerned. It should be noted that the association agreement applies in principle to all EU Member States (ie even those which do not (yet) participate fully in the Schengen *acquis*), but *not* to the non-Member States associated with Schengen.

Nevertheless, the territorial scope of the standstill obligation is still not clear. The relevant Additional Protocol applied to the first nine Member States from the start of 1973. But for the other Member States, the relevant date is not absolutely certain, because no Protocols extending the EU–Turkey agreement to other Member States have yet entered into force. Nonetheless, in practice the Court of Justice and the national courts of Austria and Spain have assumed that the EU–Turkey agreement is applicable there.[136] If the Additional Protocol has entered into force for some or all other Member States, when did this happen exactly?

Moreover, the precise date at which some Member States applied visa requirements to Turkey is not known either. The twelve Member States which joined the EU in 2004 and 2007 had an obligation to impose visa requirements on Turkish nationals as from the beginning of their membership,[137] so even if the Additional Protocol applied to those Member States, its standstill clause could not be invoked to object to their imposition of a visa requirement upon Turkish nationals. As for the other Member States, ten of them had ratified a Council of Europe treaty abolishing short-stay visa requirements for the other contracting parties, which includes Turkey.[138] However, this treaty allows for suspension of visa abolition as

movement of persons, [2002] OJ L 114/6). Of course, due to Swiss participation in the Schengen area from Dec 2008 (see 4.2.5 above), the visa requirement for third-country national family members now applies only for travel between Switzerland and EU Member States which do not (yet) apply the Schengen rules.

[133] [1977] OJ L 261/60.

[134] Case C-37/98 *Savas* [2000] ECR I-2927 (self-employed persons); Joined Cases C-317/01 and C-369/01 *Abatay and others* [2003] ECR I-12301 (services).

[135] Case C-228/06 *Soysal* [2009] ECR I-1031. The same rule applies to entry control: see Case C-16/05 *Tum and Dari* [2007] ECR I-7415 and 3.4.2 above. The following discussion draws upon S Peers, 'EC Immigration Law and EC Association Agreements: Fragmentation or Integration?' (2009) 34 ELRev 628.

[136] As regards Austria, see Cases: C-65/98 *Eyup* [2000] ECR I-4747; C-171/01 *Birlikte* [2003] ECR I-4301; C-465/01 *Commission v Austria* [2004] ECR I-8291; C-373/02 *Ozturk* [2004] ECR I-3605; C-136/03 *Dorr* [2005] ECR I-4759; and C-383/03 *Dogan* [2005] ECR I-6237. As regards Spain, see Case C-152/08 *Kahveci* [2008] ECR I-6291.   [137] See 4.2.5 above.

[138] European Agreement on Regulations governing the Movement of Persons between Member States of the Council of Europe (ETS 25, 1957). The Member States in question are Austria,

against other contracting parties.[139] Five of the first six Member States[140] suspended their visa abolition commitment regarding Turkey in 1980—but this was after the Additional Protocol came into force for those Member States. Italy never suspended the agreement as regards Turkey; nor did Spain, which joined the EU later. Portugal suspended the agreement as regards Turkey only from 1991, after its membership of the EU, while Greece never applied it to Turkey in the first place, and Austria suspended it as regards Turkey before it joined the EU.[141] But a further complication is the personal scope of the Council of Europe treaty, because it permits (but does not require) signatories to impose a visa requirement when a person enters the territory 'for the purpose of pursuing a gainful activity'.[142]

This brings us to the personal scope of the standstill rule. Does it cover both service providers (who would generally fall within the scope of the exception in the Council of Europe treaty) and also service *recipients* (who generally would not fall within the scope of that exception)? The Court of Justice has ruled that the concept of 'services' in the standstill clause in the Additional Protocol is meant to be interpreted in accordance with the EU free movement law definition 'as far as possible'.[143] This must mean that at least persons providing services from Turkey are covered by the standstill, but does this also mean that Turkish service *recipients* are covered by the standstill? In light of the case law of the Court on the EU Treaty right of free movement of services, Turkish service recipients would include not only tourists,[144] but also any Turkish nationals merely present on the territory.[145] But would the extension of the standstill to cover all Turkish service recipients go beyond the requirement to apply free movement concepts to the association agreement 'as far as possible'? In light of the Court's application of this principle in other cases, it would not.[146]

In the *Soysal* judgment, the Court of Justice expressly rejected the argument that (most) Member States were now exempt from compliance with the standstill clause as regards visas, because the visa obligation was now established by EU

Belgium, France, Germany, Greece, Italy, Luxembourg, the Netherlands, Portugal, and Spain. Also two of the newer Member States (Malta and Slovenia) have ratified this treaty.

[139] Art 7 of the agreement (ibid).   [140] Germany, the Benelux countries, and France.

[141] So did Malta and Slovenia. As for Schengen associates, Switzerland suspended the agreement as against Turkey before its participation in the Schengen *acquis*, while Norway and Iceland never ratified it. Liechtenstein has ratified it, without any limitation as regards Turkey, but does not yet apply the Schengen *acquis*.

[142] Art 1(3) of the agreement. It is not known when each Member State imposed visa requirements on this category of Turkish visitors, although again the Member States joining in 2004 and 2007 had to impose visa requirements on this category of Turkish visitors as soon as they joined the EU. The *Soysal* judgment (n 135 above) provides some information on the German position.

[143] *Abatay* (n 134 above).

[144] Cases: 286/82 and 26/83 *Luisi and Carbone* [1984] ECR 377; 186/87 *Cowan* [1989] ECR 195; and C-348/96 *Calfa* [1999] ECR I-11.

[145] Case C-274/96 *Bickel and Franz* [1998] ECR I-7637.

[146] Compare in particular the opinions to the judgments on this point in *Tum and Dari* (n 135 above) and Cases C-275/02 *Ayaz* [2004] ECR I-8765 and C-294/06 *Payir* [2008] ECR I-203.

law, not national law. The Court could have rebutted this argument by pointing out that the Community (as it then was), along with its Member States, is a party to the association agreement, and moreover that most Member States have transferred competence over this issue to the Community, but it did not.[147] Instead, the Court looked solely at the question of whether service providers now faced more restrictions in each particular Member State than they did when the Additional Protocol entered into force for each Member State. This approach fragments the concept of a Schengen visa by requiring at least some Member States to revert to the different national rules which were applicable when the Additional Protocol entered into force for each of them.

Furthermore, it should also be pointed out that while the *Soysal* judgment concerned the core question of a visa obligation, various changes in the visa regimes of Member States, and subsequently also the EU, must also be covered by the standstill clause, to the extent that they make the provision of services and establishment from Turkey more difficult than it was when the Additional Protocol entered into force. So, for instance, increases in the visa fee, the requirement for visa applicants to pay a fee, and the requirement to attend at consulates in order to provide biometric information, are all prima facie breaches of the standstill clause.[148]

Finally, as regards the right to establishment set out in the Europe Agreements with ten Central and Eastern European states which later joined the EU, the Court of Justice ruled that nationals of associated States who had legally entered on a short-term visa or for a short period without being subject to a visa obligation did not have the right to make an in-country application for establishment.[149] Presumably the same will be true as regards Western Balkans states, once the provisions on the right to establishment in the Stabilization and Association Agreements with those states are activated.[150]

4.4.3. Other issues

It has been assumed in practice that the EU's data protection Directive[151] applies to the issue of visas.[152] For the reasons set out in the previous chapter, it is submitted

---

[147] Of course, the temporal scope of the EU's obligations under the agreement might be an issue, because, as noted above, of the different dates at which the association agreement applied (if at all) for different Member States.   [148] See 4.7 below.

[149] Case C-327/02 *Panayotova* [2004] ECR I-11055.

[150] [2004] OJ L 84 (Former Yugoslav Republic of Macedonia (FYROM)), [2005] OJ L 26 (Croatia), [2009] OJ L 107 (Albania); and [2010] OJ L 108 (Montenegro). SAAs have also been signed with Bosnia-Herzegovina (COM (2008) 182, 8 Apr 2008), and Serbia (COM (2007) 743, 20 Nov 2007), but these two SAAs are not yet in force.

[151] Dir 95/46 ([1995] OJ L 281/31) applies to Member States' processing of data, while Reg 45/2001 ([2001] OJ L 8/1) applies to EU bodies' processing of data. For more on EU data protection law, see 12.3.2 and 12.6.4 below.

[152] The Regulation establishing the visa code (Reg 810/2009, [2009] OJ L 243/1) refers to Dir 95/46 at several points (recital 12–14 in the preamble, Art 43(9), and point A(g) in Annex X). So

that this practice is correct.[153] However, as argued above, the amount of data which will be kept in the VIS on third-country national family members of EU citizens who have exercised free movement rights will amount to a violation of both free movement law and data protection law.[154]

4.5. Visa list

4.5.1. Overview

The EC (as it then was) first adopted a visa list Regulation, pursuant to the powers granted by Article 100c EC, in 1995.[155] This Regulation included a list of States whose nationals would require visas to visit any Member State (a 'blacklist'), but it left to Member States whether or not to impose visa requirements on the nationals of any State not on the list. However, the Regulation was annulled in 1997 for procedural reasons.[156] It was subsequently adopted again in 1999, without any substantive amendment.[157]

In the meantime, the EU adopted a Joint Action in 1996 on the issue of airport transit visas, requiring all Member States to impose an obligation on the nationals of certain States to obtain an airport transit visa (ATV) merely for staying in an airport to switch between flights.[158] The Commission challenged the validity of this Joint Action, arguing that the issue of ATVs fell within the EC's powers at the time to establish a visa blacklist, but the Court of Justice ruled that the Joint Action was not within the scope of Article 100c EC.[159]

Furthermore, the Schengen States were proceeding during the 1990s to harmonize their visa lists more fully than the EC as a whole, pursuant to Article 9 of the Schengen Convention, which required a general harmonization to take place. To that end, the Schengen Executive Committee adopted decisions in 1997 and 1998, almost entirely harmonizing the visa lists of Schengen states.[160]

---

does: Reg 333/2002, which concerns visa formats for unrecognized entities ([2002] OJ L 53/4, recital 8 in the preamble); Reg 390/2009, which concerns the taking of biometrics from visa applicants ([2009] OJ L 131/1, recitals 9 and 13 in the preamble) and the Regulation establishing the VIS (Reg 767/2008, [2008] OJ L 218/60), recital 17 in the preamble and Arts 31(2)(a), 37(4), and 38(1); also recital 19 in the preamble and Arts 39(2), 41(1), and (4) refer to Reg 45/2001). According to the latter Reg (recital 17 in the preamble), the Directive is clarified on several points as regards the VIS: responsibility for the processing of data; safeguarding the rights of the data subjects; and supervision on data protection.

[153] See 3.4.3 above.   [154] See 4.4.1 above.   [155] Reg 2317/95, [1995] OJ L 234/1.

[156] Case C-392/95 *Parliament v Council* [1997] ECR I-3213. See further 4.2.1 above.

[157] Reg 574/99, [1999] OJ L 72/2. For Commission communications on implementation of the 1995 and 1999 visa list Regs, see: [1996] OJ C 379; [1997] OJ C 180; [1998] OJ C 101; [1999] OJ C 133; and [2000] OJ C 272.   [158] [1996] OJ L 63/8.

[159] Case C-170/96 *Commission v Council* [1998] ECR I-2763. For the context, see 4.2.1 above.

[160] Decisions SCH/Com-ex (97)32 and SCH/Com-ex (98)53 rev 2 ([2000] OJ L 239/186 and 206).

Following the entry into force of the Treaty of Amsterdam, the EC (now without the participation of the UK and Ireland) adopted a new visa list Regulation in 2001, which established a fully harmonized blacklist as well as a fully harmonized list of States whose nationals would *not* need a visa to cross the external borders of the Member States (a 'whitelist').[161] The 1999 EC Regulation and the two previous Schengen Executive Committee Decisions were repealed.[162] This Regulation was subsequently amended in 2001, 2003, 2005, 2006, and 2009,[163] as well as by the Treaties of Accession in 2003 and 2005.[164] Two further amendments were proposed in 2010, but they have not yet been adopted.[165] In the meantime, the Commission proposed a codified version of the much-amended visa list Regulation in 2008,[166] but this proposal has not been adopted. Finally, the list of States subject to an airport transit visa requirement is now set out in the visa code Regulation.[167]

In addition to the visa list legislation, the EU has also agreed treaties specifically providing for visa waivers, and more general association agreements which provide for visa waivers among other commitments.[168]

4.5.2. Visa lists

The original 1995 visa list Regulation, and its 1999 replacement,[169] obliged Member States to impose a visa obligation upon most States in Africa and Asia,[170] plus a number of States in Central and Eastern Europe,[171] and a small number of States in Latin America, the Caribbean, and the Indian and Pacific Oceans.[172] The priority criteria for inclusion on the list, according to the preamble to the Regulation, were 'risks relating to security and illegal immigration', although 'Member States' international relations with third countries also play a role'.[173] For its part, the 1996 Joint Action placed an ATV obligation on ten States.[174] As

---

[161] Reg 539/2001, [2001] OJ L 81/1.

[162] Art 7. On the question of whether the UK and Ireland are still bound by the 1999 EC Regulation, see 2.2.5.1.5 above.

[163] Respectively Regs 2414/2001 ([2001] OJ L 327/1), 453/2003 ([2003] OJ L 69/10), 851/2005 ([2005] OJ L 141/3), 1932/2006 ([2006] OJ L 405/23), and 1244/2009 ([2009] OJ L 336/1).

[164] Annex II, part 18.B.2, to the 2003 Accession Treaty (ibid); Reg 1791/2006, [2006] OJ L 363/1, point 11.B.3. These amendments merely removed the names of the new Member States from the Regulation.   [165] COM (2010) 256, 27 May 2010 and COM (2010) 358, 5 July 2010.

[166] COM (2008) 761, 28 Nov 2008.   [167] See 4.7.2 below.

[168] See respectively 4.4.2 above and 4.11.1 below.

[169] Regs 2317/95 and 574/99, nn 155 and 157 above.

[170] The exceptions were the Commonwealth States of southern Africa (except Zambia) and, in Asia, Israel, Japan, South Korea, Singapore, Malaysia, and Brunei.

[171] Albania, Romania, Bulgaria, Turkey, the Federal Republic of Yugoslavia, the Former Yugoslav Republic of Macedonia, and all the former Soviet Union States except for the Baltic States.

[172] Peru, Guyana, Surinam, Cuba, the Dominican Republic, Haiti, Mauritius, the Maldives, and Fiji.   [173] Para 3 of the preamble.

[174] Afghanistan, Sri Lanka, Iran, Iraq, Ethiopia, Eritrea, Somalia, Nigeria, Ghana, and Congo.

noted above, both measures left it to Member States to decide whether other third countries would, or would not, be subject to visa obligations.

The Schengen countries had agreed by 1997 on a harmonized visa list in respect of almost all countries,[175] and then by 1998 on a harmonized list in respect of all but one country (Colombia).[176] These rules required Schengen States to impose visa requirements on all the States in Africa, the Caribbean, and the Indian Ocean, as well as most States in Asia and the Pacific,[177] and to waive visa requirements for most States in Europe and Latin America.[178] There was also a Schengen blacklist regarding ATVs, consisting of twelve States.[179]

The 2001 EC Regulation fully harmonized the visa list policy, by adding Colombia definitively to the blacklist.[180] It also set out revised criteria for defining which states would go on the blacklist or whitelist; this decision was based on:[181]

...a considered, case-by case assessment of a variety of criteria relating *inter alia* to illegal immigration, public policy and security, and to the European Union's external relations with third countries, consideration also being given to the implications of regional coherence and reciprocity.

To this end, the 2001 Regulation moved three states or other entities from the blacklist to the whitelist: Hong Kong, Macao, and Bulgaria, along with Romania (provisionally). Hong Kong and Macao received this benefit in return for agreeing readmission treaties with the EC (as it was then), which covered also the readmission of at least some persons who had merely transited through their territory (in practice, Chinese citizens).[182] Bulgaria and Romania received this waiver partly in the interests of regional coherence, since those two States had just begun negotiations to join the EU, and all other countries which were then negotiating were already on the whitelist. But the Council also asked the Commission to prepare

---

[175] Decision SCH/Com-ex (97)32 (n 160 above), which placed thirteen States on the Schengen whitelist and four States on the Schengen blacklist.

[176] Decision SCH/Com-ex (98)53 rev 2 (ibid), which placed Bolivia, Ecuador, and the three Baltic states on the Schengen whitelist.

[177] The exceptions were Israel, Japan, South Korea, Singapore, Malaysia, Brunei, Australia, and New Zealand.

[178] The European exceptions were Albania, Romania, Bulgaria, Turkey, the Federal Republic of Yugoslavia, the Former Yugoslav Republic of Macedonia, Bosnia-Herzegovina, and all the former Soviet Union States except for the Baltic States. The Latin American exceptions were Peru, Guyana, Surinam, Cuba, the Dominican Republic, and Haiti.

[179] The list appeared in Annex 3, part of the Common Consular Instructions (Decision SCH/Com-ex (99)13, [2000] OJ L 239/317). These were the same States listed in the EU Joint Action (n 174 above), plus Pakistan and Bangladesh. This list of countries has now been incorporated in the visa code (see 4.7.2 below).   [180] Reg 539/2001 (n 161 above).

[181] See para 5 of the preamble.

[182] See 7.9.1 below. Note that this was the last time that third States or entities received a visa *waiver* in return for signing readmission treaties; the EU subsequently offered visa *facilitation* treaties in return for signing (some) readmission treaties. See 4.11.2 below.

a prior report on Bulgaria's and Romania's attempts to prevent illegal residence of their nationals in the Member States and readiness to accept their readmission, as a quid pro quo for visa abolition.[183] The report, issued early in 2001,[184] satisfied the Council as regards Bulgaria, but Romania was placed in a 'waiting room', pending a further report on 'the undertakings it is prepared to enter into on illegal immigration and illegal residence, including repatriation of persons from that country who are illegally resident'.[185] This report was submitted in June 2001, and recommended abolition of the visa requirement for Romanians, in light of Romania's undertakings.[186] So following a further Commission proposal, the Council amended the visa list Regulation to place Romania definitively on the white list from 1 January 2002.[187]

The next amendment to the list of countries dated from 2003, when the Council moved Ecuador from the whitelist to the blacklist due to concerns about illegal immigration, Switzerland was deleted from the lists altogether following the entry into force of its treaty with the EU on free movement of persons,[188] and East Timor was designated a State, rather than an entity only recognized by some Member States, after it had gained independence (although it remained on the blacklist).[189]

Next, in 2006 the Council moved Bolivia to the blacklist, on grounds of illegal immigration and crime, and moved six micro-States in the Pacific and Indian Ocean from the whitelist to the blacklist, on the grounds that there was limited migration pressure from those States and few or no Member States had consulates there.[190] However, the latter waiver was made subject to the conclusion of treaties establishing a reciprocal visa waiver between the EC (as it then was) and each of those countries; these treaties were not agreed until 2009.[191] The Council also decided in 2006 to adopt harmonized rules concerning various categories of quasi-British citizens. So a visa waiver applies to all 'British Nationals (Overseas)', while a visa requirement applies to four other such categories.[192]

In the meantime, in June 2003, the Council agreed criteria for potential abolition of the visa requirement for Western Balkan states,[193] comprising 'major reforms in areas such as' strengthening the rule of law; combating organized crime; corruption; and irregular migration; and strengthening

---

[183] See JHA Council press release of JHA Council, 30 Nov and 1 Dec 2000.

[184] COM (2001) 61, 2 Feb 2001.   [185] Art 8(2), Reg 539/2001 (n 161 above).

[186] COM (2001) 361, 29 June 2001.

[187] Reg 2414/2001 ([2001] OJ L 327/1). On the legal questions resulting from the 'waiting period' for visa abolition for Romanians, see the order in Case C-51/03 *Georgescu* [2004] ECR I-3203.

[188] See 4.4.2 above.   [189] Reg 453/2003 (n 163 above).

[190] The States concerned were Antigua and Barbuda, the Bahamas, Barbados, Mauritius, Saint Kitts and Nevis, and the Seychelles.   [191] See 4.11.1 below.

[192] These categories are: 'British Overseas Territories Citizens who do not have the right of abode in the United Kingdom'; 'British Overseas Citizens'; 'British Subjects who do not have the right of abode in the United Kingdom'; and 'British Protected Persons'.

[193] Other than Croatia, which was always on the EU whitelist.

administrative capacity regarding border control and document security.[194] This process encompassed visa facilitation treaties, in force from the start of 2008,[195] and then in November 2009, the Council adopted the most recent amendment to the visa list Regulation, moving Serbia, Montenegro, and the Former Yugoslav Republic of Macedonia (FYROM) from the blacklist to the whitelist,[196] in light of the Commission's assessment that these States had sufficiently met the relevant criteria. Subsequently, in May 2010, the Commission suggested moving Albania and Bosnia-Herzegovina to the whitelist, on the grounds that they too would have sufficiently met the criteria by the time the legislative proposal would be adopted.[197] In each case, the visa waiver only applies (or will apply) to holders of biometric passports. Also, the holders of passports issued in Kosovo are not covered.[198] The EU has, however, opened a visa dialogue with Kosovo with a view to waiving visa requirements when the criteria are met.[199]

As for the future, the Commission suggested in July 2010 the removal of the visa requirement for Taiwan.[200] In the longer term, the EU has opened a visa dialogue with 'eastern partnership' countries (Ukraine, Belarus, Moldova, Armenia, Azerbaijan, and Georgia), expressing a willingness to remove visa requirements on the basis of a 'roadmap' addressing issues such as 'document security; fight against irregular migration, including readmission; public order issues; and external relation issues, including human rights of migrants and other vulnerable groups'. There is also a visa dialogue with Russia.[201]

4.5.3. Exceptions

The 1995 and 1999 visa list Regulations permitted Member States to decide on the visa requirements for stateless persons and refugees, and to exempt various categories of persons from the visa requirement (transport and rescue workers and holders of diplomatic or official passports).[202] The 2001 visa list Regulation, after

---

[194] See the Press Release of the External Relations Council, 16 June 2003, and subsequently the Commission communication on the Western Balkans (COM (2006) 27, 27 Jan 2006). For detailed documentation of the visa liberalization process in the Western Balkans, see <http://www.esiweb.org>.   [195] See 4.11.2 below.

[196] Reg 1244/2009, n 163 above.   [197] See n 156 above.

[198] See recital 4 in the preamble to Reg 1244/2009 (n 163 above).

[199] COM (2009) 534, 14 Oct 2009.   [200] COM (2010) 358, 5 July 2010.

[201] See COM (2008) 823, 2 Dec 2008 (eastern partnership), and the St Petersburg statement on EU–Russia relations: <http://www.delrus.ec.europa.eu/en/p_234.htm>. Note that for now, the EU has—or plans to have—visa facilitation treaties with all of these countries: see 4.11.2 below. See also the conclusions of the Foreign Affairs Council on relations with the South Caucasus, 14 June 2010.

[202] Arts 2 and 4 of the Regulations. For information on Member States' decisions on these issues, see n 157 above.

amendment in 2006, includes both mandatory and optional exceptions, which appear to be exhaustive.[203]

The mandatory exceptions require a waiver for people covered by the EU's local border traffic legislation, school pupils residing in a Member State which applies the EU Joint Action on liberalizing school trips, and recognized refugees and stateless persons who reside in a Member State and hold a travel document issued by that State.[204] The optional exceptions permit Member States to waive visa requirements for: school pupils taking part in a school trip from a non-Member State (including Switzerland and Liechtenstein) on the whitelist; refugees and stateless persons living in a whitelist country;[205] and members of the armed forces of NATO members or of countries linked to NATO. Member States may *either* waive *or* impose a visa requirement on transport and rescue personnel, diplomats, and international officials; and they may impose a visa requirement on a person from a positive list State who seeks to carry out a paid activity. The 'paid activity' exception is not defined in the Regulation, but the EU's visa waiver treaties clarify the meaning of the concept.[206] There is no harmonization of visa policy in relation to workers posted from third countries pursuant to the General Agreement in Trade in Services.[207]

It should also be recalled that there are special rules, which have been amended over the years, concerning visa waiver for persons holding a long-stay visa,[208] and persons covered by EU rules on transit through Cyprus, Romania, Bulgaria, and Liechtenstein.[209]

4.5.4. Visa reciprocity

The 2001 visa list Regulation set out, for the first time, a form of reciprocity system for re-imposing visa requirements on any third States which impose visa requirements on the citizens of any EU Member State.[210] If a third country not subject to any EU visa requirement imposed a visa requirement on one or more Member States, those Member States could notify this to the Commission and Council, with the effect that the EU would have imposed a visa requirement on that State automatically, unless the Council voted otherwise by a QMV or the non-Member State dropped its visa requirement. This procedure was never used.

---

[203] Arts 1 and 4 of Reg 539/2001, as amended by Reg 1932/2006 (nn 161 and 163 above). On the implementation of these exceptions, see [2001] OJ C 363/21, [2003] OJ C 68/2, [2006] OJ C 311/16, and [2008] OJ C 74/40.

[204] On these categories, see further respectively 3.8 above and 4.9 and 5.5 below.

[205] Member States are obliged to impose visa requirements on refugees and stateless persons living in *blacklist* countries, but the Regulation is 'without prejudice to' the 1959 Council of Europe treaty on the abolition of visa requirements for refugees (CETS 31), which requires a visa exemption for lawfully resident refugees who hold travel documents issued by one of the Contracting Parties to that treaty. See Appendix I for ratification details.   [206] See 4.11.1 below.

[207] On this issue, see 6.4.6 below.   [208] See 4.9 below.   [209] See 4.2.5 above.

[210] Art 1(4).

The 2003 amendment to the visa list Regulation required the Commission to draw up a report on this issue, and this report documented that several countries benefiting from visa-free entry into the EU in fact imposed visa requirements on one or more of the first fifteen Member States; moreover, the large majority of such countries imposed visa requirements on one or more of the Member States which joined the EU in 2004.[211] There were also cases in which non-EU States arguably breached the reciprocity principle by imposing limitations on entry, such as limitations on the period of entry, that are not matched by the EU.

The Council subsequently adopted an amendment to the visa list Regulation in 2005 to institute a new system regarding reciprocity.[212] This instituted a more diplomatic procedure. Instead of a semi-automatic imposition of an EU visa requirement against a third State not applying reciprocity, the Commission must enter into discussions with the third State with a view to ensuring visa-free travel. The Commission must subsequently report to the Council, possibly proposing re-imposition of the visa requirement. In a series of reports on the application of these rules, the Commission has described some success in encouraging third States to drop visa requirements for all EU Member States, with greater difficulties as regards Canada, Australia, and the US.[213] In fact, Canada *re-imposed* visa controls on Czech citizens in 2009, due to concerns about asylum applications by Czech Roma, and the EU is considering possible countermeasures.[214] Finally, it should be noted that in some cases visa reciprocity is confirmed by visa waiver treaties agreed or under negotiation between the EU and the third States concerned.[215]

4.5.5. Analysis

The Schengen and EU visa lists have been strongly criticized on a number of grounds,[216] in particular the imprecise criteria used to determine which States are subject to the visa requirement and the highly discretionary application of those criteria in practice, with (for example) the absence of any published evidence offered to justify placing Ecuador on the blacklist and the failure to institute a

---

[211] Document JAI-B-1 (2004) 1372, Rev, 18 Feb 2004.

[212] Reg 851/2005 (n 163 above), amending Art 1(4) and adding a new Art 1(5). See also Council and Commission statement ([2005] OJ C 172/1).

[213] COM (2006) 3, 10 Jan 2006; COM (2006) 568, 3 Oct 2006; COM (2007) 533, 13 Sep 2007; COM (2008) 486, 23 July 2008; and COM (2009) 560, 19 Oct 2009.

[214] See COM (2009) 562, 19 Oct 2009.   [215] See 4.11.1 below.

[216] See R Cholewinski, *Borders and Discrimination in the European Union* (ILPA/MPG, 2002), 20–37; E Guild, 'The Border Abroad—Visas and Border Controls', in E Guild, P Minderhoud, and K Groenendijk, eds, *In Search of Europe's Borders* (Kluwer, 2003), 87; E Jileva, 'Insiders and Outsiders in Central and Eastern Europe: the Case of Bulgaria' in *idem*, 273; and P Boeles, 'Schengen and the Rule of Law', in H Meijers, et al, *Schengen: Internationalisation of Central Chapters of the law on aliens, refugees, privacy, security and the police* (2nd edn, Stichting NJCM-Boekerij, 1992).

regular review to see whether States really should remain on the blacklist.[217] Also, despite some liberalization, the EU visa blacklist arguably breaches the principle of non-discrimination, particularly given the application of the visa requirement to nearly all countries with a majority black or Muslim population; the airport transit visa list arguably similarly breaches the principle of non-discrimination.[218] Furthermore, the pressure placed on certain non-Member States to amend their immigration laws in order to secure visa abolition is disproportionate to the EU's legitimate interest in ensuring that citizens of those States do not abuse the abolition of the visa requirement; the EU's interests would be satisfied if readmission of *those States' nationals* was guaranteed and if passports issued by those States contained sufficient security features to ensure that passport-holders were genuine citizens. In particular, the EU's pressure has resulted in the application of national rules that arguably breach the human right to leave one's own country.[219]

4.6. Visa format

The Council first used the powers originally conferred by the former Article 100c EC to adopt an initial Regulation establishing a standard visa format in 1995.[220] Member States must issue visas for intended stays in that Member State or several Member States of no more than three months or transit through the territory or airport transit zone of that Member State or several Member States in the standard format set out in the Annex to the Regulation.[221] Further technical details making the visa difficult to counterfeit or falsify have been established in (secret) implementing measures adopted by the Commission, assisted by a committee of Member States' representatives (a 'comitology' committee).[222] Individuals to whom visas are issued have the right to verify the data on the visa and to ask for any corrections or deletions to be made, and only the data set out in the Annex to the Regulation or mentioned in that person's travel document can be included in machine-readable form on the visa.[223]

This Regulation was amended in 2002,[224] for two reasons. First of all, the amendment updated the 'comitology' rules in the Regulation concerning Member States' control of the Commission's use of implementing powers, since the general rules governing 'comitology' procedures had been amended in 1999.[225] Secondly,

---

[217] R Cholewinski and E Guild, ibid.   [218] R Cholewinski, ibid.
[219] R Cholewinski, ibid.   [220] Reg 1683/95 ([1995] OJ L 164/1).
[221] Arts 1 and 5 and Annex, Reg 1683/95.

[222] Arts 2, 3, and 6, Reg 1683/95. The secret implementing measures are set out in Commission Decisions 2/96, 7 Feb 1996 and COM (2000) 4332, 27 Dec 2000 (both unpublished; see COM (2001) 157, 23 Mar 2001, p 2). The standard visa format therefore became applicable on 7 Aug 1996 (see Art 8, Reg 1683/95).   [223] Art 4, Reg 1683/95.

[224] Reg 334/2002 ([2002] OJ L 53/7).

[225] On the issue of 'comitology', see 2.2.2.1 above.

the amended Regulation requires Member States to include a photograph in visas in order to increase security and to pave the way for the introduction of the VIS.[226] Member States have had an obligation to introduce photographs in visas from 3 June 2007.[227]

In 2003, the Commission proposed a further amendment to the Regulation,[228] in order to store further 'biometric' data (ie fingerprints) in relation to visas, in parallel with comparable changes then planned (and subsequently implemented) as regards residence permits and passports.[229] However, the proposed Regulation was not adopted due to technical difficulties, and the Commission withdrew the proposal early in 2006.[230] Instead of storing biometric data on visa applicants in a computer chip integrated into each visa sticker, this biometric data will be stored in the central computer system which will service the VIS, when the VIS begins operations. The process of taking and storing biometric data is therefore regulated by amendments to the Common Consular Instructions (CCI) adopted in 2009, which have now been integrated into the EU's visa code.[231]

A second amendment to the original Regulation was nonetheless adopted in 2008,[232] in order to ensure that the standard format was consistent with the planned introduction of the VIS, so that visa sticker numbers could be searched easily via the VIS.

In addition to these two substantive amendments, the visa format Regulation has also been amended twice following the accession of new Member States to the EU.[233] In light of these numerous amendments to the Regulation, late in 2008, the Commission proposed a codified version of it.[234] This proposal (which is now subject to the ordinary legislative procedure, following the entry into force of the Treaty of Lisbon),[235] has not yet been adopted.

A separate Regulation establishing a form of visa format where persons are travelling on a travel document issued by an entity which is not recognized by the Member State drawing up the form was adopted in March 2002.[236] It follows the structure of the main visa format Regulation.

---

[226] On the VIS, see further 4.8 below.

[227] See Art 1(3), Reg 334/2002 and the secret implementing Commission Decision C (2002) 2002, 3 June 2002 (unpublished; see COM (2003) 558, 24 Sept 2003, p 2).

[228] COM (2003) 558, 24 Sept 2003.

[229] On the formats of residence permits, long-stay visas, and passports, see 6.9 below and 3.9 above.

[230] COM (2006) 110, 10 Mar 2006. On the technical difficulties, see Council doc 6492/05, 17 Feb 2005, online at: <http://www.statewatch.org/news/2005/feb/6492.05.pdf>; and see the Statewatch story with further documentation online at: <http://www.statewatch.org/news/2004/dec/07visas-residence-biometrics.htm>.   [231] See further 4.7 below.

[232] Reg 856/2008 ([2008] OJ L 235/1), applicable at the latest on 1 May 2009 (Art 2).

[233] See the 2003 Act of accession, Annex II, part 18.B ([2003] OJ L 236/1) and Reg 1791/2006 ([2006] OJ L 363/1); see further 4.2.5 above.   [234] COM (2008) 891, 19 Dec 2008.

[235] See 4.2.3 above.

[236] Reg 333/2002 ([2002] OJ L 53/4), applicable from 23 Feb 2002.

Similarly, several other EU measures provide for a distinct form of visa format,[237] but on the other hand, a number of measures provide for the application of the standard visa format in other contexts.[238] In particular, a Regulation adopted in 2010 provides for the use of the common visa format for all long-stay visas also.[239]

4.7. Conditions for issuing visas

4.7.1. Overview and background

The basic conditions governing the issue of Schengen visas were initially set out in Articles 9–17 of the 1990 Schengen Convention, as supplemented by a number of decisions of the Schengen Executive Committee, particularly establishing the CCI.[240] Following the integration of the Schengen *acquis* into the EC and EU legal order, the Council adopted a Regulation in 2001 which conferred powers to amend the CCI, along with four other Schengen measures concerning visas,[241] in part upon itself, and in part upon individual Member States.[242] The Commission brought a legal

---

[237] The Regulations regarding the Kaliningrad visa format (Reg 694/2003, [2003] OJ L 99/15) and the issue of collective visas to seamen (see originally Reg 415/2003, [2004] L 64/1, and now Art 36 and Annex IX to the visa code (Reg 810/2009, [2009] OJ L 243/1)). The Olympic visa regulations provide instead for insertion of numbers into the Olympic accreditation card as the format of the visa (Art 6, Reg 1295/2003, [2003] OJ L 183/1 and Art 6, Reg 2046/2005, [2005] OJ L 334/1). The same rule will apply to any future Olympics held in the Schengen area (see Art 49 and Annex XI, Art 6 of the visa code (*idem*)). On these measures, see further 4.7.3 below.

[238] The Joint Action on airport transit visas ([1996] OJ L 63/8) provided explicitly for use of the standard format (see Art 2(3)), although the visa code (ibid), which repealed this Joint Action, no longer contains an express rule to this effect; while the ADS treaty with China (see 4.11.3 below) provides implicitly for the use of the standard visa format.

[239] Art 18 of the Schengen Convention, as amended by Reg 265/2010 ([2010] OJ L 85/1). See further 6.9.2 below. Note that biometric data is *not* taken from long-stay visa applicants, but this issue is due to be reviewed by July 2011 (see the Joint Statement in the summary of Council acts for Mar 2010: Council doc 8252/10, 13 Apr 2010).

[240] [2000] OJ L 239/17 (Convention). The consolidated text of the CCI as of 1 May 1999, as integrated into the EC legal order, was set out in SCH/Com-ex (99) 13, [2000] OJ L 239/307. For a summary of the Schengen Convention and CCI visa rules, see the second edition of this book, at 151–155.

[241] The other four measures were: Executive Committee Decisions SCH/Com-ex (98) 56 and SCH/Com-ex (99) 14 ([2000] OJ L 239/207 and 298), which both concerned a manual of travel documents to which a visa could be affixed; a manual concerning the issuance of Schengen visas in third States where all the Schengen States are not represented (Document SCH/II (95) 16, 19th revision, referred to in point III of the Decision consolidating the text of the CCI (ibid), but not published in the OJ); and document SCH/II-Vision (99) 5 ('Schengen Consultation Network (Technical Specifications)'), referred to in Executive Committee Decision SCH/Com-ex (94) 15 rev ([2000] OJ L 239/165, as corrected by a later Council Decision ([2000] OJ L 272/24)), which concerns a computerized procedure for consulting the central authorities of other Member States on visa applications. The latter measure was initially confidential, but then was largely declassified by the Council (see Decision, [2003] OJ L 116/22).

[242] Reg 789/2001 ([2001] OJ L 116/2). On the parallel Regulation governing amendments to the Schengen Borders Manual, see 3.6.1 above.

challenge to this Regulation, on the grounds that the Regulation did not adequately explain why implementing powers had not been conferred on the Commission (which is the normal legal rule), but the Court of Justice dismissed the challenge.[243]

This Regulation was used a number of times by the Council to amend the CCI up until January 2010,[244] in particular: to oblige applicants to pay a fee for a visa *application*, not just when the visa is issued;[245] to provide for a standard form for Schengen visa applications;[246] to set out harmonized rules on the use of travel agents in the visa process;[247] to establish a standard fee of €35 for Schengen visa applications;[248] to strengthen the normal obligation to interview visa applicants in consulates;[249] to liberalize the rules on the representation of one Member State by another, as regards visa applications;[250] to impose an obligation in principle for visa applicants to have medical insurance;[251] and to increase the standard fee for an application to €60 as from the start of 2007, in order to fund the VIS.[252] The Council made a number of other more technical amendments,[253] and the CCI was also amended following enlargement of the EU.[254] It was also still possible to amend the CCI by means of legislation, and indeed several legislative acts amended the Instructions.[255] In particular, a major amendment to the CCI adopted in 2009 regulated the process of taking biometric data from visa applicants, pursuant to the planned operation of the VIS.[256] Due to all these changes, the CCI were frequently consolidated informally.[257]

The Decision setting out the CCI was not the only Decision of the Schengen Executive Committee relating to visas. There were a further thirteen Decisions wholly related to visas and five Decisions partly related to visas (setting aside

---

[243] Case C-257/01 *Commission v Council* [2005] ECR I-345. On the issue of implementing measures, see generally 2.2.2.1 above.

[244] The amendments made by Member States to the CCI (see Art 2, Reg 789/2001) were not published in the OJ.   [245] Decision 2002/44 ([2002] OJ L 20/5).

[246] Decision 2002/354 ([2002] OJ L 123/50).   [247] [2002] OJ L 187/44.

[248] [2003] OJ L 152/82.   [249] [2004] OJ L 5/74.

[250] [2004] OJ L 5/76. This Decision also replaced the manual on the issuance of Schengen visas in third States where all the Schengen States are not represented (Document SCH/II (95) 16, 19th revision, n 241 above) with an Annex to the CCI.   [251] [2004] OJ L 5/79.

[252] [2006] OJ L 175/77.

[253] Decision 2001/329/EC ([2001] OJ L 116/32) amended the CCI consequential to the enlargement of the Schengen zone to Nordic countries. Decision 2001/420/EC ([2001] OJ L 150/47) adjusted the CCI to the creation of a new D+C visa for holders of long-stay visas (see further 4.9 below). Another Decision ([2002] OJ L 187/48) related to amended rules on the standard visa format (see 4.6 above). The remaining decisions concern holders of Pakistani, Indonesian, and Saudi diplomatic and service passports ([2003] OJ L 198/13, [2006] OJ L 280/29, [2009] OJ L 61/17, and [2010] OJ L 26/22), airport transit visa requirements ([2003] OJ L 198/15, [2008] OJ L 129/46, [2008] OJ L 303/11, and [2009] OJ L 348/51) and changes to the rules regarding filling in visa stickers ([2008] OJ L 327/19 and L 345/88).   [254] See 4.2.5 above.

[255] Art 7(2) of Reg 539/2001 ([2001] OJ L 81/1); Art 2 of Reg 1091/2001 ([2001] OJ L 150/4); Art 2 of Reg 334/2002 ([2002] OJ L 53/7); Art 5(4) of Reg 415/2003 ([2003] OJ L 64/1); Art 11(1) of Reg 693/2003 ([2003] OJ L 99/8); and Art 39(2)(c) of the Schengen Borders code ([2006] OJ L 105/1).

[256] Reg 390/2009 ([2009] OJ L 131/1).

[257] [2002] OJ C 313/1, [2003] OJ C 310/1, and [2005] OJ C 326/1.

measures which were not allocated to the EC legal order, pursuant to the Schengen Protocol, when the Treaty of Amsterdam entered into force). The former comprised Decisions on: extending the uniform visa;[258] procedures for cancelling the uniform visa;[259] issuing uniform visas at the border;[260] introducing a computerized procedure for the consultation provided for in Article 17(2);[261] a common visa policy;[262] representation of other Member States when issuing visas;[263] issuing visas at the borders to seamen in transit;[264] harmonization of visa policy;[265] exchange of visa statistics at local level;[266] stamping of passports of visa applicants;[267] abolition of the visa 'grey list';[268] a manual of documents to which a visa may be affixed;[269] and the introduction of a harmonized form for sponsorship.[270] The latter comprised Decisions on: the acquisition of common entry and exit stamps;[271] exchanges of statistical information on visas;[272] an action plan to combat illegal immigration;[273] the coordinated deployment of document advisers;[274] and a manual of documents to which a visa may be affixed.[275]

Of these further eighteen decisions, two related to visa lists, and so were repealed by the EC's visa list Regulation in 2001.[276] Two further Decisions—concerning the issue of visas to seamen, and the issue of visas at the border—were repealed when the EC adopted updated rules on these issues in 2003.[277]

The EC also adopted some separate measures setting out exceptions from the normal rules on issuing visas following the entry into force of the Treaty of Amsterdam. First of all, to assuage Russian concerns about the transit of Russian citizens between the enclave of Kaliningrad, which became surrounded by EU Member States after enlargement of the EU, and the rest of Russia, the EU came to an arrangement with Russia and the Council adopted two special Regulations

[258] SCH/Com-ex (93) 21 ([2000] OJ L 239/151).

[259] SCH/Com-ex (93) 24 ([2000] OJ L 239/154).

[260] SCH/Com-ex (94) 2 ([2000] OJ L 239/163).

[261] SCH/Com-ex (94) 15 ([2000] OJ L 239/165), corrected by the Council in 2000 ([2000] OJ L 272/24). As noted above, Reg 789/2001 set out a procedure for amending this Decision.

[262] SCH/Com-ex (95) PV 1 rev ([2000] OJ L 239/175).

[263] SCH/Com-ex (96) 13 rev 1 ([2000] OJ L 239/180).

[264] SCH/Com-ex (96) 27 ([2000] OJ L 239/182).

[265] SCH/Com-ex (97) 32 ([2000] OJ L 239/186).

[266] SCH/Com-ex (98) 12 ([2000] OJ L 239/196).

[267] SCH/Com-ex (98) 21 ([2000] OJ L 239/200).

[268] SCH/Com-ex (98) 53 rev 2 ([2000] OJ L 239/206).

[269] SCH/Com-ex (98) 56 ([2000] OJ L 239/207). As noted above, Reg 789/2001 set out a procedure for amending this Decision.   [270] SCH/Com-ex (98) 57 ([2000] OJ L 239/299).

[271] SCH/Com-ex (94) 16 rev ([2000] OJ L 239/166).

[272] SCH/Com-ex (94) 25 ([2000] OJ L 239/173).

[273] SCH/Com-ex (98) 37 def 2 ([2000] OJ L 239/203).

[274] SCH/Com-ex (98) 59 rev ([2000] OJ L 239/308).

[275] SCH/Com-ex (99) 14 ([2000] OJ L 239/298). As noted above, Reg 789/2001 set out a procedure for amending this Decision.

[276] SCH/Com-ex (97) 32 and SCH/Com-ex (98) 53 rev 2 (nn 265 and 268 above).

[277] SCH/Com-ex (94) 2 and SCH/Com-ex (96) 27 (nn 260 and 264 above).

providing for facilitated transit between Kaliningrad and the rest of Russia.[278] The first Regulation provides for a special facilitated transit procedure, subject to fewer conditions and a lower fee than those applicable to Schengen visa applications, while the second Regulation provides for a standard format for the facilitated transit documents. Secondly, the EC adopted two Regulations governing the issue of visas to the 'Olympic family': first, for the summer 2004 Olympics, held in Greece, and secondly, for the Winter 2006 Olympics, held in Turin.[279] These Regulations exempted athletes, coaches, and others closely related to the running of the Olympics from any requirements for a visa, except for the requirement to hold travel documents and checks in national and EU databases, and waived the fee for visa applications entirely.

Finally, the EC also adopted two 'soft law' measures concerning special visa regimes. First of all, Council conclusions from 2003 suggested a special regime for granting visas to participants in the 'Barcelona process',[280] and secondly the EP and Council adopted a Recommendation on the issue of short-term visas to researchers in 2005, as one part of a three-part package designed to encourage third-country national researchers to visit or reside in the EU.[281] According to the Recommendation, the Member States should: expedite the examination of visa applications from third countries subject to a visa obligation; promote international mobility by issuing multiple entry visas, taking account of the duration of the research programmes when determining the period of the visa's validity; attempt to harmonize their approach to supporting evidence regarding researchers' visa applications; encourage the issue of visas without fees to researchers, in accordance with the *acquis*; exchange best practice on the issue of visas to researchers within the framework of local consular cooperation; and inform the Commission by September 2006 about the best practices developed, to enable the Commission to evaluate the progress made. Depending on the evaluation, the EU should examine the possibility of making the Recommendation legally binding.[282]

4.7.2. The visa code

The visa code Regulation was adopted in June 2009,[283] and has applied since 5 April 2010.[284] From that date, the Regulation repealed almost all of the prior

---

[278] Regs 693/2003 and 694/2003 ([2003] OJ L 99/8 and 15). See previously: COM (2001) 26, 18 Jan 2001; SEC (2002) 49, 15 Jan 2002; and COM (2002) 510, 18 Sept 2002.

[279] See respectively Regs 1295/2003 ([2003] OJ L 183/1) and 2046/2005 ([2005] OJ L 334/1). The two Regulations are essentially identical.   [280] Council doc 6254/03, 13 Feb 2003.

[281] [2005] OJ L 289/23. On the two other measures, see 6.5.3 below.

[282] In practice, the Commission has not yet released any evaluation of the Recommendation.

[283] Reg 810/2009, [2009] OJ L 243/1. All the references in this section are to the code, unless otherwise indicated.

[284] Art 58(2). However, the rules concerning appeals (see discussion below) will apply from 5 Apr 2011 (Art 58(5)).

measures governing the conditions for the issue of Schengen visas:[285] Articles
9–17 of the Schengen Convention; the Schengen Executive Committee Decision
establishing the CCI, along with the measures amending the CCI adopted within
the EC framework, including the 2009 Regulation amending the CCI as regards
obtaining biometric data from visa applicants; five of the remaining Schengen
Executive Committee Decisions, concerning a harmonized form for sponsorship
of visa applicants, extending or shortening the validity of a visa, and the exchange
of statistics; the Joint Action on airport transit visas; the 2001 Regulation conferring power on the Council to amend the CCI; another 2001 Regulation concerning freedom to travel with a long-stay visa; and the 2003 Regulation concerning
visas issued at the border. A small number of prior measures relating to Schengen
visas are still in force; these are examined separately below.[286]

The Commission has the power to amend nine of the thirteen Annexes to the
Code, by means of the 'regulatory procedure with scrutiny' (involving a form
of control by the EP), as well as the power to adopt operational instructions for
consular authorities, by means of the 'regulatory procedure'; the former rules will
likely be replaced at some point with a procedure for the adoption of 'delegated
acts'.[287] So far, the Commission has not adopted any measures implementing
the Code, although a draft operational handbook has been agreed within the
comitology committee.[288] Member States are also obliged to notify a number of
national decisions to the Commission, which is obliged to publish them.[289]

Title I of the visa code concerns respectively the objective and scope of the
code, and the relevant definitions.[290] The code is 'without prejudice' to the position of third-country nationals as regards EU free movement law and agreements
extending EU free movement law to non-EU states.[291]

Title II of the code concerns airport transit visas (ATVs).[292] There is a standard list of countries whose nationals require ATVs to cross through the international transit areas of airports, in place of the lists in the CCI and in the
Joint Action of 1996 (now repealed) which had addressed this issue.[293] Member
States may decide that the nationals of additional States will require ATVs (ie
a purely national list) in the event of 'urgent cases of massive inflow of illegal

---

[285] Art 56. Annex XIII to the Code sets out a correlation table comparing the visa code and the
prior measures.   [286] See 4.7.3.
[287] Arts 50–52. For a list of the Annexes, see below. On 'comitology', see 2.2.2.1 above, and on
delegated acts, see 2.2.3.1 above.
[288] See: <http://www.statewatch.org/news/2010/jan/eu-com-draft-visas-handbook.pdf>.
[289] Art 53.   [290] Arts 1 and 2.
[291] Art 1(2). On the relationship between EU free movement law and EU visa legislation in general, see 4.4.1 above. See also Art 3(5)(d) of the Code, which exempts family members of EU citizens
from any airport transit visa requirement, and also Art 24(2)(a) and Annex XI, Art 4.
[292] Art 3. For the definition of 'airport transit visa', see Art 2(5); see also Art 1(3) on the scope
of the code.
[293] Art 3(1), referring to Annex IV. The Annex consists of the same twelve countries which were
subject to a common ATV requirement under the CCI (see 4.5.2 above).

immigrants', subject to prior notification of the Commission before introducing or withdrawing such a national requirement.[294] These national lists are
subject to annual review in the 'comitology committee' established by the visa
code Regulation, in order to decide whether to add the countries concerned
to the uniform EU list of states requiring ATVs.[295] If the countries concerned
are not added to the uniform EU list, the Member State which listed them can
either keep those countries on its national list (if the criteria for listing them
are still met) or withdraw the ATV requirement.[296] There could presumably be
a judicial review of whether the criteria are met for a national decision to place
(or retain) a country on an ATV list in light of the criteria in the visa code.
However, it should be noted that there are no express criteria governing the
addition or removal of countries to the common EU list, other than a reference
to combating 'illegal immigration'.[297]

In any event, neither the EU common list nor any national list can apply an
ATV requirement to six categories of persons: those holding a Schengen visa,
national long-stay visa, or residence permit issued by a Member State; those
holding a valid residence permit issued by the US, Japan, Canada, San Marino,
or Andorra, if the permit is listed in Annex V to the visa code and guarantees
unqualified readmission; those holding a visa issued by a Member State, an EEA
State, or by the US, Canada, or Japan, or when they return from those countries having used the visa; family members of EU citizens who have exercised
free movement rights; holders of diplomatic passports; and flight crew members
who are nationals of States which are party to the Chicago Convention on civil
aviation.[298]

Title III of the visa code concerns the conditions and procedures for issuing visas. Chapter I defines the authorities taking part in the application procedure.[299] As a general rule, subject to limited exceptions, visa applications
must be decided upon by consulates.[300] The visa code then specifies which
Member State is responsible for considering applications for different types of
visa;[301] Member States are obliged to cooperate to prevent situations in which
an application cannot be processed because the Member State responsible does
not have a consulate or representation from another Member State in the third
State concerned.[302] There are also rules for visa applicants residing in Member
States.[303] Member States are encouraged to represent other Member States,
where the latter do not have a consulate, for the purpose of processing visa
applications or for taking biometric information for applicants.[304] There is,
however, no guarantee that a nearby consulate which is able to process applications will be available for all visa applications; the radical solution of a move

---

[294] Art 3(2). These decisions also have to be notified to the Commission: see Art 53(1)(b).
[295] Art 3(3).   [296] Art 3(4).   [297] Point 5 in the preamble.   [298] Art 3(5).
[299] Arts 4–8.   [300] Art 4.   [301] Art 5(1)–(3).   [302] Art 5(4).   [303] Art 7.
[304] Art 8. These arrangements have to be notified to the Commission: see Art 53(1)(a).

toward common EU consulates, perhaps constituting part of the EU External Action Service which was established pursuant to the Treaty of Lisbon,[305] is not mentioned in the visa code.

Chapter II of Title III of the visa code concerns the application process.[306] Visa applications cannot be made more than three months before the date of travel, except as regards multiple-entry visas, where the application can be made up to six months before the date of travel.[307] Applicants normally have to appear in person to apply for a visa, but this is subject to a number of exceptions.[308] Each applicant must fill out the standard application form, even children who are listed on their parent's passport.[309] Applicants must also present a valid travel document,[310] as well as biometric data (a photograph and ten fingerprints).[311] Fingerprints can be taken by honorary consuls or private service providers (see discussion below).[312] There are uniform exemptions from the fingerprinting requirement: children under twelve; persons for whom fingerprinting is physically impossible; heads of state, senior politicians, and their spouses and delegations on official visits; and senior royal family members on official visits.[313]

The Code then details the rules concerning supporting documents to be submitted by applicants;[314] the requirement of medical insurance;[315] the fee for visa applicants;[316] and the service fee for the use of private companies to collect biometric data (see further below).[317] The application fee remains €60, and the maximum service fee is half that amount.[318] However, the application fee must be reduced to €35 for children between six and twelve years old.[319] The fee must also be waived for: children under six years old; students, pupils, and teachers on study trips; researchers as defined by an EC recommendation; and representatives of non-profit organizations attending seminars and similar events.[320] Also, the fee *may* be waived for children between six and twelve, holders of diplomatic and service passports, and participants in non-profit seminars and similar events who are under twenty-five years old.[321] The fee may also be waived or reduced in individual cases, if this 'serves to promote cultural or sporting interests as well as interests in the field of foreign policy, development policy and other areas of vital public interest or for humanitarian reasons'.[322]

Chapter III of Title III of the visa code concerns the examination of and decisions taken upon applications.[323] This includes rules on verification of consular

---

[305] See Art 27(3), revised TEU and the Decision establishing the Service ([2010] OJ L 201/30).
[306] Arts 9–17.   [307] Art 9.   [308] Art 10.
[309] Art 11. The standard application form is set out in Annex I to the Code.   [310] Art 12.
[311] Art 13. However, fingerprints normally only need to be taken once every five years (Art 13(3)).   [312] Art 13(6), referring to Arts 42 and 43.
[313] Art 13(7).   [314] Art 14 and Annex II.   [315] Art 15.   [316] Art 16.
[317] Art 17.   [318] Arts 16(1) and 17(4).   [319] Art 16(2).   [320] Art 16(4).
[321] Art 16(5).
[322] Art 16(6). The fee is also reduced or abolished by the EU's visa facilitation treaties: see 4.11.2 below.   [323] Arts 18–23.

competence, admissibility of applications, and the stamping of applicants' travel documents.[324]

The key issue is of course the substantive grounds for deciding on the application for a visa. The visa code specifies that consulates are to apply the criteria for admission set out in the Schengen Borders Code.[325] In this context, 'particular consideration shall be given to assessing whether the applicant presents a risk of illegal immigration or a risk to the security of the Member States and whether the applicant intends to leave the territory of the Member States before the expiry of the visa applied for'.[326] The VIS (when operational) must be checked for each application,[327] and consulates must also check for the veracity of documents, the intentions of the applicant, sufficient means of the applicant for subsistence, a listing for refusal of entry in the SIS, that the applicant is not 'a threat to public policy, internal security or public health' as defined in the Borders Code, and that the applicant has sufficient medical insurance.[328] The consulate must also assess whether the applicant has overstayed the permitted length of stay on the territory at present, or in the past.[329] There are separate criteria relating to applications for ATVs.[330] Decisions on the application have to be based on the 'authenticity and reliability' of the documents submitted, and the 'veracity and reliability' of the applicant.[331] If necessary, further documents or a personal interview can be requested.[332] Finally, the visa code specifies that a previous refusal of a visa application will not automatically mean a refusal of a new application; rather, a new application 'shall be assessed on the basis of all available information'.[333] However, it remains to be seen whether the introduction of the VIS will in practice nonetheless lead to an increased tendency to reject applications due to prior refusals, because information on prior refusals will be more readily available to consulates.[334]

The visa code then sets out rules for the controversial system of 'prior consultation', according to which one Member State may require the authorities of all other Member States to inform them of all visa applications from nationals of particular third countries or from particular categories of such nationals.[335] The consulted State's authorities must reply within seven days of the consultation, or they are deemed to have no objections to the application.[336] If they do

---

[324] Respectively Arts 18–20.

[325] Art 21(1) of the visa code, referring to Art 5 of the Borders Code (Reg 562/2006, [2006] OJ L 105/1). On the Borders Code, see further 3.6.1 above.   [326] Art 21(1).

[327] Art 21(2). For details of the VIS, see 4.8 below.

[328] Art 21(3). These are the same grounds set out in Art 5(1) of the Borders Code (n 325 above), with the addition of the medical insurance requirement. Art 21(5) sets out more rules relating to subsistence, including a further cross-reference to the Schengen Borders Code as regards subsistence criteria set by Member States.

[329] Art 21(4). This will obviously be facilitated if EU plans to establish an entry-exit system become operational: see 3.6.2 above.   [330] Art 21(6).

[331] Art 21(7).   [332] Art 21(8).   [333] Art 21(9).   [334] On the VIS, see 4.8 below.

[335] Art 22(1).   [336] Art 22(2).

have objections, this is not a ground as such for refusing a visa application, but obviously it is far more likely in practice that the application will be rejected. But in the event of an objection (or, in an emergency, pending the response to the consultation), the consulting Member State can still decide 'exceptionally' to issue a visa with limited territorial validity (an 'LTV visa').[337] The code does not specify expressly whether the applicant (or indeed the consulting Member State) must be told of the consulted Member State's reasons for objecting to an application. In practice, the consultation process is carried out in accordance with the 'Schengen Consultation Network' established by previous Schengen Executive Committee Decisions; this Network will be phased out as the VIS is phased in, for the VIS will integrate a new system for such consultations.[338] Member States shall inform the Commission of any new consultation requirements, or any withdrawal of existing requirements; it shall inform other Member States and the public.[339] The requirement to inform the public of the consultation requirement is a major change from the position under the CCI, when such arrangements were kept secret.[340]

Another change from the prior rules is the possibility to replace the consultation requirement with a less onerous information requirement, which is identical to the consultation requirement except for the lack of any facility for the informed Member State to comment on the visa application.[341]

A decision (whether positive or negative) on visa applications must be made within fifteen days, although extensions of this period to thirty or sixty days are permissible under certain conditions.[342]

Chapter IV of Title III of the visa code concerns issuing a visa.[343] It specifies that visas can be valid for one entry, two entries, or multiple entries, with a maximum validity of five years and (normally) a period of grace of fifteen days.[344] Multiple-entry visas 'shall' be issued where there is both a proven need to travel frequently and the applicant has proven his or her 'integrity and reliability'.[345]

Next, there are rules on LTV visas, ie visas which are valid only for one or possibly more, but less than all, of the Schengen States.[346] LTV visas are issued 'exceptionally', either where a Member State 'considers it necessary on humanitarian grounds, for reasons of national interest or because of international obligations', to derogate from the criteria for entry set out in the Schengen Borders Code, to issue a visa despite the objections of a Member State which had to be consulted in accordance with the consultation procedure (see above), or to issue a visa 'for

---

[337] Art 25(1)(a).

[338] On the Decisions, see 4.7.1 above and 4.7.3 below; on the relationship with the VIS, see Arts 16 and 46 of the VIS Reg (Reg 767/2008, [2008] OJ L 218/60), and the 2009 Commission Decision implementing the VIS Reg on this point ([2009] OJ L 117/3).

[339] Art 22(3) and (4), and Art 53(1)(d) and (2).

[340] See Annex 5 to the consolidated CCI (n 240 above).   [341] Art 31.   [342] Art 23.

[343] Arts 24–32.   [344] Art 24(1).   [345] Art 24(2).

[346] On the territorial scope of LTV visas, see Art 25(2).

reasons of urgency' even though such a consultation has not been carried out;[347] or where a new visa is to be issued to a person who has already used a visa within the same six-month period.[348] There is also a special rule for cases where a travel document is not recognized by all Member States.[349]

There are comparable specific rules on the issue of ATVs,[350] as well as detailed technical rules on filling in, invalidating, and fixing visa stickers.[351] The visa code confirms that simple possession of a visa 'shall not confer an automatic right of entry'.[352]

The visa code also contains key provisions on the grounds for refusing a visa and the procedural rights for visa applicants in the case of refusal.[353] An application 'shall' be refused: if the applicant does not meet the conditions for obtaining a visa;[354] if the applicant has already stayed for three of the last six months on the basis of a visa;[355] or if there are 'reasonable doubts' about the authenticity, veracity, or reliability of the applicant's documents or statements.[356] The visa code is silent as to whether Member States may also invoke other grounds for refusing an application, but given the uniform nature of Schengen visas and the lack of any space for 'other' grounds for refusal on the standard notification form, it should be concluded that they cannot.

Following a refusal of an application, in a major change from the rules in the CCI, the applicant must be informed of the refusal and the grounds for it (by use of a standard form),[357] and applicants whose applicants are refused have the 'right to appeal' in accordance with the national law of the Member State which refused their application.[358] The rules on notification and appeal also apply to visa applications at the border, and to decisions on annulment and revocation of visas.[359] However, as noted above, none of the provisions on notification and appeal rights will apply until 5 April 2011.[360]

Chapter V of Title III of the visa code concerns modification of an issued visa.[361] First, a visa 'shall' be extended (free of charge) where there is 'proof of

---

[347] Art 25(1)(a). There is a requirement to inform other Member States in such cases: see Art 25(4).

[348] Art 25(1)(b). Compare to the general rules on extending visas, as set out in Art 33 of the Code (see below).   [349] Art 25(3).

[350] Art 26.   [351] Arts 27–29 and Annexes VII and VIII.   [352] Art 30.

[353] Art 32. These rules are 'without prejudice' to the possibility of issuing an LTV visa (see above).

[354] Art 32(1)(a)(i)–(iii) and (v)–(vi); these mirror the conditions for obtaining a visa set out in Art 21(3) (see above).   [355] Art 32(1)(a)(iv).

[356] Art 32(1)(b).   [357] Art 32(2). The standard form is set out in Annex VI.

[358] Art 32(3). The provisions on notification and appeal can be compared to the similar provisions in the Schengen Borders Code (see 3.6.1 above) and to the right of access to information in the VIS (see 4.8 below), considering that in the first case, the grounds for refusal of entry and refusal of a visa are nearly the same, and in the second case that information on refusals of, for example visa applications, will be inserted into the VIS (see Arts 32(5) and 34(8)) and therefore subject to the right of access to VIS data anyway.   [359] Arts 34(6) and (7) and 35(7).

[360] Art 58(5).   [361] Arts 33–34.

force majeure or humanitarian reasons preventing [the visa holder] from leaving the territory of the Member States';[362] a visa *may* be extended (for a fee of €30) where there is 'proof of serious personal reasons' justifying this.[363] On the other hand, a visa shall be annulled (presumably with retroactive effect) 'where it becomes evident that the conditions for issuing it were not met at the time when it was issued, in particular if there are serious grounds for believing that the visa was fraudulently obtained',[364] and a visa shall be revoked 'where it becomes evident that the conditions for issuing it are no longer met'.[365]

Chapter VI of Title III of the visa code concerns issuing a visa at the border.[366] Visas can only be issued at the border in 'exceptional' cases, where the applicant meets the conditions for entry in the Schengen Borders Code, is certain to return to the country of origin or transit, and 'the applicant has not been in a position to apply for a visa in advance and submits, if required, supporting documents substantiating unforeseeable and imperative reasons for entry'.[367] The medical insurance requirement may be waived in certain cases for such visas,[368] but in these circumstances visas can only be issued for a maximum of fifteen days.[369] Where the conditions for entry at the border are not met, or the applicant is part of a category of persons whose application should be subject to prior consultation, an LTV visa can be issued.[370] There are special rules relating to the issue of visas to seafarers at the border.[371]

Title IV of the visa code concerns the organization and management of visa sections.[372] It includes basic rules on the security and confidentiality at consulates, the resources of consulates, and the conduct of staff.[373] Member States are encouraged to cooperate via various means, in particular as regards collection of biometric information, in the form either of representation (see further above), co-location, Joint Application Centres, honorary consuls, or, as a last resort, the use of external service providers (ie private companies) to collect biometric information.[374] The visa code also sets out detailed rules on the collection of statistics and the provision of information to the general public.[375]

Title V of the visa code concerns local consular cooperation.[376] Local consulates and the Commission must consult as to whether there should be harmonized rules on the local level, which would then be drawn up in accordance with a 'comitology' procedure, without any special involvement of the EP.[377] Local consular cooperation must also lead to the drawing up of common information sheets

---

[362] Art 33(1).   [363] Art 33(2).   [364] Art 34(1).   [365] Art 34(2).
[366] Arts 35–36.   [367] Art 35(1).   [368] Art 35(2).   [369] Art 35(3).
[370] Art 35(4) and (5).   [371] Art 36 and Annex IX.   [372] Arts 37–47.

[373] See respectively Arts 37–39. The rules on conduct of staff are identical to those set out in Art 6 of the Schengen Borders Code (n 235 above; see 3.6.1 above), with the addition of a requirement to treat applicants courteously (Art 39(1)).

[374] Arts 40–45. For an explanation of the concepts of co-location and Common Application Centres, see Art 41(1) and (2).   [375] Arts 46 and 47.

[376] Art 48.   [377] Art 48(1), referring to Art 52(2).

for applicants, the exchange of local information and statistics, and discussion of operational issues.[378] Local reports shall be drawn up, followed by an annual report by the Commission regarding each jurisdiction.[379] Interestingly, Member States not applying the Schengen *acquis*, or third States, may be invited to participate in local consular cooperation.[380]

Lastly, Title VI of the visa code sets out final provisions.[381] These concern: the standard special rules applicable to participants in the Olympic Games;[382] the procedures for amending most of the Annexes to the Regulation and for drawing up operational instructions regarding the code;[383] notifications to the Commission by Member States;[384] amendments to the VIS Regulation and the Schengen Borders Code;[385] repeal of prior measures;[386] monitoring and evaluation of the visa Code;[387] and the entry into force of the Code.[388]

There are thirteen Annexes attached to the Code, concerning in turn:

(a) the harmonized visa application form (Annex I);

(b) a non-exhaustive list of documents supporting a visa application (Annex II);

(c) a uniform format and use of the stamp indicating that an application is inadmissible (Annex III);

(d) a list of the countries subject to a common EU ATV requirement (Annex IV);

(e) a list of the non-Member State residence permits that, if held, will waive the ATV requirement (Annex V);

(f) the standard form for notifying and giving reasons for refusing a visa application (Annex VI);

(g) rules on filling in the visa sticker (Annex VII);

(h) rules on affixing the visa sticker (Annex VIII);

(i) rules on issuing visas to seafarers (Annex IX);

(j) a list of minimum requirements to apply to external service providers (Annex X);

(k) specific procedures relating to Olympic participants (Annex XI);

(l) the requirements relating to annual statistics to be send to the Commission (Annex XII); and

(m) a correlation table comparing the code to the previous measures in force (Annex XIII).

Nine of the Annexes can be amended by the specific comitology process giving fuller powers to the EP (the 'regulatory procedure with scrutiny').[389] The exceptions are Annexes IX, X, XI, and XIII, which can only be amended by the full

---

[378] Art 48(2)–(4).   [379] Art 48(5).   [380] Art 48(6).   [381] Arts 49–58.

[382] Art 49, referring to Annex XI.

[383] Arts 50–52; see the discussion of these processes above. For a list of the Annexes, see below.

[384] Art 53.   [385] Arts 54 and 55.   [386] Art 56.   [387] Art 57.   [388] Art 58.

[389] Art 50, referring to Art 52(3).

legislative process, although this point is moot for Annex XIII, since it consists only of a correlation table.

4.7.3. Other rules governing the issue of visas

Even after the adoption of the visa code, nine of the eighteen Schengen Executive Committee Decisions relating to visas (other than the CCI) remain in force. Two of these Decisions concern a manual of travel documents (ie passports and equivalent documents) to which a visa can be affixed.[390] This manual can no longer be updated because of the entry into force of the visa code, and the Commission plans to propose its replacement by an EU Regulation.[391] A third Executive Committee Decision establishes the Schengen Consultation Network,[392] as amended by the Council pursuant to the 2001 Regulation conferring the power upon it to amend the Network.[393] However, this Network will be replaced once all consulates issuing Schengen visas implement the VIS.[394]

The remaining six Executive Committee Decisions relating to visas still in force concern: harmonizing visa policy as regards Indonesia;[395] the principles for issuing Schengen visas as regards representation;[396] the stamping of passports of visa applicants;[397] an Action Plan to combat illegal immigration;[398] the coordinated deployment of document advisers;[399] and the acquisition of common entry and exit stamps.[400] It may be questioned how much, if at all, these remnants of the Schengen *acquis* are still relevant in practice.[401]

---

[390] SCH/Com-ex (98) 56 and SCH/Com-ex (99) 14 ([2000] OJ L 239/207 and 298).

[391] This is because the legal basis for amending these Decisions (Reg 789/2001, [2001] OJ L 116/2), was repealed by Art 56(2)(d) of the visa code (Reg 810/2009, [2009] OJ L 243/1).

[392] SCH/Com-ex (94) 15 ([2000] OJ L 239/165), corrected by the Council in 2000 ([2000] OJ L 272/24).

[393] This power was conferred by Reg 789/2001 (n 391 above), and the visa code has retained the power to amend the Schengen Consultation Network pursuant to this Regulation until the Network is fully replaced by the VIS (Arts 56(2)(d) and 58(4) of the code; see the following note). The amending Decisions adopted to date have been published in [2007] L 192/26, [2007] OJ L 340/92, [2008] OJ L 328/38, and [2009] OJ L 353/49.   [394] See n 338 above.

[395] SCH/Com-ex (95) PV 1 Rev ([2000] OJ L 239/175).

[396] SCH/Com-ex (96) 13 Rev ([2000] OJ L 239/180).

[397] SCH/Com-ex (98) 21 ([2000] OJ L 239/200).

[398] SCH/Com-ex (98) 37 def 2 ([2000] OJ L 239/203).

[399] SCH/Com-ex (98) 59 Rev ([2000] OJ L 239/308).

[400] SCH/Com-ex (94) 16 Rev ([2000] OJ L 239/166).

[401] For instance, the issue of stamping the travel documents of visa applicants is addressed in detail in Art 20 and Annex III of the visa code—which conflicts in part with the Executive Committee Decision on this issue. Moreover, stamping the travel documents of visa applicants is a 'low-tech' method of preventing applicants from making multiple applications for Schengen visas from different Member States' consulates, and it is due to be phased out anyway when the VIS is fully operational (see Art 20(3), visa code). As for the Decision on representation, it is not clear how it relates to Art 8 of the visa code. On the other hand, the Decision on common entry and exit stamps is still referred to in Annex IV of the Schengen Borders Code (Reg 562/2006, [2006] OJ L 105/1).

Furthermore, although the visa code repealed a number of EU measures relating to the issuing of visas, the legislation and soft law setting out specific rules in relation to Kaliningrad, researchers' visas, and participants in the 'Barcelona process' is still in force.[402] The recommendation relating to researchers' visas has not been made legally binding, but the visa code requires Member States to waive visa fees for researchers as defined in the Recommendation.[403] On the other hand, the legislation relating to visas for Olympics participants has lapsed. As noted above, there are now standard rules on this issue inserted into an Annex to the visa code in the event that the Olympics are held again in future in the Schengen zone.

4.7.4. Analysis

Before the adoption of the visa code, the EU rules on the conditions for issuing visas were vague, complex, and highly discretionary, and failed to ensure a sufficient level of procedural rights in the event of refusal.[404] However, the visa code has clearly improved the position as regards procedural rights, and also contains useful provisions on inadmissible applications, which will ensure that rejections of applications not based on the merits of the application are listed separately in the VIS and so should not be used against applicants when they make subsequent applications. The provisions on multiple-entry visas and the further provisions for reduction or waiver of visa fees (although limited) provide for further useful facilitation of the issue of visas, and the abolition of the secrecy relating to the rules on consultations was long overdue. Finally, the visa code has resulted in a significant simplification of the legislative framework as compared to the prior rules, which can only be welcomed from the point of view of clarity, transparency, and legal certainty.

4.8. Visa Information System

4.8.1. Legal framework

The VIS, which will collect extensive personal data on all applicants for Schengen visas, was originally conceived as a reaction to the 2001 terrorist attacks on the US. It has been established by two measures. The first measure,

---

[402] For details of these measures, see 4.7.1 above.

[403] Art 16(4)(c) of the visa code (n 391 above).

[404] See criticisms in R Cholewinski, *Borders and Discrimination in the European Union* (ILPA/MPG, 2002), 20–37 and P Boeles, 'Schengen and the Rule of Law', in H Meijers, et al, *Schengen: Internationalisation of Central Chapters of the Law on Aliens, Refugees, Privacy, Security and the Police* (2nd edn, Stichting NJCM-Boekerij, 1992).

adopted in 2004,[405] was a Council Decision which established the system in principle and authorized the Commission to manage the development of the VIS project,[406] including the adoption of implementing measures,[407] with funding from the EU budget. But it was also necessary to adopt a second, more detailed, measure which sets out the precise functioning of the system. To that end, the second measure, Regulation 767/2008 (the 'VIS Regulation') was adopted in June 2008.[408] It should be noted that the VIS will not apply to applicants for long-stay visas, but will apply to third-country national family members of EU citizens who apply for visas.[409]

The VIS has also been the subject of a number of other EU and EC measures. First of all, at the same time as adopting the VIS Regulation, the Council also adopted a third-pillar measure giving police access to the VIS (the 'third-pillar VIS Decision').[410] As noted above, this latter measure is now subject to an annulment action by the UK, on the grounds that the UK should have been given fuller access to VIS data for policing purposes.[411] The Council also subsequently adopted measures amending the visa format rules, the CCI, and the Schengen Borders Code in order to ensure consistency with the VIS.[412] Furthermore, the VIS Regulation itself has already been amended by the Regulation establishing the visa code, again in order to ensure consistency between the two measures.[413] Finally, the Commission has proposed legislation to establish an agency to manage the VIS, the second-generation Schengen Information System (SIS II), and Eurodac.[414]

According to the VIS Regulation, the VIS will become operational following a decision adopted by the Commission, once the Commission has adopted all of

---

[405] [2004] OJ L 213/5.

[406] The Commission has released regular reports, pursuant to the Decision, on the development of the VIS: SEC (2005) 439, 4 Mar 2005; SEC (2006) 610, 10 May 2006; SEC (2007) 833, 13 Jun 2007; COM (2008) 714, 10 Nov 2008; and COM (2009) 473, 15 Sep 2009.

[407] The Commission has adopted several implementing measures pursuant to the powers conferred by this Decision: see [2006] OJ L 267/41 (laying down technical specifications for standards for biometric features), [2006] OJ L 305/13 (establishing VIS sites during the development phase), and [2008] OJ L 194/3 (on interfaces with national systems).

[408] [2008] L 218/60. The Commission has adopted five measures implementing the VIS Reg, concerning: the consultation mechanism in the VIS (see below; Decision in [2009] OJ L 117/30); the specifications for the use of fingerprints in the VIS ([2009] OJ L 270/14); data processing ([2009] OJ L 315/30); the regional roll-out of the VIS ([2010] OJ L 23/62); and security ([2010] OJ L 112/25).

[409] See the discussion in 4.4.1 above.

[410] [2008] OJ L 218/129. This measure is discussed in more detail in 12.6.1.3 below.

[411] Case C-482/08 UK v Council, pending; the opinion of 24 June 2010 suggests that the challenge should be dismissed. On the broader issue of UK participation in visa measures, see 4.2.5 above.

[412] See respectively Regs 856/2008 ([2008] OJ L 235/1), 390/2009 ([2009] OJ L 131/1), and 81/2009 ([2009] OJ L 35/56). Reg 390/2009 has since been subsumed into the visa code (Reg 810/2009 ([2009] OJ L 243/1).

[413] Art 54 of the visa code (ibid). The amended VIS Reg has not been consolidated. All references in this section are to the VIS Reg as thereby amended, unless otherwise indicated.

[414] See 12.6.1 below.

the necessary implementing measures and tested the system successfully (along with Member States), and the Member States have notified the Commission that they are ready to transmit the necessary data from the first region in which the VIS is to become applicable.[415] This region will be decided by the Commission by means of a comitology process, subject to the criteria of the risk of illegal immigration, threats to internal security, and the feasibility of collecting biometrics.[416] The roll-out to subsequent regions will be decided by the same process and the same criteria, subject to the possibility of individual Member States applying the VIS to those further regions in advance, if they are capable of transmitting 'at least' the alphanumeric data and photograph data connected to applications.[417] In practice, Member States decided that the VIS should begin operations in North Africa and the Middle East, with the 'roll-out' of the VIS completed worldwide within two years from the start of operations.[418] To this end, the decision on the roll-out to that first group of countries was adopted at the end of 2009.[419] The latest information available suggests that the VIS will become operational in December 2010.[420]

Chapter I of the VIS Regulation sets out its general provisions.[421] These comprise a brief description of the subject matter and scope of the VIS Regulation,[422] as well as a longer description of its purpose.[423] The VIS 'has the purpose of improving the implementation of the common visa policy, consular cooperation and consultation between' Member States' visa authorities by facilitating the exchange of data in order to achieve seven purposes: to facilitate the application procedure; to avoid bypassing the rules concerning the responsible Member State for considering the application;[424] to facilitate the fight against fraud; to facilitate checks at external borders and within the territory; to assist in identifying irregular migrants; to facilitate application of the 'Dublin' rules on responsibility for asylum applications;[425] and to contribute to preventing 'threats to internal security' of any Member States.

Next, the VIS Regulation contains a 'bridging' clause linking it to the parallel third pillar VIS Decision, giving the police authorities access to VIS data.[426] Those authorities can access VIS data in individual cases following a specific request 'if there are reasonable grounds to consider that access to VIS data will substantially contribute to the prevention, detection or investigation of terrorist offences and of other serious criminal offences'. Europol, the EU's police agency, may also access VIS data 'within the limits of its mandate and when

---

[415] Arts 51(2) and 48(1).   [416] Art 48(4).

[417] Art 48(3). It follows that transmission of fingerprint data will be an option for those Member States who are 'early adopters' of the VIS in additional regions, until the full roll-out of the VIS to those regions.   [418] See JHA Council conclusions of 1–2 Dec 2005.

[419] Commission decision ([2010] OJ L 23/62).

[420] See JHA Council press release, 30 Nov/1 Dec 2009.   [421] Arts 1–7.   [422] Art 1.

[423] Art 2.   [424] For those rules, see Art 8 of the visa code Reg.

[425] On these rules, see 5.8 below.   [426] Art 3; for the Decision, see n 410 above.

necessary for the performance of its tasks'.[427] Access by police authorities can only be obtained through central access points, which will check first whether the criteria for access are satisfied,[428] and VIS data accessed by this procedure cannot be made available to third countries or international organizations, other than in 'an exceptional case of urgency' as provided for in the third pillar VIS Decision.[429] The VIS Regulation is also 'without prejudice' to the obligation under national law for visa authorities to inform national police or prosecution authorities about suspected criminal offences.[430]

The VIS applies to the various forms of short-stay visas as defined in the visa code, but not to long-stay visas of any sort.[431] The only data which can be recorded in the VIS are:[432] alphanumeric data (eg letters and numbers) on the applicant and on visas requested, issued, refused, annulled, revoked, or extended;[433] photographs; fingerprints; and links to other visa applications by the applicant or persons who will be travelling with the applicant.[434] Only visa authorities can enter, delete, or amend data,[435] but other authorities (as well as visa authorities) can access the data for the purposes provided for in the VIS Regulation (see below).[436] A list of all authorities with powers to alter or access data must be published and regularly updated.[437] Member States must ensure that use of the VIS is 'necessary, appropriate and proportionate',[438] that there is no discrimination when using the VIS on grounds of 'sex, racial or ethnic origin, religion or belief, disability, age or sexual orientation', and that VIS use 'fully respects the human dignity and the integrity' of the applicant or visa holder.[439]

Chapter II of the VIS Regulation sets out rules on use of the VIS by visa authorities.[440] A national visa authority must create a file in the VIS without delay following an admissible visa application.[441] The authority has to check whether that applicant has made a previous visa application which is registered in the VIS,[442] and if so, to link the new application with the previous application(s).[443] Applications must also be linked to parallel applications by family members and members of a group.[444]

---

[427] Art 3(1). On Europol, see 12.8 below.

[428] Art 3(2). In 'an exceptional case of urgency' the access can take place without a prior check.

[429] Art 3(3); on the position where VIS data is accessed by other authorities, see below.

[430] Art 3(4).   [431] Art 4(1), VIS Reg, as amended by Art 54(1) of the visa code.

[432] Art 5(1).   [433] See the definition of 'alphanumeric data' in Art 4(11).

[434] See Art 8(3) and (4), which refer to group applications and applications by the applicant's spouse and children. A 'group' application is defined in Art 4(6) as a group of persons who are required for legal reasons to travel together.   [435] Art 6(1).

[436] Art 6(2).   [437] Art 6(3).   [438] Art 7(1).

[439] Art 7(2). The list of prohibited grounds for discrimination matches the list in Art 13 EC (now Art 19 TFEU).   [440] Arts 8–17.

[441] Art 8(1), as amended by Art 54(2) of the visa code.

[442] Art 8(2). Obviously visa applications made before the VIS becomes operational will not be registered in the VIS.   [443] Art 8(3).

[444] Art 8(4).

The following six Articles of the VIS Regulation then set out the data that must be entered in different circumstances: when a visa application is first lodged; if a visa is issued; if a visa application is discontinued; if a visa application is refused; if a visa is annulled or revoked, or has its validity shortened; or if a visa is extended.[445] For example, when a visa application is first lodged,[446] the data entered must comprise: the application number; the status information (the fact that a visa has been requested); the authority with which the application was lodged; thirteen items of data from the application form (concerning name, nationality,[447] travel document information, date of the application, information on the sponsor,[448] Member State(s) of destination and the duration of the intended stay or transit, the main purpose(s) of the journey, date of arrival and departure in the Schengen area, the Member State of first entry, applicant's home address, occupation and employer or educational establishment, and the names of minors' parents (with parental responsibility) or legal guardian); photographs; and fingerprints.[449]

Where a visa is refused, the authority concerned must enter data as to the reasons why, which match the grounds for refusal of a visa application set out in the visa code.[450] There is no provision for entering data into the VIS when a person overstays a visa or otherwise breaches immigration rules (for example, by taking up employment without authorization). Instead, the Commission was invited to make proposals on this issue after the adoption of the visa code,[451] although it has not yet done so. However, this issue will likely be addressed in the context of developing an 'entry-exit' system for the EU, which would generate information automatically (assuming it works as planned) on any visa holder's failure to leave the territory of the Member States on time.[452]

It should be noted that there is no ban on processing of 'sensitive' categories of personal data.[453]

As for the use of the VIS by visa authorities after information is entered, the VIS must be used when examining visa applications, including when taking decisions on whether to annul, revoke, or extend the validity of a visa.[454] Access to

---

[445] Respectively Arts 9–14.   [446] Art 9, as amended by Art 54(3) of the visa code.

[447] This includes both current nationality and nationality at birth.

[448] This is restricted to the name and address of natural persons, and to the name and address of legal persons, plus the name of a contact person at the legal person.

[449] The process of taking the fingerprints is set out in the visa code (see 4.7.2 above). An implementing Decision sets out technical requirements for taking fingerprints (n 408 above).

[450] Art 12(2), as amended by Art 54(6)(b) of the visa code (for more on these grounds, see 4.7.2 above). See also Art 13(2), as amended by Art 54(7) of the visa code, which requires the grounds for annulling or revoking a visa to be entered in the VIS.

[451] Joint Statement in the summary of Council acts for June 2008 (Council doc 12750/2/08, 13 Mar 2009). The Commission was also invited to make proposals three years after the VIS begins operations (so by Dec 2013, if the VIS begins operations as planned in Dec 2010) on the issue of misuse by persons issuing invitations.   [452] See 3.6.2 above.

[453] cf Art 40, SIS II Reg, referring to Art 8(1) of the data protection Directive (Reg 1987/2006, [2006] OJ L 381/4).

[454] Art 15(1), as amended by Art 54(9) of the visa code.

the VIS for this purpose must initially concern only specified data;[455] in the event of a 'hit', then the entire file of the applicant and all linked files can be examined for the purpose of deciding on the visa application.[456] The VIS shall also be used by visa authorities when applying the 'consultation' procedure discussed above,[457] and may also be used to transmit information and messages related to consular cooperation, to send requests for documents relating to visa applications, and to transmit such documents.[458] Finally, visa authorities can consult specified data in the VIS for the purposes of reporting and statistics, without identifying individual applicants.[459]

Chapter III of the VIS Regulation sets out rules on use of the VIS by other authorities, in five circumstances.[460] First of all, the VIS can be used by external border authorities, using the visa sticker number and fingerprints, for the purposes of checking the authenticity of the visa, verifying the identity of the visa holder (a 'one-to-one' search),[461] and confirming that the conditions for entry are satisfied.[462] However, fingerprints cannot be used for these purposes for a three-year period after the VIS begins operations, although this waiting period can be reduced to one year by the Commission as regards air borders.[463] As noted above, a separate Regulation amending the Schengen Borders Code sets out more detail of how the VIS will be used at external borders.[464]

Before the end of these one-year and three-year periods, the Regulation provides for the Commission to report on 'technical progress' regarding the use of fingerprints at external borders, including the question of whether the use of fingerprints for searches at external borders would entail 'excessive waiting time at border crossing points'. This evaluation must be transmitted to the EP and the Council, either of which may then request the Commission to make a proposal to amend the Regulation.[465]

Secondly, immigration authorities may have access to VIS data *within* the territory of a Member State, in order to verify the identity of a person, to check the authenticity of the visa, or to confirm that the conditions for entry are satisfied, either by using the visa sticker number in combination with fingerprints, or by using the visa sticker number alone.[466] Thirdly, in order to *identify* a person (a 'one-to-many' search) who may be an irregular migrant, national immigration authorities or border guards may search the VIS using fingerprints.[467]

---

[455] Art 15(2).   [456] Art 15(3).

[457] See 4.7 above, and the relevant implementing decision (n 408 above).   [458] Art 16.

[459] Art 17, as amended by Art 54(10) of the visa code.   [460] Arts 18–22.

[461] On the definition of 'verification', see Art 4(9).   [462] Art 18(1).

[463] Art 18(2). The Commission could also reduce the waiting period to an intermediate date between one and three years.   [464] Reg 81/2009, n 412 above. For details, see 3.6.1 above.

[465] Art 50(5).   [466] Art 19.

[467] Art 20. On the definition of 'identification', see Art 4(10). This Art also applies if an attempt to verify identity at the borders or on the territory by means of a one-to-one search has failed, or

Fourthly, in order to apply the rules on responsibility for asylum applications, a national asylum authority can search the VIS using fingerprint data.[468] Finally, national asylum authorities can search the VIS using fingerprint data in order to assist them with examining the merits of an asylum application.[469]

In each of these cases, in the event of a 'hit', the relevant national authorities will be given access to more data from the VIS, for the specific purposes referred to in each case.[470]

Chapter IV of the Regulation sets out rules on retention and amendment of VIS data.[471] Each file must be kept for a period of five years from a specified date, for example the expiry date of a visa, if one has been issued.[472] After that point, the file is deleted automatically. Only the Member State responsible for entering the data may delete or alter it, although another Member State may bring apparent errors to the attention of the responsible Member State.[473] Data shall be deleted in advance if a person gains the nationality of a Member State, or (as regards data on refusal of a visa) if the refusal is overturned.[474]

Chapter V of the Regulation sets out rules on the operation of the VIS and responsibilities for operation and use of the system.[475] In particular, the VIS (like SIS II and Eurodac) is to be managed by a management authority after a transitional period;[476] but in the meantime, the VIS will be managed by the Commission, which may delegate its powers to one or two Member States.[477] The intention is that the Commission will delegate its powers to France and Austria; this is consistent with the decision to locate the central VIS in France with a back-up system in Austria.[478]

Next, the VIS Regulation describes the relationship between the central VIS and the national systems,[479] and allocates responsibility as between the management authority and the national authorities.[480] It should be emphasized that the Member States, not the management authority, have the key responsibility of ensuring that data is collected, processed, and transmitted lawfully, and that the data are accurate and up to date when transmitted; the management authority is responsible for ensuring data security at its end as well as control of its staff.

VIS data can be kept in national files if necessary in specific cases, or where the data was entered by that Member State.[481] In principle, data from the VIS cannot

---

if there are otherwise doubts about, inter alia, the identity of the person concerned: see Arts 18(5) and 19(3).

[468] Art 21.   [469] Art 22.

[470] Arts 18(4), 19(2), 20(2), 21(2), and 22(2). In the event of a search regarding responsibility for asylum applications, further data can only be accessed if additional conditions are met, corresponding to the criteria for responsibility under the Dublin rules: see Art 21(2).   [471] Arts 23–25.

[472] Art 23.   [473] Art 24.   [474] Art 25.

[475] Arts 26–36. Many of these rules are similar to those in the SIS II Reg (see 3.7 above).

[476] The Commission has now proposed the legislation to establish the agency concerned: see 12.6.1 below.   [477] Art 26.

[478] Art 27; see the relevant implementing Decision ([2006] OJ L 305/13).   [479] Art 28.

[480] Art 29.   [481] Art 30.

be transferred to third countries or international organizations,[482] but 'by way of derogation',[483] certain data can be transferred to third countries or international organizations listed in the Annex to the Regulation,[484] 'if necessary in individual cases for the purpose of proving the identity of third-country nationals, including for the purpose of return', 'only' where a list of four conditions is fulfilled. First of all, one of the following three situations must exist: the Commission has decided on the adequacy of personal data protection in the relevant third State, in accordance with the data protection Directive,[485] or an EU readmission agreement is in place,[486] or the transfer of data 'is necessary or legally required on important public interest grounds, or for the establishment, exercise of defence of legal claims', again in accordance with the data protection Directive.[487] Secondly, the third country or international organization must have agreed only to use the data for the purpose for which they were transmitted. Thirdly, the data must have been transferred in accordance with the relevant provisions of EU and national law.[488] Finally, the Member State which entered the data in the VIS must have given its consent.

The VIS Regulation also provides that such transfers of data 'shall not prejudice the rights of refugees and persons requesting international protection, in particular as regards non-refoulement',[489] but it is not clear in concrete terms how this principle will be observed when data is transferred. It should be noted that only certain specific categories of alphanumeric data can be transferred—not photographs, fingerprints, or any other category of alphanumeric data.[490]

Chapter V also contains rules on data security, liability for breach of the Regulation, the keeping of records, self-monitoring, and penalties for the misuse of data.[491]

Chapter VI of the Regulation sets out data protection rights and rules on data protection supervision of the VIS.[492] Applicants and sponsors have the right to information about the processing of their data.[493] They also have the right of access, correction, and deletion of their data;[494] Member States must cooperate

---

[482] Art 31(1). The status of non-Schengen EU Member States is not clear.   [483] Art 31(2).

[484] These are UN organizations (such as the UNHCR); the International Organization for Migration; and the International Committee of the Red Cross.

[485] Such adequacy decisions have been adopted as regards Canada, certain private bodies in the US, Switzerland (which is a Schengen State in any event), and Argentina. See: <http://ec.europa.eu/justice_home/fsj/privacy/thirdcountries/index_en.htm>. On the Directive, see generally 12.3.2 below.

[486] For the list of States which have a readmission agreement with the EU, see 7.9.1 below.

[487] Art 26(1)(d) of the data protection Dir ([1995] OJ L 281/31).

[488] Art 26(1) of the data protection Directive gives Member States an option not to apply (inter alia) Art 26(1)(d) of the Directive if provided for by 'domestic law governing particular cases'.

[489] Art 31(3).

[490] The *chapeau* of Art 31(2) refers only to the data in Arts 9(4)(a), (b), (c), (k), and (m).

[491] Arts 32–36 respectively.   [492] Arts 37–44.   [493] Art 37.   [494] Art 38.

as regards the enforcement of these rights.[495] There is a right of action before national courts to enforce the rights of access, correction, and deletion.[496] As for the collective enforcement of rights, the Regulation contains rules on supervision of national authorities by national supervisory bodies;[497] on supervision of the Management Authority by the European Data Protection Supervisor (EDPS);[498] on cooperation between national supervisory bodies and the EDPS;[499] and on data protection during the transitional period.[500]

Lastly, Chapter VII of the Regulation sets out final provisions, which concern: implementing powers for the Commission; the integration of the 'Schengen Consultation Network' into the VIS; notification of readiness to transmit data; the start of operations of the VIS (summarized above); the comitology process; rules on monitoring and evaluation; and the entry into force of the Regulation.[501]

4.8.2. Analysis

Once it is operational and fully rolled out, the VIS will probably be the largest biometric database in the world. The VIS is problematic in several respects, to be considered in turn. But its existence will be even more problematic if it does not work accurately or if there is any human error in its application.

First of all,[502] the application of the VIS to the third-country national family members of EU citizens is objectionable in principle, for the reasons set out above.[503] The absence of a sponsors' database and provisions on the 'misuse' of visas are welcome, given that there was no impact assessment which would have demonstrated the need and properly examined the practical implications of entering such data into the VIS.[504]

The VIS Regulation needed to be supplemented by rules ensuring essential procedural rights in relation to visas, guaranteeing that a record of refusal or revocation of visas is not unduly taken into account when a later application is made, and that an appeal against such decisions is possible. Although the visa code now guarantees these rights, it remains to be seen how effective these will be.[505]

Next, the idea that VIS information might be used to determine the merits of asylum applications is highly questionable. A record of refused visa applications, even on prima facie serious grounds like the use of a forged passport, could arguably show that a person is intent on entering and staying in the EU in order to work without authorization—but it could equally arguably prove the

---

[495] Art 39.   [496] Art 40.   [497] Art 41.   [498] Art 42.   [499] Art 43.
[500] Art 44.   [501] Respectively Arts 45–51.
[502] See also the comments on police access to VIS, in 12.6.1.3 below.   [503] See 4.3.1 above.
[504] See the subsequent developments regarding an entry-exit system (3.6.2 above).
[505] See 4.7.2 above.

genuineness of that person's desperation to flee persecution.[506] The risk is that an asylum authority that sees such a record in the VIS will assume the former, not the latter, and that procedural standards could be curtailed as a result, leaving it difficult for an asylum seeker to rebut the authority's conclusion effectively.

As compared to SIS II,[507] the VIS Regulation is certainly much clearer as regards the grounds for including data in the system, and as regards who can access the data for which purpose. There are also better provisions in the VIS Regulation as regards the right of information. But the SIS II Regulation has a provision regarding an information campaign for the public, and better provisions regarding the publication of annual statistics, the notification of inaccurate data in the system and remedies (as the SIS II rules apply also to compensation and the right to obtain information, and contain a mutual recognition obligation and a review clause). In fact, it is the VIS Regulation rules on remedies that need to be reviewed, not the SIS II rules.

On other points, it is unfortunate that data subjects are not informed when one Member State informs another that data in the VIS appears to be inaccurate. The rule that data on a visa refusal must be removed if that visa refusal is overturned is very welcome. The key issue regarding the planned management authority will be the accountability of that body; it remains to be seen whether the legislation on this issue, and the operation of that body in practice, will satisfy the necessary standard.

As for external transfers of VIS data, one of the conditions allows transfers on grounds of the general public interest; this could obviously be interpreted broadly by Member States. It is unfortunate that there is no general requirement of adequate data standards applicable to all external transfers of VIS data. And, as noted above, how exactly will the provision on non-refoulement work on this context? The one undeniably useful limit on the external transfer of VIS data in the Regulation is that only certain categories of data are covered.

Next, as regards data protection issues, the penalties clause in the Regulation could be better. It should also have applied to data security and to breaches of all data protection rules, and there should have been criminal penalties not only for serious infringements but also perhaps for serious stupidity—such as posting CD-Roms containing the VIS database or drunkenly leaving a computer containing a copy of the VIS on a train.[508] The data security rules in the VIS Regulation are good but can only work fully if we assume that the humans who use the VIS will be infallible. The rules on collective enforcement of the data protection rules are also good on paper, but in practice the resources of supervisory authorities are a crucial issue.

---

[506] cf the recognition in Art 31 of the Geneva Convention on refugee status that unauthorized or clandestine means of entry and stay might be necessary for genuine refugees. See further 7.3 below. On asylum procedures generally, see 5.7 below.

[507] See 3.7.2 above.

[508] Both these examples are taken from the practice of the British civil service.

The monitoring provisions of the VIS Regulation have useful provisions as regards reviews on external transfers and the use of fingerprints, as well as data security. But it is unfortunate that there is no obligation to publish annual statistics or to review to what extent the VIS is being used lawfully.

In general it can be expected that the VIS Regulation, if it works as planned, will be practically useful in identifying (or deterring) a significant number of persons who make multiple or fraudulent visa applications, or who present a fraudulent visa at an external border. But the consequence of this might of course be a greater use of irregular methods of entry across the external borders. Conversely the greater ease of identifying persons making fraudulent applications could likely lead in practice to facilitation of the visa applications of bona fide travellers, since authorities will have available a full record of the 'clean sheets' maintained by such travellers. The more problematic use of the VIS will be for the 'in-between' cases—where applications were refused on more questionable (or non-existent) grounds, or where circumstances have changed (ie an applicant was unemployed before, but now has a job), but the record of prior refusal or revocation in the VIS is used to justify subsequent refusals of applications indefinitely. As noted above, it remains to be seen whether the visa code will in practice effectively address these problems.

4.9. Freedom to travel

The core rules on freedom to travel within the Schengen area for non-EU citizens were initially set out in Articles 19–24 of the Schengen Convention (Chapter IV of Title II of the Convention), which were integrated into the Community legal order (as it was then) by the Treaty of Amsterdam,[509] along with several related Decisions of the Schengen Executive Committee. These Decisions concerned: renegotiation of the treaties referred to in Article 20(2) of the Convention (see below);[510] principles and means of proof for readmission between Member States;[511] cooperation regarding returning third-country nationals by air;[512] measures to be

---

[509] The Council allocated all of these provisions to a legal base in the EC Treaty, except for Art 19(2), a clause concerning the transitional period before introduction of the Schengen visa, which had become redundant. See Decision 1999/435 ([1999] OJ L 176/1). It allocated the rest of Arts 19–22 and 23(1) of the Convention to Art 62(3) EC, the legal base concerning freedom to travel, but it gave Arts 23(2)–(5) and 24 of the Convention the 'dual' legal base of Arts 62(3) and 63(3) EC (immigration policy), presumably because they concerned expulsion as well as the freedom to travel (Decision 1999/436 ([1999] OJ L 176/17)).

[510] SCH/Com-ex(98) 24, 23 June 1998, not allocated to an EC Treaty legal base on the grounds that this Decision concerned an issue not covered by the EC or EU Treaty (Decision 1999/435, ibid).

[511] SCH/Com-ex (97) 39 rev ([2000] OJ L 239/188), allocated to Arts 62(3) and 63(3) EC.

[512] SCH/Com-ex (98) 10 rev ([2000] OJ L 239/193), allocated to Art 62(3) EC. See 7.7.3.1 below.

taken regarding countries refusing readmission;[513] and treating residence permits issued by Monaco as if they were French residence permits.[514] There was also a declaration made by Portugal, when it acceded to the Schengen Convention, relating to the readmission of Brazilians.[515]

Articles 23 and 24 of the Convention, which related to expulsion, were subsequently repealed and replaced by the more comprehensive returns Directive,[516] as has one relevant Executive Committee Decision,[517] but the remaining provisions of the Schengen *acquis* in this area have been amended once,[518] as regards the freedom to travel of long-stay visa holders.[519] This is the only area of the Schengen *acquis* regarding visas and borders which has not been entirely replaced by EU law.

As for the substantive rules, first of all, according to Article 19 of the Convention, persons with a Schengen visa who have legally entered a Member State may move freely throughout the Member States during the period of validity of their visas, as long as they meet the requirements for entry at the external borders (except the requirement to hold a visa, which they meet by definition).[520] However, persons whose visas are subject to limited territorial validity cannot exercise the right.[521]

Next, Article 20 of the Convention provides that persons who do not need a visa to enter the Schengen area may move freely throughout the Member States for a maximum of three months following the six months after their 'first entry', again as long as they meet the requirements for entry at the external borders (except the requirement to hold a visa, which they are exempt from by definition).[522] The Court of Justice has clarified that the 'date of first entry' for this purpose is the date of the initial entry of the person concerned, which then triggers a six-month period during which a person can travel to and within the Schengen area for either a single journey of three months or a number of journeys,

---

[513] SCH/Com-ex (98) 18 rev ([2000] OJ L 239/197), allocated to Arts 62(3) and 63(3) EC.

[514] SCH/Com-ex (98) 19 rev ([2000] OJ L 239/199), allocated to Art 62(3) EC.

[515] [2000] OJ L 239/76, Part III, Declaration 1, of the Final Act, allocated to Art 62(3) EC.

[516] Art 21 of Dir 2008/115 ([2008] OJ L 348/98). On Arts 23 and 24 of the Convention, and that Directive, see 7.7 and 7.7.1 below. On the interpretation of Art 23, see Joined Cases C-261/08 *Zurita Garcia* and C-348/08 *Choque Cabrera*, judgment of 22 Oct 2009, not yet reported.

[517] SCH/Com-ex(98) 10 rev (n 512 above), repealed by Art 11 of Dir 2003/110 on expulsion by air ([2003] OJ L 321/26). On that Directive, see 7.7.3 below.

[518] A Commission proposal from 1995 to adopt an amended version of the Schengen freedom to travel rules as part of EC law (as it was then) was rejected: see 4.2.1 above. A Portuguese initiative from 2000 and a Commission proposal from 2001 were also unsuccessful (see discussion below).

[519] Reg 265/2010, [2010] OJ L 85/1, amending Art 21 of the Convention.

[520] Art 19(1), Schengen Convention. This provision refers to Art 5 of the Convention, which has since been replaced by Art 5 of the Schengen Borders Code (Reg 562/2006, [2006] OJ L 105/1). It should be noted that the time limits concerned are enforced by an obligation to stamp documents at the external borders, and a presumption of irregular stay if the documents are not stamped (Arts 10 and 11 of the Code, *idem*). On the Borders Code, see further 3.6.1 above.

[521] Art 19(3), Schengen Convention. On LTV visas, see 4.7.2 above.

[522] Art 20(1), Schengen Convention. On the question of who needs a visa to enter, see 4.5 above.

which cannot cumulatively exceed three months in total during that six-month period. Following the end of that six-month period, the date of the next entry of the person concerned into the Schengen area will trigger a further period of six months, during which the person concerned has the freedom to travel for a further period (or periods) of six months.[523]

The Convention also specifies that Member States may permit a third-country national to stay for another three months in exceptional circumstances or on the basis of bilateral agreements with third States concluded prior to entry into force of the Convention.[524] However, as noted above, a Schengen Executive Committee Decision, which was not allocated to the EC or EU Treaty (as they then were), requires Member States to denounce such pre-existing treaties, so that nationals of third states could enjoy only a maximum three-month stay in the entire Schengen zone, rather than three months in *each* Member State successively as they had been accustomed to. This issue would have been addressed by a Portuguese initiative for a Regulation which would have given the EC power to negotiate treaties with third States, permitting an extended period of freedom to travel over three months for those non-resident third-country nationals who do not need a visa to enter.[525] Alternatively, the Commission had proposed a Directive in 2001, which would have replaced most of the Schengen Convention rules on freedom to travel with an amended text that would, inter alia, have provided for a 'specific travel authorisation' to permit persons to stay in the Schengen area for longer, up to six months (but no more than three months in each Member State),[526] in place of national treaties dealing with this issue. But due to legal disputes about the Community's competence to deal with stays of over six months, the Council was not able to agree on either measure. In any event, the Portuguese initiative lapsed on 1 May 2004 (the end of the Title IV transitional period),[527] and the Commission subsequently withdrew its proposal.[528] The legal issues arising from Article 20(2) of the Convention are considered elsewhere.[529]

Thirdly, as regards persons with a residence permit issued by a Member State, Article 21 of the Convention provides that they may travel on the cover of that permit and a valid travel document for a period of up to three months, as long as they meet the requirements for entry at the external borders, excepting not only the requirement to hold a visa but also the requirement to be checked in the Schengen Information System (SIS), although they may be checked in national blacklists.[530] The freedom to travel also applies to persons who have a

---

[523] Case C-241/05 *Bot* [2006] ECR I-9627.   [524] Art 20(2), Schengen Convention.
[525] [2000] OJ C 164/6.
[526] COM (2001) 388, 10 July 2001. For further detail on this proposal and the Portuguese initiative, see the second edition of this book, at 172–173.   [527] See 2.2.1.1 above.
[528] COM (2005) 462, 27 Sept 2005 and [2006] OJ C 64/3.   [529] See 4.11.3 below.
[530] Art 21(1), Schengen Convention. On the implications of this for the free movement of services using posted third-country national employees, see 4.4.1 above. Art 21(1) was amended as from 5 Apr 2010 by Reg 265/2010 (n 519 above), purely to update the cross-references to other EU measures.

provisional residence permit from a Member State and a travel document issued by that State.[531] But it is for Member States to determine what constitutes valid travel documents, residence permits, and provisional residence permits for this purpose.[532] The valid documents are notified by Member States pursuant to the Schengen Borders Code.[533]

A fourth category of persons enjoys freedom to travel rights: holders of long-stay visas. Initially, those rights were extended only to a small proportion of long-stay visa holders, pursuant to an amendment to Article 18 of the Schengen Convention set out in Council Regulation 1091/2001, adopted in May 2001.[534] Prior to the adoption of this Regulation, Article 18 of the Convention had speci-fied only that persons who had a long-stay visa issued by a Member State could cross an external border without a short-stay visa, if they were in transit to the State which issued them the long-stay visa.[535] After the 2001 amendment, Article 18 provided that such persons also had the right to freedom to travel, for a period of up to three months following the initial date of validity of the long-stay permit, if their long-stay visas were issued in accordance with the rules on the issue of uniform visas and provided that they met the requirements for entry at external borders (except the requirement to hold a visa).[536] Such visas are issued as 'D+C visas'.[537] However, in practice few Member States issued D+C visas, because most Member States preferred to continue to issue ordinary long-stay visas which were *not* valid concurrently as short-stay visas;[538] some Member States did not even provide for the possibility of issuing D+C visas, and many consulates and visa applicants were not aware of the relevant rules.[539] Therefore, the EU visa code abolished D+C visas once the code became applicable in April 2010,[540] and at the same time a separate Regulation amended Article 21 of the Convention to provide that it applied to *all* holders of long-stay visas.[541]

---

[531] Art 21(2), Schengen Convention.   [532] Art 21(3), Schengen Convention.

[533] Art 34(1)(a) of the Code (Reg 810/2009, [2009] OJ L 243/1), which replaced Annex 7 to the Common (Borders) Manual ([2002] OJ C 313/97), where this information was previously listed. Prior to the adoption of the visa code, this information was also listed in Annex 4 to the CCI ([2005] OJ C 326/1); the visa code repealed this Annex, along with the rest of the CCI (see 4.7 above). For the notifications, see: <http://ec.europa.eu/justice_home/doc_centre/freetravel/rights/doc_freetravel_rights_en.htm>.

[534] [2001] OJ L 150/4; the Regulation entered into force on 7 June 2001 (Art 3). On the compe-tence issues deriving from this Regulation, see 4.2.4 above.   [535] See further 3.6.1 above.

[536] Art 1 of the Regulation.

[537] See the relevant amendments to the CCI ([2001] OJ L 150/47).

[538] Out of over one million D visas (long-stay visas) issued in 2004, only about 21,000 (2.1% of the total) were D+C visas (see COM (2006) 403, 19 July 2006, p 12).   [539] Ibid.

[540] Art 56(2)(e) of the visa code (n 533 above), repealing Reg 1091/2001. At the same time, Reg 265/2010 (n 519 above) amended the wording of Art 18 of the Schengen Convention again (see 4.6 above and 6.9 below).

[541] Reg 265/2010 (ibid), which inserted a new Art 21(2a) into the Schengen Convention. This Regulation also made amendments to the Schengen Convention as regards visa formats (see 4.6 above) and checks in the SIS (see below in this section), and to the Schengen Borders Code (see 3.6.1 above). For an overview of the EU rules relating to residence permits and long-stay visas, see 6.9 below.

Another category of persons who enjoy freedom to travel is established by a 1994 Joint Action on schoolchildren's visas, which provides that Member States shall exempt from a visa requirement a third-country national schoolchild who is resident in another Member State and travelling on a school trip, subject to certain formalities.[542] Since the pupils concerned would in any event be entitled to freedom to travel within the Schengen area, if they hold a designated residence permit or long stay-visa, the Joint Action is in practice relevant mainly for travel between the Schengen area and non-Schengen Member States, and between non-Schengen Member States.

The rules on freedom to travel in the Schengen Convention are 'without prejudice' to an obligation for the persons concerned to declare entry to the authorities of the Member State they are visiting, in accordance with that Member State's conditions.[543] They must report either on entry or within three days of entry, at the discretion of the Member State they have entered; each Member State 'shall' lay down its exemptions from the reporting requirement. The Schengen Borders Code requires Member States to inform the Commission of the relevant national rules,[544] and it is clear that there is a wide variation between national practices, with some Member States not enforcing any reporting requirement and others enforcing it without exception.[545]

Finally, a separate Chapter of Title II of the Schengen Convention, consisting of Article 25 of the Convention,[546] concerns the issue or renewal of residence permits and (from April 2010) long-stay visas. This issue is linked to the freedom to travel because, as we have seen, the issue of a residence permit or a long-stay visa by a Member State confers that freedom within all Member States. According to Article 25, when a Member State plans to issue a residence permit or long-stay visa, it must systematically check the SIS, and if it finds that the person concerned is listed on the SIS as a person to be denied entry, it must consult the Member State that issued the relevant 'alert' and take account of its interests; the permit or long-stay visa shall then be issued 'for substantive grounds only, notably on humanitarian grounds or by reason of international commitments'.[547] Prior to issuing

---

[542] [1994] OJ L 327/1.

[543] Art 22, Schengen Convention. Compare with the rules on reporting requirements and EU free movement law, discussed in 7.4.1 below.

[544] Arts 21(d) and 37 of the code (n 533 above).

[545] See the information reported in [2008] OJ C 18/25, [2008] OJ C 207/10, and [2009] OJ C 3/11, with online updates at: <http://ec.europa.eu/justice_home/doc_centre/freetravel/rights/doc_freetravel_rights_en.htm>.

[546] This provision was previously supplemented briefly by the CCI (point 3 of Annex 14, n 533 above), but that CCI provision has now been repealed by the visa code (n 533 above) without replacement.

[547] Art 25(1), Schengen Convention. Reg 265/2010 (n 519 above) amended Art 25(1) to add the express requirement to check the SIS, and extended the rules to long-stay visa applications (inserting a new Art 25(3) into the Convention). As noted above (see 4.8), the *Visa* Information System will not apply to long-stay visa applicants. See also the conclusions of the Council and the Member States

an alert in the SIS for refusal of entry, Member States must check their national records of residence permits and long-stay visas which have been issued.[548] If it transpires that such an alert has been issued regarding a person who already has a residence permit or long-stay visa, then the Member State issuing the alert shall consult the State which issued the permit or long-stay visa 'to determine whether there are sufficient reasons for withdrawing the residence permit' or long-stay visa.[549] In either case, if the residence permit or long-stay visa is issued or withdrawn, the Member State which issued the alert must withdraw it from the SIS, but may keep the name on its national list of persons to be refused entry.[550] The legislation establishing SIS II, when it becomes applicable, contains no express reference to Article 25 of the Convention, which will therefore remain in force (as amended in 2010) in the absence of any further amendment.[551]

The provisions on freedom to travel are one of the most valuable features of the Schengen system, and the full extension of the freedom in 2010 to persons holding long-stay visas was welcome. But there are nonetheless still several weaknesses. The freedom is limited to those holding only long-stay visas or specified permits, not all those permitted to stay in a Member State. The rules on reporting presence are disproportionate, but it has not yet been possible to change them.[552] It is also unfortunate that the complex legal issues relating to the possible creation of an extended travel period for over three months prevented the adoption of a useful Commission proposal on this issue.

In contrast to the freedom to travel rules, Article 25 of the Schengen Convention (as amended) is highly problematic,[553] as it constitutes the main application of the SIS to persons already resident on Member States' territory. There is therefore a particular risk that the use of this Article will breach EU free movement law (if national officials forget that EU free movement law takes precedence over the Schengen *acquis*) as well as human rights obligations of Member States, in particular where Article 8 ECHR or EU immigration or asylum legislation protects against expulsion.[554] The wording of the Article is particularly unfortunate, as it assumes that the question of granting or withdrawing a residence permit or long-stay visa is an issue to be agreed by interstate cooperation, without

---

on information exchange as regards admission of persons held in the Guantánamo Bay detention centre by the US (JHA Council press release, 4–5 June 2009).

[548] Art 25(1a), inserted by Reg 265/2010 (ibid).

[549] Art 25(2), first sub-paragraph, Schengen Convention, extended to long-stay visas from 5 Apr 2010 pursuant to Art 25(3) of the Convention, which was inserted by Reg 265/2010.

[550] Art 25(2), second sub-paragraph, Schengen Convention.

[551] On the substance of the SIS II Reg, see 3.7.2 above.

[552] The Commission's 2001 proposal (n 526 above) would have amended these rules.

[553] See P Boeles, 'Schengen and the Rule of Law', in H Meijers, et al, *Schengen: Internationalisation of Central Chapters of the Law on Aliens, Refugees, Privacy, Security and the Police* (2nd edn, Stichting NJCM-Boekerij, 1992), and the general criticisms of the SIS set out in 3.7.3 above.

[554] See 6.3.1 below on Art 8 ECHR, as well as the discussion of specific legislation in chs 5 and 6.

any requirement to give consideration to the substantive rights and interests of the person concerned or of any procedural rights of the individual (particularly rights in relation to the discussions between Member States' authorities). Again, however, the general principles of EU law and the EU Charter of Rights ensure remedies for the individuals concerned.[555]

4.10. Administrative cooperation and EU funding

In contrast to other areas of EU law, administrative cooperation and EU funding as regards visas has never been addressed as a separate issue. The cooperation and funding concerned has either formed a subset of measures relating to immigration issues in general or border controls in particular,[556] or been addressed by ancillary rules in legislation which concerns substantive issues relating to visas.[557]

There are obligations to collect statistics on visas, deriving originally from Schengen Executive Committee Decisions,[558] and now incorporated into the visa code.[559] Unfortunately, there are no obligations to produce statistics as regards the operation of the VIS.

4.11. External relations[560]

The EU's visa rules have been developing in a broader external context. Most obviously, the decision whether to impose or remove a visa requirement for third States is a significant political issue, as are (to a lesser degree) other aspects of the EU's visa rules: visa facilitation, including fees charged for visa applicants; exceptions for certain categories of persons from select third States; the possible re-imposition of visas for lack of reciprocity; the consultation procedure for certain third states; the gradual roll-out of the VIS; the imposition of airport transit visas; and the imposition of visa requirements on foreign policy grounds.[561] There are also some specific references to certain micro-states in EU visa legislation.[562]

---

[555] See also the procedural rights conferred by the ECHR and those forming part of the general principles in EU law and recognized in the EU Charter of Fundamental Rights (see 6.3 below), as well as the effect of the SIS II Reg, when it becomes applicable (3.7.2 above).

[556] See, for instance, the programmes discussed in 3.11 above.

[557] For example, see the provisions on statistics and consular cooperation in the visa code (Arts 46 and 48 of the code (Reg 810/2009, [2009] OJ L 243/1)). The agency which will be established to manage, inter alia, the VIS will also play a role in administrative cooperation (see 12.6.1 below).

[558] Decisions SCH/Com-ex (94) 25 and SCH/Com-ex (98) 12 ([2000] OJ L 239/173 and 196). See most recently Council doc 10002/1/10, 9 June 2010.

[559] Art 46 and Annex XII (Reg 810/2009, [2009] OJ L 243/1).

[560] For an overview of the basic principles of EU external relations law, see 2.7 above.

[561] See 4.5 and 4.7 above.

[562] For instance, see the Executive Committee decision relating to Monaco as regards freedom to travel: SCH/Com-ex (98) 19 Rev ([2000] OJ L 239/199).

At the same time, there are close and growing links between the EU's developing visa policy and its broader external policies, in particular the development of its neighbourhood policy and the accession process, but also there are links with its broader external migration policy, in the form of mobility partnerships.[563] Because of these developments, the EU's external visa policy has become highly nuanced and differentiated, like many of the EU's other highly developed external policies (notably its trade policy).

Unlike EU trade policy, the extent of EU external competence over visas has not been litigated, although there is a strong argument that given the degree of uniformity achieved by EU visa legislation, and the overall context of the visa rules (particularly freedom to travel between Member States), EU competence has become prima facie exclusive by exercise, except where EU legislation gives express competence to Member States—for example, as regards specific categories of persons who can be exempted from a visa obligation, or the (limited) discretion granted by the visa code for Member States to waive or reduce fees for visa applicants.[564] The same presumption arguably arises as regards the freedom to travel rules themselves. Indeed it is striking that there are no 'mixed' agreements in the area of visas, only agreements concluded solely by the Community (now the Union).

Moving on to the specific treaties relating to visas which the EU has concluded, the most important of these are obviously the Schengen association treaties with Norway, Iceland, Switzerland, and Liechtenstein.[565] The EEA and EU–Turkey association agreements are also highly significant.[566]

As for the EU's treaties solely relating to visas, the Community (now the Union) has concluded a number of treaties concerning visa abolition and visa facilitation. The EU has also concluded, or authorized Member States to conclude, certain other treaties. Finally, the issue of freedom to travel is subject to particular complications relating to external competence. These issues are examined in turn.

4.11.1. Visa waiver treaties

First of all, visa waiver treaties were concluded between the Community (as it then was) and six micro-states (Barbados, Seychelles, Mauritius, the Bahamas, Antigua, and St Kitts) following the decision to place those states on the EU's visa 'whitelist' in 2006. A condition of application of this exemption was the

---

[563] See 7.9.2 below.

[564] See 4.7.2 above. On the issue of external competence in this area, see B Martenczuk, 'Visa Policy and EU External Relations,' in B Martenczuk and S van Thiel, eds, *Justice, Liberty, Security: New Challenges for EU External Relations* (VUBPress, 2008), 21.   [565] See 4.2.5 above.

[566] See 4.4.2 above.

willingness of the third countries concerned to sign reciprocal agreements on visa abolition with the EU.[567] Two visa waiver treaties were also agreed with Brazil in 2010.[568] Negotiations for visa waiver treaties are also underway with the US.

The treaties with the microstates were concluded by the Council in November 2009.[569] The treaties concerned each provide that EU citizens and the nationals of each other party can travel visa-free to the other party for three months within a six-month period,[570] subject only to holding a 'valid ordinary, diplomatic or service/official passport'.[571] Within the EU, this means a three-month stay in the Schengen area as a whole within the six months after first entry,[572] or three-months' stay within six months in each Member State not yet applying the Schengen *acquis* in full.[573] The agreements are without prejudice to the possibility of stays for longer periods in accordance with national law or EU law.[574]

However, the Member States and the microstates each reserve the right to require a visa if the person concerned wishes to carry out a 'paid activity'.[575] A joint declaration attached to each visa waiver treaty states the agreed interpretation that this means 'entering for the purpose of carrying out a gainful occupation/remunerated activity in the territory of the other Contracting Party as an employee or as a service provider'. But it does not include business persons who travel for business without being employed in the territory of another state; sports-persons and artists performing ad hoc activity; journalists sent by the media of their country of residence; and intra-corporate trainees.[576]

---

[567] See 4.5 above.

[568] COM (2010) 409 and 410, 6 Aug 2010 (as regards holders of, for example diplomatic passports) and COM (2010) 419 and 420, 6 Aug 2010 (as regards ordinary passport holders). Note that the latter treaty waives the visa requirement for tourists and business people (as defined in the treaty), but not for other categories of ordinary visa holders. Bilateral visa waiver agreements, where they exist, will continue to apply to the excluded categories as regards visits of EU citizens to Brazil, while Brazilians falling within the excluded categories visiting the EU will not be subject to a visa requirement, pursuant to the EU's internal legislation (see 4.5 above).

[569] [2009] OJ L 169 (text of treaties); [2009] OJ L 321/38 to 43 (Council decisions on conclusion). The treaties were provisionally in force as from their signature on 28 May 2009, and formally entered into force (see [2010] OJ L 56/1) on 1 Jan 2010 (Seychelles), 1 Mar 2010 (Barbados and Mauritius), 1 Apr 2010 (Bahamas), and 1 May 2010 (Antigua). The treaty with St Kitts is not yet formally in force.

[570] Arts 1 and 4, EU–Mauritius treaty (ibid). A Joint Declaration specifies that the three-month stay can constitute either a single visit or multiple visits totalling three months within a six-month period. This is not explicitly set out in the definition of 'visa' in the visa code (Art 2(2)(a) of Reg 810/2009, [2009] OJ L 243/1), but reflects the previous Art 11(1)(a) of the Schengen Convention ([2000] OJ L 239).   [571] Art 3(1).

[572] On the meaning of 'first entry' in this context, see the *Bot* case, discussed in 4.9 above.

[573] Art 4(2). The respective periods are to be calculated independently of each other. So it will be possible, for example, to spend three months in Romania and then three months in the Schengen area—until Romania joins the Schengen area in full.   [574] Art 4(3).

[575] Art 3(2). This is consistent with the possibility of each Member State to require a visa in such cases, according to the EU's visa list legislation: see 4.5 above. The treaties refer to the *national law* of Member States and the micro-states, rather than the possibility to negotiate treaties to this effect.

[576] The various categories of persons are not further defined.

Moreover, the visa waiver is 'without prejudice to the laws of the Contracting Parties relating to the conditions of entry and short stay', and the possibility to deny entry and stay in accordance with those laws.[577] The visa waiver applies regardless of the mode of transport used for entry—although there will surely be few journeys by sea or land between the EU and the microstates.[578] Issues not addressed by the agreement are covered by the national law of the microstates or the Member States or by EU law.[579]

The agreements only apply to the European territory of France and the Netherlands;[580] there is a joint committee to manage each agreement;[581] and each agreement takes precedence over any bilateral agreements with Member States that cover the same issue.[582] Each party may suspend each treaty in whole or part 'in particular, for reasons of public policy, protection of national security or protection of public health, illegal immigration or the reintroduction of the visa requirement by either Contracting Party',[583] or each treaty may be terminated entirely.[584] Suspension and termination is only valid by, or as against, the entire EU.[585] A final joint declaration specifies that the parties will provide information to the public about the agreement and related issues, such as entry conditions.

4.11.2. Visa facilitation treaties

There are EU visa facilitation treaties in force with Russia, Ukraine, the Western Balkan states (apart from Croatia, which was always on the EU's visa whitelist), and Moldova.[586] An agreement has been reached with Georgia, but is not yet in force,[587] and negotiations are underway with Cape Verde. In each case, a readmission agreement has also been negotiated or is under negotiation in parallel.[588] The EU has also committed itself in principle to negotiate visa facilitation and readmission agreements with the three other ex-Soviet states in the 'Eastern partnership' (Belarus, Armenia, and Azerbaijan), provided that there is sufficient commitment by these countries to the values and principles espoused by the EU.[589]

---

[577] Art 3(3). For the EU, this obviously refers principally to the Schengen Borders Code.

[578] Art 3(4). It is possible, however, that visitors from the micro-states might visit the UK or (say) Russia first and then travel to the Schengen area via ferry or rail.   [579] Art 3(5).

[580] Art 5.   [581] Art 6.   [582] Art 7.

[583] Art 8(4). There must be at least two months' prior notice.

[584] Art 8(5). There must be at least ninety days' prior notice.   [585] Art 8(6) and (7).

[586] EC–Russia treaty ([2007] OJ L 129/25); EC–Ukraine treaty ([2007] OJ L 332/ 68); Western Balkans treaties ([2007] OJ L 334). The EC–Russia treaty entered into force on 1 June 2007 ([2007] OJ L 173/34), while the remaining treaties entered into force on 1 Jan 2008.

[587] The JHA Council agreed to sign the treaty on 4 June 2010. For the proposal to conclude the treaty, see COM (2010) 198, 5 May 2010.

[588] On those treaties, see 7.9.1 below. In the specific case of Albania, the readmission agreement was negotiated several years before the visa facilitation agreement.

[589] See declaration annexed to the European Council conclusions of March 2009.

These agreements have less relevance now for Western Balkan States given the visa waivers now applied or proposed for those countries, but are still relevant for those categories of persons who do not benefit from those waivers (for instance, because they do not have biometric passports).[590] It should also be recalled that even for third States whose nationals are generally still subject to visa requirements, certain categories of persons are exempt from that requirement.[591]

Taking the agreement with Ukraine as a typical example, the agreement applies to visas for a stay of three months within a six-month period, ie the standard period applicable to Schengen visas.[592] The agreement is in principle reciprocal, although this point is moot for the time being as Ukraine does not impose a visa obligation on EU citizens.[593] For a number of categories of persons, visas shall be issued according to a simplified procedure, subject only to the requirement to submit specified documents.[594] Multiple-entry visas with a term of validity of up to five years must be issued to: members of governments, parliaments and the highest courts; permanent members of official delegations who regularly participate in, for example, meetings, in the EU; specified close family members visiting Ukrainians who are legally resident in the EU;[595] business people; and journalists.[596] Multiple-entry visas with a term of validity of up to one year must be issued, subject to certain conditions, to: professional drivers; train crews; participants in 'scientific, cultural and artistic activities'; participants in sports events and professionals accompanying them; and participants in 'twin cities' exchange programmes.[597] Subsequently the latter category of persons can obtain a multiple-entry visa valid between two and five years.[598]

The fee for a visa application is fixed at €35, and is waived altogether for a long list of categories of persons.[599] The treaty requires visa decisions to be taken within ten days, with a reduction to two days in urgent cases and a possible extension to thirty days in individual cases, in particular if further scrutiny of the application is necessary.[600] In the event of lost or stolen travel documents, EU or Ukrainian citizens can leave the territory on the basis of valid replacement documents without the requirement to obtain a visa.[601] If a Ukrainian citizen cannot leave within the period of validity of the visa due to *force majeure*, the visa must be extended free of charge.[602] For persons with valid diplomatic passports, the visa

---

[590] See 4.5 above.   [591] See ibid.

[592] Arts 1(1) and 3(d) of the EC–Ukraine treaty (n 585 above).

[593] See Art 1(2) of the treaty. Note that the treaty does not *oblige* Ukraine to waive the visa requirement. Of the States which have concluded visa facilitation agreements with the EU, only Russia imposes a visa requirement on EU citizens.   [594] Art 4 of the treaty.

[595] For the definition of legal residence, see Art 3(e) of the treaty.

[596] Art 5(1) of the treaty.   [597] Art 5(2) of the treaty.   [598] Art 5(3) of the treaty.

[599] Art 6 of the treaty. A higher fee of €70 applies to urgent applications, but that is either waived entirely or set at €35 only for the various special categories.

[600] Art 7 of the treaty. The consequence of a failure to decide within these time limits is not specified.   [601] Art 8 of the treaty.

[602] Art 9 of the treaty.

requirement is waived altogether.[603] Ukrainians can travel within the territory of the Member States on an equal footing with EU citizens, subject to Member States' national rules on 'national security' and the EU rules on the limited territorial validity of visas.[604] There is a joint committee for the management of the agreement and the agreement takes precedence over any Member State's national treaties falling within the same scope.[605] Issues outside the scope of the treaty, such as 'the refusal to issue a visa, recognition of travel documents, proof of sufficient means of subsistence and the refusal of entry and expulsion measures', are addressed by the national law of Ukraine or the Member States, or by EU law.[606] Finally, there is a joint declaration on the issues of visits to burial grounds;[607] a Commission declaration on the reasons for refusing a visa;[608] a Community declaration on information for visa applicants;[609] and a declaration by four Member States on local border traffic.[610] There are also further joint declarations relating to the position of the UK, Ireland, Denmark, Schengen associates, and Member States not yet fully applying the Schengen *acquis*.[611]

As for the application of these agreements, a Commission assessment released in 2009[612] pointed out that the visa facilitation treaties applied to over half of visa applicants.[613]

The report states that visa applications increased in some of the countries concerned, but decreased in others; it should be recalled that the application of most of these treaties broadly coincided with the extension of the Schengen zone. There were small drops in the refusal rate of applications, and there appeared to be a large increase in the numbers of visas issued free of charge and of multiple-entry visas. While the EU's neighbours continued to complain about a number of aspects of the visa-issuing process, the Commission argued that many of these complaints would be addressed by the (then) forthcoming application of the visa code. However, the Commission did suggest the renegotiation of the relevant treaties, to address the specific issues of the simplification of supporting documents, broader fee waivers, the possibility for external service providers to charge a service fee, and a ban on the discriminatory introduction of a visa obligation

---

[603] Art 10 of the treaty. This applies for the standard period of ninety days within a 180-day period.   [604] Art 11 of the treaty.

[605] Arts 12 and 13 of the treaty.   [606] Art 2(2) of the treaty.

[607] The standard period of validity for visas in this case will only be 'up to 14 days'.

[608] The declaration refers to the proposal for the EU visa code, then under discussion.

[609] Again, the declaration refers to the proposal for the EU visa code, but also states some elements of what an information policy should entail.

[610] These four states (Poland, Hungary, Slovakia, and Romania) each state a willingness to negotiate border traffic treaties with Ukraine in accordance with the EU's border traffic legislation (on which, see 3.8 above).   [611] For more on this issue, see 4.2.5 above.

[612] SEC (2009) 1401, 15 Oct 2009.

[613] This percentage will have dropped since, due to the subsequent waiver of visa requirements for three of the third States with visa facilitation agreements (see 4.5.2 above).

on citizens of only one EU Member State. So far, there have been no steps taken to renegotiate the treaties.

4.11.3. Other EU measures

The EC (as it then was) concluded a treaty with China (the 'ADS treaty'), in force 1 May 2004,[614] which provides for procedures for China to designate the entire Schengen territory as an 'Approved Destination' for tourists, as a result of which Schengen visas are issued to designated tourists following a special procedure of certification of travel agencies. China is obliged to readmit any persons who do not comply with the scheme.[615]

Member States have also negotiated a treaty that falls within EC competence (as it then was) because it addresses the issue of seafarers' visas. But because it was too late to arrange for the EC to become a party to the treaty, the Council adopted a Decision authorizing the Member States to sign the treaty, effectively as trustees of the EC's external power.[616]

Finally, as regards the issue of freedom to travel, there are complex external relations issues, deriving from the existence of Member States' bilateral treaties with third States, which give nationals of those third States extra time to reside in the Member State in question, and therefore in the Schengen area as a whole.[617] Article 20(2) of the Schengen Convention specifies that Member States can retain such agreements, and Article 307 EC (now Article 351 TFEU) generally permits Member States to keep all pre-existing treaties in force, although in the latter case there could be an obligation to amend or denounce the relevant treaties eventually.[618] There is a Schengen Executive Committee Decision requiring amendment of such bilateral treaties, but this was not, as it should have been, defined by the Council in 1999 as forming part of the Schengen *acquis* for the purposes of allocation and then allocated to the EC Treaty (as it then was). The legal position on this issue therefore remains unclear.[619]

4.12. Conclusions

The basically unsatisfactory rules deriving from the Schengen *acquis* in this area have been significantly changed since 1999, in particular by means of the adoption of the visa code, which has ensured procedural rights for visa applicants

---

[614] [2004] OJ L 83/12.   [615] On the issue of readmission, see 7.9.1 below.

[616] [2005] OJ L 136/1.   [617] For the background to this issue, see 4.9 above .

[618] On Art 351 TFEU, see 2.7 above. The Court of Justice has not addressed the question as to whether this Art, or at least the principle underlying the Art, also applies when a Member State concluded a treaty *after* joining the EU, but before the adoption of the relevant EU legislation, or before the Member States first conferred competence upon the EU in a particular area.

[619] See the discussion in the second edition of this book, at 177–178.

and made some other useful changes to the rules. Other positive developments are the waiver of visa requirements for a number of third States; visa facilitation agreements with a number of countries; and the greater flexibility to waive visa requirements for certain categories of persons. However, it remains to be seen whether the visa code lives up to the expectations concerning it, and the application of the Visa Information System, and the future development of an entry-exit system, could potentially be highly problematic, particularly if there are significant flaws in the operation of either system. Also, despite the liberalization of the EU's visa lists, there is still a strong argument for developing a more objective system for assessing whether third States should be subject to a visa obligation or not.

5

Asylum

5.1. Introduction

Asylum law is one of the most complex areas of JHA cooperation, although one of the most high-profile and controversial. The complexity arises because of the number of different issues addressed by asylum law, in conjunction with the growing interconnection between national law, EU harmonization, and international human rights obligations. This chapter begins with an overview of the asylum process in the EU from an asylum seeker's point of view, and then examines specific issues in more detail. It will be seen that while the EU has the potential to ensure effective protection of the right to asylum in the Member States, in practice the results of conferring asylum powers on the Union have been rather modest at best to date.

The journey through the labyrinth of EU asylum law begins in the territory of the asylum seeker's country of origin—usually the country of his or her nationality. At this point EU external relations law plays a large role. EU foreign policy affects developments relevant to asylum seekers, and the Community's development policy often addresses refugee issues explicitly through funding programmes and clauses in development policy agreements with third States.[1] The legality of including refugee assistance within development policy was indirectly addressed in *Portugal v Council*, in which the Court of Justice upheld the validity of a development policy agreement between the EC (as it then was) and India.[2] Refugee clauses were not specifically at issue in this case, but the Court of Justice's broad definition of 'development policy' in its judgment left little doubt that financial support to aid refugees in developing countries fell within it. Many persons fleeing persecution are able to find refuge in a neighbouring developing state or within the same state, in which case the EU's development funds are often spent on their behalf. Furthermore, the EU has elaborated a policy designed to assist neighbouring or transit States with large number of refugees on their territory, with a view to discouraging the refugees from contemplating travel onwards to the EU.

---

[1] A detailed analysis is beyond the scope of this book. Development policy is governed by Arts 208–211 TFEU (previously Arts 177–181 EC). See 7.9.2 below on external relations and irregular migration policy.　　　　　　　　　　　　[2] Case C-268/94 [1996] ECR I-6177.

Those asylum seekers who do attempt entry into the EU will obviously be most directly affected by EU rules. They will likely have to obtain a visa as a first hurdle, as EU legislation requires visas for most or all countries generating significant numbers of asylum seekers, and there is no special procedure for persons requesting visas as asylum seekers. The imposition of carrier sanctions will make it difficult for asylum seekers to get a plane ticket (or other legal transport) without a visa and other travel documents—but some asylum seekers do not have passports or other travel documents because they have been denied them in their country of origin. If they attempt to enter the territory illegally, the EU rules enhancing border controls and criminalizing smugglers of persons, along with the EU's external policy on irregular migration (including readmission agreements), is intended to erect a significant barrier.

If asylum seekers do reach EU Member States' territory and attempt to make an asylum application, their claim could be dismissed without consideration of its merits by a Member State on the grounds that they should have applied for asylum in a country which they transited through (or perhaps even a country they did *not* transit through), on the grounds that that country is to be considered a 'safe third country'. Alternatively (or additionally), the Member State where the asylum seekers apply could enforce EU rules according to which another Member State is responsible for considering their applications.

If the asylum claim is considered on its merits, the Member State in question has a number of grounds on which it can conclude that the claim is 'unfounded' (or even 'manifestly unfounded') and thus subject the claim to a 'fast-track' procedure accompanied by limited procedural rights to appeal the Member State's decision. This can include a presumption that the asylum seeker comes from a 'safe country of origin'. If the application is deemed to have some substantive merit, it will be processed instead in a 'regular' procedure.

While the claim is being considered, the asylum seeker can enjoy certain minimum treatment as regards issues such as health, welfare, and accommodation ('reception conditions'). At the end of the determination procedure, the Member State's authorities decide whether the asylum seeker has a well-founded claim for refugee status, interpreting the 1951 Geneva Convention on refugees, as amended by the New York Protocol of 1967 and as interpreted by EU legislation. Alternatively, the asylum seeker might fall outside the definition of 'refugee' in the Geneva Convention, but still have a well-founded claim to international protection on some other basis. This is usually known in practice as a claim for 'subsidiary protection', and EU legislation also defines the circumstances in which such a claim can be made. If the claim for 'Convention refugee' status or subsidiary protection status is successful, the legal position of a successful claimant as regards issues such as access to employment, health, welfare, and (for refugees) family reunion is governed by EU law. Unsuccessful claimants have rights to appeal as defined in EU legislation, and if their appeals are unsuccessful, EU law on irregular migration, including the Returns Directive,[3] will facilitate their removal. Finally, in the event of a major crisis resulting in a mass influx into the EU or persons needing protection, the EU has established a framework for offering an ad hoc status, known as 'temporary protection', to large groups of persons.

There is an obvious tension between the objective of ensuring full protection for the rights of refugees, asylum seekers, and other persons seeking international protection and the objectives of limiting irregular migration (and indeed, managing legal migration) and more effectively controlling the external borders of the EU's Member States, in particular because asylum seekers often have to resort to irregular means to enter or stay on the territory of the Member States. EU asylum law is therefore linked to EU visa policy (as regards particularly the list of States whose nationals need visas, the conditions for obtaining a visa, the creation of a Visa Information System (VIS) and the further development of the Schengen Information System (SIS), and the link between the issue of a visa and the grounds for deciding on responsibility for asylum applications) and EU rules on external border controls (as regards the entry of asylum seekers onto the territory and further grounds for deciding on responsibility for asylum applications).[4] The policy is also linked closely to EU law on irregular migration, as regards attempts to ensure that persons never reach EU Member States' territory, the criminalization of the smuggling of persons, and the EU's desire to 'externalize' its policies on irregular migration.[5] Finally, for those whose claim for international protection is successful, EU legislation on social security coordination, family reunion, and (in future) the status of long-term residents may apply.[6]

5.2. Institutional framework and overview

5.2.1. Cooperation prior to the Treaty of Amsterdam

Even before the Maastricht Treaty formalized JHA cooperation between the EU Member States, those Member States had begun cooperating on asylum issues. The most visible sign of this was the agreement on the Dublin Convention on responsibility for asylum applications in 1990.[7] This Convention was followed by the three 'London Resolutions' of Member States' immigration ministers in 1992, on the important and controversial procedural issues of 'safe third countries', 'safe countries of origin', and 'manifestly unfounded applications'.[8] Also, a

---

[3] See 7.7.1 below.   [4] See chs 3 and 4. On the SIS, see 12.6.1.1. below.   [5] See ch 7.
[6] See ch 6.   [7] See 5.8.1 below.
[8] Unpublished in the OJ; see Bunyan, *Key Texts on Justice and Home Affairs in the European Union, Volume I* (1997), 64 and 66; E Guild and J Niessen, *The Emerging Immigration and Asylum Law of the European Union* (Kluwer, 1996), 141, 161, and 177.

'clearing-house' for asylum information, known as 'CIREA', was set up within the Council.[9]

Following the entry into force of the Maastricht Treaty, Member States began protracted negotiations on another Convention, to establish a system of taking and comparing asylum seekers' fingerprints, dubbed 'Eurodac'. They were able to agree this Convention, and a connected Protocol, just before the Treaty of Amsterdam entered into force.[10] During this period, the Council adopted a Resolution on asylum procedures,[11] a Joint Position on the definition of refugee,[12] and some very modest funding programmes.[13] However, it was not able to agree any measure dealing with subsidiary protection, reception conditions for asylum seekers, or the status of refugees,[14] and could agree only on very modest measures concerning the issue of temporary protection.[15] A Resolution on unaccompanied minors concerned asylum as well as migration issues.[16]

5.2.2. Treaty of Amsterdam

The Treaty of Amsterdam inserted Article 63(1) and (2) into the EC Treaty, conferring powers upon the Community (as it then was) to adopt measures concerning asylum and other forms of international protection:

The Council, acting in accordance with the procedure referred to in Article 67, shall, within a period of five years after the entry into force of the Treaty of Amsterdam, adopt:
(1) measures on asylum, in accordance with the Geneva Convention of 28 July 1951 and the Protocol of 31 January 1967 relating to the status of refugees and other relevant treaties, within the following areas:
    (a) criteria and mechanisms for determining which Member State is responsible for considering an application for asylum submitted by a national of a third country in one of the Member States,

---

[9] Centre for Information, Discussion, and Exchange on Asylum. See doc SN 2781/92 WGI 1107, 21 May 1992, published in Bunyan, ibid, 68 (setting up CIREA) and activity reports published at *idem*, 72; [1996] OJ C 274/55; [1997] OJ C 191/29 and 33. On the parallel CIREFI body, see 7.8 below.

[10] On the draft Convention and Protocol, see the first edition of this book, at 116–117.

[11] [1996] OJ C 274/13. See the first edition of this book, at 119.

[12] [1996] OJ L 63/2. See the first edition of this book, at 119–120. There was also a Decision on monitoring implementation of EU asylum measures ([1997] OJ L 178/6).

[13] [1997] OJ L 205/3; [1998] OJ L 138/8; [1997] OJ L 205/5; [1998] OJ L 138/6; and [1999] OJ L 114/2. For more detail, see the first edition of this book, at 124.

[14] See the first edition of this book, at 120–22.

[15] The agreed measures comprised ministers' Resolutions in 1992 on the conflict in the former Yugoslavia (unpublished in the OJ; see Bunyan, n 8 above, 74 and 76), and a Council Resolution and Decision setting up a decision-making procedure to deal with potential crises ([1995] OJ C 262/1 and [1996] OJ C 63/10). Conversely, the Council failed in particular to agree an ambitious Joint Action proposed by the Commission. See the original version of this proposal in COM (97) 93, 5 Mar 1997 ([1997] OJ C 106/13) and the revised version in COM (1998) 372, 24 June 1998 ([1998] OJ C 268/13 and 22). For more detail, see the first edition of this book, at 122–123.

[16] [1997] OJ C 221/23.

(b) minimum standards on the reception of asylum seekers in Member States,

(c) minimum standards with respect to the qualification of nationals of third countries as refugees,

(d) minimum standards on procedures in Member States for granting or withdrawing refugee status;

(2) measures on refugees and displaced persons within the following areas:

(a) minimum standards for giving temporary protection to displaced persons from third countries who cannot return to their country of origin and for persons who otherwise need international protection,

(b) promoting a balance of effort between Member States in receiving and bearing the consequences of receiving refugees and displaced persons.

Another potentially relevant provision was Article 64(2) EC, which was never used in practice, but which provided as follows:

In the event of one or more Member States being confronted with an emergency situation characterised by a sudden inflow of nationals of third countries and without prejudice to paragraph 1 [concerning national responsibilities for law and order and internal security], the Council may, acting by qualified majority on a proposal from the Commission, adopt provisional measures of a duration not exceeding six months for the benefit of the Member States concerned.

The asylum powers were subject initially to the standard rules applying to Title IV of Part Three of the EC Treaty, with unanimous voting in the Council and consultation of the European Parliament (EP), and a restricted jurisdiction of the Court of Justice. Also, the Treaty of Amsterdam attached a Protocol on asylum applications by EU citizens to the EC Treaty.[17]

As with other areas of JHA law, soon after the entry into force of the Treaty of Amsterdam, the priorities and principles for use of the new provisions were set out by the Tampere European Council in October 1999. The Tampere conclusions set out an ambitious agenda for developing a 'Common European Asylum System':

II. A Common European Asylum System

13. The European Council reaffirms the importance the Union and Member States attach to absolute respect of the right to seek asylum. It has agreed to work towards establishing a Common European Asylum System, based on the full and inclusive application of the Geneva Convention, thus ensuring that nobody is sent back to persecution, i.e. maintaining the principle of non-refoulement.

14. This System should include, in the short term, a clear and workable determination of the State responsible for the examination of an asylum application, common standards for a fair and efficient asylum procedure, common minimum conditions of reception of asylum seekers, and the approximation of rules on the recognition and content of the refugee status. It should also be completed with measures on subsidiary forms of protection offering an appropriate status to any person in need of such protection. To that

---

[17] See 5.4.1 below.

end, the Council is urged to adopt, on the basis of Commission proposals, the necessary decisions...

15. In the longer term, Community rules should lead to a common asylum procedure and a uniform status for those who are granted asylum valid throughout the Union...

Following a initial discussion paper on the nature of the Common European Asylum System (CEAS),[18] the legislation to establish the first phase of the CEAS was proposed by the Commission in 2000 and 2001. All of the 'first phase' measures were then adopted by December 2005.

Taking the EC's original asylum law powers in turn, first of all, Article 63(1)(a) EC was implemented by two first-phase measures: a Regulation establishing the 'Eurodac' system, adopted in December 2000, based on the agreement reached on the draft Eurodac Convention just prior to the entry into force of the Treaty of Amsterdam, and a Regulation setting out rules on responsibility for asylum applications, adopted in February 2003.[19] Both measures have applied in practice since 2003.

Secondly, the Council implemented Article 63(1)(b) EC with the adoption in January 2003 of Directive 2003/9, which set out first-phase minimum standards on reception conditions for asylum seekers.[20]

Thirdly, the Council adopted in April 2004 a first-phase Directive defining the meaning of 'refugee' and subsidiary protection (along with the content of the connected status).[21] This Directive implemented Article 63(1)(c) EC and the second line of Article 63(2)(a) EC, and also used the 'legal base' for legal migration law (Article 63(3)(a) EC). It is generally known as the 'qualification Directive'.

Fourthly, in December 2005, the Council adopted a first-phase Directive on asylum procedures, implementing Article 63(1)(d) EC.[22] A portion of this Directive was annulled by the Court of Justice following a successful challenge by the EP.[23]

Fifthly, in July 2001, the Council adopted a Directive setting out a model temporary protection system which the EU can take 'off the shelf' and use in the event of a future perceived crisis.[24] So far, it has not been considered necessary to use the model set out in the Directive.

The EC's sixth power concerned subsidiary protection, and as noted above, the Council adopted first-phase legislation concerning the definition and content

---

[18] COM (2000) 755, 22 Nov 2000. See also later reports: COM (2001) 710, 28 Nov 2001 and COM (2003) 152, 26 Mar 2003.

[19] Respectively Regs 2725/2000 ([2000] OJ L 316/1) and 343/2003 ([2003] OJ L 50/1). For detailed discussion, see 5.8 below.

[20] Dir 2003/9 ([2003] OJ L 31/18); see further 5.9 below.

[21] Dir 2004/83 ([2004] OJ L 304/12); see further 5.5 below.

[22] Dir 2005/85 ([2005] OJ L 326/13); see further 5.7 below. Also, Austria tabled a proposal for a Regulation on 'safe third countries' late in 2002 ([2003] OJ C 17/6), but this proposal lapsed on 1 May 2004.   [23] Case C-133/06 *EP v Council* [2008] ECR I-3189.

[24] Dir 2001/55 ([2001] OJ L 212/12). See further 5.6 below.

of subsidiary protection status. However, the first-phase of the legislation establishing the Common European Asylum System did not include any rules concerning responsibility for considering applications for this status, reception conditions for applicants for this status, or procedures applicable to considering such applications.

Finally, the EC used its seventh power during the initial period of developing the CEAS by adopting a Decision establishing a 'European Refugee Fund' in September 2000. A subsequent Decision of December 2004 extended the application of the Fund (with some amendments) to 2005–10.[25]

By the time that the initial first-phase CEAS legislation was adopted, the institutional framework for decision-making concerning EC asylum law had been changed, as from the entry into force of the Treaty of Nice on 1 February 2003. This Treaty had inserted a new Article 67(5) into the EC Treaty, which provided that qualified majority voting (QMV) in the Council and co-decision with the EP would apply once the Council adopted, by unanimity, Community rules which set out 'common rules and basic principles' on asylum. The Court of Justice subsequently confirmed that, as regards the asylum procedures Directive, sufficient common rules and basic principles had been established to trigger the application of Article 67(5) as from the adoption of that Directive; no doubt the same was true as regards other areas of asylum law.[26] Although Article 67(5) did not apply to 'burden-sharing' measures adopted pursuant to the powers conferred upon the EC by Article 63(2)(b) EC, a separate Council decision shifted decision-making on those matters to QMV and co-decision as from 1 January 2005.[27]

The basis for the second-phase of the development of the Common European Asylum System was the Hague Programme on the development of JHA policy from 2005–09, adopted in November 2004. According to the Hague Programme, the second phase of the CEAS should be achieved by the end of 2010, following the adoption of legislative proposals made by the Commission following a review of the existing asylum measures in 2007.[28] To this end, the Commission issued a Green Paper on the review of the CEAS in 2007,[29] and followed this up with a policy plan on asylum in 2008.[30] In the meantime new legislation concerning the European Refugee Fund was adopted.[31]

A main feature of the policy plan was the review and update of existing legislation, with the twin objectives of increasing the degree and raising the level of harmonization. The rationale for this was the continued wide divergence in recognition rates (ie rates of successful asylum applications) as between Member

---

[25] [2000] OJ L 252/12.   [26] Case C-133/06, n 23 above.
[27] [2004] OJ L 396/45.
[28] [2005] OJ C 53/1, points 1.3 and 1.6. See also the subsequent implementation plan: [2005] OJ C 198/1.   [29] COM (2007) 301, 6 June 2007.
[30] COM (2008) 360, 17 June 2008.   [31] [2007] OJ L 144/1.

States, both in general and in respect of particular nationalities, and also as regards the breakdown between the grant of refugee status and the grant of subsidiary protection status.[32] In fact, the wide divergence between national recognition rates was recognized by the 2008 Immigration and Asylum Pact adopted by EU leaders, which also set the aim of raising standards.[33]

To implement these objectives, first of all, in December 2008, the Commission proposed amendments to the Eurodac Regulation, the Dublin II Regulation, and the reception conditions Directive.[34] Secondly, the Commission proposed amendments to the qualification Directive and the asylum procedures Directive in October 2009.[35] However, there were great difficulties in the Council negotiating the proposed legislation, and the target date for completion of the second-phase of the CEAS was in any event moved from 2010 to 2012 by the Immigration and Asylum Pact adopted by the European Council in 2008.[36] The Commission also proposed legislation in 2009 to establish a European Asylum Support Office and to establish an EU-wide resettlement scheme,[37] and a proposal to establish an agency to operate the EU's JHA databases was relevant to Eurodac (inter alia).[38]

Furthermore, in 2007 the Commission proposed an immigration Directive particularly relevant to asylum law, which would have applied the long-term residents' Directive to refugees and beneficiaries of subsidiary protection.[39] However, the Council was unable to agree on this proposal before the Treaty of Lisbon entered into force, given that (as a migration law proposal) it remained subject to unanimous voting in Council and consultation of the EP.[40] Similarly, the Council was unable to agree before the Treaty of Lisbon on a proposal for extending new social security coordination rules to third-country nationals, including persons with subsidiary protection, as it was also subject to the same decision-making rules.[41]

As for role of the Court of Justice, its role remained restricted before the entry into force of the Treaty of Lisbon, due to the restrictions on its jurisdiction imposed by Article 68 EC before that date.[42] However, the Court began to

---

[32] See Annex 6 to the impact assessment on the proposal to amend the asylum procedures Dir (SEC (2009) 1376, 21 Oct 2009, Part II).

[33] Council doc 13440/08, 24 Sep 2008.

[34] COM (2008) 815, 820, and 825, 3 Dec 2008. See further 5.8 and 5.9 below. The Eurodac proposal was subsequently amended (COM (2009) 342, 10 Sep 2009) and a parallel third pillar proposal was also then tabled to give police access to the Eurodac system (COM (2009) 344, 10 Sep 2009).

[35] COM (2009) 551 and 554, 21 Oct 2009. See further 5.5 and 5.7 below.

[36] See n 33 above.

[37] COM (2009) 66 and 67, 18 Feb 2009, and COM (2009) 456, 2 Sep 2009. The former proposals were subsequently adopted after the entry into force of the Treaty of Lisbon: see 5.2.3 below.

[38] COM (2009) 293, 24 June 2009.   [39] COM (2007) 298, 6 June 2007.

[40] On the substance of the proposal, see 6.7.2 below.

[41] COM (2007) 439, 23 July 2007. On the substance of the proposal, see 5.4.2 below.

[42] See 2.2.2.1 above.

receive a number of requests for a preliminary ruling on asylum legislation as from 2007,[43] and it also received a number of infringement actions concerning EU asylum legislation, along with an annulment action concerning the asylum procedures Directive.[44]

5.2.3. Treaty of Lisbon

The issue of asylum is now addressed in Article 78 TFEU, as follows:

1. The Union shall develop a common policy on asylum, subsidiary protection and temporary protection with a view to offering appropriate status to any third-country national requiring international protection and ensuring compliance with the principle of *non-refoulement*. This policy must be in accordance with the Geneva Convention of 28 July 1951 and the Protocol of 31 January 1967 relating to the status of refugees, and other relevant treaties.

2. For the purposes of paragraph 1, the European Parliament and the Council, acting in accordance with the ordinary legislative procedure, shall adopt measures for a common European asylum system comprising:

(a) a uniform status of asylum for nationals of third countries, valid throughout the Union;

(b) a uniform status of subsidiary protection for nationals of third countries who, without obtaining European asylum, are in need of international protection;

(c) a common system of temporary protection for displaced persons in the event of a massive inflow;

(d) common procedures for the granting and withdrawing of uniform asylum or subsidiary protection status;

(e) criteria and mechanisms for determining which Member State is responsible for considering an application for asylum or subsidiary protection;

(f) standards concerning the conditions for the reception of applicants for asylum or subsidiary protection;

(g) partnership and cooperation with third countries for the purpose of managing inflows of people applying for asylum or subsidiary or temporary protection.

3. In the event of one or more Member States being confronted by an emergency situation characterised by a sudden inflow of nationals of third countries, the Council, on a proposal from the Commission, may adopt provisional measures for the benefit of the Member State(s) concerned. It shall act after consulting the European Parliament.

---

[43] Cases: C-19/08 *Petrosian* [2009] ECR I-495; C-465/07 *Elgafaji and Elgafaji* [2009] ECR I-921; C-175/08, C-176/08, C-178/08, and C-179/08 *Abdulla and others*, judgment of 2 Mar 2010 (not yet reported); C-31/09 *Bolbol*, judgment of 17 June 2010 (not yet reported); and C-57/09 and C-101/09 *B and D*, pending (opinion of 1 June 2010). *Petrosian* concerned the Dublin II Regulation, while the other cases concerned the qualification Directive. On the substance of these cases, see 5.5 and 5.8 below.

[44] On the infringement actions, see 5.5, 5.6, 5.8, and 5.9 below; on the annulment action, see n 23 above.

Article 80 TFEU, concerning the principle of solidarity as regards EU immigration and asylum law, is also relevant:

The policies of the Union set out in this Chapter and their implementation shall be governed by the principle of solidarity and fair sharing of responsibility, including its financial implications, between the Member States. Whenever necessary, the Union acts adopted pursuant to this Chapter shall contain appropriate measures to give effect to this principle.

Comparing Article 78 TFEU to the previous Article 63(1) and (2) EC, there is no change in the relevant decision-making rule, which remains the co-decision procedure (now known as the 'ordinary legislative procedure').[45] Article 78(3) TFEU has replaced the previous Article 64(2) EC, and now includes a requirement to consult the EP before such measures are taken.[46] Unlike the previous rules, Article 78(1) states that the EU acts in this area 'with a view to offering 'appropriate status to any third-country national requiring international protection' and requires 'compliance with the principle of non-refoulement'. As with the previous Treaty Article, the policy has to be 'in accordance with' the Geneva Convention, the New York Protocol, and 'other relevant treaties'. The EU must therefore continue to ensure compliance with these treaties (and now also with the principle of non-refoulement and with a view to offering appropriate status) as an obligation deriving from the Treaty, not merely from Member States' treaty obligations, customary international law, or *jus cogens*. Moreover, this power now explicitly applies to all aspects of the EU's protection-related policies, not just (as previously) to the competences related to the Geneva Convention.

With the advent of the 'normal' jurisdiction of the Court of Justice in this area, we might expect a significant increase in the number of cases concerning asylum reaching the Court, but there were only two further references to the Court of Justice in the first few months following the entry into force of the new Treaty, and one of these cases was withdrawn soon afterward.[47] The strengthened status of the EU Charter of Rights and the EU's accession to the ECHR could also have an impact on EU asylum law in practice,[48] as could the amended rules on the British and Irish opt-outs from JHA matters.[49]

Apart from these horizontal changes to JHA rules, the most significant change in this specific area is the amendment of the competence of the EU regarding asylum issues, in particular to include the objective of creating a 'common' policy,

---

[45] For the details of that procedure, see Art 294 TFEU (ex-Art 251 EC).

[46] On Art 78(3), see further 5.2.4 below. Like the previous Art 64(2) EC, this provision has never been used.

[47] Cases C-69/10 *Diouf*, pending, and C-105/10 PPU *Gataev and Gataeva*, withdrawn. However, the UK and Irish courts also intend to refer cases concerning the Dublin II rules (see 5.8 below).

[48] For more on these issues, see 5.3 below.   [49] See 5.2.5 below.

with the components of that policy taken from the Tampere conclusions and fully including subsidiary protection.[50]

The entry into force of the Treaty of Lisbon did not impact upon pending proposals for asylum legislation,[51] given that the decision-making process remained unchanged, and the Commission maintained its suggestion that the proposals for new legislation on qualification for international protection, procedures for applications, and reception conditions set minimum standards only.[52] Discussions on these proposals, and on the new rules concerning responsibility for applications for international protection and Eurodac, remained difficult.[53] Nor was there agreement on the proposal for an EU-wide resettlement scheme within the first few months of the entry into force of the Treaty.[54]

On the other hand, shortly after the new Treaty entered into force, the Council and EP adopted legislation proposed beforehand, in order to establish the European Asylum Support Office (EASO).[55] As for measures which were now subject to new decision-making rules (the ordinary legislative procedure, consisting of QMV and the former co-decision process, instead of unanimity and consultation), the Council adopted its first-reading position on the proposal on social security for third-country nationals in July 2010,[56] and in the same month discussions on the proposed extension of long-term residence status to refugees and persons with subsidiary protection were also restarted.[57]

As for the Stockholm programme,[58] it states that the CEAS 'should be based on high protection standards', with 'due regard' also for 'fair and effective procedures capable of preventing abuse'. It is 'crucial' that applicants are offered in each Member State an 'equivalent level of treatment as regards reception conditions, and the same level as regards procedural arrangements and status determination.

---

[50] For more on the issue of competence, see 5.2.4 below.

[51] See 5.2.2 above. However, the proposal to establish an agency to manage the EU's JHA databases (COM (2009) 293, n 38 above) was amended after the entry into force of the Treaty of Lisbon in order to include provisions relating to access to the data by law enforcement bodies (COM (2010) 93, 19 Mar 2010).

[52] Respectively COM (2009) 551, COM (2009) 554, and COM (2008) 815 (nn 34 and 35 above).

[53] See COM (2008) 820 and COM (2009) 342 (n 34 above). The proposal for law enforcement access to Eurodac (COM (2009) 344, *idem*) lapsed with the entry into force of the Treaty of Lisbon (COM (2009) 665, 2 Dec 2009, Annex 2), but a replacement proposal is planned for autumn 2010.

[54] COM (2009) 456, n 37 above.

[55] Reg 439/2010 ([2010] OJ L 132/11) and the accompanying amendment to the Refugee Fund ([2010] OJ L 129/1). See 5.10.1 below.

[56] Council doc 11160/10, 16 July 2010. This text must still be agreed with the EP.

[57] COM (2007) 298, n 39 above. It should be noted that this proposal does not address the issue of transfer of protection, which is specifically referred to in the Stockholm programme, although obviously the issues of movement between Member States and transfer of protection are linked as far as the beneficiaries of international protection are concerned.

[58] [2010] OJ C 115, s 6.2.

The objective should be that similar cases should be treated alike and result in the same outcome.' Noting the 'significant differences' between national policies, the creation of the CEAS 'should remain a key policy objective for the EU', '[i]n order to achieve a higher degree of harmonisation'. The underlying principle is that '[c]ommon rules, as well as a better and more coherent application of them, should prevent or reduce secondary movements within the EU, and increase mutual trust between Member States'.

According to the Stockholm programme, in accordance with the Tampere principles, the CEAS 'should be based on a full and inclusive application of the Geneva Convention on the status of refugees and other relevant international treaties'. This 'is necessary in order to maintain the long-term sustainability of the asylum system and to promote solidarity within the EU'. For the first time, the Stockholm programme calls upon the EU to seek accession to the Geneva Convention on refugee status and its 1967 Protocol, following 'a report from the Commission on the practical and legal consequences'.

To this end, the Stockholm programme invited:

– the Council and the European Parliament to intensify the efforts to establish a common asylum procedure and a uniform status in accordance with Article 78 [TFEU] for those who are granted asylum or subsidiary protection by 2012 at the latest,
– the Commission to consider, once the second phase of the CEAS has been fully implemented and on the basis of an evaluation of the effect of that legislation and of the EASO, the possibilities for creating a framework for the transfer of protection of beneficiaries of international protection when exercising their acquired residence rights under EU law,[59]
– the Commission to undertake a feasibility study on Eurodac as a supporting tool for the entire CEAS, while fully respecting data protection rules,
– the Commission to consider, if necessary, in order to achieve the CEAS, proposing new legislative instruments on the basis of an evaluation,
– [and] . . . the Commission to finalise its study on the feasibility and legal and practical implications to establish joint processing of asylum applications.

The action plan for implementing the Stockholm programme includes communications on Eurodac (2012), EU accession to the Geneva Convention (2013), joint processing and transfer of protection (both 2014), and solidarity between Member States (2011).[60] It can be noted that there is no express reference in the Stockholm programme or the action plan to the existing proposals for asylum legislation, although it can be presumed that the second phase of the CEAS could not be completed without their adoption. However, it is striking that neither the programme nor the action plan include *further* proposals for legislation.

---

[59] See the study on this issue, online at: <http://ec.europa.eu/justice_home/doc_centre/asylum/studies/doc_asylum_studies_en.htm>.   [60] COM (2010) 171, 20 Apr 2010.

The Stockholm Programme also contained certain commitments relating to the EASO and the external aspects of asylum, which are each considered further below.[61]

5.2.4. Competence issues

Although the Treaty of Lisbon has altered the rules on EU competence regarding asylum issues, in particular to remove the requirement that the EC (as it then was) could only set minimum standards as regards asylum, except as regards the rules on responsibility for applications, it is still necessary to examine first of all the prior rules on competence, since they affect the interpretation and possibly the validity of legislation adopted before the Treaty of Lisbon entered into force.

While the qualification Directive, the procedures Directive, and the reception conditions Directive all permit Member States to set higher standards,[62] they equally in turn require that any higher standards must nevertheless be 'compatible' with each Directive (the 'compatibility clauses'). According to the opinion in the *B and D* case,[63] as regards the provisions in the qualification Directive which require exclusion from refugee status (the 'exclusion clauses'), it would violate the 'compatibility' clause in the Directive and the exclusion clauses found in the Geneva Convention to give a person who falls within the scope of those exclusion clauses refugee status on the basis of higher national standards. However, it is permissible to give a person a different form of status on the basis of national law, provided that it cannot be confused with refugee status on the basis of the Directive.

Notwithstanding this interpretation, the scope and content of secondary EU measures cannot exceed the powers conferred by the legal base on which they were adopted. It follows that the EU legislation in this field adopted before the Treaty of Lisbon always *had* to leave Member States the power to set higher standards.[64] Moreover, in light of the human rights context in which the EU asylum legislation was adopted, those higher standards must constitute *higher standards of protection for the persons concerned*. The practical application of this principle is that, with respect, the Advocate General's opinion in *B and D* is wrong

---

[61] See respectively 5.10.1 and 5.11 below.

[62] See: Art 3, Dir 2004/83 ([2004] OJ L 304/12); Art 5, Dir 2005/85 ([2005] OJ L 326/13); and Art 4, Dir 2003/9 ([2003] OJ L 31/18).

[63] Opinion of 1 June 2010 in Joined Cases C-57/09 and C-101/09 *B and D*, pending.

[64] For a fuller version of the analysis on this point, see S Peers, 'EU Immigration and Asylum Law: Internal Market Model or Human Rights Model?' in T Tridimas and P Nebbia, eds, *EU Law for the Twenty-First Century: Rethinking the New Legal Order, Vol 1* (Hart, 2004), 345.

on this point,[65] and the Council legal service was also wrong to argue that the qualification Directive required Member States to harmonize fully their laws regarding the relevant definitions (with no scope for a more generous definition of those concepts).[66] If necessary, the 'compatibility' requirements must simply be regarded as invalid.

Following the entry into force of the Treaty of Lisbon, with the removal of the 'minimum standards' clause, the Union has the power to harmonize national asylum law as fully as it wishes, subject to the principles of subsidiary and proportionality. This is confirmed by the references to the creation of a 'common policy on asylum' and related issues[67] and to a 'common European asylum system', involving a 'uniform status' of asylum and subsidiary protection, a 'common system' of temporary protection, and 'common rules' on procedures for deciding applications,[68] along with the absence of any limitation on the scope of Article 78 TFEU. Three further powers are not described as 'common' or 'uniform' by the Treaty, but still fall within the scope of the general objective of developing a 'common' policy and system: the criteria and mechanisms for determining responsibility for applications; the reception standards for applicants; and relations with third countries. However, the EU does not have the *obligation* to harmonize asylum law fully, since competence regarding asylum law, along with the rest of JHA law, is shared between the EU and the Member States.[69] It is therefore possible (although no longer *obligatory*) for the EU to continue to set minimum standards only in its asylum legislation—which is indeed what the Commission has proposed as regards the second-phase asylum legislation.[70]

But this is not the end of the story. Since the EU is no longer obliged to set minimum standards only, the requirement (if retained in the second-phase legislation, as the Commission proposes) that national law can set higher standards only if compatible with the relevant Directives would have a different meaning after the entry into force of the Treaty of Lisbon, given the different legal framework. First of all, in light of the human rights framework of asylum law, the 'more favourable' provisions in the future Directives would still have to be understood as referring to more favourable provisions for the persons concerned. Secondly, the requirement of compatibility now would have to be understood as requiring Member States to comply with any fully uniform provisions of the relevant legislation,

---

[65] To the extent that the exclusion clauses in the *Geneva Convention* are mandatory, a Member State would arguably violate its *international* obligations by breaching them (although see Art 5 of the Convention), but not its *EU* obligations at the same time.

[66] Council doc 14348/02, 15 Nov 2002. The full text of this opinion can be found at: <http://www.statewatch.org/news/2002/dec/14348.02.doc>. Equally the Commission's discussion of this issue in its 2009 impact assessment reports on the qualification Directive and the procedures Directive wrongly begs this question (SEC (2009) 1373, 21 Oct 2009, p 9, and SEC (2009) 1376, 21 Oct 2009, p 9).   [67] Arts 67(2) and 78(1).

[68] Art 78(2).   [69] Art 4(2)(j) TFEU.

[70] See: Art 3, COM (2009) 551, 21 Oct 2009; Art 5, COM (2009) 554, 21 Oct 2009; and Art 4, COM (2008) 815, 3 Dec 2008.

ie any measures which clearly left no room for national variations as regards the application of the relevant rules.[71] In light of the overall human rights context and the continued references to minimum standards in the legislation, it is submitted that in case of any uncertainty about the application of this principle in a particular case, the doubt should be resolved in favour of Member States' ability to set higher standards. However, it would be preferable, in the interests of legal certainty, to set out precisely in each measure which rules were fully uniform, depriving Member States of any competence to set higher standards. In any event, it should be recalled that as long as the EU has not fully harmonized all aspects of immigration and asylum law, Member States would remain competent to permit a person to stay on the territory on grounds falling outside the scope of EU asylum legislation, and to adopt national procedural rules and reception conditions rules to that end.[72] It should also be recalled that any restraint which might be set in EU law on Member States' powers to set higher standards regarding asylum could not breach the human rights obligations of the EU, as enshrined in primary EU law.[73]

Another important change brought about by the Treaty of Lisbon relates to the personal scope of EU asylum powers.[74] Before the entry into force of the Treaty of Lisbon, EC powers over asylum responsibility, the definition of 'refugee', and temporary protection were expressly limited to non-EU citizens, while the EC's powers over reception conditions, asylum procedures, subsidiary protection, and burden-sharing were not limited in personal scope. However, in practice EC asylum legislation adopted before the entry into force of the Treaty of Lisbon only addressed third-country nationals, presumably because the EC Treaty in principle ruled out asylum applications from EU citizens.[75] Following the entry into force of the Treaty of Lisbon, the EU's asylum powers only concern third-country nationals, and so therefore cannot be used to regulate asylum applications from EU citizens. The use of any alternative Treaty bases to regulate this issue would moreover be problematic in light of the relevant Protocol. So the impact of the Protocol can only be circumvented by making claims for subsidiary protection, or by arguing that the Protocol is in breach of the pre-existing Treaty commitments of the Member States (ie the Geneva Convention), and so must be disapplied pursuant to Article 351 TFEU.[76]

---

[71] Compare with the judgment in Case C-510/99 *Tridon* [2001] ECR I-7777, which interpreted the rule in Art 176 EC (now Art 192 TFEU) that Member States could apply higher standards in environmental law as long as such rules were compatible with the EC Treaty (as it then was). However, that Treaty rule regulates the possible conflict between environmental law and a different set of rules (internal market law), whereas the compatibility rule in the future EU asylum legislation would regulate the different issue of the intensity of harmonization within the same area.

[72] See, for instance, recital 14 of the proposed recast of the qualification Directive (COM (2009) 551, 21 Oct 2009). [73] On the content of those obligations, see 5.3 below.

[74] The remaining discussion in this section is largely adapted from S Peers, 'EU Immigration and Asylum Competence and Decision-Making in the Treaty of Lisbon' (2008) 10 EJML 219 at 235–238. [75] See 5.4.1 below.

[76] See further ibid.

One specific amendment made by the Treaty of Lisbon worth considering further is the power to regulate the *status* of asylum (and subsidiary protection), instead of *qualification* as refugees. This wording reflects the full title of the Geneva Convention and could therefore be understood as encompassing the main content of that Convention—both the definition ('qualification') of refugees and their status on the territory (in terms of, for example, residence and access to employment and benefits). Within the previous legal framework, the latter issues were dealt with by using the EC's immigration powers,[77] but this should not be necessary after the entry into force of the Treaty of Lisbon.[78] It might also be argued that EU legislation regulating long-term residents' status and movement between Member States should, as regards at least refugees, be adopted after the entry into force of the Treaty of Lisbon on the basis of the EU's asylum powers, since that (proposed) legislation regulates the status of refugees and persons with subsidiary protection as regards immigration law (although not the distinct protection aspects of the status of such persons).[79] In any event, in future there would be no conflict between the decision-making rules applicable to asylum on the one hand and legal migration on the other. The most important point is to avoid regulating the immigration status of persons with international protection purely on the basis of their protection need, because then they would lose their status if that need ceased, even if they were long-term residents.

Furthermore, what is the scope of the provision concerning 'a status of asylum...valid throughout Union'? This should entail some degree of recognition by each Member State of other Member States' recognition of refugee status, but the full extent of that requirement is not clear. Could it be confined to recognition of the *non-refoulement* obligation, with the consequence that a refugee recognized by one Member State who is irregularly on the territory of another Member State must be returned to the Member State which first recognized that person's refugee status? Does it extend as far as to provide for a right of residence, valid in any Member State, entailing also all of the benefits (access to welfare, housing, and employment) accorded to legally resident Geneva Convention refugees, to the extent required by that Convention (and/or the qualification Directive)? Or would it entail something in-between?

---

[77] As noted above (see 5.2.2), Dir 2004/83 (n 62 above) was adopted on the basis of both asylum and immigration legal bases.

[78] Note that when the Treaty of Lisbon entered into force, the Commission stated, in accordance with this interpretation, that the proposal to amend the qualification Dir (COM (2009) 551, 21 Oct 2009) fell from that point onward entirely within the scope of the EU's asylum law powers (COM (2009) 665, 2 Dec 2009, Annex 4).

[79] See the proposal to extend the long-term residents' directive (Dir 2003/109, [2004] OJ L 16/44) to refugees and persons with subsidiary protection (COM (2007 298, 6 June 2007), which had the previous immigration powers as a 'legal base'. However, the Commission communication on the effect of the Treaty of Lisbon on decision-making procedures retained the (revised) Treaty immigration provisions as the legal base of this proposal (COM (2009) 665, ibid).

The best interpretation, in the absence of any clear indication in the Treaty, is that the EU institutions have a degree of discretion between different interpretations of this provision, and can choose to develop the Union-wide validity of that status gradually. It will always have to be kept in mind, however, that the Treaty does not refer expressly to a Union-wide validity of subsidiary protection status. But it is arguable that even though the EU institutions are not *required* to provide for EU-wide validity of subsidiary protection status, they still have the *option* to provide for it, in the absence of a provision in the Treaty expressly limiting EU competence on this point.

As for temporary protection, the power following the entry into force of the Treaty of Lisbon not only constitutes a power to establish a 'common' policy, as noted above, but also it is limited, unlike the previous Treaty, to cases where there is a 'massive inflow'. However, it should be noted that the EU's current temporary protection Directive is in any event limited to cases of a 'mass influx'.[80]

Next, the new provision relating to 'partnership and cooperation' with third countries more clearly confers powers on the EU as regards this issue as compared to the previous Treaty, which expressly referred in most cases only to powers to regulate protection issues within or between Member States.[81] Furthermore, Article 78 TFEU is a *lex specialis* on this issue, which arguably therefore does not fall within the scope of the EU's development policy. The importance of this is that the EU has powers to harmonize asylum law fully, whereas EU development policy remains (as it was before the Treaty of Lisbon) a shared and parallel competence, meaning that the EU can never pre-empt national policy.[82]

The previous 'burden-sharing' power set out in the prior Article 63(2)(b) TEC was retained as such. However, the new Article 80 TFEU refers to the principles of solidarity and fair sharing of responsibility, and specifies that EU immigration and asylum legislation 'shall contain appropriate measures to give effect to this principle' whenever this is 'necessary'. The objectives set out in Article 67(2) TFEU also provide that EU immigration and asylum policy shall be 'based on solidarity between Member States'. Article 80 is not a legal base in itself, but provides justification for the adoption of measures in future such as the European Refugee Fund,[83] and possibly for non-financial measures concerning 'burden-sharing' as well.

Finally, Article 78(3) TFEU, which confers power to address an 'emergency situation' constituting a 'sudden inflow' of third-country nationals, is identical to the previous Article 64(2) EC, except for the requirement to consult the EP, its placement in an Article dealing with asylum issues, the absence of a

---

[80] Art 1 of Dir 2001/55 ([2001] OJ L 212/12). For the definition of 'mass influx', see Art 2(d) of the Directive.

[81] See the previous Art 63(1)(a), (b), and (d), and 2(b). The exceptions were Art 63(1)(c) and 2(a), concerning the qualification of refugees and temporary protection.   [82] Art 4(4) TFEU.

[83] See 5.10.2 below.

cross-reference to the general 'law and order' clause (which is now Article 72 TFEU), and the abolition of the requirement that measures should not exceed six months in duration.

What is the impact of these changes, as regards EU competence? First, the abolition of the cross-reference to the 'law and order' clause is immaterial, since this 'law and order' clause expressly applies in any event to the entire Title V. However, the placement of this emergency provision inside an Article solely concerned with asylum is new. Logically, this must mean that, after the Treaty of Lisbon entered into force, the 'sudden influx' clause is limited in its application to asylum-related issues, and moreover that its application is now governed by the general obligations set out in Article 78(1) TFEU as regards offering 'appropriate status' to persons needing international protection, along with compliance with the principle of *non-refoulement*, the Geneva Convention, and other relevant treaties. As for the abolition of the six-month limit, this can only mean that measures could, if necessary, last longer than six months; but the requirement that they be 'provisional' in nature obviously means that the measures could not apply indefinitely or for a very lengthy fixed period either. Also, it is arguable that the previous Article 64(2) EC could not have been used to amend existing EC legislation; this interpretation applies *mutatis mutandis* to Article 78(3) TFEU. If this interpretation is correct, then Article 78(3) TFEU cannot be used to establish a temporary protection regime as long as the EU has temporary protection legislation 'on the shelf' and available for use, which of course it does.[84] Instead, the 'sudden influx' power could be used to provide, for example, immediate financial assistance to Member States which are affected particularly by such an 'influx'.

5.2.5. Territorial scope

The UK opted in to all first-phase asylum measures, while Ireland opted in to all first-phase measures except the temporary protection Directive and the reception conditions Directive. It subsequently opted into the temporary protection Directive.[85] However, as regards second-phase measures, the UK and Ireland only opted in to the Dublin and Eurodac rules regarding asylum responsibility, and the proposals concerning the EASO and the EU resettlement scheme.[86] This means that the UK and Ireland have opted out of the key proposals for second-phase legislation on qualification, procedures, and reception conditions.[87] Since these proposals, would if adopted, not only *amend* the first-phase legislation but

---

[84] See Dir 2001/55 (n 80 above), discussed in 5.6 below.

[85] See Commission Decision 2003/690, [2003] OJ L 251/23. On the process of opting in after the adoption of a measure, see 2.2.5.1.2 above.

[86] On the substance of these measures, see 5.8.4, 5.10.1, and 5.11 below.

[87] On the substance of these measures, see 5.5.2, 5.7.2, and 5.9.2 below.

also *repeal* it, the question would then arise whether the UK and Ireland still remain bound by the first-phase legislation, given that it would be repealed, but considering that those Member States would not be participating in the measure which repeals the prior act.[88]

As for Denmark, it is automatically excluded from all EU asylum measures, although it remains a party to the 1990 Dublin Convention, which continued to govern the allocation of asylum applications between itself and all of the 'old' Member States, until the Community and Denmark concluded a treaty which extended the Eurodac and Dublin II Regulations to Denmark.[89] If Denmark does not agree to apply measures implementing or amending this legislation, the agreement will terminate unless the parties agree otherwise.[90] Pursuant to the revisions to the rules on Danish participation in JHA measures made by the Treaty of Lisbon, Denmark could in future decide to avail itself of an option to participate in EU asylum legislation on a case-by-case basis.[91]

Norway and Iceland are associated with the EU rules on responsibility for asylum applications (including Eurodac), due to a treaty between the EC (now the EU) and those States which has been in force since 1 April 2001.[92] This treaty requires Norway and Iceland to apply the Dublin Convention, the replacement EU rules (ie the Dublin II Regulation, and in future the proposals to amend that Regulation and the Eurodac Regulation, once adopted), and any measures implementing them.[93] Member States of the EU have reciprocal obligations,[94] except for Denmark, which was permitted to sign up to the treaty if it agreed a Protocol to that effect with the parties to the treaty.[95] Such a Protocol entered into force in 2006.[96]

The treaty can be suspended if Norway and Iceland fail to agree to new EU measures,[97] if major difficulties follow a substantial change in circumstances,[98] or if a divergence develops between the case law of the Norwegian and Icelandic courts and the Court of Justice's interpretation of the relevant rules, if the Joint Committee established by the treaty proves unable to agree a solution in either case.[99] To ensure future homogeneity of interpretation, Norway and Iceland have the right to comment on EU draft measures,[100] and to submit observations before the Court of Justice in relevant cases.[101] The practice of Norwegian and Icelandic courts and authorities should be kept under regular review.[102]

---

[88] This important issue is examined in detail in 2.2.5.1.5 above.

[89] [2006] OJ L 66/37, in force 1 Apr 2006 ([2006] OJ L 93/9). For discussion of the institutional features of the agreement, see 2.2.5.2 above.			[90] Arts 3 and 4 of the agreement.

[91] See 2.2.5.2 above. In that case, the 2006 agreement will terminate (see Art 10).

[92] Decision 2001/258 ([2001] OJ L 93/38). On the date of entry into force, see [2001] OJ L 112/16.			[93] On the substance of these measures, see 5.8 below.

[94] Art 1(2) and (5).		[95] Arts 12 and 13(3).

[96] [2006] OJ L 57/15, in force 1 May 2006. On the date of entry into force, see [2006] OJ L 112/12.			[97] Art 4(2)–(7).

[98] Art 5; compare with Art 17 of the Dublin Convention.		[99] Arts 7 and 8.

[100] Art 2; see also second and fourth Declarations to the treaty.		[101] Art 6(2).

[102] Art 7(1).

A treaty extending the responsibility rules (including Eurodac) to Switzerland entered into force on 1 March 2008, in parallel to the agreements on Swiss participation in the Schengen *acquis*.[103] This treaty is essentially identical to the EU treaty with Norway and Iceland, except that there was no need to associate Switzerland with the Dublin Convention (since it had already been replaced by an EU Regulation) and Switzerland has up to two years to implement its decision to apply new EU measures (in order to provide for a possible Swiss referendum). There are specific provisions for additional protocols regards extension of this treaty to Denmark and Liechtenstein.[104]

The various treaties associating countries with the EU asylum responsibility rules are suspect because they set out conflict rules in the absence of harmonization of substantive asylum law, and because, like the internal EU responsibility rules, they force some families apart and ignore the 'applicants' choice' principle set out in UNHCR Executive Committee conclusions, leading to an increase of destroyed documents (and therefore deemed 'unfounded' or 'manifestly unfounded' applications).[105]

It should be noted that, notwithstanding the above rules on territorial scope, the special Protocol precluding EU citizens from applying for asylum in other Member States applies to all EU Member States, but not to any non-Member States.[106] In other words, this Protocol does not prevent an EU citizen from applying for asylum in Norway or Switzerland, or a citizen of one of the latter countries from applying for asylum in an EU Member State.

5.3. Human rights

5.3.1. International human rights and refugee law

The starting point of international refugee law is the 1951 Geneva Convention on the status of refugees, together with the 1967 New York Protocol to that Convention.[107] The key provision of the Convention is Article 1.A(2), which defines a refugee (hereinafter a 'Convention refugee') as a person who:

... owing to a well-founded fear of being persecuted for reasons of race, religion, nationality, membership of a particular social group or political opinion, is outside the country

---

[103] [2008] OJ L 53/5; on the entry into force of the treaty, see [2008] OJ L 53/18. On Swiss participation in the Schengen rules, see 2.2.5.4 above.

[104] Arts 11 and 15 of the treaty. A Protocol regarding Danish participation in this treaty entered into force on 1 Dec 2008: see [2009] OJ L 161/6 and 8. A Protocol on Liechtenstein's participation has been signed, but has not yet entered into force: for the text, see COM (2006) 754, 3 Dec 2006.

[105] See criticisms in 5.8 below.   [106] On the Protocol, see further 5.4.1 below.

[107] All Member States are parties to both instruments. The Protocol removed the temporal limitation on the Convention, which was initially limited to persons fleeing developments which occurred before 1951. From a huge literature, see G Goodwin-Gill and J McAdam, *The Refugee in International Law* (3rd edn, OUP, 2007) and E Feller, V Turk, and F Nicholson, eds, *Refugee Protection in International Law: UNHCR's Global Consultations on Refugee Protection* (CUP, 2003).

of his [or her] nationality and is unable or, owing to such fear, is unwilling to avail himself [or herself] of the protection of that country, or who, not having a nationality and being outside of the country of his [or her] former habitual residence as a result of such events, is unable or, owing to such fear, unwilling to return to it.

Article 1.B of the Convention permits Contracting States to limit their obligations to events occurring within Europe, but no Member State now applies the geographical limitation and invoking it would be inconsistent with EC asylum legislation, which makes no provision for it. Article 1.C, the 'cessation' clause, sets out the grounds upon which persons cease to be Convention refugees, inter alia where a person 'can no longer, because the circumstances in connexion with which he [or she] has been recognised as a refugee have ceased to exist, continue to refuse to avail himself [or herself] of the protection of the country of his [or her] nationality'.[108] The cessation clause does not apply to those categories of refugees who held status under prior international arrangements and who were 'able to invoke compelling reasons arising out of previous persecution' to object to the application of the cessation clause.[109]

Article 1.D specifies that:

This Convention shall not apply to persons who are at present receiving from organs or agencies of the United Nations other than the United Nations High Commissioner for Refugees protection or assistance.

When such protection or assistance has ceased for any reason, without the position of such persons being definitively settled in accordance with the relevant resolutions adopted by the General Assembly of the United Nations, these persons shall *ipso facto* be entitled to the benefits of this Convention.

Article 1.F states that a person is excluded from being a Convention refugee if 'there are serious reasons for considering that':[110]

(a) he [or she] has committed a crime against peace, a war crime, or a crime against humanity, as defined in the international instruments drawn up to make provision in respect of such crimes;

(b) he [or she] has committed a serious non-political crime outside the country of refuge prior to his [or her] admission to that country as a refugee;

(c) he [or she] has been guilty of acts contrary to the purposes and principles of the United Nations.

The Convention is largely concerned with setting out the legal status of refugees, for example specifying the extent of their access to employment and welfare benefits in the state of refuge and providing for freedom of movement and the issue of travel documents to them.[111] Article 31 provides that in certain circumstances,

---

[108] Art 1(C)(5); Art 1(C)(6) applies the same principle to stateless persons.
[109] Art 1(C)(5) and (6).   [110] Art 1(E) also provides for an exclusion.
[111] Arts 12–30 of the Convention.

refugees who enter or stay on a territory irregularly cannot be subject to penalties.[112] Article 32 specifies that a refugee who is 'lawfully in [the] territory' can only be expelled on 'grounds of national security or public order', and is furthermore entitled to procedural rights to contest the expulsion. Article 33, the *non-refoulement* clause, is regarded as the most important principle in the Convention, providing that:

No Contracting State shall expel or return ('refouler') a refugee in any manner whatsoever to the frontiers of territories where his life or freedom would be threatened on account of his [or her] race, religion, nationality, membership of a particular social group or political opinion.

However, Article 33(2) of the Convention allows for an exception to this principle, where 'there are reasonable grounds for regarding [the refugee] as a danger to the security of the country in which he [or she] is, or' where, 'having been convicted by a final judgment of a particularly serious crime, [the refugee] constitutes a danger to the community of that country'.

Article 35 of the Convention requires Contracting States to cooperate with the United Nations High Commission for Refugees (the UNHCR), which has the duty of 'supervising the application' of the Convention. However, the UNHCR is not a dispute settlement body; any disputes between Contracting Parties may be referred to the International Court of Justice for settlement (Article 38). There is no mechanism for individuals to bring a dispute about a State's application of the Convention before any international organ. In practice, the UNHCR has played a key role as regards the operational aspects of refugee protection (for example, helping to establish refugee camps or resettlement programmes) and a role developing 'soft law' regarding the interpretation of the Geneva Convention and issues associated with it, in particular developing a Handbook on refugee protection and adopting Conclusions of its Executive Committee on refugee issues.[113]

The Convention does not expressly address the issues of the procedures for determining whether a claim to be recognized as a refugee is well-founded (asylum procedures), the conditions applicable to a person claiming recognition as a refugee (an asylum seeker) while a determination procedure is underway (reception conditions), or the issue of which State is responsible for the determination of a claim for recognition as a refugee. In fact, the Convention does not expressly state whether States can refuse to consider a claim for recognition as a refugee on the grounds that another State should be responsible for considering that claim. Nor does the Convention expressly deal with some key aspects of the legal status

---

[112] On this principle, see 7.3.2 below.

[113] See generally: <http://www.unhcr.org>. For the Executive Committee conclusions, see: <http://www.unhcr.org/refworld/docid/4a7c4b882.html>. For the Handbook, see: <http://www.unhcr.org/cgi-bin/texis/vtx/search?page=search&docid=3d58e13b4&query=handbook%20on%20refugee%20status%20determination>.

of refugee, in particular the right of residence of a person recognized to be a refugee and a refugee's right to family reunion. However, the *non-refoulement* clause gives rise to an implied right to remain on the territory if the conditions for application of that clause are met; and the conference which drew up the Convention agreed on a recommendation relating to family reunion.

The United Nations Convention against Torture, which has been ratified by all EU Member States, also deals with the question of the removal of people to face unsafe conditions. Article 3 of that Convention specifies that:

1. No State Party shall expel, return ('refouler') or extradite a person to another State where there are substantial grounds for believing that he [or she] would be in danger of being subjected to torture.

2. For the purpose of determining whether there are such grounds, the competent authorities shall take into account all relevant considerations including, where applicable, the existence in the State concerned of a consistent pattern of gross, flagrant or mass violations of human rights.

A Committee against Torture, established to supervise the application of the Convention, can hear petitions from individuals, and has built up a considerable jurisprudence on the interpretation of Article 3.[114]

The International Covenant on Civil and Political Rights (ICCPR) contains no express provisions preventing persons from return to unsafe conditions, but the Human Rights Committee, which supervises the application of the Covenant, has ruled that the Covenant contains implicit protection against removal to face treatment which would amount to a breach of standards set out in the Covenant.[115] It is also arguable that protection against non-refoulement constitutes a rule of customary international law, or even a *jus cogens* rule that would trump any contrary international rule.[116] The right to asylum and related rights also appear in a number of national constitutions of Member States, in particular Germany and France.

As for the European Convention on Human Rights (ECHR), it does not contain any express provision relating to asylum or refugees, or limiting the substantive

---

[114] On the Convention, see C Ingelse, *The UN Committee Against Torture: An Assessment* (Kluwer, 2001). For a critical view of the jurisprudence of the Committee, see J Doerfel, 'The Convention Against Torture and the Protection of Refugees' (2005) 24:2 RSQ 83.

[115] For an analysis of and excerpts from this jurisprudence, see J Schultz, S Joseph, and M Castan, *The International Covenant on Civil and Political Rights* (2nd edn, OUP, 2004), 194–293.

[116] See E Lauterpacht and D Bethlehem, 'The Scope and Content of the Principle of *Non-refoulement*: an Opinion', in Feller, Turk, and Nicholson (n 107 above), 87; N Coleman, 'Non-Refoulement Revised. Renewed Review of the Status of *Non-refoulement* as Customary International Law' (2003) 5 EJML 23; and J Allain, 'The *jus cogens* nature of *non-refoulement*' (2002) 4 IJRL 533. The EU courts recognize customary international law and *jus cogens* as sources of law relevant to the interpretation and validity of Community measures: see respectively Cases C-162/96 *Racke* [1998] ECR I-3655, C-286/90 *Poulsen and Diva* [1992] ECR I-6019, and T-115/94 *Opel Austria* [1997] ECR II-39 (as regards customary international law), and Cases T-306/01 *Yusuf* [2005] ECR II-3533 and T-315/01 *Kadi* [2005] ECR II-3649 (as regards *jus cogens*).

grounds upon which a person can be removed from a country. However, the jurisprudence of the European Court of Human Rights has addressed this issue in detail.[117] First of all, the Strasbourg Court has developed principles concerning the substance of international protection. Starting with its judgment in *Soering v UK*,[118] it established that a person could not be removed to a country where he or she faced a real risk of torture or inhuman or degrading treatment, in contravention of Article 3 ECHR. It did not matter whether the country of intended destination was a party to the ECHR or not, since the expelling State was liable to ensure that the removal did not breach Article 3. Although the *Soering* judgment concerned extradition, the Court soon confirmed that the principle applied equally to expulsions or other forms of removal, therefore including protected persons claiming refugee status or some other form of international protection.[119] However, it was clear from these and subsequent judgments that the threshold to show that a sufficiently high risk existed was not simple to meet.[120]

Subsequently, the Human Rights Court established the important principle that unlike Articles 32 and 33 of the Geneva Convention, Article 3 ECHR is absolute, precluding the application of limitations or derogations on the right not to be removed to face treatment in violation of Article 3, even in times of national emergency or where the person concerned was allegedly a terrorist.[121] This judgment was subsequently affirmed even after the terrorist attacks of September 11, 2001; moreover, the Human Rights Court has also consistently ruled that diplomatic assurances by the State of destination that torture will not be carried out are not in themselves sufficient to avoid the risk of it occurring, and equally the existence of domestic law safeguarding human rights and the ratification of international human rights treaties is not relevant if there is evidence of, for example actual torture, in the State concerned.[122]

---

[117] See H Lambert, 'Protection Against Refoulement from Europe: Human Rights Law Comes to the Rescue' (1999) 48 ICLQ 515 and 'The European Convention on Human Rights and the Protection of Refugees: Limits and Opportunities' (2005) 24:2 RSQ 39.   [118] A-161.

[119] See judgments in *Cruz Varas and Others v Sweden* (A-201) and *Vilvarajah and Others v UK* (A-215).

[120] See, for instance, the unsuccessful arguments in the cases of: *Venkadajalasarma v Netherlands* and *Thampibillai v Netherlands* (17 Feb 2004); *Mamatkulov and Askarov v Turkey*, chamber judgment of 6 Feb 2003, and Grand Chamber judgment (ECHR 2005-I); *Muslim v Turkey* (24 Apr 2005); *Aoulmi v France* (17 Jan 2006); *FH v Sweden* (20 Jan 2009); and *Puzan v Ukraine* (18 Feb 2010). On the other hand, see, for instance, the successful arguments in the cases of: *Jabari v Turkey* (Reports 2000-VIII); *Hilal v UK* (Reports 2001-II); *Said v Netherlands* (5 July 2005); *N v Finland* (26 July 2005); *Klein v Russia* (1 Apr 2010); and *SH v UK* (15 June 2010). Note in particular the gender-related issues considered in *N v Sweden* (20 July 2010).

[121] See particularly *Chahal v UK* (Reports 1996-V), followed by *Ahmed v Austria* (Reports 1996-VI) and *N v Finland* (ibid).

[122] *Saadi v Italy*, 28 Feb 2008. See subsequently *Ismoilov v Russia*, 24 Apr 2008, *Muminov v Russia*, 11 Dec 2008, *Ben Khemais v Italy*, 24 Feb 2009, *O and others v Italy*, 24 Mar 2009, *Abdolkhani and Karimnia v Turkey*, 22 Sep 2009, *Khodzhayev v Russia*, 12 May 2010, *Khaydarov v Russia*, 20 May 2010, *Garayev v Azerbaijan*, 10 June 2010, and *A v Netherlands*, 20 July 2010.

Moreover, although some Member States traditionally limited the application of the Geneva Convention to cases where persecution emanated from the State, Article 3 ECHR covers cases where the person concerned fears violence from non-State actors, on the condition that the relevant State is unable to provide the person with protection.[123] While the ECHR case law does not generally accept that generalized violence in the country of origin gives rise per se to an Article 3 risk for any person returned there, it is possible in principle that an exceptional situation might exist where all persons returning there are at risk. Otherwise an applicant must show that there are special distinguishing features in his or her case, unless the applicant argues that he or she is 'a member of a group systematically exposed to a practice of ill-treatment', and 'there are serious reasons to believe the existence of that practice and his or her membership of the group concerned'. The need to show special distinguishing features is assessed in light of whether the situation of overall violence means that it is more likely that the group in question will be ill-treated.[124]

While the Human Rights Court has not answered definitively the question of whether the ECHR applies to asylum applications addressed to a Member State's authorities operating outside its territory (including on the high seas), the case law on the general issue of the extraterritorial application of the Convention suggests that it does, by analogy.[125] As for the position *within* the third State concerned, the Human Rights Court has ruled that while in principle an 'internal flight alternative' principle could apply (ie the asylum seeker might conceivably be safe in a *different* part of the country of origin that he or she fled from), there had to be guarantees that 'the person to be expelled must be able to travel to the area concerned, gain admittance and settle there'.[126]

Is there a '*Soering* effect' to other provisions of the ECHR besides Article 3?[127] The *Soering* judgment itself also stated that a person could not be removed to face a manifest breach of the right to a fair trial as guaranteed by Article 6 ECHR in the destination State. However, to date the Strasbourg Court has not yet ruled in favour of an applicant who was arguing that such a risk exists. In *Bader*, the Court ruled that it would be a breach of Article 2 ECHR to send a person to a State of destination where he or she faced a death penalty imposed following an unfair trial,[128] and the Court has since confirmed that a *Soering* effect applies as regards expulsion to face the death penalty.[129] As for other ECHR articles, the Court

---

[123] *HLR v France* (Reports 1997-III), *N v Finland* (n 120 above), and *Salah Sheekh v Netherlands* (ECHR 2007-I).

[124] See *Saadi* (n 122 above), *NA v UK*, 17 July 2008, and *Soldatenko v Ukraine*, 23 Oct 2008.

[125] See particularly *Medvedyev v France*, 29 Mar 2010 and *Al-Saadoon and Mufdhi v UK*, 2 Mar 2010.

[126] *Salah Sheekh* (n 123 above), para 141. On the facts of this case, the guarantees were not present, since the person concerned was from a minority group which could not expect 'clan protection' even in the 'safe' parts of Somalia.   [127] See further the discussion in 9.3.1 below.

[128] *Bader v Sweden* (2005 ECHR-XI).   [129] *Al-Saadoon and Mufdhi* (n 125 above).

hinted in its *Bankovic* decision that Article 5 ECHR conferred a *Soering* effect,[130] and the UK House of Lords has taken the view that any provision of the ECHR could in principle confer such an effect.[131]

A number of cases also concern procedural rights in relation to international protection, applying Article 3 in conjunction with Article 13 ECHR, which guarantees an 'effective remedy' in respect of the substantive rights set out in the Convention. Although the Court has repeatedly held that the standard system of judicial review applied in English law is adequate to meet the 'effective remedies' requirement,[132] except where the usual standard is substantially lower due to alleged security risks,[133] it has criticized particular procedural rules in other countries. In *Jabari v Turkey*,[134] it stated that the ECHR will be violated if there is no consideration of the merits of an asylum request for procedural reasons, where there is also no suspensive effect of an appeal or consideration of the merits on appeal. More broadly, States have obligations to ensure 'independent and rigorous scrutiny' of claims, entailing the 'possibility of suspending' a removal.

The Court returned to some of these issues in its judgment in *Conka v Belgium*, stating that Article 13 ECHR would be breached if national authorities carry out an expulsion before it is determined whether that expulsion is compatible with the ECHR, and ruling that the Belgian system denying suspensive effect (but permitting an application to a court which might grant it) was in particular a breach of Article 13, since only automatic suspensive effect will satisfy the requirements of the Convention; arguments about the overload of the courts and the 'risks of abuse of process' did not convince the Human Rights Court.[135] Although this judgment concerned collective expulsions, not Article 3 ECHR, the Court subsequently confirmed its applicability to Article 3 in the case of *Gebremedhin v France*, ruling that 'this finding obviously applies in a case where a State Party decides to remove an alien to a country where there are substantial grounds for believing that he or she would run [an Article 3] risk'.[136] Again, it was essential either that the asylum seeker be permitted to stay on the territory pending a final decision, or that at least an application for an emergency ruling challenging an expulsion decision must have automatic suspensive effect.

Moreover, other procedural rights are conferred by the ECHR in asylum cases. It is clear from *Jabari* that an absolute and rigid time limit for presenting

---

[130] Decision in *Bankovic v UK and others* (Reports 2001-XII).

[131] *R v Special Adjudicator ex parte Ullah and Do* [2004] UKHL 26. See also the analysis by R Piotrowicz and C van Eck, 'Subsidiary Protection and Primary Rights' (2004) 53 ICLQ 107.

[132] See *Soering, Vilvarajah, Hilal,* and *NA v UK* (nn 118–120 and 124 above).

[133] See *Chahal* (n 121 above).   [134] Paras 49 and 50 (n 120 above).

[135] Paras 79–85 of the judgment (Reports 2002-I).

[136] Para 58 of the judgment, 26 Apr 2007. See subsequently *Muminov* and *Abdolkhani and Karimnia* (both n 122 above), and *Baysakov v Ukraine*, 18 Feb 2010.

applications is a procedural defect that violates Article 3 ECHR, although it might be remedied if the merits of a case were nonetheless considered in an appeal which entailed suspensive effect. In *Abdolkhani and Karimnia*, the Turkish government violated Article 13 ECHR due to failing to respond to an asylum application, failing to notify the reasons for not responding and for deporting the applicants, and failure to ensure legal assistance.[137] Other procedural issues were considered in a decision of the European Human Rights Commission in *Hatami v Sweden*,[138] a case subsequently settled. In this case, the government rejected an asylum application, inter alia on the grounds that the applicant's story about his transit route was not credible. The Commission concluded that a government refusal to recognize a refugee due to alleged inconsistencies resulting from a short interview conducted with inadequate interpretation facilities, resulting only in a short report lacking any detail and not explained to the applicant, led to a breach of Article 3 ECHR due to inadequate procedural safeguards in the State concerned. Moreover, the Commission explicitly placed great stress on the medical evidence presented by an applicant, where it is consistent with the applicant's statements concerning torture. It is also clear that, to avoid an Article 3 violation, instead of an obsessive focus by the authorities on alleged inconsistencies concerning an applicant's travel, the asylum determination process should focus on an applicant's assertions concerning the threat of torture, derived from an applicant's 'political affiliations...and his activities, his history of detention and ill-treatment'. Finally, the Commission made the important general observation that 'complete accuracy is seldom to be expected by victims of torture'. In later cases, the Human Rights Court ruled that lack of credibility in an applicant's story regarding his or her transit should be overlooked where there was nonetheless a sufficiently strong argument that Article 3 risk would materialize upon return to the country of origin,[139] and that minor inconsistencies could not detract from the underlying credibility of the applicant, given the evidence that backed up his account of events.[140]

One decision of the Human Rights Court concerns the important issue of responsibility for asylum applications. An admissibility decision in the case of *TI v UK* concerned the application of the EU's Dublin Convention (as it then was), which in the relevant case provided that the responsible State to consider the asylum application would be Germany, not the UK.[141] The applicant argued that removal from the UK to Germany would breach Article 3 ECHR, on the grounds that Germany would in turn remove him to an unsafe country. In return, the UK argued that removal of an asylum seeker pursuant to the Dublin

---

[137] *Abdolkhani and Karimnia* (ibid). See also *Baysakov* (ibid),
[138] Report, 23 Apr 1998 (unreported), paras 96–109.   [139] *N v Finland* (n 120 above).
[140] *RC v Sweden*, 9 Mar 2010.   [141] Reports 2000-III.

Convention should not engage its responsibility under Article 3 ECHR. The Human Rights Court decisively rejected that argument:

The Court finds that the indirect removal in this case to an intermediary country, which is also a Contracting State, does not affect the responsibility of the United Kingdom to ensure that the applicant is not, as a result of its decision to expel, exposed to treatment contrary to Article 3 of the Convention. Nor can the United Kingdom rely automatically in that context on the arrangements made in the Dublin Convention concerning the attribution of responsibility between European countries for deciding asylum claims. Where States establish international organisations, or *mutatis mutandis* international agreements, to pursue co-operation in certain fields of activities, there may be implications for the protection of fundamental rights. It would be incompatible with the purpose and object of the Convention if Contracting States were thereby absolved from their responsibility under the Convention in relation to the field of activity covered by such attribution...The Court notes the comments of the UNHCR that, while the Dublin Convention may pursue laudable objectives, its effectiveness may be undermined in practice by the differing approaches adopted by Contracting States to the scope of protection offered.

The Human Rights Court has applied this judgment in the context of removals to other (non-European) transit countries, setting out a test as to the application of the rule: whether there is a legal framework providing adequate safeguards against removal to the country of origin from the third State concerned.[142] The Court has also applied the principle by analogy to removals to part of the country of origin (ie assessing whether the person concerned would be compelled to move from the 'safe' part of that country to the unsafe part).[143]

As regards removals to other EU States, the Human Rights Court has ruled that the *TI* decision 'must apply with equal force to the Dublin Regulation'. However, on the facts of the case, even though the UNHCR and some NGOs had criticized Greece's application of EU asylum legislation, a removal from the UK to Greece would not violate Article 3, because in practice the Human Rights Court was convinced that Greece would not remove an asylum seeker without a review of the case and the opportunity to apply to the Strasbourg Court to postpone the removal if necessary. Moreover, the Dublin II Regulation was part of a package of measures, with which Greece should be presumed to comply.[144] However, this issue has been reopened in a case pending before the Grand Chamber of the Court.[145]

Finally, the Strasbourg Court has briefly touched on the issue of reception conditions for asylum seekers. In its *Muslim* judgment, the Court stated that Article 8 ECHR (concerning the right to private and family life) did not go so far as to impose a general obligation on States to provide refugees with

---

[142] *Abdolkhani and Karimnia* (n 122 above), para 89. This judgment has been followed in *Tehrani v Turkey* and *Keshmiri v Turkey*, both 13 Apr 2010.   [143] *Salah Sheekh* (n 123 above), para 141.
[144] *KRS v UK*, decision of 2 Dec 2008.   [145] *MSS v Belgium and Greece*.

financial assistance to enable them to maintain a certain standard of living.[146] In that case, the applicant's situation did not appear to be so desperate as to force him to leave Turkey because it was no longer tenable. This suggests *a contrario* that an asylum seeker in a desperate situation due to deprivation of any significant state support for his or her health, welfare, or housing, coupled with a denial of access to employment, could claim that rights under Article 8 or even Article 3 were violated. The UK's House of Lords has held that Article 3 can be violated where there is a withdrawal of state support sufficient to result in such conditions.[147]

It should be stressed that protection against removal pursuant to Article 3 ECHR or other provisions of the ECHR does not necessarily guarantee that refugee status, or any other formal legal status conferring rights such as social assistance or access to employment will be conferred. In the *Ahmed* case,[148] Austria in fact withdrew any form of government support from Mr Ahmed, with the result that he wandered penniless on the streets—and ultimately committed suicide.

Finally, the Human Rights Court has also addressed the issue of detention of asylum seekers pursuant to Article 5 ECHR, and the protection of private and family life pursuant to Article 8 ECHR has implications for the admission of family members of persons in need of international protection, and for the expulsion of those persons or their family members.[149]

5.3.2. Application to EU law

The Court of Justice has ruled that the general principles of EU law include the rights guaranteed by Article 3 ECHR, including the relevant jurisprudence of the Strasbourg Court.[150] However, the Court of Justice has not yet ruled on whether the general principles incorporate a right to asylum or other form of protection from removal. Furthermore, in this area the primary law of the EU refers to the protection guaranteed by the Geneva Convention and other international treaties,[151] and the Court of Justice has duly ruled that these sources must be taken into account when interpreting EU legislation.[152] The protection guaranteed by the ECHR would be strengthened once the EU accedes to that Convention,

---

[146] See n 120 above.

[147] *R (on the application of Adam and others) v Secretary of State for the Home Department* [2005] UKHL 66.   [148] Seen 121 above.

[149] See respectively 6.3.1 and 7.3.2 below.

[150] Case C-465/07 *Elgafaji and Elgafaji* [2009] ECR I-921, referring to *NA v UK* (n 124 above).

[151] Art 78 TFEU (previously Art 63 EC).

[152] Joined Cases C-175/08, 176/08, 178/08, and 179/08 *Abdulla and others*, judgment of 2 Mar 2010 (not yet reported) and C-31/09 *Bolbol*, judgment of 17 June 2010 (not yet reported); see also the opinion of 1 June 2010 in Joined Cases C-57/09 and C-101/09 *B* and *D*, pending.

and as noted above, the Stockholm Programme also calls for the EU to consider acceding to the Geneva Convention.[153]

As for the EU's Charter of Rights, it includes the right to asylum and a ban on expulsion to face such as torture, or the death penalty;[154] the Court of Justice has also referred to the Charter in the context of asylum judgments.[155] The EU's general principles and the Charter also include rights, such as the right to dignity, that are not set out as such in the ECHR but which could be relevant to asylum issues, for example in the context of reception conditions or as a substantive ground for resisting expulsion when the right to dignity would be infringed in the destination State.[156]

5.4. The impact of other EU law

5.4.1. Asylum and EU citizens

The Protocol on asylum applications by EU citizens was initially attached to the EC Treaty by the Treaty of Amsterdam, and the Treaty of Lisbon subsequently made technical amendments to the Protocol, inter alia to refer to the EU Charter of Rights and the general principles of EU law, and to take account of the restructuring of the Treaties, by attaching the Protocol to both the revised TEU and to the TFEU. The Protocol begins with a lengthy preamble, referring to the protection of human rights guaranteed by the Treaties (and now the Charter), including the Court of Justice's jurisdiction to interpret these principles. It also refers to the obligation of Member States acceding to the EU to protect human rights and the possibility, introduced by the Treaty of Amsterdam, of suspending Member States which commit a 'serious and persistent' breach of human rights, democracy, and the rule of law.[157] Taking account of the 'special status and protection' which EU citizens have under the Treaties, and 'respect[ing] the finality and the objectives of the Geneva Convention', each Member State 'shall be regarded as' a safe country of origin by the others for 'all legal and practical purposes'.

However, an asylum application made by a national of one Member State in another 'may be taken into consideration or declared admissible for processing…only' if: the Member State of which the applicant is a citizen uses the 'national security' derogation of Article 15 ECHR after the entry into force of the Treaty of Amsterdam; or the Council or the European Council is considering punishing or has punished the applicant's Member State for human rights

---

[153] See respectively 2.3 and 5.2.3 above.

[154] Arts 18 and 19 of the Charter ([2007] OJ C 303).

[155] Judgments in *Abdulla* and *Bolbol* (n 151 above).

[156] See generally 2.3 above and in the context of asylum, S Peers, 'Human Rights, Asylum and European Community Law' (2005) 24:2 RSQ 24.   [157] See Art 7 EU.

abuses pursuant to the procedure described in the preamble to the Protocol; or 'if a Member State should so decide unilaterally', in which case it must inform the Council and presume that this application is 'manifestly unfounded' (although this presumption cannot bind the national decision-making bodies).

The background to the Protocol indicates that it is an extradition measure in disguise. Its sole purpose was to prevent Belgium from considering asylum claims from persons whom Spain wished to try for terrorist offences. However, the Protocol is couched in more general terms and it might have broader effect, particularly for a period after enlargement of the EU, when citizens of the newer Member States might still wish to make asylum claims in the old Member States because they will not have the right of free movement of workers for a transition period of up to seven years.[158] The Protocol is attached to the Treaties generally, not specifically to Title V of the TFEU, so it applies to all Member States.[159]

In a unilateral Declaration to the Treaty of Amsterdam, Belgium declared that it would use the final option and 'carry out an individual examination of any asylum request made by a national of another Member State', while a Declaration to the Treaty of Amsterdam states that the Protocol does not prevent Member States from taking organizational measures which they deem necessary to apply the Geneva Convention. In light of these provisos, the Declaration was not likely to have much effect, although there is no information available on its implementation in order to test it. It should also be noted that the Protocol is not applicable to claims for subsidiary protection, so its effect is easy to avoid for any EU citizen who wishes to apply specifically for that form of protection, rather than for recognition of refugee status, in another Member State. But in light of the changes to extradition law brought about by the European Arrest Warrant (in particular the abolition of the protection against extradition traditionally enjoyed by a State's own nationals), the objectives of the Protocol may now have been achieved by other means.[160]

The validity of the Protocol may be doubted in light of the wording of the Geneva Convention, which expressly requires the Convention to be applied on a non-discriminatory basis.[161] Although the Court of Justice does not have the jurisdiction to rule on the validity of the founding Treaties (including Protocols to the Treaties), Article 351 TFEU (previously Article 307 EC) does preserve the pre-existing obligations of Member States under prior treaties concluded with third countries, so it is still open to a national court to rule that the Protocol is inapplicable due to its incompatibility with Member States' obligations under the Convention. Although Article 351 requires Member States ultimately to amend or denounce their pre-existing treaty obligations to conform to EU rules,[162] it

---

[158] For these limitations, see, for instance, Annex V to the 2003 Accession Treaty ([2003] OJ L 236).
[159] There have been no references to the Court of Justice about the Protocol to date.
[160] See 9.5.2 below.   [161] Art 3 of the Convention.   [162] See 2.7 above.

should be noted that the Court of Justice has ruled that the basic human rights rules in EU law prevail over Article 307 EC (now Article 351 TFEU).[163]

In any event, the dubious validity of the Protocol in light of the Geneva Convention entails a requirement to interpret it narrowly, with the consequence that a person holding the dual citizenship of a Member State and a non-Member State would not be prevented by the Protocol from relying on his or her non-Member State nationality to apply for asylum.[164] This derogation from the normal rule that a person with the dual nationality of a Member State and a non-Member State is not able to rely on his or her non-EU nationality is justified also by the broader human rights context.[165] Anyway, there can surely be no doubt that in the event that a person *loses* the nationality of a Member State (and does not retain or reacquire the nationality of another Member State),[166] then the Protocol no longer presents any bar to applying for asylum in a Member State.[167] Finally, there is nothing in the Protocol to question the validity of refugee status that was *already* granted to an EU citizen before the entry into force of the Treaty of Amsterdam, or (in respect of nationals of newer Member States) before the entry into force of the 2003 and 2005 Accession Treaties, or any future accession treaties. On the other hand, the position of a third-country national who obtains refugee status and then later acquires the citizenship of a Member State is addressed by a specific rule in the Geneva Convention.[168]

5.4.2. Other issues

The 1971 Regulation on social security for EU citizens and their family members who exercised free movement rights also expressly covered refugees and stateless persons (some of whom will be beneficiaries of subsidiary protection status in Member States).[169] In 2001, the Court of Justice ruled that this provision of the Regulation was valid, but stated that the Regulation only applied to refugees who

---

[163] See Joined Cases C-402/05 P and C-415/05 P *Kadi and Al Barakaat* [2008] ECR I-6351, para 304. In that case, the Court was rejecting the argument that a pre-existing treaty obligation took preference over human rights obligations; but by analogy the judgment must also mean that an EU obligation for a Member State to denounce its pre-existing treaty obligations cannot apply where that EU obligation would lead to a breach of human rights principles.

[164] He or she would surely still have to show, however, that the criteria for the refugee definition were not satisfied as regards *either* State of which he or she was a citizen.

[165] See Case C-179/98 *Mesbah* [1999] ECR I-7955 and the discussion in 6.4.1 below.

[166] See Case C-135/08 *Rottmann*, judgment of 2 Mar 2010, not yet reported, discussed ibid.

[167] Presumably, in such a case, the responsibility criteria could only take into account factors which post-dated the *de jure* loss of EU citizenship by the person concerned.

[168] See Art 1.C(3) of the Convention, which provides for refugee status to cease in the case that a person acquires the nationality of another country and enjoys the protection of that country. See also Art 11(1)(c) of the qualification Directive (Dir 2004/83, [2004] OJ L 304/12).

[169] Reg 1408/71 ([1971] OJ L 149/2). See further 6.4.2 below.

had moved between Member States.[170] Subsequently, the 1971 Regulation was replaced as from 1 May 2010 by revised legislation, which also changed the rules as regards refugees and stateless persons.[171]

In the meantime, as from 1 June 2003, EU immigration legislation extended most of the 1971 Regulation on social security coordination for persons exercising free movement rights to third-country nationals other than refugees or stateless persons,[172] with the consequence that all persons with subsidiary protection or temporary protection have also been covered by the 1971 rules as from that date. However, these other categories of third-country nationals are not yet covered by the free movement rules applicable from 1 May 2010, until the adoption of legislation to that effect;[173] the Council adopted its first-reading position on the proposed legislation to this end in July 2010.[174]

Of course, in the absence of any right for refugees or persons with subsidiary protection to move between Member States,[175] the application of the social security rules is of limited relevance. However, it should be recalled that EU employers have the right to post *any* third-country national employees to carry out a contract in another Member State,[176] regardless of any protection status they may have, as long as the employees are legally and habitually employed, so the application of the EU social security rules is at least relevant to refugees and persons with subsidiary or temporary protection who are posted workers.

An important question is the overlap between refugee status (or other protection status) and status under EU free movement legislation (whether as an EU citizen or the family member of an EU citizen) or under an EU association agreement. The Court of Justice has confirmed that failed asylum seekers (and presumably also failed applicants for subsidiary protection, persons whose protection claims are pending, or persons whose protection claims have been successful) can benefit from EU free movement law if they become a family member of an EU citizen, even if their entry onto the territory was never authorized or became unauthorized following the failure of their asylum application.[177] Also, at least as

---

[170] Joined Cases C-95/99 to 98/99 *Khalil and others* and C-180/99 *Addou* [2001] ECR I-7413. See case note by S Peers (2002) 39 CMLRev 1395.

[171] Reg 883/2004, [2004] OJ L 166/1. This Regulation only applied as from the date of effect of a subsequent implementing Regulation, namely Reg 987/2009, [2009] OJ L 284/1 (see Art 91 of Reg 883/2004, and subsequently Art 97 of Reg 987/2009 on the latter Regulation's date of entry into effect).

[172] Reg 859/2003 ([2003] OJ L 124/1). See 6.8 below.

[173] See Art 90(1)(a) of Reg 883/2004 and Art 96(1)(a) of Reg 987/2009 (both n 170 above).

[174] Council doc 11160/10, 16 July 2010. This Regulation still has to be agreed with the EP.

[175] They are excluded, for now, from the scope of the Directive on long-term residents (Dir 2003/109, [2004] OJ L 16/44), until and unless the 2007 proposal to extend that Directive to cover them is adopted (COM (2007) 298, 6 June 2007): see 6.7 below.

[176] See Cases C-43/93 *Van der Elst* [1994] ECR I-3803; C-445/03 *Commission v Luxembourg* [2004] ECR I-10191; C-244/04 *Commission v Germany* [2006] ECR I-885; C-168/04 *Commission v Austria* [2006] ECR I-9041; and C-219/08 *Commission v Belgium* [2009] ECR I-9213. For further details of the principle, see 6.4.4 below.   [177] Case C-127/08 *Metock* [2008] ECR I-6241.

regards the EU–Turkey association agreement, a refugee (and the refugee's family members) can rely on that agreement,[178] as can an asylum seeker whose asylum application was potentially subject to the rules in the Dublin Convention (before its replacement by a Regulation) concerning responsibility for applications.[179] It is arguable by analogy that in the absence of anything to the contrary, there is nothing to preclude an individual relying on either protection status or the status under free movement law or an EU association agreement, depending on which status is more favourable.[180]

5.5. Uniform status

5.5.1. Current qualification Directive

Directive 2004/83 on the definition of 'refugee' and subsidiary protection status and the content of that status was adopted in April 2004,[181] Member States had to implement the Directive by 10 October 2006,[182] but the Commission had to bring cases against eight Member States for failure to implement the Directive on time. In four of these cases, the Court of Justice gave judgment against Member States,[183] while the Commission withdrew the other four complaints, presumably after tardy compliance by the Member States concerned.[184] Furthermore, there have been four references from national courts on the interpretation of the Directive.[185] The Commission has reported on the implementation of the

---

[178] Case C-337/07 *Altun* [2008] ECR I-10323.

[179] Case C-16/05 *Tum and Dari* [2007] ECR I-7415.

[180] The point was also relevant in *Khalil* and *Addou*, n 169 above, but was not referred by the national court.

[181] [2004] OJ L 304/12. All references in this subsection are to the Directive unless otherwise indicated. On the Directive, see UNHCR, *Asylum in the European Union, A study on the implementation of the Qualification Directive*, Nov 2007 (<http://www.unhcr.org/cgi-bin/texis/vtx/refworld/rwmain?docid=473050632&page=search>); ELENA/ECRE, *The impact of the EU Qualification Directive on International protection*, Oct 2008 (<http://www.ecre.org/files/ECRE_QD_study_full.pdf>); K Zwaan, ed, *The Qualification Directive: Central themes, Problem issues, and Implementation in selected Member States* (Wolf Legal Publishers, 2007); J McAdam, 'The European Union Qualification Directive: The Creation of a Subsidiary Protection Regime' (2005) 17 IJRL 461; MT Gil-Bazo, 'Refugee Status and Subsidiary Protection under EC Law: The Qualification Directive and the Right to Be Granted Asylum', in A Baldaccini, E Guild, and H Toner, eds, *Whose Freedom, Security and Justice? EU Immigration and Asylum Law and Policy* (Hart, 2007), 229; and H Battjes, *European Asylum Law and International Law* (Martinus Nijhoff, 2006), ch 5.

[182] Art 38(1). All references in this section are to Dir 2004/83 unless otherwise indicated.

[183] Cases: C-256/08 *Commission v UK*, judgment of 30 Apr 2009; C-293/08 *Commission v Finland*, judgment of 5 Feb 2009; C-322/08 *Commission v Sweden*, judgment of 14 Jun 2009; and C-272/08 *Commission v Spain*, judgment of 9 July 2009 (all unreported).

[184] Cases: C-190/08 *Commission v Netherlands*; C-191/08 *Commission v Portugal*; C-220/08 *Commission v Greece*; and C-269/08 *Commission v Malta*.

[185] Cases: C-465/07 *Elgafaji and Elgafaji* [2009] ECR I-921; C-175/08, 176/08, 178/08, and 179/08 *Abdulla and others*, judgment of 2 Mar 2010 (not yet reported); C-31/09 *Bolbol*, judgment of

Directive (the 'implementation report'),[186] and furthermore the impact assessment accompanying its 2009 proposal for amendments to the Directive (the '2009 impact assessment') contains some additional information on the application of the Directive in practice, and so is also referred to below.[187] A key general point is that despite the adoption of the Directive, there are still significant divergences in recognition rates between Member States,[188] although neither the implementation report nor the impact assessment assess whether or not the differences in recognition rates have at least been *reduced* since the implementation of the Directive,[189] or whether recognition rates in general have increased due to the Directive.

First of all, as a general point, the Court of Justice has ruled that as regards refugee status, the Directive's preamble makes clear 'that the Geneva Convention constitutes the cornerstone of the international legal regime for the protection of refugees' and the rules on refugee status in the Directive 'were adopted to guide the competent authorities of the Member States in the application of that convention on the basis of common concepts and criteria'.[190] So the Directive must be interpreted 'while respecting the Geneva Convention and the other relevant treaties' referred to in Article 63(1) EC (now Article 78(1) TFEU), as well as the relevant provisions of the EU's Charter of Fundamental Rights in particular.[191] The Court has also touched upon the relationship between the two different systems of international protection provided for in the Directive.[192]

Moving on to the substance of the Directive, Chapter I sets out general provisions, including definitions and permission for Member States to apply more favourable rules, provided that they are 'compatible' with the Directive.[193] The interpretation of that provision, an issue which is relevant generally to EU asylum legislation, is discussed further above.[194]

Chapter II then sets out standard rules on assessment of applications,[195] which are applicable to claims for either refugee or subsidiary protection status. Member States *may* require the applicant to submit all the elements needed to substantiate the application, including the applicant's statements and all elements at the applicant's disposal, although it is the job of Member States (in cooperation with the

---

17 June 2010 (not yet reported); and C-57/09 and C-101/09 *B* and *D*, pending (opinion of 1 June 2010).

[186] COM (2010) 314, 16 June 2010.

[187] SEC (2009) 1373, 21 Oct 2009. On the content of the proposal to amend the Directive, see 5.5.2 below.

[188] See Annex 13 to the 2009 impact assessment and the conclusions to the implementation report.

[189] Note that the evidence in the 2009 impact assessment is that the rate of secondary movements of asylum seekers have not reduced following the implementation of the qualification Directive.

[190] *Abdulla*, (n 184 above), para 52, and *Bolbol* (*idem*), para 37.

[191] *Abdulla*, paras 53 and 54, and *Bolbol*, para 38 (ibid).

[192] Paras 77–80 of the *Abdulla* judgment, ibid; see the comments in 5.7 below.

[193] Arts 1–3.   [194] See 5.2.4.   [195] Arts 4–8.

applicant) to consider that application.[196] The Member State's assessment 'must be carried out on an individual basis' and 'includes' taking account of the relevant facts in the country of origin; the statements and documentation submitted by the applicant; the position and circumstances of the applicant (including gender); whether the applicant's activities since leaving the country of origin were for the 'sole or main purpose of creating the conditions' for an application; and whether the applicant could 'reasonably be expected' to seek protection in another country where he or she could obtain citizenship.[197] If the applicant has been subjected to prior persecution or serious harm as defined in the Directive, or 'direct threats' of such action, that is a 'serious indication' that that claim is well-founded.[198] The implementation report is critical of Member States' divergences and errors when transposing this provision. In the *Abdulla* judgment, the Court of Justice clarified the application of this principle when refugee status ceased on the grounds of change of a circumstances (on which, see further below), but where arguably there was now a different set of circumstances in the country of origin justifying the continuation of that status. If, in contrast, the refugee was arguing that the original circumstances had not changed enough for the cessation principle to apply, then the national authorities and courts concerned had to apply the cessation rules instead.[199]

The Directive provides that a protection need may arise *sur place*, in other words following the applicant's departure from the country of origin, but Member States may provide that applicants who file a subsequent application shall not normally be granted refugee status if they have created the circumstances for that status themselves since they left the country of origin.[200] It also requires a fundamental change to the traditional interpretation of the Geneva Convention applied in some Member States (in particular France and Germany) by stating that the 'actors of persecution' need not be the State, but may also be private parties, if it can be 'demonstrated' that the State, or parties controlling the State, is 'unable or unwilling' to provide protection against non-state agents.[201] The implementation report criticizes several Member States' restrictive application of this rule.

Next, the Directive addresses the issue of 'actors of protection', stating that parties, including international organizations, controlling all or part of a State can provide protection, such bodies 'take reasonable steps to prevent the persecution or suffering of serious harm, inter alia, by operating an effective legal system for the detection, prosecution and punishment of acts constituting persecution or serious harm, and the applicant has access to such protection'; Council acts can give guidance as to whether effective protection is provided by such bodies.[202] The Commission's 2009 impact assessment indicates that there are wide divergences between the Member States as regards the application of this principle,[203]

---

[196] Art 4(1) and (2).   [197] Art 4(3).   [198] Art 4(4).
[199] Paras 94–100 of the judgment (n 184 above).   [200] Art 5.   [201] Art 6.
[202] Art 7.   [203] See Annex 5 to the 2009 impact assessment.

and the implementation report criticizes those Member States which consider that clans, tribes, or NGOs can offer such protection, because 'in practice, protection provided by these actors proves to be ineffective or of short duration'.

In the *Abdulla* judgment, which concerned the situation in Iraq, the Court of Justice stated that 'the Directive does not preclude the protection from being guaranteed by international organisations, including protection ensured through the presence of a multinational force in the territory of the third country'. The adequacy of the protection provided must be verified on an individual basis, considering 'in particular, the conditions of operation of, on the one hand, the institutions, authorities and security forces and, on the other, all groups or bodies of the third country which may, by their action or inaction, be responsible for acts of persecution against the recipient of refugee status if he returns to that country', as well as the application of the law in practice in that country and 'the extent to which basic human rights are guaranteed' there.[204]

There is also an optional 'internal protection alternative', which may apply where there is a risk-free part of the country of origin where the applicant 'can reasonably be expected to stay'.[205] Although Member States must have regard to the general conditions in that country and to the applicant's personal circumstances, the principle can apply in spite of 'technical obstacles to return'. According to the 2009 impact assessment and the implementation report, there are again great differences in the national application of this principle, as well as some errors applying the conditions for the application of this rule. While only eight Member States apply the exception relating to technical obstacles to return, there are also differences in how they apply this rule.[206]

The rules on qualification for refugee status are set out in Chapter III.[207] 'Acts of persecution' are defined by reference to the severity of the acts, and there is a non-exhaustive list of the forms such acts can take, along with an obligation to find a link between the acts and the grounds of persecution.[208] Member States take different approaches as to whether the Directive applies when private groups persecute individuals for reasons *not* based on the Geneva Convention, but where States then *fail to protect* the persons concerned on 'Convention grounds'.[209]

To constitute persecution, the acts in question must be 'sufficiently serious by their nature or repetition as to constitute a severe violation of basic human rights', particularly the non-derogable rights under Article 15 ECHR, or be 'an accumulation of various measures, including violations of human rights which [are] sufficiently severe' as to fall within the first criterion. Six examples are given: acts

---

[204] Paras 70–75 of the judgment (n 184 above).   [205] Art 8.

[206] See Annex 6 to the 2009 impact assessment, and point 5.1.5 of the implementation report. See also the ECHR jurisprudence discussed in 5.3.1 above.   [207] Arts 9–12.

[208] Art 9(2) and (3). According to the implementation report, some Member States do not insist on a causal link; this is (rightly) regarded as an acceptable higher standard for the persons concerned.

[209] See Annex 18 to the 2009 impact assessment, point 1.1.

of violence; legal or similar measures which are discriminatory; disproportionate or discriminatory prosecution or punishment; denial of judicial redress resulting in the same outcome; prosecution or punishment for refusal to serve in a military conflict which would lead to acts falling within the scope of the exclusion clause; and 'acts of a gender-specific or child-specific nature'.[210]

As for the grounds of persecution set out in Article 1.A of the Geneva Convention, the Directive sets out detailed definitions of the concepts of 'race', 'religion', 'nationality', 'particular social group', and 'political opinion'.[211] For the 'particular social group' ground to apply, it must be shown 'in particular' that the group members have an innate characteristic, common background, or characteristic that it would be unjust to force to change *and* that the group has a distinct identity; sexual orientation might be a common characteristic but this cannot apply where the acts would be criminal under the 'national law of the Member States'. The prospect of 'gender' as an example of social group is addressed by stating that 'gender-related aspects can be considered, without by themselves alone creating a presumption' of persecution. According to the 2009 impact assessment and the implementation report, Member States are split as to whether these criteria to define a 'particular social group' are alternative or cumulative, and take different approaches as regards gender-based persecution.[212] As for 'political opinion', it includes any opinion related to the *persecutors*, not just the policy of a *state*.

Refugee status shall cease in particular where there has been a change of circumstances in the country of origin,[213] and in such cases, Member States 'shall have regard to whether the change of circumstances is of such a significant and non-temporary nature that the refugee's fear of persecution can no longer be regarded as well-founded'.[214] The implementation report stated that some Member States were less generous—or more generous—than the Directive provides for on this point. However, the Directive does not contain a reference to the provisions in Article 1.C(5) and (6) of the Geneva Convention, which specifies that the cessation clause does not apply, for persons who were covered by prior international arrangements concerning refugees, where there are 'compelling reasons arising out of previous persecution' which justify a continuation of refugee status even though the criteria for cessation of status otherwise apply. The 2009 impact assessment was not able to examine whether this proviso was applied in practice or not, despite this omission in the Directive.[215]

The issue of cessation was addressed by the Court of Justice in the *Abdulla* judgment, which concerned Iraqi refugees who were potentially subject to cessation of refugee status due to the changed situation in Iraq after the removal of

---

[210] Art 9(1) and (2).   [211] Art 10.   [212] See Annex 7 to the 2009 impact assessment.
[213] Art 11(1). See Art 1.C of the Geneva Convention (5.3.1 above).   [214] Art 11(2).
[215] See Annex 18 to the 2009 impact assessment, point 1.2.

Saddam Hussein's regime.[216] According to the Court of Justice, the test for the application of the cessation principle is the same test as that applicable to the original determination of the well-foundedness of the claim for recognition as a refugee.[217] If the person concerned argues that, following the change in circumstances leading to the cessation of the *original* refugee status, there are now other factors indicating that a *separate* threat of persecution now exists in the country of origin, the substance of this claim must be considered as far as possible in the same way that an initial application for recognition of refugee status must be considered.[218] As for the question as to whether the change of circumstances is sufficiently significant and non-temporary, the Court ruled that this principle applied 'when the factors which formed the basis of the refugee's fear of persecution may be regarded as having been permanently eradicated'. Therefore, '[t]he assessment of the significant and non-temporary nature of the change of circumstances thus implies that there are no well-founded fears of being exposed to acts of persecution amounting to severe violations of basic human rights within the meaning of Article 9(1) of the Directive'.[219]

The Directive provides for exclusion from refugee status, first of all by explicit reference to Article 1.D of the Geneva Convention,[220] excluding persons receiving protection or assistance from UN organs other than the UNHCR, but also rephrasing the rule from Article 1.D of the Convention that '[w]hen such protection or assistance has ceased for any reason, without the position of such persons being definitely settled in accordance with the relevant resolutions adopted by the General Assembly of the United Nations, these persons shall ipso facto be entitled to the benefits of this Directive'. In practice, this exclusion relates only to Palestinian refugees, and a national court requested the Court of Justice to interpret it in the *Bolbol* case.[221]

According to the judgment of the Court of Justice in this case, since this rule 'must be...construed narrowly', a person is not covered by this provision unless he or she *actually* received protection or assistance from the relevant UN agency, rather than merely being *entitled* to receive it. However, the judgment confirmed that Article 1.D of the Geneva Convention would apply not just to persons displaced by the original 1948 conflict regarding Israel and Palestine, but also the 1967 conflict and any further conflict, and could apply not just to persons actually registered with the relevant UN body, but also to persons who were receiving benefits from that body de facto. An application for refugee status by a person not covered by this exclusion must be assessed in accordance with the normal rules in the Directive. The Court did not comment on several other issues examined

---

[216] See n 184 above.   [217] Paras 55–71 of the judgment, ibid.
[218] Paras 84–91 of the judgment, ibid.   [219] Para 73 of the judgment, ibid.
[220] Art 12(1)(a). On Art 1.D of the Convention, see 5.3.1 above. The Directive also contains a provision corresponding to the exclusion clause in Art 1.E of the Convention (Art 12(1)(b)).
[221] Case C-31/09, n 184 above.

in the opinion of the Advocate General in this case, who had argued that: the reference to cessation of assistance means that the person concerned is no longer in the relevant geographical area, and has ceased to receive assistance otherwise than of his or her own volition; and the reference to the 'benefits' of the Directive means the automatic recognition as being a refugee and grant of refugee status, ie without being subject to an asylum procedure.

Another provision in the Directive corresponds broadly to the exclusion clauses of Article 1.F of the Geneva Convention,[222] but includes several elements not expressly found in Article 1.F, in particular the exclusion of those who have committed 'particularly cruel' crimes with an allegedly political objective and of those who 'instigate or otherwise participate' in Article 1.F activities.[223] The interpretation of this provision is pending before the Court of Justice in the *B and D* cases,[224] which ask the Court whether a person is subject to the exclusion clause if he or she is a member of an organization which the Council has determined to be a terrorist entity pursuant to the relevant rules,[225] and has actively supported that organization's armed struggle, along with further questions connected to the interpretation of the exclusion clause.

According to the Advocate General's opinion in this case, the exclusion for committing a 'serious non-political crime' requires a high degree of seriousness, to be assessed on a case-by-case basis, taking into account such issues as the extent of the damage caused and the severity of the applicable penalty. The threshold set by an extradition treaty was not decisive on the latter point. As to the 'political' nature of the crime, this should be assessed by examining the motive for it, subject also to a principle of proportionality—ie the crime should not be regarded as 'political' if the (violent) means used were disproportionate to the political objective. This justifies the specific clause on 'particularly cruel' actions in the Directive, which should apply where the acts violate international human rights or humanitarian law, or target civilians. As for the exclusion for 'acts contrary to the aims and principles of United Nations', the opinion argues that this concept is vague, can only apply in exceptional cases where action threatens the world community, but can apply to persons other than those controlling the State.

Applying these principles to terrorist acts, the Advocate General argues that the EU's Framework Decision on the definition of terrorism should not be applied as such,[226] and that an EU listing of a group as a 'terrorist' group should not as such be decisive. Rather the exclusions apply to a person who implements indiscriminate violence against civilians or persons who have no connection with

---

[222] Art 12(2) and (3); on Art 1.F of the Convention, see 5.3.1 above.

[223] Also, the scope of the exclusion for 'serious non-political crime' is more precisely defined by reference to acts committed prior to obtaining a residence permit based on refugee status; and the exclusion for acts contrary to UN principles is defined by reference to specific provisions of the UN Charter.   [224] Joined Cases C-57/09 and C-101/09, opinion of 1 June 2010.

[225] On those rules, see 12.4.5 below.   [226] On that measure, see 10.5 below.

the objectives pursued. Furthermore, the individual responsibility of the person concerned must always be established; an affiliation to a group which commits such activities is not sufficient. The Opinion also argues that there is no requirement to assess whether the person concerned still constitutes a danger, and that the application of the exclusion clause in individual cases must be in accordance with the principle of proportionality.

Member States are obliged to grant refugee status to persons meeting the definition of 'refugee',[227] but are obliged to 'revoke, end or refuse to renew' the refugee status of any refugee whose refugee status has ceased, applicable to all applications filed after the Directive entered into force.[228] The Court of Justice has, however, ruled that it will still exercise jurisdiction as regards the cessation provision of the Directive even if a Member State decides to apply the cessation rules to persons who obtained refugee status before that date.[229]

Also, Member States must revoke, end, or refuse to renew refugee status if it is 'established' that a person is subject to the exclusion clause or misrepresented or omitted key facts which were decisive for the grant of refugee status.[230] They *may* end refugee status if a person falls within the scope of the exceptions to the *non-refoulement* rule set out in Article 33(2) of the Geneva Convention, but in that case certain rights 'set out in or similar to' those in the Geneva Convention would still apply, as regards non-discrimination, religion, court access, education, restrictions on expulsion, and *non-refoulement*.[231] This would entail the loss of Geneva Convention rights to protection of property; the right of association; access to employment, self-employment and the professions; housing; public assistance; social security; freedom of movement; and travel documents. The implementation report concludes that some Member States do not secure these rights in such cases.

Next, the definition of subsidiary protection provides that the risk of 'serious harm' necessary to establish a subsidiary protection claim is defined by reference to the death penalty or execution, or to torture or other inhuman or degrading treatment or punishment, or to a 'serious and individual threat to a civilian's life or person by reason of indiscriminate violence in situations of international or internal armed conflict'.[232] The latter provision was interpreted by the Court of Justice in the *Elgafaji* judgment,[233] concerning the position of Iraqi nationals who feared violent retaliation due to their association with the American forces occupying Iraq. This judgment confirmed that this provision has a separate field of application from the other two aspects of the definition of subsidiary protection,

---

[227] Art 13.
[228] Art 14(1). In accordance with Art 39, the Directive entered into force on 20 Oct 2004. The point must be demonstrated on an individual basis (Art 14(2)), and is subject to procedural rights set out in the asylum procedures Directive (see 5.7 below).
[229] Judgment in *Abdulla* (n 184 above), paras 45–50.   [230] Art 14(3).
[231] Art 14(4)–(6).   [232] Art 15.   [233] See n 184 above.

given that its application was more general (as regards the types of violence and the circumstances in which the violence takes place) and also that the violence in question 'may extend to people irrespective of their personal circumstances'.[234] The Court defined the term 'individual' as meaning that it covered:[235]

... harm to civilians irrespective of their identity, where the degree of indiscriminate violence characterising the armed conflict taking place—assessed by the competent national authorities before which an application for subsidiary protection is made, or by the courts of a Member State to which a decision refusing such an application is referred—reaches such a high level that substantial grounds are shown for believing that a civilian, returned to the relevant country or, as the case may be, to the relevant region, would, solely on account of his presence on the territory of that country or region, face a real risk of being subject to the serious threat referred in Article 15(c) of the Directive.

The Court went on to clarify that although risks to which the population of a country is exposed to do not *normally* constitute 'serious harm', this left open the 'possibility of an exceptional situation which would be characterised by such a high degree of risk that substantial grounds would be shown for believing that that person would be subject individually to the risk in question'.[236] However, this judgment does make clear that there has to be a degree of individual, rather than general risk, concluded that 'the more the applicant is able to show that he is specifically affected by reason of factors particular to his personal circumstances, the lower the level of indiscriminate violence required for him to be eligible for subsidiary protection.'[237]

Subsidiary protection can cease in essentially the same circumstances as refugee status.[238] As for exclusion from subsidiary protection status,[239] the Directive is wider in scope than Article 1.F of the Geneva Convention. Along with the exclusions for, for example war crimes, and acts against the principles of the UN, persons must be excluded where they have 'committed a serious crime' without geographical limitation, in place of exclusion for committing a 'serious non-political crime' prior to admission, or where they are considered 'a danger to the community or to the security' of that Member State. The rule on 'participation' or 'instigation' also applies. Moreover, Member States may also exclude persons who have committed *petty crimes*, if they would be punishable by imprisonment in that Member State and if the person in question fled to avoid imposition of sanctions.[240] There is no link made with the possibility of disproportionate or

---

[234] Para 34 of the judgment.   [235] Para 35 of the judgment.

[236] Paras 36 and 37 of the judgment.   [237] Paras 38 and 39 of the judgment.

[238] Art 16. Presumably, therefore, the case law on Art 11 is relevant by analogy (see *Abdulla and others*, discussed above).

[239] Art 17. Presumably, the case law on Art 12(2) is relevant by analogy, to the extent that the two provisions correspond (see the opinion in the pending *B and D* cases, discussed above).

[240] According to the implementation report, about half of the Member States apply this exception.

discriminatory punishment. Member States are obliged to revoke subsidiary protection status where the cessation or mandatory exclusion clauses apply, although revocation is only optional where the 'petty crime' ground applies.[241] Also, there is no 'fallback' in the Directive for persons with subsidiary protection status who lose that status.[242]

As for the content of status, Member States may reduce benefits to persons who created their refugee or subsidiary protection status by their actions after leaving the country of origin.[243] According to the Commission's 2009 impact assessment and the implementation report, only three Member States apply this provision.[244] Beneficiaries of refugee or subsidiary protection status must be given information about their status.[245] Member States are obliged to apply the non-refoulement principle 'in accordance with their international obligations'; they can refoule a refugee, '[w]here not prohibited by [those] international obligations' on the grounds set out in Article 33(2) of the Geneva Convention. In such a case, Member States can revoke or refuse to renew the refugee's residence permit.[246]

A key issue in the Directive is the possibility for Member States to distinguish between beneficiaries of subsidiary protection and persons with refugee status, as regards the content of the rights which Member States must guarantee.[247] Member States are obliged to ensure 'family unity', and family members can claim the content of refugee or subsidiary protection status as set out in the Directive,[248] although Member States may 'define the conditions' applicable to family members of persons with subsidiary protection status.[249] Residence permits for refugees must be for at least three years and renewable, but permits for their family members may be valid for a lesser period. Persons with subsidiary protection should get renewable residence permits with at least one year's validity. Residence permits can be refused where there are 'compelling reasons of national security or public order'.[250]

Refugees have the right to a Convention travel document, except again for 'compelling reasons of national security or public order'. Persons with subsidiary protection must be given, subject to the same proviso, 'documents which enable

---

[241] Art 19.   [242] Compare Art 19 to Art 14(6).   [243] Art 20(6) and (7).

[244] Annex 18 to the impact assessment, point 1.3.   [245] Art 22.   [246] Art 21.

[247] On the approaches of Member States to this issue, see Annex 8 to the 2009 impact assessment.

[248] Art 22. 'Family members' are defined in Art 2(h). It should be recalled that the EU's family reunion Dir gives refugees a right to family reunion (see 6.6 below). On the issue of family members of refugees, etc see H Lambert, 'The European Court of Human Rights and the Right of Refugees and Other Persons in Need of Protection to Family Reunion' (1999) 11 IJRL 427, and S Peers, 'EC Law on Family Members of Persons Seeking or Receiving International Protection' in P Shah, ed, *The Challenge of Asylum to Legal Systems* (Cavendish, 2005), 83.

[249] According to the 2009 impact assessment, only one Member State (Poland) applies this rule (Annex 18, point 1.4).   [250] Art 24.

them to travel, at least when serious humanitarian reasons arise that require their presence in another State'.[251]

As for employment and self-employment, it must be authorized subject to national rules for refugees or beneficiaries of subsidiary protection immediately. Member States have an option to apply priority labour-market rules for a limited (but undefined) period to persons with subsidiary protection.[252] Education for minors with status must be offered on the same basis as nationals, but access to general education for adults must be offered only on the same basis as for legally resident third-country nationals.[253] There are special rules for the protection of unaccompanied minors.[254] Access to social assistance and health care must be offered on the same basis as nationals, with a possible limit to 'core benefits' for persons with subsidiary protection, but access to housing and freedom of movement in the host Member State must be offered on the same basis as for other third-country nationals.[255] Member States must admit refugees to integration programmes, but this is optional for persons with subsidiary protection status.[256]

The Directive raises a number of legal issues. There is no express wording in the Directive setting out its temporal scope, except as regards cessation of status; it seems obvious in light of that clause that the Directive applies to the exclusion, revocation, or *refoulement* of any persons who already have status at the time of its transposition.[257] But this leaves three issues open: the examination of claims by all those persons who had an application *pending* (including applications on appeal) at the time of the transposition of the Directive;[258] the application of the Directive to persons who already had some form of protection status at the time of the transposition, but who might argue in light of the Directive that they should be 'upgraded' to a different status; and the application of the Directive to persons who already had a protection status at the time of transposition,[259] where that status conferred fewer benefits upon them than those set out in the Directive.

In light of the objective of harmonizing standards within the context of a Common European Asylum System,[260] including the avoidance of 'secondary movements' of asylum seekers (who could include persons who already have

---

[251] Art 25. According to the 2009 impact assessment, only three Member States have made use of this proviso (Annex 18, point 1.4).

[252] Art 26. The draft Directive on third-country national workers would also confer equal treatment rights on family members of refugees and persons with subsidiary protection, in the latest version of that Directive (see 6.5.1 below).   [253] Art 27.

[254] Art 30. See now the action plan on unaccompanied minors (COM (2010) 213, 6 May 2010).

[255] Arts 28, 29, 31, and 32.   [256] Art 33.   [257] Arts 14(1) and 19(1).

[258] This point logically applies *mutatis mutandis* to cases where a dispute over a decision to revoke, end, or refuse to renew status is pending (Arts 14 and 19 of the Directive). It could also apply to those whose prior application was definitively rejected, without receiving any form of alternative status.

[259] This point applies *mutatis mutandis* to family members (see Art 23, discussed below).

[260] See points 1, 2, 4, 6, 7, 17, 18, 24, and 25 of the preamble.

protection in a Member State),[261] along with the objective of respecting and ensuring human rights,[262] and by *a contrario* reasoning from the temporal scope provisions of the Directive itself,[263] and from other EU legislation on asylum procedures, responsibility, and temporary protection,[264] the Directive should apply to all such cases.[265] The basic principle that new legislation applies to pending procedures unless otherwise indicated has been expressly confirmed by the Court of Justice to apply to EU immigration and asylum law.[266]

As for the substance of the Directive, first of all, as with other provisions of EU immigration and asylum law, the reference to national law to define the conditions of a benefit should not be taken as a carte blanche for Member States to do as they wish; such conditions cannot make the rights conferred by the Directive impossible or excessively difficult to apply.[267] Also, while there is no reference to procedural rights as regards access to benefits, the general principles of EU law and the EU Charter of Fundamental Rights confer procedural rights in respect of any benefits which EU law confers.[268] Furthermore, while there is no express protection against expulsion of refugees, persons with subsidiary protection, or their family members, such protection (including related procedural rights) should be seen as a corollary of the right to have a residence permit granted and renewed except where highly limited substantive grounds for refusal exist.[269] In any event, Article 8 ECHR will protect persons who are established in the territory against removal.[270]

The Directive's provisions on the definition of status contains a relatively liberal approach to the definition of protection. But this was at the expense of stronger cessation and exclusion clauses, the latter of which arguably contradicts the Geneva Convention, and the creation of a concept of 'revocation' of status. In particular, the 'revocation' clause permits Member States to circumvent the *Chahal* ruling of the European Court of Human Rights, which held that Article 3 ECHR may prevent the removal of a person within the scope of the exceptions to *non-refoulement* in Article 33(2) of the Geneva Convention.[271] According to the Directive, certain limited protection would still apply to such persons,

---

[261] Point 7 in the preamble; this issue is relevant to 'upgrades' between statuses and the argument for increasing standards within each status. As discussed below, the Eurodac Regulation makes express reference to the issue of refugees recognized in one Member State possibly applying for asylum in another (5.8.3 below).   [262] Point 10 in the preamble.

[263] See Arts 14(1) and 19(1).   [264] See 5.6, 5.7, and 5.8 below.

[265] For more detailed arguments, see the second edition of this book, at 331–334 and, by analogy, 6.6 below.   [266] Case C-357/09 PPU *Kadzoev*, 30 Nov 2009, not yet reported.

[267] See further ch 1 of S Peers and N Rogers, eds, *EU Immigration and Asylum Law: Text and Commentary* (1st edn, Martinus Nijhoff, 2006).

[268] See further ch 5 of Peers and Rogers (ibid).

[269] Procedural rights are a corollary of substantive rights in EU law: for example, see Case C-136/03 *Dorr and Unal* [2005] ECR I-4759. In any event, Art 32 of the Geneva Convention limits expulsion of refugees lawfully in the territory.   [270] See 6.3.1 below.

[271] See 5.3.1 above.

so while (in accordance with *Chahal*) they could stay in the country, Member States could eliminate their rights to move, earn an income, receive benefits, or obtain housing. The risk is that it will be effectively impossible for these persons to survive—as seen in the *Ahmed* case.[272]

As for the content of status, various vague provisions leave some possibility for Member States to provide for a low level of protection, particularly for persons with subsidiary protection and to their family members. For refugees, the Directive is in accordance with the minimum standards in the Geneva Convention, but at least it should be easier to enforce those standards in the form of a Directive. For persons with subsidiary protection, any binding text is an improvement on the previous position at international or EU level, but the low standards in the Directive as regards the level of benefits for persons with subsidiary protection and their family members are disappointing, and arguably breach the ECHR ban on non-discrimination in regard to the rights protected by the Convention (taking Article 14 ECHR together with Article 3 ECHR) as well as the principle of equality protected as one of the general principles of EU law.

5.5.2. Proposal for amendment

In October 2009, the Commission made a proposal for a second-phase Directive on qualification procedures, which would recast the current Directive (ie amend it and then repeal the existing Directive, replacing it with the consolidated text including the amendments).[273] So far the EP and Council have not reached agreement on the text of this Directive, but the proposal is summarized in the following paragraphs.

First of all, the 2009 proposal would widen the definition of 'family members' to include married children, parents, and siblings.[274] There would be amendments to the concept of actors of protection, to include the requirement that protection must be 'effective and durable' and to clarify that actors of protection must be 'willing and able to enforce the rule of law'.[275] The provisions on the internal protection alternative would be amended to confirm that, for the exception to apply, the person concerned must have 'access to protection against persecution or serious harm' and 'can safely and legally travel, gain admittance and settle' in that part of the country; this reflects Strasbourg case law on this issue.[276] Also, there would be new provisions on obtaining country-of-origin information in such

---

[272] See 5.3 above.

[273] COM (2009) 551, 21 Oct 2009. All references in this subsection are to this proposal, unless otherwise indicated.   [274] Revised Art 2(j).

[275] Revised Art 7.

[276] *Salah Sheekh v Netherlands* (ECHR 2007-I), discussed in 5.3.1 above.

cases, and the rule permitting the application of the internal alternative principle notwithstanding 'technical obstacles to return' would be deleted.[277]

As for the substance of refugee status, the revised Directive would clarify that the absence of protection against private attacks by the State, or other actors of protection, *for (Geneva) Convention reasons* would constitute persecution.[278] The protection against gender-related persecution would also be strengthened.[279] Furthermore, the cessation clause would be amended so that refugees could 'invoke compelling reasons arising out of previous persecution' to prevent the application of the cessation clause.[280]

A number of changes would be made to the rules on the content of protection status. First, there would be new references to additional categories of vulnerable persons (victims of trafficking and persons with mental health problems),[281] and Member States' power to reduce benefits for persons whose claims were supposedly manufactured would be deleted.[282] Secondly, the power to define special conditions for family members of persons with subsidiary protection would be deleted.[283] Thirdly, the possible distinctions between refugees and persons with subsidiary protection as regards residence permits, travel documents, employment, education, social welfare, health care, and integration facilities would be deleted.[284] Fourthly, there would be sundry other changes to the rules on content of status, as regards training and counselling for employment, grants and loans for employment-related education, recognition of professional qualifications, mental health care, tracing unaccompanied minors, access to accommodation, and integration programmes.[285]

The proposal for amendment of the Directive addresses many of the key issues identified as failings by the Commission,[286] although it is hard to assess whether it would reduce gaps in recognition rates given that the Commission has not assessed to what extent those gaps have already been reduced as a result of the adoption of the original qualification Directive. Logically, the proposal would raise recognition rates, given its clarification of the rules and tightening of the exclusions relating to this issue. The changes in the rules relating to the content of status, in particular the abolition of distinction between refugees and persons with subsidiary protection, would be particularly welcome. However,

---

[277] Revised Art 8.   [278] Revised Art 9(3).   [279] Revised Art 10(1)(d).

[280] New Art 11(3). A parallel amendment would apply to cessation of subsidiary protection status (new Art 16(3)).   [281] Revised Art 20(3).

[282] The current Art 20(6) and (7) would be deleted.   [283] Revised Art 23(2).

[284] Revised Arts 25(2), 26(1), 27(1), 29(1), 30(1), and 34(1); the current Arts 24(2), 26(3) and (4), 27(3), 28(2), 29(2), and 33(2) would be deleted.

[285] Revised Arts 26(2), 30(2), 31(5), 32, and 34, and new Arts 26(3) and 28 .

[286] See also the comments by ECRE, *Comments from the European Council on Refugees and Exiles on the European Commission proposal to recast the Qualification directive*, Mar 2010, online at: <http://www.ecre.org/files/ECRE_Position_Recast_Qualification_Directive.pdf>, and of the Meijers Committee, online at: <http://www.statewatch.org/news/2010/feb/eu-meijers-cttee-qual-proced.pdf>.

it would have been preferable also to clarify the definition of 'particular social group' (ie whether it is cumulative or alternative), to address the incompatibilities between the exclusion clauses and the Geneva Convention, and to improve the revocation clauses. In any event, if the proposal is adopted, it would remain to be seen how well the national authorities and national courts would apply its rules.

5.6. Temporary protection

Directive 2001/55 establishing a model EU-wide temporary protection scheme was adopted in July 2001,[287] and Member States had to implement the Directive by 31 December 2002. Three Member States were condemned by the Court of Justice for their failure to implement the Directive on time.[288] To date, the model temporary protection scheme set out in the Directive has never been used in practice, and the Commission has not suggested its amendment in the context of establishing the second phase of the Common European Asylum System. As noted above, the power to adopt emergency measures in the event of a mass influx on the basis of Article 78(3) TFEU (former Article 64(2) EC) has not been invoked either.[289]

Chapter I of the Directive sets out its purpose, scope, and definitions.[290] The Directive applies to either a 'mass influx' or an 'imminent mass influx' of persons; it applies to persons who have been evacuated, as well as spontaneous arrivals; and it applies even where there is *no* risk that the asylum system will be unable to process the number of applications.[291] Temporary protection 'shall not prejudge' refugee recognition pursuant to the Geneva Convention.[292] Member States may adopt more favourable rules for persons covered by temporary protection.[293] The Directive does not apply to persons admitted on national temporary protection schemes before its entry into force;[294] it appears from the Directive and other provisions of EU asylum law that Member States are now precluded from establishing new national temporary protection schemes.[295]

---

[287] Dir 2001/55 ([2001] OJ L 212/12). All references in this section are to this Directive, unless otherwise indicated. On the Directive, see generally K Kerber, 'The Temporary Protection Directive' (2002) 4 EJML 193. Ireland, which opted in after the adoption of the Directive and had to apply it by 31 Dec 2003 (Commission Decision 2003/690, [2003] OJ L 251/23).

[288] Cases: C-454/04 *Commission v Luxembourg*, judgment of 2 Jun 2005; C-476/04 *Commission v Greece*, judgment of 17 Nov 2005; and C-455/04 *Commission v UK*, judgment of 23 Feb 2006 (all unreported). Three cases were withdrawn, presumably because the Member States concerned finally complied with the legislation: Cases C-461/04 *Commission v Netherlands*; C-515/04 *Commission v Belgium*; and C-451/04 *Commission v France*.   [289] See 5.2.2 and 5.2.3.

[290] Arts 1–3.   [291] Art 2(a), (c), and (d).   [292] Art 3(1) and (2).   [293] Art 3(5).

[294] Art 3(4). The date of entry into force was 7 Aug 2001 (see Art 33).

[295] In particular, the asylum procedures Dir, the qualification Dir, and the reception conditions Dir make no allowance for such national schemes, and the 2004 and 2007 legislation of the European Refugee Fund ([2004] OJ L 381/52 and [2007] OJ L 144/1; see 5.10.2 below) refer only to the Directive, rather than national law, as regards temporary protection.

Chapter II concerns the duration and implementation of temporary protection.[296] In principle, temporary protection is one year long, extended for further periods of six months to a two-year maximum, with a possible further extension for a third year.[297] A temporary protection regime can only be established if the Council, acting by a qualified majority on a proposal from the Commission and considering certain specified factors, agrees that there is a mass influx of displaced persons.[298] Such a decision will specify, inter alia, the groups of persons covered, although Member States can extend the regime to other groups displaced for the same reasons and from the same country or region of origin.[299] The regime would end at the time of the maximum duration or upon early termination by the Council adopted by qualified majority after a Commission proposal, if the Council has established that conditions in the country of origin have improved sufficiently so 'as to permit the safe and durable return' of the beneficiaries.[300]

Chapter III sets out obligations of the Member States regarding persons enjoying temporary protection.[301] Member States must issue residence permits and visas,[302] register personal data on beneficiaries and take back a person enjoying temporary protection if that person remains on or seeks to enter the territory of another Member State without authorization during the temporary protection period.[303]

As for access to employment or self-employment, Member States are required to permit temporary protection beneficiaries to take up employment or self-employment, but they may give priority to EU citizens and EEA nationals, as well as legally resident third-country nationals receiving unemployment benefit. The Directive provides that the 'general law' regarding remuneration, social security, and other conditions of employment in each Member State applies.[304] There are rules regarding housing and social assistance, along with education;[305] the Directive leaves Member States the option as to whether to allow adults access to the general education system. Also, there are detailed rules on the status of unaccompanied minors.[306] There are no provisions on detention in this Directive, so presumably the relevant provisions of other EU asylum legislation would apply, if the person concerned has the status of asylum seeker.[307] If he or she does not have that status, then the provisions in the Returns Directive would apply, if the person concerned otherwise fell within the scope of that Directive.[308]

---

[296] Arts 4–7. [297] Art 4. [298] Art 5(2).

[299] Art 7. However, the financial support provided for in the Directive will not apply to such groups (Art 7(2)). [300] Art 6.

[301] Arts 8–15. [302] Art 8. [303] Arts 10 and 11. [304] Art 12.

[305] Arts 13 and 14 respectively.

[306] Art 16. See now the action plan on unaccompanied minors (COM (2010) 213, 6 May 2010).

[307] See 5.7 and 5.9 below.

[308] See the judgment in Case C-357/09 PPU *Kadzoev*, 30 Nov 2009, not yet reported; on the Returns Dir, see 7.7.1 below.

Member States have to authorize entry of the 'core' family of the spouse and children; entry of other family members, comprising close relatives who lived with *and* were wholly or largely dependent on the sponsor, is discretionary.[309] Moreover, the *Member States* shall decide which Member State family members will enter,[310] and there are no provisions on the status of family members.[311]

Chapter IV concerns access to the asylum procedure.[312] Member States may delay consideration of an application for Convention refugee status until the temporary protection has ended;[313] the effect of such delay will be magnified by the possible application of the Directive to cases where the asylum system is *not* under pressure and by the possible lengthy period of temporary protection. Member States can also provide that a person cannot hold temporary protection status simultaneously with the status of asylum seeker, although if an application for asylum or other protection status fails, a Member State must continue to extend temporary protection status to the beneficiary.[314] The criteria for responsibility for asylum seekers apply, but '[i]n particular', a Member State shall be responsible for examining an asylum application if it has accepted that person's transfer onto its territory.[315] This clause is vague and appears to contradict both the Dublin Convention and the Dublin II Regulation, which do not expressly contain such a criterion for assigning responsibility.[316] Moreover, the Dublin II Regulation (and its proposed replacement) do not take account of the Directive's rules on family members.

Chapter V concerns return.[317] Once the temporary protection regime ends, the 'general laws' on protection and on foreigners apply, 'without prejudice' to certain specific provisions in the Directive;[318] presumably the reference to the 'general laws' must now be understood as a reference not only to the relevant national legislation, but also to EU rules on asylum and the EU's Returns Directive.[319] The specific rules in the temporary protection Directive concerning return first of all provide for rules on voluntary return.[320] There is an express possibility of enforced return of persons after the regime has ended, but such return must be 'conducted with due respect for human dignity',[321] and Member States

---

[309] Art 15.

[310] It is not clear whether this applies only where the family have been scattered between Member States, or also when family members have been left outside the Union.

[311] If the family members are permitted to work, the draft Directive on third-country national workers would also confer equal treatment rights on the family members with temporary protection, in the latest version of that Directive (see 6.5.1 below). [312] Arts 17–19.

[313] Art 17.   [314] Art 19.   [315] Art 18.   [316] See 5.8 below.   [317] Arts 20–23.

[318] Art 20, referring to Arts 21–23.

[319] For more on the Returns Dir (Dir 2008/115, [2008] OJ L 348/98), see further 7.7.1 below. It should be noted that the Returns Dir is 'without prejudice to' more favourable rules in other EU immigration and asylum legislation (Art 4(3)), or in national law (Art 4(4)). It should also be noted that the Returns Dir does not apply to persons currently claiming asylum (Case C-357/09 PPU *Kadzoev*, judgment of 30 Nov 2009, not yet reported).

[320] Art 21; compare to Art 7 of the Returns Dir.

[321] Art 22(1); compare to Arts 8–10 of the Returns Dir.

'shall consider any compelling humanitarian reasons which may make return impossible or unreasonable in specific cases'.[322] They must also 'take the necessary measures concerning' residence status of former beneficiaries of temporary protection 'who cannot, in view of their state of health, reasonably be expected to travel; where for example they would suffer serious negative effects if their treatment was interrupted'. Specifically, those persons 'shall not be expelled so long as that situation continues'.[323] Finally on the issue of return, Member States have discretion over whether to let children complete their school year.[324]

Chapter VI concerns solidarity between Member States, and sets out rules concerning indication of reception capacity and transfer of beneficiaries (with their consent).[325] Finally, the Directive contains rules on administrative cooperation,[326] exclusion from the benefit of temporary protection (in parallel to the Geneva Convention exclusion clauses),[327] and final provisions, including the right to challenge exclusion from temporary protection or family reunion in the courts.[328]

This Directive represented a potential risk to the Geneva Convention, as its potentially wide scope of application could have been attractive to Member States who might have wished to grant considerable numbers of people the lower standards of protection in this Directive, which were weakened considerably during negotiations, instead of refugee status. However, the unwillingness to apply the Directive in practice, coupled with the apparent ban on Member States establishing national temporary protection regimes, is in fact quite a positive result for the system of international protection in the EU.

5.7. Common procedures

5.7.1. Current asylum procedures Directive

The first-phase Directive on this subject is Directive 2005/85, adopted in December 2005 after particularly difficult negotiations.[329] Member States had to

---

[322] Art 22(2); see Art 9 of the Returns Dir.

[323] Art 23(1); compare in particular to Art 9(2) of the Returns Dir, which provides only for an *option* to postpone the removal of persons in such circumstances.   [324] Art 23(2).

[325] Arts 24–26.   [326] Chapter VII (Art 27).

[327] Chapter VIII (Art 28). There is no mention of the relevance of Art 3 ECHR in such cases.

[328] Chapter IX (Arts 29–34), particularly Art 29. Compare with the exclusion clauses in the qualification Directive (Arts 12 and 17 of Dir 2004/83, [2004] OJ L 304/12; see discussion in 5.5 above).

[329] Dir 2005/85 ([2005] OJ L 326/13). All further references in this section are to this Directive, unless otherwise noted. On the Directive, see: K Zwaan, ed, *The Asylum Procedures Directive: Central themes, Problem issues, and Implementation in selected Member States* (Wolf Legal Publishers, 2008); C Costello, 'The Asylum Procedures Directive in Legal Context: Equivocal Standards Meet General Principles', in A Baldaccini, E Guild, and H Toner, eds, *Whose Freedom, Security and Justice? EU Immigration and Asylum Law and Policy* (Hart, 2007), 151; H Battjes, *European Asylum Law and International Law* (Martinus Nijhoff, 2006), chs 6 and 7; and S Peers and N Rogers, *EU Immigration and Asylum Law: Text and Commentary* (1st edn, Martinus Nijhoff, 2006), ch 14.

implement the Directive by 1 December 2007, except as regards legal aid, where the deadline was 1 December 2008.[330] So far there have been two references from national courts to the Court of Justice on the Directive, although one of these cases was withdrawn;[331] there have been no infringement proceedings yet. Also, the European Parliament brought a successful annulment action against certain provisions of the Directive;[332] the consequences of this judgment are discussed further below. The Commission has produced a report on the application of the Directive,[333] and further information on its application in practice is available in the Commission's impact assessment on the 2009 proposal to amend the Directive (the '2009 impact assessment'),[334] and in the UNHCR's report on the implementation of the Directive (the 'UNHCR report').[335] Both reports are referred to below.

The Directive's scope is limited to the minimum standards necessary for the granting and withdrawing of refugee status under the 1951 Geneva Convention on the status of refugees.[336] It includes any application for asylum made at the border or on the territory of a Member State,[337] but it does not include determination of qualification under other international instruments or for persons otherwise in need of protection, in particular subsidiary protection or temporary protection. However, Member States are obliged to apply the Directive if they apply a single procedure for determining refugee claims and claims for subsidiary protection,[338] and they may opt to apply the Directive to applications for any other kind of international protection.[339] Member States are free to provide for more favourable standards on asylum procedures, provided that such standards are 'compatible' with the Directive.[340]

The Directive does not explicitly set out any hierarchy between applications for asylum and applications for subsidiary or temporary protection status.[341] On this point, in the *Abdulla* judgment, the Court of Justice noted that the qualification Directive 'governs two distinct systems of protection' (ie refugee and subsidiary protection status), noting that that Directive defines subsidiary protection by opposition to refugee status, and stated that 'the cessation of refugee status cannot be made conditional on a finding that a person does not qualify for subsidiary protection status', for 'there would otherwise be a failure to have regard for the respective domains of the two systems of protection'. So 'the possible cessation of

---

[330] Art 43.

[331] Cases C-69/10 *Diouf*, pending, and C-105/10 PPU *Gataev and Gataeva*, withdrawn.

[332] Case C-133/06 *EP v Council* [2008] ECR I-3189.   [333] COM (2010) 465, 8 Sep 2010.

[334] SEC (2009) 1376, 21 Oct 2009. On the proposal to amend the Directive, see 5.7.2 below.

[335] *Improving Asylum Procedures: Comparative Analysis and Recommendations for Law and Practice* (UNHCR, 2010). The key findings and recommendations are online at: <http://www.unhcr.org/4ba9d99d9.html>.   [336] Art 3.

[337] Art 3(2).   [338] Art 3(3).   [339] Art 3(4).

[340] Art 5. On the issue of 'compatible' higher standards, see 5.2.4 above.

[341] On the *implicit* hierarchy set out in the Dir, see Peers and Rogers (n 328 above), ch 14.

refugee status occurs without prejudice to the right of the person concerned to request the granting of subsidiary protection status'.[342]

Chapter II of the Directive sets out basic procedural principles and guarantees for assessing asylum claims.[343] Access to the procedure must be ensured.[344] Member States shall not reject or exclude applications on the grounds that they have not been made as soon as possible, although this is 'without prejudice to' another rule which provides that Member States might consider an application 'unfounded' if an applicant has failed without reasonable cause to make an application earlier, where he or she had an opportunity to do so.[345]

There are specific rules on the position of family members of an asylum application during the determination process.[346] Applicants for asylum must be allowed to remain at the border or in the territory until such time as an initial decision has been made, with the exception of 'subsequent applications' and cases where a person is surrendered or extradited to another Member State, a non-EU State, or an international criminal court or tribunal.[347] A reference from a national court asking the Court of Justice to clarify the interpretation of this provision as regards the execution of a European Arrest Warrant issued by another Member State was withdrawn.[348]

The requirements for the examination of applications include the need for precise and up to date country of origin information, the obligation to examine applications 'individually, objectively and impartially', and the necessity to ensure that decision-makers have appropriate expertise.[349]

Guarantees for applicants include the right to have a decision on the asylum application in writing, the right to have reasons for a negative decision, the right to be informed of the procedure in a language that it is 'reasonably supposed' that they understand, a right to an interpreter, and a right to notification of decisions in a reasonable time.[350] There are detailed rules on the procedures and conditions for personal interviews, which specify that in principle, all applicants must be given an interview, subject to a number of exceptions.[351] According to the 2009 impact assessment, many personal interviews are defective in practice, as 'factual mistakes or misunderstandings are common' since applicants are not allowed to comment on or provide clarification of the reports. The UNHCR report, after

---

[342] Paras 77–80 of the judgment (Joined Cases C- C-175/08, C-176/08, C-178/08, and C-179/08, judgment of 2 Mar 2010 (not yet reported)). Note that the Advocate General's opinion in this case asserted (in note 24) that 'Member States may since the entry into force of [the qualification Directive] opt to grant subsidiary protection to individuals to whom, in the absence of that form of protection, refugee status would have been granted'. However, the Court did not expressly address this issue.   [343] Arts 6–22.

[344] Art 6.   [345] Art 8(1), referring to Art 23(4)(i).   [346] Art 6(2)–(4).   [347] Art 7.

[348] Case C–105/10 PPU, *Gataev and Gataeva*.

[349] Art 8. Note that the European Asylum Support Office will play a role in the future as regards country-of-origin information: see 5.10.1 below.   [350] Arts 9 and 10.

[351] Arts 12 and 13. According to the 2009 impact assessment, ten Member States invoked a derogation. See Annex 9 to the impact assessment for details.

examining a selection of written decisions in actual cases, concluded that in a number of cases 'there was no evidence that these applications were examined and these decisions taken individually, objectively and impartially'.

There is a right to legal assistance, but with possible exceptions to the right to legal aid.[352] In particular, the right to legal aid arises only after a negative decision,[353] although Member States remain free to apply a higher standard of granting legal assistance from the very beginning of the application process. The 2009 impact assessment concludes that in general, Member States which grant legal assistance from the beginning of the process have a higher rate of positive decisions on asylum applications.[354] There are specific provisions on the rights of access to information that an asylum seeker's legal adviser should have, along with rules on the legal adviser's access to the applicant and to interviews.[355]

Unaccompanied minors enjoy certain procedural guarantees, including the right to a representative.[356] As regards detention, Member States 'shall not' hold an applicant for asylum in detention for the sole reason that he or she is an applicant for asylum, and there must be the possibility of 'speedy judicial review' in detention cases.[357] The Directive does not define the word 'detention'.

Next, the Directive sets out a specific procedure in cases where an application for asylum is explicitly or implicitly withdrawn.[358] It also provides for the role of UNCHR in asylum proceedings, including the rights of access to detention facilities and to information on individual cases.[359] Disclosure of certain information relating to the asylum application to the authorities of the country of origin is prohibited.[360]

Chapter III is concerned with procedures at first instance for asylum applications, including accelerated and inadmissibility procedures.[361] Member States are permitted to have special or accelerated procedures for a wide range of applications, including unfounded claims, manifestly unfounded claims, admissibility claims, and repeat applications, along with two types of special procedures for applications made at the borders.[362] According to the 2009 impact assessment report, all but one Member State had put in place some accelerated procedures, with at least one Member State applying grounds not referred to in the

---

[352] Art 15.   [353] Art 15(2).

[354] For tables of recognition rates compared to the basic features of national asylum systems, see Annex 13 to the 2009 impact assessment.   [355] Art 16.

[356] Art 17. See now the action plan on unaccompanied minors (COM (2010) 213, 6 May 2010). For details of the numbers of unaccompanied minor asylum seekers in practice, see Annex 27 to the 2009 impact assessment.

[357] Art 18. It should be noted that the detention of asylum seekers is governed by this clause, and the relevant provisions in the reception conditions Directive (see 5.9.1 below), rather than the Returns Directive: see Case C-357/09 PPU *Kadzoev*, 30 Nov 2009, not yet reported, and 7.7.1 below.

[358] Arts 19 and 20.   [359] Art 21.   [360] Art 22.   [361] Arts 23–35.

[362] Arts 23, 24, and 28.

Directive,[363] and the use of such procedures in practice varying from 1% to 17% of all applications. The UNHCR report stated that in some Member States, accelerated procedures were 'the norm', and concluded that in some cases, the time limits applying to accelerated procedures made it 'extremely difficult' to ensure that basic procedural safeguards were upheld.

Next, the Directive sets out circumstances in which a claim may be rejected as inadmissible,[364] including applications for which there is another country which can be considered as the first country of asylum to which applicant has been admitted,[365] or a 'safe third country'.[366] Member States are allowed to retain or introduce lists of designated 'safe third countries', subject to certain requirements.[367] The UNHCR report notes that the principles of 'first country of asylum' and 'safe third country' are rarely if ever applied in the Member States studied, and that argues that several Member States have not implemented these provisions correctly.

The Directive originally set out the principle of a common EU list on 'safe countries of origin', along with a procedure for adopting such a list (a QMV of the Council on a proposal from the Commission after consulting the EP).[368] However, this provision was struck down by the Court of Justice, on application by the EP, because it amounted to a form of 'secondary legislative procedure' which was not provided for by the EC Treaty.[369] Member States may still however introduce national laws regarding 'safe countries of origin'. These must prima facie be governed by a list of common principles,[370] but there is a derogation for existing national lists drawn up according to less stringent requirements (Article 30(2)).[371] According to the 2009 impact assessment, one group of six Member States did not apply this rule at all; three Member States applied it on a case-by-case basis; ten Member States applied national lists of 'safe countries of origin' pursuant to the criteria in the Directive; and three large Member States applied pre-existing national law which did not meet the usual criteria (Germany, France, and the UK).[372] Most Member States did not permit a challenge to the presumption of safety, and several designated such cases as manifestly unfounded or did not allow for the suspensive effect of appeals. The UNHCR report found a similar degree of divergence among Member States, including large variations in the actual rules applicable, some of which fell short of the Directive's requirements.

---

[363] For the details of the national variations, and the numbers and proportions of asylum seekers subject to them in practice, see Annex 22 to the 2009 impact assessment.   [364] Art 25.

[365] Art 26.   [366] Art 27.   [367] Ibid.   [368] Art 29.

[369] Case C-133/06, n 331 above. The same principle must apply *a fortiori* after the subsequent entry into force of the Treaty of Lisbon, given its systemization of the legislative and non-legislative decision-making processes of the EU (see Arts 289–297 TFEU).

[370] Annex II.   [371] Art 30(2).

[372] For the content of the national lists of safe 'countries of origin', see Annex 12 to the 2009 impact assessment.

Member States may have specific procedures derogating from the rules in Chapter II to deal with fresh applications for asylum after a first application has been rejected or withdrawn, or where an applicant has failed to go to a reception centre or to appear before authorities.[373] Furthermore, Member States may also derogate from the normal procedural rules to put in place particular procedures for border applications, subject to certain safeguards.[374] According to the 2009 impact assessment, twelve Member States have such procedures in place; some of these procedures do not permit asylum seekers to present their views or to appeal against negative decisions with suspensive effect.

A further derogation is allowed from the basic procedural rights where persons seek irregular entry or have already entered irregularly from a State which has ratified and observes the Geneva Convention and the ECHR (this is known informally as the 'supersafe third countries' rule).[375] Again, the Court of Justice struck down the provisions which provided for a secondary legislative procedure to adopt a common EU list of such countries,[376] but Member States are free to apply this concept in their national law if they already did so on the day when the Directive was adopted.[377]

Chapter IV sets out specific procedures concerning withdrawal of refugee status.[378] Chapter V sets out rules on appeals,[379] confirming the principle that applicants for asylum are entitled to an effective remedy before a court or tribunal as regards 'a decision taken on their application for asylum'. The pending *Diouf* case before the Court of Justice asks whether this rule applies also to decisions made following an accelerated procedure;[380] the answer is obviously that it does, in the absence of any provision permitting Member States to exclude any category of decisions on asylum applications from judicial review and in light of the principles of international human rights law.[381] The practical importance of appeals is confirmed by the 2009 impact assessment, which reports that 28% of appeals overturned a negative decision in asylum cases in 2008,[382] and that in 2007, 77% of negative decisions were subject to appeal. The 2009 impact assessment also observes that five Member States grant a period to appeal of only one to three days, raising obvious questions as to whether the remedy is 'effective'.[383] The UNHCR report is critical of these time limits, and also of barriers to effective remedies due to limited access to legal aid and translation assistance.

Member States must set out rules 'where appropriate' dealing with the question of the suspensive effect of appeals, or the right to apply for protective measures

---

[373] Art 32.   [374] Art 35.   [375] Art 36.   [376] Case C-133/06; see n 331 above.
[377] See in particular Art 36(7).   [378] Arts 37–38.   [379] Art 39.
[380] C-69/10, n 330 above.   [381] See 5.3.1 above.
[382] See Annex 25 to the 2009 impact assessment.
[383] See Case C-63/08 *Pontin*, judgment of 29 Oct 2009, not yet reported, in which the Court of Justice was critical of a fifteen-day time limit to bring actions as regards an action for reinstatement of a pregnant worker who had been dismissed.

in the absence of automatic suspensive effect of appeals; these rules 'must be in accordance with [Member States'] international obligations'.[384] According to the 2009 impact assessment, two Member States did not permit suspensive effect of some appeals, and three Member States did not allow, in their national law, applicants to stay on the territory pending a decision on a request for interim measures.

The final provisions are set out in Chapter VI.[385] Apart from the later date to transpose the provisions on legal aid (see above), a notable point here is the temporal scope: the Directive only applies to applications (and to procedures for withdrawal of status) which were made after the deadline for transposition, ie 1 December 2007.[386]

This Directive raises a large number of complex legal issues and moreover has led to great concern among non-governmental organizations and the UNHCR that the Directive is not compatible with human rights obligations binding the Community and its Member States.[387]

Examining the major issues in turn, the first issue that arises is the question of hierarchy between applications for Geneva Convention status and applications for subsidiary protection status. Although neither this Directive nor any other first-phase EU asylum measures explicitly address the point, a number of provisions in the preamble and the main text, as well as provisions of other EU asylum legislation, suggest that a decision-maker must first consider the possibility of granting Geneva Convention refugee status, before considering granting subsidiary protection status.[388] This interpretation is also consistent with the EC Treaty obligation (now found in Article 78 TFEU) to adopt legislation 'in accordance' with the Geneva Convention and with the objectives of avoiding secondary movements of asylum seekers and of creating a Common European Asylum System. It follows that a person who is denied refugee status but has obtained subsidiary protection status can appeal against the denial of the former status, except where the Directive expressly provides otherwise.[389]

Next, the possible removal of an asylum seeker from the territory before an initial decision on the application when an extradition or similar request is

---

[384] Art 39(2).   [385] Arts 40–46.

[386] On the issue of the temporal scope of EU immigration and asylum law in general, see 5.5 above, and in particular the judgment in *Kadzoev* (n 356 above).

[387] For a full examination of all these issues, with further references, see Peers and Rogers (n 328 above), ch 14.

[388] For example, Art 2(e) of Dir 2004/83 (n 327 above) defines a person eligible for subsidiary protection status as a person 'who *does not qualify as a refugee*'. See also Art 3(4) of Directive 2003/9 ([2003] OJ L 31/18) and now the wording of Art 78(2)(b) TFEU, referring to subsidiary protection as regards persons who, '*without obtaining European asylum*, are in need of international protection' (emphasis added). The proposal for a replacement Directive addresses this issue expressly (5.7.2 below).

[389] The Directive only extends that permission where the person concerned has a status in that Member State entirely identical to that set out for Geneva Convention refugees in Dir 2004/83: see Arts 9(2), 25(2)(d) and (e), and 39(5).

accepted is particularly suspect where the extradition request comes from the country of origin.[390] Since the grounds for resisting extradition overlap with the grounds for requesting recognition as a refugee,[391] it is arguably in breach of the Geneva Convention to accede to an extradition request before determining an asylum claim. In any case, it should always be recalled that extradition will be in violation of the ECHR where there is a sufficiently serious risk of violation of ECHR standards in the destination country.[392] The Directive should also be understood to impose implied obligations to readmit an asylum seeker and continue with the asylum determination process after the criminal trial is concluded or the relevant sentence is served (if imposed) following the extradition.

The exclusions and limitations on the right to a personal interview are questionable, particularly the possibility for a Member State not to hold a personal interview where the national authorities have already determined that the application is unfounded on certain grounds.[393] In the absence of other procedural protection in such cases, and given the stress laid by the Strasbourg organs on the importance of a full consideration of an asylum claim,[394] it is doubtful whether this provision is valid. Similarly, it is doubtful whether the possibility of not receiving a report of the personal interview until after the first-instance decision is valid,[395] again because of the absence of other procedural protection; coupled with the lack of suspensive effect of an appeal decision, this could mean that asylum seekers could be removed before seeing a report of their personal interview and being given an opportunity to dispute or clarify its content.

Although the Directive provides for legal aid and legal assistance, it allows for questionable restrictions upon legal aid.[396] While the European Court of Human Rights has not had the opportunity to rule on the issue of legal aid in asylum proceedings, a right to legal aid surely exists as a corollary of the right not to be removed to face such as torture, or other breaches of the ECHR following removal to another State.[397] It must follow that the limitation of legal aid to appeals and the possible limitation of legal aid to cases considered likely to succeed (in the absence of any procedural rights or guarantees of competence and independence as regards legal aid applications) are arguably invalid.[398]

As for detention, the Directive does preclude detention of all asylum seekers, but does not preclude the detention of specific categories of asylum seekers or provide for any protection against detention other than the requirement for speedy judicial review.[399] It is arguable that the general principles of EU law and the EU Charter of Fundamental Rights incorporate the full panoply of

---

[390] See Art 7(2).   [391] See 9.5.2 below.   [392] See 5.3.1 above.   [393] Art 12(2)(c).

[394] See the case law discussed in 5.3.1 above.   [395] Art 14(2).   [396] Art 15.

[397] See, by analogy, the judgments in *Airey v Ireland* (A-32) and *Steel and Morris v UK* 15 Feb 2005.   [398] Art 15(2) and (3)(d).

[399] Art 18. See also the relevant provisions of the reception conditions Dir (discussed in 5.9 below).

protections regarding detention set out in Article 5 ECHR and the ICCPR.[400] So the Directive cannot be interpreted to permit detention for any purposes which are incompatible with ECHR or ICCPR standards.[401]

Moving on to the accelerated procedures provided for by the Directive, it should be stressed that apart from the express exceptions set out in the Directive for border procedures and procedures for repeat applications,[402] and the exceptions from the right to a personal interview mentioned above, the basic procedural guarantees in the Directive expressly apply even where a case is accelerated or considered inadmissible—although in the latter case, the guarantees will necessarily only apply to the consideration of admissibility. But in the 'real world', truncated proceedings, which will likely often be coupled with a lack of suspensive effect for appeals, will often mean great difficulty for asylum applicants in obtaining a fair hearing for arguing their claim.

As regards inadmissible applications,[403] the most important provisions concern the 'first country of asylum', which can be either a country which has granted the person refugee status or which otherwise grants him or her 'sufficient protection', and the 'safe third country' concept, which permits Member States not to consider a claim where the person concerned had a sufficient link to another country where sufficient protection *could* have been claimed.[404] Both concepts should be interpreted in light of the principles of the relevant international treaties, which require: an agreement to readmit the person in the other State and to accord that person a fair refugee status determination or other 'effective protection'; no Convention fear of persecution for the person in the other State; no risk of *refoulement* from the other State; no risk of removal from the other State to face a violation of the other rights in the Geneva Convention; no risk of violation of any human rights protected by a treaty to which the removing State is a party; willingness and ability in the other State to provide effective protection for as long is the person is a refugee or can find another source of durable effective protection; no violation of the person's right to family unity; and an application of these principles on an individual basis, including suspensive effect of appeals.[405] To the extent that the Directive does not require Member States to consider the safety of individual applicants *and* the safety of particular third countries, and does not require Member States to consider the possible ECHR breaches other than those

---

[400] For a detailed examination and comparison of the ICCPR and ECHR jurisprudence, see D Wilsher, 'Detention of Asylum-Seekers and Refugees and International Human Rights Law' in P Shah, ed, *The Challenge of Asylum to Legal Systems* (Cavendish, 2005), 145.

[401] See the case law on immigration detention, discussed in 7.3.2 below.   [402] See Art 24.

[403] Art 25.   [404] Respectively Arts 26 and 27.

[405] S Legomsky, 'Secondary Refugee Movements and the Return of Asylum Seekers to Third Countries: the Meaning of Effective Protection' (2003) 15 IJRL 567 at 673–675. See also the analysis and critique by C Costello, 'The Asylum Procedures Directive and the Proliferation of Safe Third Countries Practices: Deterrence, Deflection and the Dismantling of International Protection?' (2005) 7 EJML 35.

relating to Article 3 ECHR which might occur in the relevant 'safe third country', it should be considered invalid for breach of human rights principles.[406]

The next controversial issue is the rule on 'safe countries of origin', which provides for the possible adoption of national lists of such countries and maintaining existing national lists of such countries (or parts of countries) using *different* criteria, entailing lower standards for judging the States concerned.[407] The problem with all such rules is that they increase the standard of proof which the applicant must discharge, and are either dangerous, because the list includes countries that are still refugee producing, or meaningless, because if the country is no longer refugee producing then there are unlikely to be more than a handful of applicants from the country at any one time. Such lists are of dubious validity in light of the Geneva Convention. Moreover, the derogation for national lists to be maintained on the basis of criteria setting lower standards is arguably invalid, because of: the absence of a criterion regarding the threat of indiscriminate violence in armed conflict directly contradicts one of the main grounds for considering whether a person is entitled to subsidiary protection status in accordance with the qualification Directive;[408] the absence of a requirement to consider the consistency of State practice as regards torture and persecution, which is obviously relevant to a consideration of the 'safety' of a country; and the absence of obligations to consider all of the factors of assessment set out in Annex II to the Directive and the existence of a democratic system, which are obviously good indicators as to whether persecution and/or torture or other inhuman or degrading treatment are generally carried out.

The provision for special procedures permitted at national borders is arguably invalid, because many key procedural safeguards are omitted (particularly access to the procedure, requirements for examinations and decisions, guarantees on appeal, legal aid, lawyers' access to the file, protection regarding detention, contact with the UNHCR, and confidentiality).[409]

This brings us to perhaps the worst provision of the Directive: the possibility to maintain national lists, on 'European safe third countries'.[410] Fundamentally, this clause violates the Geneva Convention and the ECHR, by providing that 'no, or no full' examination need be carried out of an asylum application as regards applications from the countries meeting the criteria.

The special rules on withdrawal of refugee status are also questionable, to the extent that some key procedural safeguards in the Directive do not fully apply,[411]

---

[406] Art 27(2)(b) and (c).

[407] Given the annulment by the Court of Justice of the provisions allowing for adoption of a common EU list of such third States (Case C-133/06, n 331 above), the human rights aspects of such a common list will not be further considered here.

[408] See 5.5 above, and the interpretation of this provision in Case C-465/07 *Elgafaji* [2009] ECR I-921.   [409] Art 35.

[410] Art 36.   [411] In particular, Arts 7, 10, 15, 16, and 17.

along with the full right to a personal interview, to the extent that withdrawal of status will in practice lead to removal of the territory.

Finally, the possible lack of suspensive effect quite clearly seems to breach the minimum safeguards developed by the Human Rights Court for asylum appeals, at least as regards appeals at first instance.[412]

The asylum procedures Directive is clearly at or below the lowest common denominator as regards most aspects of procedural rights of asylum seekers, as evidenced by the long list of provisions which could be considered invalid for breach of human rights law. It is doubtful that any piece of EU legislation has ever been responsible for so many human rights breaches. The legitimacy of EU asylum law and of the EU's claims to support the Geneva Convention and fundamental human rights is therefore dependent on finding key provisions of the Directive invalid or radically reinterpreting or amending them, or adopting major amendments to the Directive as soon as possible.

Moreover, the position will be exacerbated once, as planned, the relevant national authorities have access to certain information in the Visa Information System (VIS) in order to assist with determining the merits of asylum claims.[413] Without detailed rules on fuller subsequent exchange of information between national authorities and governing the relevance and use of such data in asylum proceedings, ensuring that the data are fully disclosed to asylum applicants before the authorities' decision, and requiring national authorities to explain the extent of the reliance which they placed upon such data, access to this data to determine refugee claims is highly objectionable.

5.7.2. Proposal for amendment

A large number of the concerns about the procedures Directive would be addressed by the Commission's 2009 proposal to recast the Directive,[414] if it is adopted by the EP and the Council as proposed by the Commission. First of all, as with the proposed recast of the Regulation on responsibility for asylum applications and the Directive on reception conditions,[415] the scope of the procedures Directive would be extended to include applications for subsidiary protection status.[416]

---

[412] Art 39(3)(a) and (b); see discussion of the case law in 5.3.1 above. On this issue, see also R Byrne, 'Remedies of Limited Effect: Appeals under the forthcoming Directive on EU Minimum Standards on Procedures' (2005) 7 EJML 71.

[413] Art 22 of Reg 767/2008 ([2008] OJ L 218/60). See also 5.8 below, on access to the VIS to decide on responsibility for asylum claims.

[414] COM (2009) 554, 21 Oct 2009. All references in this subsection are to this proposal, unless otherwise indicated. For comments on the proposal, see the view of the Meijers Committee, online at: <http://www.statewatch.org/news/2010/feb/eu-meijers-cttee-qual-proced.pdf>.

[415] See respectively 5.8 and 5.9 below.

[416] See in particular the revised Arts 1 and 2(b), (c), (h), (i), and (k).

The territorial scope of the Directive would now expressly include Member States' territorial waters,[417] although arguably the 2005 Directive already covers such applications, since territorial waters form part of a Member State's territory. There would be new provisions requiring Member States to ensure that they have sufficient numbers of staff to process asylum applications, along with relevant staff training.[418]

There would be more precise rules on access to the asylum procedure,[419] including at border crossing points.[420] The Directive would now expressly rule out extradition to the applicant's country of origin during the asylum process,[421] and would explicitly set out standards which would apply before extradition to any other third state.[422] A new provision would explicitly address the issue of hierarchy between claims for refugee status and subsidiary protection, requiring Member States' authorities to examine the former claim first.[423] There would also be new rules on translation of documents, obtaining information from the European Asylum Support Office, the use of expert advice, and disclosing information used to the applicant's lawyer.[424]

The rules on personal interviews would be improved by deleting the most problematic exceptions from the obligation to hold such interviews,[425] by improving the standards relating to personal interviews,[426] by adding detailed provisions on the content of interviews to the Directive,[427] and by amending the rules on transcripts and reports of the interviews.[428] Equally, the right to legal aid and assistance would be enhanced, by deleting the most problematic exceptions to this right and extending the scope of the right to all stages of the procedure.[429] The legal adviser would have enhanced access to information, and would also be able to attend the personal interview.[430] There would be a new provision concerning applicants with special needs,[431] along with higher standards for unaccompanied minors.[432] The rules on withdrawal of applications would be amended modestly to reduce divergences between Member States.[433]

As for procedures at first instance, the proposal would require Member States to conclude examinations of applications within six months, with a possible further extension for six months if necessary 'in individual cases involving complex

---

[417] Revised Art 3(1).   [418] Revised Art 4(1) and (2).   [419] Revised Art 6.

[420] New Art 7.   [421] Revised Art 8(2) (current Art 7(2)).   [422] New Art 8(3).

[423] New Art 9(2). See also the new Art 41(2), which would permit a person granted subsidiary protection to appeal the decision to refuse refugee status.

[424] Revised Art 9(3) and (5) (current Art 8(2) and (4)).

[425] Revised Art 13(2) (current Art 12(2)).   [426] Revised Art 14(3) (current Art 14(3)).

[427] New Art 15.   [428] New Art 16, replacing current Art 14.

[429] Revised Art 18 (current Art 15).   [430] Revised Art 19 (current Art 16).

[431] New Art 20.   [432] Revised Art 21 (current Art 17).

[433] Revised Art 24 (current Art 20).

issues of fact and law'.[434] The list of circumstances in which Member States can apply accelerated procedures would be cut from fifteen cases to just six.[435]

The rules on inadmissible cases would include a new provision requiring a special interview before ruling a case inadmissible.[436] As for the 'safe third country' concept, it would be revised to require Member States to assess the risk of 'serious harm' in the relevant third State and to allow the applicant to challenge both the presumption of safety and of the connection with the third State concerned.[437] The 'safe country of origin' rules would be amended to delete the possibility of treating only part of a country as safe and to repeal the option for Member States to retain pre-existing lower standards on this issue.[438] Furthermore, the standards relating to repeat applications would also be modestly raised,[439] and the derogations relating to border procedures would be deleted.[440]

Finally, as regards the issue of remedies, the proposal would require Member States to let applicants stay on the territory as a general rule, and would require an appeal of the merits as well as the law.[441]

The proposed Directive is very welcome inasmuch as it addresses a large majority of the criticisms of the existing Directive, as regards in particular territorial scope, access to procedures, extradition, the supremacy of refugee law, personal interviews, legal aid and assistance, time limits, accelerated procedures, safe third countries, safe countries of origin, and remedies. It is unfortunate, however, that the Commission has not proposed an absolute time limit on detention (which should obviously match the time limit for taking a decision on an application, at the very latest), or proposed the abolition of the 'super-safe countries' rule.

5.8. Responsibility for applications

The rules on responsibility for asylum applications were first of all set out in the 1990 Schengen Convention and the Dublin Convention of the same year.[442] These rules were subsequently replaced by the Dublin II Regulation, as from September 2003,[443] as supplemented by the Eurodac Regulation, adopted in 2000 and applicable from January 2003.[444] The Commission has released one report on

---

[434] New Art 27(3). For the current practice of Member States as regards the time required to make first-instance decisions, see Annex 23 to the 2009 impact assessment.

[435] Revised Art 27(6) (current Art 23(4)). The new Art 27(9) would provide for cases which could not per se justify the application of an accelerated procedure.   [436] New Art 30.

[437] New Art 32(1)(b) and revised Art 32(2)(c) (current Art 27(3)(c)).

[438] Revised Art 33 (current Art 30).

[439] Revised Arts 35 and 36 (current Arts 32 and 34); the current Art 33 would be repealed.

[440] Revised Art 37 (current Art 35); the current Art 35(2) and (3) would be repealed.

[441] Revised Art 41 (current Art 39).   [442] See 5.8.1 below.   [443] See 5.8.2 below.

[444] See 5.8.3 below.

the application of the 'Dublin system' (ie the 'Dublin II' Regulation along with the Eurodac Regulation) in practice,[445] and has submitted proposals for amendment of both Regulations,[446] as part of the development of the second phase of the Common European Asylum System.

5.8.1. The Schengen Convention and the Dublin Convention

Articles 28–38 of the 1990 Schengen Convention set out rules on responsibility for asylum applications between the Schengen States, with effect from March 1995.[447] These rules were replaced by the essentially identical rules applicable to all Member States set in the Dublin Convention, in force from 1 September 1997.[448] The Dublin Convention was, like the Schengen Convention, explicitly related to the goal of abolishing internal borders within the EU, as set out in Article 14 EC (now Article 26 TFEU). The Convention was agreed because Member States feared that loosening or abolishing internal border checks would lead to an increase in multiple asylum applications (ie applications by the same person in more than one Member State). However, without common rules on how to determine which Member State was responsible for an application, Member States would inevitably take different approaches to determining which other Member State was responsible, and many applications would likely fall within the jurisdiction of two (or possibly more) Member States. To solve this problem, the Convention drew up a list of conflict rules for determining the Member State with jurisdiction over an application. These were to be applied in the following order:[449]

(a) the Member State where the applicant has a specified family member (spouse, parent, or child) who already has been recognized as a Geneva Convention refugee;[450]
(b) the Member State which has issued the applicant a residence permit;[451]
(c) the Member State which has issued the applicant a visa, with certain specified exceptions;[452]
(d) the Member State which the applicant first entered illegally, unless the applicant has been living in the Member State where he or she has applied for over six months;[453]
(e) the Member State responsible for controlling entry of the applicant, unless the applicant is a non-visa national who does not require a visa to enter either the Member State of first entry or the Member State in which he or she subsequently applies;[454]

---

[445] COM (2007) 299, 6 June 2007.   [446] See 5.8.4 below.   [447] [2000] OJ L 239.
[448] [1997] OJ C 254/1.   [449] Art 3(2).   [450] Art 4.   [451] Art 5(1).
[452] Art 5(2). If the applicant had multiple residence permits or visas, special rules in Art 5(3) and (4) applied.   [453] Art 6.
[454] Art 7(1). The responsible State for a non-visa national was the State in which he or she applied.

(f) the Member State in which an application is made in an airport transit zone;[455] or

(g) as a default, the Member State in which the application is made.[456]

It was also open to a Member State to decide that a non-EU country was responsible for the application,[457] or to either offer or accede to a request from another Member State to examine an application regardless of these conflict rules.[458] Detailed procedures on the transfer of asylum seekers and the exchange of information were set out.[459] The treaty was implemented by a body established by Article 18 of the Convention (the 'Article 18 Committee'), which adopted a number of measures in 1997, 1998, and 2000.[460]

The Convention was heavily criticized for forcing apart family members, for ignoring the differences in national interpretation of the Geneva Convention, and for inducing asylum seekers to destroy travel documents— thus avoiding the application of the conflict rules (due to an absence of proof about the countries they had previously entered) but raising a suspicion that their submissions about the persecution they faced would be disbelieved by authorities because of their lack of full disclosure of their prior travel details.[461] From the perspective of national authorities, the Convention was also disappointing, because only about 6% of asylum applications were identified as subject to it; since only two-thirds of those cases were accepted by the Member State identified as responsible and only 40% of the remaining cases actually resulted in the transfer of an asylum only 1.7% of all asylum applications made in the EU were ultimately subject to the transfer of an asylum seeker pursuant to the rules in the Convention.[462] In 2001, only 4.2% of asylum applications were subject to requests to take responsibility according to the Convention, and 71.4% of these requests were accepted (3% of the total asylum applications).[463]

---

[455] Art 7(3).   [456] Art 8.   [457] Art 3(5).   [458] Respectively Arts 3(4) and 9.

[459] Respectively Arts 10–15.

[460] Decisions 1/97 and 2/97 ([1997] OJ L 281/1 and 26); Decision 1/98 ([1998] OJ L 196/49); and Decision 1/2000 ([2000] OJ L 281/1). On implementation of the Convention up to 1998, see the first edition of this book, at 114–116.

[461] On the Convention, see C Marinho, ed, *The Dublin Convention on Asylum* (EIPA, 2000); K Hailbronner and C Thiery, 'Schengen II and Dublin: Responsibility for Asylum Applications in Europe' (1997) 34 CMLRev 957; A Hurwitz, 'The 1990 Dublin Convention: A Comprehensive Assessment' (1999) IJRL 646; and S Da Lomba, *The Right to Seek Refugee Status in the European Union* (Intersentia, 2004), 117–131.

[462] The statistics are for 1998–99, and were taken from the Commission evaluation of the Convention (SEC (2001) 756, 12 June 2001, p. 2).

[463] There were 371,680 asylum applications, 15,776 outgoing requests under the Convention and 11,268 acceptances of those requests. The statistics do not indicate what percentage of asylum seekers were subsequently transferred. These statistics are taken from the Commission annual report on migration and asylum statistics: <http://ec.europa.eu/justice_home/doc_centre/asylum/statistics/doc_annual_report_2001_en.htm>.

5.8.2. The 'Dublin II' Regulation

The Dublin Convention was replaced as from 1 September 2003 by Regulation 343/2003, known in practice as the 'Dublin II' Regulation.[464] This Regulation set out certain additions and amendments to the hierarchy of criteria for responsibility in the Convention along with an acceleration of the procedure for transferring asylum seekers between States, and has been implemented by a Commission Regulation, pursuant to powers which the Regulation conferred upon the Commission to adopt implementing measures.[465] The Regulation still leaves Member States free to decide that a non-Member State should take responsibility, or to take responsibility even where the Regulation does not require it.[466] It has been amended once, in order to change the rules relating to the adoption of implementing measures.[467] As noted above, in 2007 the Commission released a report on the operation of the 'Dublin system',[468] which is considered also below.

As for the Court of Justice, the Commission brought one infringement action against a Member State (Greece) for incorrect application of the Regulation, because Greece refused to consider the merits of asylum applications brought by persons who had initially made applications there, made later applications in other Member States, and then were transferred back to Greece, on the grounds that the applications had been withdrawn.[469] In fact, because of concerns about 'very low material reception standards', the Commission has reported that 'at least four Member States have refused to return asylum seekers to Greece despite the fact that Greece is responsible for processing their claim'.[470] The Court of Justice has also received one reference from a national court on the interpretation of the Regulation,[471] and two national courts have agreed to send further references concerning the validity of transfers of asylum seekers to Greece.[472]

In common with the Dublin Convention, the Regulation still leaves Member States free to decide that a non-Member State should take responsibility, or to take

---

[464] [2003] L 50/1; see Art 29 on the date of application. On the Regulation, see: S Da Lomba, *The Right to Seek Refugee Status in the European Union* (Intersentia, 2004), 131–141; A Nicol, 'From Dublin Convention to Dublin Regulation: A Progressive Move?', in A Baldaccini, E Guild, and H Toner, eds, *Whose Freedom, Security and Justice? EU Immigration and Asylum Law and Policy* (Hart, 2007), 265; and H Battjes, *European Asylum Law and International Law* (Martinus Nijhoff, 2006), ch 7.

[465] Reg 1560/2003, [2003] OJ L 222/3.   [466] Arts 3(2) and 15 of the Regulation.

[467] Reg 1103/2008 ([2008] L 304/80), changing the rules to apply the 'regulatory procedure with scrutiny' for the adoption of implementing measures. See further 2.2.2.1 above.

[468] COM (2007) 299, 6 June 2007.

[469] Case C-130/08 *Commission v Greece*. See now the proposal for a revised Regulation, which addresses this issue (5.8.4 below). On the concept of withdrawn applications, see also the asylum procedures Directive, discussed in 5.7 above.

[470] See the impact assessment for the proposed reception conditions Dir (SEC (2008) 2944, 3 Dec 2008, p 15).   [471] Case C-19/08 *Petrosian* [2009] ECR I-495.

[472] *Saeedi* (a UK reference) and *Edris and others* (an Irish reference). For a survey of national court practice on this issue, see: <http://www.unhcr.gr/dt/dublinIIreg.pdf>.

responsibility even where the Regulation does not require it.[473] The first criterion for responsibility is now the new criterion relating to unaccompanied minors; the Member State responsible for them is the Member State where a family member can take care of them, or failing that the Member State where they lodged their application.[474] The second criterion, family reunion with recognized refugees, was unchanged from the Dublin Convention.[475] The third criterion is new: a Member State is responsible for the family members of an asylum seeker if the latter is still waiting for a decision on the substance of the application in that Member State.[476]

The second criterion in the Convention rules (issue of a visa or a residence permit) became the fourth criterion in the Regulation, but it was not significantly changed in substance.[477] It should be noted that the Visa Information System, once operational, will be used in order to check more effectively whether a visa has been issued to an asylum seeker.[478] The third criterion in the Convention (crossing the border irregularly) became the fifth criterion in the Regulation, but responsibility now terminates after twelve months.[479] In order to enforce this provision, the Eurodac Regulation requires Member States to take fingerprints of persons who are stopped crossing the external borders irregularly.[480] Also, a further new provision specifies that if a Member State cannot or can no longer be held responsible on grounds of irregular border crossing, another Member State will become responsible if a person has resided there, having initially entered irregularly, for more than five months.[481] The political context of this provision was the settlement of a dispute between the UK and France concerning asylum seekers residing in France but who attracted little or no interest from the French authorities, who frequently attempted to enter the UK. Next, the sixth criterion (formerly the fourth) is the State responsible for controlling the entry of a non-visa national, with the wording of the Dublin Convention rules in effect retained.[482] The seventh criterion (formerly the fifth) is the Member State where the asylum seeker applied for asylum in the airport transit zone.[483] Finally, as before, the default criterion is the Member State where the asylum seeker submitted his or her application.[484]

There is a new 'tie-break' clause in the event of family members submitting an application in the same Member State close together,[485] but no such clause to govern the position where the family members submit applications in *different* Member States. The old 'humanitarian' clause was retained and expanded, now focusing on family reunion alone.[486] Although this clause remains optional for Member States, it might well be possible in national law to argue about how the authorities have exercised their discretion.

---

[473] Arts 3(2) and 15 of the Regulation.
[474] Art 6. See now the action plan on unaccompanied minors (COM (2010) 213, 6 May 2010).
[475] Art 7.   [476] Art 8.   [477] Art 9.
[478] Reg 767/2008, [2008] OJ L 218/60, Art 21. See further 4.8 above.
[479] Art 10(1).   [480] See 5.8.3 below.   [481] Art 10(2).   [482] Art 11.   [483] Art 12.
[484] Art 13.   [485] Art 14.   [486] Art 15.

The procedural rules and provisions on administrative cooperation were amended, in particular to accelerate the transfer of asylum seekers and to include some of the details of the previous implementing measures in the text of the Regulation (with the result that the Commission cannot amend those provisions via means of a 'comitology' procedure).[487] The suspensive effect of an appeal against the application of the Regulation is permitted on a case-by-case basis, although it is only optional for Member States.[488] According to the Court of Justice, the time limit of six months to take an asylum seeker back following the agreement to do so by a Member State only starts to run from the date of a final court decision on a challenge to a transfer decision, not from the date on which a court or tribunal suspended that transfer pending its judgment.[489]

As for the implementation of the Regulation,[490] the Commission's 2007 report indicates that over 2003–05, the number of asylum applications subject to requests to apply the Dublin II rules rose to 11.5%, as compared to 6% for the Dublin Convention. The acceptance rate of transfers was similar (72%) and the rate of transfers carried out rose to 52%, although the Commission still considered this disappointing. Overall 4.1% of asylum seekers were transferred under the rules, also a rise compared to the previous period, but still quite a modest percentage of the overall number of asylum seekers. The Commission did not suggest the reasons why such a low percentage of asylum seekers was still covered by the Dublin rules, given that the Eurodac system had started operations and the EU had been enlarged in the meantime.

On the criteria in the Dublin rules, the Commission reported that: unaccompanied minors made up perhaps 1–2% of requests; the family members' provisions were 'rarely applied' due to evidence problems; the criteria regarding visas and residence permits were 'applied frequently', particularly as regards visas (about 6–20% of requests); the requests for the application of the irregular entry criterion 'far exceed transfers', because of the low rate of fingerprinting under the Eurodac system (see below) and the difficulty proving irregular entry without such data; the 'illegal stay' criterion was 'less often' used, again due to evidence problems; and the 'legal entry' criterion made up only a 'small proportion' of requests. The failure to carry out half of the agreed transfers was due to asylum seekers absconding (the evidence that detention was necessary to avoid this was mixed), the suspensive effect of an appeal (although few Member States allowed this), illness or humanitarian reasons, or voluntary return to the country of origin.

This evidence suggests that the Dublin rules remain an expensive waste of time, ultimately still applying to only a small percentage of asylum seekers and imposing an extra cost on top of the cost of considering each asylum application. The application of the Eurodac system and the increase in EU border controls

---

[487] Arts 16–23.   [488] Art 20(1)(e).   [489] See the judgment in *Petrosian* (n 470 above).
[490] COM (2007) 299 and SEC (2007) 742, 6 June 2007.

have not altered the situation profoundly. Yet, as we shall see, the Commission's subsequent proposal to amend the Dublin system tries to improve it, rather than overthrow it.

From a human rights perspective, there was some improvement in the Regulation as regards the issue of family reunion, although with a narrow definition of 'family' in the Regulation and the limitation of reunion to certain categories (leaving out, for instance reunion with an irregularly resident family member, a family member enjoying or applying for subsidiary protection, or a family member with legal residence on other grounds) many families could still be separated by the revised rules. It is arguable that the fundamental objection to allocating responsibility for asylum claims in the absence of a common definition of the Geneva Convention should have been overcome after the qualification Directive took effect, from October 2006—although it has transpired that in practice there is still great divergence in Member States' asylum law, in spite of the latter Directive.[491] In any case, the negative impact of the Dublin Convention rules as regards the destruction of documents by asylum seekers was not reduced by the Regulation.

5.8.3. Eurodac

The Eurodac Regulation was adopted in December 2000,[492] and took effect on 15 January 2003, when Eurodac began operations following the satisfaction of complex technical requirements by the Commission and the Member States.[493] It should be noted that the Commission's operational management of Eurodac would in future be transferred to a new agency responsible for EU JHA database management, if the Commission's proposal to this end is adopted.[494]

The Regulation requires fingerprints of all asylum seekers over fourteen to be taken and transmitted to a 'Central Unit' which compares them with other fingerprints previously (and subsequently) transmitted to see whether the asylum seeker has made multiple applications in the EU.[495] Similarly, Member States must take the fingerprints of all third-country nationals who cross a border irregularly,[496] and transmit them to the Central Unit to check against fingerprints

---

[491] See 5.5 above.

[492] Reg 2725/2000, [2000] OJ L 316/1. On the Regulation, see E Brouwer, 'Eurodac: Its Temptations and Limitations' (2002) 4 EJML 231.

[493] See Art 27(2) and the Communication on start of operations ([2003] OJ C 5/2).

[494] COM (2009) 293, 24 June 2009; revised: COM (2010) 93, 19 Mar 2010.

[495] Chapter II (Arts 4–7).

[496] Rather dubiously, this concept is extended in an unpublished statement in the Council minutes to include cases where a third-country national 'is apprehended beyond the external border, where he/she is still en route and there is no doubt that he/she crossed the external border irregularly' (Council doc 12314/00 Add 1, 15 Nov 2000).

subsequently taken from asylum seekers.[497] Member States may also take finger-prints of third-country nationals 'found illegally present' and transmit them to the Central Unit to see whether such persons have previously applied for asylum in another Member State. There are provisions on data protection, data security, and rights of the data subject.[498] For a transitional period, the data on recognized refugees is blocked once the refugee status of a person is granted.[499] At the end of that period (January 2008), the EU institutions had to decide either to store the data and use it in the same way as data on asylum seekers, or to erase all data as soon as a person has been recognized as a refugee. No such decision has yet been taken, although the subsequent proposal to amend the Regulation addresses this issue.[500]

The EU institutions disagreed as to which institution should have the power to adopt implementing measures. Ultimately, although Article 202 EC (now, after the Treaty of Lisbon, Article 291 TFEU) required implementing power to be delegated to the Commission, with a limited possibility of delegating power to the Council, the Council decided that it would retain power to adopt the measures concerning the detailed operations of the Central Unit and concerning the 'blocking' of the fingerprints of recognized refugees, while leaving other measures to be adopted by the Commission following a form of 'comitology' procedure.[501] Applying this procedure, the Eurodac Regulation was subsequently implemented by Council Regulation 407/2002.[502] This Regulation sets out rules on transmission of data by Member States, carrying out comparisons by the Central Unit, communication between Member States and the Central Unit, and other tasks of the Central Unit, which concern the separation of data on different categories of fingerprints and gathering statistics on the number of recognized refugees who request asylum in other Member States.

The Commission is required to report annually on the operation of Eurodac and to evaluate Eurodac generally at regular periods, beginning in January 2006.[503] According to these annual reports,[504] in 2003 Eurodac registered 271,573 sets of fingerprints: 246,902 from asylum seekers, 7,857 from irregu-lar border-crossers, and 16,814 from irregular residents. In 2004, the ten new Member States began operating the Eurodac system, most immediately upon accession and the last two by July 2004. Eurodac registered 287,938 sets of fin-gerprints: 232,205 from asylum seekers, 16,183 from irregular border-crossers,

---

[497] Chapter III of the Regulation (Arts 8–10).   [498] Chapter VI (Arts 13–20).   [499] Art 12.
[500] See 5.8.4 below.   [501] Art 23. On the issue of comitology, see 2.2.2.1 above.
[502] [2002] OJ L 62/1.
[503] Art 24 of Reg 2725/2000. On the first general evaluation, see 5.8.2 above.
[504] SEC (2004) 557, 5 May 2004 (for 2003); SEC (2005) 839, 20 June 2005 (for 2004); SEC (2006) 1170, 15 Sep 2006 (for 2005); SEC (2007) 1184, 11 Sep 2007 (for 2006); COM (2009) 13, 26 Jan 2009 (for 2007); COM (2009) 494, 25 Sep 2009 (for 2008); and COM (2010) 415, 2 Aug 2010 (for 2009).

and 39,550 from irregular residents. In 2005, there were 258,684 sets of fingerprints: 187,223 from asylum seekers, 25,162 from irregular border-crossers,
and 46,299 from irregular residents. In 2006, there were 270,611 sets of fingerprints: 165,958 from asylum seekers, 41,312 from irregular border-crossers, and
63,341 from irregular residents. In 2007, there were 300,018 sets of fingerprints:
197,284 from asylum seekers, 38,173 from irregular border-crossers, and 64,561
from irregular residents. In 2008, there were 357,421 sets of fingerprints: 219,557
from asylum seekers, 61,945 from irregular border-crossers, and 75,919 from
irregular residents. Finally, in 2009, there were 353,561 sets of fingerprints:
236,936 from asylum seekers, 31,071from irregular border-crossers, and 85,554
from irregular residents.

It can be seen that over 2003–08, the total number of asylum seekers' fingerprints registered dropped and then increased again (with a minor drop in
2009), in line with the trend for asylum applications. On the other hand, the
number of fingerprints registered from irregular border-crossers and irregular
residents has overall risen significantly, although there was a sharp drop for
the former category in 2009 (understood to be the consequence of an agreement between Italy and Libya). For several years, the Commission suggested
that many cases of irregular border crossing may be missing from the Eurodac
system, but it has not repeated this suggestion since the 2007 general evaluation. In any event, the statistics regularly show that over half of the irregular border-crossers who made a subsequent asylum claim did so in the *same*
Member State—which is irrelevant for the purposes of the Dublin system.
About 20–25% of the persons who were irregularly staying had made prior
asylum claims, one-third of these in the same Member State. The percentage of multiple asylum applications detected was 7% in 2003, 13.5% in 2004,
and 16% in 2005, and then stabilized: 17% in 2006, 16% in 2007, and 17.5%
in 2008 (these figures include some comparisons with fingerprints submitted
by the same Member State). The Commission frequently observed that there
were a high number of 'special searches' of the system, which were supposed
to be exceptionally rare.

Neither the annual reports nor the general evaluation of the Dublin system
(see above) have been able to draw comprehensive conclusions about the link
between Eurodac data and the application of the Dublin II Regulation, except to
show that Member States rarely accept responsibility for irregular border-crossers
in the absence of such data. But it is clear, as discussed above, that since Eurodac
began operations, the numbers of persons covered by the Dublin rules has only
increased modestly. So it might be questioned whether Eurodac has contributed
to the operation of the Dublin rules sufficiently to justify the cost of the system
for the EU and its Member States.

It remains to be seen whether this situation changes once national authorities
have access to certain information in the Visa Information System (VIS) in order
to assist with determining the country responsible for determining the asylum

claim.[505] The future is likely to include interlinks between Eurodac and other EU information systems.[506]

The operation of Eurodac is subject to the principles of data protection and the right to privacy, in particular requiring a link with the data collected and a legitimate aim and the application of the principle of proportionality (including the 'purpose limitation' principle of data protection law, ie giving access to the data only for the purposes it was originally collected for). In fact, the Eurodac system already infringes this principle to the extent that data on irregular border-crossers is kept for a longer period than the period during which a Member State could be held responsible under the Dublin II rules.

5.8.4. Proposals for amendment

In December 2008, the Commission proposed parallel measures to amend both the Dublin II Regulation and the Eurodac Regulation.[507] The Eurodac proposal was replaced by a new proposal in September 2009,[508] at which point the Commission also proposed a parallel third pillar Decision to give law enforcement services access to Eurodac data.[509] The latter proposal lapsed with the entry into force of the Lisbon Treaty, and has not yet been replaced by a new proposal, although a replacement proposal will likely be made in 2010.[510]

The proposed amendments to the Dublin II Regulation would first of all extend the scope of that Regulation to persons who make applications for subsidiary protection.[511] Next, the scope of 'family members' would be enlarged to include married minor children, the parents of married minor children, and minor siblings.[512] The provision permitting Member States to determine that a third State is responsible for the application would be amended to confirm

---

[505] Art 18 of Reg 767/2008 ([2008] OJ L 218/60); see generally 4.8 above. See also 5.5 above, on access to the VIS to decide on the merits of asylum claims.

[506] See Commission Communication (COM (2005) 597, 24 Nov 2005).

[507] COM (2008) 820 and 825, 3 Dec 2008. For comments on the proposals, see: ECRE, online at: <http://www.ecre.org/files/ECRE_Response_to_Recast_Dublin_Regulation_2009.pdf>; Caritas Europa and others, online at: <http://www.caritas-europa.org/module/FileLib/ChrGrp_CommonpaperonECproposalsforDublinII_FINALd.pdf>; the Meijers Committee, online at: <http://www.statewatch.org/news/2009/mar/eu0dublin-reception-meijers-cttee.pdf>; and the UNHCR, online at: <http://www.unhcr.org/4a0d6a6710.html>.

[508] COM (2009) 342, 10 Sep 2009.

[509] COM (2009) 344, 10 Sep 2009. See also the 'bridging clause' in the proposed Regulation (new Art 3, ibid).

[510] The correct legal base for this proposal would now be Art 87(2)(a) TFEU. See 12.2.4 below.

[511] See, for instance, the revised Arts 1 and 2(b). This would also mean that responsibility for applications would lie with a Member State where a family member has received or applied for *international protection*, not merely refugee status (revised Arts 9 and 10).

[512] Revised Art 2(i).

expressly that such a State must be a 'safe third country' as defined in the asylum procedures legislation.[513] There would be expanded procedural rights concerning the protection-seekers' right to information, the right to a personal interview, and special guarantees for minors.[514]

The main criteria for responsibility would not be amended, except to: change the rules on timing of applications where the interests of family unity or the best interests of the child were an issue;[515] make assorted changes to the rules applicable to responsibility for unaccompanied minors;[516] and provide for a different status for the rules relating to dependent relatives and potentially separated families.[517] All of the humanitarian provisions would require the applicant's consent.[518] The procedural rules would be amended in order to provide further information to the applicant, a stronger right to a remedy, and detailed rules regulating detention of applicants.[519] There would be new rules concerning costs and the exchange of information before transfers are carried out.[520] Finally, there would be the possibility of suspending the entire Dublin system as regards (a) particular Member State(s) for a limited period.[521]

As for the Eurodac Regulation, first of all its scope would also be extended to cover persons who make applications for subsidiary protection.[522] As noted above, Eurodac would be managed by a new agency, rather than the Commission.[523] There would now be a deadline to take the fingerprints within seventy-two hours after an application for international protection was made, or after apprehension in connection with irregular crossing of an external border.[524] The database would include additional information on the status of the data subject.[525] Data on irregular border-crossers would only be kept for one year, consistently with the responsibility rules in the Dublin II (and III) Regulation.[526] However, data on persons who have received international protection status would now be unblocked.[527] The rights of data subjects would be enhanced,[528] and there would be new provisions on the role of the European Data Protection Supervisor (EDPS).[529] Finally, the provisions concerning the adoption of implementing measures by the Council

---

[513] Revised Art 3(3); on the procedures Directive, see 5.7 above. Arguably this is already implicitly the correct interpretation of the current provision.　　　　[514] New Arts 4–6.

[515] New Art 7(3).　　　[516] Revised Art 8.

[517] Revised Arts 11 and 12. These rules would now be part of the main hierarchy, not ancillary rules; the substance of the former rules would also be amended.　　　[518] Art 17.

[519] Revised Art 25 (see also revised Art 32) and new Arts 26 and 27. On the issue of detention, it should be recalled that the detention of asylum seekers falls outside the scope of the EU's Returns Directive (Dir 2008/115, [2008] OJ L 348/98): see Case C-357/09 PPU *Kadzoev*, judgment of 30 Nov 2009, not yet reported.　　　[520] New Arts 29 and 30.

[521] New Art 31.　　　[522] See, for instance, the revised Art 1(1).

[523] New Art 5; see n 492 above.　　　[524] Revised Arts 7(1) and 12(2).

[525] New Art 8 and revised Art 9(h)–(k).　　　[526] Revised Art 14(1).

[527] New Arts 16 and 33.　　　[528] Revised Art 25.

[529] New Arts 27 and 28. On the EDPS, see further 12.3.2 below.

or the Commission would be repealed,[530] and the current implementing measure would be inserted into the text of the main Regulation.

The Dublin III proposal is welcome to the extent that it enlarges the possibility of family reunion, strengthens the procedural rights of asylum seekers who challenge transfers, and ensures that basic rights are secured during detention— although an express (short) time-limit on the maximum period of detention should be added. The Eurodac proposal includes a necessary reduction in the time period for accessing data on irregular border-crossers, but the Commission has not sufficiently justified its suggestion to unblock the fingerprints of recognized refugees. It remains to be seen whether, when, and if law enforcement authorities obtain access to Eurodac data, this will be subject to sufficient safeguards.

5.9. Reception conditions

The first-phase Directive 2003/9 on reception conditions for asylum seekers was adopted in January 2003.[531] Member States had to implement the Directive by 6 February 2005,[532] but some of them missed this deadline.[533] The Commission has issued a report on the application of the Directive, which is considered below as part of the discussion of the Directive.[534] There has subsequently been a proposal to amend the Directive, still under discussion, which is discussed separately below.[535]

5.9.1. Current reception conditions Directive

The Directive applies to applications for Geneva Convention refugee status made at the border or on the territory of Member States, and to asylum seekers' family

---

[530] Current Arts 21 and 22.

[531] Dir 2003/9 ([2003] OJ L 31/18). On the Dir, see S Da Lomba, *The Right to Seek Refugee Status in the European Union* (Intersentia, 2004), 219–262 and J Handoll, 'Directive 2003/9 on Reception Conditions of Asylum Seekers: Ensuring "Mere Subsistence" or a "Dignified Standard of Living"?', in A Baldaccini, E Guild, and H Toner, eds, *Whose Freedom, Security and Justice? EU Immigration and Asylum Law and Policy* (Hart, 2007), 195. All references in this section are to this Directive, unless otherwise indicated.   [532] Art 26(1).

[533] The Court of Justice ruled against two Member States that failed to meet the deadline: Cases C-72/06 *Commission v Greece*, judgment of 19 Apr 2007; and C-102/06 *Commission v Austria*, judgment of 26 Oct 2006 (both unreported). Four other cases were withdrawn by the Commission, presumably because the Member States concerned complied with their obligations during the proceedings. These were Cases: C-47/06 *Commission v Luxembourg*; C-75/06 *Commission v Portugal*; C-389/06 *Commission v Belgium*; and C-496/06 *Commission v Germany*.

[534] COM (2007) 745, 26 Nov 2007. See also ECRE, 'The EC Directive on the Reception of Asylum Seekers: Are Asylum Seekers in Europe Receiving Material Support and Access to Employment in Accordance with European Legislation?' November 2005, and A Baldaccini, *Asylum Support: A Practitioners' Guide to the EU Reception Directive* (Justice, 2005).   [535] See 5.9.2.

members if they are covered by the asylum seekers' applications according to national law.[536] Member States have an option to apply the Directive to persons claiming other forms of status.[537] The Directive applies to asylum seekers as long as a 'final decision' has not been taken on their application, 'as long as they are allowed to remain on the territory as asylum seekers'.[538] According to the Commission's report, some Member States failed to apply the Directive at all stages of the asylum procedure (not in transit zones, or during the admissibility stage, or during the determination of whether the Dublin rules apply), or applied the Directive only to certain categories of asylum seekers (holding a certain ID card, or who have already registered), and a significant number of Member States failed to apply the Directive in detention centres.

The reception conditions Directive does not apply when the EU's temporary protection Directive applies,[539] which suggests *a contrario* that the former Directive *will* apply when a purely national temporary protection regime is in force, rather than the EU system provided for in the temporary protection Directive—assuming that new national temporary protection regimes can still be established.[540] As with other first-phase asylum Directives, Member States may apply more favourable provisions as regards reception conditions, provided that they are 'compatible' with the Directive.[541]

Asylum seekers must be informed within fifteen days of lodging their application of the rights and benefits to which they are entitled and the obligations placed upon them by Member States.[542] According to the Commission's report, the 'vast majority' of Member States complied with this obligation, but some Member States did not make sufficient information available, or did not make it available in many languages. Also, asylum seekers must be given, within three days of their application, a document certifying their status or the legality of their presence on the territory (subject to certain exceptions), and Member States 'may' supply asylum seekers with a travel document permitting them to travel to another State.[543] The Commission's report indicates that while all Member States issue the required documentation, many do not issue it by the required deadline. However, in practice the form and content of the documents vary, and because the documents often do not certify identity,[544] this causes some problems for asylum seekers in daily life. The Commission suggests that

---

[536] Art 3(1).

[537] According to the Commission report, the 'vast majority' of Member States chose to apply the Directive to persons applying for subsidiary protection status.

[538] Arts 2(c) and 3(1). The Directive does not define 'final decision'. On the issue of whether asylum seekers can remain on the territory, see the asylum procedures Directive (5.7 above). Note that the proposal to amend the Directive (see 5.9.2 below) still does not define a 'final decision'.

[539] Art 3(3) and (4).   [540] See 5.6 above.

[541] Art 4. On the issue of 'compatible' higher standards, see 5.2.4 above.   [542] Art 5.

[543] Art 6.   [544] There is no requirement that the documents must do so: see Art 6(3).

a standard model document, which would certify identity, would address these problems.[545]

Next, asylum seekers are entitled to freedom of movement within a Member State, or at least within an assigned area, but Member States can decide on asylum seekers' residence on grounds of public order, public interest, or the necessity to decide on applications quickly; Member States may also 'confine' an asylum seeker 'to a particular place' where this 'proves necessary' in accordance with national law.[546] According to the Commission report, most Member States apply the Directive correctly to non-detained applicants, given the wide discretion that the Directive permits them. However, the Commission convincingly argues that since detention of applicants is governed by a necessity requirement, detention without an individual evaluation is a breach of the Directive. The Commission also takes the view that detention for an indefinite period, except for 'duly justified' reasons, is a breach of the Directive, since it prevents the applicants from enjoying the rights granted by it, and that detention of minors, including unaccompanied minors, must take account of the special rules applicable to this group, including the best interests of the child.[547]

Member States must maintain family unity 'as far as possible' if the asylum seeker is provided with housing by the Member State.[548] The Commission report questions whether the additional procedural requirements in relation to family housing in two Member States are compatible with the Directive.

Asylum-seeking minors, and asylum seekers' minor children, must be given access to education under 'similar' conditions as nationals of the host state until an expulsion order is actually enforced, although the access to education can be delayed or offered in accommodation centres.[549] According to the Commission report, access to primary schools is not an issue, but access to secondary school is complicated because access to school is only granted at certain times of the school year, or because access is dependent on places available or decisions by local authorities. Also, 'many Member States deny detained minors access to education or make it impossible or very limited in practice'; only 'a few' Member States give effect to this right for such detainees.

---

[545] It should be noted that the proposal to amend the Directive (see 5.9.2 below) does not take up this suggestion.

[546] Art 7. It should again be recalled that the detention of asylum seekers falls outside the scope of the EU's Returns Dir (Dir 2008/115, [2008] OJ L 348/98): see Case C-357/09 PPU *Kadzoev*, judgment of 30 Nov 2009, not yet reported. On the human rights rules relating to immigration detention, see 7.3.2 below.

[547] See Arts 18 and 19; Art 18(1) states that '[t]he best interests of the child shall be a primary consideration' when applying the Directive to minors. See also by analogy the requirement to take account of the best interests of the child set out in the family reunion Dir (Dir 2003/86, [2003] OJ L 251/12), as interpreted by the Court of Justice in Case C-540/03 *EP v Council* [2006] ECR I-5769 (see further 6.6 below).   [548] Art 8.

[549] Art 10.

Member States must set out conditions on access to employment for asylum seekers whose application has been the subject of a first-instance decision within one year, but they may give priority to EU and EEA citizens and legally resident third-country nationals; access to employment cannot be withdrawn during an appeal against a negative decision if that appeal has suspensive effect.[550] Again, due to the flexibility of the Directive, the Commission did not find 'major' problems with the application of this rule by Member States, except that one Member State did not permit any labour market access at all for asylum seekers,[551] and the requirement to obtain a work permit and limits on labour market access and hours of work were questioned. Access to vocational training is at the discretion of Member States, although applicants must have access to vocational training which is linked to an employment contract, to the extent that they have access to the labour market.[552]

As for State assistance, Member States must provide for 'material reception conditions' which are sufficient 'to ensure a standard of living adequate for the health of applicants and capable of ensuring their subsistence', although assistance may be reduced or eliminated for asylum seekers with means or who have been working.[553] Assistance can be provided in kind or in the form of money or vouchers.[554] Member States have similar flexibility as regards the forms of housing offered to asylum seekers: this may include border accommodation, accommodation centres, or private housing.[555] According to the Commission report, there were 'no major problems' where the assistance was provided in kind or in reception centres, although in some Member States there were still shortages of housing places, or problems regarding clothes for asylum seekers or the 'generally low level of reception conditions'. However, the 'main problems' were in 'Member States where asylum seekers are given financial allowances', since these allowances were 'often too low to cover subsistence', were 'only rarely commensurate with the minimum social support granted to nationals', and might be insufficient even where they matched social support for nationals.

Health care provided to asylum seekers must include as a minimum essential treatment of illness and emergency care.[556] The Commission reports that all Member States comply with this minimum requirement, and some Member States go beyond it.

Member States are allowed to reduce or withdraw reception conditions in certain cases, for example where rules on reporting or residence have been breached, or where 'an asylum seeker has failed to demonstrate that the asylum claim was made as soon as reasonably practicable after arrival in that Member State'.[557]

---

[550] Art 11.
[551] Conversely, nine Member States gave asylum seekers access to labour markets less than one year after making their application. [552] Art 12.
[553] Art 13(2)–(4). [554] Art 13(5). [555] Art 14. [556] Art 15.
[557] Art 16(1) and (2).

According to the Commission report, 'only a few' Member States apply the latter exception, but '[s]ome Member States withdraw reception conditions in situations not authorised by the Directive'. Before reception conditions can be reduced or withdrawn, applicants have procedural rights, and in any case, access to emergency health care must always be guaranteed.[558]

There are special rules concerning groups with special needs, such as minors, in particular unaccompanied minors, the elderly, disabled persons, and victims of torture.[559] The Commission report on implementation of the Directive concludes that Member States are under an obligation to identify such persons (which many of them fail to do) and that some of the specific standards relating to vulnerable persons are not properly applied in some Member States (as regards health care, minors with special needs, and detention).

Finally, Member States must allow an appeal or review, ultimately before a judicial body, of negative decisions on benefits and of decisions concerning freedom of movement; '[p]rocedures for legal assistance in such cases shall be laid down by national law'.[560] The Commission rightly argues that some Member States breach the Directive when they do not allow appeals against decisions regarding freedom of movement, or withdrawing or reducing reception conditions, or any other decision other than detention. In some cases, the Commission reports that there are poorly justified or orally notified withdrawal decisions,[561] and the provision of legal aid in some Member States is queried.

The Commission's general conclusion in its report on application of the Directive is that '[o]verall, the Directive has been transposed satisfactorily in the majority of Member States', with '[o]nly a few' issues of misapplication arising; the Commission promised to pursue these. Furthermore, the report asserted that contrary to predictions, 'it appears that Member States have not lowered their previous standards of assistance to asylum seekers'. Finally, the Commission considered that the wide discretion granted to Member States by the Directive in key areas of reception conditions 'undermines the objective of creating a level playing field' in this area, and could only be addressed by a revision of the Directive.

By and large the standards set out in the Directive are imprecisely worded, leaving considerable scope for argument as to their correct application. It is particularly regrettable that the Directive did not more precisely limit the detention of asylum seekers and provide for more extensive access to employment, education, and vocational training. The provisions on possible withdrawal or reduction

---

[558] Art 16(4) and (5).

[559] Arts 17–20. See now the action plan on unaccompanied minors (COM (2010) 213, 6 May 2010).   [560] Art 21; see also Art 16(4).

[561] A poorly justified withdrawal decision will probably breach Art 16(4), but neither Art 16(4) nor Art 21 expressly requires decisions to be in writing.

of benefits are dubious on human rights grounds, in light of the case law of the UK courts.[562]

Some of the conclusions of the Commission's report on the application of the Directive are questionable. There is no evidence offered for the assertion that the Member States have not lowered their standards as regards reception conditions, and the report does not assess to what extent the Directive has led to a rise in standards. The overall assessment that transposition has been satisfactory overall is unconvincing, given the evidence that a number of Member States are not correctly applying the rules on making sufficient information available; issuing documentation in time; justification for detention; housing families together; ensuring access to education; giving sufficient access to employment and benefits; protecting vulnerable persons; withdrawing benefits; and providing effective remedies as regards alleged violations of the Directive. The Commission's promise to enforce the Directive has not been followed up to date by further infringement actions against Member States before the Court of Justice, and there has been no further report on the application of the Directive in order to assess whether more Member States have applied the Directive correctly in light of the threat of Court action.[563]

5.9.2. Proposal for amendment

As noted above, in December 2008, the Commission proposed a second-phase version of the reception conditions Directive,[564] which would 'recast' the existing Directive (ie make amendments to the existing text and then repeal that text after the amendments were consolidated). This proposal remains under discussion in the Council and EP.

First of all, the proposal would extend the existing Directive to include applications for subsidiary protection, which would confirm the current practice of almost all Member States.[565] The definition of 'family members' would also be widened, in common with the proposals to amend the qualification Directive and the Dublin rules.[566] The scope of the Directive would expressly include transit zones, although arguably this is already implicit in the current Directive.[567] There would be detailed rules on detention, in particu-

---

[562] *R (on the application of Adam and others) v Secretary of State for the Home Department* [2005] UKHL 66.

[563] The next report on implementation is due in Aug 2011 (Art 25).

[564] COM (2008) 815, 3 Dec 2008. All of the references in this subsection are to this proposal, unless otherwise indicated. See comments on the proposal by: ECRE, online at: <http://www.ecre.org/files/ECRE_Comments_on_Reception_Conditions_Directive_recast_2009.pdf>; UNHCR, online at: <http://www.unhcr.org/4a0d6bf86.html>; the Meijers Committee, online at: <http://www.statewatch.org/news/2009/mar/eu0dublin-reception-meijers-cttee.pdf>.

[565] See, for instance, the new Art 2(a) and the revised Art 3(4).   [566] Revised Art 2(c).

[567] Revised Art 3(1).

lar setting out the circumstances in which asylum seekers can be detained; specifying guarantees for detained asylum seekers; regulating detention conditions; and establishing requirements relating to the detention of vulnerable persons.[568] While there would be no time limit placed on detention,[569] the separate proposal on asylum procedures would set a time limit to decide on the *application*.[570] In particular, unaccompanied minors could never be detained.[571] These provisions are largely similar to the relevant provisions of the Returns Directive,[572] but would generally set higher standards than that Directive, although unlike that Directive they would not set any ultimate time limit on detention (or a requirement for special justification if detention lasts longer than six months).

The rules on access to education would be amended to set higher standards, in particular to eliminate the possible one-year waiting period for access to education, to require that Member States offer preparatory classes if necessary, and to require Member States to offer alternative forms to education if access to the regular education system is not possible.[573] Access to employment would also be enhanced, by reducing the maximum waiting period to six months rather than one year (regardless of whether a first-instance decision has been taken or not), and by specifying that any national conditions applicable shall not 'unduly' restrict access to employment.[574]

As for material reception conditions, the proposal specifies that financial support should be equal to the level of social assistance for nationals, but then specifies that any differences 'shall be duly justified'.[575] There would be stronger protection against gender-based violence, and fewer possibilities for exceptions from the normal modalities of providing support.[576] The obligation to provide health care would be extended to include mental health care.[577]

The possibility to withdraw reception conditions where an applicant had not made an application as soon as reasonably practicable would be deleted, and any withdrawal of benefits could not extend to withdrawal of subsistence, essential medical care, or care for mental disorder.[578] The definition of persons with special needs would be expanded, and there would be an express obligation to identify such persons.[579] Also, the factors to take into account when considering the best interests of the child would be defined in further detail,[580] the rules concerning

---

[568] New Arts 8–11; the current Art 7(3) would be repealed.

[569] Compare to the Returns Dir (7.7.1 below).   [570] See 5.7.2.

[571] New Art 11(1), second sub-paragraph.

[572] Arts 15–18 of Dir 2008/115 ([2008] OJ L 348/98); see 7.7.1 below.

[573] Revised Art 14.

[574] Revised Art 15. It should be noted that the six-month maximum waiting period matches the proposed normal time period to take a first-instance decision in the ordinary asylum procedure, in the proposal to amend the asylum procedures Dir (see 5.7.2 above).   [575] New Art 17(5).

[576] Revised Art 18(2) and (8).   [577] Revised Art 19.   [578] Revised Art 20.

[579] Revised Art 21.   [580] Revised Art 22.

unaccompanied minors would be amended to strengthen the obligation to trace family members,[581] and the provisions on victims of torture would be amended, as regards access to rehabilitation services and training of persons who work with torture victims.[582] Finally, there would be a clearer obligation to grant legal aid and an express obligation to ensure review of both the facts and the law when an appeal is brought.[583]

Compared to the current Directive, the revised text would significantly increase standards as regards in particular detention, access to education, access to employment, the position of vulnerable persons, standards in the event of reduction of benefits, and the appeal process. The provisions on material reception conditions would remain relatively vague, however, and the absence of any provision setting time limits on detention is indefensible—particularly in light of the time limits on detention in the Returns Directive,[584] and the general time limit of six months to take a first-instance decision on an asylum application which the Commission has proposed separately.[585] Time will tell whether there will be enough support in the Council to accept the more ambitious elements of the Commission's proposal.

5.10. Administrative cooperation and EU funding

The most significant EU action to assist administrative cooperation in the field of asylum is the creation of a European Asylum Support Office. Furthermore, there is a long-established European Refugee Fund, and also EU measures on (inter alia) asylum statistics and information exchange.

5.10.1. European Asylum Support Office

In February 2006, the Commission released a Communication on cooperation between national administrations as regards asylum,[586] followed by Council conclusions.[587] The next step was the creation of a European Asylum Support Office, by means of a Regulation adopted in 2010.[588] The seat of the Asylum Support Office is in Valetta, Malta.[589]

---

[581] Revised Art 23.   [582] Revised Art 24.   [583] Revised Art 25.

[584] The proposal has also missed the opportunity to address the question of whether detention of asylum seekers counts toward the maximum time limits in the Returns Dir (see 7.7.1 below).

[585] See comments in 5.7.2 above.

[586] COM (2006) 67 and SEC (2006) 189, both 17 Feb 2006.

[587] See JHA Council press release, 27–28 Apr 2006.

[588] Reg 439/2010, [2010] OJ L 132/11. All further references in this subsection are to this Regulation unless otherwise noted. There was also a parallel amendment to the European Refugee Fund ([2010] OJ L 129/1). On the Fund, see 5.10.2 below.   [589] Council doc 5879/2/10, 23 Feb 2010.

The Agency was established in order to 'improve the implementation of the Common European Asylum System...to strengthen practical cooperation among Member States on asylum and to provide and/or coordinate the provision of operational support to Member States subject to particular pressure on their asylum and reception systems'.[590] Its main purposes are to 'provide effective operational support to Member States subject to particular pressure on their asylum and reception systems' and 'provide scientific and technical assistance in regard to [EU asylum] policy and legislation', in particular as 'an independent source of information'.[591] The Office's tasks are without prejudice' to those of the EU Fundamental Rights Agency, and it shall 'work closely' with that Agency and with the UNHCR.[592]

As for the practical cooperation tasks, the Office shall in particular 'organise, promote and coordinate' the exchange of information and identify and pool good practice; 'organise, promote and coordinate' activities relating to country-of-origin information (ie information about conditions in asylum seekers' countries of origin), including gathering and analysis of that information and drafting reports on that information; assist with the voluntary transfer of persons granted international protection status within the EU; support training for national administrations and courts, including the development of an EU asylum curriculum; and coordinate and exchange information on the operation of EU external asylum measures.[593] For Member States under 'particular pressure', the Office will gather information concerning possible emergency measures, set up an early warning system to alert Member States to mass influxes of asylum seekers, help such Member States to analyse asylum applications and establish reception conditions, and set up 'asylum teams' (see further below).[594]

For its contribution to the implementation of the Common European Asylum System, the Office will gather information on national authorities' application of EU asylum law, as well as national legislation and case law on asylum issues. It must also draw up an annual report on the situation regarding asylum in the EU. At the request of the Commission, the Office may draw up 'technical documents on the implementation of the asylum instruments of the Union, including guidelines and operating manuals'.[595]

The Office can also deploy 'asylum support teams' on the territory of a requesting Member State, in order to provide 'in particular expertise in relation to interpreting services, information on countries of origin and knowledge of the handling and management of asylum cases'.[596] The Regulation provides further detail on the process of deciding on the number of members and profiles of such teams, and on their deployment.[597]

---

[590] Art 1.   [591] Art 2(2) and (3).   [592] Arts 50 and 52.
[593] Arts 3–7.   [594] Arts 8–10.   [595] Arts 11 and 12.   [596] Arts 13 and 14.
[597] Arts 15–23. Compare with the rules on border support teams, as set out in the Frontex Reg (3.10.1 above).

As for the organization of the Office, it has a Management Board,[598] consisting of one member appointed by each Member State and two members appointed by the Commission, with the UNHCR as a non-voting Board member. The Board meets at least twice a year, or more if convened by its Chairman. It votes by an absolute majority, but Member States which did not participate in a particular EU asylum measure have to abstain from a vote relating solely to that measure. The main roles of the Board are to: appoint the Executive Director; adopt an annual report on the Office's activities; establish the staff policy of the Office; set up information systems; adopt an annual work programme; and take all (other) decisions necessary to fulfil the Office's terms of reference.

The Office's Executive Director is appointed by the Management Board for a five-year term from a list of candidates suggested by the Commission, after a hearing before the European Parliament. His or her term of office can be extended once for a three-year period. The job of the Executive Director is to manage the day-to-day running of the Office, including drafting reports on countries of origin.[599] Finally, there is a Consultative Forum which liaises between NGOs, civil society, and the Agency, and the Office can establish expert working parties.[600] There are also detailed provisions on the Office's budget, staff, legal status, languages, access to documents, security rules, liability, evaluation, and administrative control by the EU ombudsman.[601]

As for the Office's external relations, the Office is open to participation by countries which have agreements concerning the application of EU asylum legislation.[602] The Office also facilitates cooperation between the EU and third countries within the framework of EU external relations policy, and cooperates with other third countries as regards 'technical aspects' of policy, 'within the framework of working arrangements concluded with those countries'.[603] Furthermore, the Office has to collaborate with the UNHCR, Frontex, the EU's Fundamental Rights Agency, and other international organizations.[604]

5.10.2. Other measures

The most prominent form of 'burden-sharing' between the Member States is the European Refugee Fund, which was first established in September 2000,[605] replacing ad hoc agreements on modest short-term funding of asylum measures during the 'Maastricht era'.[606] This Fund expired in 2004, and a Decision establishing a second

---

[598] Arts 24–29.   [599] Arts 30–31.   [600] See respectively Arts 51 and 32.
[601] Arts 33–47.   [602] Art 49(1). For more on this association, see 5.2.5 above.
[603] Art 49(2).   [604] Arts 50 and 52.
[605] Decision 2000/596/EC, [2000] OJ L 252/12. For more on the fund, see the second edition of this book, at 345–348.
[606] [2000] OJ L 252/12. The first Fund made €216 million available over five years from 1 January 2000 to 31 December 2004 (or €43.2 million/year).

European Refugee Fund for 2005–10 was adopted in December 2004.[607] A third Fund Decision was adopted in 2007, to cover the years 2008–13.[608] This measure was amended in 2010, in parallel with the establishment of the European Asylum Office,[609] and another amendment relating to an EU resettlement programme is under discussion.[610] The EU's ARGO funding programme also supported activities of Member States in areas falling within the scope of EU asylum policy.[611]

As for asylum statistics and information, a body known as CIREA, a clearing house for asylum information, was initially established during the intergovernmental period of cooperation on immigration and asylum.[612] Subsequently, CIREA was terminated in 2002, and was replaced by the Commission's Immigration and Asylum Committee (a body for consulting Member States' experts), Eurasil (a body made up of asylum practitioners in national bodies), and Eurostat, the Commission's statistics body, which had taken over the role of drawing up immigration and asylum statistics in 1998.[613]

Eurostat's role has been placed on a more formal footing since EU legislation concerning asylum and migration statistics was adopted in 2007.[614] This legislation requires Member States to provide statistics on: the numbers claiming international protection, the number of pending claims, and withdrawn applications; the first-instance or final decisions on the rejection, granting, or withdrawal of refugee, subsidiary protection, and temporary protection status, as well as the granting or withdrawal of humanitarian status under national law; the number of applicants who are unaccompanied minors or who have been admitted under a resettlement scheme; and (as regards the Dublin rules) the number of requests for transfer of an asylum seeker, the reasons for those requests, the response to those requests, the number of transfers, and the number of requests for information.[615] Except for the Dublin statistics, this information must be disaggregated by age, sex, and country of origin.

Furthermore, current EU asylum legislation requires Member States to inform the Commission of the number of people covered by reception conditions,[616] and

---

[607] [2004] OJ L 381/52. The second Fund made available €114 million to disburse over the first two years (€57 million/year): see Art 2(1), 2004 Decision.

[608] [2007] OJ L 144/1. The third Fund made available €628 million to disburse over six years (€104.7 million/year): see Art 12(1), 2007 Decision.

[609] [2010] OJ L 129/1. See 5.10.1 above.

[610] COM (2009) 456, 2 Sep 2009. See 5.11 below.

[611] [2002] OJ L 161/11 (Art 6) and [2004] OJ L 371/48; see further 3.11 above.

[612] See 5.2.1 above.

[613] See COM (2003) 152, 26 Mar 2003, and, as regards statistics: JHA Council conclusions of Mar 1998 and May 2001; Communication (SEC (2001) 602, 9 Apr 2001); and Action Plan (COM (2003) 179, 15 Apr 2003). For the first annual EU report on asylum and migration statistics, see: <http://ec.europa.eu/justice_home/doc_centre/immigration/statistics/doc_immigration_statistics_en.htm>.

[614] Reg 862/2007, [2007] OJ L 199/23.

[615] Art 4, Reg 862/2007 (ibid); for the definitions, which refer back to EU asylum legislation, see Art (2)(1)(j)–(o) of the Reg.   [616] Art 22 of Dir 2003/9 ([2003] OJ L 31/18).

the proposed legislation on the same issue would require Member States to supply significantly more information, for example as regards labour market access and the amount of social assistance for asylum seekers.[617]

The role of official asylum statistics is absolutely crucial as regards public understanding of the nature of the asylum issue: in particular, there appears to be wide misunderstanding as to the numbers of persons claiming asylum in the EU and its Member States and the percentage of asylum seekers who are subsequently allowed to stay on one ground or another. Time will tell whether the increased information available on the basis of the statistics legislation will be useful in assessing the application of EU asylum law. For that purpose, it would also be useful to have data on the success rate of appeals and on the precise grounds why applications are unsuccessful (to evaluate, for example, how widely the 'safe third country' concept is applied to rule applications inadmissible), and to have further public data on issues such as detention of asylum seekers.

Finally, the EU measures on the exchange of information as regards asylum and immigration policy, the Migration Network, and the annual report on asylum and immigration also play a role in this field.[618]

5.11. External relations

Following growing interest in the external aspects of asylum law, in particular the question of processing asylum applications outside the EU, the Commission released a series of communications on this controversial issue.[619] An initial communication of 2003 suggested that the EU should: develop a policy on an EU-wide 'protected entry' system and an EU resettlement scheme (ie a policy to admit persons staying in third States who had already been determined to have protection needs); develop burden-sharing within the EU and between the EU and third countries, in particular to place EU external migration funding on a formal legal basis, in order to support regions which housed a large number of asylum seekers who might wish to travel to EU Member States; and further speed up asylum procedures within the EU.[620] A seminar held by the Italian presidency found that Member States were more interested in a resettlement scheme than a

---

[617] Annex I to the proposed Directive on reception conditions (COM (2008) 815, 3 Dec 2008). Note that the Commission has reported that Member States are not complying with their obligations to supply information under the existing Directive (see p 14 of the impact assessment on the proposal: SEC (2008) 2944, 3 Dec 2008). See also Art 42 of the proposed asylum responsibility Regulation (COM (2008) 820, 3 Dec 2008), which simply refers to the immigration statistics Regulation.

[618] For details, see 6.11 below.

[619] For a detailed analysis of the issues, see G Noll, 'Visions of the Exceptional: Legal and Theoretical Issues Raised by Transit Processing Centers and Reception Zones' (2003) 5 EJML 303.

[620] COM (2003) 315, 3 June 2003; see also the conclusions of the June 2003 Thessaloniki European Council. For studies on these issues, see: <http://ec.europa.eu/justice_home/doc_centre/asylum/studies/doc_asylum_studies_en.htm>.

protected entry scheme at EU level.[621] Subsequently, a Commission communication of 2004 endorsed the creation of an EU resettlement scheme, the possible future development of further support for non-EU states,[622] and the creation of Regional Protection Programmes to develop an integrated approach to asylum and migration issues in certain third countries or regions.[623]

In view of the initial lack of interest among Member States in an EU-wide resettlement scheme, the Commission proposed the creation of pilot Regional Protection Programmes, in East Africa and the Western ex-Soviet States.[624] Subsequently, the EU's Refugee Fund provided a source of finance for national resettlement schemes as from 2008,[625] and in 2009, the Commission proposed the creation of a European resettlement policy, along with corresponding changes to the legislation establishing the Refugee Fund.[626] The Commission aims in particular to encourage more Member States to take part in resettlement activities (which would remain voluntary): already more Member States have got involved in resettlement activities since the Refugee Fund started to provide funding.

As for the future, the Stockholm programme encourages the EU's accession to the Geneva Convention, the development of further Regional Protection Programmes, a review of the EU's resettlement activities, and the exploration by the Commission of the possible creation of protected entry procedures or joint external processing of asylum claims.[627]

5.12. Conclusions

The development of EU competence on asylum initially promised much. It was an opportunity to break out of the cycle of competitive lowering of standards relating to asylum, by adopting EU-wide rules setting a high level of standards applicable and enforceable across the entire EU, taking into account also the involvement of the Commission and the European Parliament, traditionally supporters of high standards in this area.

The outcome has, so far, been rather more disappointing. As we have seen, minimum standards were set at rather low levels, and indeed very low levels in the case of asylum procedures, to the point where the Directive on this issue arguably

---

[621] Council doc 14987/03, 18 Nov 2003.

[622] See also the development of the external aspects of migration policy, including the impact of readmission agreements on asylum seekers (7.9 below).

[623] COM (2004) 410, 4 June 2004; see also the conclusions of the Nov 2004 General Affairs/External Relations Council.

[624] COM (2005) 388, 1 Sep 2005; see the conclusions of the Nov 2005 General Affairs/External Relations Council.

[625] Arts 3(1)(d), 6(e), and 13(3), (4), and (6) of the 2007 Decision establishing the Fund ([2007] OJ L 144/1).

[626] COM (2009) 456 (proposed legislation) and COM (2009) 447 (communication), both 2 Sep 2009.   [627] [2010] OJ C 115, s 6.2.

seriously breaches international human rights law in a number of respects. The legislation establishing the first phase of the Common European Asylum System does not seem to have resulted in major changes in national law or practice, and the proposals to establish the second-phase legislation, while generally welcome, are not progressing quickly, despite the application of qualified majority voting in the Council and a joint decision-making role for the European Parliament, as well as the Treaty commitment to adopt a common policy. The Court of Justice has to date played a modest role, and it remains to be seen whether the wider jurisdiction established by the Treaty of Lisbon will enhance its role in practice. As regards external asylum policy, the controversial ideas of some Member States to remove some or all asylum processing to locations outside the Union have fortunately not been taken forward. More positively, the EU has encouraged national resettlement policies, with some success, and plans to develop an EU-wide policy on this issue.

For the initial promise of EU competence in this area to be fulfilled, the EU needs to adopt second-phase legislation enshrining fair standards at the very heart of the Common European Asylum System. Time will tell whether Member States have the political will to live up to the commitments to high standards in this area which they have frequently made within the EU context.

6

Legal Migration

6.1. Introduction

Migration poses fundamental issues for the economic, social, and cultural development of Europe. Certainly migrants have made substantial contributions of every kind to EU Member States throughout history, and continue to do so today, but migration still remains highly controversial, because of fears that significant migration flows would damage national economies, threaten social harmony, and challenge established national values. There are sharp differences within and between Member States on the issues related to migration, due not only to economic, social, and cultural divergences but also because Member States' different histories have resulted in diverse patterns of migration.

As a result, the EU's legal framework for legal migration issues has developed only gradually. The key issue of migration for economic purposes been addressed very partially, and legislation on other issues has left considerable discretion to Member States, although the initial indication from the case law is that the Court of Justice may curtail that discretion somewhat. As with other areas addressed in this book, legal migration raises some important human rights issues and intersects with important aspects of non-JHA EU law, in particular free movement law and external relations, as regards association agreements, commercial policy, and development policy (the latter issue is addressed further in Chapter 7). The relationship between EU migration law and both human rights law and other areas of EU law has been the subject of continued controversy.

This chapter, like the others in this book, begins with a historical overview of the substance and institutional framework of the subject, including issues of legal competence and the territorial scope of the rules, followed by an analysis of the relevant rules of human rights law and other areas of EU law. Then it examines in detail the EU rules relating to admission of migrants, first of all primary admission and then secondary admission (for family reunion purposes), followed by the rules relating to long-term residence and integration, examining also the issue of administrative cooperation in this field.

The issues addressed in this chapter have close links with the issues discussed in other chapters, particularly Chapter 7 concerning irregular migration, since the definition of irregular migration is in part shaped by the rules relating to legal migration. There are also important links with asylum law (the subject of

Chapter 5), in particular where a person has been granted refugee status and the EU's migration powers are used to regulate topics such as the issue of residence permits and access to employment. However, the issue of family reunion for refugees and possible long-term residence status for refugees and persons with subsidiary protection are addressed in this chapter. The grant of a residence permit or a long-stay visa or the admission of family members can also trigger the EU's rules on responsibility for asylum applications.[1] Finally, certain issues concerning long-stay visas and residence permits that are indissolubly linked to the issues of short-term visas and external border control are dealt with in Chapters 3 and 4, concerning border controls and visas respectively, due to their close link with the issues in those chapters.[2] It should also be recalled that some issues principally dealt with in this chapter, such as the provision of services by third-country nationals from either inside or outside the EU and the movement of third-country national family members of EU citizens, are in part also affected by border control and visa rules, and so partly dealt with in Chapters 3 and 4.[3]

6.2. Institutional framework and overview

As pointed out in Chapter 3,[4] several important aspects of the rules governing third-country nationals were part of Community law (as it then was) even before the entry into force of the Treaty of Amsterdam. These issues have remained within the framework of other EU law rules, rather than the specific rules for Justice and Home Affairs (JHA) set out (now) in Title V of the Treaty on the Functioning of the European Union (TFEU), or previously (before the Treaty of Lisbon entered into force) in Title IV of Part Three of the EC Treaty. However, this chapter considers those issues,[5] to the extent that they are connected to EU immigration law based on the specific JHA rules.

6.2.1. Cooperation prior to the Treaty of Amsterdam

Prior to the entry into force of the Maastricht Treaty, the Member States' interior ministries adopted a resolution on family reunion.[6] Subsequently, pursuant to

---

[1] See 5.8 above.

[2] As regards crossing external borders, see 3.6.1 above; as regards freedom to travel and checks in the Schengen Information System, see 4.9 above.   [3] See 3.4.1 and 4.4.1 above.

[4] See 3.2.1 above.   [5] See 6.4 below.

[6] SN 2828/1/93, not published in the OJ; see E Guild and J Niessen, *The Developing Immigration and Asylum Policies of the European Union: Adopted Conventions, Resolutions, Recommendations, Decisions and Conclusions* (Kluwer, 1996), 250–257; T Bunyan, ed, *Key Texts on Justice and Home Affairs in the European Union* (1997), 98.

the 'third pillar' arrangements established by the Maastricht Treaty, the Council adopted a number of 'soft-law' measures on migration law. These measures concerned family reunion, admission of workers, admission of the self-employed, admission of students, the status of long-term residents, and marriages of convenience.[7] In order to convert these rules into 'hard law', the Commission proposed a migration law Convention in 1997, but this was not agreed by the Council.[8] Therefore the only 'hard law' on migration adopted before the entry into force of the Treaty of Amsterdam was a Joint Action on a uniform residence permit, adopted by the Council in 1996.[9]

6.2.2. Treaty of Amsterdam

The Treaty of Amsterdam conferred migration law competence upon the Community in Article 63(3) and (4) EC to adopt the following:

(3) measures on immigration policy within the following areas:
   (a) conditions of entry and residence, and standards on procedures for the issue by Member States of long term visas and residence permits, including those for the purpose of family reunion,
   (b) illegal immigration and illegal residence, including repatriation of illegal residents;[10]
(4) measures defining the rights and conditions under which nationals of third countries who are legally resident in a Member State may reside in other Member States.

---

[7] See respectively [1994] OJ C 274/7; [1996] OJ C 274/10; [1996] OJ C 80/2; and [1997] OJ C 382/1. There was a further Resolution on unaccompanied minors ([1997] OJ C 221/23) and a Decision on monitoring implementation ([1997] OJ C 11/1). These Resolutions, and the earlier Resolution on family reunion, are not covered further in this book; see the first edition of this book, at 84–90; E Guild and J Niessen, ibid; S Peers, 'Building Fortress Europe: The Development of EU Migration Law' (1998) 35 CMLRev 1235; M Hedemann-Robinson, 'Third-Country Nationals, European Union Citizenship and Free Movement of Persons: A Time for Bridges Rather Than Divisions?' (1996) 16 YEL 321; K Hailbronner, 'Migration Law and Policy Within the Third Pillar of the European Union' in R Bieber and J Monar, eds, *Justice and Home Affairs in the European Union* (European University Press, 1995); and P Boeles, et al, *A New Immigration Law for Europe: the 1992 London and 1993 Copenhagen Rules on Immigration* (Standing Committee of Experts on Immigration, 1994).

[8] COM (97) 387, 30 July 1997; [1997] OJ C 337/9. For more on the proposed Convention, see the first edition of this book, at 90–92; M Hedemann-Robinson, 'From Object to Subject? Non-EC Nationals and the Draft Proposal of the Commission for a Council Act Establishing the Rules for Admission of Third-Country Nationals to the Member States' (1998) 18 YEL 289; and S Peers, 'Raising Minimum Standards or Racing to the Bottom? The Commission's Proposed Migration Convention', in E Guild, ed, *The Legal Framework and Social Consequences of Free Movement of Persons in the European Union* (Kluwer, 1999), 149.

[9] [1997] OJ L 7/1. See 6.9 below.

[10] This sub-paragraph and measures based on it are considered separately in ch 7.

However, the final provisions of Article 63 provided that:

Measures adopted by the Council pursuant to points 3 and 4 shall not prevent any Member State from maintaining or introducing in the areas concerned national provisions which are compatible with this Treaty and with international agreements.

It was also specified, by implication, that there was no deadline to adopt measures pursuant to Article 63(3)(a) and (4) within the five-year deadline applicable to all of Article 62 (as regards visas and border controls) and almost all of the remaining provisions of Article 63 (as regards asylum and irregular migration). The immigration provisions were also subject to the 'emergency powers' derogation and the reserve of Member States' powers set out in Article 64 EC, and the possible adoption of measures to assist administrative cooperation in Article 66 EC.[11]

The Tampere European Council, held in October 1999, set out basic principles which EC migration law should uphold. In fact, the conclusions of the European Council contained an entire section on 'Fair treatment of third-country nationals':

18. The European Union must ensure fair treatment of third country nationals who reside legally on the territory of its Member States. A more vigorous integration policy should aim at granting them rights and obligations comparable to those of EU citizens...

20. The European Council acknowledges the need for approximation of national legislations on the conditions for admission and residence of third country nationals, based on a shared assessment of the economic and demographic developments within the Union, as well as the situation in the countries of origin. It requests to this end rapid decisions by the Council, on the basis of proposals by the Commission. These decisions should take into account not only the reception capacity of each Member State, but also their historical and cultural links with the countries of origin.

21. The legal status of third country nationals should be approximated to that of Member States' nationals. A person, who has resided legally in a Member State for a period of time to be determined and who holds a long-term residence permit, should be granted in that Member State a set of uniform rights which are as near as possible to those enjoyed by EU citizens; e.g. the right to reside, receive education, and work as an employee or self-employed person, as well as the principle of non-discrimination vis-à-vis the citizens of the State of residence...

This ambitious programme led to a Commission proposal for a Directive on family reunion before the end of 1999,[12] followed by further proposals in 2001 on the status of long-term residents and admission for employment or self-employment;[13] a proposal in 2002 on the admission of students, school pupils, unremunerated trainees, and volunteers;[14] and a proposal early in 2004 for specific

---

[11] See further 3.2.4 above on Art 64 (now Art 72 TFEU), and 6.12 below on Art 66 and legal migration issues.   [12] COM (1999) 638, 1 Dec 1999.
[13] See respectively COM (2001) 127, 13 Mar 2001 and COM (2001) 386, 11 July 2001.
[14] COM (2002) 548, 7 Oct 2002.

rules on admission of research workers.[15] It proved initially difficult to agree on most of these proposals, but eventually the Council finally adopted the Directives on family reunion and long-term residents in 2003,[16] on students, pupils, trainees, and volunteers in 2004,[17] and on researchers in 2005.[18] But the cost of reaching agreement on the various measures was a huge reduction in the standards proposed by the Commission, particularly in the family reunion Directive. The result was that the European Parliament sued to annul parts of the family reunion Directive for breach of the human rights principles forming part of EC law.[19] While the EP's challenge was unsuccessful, the Court of Justice's judgment clarified a number of important points as regards the interpretation of the Directive.

As for labour migration, the Council did not hold extensive discussions on the Commission's 2001 proposal concerning admission for migration for employment and self-employment, and it became clear that there was no prospect of the Council adopting it. A Directive on the legal status of victims of trafficking or smuggling or persons was adopted in 2004, but this is considered in detail in Chapter 7, along with other EC measures concerning irregular migration.[20]

In the meantime, the Council adopted two Regulations on other aspects of migration law. First, it agreed in 2002 to 'communitarize' the Joint Action on residence permits.[21] Secondly, following a judgment of the Court of Justice in 2001 on the application of EC legislation on social security coordination to refugees and stateless persons,[22] the Council adopted in 2003 a Regulation extending these rules to other third-country nationals.[23]

The integration of the migration-related aspects of the Schengen *acquis* into EC law from 1 May 1999 had little impact on legal migration law. These provisions of the *acquis* consisted of Articles 18 and 25 of the Schengen Convention,[24] and a Decision of the Schengen Executive Committee relating to implementation of the EU's Joint Action on residence permits.[25]

The particular political difficulties agreeing measures on legal migration were underlined when the Hague Programme outlining future JHA policy was adopted in November 2004.[26] That Programme did not call for an immediate shift to a qualified majority vote (QMV) in the Council and co-decision with

---

[15] COM (2004) 178, 16 Mar 2004.

[16] Respectively Dirs 2003/86 ([2003] OJ L 251/12) and 2003/109 ([2004] OJ L 16/44). See 6.6 and 6.7 below.   [17] Dir 2004/114 ([2004] OJ L 375/12). See 6.5.4 below.

[18] Dir 2005/71 ([2005] OJ L 289/15). See 6.5.3 below.

[19] Case C-540/03 *EP v Council* [2006] ECR I-5769. For discussion of this judgment, see 6.6 below.   [20] Directive 2004/81 ([2004] L 261/19); see 7.6.2 below.

[21] Reg 1030/2002 ([2002] OJ L 157/1). See 6.9 below.

[22] Joined Cases C-95/99 to 98/99 *Khalil and others* and C-180/99 *Addou* [2001] ECR I-7413. See further 5.4.2 above and 6.4.2 below.

[23] Reg 859/2003 ([2003] OJ L 124/1). See further 6.8 below.

[24] [2000] OJ L 239/1. On the original version of Art 18, see 3.6.1 above; on the current version of Art 18, see 6.9.2 below. On Art 25, as amended subsequently, see 4.9 above and 6.9 below.

[25] [2000] OJ L 239/187. See further 6.9 below.   [26] [2005] OJ C 53/1.

the European Parliament (EP) regarding legal migration, and as a result, from 1 January 2005, until the entry into force of the Treaty of Lisbon, legal migration remained the only immigration-related topic area still subject to unanimous voting in the Council and consultation of the EP. Furthermore, the Hague Programme, unlike the Tampere conclusions, failed to outline any substantial future programme of EC legislation concerning legal migration. It merely invited the Commission to draw up a policy plan on legal migration by the end of 2005, taking account of a Green Paper which the Commission was then planning, without any commitment to adopt legislation or invitation to the Commission to propose any.

However, the subsequent June 2005 implementation plan for the Hague Programme did refer to some further measures,[27] in particular a Directive to extend the scope of the long-term residents' Directive to refugees and persons with subsidiary protection status; measures on a European migration observatory; a mutual information system on national immigration law; a proposed integration fund; and a measure on migration and asylum statistics.

These plans were implemented by Commission proposals, subsequently adopted by the Council between 2006 and 2009, establishing an EU integration fund;[28] a Decision on exchange of information on immigration and asylum policy;[29] a Regulation on immigration and asylum statistics;[30] and a Decision formally establishing a European Migration Network.[31] The Council also adopted an amendment to the EU rules on harmonized residence permit formats, in order inter alia to insert biometric identifiers into residence permits.[32] On the other hand, the Council was not able to agree, before the entry into force of the Treaty of Lisbon, on a Directive applying the long-term residents' Directive to refugees and beneficiaries of subsidiary protection;[33] a Regulation to extend the revised social security rules for EU citizens to third-country nationals who move within the EU;[34] or a proposal concerning aspects of long-term visas.[35]

Again, labour migration proved a difficult issue. In light of the deadlock on its 2001 proposal for a Directive on economic migration,[36] the Commission released a Green Paper on this issue in January 2005, in order to launch a wide discussion on the topic, as a likely precursor to fresh proposals for legislation.[37] Subsequently, the Commission withdrew the 2001 proposal.[38] In December 2005, taking account of the response to the Green Paper on economic migration mentioned above, the

---

[27] [2005] OJ C 198/1.   [28] [2007] OJ L 168/16; see 6.10 below.
[29] [2006] OJ L 283/40; see 6.11 below.
[30] Reg 862/2007 ([2007] OJ L 199/23); see 6.11 below.
[31] [2008] OJ L 131/7. See 6.11 below.
[32] Reg 330/2008 ([2008] OJ L 115/1), amending Reg 1030/2002 (n 21 above). See 6.9.1 below.
[33] COM (2007) 298, 6 June 2007. See 6.7 below.
[34] COM (2007) 439, 23 July 2007. See 6.8 below.   [35] COM (2009) 90, 27 Feb 2009.
[36] COM (2001) 386, n 13 above.   [37] COM (2004) 811, 11 Jan 2005.
[38] [2006] OJ C 64/3.

Commission issued a policy plan on legal migration into the EU.[39] The legislative aspects of the policy plan comprised first of all proposals (issued in 2007) for legislation on highly skilled workers and on a single procedure for admission of third-country national workers.[40] The Council was able to agree on the first of these proposals (known generally as the 'Blue Card' Directive) in 2009,[41] but was not able to agree on the second proposal before the Treaty of Lisbon entered into force.

The 2008 immigration and asylum pact contained provisions on legal immigration,[42] making a commitment 'to organise legal immigration to take account of the priorities, needs and reception capacities determined by each Member State, and to encourage integration'. In particular, the pact agreed: 'to increase the attractiveness' of the EU for highly qualified workers, and to take new measures regarding reception and movement of students and researchers; 'to regulate family migration more effectively by inviting each Member State, in compliance with' the ECHR, to take into consideration in its national legislation, except for certain specific categories, its own reception capacities and families' capacity to integrate, as evaluated by their resources and accommodation in the country of destination and, for example, their knowledge of that country's language'; to strengthen existing systems for information exchange; and to develop integration policy further. There was no express reference to any EC legislation concerning any of these issues.

In addition to 'hard law', the EC developed a body of 'soft law' on the particular topic of integration of third-country nationals.[43] There were also a number of measures adopted relating to EU funding and to cooperation between administrations.[44] As in other areas of immigration and asylum law, there was an important external dimension to EC migration policy.[45]

As for the Court of Justice, the limitations on its jurisdiction prior to the entry into force of the Treaty of Lisbon meant that it only received one reference from national courts during this time concerning legal migration legislation.[46]

6.2.3. Treaty of Lisbon

The issue of migration, including legal migration, is now regulated by Article 79 TFEU:[47]

1. The Union shall develop a common immigration policy aimed at ensuring, at all stages, the efficient management of migration flows, fair treatment of third-country nationals

---

[39] COM (2005) 669, 21 Dec 2005.   [40] COM (2007) 637 and 638, 23 Oct 2007.

[41] Dir 2009/50 ([2009] OJ L 155/17). See 6.5.2 below.

[42] Council doc 13340/08, 24 Sep 2008.   [43] See further 6.10 below.

[44] See further 6.11 below.

[45] See further 7.9.2 below; as regards association agreements and commercial policy, see 6.4.3 and 6.4.6 below.

[46] Case C-578/08 *Chakroun*, judgment of 4 Mar 2010, not yet reported, concerning interpretation of Dir 2003/86 on family reunion (n 16 above).

[47] Art 79(2)(c) and (d) and (3) TFEU concern irregular migration, and so are examined in 7.2.3 below.

residing legally in Member States, and the prevention of, and enhanced measures to combat, illegal immigration and trafficking in human beings.

2. For the purposes of paragraph 1, the European Parliament and the Council, acting in accordance with the ordinary legislative procedure, shall adopt measures in the following areas:

(a) the conditions of entry and residence, and standards on the issue by Member States of long-term visas and residence permits, including those for the purpose of family reunification;

(b) the definition of the rights of third-country nationals residing legally in a Member State, including the conditions governing freedom of movement and of residence in other Member States...

4. The European Parliament and the Council, acting in accordance with the ordinary legislative procedure, may establish measures to provide incentives and support for the action of Member States with a view to promoting the integration of third-country nationals residing legally in their territories, excluding any harmonisation of the laws and regulations of the Member States.

5. This Article shall not affect the right of Member States to determine volumes of admission of third-country nationals coming from third countries to their territory in order to seek work, whether employed or self-employed.

It can be seen first of all that the EU's powers as regards migration are now more intensive than before, given the obligation to develop a 'common' policy and the abolition of the penultimate paragraph of the previous Article 63 EC, reserving to Member States the power to maintain or introduce national provisions alongside EC legislation. It is not clear what the previous proviso meant,[48] but arguably it remains relevant to any immigration measures adopted before the Treaty of Lisbon, until they are amended after the entry into force of that Treaty. Moreover, the obligation to establish a 'common' immigration policy is now referred to in the general provisions of Title V.[49]

Furthermore, Article 79(1) TFEU, unlike the previous Article 63 EC, sets out objectives specific to immigration policy: 'efficient management', 'fair treatment' of legal residents, and prevention and combating of illegal immigration and human trafficking. Of these objectives, fairness is also mentioned in part of the general Title V objectives in Article 67(2) TFEU.

As for the specific provisions on legal migration, Article 79(2)(a) TFEU is identical to the previous Article 63(3)(a) EC, although since the overall legal framework of the EU's immigration powers has changed, as described above, there might be a case for a different interpretation of the same provision. On the other hand, Article 79(2)(b) TFEU now sets out a wider express competence as regards the rights of third-country nationals legally resident in a Member State than the prior Treaty, and a different wording as regards third-country nationals' movement to other Member States (including an express reference

---

[48] See 6.2.4 below.   [49] Art 67(2) TFEU; on the general provisions, see 2.2.3.2 above.

to 'freedom of movement', which is obviously distinct from the 'freedom to travel for a short period' referred to in Article 77 TFEU).[50] However, it should be noted that the EC's previous powers were already used to define the rights of third-country nationals.[51] Furthermore, given that Article 77 TFEU is now less precise as regards the time limit for short-term entry of third-country nationals (as compared to the previous three-month limit), the dividing line between that Article and Article 79 TFEU is now less precise than the division between the previous Articles 62(3) and 63(3) and (4) EC.

Article 79(4) constitutes a new express 'legal base' providing for the adoption of EU measures 'to provide incentives and support' for Member States' action 'promoting the integration' of legally resident third-country nationals. Again, the EU was already active on this issue within the previous legal framework, in particular by establishing a 'European integration fund' which now obviously falls within the scope of the EU's new competence to support Member States' integration policies.[52]

But the biggest change in this area is the extension of QMV to legislation, along with the extension of co-decision powers (now the 'ordinary legislative procedure') for the EP. The impact of this change is that the Council (now together with the EP) was able to adopt the previously proposed legislation on long-term visas,[53] and the Council was able to agree on the single permit for third-country national workers,[54] and the extension of the revised social security rules to third-country nationals.[55] It remained to be seen whether the Council and EP could agree on the proposal to extend the long-term residents' Directive to refugees and beneficiaries of subsidiary protection.[56] It will presumably be easier than it would otherwise have been to agree on subsequent proposals as well.

As for such further proposals, the Stockholm Programme,[57] in the field of labour migration, calls for: the continued implementation of the policy plan on legal migration; consideration of more effective use of existing information sources and networks; evaluation of existing policies; and consideration of possible consolidation of legislation, 'including regarding categories of workers currently not covered by Union legislation'. Regarding other aspects of immigration law, the Union should complete its objective of granting third-country nationals rights comparable to those of EU citizens by 2014 at the latest. In particular, the Commission should submit proposals for consolidation of immigration legislation, starting with legal migration, which would 'include amendments needed

---

[50] On Art 77, see 4.2.4 above.

[51] See, for instance, Dir 2003/109 on long-term residents (n 16 above), although in this Directive, there is a link between the regulation of the status of long-term resident in a first Member State and the right to move to another Member State.   [52] See 6.10 below.

[53] Reg 265/2010, [2010] OJ L 85/1. See 3.6.1 and 4.9 above and 6.9.2 below.

[54] COM (2007) 638, 23 Oct 2007.   [55] COM (2007) 439, 23 July 2007.

[56] COM (2007) 298, 6 June 2007.

[57] [2010] OJ C 115, points 6.1.3 and 6.1.4.

to simplify and/or, where necessary, extend the existing provisions and improve their implementation and coherence', as well as 'evaluation and, where necessary, review of the directive on family reunification, taking into account the importance of integration measures'. It is not clear whether the separate calls for consolidation of legislation would be dealt with together, or whether the review of the family reunion Directive would form part of the consolidation process. There are also commitments regarding integration policy and the external relations aspects of immigration policy.[58]

The Commission's work programme for 2010 and beyond and the action plan to implement the Stockholm Programme provide for: proposals on intra-corporate transferees and seasonal workers, in order to implement the policy plan on legal migration (proposals made in 2010); a Green Paper on family reunion (in 2010) and an eventual legislative proposal on this issue (2012); an action plan on unaccompanied minors (2010, since released); annual reports on immigration and asylum policy (to follow up the immigration and asylum pact and the Stockholm Programme; the first of these has also since been released); a report (2010) and legislative amendments to the Directive on non-economic migration, inter alia concerning unpaid trainees and au pairs (2011); a communication on integration (2011); further measures on immigration statistics (2011–12); reports on the implementation of the researchers' and long-term residents' Directives, with possible follow-up (both in 2011); a communication on addressing labour shortages through migration (2012); a report on the operation of the Blue Card Directive (2014); further development of the European Migration Network (ongoing); and the development of an immigration code (2013).[59]

The entry into force of the Treaty of Lisbon has also meant an expansion in the jurisdiction of the Court of Justice in this area. It remains to be seen whether there will be a significant increase in the references from national courts, although there were none in the first few months after the Treaty entered into force. The Treaty of Lisbon has also amended the rules relating to opt-outs from this area of law.[60]

6.2.4. Competence issues

Prior to the entry into force of the Treaty of Lisbon, there were several disputes about the extent of the EC's competence over legal migration. These arguments remain potentially relevant as regards the validity of legislation adopted before

---

[58] Points 6.1.5 and 6.1.1 and 6.1.2 of the programme. See 6.10 and 7.9.2 below.

[59] COM (2010) 135, 31 Mar 2010 (2010 work programme) and COM (2010) 171, 20 Apr 2010 (proposed action plan). For the measures released already, see COM (2010) 214, 6 May 2010 (annual report), COM (2010) 213, 6 May 2010 (unaccompanied minors), and COM (2010) 378 and 379, both 13 July 2010 (intra-corporate transferees and seasonal workers).   [60] See 6.2.5 below.

the Treaty of Lisbon entered into force, at least until that legislation is amended by post-Lisbon measures.

First of all, as regards competence to regulate labour migration,[61] although the previous Article 63(3)(a) and 63(4) EC did not mention migration for employment as such, conversely those provisions did not exclude any form of legal migration from their scope. Furthermore, the prior Article 39 EC governed the movement of 'workers' of the Member States, without any restriction based on nationality, while the prior Article 137 EC granted competence to the Community to adopt measures concerning the 'conditions of employment' of third-country nationals. Between them, these provisions were sufficient to confer competence to regulate labour migration of third-country nationals, although complications could arise from their potential overlap.

Next, it was necessary to distinguish, after the change in Title IV decision-making rules which took effect on 1 January 2005,[62] between the legal base for the adoption of measures concerning legal migration and the legal base for the adoption of measures concerning irregular migration. The best interpretation is that the EC Treaty power over legal migration conferred competence to adopt rules concerning the acquisition and loss of legal migration status, while the power over irregular migration conferred power to adopt rules concerning persons who were not entitled to enter and stay or who had definitively lost their power to enter and stay. This particular dispute is clearly irrelevant to measures adopted after the entry into force of the Treaty of Lisbon, given the identical decision-making rules applicable to these issues. Another argument concerned whether the EC had power to regulate limited stays of up to six months; this point is now moot since the adoption of the Treaty of Lisbon.[63]

Finally, to what extent did the closing words of the prior Article 63 EC limit the scope of the EC's power to harmonize legal migration law? These words could possibly have been interpreted to mean that Member States could do whatever they wanted regardless of whether the EC had acted or not. But in order to give the EC's powers some practical effect, the best interpretation of those was that EC powers were not automatically exclusive, immediately precluding any national competence over immigration; but Member States were (and still are) obliged to comply with EC law to the extent that the EC has acted, and that it was open to the EC to harmonize national law fully in the field of immigration if it had desired, subject to the principle of subsidiarity.[64] This was also consistent

---

[61] For more detailed analysis, see the second edition of this book, at 187–188; S Peers, 'The The EU Institutions and Title IV' and E Guild and S Peers, 'Out of the Ghetto? The Personal Scope of EU Law', both in S Peers and N Rogers, eds, *EU Immigration and Asylum Law: Text and Commentary* (1st edn, Martinus Nijhoff, 2006).   [62] See 6.2.2 above.

[63] See 4.2.4 above.

[64] See further: the opinion in Case C-540/03 *EP v Council* [2006] ECR I-5769; G Brinkmann, 'Family Reunion, Third-Country Nationals and the Community's New Powers', in E Guild and C Harlow, *Implementing Amsterdam: Immigration and Asylum Rights in EC Law* (Hart, 2001), 241 at 265;

with a declaration to the Treaty of Amsterdam, concerning the EC's external competence in this field. It should be noted that EU legislation on legal immigration generally permits Member States to establish higher standards as regards most or all provisions of each measure, without requiring that such national measures be 'compatible' with the Directive in question.[65]

Following the entry into force of the Treaty of Lisbon, immigration still remains a shared competence of the EU and its Member States.[66] However, the wording of the new provisions (in particular the references to a 'common immigration policy' and the removal of the final words of Article 63 EC) suggests that it is now easier to justify more intensive EU action pursuant to the principles of proportionality and subsidiarity, and harder to argue that any particular area of immigration law is outside EU competence—apart from the express restriction on competence in Article 79(5) TFEU, which (as seen above) reserves competence of Member States over volumes of third-country nationals coming from third countries to seek work, including self-employed work. Arguably, this is a new restriction on competence as compared to the previous Article 63 EC, although this limit on competence had been incorporated into one relevant Directive adopted even before the Treaty of Lisbon entered into force.[67] In any event, in practice no legislation was adopted prior to the Treaty of Lisbon which restricted Member States from adopting such measures.

First of all, as for the competence to regulate the economic migration of third-country nationals after the Treaty of Lisbon, the power to adopt measures regarding a 'common immigration policy' and the express restriction regarding economic migration in Article 79(5) TFEU both point to a power to regulate economic migration within the scope of Article 79(2) TFEU, as does the addition of the express power to regulate 'the rights of third-country nationals residing legally in a Member State'. Taking these provisions in turn, a 'common immigration policy' would obviously be incomplete without regulation of economic migration; a restriction relating to volumes of admission of economic migrants would be meaningless unless the EU had competence to regulate such migration in the first place; and the regulation of the 'rights' of resident third-country

---

G Papagianni, *Institutional and Policy Dynamics of EU Migration Law* (Martinus Nijhoff, 2006), 49; and S Peers, 'EU Immigration and Asylum Law: Internal Market Model or Human Rights Model?', in Tridimas and Nebbia, eds, *EU Law for the Twenty-First Century: Rethinking the New Legal Order, Vol. 1* (Hart, 2004), 345 at 358–359.

[65] See the legislation discussed in 6.5–6.7 below. On the concept of the 'compatibility' of higher national standards, see 5.2.4 above.

[66] See Art 4(2)(j) TFEU. On the concept of shared competence, see Art 2(2) TFEU and the discussion in 2.2.4 above. The remainder of this subsection is adapted from S Peers, 'EU Immigration and Asylum Competence and Decision-Making in the Treaty of Lisbon' (2008) 10 EJML 219 at 241–246.

[67] See Art 6 of Dir 2009/50 ([2009] OJ L 155/17), which reserves competence as regards volumes of all third-country nationals 'entering the territory' for highly qualified employment, not just those entering from third countries.

nationals would logically include the regulation of their access to employment, in the absence of any indication to the contrary.

It must therefore be concluded that Article 79 TFEU includes the power to regulate economic migration of third-country nationals, limited only by the express restriction on competence in Article 79(5) TFEU. As compared to other Treaty Articles, it could no longer be argued that any power to regulate this issue would be contained within Article 40 EC (now Article 46 TFEU), because Article 79 TFEU is now a *lex specialis*. On the other hand, Article 153 TFEU (previous Article 137 EC) is still a *lex specialis* as regards 'conditions of employment' of third-country nationals. The distinction between Articles 79 and 153 TFEU still matters because the social policy competence has remained subject to unanimous voting in the Council and consultation of the EP (ie a 'special legislative procedure'),[68] with no facility for the UK, Ireland, or Denmark to opt out of legislation.

The best approach to the relationship between Articles 79 and 153 TFEU is that the former Article confers competence to regulate the conditions of employment of third-country nationals (or categories of third-country nationals) generally,[69] if the regulation of this issue were ancillary to a measure regulating the rights of third-country nationals (or a category of them) generally, while the latter Article would be the correct legal base for a matter solely concerning the conditions of employment of third-country nationals.[70]

Three other provisions of the Treaties also need to be considered as regards the EU's competence to regulate economic migration. First, Article 56 TFEU (former Article 49 EC) explicitly gives (as it did before) the EU competence to regulate the provision of services in one Member State by third-country nationals who are legally resident in another Member State.[71] The Treaty of Lisbon has changed the decision-making rules as regards this issue, but the competence itself has not been altered.[72] So it must be concluded that Article 56 TFEU would continue to be a *lex specialis* as regards this issue.

Next, Article 217 TFEU (previous Article 310 EC) continues to confer competence as regards the negotiation and conclusion of association agreements.[73] As the Court of Justice has confirmed, this Treaty Article confers competence upon the EC/EU to extend the entirety of the Treaty rules to non-member countries.[74] Indeed, the EC (as it then was) has used this power to extend the full

---

[68] See Art 289(2) TFEU.

[69] Except for persons seeking or obtaining protection status, who fall within the scope of Art 78 TFEU. On this point, see 5.2.4 above.

[70] See by analogy *Opinion 1/94* [1994] ECR I-5273, as regards the relationship at the time between the commercial policy powers of the EC and the European Coal and Steel Community.

[71] On the substance of this issue, see further 6.4.4 below.

[72] See ibid. On the scope of this competence, see Guild and Peers (n 61 above), 105–109.

[73] On the substance of this issue, see further 6.4.3 below.

[74] See Case 12/86 *Demirel* [1987] ECR 3719.

free movement of persons to some non-EU States.[75] Since Article 217 TFEU has not significantly amended the previous Article 310 EC, the relationship between this provision and the EU's express immigration competence (by virtue of the extension of the internal market rules, inter alia, which association agreements may provide for) has presumably remained the same.[76]

Finally, the Treaty of Lisbon has revised the EC's (now the EU's) commercial policy powers (Article 207 TFEU; previous Article 133 EC) in order, inter alia, to extend the EU's powers to regulate the movement of services from *third states*.[77] Article 207 TFEU needs to be distinguished from the EU's powers over labour migration because the commercial policy power is fully exclusive and uniform, with no opt-outs for Member States. The definition of 'services' for the purpose of Article 207 TFEU includes the short-term movement of persons within the context of service provision,[78] so such movement falls within the concept of the common commercial policy, not the immigration policy. However, the issue of transition to a long-term stay, and arguably also the specific regulation of visas for entry of service providers, would fall within the scope of the immigration and visa powers of the EU.

It remains to be determined to what extent Article 79(5) restricts the EU's competence. The starting point for the interpretation of the exclusion should be that as an exception from the EU's competence to establish a 'common' policy, it should be narrowly interpreted.[79] Then the four specific aspects of the restriction need to be considered in turn. First of all, the provision would only restrict competence in respect of '[t]his Article', ie Article 79 TFEU. So the competence regarding economic migration conferred by Articles 153, 207, and 217 TFEU is unaffected.[80] Furthermore, from an external relations point of view, volumes of economic migrants coming to Member States from third countries could be regulated in mixed agreements, to which the EU together with the Member States was a party, presuming (in order to justify the EU's participation in the agreement concerned) that the treaty in question also concerned another issue within the EU's competence.

---

[75] See the treaties establishing the European Economic Area ([1994] OJ L 1/1) and the EU–Swiss treaty concerning the free movement of persons ([2002] OJ L 114).

[76] On the scope of this competence, see Guild and Peers (n 61 above), 98–100.

[77] For further detail, see 6.4.6 below.

[78] See further ibid, and particularly *Opinion 1/2008*, 30 Nov 2009.

[79] See, by analogy, the judgments in Cases C-307/05 *Del Cerro Alonso* [2007] ECR I-7109 and C-268/06 *Impact* [2008] ECR I-2483 as regards the exclusions from competence in the previous Art 137(5) EC (now Art 153(5) TFEU) which, moreover, does not concern a limitation on competence to establish a 'common' policy. On the former Art 137(5) EC, see also Cases C-341/05 *Laval* [2007] ECR I-11767 and C-438/05 *Viking Line* [2007] ECR I-10779.

[80] This analysis is consistent with the 'anti-circumvention' argument relating to the previous ban on harmonizing passport legislation (see 3.2.4 above), because the relevant legal bases confer more specific legal powers.

Secondly, the restriction only concerns *volumes* of admissions, rather than the question of access to employment for persons who have already been admitted or other aspects of the admission of economic migrants (such as the technical aspects of the admissions process or the grounds for admission, which could be separated from the question of permitted volumes per Member State).[81]

Thirdly, the restriction only applies to third-country nationals who come directly from third countries. Therefore, third-country nationals who are already resident, or at least legally resident, in a Member State (including presumably a Member State which has opted out of some EC/EU immigration legislation) are not covered by the exclusion. So the EU would be competent, for example, to abolish Member States' ability to restrict the movement of long-term residents between Member States by means of quotas.[82]

Fourthly, the limitation on competence only concerns people who *seek* employment or self-employment. It would be possible to interpret this aspect of the limitation on competence very restrictively indeed, so that the EU competence is restricted only as regards the volumes of work-seekers, as distinct from the volumes of persons who already have work contracts or arrangements for self-employment. But such a highly restrictive interpretation would go too far, because it would leave Member States with a highly ineffective reserve of competence.

The EU would be able to nullify that national reserve of competence entirely by simply requiring any third-country nationals admitted for employment or self-employment in a Member State to have a contract of employment or to have made arrangements for self-employment beforehand.[83] On the other hand, the limitation on competence should not be construed so widely as to reserve to Member States a power to regulate the volumes of third-country nationals from third countries who might seek employment or self-employment on an ancillary basis, where the main reason for admission is for a non-economic purpose such as family reunion, study, or seeking international protection, but where EU legislation nevertheless regulates access to employment for the persons concerned.[84]

Finally, the new Treaty provisions have not expressly settled the question as to whether the EC/EU's migration powers extend to the regulation of social security for all third-country nationals who move between Member States.[85] Previously it was assumed by the EU institutions that the EC's migration powers

---

[81] These two issues have been the subject of the Blue Card Dir (Dir 2009/50, [2009] OJ L 155/17), adopted before the Treaty of Lisbon, and the proposal relating to a single permit for third-country national workers (6.5.1 below).

[82] See Art 14(4) of Dir 2003/109 ([2004] OJ L 16/44).

[83] For example, see Art 5(1)(a) of the 'Blue Card' Dir (n 81 above).

[84] See, for instance, Dirs 2003/86 and 2004/83 ([2003] OJ L 251/12 and [2004] OJ L 304/12). Indeed, as discussed in 5.2.4 above, the employment status of persons seeking or obtaining protection falls within the scope of Art 78 TFEU, not Art 79 TFEU.

[85] On the substance of this issue, see 6.4.2 below.

applied to this issue, rather than its powers to regulate social security for EC workers pursuant to the previous Article 42 EC.[86] However, a Declaration to the Treaty of Lisbon clearly assumes that the immigration powers (continue to) apply.[87] It should be noted that under the Treaty of Lisbon, the social security legal base (unlike any of the migration legal bases) is now subject to an 'emergency brake' which any Member State can pull in certain cases; but it is not subject to any opt-outs.[88] Given the Treaty power to develop a 'common' policy on migration and the absence of any exclusion for social security from that power, and by *a contrario* reasoning from the exclusion set out in Article 79(5) TFEU, it follows that Article 79 TFEU confers powers on the EU as regards social security for third-country nationals.[89]

6.2.5. Territorial scope

The UK has opted into:[90] the Regulation on the uniform residence permit and its 2008 amendment;[91] the 2003 Regulation on social security coordination, but not the 2007 proposal on the same issue (agreed by the Council in 2010);[92] the 2006 Decision on exchange of information on migration policy;[93] the 2007 Decision adopting the Integration Fund;[94] and the 2008 Decision on the European Migration Network.[95]

Ireland has opted into: the 2003 Regulation on social security coordination and the 2007 proposal on the same issue (agreed by the Council in 2010);[96] the 2006 Decision on exchange of information on migration policy;[97] the 2007 Decision adopting the Integration Fund;[98] the Directive on researchers;[99] and the proposed Directive on economic migration (later withdrawn).[100] Also, Ireland opted in to the 2002 Regulation on the uniform residence permit after its adoption,[101] and then into the 2008 amendment to this Regulation in the ordinary way.[102] Ireland also opted into the Decision on the European Migration Network after its adoption.[103]

---

[86] For detailed comments, see ch 23 of Peers and Rogers (n 61 above).   [87] Declaration 22.
[88] Art 48 TFEU.
[89] This has also been the Council's practice: see the agreed text of the Reg on social security for third-country nationals (Council doc 10442/10, 2 June 2010).
[90] On the UK and Irish position, see 2.2.5.1 above.
[91] Regs 1030/2002 ([2002] OJ L 157/1) and 380/2008 ([2008] OJ L 115/1). See 6.9 below.
[92] Respectively Reg 859/2003 ([2003] OJ L 124/1) and Council doc 11160/10, 16 July 2010. This measure still has to be agreed with the EP before it becomes law. On the substance, see 6.8 below.
[93] [2006] OJ L 283/40. See 6.11 below.   [94] [2007] OJ L 168/18. See 6.10 below.
[95] [2008] OJ L 131/7. See 6.11 below.   [96] See n 92 above.   [97] See n 93 above.
[98] See n 94 above.   [99] Dir 2005/71 ([2005] OJ L 289/15).
[100] COM (2001) 386, 11 July 2001.
[101] Commission Decision C(2007)4589/F of 11 Oct 2007, not published in the OJ.
[102] Reg 380/2008 (n 91 above).   [103] See Commission Decision ([2009] OJ L 108/53).

The main provisions of the Schengen *acquis* relating to legal migration are Articles 18 and 25 of the Schengen Convention. The substance and territorial scope of these measures is discussed in detail in Chapter 4, as are measures building upon those provisions of the *acquis*,[104] except for the issue of the format and validity period of long-stay visas, which are discussed in this chapter.[105] Also, the EU measures concerning the uniform residence permit format (a Joint Action, replaced by a 2002 EC Regulation, as amended in 2008) fall within the scope of the Schengen *acquis*.[106]

Applying the special provisions on the Schengen *acquis*, Denmark decided to apply the original residence permit Regulation in its national law;[107] the Regulation and its amendment are also applicable to Norway, Iceland, and Switzerland;[108] and Liechtenstein will have to apply this Regulation and its amendment once the Schengen *acquis* becomes binding upon that country.[109]

Finally, it should be recalled that the immigration provisions derived from other areas of EU law, as well as the legislation on immigration statistics, apply to all Member States (but not to any non-Member States).[110]

6.3. Human rights

6.3.1. The right to family reunion, family life, and private life

The most important human rights protection offered to legal migrants in practice is the obligation to ensure the right to 'private and family life'. These rights are protected in a number of international human rights instruments, and furthermore several treaties recognize the family as a fundamental unit of society.[111] Of these, the European Convention of Human Rights (ECHR) and the relevant case law of the European Court of Human Rights is referred to expressly in the EU Charter of Rights, and is best known and most influential source of human rights principles forming part of the general principles of EU law.[112] Article 8 ECHR guarantees the right to respect for private and family life, but Article 8(2) ECHR allows interference with that right, 'in accordance with the law' and if 'necessary in a democratic society', on a number of grounds, including public safety,

---

[104] See 4.9 above.   [105] See 6.9 below.   [106] See ibid.

[107] See Danish letter of 9 Dec 2002 (Council doc 14807/03, 14 Nov 2003), and further 2.2.5.2 above.   [108] See further 2.2.5.4 above.

[109] See ibid.   [110] See respectively 6.4 and 6.11 below.

[111] See generally, R Cholewinski, *Migrant Workers in International Human Rights Law* (OUP, 1997), 68–70, 171–173, and 335–336; and ibid, 'The Protection of the Right of Economic Migrants to Family Reunion in Europe' (1994) 43 ICLQ 568. On the UN International Covenant on Civil and Political Rights, see S Joseph, J Schultz, and M Castan, *The International Covenant on Civil and Political Rights: Cases, Materials and Commentary* (2nd edn, OUP, 2004), 585–609.

[112] See 2.3 above.

national security, the economic well-being of the country, and the prevention of disorder or crime.[113]

The judgments of the European Court of Human Rights relevant to Article 8 and immigration can be broken down between those judgments concerning admission, those governing removal, and those governing status while in the country. A further distinction can be drawn in the 'expulsion' category between those persons to be expelled on public safety, public security, or similar grounds and those to be expelled in the economic interests of the host State.

First of all, the admission cases are relatively few; here the Strasbourg Court has consistently ruled that there is in principle no interference with the right to respect for family life if it is possible for the family to live elsewhere. This even applies in cases where the mother of the child has died and the father (after some years' residence abroad) wishes the child to join him, or where the parents have difficulty leaving a host State because of the illness of the mother.[114] However, the Convention can entail a right of admission in some cases: the Court has ruled that where some children are living in the host State with their parents and some have been left in the country of origin, the latter must be reunified in the host State of their parents if it is impractical for their siblings to leave school there.[115]

In recent years, the Court has developed a line of case law concerning persons who did not acquire a legal right to enter and stay, but who formed a family life during their period of residence on the territory. The factors to take into account in such cases are 'the extent to which family life is effectively ruptured, the extent of the ties in the Contracting State, whether there are insurmountable obstacles in the way of the family living in the country of origin of one or more of them and whether there are factors of immigration control (for example, a history of breaches of immigration law) or considerations of public order weighing in favour of exclusion'. But if family life develops while a person was contesting or avoiding expulsion, and the family knew all along that the immigration status of one person was precarious, then Article 8 ECHR will benefit them only exceptionally.[116]

---

[113] For a detailed analysis, see J van Dijk, 'Protection of 'Integrated' Aliens against Expulsion under the European Convention on Human Rights', in E Guild and P Minderhoud, eds, *Security of Residence and Expulsion: Protection of Aliens in Europe* (Kluwer, 2001), 23; C Harvey, 'Promoting Insecurity: Public Order, Expulsion and the European Convention on Human Rights (idem) 41; J Marin and J O'Connell, 'The European Convention and the Relative Rights of Resident Aliens' (1999) 5 ELJ 4 at 4–14; and H Storey, 'The Right to Family Life and Immigration Case Law at Strasbourg' (1990) 39 ICLQ 329.

[114] See *Ahmut v Netherlands* (Reports 1996-VI) and *Gul v Switzerland* (Reports 1996-I).

[115] *Sen v Netherlands*, 21 Dec 2001, and *Tuquabo-Tekle v Netherlands*, 1 Dec 2005.

[116] *Da Silva and Hoogkamer v Netherlands*, 31 Jan 2006, para 39. See subsequently *Konstantinov v Netherlands*, 26 Apr 2007; *Omoregie v Norway*, 31 July 2008, and *Y v Russia*, 4 Dec 2008. In the *Konstantinov* judgment (para 50), the Court acknowledges that a sufficient income requirement for family reunion is acceptable. Compare with the discussion of the relevant provisions of EU legislation on this issue (6.6.1 below). See also *Kawala v Netherlands*, 1 June 2010, where the importance of legal residence is confirmed expressly. The Court has also found that separating asylum-seeking

States are entitled to have a separate regime for persons with special links with that State that treats such persons more favourably as compared to other sponsors, but a distinction between men and women as regards family reunion is a breach of Articles 8 and 14 ECHR (the latter Article guarantees equality in respect of the rights set out in the Convention).[117]

As for expulsion, in principle there is an interference with family life where States seek to expel persons who have established family life in that State, and an interference with private life to the extent that even a person without a family life in a State has developed there a 'network of personal, social and economic relations' and property rental or ownership.[118] Where States simply wish to expel persons solely in their economic interest of the State, the Court is unwilling to accept an interference with family life, ruling that the State's interest was outweighed by the interest of an active father in continuing a relationship with his young daughter.[119] Also, where a father showed signs of wishing to develop a relationship with his child but faced difficulties due to the opposition of the child's mother, the State could not pre-empt the conclusion of the family law proceedings by expelling the father before those proceedings were properly completed.[120]

The position changes in cases where the State wishes to expel a person following a criminal conviction for a serious crime. In such cases, there must be a balancing test, which takes into account on the one hand the extent, timing, and seriousness of the criminal offences committed, and on the other hand, the difficulties that expulsion from that State would cause for the family life of the person concerned.[121] This aspect of the test entails assessing whether a family life could be maintained in the State of origin, taking into account such factors as the number of family members living in the State of origin as compared to the host State, along with the language skills and other connections with the State of origin which the expellee still maintains.

The principles derived from this case law were summarized in the *Boultif v Switzerland* judgment of 2001, which looked in particular at an extra factor:

---

family members can amount to a breach of the Convention, taking into account the impossibility of removal: *Kimfe v Switzerland* and *Agraw v Switzerland*, 29 July 2010.

[117] *Abdulaziz and others v UK* (Series A, no 94).

[118] See, for instance, *Slivenko v Latvia* (Reports 2003-X), para 96.

[119] *Berrehab v the Netherlands* (Series A, no 138).

[120] *Ciliz v the Netherlands* (Reports 2000-VIII). See subsequently *Da Silva and Hoogkamer v Netherlands* (n 116 above).

[121] Case law beginning with *Moustaquim v Belgium* (Series A, no 193). See further: *Beldjoudi v France* (Series A, no 234); *Nasri v France* (Series A, no 320); *C v Belgium* (Reports 1996-III); *Bouchelkia v France* (Reports 1997-I); *El-Boujaidi v France* (Reports 1997-VI); *Boujlifa v Belgium* (Reports 1997-VI); *Mehemi v France I* (Reports 1997-VI); *Dalia v France* (Reports 1998-I); *Baghli v France* (Reports 1999-VIII); *Ezzouhdi v France*, 13 Feb 2001; *Yildiz v Austria*, 31 Oct 2002; *Jakupovic v Austria*, 6 Feb 2003; and *Yilmaz v Germany*, 17 Apr 2003.

the difficulties which the family members with the nationality of the host State might have adjusting to life in the expellee's home State.[122] Those basic rules were restated and clarified in the Grand Chamber judgment of 2006 in *Uner v Netherlands*, as follows:[123]

- the nature and seriousness of the offence committed by the applicant;
- the length of the applicant's stay in the country from which he or she is to be expelled;
- the time elapsed since the offence was committed and the applicant's conduct during that period;
- the nationalities of the various persons concerned;
- the applicant's family situation, such as the length of the marriage, and other factors expressing the effectiveness of a couple's family life;
- whether the spouse knew about the offence at the time when he or she entered into a family relationship;
- whether there are children of the marriage, and if so, their age; and
- the seriousness of the difficulties which the spouse is likely to encounter in the country to which the applicant is to be expelled;
- the best interests and well-being of the children, in particular the seriousness of the difficulties which any children of the applicant are likely to encounter in the country to which the applicant is to be expelled; and
- the solidity of social, cultural, and family ties with the host country and with the country of destination.

These principles have been applied in a number of subsequent cases.[124] There seem to be special considerations for children, as it is not permissible to return them alone to a State of origin where they have no close family and there has been recent fighting when they have only committed a less serious crime.[125]

There have also been cases concerning expulsion on grounds of 'national security'; this concept can include the removal of foreign military and their family members, but it is nonetheless not 'necessary' to expel such persons where they have spent their entire lives in the country, have integrated to a sufficient degree into the civilian life of the host State, and do not represent an individual security threat.[126]

---

[122] Reports of Judgments and Decisions, 2001-IX. See subsequently: *Amrohalli v Denmark*, 11 July 2002; *Benhebba v France*, 10 July 2003; *Mokrani v France*, 15 July 2003; *Radovanovic v Austria*, 22 Apr 2004; *Keles v Germany*, 27 Oct 2005; *Aoulmi v France*, 17 Jan 2006; and *Sezen v Netherlands* 31 Jan 2006.   [123] Judgment of 18 Oct 2006, paras 57–58.

[124] Expulsions were justified in: *Kaya v Germany*, 28 June 2007; *Chair and JB v Germany*, 6 Dec 2007; *Grant v UK*, 8 Jan 2009; *Onur v UK*, 17 Feb 2009; and *Mutlag v Germany*, 25 Mar 2010. Expulsions were not justified in: *Emre v Switzerland*, 22 May 2008; *Maslov v Austria*, 23 June 2008; *Omojudi v UK*, 24 Nov 2009; and *Khan v UK*, 12 Jan 2010.

[125] *Jakupovic v Austria* (n 121 above). See also *Maslov v Austria* (ibid).

[126] See *Slivenko v Latvia*, n 118 above. A series of other 'national security' cases have been decided on the grounds that the restrictions were not 'prescribed by law': case law beginning with *Al-Nashif v*

The concept of family member for the purposes of the ECHR initially appeared to be broad, encompassing not just the nuclear family but also co-habitees (at least in cases involving children), parents' relationship with children (and vice versa) after divorce or separation from the parent carer or adulthood of the children, and siblings, aunts, and uncles.[127] More recently, the Court has come to focus on 'core' family members, ruling that elderly non-dependent parents do not fall into this category, although relations with such persons still fall within the scope of 'private life';[128] it has also repeatedly emphasized that relations between adults do not normally fall within the scope of 'family life', except where there is a condition of dependence.[129]

Another aspect of the case law is the finding in several cases that while the offences committed by an applicant justified some period of expulsion, Article 8 ECHR was violated by the imposition of an unlimited period of expulsion, which violated the principle of proportionality in light of strength of the migrant's family links, weighed against the severity of his or her offences.[130]

Moreover, there are minimum procedural requirements for Member States where Article 8 rights may be involved; they cannot simply disrupt family life without considering objections by the individuals concerned, as 'the concepts of lawfulness and the rule of law in a democratic society require that measures affecting fundamental human rights must be subject to some form of adversarial proceedings before an independent body competent to review the reasons for the decision and relevant evidence, if need be with appropriate procedural limitations on the use of classified information'.[131] In conjunction with Article 13 ECHR, which guarantees effective remedies for breaches of rights guaranteed by the Convention, 'States must make available to the individual concerned the effective possibility of challenging the deportation or refusal-of-residence order and of having the relevant issues examined with sufficient procedural safeguards and thoroughness by an appropriate domestic forum offering adequate guarantees of independence and impartiality'.[132] Even in alleged 'national security' cases:

... the guarantee of an effective remedy requires as a minimum that the competent independent appeals authority must be informed of the reasons grounding the deportation

Bulgaria (10 June 2002), discussed further below. For a case where the national security argument justified expulsion, see *Cherif v Italy*, 7 Apr 2009.

[127] See, for example, *Abdulaziz* (n 117 above) and *Moustaquim* (n 121 above).

[128] See *Slivenko* (n 118 above), para 97.

[129] For instance, see *Uner* (n 123 above). The Court does not appear to be suggesting that relations between *spouses* fall outside the scope of 'core' family relationships. Relationships with an unmarried partner are covered, at least where there is a joint child—see, for instance, *Yildiz v Austria* (n 121 above).

[130] See, for instance, the judgments in *Yilmaz* (n 121 above), *Radovanovic*, and *Keles* (both n 122 above).   [131] *Al-Nashif v Bulgaria* (n 126 above), para 123.

[132] *Al-Nashif* (ibid), para 133. For a simpler violation of the requirement that expulsions must be in accordance with the law in Art 8 cases, see *Estrikh v Latvia*, 18 Jan 2007.

decision, even if such reasons are not publicly available. The authority must be competent to reject the executive's assertion that there is a threat to national security where it finds it arbitrary or unreasonable. There must be some form of adversarial proceedings, if need be through a special representative after a security clearance. Furthermore, the question whether the impugned measure would interfere with the individual's right to respect for family life and, if so, whether a fair balance is struck between the public interest involved and the individual's rights must be examined.[133]

Even where judicial review exists, an interference with Article 8 rights will not be 'in accordance with the law' in such cases, if the extent of the judicial review is entirely inadequate.[134]

The consequence of a ruling that a person has been wrongly expelled in breach of Article 8 ECHR is that the State must ensure family reunion (or the right to a private life) by readmitting a person who has been expelled 'with special expedition'.[135] However, three and a half months is not unduly long for this purpose, and States are not required to give a person any particular form of residence permit upon their return.[136]

This brings us to the third category of cases, concerning the legal status of migrants. Although the judgment just mentioned appeared to suggest that, in the absence of expulsion, the regulation of a person's migration status could not infringe Article 8, the Human Rights Court has ruled that a lengthy period of uncertain and precarious migration status could violate Article 8, with the consequence that States are obliged to regularize the position of the person concerned.[137] The Human Rights Court has applied this principle particularly strongly in the context of EU free movement law.[138]

Although it has been argued that foreign nationals should not be subject to expulsion when nationals are not, and that EU Member States should not subject nationals of non-EU states to discrimination as regards expulsion compared to nationals of EU states, the Strasbourg Court has rejected these arguments, on the grounds that in principle a State's nationals cannot be expelled at all, and that the EU has created a 'special legal order', so there is an 'objective and reasonable justification' for treating them better than persons from non-EU States.[139] A subsequent judgment updates this conclusion by referring to the subsequent

---

[133] *Al-Nashif* (ibid), para 137. See subsequently: *Liu v Russia*, 6 Dec 2007; *Musa and Others v Bulgaria*, 11 Jan 2007; and *Bashir and Others v Bulgaria* and *Hasan v Bulgaria*, 14 June 2007.

[134] See *CG and others v Bulgaria*, 24 Apr 2008; *Raza v Bulgaria*, 11 Feb 2010; and *Kaushal v Bulgaria*, 2 Sep 2010. A violation of Art 13 ECHR (the right to an effective remedy) was also found in these cases. See also *Kaya v Romania*, 12 Oct 2006; *Gulijev v Lithuania*, 16 Dec 2008; and *Nolan v Russia*, 12 Feb 2009.   [135] *Mehemi v France (II)*, 10 Apr 2003.

[136] Ibid.

[137] *Sisojeva v Latvia*, Grand Chamber judgment of 15 Jan 2007, along with *Kaftailova v Latvia* and *Shevanova v Latvia*, both Grand Chamber judgments of 7 Dec 2007. See also *Liu v Russia* (n 133 above) and *Zakayev and Sofanova v Russia*, 11 Feb 2010.

[138] *Mendizabal v France*, 17 Jan 2006; see further 6.3.4 below.

[139] See *Moustaquim* (n 121 above) and earlier *Abdulaziz* (n 117 above).

creation of citizenship of the Union, failing to take account of the prospect that
'citizens' of the Union outside their Member State of nationality can be expelled
from other Member States, unlike the citizens of the relevant Member State.[140]
However, this is hard to reconcile with another line of case law from the Court,
which rules that nationality discrimination as regards the rights set out in the
Convention cannot easily be justified.

6.3.2. The right to non-discrimination

As observed above, Article 14 ECHR requires States to secure the rights set out
in the Convention without discrimination on the grounds set out in that Article.
The list of grounds set out is non-exhaustive, and Article 14 also applies to discrimination on grounds of nationality; indeed, 'very weighty reasons' must be
given to justify discrimination on grounds of nationality.[141]

The Human Rights Court has ruled several times that emergency assistance
benefits fall within the scope of Article 1 of Protocol 1 to the ECHR, which
concerns the right to property. It follows that such benefits must be granted
on the basis of non-discrimination on the grounds of nationality, whether the
benefits are contributory or non-contributory, and so far the Court has not
accepted justifications for discrimination based on the principle of reciprocity
or States' desire to control their social benefits budgets.[142] The same principles
apply to access to child benefits, where the benefit is linked to ECHR rights
because child benefits aim to support family life, and where the discrimination
is between the holders of different types of residence permits and therefore not
on the grounds of nationality as such.[143] It is also a violation of Article 14 to
refuse legal aid to persons on the ground that their residence is irregular, at least
in certain circumstances.[144]

It should also be observed that Article 26 of the ICCPR also contains
a non-discrimination clause, which also applies to non-discrimination on
grounds of nationality and which secures equality as regards all rights (including particularly social and economic rights), not just the rights set out in the
Covenant.[145]

---

[140] *C v Belgium* (ibid).   [141] *Gaygusuz v Austria* (Reports 1996-IV).

[142] See *Gaygusuz* (ibid); *Poirrez v France* (ECHR 2003-X); *Luczak v Poland* (ECHR 2007-XIII);
and *Andrejeva v Latvia*, 18 Feb 2009. All EU Member States have ratified the First Protocol. The
Court has definitively confirmed that non-contributory benefits fall within the scope of the right
to property: decision in *Stec and others v UK* (Reports 2005-X).

[143] *Niedzwiecki v Germany* and *Okpisz v Germany*, 25 Oct 2005.

[144] *Yula v Belgium*, 10 Mar 2009.

[145] See Joseph et al (n 111 above), 679–751.

6.3.3. Other human rights of migrant workers

Article 6 ECHR, which guarantees the right to a fair trial, does not cover immigration proceedings.[146] However, Article 6 *does* apply to disputes concerning foreigners' (or their would-be employers') applications for work permits,[147] and it should be recalled that if an immigration dispute can be brought within the other substantive provisions of the Convention, then procedural rights must nonetheless be guaranteed.[148] Specific procedural rights concerning expulsion are set out in the Seventh Protocol to the ECHR and in the ICCPR, but these are considered in detail in Chapter 7, along with the rules concerning detention in the context of immigration proceedings.[149] The rights to free movement within a State's territory and to enter and leave countries are considered in detail in Chapter 3.[150] There seems little doubt that, where no issues of nationality or immigration status are relevant, foreign nationals can generally assert the same human rights as nationals.[151] Migrant workers (or their children) may also be apply to invoke the right to education (for example, under the First Protocol to the ECHR), either alone or in conjunction with non-discrimination provisions of international treaties.

Specific rights for migrants, and particularly migrant workers, are guaranteed by a number of treaties, in particular the UN Convention on Migrant Workers, conventions adopted by the International Labour Organization, and certain Council of Europe conventions (regarding migrant workers, establishment, and social and medical assistance). However, these conventions have attracted little or no ratifications from EU Member States to date.[152] They are particularly concerned with regulating the legal status of migrant workers, including issues such as access to employment and equality as regards social and economic rights.

6.3.4. Application to EU law

The Strasbourg Court has ruled that the ECHR rules on the right to private life and family apply to cases within the scope of EU free movement law. In particular, a Member State that issues a series of short-term residence permits

---

[146] *Maaouia v France* (Reports 2000-X).

[147] *Jurisic and Collegium Mehrerau v Austria* and *Coorplan-Jenni GMBH and Hascic v Austria*, 27 July 2006, and *Koottummel v Austria*, 10 Dec 2009.

[148] See *Al-Nashif v Bulgaria* (n 126 above); as regards asylum proceedings, see 5.3.1.

[149] See 7.3 below.   [150] See 3.3 above.

[151] For example, see *Djaid v France*, 29 Sep 1999, regarding the right to 'trial within a reasonable time' set out in Art 6 ECHR.

[152] For detailed analysis, see Cholewinski (n 111 above). On the UN Convention, in force 1 July 2003 and ratified by over forty States, but no EU Member States, see: <http://www.december18.net> and further links.

to the family member of a migrant EU citizen instead of the permits required by EU law is interfering with the right to family life, and the interference is not 'prescribed by law' if it does not comply with EU or national law.[153] Previously the Human Rights Court had examined in several judgments whether a non-EU national could move with an EU spouse to another EU country besides other than that wishing to expel the non-EU spouse,[154] but it never drew the obvious connection with EU free movement law in such cases. In fact, it might be questioned whether the crimes committed in these particular cases would be serious enough to permit another Member State to refuse the entry of such persons.[155] The Strasbourg Court instead focused in these cases on the extent of family life enjoyed by the expellee in the host Member State. In cases involving admission of a non-EU national to live with an EU national, free movement law could also be relevant.[156] The free movement of long-term resident third-country nationals in the EU could also be relevant to family reunion cases.

Also, there is one Strasbourg judgment involving application of an EU association agreement with a non-EU country, in which the Court of Human Rights left it to national courts to determine whether the association agreement with Turkey had been correctly applied.[157] Conversely, the Court of Justice has on a number of occasions referred to the right to family life when ruling on family reunion cases governed by EU free movement law and the EU's family reunion Directive, often referring to Article 8 ECHR and even, in several cases, to Strasbourg Court judgments.[158]

---

[153] *Mendizabal v France* (n 66 above).

[154] See particularly *Mehemi v France* (n 135 above), where the spouse of the expellee was actually a national of Italy, not France. In *Amrohalli v Denmark* (n 122 above), the Court rejected the possibility that the expellee could live in Greece or Turkey on grounds of insufficient links there, not considering the prospect of the Danish spouse exercising free movement rights to live in Greece.

[155] See 6.4.1 below.   [156] See ibid.

[157] *Yildiz* (n 121 above) concerning the EU–Turkey agreement; compare with the case law of the Court of Justice limiting expulsion of Turkish workers and their family members, discussed in 6.4.3 below. The possible application of the EU–Turkey agreement was not referred to in the judgments in *Yilmaz, Uner, Keles, Kaya,* and *Onur* (nn 121–124 above).

[158] As regards EU free movement law, see: Cases 249/86 *Commission v Germany* [1989] ECR 1263; C-60/00 *Carpenter* [2002] ECR I-6279 (applying the *Boultif* judgment); C-459/99 *MRAX* [2002] ECR I-6591; C-413/99 *Baumbast and R* [2002] ECR I-7091; C-257/00 *Givane* [2003] ECR I-345; C-109/01 *Akrich* [2003] ECR I-9607 (referring to *Boultif* and *Amrohalli*); C-482/01 and C-493/01 *Orfanopolous and Olivieri* [2004] ECR I-5257 (referring to *Boultif*); C-157/03 *Commission v Spain* [2005] ECR I-2911; C-503/03 *Commission v Spain* [2006] ECR I-1097; Case C-441/02 *Commission v Germany* [2006] ECR I-3449 (referring to *Boultif*); Case C-127/08 *Metock* [2008] ECR I-6241; and Cases C-310/08 *Ibrahim* and C-480/08 *Teixeira*, judgments of 23 Feb 2010, not yet reported. As regards the EU family reunion directive, see Case C-540/03 *EP v Council* [2006] ECR I-5769 (referring to *Sen, Ahmut, Gul,* and *Rodrigues da Silva and Hoogkamer*) and C-578/08 *Chakroun*, judgment of 4 Mar 2010, not yet reported. On the links between the ECHR and EU free movement law, see also the Commission's report on the derogations from free movement law (COM (1999) 372, 19 July 1999), at 7–9 and 20–21.

As for association agreements, the Court of Justice has ruled that it can only rule on human rights issues falling within the scope of EU law,[159] but it has nonetheless indicated that Member States must take account of the right to family life and the right to property of persons who do not meet the criteria for admission and stay pursuant to the Europe Agreements with Central and Eastern European countries.[160]

Also, it has ruled that persons who wish to enter and stay pursuant to those agreements have a right to effective remedies stemming from the general principles of EU law:

It follows in particular that the scheme applicable to...temporary residence permits [issued in order to exercise the rights conferred by the Europe Agreements] must be based on a procedural system which is easily accessible and capable of ensuring that the persons concerned will have their applications dealt with objectively and within a reasonable time, and refusals to grant a permit must be capable of being challenged in judicial or quasi-judicial proceedings...It should be remembered, in this last respect, that Community law requires effective judicial scrutiny of the decisions of national authorities taken pursuant to the applicable provisions of Community law, and that this principle of effective judicial protection constitutes a general principle which stems from the constitutional traditions common to the Member States and is enshrined by the European Convention for the Protection of Human Rights and Fundamental Freedoms, signed at Rome on 4 November 1950, in Articles 6 and 13 of the Convention...[161]

This general principle is also reflected in the EU Charter of Rights,[162] which has become binding in the meantime.[163] The ruling indicates indisputably that, at least as regards the right to a fair trial and effective remedies in immigration proceedings, the scope of the general principles of EU law is wider than the scope of the corresponding ECHR rights.[164] Rather the procedural rights apply whenever there is a link to a right conferred by EU, with the consequence that all immigration and asylum proceedings linked to EU legislation are covered by the right to a fair trial and an effective remedy. Even where EU legislation sets out a minimum set of procedural rules, the general principles nevertheless (and now presumably also the Charter) require Member States to set a higher standard if necessary to ensure effective procedural protection.[165]

So far the Court of Justice has not had an opportunity to rule on whether the general principles of EU law include other human rights applicable to migrants whose position falls within the scope of EU law. In particular the Court has

---

[159] Case 12/86 *Demirel* [1987] ECR 3719. Conversely, see the Opinion in Case C-65/98 *Eyup* [2000] ECR I-4747.

[160] Cases C-63/99 *Gloszczuk* [2001] ECR I-6369, para 85, and C-235/99 *Kondova* [2001] ECR I-6427, para 90.   [161] Case C-327/02 *Panayotova* [2004] ECR I-11055, para 27.

[162] Art 47 of the Charter ([2007] OJ C 303).   [163] See 2.3 above.

[164] Compare with *Maaouia v France* (n 146 above).

[165] Case C-185/97 *Coote* [1998] ECR I-5199.

not ruled on the equality rights of non-EU citizens in general.[166] As for the EU
Charter of Rights, it includes the right to private and family life, plus equality in
working conditions for third-country nationals, non-discrimination on grounds
of nationality, and the possibility of free movement for third-country nationals.[167]
So far, the Court of Justice has applied the Charter rules on private and family life (both before and after the Charter gained binding force with the Treaty
of Lisbon),[168] but has not yet had the opportunity to rule on the other relevant
Charter rights. Finally, it should be recalled that when the EU becomes party to
the ECHR, it will have the obligation to protect family and private life in that
context.[169]

6.4. Impact of other EU law[170]

The distinction between EU immigration law and other (ie non-JHA) provisions
of EU law is of less importance since the entry into force of Treaty of Lisbon,
given that legal migration issues are subject now to QMV and the ordinary legislative procedure, along with the full jurisdiction of the Court of Justice. However,
it is still necessary to distinguish between the relevant legal bases because of the
opt-outs from EU immigration law,[171] and because the limitation on EU competence over volumes of admission of third-country national economic migrants
coming from third countries, as set out in Article 79(5) TFEU, only applies, as
noted above, to the immigration competence in Article 79 itself.[172] Put another
way, the national competence reserved by Article 79(5) cannot be used to limit
the numbers of third-country nationals admitted for economic purposes coming
from third countries when another legal base in the Treaties is validly used to
regulate the issue in question.

---

[166] A number of judgments on the EU–Turkey agreement (6.4.3 below) make reference to a
non-discrimination clause expressly set out in the EU–Turkey agreement. On the application of
the non-discrimination clause in Art 12 EC (now Art 18 TFEU) to non-EU citizens, see E Guild
and S Peers, 'Out of the Ghetto? The Personal Scope of EU Law', in S Peers and N Rogers, eds,
EU Immigration and Asylum Law: Text and Commentary (1st edn, Martinus Nijhoff, 2006) and 3.4.3
above.

[167] Arts 7, 15(3), 21(2), and 45(2) of the Charter (n 162 above). On the status of the Charter, see
2.3 above; on its impact on EU immigration and asylum law, see S Peers, 'Immigration, Asylum
and the European Union Charter of Fundamental Rights' (2001) 3 EJML 141. The provision on
non-discrimination on grounds of nationality is identical to Art 12 EC (now Art 18 TFEU), on
which see ibid.   [168] See *EP v Council* and *Chakroun* (n 158 above).

[169] See 2.3 above.

[170] For a detailed analysis of the position of third-country nationals under other provisions of EC
and EU law (before the Treaty of Lisbon), see Guild and Peers (n 166 above).

[171] For the details of these rules, see 6.2.5 above.   [172] See further 6.2.4 above.

In any event, it is necessary to set out an overview of the other EU rules impacting upon immigration in order to get a fuller picture of the legal status of third-country nationals pursuant to EU law as a whole.[173]

6.4.1. EU free movement law

The most important case of a non-JHA area of EU law applying to third-country nationals is EU free movement law—namely, where third-country nationals are family members of EU citizens. However, such family members can only claim status under EU free movement law if the EU citizen sponsor has exercised free movement rights; this will usually entail the EU citizen residing in an EU Member State other than that of his or her nationality.[174] However, at least in some cases it is enough for an EU citizen to exercise some economic activity in another Member State, even while still resident in the Member State of his or her nationality, for EU free movement law to apply to that citizen's family members.[175] Also, it is enough for the purposes of EU free movement law that the EU citizen is a small child, even if he or she has never moved and is a citizen of the Member State in question, along as he or she is (also) a citizen of another Member State.[176] This could even entail corollary rights for the third-country national parent of that child to stay in the country, as long as the family is not a financial burden on the host State.[177] EU free movement law will also apply to the family members where the EU citizen has exercised free movement rights and then returned to his or her home Member State.[178] In particular, it should be emphasized that the third-country national family member can benefit from EU free movement law even if he or she was not previously resident in any Member State, and even if he or she was an unauthorized migrant before forming a family relationship with an EU citizen.[179]

---

[173] For the impact of non-JHA EU law in other contexts, see further 3.4, 4.4, and 5.4 above and 7.4 below.

[174] See particularly Joined Cases 35 and 36/82 *Morson and Jhanjan* [1982] ECR 3723 and Joined Cases C-64/96 and 65/96 *Uecker and Jacquet* [1997] ECR I-3171. The position was confirmed in Case C-212/06 *Gouvernement de la Communauté française and Gouvernement wallon* [2008] ECR I-1683. However, see now Case C-34/09 *Ruiz Zambrano*, pending.

[175] C-60/00 *Carpenter* [2002] ECR I-6279.

[176] Case C-148/02 *Avello* [2003] ECR I-11613. On the position of a dual citizen of two Member States who has never left one of them, see also Case C-434/09 *McCarthy*, pending.

[177] See Case C-200/02 *Chen and Zhu* [2004] ECR I-9925. See also *Ruiz Zambrano* (n 174 above), pending.

[178] Case C-370/90 *Surinder Singh* [1992] ECR I-4265; see also Case C-291/05 *Eind* [2007] ECR I-10719.

[179] See particularly Case C-127/08 *Metock* [2008] ECR I-6241 (followed in Case C-551/07 *Sahin* [2008] ECR I-10453), overturning Case C-109/01 *Akrich* [2003] ECR I-9607. See earlier *Carpenter*

Fundamental questions arise as regards the application of free movement law and EU immigration law when a person either has dual nationality of a Member State and a non-Member State, or loses the nationality of a Member State and either retains (or automatically reacquires) the nationality of a third State or thereby becomes stateless.[180]

In the first scenario, the Court of Justice has made clear that there is an absolute obligation of other Member States to recognize and give effect to a person's acquisition of a Member State's nationality.[181] The complication arises where the person concerned instead seeks to rely, at least for some purposes, on his or her third-country nationality, rather than his or her EU citizenship. This would most likely occur where the person concerned has not exercised EU free movement rights, so could not rely on EU free movement law, and where the Member State where that person is a national treats its nationals worse than third-country nationals, at least for some purposes. This is the case, for instance, in some Member States as regards family reunion.[182] In that scenario the person concerned would likely find it easier in practice simply to 'stay put' in his or her 'own' Member State and invoke his or her third-country nationality in order to fall within the scope of the relevant rules, rather than trigger EU free movement law by moving to another Member State (if only for a limited period).

However, the Court of Justice has ruled in the *Mesbah* judgment that in such cases, a person with the nationality of a Member State and of a non-Member State can *only* rely on his or her EU citizenship, not on his or her third-country nationality, in particular because a free movement right is not being invoked.[183] It is arguable, however, that the position is different where the person concerned is relying on a free movement right under the EEA or Swiss treaties, or on rights under the EU–Turkey association agreement, given the stronger link with the EU internal market exhibited in such cases, and especially in light of the obligation to interpret the EU–Turkey association rules the same as the EU free movement law rules 'as far as possible'.[184] More broadly, it is arguable that the position in the *Mesbah* case might have to be reconsidered in light of the subsequent development of EU immigration and asylum law, and/or particularly where there is a link with a human right such as family reunion or asylum, given the central role

(n 175 above) and Case C-459/99 *MRAX* [2002] ECR I-6591; and see also Case C-1/05 *Jia* [2007] ECR I-1. See further 7.4.1 below.

[180] On this issue as regards criminal law, see 9.5.2 below; as regards civil law, see Case C-168/08 *Hadadi* [2009] ECR I-6871.

[181] Case C-369/90 *Micheletti and Others* [1992] ECR I-4239.   [182] See 6.6 below.

[183] Case C-179/98 *Mesbah* [1999] ECR I-7955. Although technically this judgment only considered the position of third-country national family members of such persons, the principle developed in this case must logically also apply to the dual citizens themselves.

[184] As regards the EU–Turkey agreement, this issue is pending before the Court of Justice: Joined Cases C-7/10 and 9/10 *Kahveci and Inan*, pending. On these association agreements, see 6.4.3 below.

of human rights within the EU legal order.[185] It should be noted that the *Mesbah* case explicitly applies to the position of third-country national family members of dual citizens of a Member State and a non-Member State.

In the second scenario,[186] the person concerned would obviously be entitled to rely, as from the loss of his or her EU citizenship,[187] on any rights that derived from the third-country nationality which he or she retained or reacquired, or failing that, from the status of statelessness, which is a form of third-country nationality as far as EU immigration law is concerned.[188] The more challenging question is whether the person concerned could rely on their third-country even before the date of losing their EU citizenship status, in particular in order to qualify themselves for (or toward) long-term residence status or status as a Turkish worker or Turkish worker's family member.[189] The answer to that question is arguably dependent on the position under the first scenario, ie whether it had been possible to rely on third-country nationality while also an EU citizen (although it is obviously not possible to rely simultaneously on EU citizenship and the status of statelessness). If so, then obviously reliance on the third-country nationality can simply continue after the loss of EU citizenship. If not, then reliance on the third-country nationality (or statelessness status) can only start once the EU citizenship was lost.

A particular issue obviously arises as regards the position of family members of EU citizens who lose their EU citizenship, if the family members are third-country nationals.[190] Arguably, following the loss of EU citizenship by their sponsor, the family members would still retain any status which they had already acquired under EU free movement law, by analogy with the case law on the EU–Turkey association agreement and the free movement law rules governing other circumstances in which the link between EU citizens and family members is broken.[191] As to whether the family members could rely on their third-country nationality, the question is whether the principle in the *Mesbah* case would apply, ie whether they, like EU citizens, could not rely on their

---

[185] See generally 2.3 above. On the position of persons with the dual nationality of a Member State and a non-Member State as regards asylum, including cases in which the EU citizenship is lost, see 5.4.1 above.

[186] On the limits to withdrawal of a Member State's nationality deriving from EU law, see the judgment of 2 Mar 2010 in Case C-135/08 *Rottmann*, not yet reported.

[187] If the loss of EU citizenship was retroactive, reliance on third-country citizenship or statelessness status would take effect from the date on which citizenship was lost *de jure*.

[188] See Art 67(2) TFEU.   [189] See 6.7 and 6.4.3 below.

[190] If the family members are EU citizens, then they can continue to claim EU citizenship status in their own name, and the person who has lost EU citizenship moreover then has the right to be treated as the family member of an EU citizen. If the family members of the EU citizen who has lost his or her citizenship lose *their* EU citizenship in turn, as a direct result of the sponsor's loss of EU citizenship (ie because the family members only acquired their citizenship because of the sponsor's citizenship), then the principles set out above apply *mutatis mutandis*.

[191] On the former point, see Case C-337/07 *Altun* [2008] ECR I-10323; on the latter point, see discussion further below in this section.

third-country nationality as such to obtain rights;[192] the *Mesbah* rule might even apply where the family members retain rights as family members of EU citizens which they had obtained before the EU citizen's loss of nationality. If the *Mesbah* principle does apply, the family members would nevertheless at least be able to rely on their third-country nationality once their sponsor had lost his or her EU citizenship, if those family members were not able to claim acquired rights under EU free movement law.[193]

The four central issues regarding family reunion are: the definition of sponsors; the definition of family members; the conditions attached to family reunion (for example, waiting periods and financial requirements); and the treatment of family members after reunion (referred to as the issue of the 'status of family members'), concerning such issues as the grounds on which family members can be expelled, their access to education and employment, and their status in the event of family breakdown.[194] Although the rules governing the free movement of EU citizens and their family members used to be set out in the EC Treaty (as it then was),[195] and a number of different secondary legislative measures,[196] most of that legislation was consolidated and updated by Directive 2004/38, as of 30 April 2006.[197] The Court of Justice has confirmed that this Directive does not reduce the rights conferred by the prior legislation,[198] so it is therefore assumed in the following discussion that the Court's case law concerning the prior legislation is still relevant, *mutatis mutandis,* to the 2004 Directive.

Firstly, for an initial three-month period, the sponsors of third-country national family members can be *any* EU citizens.[199] After that period, sponsors can be

---

[192] Although the *Mesbah* judgment decided that third-country national family members of dual citizens could not rely on the non-EU citizenship of the *sponsor,* arguably this can be distinguished from the question of whether those family members can rely on *their own* (single) third-country nationality in its own right.

[193] Note that in either case, there might be practical complications, if the person who lost EU citizenship was the 'breadwinner', while his or her family members are not economically active.

[194] See S Peers, 'Family Reunion and Community Law', in N Walker, ed, *Towards an Area of Freedom, Security and Justice* (OUP, 2004), 143.

[195] The relevant EC Treaty Articles, now TFEU Articles, are Arts 45 (workers; ex-Art 39 EC), 49 (self-employed; ex-Art 42 EC), and 56 (service providers and recipients; ex-Art 49 EC). Also, Arts 18 and 166 (ex-Arts 12 and 150 EC), taken together, give free movement rights to students (Case C-357/89 *Raulin* [1992] ECR I-1027), and Art 21 TFEU (ex-Art 18 EC) on EU citizens' right to 'move and reside' freely can also confer free movement rights in certain cases (C-413/99 *Baumbast and R* [2002] ECR I-7091; *Chen and Zhu,* n 177 above).

[196] The relevant legislation comprised Regs 1612/68 ([1968] OJ Spec Ed L 257/2, p 475) and 1251/70 ([1970] OJ Spec Ed L 142/24, p 402), along with Dirs 64/221 ([1963–64] OJ Spec Ed L 117), 68/360 ([1968] OJ Spec Ed L 257/13, p 485), 72/194 ([1972] OJ L 121/32), 73/148 ([1973] OJ L 172/14), 75/34 ([1975] OJ L 14/10), 75/35 ([1975] OJ L 14/14), 90/364 ([1990] OJ L 180/26), 90/365 ([1990] OJ L 180/28), and 93/96 ([1993] OJ L 317/59).

[197] [2004] OJ L 229/35. Arts 1–9 and 12 of Reg 1612/68 (ibid) remain in force (see Art 38 of the Directive). Also, the relevant TFEU (ex-EC Treaty) Articles remain in force.

[198] See *Metock* (n 179 above), and subsequently Cases C-310/08 *Ibrahim* and C-480/08 *Teixeira,* judgments of 23 Feb 2010, not yet reported.   [199] Art 6, Dir 2004/38.

workers, self-employed persons, students, or others with sufficient resources and sickness insurance,[200] as defined relatively broadly by the Court of Justice's interpretation of the Treaty free movement rights and the prior secondary legislation. Secondly, the family members who can 'accompany or join'[201] an EU citizen in another Member State are: a spouse; a registered partner (in accordance with a Member State's law) if the national law of the host State treats registered partnerships equally to marriage and in accordance with the national conditions in the host State;[202] direct descendants under twenty-one or dependants of the sponsor and of the spouse or partner; and dependent ascending relatives of sponsor and of the spouse or partner.[203] Member States are also obliged to facilitate, in accordance with national law, the entry and residence of persons who are dependants or members of the household in the country of origin, or a person requiring medical care from EU citizen, or the partner of an EU citizen with a durable relationship which is duly attested.[204] According to the Court's case law, a 'spouse' refers only to a relationship of marriage, although Member States must extend to citizens of other EU Member States the same treatment that they extend to their own citizens as regards admission of unmarried partners.[205] Spouses retain their status during marital separation and in the different stages of divorce proceedings falling short of the final legal termination of the marriage, as long as they reside in the same EU Member State as the sponsor.[206] Children also include stepchildren of the sponsor.[207]

Thirdly, EU free movement rules do not set waiting periods or other conditions of admission of family members above and beyond the restrictions inherent in the definitions of sponsors and family members, except for a 'dependence' requirement as regards certain (not all) family members,[208] and some limited possibilities to require a short-term visa.[209] Directive 2004/38 repealed the accommodation requirement which had previously applied to workers' family members.[210]

---

[200] Art 7(1)–(3), Dir 2004/38.

[201] Art 3(1), Dir 2004/38; see also Art 7(1)(d) and (2).

[202] On such national conditions, see by analogy Case C-267/06 *Maruko* [2008] ECR I-1757.

[203] Art 2(2). Students still lack the right to bring in ascending relatives (Art 7(3)).

[204] Art 3(2). The interpretation and extent of this 'facilitation' obligation (or the earlier version of this rule in the prior legislation) has not yet been clarified by the Court of Justice.

[205] Case 59/85 *Reed* [1987] ECR 1283. This interpretation of the prior legislation is arguably confirmed by the explicit distinction between spouses and partners in Dir 2004/38.

[206] Case 267/83 *Diatta* [1985] ECR 567 and *Singh* (n 178 above).

[207] See *Baumbast* (n 195 above).

[208] On the definition of dependency, see: Case 316/85 *Lebon* [1987] ECR 2811; *Chen and Zhu* (n 177 above); and *Jia* (n 179 above).

[209] For details, see 4.4.1 above. Member States cannot impose a long-term visa requirement for EU citizens' family members: see C-157/03 *Commission v Spain* [2005] ECR I-2911. For the position as regards border controls, see 3.4.1 above.

[210] On that prior requirement, see Case 249/86 *Commission v Germany* [1989] ECR 1263.

As for the status of family members after admission, Directive 2004/38 grants permanent residence for EU citizens and family members after five years' legal residence.[211] Before that point, there is one set of rules regarding the position of family members in the event of the death or departure of the EU citizen sponsor,[212] and a second set of rules governing the position after divorce, marriage annulment, or termination of a registered partnership.[213] However, it should be noted that some family members can rely in such cases on the more favourable rules set out in prior legislation, which continues to confer upon migrant worker's children a right to reside in order to obtain education even where the parent who is an EU citizen has left or divorced the other parent, along with a corollary right for the parent caring for that child to stay on the territory.[214] Also, there is a special rule governing the acquisition of permanent residence in the event of retirement or disability of the sponsor who is a worker or in self-employment, or the death of such a sponsor during his or her working life.[215]

Family members have the right to take up employment or self-employment in all cases where an EU citizen is a resident or permanent resident,[216] along with a general right to equal treatment, including as regards social assistance, with derogations concerning social assistance and student support.[217] Member States may refuse admission to EU citizens' family members, or expel them, on grounds of public policy, public security, or public health, but such decisions are subject to strict substantive thresholds and procedural requirements identical to those applicable to EU citizens.[218]

[211] Arts 16–21, Dir 2004/38. On the acquisition of that status, see Case C-162/09 *Lassal*, pending (opinion of 11 May 2010), Case C-325/09 *Dias*, pending, and the opinion in *Teixeira* (n 198 above). On the loss of the extra status conferred after *ten* years' residence, see C-145/09 *Tsakouridis*, opinion of 8 June 2010, pending. The Court of Justice has confirmed that the issue of documentation proving this status is purely declaratory, ie the status is obtained even if such documents are not issued: Case C-123/08 *Wolzenburg* [2009] ECR I-9621.   [212] Art 12, Dir 2004/38.

[213] Art 13, Dir 2004/38.

[214] *Ibrahim* and *Teixeira* (n 198 above), decided on the basis of Art 12 of Reg 1612/68, which was not repealed by Dir 2004/38 (n 197 above), as interpreted previously in the judgment in *Baumbast* (n 195 above). See earlier Joined Cases 389/87 and 390/87 *Echternach and Moritz* [1989] ECR 723, on the position of older children remaining to complete their education after their parents leave the country. On the scope of the right to education, see Case 9/74 *Casagrande* [1974] ECR 773.

[215] Art 17. See Case C-257/00 *Givane* [2003] ECR I-345.

[216] Art 23. See in particular Cases 131/85 *Gul* [1986] ECR 1573 and C-165/05 *Commission v Luxembourg*, judgment of 27 Oct 2005, unreported. Third-country national family members only have access to employment in the Member State where the EU citizen is resident: see Case C-10/05 *Mattern and Cikotic* [2006] ECR I-3145.

[217] Art 24. See Case 32/75 *Christini* [1975] ECR 1085 (social benefits), applied to third-country national family members in Case 94/84 *Deak* [1985] ECR 1873. Equal treatment does not appear to extend to independent residence status: Cases C-356/98 *Kaba I* [2000] ECR I-2625 and C-466/00 *Kaba II* [2003] ECR I-2219, although it might be arguable that this issue could be revisited pursuant to Dir 2004/38.

[218] Arts 26–33. See further *MRAX* (n 179 above), Case C-503/03 *Commission v Spain* [2006] ECR I-1097, and the further discussion in 3.4.1 above and 7.4.1 below.

Finally, there was a special rule applicable to family members of workers from the newer Member States, but this has now expired (as from 1 May 2007 for eight Member States joining on 1 May 2004, and as from 1 January 2010 for Romania and Bulgaria).[219]

According to the Commission report on the application of Directive 2004/38,[220] Member States' transposition of the definition of core family members in the Directive was 'satisfactory'. However, the transposition of the requirement to 'facilitate' entry of extended family members was 'less satisfactory', with thirteen Member States applying the law incorrectly (although ten Member States go further than required, and admit all such family members). Thirteen Member States admit same-sex registered partners.

Residence rights for family members were restricted by the eleven Member States which required prior lawful entry in another Member State (following the Court's case law, later overturned), and by one Member State which imposed an accommodation requirement regarding family members. Twelve Member States did not opt to restrict the admission of students' family members beyond spouses and children, but eight of the other fifteen Member States applied the obligation to facilitate the admission of students' other family members incorrectly. In some Member States, the 'residence card' for family members had a different title, which could cause complications, and six Member States did not apply the rules on the position of third-country national family members after death, divorce, etc correctly.

In its subsequent guidance on the correct application of the Directive,[221] the Commission asserts that in principle Member States must recognize marriages to EU citizens contracted anywhere in the world, with an exception for forced marriages (as distinct from arranged marriages). As to the definition of a 'durable partnership', a Member State could examine the length of time that the partnership had lasted, but had to consider other factors as well. The concept of 'family' includes adoptive relationships, guardians with custody of children, and possibly even foster children. Finally, while Member States may offer integration courses for EU citizens and their family members, no consequence could be attached to a refusal to attend these courses.[222]

6.4.2. Social security coordination

The second case where non-JHA EU law applies to third-country nationals in part in the context of immigration is EU law on coordination of social security.

---

[219] See Annex V to the 2003 Accession Treaty ([2003] OJ L 236) and Annex VI to the 2005 Accession Treaty ([2005] OJ L 157). Citizens of Malta and Cyprus are not subject to any transitional restrictions.   [220] COM (2008) 840, 10 Dec 2008.

[221] COM (2009) 313, 2 July 2009.

[222] Compare with the position under EU immigration law (6.6 and 6.7 below).

This subject is closely connected to free movement law, but a separate Regulation (dating previously from 1971, then replaced by a Regulation adopted in 2004) sets out detailed rules on social security coordination for all EU citizens who exercise rights of free movement within the EU, and all of their family members.[223] Family members of EU citizens, including third-country national family members, used to be covered by a rule—known as the 'derived rights' rule—that restricted their ability to rely on the legislation in their own name. However, in 1996 the Court of Justice largely scrapped that rule, and thus enhanced the application of the legislation to family members of EU citizens.[224]

Both the 1971 Regulation and the 2004 Regulation also apply to stateless persons and refugees, and in 2001 the Court of Justice delivered its *Khalil and Addou* judgment on the scope and validity of the application of the 1971 Regulation to these groups.[225] In this judgment, the Court concluded that the Council had validly included such categories of persons within the scope of the EC's then-existing social security Regulation by using what was originally Article 51 EEC (later Article 42 EC, and now Article 48 TFEU) as a 'legal base' for adoption of the legislation. But the Court also ruled that the legislation only governed the position of refugees and stateless persons when they *moved within the Community* (now the Union). It followed that refugees and stateless persons did not have the right to equal treatment in a single Member State. However, since, unlike EU citizens and their family members, refugees and stateless persons have (for now, at least) no right to move between Member States pursuant to EU law, the EU social security rules are therefore of little use to them, although they do apply to any refugees and stateless persons posted to another Member State by their employer to carry out services.[226]

Apart from the categories of family members of EU citizens exercising free movement rights, and stateless persons and refugees, there are also social security rules for some categories of persons covered by association agreements and 'immigration law' legislation applying to for third-country nationals in general; arguably the latter rules were adopted using the wrong 'legal base' (the immigration provisions of the EC Treaty (now Title V of Part Three of the TFEU), instead of Article 42 EC (now Article 48 TFEU)).[227] It is not clear whether persons with

---

[223] Until 1 May 2010, the applicable law was Reg 1408/71 [1971] OJ L 149/2. This Regulation was replaced from that date by Reg 883/2004 ([2004] OJ L 166/1), when Reg 987/2009 ([2009] OJ L 284/1) implementing Reg 883/2004 entered into force (see Art 91, Reg 883/2004, and Art 97, Reg 987/2009).

[224] Case C-308/93 *Cabanis-Issarte* [1996] ECR I-2097. See comments by S Peers, 'Equality, Free Movement and Social Security' (1997) 22 ELRev 342. The 'derived rights' rule still applies to unemployment benefits: see Case C-189/00 *Ruhr* [2001] ECR I-8225.

[225] Joined Cases C-95/99 to 98/99 *Khalil and others* and C-180/99 *Addou* [2001] ECR I-7413.

[226] On the position of refugees and stateless persons as regards movement between Member States, see 6.7 below; on posted third-country national workers, see 6.4.4 below.

[227] See respectively 6.4.3 and 6.8 below; on the legal base argument, see ch 23 of Peers and Rogers (n 166 above).

refugee status can rely on the association agreements as regards social security, if they have the relevant nationality, other than the agreement with Turkey.[228] However, it seems clear that persons with dual nationality of an EU Member State and a non-EU country cannot rely on the association agreements as regards social security, except arguably where the relevant agreement creates or is linked to free movement rights (ie the EEA and the treaties with Switzerland and Turkey).[229]

6.4.3. Association agreements

The third category of cases where non-JHA EU law applies to third-country nationals is the case of association agreements concluded by the Community (now the Union) and (usually) its Member States with non-EU countries. The Court of Justice has ruled that such agreements form an integral part of EC (now EU) law;[230] that it can interpret their provisions, even those relating to immigration;[231] that provisions in these agreements can have 'direct effect' allowing individuals to rely on them in their national courts, where those provisions are clear, precise, and unconditional;[232] and that where the agreements have similar or identical wording to EU free movement rules, the agreements will not *necessarily* be interpreted the same way.[233] A number of these agreements contain provisions on immigration, or at least some aspects of the status of migrants, but these specific clauses vary widely in scope. It is therefore necessary to consider the relevant migration provisions of each agreement in turn.

First of all, the European Economic Area (EEA) agreement with Norway, Iceland, and Liechtenstein essentially fully extends the EU rules on free movement of persons, including rules on mutual recognition of qualifications and social security, to these States.[234] Secondly, most of the EU free movement rules (except for the imposition of transitional periods and certain limitations on the right to provide services) also apply to Switzerland, pursuant to a bilateral treaty on free movement of persons which entered into force on 1 June 2002.[235] The

---

[228] This point was relevant in *Khalil and Addou* (n 225 above), but was not referred by the national court, which assumed that refugees could not rely on the EU–Morocco agreement. For the argument that refugees *can* rely on such agreements, see S Peers, case note on *Khalil and Addou*, (2002) 39 CMLRev 1395. The Court of Justice has since confirmed, in Case C-337/07 *Altun* [2008] ECR I-10323, that the family members of a Turkish worker with refugee status are covered by the relevant rules in the EU–Turkey agreement. This judgment obviously strengthens the general argument that persons governed by association agreements can rely on the rules in the agreements even if they have refugee status.

[229] See Case C-179/98 *Mesbah* [1999] ECR I-7955 and the discussion in 6.4.1 above.

[230] Case 181/73 *Hagemann* [1974] ECR 449.   [231] Case 12/86 *Demirel* [1987] ECR 3719.

[232] *Demirel*, ibid; see also Case 104/81 *Kupferberg* [1982] ECR 3641.

[233] Case 270/80 *Polydor* [1982] ECR 329.

[234] [1994] OJ L 1/1. See Case C-92/02 *Kristiansen* [2003] ECR I-14597, para 24.

[235] [2002] OJ L 114. See S Peers, 'The EC-Switzerland Agreement on Free Movement of Persons: Overview and Analysis' (2000) 2 EJML 127.

Court of Justice has ruled on the provisions of this treaty as regards self-employed frontier workers, but has also confirmed that legal persons cannot derive rights from it.[236] As regards social security, these treaties mean that nationals of Norway, Iceland, Liechtenstein, and Switzerland are covered both by the right to equal social security treatment in one EU Member State and by the coordination rules if they move to another EU Member State.

Thirdly, the position of Turkish citizens is particularly complex. Their status in EU law is governed by several instruments: the original 1963 Association Agreement with Turkey; a 1970 Protocol to that Agreement; Decisions 2/76 and 1/80 of the Association Council established by that Agreement concerning the access to employment of Turkish workers and their family members; and Decision 3/80 of the Association Council, concerning Turkish workers' social security.[237] First of all, the original Association Agreement sets out a goal of full free movement of workers, services, and self-employed persons. The Court of Justice has ruled that these provisions set out only a goal to be achieved and therefore do not confer 'directly effective' rights on individuals which can be enforced in the national courts.[238] Next, the 1970 Protocol sets a deadline to achieve the goal of free movement of workers and sets a standstill barring any new national rules which make establishment of the provision of services between the parties more difficult than it was before that Protocol entered into force. The Court of Justice has ruled that the 'workers' provisions in the Protocol are not directly effective, but that the two standstill clauses are.[239]

Next, Decisions 2/76 and 1/80 (which replaced Decision 2/76) set out detailed rules regarding Turkish workers and their family members, falling short of full free movement rights. The Court of Justice has delivered no fewer than thirty-seven judgments on these provisions.[240] For Turkish workers, the key provision

---

[236] Cases: C-13/08 *Stamm* [2008] ECR I-11087; C-351/08 *Grimme*, judgment of 12 Nov 2009, not yet reported; and C-541/08 *Fokus Invest*, judgment of 11 Feb 2010, not yet reported. See also Case C-70/09 *Hengartner and Gasser* (judgment of 15 July 2010, not yet reported), the pending Case C-257/10 *Bergstrom*, and the discussion of the Court's jurisdiction over and legal effect of the agreement in the Opinion in the withdrawn case of *Zentralbetriebsrat der Landeskrankenhäuser Tirols and Land Tirol* (Case C-339/05 [2006] ECR I-7097).

[237] The Agreement is published in [1977] OJ L 261/60; the Protocol is published [1972] JO L 293/1; Decision 3/80 is published at [1983] OJ C 110/60; the other Decisions are unpublished in the OJ.

[238] *Demirel*, n 231 above (workers), Case C-37/98 *Savas* [2000] ECR I-2927 (self-employed persons). The same is undoubtedly true as regards services.

[239] *Demirel*, ibid (workers), *Savas*, ibid (self-employed persons); Joined Cases C-317/01 and C-369/01 *Abatay and others* [2003] ECR I-12301 (services).

[240] Cases: C-192/89 *Sevince* [1990] ECR I-3461; C-237/91 *Kus* [1992] ECR I-6781; C-355/93 *Eroglu* [1994] ECR I-5113; C-434/93 *Bozkurt* [1995] ECR I-1475; C-171/95 *Tetik* [1997] ECR I-329; C-351/95 *Kadiman* [1997] ECR I-2133; C-386/95 *Eker* [1997] ECR I-2697; C-285/95 *Kol* [1997] ECR I-3095; C-36/96 *Günaydin* [1997] ECR I-5143; C-98/96 *Ertanir* [1997] ECR I-5179; C-210/97 *Akman* [1998] ECR I-7519; C-1/97 *Birden* [1998] ECR I-7747; C-340/97 *Nazli* [2000] ECR I-957; C-329/97 *Ergat* [2000] ECR I-1487; C-65/98 *Eyup* (n 87 above); C-188/00 *Kurz* [2002] ECR I-10691; C-171/01 *Birklite* [2003] ECR I-1487; *Abatay and others*, ibid; C-275/02 *Ayaz* [2004] ECR I-8765; C-467/02 *Cetinkaya* [2004] ECR I-10895; C-136/03 *Dorr and Unal*

in Decision 1/80 is Article 6(1), which provides that 'a Turkish worker duly registered as belonging to the labour force of a Member State': is entitled to a renewed work permit after one year's 'legal employment' in order 'to work for the same employer, if a job is available'. That worker is then entitled to respond to another job offer 'in the same occupation' after three years' legal employment, subject to priority for EU workers. Finally, the Turkish worker has free access to any paid employment after four years' legal employment. Article 6(2) provides that annual holidays, maternity absences, work accidents, and short sicknesses count as 'legal employment', and that involuntary unemployment duly certified and long absences due to sickness 'shall not affect rights acquired as the result of the preceding period of employment'. For family members, Article 7(1) of Decision 1/80 provides that '[t]he members of the family of a Turkish worker duly registered as belonging to the labour force of a Member State, who have been authorized to join him' are entitled to respond to offers of employment after three years legal residence, subject to EU nationals' priority, and then have free access to any paid employment after five years' residence. Article 7(2) provides that '[c]hildren of Turkish workers who have completed a course of vocational training in the host country may respond to any offer of employment there, irrespective of the length of time they have been resident in that Member State, provided one of their parents has been legally employed in the Member State concerned for at least three years'. Article 9 states that Turkish children resident with parents who are or have been legally employed in a Member State have equal treatment in access to education in that State (compared to that State's nationals) as regards their qualifications, and 'may' be able to take advantage of the relevant benefits. Article 10 provides for a right to equal treatment in working conditions; Article 13 provides for a standstill on any new restrictions on access to employment for legally resident Turkish workers and their family members; and Article 14(1) specifies that the provisions of the Decision are 'subject to limitations justified on grounds of public policy, public security or public health'.

The key points established in the jurisprudence are that the Court of Justice has the competence to interpret Decision 1/80;[241] that Articles 6, 7, 9, 10, and 13 of

---

[2005] ECR I-4759; C-373/03 *Aydinli* [2005] ECR I-6181; C-374/03 *Gurol* [2005] ECR I-6199; C-383/03 *Dogan* [2005] ECR I-6237; C-230/03 *Sedef* [2006] ECR I-157; C-502/04 *Torun* [2006] ECR I-1563; C-4/05 *Guzeli* [2006] ECR I-10279; C-325/05 *Derin* [2007] ECR I-6495; C-349/06 *Polat* [2007] ECR I-8167; C-294/06 *Payir and others* [2008] ECR I-203; C-152/08 *Kahveci* [2008] ECR I-6291; C-453/07 *Er* [2008] ECR I-7299; C-337/07 *Altun* [2008] ECR I-10323; C-242/06 *Sahin* [2009] ECR I-8465; C-462/08 *Bekleyen*, judgment of 21 Jan 2010, not yet reported; C-14/09 *Genc*, judgment of 4 Feb 2010, not yet reported; and C-92/07 *Commission v Netherlands*, judgment of 29 Apr 2010, not yet reported. There are several pending cases: C-484/07 *Pehlivan* (opinion of 8 July 2010); C-303/08 *Bozkurt* (opinion of 8 July 2010); C-371/08 *Ornek*; C-420/08 *Erdil*; C-300/09 and C-301/09 *Toprak and Oguz*; C-436/09 *Belkiran*; C-7/10 and 9/10 *Kahveci and Inan*; and C-187/10 *Unal*. See also Case C-465/01 *Commission v Austria* [2004] ECR I-8291.

[241] *Sevince*, ibid.

the Decision are directly effective;[242] and that the right to employment brings with it a right to residence.[243] However, the Court has constantly made clear that the Decision does not affect national control over initial entry and employment of Turkish workers or family members,[244] and does not grant right to free movement between Member States.[245] Also, the Decision should be interpreted consistently with EU free movement case law 'as far as possible',[246] as should the standstill on establishment and services.[247]

The case law has made clear that the definition of a 'Turkish worker' follows the same broad definition applicable in EU free movement law.[248] The concept of registration in labour force simply means that Turkish workers must comply with rules on entry to the Member States' territory and initial access to employment,[249] plus maintain a territorial link with a Member State;[250] it does not permit Member States to establish distinct labour markets on which Turkish workers cannot participate.[251] Next, the requirement of 'legal employment' means that the Turkish worker must have a 'stable and secure situation on the labour force', or in other words authorized residence.[252] However, it is clear that Turkish workers can obtain rights under Article 6 of Decision 1/80 even if their entry and employment was authorized on grounds other than entry for employment, such as to marry a host State national,[253] where the worker was permitted to enter for a limited period only,[254] as a refugee,[255] or as a student.[256]

Regarding the time periods set out in Article 6, the Court has established that Turkish workers cannot claim rights under the first indent of that Article if they changed their employers during the first year,[257] and similarly cannot claim rights after three or four years if they changed employers before that point.[258] However,

---

[242] See *Sevince and Kus* (Arts 6 and 13); *Kadiman* (Art 7(1)); *Eroglu* (Art 7(2)); *Gurol* (Art 9); and *Birklite* (Art 10) (all n 240 above).

[243] See *Sevince and Kus* (Art 6); *Kadiman* (Art 7(1)); and *Eroglu* (Art 7(2)).

[244] The case law in recent years has failed to point out that EU legislation now impacts upon national competence in these areas: see the legislation discussed in 6.5 and 6.6 below.

[245] See particularly *Tetik*, n 240 above. Again, the EU's long-term residence Directive (6.7 below) now addresses this issue, as does the legislation on researchers, students, and Blue Card holders (6.5 below).

[246] Case law starting with *Bozkurt*. On the question of whether dual nationals of a Member State and Turkey can benefit from the rules, see Cases C-7/10 and C-9/10 (n 240 above), pending, and the broader discussion in 6.4.1 above.

[247] See the judgment in *Abatay*, n 239 above, paras 101 and 110. On the scope of the standstill, see Cases C-16/05 *Tum and Dari* [2007] ECR I-7415 and C-228/06 *Soysal* [2009] ECR I-1031, discussed in 3.4.2 and 4.4.2 above, C-92/07 *Commission v Netherlands*, judgment of 29 Apr 2010, not yet reported, and C-186/10 *Oguz*, pending.

[248] See particularly *Ertanir, Gunaydin, Birden,* and *Kurz, Payir,* and *Genc* (n 240 above).

[249] See *Birden* (n 240).   [250] See *Bozkurt* (n 240).   [251] See *Birden* (n 240).

[252] See *Sevince and Kus*, in which the Court made clear that a Turkish worker cannot gain the status of legal employment just because national law allowed the worker to work while contesting a deportation order, and *Kol*, in which the Court established that Turkish workers could not obtain rights under the Decision if it was proven that they entered on the basis of fraud (all n 240 above).

[253] *Kus* (n 240).   [254] *Ertanir* (n 240).   [255] *Altun* (n 240). See 5.4.2 above.

[256] *Payir* (n 240).   [257] *Eker* (n 240).   [258] *Eroglu* and *Sedef* (n 240).

after four years, their access to employment must be fully equal to that of EU citizens.[259] Turkish workers lose status under Article 6 once they have completely retired or become permanently disabled,[260] but they do not lose status immediately upon voluntary unemployment, but have a 'reasonable period' to find work.[261] Moreover, they do not lose status under Article 6 just because they have been in prison for any reason.[262] The list of circumstances set out in Article 6(2) where the clock either 'keeps ticking' for the acquisition of a Turkish worker's rights under Article 6 or where the clock is 'stopped' is non-exhaustive; rights can also be acquired or frozen where comparable legitimate reasons for interruption of employment exist.[263]

As for Article 7(1),[264] during the first three years of the family member's residence in the host Member State, it only confers rights to stay if that family member stays with the Turkish worker that he or she was 'authorized to join', unless there is an objective reason such as work or education to live apart.[265] However, after that point, the family member has independent rights to seek employment, with the corollary right to reside, even if he or she spends some time in prison and/or ceases employment or does not actually take up employment, or becomes independent of his or her parents, or the sponsor's residence right is called into question retroactively, and even if the worker which the family member joined is no longer employed in the host Member State.[266] A 'family member' includes a spouse and child,[267] comprising also stepchildren and children born on the territory of the relevant Member State;[268] it can even include an unmarried partner, at least where a married couple divorced, stayed together, and then remarried.[269] Article 7(2) applies independently of Article 7(1), so can confer rights on Turkish graduates even if they entered a Member State as a student, not as a family member of a Turkish worker.[270] The Court has also established that the condition of three years' residence for one of the graduate's parents set out in Article 7(2) can be fulfilled before the graduate's entry into the workforce; Article 7(2) will even benefit the graduate if the parent has returned to Turkey, if the graduate has become independent of his or her parents or began education after the parent left the country, or if the graduate does not in fact take up employment.[271] Following five years' residence pursuant to Article 7(1) of the Decision, or upon graduation pursuant to Article 7(2) of the Decision, family members must be treated equally to EU citizens as regards access to employment.[272]

---

[259] *Tetik* (n 240).   [260] *Bozkurt* (n 240).   [261] *Tetik* (n 240).

[262] *Nazli* and *Dogan* (n 240).   [263] *Sedef* (n 240).

[264] On the relationship between Arts 6 and 7, see *Aydinli* (n 240).

[265] *Kadiman* (n 240). On the question as to whether other circumstances can break the family link, see the opinions in *Pehlivan* and C-303/08 *Bozkurt*, pending.

[266] *Ergat, Cetinkaya, Aydinli, Derin, Altun,* and *Er* (n 240).   [267] *Kadiman* and *Ergat* (n 240).

[268] See respectively *Ayaz* and *Cetinkaya* (n 240).   [269] *Eyup* (n 240).

[270] *Eroglu* and *Bekleyen* (n 240).   [271] See *Akman, Torun, Derin,* and *Bekleyen* (all n 240).

[272] *Ergat* and *Akman* (n 240).

Article 9 applies even if the children are no longer residing with their parents due to attendance at an educational institution, and gives a right to equal treatment as regards educational grants, even when pursuing higher education in Turkey. Also, by analogy with the case law on Articles 6 and 7 of the Decision, it seems likely that children falling within the scope of Article 9 have a right of residence corollary to their right to equal treatment to education.[273]

Next, the Court has ruled that Article 10 of the Decision, which sets out the right to equal treatment in working conditions, is directly effective and has a similar meaning to the equivalent right which EU free movement law extends to EU citizens and their family members. In particular, it gives a right to equal treatment as regards elections to works councils, access to professional sports matches, and further rights of residence.[274]

As for the standstill on new restrictions on access to employment for legally employed workers and their family members in Article 13, this rule is not restricted in scope to those Turkish workers and family members who were resident when Decision 1/80 entered into force, but also covers persons who have entered the host Member State since then. However, it does not cover Turkish workers unless they have an intention to integrate into the host Member State.[275] The persons concerned must be lawfully resident, but status under Article 10 of the Decision is not lost just because of technical difficulties, for example renewing residence permits, where the person's underlying residence status remains legal.[276] To benefit from the standstill, the persons concerned need not have qualified for status under Article 6 of Decision 1/80; indeed the Court has apparently suggested that only persons *not* covered by Article 6 of the Decision are covered by Article 13.[277] With respect, it is submitted that the Court of Justice should rethink this case law, since the wording of Article 13 of the Decision does not restrict its scope either to persons with an intention to integrate into the host Member State or to persons who are not covered by Article 6 of the Decision.[278] Excluding the latter category of persons from the scope of Article 13 of the Decision could prevent a significant number of people from relying on that Article, and either exclusion frustrates

---

[273] See the reasoning of the Court of Justice as regards EU citizens' residence rights derived from the rights of access to education in *Raulin* (n 195 above).

[274] *Birklite, Kahveci*, and *Guzeli* (all n 240 above).   [275] *Abatay and others* (n 239 above).

[276] See *Sahin*, n 240 above, applying case law concerning Art 7 of the Decision (*Ergat, idem*).

[277] *Sahin* and *Commission v Netherlands*, ibid. The same principle should *not* apply by analogy to family members, since they are covered by Art 7 of the Decision from the outset (see *Kadiman, idem*).

[278] This means that the standstill should apply also to pre-existing rules which benefited persons who had already obtained some status pursuant to Art 6 of Decision 1/80. For example, Art 13 should cover a national rule which applied when Decision 1/80 entered into force in the Member State concerned, and which allowed access to the entire labour market after *two* years' work with the same employer.

the underlying objective of interpreting the Turkish rules the same as the EU free movement rules as far as possible.[279]

Furthermore, the case law establishes that the standstill cannot result in Turkish nationals being treated better than EU citizens, although any difference between the two categories must be proportionate.[280] Finally, the Court of Justice has been asked whether the standstill covers cases where the national rules in question became more favourable after the standstill date, but then the Member State purported to make those national rules more restrictive again.[281] On this point, it is submitted that the standstill should in such cases freeze the later more favourable national rules, since this interpretation would best respect the obligation of applying the EU free movement rules to Turkey as far as possible.[282]

Finally, the Court has ruled that Article 14(1) of the Decision must be interpreted consistently with the former Article 39(3) EC (now Article 45(3) TFEU), meaning that Turkish workers and their family members cannot be expelled as part of a policy of treating foreigners harshly for commission of crimes as a deterrent or imposing automatic expulsions; they can only be expelled where their personal conduct is a serious present threat to one of the fundamental interests of society.[283] The question now arises whether the higher standards established by Directive 2004/38 to limit expulsion of long-settled EU citizens and their family members also apply to Turkish workers and their family members.[284]

As for the social security rights of Turkish workers and their family members, the Court of Justice has ruled that while the equal treatment provisions of Decision 3/80 are directly effective, the coordination rules in that Decision cannot apply until the EU adopts internal legislation to apply them.[285] But in light of the adoption of internal EU legislation coordinating the social security rights of

---

[279] See the example in the previous footnote. If Art 13 of Decision 1/80 did not apply to such a rule, all persons who have worked between two and four years for the same employer would be unable to rely on the continued application of such a rule. There might even be paradoxical cases where persons who had worked for less than one year with the same employer would be better off than people who had worked for the same employer for longer periods. Moreover, unlike Art 7 of the Decision (see *Aydinli*, n 240 above) Art 13 is not 'subject to' Art 6.

[280] See *Sahin* and *Commission v Netherlands*, both n 240 above.

[281] *Toprak* and *Oguz* (n 240).

[282] Note that such a rule applies to the Treaty standstill concerning national restrictions on external free movement of capital: see C-101/05 *A* [2007] ECR I-11531.

[283] Case law beginning with *Nazli*, n 240 above. See further 7.4.2 below.

[284] Cases: C-371/08 *Ornek*; C-420/08 *Erdil*; and C-436/09 *Belkiran*, all pending (n 240 above). An earlier reference on this issue pre-dated the application of Directive 2004/38 (*Polat* (n 240)). On the substance of these higher levels of protection, see 7.4.1 below.

[285] Respectively Cases C-262/96 *Surul* [1999] ECR I-2685 and C-277/94 *Taflan-Met* [1996] ECR I-4085. See further Joined Cases C-102/98 *Kocak* and C-211/98 *Ors* [2000] ECR I-1287 and Case C-485/07 *Akdas*, pending; on the distinction between equal treatment rules and coordination rules, Case C-373/02 *Ozturk* [2004] ECR I-3605. See S Peers, 'Equality, Free Movement and Social Security' (1997) 22 EL Rev 342 and 'Social Security Equality for Turkish Nationals' (1999) 24 EL Rev 627.

all third-country nationals who move within the EU,[286] such a measure is prob-ably now unnecessary.

A general point arises as regards the potential cross-over between rules in EU immigration legislation and the rights derived from the Association Agreement. Since treaties concluded by the EU take precedence over secondary EU legisla-tion, the latter cannot set standards lower than the former.[287] But conversely, where the legislation sets higher standards than the association agreement, it would not conflict with the agreement to apply those higher standards to Turkish workers and their family members, since applying such higher standards would be consistent with the objective of enhancing the position of Turkish workers and their family members as much as possible with a view to applying the full internal market rules in future.[288]

Next, the Europe Agreements with Central and Eastern European countries are no longer in force, but contained four key provisions on migration: the right of establishment; the right to equal treatment in working conditions; the right of specified legally resident family members of a worker to take up employment in a Member State; and the right of corporations to send certain key employees to an establishment in a Member State.[289] These provisions could be relevant by analogy to the interpretation of the Stabilization and Association Agreements (SAAs) in force with four Western Balkans states (Croatia, the Former Yugoslav Republic of Macedonia, Albania, and Montenegro).[290] These agreements are similar to the Europe Agreements, except that rules on the self-employed will not be discussed or adopted until five years after the agreements entered into force.[291] Commission proposals for Association Council decisions to implement the social security rules as regards Croatia and the former Yugoslav Republic of Macedonia have been agreed.[292]

The case law on the Europe Agreements held that the right to establishment was directly effective and carried with it a corollary right of entry and residence; it precluded the imposition of 'economic needs' tests upon nationals of Central

---

[286] See 6.8 below.

[287] The Court of Justice has confirmed this point: see the judgments in *Payir* and *Soysal* (nn 240 and 247 above). Moreover, the principle is expressly set out in the relevant EU immigration legisla-tion (see 6.5–6.7 below), although not in EU asylum legislation, which might also interact with the EU–Turkey rules in practice (see *Altun*, n 240 above).

[288] See S Peers, 'EU Migration Law and Association Agreements', in B Martenczuk and S van Thiel, eds, *Justice, Liberty, Security: New Challenges for EU External Relations* (VUBPress, 2008), 53.

[289] Europe Agreements with Poland, Hungary, the Slovak and Czech Republics, Latvia, Lithuania, Estonia, Slovenia, Romania, and Bulgaria (respectively [1993] OJ L 347 and 348; [1994] OJ L 359 and 360; [1998] OJ L 26, 51, and 68; [1999] OJ L 51; and [1994] OJ L 357 and 358).

[290] [2004] OJ L 84 (Former Yugoslav Republic of Macedonia); [2005] OJ L 26 (Croatia); [2009] OJ L 107 (Albania); and [2010] OJ L 108 (Montenegro). SAAs have also been signed with Bosnia-Herzegovina (COM (2008) 182, 8 Apr 2008), and Serbia (COM (2007) 743, 20 Nov 2007), but these two SAAs are not yet in force.　　　　　　　　　　　　　　[291] See further 3.4.1 above.

[292] COM (2007) 787 and 789, 11 Dec 2007 (proposals); see the press release of the employment Council, 7–8 June 2010.

and Eastern Europe who wished to enter the EU to create a company or work as a self-employed person. The concept of 'establishment' had the same broad meaning as it does under EU free movement law as regards the types of activities covered (even potentially prostitution), but since the Europe Agreements permitted EU Member States to maintain immigration law restrictions, checks could be imposed in advance of taking up self-employment to ensure that the planned activity did not constitute disguised employment, and Member States could oblige persons without existing residence rights to submit an application from outside the territory.[293] As regards equality in working conditions, the Court of Justice held that this was a directly effective right and should be interpreted the same way as the equivalent right guaranteed by EU free movement law; therefore it precluded indirect discrimination in state-sector employment contracts and rules of private associations which restricted the number of Eastern European nationals who can play at any given time for a professional sports team.[294] There was never any case law on the other two migration rights guaranteed by the Europe Agreements, and the powers to adopt social security rules provided for in each Europe Agreement were not exercised.[295]

Also, there are Partnership and Cooperation Agreements (PCAs) in force with Russia and all other ex-Soviet states except Belarus and Turkmenistan.[296] These agreements provide for the right to equal treatment in working conditions, and the Court of Justice has ruled that at least in the agreement with Russia, this right has direct effect and has the same meaning as the Europe Agreement treaties.[297]

Next, treaties with the three Maghreb States (Algeria, Morocco, and Tunisia) provide for equal treatment in social security for workers and family members and equality in working conditions.[298] The case law of the Court of Justice makes

---

[293] See Cases: C-63/99 *Gloszczuk* [2001] ECR I-6369; C-235/99 *Kondova* [2001] ECR I-6427; C-257/99 *Barkoci and Malik* [2001] ECR I-6557; C-268/99 *Jany* [2001] ECR I-8615; C-327/02 *Panayotova* [2004] ECR I-11055; and C-101/10, *Pavlov and Famira*, pending. For more on the border control and visas aspects of the Europe Agreements, see 3.4.2 and 4.4.2 above.

[294] See Cases C-162/00 *Pokrzeptowicz-Meyer* [2002] ECR I-1049 and C-438/00 *Calpak* [2003] ECR I-4135.

[295] Commission proposals to use these powers (COM (1999) 675–684, 20 Dec 1999) were not agreed. The Commission has withdrawn the proposals ([2006] OJ C 64/3 and COM (2007) 640, 23 Oct 2007).

[296] See [1997] OJ L 327 (Russia); [1998] OJ L 49 (Ukraine); [1998] OJ L 181 (Moldova); [1999] OJ L 196 (Kazahkstan); [1999] OJ L 196 (Kyrgyz Republic); [1999] OJ L 205 (Georgia); [1999] OJ L 229 (Uzbekistan); [1999] OJ L 239 (Armenia); [1999] OJ L 246 (Azerbaijan); and [2009] OJ L 350 (Tajikistan). An agreement with Turkmenistan (COM (97) 693, 6 Feb 1998) has been signed, but not yet ratified, while an agreement with Belarus (COM (95) 44, 22 Feb 1995) was signed but ratification was frozen due to EU concerns about human rights.

[297] Case C-265/03 *Simutkenov* [2005] ECR I-2579, regarding limits on the fielding of foreign football players during professional matches.

[298] Agreements with these States initially entered into force in 1978 ([1978] OJ L 263, 264, and 265). Replacement treaties were agreed between 1995 and 2002. They have all now entered into force (Tunisia: [1998] OJ L 97; Morocco: [2000] OJ L 70; Algeria: [2005] OJ L 265). However, the migration provisions in these treaties are not different in substance to the 1978 rules.

clear that both of these rights are directly effective. However, the right to equal treatment in 'working conditions' does not entail a continuing right to reside in order to work, although it does prevent Member States from terminating legal residence as long as a Maghreb worker is legally employed, except on grounds of public security, public policy, or public health.[299] The extensive case law of the Court of Justice on the right to equal treatment in social security makes clear that 'workers' can claim the benefit of the equal treatment rule even after retirement, disability, or unemployment; that the definition of 'family members' of workers has a wide scope, including even parents and mothers-in-law residing with the worker; that family members can claim benefits independently, even after the worker has ended employment or died; and that the definition of 'social security' is the same as that in the EU free movement rules.[300] Commission proposals for Association Council decisions to implement the social security rules further have been agreed in principle.[301]

As for the EU's agreements with Latin American States the Association Agreement with Chile contains provisions on free trade in services, including rules on the admission of employees of service providers,[302] and on the establishment of companies (although not establishment by self-employed persons).[303] In 2010, the EU concluded negotiations on a free trade agreement with Colombia and Peru which will also liberalize the movement of business persons, if it enters into force.[304] In Asia, the EU has agreed a treaty with Korea, including provisions on trade in services.[305]

Finally, the EU's relations with the African, Caribbean, and Pacific (ACP) States were governed from 1976–2003 by the Lomé Convention, which has now been replaced by the Cotonou Convention. Annexes to the Lomé Conventions (starting with Lomé II) referred to equal treatment in social security and working conditions

---

[299] C-416/96 *El-Yassini* [1999] ECR I-1209. A subsequent judgment appears to suggest that this rule has the same meaning as in EU free movement law (Case C-97/05 *Gattoussi* [2006] ECR I-11917).

[300] Cases: C-18/90 *Kziber* [1991] ECR I-119; C-58/93 *Yousfi* [1994] ECR I-1353; C-103/94 *Krid* [1995] ECR I-719; C-126/95 *Hallouzi-Choho* [1996] ECR I-4807; C-113/97 *Babahenini* [1998] ECR I-183; C-314/96 *Djabali* [1998] ECR I-1149; C-179/98 *Mesbah* (n 229 above); C-33/99 *Fahmi and Cerdeiro-Pinedo Amadao* [2001] ECR I-2415; C-23/02 *Alami* [2003] ECR I-1399; C-336/05 *Echouikh* [2006] ECR I-5223; and C-276/06 *El-Youssfi* [2007] ECR I-2851.

[301] COM (2007) 788, 790, and 792, 11 Dec 2007. See also the parallel proposal as regards Israel: COM (2007) 793, 11 Dec 2007. For the agreement on these proposals, see the press release of the employment Council, 7–8 June 2010.

[302] See Arts 95–115, particularly 95(1)(d) and 101, and Annex VII to the Agreement, and the special rules for financial services in Arts 116–129 and Annex VIII to the Agreement ([2002] OJ L 352/3). The services provisions entered into force on 1 Mar 2005 ([2005] OJ L 84/21). For the context, see the discussion of World Trade Organization commitments in 6.4.6 below. The agreement with Chile goes further establishing free trade in services than the EU's WTO commitments.

[303] See Arts 130–135 and Annex X to the Agreement (ibid).

[304] Arts 122–126 of the treaty, online at: <http://www.bilaterals.org/IMG/doc_100330_full_text.doc>.   [305] Chapter 7 of the agreement (COM (2010) 136, 7 Apr 2010).

for ACP nationals.[306] However, the legal effect of these Annexes was not clear, as the Court of Justice never ruled on their legal effect,[307] although the Court did rule that at least some provisions of the Lomé Conventions could be directly effective.[308] The Cotonou Convention now contains a right to equal treatment in working conditions in the main text of the Convention.[309] By analogy with the case law on the Lomé Convention and the EU's other association agreements, this provision is directly effective and comprises at least the right to be treated equally as regards public-sector employment contracts, rules of private associations on the nationality of persons who can play at any given time for a professional sports team, and rules about elections to chambers of workers.[310] Other types of discrimination as regards working conditions falling within the scope of the ban could also be imagined. However, again by analogy from the case law on other agreements, there are also limits on the right: the equal treatment rule does not entail a continuing right to reside in order to work, although it does prevent Member States from terminating legal residence as long as an ACP worker is legally employed, except on grounds of public security, public policy, or public health.[311] Also the right to equal treatment in working conditions should be distinguished from initial access to the territory and the rules on access to employment,[312] which remain (to the extent that there is no EU legislation on the issue) within the competence of Member States.[313]

The EU plans to agree full Economic Partnership Agreements with ACP states, which would include provisions on services, addressing inter alia the movement of natural persons. So far, the EU has agreed such a treaty with Caribbean States.[314]

6.4.4. Posting of workers

Article 56 TFEU (formerly Article 49 EC) provides that EU citizens established in a Member State have the right to provide services to persons in another Member State.[315] This right affects third-country nationals in two ways. First of all, the Court of Justice has ruled that EU employers have the right under Article 56

---

[306] See Lomé II ([1980] OJ L 347); Lomé III ([1986] OJ L 86); Lomé IV ([1991] OJ L 229); and revision of Lomé IV ([1998] OJ L 156).

[307] But see Case C-206/91 *Poirrez* [1992] ECR I-6685, where the facts fell just outside the scope of both the Convention rules and EU free movement law. On the human rights aspects of the *Poirrez* case, see 6.3.2 above. On the right to non-discrimination in establishment in Lomé I, see Case 65/77 *Razanatsimba* [1977] ECR 2229. This right was removed from later Lomé Conventions.

[308] Case C-469/93 *Chiquita Italia* [1995] ECR I-4533. See further Cases C-280/93 *Germany v Council* [1994] ECR I-4973 and C-369/95 *Somalfruit* [1997] ECR I-6619.

[309] Art 13 of Cotonou Convention ([2000] OJ L 317), in force 1 Apr 2003.

[310] *Pokrzeptowicz-Meyer* and *Calpak* (both n 294 above); *Birklite* (n 240 above).

[311] *El-Yassini* (n 299 above).   [312] *Calpak* (n 294 above).

[313] On the relevant EU legislation, see 6.5 below.

[314] [2008] OJ L 289; see Arts 80–84 of the agreement.

[315] The issue should be distinguished from that of persons posted from *outside* the EU to provide services: see 6.4.6 below.

TFEU to send all of their 'legal and habitual' employees, regardless of those employees' nationality, to another Member State in order to enable the employer to provide services there (for example, by carrying out a construction or demolition contract).[316] The host Member State cannot require work permits for these workers. In subsequent infringement actions brought by the Commission against four Member States, the Court of Justice ruled that a Member State may not insist on a prior authorization of such postings (even if such decisions are subject to judicial review), or a requirement that the employee be hired on an indefinite contract at least six months or a year earlier, or any particular period of work or residence in the host Member State, or the furnishing of a bank guarantee, or the automatic refusal to issue an entry and residence permit if a worker has entered without a visa.[317] The Court has not yet delivered a judgment on whether Article 56 could also preclude other restrictions imposed by the host State on such employees (for example, a long-stay visa or residence permit requirement).[318] However, it is arguable that for the right to provide services to be effective, the workers concerned must be allowed to reside on the territory, and therefore any such documents would be purely declaratory. They must be issued by the Member State concerned and any failure to obtain them by the workers concerned cannot be punished by disproportionate penalties such as exclusion for the territory or imprisonment, which would negate the freedom to provide services.

Secondly, Article 56 TFEU expressly provides that the Council, by means of the ordinary legislative procedure,[319] can extend the freedom to provide services to third-country nationals established in the EU. In 1999, the Commission proposed legislation (based on Articles 57 and 66 EC, later Articles 47 and 55 EC, now Articles 53 and 62 TFEU) to facilitate the exercise of the right of EU service providers to send third-country national employees to other Member States, and (based on Article 49 EC, now Article 56 TFEU) to extend free movement of services to established third-country nationals.[320] The Council did not adopt these proposals, and they were withdrawn in 2004.[321]

---

[316] Case C-43/93 *Van der Elst* [1994] ECR I-3803. See similarly, as regards the nationality of directors of companies exercising the right to establishment, Case C-299/02 *Commission v Netherlands* [2004] ECR I-9761.

[317] Cases C-445/03 *Commission v Luxembourg* [2004] ECR I-10191; C-244/04 *Commission v Germany* [2006] ECR I-885; C-168/04 *Commission v Austria* [2006] ECR I-9041; and C-219/08 *Commission v Belgium* [2009] ECR I-9213.

[318] For further implications of the case law, see 3.4.1, 4.4.1, and 5.4.2 above, and 7.4.1 below.

[319] Before the entry into force of the Treaty of Lisbon, the relevant voting procedure was a QMV in Council on a proposal from the Commission (with no involvement of the EP).

[320] For the text of the proposals, see COM (1999) 3, 26 Feb 1999, amended in 2000 (COM (2000) 271, 8 May 2000). For discussion of the 'legal base' of the proposals, see E Guild and S Peers, 'Out of the Ghetto? The Personal Scope of EU Law', in S Peers and N Rogers, eds, *EU Immigration and Asylum Law: Text and Commentary* (1st edn, Martinus Nijhoff, 2006).

[321] COM (2004) 542, 6 Aug 2004.

However, the EU's general Directive on services permits Member States to impose visa and residence permit requirements on third-country nationals who move to another Member State in the context of service provision,[322] if they are not covered by the Schengen rules on freedom to travel,[323] along with reporting requirements on such persons.[324] It must be noted that as secondary legislation, the Services Directive cannot restrict rights which the employers of posted workers derive directly from Article 56 TFEU, and so the application of any such requirements imposed by Member States on posted workers must respect the underlying Treaty right, as discussed above.[325]

6.4.5. Social policy

Article 153(1)(g) TFEU (previously Article 137(1)(g) EC) expressly provides that the Council can adopt legislation on the 'conditions of employment for third-country nationals legally residing in Union territory'.[326] According to Article 153(2) TFEU (previously Article 137(2) EC), this power can only be exercised following a 'special legislative procedure', namely a unanimous vote in the Council, acting on a proposal from the Commission and after consulting the EP.[327] Although this power has existed since the entry into force of the Maastricht Treaty in November 1993,[328] the Commission has never proposed legislation to implement this power and therefore the Council has never adopted any such legislation. It should also be recalled that the EU Charter of Fundamental Rights states that third-country nationals who are authorized to work on Member States' territories 'are entitled to working conditions equivalent to citizens of the Union';[329] this differs from a mere *power* to adopt *some* rules on this issue (which might not necessarily guarantee equality), as set out in Article 153 TFEU. It is also not clear whether the Treaty powers over 'conditions of employment' are wider than rules relating to 'working conditions', and in particular whether these powers extend to issues of access to employment for third-country nationals.[330] Another issue is whether EU

---

[322] This appears to cover both self-employed persons and posted workers.

[323] See 4.9 above.   [324] Art 17(9), Dir 2006/123 ([2006] OJ L 376/36).

[325] Note that the services Dir does not expressly permit Member States to require visas or residence permits *as a condition of* entry, residence, or service provision.

[326] See previously Joined Cases 281–283, 285, and 287/85 *Germany and others v Commission* [1987] ECR 3203, discussed in 3.2.4 above.

[327] The same provision also permits the Council, acting by the same procedure, to extend QMV and the 'co-decision' procedure to adoption of such measures. No such change in the decision-making procedure has been adopted or proposed.

[328] Initially, this power was contained in the Agreement on Social Policy attached to a Protocol to the EC Treaty. This Agreement did not apply to the UK. However, the Treaty of Amsterdam integrated the Protocol into the EC Treaty (as it then was) and since then these provisions are applicable to all Member States.

[329] Art 15(3) of the Charter ([2007] OJ C 303). See further 6.3.4 above.

[330] For a discussion of the 'legal base' issue, see 6.2.4 above.

social policy legislation in general applies to third-country nationals: in practice, it has apparently been assumed that it does, in the absence of any indication of the contrary, but the issue has not yet been explicitly addressed by case law.

6.4.6. Commercial policy

The World Trade Organization (WTO) agreements, in force since January 1995, contain a General Agreement on Trade in Services (GATS).[331] Under this agreement, the EC (as it was then) and its Member States made commitments to allow temporary entry of intra-company transferees (managers or specialists being transferred within a company); business visitors (persons entering temporarily in order to sell services or to establish a commercial presence for a services company); and contractual service suppliers (companies providing services by sending their employees to perform the service in the host State).[332] The latter is, in effect, the external equivalent of EU companies' free movement right to post such employees within the EU.[333] Member States' legal obligations to accept such employees under the WTO rules are much more limited than under the EU free movement rules, as the obligations are limited to certain services sectors and to a limit of three months within any year. However, the EU, along with a number of other WTO Members, is seeking to widen the scope of the WTO obligations in this area.[334] The EU's GATS offer includes particularly: the addition of graduate trainees to the category of intra-corporate transferees; setting standard rules on admission of intra-corporate transferees (three years, or one year for graduate trainees) and business visitors (three months a year) to the EU; an increase in the services sectors covered and the time limit applicable to admission of contractual service supplies; and the admission of independent self-employed service suppliers in a small number of sectors. Also, it is open to WTO Members to conclude services liberalization or labour market liberalization agreements with each other, subject to certain conditions;[335] the EU's services agreements with various countries are an example of this.[336]

The framework governing international trade in services within the EU legal order has been evolving for a number of years. First of all, before amendments were made to the rules governing the EC's common commercial policy,[337] the

---

[331] [1994] OJ L 336/191.

[332] This form of service provision is known as 'Mode 4' of service supply pursuant to the GATS.   [333] See 6.4.4 above.

[334] On the EU's current commitments and its proposed offer, see the EC's GATS offer of 1 Apr 2005, online at: <http://trade.ec.europa.eu/doclib/docs/2008/september/tradoc_140501.pdf>.

[335] See Arts V and Vbis of GATS.

[336] See 6.4.3 above. In particular, as noted above, these agreements liberalize the posting of workers considerably as compared to the EU's GATS commitments to other WTO members.

[337] See Art 113 EC, before the Treaty of Amsterdam.

Court of Justice ruled in 1994 that competence to conclude GATS initially was shared between the Community (as it then was) and the Member States, inter alia because the EC had not fully harmonized the rules relating to entry of service providers' employees.[338] However, the Court of Justice nevertheless ruled later that it had jurisdiction to give a ruling on any dispute concerning provisions of the GATS, even if that dispute involves issues within Member States' competence, as long as the provision in question could also apply to an issue within the EC's competence.[339] This means that, during this period, the Court likely had jurisdiction to rule on most or all disputes involving admission of service providers' employees pursuant to GATS. But, during this period, WTO rules lacked direct effect in EC law and could not be used to attack the validity of EC acts, except where the EC act aimed to implement WTO obligations or referred to WTO obligations.[340] On the other hand, the Court also ruled that EC legislation (and national law within the scope of EC legislation) had to be interpreted consistently with WTO rules,[341] but if the EC had not yet adopted legislation within the scope of a particular WTO obligation, it was up to Member States to determine what legal effect their WTO obligations had.[342]

Following amendments to the EC's commercial policy powers brought about by the Treaty of Nice,[343] the common commercial policy included all issues related to services (and trade-related intellectual property), as defined in the GATS.[344] Although the EC's power over the 'classic' common commercial policy issues (goods and limited aspects of services and intellectual property) was exclusive, in these new areas, Member States remained free to maintain and conclude agreements as long as they 'compl[ied] with Community law and other relevant international agreements'. Moreover, where a treaty related to 'trade in cultural and audiovisual services, educational services, and social and human health services', it fell within the shared competence of the EC and its Member States and

---

[338] *Opinion 1/94* [1994] ECR I-5273.

[339] See Cases: C-53/96 *Hermes* [1998] ECR I-3603; C-300/98 and 392/98 *Christian Dior and Layher* [2000] ECR I-11307; and C-245/02 *Anheuser-Busch* [2004] ECR I-10989. For the limits of this approach, see Case C-431/05 *Merck* [2007] ECR I-7001. These cases concern the WTO's intellectual property agreement, but there is no reason to doubt their applicability to the GATS. In fact, the Court of Justice has touched on the interpretation of the GATS in one reference for a preliminary ruling: Case C-335/05 *Rizeni Letoveho Provozu UR SP* [2007] ECR I-4307.

[340] Case C-149/96 *Portugal v Council* [1999] ECR I-8395 and *Dior*, ibid. But see the more flexible approach in Case C-377/98 *Netherlands v Council* [2001] ECR I-7079, para 55: the Court can review the validity of an EC act if it arguably requires Member States to breach their WTO obligations, while expressly claiming not to do so. This judgment was subsequently interpreted narrowly in the judgment in Case T-19/01 *Chiquita Italia* [2005] ECR II-315.

[341] See Case T-256/97 *BEUC* [2000] ECR II-101, paras 66 and 67 and Case C-76/00 P *Petrotub* [2003] ECR I-79, para 57.   [342] *Dior* (n 339 above).

[343] Revised Art 133 EC.

[344] For a full analysis of the position, see *Opinion 1/2008*, 30 Nov 2009, not yet reported; see also Case C-13/07 *Commission v Council*, withdrawn (opinion of 26 Mar 2009).

had to be concluded by both of them.[345] Arguably this covered any agreement concerning the posted workers of companies providing services in these fields. In any event, the Council had to act unanimously regarding treaties in these fields where the EC has not yet acted internally or had to act unanimously to adopt internal rules.

The position changed again with the entry into force of the Treaty of Lisbon.[346] The Treaty now provides that the entirety of the area of the common commercial policy, including all aspects of services and intellectual property, is an exclusive competence of the EU, although the EU can delegate some of this competence to Member States.[347] This competence includes not only treaty-making, in the context of the WTO or bilaterally, but also internal legislation, which is now adopted by means of the ordinary legislative procedure.[348] But for treaty-making, the Council is still obliged to act unanimously 'where such agreements include provisions for which unanimity is required for the adoption of internal rules', or 'in the field of trade in cultural and audiovisual services, where these agreements risk prejudicing the Union's cultural and linguistic diversity', or 'in the field of trade in social, education and health services, where these agreements risk seriously disturbing the national organisation of such services and prejudicing the responsibility of Member States to deliver them'.[349] Also, transport services treaties are still subject to the transport Title of the Treaty, which is a shared competence, not an exclusive one.[350] While the first of the general exceptions would not require the use of unanimous voting as regards the movement of service providers—since QMV applies to this area internally—it might be possible to argue that, depending on the extent of the liberalization, the movement of persons in the fields of cultural and audiovisual services, and social, education, and health services, will require unanimous voting. It is also possible that unanimous voting will be required as regards the movement of service providers in the field of transport, depending on the adoption of legislation in that area.[351]

As for the legal effect of the treaties concerned and the Court's jurisdiction over services agreements, it is now arguable that the issue of legal effect of the WTO agreements needs to be revisited after new provisions on the

[345] For interpretation of these provisos, see *ibid*.

[346] On the distinction between commercial policy competence and immigration competence after the Treaty of Lisbon, see 6.2.4 above.

[347] Arts 2(1) and 3(1)(e) TFEU. The EU has not yet delegated any competence to Member States as regards services.   [348] See Art 207 TFEU.

[349] Art 207(4) TFEU.

[350] Art 207(5) TFEU; see Art 4(2)(g) TFEU. Presumably this exception must be interpreted the same way as the previous very similar provision (Art 133(7) EC): see *Opinion 1/2008* and Case C-13/07 (n 344 above). In any case the EP will have the power of consent over such treaties: see Art 218(6)(a)(v) TFEU, read with Art 207(2).

[351] On the exclusive treaty-making competence of the EU derived from the adoption of internal legislation, see Art 3(2) TFEU.

role of international law generally have been inserted into the Treaties by the Treaty of Lisbon.[352] The Court's jurisdiction over treaties regulating service provision is now arguably unlimited in light of the extension of the exclusive competence of the Union; and as a further consequence of exclusive competence there must be a uniform EU-wide rule governing the legal effect of all such treaties within the EU legal order. But it should be noted that the EU could always delegate some or all of this exclusive power back to Member States for a period,[353] much as the Community (as it then was) for many years delegated aspects of its 'classic' commercial policy competence to the Member States, subject to conditions which the Court of Justice had attached to such delegation.[354]

6.5. Primary migration

As noted in the overview,[355] the EU has found it difficult to agree on rules governing the initial admission of migrants to enter and reside on the territory of Member States. In particular, it has found it difficult to agree on the key issue of labour migration, in light of its significant social and economic impact. So the Council was not able to agree on the Commission's 2001 proposal for a Directive on migration for employment and self-employment,[356] and was not interested in a parallel communication on applying an 'open method of coordination' to labour migration policy.[357] Subsequently, as noted above, the Commission attempted to restart discussion on the issue by means of a Green Paper released in early 2005,[358] announcing in September 2005 that it would withdraw the 2001 proposal for a Directive,[359] and issuing a 'policy plan' on legal migration in December 2005.[360] The legislative aspects of the 'policy plan' included two Directives proposed in 2007 (on the admission of highly skilled workers and for a general framework on the status of all persons admitted for employment), which were adopted and agreed by the Council in 2009 and 2010 respectively, and two further Directives (on seasonal workers and intra-corporate transferees) which were proposed in 2010.[361]

---

[352] See Art 3(5), revised TEU ('the strict observance and the development of international law'), along with Art 21(1) and (2)(b), revised TEU.   [353] See Art 2(1) TFEU.

[354] See M Cremona, 'The Completion of the Internal Market and the Incomplete Commercial Policy of the European Community' (1990) 15 ELRev 283 and the further references in S Peers, 'EU Borders and Globalisation' in Groenendijk, Guild, and Minderhoud, eds, *In Search of Europe's Borders* (Kluwer, 2003), 45 at 48, note 29. The Commission has proposed such a delegation as regards foreign investment, but not services: COM (2010) 344, 7 July 2010.   [355] See 6.2.2 above.

[356] COM (2001) 386, 11 July 2001.   [357] COM (2001) 387, 11 July 2001.

[358] COM (2004) 811, 11 Jan 2005.

[359] COM (2005) 462, 27 Sep 2005. For confirmation of withdrawal, see [2006] OJ C 64/3.

[360] COM (2005) 669, 21 Dec 2005.   [361] COM (2010) 378 and 379, 13 July 2010.

In addition to the rules on labour migration, the EU has proved able to agree on legislation concerning the admission of researchers and of students and others seeking admission for non-economic purposes.

The following section examines in turn the agreed general rules governing admission of workers on to the territory and then the specific rules governing specific categories of workers, researchers, and non-economic migrants.

6.5.1. General rules on labour migration

General rules on labour migration are set out in the Directive on a single permit proposed in 2007 and agreed by the Council in 2010.[362] The Directive will have to be applied two years after adoption.[363]

The Directive has the twin goals of regulating procedural aspects of admission for employment and of setting out rules concerning equal treatment of third-country national workers generally, whether those workers were admitted for employment as such or whether they were admitted for another purpose and nevertheless permitted to take up employment.[364] It will not alter the rules regarding the substantive grounds of admission of third-country nationals to national labour markets.[365]

Moreover, the Directive will not apply to: persons with free movement rights as family members of EU citizens or pursuant to association agreements which extend EU free movement rights;[366] workers posted from inside or outside the EU, or who enter pursuant to an agreement on trade-related movements of persons;[367] persons who have applied for or received some form of protection status under national or EU law;[368] persons who have status as a long-term resident of the EU;[369] persons whose expulsion has been suspended for reasons of fact and law;[370] persons who have applied for or been accepted for admission as

---

[362] Council doc 10708/10, 8 June 2010. The text has not yet been agreed with the EP, so might change before adoption. All further references in this subsection are to this agreed text unless otherwise indicated.   [363] Art 16(1).

[364] Arts 1 and 3(1). On the definition of the latter category, see Arts 2(b) and 3(1)(b). On the specific employment rights of various categories of persons within the scope of the Directive, see 6.5.2 (Blue Card holders), 6.5.3 (researchers), 6.5.4 (students), and 6.6 (family reunion) below, as well as 6.4.3 above (association agreements, particularly with Turkey).

[365] Art 1, second sub-paragraph.

[366] Art 3(2)(a) and (b). On these categories of persons, see 6.4.1 and 6.4.3 above.

[367] Art 3(2)(c) and (d). On these categories of persons, see 6.4.4 and 6.4.6 above.

[368] Art 3(2)(f)–(h). On these categories of persons, see 5.5, 5.6, and 5.9 above.

[369] Art 3(2)(i), referring to Dir 2003/109 ([2004] OJ L 16/44), on which, see 6.7 below.

[370] Art 3(2)(j). The Dir on sanctions against employers of irregular migrants (Art 3(3) of Dir 2009/52, [2009] OJ L 168/24) leaves it to Member States to decide whether such persons are permitted to be employed; on this Directive, see 7.6.1 below.

a self-employed person;[371] or persons who work in certain sectors of the labour market (as au pairs, seafarers, or seasonal workers).[372] Also, the rules on the single permit process do not apply to persons admitted on the basis of a visa,[373] and Member States may *opt* to exclude persons who have been authorized to work for less than six months, and who have been admitted for the purpose of study, from the rules on the single permit process.[374] The Directive is without prejudice to more favourable rules in national or EU law, or in treaties concluded by the EU and/or the Member States.[375]

As to the procedure of applying for work in the Member States, applications will have to be made for a single permit (ie a combined work and residence permit) on the basis of a single procedure.[376] The single permit will also have to be issued when pre-existing permits are renewed or modified after the Directive is implemented by Member States.[377] It is up to Member States to decide whether applicants will have to be outside their territory when applying for a permit, and whether the application will have to be made by the employer and/or the worker.[378] The national authority will have to decide on the application for a single permit within four months, but will be allowed to delay its decision past this date if the application is particularly complex.[379] The single permit will have to be issued in the EU's standard residence permit format, and both the single permits and any residence permits issued for other purposes will have to indicate the extent of the person's permitted labour market access.[380] Member States will have to grant procedural rights if the single permit is not issued or renewed, or is withdrawn, including the right to bring a 'legal challenge' against such a decision,[381] but it will be open to Member States to declare an application inadmissible on the grounds that a quota has already been filled.[382] The Directive does not set out substantive grounds for refusing, withdrawing, or not renewing a permit. There are no common rules on the validity of single permits, but there are rules on the information to be made available to applicants and employers and on the fees to be charged.[383] The single permit shall entitle the holder to enter and stay on the territory of the Member State issuing it, to have free access

---

[371] Art 3(2)(k). The EU's GATS commitments do not (yet) extend to self-employed persons, so this category of persons is currently entirely regulated by national law, except for certain association agreements (see 6.4.3 above).   [372] Art 3(2)(e) and (1). On seasonal workers, see 6.5.2 below.

[373] Art 3(4), referring to Arts 4–10.

[374] Art 3(3), referring to Arts 4–10. On persons admitted as students, see Dir 2004/114 ([2004] OJ L 375/12, discussed in 6.5.4 below.

[375] Art 13. On the more favourable rules in the Blue Card Dir (Dir 2009/50, [2009] OJ L 155/17), see discussion in 6.5.2 below.   [376] Art 4.

[377] Art 4(5).   [378] Art 4(1) and (3).   [379] Art 5.

[380] Arts 6 and 7. On the standard format for residence permits, see further 6.9.1 below.

[381] In light of the ECHR judgments relating to work permit applications (see 6.3.3 above) and the case law on the similar provision in the family reunion Directive (see Case C-540/03 *EP v Council* [2006] ECR I-5769), this entails a right of access to court.   [382] Art 8(2).

[383] Arts 9 and 10.

to the territory of that Member State,[384] to exercise the authorized employment activity, and to be informed about his or her rights linked to the single permit and/or national law.[385]

The remaining provisions of the Directive apply both to single permit holders and to persons who were admitted for other purposes, but who were permitted to work (if they are not excluded from the scope of the Directive).[386] These rules concern equal treatment,[387] the power to set more favourable standards,[388] and the obligation to make information on labour migration conditions available to the general public.[389] The equal treatment clause entitles both single permit holders and other persons permitted to work to equal treatment with nationals in seven areas: 'working conditions', which includes pay, dismissal, and health and safety rules in the workplace; 'freedom of association' as regards bodies such as trade unions, 'without prejudice to the national provisions on public policy and public security'; 'education and vocational training'; recognition of diplomas, etc in accordance with national procedures; access to social security as defined by EU free movement rules, subject to the special rules applicable to most third-country nationals;[390] access to goods and services including procedures for obtaining housing; and counselling services offered by national employment offices. There is also a separate provision requiring equal treatment as regards the payment of pensions for workers or their survivors who move to a third country.[391] The equal treatment right is without prejudice to a Member State's right to refuse to renew or withdraw any residence permit or authorization to work.[392] Furthermore, Member States are permitted to set several limitations on equal treatment rights.[393] In particular, Member States may limit equal treatment regarding grants or loans as concerns housing; they also retain a more general power to restrict equal treatment regarding housing. Member States may also restrict equal treatment as regards grants and loans for 'secondary and higher education and vocational training'; more generally Member States may either restrict equal treatment in this area for persons admitted as students, and/or restrict equal treatment in this area (along with equal treatment as regards all goods and serv-

---

[384] On the human rights context of this provision, see 3.3 above.

[385] Art 11. Note that this Art, unlike Arts 4–10, applies to those admitted as students, allowed to work on the basis of a visa, or admitted as students (see Art 3(3) and (4)).

[386] These rules therefore also apply to persons admitted to work before the implementation of the Directive, and who have not yet obtained a single permit because their prior permit has not yet been renewed or modified after the Directive was implemented (see Art 4(5)).   [387] Art 12.

[388] Art 13, referred to above.

[389] Art 14. In fact, the wording of this provision only covers persons admitted for the purpose of work.

[390] On the EU free movement rules applicable to social security and their scope, see 6.4.2 above; on the general social security rules applicable to third-country nationals who move within the EU, see 6.9 below.   [391] Art 12(4).

[392] Art 12(3). It should be recalled that several association agreements limit Member States' right to withdraw residence permits for persons with work permits: see 6.4.3 above.   [393] Art 12(2).

ices) to persons who are in employment only. Access to education and vocational training may also be subject to proof of language proficiency or other 'specific prerequisites', including payment of fees. Social security rights may be restricted to those who are either in employment or whose entitlements derive from prior employment in the Member State concerned. Finally, equal treatment as regards counselling services may be restricted to persons who have the right to work without any restriction.

This Directive, as agreed by the Council, will make a useful contribution towards ensuring equal treatment for migrant workers and streamlining Member States' processes relating to admission. However, it does not go far enough to ensure their fair treatment as regards issues such as access to employment and grounds for the non-renewal of permits. It can only be hoped that further EU measures will address these issues.

6.5.2. Specific categories of workers

6.5.2.1. Highly-skilled workers

Directive 2009/50 was adopted by Council in May 2009,[394] and must be implemented by Member States by 19 June 2011.[395] Although the purpose of the Directive is to regulate 'highly qualified employment' by third-country nationals in the Member States, it is widely known as the 'Blue Card' Directive, because it creates an EU 'Blue Card' to compete with the well-known American 'Green Card' for labour migrants.[396] In order to enhance the attractiveness of the EU for highly qualified workers, the Directive contains derogations from the family reunion Directive and the long-term residents Directive, which are examined separately below.[397]

The core of the Directive is the definition of 'highly qualified employment', since it applies only to admission for such employment.[398] This definition has three parts.[399] Firstly, the person concerned must be 'protected as an employee under national employment law and/or' practice, 'irrespective of the legal relationship, for the purpose of exercising genuine and effective work for, or under the direction of, someone else'. This definition is similar to the definition of 'worker' under EU free movement law.[400] Secondly, this employee must be 'paid' (with no further definition).[401] Thirdly, the person concerned must have 'the

---

[394] [2009] OJ L 155/17. All further references in this subsection are to this Directive unless otherwise indicated.   [395] Art 23(1).

[396] See Art 2(c).

[397] See respectively Arts 15 and 19, examined in 6.6.2 below, and Arts 16 and 17, examined in 6.7.2 below.   [398] Art 3(1).

[399] Art 2(b).   [400] See, for instance, Case 66/85 *Lawrie-Blum* [1986] ECR 2121.

[401] On this point, as regards EU free movement law, see for instance Case C-3/87 *Agegate* [1989] ECR I-4459.

required adequate and specific competence, as proven by higher professional qualifications'. In turn, 'higher professional qualifications' are defined either as 'qualifications attested by evidence of higher education qualifications' or alternatively, 'by way of derogation, when provided for by national law, attested by at least five years of professional experience of a level comparable to higher education qualifications and which is relevant in the profession or sector specified in the work contract or binding job offer'.[402]

Next, the Directive defines a 'higher education qualification' as 'any diploma, certificate or other evidence of formal qualifications issued by a competent authority attesting the successful completion of a post-secondary higher education programme, namely a set of courses provided by an educational establishment recognised as a higher education institution by the State in which it is situated'; the course concerned must last at least three years to be covered by the definition in the Directive.[403] As for the alternative option of attesting higher qualifications by means of 'professional experience', the latter term is defined simply as 'the actual and lawful pursuit of the profession concerned'.[404]

As for its scope,[405] the Directive does not apply to persons who have obtained or who are seeking temporary protection, 'international protection' under EU legislation, or who are 'beneficiaries of protection in accordance with national law, international obligations or practice of the Member State' or who are seeking such status.[406] Also, it does not apply to the family members of EU citizens who have free movement rights, or to the citizens of countries (or the family members of those citizens) which have a free movement agreement with the EU.[407] Furthermore, the Directive does not apply to persons covered by the researchers' Directive, the Directive on long-term residents (if they have moved to another Member State), or the EU Directive on posted workers,[408] who enter pursuant to 'an international agreement facilitating the entry and temporary stay of certain categories of trade and investment-related natural persons' (most obviously the GATS), who have been admitted as seasonal workers, or whose expulsion has been suspended for reasons of fact or law.[409]

The EU and/or the Member States can also exempt certain professions from the Directive by means of international agreement, 'in order to assure ethical recruitment, in sectors suffering from a lack of personnel, by protecting human resources in the developing countries which are signatories to these agreements'.[410]

---

[402] Art 2(g).   [403] Art 2(h).   [404] Art 2(i).

[405] The relevant exclusions are nearly identical to the agreed single permit Dir (Art 3(2)); see further 6.5.1 above.   [406] Art 3(2)(a)–(c).

[407] Art 3(2)(e) and (2), second sub-paragraph.

[408] Art 3(2)(d), (f), and (j). The posted workers Dir is Dir 96/71 ([1997] OJ L 18/1). On the researchers' Dir (Dir 2005/71, [2005] OJ L 289/15), see 6.5.3 below.

[409] Art 3(2)(g), (h), and (i).   [410] Art 3(3). The EU has not concluded any such agreements.

Member States may also reject an application on similar grounds on the basis of their domestic law.[411]

Most significantly, the Directive is without prejudice to the right of Member States to issue permits *other than* in the form of a Blue Card for 'any purpose of employment'.[412] Such national permits will not confer the right of residence in other Member States. It is implicit that such national rules can either set higher standards or lower standards than the Directive, or some combination of *both* higher and lower standards.[413] The Directive does not address the question of the relationship between such purely national rules on admission and the EU rules. For example, if a Member State has a quota on admission of labour migrants, or on certain categories of labour migrants within the scope of the Directive, how will the quota be divided between the national rules and the Blue Card rules? Will employees and employers, whichever is applicable,[414] have a choice as to whether to apply under the national rules or under the Blue Card rules? Logically, they must have a choice,[415] and any national quotas must be open to both Blue Card and applicants applying pursuant to different rules established by national law, otherwise the effectiveness of the Directive would be seriously undermined.

In any event, Member States retain a general power to control the overall volumes of admission of third-country nationals entering the territory for the purpose of highly qualified employment.[416] This explicitly applies regardless of whether the third-country nationals concerned come from outside the EU or within it,[417] and so is broader in scope than the national reserve of competence which was subsequently inserted into the Treaties.[418]

Furthermore, even within the scope of the Directive, Member States retain power to establish 'more favourable provisions' in bilateral or multilateral treaties, as does the EU, either by itself or with the Member States.[419] Member States may also retain or adopt more favourable provisions in their national law, as regards particular issues: the salary criteria for admission, as regards admission to a second Member State; procedural safeguards; the option to grant equal treatment with nationals as regards employment access after two years; changes of employer within the first two years; the consequences of temporary unemployment; equal treatment with nationals; the admission of family members; and the possible

---

[411] Art 8(4) gives Member States an option to refuse applications 'in order to ensure ethical recruitment in sectors suffering from a lack of qualified workers in the countries of origin'.

[412] Art 3(4).   [413] This is an interpretation of Art 3(4) *a contrario* Art 4(2).

[414] See Art 10(1).

[415] This is confirmed (as regards employees) by recital 7 in the preamble to the Directive.

[416] Art 6. An application for a Blue Card may be considered inadmissible on such grounds (Art 8(3)).   [417] Art 18(7).

[418] Art 79(5) TFEU, discussed in 6.2.4 above. On the similarly broad clause in the long-term residents' Directive (Art 14(4) of Dir 2003/109, [2003] OJ L 16/44), see 6.7 below.

[419] Art 4(1).

extension of the period of absence from the EU allowed before long-term resident status will lapse.[420] In either case, there is no requirement that the more favourable rules must be 'compatible' with the rules in the Directive.[421] Also, there are other specific derogations permitted in the Directive.[422]

The next key issue in the Directive is the criteria for admission. Member States decide whether applications can be made by the employer and/or the employee.[423] The mandatory conditions for Blue Card applications are:[424] a 'valid work contract' or, if specified under national law, a 'binding job offer', for 'highly qualified employment' for at least one year; proof that the applicant meets the conditions set out by national law as regards EU citizens' exercise of a 'regulated profession';[425] as regards unregulated professions, proof that the applicant has 'the relevant higher professional qualifications in the occupation or sector'; a valid travel document and possibly a short-term or long-term visa or residence permit (or application for one) as determined by national law; evidence of having, or having applied for, sickness insurance, if such sickness insurance would not be a benefit pursuant to the employment contract; and the absence of a threat to public policy, public security, or public health. Each Member State may also opt to require the applicant to provide his or her address on the territory of the Member State.[426] A further mandatory condition is a requirement to set a salary threshold of *at least* 1.5 times the average gross annual salary in the Member State concerned.[427]

However, the threshold set by the latter mandatory condition may be reduced to 1.2 times the average gross annual salary by way of derogation, for 'professions which are in particular need of third-country national workers and which belong to the major groups 1 and 2 of ISCO'.[428] This derogation refers to managers and professionals.[429] On the other hand, Member States may insist that meeting the salary threshold must also entail ensuring that 'all conditions in the applicable laws, collective agreements or practices in the relevant occupational branches for

---

[420] Art 4(2), referring to: Art 5(3) in conjunction with Art 18; Art 11; Art 12(1), second sentence; Art 12(2); Arts 13–15; and Art 16(4). There is an unlimited power for other EU legislation to set higher standards (Art 4(1)(a)).   [421] See 6.2.4 above.

[422] Arts 2(g), 5(1)(a), (d), and (e) (to an extent), (2), (5), 6, 8(3), (4), (5), 10(3), (4), 14(2), (4), 15(7), 16(5), 18(2), (5), (7), 19(3), and (4). Furthermore, various provisions provide for options for Member States (Arts 5(3), 7(2), 8(2), 9(3), 10(1), and 12(1), (3), and (4)), and Arts 2(b), (g), 3(2)(c), 5(1)(b), (c), and (d), 8(2), 11(1), (3), 12(2), 14(1)(e), (f), and (h), (4), 18(2), (4)(b), (5), and 19(2) refer to 'national law' as regards some issues.   [423] Art 10(1).

[424] Art 5(1).   [425] See the definition of 'regulated profession' in Art 2(j).   [426] Art 5(2).

[427] This is to be calculated in accordance with EU statistical data and national data 'where appropriate': see Art 20(3).   [428] Art 5(5). For the calculation rule, see ibid.

[429] More precisely, group 1 consists of: chief executives, senior officials, and legislators; administrative and commercial managers; production and specialized services managers; and hospitality, retail, and other services managers. Group 2 consists of science and engineering professionals; health professionals; teaching professionals; business and administration professionals; information and communications technology professionals; and legal, social, and cultural professionals. See: <http://www.ilo.org/public/english/bureau/stat/isco/docs/resol08.pdf>, last accessed 25 March 2009.

highly qualified employment are met'.[430] Presumably this means that any applicable legally required minimum salaries for certain jobs could not be circumvented. More generally the rules on admissions criteria are 'without prejudice to the applicable collective agreements or practices in the relevant occupational branches for highly qualified employment.'[431]

If an applicant meets the criteria for obtaining a Blue Card, and the national authorities have taken a positive decision on the application, an EU Blue Card shall be issued.[432] The Directive does not expressly address the question of whether or not the authorities are *obliged* to issue a Blue Card if the conditions are satisfied. The person concerned must be granted 'every facility to obtain the requisite visas'.[433] A Blue Card shall be valid for a 'standard' period, which must be between one and four years; if the work contract is for a shorter period, the Blue Card shall be valid for that period plus four months.[434] The Blue Card shall be issued in the EU's standard residence permit format,[435] and shall entitle the holder to 'enter, re-enter and stay in the territory of the Member State issuing the EU Blue Card',[436] as well as the rights recognized by the Directive.[437]

Next, the Directive sets out grounds for refusal of a Blue Card application. Member States are obliged to reject an application if the criteria for obtaining a Blue Card are not satisfied, or if 'the documents presented have been fraudulently acquired, or falsified or tampered with'.[438] Member States have an option, as regards the initial application or during the first two years of legal employment of the Blue Card holder, to apply national rules giving priority to their own citizens, other EU citizens, legally resident third-country nationals already part of its labour market, or long-term residents moving from another Member State.[439] As noted above, applications can also be rejected because of a quota on labour migration, a ban on hiring to protect against a 'brain drain' from third States, or because the relevant employer has breached the rules on undeclared work or illegal employment.[440] The Directive does not expressly state whether or not these grounds for refusal of a Blue Card, taken together with the criteria for grant of a Blue Card,[441] are the only criteria relating to the grant or refusal of a Blue Card, but given Member States' express powers to apply different rules as regards certain provisions of the Directive, or the Directive in general,[442] it should follow that they are, by *a contrario* reasoning. By reducing the number of options to refuse

---

[430] Art 5(4).   [431] Art 5(6).   [432] Art 7(1), first sub-paragraph.

[433] Art 7(1), second sub-paragraph. On long-stay visas and EU law, see generally 6.9.2 below.

[434] Art 7(2). On residence permits and EU law, see generally 6.9.1 below.

[435] Art 7(3). On this standard format, see further ibid.   [436] Art 7(4)(a).

[437] Art 7(4)(b). Chapter IV of the Directive (Arts 12–17) is entitled 'Rights'.   [438] Art 8(1).

[439] Art 8(2).

[440] Art 8(3)–(5). As regards the latter rule, see the employer sanctions Dir (Dir 2009/52, [2009] OJ L 168/24; see 7.6.1 below); but note that 'undeclared work or illegal employment' has a wider scope than the prohibition on employment of irregular migrants.   [441] Art 5, discussed above.

[442] In particular, in Arts 3(4) and 4(2).

applications and criteria for grant of a Blue Card, this interpretation would also best reflect the Directive's objective of encouraging highly skilled workers to come to the EU.

Member States are obliged to withdraw or to refuse to renew the Blue Card when: the Blue Card 'has been fraudulently acquired, or has been falsified or tampered with'; if the holder did not meet or no longer meets the criteria for a Blue Card or is residing for purposes other than the grounds for authorization to reside; or where the holder has breached the rules on the Directive concerning changing employment or becoming unemployed (discussed further below).[443] A lack of communication concerning unemployment or changes in employer shall not be a reason for withdrawal or non-renewal of the Blue Card, if the Blue Card holder can prove that the Card was not received for reasons other than his or her will.[444] Member States *may* withdraw or refuse to renew the Blue Card: for 'reasons of public policy, public security or public health'; where the Blue Card holder lacks 'sufficient resources' to maintain him or herself or family members without recourse to social assistance; for failure to communicate an address; or because of an application for social assistance.[445] As with the rules on the criteria for applications and refusals of applications, the Directive does not expressly state whether or not these are the only grounds for withdrawal or non-renewal of a permit, but it should follow that they are for the reasons set out above.

The latter issue raises the question as to whether the Directive *implicitly requires* Member States to renew Blue Card permits, by way of necessary corollary from the exhaustive nature of the list of grounds for non-renewal of the permit. While the Directive does not *expressly require* Member States to renew Blue Card permits,[446] neither is such an obligation expressly ruled out.[447] The Directive obviously contemplates that permits should be renewed, given a number of references to their renewal,[448] and the (facilitated) possibility of obtaining long-term residence status necessarily assumes that permits can be renewed.[449] An obligation to renew permits would obviously also facilitate the attainment of the Directive's

---

[443] Art 9(1).   [444] Art 9(2).

[445] Art 9(3). The 'sufficient resources' provision is similar to one of the conditions for admission of family members in the family reunion Directive (Art 7(1)(c) of Dir 2003/86, [2003] OJ L 251/12), and arguably the case law on the interpretation of that provision is relevant by analogy (Case C-578/08 *Chakroun*, judgment of 4 Mar 2010, not yet reported). However, note that the Blue Card Dir, unlike the family reunion Dir, does not require that these resources be 'stable and regular', and that this requirement cannot be imposed during the period of unemployment permitted by Art 13 (on which, see below).   [446] See, for instance, Art 8 of the researchers Dir (n 408 above).

[447] There is certain no obligation to *refuse* to renew permits.

[448] As well as Art 9(1), (2), and (3), see Arts 7(2), 8(2), 11(2), 14(3), and 20(2).

[449] The five-year qualification period for long-term residence status exceeds the four-year maximum validity of a Blue Card. It would also be bizarre for the Directive to provide for the possibility of movement to another Member State even before obtaining long-term residence status, if there was no possibility of renewal of a residence permit in the *first* Member State during the same time period.

objectives, since highly skilled workers would hardly be attracted to the EU if there were no guarantee of renewal of their initial Blue Card. This interpretation also follows from the absence of wording to the contrary, given the large number of derogations that Member States expressly inserted in the Directive. Therefore Blue Card permits *must* be renewed unless one of the express grounds for non-renewal apply; it follows that Member States cannot refuse to renew Blue Card permits (inter alia) on grounds of labour market admission quotas, EU preference, or brain drain.[450]

As regards the application process, the applicant must either be outside the territory of the Member State concerned, or legally resident on that territory as the holder of a long-stay visa or residence permit.[451] However, Member States can derogate either to set a more favourable rule (admitting applications from any applicant who is otherwise legally present),[452] or a less favourable rule (requiring all applicants to be abroad when the application is made).[453]

Procedurally, national authorities must adopt a decision in writing on the application and inform the applicant no more than ninety days after the application is made. The consequences of missing the deadline are laid down in national law.[454] If further documents are needed, the national authorities shall inform the applicant and set a reasonable deadline to receive the further documents; the ninety-day deadline to reply to the application will then be suspended. If the applicant does not send the further documents within the time required, the application may be rejected.[455] A refusal of an application, a refusal to renew a Blue Card, or a withdrawal of a Blue Card must be notified in writing to the holder or applicant and, where relevant, the employer. This decision must be open to legal challenge in accordance with national law, and the notification must 'specify the reasons for the decision, the possible redress procedures available and the time limit for taking action'.[456] As with other EU immigration legislation, the right to a legal challenge should be understood as a right of access to court.[457] All of the rules relating to procedural standards are 'minimum standards' provisions.[458]

---

[450] Art 9 *a contrario* Art 8.

[451] Art 10(2). As a matter of EU immigration law, students, researchers, family members, and (in future) single permit holders would all hold such permits (see 6.5.1, 6.5.3, 6.5.4, and 6.6).

[452] Art 10(3). This would obviously cover the situation where either the applicant holds a valid short-term visa, or where the applicant has legally entered for a short-term stay and is not subject to a visa obligation because his or her country of origin is on the EU visa 'whitelist' (see 4.5 above).

[453] Art 10(4). This option is only valid where this restriction (for all third-country nationals or for certain categories of them) existed already at the time of adoption of the Dir (25 May 2009).

[454] Art 11(1). This compares with a four-month deadline as regards applications for single permits (see 6.5.1 above).   [455] Art 11(2).

[456] Art 11(3).

[457] See the relevant ECHR case law (6.3.3 above), the relevant case law on the general principles of EU law (6.3.4 above) and, by analogy, Case C-540/03 *EP v Council* [2006] ECR I-5769.

[458] Art 4(2)(b).

Chapter IV of the Directive sets out provisions concerning access to employment, unemployment, equal treatment, family reunion, and long-term residents' status.[459] First, for the first two years of their legal employment as a Blue Card holder, Blue Card holders are restricted to employment that meets the criteria of their initial admission.[460] They may not change employers without prior authorization of the national authorities, and any changes 'that affect the conditions for admission shall be subject to prior communication or, if provided for by national law, prior authorisation'.[461]

After the first two years, Member States *may* grant equal treatment with nationals as regards to access to highly qualified employment.[462] If a Member State does not take up this option, the Blue Card holder must communicate any changes affecting the conditions for admission to national authorities.[463] In any event, Member States may retain restrictions on access to employment (presumably after the two-year period), where 'such employment activities entail occasional involvement in the exercise of public authority and the responsibility for safeguarding the general interest of the State', *and* such activities were restricted to nationals in accordance with 'existing' law;[464] or more generally, where in accordance with existing law, any category of employment activities is 'reserved to nationals, Union citizens or EEA citizens'.[465] Finally, the rules on access to employment are without prejudice to the rules in the 2003 and 2005 Accession Treaties as regards the employment of nationals of newer Member States.[466]

Unemployment will not lead instantly to the withdrawal of the Blue Card, unless it lasts longer than three consecutive months or occurs more than once during each period of validity.[467] During this three-month period, the Blue Card holder may search for other work, subject to the general rules on access to employment.[468] The Blue Card holder may remain on the territory while waiting for authorization. Alternatively, where a Member State requires prior communication of change of employment, that communication shall end the period of unemployment of the Blue Card holder.[469] A Blue Card holder must

---

[459] Arts 12–17. As noted above, the latter two issues are examined further below (6.6.2 and 6.7.2).

[460] Art 12(1), first sentence. Member States do *not* have the power to set higher standards on this point (see Art 4(2)(b) *a contrario*).

[461] Art 12(2). In accordance with Art 4(2)(b), this clause is a 'minimum standards' rule. National authorities must reply to applications to change employer within ninety days.

[462] Art 12(1), second sentence. In accordance with Art 4(2)(b), this is a 'minimum standards' rule.

[463] Art 12(2). Again, in accordance with Art 4(2)(b), this is a 'minimum standards' rule.

[464] Art 12(3). It is not clear when such rules had or have to be 'existing'. By *a contrario* comparison with Art 12(4), these two conditions are cumulative, not alternative.

[465] Art 12(4). Again, it is not clear when such rules had or have to be 'existing'.

[466] Art 12(5).

[467] Art 13(1). As noted above, the period of validity of the Blue Card will be between one and four years, depending on the Member State (Art 7(2)).

[468] Art 13(2), referring to Art 12, discussed above.   [469] Art 13(3).

in any event communicate the start of the unemployment period to the national authorities.[470] All of the rules relating to unemployment are 'minimum standards' provisions.[471]

The Blue Card Directive also contains important provisions concerning equal treatment. Blue Card holders are entitled to equal treatment with nationals in eight areas: 'working conditions', which includes pay, dismissal, and health and safety rules in the workplace; 'freedom of association' as regards bodies such as trade unions, 'without prejudice to the national provisions on public policy and public security'; 'education and vocational training'; recognition of diplomas, etc in accordance with national procedures;[472] access to social security in accordance with EU free movement rules, subject to the special rules applicable to most third-country nationals;[473] payment of pensions when moving to a third country; access to goods and services including procedures for obtaining housing; and free access to national territory, 'within the limits provided for by national law'.[474]

Limitations are permitted, however. Member States may limit equal treatment regarding grants or loans as concerns housing and 'secondary and higher education and vocational training'. Access to education and vocational training may also be subject to 'specific prerequisites in accordance with national law', and Member States may restrict equal treatment to cases where the Blue Card holder or family member has his or her 'registered or usual place of residence' on national territory.[475] The right to equal treatment to goods and services is without prejudice to the freedom to contract.[476] Moreover, the right to equal treatment does not prejudice Member States' power to withdraw or refuse to renew a Blue Card under the applicable conditions.[477] There is also a specific rule concerning the limitation of equal treatment after a Blue Card holder moves to another Member State.[478] Compared to the general rules set out in the single permit Directive, the right to equal treatment is the same but the possible derogations are less far-reaching.[479] On the other hand, the rules are less generous than for long-term residents, who (subject to certain exceptions) have a right of equal treatment to employment or self-employment, as well as social assistance and social protection.[480]

---

[470] Art 13(4).   [471] Art 4(2)(b).

[472] The Directive does not expressly address recognition of qualifications in the context of an *application* for a Blue Card.

[473] On the applicable social security rules, see 6.4.2 above and 6.8 below.

[474] On the human rights context of access to the territory, see 3.3 above.

[475] Art 14(2). It is not clear whether the 'specific requisites' can amount to an infringement of the equality rule.   [476] Ibid.

[477] Art 14(3).   [478] Art 14(4), discussed further below.

[479] Art 12 of the agreed single permit Dir; see 6.5.1 above.

[480] Art 11 of Dir 2003/109 ([2004] OJ L 16/44); see 6.7 below.

There are provisions on the possibility of Blue Card holders moving between Member States, even before they have the status of long-term residents.[481] The basic rule is that after 18 months of legal residence in the first Member State as a Blue Card holder, a Blue Card holder can move with his or her family members to take up highly qualified employment in another Member State.[482] To exercise this possibility, the Blue Card holder and/or his or her employer must make an application within one month of moving to the second Member State; that State may decide that the Blue Card holder cannot work until its authorities take a decision on the application.[483] The application could also be submitted to the second Member State while the Blue Card holder still resides in the first Member State.[484] In accordance with the general procedural safeguards, the second Member State shall either accept the application or refuse to issue the Blue Card; in the latter case the first Member State must readmit the applicant and family members, and the rules on temporary unemployment apply.[485] It is not clear whether the second Member State *must* accept the application if the criteria for admission as a Blue Card holder are satisfied, but the Directive does preserve Member States' power to control volumes of admission during this process.[486] If the Blue Card expires during the application process, Member States *may* issue a temporary residence permit or equivalent authorization to stay.[487] There are also provisions on the movement of family members with the Blue Card holder who has not yet obtained long-term residence status, discussed further below.[488]

Finally, the Blue Card Directive requires Member States to report to other Member States and the Commission if they make use of certain options set out in the Directive,[489] and to communicate statistics concerning Blue Card applications and renewals.[490] The Commission must report on the application of the Directive every three years, starting from 19 June 2014, examining particularly the national power to set entirely different rules for skilled workers, the criteria for admission, and the rules on early free movement between Member States; it is particularly encouraged to examine the application of the salary threshold and the derogations granted from it.[491] This reporting obligation is repeated in the action plan for implementing the Stockholm programme.[492]

Since the purpose of the Blue Card Directive, according to its preamble, is to 'attract and retain highly qualified third-country workers' in the context of enhancing the relative competitiveness of the EU economy, it should be assessed in that light.[493] The broader context of the Directive is the evidence that the EU

---

[481] Compare to the provisions of Dir 2003/109, discussed ibid.   [482] Art 18(1).

[483] Art 18(2). If a Member State permits work, then the equal treatment rules are applicable, otherwise most of the equal treatment rules can be disapplied (Art 14(4)).   [484] Art 18(3).

[485] Art 18(4).   [486] Art 18(7).   [487] Art 18(5).   [488] See 6.6.2.

[489] Art 20(1).   [490] Art 20(2); see further 6.11 below.   [491] Art 21.

[492] COM (2010) 171, 20 Apr 2010.

[493] Recital 3 in the preamble. See also recital 7 in the preamble. It should also be noted that the impact assessment prepared by the Commission when it originally proposed the Dir (SEC (2007)

is less likely than other advanced economies to attract highly skilled workers from third countries,[494] coupled with the argument that the immigration regime is a significant factor in attracting such persons, in particular as regards routes to permanent residence.'[495] Furthermore, it was also argued that geographic mobility for such persons needed to be improved within the EU in order to attract highly skilled workers,[496] and that the collective development of an EU policy on this issue would have a sort of collective 'publicity effect'.[497]

To this end, the preferred option set out in the impact assessment, reflected in the original proposal for the Blue Card directive, included: decision-making on applications within thirty/sixty days; a special derogation for the scheme for young workers (ie a lower salary threshold); validity of residence permits for over one year; in-country applications; and internal job mobility after two years.[498] It is remarkable that all of these features of the proposal were either removed in the final text (as regards the young workers' derogation) or watered down by permitting national derogations (as regards the valid period of permits, in-country applications, and job mobility) or less favourable standards (as regards the period for processing applications). Due to the legitimate concern that the Directive might contribute to a 'brain drain' from a developing country, the impact assessment report also referred to the possibility of '*obliging* Member States to pursue ethical recruitment policies by not actively recruiting in countries suffering from recognised situations of brain drain',[499] but neither the proposal nor the final Directive contains an obligation to this effect. There was no examination of the alternative or parallel possibilities of using the existing EU third-country national workforce more intensively, by means of removing the restrictions which still remain on the employment of legal residents, or of facilitating labour migration from Turkey, in light of its negotiations for EU accession.

Taking account of the information and arguments in the impact assessment report, and assuming them to be correct for the sake of argument, to what extent is the Blue Card Directive likely to achieve the aims of attracting more highly skilled third-country national workers to the EU?[500] First of all, the deletion of the special rule (proposed by the Commission) for facilitating younger highly skilled workers will not help achieve its aims, precisely because younger workers

1403, 23 Oct 2007) also justified it by reference to the demographic issue, ie the effect of an expected decline in the EU working age population on the sustainability of economic growth and the welfare state. There is no reference to these demographic justifications as such in the preamble to the final text of the Directive, which contains purely economic explanations.

[494] See pp 14 and 113 of the impact assessment report.

[495] See pp 14–15 of the impact assessment report.

[496] See pp 12–15 of the impact assessment report.

[497] See pp 18, 56, and 69 of the impact assessment report.

[498] See p 55 of the impact assessment report. For the original proposal, see COM (2007) 637, 23 Oct 2007.   [499] See p 65 of the impact assessment report, ibid.

[500] See also the comments on the provisions on family reunion and long-term residents (6.6.2 and 6.7.2 below).

are likely to be earning lower salaries and therefore are less likely to satisfy the salary threshold in the Directive. The salary threshold of 1.5 times average earnings (with a possible derogation to 1.2 earnings for some professions) is reasonable enough, but if many Member States take advantage of the opportunity to set a higher threshold then the Directive will have a very limited impact. It would have been more useful also to set a *maximum* salary threshold which Member States could apply, given that Member States have other possibilities available (EU preference, overall, or sectoral quotas) to protect their workforce if this is deemed desirable.

As for the existence of the power to establish national quotas, this is understandable in political terms and also (as regards workers coming from outside the EU) in legal terms, in light of the wording of the Treaty of Lisbon. Of course if many Member States use this power to prevent admission of Blue Card holders altogether or to admit only very low numbers, the Directive has no chance of achieving its objectives. It should be observed that there is no guarantee that the quotas will be set rationally and objectively, only in light of economic conditions. Given Member States' power to apply an EU preference test for admission under the Directive, a national quota is an overly crude way of managing the effect of immigration upon the employment market, because it might mean that an vacancy for highly skilled employment that an EU employer needs to fill will not be filled, even if no suitable EU citizen applicant for the job can be found. In particular, the continued possible application of national quotas to Blue Card holders who *move between* Member States, even after they obtain long-term residence status, goes beyond the wording of the Treaty of Lisbon,[501] and could obviously prove to be a hindrance to the attractiveness of the Blue Card regime. Furthermore, the possible obligation for Blue Card applicants to leave a Member State where they are legally resident already and apply from outside the territory is truly absurd from the point of view of encouraging applications, given the extra travel and accommodation costs that this will obviously entail.

A further hindrance to the attractiveness of the Blue Card regime which Member States are allowed to retain is the possible restriction on equal access to highly qualified employment after a two-year period, given that the Blue Card holder might well be able to add value to other EU employers. The ambiguity of the Directive on the question of the renewal of permits might also prove problematic, if some Member States (wrongly) take the view that they have the power to refuse all renewals (see the discussion on this issue above). Moreover, it should also be noted that the Directive is silent on the question of access to self-employment or *less* skilled employment by Blue Card holders, before they obtain long-term residence status. The silence on the former issue is also likely to deter Blue Card holders who might be interested in setting up a (job-creating) business

---

[501] See 6.2.4 above.

after a period of employment. Equally, if the EU is concerned to attract highly skilled individuals to the EU, why focus only on employees, and not also establish a parallel EU system for the initial admission of self-employed persons who meet requirements comparable to those set out in the Blue Card directive?

It is possible that the Blue Card regime may prove more attractive to Turkish workers than others, due to the interaction between the rules in the Directive and the rules in the EU–Turkey association agreement. In particular, the obligation to renew the original Blue Card will be stronger as regards Turkish workers,[502] due to the obligation to renew their work permit (and therefore their residence permit) with the same employer after one year's employment; also any restrictions on labour market access which Member States apply pursuant to the Directive cannot apply to Turkish workers (as regards the same occupation) after three years with the same employer, and after four years overall. Presumably if Turkish Blue Card holders move to another Member State, whether before or after gaining long-term residence status, they will obtain a second 'Turkish worker' status under the Ankara Agreement from scratch.

The possibility of moving between Member States even before obtaining long-term residence status should be attractive in principle, but the capacity to apply national employment quotas may prevent this movement altogether and the lack of clarity as to whether an application must be accepted if it meets the relevant criteria is obviously unhelpful. The exclusion of refugees and persons with other forms of international protection from the Blue Card system is hard to justify, given the under-use (as the impact assessment pointed out) of highly skilled resident third-country nationals, and that some of those forced to flee their home countries may have considerable skills to offer employers in various Member States, but are not able to qualify for long-term residence status in order to move between Member States. Also, there can be no 'brain drain' argument as regards people who were forced to flee their countries of origin.

The genuine concerns about a possible 'brain drain' were not, as noted above, properly addressed in the Directive, although as the impact assessment pointed out, at least some developing countries (the Middle East and North Africa), graduates are often unemployed anyway, so they are therefore not leaving vital jobs vacant if they move to the EU. Moreover, the EU's international competitors are already draining brains from poorer countries, and any assessment of this issue has to take into account the huge amounts of remittances sent back to developing

---

[502] See the discussion of Art 9 of the Directive above. The analysis there as to whether there is an obligation to renew Blue Cards is also entirely moot as regards Turkish workers who hold one. On the interaction between the EU–Turkey rules and EU immigration law in general, see Case C-294/06 *Payir and others* [2008] ECR I-203 and the discussion in S Peers, 'EU Migration Law and Association Agreements', in B Martenczuk and S van Thiel, eds, *Justice, Liberty, Security: New Challenges for EU External Relations* (VUBPress, 2008), 53. For more on the substance of the EU–Turkey rules, see 6.4.3 above.

countries by migrant workers.[503] Anyway, the issue will not arise much in practice in the first place, if many Member States exploit the many opportunities granted by the Directive to restrict its impact.

It is not clear if the maintenance of parallel national immigration regimes will hinder or assist the objectives of the Blue Card system. This will be dependent on how many Member States maintain or develop such regimes, whether they are less or more attractive than the Blue Card system, and how they interact with the Blue Card system (which will certainly be problematic if the interpretation of the Directive on this issue advocated above is not followed). More generally, the level of complexity of the interaction between the EU and national regimes and between the different EU rules, along with the high number of derogations allowed to Member States, may itself reduce the attractiveness of the EU to highly skilled migrants. Any 'publicity effect' of the new EU rules on attracting highly skilled migrants could well be undercut by the complexity of the interacting systems.

Having said that, it is possible that the symbolic (and literally emblematic) effect of the new Directive will establish itself in the minds of would-be highly skilled migrants worldwide, in the same way that the American Green Card and the EU's own Schengen visa system have become well known. Certainly, back in 1994 when the EU adopted its highly negative resolution on admission of workers,[504] and after 2001 when the Commission's proposal for a regime on labour migration was 'dead on arrival' in the Council,[505] it was hard to imagine the EU adopting, just a few years later by unanimity, a Directive which explicitly aims to encourage significant levels of labour immigration to the Union. Whether the Directive will nevertheless have the impact of raising the number of highly skilled labour migrants to the EU remains to be seen.

6.5.2.2. Other workers

The 2010 proposals for Directives to regulate the admission of intra-corporate transferees and seasonal workers would, if adopted, mean that a significant proportion of labour migration was harmonized by EU law.[506] However, it remains to be seen if the Council and EP can agree on these measures and, if so, how much of the original proposals will remain intact. First of all, the proposal on intra-corporate transferees would apply where the person concerned has worked for the corporate group for at least 12 months before the application for admission to the EU, subject also to other requirements such as rules on qualifications. Member States may establish simplified procedures for certain companies under specified conditions. The persons concerned would have procedural rights as well as certain equal treatment rights. There would be derogations from the family

---

[503] See generally 7.9.2 below.   [504] [1996] OJ C 274.
[505] COM (2001) 386, 11 July 2001.
[506] COM (2010) 378 and 379, 13 July 2010.

reunion Directive as well as rules on mobility between Member States, in order to facilitate international business.

Secondly, the proposal on seasonal workers would similarly set out standard rules on admission as well as provisions on procedural rights and equal treatment rights. There would be no special provisions on mobility or family reunion, however, Seasonal workers could only be admitted for a maximum period of six months per calendar year.

6.5.3. Researchers

In order to increase the number of research workers in the EU with a view to meeting the 'Lisbon agenda' objective of making the EU the world's most competitive and dynamic knowledge economy by 2010, the Council adopted in 2005 a Recommendation on the issue of short-term visas to third-country national researchers,[507] and subsequently in parallel a Directive and a Recommendation on admission of third-country national researchers.[508] Member States had to apply the Directive by 12 October 2007,[509] and one Member State was condemned by the Court of Justice for failure to meet this deadline.[510] The Commission was due to report on the application of this Directive by November 2008, but has not yet done so.[511] According to the action plan on implementation of the Stockholm programme, the report will be released in 2011.[512]

Directive 2005/71 applies to admission as a researcher for periods of more than three months.[513] It contains definitions of 'researcher', 'research', 'research organisation', and 'residence permit', with a special 'researcher' residence permit to be issued to beneficiaries of the Directive.[514] 'Research' is broadly defined to mean 'creative work undertaken on a systematic basis in order to increase the stock of knowledge'. The definition incorporates the social sciences, not just the physical sciences, as it includes 'knowledge of man, culture and society'; and the definition also includes applied research ('and the use of the stock of knowledge to devise new applications'). A 'research organisation' could include not just a public organization, but also a private organization.

As for the scope, the Directive applies to persons applying for admission to carry out a research project.[515] But the Directive does not apply to: applicants for international protection; persons on a temporary protection scheme; persons applying for admission as students under Directive 2004/114 on the admission

---

[507] [2005] OJ L 289/23. This Recommendation is discussed in 4.7.1 above.

[508] [2005] OJ L 289/15 (Directive); [2005] OJ L 289/26 (Recommendation). All references in this subsection are to Dir 2005/71 unless otherwise noted.   [509] Art 17(1).

[510] Case C-523/08 *Commission v Spain*, judgment of 11 Feb 2010, unreported.

[511] Art 16 (read with Art 20).   [512] COM (2010) 171, 20 Apr 2010.   [513] Art 1.

[514] Art 2.   [515] Art 3(1).

of students and other categories of persons to take up doctoral studies;[516] persons whose expulsion is suspended for reasons of fact or law; or researchers seconded by a research organization to another research organization in a different Member State.[517] The Directive is without prejudice to more favourable provisions in treaties concluded by the Member States, the EU, or both together; and it leaves Member States the power to adopt more favourable provisions of national law, without a requirement that such measures be 'compatible' with the Directive.[518]

The core of the Directive is a special procedure for admitting researchers, which entails a significant delegation of power from national immigration authorities to research institutions as regards the admission of researchers. First of all, there are detailed rules on the process of Member States' approval of the research institutions.[519] Then, the Directive sets out rules concerning the 'hosting agreement' to be agreed between the institution and the researcher.[520] These agreements provide for the institution to host the researcher while the researcher works on a research project for the institution, subject to the issue of a residence permit to the researcher. An agreement can only be signed if: the research project has been accepted by the institution, in light of the purpose and duration of the research and financial resources to fund it, and of the researchers' qualifications, and if the researcher can meet resources and sickness insurance conditions. The institution will then issue a statement to the researcher that it assumes responsibility for his or her health, residence, and return costs. Member States may require the institution to assume responsibility for the researcher's stay and return costs if he or she becomes an irregular resident. Also, the agreement will lapse if the legal relationship between the researcher and the institution is terminated, or if the researcher is not admitted.

As for the immigration process, Member States are obliged to admit researchers following the mandatory conclusion of checks to ensure that the conditions for admission are met.[521] The conditions are fourfold: possession of a valid travel document, as determined by national law; a hosting agreement; a statement of financial responsibility from the host institution; and a lack of threat to public policy, public security, or public health.[522] Member States must issue residence permits for at least one year, unless the period of project is less than one year's duration, and the permit must be renewed if the conditions for its renewal are still met.[523] A provision on family members specifies that their residence permit shall have the same validity as that of the researcher, if the validity of their travel documents allows it; but Member States may shorten such permits' validity in 'duly justified' cases.[524] Moreover, the period of residence of family members shall not be made dependent on a minimum period of residence of the researcher.

---

[516] [2004] OJ L 375/12. On this Directive, see 6.5.4 below.   [517] Art 3(3).   [518] Art 4.
[519] Art 5.   [520] Art 6.   [521] Art 7(3).   [522] Art 7(1).
[523] Art 8. For more on residence permits generally, see 6.9.1 below.
[524] Art 9. There is no definition of 'family members'.

However, there is no explicit right of family reunion, although a recital to the preamble encourages family members' admission. Member States may withdraw or refuse to renew a permit if it was acquired by fraud, if the holder no longer meets the conditions of the permit or is residing for other purposes, or on grounds of public policy or public security.[525]

Chapter III of the Directive concerns researchers' rights. Researchers admitted under the Directive may teach in accordance with national law, although Member States may set a maximum number of teaching hours per year.[526] They have the right to equal treatment as regards recognition of diplomas; certificates and qualifications; working conditions (including pay and dismissal); social security as defined under EU free movement legislation, subject to the limitations allowed by the Regulation extending those rules to third-country nationals; tax benefits; and access to goods and services made available to the public.[527] Finally, a researcher has the right of mobility to other Member States to conduct part of his or her research project there.[528] If the period of mobility is less than three months, the second Member State cannot insist on a new hosting agreement, although the mobility is subject to meeting a sufficient resources test and requirements of, for example public policy, in the second Member State. After three months, the second Member State may insist on the negotiation of a new hosting agreement. Any necessary visas or residence permits must be issued 'in a timely manner' and Member States cannot require the researcher to leave their territory while the application is processed.

The procedural rules in Chapter IV of the Directive comprise first of all an option for Member States to determine whether the researcher or the research organization submits the application. An application must be submitted while the researcher is outside the Member States which he or she wishes to enter, although Member States have an option to consider applications made by persons who are already present.[529] If an application is successful, Member States must grant the person concerned 'every facility' to obtain the necessary visas.[530] Member States must respond to applications 'as soon as possible', but with no deadline set.[531]

---

[525] Art 10.   [526] Art 11.

[527] Art 12. On the social security legislation applicable to third-country nationals, see 6.4.2 above and 6.8 below (and, as regards association agreements, 6.4.3 above). Note also that the subsequent agreed Dir on single permits furthermore confers equal treatment rights on researchers in the context of employment; see recital 17 in the preamble and Art 12 of the agreed text, discussed in 6.5.1 above. To some extent, the researchers' Dir is more favourable to the persons concerned, since it lacks the exceptions to the equal treatment rules found in the single permit Dir; but the latter Dir expressly allows for other EU immigration legislation to set higher standards (Art 13(1)(a), single permit Dir).   [528] Art 13.

[529] Art 14. A clause in the preamble states that holders of residence permits 'should' be able to make an application for researcher status without leaving the territory.

[530] Art 14(4). On long-stay visas generally, see 6.9.2 below.

[531] Art 15(1). Compare with the four-month deadline set in the agreed single permit Dir, discussed in 6.5.1 above, which presumably will apply once that Dir becomes applicable if the would-be researcher would obtain an employment contract.

Persons must be notified of negative decisions and have a right to 'mount a legal challenge before the authorities' of the relevant Member State in the event of a dispute.[532]

In the absence of the Commission's overdue report on the application of this Directive, it is difficult to assess its practical impact. However, the Directive should in principle have made a contribution towards achieving the objective of increasing admission of a category of migrants whose admission would be in the economic interests of the EU, particularly in light of the special procedure for admission, the implied abolition of work permit requirements and quotas, the provisions on family members, the rights to equal treatment, mobility and (arguably) academic employment, the right to renewal of residence permits, and the absence of any economic needs test. Several provisions of the Directive are sufficiently clear, precise, and unconditional to confer directly effective rights,[533] so the Directive inter alia provides a right of entry and residence for researchers once the criteria for admission are met initially, and a right of continued residence if the conditions for admission are still met.

However, in the absence of provisions on speedy responses to applications and the right to submit in-country applications, there will remain a prospect that delays in issuing long-stay visas or residence permits could frustrate the intention of the Directive. Furthermore, the absence of any provision granting a right to family reunion (or any status for family members after entry, such as the right to work) could deter researchers from seeking entry, if the family reunion rules are set at the lowest standard permitted by Directive 2003/86,[534] or if the Member State in question takes the view that the researchers, when they are initially admitted, do not even meet the conditions for application of that Directive at first, given its application only to persons with a 'reasonable prospect' of obtaining permanent residence.[535] In that case, even lower national standards on family reunion, perhaps even entailing a complete ban on entry and admission of family members, could apply, although the researchers' Directive clearly at least precludes banning entry of family members based solely on the time period of the researchers' entry. The miserly attitude of the researchers' Directive to this issue compares with the provisions of the Blue Card Directive, which made a point of waiving a number of restrictions in the family reunion Directive.[536]

The next question to consider is the application of the long-term residents' Directive to researchers. There is no provision in the researchers' Directive on its relationship with Directive 2003/109. However, it can be assumed that in the absence of any explicit derogation in either Directive that researchers will ultimately be able to qualify for long-term residence status, particularly because their residence permits under the researchers' Directive are expressly renewable

---

[532] Art 15.   [533] Arts 7(3), 8, 9(1) (first sentence), 11, 12, 13, and 15.
[534] [2003] OJ L 251/12; see 6.6 below.   [535] Art 3(1), Dir 2003/86 (ibid).
[536] Art 15 of Dir 2009/50 ([2009] OJ L 155/17); see 6.6.2 below.

as long as the conditions for their issue are still met, and therefore should not be considered as 'limited' permits taking them outside the scope of the long-term residents' Directive.[537] Indeed, conversely, it will be possible for long-term residents settled in one Member State to become researchers covered by this Directive in another Member State; this could be appealing where the second Member State is applying restrictions on movement of long-term residents permitted by Directive 2003/109. Eventual long-term resident status for researchers would offer the added attraction of enhanced long-term movement between Member States, expanded equality rights (except as regards social security in the first Member State, where the researchers' Directive is more beneficial), and the ability to switch status. For example, researchers might wish to take up a relevant job in a university or private industry that falls outside the scope of the 'researcher' category defined by this Directive, or to establish a company that makes use of their expertise. Also, as argued below, the acquisition or prospect of long-term resident status would be sufficient to trigger application of the family reunion Directive,[538] and indeed it could be argued that the right to a renewable permit under the researchers' Directive offers researchers a strong argument that they have a 'reasonable prospect' of permanent residence, as required for the family reunion Directive to apply, not long after their initial entry.

Like the Blue Card Directive, Directive 2005/71 could also interact with the Association Agreement with Turkey. Since the latter Directive is 'without prejudice to more favourable provisions' of such agreements,[539] it should follow that the two sets of rules both apply to Turkish workers, with the highest standard of protection applying in the event of overlap, as any Turkish nationals admitted as researchers pursuant to the researchers' Directive will be considered 'workers' under the EU-Turkey agreement if they have an employment relationship as defined by EU free movement law.[540]

As for the clause on family members, it is hard to see when it would be 'duly justified' to limit the duration of residence of family members. In the absence of a reference to national law, the concept should be considered a concept of EU law. The obligation for due justification implies a duty to give objective reasons to the person concerned and since the potential limitation would amount to an exception to a rule in the Directive, it should be interpreted narrowly.

While the Directive appears equivocal about another right for researchers, the right to teach, it is arguable that the reference to national law allows Member States to place reasonable and proportionate limits on the right to teach, but that a complete or nearly complete ban on teaching would violate the Directive. As a purely practical matter, it may not be realistic for research institutions to sign

---

[537] Art 3(2)(e), Dir 2003/109 ([2004] OJ L 16/44). See further 6.7 below.
[538] See 6.6 below.   [539] Art 4(1)(a).
[540] See the relevant case law discussed in 6.4.3 above. In particular the case law concerning students (Case C-294/06 *Payir* [2008] ECR I-203) should apply by analogy.

non–EU citizens to research agreements unless the researchers can take up some
of the teaching load of the institution (if the institution has students); and any
deterrent to signing such agreements will make the objectives of the Directive
harder to achieve.

Finally, as in other EU immigration law measures, the weak procedural standards are objectionable in principle. But given that the Directive appears to create
a right to entry and stay, and in light of the procedural rights inherent in the
general principles of EU law (and now the EU Charter of Rights),[541] Member
States' authorities nevertheless have a duty to give reasons for negative decisions,
and Member States must allow challenges to such decisions in the courts. The
latter part of this interpretation is confirmed, by analogy, by the Court of Justice
ruling in the EP challenge to the family reunion Directive.[542]

6.5.4. Non-economic migrants

In December 2004, the Council adopted Directive 2004/114 on admission of
students, pupils, trainees, and volunteers.[543] Member States had to comply with
the Directive by 12 January 2007.[544] So far, there is no case law of the Court
of Justice concerning the Directive, other than a judgment touching on its
relationship with the EU–Turkey association agreement.[545] The Commission
has not yet released the report on the application of the Directive that was
due in January 2010,[546] but the action plan on implementing the Stockholm
programme refers to a report in 2010 and a proposal to amend the legislation
in 2011.[547]

Chapter I of the Directive sets out general provisions, comprising the purpose
of the Directive, definitions, and scope.[548] The Directive only covers stays of
over three months.[549] As for the scope, Member States are only obliged to apply
the Directive to students; application of the rules in the Directive to the other
three categories of persons remains optional. Member States are free to provide
for more favourable rules in national law or by international treaties; the EU
(alone or with the Member States) is also empowered to adopt more favourable
rules by means of treaties. Employed or self-employed persons; asylum seekers;
persons on temporary protection or subsidiary protection schemes; persons whose
expulsion is suspended; long-term residents within the scope of the long-term
residents' Directive; and third-country nationals who are the family members of

[541] See 6.3.4 above.   [542] Case C-540/03 *EP v Council* [2006] ECR I-5769.
[543] [2004] OJ L 375/12. All references in this subsection are to this Directive, unless otherwise
indicated.   [544] Art 22.
[545] Case C-294/06 *Payir* [2008] ECR I-203; see the discussion below.   [546] Art 21.
[547] COM (2010) 171, 20 Apr 2010.   [548] Arts 1–3.   [549] Art 1(a).

EU citizens who have moved within the EU are all excluded from the scope of the Directive.[550]

Chapter II sets out conditions of entry and residence.[551] A person can only enter if he or she meets the specific conditions set out for various categories of persons set out in the Directive. There are general rules applying to all four categories of migrant: presentation of a travel document; parental authorization if the migrant is a minor; sickness insurance; requirements of public policy, public security, or public health; and proof of fee payment. Next, there are specific conditions and specific limits on residence status for each of the four groups; it is not possible for anyone to obtain an indefinite residence status pursuant to the Directive. Member States must facilitate admission for persons participating in EU education schemes, and permit mobility between Member States for students.

Residence permits may be terminated on grounds of, for example public policy, or fraud, and students are entitled to work, subject to certain limits.[552] There are limited procedural rights regarding time limits for taking decisions and appeals against negative decisions.[553]

Assessing the Directive,[554] its extended scope as compared to the prior Resolution on students is welcome,[555] but it would have been preferable to include all persons not covered by other EU migration legislation. Such an approach would have guaranteed that minimum standards on entry and residence apply to all persons who have been legally authorized to reside by a Member State.

The result is that, in at least those Member States that opt out of this Directive's rules on the three additional categories, the EU has not fundamentally achieved any more harmonization of the rules on admission of 'other' categories than it had following its failed attempts to agree soft law on such admission in 1995.[556] Also, it is disappointing that family members, at least of students, are not included within the scope of the Directive, as the presence of family members could facilitate students' integration into the life of the host State and provide them with financial and emotional support; some of the best students might be deterred from entry if they cannot bring their family members with them.

A fundamental question regarding the Directive is the extent of discretion left to Member States to control the numbers of persons entering pursuant to it, or to set conditions for entry other than those specified within the Directive (on top of

---

[550] Most of these categories of persons are also excluded from other EU immigration legislation: see 6.5.1 above.   [551] Arts 5–11.

[552] Arts 16 and 17. The agreed Dir on single permits furthermore confers equal treatment rights on students in the context of employment; see recital 17 in the preamble and Art 12 of the agreed text, discussed in 6.5.1 above.   [553] Art 18.

[554] For more detailed comments on the Directive, see ch 22 of S Peers and N Rogers, eds, *EU Immigration and Asylum Law: Text and Commentary* (1st edn, Martinus Nijhoff, 2006).

[555] See 6.2.1 above.   [556] On this, see Peers, n 553 above.

the discretion Member States have as to whether to apply the Directive at all to three of the categories of persons within its scope). The most convincing interpretation is that while Member States may in principle impose rules such as an overall limit on persons admitted as students or for other purposes, such rules could be struck down if they infringe the general principles of EU law. Alternatively it could be argued that such rules fall within the 'public policy' exception permitted by the Directive. In any case, an absolute discretion for authorities over admission would not be permissible.

In any case, it is clear from the wording of the Directive that Member States must permit mobility of students if the relevant conditions are met,[557] and must also renew students' residence permits if the conditions set out in the Directive are still met.[558]

A closely connected issue is the question of whether the Directive obliges Member States to permit the entry and residence of persons covered by the Directive in any other cases. It could be argued that there is an implied obligation to ensure the entry and residence of all persons who meet the criteria for admission set out in the Directive (and who also meet any further national criteria for admission, if such criteria are permitted), as a corollary of the rules set out within it; otherwise the Directive would lose much of its *effet utile*.

As for expulsion or refusal to admit on grounds of, for example public policy, it would have been preferable to include limits on the use of such criteria in order to provide for 'fair' treatment of third-country nationals 'comparable' to that of EU citizens, in line with the Tampere conclusions. Nevertheless, in the absence of a reference to national law for interpreting such concepts, it could still be argued that the restrictions for, for example public policy, have an EU-wide meaning, possibly even a meaning identical or comparable to that applicable to EU citizens. In any event, it could be argued that the EU law principle of proportionality would limit a Member State's expulsion. For example, if a Member State refuses to renew a residence permit where the student is not making sufficient progress in studies, the decision could be disproportionate if the student's lack of progress is due to extenuating circumstances, or a change in course; and it should in any event be sufficient to meet this criterion that the student is passing his or her studies, or at least willing to switch to another course if having difficulty with the original course of studies.

The right of employment for students is welcome, but the Directive is very vague on this point. They do not appear to enjoy a right of equal access to employment; but it would breach the principle of proportionality to interpret the Directive to mean that Member States' power to 'take account' of their labour market can justify an absolute ban on any employment or self-employment by students, in light

---

[557] Arts 8 and 12.   [558] Arts 6 and 7; see Art 12(1).

of the various options to restrict students' economic activities that the Directive sets out.[559] An interesting issue here is the link with the EU–Turkey agreement, where the Court of Justice has ruled that since the Directive is without prejudice to higher standards set out in treaties concluded by the EU, 'Directive 2004/114 cannot justify a narrow construction of Article 6(1) of Decision No 1/80 and no interpretation of that provision can be inferred from it'.[560] The Court did not expressly rule on whether Turkish students authorized to work pursuant to the Directive could benefit from the EU–Turkey agreement, but this is unsurprising since the student concerned in this case was outside the temporal and geographic scope of the Directive.[561]

Finally, the weak provisions on procedural rights in the Directive are objectionable, given the basic principles of the rule of law and judicial protection underlying EU law, the basic procedural standards of international human rights law regarding expulsion of lawful migrants, and the effects of expulsion upon the individuals concerned. As with the procedural rules in other immigration Directives, it is arguable that notwithstanding the wording of the Directive, persons who wish to contest decisions taken in the context of this Directive have a right to a sufficiently reasoned and objective decision and the right to contest the merits of that decision in the courts of the Member State concerned.[562] This should also apply to disputes over the access to employment of students and unremunerated trainees, and disputes with private bodies when they are able to take decisions affecting entry and residence under a 'fast-track' procedure or send progress reports on students to the State authorities.

6.6. Family reunion

The issue of family reunion is important for a large number of third-country nationals and EU citizens alike, and is closely linked to the right to family life,[563] but remains controversial as regards third-country national family members, largely due to the broader economic, social, and cultural concerns about immigration into the EU.[564] The legal rules governing this issue in part derive from

---

[559] See the comparable comments on the researchers' Dir (6.5.3 above).

[560] Para 48 of the *Payir* judgment, n 543 above.

[561] See generally the discussion of the interaction between the two sources in S Peers, 'EU Migration Law and Association Agreements', in B Martenczuk and S van Thiel, eds, *Justice, Liberty, Security: New Challenges for EU External Relations* (VUB Press, 2008), 53.

[562] See the comments on the comparable provisions in 6.5.1, 6.5.2, and 6.5.3 above, and 6.6 and 6.7 below, and in particular Case C-540/03 *EP v Council* [2006] ECR I-5769, as regards access to a court.   [563] See 6.3.1 and 6.3.4 above.

[564] See S Peers, 'Family Reunion and Community Law', in N Walker, ed, *Towards an Area of Freedom, Security and Justice* (OUP, 2004), 143.

EU free movement law and association agreements,[565] but are largely set out in the EU's family reunion Directive, adopted in 2003, which governs the admission of family members of third-country nationals residing in the EU.[566] In addition, there are several special regimes in EU law for family reunion with special categories of third-country nationals, which derogate from the family reunion Directive, namely those for refugees and Blue Card holders, including Blue Card holders who move to another Member State before obtaining long-term residence status. These special regimes are discussed separately in this section.[567] The equal treatment rules in the EU legislation on single permits for migrant workers, once adopted, will also apply to family members.[568] Finally, there is also some reference to family reunion in the EU legislation on long-term residence status, researchers, and international protection,[569] but these measures do not derogate from the family reunion Directive as such.

6.6.1. General rules

Directive 2003/86 on family reunion for third-country nationals was adopted by the Council in September 2003.[570] Member States had to comply with the Directive by 3 October 2005,[571] but several Member States failed to implement the Directive on time.[572] As noted several times already, the EP challenged parts of this Directive for breach of the human rights principles of EU law,[573] and the Court of Justice has also ruled on one reference from a national court concerning the Directive.[574] Moreover, the Commission has released a report on national implementation of the Directive (the 'Commission report', discussed below).[575] The Commission furthermore plans to issue a Green Paper on family reunion in

---

[565] For details, see 6.4.1 and 6.4.3 above. Note that only the EEA and the EU–Swiss agreement on free movement of persons fully extend EU free movement rules to third States; other association agreements, such as the EU–Turkey agreement, only touch on aspects of family reunion.

[566] Dir 2003/86, [2003] OJ L 251/12, discussed in 6.6.1 below.

[567] See 6.6.2 below. The proposed special family reunion regime for intra-corporate transferees (see Art 15 of COM (2010) 378, 13 July 2010) is not discussed, because it remains to be seen whether this proposal is agreed.

[568] See the agreed text of the Dir, discussed in 6.5.1 above, particularly point 10 in the preamble.

[569] See respectively 6.7 below, 6.5.3 above, and 5.5 and 5.6 above. On the latter category of rules, see also S Peers, 'EC Law on Family Members of Persons Seeking or Receiving International Protection' in P Shah, ed, *The Challenge of Asylum to Legal Systems* (Cavendish, 2005).

[570] [2003] OJ L 251/12. All references in this section are to this Directive unless otherwise indicated.

[571] Art 20.

[572] The Court of Justice gave one judgment against a Member State for failure to apply this Directive on time: C-57/07 *Commission v Luxembourg* (judgment of 6 Dec 2007, unreported). Three cases were withdrawn following tardy implementation—Cases: C-87/07 *Commission v Malta*; C-91/07 *Commission v Italy*; and C-192/07 *Commission v Germany*.

[573] Case C-540/03 [2006] ECR I-5769. The EP had attacked the validity of Arts 4(1), last sub-paragraph, 4(6), and 8(2). See discussion below.

[574] Case C-578/08 *Chakroun*, judgment of 4 Mar 2010, not yet reported.

[575] COM (2008) 610, 8 Oct 2008.

2010, and the action plan on implementation of the Stockholm programme calls for amendments to the Directive in 2012.[576]

As regards the Directive in general, the Court of Justice has ruled that:[577]

Since authorisation of family reunification is the general rule, the faculty provided for in Article 7(1)(c) of the Directive [ie the condition relating to social assistance] must be interpreted strictly. Furthermore, the margin for manoeuvre which the Member States are recognised as having must not be used by them in a manner which would undermine the objective of the Directive, which is to promote family reunification, and the effectiveness thereof.

While this analysis addresses a specific provision of the Directive, it should follow by analogy that all exceptions and derogations from the general rule of authorization of family reunion should be interpreted strictly, including the rules relating to the scope of the Directive and the definition of family members. In particular, this approach to interpretation must mean that the lists of the exceptions, derogations, and conditions in the Directive which might restrict family reunion must all be regarded as exhaustive.

Chapter I of the Directive concerns its purpose, definitions, and scope.[578] The scope of the Directive is limited to those third-country national sponsors who have 'reasonable prospects of obtaining the right of permanent residence', and who hold a residence permit issued by a Member State and is valid for one year or more.[579] The prospect of obtaining permanent residence must surely be interpreted as referring, where relevant, to potential status under the EU long-term residents' Directive or to the EU's association agreement with Turkey.[580] According to the Commission report, most Member States allow for family reunion with a temporary residence permit, but subject to a minimum period of residence on the territory. In light of the obligation to interpret derogations from the scope of the Directive strictly, this approach is objectionable if sponsors are not given any opportunity to prove that they have in fact a reasonable prospect of becoming a permanent resident even if they do not meet these criteria. Another group of Member States require the sponsor to *have* a permanent residence permit; this is a clear breach of the Directive, unless (and to the extent that) those Member States issue a permanent residence permit upon entry. A third group of Member States simply transpose the Directive literally, which is not problematic as such, although the Commission objects to one Member State (Cyprus) which in principle does not renew residence permits for longer than four years (except for employees of an international company). While this should not be considered a breach of the family reunion Directive, since this

---

[576] See the Commission's 2010 work programme (COM (2010) 135, 31 Mar 2010) and the action plan to implement the Stockholm programme (COM (2010) 171, 20 Apr 2010).

[577] Judgment in *Chakroun* (n 573 above), para 43.   [578] Art 1(3).   [579] Art 3(1).

[580] See 6.7 below and 6.4.3 above.

Directive does not regulate the issue of the renewal of the sponsor's residence permit, it is a breach of the obligations in other EU legislation to renew residence permits for refugees, researchers, and (in future) Blue Card holders.[581] A refusal to renew a residence permit after several years' residence might also amount to a breach of the ECHR in some cases,[582] although (in the absence of EU regulation of this issue) this would fall outside the scope of EU law. For Turkish workers, depending on the circumstances, it would in some cases also amount to a breach of the EU–Turkey association agreement,[583] although in practice of course there are few if any Turkish nationals resident in the southern part of Cyprus.[584]

Sponsors applying for or receiving protection status are excluded from the scope of the Directive, except for recognized refugees.[585] Members of the family of an EU citizen are also excluded, whether that EU citizen has moved within the EU or not.[586] It is open to the EU, with or without the Member States, to sign more favourable bilateral treaties with third countries;[587] three specified multilateral treaties signed by Member States can also set higher standards.[588] Member States can also set higher standards unilaterally in domestic law,[589] and there is no requirement that such standards be 'compatible' with the Directive.[590] However, there is no general 'standstill' requirement applicable to national law falling within the scope of the Directive.

'Family reunification' is defined as 'the entry into and residence in a Member State by family members of a third country national residing lawfully in that Member State in order to preserve the family unit, whether the family relationship arose before or after the resident's entry'.[591] The Court of Justice has ruled that this includes the concept of 'family formation' (ie where the family was only formed after the sponsor was admitted to the territory).[592]

---

[581] See respectively: Art 24(1) of Dir 2004/83 ([2004] OJ L 304/12; see further 5.5 above); Art 8 of Dir 2005/71 ([2005] OJ L 289/15); and Art 9 of Dir 2009/50 ([2009] OJ L 155/17), discussed in 6.5.2 above.   [582] See 6.3.1 above.

[583] See 6.4.3 above.

[584] If EU law is extended to the northern part of Cyprus (see 2.2.5.3 above), the position would obviously be different.

[585] Art 3(2). As noted above, some EU asylum legislation governs the position of family members of persons seeking or receiving international protection (n 568 above). According to the Commission report, nine Member States have decided anyway to apply the Directive to sponsors who have subsidiary protection.

[586] Art 3(3). On the family members of EU citizens who do move, see 6.4.1 above. The family members of EU citizens who do not move will have rights to equal treatment pursuant to Art 12 of the single permit Dir (n 567 above), and can qualify for long-term residence status (see 6.7 below).

[587] Art 3(4)(a).

[588] Art 3(4)(b). Note that it is implicitly not permissible for the Member States to set higher standards via any *other* international treaties, unless the EC (now the EU) concludes those treaties alongside the Member States.   [589] Art 3(5).

[590] On this issue, see 6.2.4 above.   [591] Art 2(d).

[592] Paras 59–62 of the *Chakroun* judgment, n 573 above.

Chapter II of the Directive specifies the family members who must or may be admitted to join a sponsor.[593] The spouse and minor unmarried children must be admitted,[594] subject to certain qualifications regarding adopted children and children whose custody is shared. Member States also have an option, subject to certain conditions, to admit dependent parents of the sponsor or the spouse, adult disabled children of the sponsor or the spouse, or unmarried partners of the sponsor, along with relevant children.[595]

However, there are a number of derogations from these rules. First of all, Member States have an option to retain legislation which existed on the date of implementation of the Directive which imposes a special 'integration require-ment' for children over twelve years old, if they arrive separately from the rest of their family.[596] Arguably Member States which liberalize their law cannot later revert back to the original more restrictive provision.[597] Next, in the event of polygamy, Member States cannot admit additional spouses once one spouse is res-ident within the EU, but have the option to admit (or not admit) the children of the additional spouse(s).[598] It is presumably up to the sponsor to determine which of his wives will have the honour of joining him, although arguably the sponsor has the right to rotate the spouses which do so.[599] Thirdly, Member States can set age limits for the sponsor and the spouse before authorizing admission, '[i]n order to ensure better integration and to prevent forced marriages'; the maximum age limit is twenty-one.[600] Finally, a Member State can optionally require that applications concerning children must be made before the children turn fifteen, if provided for by its existing law on the date of implementation of the Directive; Member States applying this derogation 'shall authorise the entry and residence of such children on grounds other than family reunification'.[601]

According to the Court of Justice, although the ECHR, the Convention on the Rights of the Child, and the EU's Charter of Fundamental Rights 'stress the importance to a child of family life and recommend that States have regard to the child's interests... they do not create for the members of a family an individual right to be allowed to enter the territory of a State and cannot be interpreted as denying States a certain margin of appreciation when they examine applications for family reunification'.[602] With respect, this assessment understates the effect of the line of case law of the European Court of Human Rights beginning with *Sen v the Netherlands*, according to which there are certain circumstances in which a State must admit children;[603] it also makes no references to the other circumstances

---

[593] Art 4.   [594] Art 4(1).   [595] Art 4(2) and (3).   [596] Art 4(1), final sub-paragraph.
[597] See by analogy Case C-101/05 *A* [2007] ECR I-11531.   [598] Art 4(4).
[599] The Directive only prohibits admission of further spouses when the first spouse 'has a spouse *living with him* in the territory of a Member State' (emphasis added). If that spouse *ceases* to live with him, the sponsor could then invoke the right to family reunion with another spouse.   [600] Art 4(5).
[601] Art 4(6).   [602] Para 59 of *EP v Council* judgment, n 572 above.
[603] See further 6.3.1 above.

in which a State should be considered as obliged to admit family members because the 'elsewhere' test is not applicable, for instance because the State of one family member refuses to admit the other family members, or because of reasons connected to international protection. On the other hand, the Court stressed that the Directive '[goes] beyond those provisions', since it 'imposes precise positive obligations, with corresponding clearly defined individual rights, on the Member States, since it requires them, in the cases determined by the Directive, to authorise family reunification of certain members of the sponsor's family, without being left a margin of appreciation'.[604]

As for the exceptions to the rules challenged by the EP, according to the Court of Justice, the optional integration requirement for children over twelve simply 'partially preserv[es] the margin of appreciation of the Member States' in 'strictly defined circumstances'.[605] Indeed, that margin of appreciation 'is no different from that accorded to [Member States] by the European Court of Human Rights, in its case-law relating to that right, for weighing, in each factual situation, the competing interests' and so 'cannot be regarded as running counter to the right to respect for family life'.[606] Moreover, when applying this provision, Member States had to take account of other provisions of the Directive regarding the best interests of the child and setting out factors to take into account when refusing applications for admission;[607] permitting Member States to impose an integration requirement does not as such violate human rights principles.[608] According to the Commission report, only Cyprus and Germany have invoked this derogation, and the Cypriot derogation was adopted after the date of implementation of the Directive. It is therefore invalid.

Similarly, the Court of Justice upheld the other challenged derogation, concerning a requirement to apply for reunion with children before they turn fifteen, on the grounds that this provision 'cannot...be interpreted as prohibiting the Member States from taking account of an application relating to a child over 15 years of age or as authorising them not to do so', and that like the first derogation challenged by the EP, this rule must be applied in conjunction with the Directive's provisions regarding the best interests of the child and setting out factors to take into account when refusing applications for admission.[609] However, the Commission report states that no Member State has invoked this derogation, and since this derogation could only be validly invoked prior to the implementation date, any attempt to invoke it in future would be invalid.

---

[604] Para 60 of *EP v Council* judgment (n 572 above).   [605] Para 61, ibid.

[606] Para 62, ibid.

[607] Paras 63 and 64, ibid, referring to Arts 5(5) and 17, set out below. The Court also links Art 17 to the case law of the European Court of Human Rights on admission of family members, and refers to Strasbourg case law taking account of the child's age and independent entry when considering a possible obligation to admit the child (para 65, ibid).   [608] Paras 66–76, ibid.

[609] Paras 84–90, ibid.

As for the other derogations from the obligation to admit family members, the Commission report states that most Member States set a minimum age for spouses, five of them setting it at the highest possible age of twenty-one. Cyprus also requires that the marriage took place a year before admission; the Commission rightly doubts the validity of this provision, since (as argued above) it follows from the requirement to interpret the exceptions from the Directive strictly that the list of derogations from the obligations to admit family members is exhaustive. Furthermore, the Commission report indicates that seven Member States permit entry of unmarried partners, while over half admit parents of the sponsor and/or the spouse.

Chapter III sets out procedural rules on the submission and consideration of applications.[610] This includes a proviso that applications should normally be submitted when the family member is outside the territory of the Member State in which the sponsor resides, although as a 'derogation', Member States can accept an in-country application 'in appropriate circumstances'.[611] This particular derogation should *not* be interpreted strictly, since it facilitates family reunion, rather than hinders it. So it must follow that it is entirely up to Member States to determine how often they will consider in-country applications. Although this provision of the Directive could, on its face, be interpreted to rule out the possibility of *always* permitting in-country applications, Member States must be regarded as retaining the power to provide for this pursuant to their power to set higher standards as regards family reunion, given that the power to set higher standards is not constrained by a requirement that such standards must be 'compatible' with the Directive. The Commission report is therefore wrong to complain that 'five Member States...impede this provision as they do not even enact the primary rule of family members having to reside outside their territory'. It should be noted that according to the report, all Member States except one (Cyprus) permit some in-country applications, subject to differing rules.

Next, the Directive establishes a time limit of nine months to make a decision on an application, although this deadline can be exceeded in 'exceptional' cases; there is an obligation to issue a written decision on an application, and to give reasons for the rejection of an application.[612] Finally, Chapter III of the Directive also specifies that 'Member States shall have due regard to the best interests of minor children' when examining applications.[613] As noted already, as interpreted by the Court of Justice, this provision is not merely an empty gesture, but is an obligation which pervades the interpretation of all of the derogations and conditions in the Directive which were challenged by the EP; it must follow that the obligation to consider the best interests of the child equally applies to the interpretation of *any* provisions of the Directive.

---

[610] Art 5.   [611] Art 5(3).

[612] Art 5(4). According to the Commission report, all Member States comply with the latter rules.   [613] Art 5(5).

Next, Chapter IV sets out additional conditions which *may* be imposed by Member States before entry of family members is authorized.[614] These concern requirements of 'public policy, public security or public health', as clarified by the preamble; accommodation, sickness insurance, and resources requirements; an integration requirement; and a waiting period. As regards the resources requirement, the Directive states that Member States may require the sponsor to have 'stable and regular resources which are sufficient to maintain himself/herself and the members of his/her family, without recourse to the social assistance system of the Member State concerned'. Also, 'Member States shall evaluate these resources by reference to their nature and regularity and may take into account the level of minimum national wages and pensions as well as the number of family members'.[615]

On this condition, the Court of Justice ruled in its *Chakroun* judgment that 'the concept of "social assistance system of the Member State" is a concept which has its own independent meaning in European Union law and cannot be defined by reference to concepts of national law'. The concept has to be 'understood as referring to social assistance granted by the public authorities, whether at national, regional or local level'.[616] Because the Directive contrasts the concept of 'social assistance' with that of 'stable and regular resources', the former concept 'refers to assistance granted by the public authorities, whether at national, regional or local level, which can be claimed by an individual, in this case the sponsor, who does not have stable and regular resources which are sufficient to maintain himself and the members of his family and who, by reason of that fact, is likely to become a burden on the social assistance system of the host Member State during his period of residence'.[617] Member States are entitled to 'indicate a certain sum as a reference amount', but this does not mean that Member States 'may impose a minimum income level below which all family reunifications will be refused, irrespective of an actual examination of the situation of each applicant'.[618] In this case Dutch law, which applied a reference amount of 120% of the minimum income of a worker aged twenty-three in cases of family formation, breached the Directive because the concept of social assistance could only refer to cases of *ongoing* need for State support, not the level of support 'which enables exceptional or unforeseen needs to be addressed'.[619] Furthermore, there was a breach of the Directive because the income threshold applied in cases of family formation was higher than the threshold applied where the family had already been established prior to the admission of the sponsor.[620] According to the Commission report,

---

[614] Arts 6–8.   [615] Art 7(1)(c).   [616] Para 45 of the judgment, n 573 above.

[617] Para 46, ibid.

[618] Para 48, ibid, referring again to Art 17. Presumably, where relevant, Member States must also consider the best interests of the child when applying this condition (the *Chakroun* case only concerned a spouse).   [619] Para 49, ibid.

[620] Paras 51 and 64, ibid.

all except one Member State (Sweden) applies this condition, and some (rightly) could be criticized, either due to the high increases in the reference amounts due to additional family members or due to de facto discrimination on grounds of age (cf the Dutch rules).

As regards the other conditions, the Commission report indicates that most Member States (all except four) apply an accommodation requirement, and rightly criticized the two Member States which required the sponsor to satisfy the accommodation requirements before entry of the family members. About half of the Member States apply a sickness insurance requirement; the Commission criticism of one Member State which requires applicants to have either sickness insurance *or* sufficient resources is not convincing, since that rule facilitates family reunion by refraining from requiring applicants to satisfy both conditions. As for integration measures, the Commission report refers to three Member States which insist upon an integration requirement before entry, and four others which impose that requirement after entry; the report rightly argues that integration requirements can only be imposed if they are in line with the principle of proportionality (for example, as regards the accessibility of the courses and tests and the applicable fees). The Commission also rightly criticizes some Member States which impose conditions outside the scope of the condition of, for example public policy, or which permit non-renewal or withdrawal of a residence permit on public health grounds after admission, which is a breach of the express provisions of the Directive.[621]

Although the limitation of entry and possible expulsion of family members on grounds of 'public policy, public security and public health' makes no reference to the substantive rules applied to migrant EU citizens and their family members pursuant to EU free movement law,[622] it is nonetheless arguable that equal treatment is required. The argument for this interpretation is that the Council has in a number of cases inserted into the Directive additional grounds for admission of third-country national family members as compared to EU citizens (such as an integration requirement), different wording regarding conditions of entry, and different wording on the *procedures* to dispute an expulsion or a refusal to admit. Logically the failure to insert additional or different wording as regards the *substance* of the exception for, for example public policy, suggests that this exception has the same substantive meaning as it does under EU free movement law.

Next, as regards the waiting period, the Directive specifies that the maximum period possible is two years' lawful stay by the sponsor, subject to a derogation permitting Member States to retain an existing three-year waiting period following submission of the application, if legislation in force on the date of adoption of the Directive took account of that Member State's reception capacity.[623] This provision was the third clause challenged by the EP, and again the Court

---

[621] See Art 6(3).   [622] See 6.4.1 above.   [623] Art 8.

of Justice upheld its validity,[624] ruling that this provision does not prevent family reunion, but merely permits Member States to delay it, in accordance with the 'margin of appreciation' granted to them by the case law of the European Court of Human Rights, in the interests of ensuring better integration by family members. Moreover, Member States could not simply reject an application due to a waiting period, but still had to consider the best interests of the child and all of the other factors referred to in the Directive when imposing such a requirement.[625] In particular, the Directive could not be interpreted as authorizing a quota system.

The Commission report does not give much information on the specific waiting periods applied by Member States, but rightly criticizes four Member States that calculate the two-year waiting period from the date of *application*, given that the literal wording of the Directive (never mind the requirement to interpret the conditions strictly) makes clear that the two-year waiting period (as distinct from the three-year derogation) can be calculated only as regards the period of the sponsor's *lawful stay* on the territory, not from the date of the application.[626] The report also states that only Austria applied the derogation permitting a three-year waiting period, and that in light of the Court's judgment, Austria has now eliminated a quota system that applied to applications for family reunion at this point. The report rightly states that this provision of the Directive 'precludes the introduction of the notion of reception capacity as a condition in national law'.

Specific rules for refugees are set out in Chapter V, and are addressed further below.[627] Chapter VI then deals with the entry and residence of family members, including the status of family members after entry.[628] They must be given the 'facility' to obtain the necessary visas,[629] and a renewable residence permit of at least one year's validity to start with.[630] The Commission report rightly criticizes the Netherlands for double-checking an application again later (when a residence permit is applied for) and for limiting the locations where an entry visa can be applied for.

Next, the Directive gives family members the right of access to education, employment, self-employment, and training on the same footing as the sponsor,[631] although access to employment and self-employment can be restricted for non-nuclear family members,[632] or subjected to a waiting period of up to a year for all

[624] *EP v Council* judgment (n 572 above), paras 97–103.

[625] Again the Court referred to Arts 5(5) and 17.

[626] Note also that the special rules which disapply this provision (Art 12(2) of Dir 2003/86, and Art 15(2) of the Blue Card Dir) refer to '*residence*' of the sponsor (emphasis added).

[627] Arts 9–12; see 6.6.2 below.   [628] Arts 13–15.

[629] Art 13(1). On long-stay visas, see generally 6.9.2 below.

[630] Art 13(2). These take the form of the EU's standard residence permit format: see Art 2(e) and further 6.9.1 below.

[631] Art 14(1). As noted above, a broader right to equal treatment will be conferred pursuant to Art 12 of the single permit Dir (Council doc 10708/10, 8 June 2010). See also recital 10 in the preamble to that Directive.   [632] Art 14(3).

family members, during which the Member State concerned 'may examine the situation of [its] labour market before authorising' the exercise of an activity.[633] According to the Commission report, five Member States impose no restrictions on labour market access, seven apply a labour market test, and three breach the Directive by imposing a blanket ban on employment for one year. Some Member States breach the Directive by requiring family members to have a work permit even if the sponsor does not need one. It should be recalled that the EU–Turkey association agreements with Turkey and the Western Balkans contain rules on employment of family members, which prevail to the extent that they set higher standards or interact with the rules in the Directive.[634] These rights might also interact with other EU legislation which defines, inter alia, the labour market access of the sponsor.[635]

After five years' residence at the latest, the spouse or partner, and a child who has reached majority, must be given an autonomous residence permit.[636] Such permits *may* be granted earlier in the event of 'widowhood, divorce, separation, or death', and *must* be granted earlier in the event of 'particularly difficult circumstances'.[637] They may also be granted to other family members.[638] The conditions concerning the granting and duration of the permit are laid down in national law.[639] Note that if the sponsor's residence comes to an end and the family members do not (yet) have an autonomous right of residence, Member States may withdraw or refuse to renew the family member's residence permit.[640]

According to the Commission report, most Member States do not issue an autonomous permit before five years' residence, although four Member States offer autonomous permits after three years. In one Member State the five year period is counted from the issue of a residence permit, which is a breach of the Directive if the person concerned held a visa beforehand,[641] since the Directive only refers to five years' *residence*. Other Member States breached the Directive by defining the beneficiaries of the autonomous permit too narrowly, or by not making issue of the permit obligatory. Eleven Member States limit the grant of the permit in cases of family breakdown. As for the early grant of a permit,

---

[633] Art 14(2).

[634] Eg, the family members of Turkish workers must be entitled to the same labour market access as the Turkish worker as defined in the EU–Turkey rules as interpreted by the Court of Justice; this is a dynamic concept since the rules permit progressively greater labour market access for the worker (see 6.4.3 above).

[635] For instance, the long-term residents' Dir (see 6.7 below).

[636] Art 15(1), although Member States may limit this obligation 'to the spouse or unmarried partner in cases of breakdown of the family relationship'.   [637] Art 15(2).

[638] Art 15(3).   [639] Art 15(4).

[640] Art 16(3). This provision refers to a 'right of residence' rather than a 'residence permit'; the implication is that a person who is *entitled* to an autonomous residence permit but who does not yet hold one is also protected from removal on this ground.

[641] According to other EU legislation, a long-stay visa can be valid for up to one year before it is replaced by a residence permit: see 6.9.2 below.

sixteen Member States grant the permit early in the event of, for example widowhood; the Commission report does not refer to the provision requiring issue of a permit early in 'particularly difficult circumstances'. Seven Member States either do not lay down the conditions for granting the permit or do so by giving too much leeway to the authorities. On this point, it should be recalled that EU measures which refer to Member States' competence to establish 'conditions' cannot be applied in such a way as to limit the underlying substantive rights which are granted by the provision in question.[642] In particular, the Directive does not regulate how to take account of absences from national territory as regards calculating the five-year period,[643] but the principle of proportionality must mean that short absence periods which occur in the ordinary course of life (ie for annual holidays) must still count toward the five-year period, and that longer periods of absence which are essentially unavoidable (ie due to obligatory military service or the serious illness of a parent in the country of origin) must at least mean that the family members do not have to start accruing the right to an autonomous residence permit from scratch. It should also be kept in mind that family members might be eligible to obtain long-term residence status under EU or national law, and that the family members of Turkish workers benefit from special rules in this regard.[644]

Chapter VII of the Directive concerns penalties and redress.[645] Status may be removed in the event of, inter alia, changed circumstances or fraud.[646] However, there are substantive limits, clearly based on ECHR jurisprudence, regarding both the admission of family members and the termination of their residence, including removal of the sponsor:[647]

Member States shall take due account of the nature and solidity of the person's family relationships and the duration of his residence in the Member State and of the existence of family, cultural and social ties with his/her country of origin where they reject an application, withdraw or refuse to renew a residence permit or decide to order the removal of the sponsor or members of his family.

As noted already, the Court of Justice has ruled that this principle applies as regards the application of the three derogations and conditions challenged by

---

[642] See, for instance, the case law on Art 6 of EU–Turkey Association Council Decision 1/80, referred to in 6.4.3 above.

[643] For comparison, see the rules on the calculation of: the waiting period for permanent residence for EU citizens and their family members (6.4.1 above); the waiting period for long-term residence status (6.7 below); and the various time periods applicable to Turkish workers and their family members (6.4.3 above).　　　　[644] See respectively 6.7 below and 6.4.3 above.

[645] Arts 16–18.

[646] Art 16. The Commission report only examines implementation of Art 16(4), arguing rightly that Member States which systematically suspect all applicants of fraud, etc breach the Directive, which refers only to 'reason to suspect' such activity (emphasis added). As regards change of circumstances, there are again particular rules deriving from the EU–Turkey agreement: see, for instance, Case C-337/07 Altun [2008] ECR I-10323.　　　　[647] Art 17.

the EP, as well as the 'sufficient resources' condition.[648] It must follow that this principle applies to all other derogations and conditions, and furthermore (in accordance with its wording and the ECHR case law) to any removal from the territory. The Commission report has rightly pointed out that those Member States which strictly apply the national rules relating to family reunion are violating this principle.

There is also a parallel procedural right, namely the 'right to mount a legal challenge' for the sponsor and/or the family members if an application for family reunion is rejected, removal is ordered, or a residence permit is withdrawn or not renewed.[649] While there is no explicit requirement that such legal challenges must be brought before the *courts*, such a principle follows from the human rights protection forming part of EU law,[650] and has been implicitly conformed by the Court of Justice, which has ruled, interpreting the relevant provision, that '[i]mplementation of the Directive is subject to review by the national courts'.[651] Also, while the Directive does not specify that there must be a right to bring legal challenges as regards other aspects of the Directive (such as a refusal to permit employment, to issue an autonomous residence permit, or to challenge the refusal of a visa),[652] such a right must also follow from the human rights principles of EU law and the EU Charter of Fundamental Rights. It is also arguable that the general principles and the Charter, along with the principle of effectiveness,[653] guarantee other procedural rights, for example judicial review of the *merits* of decisions and effective time limits to challenge decisions, as well as legal aid.[654]

The first point to consider regarding the Directive is its temporal scope, a point of broader relevance to EU immigration and asylum law.[655] Does the Directive only apply to persons who submitted applications for family reunion after 5 October 2005, or did it also apply to applications pending on that date, and to persons already admitted prior to that date? The latter group might have an interest in relying, for instance, on the Directive's provisions on protection against expulsion or access to employment. The answer, according to the case law of the Court of Justice, is that in the absence of explicit provisions to the contrary, EU legislation applies to the future effects of past situations, including

---

[648] *EP v Council* and *Chakroun*, nn 572 and 573 above.

[649] Art 18. The 'procedure and competence' for such challenges are established by each Member State. As noted already (n 641 above), national competence over procedure cannot be used to empty rights guaranteed by EU law of their substance.   [650] See 6.3.1 and 6.3.4 above.

[651] *EP v Council* (n 572 above), para 106.

[652] According to the Commission report, four Member States do not permit a challenge to the refusal to issue a visa. Since such a refusal entirely prevents family reunion from taking place, this is a particularly blatant breach of procedural rights. See further 6.9.2 below.

[653] The principle of effectiveness as regards the Directive is expressly referred to in the *Chakroun* judgment.

[654] According to the Commission report, five Member States deny or restrict judicial review of the merits of decisions, and seven deny legal aid.   [655] See also 5.5 above.

to proceedings that are already underway when the new rules come into force.[656] This has been explicitly confirmed as regards the calculation of detention conditions in the returns Directive,[657] and so this principle should obviously apply by analogy as regards other provisions of EU immigration and asylum legislation.

Moving on to an assessment of the Directive, its scope is severely restricted as compared to the original proposal, which had included family members of EU citizens, of persons with subsidiary protection, and of any other third-country nationals who had been admitted for more than one year.[658] Moreover, there is no plan to propose amendments to the Directive before 2012. The limitation to sponsors with a prospect of 'permanent residence' is very similar to the threshold in the 1993 Ministers' resolution on family reunion, and violates principles of clear and precise drafting.

As for the scope of family members, the absence of a requirement to admit extended family and unmarried partners has obviously limited the numbers of family members who will be able to enter, discriminating on grounds of culture and sexual orientation against those groups who traditionally live with extended family and those with same-sex partners. The 'knock-on' effect on the long-term residents' Directive (which, as discussed below, permits Member States to prevent movement of third-country nationals' family members other than spouses and children between Member States)[659] will in turn hinder movement of third-country nationals within the EU. The various possible age limits are contradictory, assuming that teenagers are too mature to integrate into the host State but too immature to decide on marriage.

Next, the conditions attached to entry could mean an indefinite delay in receiving a reply to an application and a lengthy wait for entry, with discrimination permitted as regards accommodation, resources, and sickness insurance requirements.[660] The absence of any final absolute date to reply to applications appears incompatible with Article 13 ECHR, which requires effective remedies in respect of all of the rights guaranteed by that Convention. Checks on family members after entry are permitted potentially indefinitely, raising the prospect

---

[656] See in particular: Cases C-122/96 *Saldanha and MTS* [1997] ECR I-5325; C-60/98 *Butterfly Music* [1999] ECR I-3939; C-195/98 *Österreichischer Gewerkschaftsbund* [2000] ECR I-10497; C-464/98 *Stefan* [2001] ECR I-173; C-162/00 *Pokrzeptowicz-Meyer* (n 178 above); C-28/00 *Kauer* [2002] ECR I-1343; C-290/00 *Duchon* [2002] ECR I-3567; C-224/98 *D'Hoop* [2002] ECR I-6191; C-512/99 *Germany v Commission* [2003] ECR I-845; and C-519/03 *Commission v Luxembourg* [2005] ECR I-3067.

[657] Case C-357/09 PPU *Kadzoev*, judgment of 30 Nov 2009, not yet reported. On the substance of this judgment, see 7.7.1 below.

[658] For the original proposal, see COM (1999) 638, 1 Dec 1999; later versions can be found in COM (2000) 624, 10 Oct 2000 and COM (2002) 225, 3 May 2002. For a detailed history of negotiations, see ch 19 of S Peers and N Rogers, eds, *EU Immigration and Asylum Law: Text and Commentary* (1st edn, Martinus Nijhoff, 2006).   [659] See 6.7 below.

[660] On this issue, see particularly R Cholewinski, 'Family Reunification and Conditions Placed on Family Members: Dismantling a Fundamental Human Right' (2002) 4 EJML 271.

that particularly intrusive checks could constitute an unjustified interference in private and family life.

As regards the possible conditions of accommodation, sickness insurance, and stable and sufficient resources, the Directive could be interpreted to mean that failure to satisfy any of these conditions after entry could justify removal.[661] While avoidance of an additional cost to the public could be considered justified on economic grounds under Article 8(2) ECHR, the Strasbourg case law makes clear that removals on purely economic grounds in the absence of criminal activity by the family member are very difficult to justify.[662] If family members' housing is considered inadequate after entry, but *without* a demand for public funds, it is hard to see how expulsion could be justified.[663] The Court's justification of the waiting period requirement on integration grounds is, with respect, unconvincing, given that the Directive contains a separate specific provision on integration.

While the jurisprudence of the Court of Justice on the Directive to date is broadly encouraging, it is clear from the Commission report that a number of Member States are not even correctly applying many of fairly low standards set out in the Directive, and the restrictions on the Court of Justice's jurisdiction until the Treaty of Lisbon entered into force undoubtedly deterred further challenges in this respect. While the Commission report promised to bring infringement proceedings against Member States in 2009, it has not yet done so. The same report concludes (without evidence) that due to the Directive, national standards have been raised as regards access to the labour market by family members, but in practice standards have also been lowered (although the Directive does not *require* this) as regards waiting periods, sponsors' minimum ages, the income requirement, and integration requirements. Although it is of course possible that standards would anyway have fallen, and indeed below the minimum set by the Directive, in at least some respect in some Member States, if the Directive had not been adopted, it will never be possible to know what would have happened if the Directive had not been adopted. But we can be certain that standards would not have dropped as far, and would have risen more in some Member States, if the Directive had established better standards from the outset. The continued failure to revise this inadequate Directive and to enforce it properly in the meantime is a lasting disgrace for a EU purportedly committed to high standards of human rights protection.

6.6.2. Special rules

EU legislation has established two sets of special (favourable) rules regarding family reunion. Firstly, there are some specific rules regarding refugees in the main family reunion Directive, requiring Member States to waive some of

---

[661] Art 16(1)(a).   [662] See 6.3.1 above, in particular the *Ciliz* and *Berrehab* judgments.
[663] See Case 249/86 *Commission v Germany* [1989] ECR 1263.

the restrictive rules in that Directive as regards family reunion with refugees. Secondly, with the objective of encouraging the migration of highly skilled persons, the Blue Card Directive also waives some of the restrictive rules in the family reunion Directive,[664] and moreover includes a second set of rules relating to family members who move with a Blue Card holder who has not yet obtained long-term residence status to another Member State.[665]

Starting with the special rules for refugees, the family reunion Directive defines a 'refugee' by reference to the Geneva Convention on refugee status,[666] not by reference to the EU legislation which defines refugees (known as the 'qualification Directive')[667]—for the obvious reason that the latter Directive was adopted after the former one. In light of the case law of the Court of Justice, which provides that the family reunion Directive should not be interpreted strictly, it is arguable that the definition of 'refugee' in that Directive should incorporate not just refugees as defined in the qualification Directive, but also any other person considered to be a refugee pursuant to national law.[668]

The specific rules relating to refugees are set out in Chapter V of the general family reunion Directive.[669] It should be noted at the outset that Member States can confine the scope of these rules to refugees whose family relationships predated their entry to the territory.[670] These rules are more generous than the main regime in the Directive, in that the possible special limits on children over twelve cannot apply;[671] admission of additional dependent family members may be authorized;[672] there are special rules on admission of the family or guardians of unaccompanied minors who are refugees;[673] the rules on proving a family relationship are more liberal;[674] the integration requirement cannot be

---

[664] Art 15 of Dir 2009/50 ([2009] OJ L 155/17). It will be recalled that this Directive must be implemented by 19 June 2011 (Art 23(1)). For more on this Directive, see 6.5.2 above.

[665] Art 19 of Dir 2009/50 (ibid).

[666] Art 2(b), Dir 2003/86 ([2003] OJ L 251/12); see generally 6.6.1 above.

[667] Dir 2004/83, [2004] OJ L 304/12. This Directive also includes some specific rules on the status of family members of refugees: see 5.5.1 above.

[668] Note that Art 3 of the qualification Dir (ibid) permits Member States to have higher standards, as does the proposal for amendment of that Dir (COM (2009) 551, 21 Oct 2009). Also, the Blue Card Dir (Art 3(2)(b) and (c)) refers to qualification for international protection *either* under the qualification Dir *or* pursuant to national law.

[669] Arts 9–12, Dir 2003/86. According to the Commission report on implementation of the Directive (the 'Commission report': COM (2008) 610, 8 Oct 2008), two Member States (Cyprus and Malta) do not implement these special rules at all.   [670] Art 9(2), Dir 2003/86.

[671] Art 10(1) of Dir 2003/86, disapplying Art 4(1), third sub-paragraph. On the application of this provision in practice, and its interpretation by the Court of Justice, see 6.6.1 above.

[672] Art 10(2), Dir 2003/86.

[673] Art 10(3), Dir 2003/86; 'unaccompanied minor' is defined in Art 2(f). For other rules on unaccompanied minor refugees (or asylum seekers), see 5.5–5.9 above. See now the action plan on unaccompanied minors (COM (2010) 213, 6 May 2010). According to the Commission report, this provision is not implemented in Bulgaria.

[674] Art 11, Dir 2003/86. The Commission report questions whether two Member States comply with this rule.

applied until the persons concerned have entered the country;[675] and the waiting period[676] and accommodation, sickness insurance, and resources requirements are waived.[677] It should be noted that any refugee sponsors admitted pursuant to the qualification Directive will necessarily have a residence permit valid for over one year,[678] although refugee sponsors are not exempt from the requirement to show a prospect of permanent residence.[679] Also, it must be recalled that the family members of Turkish workers who are refugees are entitled to retain that status after a certain point even if the worker's refugee status is questioned.[680] Like other family members admitted pursuant to the family reunion Directive, the family members of refugees, once authorized to work, will have additional rights pursuant to the EU's single permit Directive.[681] Finally, pursuant to the application of the family reunion Directive to persons who were already present before implementation of the Directive,[682] that Directive must also apply where the sponsors concerned obtained refugee status before it was implemented.

Secondly, the main Blue Card regime for family members contains six derogations from the family reunion Directive, which otherwise applies to family reunion with Blue Card holders.[683] First of all, the Blue Card Directive waives the waiting period of up to two or three years before family reunion is authorized, and also the requirement that the Blue Card holder show that he or she has a reasonable prospect of obtaining permanent residence.[684] Although it is likely in practice that Blue Card holders would usually have

---

[675] Art 7(2), second sub-paragraph, Dir 2003/86. According to the Commission report, the Netherlands imposes an integration condition in cases of family formation. However, it should be noted that Art 9(2) permits Member States to disapply all the special rules for refugees in such cases; a Member State is surely therefore permitted to disapply only *some* of these special rules to such cases if it chooses.

[676] Art 12(2), Dir 2003/86, waiving Art 8. On the application of this provision in practice, and its interpretation by the Court of Justice, see 6.6.1 above.

[677] Art 12(1), Dir 2003/86, waiving Art 7. Member States may however apply Art 7 either if 'family reunification is possible in a third country with which the sponsor and/or family member has special links', or where the application for family reunion was not submitted within three months of granting refugee status. According to the Commission report, Poland requires refugees to satisfy the accommodation requirement. This is an obvious breach of the Directive, except as regards those cases where the Directive still permits Member States to apply that requirement.

[678] Art 3(1), 2003/86; Art 24(1) of Dir 2004/83 requires a residence permit for refugees to be valid for at least three years.

[679] There may be a complication here because the EU's long-term residence Dir does not apply to refugees (see 6.7 below), although it is of course still open to Member States to extend national long-term residence regimes to refugees.   [680] Case C-337/07 *Altun* [2008] ECR I-10323.

[681] See Art 12 of that Directive, and the discussion in 6.5.1 above. Although that Directive excludes refugees from its scope, it does not exclude their family members from it. The same is true of family members of persons with subsidiary or temporary protection.   [682] See further 6.6.1 above.

[683] Art 15(1), Dir 2009/50. Pursuant to Art 4(2)(b) of this Directive, these rules are minimum standards rules.

[684] Art 15(2), Dir 2009/50, referring to Arts 3(1) and 8 of Dir 2003/86. It should be recalled that the latter provision was one of the clauses challenged by the EP before the Court of Justice.

found it easy to argue that they had a reasonable prospect of permanent residence, waiving this requirement will likely be useful in at least some cases. It should be noted that the requirement in the family reunion Directive to have a residence permit of at least one year's validity will almost always be met by Blue Card holders.[685]

Next, the integration requirements permitted by the Directive can only be imposed after the family members have been admitted to the territory.[686] Thirdly, permits must be granted at the latest six months after application by a Blue Card holder.[687] Fourthly, family members' residence permits shall be valid for the same period as the Blue Card holder, if those family members' travel documents are valid for long enough.[688] Fifthly, the possible waiting period for family members' access to the labour market is waived.[689] Finally, Member States have the *option* to cumulate the time periods the family member of the Blue Card holder has spent in different Member States, when calculating the time period for the acquisition of an autonomous residence permit for that family member.[690]

The second set of special rules in the Blue Card Directive applies to family members of Blue Card holders who move between Member States pursuant to that Directive even before they obtain long-term resident status.[691] These rules provide that where a family was already constituted in the first Member

---

[685] Art 7(2), Dir 2009/50 requires that the residence permit be valid for a period of between one and four years, except where the work contract is for a shorter duration.

[686] Art 15(3), Dir 2009/50. This applies to both the general possibility of integration measures, provided for in Art 7(2) of Dir 2003/86, as well as the possible particular requirements for older children who arrive separately, as set out in Art 4(1) of the latter Directive. It should again be recalled that the latter provision was one of the clauses challenged by the EP before the Court of Justice.

[687] Art 15(4), Dir 2009/50, referring to the first sub-paragraph of Art 5(4), Dir 2003/86, which sets a normal period of nine months for a decision. It should be noted that the *second* sub-paragraph of Art 5(4) of Dir 2003/86, which exceptionally permits a longer period to decide on a complex application, will still apply to Blue Card holders. However, in practice this provision should not apply to them often, since their applications will not be as complex due to the relevant waivers from the normal rules and the greater ease which Blue Card holders should have meeting the accommodation, resources, and insurance requirements.

[688] Art 15(5), Dir 2009/50, referring to Art 13(2), Dir 2003/86. The latter provision requires that family members' residence permits should be valid for at least one year, whereas the Blue Card must normally be valid for a period between one and four years (Art 7(2), Dir 2009/50).

[689] Art 15(6), Dir 2009/50, referring to Art 14(2), Dir 2003/86. This applies as of 19 Dec 2011. Note that Art 14(1) of Dir 2003/86, requiring that the family member have the same level of access to employment as the sponsor, will continue to apply. On the issue of the sponsors' access to employment before obtaining long-term residents' status, see Art 12 of Dir 2009/50, discussed in 6.5.2 above. Presumably this rule is dynamic, ie the family member will get enhanced labour market access at the same time as the sponsor.

[690] Art 15(7) of Dir 2009/50, referring to Art 15(1), Dir 2003/86. Art 15(8) of Dir 2009/50 provides that in this case, the special rules on calculating the qualification for long-term residence status for the Blue Card holder in Art 16(2) of that Dir (see 6.7.2 below) will apply *mutatis mutandis*.

[691] Art 19, Dir 2009/50. On the underlying rules allowing Blue Card holders to move between Member States, see Art 18 of that Directive, discussed in 6.5.2 above. It should be noted that Art 19 does *not* set minimum standards only (see Art 4(2) of the Directive, *a contrario*).

State, the family members in question shall be authorized to join the Blue Card holder in the second Member State.[692] They (or the Blue Card holder) must apply for residence permits in the second Member State within one month;[693] Member States *must* issue the family members with temporary authorizations if their residence permit from the first Member State has expired or no longer allows them to stay in the second Member State.[694] Member States may require the family members to present evidence of: their prior stay in the first Member State as the family member of a Blue Card holder; travel documents, visas, and residence permits; and sickness insurance in the second Member State.[695] They may also require the Blue Card holder to meet accommodation and minimum income requirements before his or her family members can be admitted[696]— but the latter criterion, in the form of the salary threshold requirement, would have had to be met anyway before the Blue Card holder was admitted into the second Member State.[697] It should be noted that the provisions on accommodation and minimum income are identical to the equivalent provisions in the family reunion Directive, and so should logically therefore be interpreted the same way.[698] Next, the derogations from the family reunion Directive that applied to the admission of family members in the first Member State shall continue to apply in the second Member State.[699] Finally, if the family members were not admitted already into the first Member State, then the specific rules on family reunion in the Blue Card Directive will apply in the second Member State.[700]

The special provisions for refugees should make it easier in practice for refugees to be reunited with family members, although the requirement of a prospect of permanent residence for the sponsors might in practice prove a difficulty, and the possible requirement to make an application within three months of the grant of refugee status in order to benefit from some of the waivers from the general rules could prove a problem for refugees who need a longer period in practice to save up in order to afford, for example the cost of travel, for their family members.

---

[692] Art 19(1).   [693] Art 19(2), first sub-paragraph.

[694] Art 19(2), second sub-paragraph.

[695] Art 19(3). Logically a visa requirement should not apply where the Blue Card holders move between Member States which fully apply the Schengen *acquis* (see 4.9 above).   [696] Art 19(4).

[697] See Art 18(2), referring to the conditions in Art 5. In practice, due to the higher than average salary which must be earned by the Blue Card holder, it should not be difficult to afford the cost of meeting the accommodation and sickness insurance requirements.

[698] Compare Art 19(4), Dir 2009/50, to Art 7(1)(a) and (c) of Dir 2003/86. This would mean that the judgment of 4 Mar 2010 in Case C-578/08 *Chakroun* (not yet reported), concerning the sufficient resources exception, would also apply. As for sickness insurance, Art 19(3)(c) of Dir 2009/50 is slightly different from Art 7(1)(b) of Dir 2003/86 (the latter refers to 'all risks normally covered for' the host State's own nationals, while the former refers to 'all risks' more generally).

[699] Art 19(5).   [700] Art 19(6); see ibid.

As for the special Blue Card rules, the underlying question (as with the Blue Card regime as a whole) is whether these rules will contribute to the objective of the Blue Card Directive—making the EU more attractive for highly skilled workers? On this point, the changes to the family reunion regime of the EU (waiting periods and permanent residence requirements abolished, longer period of validity of residence permits, immediate access to employment by family members, waiver of advance integration requirements, and shorter time limits for decision-making) may prove rather more attractive. In fact, it is even conceivable that the family reunion rules in the Blue Card Directive will induce some persons to apply for Blue Card status purely to take advantage of them, even if the applicant has few reasons to apply for Blue Card status otherwise, in particular in Member States which have a restrictive regime for family reunion for other third-country nationals. The special family reunion regime for Blue Card holders who move between Member States before they obtain long-term residence status will also facilitate that movement, although in practice these rules are likely to have an impact on much fewer people than the general Blue Card rules.

6.7. Long-term residents

The status of long-term resident third-country nationals of the EU, including their right to move between EU Member States, is regulated first of all by Council Directive 2003/109, which sets out the basic rules on this issue.[701] However, as with the issue of family reunion,[702] there are special rules set out in the Blue Card Directive, which are discussed separately below.[703] But unlike the family reunion Directive, there are not (yet) any special rules on refugees (along with persons who have subsidiary protection status), since the proposal to this end has not (yet) been adopted.[704] It should also be noted that EU legislation on researchers and students, as well as the Blue Card Directive and the proposed Directive on intra-corporate transferees, contain separate rules on the movement of third-country nationals and their family members between Member States, even before such persons have attained long-term residence status.[705]

6.7.1. General rules

Following the adoption of Directive 2003/109 in November 2003,[706] Member States had to implement the Directive by 23 January 2006.[707] The Court of Justice

---

[701] [2004] OJ L 16/44.   [702] See 6.6 above.
[703] Arts 16 and 17 of Dir 2009/50, [2009] OJ L 155/17. See 6.7.2 below.
[704] COM (2007) 298, 2 June 2007   [705] See 6.5.2–6.5.4 above.
[706] [2004] OJ L 16/44.   [707] Art 26.

gave three judgments against Member States for failure to apply this Directive on time.[708] Another three infringement cases were withdrawn following delayed implementation of legislation by Member States.[709] So far, there have been no references to the Court of Justice on the interpretation of the Directive.

Chapter I of the Directive sets out its purpose, definitions, and scope.[710] It applies to all lawful residents of a Member State, except for: diplomats;[711] persons who are seeking or who have received refugee status, temporary protection, or subsidiary protection;[712] students;[713] and temporary residents 'such as' au pairs, seasonal workers, cross-border service providers, workers posted by a cross-border service providers, or persons whose 'residence permit has been formally limited'.[714] As noted above, a 2007 proposal to extend the scope of the Directive to persons with refugee or subsidiary protection status has so far not been adopted.[715] The Directive is without prejudice to more favourable provisions of EU or mixed agreements with third States, pre-existing treaties of Member States, and certain Council of Europe migration treaties.[716]

Chapter II sets out rules concerning long-term resident status in one Member State.[717] The basic rule is that third-country nationals are entitled to such status after residing 'legally and continuously for five years in the territory of the Member State concerned' before their application for status.[718] Absences from that Member State of up to six months at a time, totalling no more than ten months during the five-year period, must be taken into account in calculating that period.[719] Member States may permit longer periods of absence for 'specific or exceptional reasons of a temporary nature and in accordance with their national law', but such absences will not count toward the qualifying period (in other words, the clock will be stopped).[720] But Member States may allow the clock to keep ticking if a person is detached for employment purposes.[721] Prior residence as a diplomat or on a temporary permit does not count at all, while prior residence as a student must be discounted 50%.[722]

Long-term resident status may be denied on grounds of insufficient resources or public policy, or public security.[723] The Directive also sets out detailed rules

---

[708] Cases: C-5/07 *Commission v Portugal* (judgment against Portugal, 27 Sep 2007); C-59/07 *Commission v Spain* (judgment against Spain, 15 Nov 2007); and C-34/07 *Commission v Luxembourg* (judgment against Luxembourg, 29 Nov 2007).

[709] Cases: C-30/07 *Commission v Hungary*, C-37/07 *Commission v France*, and C-104/07 *Commission v Italy*.   [710] Arts 1–3.

[711] Art 3(2)(f), referring to specific relevant treaties.

[712] Art 3(2)(b)–(d). On these categories of persons, see 5.5 and 5.6 above.

[713] Art 3(2)(a). On this category, see 6.5.4 above.

[714] Art 3(2)(e). On service providers, see 6.4.4 and 6.4.6 above.   [715] See n 703 above.

[716] Art 3(3). On the first category of treaties, see 6.4.3 above.   [717] Arts 4–13.

[718] Art 4(1). The Blue Card Dir provides for a derogation from this rule: see 6.7.2 below.

[719] Art 4(3), first sub-paragraph. Again, the Blue Card Dir provides for a derogation from this rule: see ibid.   [720] Art 4(3), second sub-paragraph.

[721] Art 4(3), third sub-paragraph.   [722] Art 4(2).   [723] Arts 5–6.

on the procedure for acquisition and withdrawal of long-term residence status.[724] In particular, the status 'shall' be lost due to its fraudulent acquisition, the adoption of an expulsion measure, or following absence from the EU (not just the particular Member State which granted the status) 'for a period of 12 consecutive months', although Member States *may* provide that absences for longer periods *or* for 'specific and exceptional reasons' will not lead to loss of the status.[725] Where status is lost due to departure from the EU or a lengthy stay in another Member State, Member States must establish a procedure to 'facilitate' re-acquisition of the status.[726]

Substantively, long-term residence status entitles its holders to equal treatment with nationals in a number of areas.[727] Long-term residents are also entitled to enhanced, although not absolute, protection against expulsion, which is clearly based on ECHR jurisprudence.[728] Member States may create or maintain national systems that are more favourable than the rules in Chapter II, but acquisition of status under such more favourable rules will not confer the right of residence in other Member States pursuant to Chapter III.[729]

Chapter III concerns the exercise of the right of residence for periods above three months in other Member States,[730] other than as a posted worker or provider of services.[731] Member States can impose labour market tests limiting movement on economic grounds, or an overall quota on the numbers of third-country nationals (if that quota existed at the time of adoption of the Directive), along with special rules restricting movement of seasonal workers or cross-border workers.[732] The right of residence can be exercised if the long-term resident is pursuing an economic activity or a non-economic activity, but the 'second' Member State can insist that the long-term resident has sufficient resources and sickness insurance and comply with integration measures, provided that such measures were not already complied with in the first Member State.[733] Long-term residents can bring with them their 'core' family members as defined by the family reunion Directive,[734] but the second Member State retains the option to decide whether to admit other family members.[735] Again, sickness insurance and sufficient resources tests can apply. Admission of long-term residents and their family members can also be refused not just on grounds of public policy and public security, but also public health.[736]

---

[724] Arts 7–10.

[725] Art 9(1) and (2). The Blue Card Dir provides for a derogation from the rule regarding the period of departure from the EU (Art 9(1)(c)): see 6.7.2 below.   [726] Art 9(4) and (5).

[727] Art 11(1). Compared to the equal treatment rules in other Directives (see Arts 12(1) and 14 of the Blue Card Dir and Art 12 of the single permit Dir, the long-term residence Dir guarantees equal treatment as regards access to employment and self-employment, along with social assistance and social protection, subject however to exceptions (Art 11(2)–(4)).   [728] Art 12.

[729] Art 13.   [730] Arts 14–22.

[731] Art 14(5), first sub-paragraph. On this category of persons, see 6.4.4 above.

[732] Art 14(3), (4), and (5), second sub-paragraph. Compare the two former exceptions to Art 79(5) TFEU, discussed in 6.2.4 above.   [733] Art 15.

[734] See 6.6 above.   [735] Art 16.   [736] Arts 17–18.

The potential 'second' Member State must process the application within four months, with a potential three-month extension. If the various conditions are met, the second Member State must issue the long-term resident and his or her family members with a renewable residence permit.[737] Reasons must be given if the application is rejected, and there is a 'right to mount a legal challenge' where an application is rejected or a permit is withdrawn or not renewed.[738] Once they have received their residence permit, long-term residents have the right to equal treatment in the second Member State,[739] 'with the exception of social assistance and study grants', and subject to a possible one-year delay in full labour market access.[740] Family members have the same status as family members under the family reunion Directive as regards access to employment and education, once they have received their long-term residence permit.[741]

Before the long-term resident gains long-term resident status in the second Member State, that Member State can remove or withdraw his or her residence permit and expel the long-term resident and family in accordance with national procedures on grounds of public policy or public security, where the conditions for admission are no longer met and where the third-country national 'is not lawfully residing' there.[742] The first Member State must readmit such persons, although if there are 'serious grounds of public policy or public security', the person concerned can be expelled outside the EU. Once the conditions for obtaining long-term resident status are satisfied in the second Member State, the long-term resident can apply for long-term resident status there, subject to the same procedural rules that apply to initial applications for long-term resident status.[743]

Finally, Chapter IV sets out final provisions,[744] including a 'rendez-vous' clause, which requires the Commission to propose amendments in future 'if necessary' (at the latest by January 2011) by way of priority to the Articles concerning the calculation periods for status, the conditions of resources and sickness insurance, withdrawal, or loss of status, and movement to additional Member States. The action plan on the implementation of the Stockholm programme includes a commitment to present this report.[745]

Despite its limitations, this Directive is an accomplishment simply because it facilitates the security of residence, equal treatment, and free movement of third-country nationals more than EU law previously provided for.[746] Given that the equal treatment principle as set out in the Tampere conclusions is expressly part of the preamble to this Directive, along with the objectives of ensuring integration of third-country nationals and facilitating their mobility to other

---

[737] Art 19.   [738] Art 20.   [739] As defined in Art 11.   [740] Art 21.

[741] The family members will also be entitled to equal treatment under Art 12 of the single permit Dir: see 6.5.1 above.   [742] Art 22.

[743] Art 23.   [744] Arts 24–28.   [745] COM (2010) 171, 20 Apr 2010.

[746] For more detailed comments, see and S Peers and N Rogers, eds, *EU Immigration and Asylum Law: Text and Commentary* (1st edn, Martinus Nijhoff, 2006), ch 20.

Member States, it is arguable that any ambiguity in this Directive should be resolved in favour of the long-term resident and family members. As a corollary, any exceptions to their rights should be interpreted narrowly. Having said that, the limitations in scope of this Directive and the conditions placed upon acquisition of long-term residence status and the right to move to another Member State clearly reduce its value as a contribution to ensuring equality between long-term resident third-country nationals and EU citizens, as called for in the Tampere conclusions.

The largest and most disappointing (continuing) omission from the scope of the Directive is refugees and the exclusion of persons with subsidiary protection. In the absence of adoption of the later proposal to remedy this omission,[747] the EU's commitment to ensuring a secure residence status for refugees and persons with subsidiary protection appears disturbingly weak. However, it is arguable that if a third-country national's refugee status ceases after more than five years' legal residence, he or she will be covered by this Directive anyway. Moreover, a refugee resident for a long period in a Member State will also have some protection against expulsion conferred by Article 8 ECHR if refugee status ceases.[748]

Despite the limitations of the Directive's scope, it clearly applies to all legally residing third-country nationals who are not expressly excluded, including those whose status has been regularized, family members of third-country nationals, and third-country national family members of EU citizens, whether those persons have moved within the EU with their sponsors (and are therefore covered by EU free movement law) or not. As for the exception for persons who have only a limited residence permit, the best interpretation of this exception is that it can only apply to persons whose residence permit cannot in principle be extended under the relevant applicable rules for more than a certain period. Also, in the absence of wording to the contrary the Directive should apply to persons who were already resident in the Member States at the time of its adoption (as well as those who enter later) and any persons who already meet the criteria for long-term residence as of January 2006 (or who satisfy the criteria during the following five years) should be able to claim status from January 2006 or during the following five years, rather than wait until five years have passed from the deadline date for application of the Directive.[749]

As for procedural guarantees, it is again regrettable that the Council did not follow the standards in EU free movement law, but it is again arguable that given Strasbourg jurisprudence, the general principles of EU law, and the EU Charter of Fundamental Rights, the right to 'mount a legal challenge' must inter alia

---

[747] See n 703 above.   [748] See 6.3.1 above.

[749] On the temporal scope of EU immigration and asylum law, see 5.5 above and Case C–357/09 PPU *Kadzoev*, 30 Nov 2009. See also, by analogy, the opinion of 11 May 2010 in the pending *Lassal* case (C–162/09).

include the right to argue the merits of any issue falling within the scope of the Directive before a court or tribunal.[750]

Although the provisions on equal treatment for long-term residents can be criticized, it should be noted that there is no possibility to restrict equality to 'core benefits' as regards 'social security', and it is arguable that the various references to 'national law' and 'national procedures' in the Directive should not be interpreted to permit restriction of equal treatment, except where the Directive expressly permits a restriction of substantive equality. Even in that case, the restrictions under national law could be challenged in light of the equality principles of human rights law, the general principles of EU law, and the EU Charter of Fundamental Rights.[751]

Also, while the protection against expulsion under the Directive is not expressly equal to that conferred by EU free movement law, it is still arguable that many substantive and procedural rules of free movement law could be applicable to this Directive.

As for movement to a second Member State, since there are many express possibilities for Member States to limit movement of long-term residents, it should follow that unless one of these express exceptions applies, long-term residents enjoy equal treatment as regards the initial take-up of employment, self-employment, or non-economic activities in the second Member State. Also, it appears that the Directive can be used where a long-term resident wishes to move between Member States to join a sponsoring family member in another Member State. This means that such persons will only have to satisfy the criteria for obtaining long-term residents' status, and may therefore avoid the limitations and conditions set out in the family reunion Directive or EU free movement law. For example, an American national with long-term resident status in France could rely on that status to move to Austria to join his unmarried partner (of either sex).

6.7.2. Special rules

As noted above, the only set of special rules adopted to date regarding long-term residents appears in the Blue Card Directive, applicable from 19 June 2011.[752] These special rules provide that the long-term residents' Directive will apply to Blue Card holders, with three derogations provided for in the Blue Card Directive.[753] All of the special rules will presumably apply to persons who have already spent some period of legal residence in a Member State (taking account

---

[750] See again the judgment on the analogous provision in the family reunion Dir (Case C-540/03 *EP v Council* [2006] ECR I-5769) and 6.3.1 and 6.3.4 above.   [751] See 6.3.2 and 6.3.4 above.
[752] Arts 16 and 17 of Dir 2009/50, [2009] OJ L 155/17; on the implementation date, see Art 23(1) of that Directive. All references in this subsection are to the Blue Card Dir unless otherwise indicated.
[753] Art 16(1).

of the calculation rules in the long-term residents' Directive) before they obtain a Blue Card.[754]

First of all, in order to obtain long-term residence status in the first place, Blue Card holders will not need to show five years' continuous residence in the *single* Member State where they make their application for a long-term residence permit, but can cumulate residence in *different* Member States, as long as they have *two* years' residence in that Member State just prior to their application for long-term residence status there, and have five years' 'legal and continuous' residence *within the EU* as a Blue Card holder, having made use of the possibility in the Blue Card Directive of moving between Member States even before obtaining Blue Card status.[755]

Secondly, when calculating the five-year residence period for Blue Card holders, Member States must moreover include absences from *EU* territory of up to *twelve* months, adding up to *eighteen* months' absence in total.[756] This rule applies regardless of whether the Blue Card holder has moved within the EU or not, and derogates from the rule in the long-term residents' Directive which requires Member States to include in the calculation only absences from *national* territory of up to *six* months, adding up to *ten* months in total.[757]

Thirdly, a Blue Card holder who has obtained long-term residence status (and his or her family members with long-term residence status) will be entitled to a period of two years' absence from the EU, not just one year, before Member States are entitled to withdraw his or her long-term residence permit.[758] However, Member States *may* limit the second and third derogations from the long-term residence Directive to cases in which the person concerned 'can present evidence that he has been absent from the territory of the [EU] to exercise an economic activity in an employed or self-employed capacity, or to perform a voluntary service, or to study in his own country of origin'.[759] Finally, the favourable rules in the Blue Card Directive on family reunion and on the transfer of pensions to third countries will continue to apply to former Blue Card holders who have obtained

---

[754] On the temporal scope of EU immigration and asylum law, see 5.5 and 6.6 above.

[755] Art 16(2); this is an express derogation from Art 4(1) of Dir 2003/109 ([2003] OJ L 16/44). The specific rule in Art 4(2) of Dir 2003/109 continues to apply (see Art 16(1)). Point 20 in the preamble explains the purpose of this derogation: it exists 'in order not to penalise geographically mobile highly qualified third-country workers who have not yet acquired' EU long-term resident status, and 'in order to encourage geographical and circular migration.'   [756] Art 16(3).

[757] More specifically, the derogation is from the rule in the first sub-paragraph in Art 4(3) of Dir 2003/109. On the purpose of this derogation, see again point 20 in the preamble. It follows from Art 16(1) that the rules in the second and third sub-paragraphs of Art 4(3) of Dir 2003/109 continue to apply to Blue Card holders.

[758] Art 16(4), derogating from Art 9(1)(c) of Dir 2003/109. On the purpose of this derogation, see point 21 in the preamble. It follows from Art 16(1) that the other rules on the loss or withdrawal of long-term residence status in Art 9 of Dir 2003/109 continue to apply, including the discretion to permit longer periods of absence for 'specific or exceptional reasons' (Art 9(2)) and the requirement to facilitate the re-acquisition of long-term residence status after losing it on this basis (Art 9(5)).

[759] Art 16(5).

long-term residence status.[760] Once Blue Card holders qualify for long-term residence status, they will receive a long-term residence permit in the standard format, marked 'former Blue Card holder'.[761]

It should be noted that the Council dropped an important part of the Commission's original proposal, which would have disapplied any national quotas on the total number of resident third-country nationals as regards any Blue Card holders who obtained long-term resident status, and would also have required Member States who applied priority employment rules against long-term residents who moved to their Member State to give long-term residents who held Blue Cards preference as compared to all other third-country nationals applying to reside there for the same reasons.[762]

As with the parallel derogations from the family reunion Directive, the key question is to what extent these particular provisions will contribute to the objective of the Blue Card Directive—making the EU more attractive for highly skilled workers? On this point, the removal of some restrictions on obtaining and retaining long-term resident status might have a modest impact on the attractiveness of the Blue Card system to would-be applicants. The Commission's proposals to lift quotas and weaken the local preference rule for Blue Card holders who obtained long-term status would have been more significant, but the Council rejected them entirely. The most obvious step to attract highly skilled workers to the EU would have been to shorten the period needed to obtain long-term residence status for Blue Card holders—but this idea was not even considered.[763]

6.8. Social security coordination[764]

It should first of all be recalled, as set out above, that certain third-country nationals (refugees, stateless persons, and family members of EU citizens exercising free movement rights) are covered by EU free movement legislation governing social security coordination, and certain others are governed by the EU's association agreements.[765] The social security position of other third-country nationals is governed, for now, by Regulation 859/2003, which took effect from 1 June 2003.[766] This Regulation extends the 1971 free movement legislation on

---

[760] Art 16(6). On these rules, see respectively 6.6.2 and 6.5.1 above.

[761] Art 17. On the residence permit format, see 6.9.1 below.

[762] Art 20 of the original proposal (COM (2007) 637, 23 Oct 2007), referring to Art 14(3) and 14(4) of Dir 2003/109 (on which, see 6.7.1 above).

[763] Note that Member States do retain the power to set more favourable standards (including a shorter waiting period) for highly skilled workers as regards national long-term residence regimes (Art 13, Dir 2003/109).

[764] For detailed comments on the background to this issue, see ch 23 of S Peers and N Rogers, eds, *EU Immigration and Asylum Law: Text and Commentary* (1st edn, Martinus Nijhoff, 2006).

[765] See 6.4.1, 6.4.2, and 6.4.3 above.   [766] [2003] OJ L 124/1.

social security to all third-country nationals and members of their families who are not already covered by that Regulation, on two conditions: they must be 'legally resident' and, following the *Khalil and Addou* judgment,[767] there must be a cross-border dimension within the EU.[768] Third-country nationals had to apply for equal treatment within two years (so by 1 June 2005), otherwise they were limited to equal treatment from the time of their application.[769] Finally, an Annex provides that in Germany, only persons in possession of a particular permit will qualify for certain family benefits, while Austria is permitted to set out special additional conditions for access to family allowances. A pending reference from a national court has asked the Court of Justice to clarify aspects of the Regulation.[770]

The position is complicated now that EU legislation dating from 2004 and 2009 has amended the basic rules on social security coordination for EU citizens and their family members, along with refugees and stateless persons, with effect from 1 May 2010.[771] Although the Commission proposed back in 2007 that the revised EU free movement legislation should apply in future to all other third-country nationals who move within the EU,[772] this legislation has not yet been adopted formally. However, the Council adopted its first-reading position on this proposal in July 2010.[773] But until the 2007 proposal is adopted, the 1971 free movement rules on social security coordination continue to apply to all other third-country nationals who move within the EU.[774] A further complication here is that while the UK opted in to the 2003 Regulation, it did not opt in to the 2007 proposal.[775]

Those third-country nationals who have *not* moved within the EU must look to another source of EU law if they wish to claim equal treatment as regards social security. In addition to association agreements and free movement law,[776] several JHA Directives address access to social security benefits, as regards temporary protection, refugee and subsidiary protection status, long-term residents, Blue Card holders, workers in general, and researchers.[777]

---

[767] Joined Cases C-95/99 to 98/99 *Khalil and others* and C-180/99 *Addou* [2001] ECR I-7413.

[768] On this requirement, see C-276/06 *El-Youssfi* [2007] ECR I-2851.   [769] Art 2.

[770] Case C-247/09 *Xhymshiti*, pending.

[771] Reg 883/2004, [2004] OJ L 166/1. This Regulation only applied as from the date of effect of a subsequent implementing Regulation, namely Reg 987/2009, [2009] OJ L 284/1 (see Art 91 of Reg 883/2004, and subsequently Art 97 of Reg 987/2009 on the latter Regulation's date of entry into effect).

[772] COM (2007) 439, 23 July 2007.

[773] Council doc 11160/10, 16 July 2010. This measure must still be agreed with the EP.

[774] See Art 90(1)(a) of Reg 883/2004 and Art 96(1)(a) of Reg 987/2009 (both n 770 above).

[775] On the implications of this, see 6.2.5 above.

[776] See further 6.4.2 and 6.4.3 above, and in particular *El-Youssfi* (n 767 above), where the Court pointed out that a Moroccan woman who had not moved within the EU could not claim benefits on the basis of Reg 859/2003, but could potentially rely on the EU–Morocco treaty instead.

[777] See respectively: Art 12 of Dir 2001/55 ([2001] L 212/12); Art 26(5) of Dir 2004/83 on refugee and subsidiary protection status ([2004] L 304/12); Art 11(1)(d) of Directive 2003/109 ([2004] OJ L

The 2003 Regulation and the Regulation agreed by the Council in 2010, if adopted, are useful contributions towards ensuring the effective application of free movement of third-country nationals, and is of practical use to long-term residents, posted workers, researchers, Blue Card holders, and any other third-country nationals who are allowed in practice to move between Member States.[778] These measures also help to ensure equality in respect of social security, as required by human rights law, although the derogations regarding Austria and Germany in the 2003 Regulation might be questioned in light of the Strasbourg jurisprudence.[779]

6.9. Residence permits and long-stay visas

EU legislation sets out obligations to issue residence permits and long-stay visas in many contexts, and also regulates the validity of the permits and visas, their formats, and procedural rules related to applications for their issue and renewal. The two forms of document are considered in turn. It should be noted that in the context of EU free movement law, residence permits are not issued. Instead, Member States issue 'registration certificates' to EU citizens, if they oblige them to register their presence on the territory after three months' stay,[780] and a 'residence card' to third-country national family members of EU citizens.[781] It should also be recalled that, following the entry into force of the Treaty of Lisbon, the Council has the power (not yet used), in order to facilitate EU citizens' free movement rights, to adopt measures concerning 'passports, identity cards, residence permits or any other such document'.[782]

16/44); Art 14(1)(e) of Dir 2009/50 ([2009] OJ L 155/17); the agreed single permit Dir (6.5.1 above); and Art 12(c) of Dir 2005/71 ([2005] OJ L 289/15). As regards refugee and subsidiary protection status, the proposal to amend Dir 2004/83 would not amend the relevant rules (Art 26(4) of COM (2009) 551, 21 Oct 2009). See also Art 14 of the proposed Directive on intra-corporate transferees (COM (2010) 378, 13 July 2010) and Art 16 of the proposed Directive on seasonal workers (COM (2010) 379, 13 July 2010).

[778] On these categories of persons, see respectively 6.7, 6.4.4, 6.5.4, and 6.5.2 above.

[779] See 6.3.2 above, particularly the judgments of 25 Oct 2005 in *Niedzwiecki v Germany* and *Okpisz v Germany* (not yet reported), and H Verschueren, 'EC Social Security Coordination Excluding Third-Country Nationals: Still in Line with Fundamental rights After the *Gaygusuz* judgment?' (1997) 24 CMLRev 991. Note that in the agreed text of the 2007 proposal, these special exceptions would be dropped (n 772 above).

[780] Art 8 of Dir 2004/38 ([2004] OJ L 229/35). Note that Member States cannot insist on production of these documents as a condition for exercise of a right (Art 25, Dir 2004/38).

[781] Arts 9–11, Dir 2004/38 (ibid). Note that Member States may not require a long-term visa for third-country national family members of EU citizens: Case C-157/03 *Commission v Spain* [2005] ECR I-2911. According to the Commission guidance on the Directive, Member States can define the format of the residence card as they see fit, but it must be a free-standing document, not a stamp in a passport (COM (2009) 313, 2 July 2009).   [782] Art 77(3) TFEU, discussed in 3.2.4 above.

6.9.1. Residence permits

Member States are obliged to issue residence permits to beneficiaries of refugee or subsidiary protection status, beneficiaries of EU temporary protection status, victims of trafficking or smuggling, single permit holders, Blue Card holders, researchers, students and other non-economic migrants, persons admitted for family reunion, and long-term residents.[783]

There are specific rules concerning the validity of the relevant permits. Permits for refugees must be valid for at least three years and renewable, but can have a shorter period of validity for refugees' family members.[784] Permits for persons with subsidiary protection status must be valid for at least one year and renewable; there is no express reference to permits for their family members.[785] The permits for persons admitted under an EU temporary protection scheme must be valid for the entire duration of the temporary protection.[786] For victims of trafficking, the permits shall be valid for at least six months and renewable.[787]

As for immigration legislation, there are no rules on the period of validity of single permits.[788] For Blue Card holders, the permits shall be issued for a standard period of between one and four years, or for less if the work contract covers a shorter period.[789] Researchers' permits must be issued for periods of at least one year, renewable if the conditions for admission are still met.[790] For non-economic migrants, students' permits must be valid for at least one year and renewable; school pupils' permits must be valid for a maximum period of one year; unpaid trainees' permits must be valid for a one-year maximum, and renewed only in exceptional cases; and volunteers' permits must also be valid only for a maximum period of one year, with an exceptional possibility of a longer period.[791] Persons admitted for family reunion must receive a permit valid for at least one year (renewable), and an autonomous permit, subject to certain conditions and exceptions, after five

---

[783] Note that Member States have an obligation to issue documents to all asylum seekers, subject to certain exceptions, which must be valid as long as the asylum seekers are authorized to remain on the territory (Art 6 of Dir 2003/9, [2003] OJ L 31/18).

[784] Art 24(1), Dir 2004/83 ([2004] OJ L 304/12).

[785] Art 24(2), Dir 2004/83 (ibid). See further 5.5 above. The proposal to amend this Directive would treat beneficiaries of subsidiary protection and their family members the same as refugees in this regard (COM (2009) 551, 21 Oct 2009).

[786] Art 8, Dir 2001/55 ([2001] OJ L 212/12). See further 5.6 above.

[787] Art 8(3), Dir 2004/81 ([2004] OJ L 261/19). See further 7.6.2 below.

[788] Note, however, that the issue of a residence permit in the EU standard format (see below) determines the *scope* of the Dir in some respects (Art 3(1)(b)). See further 6.5.1 above.

[789] Art 7(2), Dir 2009/50 ([2009] OJ L 155/17). See further 6.5.2 above. See also Art 16(3) of the proposed Dir on intra-corporate transferees (COM (2010) 378, 13 July 2010) and Art 11 of the proposed Dir on seasonal workers (COM (2010) 379, 13 July 2010).

[790] Art 8, Dir 2005/71 ([2005] OJ L 289/15); see also the special rule for researchers' family members (Art 9(1), Dir 2005/71). See further 6.5.3 above.

[791] Respectively Arts 12–15, Dir 2004/114 ([2004] OJ L 375/12); see further 6.5.4 above.

years.[792] Finally, for long-term residents, the permit must be valid for at least five years (renewable automatically),[793] with a special rule for cases where the long-term resident has moved to a second Member State without yet transferring his or her long-term residence status there.[794]

States fully participating in the Schengen *acquis* have procedural obligations to check the Schengen Information System (SIS) before issuing *any* residence permit; if the person concerned is already listed on the SIS, the State planning to issue the permit must consult with the State which issued the alert.[795] The holders of such permits, if they are issued, then benefit from the freedom to travel within the EU,[796] as well as a simplified process to cross the external borders.[797] Applicants for, or holders of, residence permits also have procedural rights relating to the issue or withdrawal of the permits, pursuant to much EU legislation.[798]

EU legislation has for some time established a uniform format for residence permits for third-country nationals. First of all, a 'Joint Action' was adopted in 1996,[799] during the initial 'third pillar' period, in order to increase the level of security applicable to such documents.[800] This Joint Action was subsequently replaced by a Regulation adopted in 2002,[801] which was in turn amended in

---

[792] Arts 13(2) and (3) and 15, Dir 2003/86 ([2003] OJ L 251/12); see further 6.6 above.

[793] Arts 8(2) and 23(2), Dir 2003/109 ([2004] OJ L 16/44). See further 6.7 above.

[794] Art 19(2) and (3), Dir 2003/109 (ibid).

[795] Art 25(1) of the Schengen Convention ([2000] OJ L 239), as amended by Reg 265/2010 ([2010] OJ L 85/1); see further 4.9 above. A 'residence permit' for these purposes is defined as 'an authorisation of whatever type issued by a Contracting Party which grants right of residence within its territory. This definition shall not include temporary permission to reside in the territory of a Contracting Party for the purposes of processing an application for asylum or a residence permit' (Art 1, Schengen Convention).

[796] Art 21 of the Schengen Convention, as amended by Reg 265/2010 (both ibid); see further 4.9 above.

[797] Art 5 of the Schengen Borders Code (Reg 562/2006, [2006] OJ L 105/1), as amended by Reg 265/2010 (ibid). On the substance of this rule, see 3.6.1 above.

[798] See: agreed text of single permit Dir (6.5.1 above); Art 11, Dir 2009/50 (Blue Card holders); Art 15, Dir 2005/71 (researchers); Art 18, Dir 2004/114 (non-economic migrants); Art 18, Dir 2003/86 (family reunion); and Arts 10, 20, and 23(2), Dir 2003/109 (long-term residents). See also Art 12(3) of the proposed Dir on intra-corporate transferees (COM (2010) 378, 13 July 2010) and Art 13(3) of the proposed Dir on seasonal workers (COM (2010) 379, 13 July 2010). On the interpretation of these provisions, see Case C-540/03 *EP v Council* [2006] ECR I-5769, concerning the family reunion Dir, which presumably applies by analogy. Note also the judgment in Case C-327/02 *Panayotova* [2004] ECR I-11055, discussed in 6.3.4 above, which refers to procedural rights in connection with all immigration proceedings linked to EU law.

[799] [1997] OJ L 7/1. See Communication on technical specifications ([1998] OJ C 193/1) and Decisions on sharing costs of preparing film masters and on common standards for filling in the permit ([1998] OJ L 99/1 and 333/8). A Schengen Executive Committee Decision (which has not been repealed) required Schengen States to use the standard format early if possible (Sch/Com-ex (97) 34 rev ([2000] OJ L 239/187)).

[800] For more detail on the background, see the first edition of this book, at 92–93.

[801] Reg 1030/2002 ([2002] L 157/1), which entered into force 15 June 2002 (Art 10).

2008.[802] The later measures had the particular objectives of enhancing document security by inserting photographs (2002)[803] and subsequently fingerprints (2008) into the permit. The Commission has brought legal proceedings against Italy for failing to apply the 2002 Regulation.[804]

The Regulation applies to *all* residence permits authorizing a legal stay on the territory (ie regardless of any link to EU legislation which regulates substantive immigration law), with the exception of: visas; permits issued pending examination of an application for asylum or a residence permit or for a residence permit's extension; permits issued exceptionally allowing for a further stay of one month; and (for Member States not applying the Schengen *acquis* fully) permits for an initial stay for a period defined by national law (but no longer than six months).[805] However, it does not apply to permits issued to family members of EU citizens exercising their right to free movement, nationals of EEA states, or to any non-visa nationals who are permitted to stay in a Member State for less than three months.[806] Permits must be issued in the form of a stand-alone document.[807] Member States are allowed to use the format for other purposes, as long as they avoid confusion between those purposes and the residence permit as defined in the Regulation.[808] The Regulation specifies that Member States' powers over recognition of States, territorial entities, and documents are not affected by it.[809]

Individuals to whom the permits are issued have the right to verify the data on the permit and to ask for any corrections or deletions to be made, and only the data set out in the Annex to the Regulation or mentioned in that person's travel document can be included in machine-readable form on the permit, although

---

[802] Reg 330/2008 ([2008] L 115/1), which entered into force on 19 May 2008 (Art 2). The legislation has not been consolidated. All further references in this subsection are to the 2002 Regulation as amended, unless otherwise indicated.

[803] Point 14 of the Annex to Reg 1030/2002. The Joint Action had required inclusion of a photograph only where the permit was produced as a stand-alone document.

[804] Case C-486/09, pending.

[805] Art 1(2). Note that this definition differs to some extent from that in Art 1 of the Schengen Convention, which applies to residence permits as regards checks in the SIS and freedom to travel (see n 794 above). When the 2008 Reg was published in the OJ, a Council statement was also published asking the Commission to consider 'the most appropriate and proportionate way of introducing harmonised security features of the residence permits' covered by the second and third categories of excluded documents.

[806] Art 5. Again, note the differences with Art 1 of the Schengen Convention (ibid). It should also be noted that EU citizens' family members and EEA citizens no longer need residence permits (see 6.4.1 and 6.4.3 above). Separate legislation determines which persons do not need visas to enter Member States (apart from the UK and Ireland): see 4.5 above.

[807] Art 1(1); prior to the 2008 Reg, Member States had the choice whether to issue permits in the form of a stand-alone document or a sticker. The obligation to use a stand-alone document applies from May 2011 (see Art 9, discussed below), although Member States may choose to provide that previously issued permits are still valid.   [808] Art 5a.

[809] Art 8.

Member States may store additional data on government services in the chip inserted into the residence permit.[810]

The biometric data to be stored in residence permits must consist of a photograph and two fingerprints; fingerprinting is compulsory from six years of age.[811] The Commission has powers to implement the Regulation, assisted by a 'comitology' committee of Member States' representatives, in line with the standard approach to implementing EU law.[812] It should be noted that the rules in the residence permit legislation are based on those applicable to the common EU visa format,[813] although an important difference between the two issues is that the biometric data to be included in the uniform residence permit will not be linked to any EU-wide information systems.

In order to allow Member States to adjust to their new obligations, the original Joint Action did not apply for a period of up to five years after the implementing measures were adopted.[814] Member States then had to implement the 2002 Regulation by August 2003, and had to include (non-biometric) photos in all permits by 14 August 2007.[815] As for the 2008 Regulation, Member States have to include photographs as biometric identifiers two years after adoption of the relevant implementing measures, and fingerprints three years after the adoption of those measures;[816] these obligations will therefore apply from May 2011 and May 2012 respectively.[817]

Although, as described above, much EU immigration and asylum legislation requires the issue of residence permits, that legislation does not always refer expressly to the 2002 Regulation as amended (or its precursor Joint Action). All the immigration legislation refers expressly to the Regulation,[818] but EU asylum

---

[810] Art 4.   [811] Arts 4a and 4b.

[812] Arts 2, 6, and 7. See also the possibility of secrecy (Art 3). On 'comitology', see further 2.2.2.1 above.

[813] See 4.6 above; and see also the subsequent adoption of a Reg on security features in EU passports, as later amended (3.9 above).   [814] Art 7 of the Joint Action.

[815] See Art 9, Reg 1030/2002 and the secret implementing Commission Decision C (2002) 3069, 14 Aug 2002 (unpublished; see COM (2003) 558, 24 Sep 2003, p 2).   [816] Art 9.

[817] The secret implementing decision (C(2009)3770/F) was adopted on 26 May 2009.

[818] See: Art 6, agreed single permit Dir (n 787 above); Art 7(5) of Dir 2009/50 (n 788 above); Art 2(e) of Dir 2005/71 (n 789 above); Art 2(g) of Dir 2004/114 (n 790 above); Art 2(e) of Dir 2003/86 (n 791 above); and Arts 2(g), 8(3), and 23(2) of Dir 2003/109 (n 792 above). The Blue Card Dir requires an express reference to 'Blue Card' status, and the conditions of permitted labour market access, to be indicated on the permit. In the case of Dir 2003/109, the reference only concerns the long-term residents' permit, not the other permits within the scope of the Directive (see Art 19); also, the Directive requires an express reference to the long-term residence status to be entered onto the permit (Art 8(3)). Art 7 of the agreed single permit Dir requires Member States to indicate the information regarding labour market access, regardless of the type of permit. The Annex to Reg 1030/2002, as amended, requires Member States to indicate 'family member' status in the permit for family members of EU citizens who have *not* moved within the EU, and permits Member States to indicate a specific status for the non-core family members covered by EU free movement law (Art 3(2) of Dir 2004/38, n 779 above). Dir 2003/109 refers to issue of the permit in either sticker or stand-alone format; this is now obsolete in light of the 2008 amendments to the

law and EU legislation on trafficking victims refers to national law for the definition of 'residence permit'.[819] Nonetheless, given the wording of the Regulation,
the uniform permit format has to be used for the various permits issued pursuant
to other EU legislation.

6.9.2. Long-stay visas

Member States have an obligation to 'facilitate' the issue of long-stay visas pursuant to EU legislation concerning temporary protection, Blue Cards, researchers, and family reunion.[820] This specific legislation has no rules on the validity
of long-stay visas, but there is a general rule in the Schengen Convention, as
amended in 2010: *any* long-stay visa (ie regardless of any link to substantive EU
law) shall have a period of validity of a maximum of one year.[821] If a Member
State allows a person to stay after that period, then it must issue a residence permit
before the end of that period. This rule is without prejudice to the EU legislation
which requires the issue of a residence permit, instead of a long-stay visa.[822]

The process of issuing *any* long-stay visa involves, as for residence permits, an
obligatory prior check in the SIS in States which fully apply the Schengen rules,
followed by consultation between Member States in the event that the person
concerned has already been the subject of an alert for the refusal of entry.[823]
Equally, the issue of any long-stay visa gives rise to the freedom to travel between
the Schengen States,[824] as well as a simplified process to cross the external borders.[825] However, in the case of long-stay visas, there are no express procedural

residence permit Reg (see discussion above). See also Art 11 of the proposed Dir on intra-corporate
transferees (COM (2010) 378, 13 July 2010) and Art 10 of the proposed Dir on seasonal workers
(COM (2010) 379, 13 July 2010).

[819] Art 2(j) of Dir 2004/83 (n 783 above); Art 2(g) of Dir 2001/55 (n 785 above); and Art 2(e) of
Dir 2004/81 (n 786 above).

[820] Art 8(3), Dir 2001/55 (ibid); Art 7(1), Dir 2009/50 (n 788 above); Art 14(4), Dir 2005/71 (n 789
above); and Art 13(1), Dir 2003/86 (n 791 above). Although this legislation refers to 'visas' generally,
not to long-stay visas in particular, it follows from the legal bases of the legislation concerned (Art
63 EC, not Art 62 EC) and the intention that the persons concerned stay *longer* than three months
(see the prior Art 62(2)(b) EC) that the legislation envisages the issue of long-stay visas.

[821] Art 18(2) of the Convention, as amended by Reg 265/2010 (n 794 above). A 'long-stay visa'
is not defined, other than by reference to national and EU law and a validity period of more than
three months (see Art 18(1) of the Convention, as amended by Reg 265/2010).

[822] Art 3, Reg 265/2010 (ibid). Note that Dirs 2005/71 and 2004/114 gave Member States a further
two years (now expired) before they had to issue permits pursuant to those Directives in the form of
a residence permit (Art 18 of Dir 2005/71, n 789 above, and Art 23 of Dir 2004/114, n 790 above).

[823] Art 25(3) of the Schengen Convention, as inserted by Reg 265/2010 (ibid). On the substance
of this process, see 4.9 above.

[824] Art 21(2a) of the Schengen Convention, as inserted by Reg 265/2010 (ibid). On the substance
of this freedom, see 4.9 above.

[825] Art 5 of the Schengen Borders Code (n 796 above), as amended by Reg 265/2010 (ibid). On
the substance of this rule, see 3.6.1 above.

rights in any EU legislation. But since the denial of the long-stay visa would mean that the relevant rights could not be invoked in practice, it must follow from the general principles of EU law and the EU Charter of Fundamental Rights that there are procedural rights for individuals whose application for a long-stay visa is refused, if there is any link with EU legislation.[826]

Finally, as from 2010 there is a common format for long-stay visas, namely the same format as for *short-term* visas.[827] It should be noted, however, that in the case of long-stay visas, there is no obligation to take biometric information, and therefore no obligation to store such information in the Visa Information System.[828] This issue will be addressed when the legislation on long-term visas is reviewed.[829]

6.10. Integration policy

The integration of migrants is to a large degree facilitated by EU immigration and asylum legislation, in particular to the extent that this legislation sets out rights to equal treatment and secure residence status. As set out above, the family reunion and long-term residents' legislation also allows Member States to apply an integration test as a condition for obtaining status. Integration is also facilitated by EU measures in other areas, for example the EU's equality Directives, which aim to eliminate inter alia discrimination on grounds of race and religion for EU citizens and third-country nationals alike.[830] But an EU integration *policy* has also developed, in particular following the conclusions of the Thessaloniki European Council of June 2003,[831] which called for 'the elaboration of a comprehensive and multidimensional policy on the integration of legally residing third country nationals', which would 'cover factors such as employment, economic participation, education and language training, health and social services, housing and urban issues, as well as culture and participation in social life'. This policy is to contribute to 'the new demographic and economic challenges which the EU is now facing, taking into account' certain groups such as women, children, the elderly, and persons with international protection status. Furthermore, 'integration policies should be understood as a continuous, two-way process based on

---

[826] See Case C-327/02 *Panayotova* [2004] ECR I-11055, discussed in 6.3.4 above.

[827] Art 18(1) of the Schengen Convention, as amended by Reg 265/2010 (n 794 above). On the legislation setting out the short-term visa format, see 4.6 above. As noted in the preamble to Reg 265/2010 (point 5), this obligation reflects the prior practice of Member States.

[828] For the relevant rules on short-stay visas, see 4.6–4.8 above.

[829] A review of Reg 265/2010 (ibid) is due by 5 Apr 2012: see Art 5, Reg 265/2010 (ibid). However, the Council has requested the Commission to draw up a report on the biometrics issue by 30 July 2011 (statement on adoption of the Regulation, Council doc 7392/10, 15 Mar 2010).

[830] Dirs 2000/34 ([2000] OJ L 180/22) and 2000/78 ([2000] OJ L 303/16). For further details of relevant EU policies, see the Commission's communication on employment, migration, and integration (COM (2003) 336, 3 June 2003). [831] Points 28–32 of the conclusions.

mutual rights and corresponding obligations' of third-country nationals and host States; although Member States had 'primary responsibility' for integration policies, 'such policies should be developed within a coherent European Union framework, taking into account the legal, political, economic, social and cultural diversity of Member States'. In particular, 'common basic principles' on integration should be defined. The European Council therefore welcomed the creation of contact points on integration, which had just been established, in order to develop cooperation, exchange information, and strengthen coordination on this issue.

A subsequent Commission communication urged a focus upon introduction programmes, language training, and participation in civic, political, and cultural life, and announced a pilot funding programme on integration policy.[832] In 2004, the Hague programme called again for development of common basic principles on integration and set out some basic elements of the principles.[833] Next, the JHA Council of November 2004 adopted conclusions on integration,[834] elaborating the basic principles of integration policy, comprising: integration as a two-way process; the importance of employment; the knowledge of a host State's society, language, history, and institutions; education; access to institutions, goods, and services; interaction between immigrants and host State citizens; guaranteeing the practice of diverse cultures and religions *unless* that practice conflicts with national law or European rights; participation of immigrants in the democratic process; mainstreaming integration policies; and developing goals and benchmarks regarding integration policy. At this time, the Commission also published an integration handbook for policy-makers and practitioners.[835]

In 2005, the Commission issued a communication on integration, which suggested a list of concrete actions at national and EU level to implement those principles.[836] As for the institutional framework, the communication suggested that the national contact points should focus their work on the common basic principles, and their results should be presented in other fora on some occasions. A second edition of the Handbook would be established; a website was planned;[837] an integration forum involving 'stakeholders' would be established; and national ministers should hold an annual debate on the integration issue. The JHA Council subsequently adopted conclusions supporting the Commission's suggestions for developing the framework.[838]

The next step was the Council's adoption, in 2007, of a Decision establishing a formal Integration Fund, in order to facilitate the practical application of the

---

[832] Communication on employment, migration, and integration (COM (2003) 336, 3 June 2003). [833] [2005] OJ C 53/1, point 1.6.

[834] Press release of JHA Council, 19 Nov 2004.

[835] The handbook was subsequently updated in 2007 and 2010. See: <http://ec.europa.eu/justice_home/doc_centre/immigration/integration/doc_immigration_integration_en.htm>.

[836] COM (2005) 389, 1 Sep 2005. [837] See: <http://ec.europa.eu/ewsi/en/index.cfm>.

[838] JHA Council press release, 1–2 Dec 2005.

common basic principles.[839] The main objectives of the Integration Fund are to: assist the development and implementation of admission procedures linked to the integration process, and of the integration process itself; to increase Member States' capacity to develop and implement integration policies; and to exchange information and best practices in and between Member States in this area.[840] This Decision now falls within the scope of Article 79(4) TFEU, inserted by the Treaty of Lisbon, which provides for the adoption of measures, pursuant to the ordinary legislative procedure, 'to provide incentives and support for the action of Member States with a view to promoting the integration of third-country nationals residing legally in their territories, excluding any harmonisation of the laws and regulations of the Member States'. The focus of this policy in recent years has been issues relating to employment, education, and the evaluation of integration policy.[841] It should also be recalled that Member States have the power to require compliance with integration obligations before third-country nationals can benefit from the family reunion and long-term residence Directives.[842]

As for future developments, the Stockholm programme calls for the development of a coordination mechanism; the incorporation of integration issues in other policy areas; the 'identification of joint practices and European modules to support the integration process'; the development of 'core indicators' in certain areas; improved consultation with civil society; and enhanced democratic values and social cohesion.[843] The action plan on implementing the Stockholm programme provides for a further communication on integration policy in 2011.[844]

6.11. Administrative cooperation and EU funding

The main development as regards EU funding and legal migration has been the pilot programme and subsequent adopted Decision establishing an integration fund, already mentioned above.[845] The EU's ARGO funding programme also supported activities of Member States in areas falling within the scope of EU immigration policy.[846]

As for administrative cooperation, the principal focus of EU activity has been information exchange and analysis. The first step in this area is gathering information, where the Commission's statistics body, Eurostat, took over the role of drawing up immigration and asylum statistics in 1998.[847] Eurostat's

---

[839] [2007] OJ L 168/24.   [840] Art 3 of the Decision.

[841] Council doc 8771/10, 20 Apr 2010, and the Council conclusions on the education of migrant children, [2009] OJ C 301/5.   [842] See 6.6. and 6.7 above.

[843] [2010] OJ C 115, point 6.1.5.   [844] COM (2010) 171, 20 Apr 2010.

[845] See 6.10 above.

[846] [2002] OJ L 161/11 (Art 6) and [2004] OJ L 371/48; see further 3.11 above.

[847] See: JHA Council conclusions of Mar 1998 and May 2001; Communication (SEC (2001) 602, 9 Apr 2001); and Action Plan (COM (2003) 179, 15 Apr 2003). For the first annual EU report on

role was then formalized in 2007 when EU legislation concerning asylum and migration statistics was adopted.[848] This legislation requires Eurostat to produce, starting in 2008, annual data on immigration, emigration, and population breakdown by (inter alia) citizenship, as well as annual statistics on the issue of residence permits for specific reasons and on the numbers of long-term residents (as defined by Directive 2003/109).[849] A subsequent Commission implementing measure requires Member States to disaggregate the data on residence permits by reference to admission for the purposes of family reunion, education, remunerated activities, and other reasons, referring specifically to EU legislation on students and researchers.[850] Subsequently, the EU's Blue Card Directive requires Member States to send information to Eurostat annually on the issue, renewal, or withdrawal of Blue Cards, broken down by nationality and occupation, as well as statistics on the family members of Blue Card holders and the movement of Blue Card holders between Member States.[851] Similarly, the agreed single permit Directive requires Member States to communicate annually information on the numbers of single permits issued the previous year.[852]

The statistics produced pursuant to this legislation are available on the Eurostat website.[853] It should be noted that for 2008, Member States had the option to use alternative national definitions (rather than the definition in Directive 2003/109) for the statistics on long-term residents, and until 2010, they were not yet obliged to provide statistics on researchers and students in accordance with EU law definitions.[854] There is still no obligation to link the family reunion statistics with the family reunion Directive, and (unlike the future obligation as regards Blue Card holders) there is no obligation to supply statistics regarding the movement of long-term residents between Member States.

In order to use the statistical data to assess the impact of EU policy and legislation, and its relevance for the further development of policy and legislation, there needs to be further analysis of the statistics and collection and analysis of broader information on immigration policy—and it is not Eurostat's job to provide either function. To perform these functions, first of all a European Migration Network has been gradually established in recent years. Originally, from 2002,

asylum and migration statistics, see: <http://ec.europa.eu/justice_home/doc_centre/immigration/statistics/doc_immigration_statistics_en.htm>.

[848] Reg 862/2007, [2007] OJ L 199/23.

[849] See Arts 3 and 6, Reg 862/2007, along with the definition of 'long-term residents' (Art 2(1)(h)).

[850] Commission Reg 216/2010, [2010] OJ L 66/1. This Regulation applied as from 5 Apr 2010 (Art 2), so presumably applies as from calendar year 2010.

[851] Art 20(2), Dir 2009/50, [2009] OJ L 155/17. This obligation applies as from 19 June 2013, so presumably applies as from calendar year 2012. The Directive must be implemented by 19 June 2011 (Art 23(1)).   [852] Art 15(2), agreed text of single permit Dir (6.5.1 above).

[853] See: <http://epp.eurostat.ec.europa.eu/portal/page/portal/population/data/database>.

[854] See Art 2(3), Reg 862/2007.

the Commission has used preparatory funds to establish the network, which was later formally established pursuant to a Council Decision.[855] The main tasks of the Network are, inter alia, to collect and analyse data and information relating to immigration and asylum.[856] It consists of national contact points designated by Member States and of the Commission, and is guided by a Steering Board made up of members appointed by Member States and the Commission.[857] In practice, the Network has produced very useful and detailed annual reports on both statistics and policy from each Member State, although the synthesis reports (ie the EU-wide analysis) based on the annual reports were not very timely.[858] The Network has also produced a number of interesting reports on specific issues.

Next, information on national immigration *policy* is exchanged between Member States pursuant to a Decision adopted in 2006,[859] which the Council had requested the Commission to propose following a dispute between Spain and other Member States over a Spanish decision to regularize large numbers of irregular migrants.[860] This Decision requires the exchange of information on national measures 'that are likely to have a significant impact on several Member States or on the European Union as a whole', for the purpose of preparing 'exchanges of views and debates on such measures'.[861] Member States decide which (publicly available) measures are likely to have such a significant impact, and it is possible for other Member States or the Commission to request further information (except as regards final court judgments).[862] The Commission is to prepare an annual report summarizing this information, which will serve as the basis for a debate at ministerial level.[863] According to the Commission's report on the implementation of this Decision,[864] over a two-and-a-half-year period, sixteen Member States communicated information on forty-five measures, half of which were legislation (usually adopted already), much of it concerning the implementation of EU law. The other measures communicated were policy plans or general administrative decisions or circulars. In the Commission's view, the implementation of the Decision was disappointing due to the modest number of communications, in particular as regards draft measures.

As regards the later development of the 2006 Decision, the Commission has merged its reports pursuant to the Decision with the reports which the European Council has requested in the meantime, on the application of the EU's Immigration and Asylum Pact, as adopted in 2008, and subsequently the Stockholm programme,

---

[855] [2008] OJ L 131/7. See the earlier Green Paper on the development of the Network (COM (2005) 606, 28 Nov 2005).   [856] Art 2, Council Decision.

[857] Arts 3 and 4, Council Decision.

[858] See the Network website: <http://emn.sarenet.es/html/index.html>. In particular, the synthesis report on the 2006 statistics was only produced in October 2009, and the synthesis report on the 2007 policy developments was only produced in March 2009.   [859] [2006] OJ L 283/40.

[860] See JHA Council press release, 14 Apr 2005.   [861] Art 1 of the Decision.

[862] Art 2 of the Decision.   [863] Art 4 of the Decision.

[864] COM (2009) 687, 17 Dec 2009.

which are intended to prepare the ground for an annual debate on immigration and asylum issues at European Council level.[865] The Commission's communication on the 'tracking mechanism' for gathering information to prepare this report included a draft list of questions to Member States about national policy developments.[866] This communication indicated that the Commission wanted to subsume Member States' reporting obligations under the 2006 Decision within the new process. Presumably the new process will also replace the annual reports on immigration and integration which the Thessaloniki European Council in 2003 invited the Commission to present.[867] The Commission also intends to use information provided by the European Migration Network and the statistics provided by Eurostat to prepare each report.

The first report was released in May 2010, and consisted of a very general summary of developments at EU level and in the Member States.[868] Neither the Commission nor the Council drew very detailed conclusions from this information.[869]

As for the future, the Stockholm programme has called upon the Commission 'to consider how existing information sources and networks can be used more effectively to ensure the availability of the comparable data on migration issues with a view to better informing policy choices, which also takes account of recent developments'.[870] The action plan on implementing the Stockholm programme refers to ongoing development of the European Migration Network and the statistical framework.[871]

Given the intensity of concerns about immigration policy, it is important to ensure that objective, accurate, and timely information and analysis is available to inform the debate. The EU has made important steps in that direction with the development of the European Migration Network and statistics legislation, but the statistics legislation needs to be much more focused (along the lines of the provisions in the Blue Card Directive) in order for the statistics to be more useful, and the operation of the European Migration Network needs to be much more timely. At the level of the Commission and the European Council, the initiatives taken in this field have been spasmodic and uncoordinated, with an unfortunate detour (by way of the 2006 Decision) to make a political gesture. The annual assessment of policy in this area should also be more incisive.

6.12. Conclusions

At least until the Treaty of Lisbon entered into force, it was difficult to agree rules on migration at EU level, resulting initially in only modest steps towards

---

[865] Council doc 13440/08, 24 Sep 2008.   [866] COM (2009) 266, 10 June 2009.
[867] There have been three reports: COM (2004) 408, 16 July 2004; SEC (2006) 892, 30 June 2006; and COM (2007) 512, 12 Sep 2007.   [868] COM (2010) 214, 6 May 2010.
[869] See Council conclusions on the annual report, JHA Council press release, 3–4 June 2010.
[870] [2010] OJ C 115, point 6.1.3.   [871] COM (2010) 171, 20 Apr 2010.

achieving the Tampere objectives of fair treatment for third-country nationals and equal treatment for long-term residents, which were moreover understandably criticized on human rights grounds. Nevertheless, the later agreement on the Blue Card Directive, which actually aims to attract immigration, proved an exception.

With the entry into force of the Treaty of Lisbon, the resulting changes in decision-making and expanded jurisdiction for the Court of Justice (given the Court's early liberal case law in this area), along with the objective of developing an immigration code, as implied in the Stockholm programme, appear likely to push the EU in the direction of a more uniform and modestly more liberal policy on legal migration. However, it remains to be seen whether the key Directives on family reunion and long-term residence will be amended, or further measures on labour migration will be approved. The EU is still some way off developing a fair and comprehensive policy on legal immigration, but there are clear positive signs in that direction.

7

Irregular Migration

7.1. Introduction

States' desire to control access to and stay on their territory manifests itself particularly in a desire to prevent irregular migration, to detect irregular migrants, and to remove any irregular migrants once they are detected.[1] But the exercise of this policy raises obvious questions about the human rights of the persons affected by such a policy, most obviously if they have a claim for asylum or another form of international protection, but also as regards detention (the permissibility of detention, procedural rights concerning detention, and detention conditions); the general rules governing persons subject to expulsion (procedural rights to challenge expulsion orders, living conditions); and the conduct of expulsion operations (as regards the health and human dignity of the persons being expelled).

This chapter, like the others in this book, begins with a historical overview, including issues of legal competence and the territorial scope of the rules, followed by an analysis of the relevant rules of human rights law and relevant rules deriving from other areas of EU law (ie areas of law other than Justice and Home Affairs (JHA) law). Then it examines in detail the Schengen and EU rules concerning the prevention of irregular migration, the treatment of irregular migrants inside the territory, and expulsion (including the controversial Returns Directive), along with the rules on cooperation between Member States' administrations and on the external relations aspects of irregular migration.

These issues obviously has close links with the issues discussed in other chapters, particularly Chapters 3 and 4 concerning visas and border controls, which are obviously also aimed at preventing irregular entry into the territory of the Member States and which regulate in detail the interception of irregular entrants at the border, along with the planned development of an 'entry-exit' system to identify 'overstayers' (ie those who enter the territory legally but remain after their permission to stay expires). EU law defines an irregular migrant as 'a third-country national present on the territory of a Member State, who does not fulfil,

---

[1] Since unauthorized migrants have not generally committed any criminal offences besides breaches of migration law, which is in any event often punishable by administrative sanctions, rather than criminal penalties, this chapter refers throughout to 'irregular', rather than 'illegal', migration.

or no longer fulfils, the conditions for stay or residence in that Member State';[2] those 'conditions for stay or residence' are largely shaped by the rules relating to visas, external borders, and freedom to travel, along with the rules relating to asylum (discussed in Chapter 5) and legal migration (discussed in Chapter 6). Irregular migration may also result in a listing in the Schengen Information System (SIS) blacklist for denial of further entry, an issue considered further in Chapter 3.[3] Furthermore, the EU's border agency, Frontex (also discussed in Chapter 3), has powers relating to expulsion.[4]

There are further links between the rules on irregular migration and on asylum law, in particular because of the impact of rules concerning irregular migration on asylum seekers' ability to reach refuge and on the treatment and procedural rights of rejected asylum seekers, including persons who are appealing a rejection of their asylum applications but who are nonetheless subject to expulsion because their appeal does not have suspensive effect.[5] Also, the EU's rules on responsibility for asylum applications in some cases assign responsibility for dealing with a claim based on the irregular stay of an asylum seeker on a Member State's territory,[6] and EU policy concerning external control of irregular migration impacts upon external aspects of asylum.

Finally, there are links between irregular migration and criminal law and policing, in particular as regards: the application of criminal law to aspects of irregular migration (discussed in detail in this chapter, but on the general relationship between EU law and criminal law, see Chapter 10); expedited criminal procedural rules relating to irregular migration (see Chapter 9); and the application of cross-border policing rules and the competence of EU-wide policing bodies to address irregular migration issues (see Chapter 12).

7.2. Institutional framework and overview

7.2.1. Framework prior to the Treaty of Amsterdam

Prior to the Maastricht Treaty, there was loose intergovernmental cooperation on the issue of irregular migration, as Member States did not accept the Commission's argument that the effect of irregular migration on the EEC's common market (as it was then) was sufficient to adopt a proposed Directive on the

---

[2] See, for instance, Art 2(b) of Dir 2009/52, on sanctions against irregular migrants ([2009] OJ L 168/24) and similarly Art 79(3) TFEU. Further on the issue of defining irregular migration, see E Guild, 'Who is an Irregular Migrant?' in B Bogusz, R Cholewinski, A Cygan, and E Szyszczak, eds, *Irregular Migration and Human Rights* (Martinus Nijhoff, 2004), 3.

[3] See 3.7 above. On the SIS generally, see 12.6.1.1 below. Another database, the Visa Information System, will, when operational, also be used to control irregular migration (see 4.8 above).

[4] See 3.10.1 above.   [5] See 5.7 above, on the asylum procedures Directive.

[6] See 5.8 above.

issue.[7] Starting in the period just before the Maastricht Treaty entered into force, the Member States' immigration ministers (and subsequently the Council) began to adopt a number of Recommendations on the subject of irregular immigration.[8] An initial Recommendation of 1992 set out general principles governing control of irregular migration, which were supplemented in later measures.[9] A series of three later Recommendations concerned particularly in-country detection of irregular migration and irregular employment.[10] Other Recommendations addressed operational aspects of expulsion,[11] and three further Recommendations concerned readmission,[12] setting out a standard travel document (or laissez-passer) for use in individual expulsions, a standard bilateral readmission agreement, and principles to be included in protocols to readmission agreements. The Council also adopted a Decision on monitoring the implementation of the post-Maastricht measures.[13] Finally, the EU's immigration ministers established CIREFI (the Centre for Information, Discussion, and Exchange on the Crossing of Borders and Immigration), to exchange information between national administrations on irregular migration.[14]

Within the scope of the Schengen *acquis*, Articles 23 and 24 of the Schengen Convention addressed the legal status of persons who were not lawfully on the territory; Article 26 set out rules concerning carrier sanctions to prevent irregular entry; and Article 27 concerned penalties to be imposed on persons who facilitate such entry.[15] There were also further Executive Committee decisions in the area of irregular migration.[16]

7.2.2. The Treaty of Amsterdam

7.2.2.1. Institutional framework

Following amendment of the EC Treaty by the Treaty of Amsterdam, the EC gained express powers to address the issue of irregular migration, as set out in Article 63(3)(b) EC, which gave the EC powers over 'illegal immigration and illegal residence, including repatriation of illegal residents'. This power was initially subject to the general decision-making rules governing Title IV of the EC

---

[7] See the proposed Directive in [1976] OJ C 277/2, revised in [1978] OJ C 97/9.

[8] These measures are not discussed in detail in this book; for details, see the first edition, at 94–99.

[9] Recommendation of Immigration Ministers on 30 Nov/1 Dec 2002 (SN 4678/92, WGI 1266, 16 Nov 1992), published in E Guild and J Niessen, *The Developing Immigration and Asylum Policies of the European Union: Adopted Conventions, Resolutions, Recommendations, Decisions and Conclusions* (Kluwer, 1996), and in T Bunyan, ed, *Key Texts on Justice and Home Affairs in the European Union* (1997).

[10] Recommendation of Immigration Ministers on 1–2 June 2003 (SN 3017/93, WGI 1516, 25 May 1993), published in Guild and Niessen and in Bunyan, ibid; [1996] OJ C 5/1; [1996] OJ C 304/1.   [11] [1996] OJ C 5/3, 5, and 7.

[12] [1996] OJ C 274/20, 21, and 25.   [13] [1996] OJ L 342/5.   [14] See 7.8 below.

[15] [2000] OJ L 239; see further 7.7, 7.5.1, and 7.5.3 below.   [16] See 7.7 below.

Treaty: a shared initiative of the Commission and Member States, unanimous voting in the Council, consultation of the European Parliament (EP), and restricted jurisdiction of the Court of Justice.[17] Following the end of the transitional period on 1 May 2004, the Commission gained its usual monopoly of initiative in this area; and following the agreement as part of the Hague programme to alter most of the Title IV decision-making rules, measures in this area were subject to qualified majority voting (QMV) in the Council and co-decision of the EP starting on 1 January 2005.[18] Also, the EU adopted a number of 'third pillar' criminal law measures which are relevant to irregular immigration, and so are considered in some detail in this chapter; such measures were subject to unanimous voting in the Council, shared competence among the Commission and Member States to make proposals, consultation of the EP, and a different regime of jurisdiction of the Court of Justice, until the entry into force of the Treaty of Lisbon.[19] But even before the entry into force of that Treaty, the Community adopted measures setting out criminal law obligations for Member States in this area.

The issue of irregular migration also fell within the scope of Article 66 EC, which conferred powers relating to cooperation between national administrations, or between national administrations and the Commission.[20] Also, the topic was subject to the national sovereignty safeguard and emergency powers clause set out in Article 64 EC.[21]

7.2.2.2. Overview of practice

The Council allocated Articles 26 and 27(1) of the Schengen Convention to Article 63(3)(b) of the EC Treaty, along with Article 17(3)(g) of the Convention, concerning the powers to define further the criteria for inclusion in the Schengen 'blacklist'.[22] Article 18 of the Convention, on the status of persons with long-stay visas,[23] was allocated jointly to Articles 62(2) and 63(3). Articles 23(2)–(5), 24, and 25 of the Convention, on expulsion of persons and checks in the SIS in connection with residence permits, were allocated jointly to Articles 62(3) and 63(3), while Article 23(1) was allocated only to Article 62(3).[24] Executive Committee Decisions concerning means of proof in readmission agreements and transit for expulsion were allocated jointly to Articles 62(3) and 63(3),[25] and three other Decisions were allocated jointly to Article 63(3) and other 'legal bases': an action plan on irregular migration, a measure on the coordinated deployment of

---

[17] See 2.2.2.1 above.   [18] Ibid.   [19] See 2.2.2.2 above.

[20] See 7.8 below on substantive measures in this area. On the scope of Art 66 compared to Art 63(3)(b), see (*mutatis mutandis*) 3.2.4 above (as regards Art 74 TFEU as compared to Art 77 TFEU).

[21] See 3.2.4 above (as regards Art 72 TFEU).   [22] See [1999] OJ L 176/17.

[23] On Art 18, see 3.6.1 and 4.9 above. It is assumed that the Article was only allocated to Art 63(3) EC due to its relevance to *legal* migration.

[24] On these provisions, see 4.9 above and 7.7 below. Again, it is assumed that Art 25 was only allocated to Art 63(3) EC as regards its impact on legal migration.

[25] On the latter issue, see further 7.7.3 below.

document advisers, and the Common Manual (on border controls) and Common Consular Instructions (on short-term visas).

The Tampere European Council in 1999 set out specific objectives relating to irregular migration, in particular calling for the adoption of legislation concerning trafficking in persons by the end of 2000; assistance to countries of origin and transit; an invitation to the Council to conclude readmission agreements between the EC and third States or 'standard clauses' on this issue in broader agreements with third States; and the possible adoption of rules on internal readmission (ie between Member States).

The trafficking proposal referred to was released by the Commission at the end of 2000, although not adopted until 2002.[26] Also, the Community adopted an active policy of attempting to conclude readmission agreements, including standard clauses concerning readmission in its association or cooperation agreements, and developed further the other external relations aspects of its irregular migration policy.[27]

As for other measures, a first set of Directives concerning irregular migration (carrier sanctions, facilitation of irregular entry and residence, and mutual recognition of expulsion decisions) were all adopted by the Council by 2001–02.[28]

In an attempt to develop an overall strategy for EU measures concerning irregular migration, the Commission released a Communication on irregular migration in 2001;[29] the Council duly adopted a detailed action plan early in 2002.[30] Soon afterward, the Commission issued a Green Paper on expulsion ('return') policy;[31] this too was followed by a detailed Council action plan.[32] The parallel action plan on external border control was also relevant to irregular immigration issues.[33]

A series of further measures were adopted afterward, consisting of: a Directive on assistance for expulsions via air transit;[34] conclusions on assistance for expulsions via land and sea;[35] a Regulation on a network of immigration liaison officers;[36] a Decision on financing expulsion measures;[37] a Directive on the exchange of passenger data;[38] a Decision on joint expulsion flights;[39] a Directive on the legal status of victims of trafficking in persons;[40] and a Decision establishing an information and coordination network for Member States' migration management services.[41] Measures concerning the Schengen Information System (SIS) were adopted in 2001 and 2004, and in 2006, legislation to establish a new system (SIS II) was adopted.[42] The Commission also released a discussion paper on the

---

[26] See 7.5.4 below.   [27] See 7.9 below.   [28] See 7.5.1, 7.5.3, and 7.7.2 below.
[29] COM (2001) 672, 15 Nov 2001.   [30] [2002] OJ C 142/23.
[31] COM (2002) 175, 10 Apr 2002; see later Communication on the same topic (COM (2002) 564, 14 Oct 2002).   [32] Council doc 14673/02, 25 Nov 2002.
[33] See 3.2.2.2 above.   [34] See 7.7.3.1 below.   [35] See 7.7.3.2 below.
[36] See 7.5.5 below.   [37] See 7.7.2 below.   [38] See 7.5.2 below.
[39] See 7.7.4 below.   [40] See 7.6.2 below.   [41] See 7.8 below.   [42] See 3.7 above.

link between legal and irregular migration,[43] along with several updates on the implementation of EC policy on irregular migration (as well as visas and border control).[44] In addition to the negotiation of readmission treaties and the broader external agenda concerning irregular migration, the EC concluded Protocols to the UN Convention on organized crime, concerning smuggling and trafficking in persons.[45]

The Hague programme on the JHA agenda for 2004–09 called for negotiations to start on a proposal on expulsion standards, along with further readmission agreements, the creation of a European return fund, and the adoption of a policy plan on trafficking in persons.[46] Implementing the Hague programme, the EU eventually adopted in 2008 a Directive touching on many key aspects of expulsions (known as the 'Returns Directive'), after three years of difficult negotiations.[47] In the meantime, the EU had agreed on legislation to establish a European return fund in 2007,[48] and a number of further readmission treaties were also agreed with third States.[49] Also, the Council agreed an action plan on trafficking in persons in December 2005.[50] There were also developments as regards the external aspects of migration control.[51] Finally, the Commission issued a communication on policy priorities as regards irregular migration in 2006,[52] in particular addressing the question of deterring the employment of irregular migrants. This ultimately led to legislation on this subject—a Directive adopted in 2009, which was the first EC immigration legislation (as distinct from a third pillar measure) to establish criminal law offences.[53] The only proposal in this area not agreed before the Treaty of Lisbon entered into force was a proposal to amend the rules governing immigration liaison officers,[54] although a criminal law proposal to amend the rules on trafficking in persons was not adopted in time either.[55]

Alongside the Hague programme, the decision-making rules relating to irregular migration were altered, as from 1 January 2005, so that QMV in the Council applied in this area, along with co-decision with the EP.[56] As regards the Court of Justice, due to the limitations on its jurisdiction before the Treaty of Lisbon entered into force, it received only one case referred from national courts during this period, concerning the interpretation of the rules on immigration detention set out in the Returns Directive.[57] On the other hand, the Commission

---

[43] COM (2004) 412, 4 June 2004.

[44] COM (2003) 323, 3 June 2003; SEC (2004) 1349, 25 Oct 2004; SEC (2006) 1010, 19 July 2006; and SEC (2009) 320, 9 Mar 2009.   [45] See 7.5.2 and 7.5.4 below.

[46] [2005] OJ C 53, points 1.6.4 and 1.7.1. See also the later implementation plan: [2005] OJ C 198, point 2.6.   [47] Dir 2008/115, [2008] OJ L 348/98; see 7.7.1 below.

[48] [2007] OJ L 144/45; see 7.8 below.   [49] See 7.9 below.   [50] See 7.5.4 below.

[51] See 7.9.2 below.   [52] COM (2006) 402, 19 July 2006.

[53] Dir 2009/52, [2009] OJ L 168/24. See 7.6.1 below.

[54] COM (2009) 322, 8 July 2009. See 7.5.5 below.

[55] COM (2009) 136, 25 Mar 2009. See 7.5.4 below.   [56] [2004] OJ L 396/45.

[57] Case C-357/09 PPU *Kadzoev*, judgment of 30 Nov 2009, not yet reported. See 7.7.1 below.

brought before the Court a number of infringement actions in order to ensure that Member States complied with the legislation adopted in this area.[58]

7.2.3. The Treaty of Lisbon

The former Article 63(3) and (4) EC, concerning migration, became Article 79 of the Treaty on the Functioning of the European Union (TFEU), as amended by the Treaty of Lisbon with effect from the entry into force of the latter Treaty on 1 December 2009.[59] Article 79 TFEU provides (in part) as follows:

(1) The Union shall develop a common immigration policy aimed at ensuring, at all stages, the efficient management of migration flows, fair treatment of third country nationals residing legally in Member States, and the prevention of, and enhanced measures to combat, illegal immigration and trafficking in human beings.

(2) For the purposes of paragraph 1, the European Parliament and the Council, acting in accordance with the ordinary legislative procedure, shall adopt measures in the following areas:

   . . .

   (c) illegal immigration and unauthorised residence, including removal and repatriation of persons residing without authorisation;

   (d) combating trafficking in persons, in particular women and children.

(3) The Union may conclude agreements with third countries for the readmission to their countries of origin or provenance of third-country nationals who do not or who no longer fulfil the conditions for entry, presence or residence in the territory of one of the Member States.

Paragraphs 4 and 5 and sub-paragraphs 2(a) and 2(b) of this Article concern only legal migration, and so were considered instead in Chapter 6.[60] As for the provisions concerning irregular migration, there was no change in the decision-making rules, which as noted above, were subject to QMV in Council and co-decision already from 1 January 2005. There was, however, an extension of the jurisdiction of the Court of Justice, with the likely effect in particular that more disputes concerning expulsion (once the Returns Directive is fully applicable) will reach the Court of Justice. But there was no immediate impact of this enlargement of the Court's jurisdiction in this area in the first few months after the Treaty of Lisbon entered into force.

As with legal migration, the EU's powers as regards irregular migration are now part of an obligation to develop a 'common' policy,[61] and the penultimate paragraph of the previous Article 63 EC has now been removed.[62] Article 79(1)

---

[58] See 7.5.1, 7.5.3, 7.7.2, and 7.7.3.1 below.
[59] [2007] OJ C 306. The consolidated TFEU is in [2008] OJ C 115.
[60] See 6.2.3 and 6.2.4 above.   [61] See also Art 67(2) TFEU.
[62] See further the discussion of competence issues below (7.2.4).

TFEU, unlike the previous Article 63 EC, also sets out, inter alia, the objective of the prevention and combating of illegal immigration and human trafficking. The general provisions of Title V of Part Three of the TFEU also specify that the common immigration policy includes fairness towards *all* third-country nationals, ie including irregular migrants as well as legal residents.[63]

The revised Treaty text refers now to 'unauthorised', rather than 'illegal' presence, and also refers expressly to 'removal'. There is a definition of irregular migration in the context of readmission treaties (Article 79(3)), which reflects EU legislation in this area.[64]

Article 79(2)(d) confers an express competence as regards trafficking in persons, although it should be noted that there is also an explicit reference to this issue in the criminal law provisions of the Treaty.[65] As regards other criminal law aspects of migration policy, the general power to adopt criminal law measures linked to harmonization in other areas is obviously relevant.[66]

The external power over readmission agreements became explicit, and it should be noted that the EP gained powers of consent over the conclusion of readmission agreements.[67]

As for the immediate impact of the Treaty of Lisbon on legislation in this area, it had no impact as such on the proposal to amend the legislation on immigration liaison officers, which had been pending when the new Treaty entered into force.[68] The Treaty had a bigger impact on the proposed third pillar measure on trafficking in persons,[69] which lapsed when the Treaty entered into force. The Commission instead submitted a proposal for a Directive on this subject in spring 2010, which was agreed by the Council in June 2010.[70]

The Stockholm programme largely reiterates established EU policy in this area, without calling for further legislation,[71] except for a more general call for the consolidation and amendment of all legislation in the area of migration— although this process is intended to start with legal migration measures.[72] There are specific commitments relating to trafficking in persons, as regards the adoption of new legislation, the possible appointment of an Anti-Trafficking Coordinator, special treaties with third States, and the proposal of further measures relating to protection of victims, prevention measures by consular services, and border controls.[73] The programme also calls for an evaluation of EU readmission policy in 2010, and the conclusion of readmission agreements in particular with Turkey, Morocco, Algeria, Libya, Egypt, Iraq, Afghanistan,

---

[63] Compare Art 67(2) TFEU with Art 79(1) TFEU, which refers only to fairness as regards legal residents.   [64] See n 2 above.

[65] Art 83(1) TFEU. See further 7.2.4 below.   [66] Art 83(2) TFEU. See further 7.2.4 below.

[67] On external competence in JHA matters, see generally 2.7 above.

[68] COM (2009) 322, 8 July 2009. See 7.5.5 below.   [69] COM (2009) 136, 25 Mar 2009.

[70] See 7.5.4 below. On the issue of the correct 'legal bases' for this proposal, see 7.2.4 below.

[71] [2010] OJ C 115, point 6.1.6.   [72] Ibid, point 6.1.4.   [73] Ibid, point 4.4.2.

and Bangladesh,[74] and sets out a general agenda for external policy in this area.[75] The action plan on implementation of the programme refers to an evaluation of return policy in 2011 and a proposal to amend the Directive on facilitation of unauthorized entry (possibly merging it with the Framework Decision on this subject) in 2012.[76] It should also be noted again that the EU's plans for legislation to establish an entry-exit system will impact upon regulation of irregular migration.[77]

7.2.4. Competence issues

There were a number of historic disputes, before the entry into force of the Treaty of Lisbon, over the extent of the EC's competence over irregular migration issues pursuant to the previous Article 63(3)(b) EC. These issues remain relevant if the validity of any EU measures adopted before the entry into force of the Treaty of Lisbon is challenged, and in light of the similar wording of the Treaty provisions in this area after the entry into force of the Treaty of Lisbon, the historic disputes might even still be relevant to measures adopted after that Treaty's entry into force.

The boundary between the irregular migration powers and EU free movement law and association agreements is explored further below, as is the practice and scope of the EU's external relations powers in this field.[78]

Since the Treaty of Lisbon has unified the decision-making rules applicable to the adoption of legislation on legal migration and irregular migration, it is no longer necessary to distinguish between the powers over legal migration and the powers over irregular migration.[79] This means, for instance, that there would no longer be an awkward problem if the EU wanted to amend the existing Directive concerning the legal status of victims of trafficking.[80] However, it remains necessary to distinguish between the legal base concerning irregular migration and the legal basis for cooperation between national administrations,[81] as the latter provision entails a different rule on involvement of the EP (consultation only). The most logical distinction is that the former provision governs the adoption of rules which directly regulate the issue, while

---

[74] Ibid, points 6.1.6 and 7.5. It should be noted that negotiation mandates for readmission agreements with Turkey, Morocco, and Algeria already existed before the Stockholm programme was adopted (see 7.9.1 below), whereas there were not previously any mandates to negotiate such treaties with the other countries referred to.   [75] Ibid, points 6.1.1 and 6.1.2. See further 7.9.2 below.

[76] COM (2010) 171, 20 Apr 2010.

[77] See 3.6.2 above. The Commission's 2010 work programme (COM (2010) 135, 31 Mar 2010) refers to planned legislation on this issue in 2011.   [78] Respectively 7.4 and 7.9.1 below.

[79] On this issue, see further 6.2.4 above.

[80] Dir 2004/81, [2004] OJ L 261/19; see 7.6.2 below.

[81] Now Art 74 TFEU, previously Art 66 EC.

the latter provision is confined to regulating issues such as the exchange of personnel.[82]

As for the intensity of the EC's powers to regulate irregular migration, despite the final words of Article 63, Member States did not have carte blanche to adopt measures in this field regardless of EC legislation. Member States were still obliged to comply with EC law to the extent that the EC has acted, and the EC could harmonize national law fully in this field if it wished, subject to the principle of subsidiarity; but EC powers were not prima facie exclusive.[83] This position was confirmed by the Treaty of Lisbon, which removed the final provisions of Article 63 EC, and instead subjects the entire JHA Title explicitly to the rule of shared competence.[84] This leaves Member States free to act to the extent that the EU has not acted, but it is open to the EU to harmonize the field as much as it wishes.[85]

Where the EC or EU legislation in this area adopted before *or* after the entry into force of the Treaty of Lisbon permits Member States to set higher standards if they are 'compatible' with the legislation concerned, the remaining competence of the Member States must be determined by analogy with the rules applying to asylum legislation adopted after the entry into force of the Treaty of Lisbon.[86] In a nutshell,[87] this means that: any reference to 'more favourable' provisions has to be understood as referring to more favourable provisions for the persons concerned; the requirement of compatibility means that Member States must comply with any fully uniform provisions of the relevant legislation, ie any measures which clearly leave no room for national variations as regards the application of the relevant rules, with any uncertainty about the application of this principle in a particular case to be resolved in favour of Member States' ability to set higher standards; and that any restraint on Member States' powers to set higher standards could not breach the human rights obligations of the EU, as enshrined in primary EU law.[88]

As to the material content of the EU's powers regarding irregular migration, does it extend to issues such as deportation, expulsion, and interior enforcement measures? The EP expressed doubts over the EC's powers in this area,[89] as did academics.[90] But surely powers over 'repatriation of illegal residents' logically had to include deportation measures, since the Treaty did not refer only to

---

[82] See the analysis in 2.2.3.2 and 3.2.4 above.   [83] See 6.2.4 above.

[84] Art 4(2)(j) TFEU; see 2.2.4 above.   [85] Art 2(2) TFEU; see ibid.

[86] The reason such principles apply only to asylum legislation adopted *after* the entry into force of the Treaty is that before that date, the Treaty limited EC asylum law to setting minimum standards only, whereas it did not apply such a limit as regards legislation concerning irregular migration.

[87] For the full analysis of this issue, see 5.2.4 above.

[88] On the content of those obligations in this area, see 7.3.1 below.

[89] See, for instance, the Nassauer report on the proposed Directive on mutual recognition of expulsion orders (A5-0394/2000, 11 Dec 2000).

[90] See K Hailbronner, 'European Immigration and Asylum Law after the Amsterdam Treaty', (1998) 35 CMLRev 1047 and J Monar, 'Justice and Home Affairs in the Treaty of Amsterdam: Reform at the Price of Fragmentation' (1998) 23 ELRev 320.

voluntary repatriation. Equally, mutual recognition of expulsion measures was not excluded from the scope of the EC's powers, and surely competence over 'illegal immigration and illegal residence' had to include internal enforcement measures against common breaches of immigration law such as overstays and clandestine entry. It is doubtful whether the changes made by the Treaty of Lisbon to the legal base in this area (to refer to 'unauthorised' residence, and add a reference to 'removal') have added to the EC's (now the EU's) competence, because persons who are not authorized to reside would likely be considered 'illegal' anyway, and the previous powers over irregular migration, which are expressly non-exhaustive ('including...') were obviously apt to include competence concerning removals, which presumably differ from 'repatriation' in that a 'removal' could take place other than to the country of origin. Indeed, several measures adopted before the entry into force of the Treaty of Lisbon address this issue.[91]

However, even after the entry into force of the Treaty of Lisbon, the EU (like the EC before it) still lacks the power to regulate irregular *employment* as such, as it is not mentioned in Article 79 TFEU (or in the prior Article 63(3)(b) EC), or in the social policy provisions of the TFEU (previously the EC Treaty). However, the EU (and the EC before it) can regulate this issue indirectly where it is ancillary to one of the powers which clearly has been conferred upon the EU. This allowed the EC to use the powers conferred by the prior Article 63(3)(b) EC to prohibit the employment of irregular migrants.[92] The EC could also (using the same legal base) have regulated the position of persons who had definitively lost their legal status because of irregular employment, or used its legal migration powers (as it did) to set out the circumstances in which employment may or must be authorized (thus indirectly regulating irregular employment), and/or in which unauthorized employment will terminate legal migration status.[93] The Treaty of Lisbon has now conferred these powers on the EU, pursuant to Article 79 TFEU.

As for the distinction between EU competence over criminal law as compared to immigration law,[94] first of all, the EU's express power to regulate trafficking in persons only extends to the regulation of immigration-related issues, as the *criminal* law response to trafficking in persons falls within the scope of the *lex specialis* set out in Article 83(1) TFEU. The distinction between Articles 79(2) and 83(1) TFEU is important because an 'emergency brake' applies to the adoption of legislation under the latter provision, but not the former.[95] So the agreed

---

[91] See generally 7.7 below.   [92] Dir 2009/52, [2009] OJ L 168/24.

[93] On this issue, see the more detailed argument in S Peers and N Rogers, *EU Immigration and Asylum Law: Text and Commentary* (1st edn, Martinus Nijhoff, 2006), ch 3. See also the Council resolution on irregular employment, adopted as an employment policy measure ([2003] OJ C 260/1).

[94] See further 10.2.4 and 10.4.1 below.   [95] On the 'emergency brake', see 2.2.3.4.1 above.

Directive on the criminal law aspects of trafficking in persons correctly uses legal bases concerning criminal law only.[96]

The criminal law aspects of facilitation of irregular migration, or of sanctioning employers of irregular migrants,[97] now fall within the scope of Article 83(2) TFEU, which provides for EU competence over criminal law measures if such measures are necessary to ensure the effective implementation of a Union policy, once harmonization measures have been adopted. The same decision-making procedure applies to the adoption of such measures as applied to the original Union policy, except that the 'emergency brake' is again applicable.[98]

7.2.5. Territorial scope

All of the measures discussed in this chapter build upon the Schengen *acquis*, with the exception of the readmission treaties; the measure funding external migration management; the Directive on trafficking victims; the return fund; the Directive on sanctioning employers of irregular migrants; and the Framework Decision (and the subsequent agreed Directive) on trafficking in persons.[99] Several measures build on the Schengen *acquis* in part, to the extent that they apply to persons who no longer meet the criteria for short stays within the Schengen area: the Decision on the system for exchange of operational information; the Decision on financing of expulsion decisions; the Directive on transit for expulsion; and the Returns Directive.[100] The specific rules on participating in Schengen measures (see further below) therefore applied to such measures.

Several measures discussed in this chapter do not fall within the scope of the immigration provisions of the TFEU (previously Title IV of Part Three of the EC Treaty): the Regulation on migration management funding (which fell within the scope of EC development policy and policy on cooperation with non-developing countries) and the Framework Decisions on trafficking in persons and facilitation of irregular entry (which fell within the scope of the previous third pillar). So those measures apply to all Member States, and to non-Member States.

The UK and Ireland are covered by all of the measures considered in this chapter, except for: the Directive on trafficking victims; the Decision on financing expulsions (the UK is covered in part, while Ireland is not covered at all); the 2003 Directive on transit for expulsion; the Returns Directive; the Directive on sanctions for employers of irregular migrants; the Decision on the system for exchange of operational information (which covers the UK fully, but Ireland only to the extent that it builds on the Schengen *acquis*); and EU readmission treaties

---

[96] On the substance, see 7.5.4 below. On the correctness of the *particular* criminal law legal bases on which the proposal is based, see 9.2.4 and 10.2.4 below.   [97] See 7.5.3 and 7.5.4 below.
[98] See further 10.4.1.2 below.   [99] See 7.5.4, 7.6, 7.8, and 7.9 below.
[100] See 7.7 and 7.8 below.

(the UK has opted into all of them, but Ireland has only opted in to the treaty with Hong Kong). Both Member States have also opted into to Articles 26 and 27 of the Schengen Convention.[101]

As for Denmark, its position regarding measures adopted before the entry into force of the Treaty of Lisbon follows the scope of the previous Title IV EC and the Schengen *acquis*. So it is covered by the Framework Decisions on trafficking in persons and facilitation of irregular entry (which fell outside the scope of Title IV). It decided to apply in full or in part the Decision on the system for exchange of operational information, the Decision on financing of expulsion decisions, and the Directives on mutual recognition of expulsion measures and transit for expulsion, to the extent that they built on the Schengen *acquis* (ie as regards persons who no longer meet the conditions for entry as set out in the Schengen Borders Code, or who never met those conditions).[102] It could not participate in the readmission treaties, the measure funding external migration management, the Directive on trafficking victims or the Return Fund, although a Joint Declaration to each readmission treaty encourages the EU's contracting partner to negotiate a readmission treaty separately with Denmark.

As for the newer Member States, the measures in this chapter applied immediately as from their accession (or, if they first applied later, at the same date as the other Member States), except for the Directive on mutual recognition of expulsion orders and the connected Decision on funding expulsions, which only applied (or will apply) fully when the Schengen rules were (or will be) fully applied for each of the newer Member States in turn.

Pursuant to their association with the Schengen *acquis*,[103] Norway, Iceland, Switzerland, and (in future) Liechtenstein are not covered by the measures outside the scope of that *acquis*: the readmission treaties (although each treaty contains a Joint Declaration urging the negotiation of parallel agreements with Schengen associates); the Directive on trafficking victims; the return fund Decision; the Directive on sanctioning employers of irregular migrants; the Framework Decision (and agreed Directive) on trafficking in persons; and the measures on immigration statistics. Like Denmark, they are covered in part by those measures which build on the Schengen *acquis* in part (as regards persons who no longer meet the criteria for short stays within the Schengen area): the Decision on the system for exchange of operational information; the Decision on financing of expulsion decisions; the Directive on transit for expulsion; and the Returns Directive. They are fully covered by everything else.

---

[101] See the Decisions on the UK participation in the Schengen *acquis* ([2000] OJ L 141/43, applicable from 1 Jan 2005: [2004] OJ L 395/70) and on Irish participation in the Schengen *acquis* ([2002] OJ L 64/20, not yet applied), as well as the preambles to the relevant legislation and treaties.

[102] Council docs 14261/01, 23 Nov 2001; 9963/02, 20 June 2002; 10661/04, 18 Jun 2004; 12195/04, 10 Sep 2004; and 12907/04, 29 Sep 2004.   [103] See further 2.2.5.4 above.

7.3. Human rights

7.3.1. European Convention on Human Rights

The starting point for the consideration of the human rights aspects of irregular migration is the European Convention on Human Rights (ECHR). Examining the relevant ECHR rights in turn, Articles 2 and 3 ECHR (and possibly other ECHR provisions as well) prevent persons from being expelled to a country where they would face the death penalty or a sufficient risk of torture or other inhuman or degrading treatment.[104] Article 5(1)(f) ECHR provides that a person can be deprived of liberty following a 'lawful arrest or detention . . . to prevent his [or her] effecting an unauthorized entry into the country or of a person against who action is being taken with a view to deportation'. It is considered further below.

As regards trafficking in persons, Article 4(1) ECHR prohibits holding people in slavery or servitude,[105] and Article 4(2) proscribes any requirement to perform forced or compulsory labour.[106] According to the Human Rights Court, Article 4 creates positive obligations for States, to criminalize actions by private persons; 'forced or compulsory labour' covers cases where an underage migrant who had not been authorized to reside feared police arrest and expulsion and was induced by promises of regularized status; 'slavery' means a case of actual ownership of a person; and 'servitude' is 'an obligation to provide one's services that is imposed by the use of coercion'.[107] Moreover, trafficking in persons, as defined in UN and Council of Europe instruments, falls within the scope of Article 4, and there is a positive obligation on States to take operational measures to protect persons from trafficking if their authorities 'were aware, or ought to have been aware, of circumstances giving rise to a credible suspicion that an identified individual had been, or was at real and immediate risk of being, trafficked'.[108]

Next, the right to a fair trial set out in Article 6 ECHR does not apply to immigration disputes,[109] although as discussed below, the principles of a fair trial and effective remedies have a wider scope within the context of EU law.[110]

Article 8 ECHR, which protects against expulsion where family or private life is established in a State,[111] can apply to irregular migrants. It appears that if the migrant has been convicted of serious crimes, his or her irregular status is a further aggravating factor supporting expulsion; but conversely, if the State's

---

[104] See further 5.3.1 above.
[105] It is not possible to derogate from this provision in times of emergency: see Art 15(2) ECHR.
[106] This provision *is* subject to possible derogation pursuant to Art 15 ECHR; moreover, Art 4(3) ECHR lists forms of labour which are not covered by this proscription.
[107] *Siliadin v France* (Reports of Judgments and Decisions 2005-VII).
[108] *Rantsev v Cyprus and Russia*, 7 Jan 2010. On these international instruments, see 7.5.4 below.
[109] *Maaouia v France* (2000-X).   [110] See 7.3.4.   [111] See generally 6.3.1 above.

interest in expulsion is purely economic and the migrant has established a strong family life with his or her small children, the irregular migration status must be disregarded.[112] In certain circumstances, States must regularize the status of irregular migrants.[113] Article 8 is also relevant to data protection, an issue which arises in the context of irregular migration.[114]

Next, the Fourth Protocol to the ECHR contains a number of important rights, although it has not been ratified by two Member States.[115] Article 3 of the Protocol gives nationals the right to enter the territory of their own State, and freedom from expulsion from their own State. Article 4 of the Protocol prohibits the collective expulsion of foreigners, implicitly regardless of their immigration status. These rights are not subject to any limitations, although they are subject to the 'public emergency' derogation set out in Article 15 ECHR.

The rights set out in Article 3 of the Fourth Protocol have not yet been the subject of a judgment by the Human Rights Court,[116] although admissibility decisions have made clear that Article 3 leaves intact a State's power to determine who are its own nationals.[117] Article 3 of the Fourth Protocol can be compared to Article 12(4) of the International Covenant on Civil and Political Rights (ICCPR), which all Member States have ratified. This provision states that '[n]o-one may be arbitrarily deprived of the right to enter his [or her] own country'.[118] Unlike the ECHR clause, the provision does not expressly set out a ban on expulsion (although this is surely a necessary corollary of the right to enter); the right extends beyond nationals of the country; and it sets out a possible justification for State action (it must merely be non-'arbitrary'), rather than an apparently absolute ban.

As for Article 4 of the Fourth Protocol, the Human Rights Court has issued only two judgments, defining collective expulsion as 'any measure compelling aliens, as a group, to leave a country, except where such a measure is taken on the basis of a reasonable and objective examination of the particular case of each individual alien of the group'.[119] In the *Conka* judgment, the Court ruled that even where individual decisions had been taken, it could examine the background to them; in this particular case, the stated political intention of removing a particular group of people from the territory and the standardized procedure followed to

---

[112] See respectively the cases of *Dalia v France* (Reports 1998-I) and *Da Silva and Hoogkamer v Netherlands*, 31 Jan 2006.   [113] See 6.3.1 above.

[114] See 12.3.2 below.

[115] Greece and the UK. See also Art 2 of the Protocol, which grants free movement within a territory and the freedom to leave any country, discussed further in 3.3 above.

[116] See *Denizci and others v Cyprus* (Reports 2001-V), where the Court declined to rule on an allegation that Art 3 had been breached.

[117] *Slivenko v Latvia* (23 Jan 2002) and *Nagula v Estonia* (25 Oct 2005).

[118] On the interpretation of the ICCPR provisions, S Joseph, J Schultz, and M Castan, *The International Covenant on Civil and Political Rights: Cases, Materials and Commentary* (2nd edn, OUP, 2004), 364–376.   [119] *Conka v Belgium* (Reports 2002-I).

that end amounted to a collective expulsion. Furthermore, there were extensive procedural rights which had to be observed before the expulsion could be carried out, in particular the suspensive effect of any challenges to enforcement of the expulsion decisions. On the other hand, where an asylum seeker's application had been the subject of an individual assessment of its merits, a State did not violate Article 4 simply because it expelled him on a 'joint flight' together with other expellees.[120] Article 4 has no equivalent in the ICCPR, but then the procedural rights in cases of individual expulsion decisions set out in Article 13 ICCPR (on which, see below) should necessarily prevent collective expulsions.

Finally, the Seventh Protocol to the ECHR, which four Member States have not ratified,[121] sets out procedural rights applicable to individual cases of expulsion (Article 1 of the Protocol). A lawfully resident foreigner may only be expelled following a 'decision reached in accordance with law' and has the right to submit reasons against expulsion, have the case reviewed, and be represented for this purpose before a 'competent authority'. A State may insist that these rights can be exercised only after expulsion, 'when expulsion is necessary in the interests of public order or is grounded on reasons of national security'. These procedural rights are nearly identical to those set out in Article 13 of the ICCPR,[122] and (as regards refugees lawfully on the territory) very similar to Article 32(2) of the Geneva Convention on the status of refugees.[123]

First of all, as for the personal scope of the ECHR provision, the Human Rights Court has ruled that a failed asylum seeker can no longer be regarded as lawfully in the territory.[124] As distinct from persons whose visas had expired and who had no reasonable expectation of being permitted to stay once an asylum application was turned down, Article 1 of the Seventh Protocol applied to persons who had been lawfully admitted for residence, issued a residence permit, and were eligible for and had applied for extensions of that permit,[125] as well as persons issued a valid long-stay visa who were not subject to a deportation order.[126] The application of the Protocol could not cease simply because a person who was previously legally resident had become subject to an expulsion order, and status of 'resident' is not lost simply because a person who has not established any residence in another State takes a short trip abroad from his normal State of residence.[127] An 'expulsion' has an autonomous meaning, and applies to any act

---

[120] *Sultani v France*, 20 Sep 2007.   [121] Belgium, Germany, the Netherlands, and the UK.

[122] The difference is that there is no 'public order' exception in Art 13 ICCPR. On the interpretation of this clause, see S Joseph, J Schultz, and M Castan (n 118 above) at 377–387.

[123] Art 32(1) of this Convention also sets out substantive limitations on the expulsion of such refugees, and of course Art 33 of the Convention further sets out a rule of *non-refoulement*. Art 32(3) also provides that expelled refugees must be given a 'reasonable period of time' in which to seek admission to another State. On Art 32, see J Hathaway, *The Rights of Refugees under International Law* (Cambridge University Press, 2005), 659–695.   [124] *Sultani v France*, n 120 above.

[125] *Bolat v Russia* (ECHR 2006-XI).   [126] *Nolan v Russia*, 12 Feb 2009.

[127] *Nolan*, ibid.

other than extradition which compels a person to depart from the territory, in particular to removal of a person from his home and placing him on a flight to another country,[128] and to banning re-entry to the State of residence after his next trip abroad.[129]

Secondly, as to the specific procedural rights established by Article 1 of the Seventh Protocol, the European Court of Human Rights has ruled that the right to a decision 'in accordance with the law' was violated where the relevant national law lacked sufficient basic safeguards and the national court did not examine the merits of the administration's decisions.[130] It is also not in accordance with the 'law' to expel a foreign national without a judicial order, where national law requires such an order to be issued as a condition for expulsion.[131] Furthermore, even where there was an alleged breach of 'national security', the specific rights to submit reasons against expulsion and to have the case reviewed were violated where the person concerned was not informed of the offence of which he was suspected, he did not have a copy of the order against him until the (only) day of his hearing, and the national court refused a request for adjournment.[132] The right to a review of the case was violated where a national court refused to gather evidence regarding the allegations to the expulsion decision, or to review the merits of the national decision,[133] and where there was a three-month delay in the communication of the decision on expulsion, there was no possibility to submit reasons against the expulsion and to have the case reviewed with the assistance of counsel.[134] There was no justification for preventing in-country exercise of the procedural rights where the 'national security' arguments were not genuine (the deprivation of in-country procedural rights could in any event in that case still only be justified if this were necessary and proportionate), and where there was no convincing argument for the 'public order' exception to apply.[135]

Finally, it should be recalled that Articles 2 and 3 ECHR (as regards asylum) and Article 8 ECHR (as regards family reunion and long-term residents) also contain implied procedural rights.[136]

7.3.2. Geneva Convention and detention issues

The other main source of international legal rules governing the rights of irregular migrants is the Geneva Convention on the status of refugees. Article 31(1) of this

---

[128] *Bolat*, n 125 above.   [129] *Nolan*, n 126 above.

[130] *Lupsa v Romania* (Reports of Judgments and Decisions 2006-VII); *Kaya v Romania*, 12 Oct 2006; and *CG v Bulgaria*, 24 Apr 2008. In the latter case, the Court confirmed that the 'in accordance with the law' requirement must be interpreted in the same way as other similar provisions in the ECHR, for example in Art 8(2).   [131] *Bolat*, n 125 above.

[132] *Lupsa* and *Kaya*, n 130 above.   [133] *CG*, n 130 above.   [134] *Nolan*, n 126 above.

[135] *CG* and *Nolan*, (both n 130 above). The Court also stated in *CG* that any use of the 'public order' exception would be subject to the principle of proportionality.

[136] See 5.3 and 6.3.1 above.

Convention specifies that States 'shall not impose penalties, on account of their illegal entry or presence, on refugees who, coming directly from a country where their life or freedom was threatened in the sense of Article 1 [of the Convention], enter or are present in their territory without authorization, provided they present themselves without delay to the authorities and show good cause for their illegal entry or presence'. Article 31(2) then provides that States shall only restrict the movement of such refugees if 'necessary' and only until 'their status in the country is regularized or they obtain admission to another country'. Although it is considered in this chapter because of its relevance to irregular migration, Article 31 is obviously also relevant to EU rules on visas and external borders, which were discussed in detail in Chapters 3 and 4.

A detailed analysis of Article 31(1) suggests convincingly that:[137] the provision applies to asylum seekers as well as recognized refugees; it does not apply to removal from the territory, in effect because Articles 32 and 33 of the Convention are *lex specialis* rules concerning removal (the latter applying regardless of the migration status of the refugee);[138] the refugees can present themselves to any authorities, although they cannot rely on the provision after their apprehension unless there was no reasonable possibility to contact the authorities beforehand; the 'without delay' criterion must be applied on a case-by-case basis, without the application of any inflexible deadline; the 'coming directly' criterion means that persons who have obtained refuge in another State cannot enjoy the benefit of Article 31, but that persons who have transited through other States and who feared persecution in other States can still benefit from it; and a 'good cause' explanation can be invoked by persons fleeing persecution and who needed to avoid rejection at the border. While Article 31(1) cannot be invoked by bodies that or persons who assist refugees to avoid immigration rules, it was recognized that States should refrain from initiating prosecutions in such cases. The definition of 'penalties' encompasses criminal and civil/administrative penalties, plus arguably different (lower) standards of procedural rules applicable to the consideration of the refugee claims and the denial of benefits.[139]

As for Article 31(2), the possibility of detention on grounds of irregular entry per se is only possible until an initial assessment has been made and the person concerned is admitted to the asylum determination process. The necessity test imposed by this provision also entails a proportionality requirement, so refugees must be released from detention if bail is provided or if they agree to reside in accommodation centres, and can only be detained if there are specific reasons, such as a risk of absconding.

---

[137] Hathaway, n 123 above, 370–439. See also G Goodwin-Gill, 'Article 31 of the 1951 Convention Relating to the Status of Refugees: Non-penalization, Detention and Protection', in E Feller, V Turk, and F Nicholson, eds, *Refugee Protection in International Law: UNHCR's Global Consultations on Refugee Protection* (Cambridge University Press, 2003), 185.

[138] On those provisions, see 5.3 above.   [139] On these issues, see 5.7 and 5.9 above.

This brings us to the more general issue of the detention of irregular migrants. As noted above, Article 5(1)(f) ECHR permits detention of persons in accordance with the law in order to prevent unauthorized entry or against whom action is being taken as regards deportation; this is subject to safeguards to inform that person about the grounds for detention (Article 5(2)), to permit judicial review (Article 5(4)), and to compensate persons in case of breaches of this Article (Article 5(5)). Article 5 applies to detention within immigration transit zones,[140] as well as to detention following the interception of a vessel on the high seas.[141] While the detention of children pursuant to Article 5(1)(f) is not prohibited, any immigration detention of children must be adapted to their particular vulnerability in order to be lawful.[142]

Most of the cases concern detention with a view to deportation: the Human Rights Court has ruled that in such cases, it is sufficient that expulsion proceedings are underway and are being pursued with 'due diligence' in order to justify continued detention pursuant to Article 5; there is not a separate 'necessity' requirement, even though such a requirement applies to other grounds of permissible detention.[143] Detention is therefore no longer justified if the removal is unfeasible, and if an alternative measure to prevent absconding can be applied in practice.[144]

Also, Article 5(1) is violated where authorities mislead asylum seekers and render remedies inaccessible,[145] where national law does not set out sufficiently precise details of the basis for detention,[146] or where the national law in question is breached.[147] As for detention in order to prevent unauthorized entry, the leading

---

[140] See *Amuur v France* (Reports 1996-III), *Shamsa v Poland* (27 Nov 2003), *Riad and Idiab v Belgium* (24 Jan 2008), and *Nolan* (n 126 above).   [141] *Medvedyev v France*, 29 Mar 2010.

[142] *Mayeka and Mitunga v Belgium* (Reports of Judgments and Decisions [2006] ECR-XI) and *Muskhadzhiyeva v Belgium* (19 Jan 2010).

[143] *Chahal v UK* (Reports 1996-V), *Slivenko* (n 117 above), *Singh v Czech Republic* (25 Jan 2005), and *Raza v Bulgaria* (11 Feb 2010); the 'due diligence' requirement was violated in the *Singh* and *Raza* cases. On the ECHR and ICCPR jurisprudence, see D Wilsher, 'Detention of Asylum-Seekers and Refugees and International Human Rights Law' in P Shah, ed, *The Challenge of Asylum to Legal Systems* (Cavendish, 2005), 145. On this issue, see J Hughes and F Liebaut, eds, *Detention of Asylum-Seekers in Europe: Analysis and Perspectives* (Martinus Nijhoff, 1998).

[144] *Mikolenko v Estonia*, 8 Oct 2009.   [145] *Conka* (n 119 above).

[146] Case law beginning with *Soldatenko v Ukraine*, 23 Oct 2008; see also *Sadaykov v Bulgaria*, 22 May 2008, *Khudyakova v Russia*, 8 Jan 2009 and *Abdolkhani and Karimnia v Turkey*, 22 Sep 2009. On the specific situation of cases where the European Court of Human Rights has blocked the expulsion pending its decision on the merits of an application, see *Gebremedhin v France*, 26 Apr 2007.

[147] See: *Khudyakova* (ibid); *Riad and Idiab*, n 140 above (detention continuing despite court orders for release); *Eminbeyli v Russia*, 26 Feb 2009 (no extradition of refugees permitted under national law); *SD v Greece*, 11 June 2009 (no detention of asylum seekers permitted under national law); *Hokic v Italy*, 1 Dec 2009 (where detention continued after the deportation order had been set aside); *Shchebet v Russia*, 12 June 2008; *Dzhurayev v Russia*, 17 Dec 2009; *Rusu v Austria*, 2 Oct 2008 (where a 'necessity' requirement was part of national law); and *Khaydarov v Russia*, 20 May 2010. For an example of lawful detention, see *Liu v Russia*, 6 Dec 2007.

case is *Saadi v UK*,[148] in which the Human Rights Court ruled that: the provision can apply to asylum seekers; entry can be regarded as 'unauthorised' if it has not yet been authorized, and even if the persons concerned are trying to effect an authorized entry for asylum purposes; and the principles for justifying detention are the same as those applicable to detention cases. The key test is:

... such detention must be carried out in good faith; it must be closely connected to the purpose of preventing unauthorised entry of the person to the country; the place and conditions of detention should be appropriate, bearing in mind that 'the measure is applicable not to those who have committed criminal offences but to aliens who, often fearing for their lives, have fled from their own country'; and the length of the detention should not exceed that reasonably required for the purpose pursued.[149]

On the facts of this case, detention for the purpose of fast-track processing was in good faith and was related to the prevention of unauthorized entry; the detention centre was adapted to asylum seekers and had relevant facilities, notably legal assistance; and the length of detention (seven days) was not unreasonable.

Next, the right to information about detention set out in Article 5(2) ECHR has been violated in a number of immigration detention cases, or analogous extradition cases.[150] Article 5(4) is violated where, inter alia, national security considerations preclude any judicial review of detention in expulsion cases,[151] and in a number of other immigration and/or extradition cases.[152] Finally, Article 5(5) has also been violated in some immigration and/or extradition detention cases.[153] Article 3 ECHR also protects migrants against mistreatment during detention (or during removal operations) which is sufficiently severe to amount to torture or other inhuman or degrading treatment.[154]

The position under the ECHR can be contrasted with the ICCPR, Article 9 of which protects individuals against arbitrary detention, and Article 10 of which sets standards for detention conditions.[155] Article 9 has been interpreted by the Human Rights Committee to require a necessity test for detention of asylum seekers who entered irregularly, for example requiring the State to give specific

---

[148] Grand Chamber judgment, 29 Jan 2008.

[149] Para 74 of the judgment (ibid), case law reference omitted.

[150] See: *Saadi v UK* (ibid); *Abdolkhani and Karimnia* (n 146 above); *Rusu* (idem); as regards detention at the border; *Kaboulov v Ukraine* (19 Nov 2009); and *Khodzhayev v Russia*, 12 May 2010.

[151] See *Chahal* (n 143 above) and *Al-Nashif v Bulgaria* (10 June 2002).

[152] See, for instance, *Conka* (n 119 above); *Singh* (n 143 above); *Soldatenko* (n 146 above); *SD v Greece* (n 147 above); *Eminbeyli* (n 147 above); *Shchebet* (n 147 above); *Nolan* (n 126 above); *Dzhurayev* (n 147 above); *Raza* (n 143 above); *Abdolkhani and Karimnia* (n 145 above) and *Khaydarov* (n 147 above).

[153] See: *Nolan* (ibid) and *Kaboulov* (n 150 above).

[154] For instance, see *Mogos v Romania* (17 Oct 2005), concerning treatment in a transit centre, and similarly *Riad and Idiab* (n 140 above); see also: *Dougoz v Greece* (2001 ECHR-II); *Tabesh v Greece* (26 Nov 2009); *Shchebet* (n 147 above); *SD v Greece* (n 147 above); *AA v Greece* (22 July 2010); and *Shchukin v Cyprus* (29 July 2010). There are special considerations as regards the detention conditions of children: see *Mayeka and Mitunga* and *Muskhadzhiyeva* (n 142 above).

[155] On these ICCPR provisions, see Joseph et al (n 118 above), at 303–347 and 274–293.

reasons for the detention of individuals and to demonstrate why alternative forms of control of movement are not sufficient.

7.3.3. Other rights

Rights for irregular migrants are specifically guaranteed by the UN Convention on Migrant Workers and certain conventions adopted by the International Labour Organization. However, these conventions have attracted little or no ratifications from EU Member States to date, in particular because of their provisions concerning irregular migrants, and so they are not considered in detail here.[156]

7.3.4. Application to EU law[157]

To what extent do the relevant rules discussed above form part of the general principles of EU law, and/or the EU Charter of Fundamental Rights? The Court of Justice has ruled many times that the right to family life (as manifested in family reunion) and the right to a fair trial and effective remedies for protection of rights form part of the general principles; it has more recently confirmed that the freedom from, for example torture also forms part of the general principles.[158] These rights are also set out in the Charter.[159] A crucial point is that, in the context of both the general principles and the Charter, the right to a fair trial and to effective remedies have a wider scope where there is a link to EU law, applying in particular to immigration proceedings, raising the prospect that procedural rights equivalent to those guaranteed by Articles 6 and 13 ECHR apply regardless of the limitations of the Seventh Protocol to the ECHR (non-application to some Member States, limited list of rights, restriction to lawful residents). The Court has not yet had an opportunity to rule on whether the right to life, the prohibition of slavery, etc, and the ECHR restrictions on detention are recognized part of the general principles of EU law, but it would be astounding if they were not; and in any event, there are relevant provisions in the Charter.[160]

   In the case of restrictions on detention, in light of the more favourable rules applied by the Human Rights Committee when interpreting the ICCPR, it may be necessary to revisit the issue of whether the Court of Justice can accept that the rulings of that Committee can be considered a source of the general principles

---

[156] See 6.3.3 above.

[157] On human rights in EU law, see generally 2.3 above. On human rights in this area of EU law, see R Cholewinski, 'European Union Policy on Irregular Migration: Human Rights Lost?' in B Bogusz, et al, eds, *Irregular Migration and Human Rights* (Martinus Nijhoff, 2004), 159.

[158] See 6.3.4 above and Case C-465/07 *Elgafaji* [2009] ECR I-921.

[159] Arts 4, 7 and 47 ([2007] OJ C 303).   [160] Arts 2, 5, and 6 (ibid).

of EU law,[161] although in any event the EU's Returns Directive incorporates the ICCPR jurisprudence on the 'necessity' of immigration detention.[162]

As for the ECHR Protocols, EU law also recognizes the principle set out in Article 3 of the Fourth Protocol that 'Member States have no authority to expel [their nationals] from the territory or deny them access thereto',[163] although the Court of Justice has only referred to the source of this principle as human rights law on one occasion,[164] and has not formally recognized this principle as a human right forming part of the general principles of EU law, and there is no express provision in the Charter on this point. In fact, the Court has made use of the principle only to distinguish between a Member State's own citizens and nationals of other Member States (or non-Member States) in order to legitimize the greater protection which Member States may afford to the former in certain circumstances. The reason for the limited recognition of the source of the rule in human rights law may be that EU free movement law does not grant rights to EU citizens in their 'own' Member State, unless they have previously exercised free movement rights,[165] and that EU law does not generally impinge upon Member States' rights to determine who their own citizens are.[166] Nonetheless, if a Member State tried to prevent its own citizens (as it defines them) from entering its territory from another Member State, the issue would fall within the scope of EU free movement law, and so the Court of Justice would presumably officially recognize the right as forming part of the general principles of EU law; it should be recalled that this right appears in the ICCPR, which all Member States have ratified.[167]

On the other hand, the Court of Justice has not yet ruled on whether the rights set out in Article 4 of the Fourth ECHR Protocol, or Article 1 of the

---

[161] See 2.3 above.   [162] See 7.7.1 below.

[163] Cases 41/74 *Van Duyn* [1974] ECR 1337, para 22; 115/81 and 116/81 *Adoui and Cornuaille* [1982] ECR 1665, para 7; C-370/90 *Singh* [1992] ECR I-4265, para 22; C-65/65 and 111/95 *Shingara and Radiom* [1997] ECR I-3343, para 28; C-171/96 *Roque* [1998] ECR I-4607, para 37; C-348/96 *Calfa* [1999] ECR I-11, para 20; C-235/99 *Kondova* [2001] ECR I-6557, para 83; C-257/99 *Barkoci and Malik* [2001] ECR I-6427, para 80; C-63/99 *Gloszczuk* [2001] ECR I-6369, para 78; and C-100/01 *Olazabal* [2002] ECR I-10981, para 40.

[164] In the *Singh* judgment, ibid, para 22, it referred to the Fourth Protocol to the ECHR, although not to the ICCPR, and also stated that the right was derived from national citizenship, not EU law. In *Van Duyn*, *Roque* (para 38), *Kondova* (para 84), *Barkoci and Malik* (para 81), and *Gloszczuk* (para 79), all ibid, it referred to the principle as a 'principle of international law, which the [EC] Treaty cannot be assumed to disregard in relations between Member States'.

[165] See generally 4.4.1 above; and in this field, see particularly the Opinion in Case C-192/99 *Kaur* [2001] ECR I-1237, which argued on this ground against the claim of a 'second-class' UK citizen pursuant to EU free movement law to enter the UK from outside the EU, even though she had referred to the Fourth Protocol to the ECHR.

[166] Compare the judgment in *Kaur*, ibid, to the judgment in Case C-135/08 *Rottmann*, judgment of 2 Mar 2010, not yet reported.

[167] On the rule of the ICCPR as a source of the general principles, see for instance Case C-540/03 *EP v Council* [2006] ECR I-5769.

Seventh Protocol, are protected as part of the general principles of EU law,[168] although the EU Charter refers expressly to the ban on collective expulsion in Article 4 of the Fourth Protocol.[169] Nor has the Court ruled on the status within the general principles or the Charter of Article 31 of the Geneva Convention, or indeed of any provision of that Convention, although the Court has ruled on the importance of that Convention as regards interpreting the EU legislation on the definition of refugees.[170] However, Article 31 is reflected implicitly in the provisions of the Schengen Borders Code, as regards external border control.[171]

As always, it should be recalled that the Court of Justice has also recognized the existence of other rights as part of the EU general principles, in particular the rights to dignity and integrity,[172] which may be relevant to detention conditions or the conditions of removal, or as a substantive ground to resist expulsion (ie because of the treatment the person concerned might suffer in the country of destination). These rights are also protected in the EU Charter.[173]

Finally, to the extent that some of the rights in the ICCPR and the ECHR Protocols do not appear in the EU Charter of Fundamental Rights, there is still an argument that they can be recognized as part of the general principles of EU law regardless. In any event, Member States must uphold their obligations under international human rights treaties which they have ratified.[174]

7.4. The impact of other EU law

As with other areas of immigration and asylum law, EU free movement law and EU association agreements have a considerable impact on the issue of irregular migration. EU development policy measures, EU statistics legislation, and EU data protection law are also relevant.[175]

7.4.1. Free movement law

EU free movement law applies both to EU citizens and to their family members, as long as they have exercised free movement rights within the EU. They have the right to move and reside in another Member State pursuant to the Treaty on the Functioning of the European Union (TFEU) (previously the EC Treaty) and/ or secondary legislation if they meet the relevant conditions. Since these rights

---

[168] The rule in Art 2 of the Fourth Protocol has been referred to: see 3.3.1 above.

[169] Art 19(1) of the Charter.   [170] See 5.3.2 above.   [171] See 3.6.1 above.

[172] See Cases C-36/02 *Omega* [2004] ECR I-9609 and C-377/98 *Netherlands v Council and EP* [2001] ECR I-7079.   [173] Arts 1 and 3.

[174] See generally 2.3 above.   [175] See respectively 7.9.2, 7.8, and 12.3.2 below.

are quite extensive, it is very difficult for EU citizens or their family members to be considered to be irregular migrants in another Member State. A number of specific issues are addressed by the case law and relevant legislation; the latter was consolidated and recast in Directive 2004/38, which Member States had to apply by 30 April 2006.[176]

The case law of the Court of Justice makes clear that EU citizens and their family members cannot be expelled from another Member State or imprisoned there simply for breaching formal administrative requirements, such as the obligation to hold a residence permit or to report to the authorities, if they satisfy the underlying conditions for the exercise of free movement rights.[177] In particular, third-country national family members who satisfy the underlying conditions cannot be expelled because they entered illegally or because their visa has expired.[178] Directive 2004/38, essentially codifying the prior case law, expressly states that while Member States may impose reporting obligations, sanctions for failure to breach those obligations must be 'proportionate and non-discriminatory'.[179] Also, EU citizens and their family members are entitled to stay in another Member State for up to three months on the basis only of a passport or (for EU citizens) an identity card.[180] After that point, the host Member State may require the EU citizen or family member to register with the authorities, subject again to the proviso that a failure to register can only be punished by 'proportionate and non-discriminatory' sanctions.[181] The Directive expressly states that breaches of the various administrative requirements cannot result in expulsion, and provides for procedural safeguards for persons whose free movement is restricted on grounds other than public policy, public security, and public health.[182] Again codifying the case law, the Directive specifies that possession of the various forms of residence documents mentioned in the Directive may 'under no circumstances' be a condition for exercising a right.[183]

Furthermore, the Court of Justice has ruled in several cases on the link between irregular migration status and access to social benefits, indicating that there are circumstances in which EU citizenship confers a right of access to benefits, with the result that the conditions for continued residence are satisfied and expulsion

[176] Dir 2004/38 ([2004] OJ L 229/35). For further details, see 3.4.1, 4.4.1, and 6.4.1 above.
[177] Cases: 48/75 *Royer* [1976] ECR 497; 118/75 *Watson and Bellman* [1976] ECR 1185; 8/77 *Sagulo and Others* [1977] ECR 1495; 157/79 *Pieck* [1980] ECR 2171; C-265/88 *Messner* [1989] ECR 4209; C-363/89 *Roux* [1991] ECR I-273; C-376/89 *Giagounidis* [1991] ECR I-1069; C-215/03 *Oulane* [2005] ECR I-1215; and C-408/03 *Commission v Belgium* [2006] ECR I-2647. See E Guild, 'Who is an Irregular Migrant?' in B Bogusz, et al, eds, *Irregular Migration and Human Rights* (Martinus Nijhoff, 2004), 3. See also Art 3(3) of Dir 64/221 (OJ Spec Ed, 1963–64, 117), which provided expressly that expulsion could not be ordered due to expiry of a passport or identity card.
[178] Case C-459/99 *MRAX* [2002] ECR I-6591.
[179] Art 5(5) of the Directive. See also Art 26.
[180] Art 6 of the Directive; this reproduces provisions in the prior legislation.
[181] Arts 8 and 9 of the Directive. See also Art 26.   [182] Art 15 of the Directive.
[183] Art 25(1) of the Directive.

cannot be carried out.[184] The Court has also ruled on whether third-country family members with irregular migration status can nonetheless rely on EU free movement law once they become part of the family of an EU citizen. At one point this case law was unclear,[185] but the Court has now overturned prior case law and clearly established that family members can rely on their connection with the sponsor regardless of their irregular immigration status, even if they were irregular migrants before they even met the sponsor and formed a family relationship.[186]

The 2004 Directive has substantially changed the rules concerning expulsion on grounds of public policy, public security, or public health.[187] Previously, these rules were set out in Directive 64/221.[188] The substantive provisions of the 1964 Directive, supplemented by extensive jurisprudence of the Court of Justice,[189] specified that it applied even where a person was not legally resident.[190] An expulsion could not be used to 'service economic ends'.[191] Also, expulsions on grounds of public security or public policy must be based 'exclusively' on the 'personal conduct' of the individual, and 'previous criminal convictions' must not 'in themselves' constitute grounds for expulsion,[192] although a host Member State may request another Member State to furnish the police records of a particular individual.[193] 'Personal conduct' may entail association with an organization; the organization need not necessarily be banned, although it must be subject to repressive measures by the State, and the definition of 'public policy' may differ between Member States, subject to supervision by the Court of Justice.[194] Moreover, the 'personal conduct' criterion means that Member States cannot expel persons as a general deterrent to other foreigners who might commit criminal activities, but only following a consideration of the personal circumstances of the particular individual.[195] Expulsion of non-nationals does not infringe the principle of non-discrimination, since it is generally not possible for a State to

---

[184] See particularly Cases: C-85/96 *Martinez Sala* [1998] ECR I-2691; C-184/99 *Grzelczyk* [2001] ECR I-6193; C-138/02 *Collins* [2004] ECR I-2703; C-456/02 *Trojani* [2004] ECR I-7572; C-209/03 *Bidar* [2005] ECR I-2119; C-258/04 *Ionnidis* [2005] ECR I-8275; and C-406/04 *De Cuyper* [2006] I-6947. See also Cases C-22/08 and C-23/08 *Vatsouras and Koupatantze* [2009] ECR I-4585, and E Szyszczak, 'Regularising Migration in the European Union' in Bogusz, et al (n 177 above), 407.

[185] See in particular Case C-109/01 *Akrich* [2003] ECR I-9607.

[186] Case C-127/08 *Metock* [2008] ECR I-6241; see further Case C-60/00 *Carpenter* [2002] ECR I-6279 and *MRAX* (n 178 above). In the interim see also Cases C-1/05 *Jia* [2007] ECR I-1 and C-291/05 *Eind* [2007] ECR I-10719.   [187] Arts 27–33 of the Directive.

[188] See n 177 above. See also the Commission's report on the derogations from free movement law (COM (1999) 372, 19 July 1999).

[189] See in particular *Van Duyn* (n 163 above), and Cases: 67/74 *Bonsignore* [1975] ECR 297; 36/75 *Rutili* [1975] ECR 1219; 30/77 *Bouchereau* [1977] ECR 1999; *Adoui and Cornuaille* (n 163 above); C-348/96 *Calfa* [1999] ECR I-11; C-100/01 *Olazabal* [2002] ECR I-10981; C-482/01 and C-493/01 *Orfanopolous and Olivieri* [2004] ECR I-5257; and C-441/02 *Commission v Germany* [2006] ECR I-3449.   [190] Case C-50/06 *Commission v Netherlands* [2007] ECR I-4383.

[191] Art 2(2) of the Directive.   [192] Art 3(1) and 3(2) of the Directive.

[193] Art 5(2) of the Directive. On criminal records, see further 9.6.1.4 below.

[194] *Van Duyn* and *Adoui and Cornuaille* (n 163 above).

[195] *Bouchereau*, n 189 above; see also Case C-50/06, n 190 above.

expel its own nationals.[196] A Member State may limit an individual to part of its territory only in certain circumstances, in particular where such a measure would be comparable to measures which could be imposed against its own nationals.[197] The concept of 'public policy' entails a requirement that the person concerned is a genuine and sufficiently serious threat affecting a fundamental interest of society; as the person concerned must be a 'present' threat, his or her past conduct is only decisive where it indicates a propensity to repeat the same actions in future.[198] An automatic expulsion for life following a conviction for specific crimes is therefore a breach of the EU rules.[199] As for public health, expulsion on such grounds can only take place in relation to specified illnesses and only before the issue of the first residence permit.[200]

The 1964 Directive also included procedural rights, in particular specifying that a decision to grant or refuse an initial residence permit had to be taken within six months; the individual could remain on the territory in the meantime.[201] Individuals had to be informed of the grounds of their expulsion, unless this was contrary to State security interests, and informed officially of the decision expelling them, with a period of a least fifteen days or (if they already had a residence permit) one month to leave the territory.[202] The Directive required that an expellee had remedies equal to those of a national challenging administrative acts,[203] and at the very least, where there were limited or non-existent rights of appeal, an expulsion decision could not be taken until the opinion of an independent competent authority had been obtained, except in cases of urgency.[204] These procedural rules also were also interpreted in extensive jurisprudence of the Court of Justice.[205]

The 2004 Directive amended the substantive criteria in the 1964 Directive by adding, as derived from the Court's jurisprudence, an express reference to the principle of proportionality and the requirement that the person concerned constitute a sufficiently serious individual threat to public policy.[206] Also, the later Directive expressly specifies that factors such as length of residence and degree

---

[196] See 7.3 above.   [197] *Rutili* and *Olazabal*, n 189 above.   [198] *Bonsignore*, n 189 above.
[199] *Calfa*, n 189 above.   [200] Art 4 and Annex to the Directive.
[201] Art 5(1) of the Directive. For a breach of this provision, see Case C-157/03 *Commission v Spain* [2005] ECR I-2911.   [202] Arts 6 and 7 of the Directive.
[203] Art 8 of the Directive.
[204] Art 9(1) of the Directive, concerning expulsion following the issue of a first residence permit. Where a permit had not yet been issued, Art 9(2) gave the person concerned the right to request the opinion of this competent authority.
[205] See: *Rutili* (n 189 above); *Royer* (n 177 above); Case 98/79 *Pecastaing* [1980] ECR 691; Case 131/79 *Santillo* [1980] ECR 1585; *Adoui and Cornuaille* (n 163 above); Joined Cases C-297/88 and C-197/89 *Dzodzi* [1990] ECR I-3763; Case C-175/94 *Gallagher* [1995] ECR I-4253; *Shingara and Radiom* (n 163 above); Case C-357/98 *Yiadom* [2000] ECR I-9265; *MRAX* (n 178 above); *Orfanopolous and Olivieri* (n 189 above); Case C-136/03 *Dorr and Unal* [2005] ECR I-4759; and the judgment in Case C-441/02 (n 189 above).
[206] Art 27(2) of the Directive. On proportionality, see para 99 of the judgment in *Orfanopolous and Olivieri* (ibid).

of integration must be taken into account when deciding on an expulsion.[207] A new point is that there is a more precise degree of protection for EU citizens and their family members who have resided for a longer period: permanent residents can only be expelled 'on serious grounds of public policy or public security' and minors and persons resident for over ten years can only be expelled on 'imperative grounds of public security'.[208] Expulsion on grounds of public health is now only possible within three months of arrival, although the substantive public health grounds have been amended and medical checks during the first three months are now expressly permitted.[209] The Court of Justice has ruled that, pursuant to the Directive, a Member State cannot restrict its nationals from travel to another Member State due to a breach of immigration law in that Member State prior to the former Member State joining the EU.[210]

As for procedural rules, the notification requirements have been clarified and all persons now have one month to leave the territory (except in urgent cases) if expelled.[211] Individuals are entitled to judicial (and possibly also administrative review) of the merits and legality of any expulsion decision, and subject to certain exceptions, the expulsion cannot be carried out if the expellee applies for an interim suspension of the order pending a decision on the appeal.[212] Expulsion orders have to be reviewed after three years to determine if the grounds motivating them are still valid.[213] Finally, if there is a delay in enforcement of the expulsion order of over two years, Member States must re-examine its validity before executing it.[214]

A Commission report on the application of Directive 2004/38 stated that all Member States except Ireland have set up a registration system applicable to EU citizens and their family members.[215] Thirteen Member States do not comply with the provision of the Directive which rules out expulsion as the automatic consequence of an application for social assistance, and four Member States make the right of residence conditional upon lawful entry. Implementation of the rules concerning expulsions is 'often insufficient or incomplete'; in particular, two Member States provide for automatic expulsion for certain crimes,

---

[207] Art 28(1) of the Directive. Again, see para 99 of the judgment in *Orfanopolous and Olivieri* (ibid).

[208] Art 28(2) and (3) of the Directive. On the concept of 'permanent residence', which was introduced by the Directive, see Arts 16–21, and Cases C-162/09 *Lassal* (opinion of 11 May 2010) and C-325/09 *Dias*, both pending. On the loss of permanent residence, see Case C-145/09 *Tsakouridis*, pending (opinion of 8 June 2010). On the interpretation of the substantive test for enhanced protection against expulsion, see *Tsakouridis* (*idem*) and Case C-348/09 *Infusino*, pending, and the relevant references concerning the EU–Turkey association agreement (7.4.2 below).

[209] Art 29 of the Directive.   [210] Case C-33/07 *Jipa* [2008] ECR I-5157.

[211] Art 30 of the Directive.   [212] Art 31 of the Directive.

[213] Art 32 of the Directive. See *Adoui and Cornuaille*, para 12, and *Shingara and Radiom*, paras 38–44 (both n 163 above).

[214] Art 33 of the Directive. See *Orfanopolous and Olivieri* (n 189 above), paras 77–82.

[215] COM (2008) 840, 10 Dec 2008.

and Italy increases the length of detention for irregular migrants who commit crimes. The Commission's guidance on the application of the Directive claims that 'persistent petty criminality' could in some cases provide a ground for expulsion.[216] As for the provision of the Directive that permits expulsion on grounds of 'abuse' or 'fraud',[217] the Commission guidance argues that 'fraud' constitutes a conviction for the use of forged documents or false representation of material facts, while an 'abuse' constitutes artificial conduct for the sole purpose of obtaining a right, while not complying with the purpose of EU law. A 'marriage of convenience' (also ruled out by the Directive) is a marriage agreed for the sole purpose of obtaining free movement rights, but a marriage cannot be regarded as such purely because it confers an immigration advantage. There can be no systematic checks on all third-country nationals, or all members of a particular ethnic group, but Member States' authorities can still link their checks to 'certain characteristics'. The communication offers 'indicative' lists of behaviour which suggests that a marriage is genuine on the one hand, or a marriage of convenience on the other, and of behaviour which suggests whether or not a move to another Member State has the sole purpose of evading national law. The burden of proof in asserting fraud or abuse is on national authorities. Time will tell whether the Court of Justice agrees with the Commission's analysis.

It should also be recalled that the Court of Justice has ruled that the Schengen *acquis*, and in particular the SIS, is subject to the application of Community law (as it was then), inter alia free movement law.[218] While the Court's ruling concerned the specific issue of visas and borders, the judgment would also be applicable by analogy to expulsion proceedings carried out on the basis of an SIS listing.

Finally, EU free movement law (Article 56 TFEU, formerly Article 49 EC) also grants to EU employers the right to post their third-country national employees to another Member State within the framework of the provision of services.[219] The Court has not yet delivered a judgment on whether Article 56 entails the right to post workers without the need to obtain visas or residence permits (thus preventing such workers from being considered irregular migrants in such circumstances), or whether expulsion of such workers on grounds of public policy, public security, or public health pursuant to Articles 52 and 62 TFEU (formerly Articles 46 and 55 EC) is subject to substantive and procedural rules identical to those applicable to free movement of EU citizens and their family members.

---

[216] COM (2009) 313, 2 July 2009.   [217] Art 35, Dir 2004/38.

[218] Case C-503/03 *Commission v Spain* [2006] ECR I-1097. See further 2.4.2, 3.4.1, and 3.6.1 above.

[219] Cases: C-43/93 *Van der Elst* [1994] ECR I-3803; C-445/03 *Commission v Luxembourg* [2004] ECR I-10191; C-244/04 *Commission v Germany* [2006] ECR I-885; C-168/04 *Commission v Austria* [2006] ECR I-9041; and C-219/08 *Commission v Belgium* [2009] ECR I-9213. Also, the EU's services Directive in part addresses this issue. On this Directive and other related issues, see 6.4.4 above; for further implications of the case law, see 3.4.1, 4.4.1, and 5.4.2 above.

However, the Court has ruled that an automatic refusal of entry and residence permits for a posted worker who has not obtained a visa is a breach of the Treaty rights.[220] By analogy, it is arguable that since entry and residence onto the territory is inherent in the freedom to provide services, any penalties imposed due to any failure to obtain any necessary permits must be proportionate, and in particular cannot entail expulsion or imprisonment. Logically, since the freedom to post workers derives directly from the Treaty, individual posted workers could only be expelled pursuant to substantive and procedural rules equivalent to those applying to EU citizens and their family members.

7.4.2. Association agreements

The EU's association agreements have implications for the definition of irregular migration.[221] To start with, the European Economic Area (EEA) agreement with Norway, Iceland, and Liechtenstein and the EU–Switzerland agreement on free movement of persons both essentially extend the EU rules on free movement of persons to these States.[222] It should follow that all of the relevant principles derived from EU free movement law, as discussed above, apply to these agreements.

Next, the status of Turkish nationals in the EU is governed by the initial EU–Turkey association agreement (the Ankara Agreement), a Protocol to that agreement dating from 1970, and Decision 1/80 of the EU–Turkey Association Council.[223] Although the Protocol establishes a standstill on national measures which make more restrictive the establishment of Turkish nationals or the supply of services from Turkey, the Court of Justice has ruled that this standstill cannot benefit those who have entered or stayed without authorization.[224] As for Turkish workers and their family members, they have rights to work and/or reside pursuant to Decision 1/80 following periods of employment or residence in a Member State, but that employment or residence must be authorized by the Member State in question; periods accrued solely during purely provisional residence pending expulsion or a decision on the grant of a residence permit do not qualify.[225] Furthermore, these rights cannot be acquired if the worker is convicted of fraud in relation to his or her immigration status.[226] On the other hand, if the

---

[220] See *Commission v Austria*, ibid.

[221] For an overview of the migration provisions of these agreements, see 6.4.3 above.

[222] Respectively [1994] OJ L 1/1 and [2002] OJ L 114

[223] The Agreement is published in [1977] OJ L 261/60; the Protocol is published in [1972] JO L 293/1; Decision 1/80 is unpublished in the OJ.

[224] Cases C-37/98 *Savas* [2000] ECR I-2927 (self-employed persons) and Joined Cases C-317/01 and C-369/01 *Abatay and others* [2003] ECR I-12301 (services). On the limits of this exception, see however Case C-16/05 *Tum and Dari* [2007] ECR I-7415.

[225] Cases C-192/89 *Sevince* [1990] ECR I-3461 and C-237/91 *Kus* [1992] ECR I-6781.

[226] Case C-285/95 *Kol* [1997] ECR I-3095. However, note that the link between the behaviour of the worker and the status of his or her family member is broken after a certain period: see Case

entry and residence status of the worker or family member is fundamentally legal, that person cannot be expelled merely for technical breaches of immigration law such as the failure to renew a residence permit on time;[227] the position of Turkish workers and family members on this point is therefore comparable to that of EU citizens.[228] As for the loss of residence on grounds of public policy, public security, and public health, Turkish workers and their family members within the scope of the Decision enjoy substantive and procedural protection at least equivalent to that enjoyed by EU citizens *before* the application of Directive 2004/38;[229] the question of whether they enjoy the *enhanced* protection in this regard offered by Directive 2004/38 is pending before the Court of Justice.[230]

The Europe Agreements with Central and Eastern European countries, which inter alia included provisions on the right of establishment of the self-employed,[231] have since been superseded by membership of the countries concerned, but the case law on these agreements could still be relevant to the establishment provisions of the Stabilization and Association Agreements (SAAs) with Western Balkan States, once those provisions are applied after a five-year waiting period.[232] The Europe Agreements case law specified that since those treaties allowed EU Member States could maintain immigration law restrictions, the right of establishment did not entail the right to enter and begin self-employment without prior authorization.[233] However, the Court of Justice made clear that a later application to exercise freedom of establishment pursuant to the Agreements always had to be considered, regardless of any prior irregular entry or residence.[234] If names had been placed in the SIS as a result of those prior offences, resulting in a refusal of entry to exercise the right of establishment on that ground alone,

---

C-337/07 *Altun* [2008] ECR I-10323. See now Case C-484/07 *Pehlivan*, pending (opinion of 8 July 2010).

[227] Cases C-434/93 *Bozkurt* [1995] ECR I-1475; C-351/95 *Kadiman* [1997] ECR I-2133; C-36/96 *Günaydin* [1997] ECR I-5143; C-98/96 *Ertanir* [1997] ECR I-5179; C-1/97 *Birden* [1998] ECR I-7747; and C-329/97 *Ergat* [2000] ECR I-1487.   [228] See 7.4.1 above.

[229] Cases C-340/97 *Nazli* [2000] ECR I-957, C-467/02 *Cetinkaya* [2004] ECR I-10895, and *Dorr and Unal* (n 205 above). See also Cases C-373/03 *Aydinli* [2005] ECR I-6181, C-383/03 *Dogan* [2005] ECR I-6237, C-502/04 *Torun* [2006] ECR I-1563, C-325/05 *Derin* [2007] ECR I-6495, and C-349/06 *Polat* [2007] ECR I-8167.

[230] Cases: C-371/08 *Ornek*; C-420/08 *Erdil*; and C-436/09 *Belkiran*, all pending. An earlier reference on this issue pre-dated the application of Dir 2004/38 (*Polat*, ibid).

[231] See further 6.4.3 above.

[232] [2004] OJ L 84 (Former Yugoslav Republic of Macedonia (FYROM)), [2005] OJ L 26 (Croatia), [2009] OJ L 107 (Albania), and [2010] OJ L 108 (Montenegro). SAAs have also been signed with Bosnia-Herzegovina (COM (2008) 182, 8 Apr 2008), and Serbia (COM (2007) 743, 20 Nov 2007), but these two SAAs are not yet in force. For further detail, see 3.4.1 above.

[233] See Cases C-235/99 *Kondova* [2001] ECR I-6557; C-257/99 *Barkoci and Malik* [2001] ECR I-6427; C-63/99 *Gloszczuk* [2001] ECR I-6369; C-268/99 *Jany* [2001] ECR I-8615; and C-327/02 *Panayotova* [2004] ECR I-11055.

[234] *Gloszczuk* judgment, para 85; *Kondova* judgment, para 90 (both ibid). It is not clear whether the prior breach of immigration law could be taken into account or not when reviewing the fresh application.

the Europe Agreements would arguably have been breached.[235] Furthermore, the right of establishment under the Agreements could be restricted on grounds of public policy, public security, or public health; the Court of Justice ruled that this has the same substantive meaning as the restrictions permitted by EU free movement law.[236]

Finally, the Euro–Mediterranean treaties with the three Maghreb States (Algeria, Morocco, and Tunisia) provide inter alia for equality in working conditions.[237] The Court of Justice has ruled that this right prevents Member States from terminating legal residence as long as a Maghreb worker is legally employed, except on grounds of public security, public policy, or public health, and that this apparently confers substantive and procedural protection equivalent to EU free movement law, at least before the application of Directive 2004/38.[238] This raises the question of whether all association agreements which give a right to equal treatment in working conditions must be interpreted the same way. This would mean that equivalent protection is granted pursuant to the SAAs, the EU–Turkey Agreement, the Partnership and Cooperation Agreements with ex-Soviet States, and the Cotonou Convention with African, Caribbean, and Pacific States.[239]

7.5. Prevention of irregular migration

Prevention of irregular migration is obviously more attractive to States than detecting and expelling persons once they have already arrived, provided that it can be accomplished at a reasonable cost. One method of reducing costs for the State is to transfer the liability for controlling entry to the private sector, in particular passenger transport companies, as regards the requirement to carry visas and valid travel documents.[240] But this strategy, if effective in practice, is likely to lead to an increase in entry via unofficial means of transport, in particular by means of smuggling. Smuggling of persons may in turn be connected to trafficking in persons, where there is a lack of valid consent. In order to deter the perceived increase in both smuggling and trafficking, the EU has resorted to measures setting out criminal sanctions.

It should be noted that, apart from the specific issues of smuggling and trafficking in migrants and the separate issue of sanctioning employers for hiring

---

[235] See by analogy Case C–503/03 (n 218 above).

[236] *Jany* judgment, paras 58–62 (n 233 above). Arguably, following the case law on the EU–Turkey agreement, it must also follow that the same procedural protection applies.

[237] Tunisia: [1998] OJ L 97; Morocco: [2000] OJ L 70; Algeria: [2005] OJ L 265. Previous agreements with these States with similar clauses applied from 1978.

[238] Cases C–416/96 *El-Yassini* [1999] ECR I-1209 and C–97/05 *Gattoussi* [2006] ECR I-11917.

[239] The Court has apparently confirmed that the principle applies to the EU–Turkey agreement: Cases C–4/05 *Guzeli* [2006] ECR I-10279.

[240] On visa and border control rules, see chs 3 and 4.

irregular migrants,[241] no provisions of EU law lay down express rules on criminalization *or* decriminalization in relation to immigration law; in particular there is no EU requirement to criminalize (or to decriminalize) migrants who have breached immigration law as such. It should not be forgotten, however, that Article 31 of the Geneva Convention on refugee status exempts refugees who have entered or stayed irregularly from penalties under certain circumstances.[242] Moreover, irregular migration (of whatever type) through a number of Member States consecutively falls within the scope of the EU's double jeopardy rules, which preclude in principle prosecution by more than one Member State for the same act.[243]

7.5.1. Carrier sanctions

The issue of carrier sanctions was initially addressed by Article 26(1)(a) of the Schengen Convention,[244] which requires carriers to 'take responsibility for' third-country nationals whom the carriers have brought to the external borders of the Community by air, sea, or land, but who are then refused entry. The carriers, at the border authorities' request, must return such persons to a third state as specified in the Convention, comprising either the state from which that person came, the state issuing that person a travel document, or any other state willing to guarantee entry of that person. Article 26(1)(b) of the Convention requires sea or air carriers to ensure that third-country nationals have the travel documents required for entry. To enforce this obligation, Article 26(2) of the Convention requires Member States to impose (unspecified) penalties on carriers which transport, by air or sea, third-country nationals who do not possess the necessary travel documents from a third state to their territories. Article 26(3) extends the provisions of Article 26(1)(b) and (3) to transport by coach, but not to other forms of land transport. Also, Article 26(1) and (2) are both 'subject to' the Geneva Convention on the status of refugees and its Protocol; Article 26(2) furthermore applies 'in accordance with [Member States'] constitutional law'.

Article 26 of the Convention was later supplemented by Directive 2001/51, which Member States had to implement by 11 February 2003.[245] Luxembourg was condemned by the Court of Justice for failure to implement this Directive on time,[246] and the Commission withdrew cases brought against the Netherlands and Belgium following late implementation.[247]

---

[241] See 7.6.1 below.   [242] See 7.3 above.   [243] See 11.8 below.

[244] [2000] OJ L 239.

[245] Art 7(1) of the Dir ([2001] OJ L 187/45). The Directive and the Convention provision have not been consolidated. There is no obligation to review implementation of the Directive (or the Convention provision) by Member States, and the Commission has not in fact conducted such a review.

[246] Case C-449/04 *Commission v Luxembourg*, judgment of 21 July 2005 (unreported).

[247] Cases C-460/04 *Commission v Netherlands* and C-516/04 *Commission v Belgium*.

As for the substance of the Directive, first of all it extends the personal scope of carriers' obligations as compared to the Schengen Convention. Carriers must also take responsibility for and return persons to *persons in transit to another State*, if that State refuses to admit them and sends them back, or if a carrier refused to transport them onward to that State.[248] Secondly, the Directive then extends the material scope of carriers' obligations: if they cannot effect return of persons immediately, they must find means of returning them with another carrier.[249] Failing that, they must pay for the costs of the stay and return of that person. Thirdly, the Directive harmonizes, although to a limited degree, the level of the penalties applying to carriers: Member States can opt for a maximum amount of at least €5,000 per person; or a minimum amount of €3,000 per person; or a lump sum with a maximum amount of at least €500,000.[250] A declaration in the Council minutes attempts to define carriers' obligations further; it asserts that for the purpose of applying the Directive, 'the Council has agreed that using an obvious forgery or obvious usurpation is equivalent to the absence of a travel document', although it is up to each Member State to determine whether such forgeries or usurpations are detectable.[251] But it should be recalled that for the purposes of EU law, the legal effect of statements in the minutes of Council meetings is very limited.[252]

The original French initiative had proposed an exemption from carrier sanctions for cases where a third-country national is 'admitted to the territory for asylum purposes'.[253] However, the final text provides only that the obligation to impose penalties is 'without prejudice to Member States' obligations in cases where a third-country national seeks international protection'.[254] The Directive does provide that Member States must grant 'effective rights of defence and appeal' against proceedings which may give rise to penalties,[255] but this does not apply to the other obligations imposed on carriers by the Directive and there is no obligation to ensure that procedures are in place for passengers to bring disputes against the carriers, or against the Member State.

This replacement of an enforceable asylum exception with fuzzy ambiguity is the biggest disappointment in this Directive. Although Article 26 of the Schengen Convention (and therefore presumably the 2001 Directive, which supplements it) is still expressly subject to the Geneva Convention and the New York Protocol, it remains unclear what this reference to the Geneva Convention means in practice. Furthermore, the Directive has likely led to increased difficulties for persons who wish to challenge the private enforcement of immigration

---

[248] Art 2.

[249] Art 3. This appears to apply both to persons refused entry to a Member State pursuant to Art 26(1) of the Convention, and to persons refused entry in transit pursuant to Art 2 of the Directive.

[250] Art 4(1).

[251] See Statement 75/01, in the monthly summary of Council Acts for June 2001 (Council doc 11450/01, 27 Aug 2001).   [252] See, for example, Case C-292/89 *Antonissen* [1991] ECR I-745.

[253] Art 4(3) of initial proposal ([2000] OJ C 269/8).   [254] Art 4(2).   [255] Art 6.

law, because the extension of personal and material scope of carriers' obligations has increased the complications involved. It is possible for Carrier A to bring a person to a Member State, Carrier B to deny him or her entry into another state, and then Carrier C to remove that person to another country. Also, the potential for increased costs under the Directive, without any accompanying clarity regarding asylum cases, likely further discouraged carriers from transporting likely asylum seekers and thus increased the likelihood that such persons will use illegal means to enter the EU. In fact, at least one delegation expressly admitted that its goal was to deter asylum seekers, arguing that the exemption in the initial proposal 'could make penalties for carriers ineffective and increase asylum applications'.[256]

7.5.2. Passenger data[257]

Directive 2004/82 on passenger data transmission, which further increases the role of passenger transport companies in the enforcement of immigration law, was adopted in April 2004.[258] Member States had to implement the Directive by 5 September 2006.[259]

The objective of this Directive is to improve border controls and to combat irregular immigration by means of transmission of passenger data by carriers in advance to the relevant national authorities.[260] Its core obligation is for carriers (defined as persons or companies providing passenger air transport services) to transmit specified information on passengers who will be crossing an external border (a border between the Member States and non-EU countries), at the request of external border control authorities, at the latest before the end of check-in of passengers.[261] This obligation comprises nine categories of information: the number and types of travel documents; nationality; full names; date of birth; border crossing point to be used; transport codes; departure and arrival time; total number of passengers carried; and the initial point of embarkation.[262] But compliance with the obligation to transmit information will not exempt carriers from compliance with the carrier sanctions rules in the Schengen Convention and Directive 2001/51.[263] It should be stressed that the obligation to transmit information apparently applies to information on all passengers, not just to information on non-EU nationals.

---

[256] Comments of the German delegation (Council doc 12361/00, 16 Oct 2000).

[257] For further information on the issue of passenger data transmission within the EU, see the Statewatch observatory on the issue: <http://www.statewatch.org/eu-pnrobservatory.htm>.

[258] [2004] OJ L 261/24.

[259] Art 7(1). All further references in this subsection are to this Directive. The Commission has brought proceedings against one Member State for failure to implement the Directive: Case C-304/10 *Commission v Poland*, pending.   [260] Art 1.

[261] Art 3(1). For the definitions, see Art 2(a) and (b).   [262] Art 3(2).   [263] Art 3(3).

If carriers fail in their obligations and, due to fault, do not transmit data or transmit incorrect or false data, Member States must impose penalties upon them. The penalties must comprise either a maximum of at least €5,000 per journey or a minimum of €3,000 per journey.[264] Member States are free to impose further sanctions, such as a withdrawal of an operating licence, for very serious infringements.[265] But Member States must ensure that carriers have effective rights of defence and appeal.[266] These rules can be compared to the carrier sanctions Directive, which (as outlined above) provides for a third sanctions option for Member States, requires the sanctions to be applied per individual (rather than per journey), has a lower threshold for applying further sanctions, and provides for a vague safeguard where a person seeks international protection.

As for data protection,[267] the information must be transmitted to external border control authorities for the purpose of facilitating checks with the objective of combating illegal immigration. These authorities shall save the data in a temporary file and shall delete it within twenty-four hours, unless the data are needed later for fulfilling the statutory functions of those authorities in accordance with national law and subject to the EU's data protection Directive.[268] Member States must oblige carriers to delete the information within twenty-four hours, and to inform the passengers on the information being transmitted. Furthermore, Member States may also use the data for law enforcement purposes, in accordance with national law and subject to the data protection Directive. It should be noted that the Commission has made proposals on the law enforcement use of passenger name records.[269]

This Directive is highly questionable for several reasons. It is not necessary or proportionate to require transmission of information on EU citizens or their family members, and to permit continued storage of their data for 'law enforcement' purposes. In fact, this is probably not valid pursuant to EU free movement law, given the very limited grounds upon which EU citizens or their family members can be refused entry or expelled.[270] The continued storage of data on any individual should not be permitted for 'law enforcement' purposes in general, without a specific limitation to cases where it is necessary to keep the information for an ongoing or imminent criminal investigation, or prosecution. Such a general exception, depending on the interpretation of the data protection Directive, could be interpreted to permit the compilation of a database on all travellers' movements across the EU external borders. Moreover, vague references to the collection of data for such general purposes are not permissible in light of the

---

[264] Art 4(1).   [265] Art 4(2).   [266] Art 5.

[267] Art 6.   [268] Dir 95/46 ([1995] OJ L 281/31). On this Directive, see further 12.3.2 below.

[269] Proposed framework decision on passenger name records (COM (2007) 654, 6 Nov 2007), which was not agreed before the Treaty of Lisbon entered into force. The Commission is planning to make a new proposal on this issue in 2011. See further 12.6.3 below.

[270] See 7.4.1 above and further 3.4.1 and 4.4.1 above.

case law of the European Court of Human Rights on Article 8 ECHR, requiring that accessible legislation must set out the specific cases when data is going to be collected and the uses to which the data is to be put.[271]

Finally, it should be noted that Directive 2004/82 is a separate measure from another controversial issue, an EC–US agreement on the transfer of passenger data to the US. The EP had referred this planned treaty to the Court of Justice,[272] but the Council went ahead and concluded it anyway;[273] the EP then decided to bring an annulment action against both the conclusion of the treaty and the Commission's decision that the US provided adequate protection for this transfer of personal data, but the Court of Justice rejected this argument.[274] Also, the EC (as it then was) and Canada concluded an agreement on passenger name exchange,[275] and the EU has agreed subsequent treaties with the US and Australia.[276] Because these treaties concern the use of data for the purposes of law enforcement, not immigration control, they are discussed further in Chapter 12.[277]

7.5.3. Facilitation of unauthorized entry and residence

In order to address the issue of smuggling of persons, Article 27(1) of the Schengen Convention provided that Member States 'undertake to impose appropriate penalties on any person who, for financial gain, assists or tries to assist an alien to enter or reside within the territory of one of the Contracting Parties in breach of that Contracting Party's laws on the entry and residence of aliens'. Article 27(2) and (3) were supplementary measures. According to Article 27(2), a Member State which is informed of actions as defined in Article 27(1) which are in breach of the law of another Member State had to inform that Member State. Article 27(3) provided that if one Member State asked another to prosecute actions referred to in Article 27(1) on the grounds that its laws have been breached, it had to specify by official means which provisions of its law was concerned.

Article 27 of the Schengen Convention was subsequently repealed by Directive 2002/90 and a related third pillar Framework Decision as from 5 December 2004,[278] when Member States had to implement both measures.[279] The Commission plans to propose amendments to (and possibly a merger of) these measures in

---

[271] See further 12.3.1 below.   [272] *Opinion 1/2004*, withdrawn.

[273] See [2004] OJ L 183/83 and [2004] OJ L 235/11. For more information on the EU–US agreement, see the Statewatch observatory on this issue, online at: <http://www.statewatch.org/pnrobservatory.htm>.

[274] Joined Cases C-317/04 and C-318/04, *EP v Council and Commission* [2006] ECR I-4721.

[275] [2006] OJ L 82/14; the agreement entered into force on 22 Mar 2006 ([2006] OJ L 86/19).

[276] [2007] OJ L 204/18 and [2008] OJ L 213/47.   [277] See 12.6.3 below.

[278] Dir 2002/90 ([2002] OJ L 328/17) and Framework Decision 2002/946 ([2002] OJ L 328/1). On the repeal of Art 27 of the Convention, see Art 5 of the Directive and Art 10 of the Framework Decision.   [279] Art 4(1) of the Directive and Art 9(1) of the Framework Decision.

2012,[280] and brought infringement proceedings against Member States which missed the deadline to implement the Directive.[281] It should be noted that the EU's mutual recognition measures have generally required Member States to relinquish the dual criminality principle as regards the crime of the facilitation of illegal entry or residence.[282]

Reflecting the allocation of Article 27 of the Schengen Convention between the first and third pillars, the Directive defines facilitation of illegal entry, residence, or movement, while the Framework Decision sets out the criminal penalties that must apply, along with rules on jurisdiction. However, in light of subsequent judgments of the Court of Justice on the Community's competence to adopt criminal law measures, it might be argued that aspects of the Framework Decision, as regards the definition of criminal offences, fell at the time within Community competence.[283] Following the entry into force of the Treaty of Lisbon, the entire Framework Decision is now within the scope of Article 83(2) TFEU.[284]

The Directive requires Member States to impose sanctions upon any person who intentionally assists a third-country national 'to enter or transit across' a Member State 'in breach of the laws of the State concerned on the entry or transit' of foreigners,[285] and any person 'who, for financial gain, intentionally assists' a third-country national to 'reside within' a Member State in breach of its national laws on residence.[286] Identical sanctions must also be applied to instigators or accomplices and those who attempt to commit the activities in question.[287] There is a 'humanitarian' exemption, applying 'where the aim of the behaviour is to provide humanitarian assistance to the person concerned'. But this exception is *optional*, and only applies to the first category of offence.[288] However, a subsequent Directive concerning sanctions against employers for hiring irregular migrants specifies that assistance to those migrants in order to lodge complaints against their employers must *not* be considered to be facilitation of unauthorized residence for the purpose of the 2002 Directive.[289]

The Framework Decision requires Member States to punish all the conduct defined in the Directive by 'effective, proportionate and dissuasive criminal penalties, which may entail extradition',[290] accompanied if appropriate by confiscation of transport, prohibition of practice of an occupation, or deportation.[291]

---

[280] See the action plan on implementing the Stockholm programme (COM (2010) 171, 20 Apr 2010).

[281] Cases C-48/06 *Commission v Luxembourg* (judgment of 7 Dec 2006, unreported) and C-485/06 *Commission v Germany* (withdrawn).   [282] See ch 9 below.

[283] Cases C-176/03 *Commission v Council* [2005] ECR I-7879 and C-440/05 *Commission v Council* [2007] ECR I-9097; see 10.4.1 below.   [284] See further 7.2.4 above and 10.4.1 below.

[285] Art 1(1)(a) of the Directive.   [286] Art 1(1)(b) of the Directive.

[287] Art 2 of the Directive.   [288] Art 1(2) of the Directive.

[289] Art 13(3) of Dir 2009/52 ([2009] OJ L 168/24); see further 7.6.1 below.

[290] Art 1(1) of the Framework Decision.   [291] Art 1(2) of the Framework Decision.

However, in cases of unauthorized entry or transit, there must be a maximum sentence of at least eight years if the activity was committed by a criminal organization as defined in another EU measure or if committed while endangering a would-be migrant's life.[292] Member States can reduce the maximum sentence to at least six years if necessary to preserve the coherence of national penalty systems.[293]

There are also standard provisions on liability of legal persons and jurisdiction;[294] the latter rules require Member States to take jurisdiction where an act is carried out on its territory, by one of its nationals, or for the benefit of a legal person established in its territory.[295] Member States can derogate from the second and third jurisdictional rules if they inform the Council.[296] In any event, each Member State must either prosecute or extradite when the relevant conduct has been committed by its own nationals outside its territory.[297] The provisions of Article 27(2) and (3) of the Convention were reproduced in the Framework Decision without any amendment.[298] The entire Framework Decision is 'without prejudice to the protection afforded refugees and asylum seekers in accordance with international law on refugees or other international instruments relating to human rights', in particular Articles 31 and 33 of the Geneva Convention on the status of refugees.[299]

Compared to Article 27 of the Schengen Convention, the Directive broadens the scope of the obligation to impose penalties on facilitators of irregular entry or residence. Most importantly, it requires Member States to impose penalties even where the facilitators do *not* facilitate irregular entry for financial gain. It also extends the penalty obligation to irregular transit alongside irregular entry or residence. Moreover, Member States' obligation extends beyond persons attempting to commit the infringement, to include also instigators and accomplices.[300] On top of this, the Framework Decision now defines more precisely the minimum level of sanctions which Member States must impose. But as we have seen, there is an optional exception from liability in the Directive as regards the 'entry or transit' infringement, and a general safeguard clause in the Framework Decision.

---

[292] Art 1(3) of the Framework Decision, referring to a 1998 Joint Action ([1998] OJ L 351/1) on organized crime, which has since been replaced by a Framework Decision ([2008] OJ L 300/42).

[293] Art 1(4) of the Framework Decision.

[294] Arts 2–5 of the Framework Decision. For an analysis of such standard provisions in this and other EC and EU criminal law measures, see 10.5.2 below.

[295] Art 4(1) of the Framework Decision.   [296] Art 4(2) and (3), Framework Decision.

[297] Art 5; this provision is largely irrelevant in light of the Framework Decision on the European Arrest Warrant; see further 9.5.2 below.   [298] Art 7 of the Framework Decision.

[299] Art 6 of the Framework Decision.

[300] On these extended forms of liability, see the analysis in 10.5.2 below.

According to the Commission's report on the application of the Framework Decision,[301] Member States were broadly in compliance with the measure, although some had not clearly distinguished between trafficking and smuggling in persons. However, the range of penalties imposed by Member States was wide, and the Commission therefore thought there was scope for considering a greater degree of harmonization. The Commission was not aware that any Member States had made notifications regarding derogations from the jurisdiction rules.[302] As for the safeguard clause, the Commission had no information on the application of this clause, but there was 'no indication that the international law on refugees has been violated as a result of the implementation of this Framework Decision'. Of course, if Member States were responsible for such violations, one would hardly expect them to inform the Commission. Overall, the Commission found it difficult to assess national implementation of the Framework Decision in practice in the absence of relevant statistics.[303]

Do these measures strike the right balance between a justifiable attempt to ensure the effective application of immigration control, and the need to ensure that persons needing international protection are still able to seek it effectively? An optional humanitarian exception is obviously not worth much and clearly shows some contempt for the very humanitarian principle which supposedly inspires it. Moreover, the vague 'saving clause' referring to the Geneva Convention would only assist refugees and asylum seekers, while leaving intact the effect of the two measures on the persons who facilitate the entry of those persons into the Member States. Should persons who assist persons in need of international protection be subject to criminal sanctions, in particular when they do not do so for financial gain? Without a clear exemption for all cases in which a person claims asylum, there is a high risk that these two measures will impact negatively upon refugees and asylum seekers.

The Directive and Framework Decision can be compared to the Protocol on smuggling of persons attached to the UN Convention on organized crime, which has been ratified by a large majority of Member States and also concluded by the EC (as it then was).[304] The Protocol differs from the EC/EU measures in particular in that the obligation to criminalize acts only applies where those acts are committed for financial gain, and that aggravating circumstances include the

---

[301] COM (2006) 770, 6 Dec 2006, adopted pursuant to Art 9(2) of the Framework Decision. There is no obligation to review implementation of the Directive by Member States, and the Commission has not in fact conducted such a review.

[302] In fact, two declarations are publicly available, from Denmark (Council doc 14401/05, 22 Nov 2005) and Hungary (Council doc 13754/05, 26 Oct 2005).

[303] On the statistics issue generally, see 7.8 below.

[304] [2001] OJ L 30/44 (EC signature of Protocol); [2006] OJ L 262/24 and 34 (EC conclusion of Protocol). The Protocol entered into force on 28 Jan 2004. On the details of ratification by the Member States, see Appendix I. The EC also concluded the main UN Convention on organized crime ([2004] OJ L 261/69).

inhuman or degrading treatment, including exploitation, of migrants, rather than acts carried out within the framework of a criminal organization. Also, there is no requirement to provide for specific potential sentences when the aggravating circumstances apply, States must also criminalize the creation of false documents for the purpose of smuggling, migrants cannot be criminalized for the fact of being subject to conduct to be criminalized pursuant to the Protocol, and the Protocol sets out detailed rules concerning the smuggling of migrants by sea.

7.5.4. Trafficking in persons

The parallel concern to address the issue of trafficking in persons, which also reflects obligations pursuant to international human rights law to combat slavery and forced labour,[305] led initially to the adoption of a Joint Action in 1997, which also addressed the issue of pornography and prostitution.[306] This was replaced by a Framework Decision, which Member States had to implement by 1 August 2004.[307] That Framework Decision in turn would be replaced by a Directive proposed by the Commission in March 2010,[308] which was agreed by the Council in June 2010.[309] It should be noted at the outset that neither the 2002 Framework Decision nor the 2010 proposal limit themselves to the issue of persons trafficked for the purposes of prostitution.

The EU has also addressed this issue by adopting a Directive on the status of trafficking victims who assist in prosecutions,[310] as well as a number of soft law measures,[311] and by concluding the relevant Protocol to the UN Convention on

---

[305] See 7.3.1 above.   [306] [1997] OJ L 63/2.

[307] [2004] OJ L 203/1. The other provisions of the Joint Action were replaced by a Framework Decision on sexual exploitation and child pornography ([2004] OJ L 13/44; see further 10.5 below).

[308] COM (2010) 95, 29 Mar 2010; this replaced an earlier proposal for a new Framework Decision on this subject (COM (2009) 136, 25 Mar 2009), which lapsed with the entry into force of the Treaty of Lisbon. The framework Decision on sexual exploitation and child pornography is also the subject of a parallel Commission proposal for a new text (see 10.5 below). For comments on the 2010 proposal, see the comments by UNHCR, online at: <http://www.unhcr.org/4c0f932a9.html>, by a group of UN agencies and the ILO, online at: <http://www.lastradainternational.org/lsidocs/Joint%20UN%20letter%20MEPs%20Directive%20Trafficking%20FINAL.pdf>, and by a group of NGOs, online at: <http://s3.amazonaws.com/rcpp/assets/attachments/1035_NGO_statement_for_EP_seminar_10_June_2010_original.pdf>.

[309] Council doc 10845/10, 10 June 2010. This text still has to be agreed with the EP. On the competence to adopt this measure, see 7.2.4 above.

[310] Dir 2004/81 ([2004] OJ L 261/19); see further 7.6.2 below.

[311] These comprise: Council conclusions on trafficking in persons ([2003] OJ C 137/1); Council resolution on the law enforcement response ([2003] OJ C 260/4); a Commission decision establishing an expert group of advisers ([2003] OJ L 79/25, replaced by [2007] OJ L 277/79); an Action Plan against human trafficking ([2005] OJ C 311/1); Council conclusions of Apr 2006 (JHA Council press release, 27–28 Apr 2006); reports to the Council as regards trafficking for prostitution and the 2006 World Cup (Council docs 5008/07 and 5006/1/07, 3 Jan and 19 Jan 2007); Council conclusions of Nov 2007 (JHA Council press release, 8–9 Nov 2007); Council conclusions of June 2009 on an informal

organized crime.[312] In parallel, the Council of Europe agreed a Convention on the issue in 2005, which the majority of Member States have ratified.[313] Moreover, the EU's mutual recognition measures have generally required Member States to relinquish the dual criminality principle as regards the crime of trafficking in human beings,[314] and the Framework Decision on confiscation of criminal proceeds requires Member States to take measures against the proceeds of this crime in certain circumstances.[315] There are also some relevant provisions in the EU's general Framework Decision on the status of victims in criminal proceedings.[316] For the future, the Stockholm programme calls, inter alia, for the EU to appoint an anti-trafficking coordinator.[317]

The Framework Decision requires Member States to adopt criminal sanctions to combat trafficking in human beings, a concept with a three-part definition. There must be the 'recruitment, transportation, harbouring, transfer, or subsequent reception' of a person; there must be a use of force by the person involved (in other words, the use of 'coercion, force or threat, including abduction', the use of 'deceit or fraud', an 'abuse of authority or a position of vulnerability', or payment in return for the transfer of control of a person); and the trafficking must be for the purpose of labour exploitation (including slavery, forced labour, or similar practices) or sexual exploitation (including pornography or prostitution).[318] Where the specified types of force are applied, the consent of the victim is irrelevant;[319] where a child is involved, there is no requirement that force was used.[320] There is no requirement of a cross-border element to the offence, but the issue is nevertheless considered in this chapter because a cross-border element to human trafficking is often present in practice.

It should also be noted that a subsequent Directive requires Member States to criminalize employers who use 'work or services exacted from an illegally staying third-country national with the knowledge that he or she is a victim of trafficking

---

network of national rapporteurs (JHA Council press release, 4 Jun 2009). See also the Commission's communications on human trafficking (COM (2005) 514, 18 Oct 2005 and COM (2008) 657, 17 Oct 2008) and the reports and opinions of the expert group, online at: <http://ec.europa.eu/justice_home/doc_centre/crime/trafficking/doc_crime_human_trafficking_en.htm#Experts%20Group%20on%20Trafficking%20in%20Human%20Beings>. See also the recommendations drawn up by the Commission for the 2007 Anti-Trafficking Day: <http://ec.europa.eu/justice_home/news/information_dossiers/anti_trafficking_day_07/documents_en.htm>.

[312] [2001] OJ L 30/44 (signature); [2006] OJ L 262/44 and 51 (conclusion). A large majority of Member States have also ratified the Protocol, which entered into force on 25 Dec 2003. For ratification details, see Appendix I. The EC has also concluded the main UN Convention on organized crime ([2004] OJ L 261/69).

[313] ETS 197, in force 1 Feb 2008. For ratification details, see Appendix I.

[314] See ch 9 below.

[315] Art 3 of Framework Decision ([2005] OJ L 68/49). See further 9.7.4 below.

[316] [2001] OJ L 82/1; see 9.8.3 below.   [317] [2010] OJ C 115, point 4.4.2.

[318] Art 1(1), Framework Decision.   [319] Art 1(2), Framework Decision.

[320] Art 1(3), Framework Decision; a 'child' is defined as any person under eighteen years of age (Art 1(4)).

in human beings', where the employer has not been charged or convicted of an offence pursuant to the Framework Decision on trafficking in persons.[321]

Member States must ensure that a maximum sentence of at least eight years for trafficking in persons is possible, in four particularly serious circumstances: endangering the life of the victim deliberately or by gross negligence; committing the offence against a 'particularly vulnerable' victim, including at least children below the age of sexual majority trafficked for the purpose of sexual exploitation; using serious violence in order to commit the offence or causing 'particularly serious harm to the victim'; or committing the crime within the framework of a 'criminal organisation' as defined by an EU measure on organized crime, but without the threshold for criminal liability set out in that measure.[322] There are standard provisions on the liability of legal persons and on jurisdiction;[323] the latter provision requires Member States to take jurisdiction where an act is carried out on its territory, by one of its nationals, or for the benefit of a legal person established in its territory.[324] Member States can derogate from the second and third jurisdictional rules if they inform the Council.[325] In any event, each Member State must either prosecute or extradite when the relevant conduct has been committed by its own nationals outside its territory.[326] Member States are obliged to protect child victims of trafficking, by reference to the EU's Framework Decision on crime victims' rights, and to permit investigations or prosecutions to begin in the absence of a complaint by a victim, at least in cases where the acts took place on national territory.[327]

Although there is no direct cross-over or conflict between the Framework Decisions on facilitation and trafficking, there are likely still circumstances where the two measures cross over, since the offences covered by the Framework Decision on facilitation will also fall within the Framework Decision on trafficking if the additional elements set out in the latter measure are also present. This will be particularly true in the case of children, given the absence of the 'force' element in the trafficking offence where children are involved. Comparing the two measures, there is a common maximum sentence of at least eight years when the migrant's life was endangered or a criminal organization was involved, subject

---

[321] Art 9(1)(d) of Dir 2009/52 on sanctions for employment of irregular migrants ([2009] OJ L 168/24); Member States must apply this Directive from 20 July 2011. For more details on this Directive, see 7.6.1 below.

[322] Art 3, Framework Decision, referring to a 1998 Joint Action ([1998] OJ L 351/1) on organized crime, which has since been replaced by a Framework Decision ([2008] OJ L 300/42). On those measures, see 10.5 below.

[323] Arts 4–6, Framework Decision. On the general approach of EU criminal law measures to such issues, see 10.5.2.1 and 11.5 below.   [324] Art 6(1), Framework Decision.

[325] Art 6(2) and (4), Framework Decision.

[326] Art 6(3), Framework Decision; this provision is largely irrelevant in light of the Framework Decision on the European Arrest Warrant; see further 9.5.2 below.

[327] Art 7, Framework Decision. On the Framework Decision on victims of crime, see 9.8.3 below.

to different wording of these criteria (the trafficking measure requires a further element where a life was endangered, and relaxes the penalty threshold as regards involvement of organized crime); the Framework Decision on trafficking also applies this sentence in two other circumstances. Given the comparative serious-ness of the two offences, it is rather odd that an equal sentence will apply.

The definition of trafficking in the Framework Decision is very similar to that in the UN Protocol, although the Framework Decision goes further in provid-ing for maximum sentences to be imposed in certain cases, and the UN Protocol contains a 'saving clause' for asylum cases. The Council of Europe Convention provides for a similar definition of the crime, but it also requires parties to crimi-nalize related actions concerning the forgery of travel and identity documents, and states that parties shall 'consider' criminalizing the use of services of a victim. This latter Convention also contains a different list of aggravating circumstances than set out in the Framework Decision, and does not specify what sentences must be available in such cases.[328]

According to the Commission's report on the national application of the Framework Decision,[329] most Member States implemented the definition of traf-ficking sufficiently in national law, including as regards inchoate offences. Equally Member States had applied the rules on penalties, although the Commission raised the question of whether there ought to be aggravated penalties as regards all minors (not just those under the age of consent) and the wide variation in penalties, where the Commission wanted to examine the possibility of further harmonization. The large majority of Member States apply the rules concern-ing extra-territorial jurisdiction.[330] It was difficult for the Commission to assess whether the specific provisions on victims were complied with.

Further information on the practical application of the Framework Decision is set out in the Commission's 2008 communication on the issue of trafficking in persons,[331] which states that there has been a steady increase in the number of prosecutions for trafficking related to sexual exploitation to 1,500 a year by 2006, although this fell short of estimates of 500,000 persons trafficked each year into the EU.[332] Most countries offered police protection and compensation to very few victims in practice.

As noted above, in June 2010, the Council agreed on a new Directive on traf-ficking in persons which would, if adopted after agreement with the EP, replace the existing Framework Decision on this issue.[333] The agreed Directive would, first of all, amend the definition of 'exploitation' to include the exploitation of

---

[328] For further comparisons between the EU and the international measures, see 7.6.2 below.

[329] COM (2006) 187, 2 May 2006.

[330] The only relevant declaration available in the Council's register of documents concerns Hungary (Council doc 13756/05, 26 Oct 2005).   [331] COM (2008) 657, n 311 above.

[332] For further statistics, see the impact assessment of the 2009 proposal for a new Framework Decision on this issue (n 308 above), pp 7–12 and Annex I.   [333] See n 309 above.

'begging' or of criminal activities, or the removal of organs.[334] Next, it would require Member States to introduce a maximum penalty of at least five years for *any* trafficking offence.[335] As for aggravating circumstances, there would be a 'minimum maximum' penalty of at least *ten* years (rather than eight) where the victim was particularly vulnerable (defined now to include *all* child victims), and where the offence was committed within the framework of organized crime as defined by EU law, or endangered the life of the victims, was committed by use of serious violence, or has caused particularly serious harm to the victim.[336] Member States would also have cases where a public official committed the offence in the performance of his or her duties as an aggravated circumstance.[337]

A new provision specifies that Member States shall provide for the 'possibility' of not sanctioning the victims of trafficking offences, where they were compelled to commit criminal activities due to the trafficking.[338] The requirement to permit investigations and prosecutions even where the victim did not make a complaint would be extended to all cases, not just cases where a Member State has territorial jurisdiction, and Member States would have to ensure that 'criminal proceedings may continue even if the victim has withdrawn his or her statement'.[339] New provisions would require: that the time limit to prosecute would have to be extended for a reasonable period after child victims reached the age of majority; that prosecutors and investigators received sufficient training; and that investigative tools used in organized crime or other serious crime cases are available as regards the offences of trafficking in persons.[340]

Jurisdiction over human trafficking offences would be extended also to any offences committed by nationals of a Member State, without any possibility of derogation by Member States.[341] As regards offences committed by their citizens outside their territory, Member States would not be allowed to make prosecution dependent upon the act being an offence in the territory where it was committed, upon a report by the victim, or upon a denunciation by the State where the act was committed.[342] There would also be detailed new rules on protection and assistance for victims.[343]

As compared to the international measures on this issue, the agreed text of the Directive now corresponds to or goes further than the Council of Europe and

---

[334] Agreed Art 1(3). However, the explicit reference to 'pornography' as a form of exploitation would be dropped.

[335] Agreed Art 4(1). On inchoate and accessory offences, see the agreed Art 4(4). On criminal penalties and EU law generally, see 10.6 below.

[336] Agreed Art 4(2). The only change from the Framework Decision is that all child victims would have to be considered vulnerable.

[337] Agreed Art 4(3); this is new as compared to the Framework Decision.

[338] Agreed Art 7.   [339] Agreed Art 8(1).   [340] Agreed Art 8(2)–(4).

[341] Agreed Art 9(1). On criminal jurisdiction rules generally, see 11.5 below.

[342] Agreed Art 9(3).

[343] Agreed Arts 10–14; see also Art 15 (prevention) and Art 16 (rapporteurs).

UN measures as regards the definition of trafficking, prevention of the offence, and rules concerning victim protection and assistance.

7.5.5. Immigration liaison officers

An important practical role in preventing irregular migration is played by Member States' immigration liaison officers (ILOs) posted in third countries. The creation of a framework to coordinate the activities of these national officers started with the JHA Council conclusions of 2000 on irregular immigration networks, which suggested that Member States 'improve cooperation between liaison officers operating in the same immigration source country or in the same region of the world, which could lead to mutual and reciprocal assistance or even complementarity in carrying out tasks'.[344] Next, the JHA Council of May 2001 adopted conclusions on the creation of an ILO network in the Western Balkans,[345] which set out detailed guidelines on the establishment of such a network.

In the event, the funding to establish this network was not available, but the Council's Action Plan on external borders policy, adopted in 2002, nevertheless called for the creation of a general ILO network. A report on the creation of the network indicated that common training, a common handbook, and the improvement of cooperation and information sharing were necessary.[346] This resulted in the adoption of further Council conclusions adopting most of the report's recommendations (except as regards training).[347]

The next step was the formalization of the ILO network by means of a Council Regulation adopted early in 2004.[348] Regulation 377/2004 establishes the ILO network, defines the concept of ILOs and sets out their powers, and sets out the scope of the ILO network, which includes the Member States as well as non-EU countries.[349] The ILOs collect information of use to the prevention of irregular immigration and may also assist with establishing the identity of third-country nationals and facilitating their return to their country of origin. Member States must ensure that their ILOs act in accordance with national law (particularly regarding data protection) and international agreements with the host States.[350] They must also keep each other, the Council and the Commission informed of ILO postings.[351] The tasks of ILO networks include: regular meetings; exchange of information; coordinated positions as regards commercial carriers; organization of information and training sessions for diplomatic and

---

[344] See the JHA Council press release, 30 Nov/1 Dec 2000.
[345] See the JHA Council press release, 28–29 May 2001.
[346] Council doc 13406/02, 28 Oct 2002.
[347] See the JHA Council press release, 28–29 Nov 2002.
[348] Reg 377/2004, [2004] OJ L 64/1, in force 5 Jan 2004. All references in this subsection are to this Regulation unless otherwise indicated.   [349] Art 1.
[350] Art 2.   [351] Art 3.

consular staff, when appropriate; adoption of common approaches to collecting and reporting strategic information; contribution to bi-annual reports on common activities; and establishing contacts with networks in neighbouring countries.[352] Commission staff are entitled to attend network meetings and the Member State holding the Council Presidency is to take the lead holding those meetings.[353] Member States may agree that ILOs can look after the interests of other Member States, or share tasks among each other.[354] Each Council Presidency must draw up a report, in accordance with a model and format drawn up by the Commission, on the activity of ILO networks in each country where it has a representative.[355] The Presidency must then prepare an overall evaluation report, drafted by the Commission, and a factual summary on the basis of these reports is to be included in the annual Commission report on the development of EU policy on illegal immigration, external border controls, and expulsion.[356] Finally, the entire Regulation is without prejudice to the rules on consular cooperation.[357]

According to the Commission's 2009 report on EU policy on irregular migration, visas, and border control, the ILO network had in 2006 identified four key migration routes from Africa to Europe, and four Member States started work to develop cooperation among ILOs on these routes. Links had also been created between the ILO network and Europol and Frontex. The ILO system had also received money from the EU borders fund, to promote the establishment and development of ILO networks in Africa and in eastern and south-eastern Europe.[358]

In order to develop the ILO network further, the Commission proposed to amend the ILO Regulation in July 2009.[359] This proposal would: add a reference to the use of the 'Iconet' system for transferring information;[360] entitle Frontex, the EU border agency, to send representatives to all network meetings;[361] permit Member States other than those holding the Council Presidency to call network meetings;[362] and reduce the reporting burden on the Council Presidency and Commission, since the requirements in the 2004 Regulation had proved impossible to satisfy.[363]

The Commission subsequently proposed separately that Frontex should be able to send liaison officers to non-EU States, with such officers forming part of

---

[352] Art 4(1).   [353] Art 4(2) and (3).   [354] Art 5.

[355] Art 6(1) and (2). The Commission adopted a Decision setting out the standard model in Sep 2005: [2005] OJ L 264/8.   [356] Art 6(3) and (4).

[357] Art 7. On those rules, see 4.7 above.   [358] SEC (2009) 320, 9 Mar 2009, pp 18 and 25.

[359] COM (2009) 322, 8 July 2009. The proposal has not yet been agreed between the Council and EP.   [360] Proposed amendments to Art 3 and 4(1). On Iconet, see 7.8 below.

[361] Proposed amendment to Art 4(2). On Frontex, see 3.10.1 above.

[362] Proposed amendment to Art 4(3).

[363] Proposed new version of Art 6. The explanatory memorandum to the Commission's 2009 proposal to amend the Regulation stated that Member States had ILOs in more than 130 countries (COM (2009) 322, n 359 above).

the overall ILO network.[364] It remains to be seen whether this measure, if agreed, would increase the effectiveness or accountability of EU action in this area.

There is not enough public information to judge to what extent the planned ILO network has met its objectives. But the inherent problem with the ILO network is that no regard is paid in the Regulation (including the proposed amendments to it) or the prior soft law to the human rights aspects of irregular migration, considering that some persons have a justified need to leave their country of origin by any means possible.

7.6. Treatment of irregular migrants

A number of early EU soft law measures make reference to detection of irregular migrants within Member States' territory and restrictions upon their status,[365] while the relevant International Labour Organization Convention and the UN Convention on the status of migrant workers instead set out requirements for a minimum level of social and legal protection for irregular migrants within the territory.[366] The principal binding EU measures in this area, which will be considered in turn, concern sanctions against employers for employment of irregular migrants and the legal status of victims of trafficking in persons. It should also be recalled that Member States may opt to check the fingerprints of an irregular migrant against the Eurodac database to see whether he or she has applied for asylum in any Member State,[367] and (when the Visa Information System becomes operational) check those fingerprints in that System for the purpose of verifying the identity of a possible irregular migrant or of identifying an irregular migrant.[368] The planned entry-exit system, if it is agreed and becomes operational, will also impact upon those irregular migrants who have overstayed on the territory.[369] Finally, the Returns Directive contains a number of important provisions concerning the treatment of irregular migrants pending expulsion; it is considered separately further below.[370]

7.6.1. Sanctions against employers of irregular migrants

The purpose of adopting legislation addressing employment of irregular migrants was threefold: to reduce the 'pull' factor attracting migrants to the EU; to reduce

---

[364] COM (2010) 61, 24 Feb 2010, proposing to replace Art 14 of the Frontex Reg (Reg 2007/2004, [2004] OJ L 349/1).   [365] See 7.2.1 above.

[366] See 7.3.3 above.   [367] See 5.8.3 above.

[368] Arts 19 and 20, Reg 767/2008 ([2008] OJ L 218/60). On this system, see 4.8 above.

[369] See 3.6.2 above.

[370] Dir 2008/115 ([2008] OJ L 348/98), in particular Arts 14 as regards, inter alia, education and health care, and Arts 15–18 as regards detention; see 7.7.1 below.

distortions of competition between companies in Member States that employed irregular migrants and those that did not; and to ensure that labour standards were not undercut by employment of irregular migrants. An early suggestion to adopt legislation on this issue as an internal market matter in the 1970s did not find favour.[371]

Over thirty years later, Directive 2009/52 was adopted by the EP and the Council in May 2009.[372] Member States must apply the Directive by 20 July 2011.[373] The Directive broke new ground as the first EC measure not related to environmental law to require Member States to impose criminal sanctions to enforce it.[374]

The purpose of the Directive is to prohibit the employment of irregular migrants 'in order to fight illegal immigration', and therefore 'to lay down minimum common standards on sanctions and measures' against employers who breach this prohibition.[375] Member States may set higher standards as regards employees' rights to receive back pay and as regards facilitation of employees' complaints, 'provided that such provisions are compatible with' the Directive,[376] and may also establish 'more stringent' rules relating to the liability of sub-contractors.[377] While it might be inferred from this that *other* provisions of the Directive fully harmonize national law, nonetheless the preamble to the Directive and its title suggest that it sets only 'minimum' standards through-out.[378] In light of this, the best interpretation is that the entire Directive sets minimum standards as regards enforcement, except for the specific provision which permits higher standards as regards employees' rights. In any event, it should be noted that the Directive explicitly provides for a number of options for Member States.[379]

It should be noted that the Directive does not apply to *legal* migrants who take up employment which is unauthorized, regardless of whether those migrants are prohibited from taking up any work or from taking up the particular work they have been employed to carry out.[380] In fact, the Directive could not apply to those groups of persons, due to the different decision-making procedures applying to

---

[371] Proposed Directive in [1976] OJ C 277/2, revised in [1978] OJ C 97/9.

[372] [2009] OJ L 168/24.

[373] Art 17(1). All references in this subsection are to Dir 2009/52 unless otherwise indicated.

[374] See further 7.2.4 and 10.2.4 below.   [375] Art 1.

[376] Art 15. On the meaning of the requirement of 'compatibility', see 7.2.4 above.

[377] Art 8(4). This clause is not subject to the requirement of 'compatibility' with the Directive.

[378] Recital 4 in the preamble. Again, there is no reference to 'compatibility' with the Directive here.

[379] Arts 3(3), 4(2), 5(2)(b), (3), 6(2), 7(2), 10(2), and 12. For more on these various options, see below. Moreover, the Directive refers to 'national law' (or similar phrases) in Arts 2(c), (g), (h), 3(3), 6(1), (2), (5), 8(1), (3), (4), 9(1), 10(2), 13(1), (2), and (4).

[380] Recital 5 in the preamble states that the Directive is 'without prejudice' to national law deal-ing with this issue.

the legal base for 'legal migration' at the time of the adoption of the Directive.[381] Furthermore, obviously the Directive does not apply either to self-employment by irregular migrants, or to the unauthorized self-employment of legal migrants.[382] Also, the Directive does not apply to those third-country nationals who enjoy the EU right of free movement.[383] Although the Directive fails to give express priority to any treaties concluded by the EU and/or the Member States, any treaties binding the EU nonetheless take priority over any EU secondary legislation.[384] Therefore employer sanctions cannot be imposed where a Turkish worker derives employment rights from the EU–Turkey association agreement.[385] In the case of victims of trafficking in persons, other EU legislation provides for access to employment where a Member State gives them a residence permit;[386] it must be assumed that such persons are not 'illegally staying' as long as the permit is valid, and therefore their position falls outside the scope of the prohibition in Directive 2009/52. Equally any employment carried out pursuant to other EU legislation which provides for access to employment in connection with a residence permit must also fall outside the scope of this prohibition, since such persons are not 'illegally staying' either.[387] It must also be the case that any Member States which regard asylum seekers as irregularly staying (assuming that this position is permitted as a matter of EU law) must nonetheless authorize their employment, according to the terms of the reception conditions Directive, even in the absence of a requirement to issue a residence permit to asylum seekers, because the latter Directive is a *lex specialis* on this issue.[388]

The basic obligation in Directive 2009/52 is that Member States have to prohibit the employment of irregular migrants,[389] with the Directive specifying the sanctions and other measures which apply to enforce this prohibition.[390]

---

[381] See 7.2.4 above. After the entry into force of the Treaty of Lisbon, this point is purely historic.

[382] There is no definition of 'self-employment' in the Directive, but see the definition of 'employment' in Art 2(b).

[383] See the definition of 'third-country national' in Art 2(a). Furthermore, recital 5 of the preamble states that the Directive does not apply to third-country nationals who have been posted by their employer between Member States in order to provide services. See also recital 32 in the preamble, and generally 7.4 above.

[384] See Case C-228/06 *Soysal* [2009] ECR I-1031. However, this leaves open the question of priority as between the Directive and treaties concluded only by *Member States* with third countries.

[385] See Case C-65/98 *Eyup* [2000] ECR I-4747.

[386] Art 11 of Dir 2004/81, [2004] OJ L 261/19. On this Directive, see 7.6.2 below.

[387] See 5.5, 5.6, and 6.5–6.7 above.

[388] Dir 2003/9 ([2003] OJ L 31/18), Art 11; proposed new version of Dir (COM (2008) 815, 3 Dec 2008), Art 15; see 5.9 above. It should also follow that Dir 2009/52 is inapplicable to asylum seekers to the extent that Member States authorize their employment beyond the minimum standards set out in the reception conditions Directive. See by analogy Case C-357/09 PPU *Kadzoev*, judgment of 30 Nov 2009, not yet reported, in which the Court ruled that asylum seekers fell entirely outside the scope of the Returns Dir (n 370 above; see further 7.7.1 below).

[389] Art 3(1). 'Employment' and 'illegally staying' are defined in Art 2(b) and (c).

[390] Art 3(2).

However, Member States have an option not to apply the prohibition 'to illegally staying third-country nationals whose removal has been postponed and who are allowed to work in accordance with national law'.[391] Returning again to the situation of victims of trafficking, a separate Directive provides for a mandatory postponement of removal during a period of reflection which may be granted pursuant to that Directive;[392] arguably this should entail an option for a Member State to permit the victim to work during this period.

To enforce the prohibition of employment of irregular migrants, employers have three obligations regarding each third-country national employee:[393] to ensure that each employee 'hold and present to the employer his/her valid residence permit or other authorisation for his or her stay' before starting employment;[394] to keep copies of such documents at least for the duration of the employment, for 'possible inspection' by the national authorities; and to notify those authorities of the start of employment of each third-country national by the time laid down by each Member State. The Directive does not expressly address what happens when a fixed-term contract is renewed or made permanent.

Member States may optionally *simplify* the notification requirement 'where the employers are natural persons and the employment is for their private purposes' (hereinafter 'household employers'),[395] but Member States do not have the option to *waive* the notification requirement for this category of employers. Nor do Member States have any option, as regards household employers, to simplify *or* waive the requirements to check or keep copies of the relevant documents. Of course, in some circumstances it might be possible to argue that the persons concerned should be regarded as self-employed, in which case the obligations in the Directive would not apply.[396]

A wider optional exception applies to long-term residents as defined by EU law.[397] Member States are permitted to waive the notification requirement entirely as regards such employees.[398] Again, the obligation to check and keep copies of documents cannot be waived.

---

[391] Art 3(3). See, for instance, Case C-192/89 *Sevince* [1990] ECR I-3461. On the definition of 'postponement' of expulsion in light of the Returns Dir, see 7.7.1 below. It should also be noted that some EU measures on legal migration do not apply to persons whose expulsion is suspended as a matter of fact and law (see 6.5 above).   [392] Art 6(2) of Dir 2004/81, n 386 above.

[393] Art 4(1). For the definition of 'employer', see Art 2(e). An 'employer' includes a 'temporary work agency'; for a definition of the latter concept, see Art 2(h).

[394] According to recital 9 in the preamble, this provision should apply to third-country national workers posted by EC companies; this contradicts recital 5, which excludes such persons entirely from the scope of the Directive. Recital 12 in the preamble states that 'Member States should use their best endeavours to handle requests for renewal of residence permits in a timely manner'; this does not as such exempt employers from their obligations in cases where an employee is still awaiting a decision on an application for a renewal of his or her recently expired residence permit when he or she starts work.   [395] Art 4(2), first sub-paragraph.

[396] However, Member States are free, as a matter of national law, to extend some or all of these requirements to persons contracting with self-employed third-country nationals.

[397] Dir 2003/109 ([2004] OJ L 16/44). See 6.7 above.   [398] Art 4(2), second sub-paragraph.

The consequence of employers fulfilling all their obligations is that they cannot be held liable for breach of the prohibition on hiring irregular migrants 'unless the employers knew that the document presented as a valid residence permit or another authorisation for stay was a forgery'.[399] This is clearly a subjective test (*mens rea*) only, but if the Directive must be interpreted as setting only minimum standards as regards enforcement (see above), it therefore remains an option for Member States to apply strict criminal liability for the employers of irregular migrants.[400] There is no express rule on what happens if the employee loses the right to work after employment begins, but arguably the basic rule applies *mutatis mutandis*.

The Directive then specifies the consequences if employers have infringed the prohibition on *employing* irregular migrants.[401] This is a distinct issue from the employers' obligations to check and keep documents and to notify the authorities when hiring third-country nationals, since it is conceivable that an employer that has breached one or more of these latter obligations has nonetheless employed a person who is *not* an irregular migrant. It follows that it is up to each Member State to determine whether and to what extent the penalties set out in the Directive, alternative penalties, or any penalties at all, must be applied to employers who breach the separate obligations to check and keep documents and to notify the authorities when hiring third-country nationals. For example, prima facie it is open to Member States to exempt household employers, or those employers who have breached the requirements only as regards a few employees, from any penalty. Against this, it might be argued that the Community law principle of effectiveness requires that Member States impose some penalty on employers who have breached such requirements, but on the other hand the same principle must mean that such penalties cannot apply where EU law itself permits the employment of such third-country nationals.[402]

Where employers have breached the key prohibition on employing irregular migrants, they must generally be made subject to 'effective, proportionate and dissuasive sanctions'.[403] These sanctions must include 'financial sanctions which shall increase in amount according to the number of illegally employed third-country nationals',[404] 'and' the payment of the costs of return, if return is carried out.[405] But Member States can instead 'decide to reflect at least the average costs of return in the financial sanctions' which they must impose. Member States also have an option to reduce the 'financial sanctions' applicable to household

---

[399] Art 4(3).   [400] On principles of criminal liability in EU criminal law, see 10.5.3 below.

[401] Art 5.   [402] For example, see *Eyup* (n 385 above).   [403] Art 5(1).

[404] Art 5(2)(a). The precise application of this requirement (ie the exact numbers which will entail higher penalties) is implicitly left to Member States' law. The word 'include' in Art 5(2) must mean that the list of two measures mentioned in points (a) and (b) is not exhaustive.

[405] Art 5(2)(b). See the more precise obligations regarding costs set out in the carrier sanctions Dir (Dir 2001/51, [2001] OJ L 187/45), discussed in 7.5.1 above.

employers, if 'no particularly exploitative working conditions are involved'.[406] Again, this is only an option to *reduce* penalties for this category of employers, not to waive them altogether.

Next, employers which have breached the prohibition on employing irregular migrants are liable to pay any outstanding remuneration for the employee(s),[407] any taxes or social security contributions which would have been paid in the event of legal employment,[408] and any cost arising from sending the back payments to the country which the employee has returned to.[409] As for the amount of the pay and related taxes, and social security contributions, Member States must presume a period of three months' prior employment unless either the employer or employee (or 'others') can prove differently.[410] Presumably this time period is calculated backward from the date on which the employment actually ceased.

Similarly, the level of pay 'shall be presumed to have been at least as high as the wage provided for by the applicable laws on minimum wages, by collective agreements or in accordance with established practice in the relevant occupational branches', again unless the employee or employer can prove otherwise, subject to the relevant mandatory national laws on wages.[411] There is also a definition of remuneration—'the wage or salary and any other consideration, whether in cash or in kind, which a worker receives directly or indirectly in respect of his employment from his employer and which is equivalent to that which would have been enjoyed by comparable workers in a legal employment relationship'.[412] The Directive does not specify any presumption concerning the working time of the employee concerned (ie how many hours per week the employee must be presumed to have worked during the reference period, which could be relevant for the calculation of salary), as regards holiday pay,[413] or as regards other labour law issues regulated by EU or national law. Presumably at least all issues related to pay must be subject to the Directive, *mutatis mutandis*.[414] The Directive does not specifically address

---

[406] Art 5(3). The definition of 'particularly exploitative working conditions' is set out in Art 2(i); note that prima facie it appears that even *legal* working conditions could be covered by this definition.

[407] Art 6(1)(a).

[408] Art 6(1)(b). This includes 'penalty payments for delays and relevant administrative fines'.

[409] Art 6(1)(c).   [410] Art 6(3).   [411] Art 6(1)(a).

[412] Art 2(j). The relationship between this definition and the wording of Art 6(1)(a) is not entirely clear.

[413] Four weeks' paid holiday or pro rata periods of holiday pay is guaranteed by Art 7 of Dir 2003/88 on working time ([2003] OJ L 299/9). A payment in lieu must be made upon termination of employment (Art 7(2), Dir 2003/88); presumably this will also apply when employment terminates due to the irregular migration status of the employee. Recital 20 in the preamble refers to both holiday funds and social funds as part of back pay.

[414] This includes sick pay, maternity pay, and pay (or arguably other forms of financial compensation) due from a prior employer due to redundancy, unfair dismissal, or insolvency. Some of these issues are addressed by EU legislation (for instance, back pay due following insolvency: see Dir 2008/94 ([2008] OJ L 283/36)).

what happened if the employer can prove that *some* back pay was paid to the employee; presumably that amount should be set off against the remaining amount due, in accordance with the principle of proportionality. It is also not clear how to address the situation where the employee was in fact paid in full by the employer, but the pay rate agreed between them was less than the relevant minimum wage (or the level required by a generally applicable collective agreement). In that case, it should follow from the EU law principle of effectiveness that the employer must top the employee's pay up to the level which was legally required by national law.

The level of any tax and social security payments due implicitly must also be calculated in relation to the pay.[415] There is no provision for interest to be charged on back payments or on taxes, or social security contributions; arguably Member States are under an obligation to ensure that interest is payable in order to ensure the effectiveness of the Directive.[416]

While the Directive does not expressly require Member States to impose a time limit for employers to pay the amounts due to employees and the authorities, presumably Member States have the power and even the obligation to set a time limit to pay, enforceable by further penalties, in order to ensure the effectiveness of EU law. But conversely, there is no provision for a limit to be placed on the amount of back pay which an employee could receive.[417] It should be recalled that this provision of the Directive only sets minimum standards, with Member States free to set more favourable standards 'compatible' with the Directive for the benefit of the third-country nationals concerned.[418] So Member States could establish a presumption of six months' back pay, or arguably provide that the presumption relating to periods of back pay cannot be rebutted by the *employer*.[419]

While the Directive is silent on the application of labour law rules other than pay to irregular migrants, to the extent that labour law has been harmonized by EU law, then it follows from the EU law principle of effectiveness *as regards EU social policy* that irregular migrants should be covered by the relevant EU legislation. They are not expressly excluded from any EU social legislation, and their inclusion within the scope of the legislation would further its objectives of avoiding unfair competition as between Member States and ensuring a high level of protection for employees.[420]

---

[415] This is explicit as regards the presumption of three months' back payments (Art 6(3)).

[416] Case C-271/91 *Marshall II* [1993] ECR I-4367; but see Case C-66/95 *Sutton* [1997] ECR I-2163.

[417] A time limit for *bringing* a claim can be applied in accordance with Art 6(2)(a), discussed below.   [418] Art 15.

[419] It must always be possible to permit the *employee* to rebut the presumed period, because preventing an employee from doing this would not constitute a more favourable rule for the third-country nationals concerned.

[420] On the question of the personal scope of EU social legislation as regards third-country nationals generally, see E Guild and S Peers, 'Out of the Ghetto? The Personal Scope of EU law', in S Peers

It is obviously also necessary to ensure that there are effective mechanisms for irregular migrants to recover the back pay which they are due.[421] To this end, the Directive requires Member States to 'enact mechanisms to ensure that' the migrants can either introduce a claim on their own behalf to obtain back pay, subject to time limits imposed by Member States, and then 'enforce a judgment' to this end,[422] *or* can 'call on' a national authority to collect this claim on their behalf, 'when provided for by national legislation'.[423] It must follow that when national legislation does not foresee the latter remedy, then the former remedy must be provided for, otherwise the provisions on back pay would be rendered ineffective. While the Directive refers to these remedies as alternatives, it must be open for Member States to provide for *both* measures if they wish, since the Article in question sets only minimum standards in respect of third-country nationals' rights. Member States must inform irregular migrants about these rights, and the rights concerning facilitation of complaints, before the enforcement of any return decision.[424]

The individual remedy for the applicant is necessarily a judicial remedy, as evidenced by the words 'claim' and (most obviously) 'judgment'. It must follow that the EU rules on jurisdiction and conflict of law would apply.[425] Where a proceeding to reclaim back pay can only be brought through national authorities, the same principle must mean that the national authorities must act quickly when 'called on', and that if necessary a legal action or at least an effective complaints procedure must be in place for the employee where the authorities fail to act swiftly and competently. While there is no reference to costs, it should follow from the principle of effectiveness of EU law that the winning party in a judicial action should not have to pay costs,[426] and where national authorities act to reclaim back pay, at least that the costs charged to the employee are proportionate.

---

and N Rogers, eds, *EU Immigration and Asylum Law: Text and Commentary* (1st edn, Martinus Nijhoff, 2006).

[421] Art 6(2). Recital 16 in the preamble states that 'Member States should not be obliged to involve their missions or representations in third countries in those mechanisms'.

[422] Art 6(2)(a). According to the EU principle of effectiveness, such time limits cannot render the right impossible, and must be equivalent to those applying to comparable claims under national law. See, for instance, Case C-432/05 *Unibet* [2007] ECR I-2271.

[423] Art 6(2)(b). However, the preamble states that if employees are not able to regain back pay from their employer, the State is not therefore liable to pay it (recital 14).

[424] Arts 6(2) and 13. Due to the identical terms used, these provisions must surely be interpreted consistently with the Returns Dir, to the extent that the two Directives overlap.

[425] On the substance of those rules, see 8.5 below. If the rules on conflict of law in contracts do not apply, because an employment contract with an irregular migrant is considered void (although those conflict rules would still apply in order to determine *which* national contract law requires the nullity of the contract), then arguably the rules on conflict of laws concerning non-contractual liability should apply instead. It also seems obvious that an employer/employee dispute regarding pay is a civil claim, so Art 6 ECHR would apply, as would the right to a fair trial pursuant to the general principles of EU law.

[426] According to the Court of Justice, costs rules in EU law actions should follow the national rules on costs which apply in comparable cases: Case C-472/99 *Clean Car II* [2001] ECR I-9687.

For the avoidance of any doubt, the Directive provides that Member States must ensure that the employees are able to obtain the back pay concerned, whichever procedure is in place.[427]

Next, Member States are obliged to take four further measures, 'if appropriate', against employers who breach the prohibition against employing irregular migrants: exclusion from various forms of public aid, including EU funds, for up to five years; a claw-back of such aid given in the twelve months before the irregular employment was detected; exclusion from public procurement as defined by EU law for up to five years; and closure of the establishments used or withdrawal of licences to conduct the relevant activity.[428] Moreover, Member States can optionally exempt household employers from these measures,[429] although there is no option to exempt such employers from the core requirement to pay back pay, taxes, and social security contributions, or to reduce such obligations for such employers.

Where the employer is a subcontractor,[430] Member States are obliged to ensure joint and several liability with the employer as regards back pay and financial penalties.[431] The same applies where there is a main subcontractor and an intermediate subcontractor.[432] Subcontractors shall be exempt if they have 'undertaken due diligence obligations as defined in national law',[433] but as noted at the outset, all of the rules on subcontractors' liability are minimum standards, in that Member States may set more stringent liability rules under national law.[434]

Next, Member States are obliged to criminalize the employment of irregular migrants in five cases of intentional conduct 'as defined by national law':[435] a continued or 'persistently repeated' breach; the 'simultaneous employment of a significant number' of irregular migrants; there are 'particularly exploitative working conditions';[436] the employer was aware that the employees had been trafficked, pursuant to the Framework Decision on trafficking in persons (even in the absence of a charge or conviction for a trafficking offence);[437] or the employee was a minor.[438] Member States must also criminalize inciting and aiding or abetting such offences.[439] There is no exemption as such for household employment. As compared to EU criminal law measures, there is no provision on jurisdiction.[440]

---

[427] Art 6(4).   [428] Art 7(1).

[429] Art 7(2). This is clearly an option to *exempt* such employers entirely, not merely to *reduce* the relevant sanctions.   [430] See the definition in Art 2(f).

[431] Art 8(1).   [432] Art 8(2).   [433] Art 8(3).   [434] Art 8(4).

[435] Art 9(1). National law will necessarily have to define these offences more precisely, otherwise it will infringe the obligation to define criminal obligations sufficiently clearly as set out in Art 7 ECHR (see 10.3.1 below).   [436] For the definition of this phrase, see Art 2(i).

[437] [2002] OJ L 203/1; see 7.5.4 above. This rule will presumably apply *mutatis mutandis* when that Framework Decision is replaced by a Directive. This only applies where the employer was not itself charged or convicted as regards trafficking in persons.

[438] 'Minor' is not defined in the Directive.

[439] Art 9(2).   [440] On criminal jurisdiction and EC/EU law, see further 11.5 below.

The penalties for this criminal offence are not harmonized, because the EC at the time of adoption of the Directive had no competence to harmonize criminal sanctions.[441] Rather, Member States must simply apply 'effective, proportionate and dissuasive criminal penalties' to natural persons.[442] It is notable that most of the EU's measures concerning mutual recognition in criminal law do not abolish the dual criminality requirement as regards the offence of employing irregular migrants,[443] although the obvious consequence of implementing the Directive will be that (for the participating Member States) the dual criminality requirement will be relatively easy to satisfy.[444] Member States may also apply 'other sanctions or measures of a non-criminal nature', unless this is 'prohibited by general principles of law', and may also publish the judgments relating to the case.[445] For legal persons, in common with other EU measures, Member States must ensure they are liable, without an obligation to apply criminal penalties as such,[446] although Member States must apply some form of penalty to legal persons, which may entail application of the 'other measures' referred to in the Directive (exclusion or repayment of state aid, ban from participation in public procurement, etc).[447] Obviously legal persons will also be subject to the obligation to pay back pay, tax, and social security contributions.

Member States must facilitate complaints by employees against employers as regards the obligations in the Directive, either directly or through third parties such as trade unions.[448] They must also ensure that third parties meeting 'the criteria laid down in their national law' can act on behalf or in support of employees in administrative or civil proceedings to ensure compliance with the Directive.[449] Providing assistance to third-country nationals to lodge complaints shall not be regarded as the facilitation of irregular migration within the scope of separate legislation prohibiting the facilitation of irregular migration.[450] Where there is a criminal offence involving 'particularly exploitative working conditions' or a minor, Member States 'shall define in national law the conditions under which they may grant, on a case-by-case basis, permits of limited duration, linked to the length of the relevant national proceedings' in a manner 'comparable' to

---

[441] See C-440/05 *Commission v Council* [2007] ECR I-9097, and further 7.2.4 above and 10.2.4 below.   [442] Art 10(1).

[443] See for instance, Art 2(2) of the Framework Decision establishing the European Arrest Warrant ([2002] OJ L 190/1). The exception is Art 5(1) of the Framework Decision on the mutual recognition of financial penalties ([2005] OJ L 76/16), which abolishes dual criminality as regards offences applied by a Member State in order to implement 'obligations arising from instruments adopted under the EC Treaty'.   [444] See generally ch 9.

[445] Art 10(2).

[446] Art 11. On the issue of corporate criminal liability, see further 10.5.2.1 below.

[447] Art 12, referring to Art 7.

[448] Art 13(1). As noted above, all of the obligations in Art 13 are minimum standards only (see Art 15).   [449] Art 13(2).

[450] Art 13(3), referring to Dir 2002/90 ([2002] OJ L 328/17). On that Directive, see 7.5.3 above.

the protection of the victims of trafficking in persons who cooperate with the prosecution authorities as set out in the separate Directive on the protection of the victims of such trafficking.[451] Furthermore, Member States 'shall define under national law the conditions under which the duration of these permits may be extended until the third country national has received any back payment' due under the Directive.[452]

There must be regular inspections of employers to enforce the Directive, based on a 'risk assessment' by national authorities,[453] which shall also 'regularly identify the sectors of activity in which the employment of illegally staying third-country nationals is concentrated on their territory'. Member States shall then inform the Commission annually of the numbers of inspections and their results.[454]

This Directive takes as a given the objective of decreasing the attraction of the EU as a destination for irregular migrants, even though the Commission's impact assessment concerning its original proposal for this Directive states that there are economic benefits to such employment.[455] The alternative route of legalizing it is not considered at all by the Commission. According to the impact assessment, almost all Member States had employer sanctions regarding employment of irregular migrants already in 2007, and moreover most Member States imposed criminal sanctions; the crucial issue was the *enforcement* of these obligations.[456] As to the reasons for the absence of enforcement, these stemmed from various inadequacies in the organization and financing of national administrations;[457] the EU could only add value in the form of supporting the costs of inspections or assisting coordination between different national administrations, but Directive 2009/52 does neither.

The Commission argument for EU action was to 'level the playing field' between employers in different Member States, along with the 'publicity effect' of adopting an EU-wide measure. But the first objective could only be accomplished if enforcement were actually stepped up. While the Commission's original proposal would have increased the rate of inspections from 2% to 10% of all employers annually,[458] and therefore could well prima facie have increased the level of enforcement, the final text of the Directive only requires Member States to carry out general and sectoral risk assessments. The impact assessment report had made little reference to the issue of risk assessment, but presumably national authorities were already aware that there are likely to be more irregular migrants cleaning hotel toilets than teaching EU law.

---

[451] Art 13(4), referring to Dir 2004/81 ([2004] OJ L 261/19). On that Directive, see 7.6.2 below.

[452] Art 6(5). More generally, recital 15 in the preamble states that irregular migrants should not be able to derive a right to stay from the employment or back pay, etc.   [453] Art 14(1).

[454] Art 14(2). There is no requirement for the Commission to make these statistics public.

[455] SEC (2007) 603, 16 May 2007.   [456] See p 9 of the report.

[457] See p 10 of the report. Some of these issues are referred to briefly in recital 30 of the preamble to the Directive (adequate powers to inspect, collection and processing of information, sufficient staff).

[458] COM (2007) 249, 15 May 2007, Art 15.

Even if the Commission has the resources and expertise to analyse the annual risk assessments submitted by Member States, Member States' authorities would not be obliged to follow up any suggestions which the Commission makes.

Moreover, even assuming that the Directive contained effective rules on enforcement, the 'playing field' could not be levelled and deterrence could not be assured without harmonizing to some degree the levels of penalties. But the Directive does not harmonize the levels of criminal penalties (due to limits on Community competence) or administrative penalties, even at a minimum standard. It remains to be seen whether any 'publicity effect' the Directive may have, and/or its provisions on back pay for employees and related payments to administrations, have any impact on achieving its desired objective.

7.6.2. Victims of trafficking or smuggling in persons

Due to public concern about the fate of victims of trafficking in persons and the apparent difficulties in prosecuting the perpetrators of trafficking crimes, since the victims who could testify against them were usually irregular migrants subject in principle to expulsion, the Council considered it necessary to adopt Directive 2004/81 in April 2004, addressing the issue of the immigration status of these victims.[459] Member States had to implement the Directive by 6 August 2006.[460] The Commission brought two infringement actions against Member States that did not apply this Directive by the deadline.[461] A subsequent Directive also provides that Member States shall define in national law the conditions under which they may apply comparable arrangements to Directive 2004/81, where there are criminal proceedings relating to the illegal employment of a minor or a third-country national has been illegally employed and also subject to 'particularly exploitative working conditions'.[462]

The purpose of Directive 2004/81 is to define the conditions for issuing a limited residence permit, linked to the length of the judicial proceedings, to persons who cooperate in the fight against trafficking or the facilitation of illegal

---

[459] [2004] OJ L 261/19. On the 'legal base' of the Directive, see 7.2.4 above. On the underlying issues, see D Haynes, 'Used, Abused, Arrested and Deported: Extending Immigration Benefits to Protect the Victims of Trafficking and to Secure the Prosecution of Traffickers' (2004) 26 HRQ 221 and H Askola, *Legal Responses to Trafficking in Women for Sexual Exploitation in the European Union* (Hart, 2007).

[460] Art 17, Dir 2004/81. All references in this subsection are to Dir 2004/81 unless otherwise indicated.

[461] Cases: C-209/08 *Commission v Luxembourg* (withdrawn) and Case C-266/08 *Commission v Spain* (judgment of 14 May 2009, unreported).

[462] Art 13(4) of Dir 2009/52 ([2009] OJ L 168/24), referring to Arts 9(1)(c) and (e) of that Directive; for the relevant definitions, see Art 2(b), (d) and (i) of that Directive. On Dir 2009/52, see further 7.6.1 above.

immigration.[463] The Directive defines trafficking and the facilitation of illegal immigration by reference to the EU acts concerning these issues, but the definition in the EU acts is not exhaustive.[464] It should be noted that the status of the victims as regards criminal procedure is regulated by separate EU measures.[465]

Member States are obliged to apply the Directive to victims of trafficking in persons, including those who did not enter legally.[466] They have an option to apply it to persons who have been 'the subject of an action to facilitate illegal migration'.[467] Its application to minors is also optional.[468] The preamble sets out a safeguard clause on protection for refugees, persons with subsidiary protection, and asylum seekers, along with human rights treaties, and also includes a non-discrimination clause.[469] On this point, it is conceivable that some victims might have a valid claim for international protection, if non-state persecutors (ie the criminal organizations which trafficked those victims) pose a sufficient risk of inflicting serious harm or persecution as defined by the EU Directive on qualification for refugee status or subsidiary protection.[470] Member States are free to provide for more extensive protection for persons covered by the Directive, without a requirement that such measures be 'compatible' with the Directive.[471]

Member States' authorities will usually trigger the application of the Directive by informing persons whom they believe could fall within its scope, although Member States have an option to decide if NGOs or associations specifically appointed by the Member State concerned can also trigger the process.[472] After that point, there is a reflection period for the persons concerned to decide if they wish to cooperate with the authorities; the starting point and length of this period are determined by national law.[473] During this period, expulsion orders cannot be enforced,[474] and the person concerned is entitled to minimum standards of

---

[463] Art 1.

[464] Art 2(b) and (c). See the Framework Decision and Directive on facilitation of illegal entry and residence (7.5.3 above) and the Framework Decision, and now the agreed Directive, on trafficking in persons (7.5.4 above). The definition of a 'measure to enforce an expulsion order' (Art 2(d)) presumably must in future be understood in light of the Returns Dir (Dir 2008/115, [2008] OJ L 348/98), to the extent that the victims fall within the scope of that Directive (see 7.7.1 below).

[465] The Framework Decision on trafficking in persons (ibid) as well as the Framework Decision on crime victims (see 9.8.2 below).   [466] Art 3(1).

[467] Art 3(2).   [468] Art 3(3). The Directive defines 'minors' by reference to national law.

[469] Recitals 4 and 7 in the preamble of the Directive.

[470] Dir 2004/83 ([2004] OJ L 304/12), and proposed new qualification Dir (COM (2009) 551, 21 Oct 2009). See further 5.5 above.   [471] Art 4. On the 'compatibility' issue, see 7.2.4 above.

[472] Art 5.   [473] Art 6(1).

[474] Art 6(2). Although the subsequent Returns Dir (n 464 above) will create a prima facie obligation to expel irregular migrants, there will nonetheless be a broad discretion for a Member State to refrain from issuing or to withdraw or suspend a return decision, or to postpone removal (Arts 6(4) and 9(2), Dir 2008/115). In any event, the entire Returns Dir is subject to more favourable provisions in other EU immigration and asylum law (Art 4(2), Dir 2008/115). This provision in Dir 2004/81 is obviously one example of a more favourable provision. Also, the obligation to postpone

treatment as regards subsistence, emergency medical treatment, translation and interpretation, and legal aid.[475] The reflection period does not create a right to subsequent residence,[476] and a Member State may end the period if the person concerned 'actively, voluntarily and on his/her own initiative' renews contact with the perpetrators, or on grounds of public policy or national security.[477] Following (or possibly before) the end of the reflection period, the national authorities shall consider the 'opportunity presented by' the continued stay of the victim, his or her intention to cooperate and whether he or she has severed relations with the perpetrators,[478] before issuing a residence permit. However, the Directive does not appear to create a right to a permit if the conditions are met.[479] The permit must be valid for at least six months, and may be renewed if these conditions are still met,[480] but there is no express reference to using the EU's uniform residence permit.[481] Member States are encouraged to consider authorizing the stay of the victim's family members on other grounds.[482]

The Directive also sets out rules on the treatment of the victims after the special permit is issued. Member States must continue to extend minimum standards regarding subsistence, emergency medical treatment, translation and interpretation, and (optionally) legal aid to victims, and must also give necessary medical or other assistance to victims with special needs and without sufficient resources.[483] If Member States apply the Directive to minors, they must take account of the best interests of the child, give access to education on the same basis as nationals (although this may be limited to the public education system), and establish the identity and nationality of, trace the family members of, and ensure legal representation for unaccompanied minors in accordance with national law.[484] Member States must define the rules for victims' access to the labour market, vocational training, and education during the period of the residence permit; this does not appear to grant them discretion over whether to allow such access, but only discretion as regards the extent of and procedures for exercising such access.[485] The persons concerned by the Directive must be given access to schemes designed to assist them to develop a normal social life, if such schemes exist, including courses to improve professional skills or to prepare for assisted return to their country of origin. Member States may

---

removal in Art 6(2) entitles a Member State to permit the person concerned to work (see Art 3(3), Dir 2009/52, n 464 above).

[475] Arts 6(2) and 7.   [476] Art 6(3).   [477] Art 6(4).   [478] Art 8(1).

[479] See Art 8(2).   [480] Art 8(3).

[481] See Art 11 of the initial proposal, and see further 6.9.1 above.

[482] Recital 15 in the preamble.   [483] Art 9.

[484] Art 10. Art 2(f) defines 'unaccompanied minors'.

[485] Art 11. The subsequent Dir 2009/52 on employer sanctions for employing irregular migrants (n 462 above) makes no express exception for victims of trafficking or smuggling who have such a permit, but it must be assumed that the grant of a residence permit pursuant to Dir 2004/81 means that the person concerned is not an irregular migrant as long as that permit is valid (see Art 2(b) and (d), Dir 2009/52).

also provide for special schemes designed for the persons concerned, and may make the residence permit conditional on participation in either the general or special schemes.[486] Moreover, the subsequent Returns Directive provides that an 'entry ban' as defined by that Directive shall not be issued to victims of trafficking, although this is 'without prejudice' to the obligation to issue an entry ban if an obligation to return has not been complied with, and also subject to a derogation on grounds of 'public policy, public security or national security'.[487]

The permit shall not be renewed if the proceedings are over or if the conditions for its issue cease to be satisfied. After this point, normal immigration law applies,[488] but the preamble to the Directive states that Member States 'should consider the fact that' the person concerned already has a residence permit issued on the basis of this Directive if that person applies to stay on another ground.[489] The permit may also be withdrawn on grounds of: the person concerned 'actively, voluntarily and on his/her own initiative' renewing contact with the suspected perpetrators; the authorities' belief in fraudulent cooperation or a fraudulent complaint by the person concerned; public policy or national security; the person concerned ceasing to cooperate; and discontinuation of the proceedings. These grounds are non-exhaustive ('in particular').[490]

Although the Commission has not yet produced the review of the application of the Directive that was due in August 2008,[491] there is some information available about its implementation by Member States. In 2008,[492] the Commission reported that the reflection period was not applied in practice in most Member States. Residence permits were available for periods between forty days and one year, most often for six months. Victims have access to the labour market in accordance with the Directive in every Member State except Poland. The available figures from nine Member States indicated that 2,676 victims had received permits, but 80% of those were in Italy, which had a pre-existing very generous status for trafficking victims. The Commission concluded that 'at EU level the situation is still largely unsatisfactory', but also noted that 'in countries . . . which

---

[486] Art 12.

[487] Art 11(3), Dir 2008/115 (n 464 above). Note that this protection will not apply to victims of smuggling, and also will not apply if a victim falls outside the personal scope of the Returns Dir (see further 7.7.1 below). Presumably the protection will also expire with the residence permit. Note, however, that Member States have considerable discretion as to whether to issue or withdraw an entry ban in all such cases (Arts 11(1) and (3), Dir 2008/115).

[488] Presumably the Returns Dir (ibid) would then normally apply once the deadline for its application passes, if the person concerned is within the scope of that Directive. This will trigger a prima facie obligation to issue a return decision (Art 6(1) of that Directive), but Member States retain a broad discretion to grant an 'autonomous residence permit or other authorisation offering a right to stay for compassionate, humanitarian or other reasons' (Art 6(4) of that Directive). As noted above, it is also possible that the person concerned might have a claim for international protection.

[489] Recitals 15 and 18 in the preamble.   [490] Art 14.   [491] Art 16(1).

[492] Communication on human trafficking (COM (2008) 657, 17 Oct 2008).

have a significant number of assisted victims, figures on criminal proceedings are also higher... [t]herefore, further regulation might be necessary in order to ensure more effective victim support mechanisms'.

This evidence proves that the Directive, as it currently stands, was unable to avoid the inherent tension between trying to combat irregular immigration by encouraging victims of trafficking and smuggling to testify, and the risk that the incentives offered to the victims would either be abused or have the result that the victims would be able to stay in the 'host' Member State longer than it would wish. The key changes to the text as initially proposed by the Commission made its application to smuggling cases optional and weakened the extent and precision of the obligations imposed upon Member States as regards victims.[493] The latter changes have made the scheme established by the Directive less attractive to victims, as evidenced by the higher numbers receiving permits under the more generous scheme in Italy. It has also proved hard, as might have been expected, to monitor the usefulness of the Directive in practice because the provisions on exchange of information proposed by the Commission were deleted by the Council. Moreover, the Directive contains more limited provisions on the status of victims than the UN Protocol or the Council of Europe Convention on trafficking in persons.[494] As matters stand, it does not appear that the Directive has by itself made a significant contribution to its main goal of combating trafficking in persons. It remains to be seen whether a more generous implementation by Member States, or the revision of the Directive (alongside the parallel agreed changes to the criminal law framework in this area) might have a more successful outcome.[495]

7.7. Expulsion

Of course, if persons who do not or longer have authorization to stay on the territory of a Member State are detected, the primary response of Member States is to expel them from the territory,[496] but expulsions are necessarily subject to the protection afforded by human rights or refugee law and humanitarian concerns. Expulsion often involves cross-border elements, but there is an argument that a Member State should not assist another Member State to carry out an expulsion without guarantees that human rights standards will be upheld.

---

[493] For the Commission's proposal, see COM (2002) 71, 11 Feb 2002.

[494] See Arts 6 and 7 of the Protocol ([2006] OJ L 262/51) and Arts 10–15 of the Convention (CETS 197).

[495] On the agreed criminal law measures, see 7.5.4 above. On the broader agenda on this issue set out in the Stockholm programme, see 7.2.3 above.

[496] This book generally uses the word 'expulsion' throughout, although in recent years the EU institutions have preferred the term 'return'. The word 'return' is used in this section to the extent that it is a specific legal term with a meaning defined in legislation.

The EU has become involved in expulsion issues, first of all in regulating cross-border aspects, and only subsequently in adopting minimum standards to govern expulsions, in the form of the 'Returns Directive'.[497] Due to the importance of this Directive, it is considered in detail first, and then the earlier cross-border rules relating to mutual recognition of expulsion orders, expulsion for transit, and joint flights are considered in turn. An EU expulsion fund has also been established.[498]

The initial source of rules on this issue was the Schengen Convention, Article 23 of which provides that persons who do not, or no longer, fulfil the requirements of entry within a Member State for a short stay 'shall normally be required to leave' all the Member States immediately.[499] Where the persons concerned hold 'valid residence permits or provisional residence permits' issued by another Member State, they 'shall be required to go to' that Member State immediately.[500] If they have not left voluntarily, or it may be assumed that they will not, or where 'their immediate departure is required for reasons of national security or public policy', they must be expelled immediately from the Member State where they were apprehended, 'in accordance with' the relevant national law; but if that national law does not allow for expulsion, the person concerned may be allowed to stay on the territory.[501] They may be expelled either to their country of origin or to any State where they may be admitted, in accordance with Member States' readmission agreements.[502] But the latter rule 'shall not preclude the application of' the Geneva Convention on asylum, national rules on asylum, or the Convention provision concerning the requirement to go to another Member State.[503]

Where the expulsion cannot be charged to the third-country national, Article 24 of the Schengen Convention provides that Member States must reimburse to each other the costs of such expulsions, subject to the Schengen Executive Committee's determination of the costs and practical arrangements. In fact, the Executive Committee never adopted the relevant rules.

The Court of Justice has ruled that Article 23 of the Convention applies to all persons who do not or no longer meet the legal requirements for a short stay on the territory.[504] But it does not impose a strict obligation to expel such a

---

[497] See also, as regards voluntary return, a Maastricht-era Decision ([1997] OJ L 147/3) and Council conclusions of 2005 (text in JHA Council press release, 12 Oct 2005).

[498] See 7.8 below.

[499] Art 23(1) of the Convention ([2000] OJ L 239). This subsection refers to the Schengen Convention, except where otherwise indicated. On the allocation of Arts 23 and 24 following the entry into force of the Treaty of Amsterdam, see 7.2.2.2 above.

[500] Art 23(2).   [501] Art 23(3).   [502] Art 23(4). On readmission treaties, see 7.9.1 below.

[503] Art 23(5). On asylum, see generally ch 5 above.

[504] Joined Cases C-261/08 *Zurita Garcia* and C-348/08 *Choque Cabrera*, judgment of 22 Oct 2009, not yet reported. Implicitly the Court did not limit the scope of Art 23 to persons who had moved between Member States, despite the overall context of Art 23, which appears in the Convention provisions concerning freedom to travel between Member States (see generally 4.9 above).

person, on the grounds that it 'favours the voluntary departure' of the persons concerned.[505] Even where the Convention does create an obligation to expel, this 'is subordinate to the conditions laid down in the national law of the Member State concerned'.[506] Therefore it is up to 'the national law of each Member State to adopt, particularly with regard to the conditions under which expulsion may take place, the means for applying the basic rules established in Article 23 of the' Convention.[507]

7.7.1. Returns Directive

The controversial 'Returns Directive' was adopted in December 2008 after a lengthy and difficult negotiation between the EP and the Council (and also within each institution).[508] Member States must apply the Directive by Christmas Eve 2010, with a further delay of one year to apply the provisions on legal aid.[509] The Directive replaces the provisions of Articles 23 and 24 of the Schengen Convention, which were summarized above.[510] It has already been the subject of one judgment of the Court of Justice.[511]

The Directive applies to all third-country nationals 'staying illegally' in a Member State,[512] except that Member States may decide (optionally) not to apply it to persons who: (a) were refused entry in accordance with the Schengen Borders Code, or who were 'apprehended or intercepted in connection with' irregular crossing of an external border and who were not later allowed to stay in that Member State; or (b) 'are subject to a return as a criminal law sanction or as a consequence of a criminal law sanction, according to national law, or who are the subject of extradition procedures'.[513] However, as regards persons who were

---

[505] Ibid, para 61 of the judgment, as regards Art 23(1); see equally para 62, as regards Art 23(2).

[506] Para 63 of the judgment, concerning Art 23(3).   [507] Para 64 of the judgment.

[508] Dir 2008/115 ([2008] OJ L 348/98). On the Directive, see: A Baldaccini, 'The Return and Removal of Irregular Migrants under EU Law: An Analysis of the Returns Directive' (2009) 11 EJML 1; D Acosta, 'The Good, the Bad, and the Ugly in EU Migration Law' (2009) 11 EJML 19; and the Statewatch analysis of June 2008: <http://www.statewatch.org/news/2008/jun/eu-analysis-returns-directive-june-2008-final.pdf>.

[509] Art 20(1), Dir 2008/115. All the references in this subsection are to this Directive, unless otherwise indicated.   [510] Art 21.

[511] Case C-357/09 PPU Kadzoev, judgment of 30 Nov 2009, not yet reported.

[512] Art 2(1). According to the definition in Art 3(2), this is a person who *either* 'does not fulfil, or no longer fulfils the conditions of entry as set out in Article 5 of the Schengen Borders Code' *or* who does not or no longer fulfils 'other conditions for entry, stay or residence in that Member State'. Presumably the 'other' conditions referred to here could be established by either EU or national law. The Schengen Borders Code is set out in Reg 562/2006 ([2006] OJ L 105/1); on the code, see 3.6.1 above. Note that the first category of persons covered matches the scope of Art 23(1) of the Schengen Convention, but the second category of persons concerned is wider. Equally the Directive only builds on the Schengen *acquis* as regards the first category of persons, not the latter (paras 25–30 in the preamble); this has implications for the territorial scope of the Directive (see further 7.2.5 above).

[513] Art 2(2), referring in part to Art 13 of the Borders Code (ibid).

refused entry or stopped in connection with irregular entry, Member States are nevertheless required to apply certain rules in the Directive,[514] as well as the principle of non-refoulement (on this principle, see the discussion below). Furthermore, the Directive does not apply to persons with EU free movement rights.[515] There is no express exclusion for asylum seekers, but the preamble to the Directive states that in accordance with the EU's asylum procedures Directive,[516] a third-country national asylum seeker 'should not be regarded as staying illegally on the territory of that Member State until a negative decision on the application, or a decision ending his or her right of stay as asylum seeker has entered into force'.[517] The Court of Justice has therefore reached the conclusion that asylum seekers fall outside the scope of the Directive.[518]

The exclusion relating to refusal of entry pursuant to the Borders Code is clear enough, but the exclusion relating to irregular border crossing is less clear. Since there is no reference to national law as regards this exclusion (as compared to the criminal law exclusion), and the EU law rules on borders to which it implicitly refers are subject to a high degree of harmonization, this exclusion should have an autonomous EU law meaning.[519] Quite clearly, the drafters of the Directive did not intend that Member States should have carte blanche to exclude all cases of clandestine entry from the scope of the Directive, otherwise the Directive could simply have provided for an optional exclusion regarding all persons 'who have illegally entered the territory of a Member State'—which in fact it provides for separately in relation to one specific issue.[520] This suggests a strong argument for an *a contrario* interpretation of the more general optional exclusion. Moreover, the preamble to the Directive simply states without qualification that the Directive should apply to 'all' third-country nationals who do not or no longer meet the conditions for entry, stay, or residence;[521] this necessarily means

---

[514] Art 4(4). The provisions concerned are 'Article 8(4) and (5) (limitations on use of coercive measures), Article 9(2)(a) (postponement of removal), Article 14(1) (b) and (d) (emergency health care and taking into account needs of vulnerable persons), and Articles 16 and 17 (detention conditions)'.

[515] Art 2(3). See also the definition of 'third-country national' in Art 3(1). On the relationship between irregular migration and free movement law, see 7.4.1 above.

[516] Art 7 of Dir 2005/85, [2005] OJ L 326/13; see now Art 8 of the proposed new version of the Dir (COM (2009) 554, 21 Oct 2009). On this Directive generally, see 5.7 above.

[517] Recital 9 in the preamble. It should be recalled that the current asylum procedures Dir, unlike the Returns Dir, also applies to the UK and Ireland, whereas the Returns Dir (in part), but not the asylum procedures Dir, applies to Schengen associates.

[518] *Kadzoev*, n 511 above. The Court noted that specific rules on detention appear in the EU's asylum legislation, and it should be noted that the Commission has proposed new rules on these issues: see 5.7–5.9 above. Note that the EU's Dir on temporary protection does not have specific rules on this issue, and so arguably any persons who obtain temporary protection status but who are not also asylum seekers *would* be covered by the detention rules in the Returns Dir (see 5.6 above).

[519] See by analogy Case C-578/08 *Chakroun*, judgment of 4 Mar 2010, not yet reported.

[520] Art 12(3).

[521] Recital 5. There is no mention in the preamble of any of the exclusions from the Directive's scope. On this basis of this recital, it can surely be concluded that the list of exceptions set out in Art 2(2) is exhaustive.

that any exclusions from the scope of the Directive must be interpreted narrowly. In this light, the optional exclusion for irregular border crossing should only apply where a person was stopped at or near the border, in principle by border guards carrying out border surveillance as part of their border control obligations,[522] and *not* when a clandestine entrant was later detected on the territory.

As for the optional criminal law exclusion, in principle it should have a more varied application, given the reference to national law in the Directive. However, if Member States provide in their national law for expulsion as a penalty for the criminal law offence (if one is established) of most or all cases of irregular entry and/or irregular residence, then the intention of the Directive (evidenced in the preamble) of applying to 'all' irregular migrants who are third-country nationals would clearly be circumvented. Indeed, if this interpretation were permissible, it would be possible, if a Member State makes all cases of irregular entry or residence an offence and punishes all those offences by expulsion, to exclude *everyone* from the scope of the Directive. An exception cannot become the rule. It must follow, in light of the principle of the effectiveness of EU law, that the criminal law exclusion cannot apply where the criminal offences in question relate only to irregular migration.

More favourable provisions for the persons concerned can be set out either in agreements between the EU and/or the Member States with third countries, or in other EU legislation, or in national legislation. In the case of national legislation (but not otherwise), this possibility is subject to the proviso that the more favourable rules are 'compatible' with the Returns Directive.[523] The EU legislation which sets more favourable standards includes an option (rather than an obligation) to expel a person pursuant to the Schengen Borders Code.[524] Furthermore, Directive 2004/81 on the rights of victims of trafficking[525] must entail at the very least an obligatory postponement of expulsion during the reflection period set out in that Directive,[526] and might also mean suspension or withdrawal of a return decision for that period. If a residence permit is granted under the 2004 Directive it must follow that the person concerned is, for the time being, outside the scope of the Returns Directive entirely, so either a return decision cannot be issued or any such decision must be rescinded or withdrawn,[527] and the postponement (or,

---

[522] See the definitions of 'border guard' and 'border surveillance' in Art 2(11) and (13) of the Borders Code, as well as the specific provision on border surveillance in Art 12 of the Code. The definition of 'border control' in Art 2(9) of the Code should also be used to define the scope of the exclusion in the Directive: an 'activity carried out at the border in accordance with and for the purposes of [the Code] in response exclusively to an intention to cross or the act of crossing that border'.

[523] Art 4. On such requirements of 'compatibility' in EU immigration and asylum law, see 5.2.4 above.

[524] Art 11 of the Code (n 512 above), as interpreted by the Court of Justice in Joined Cases C-261/08 *Zurita Garcia* and C-348/08 *Choque Cabrera*, judgment of 22 Oct 2009, not yet reported. See the discussion in 3.6.1 above.

[525] Dir 2004/81 ([2004] OJ L 261/19), discussed in 7.6.2 above.   [526] Art 9.

[527] Art 6(4).

by implication, the rescinding) of removal necessarily follows. Victims also have more rights to health care, employment, and social assistance during the reflection period and while residing on the basis of a residence permit than they would have under the Returns Directive.[528]

When implementing the Returns Directive, Member States 'shall take due account of' the best interests of the child, family life, and the state of health of the persons concerned, and respect the principle of non-refoulement.[529] Given the emphasis placed by the Court of Justice on the effect of similar general provisions in the EU's family reunion Directive,[530] prima facie these provisions of the Returns Directive should have a similarly strong legal impact. The Directive has no definition of 'non-refoulement' and makes no reference to the source of the principle.[531] Arguably the concept should not be defined in accordance with national law, in the absence of any reference to it,[532] but rather has a EU-wide meaning, defined either by reference to EU legislation, international obligations, some autonomous version of the concept, or a combination of these various sources. Procedurally, it is unclear whether a Member State could argue that a completed (failed) asylum procedure exempts it from its obligation under the Returns Directive to ensure non-refoulement, on the grounds that compliance with the principle has already been assessed.

These are the only substantive grounds for objecting to an expulsion set out in the Directive, if this provision is indeed to be understood as setting out grounds for resisting expulsion at all. However, it should not be forgotten that any substantive grounds for resisting expulsion set out in other EU legislation, national legislation, or international treaties will take priority over the Returns Directive anyway.[533]

Chapter II of the Directive contains six Articles concerning the 'termination of illegal stay'. First of all, there are basic rules regarding 'return decisions'.[534] Member States must issue a return decision to every third-country national staying illegally on their territory,[535] but this is 'without prejudice' to a number

---

[528] Compare Arts 7 and 9–12 of Dir 2004/81 to Art 14, Returns Dir. It should also be noted that Dir 2004/81 does not include an option to exclude persons refused entry or stopped in connection with illegal entry from its scope, whereas the Returns Dir does.   [529] Art 5.

[530] Case C-540/03 *EP v Council* [2006] ECR I-5759; see further 6.6 above.

[531] Compare to Art 23(5) of the Schengen Convention, although note that recitals 23 and 24 in the preamble refer to the Geneva Convention on refugee status and the EU Charter of Fundamental Rights respectively. For more on the concept of non-refoulement, see 5.3.1 above.

[532] However, it should be noted that the EU and relevant international sources of the principle expressly set minimum standards only, so the capacity to set higher national standards must not be prejudiced.

[533] Art 4(1) to (3). As noted above though, any higher national standards must be 'compatible' with the Directive.

[534] Art 6. For the definition of 'return decision', see Art 3(4).

[535] Art 6(1). The definition of 'return' is set out in Art 3(3): 'return' can be either to a country of origin or transit, or to another third country which the person concerned chooses to return to and in which that person will be admitted. There is no definition of 'third countries'. It is not clear

of exceptions.[536] First of all, a third-country national who holds a residence permit or other authorization to stay in a second Member State 'shall be required to go' back there instead; he or she would only be subject to a return decision in cases of non-compliance with the obligation to return to the second Member State or for reasons of 'public policy or national security'.[537] Next, a third-country national 'may' instead be sent to another Member State pursuant to a pre-existing bilateral deal, but in that case the second Member State 'shall' then issue a return decision to the person concerned.[538] Presumably, where the person concerned has a residence permit or other authorization to stay in another Member State, the first exception takes precedence over the second one.

Next, Member States have a very wide discretion to regularize stays of irregular migrants, 'at any moment . . . for compassionate, humanitarian or other reasons'.[539] In that case, no return decision shall be issued, but if a return decision has already been issued, Member States have the option of merely suspending the decision, rather than withdrawing it, for the duration of the authorized stay. The Directive is silent on the question of regularizing large numbers of persons, so in the absence of any other EU rules regulating this issue, Member States retain competence to regularize the stay of large numbers of irregular migrants collectively if they wish.[540] But equally there is no *right* to regularization as a matter of EU law,[541] or any harmonized procedural or substantive rules at EU level applicable to regularizations. It is open to Member States to limit regularization to particular categories of persons, or to regularize stay only for a limited time, at least initially, in light of the circumstances in the country of origin.[542]

whether a Member State (or a non-EU Schengen State) might be considered a 'third country', and furthermore if there is any distinction between the participating and non-participating Member States in this regard. Note that the obligation to issue a return decision is similar to the prior obligation under Art 23(1) of the Schengen Convention to oblige a person to leave the territory (see the definition of 'return decision', ibid). Compare also the definition of 'return' in the Directive to Art 23(4) of the Convention.

[536] Furthermore, the preamble to the Directive—but not the main text—states in effect that decisions on return have to be decided on a case-by-case basis, not automatically for the sole reason that a person is not legally resident (recital 6).

[537] Art 6(2). The basic rule in this paragraph is taken from Art 23(2) of the Schengen Convention, but the exception to the rule is new.

[538] Art 6(3). The agreements in question had to exist already when the Directive entered into force (this was 13 Jan 2009: see Art 22). The implication is that no further such agreements can be made after this date.

[539] Art 6(4). Presumably this discretion also exists where an irregular migrant has been sent to another Member State pursuant to Art 6(3), because the second Member State in that case has taken over the entire return procedure (including any exceptions which may apply).

[540] See by comparison Art 7(2), which provides for extension of the required period to return in individual cases.

[541] Leaving aside the possibility of becoming a family member of an EU citizen: see 7.4.1 above.

[542] If, however, some of the persons concerned wished to pursue asylum applications, the EU's asylum legislation would be applicable (see generally ch 5).

Member States are not limited as regards the grounds for regularization in individual cases, which are clearly non-exhaustive ('or other reasons'),[543] or the timing of regularization, which expressly can take place at any time—presumably even after a removal has actually taken place. They do not have to report to the EU institutions on individual regularizations, although they might have obligations to report on large-scale regularizations pursuant to the Decision on the exchange of immigration information,[544] and the Schengen Convention imposes an obligation to consult another Member State which has issued a SIS alert on an individual before issuing that person with a residence permit or a long-stay visa.[545]

Furthermore, Member States 'shall consider refraining from issuing a return decision' to persons whose applications for renewal of a permit to stay are pending, until that pending procedure is finished.[546]

As for the procedure of issuing return decisions, a return decision can be issued as a single act along with a decision terminating legal stay, a removal decision, or an entry ban, subject to the relevant safeguards in the Directive and other EU and national rules.[547] The Directive does not specify whether Member States must refrain from issuing, withdraw, or suspend removal orders and entry bans in the event that they refrain from issuing, withdraw, or suspend return decisions, but logically the former must be considered as a necessary corollary of the latter.

Next, the Directive addresses voluntary departure. The basic principle is that a return decision must allow for a possible voluntary departure within a period of between seven and thirty days, although the persons concerned are free to leave earlier.[548] Also, this rule is subject to exceptions. On the one hand, Member States 'shall, where necessary, extend the period for voluntary departure for an appropriate period' in 'individual case[s]', on grounds 'such as' family and social links, the length of stay, or children's school attendance.[549] On the other hand, if

---

[543] For that reason it does not matter that the grounds of exception from the obligation to expel irregular migrants set out in Art 6(2)–(5) are arguably exhaustive, since Art 6(4) is itself not subject to any limitations.   [544] See 7.8 below.

[545] Art 25 of the Convention; on this provision, see further 4.9 above.

[546] Art 6(5). Compare with the position of Turkish workers and their family members pursuant to the EU–Turkey association agreement (7.4.2 above).

[547] Art 6(6); see also Art 8(3). For the definition of 'removal' and 'entry ban', see Art 3(5) and (6).

[548] Art 7(1). Member States may decide that this period applies only after application by the person concerned, although in that case they must inform the eligible persons about the possibility of applying.

[549] Art 7(2). Implicitly Member States have no power to set a longer period for voluntary departure for all irregular migrants, or for a large group of collective migrants without consideration of individual circumstances, but arguably such a measure could fall within the scope of Member States' power to set higher standards pursuant to Art 4(3). In any event, Member States which wished to refrain from expelling a large group of persons could regularize their stay for a limited period, pursuant to Art 6(4).

there is a risk of absconding,[550] if an application for legal stay has been dismissed as 'manifestly unfounded' or fraudulent,[551] or if 'the person concerned poses a risk to public policy, public security or national security', Member States may refrain from permitting voluntary departure or grant a period shorter than seven days.[552] The wording of the Directive suggests that the grounds for extension of the period for voluntary departure are non-exhaustive ('such as'), whereas in the absence of similar wording, the grounds for limiting that period or refusing such an opportunity are exhaustive. Member States are able to impose obligations upon individuals during the period allowed for voluntary departure, to avoid the risk of absconding.[553]

Member States are required in principle to remove a person once the period for voluntary departure has expired, or if no such period has been granted.[554] A removal cannot be carried out while the period for voluntary departure has not yet expired, unless that period has been curtailed pursuant to the Directive.[555] Any coercive measures must be used as a 'last resort', and must be 'proportional', 'not exceed reasonable force', and be in accordance with human rights and the dignity and physical integrity of the person concerned.[556] When removing persons by air, Member States 'shall take into account' the common guidelines on security provisions for joint removals, attached to the 2004 Decision on joint flights.[557] In all cases, Member States 'shall provide for an effective forced-return monitoring system'.[558]

Member States are obliged to postpone removal where it would violate the principle of non-refoulement (see the discussion of this principle above), or where a suspensive effect of removal has been granted by a court (see below).[559] Member States *may* postpone removal in other specific cases,[560] and 'shall in particular take into account' the health of the person concerned or technical difficulties. These grounds are non-exhaustive ('in particular'). It is odd that the Directive only refers to postponement of removal, rather than the possibility of cancellation,

---

[550] The definition of 'risk of absconding' is set out in Art 3(7): the 'existence of reasons in an individual case which are based on objective criteria defined by law to believe that a third-country national who is the subject of return procedures may abscond'.

[551] It might be questioned whether the concept of a 'manifestly unfounded' application corresponds, at least for failed asylum seekers, to the equivalent concept in the asylum procedures Dir. See 5.7 above.   [552] Art 7(4).

[553] Art 7(3).

[554] Art 8(1). On the definition of 'removal', see Art 3(5). Compared to Art 23(3) of the Schengen Convention, the obligation to enforce a removal is stronger, although it should be recalled that Member States have the power to set more favourable standards (Art 4(3)).   [555] Art 8(2).

[556] Art 8(4).

[557] Art 8(5), referring to [2004] OJ L 261/28. On this Decision, see 7.7.4 below.

[558] Art 8(6).   [559] Art 9(1).

[560] Art 9(2). The definition of individual cases here is the same as set out in Art 7(2), although the examples of cases are different, and it is clear that while Art 9(2) is a discretionary exception, Art 7(2) is mandatory ('shall').

particularly as regards the non-refoulement principle,[561] but presumably the power to cancel a removal order entirely is implicit in Member States' power to grant authorized residence 'at any moment'.[562] Where removal has been postponed, there are provisions in this Directive and in the Directive on prohibition of employment of irregular migrants (discussed further below) on the status of the person concerned in the meantime. But there is no obligation in the Returns Directive to end this 'state of limbo' at any particular point.

There are specific safeguards concerning the return or removal of unaccompanied minors.[563] Before a return decision is issued to such persons, there must be assistance from bodies other than the return authorities, 'with due consideration being given to the best interests of the child'.[564] Furthermore, before removal of an unaccompanied minor, the national authorities 'shall be satisfied that he or she will be returned to a member of his or her family, a nominated guardian or adequate reception facilities in the State of return'.[565]

Next, the rules on entry bans were among the most controversial provisions of the Directive.[566] An entry ban *must* be issued where a return decision was issued without a period for voluntary departure being granted, or where an obligation for return was not complied with.[567] In other cases, an entry ban *may* be issued.[568] The length of the entry ban must be based on 'all relevant circumstances of the individual case' and 'shall not in principle exceed five years', although longer bans are possible in cases of 'serious threat to public policy, public health or national security'.[569]

Member States 'shall consider withdrawing or suspending' an entry ban if the person concerned can demonstrate that he or she in fact left in compliance with a return decision.[570] They must not apply an entry ban to victims of trafficking in persons who have been granted a residence permit pursuant to Directive 2004/81,

---

[561] While protection status is subject to the possibility of 'cessation' if circumstances change (see 5.5 above), it may be years before circumstances have changed sufficiently—or they might never change much at all.

[562] Art 6(4), discussed above. In particular, as suggested above, the suspension or withdrawal of a return decision must logically entail the suspension or withdrawal of a removal order in parallel. The general power to set higher standards pursuant to Art 4(3) must also entail a power to rescind removal orders entirely.

[563] There is no definition of 'unaccompanied minors' (or 'minors') in the Directive. For the definition in other measures, see, for instance, Art 2(f) of the family reunion Dir (Dir 2003/86, [2003] OJ L 251/12). See now the action plan on unaccompanied minors (COM (2010) 213, 6 May 2010).   [564] Art 10(1). See the discussion of this concept above.

[565] Art 10(2).

[566] Art 3(6) defines an 'entry ban' as a decision which applies to *all* the participating Member States. See also recital 18 in the preamble.

[567] Art 11(1). This matches the circumstances in which a removal decision must be carried out (Art 8(1)).

[568] Ibid. This implies that an entry ban may be issued even if a period for voluntary departure has been granted (compare to Art 8(2), prohibits a removal order in those circumstances), and even if a voluntary departure obligation has been complied with (but see Art 11(3), discussed below).

[569] Art 11(2).   [570] Art 11(3), first sub-paragraph.

which concerns the immigration status of such victims,[571] but this is 'without prejudice' to the obligation to issue an entry ban where an obligation to return was not complied with, and also subject to an exception on grounds of public policy, public security, or national security.[572] Member States may refrain from issuing, or withdraw or suspend, an entry ban 'in individual cases for humanitarian reasons', and 'may withdraw or suspend' a ban 'in individual cases or certain categories of cases for other reasons'.[573]

The Directive also provides that if a Member State intends to issue a residence permit to a person who is subject to an entry ban issued by another Member State, the first Member State should first of all consult with the Member State that issued the entry ban according to the rules set out in the Schengen Convention.[574] The Convention rules previously applied only where an alert for the purpose of refusing entry had been entered into the Schengen Information System (SIS),[575] but the Directive appears to extend these rules to cases in which an entry ban has not been entered onto the SIS. But it is hard to see how Member States will be aware of other Member State's entry bans in any case unless those bans have been entered as SIS alerts. A Commission statement issued when the Directive was adopted indicates that when the operation of the second-generation Schengen Information System (SIS II) is reviewed, that will be 'an opportunity to propose an obligation to register in the SIS entry bans issued under this Directive', although of course Member States might choose to register those entry bans in the SIS even before they are obliged to do so.[576]

As for future developments on this point, the EU's immigration and asylum pact of 2008 agreed that in the context of mutual recognition of expulsion decisions, alerts for refusal of entry in the SIS should oblige other Member States not to let the person concerned enter or reside.[577] This principle was subsequently repeated by the Stockholm programme, which referred more explicitly to recording entry bans in the SIS.[578] It is not clear, however, whether the intention is to revise the Returns Directive or the SIS II rules by bringing forward the Commission's proposals to this effect to an earlier date (perhaps to require that entry bans be listed in the *current SIS*, given the delay in implementing SIS II), or merely to endorse the principle of the planned legislation.

---

[571] [2004] OJ L 261/19. On this Directive, see 7.6.2 above.

[572] Art 11(3), second sub-paragraph.

[573] Art 11(3), third and fourth sub-paragraphs. Note that in the latter case, there is no capacity to refrain from issuing bans, but then again Member States retain a power to set more favourable standards compatible with the Directive (Art 4(3)).

[574] Art 11(4), referring to Art 25 of the Convention. On this provision of the Convention, see 4.9 above.　　　　　　　　　　　　　　　[575] On these alerts, see 3.7.1 above.

[576] Summary of Council acts for Dec 2008 (Council doc 7478/08, 11 Mar 2009). For a detailed discussion of the relationship between the Returns Dir and the SIS II Reg, see 3.7.2 above.

[577] Council doc 13440/08, 24 Sep 2008, Part II.

[578] [2010] OJ C 115, point 6.1.6.

Chapter III of the Directive concerns procedural safeguards. Return decisions, removal decisions, and decisions on entry bans must be issued in writing and contain reasons in fact and law as well as information on remedies, although the obligation to give factual reasons can be limited by national law, 'in particular in order to safeguard national security, defence, public security and for the prevention, investigation, detection and prosecution of criminal offences'.[579] The main elements of the decision must be translated upon request, including information on the available legal remedies, in a language which the person concerned understands or can be presumed to understand.[580] Member States have an option not to provide a translation where persons have entered irregularly and have not subsequently obtained authorization to stay; but in that case Member States must supply information by means of a standard form set out in national law, and must provide explanations of this form in at least five languages which are most frequently used or understood by irregular migrants who enter that Member State.[581]

The persons concerned must have an 'effective remedy' to appeal or review all types of decisions related to return before some sort of independent and impartial body, which could be (but need not be) a judicial or administrative body.[582] This entity must have the power to review the decisions related to return, including the power to suspend those decisions temporarily, unless such a power already exists in national law (ie because the legal challenge automatically suspends application of the decision concerned).[583] The person concerned must also be able to obtain 'legal advice, representation and, where necessary, linguistic assistance'.[584] As for legal aid, this must be available subject to the same limitations provided for in the asylum procedures Directive.[585]

The Returns Directive provides for safeguards pending return, in the case of voluntary departure or postponement of a removal decision.[586] The persons concerned must be given written confirmation of their position, and Member States must 'ensure that the following principles are taken into account as far as possible', except where persons are in detention: family unity; emergency health care and essential treatment of illness; minors' access to basic education; and 'special needs of vulnerable persons are taken into account'.[587]

Further on the issue of safeguards pending return, it should also be noted that the subsequent employer sanctions Directive prohibits the employment of irregular migrants, but nevertheless gives Member States an option to exempt the employment of persons 'whose removal has been postponed' from this

---

[579] Art 12(1). The list of possible grounds for restricting information appears to be non-exhaustive.   [580] Art 12(2).

[581] Art 12(3).   [582] Art 13(1).   [583] Art 13(2).   [584] Art 13(3).

[585] Art 13(4), referring to Art 15(3)–(6) of Dir 2005/85 (n 516 above). It should be noted that the proposal to amend the asylum procedures Dir would raise the relevant standards (Art 18 in COM (2009) 554, *idem*). On the substance of these rules, see 5.7 above.   [586] Art 14.

[587] The definition of 'vulnerable persons' is set out in Art 3(9).

prohibition.[588] Arguably this only applies to the rules in the Returns Directive on the obligation or possibility of postponing removal,[589] but the alternative interpretation is that any national decision under the Returns Directive which amounts de facto to a postponement of removal (ie because of the absence, withdrawal, or suspension of a return decision, even if the immigration status of the person concerned is *de jure* irregular), also triggers the option for Member States to authorize employment under the employer sanctions Directive.

In any event, it should be recalled that the employer sanctions Directive has a wider personal scope than the Returns Directive, because there are no options to exclude cases relating to border crossing or criminal law from the scope of the employer sanctions Directive.[590]

The Directive next addresses the controversial issue of immigration detention.[591] Persons subject to return procedures 'may only' be detained 'in order to prepare return and/or to carry out the removal process in particular when' there is a risk of absconding or if the person concerned 'avoids or hampers' the return or removal process. Detention is only justified while removal arrangements 'are in process and executed with due diligence'. It can be ordered by administrative or judicial authorities, and must be 'ordered in writing with reasons in fact and law'. If the detention was ordered by administrative authorities, there must be some form of 'speedy' judicial review. There must be regular reviews of detention, either automatically or at the request of the person concerned. If there is no 'reasonable prospect of removal' or the conditions for detention no longer exist, the person concerned must be released immediately. Conversely, detention shall been maintained as long as the conditions exist; this shall not exceed six months, except where national law permits a further period of up to one extra year because the removal operation is likely to last longer due to lack of cooperation by the person concerned or delays in obtaining documentation.

These provisions have been interpreted in the Court of Justice's *Kadzoev* judgment.[592] First of all, the Court ruled that the relevant time limits for detention must take into account also time served already before the application of the Directive. The Court did not, however, explain how to address the situation where the detention was interrupted, either by periods which do not count because the person concerned applied for asylum, or for some other reason. It would obviously be problematic if the Member States could evade the time limits in the Directive by releasing a person for one day at the end of the applicable time

---

[588] Art 3(3) of Dir 2009/52 ([2009] OJ L 168/24), discussed in 7.6.1 above. However, the EU rules on legal migration will not generally apply in such cases, as they do not apply where expulsion has been suspended for reasons of fact and law (see 6.5 above).

[589] Art 9, discussed further above.

[590] It should be recalled, however, that persons subject to the optional 'border crossing' exclusion from the scope of the Returns Dir (but not the 'criminal law' exclusion) can rely on *parts* of Art 9 (see Art 4(4)). [591] Art 15.

[592] See n 511 above.

limit, and then re-arresting that person the next day to start a fresh lengthy period of detention. Next, the Court ruled that the period of detention spent while the removal decision was subject to judicial review could not be deducted from the relevant time limits, but had to count against them.

As for the question of whether there is a 'reasonable prospect of removal', the Court ruled that this criterion for releasing the person concerned is irrelevant where the time limits on detention have in any event expired. Where the criterion does apply, it means that a 'real prospect exists that the removal can be carried out successfully, having regard to' the relevant time limits, and that this prospect 'does not exist where it appears unlikely that the person concerned will be admitted to a third country, having regard to' those time limits.[593] The Court also ruled that Member States could not keep a person in detention, once the relevant time limit had expired, merely because the person concerned does not possess valid documents, his conduct is aggressive, and he has no financial support or accommodation.

Finally, the Directive's rules on detention conditions address in turn: the place of detention (special facilities 'as a rule', separation from ordinary prisoners if detained in prison); the right to contact legal representatives, family members and consular authorities; the situation of vulnerable persons; the possibility for independent bodies to visit detention facilities; and information to be given to the persons concerned.[594] There are more detailed rules on the detention of minors and families,[595] although Member States may derogate from certain aspects of the rules concerning speedy judicial review and detention conditions in 'exceptional' situations.[596]

Comparing the detention rules with human rights standards,[597] the Directive includes the 'necessity' principle set out in the ICCPR jurisprudence on immigration detention,[598] along with a number of principles derived from ECHR case law (such as due diligence in pursuing expulsion and the requirement to end detention if removal efforts are no longer underway). The time limits in the Directive regarding detention exceed ECHR standards, given that there is no fixed time limit on immigration detention set out in the ECHR, and the rules on judicial review reflect the ECHR and relevant case law as well. While it is understandable that asylum seekers are generally excluded from the Directive in that they should not be regarded as illegally present, it is unfortunate that the detention standards in the Directive do not apply to them, at least until more favourable standards can be agreed in EU asylum legislation.[599]

How should this controversial Directive be assessed? Although the EP, in its negotiations with the Council, was able to insist on higher standards on a

---

[593] Paras 65 and 66 of the judgment, ibid.   [594] Art 16.   [595] Art 17.   [596] Art 18.
[597] See 7.3 above, and particularly 7.3.2 as regards detention.   [598] Art 15(5).
[599] See the proposed revision of that legislation (5.7–5.9 below), which, however, does not suggest maximum time limits on detention of asylum seekers.

number of points, it accepted a significantly higher period of detention than can be justified, and the Directive also falls short of desirable standards as regards the substantive safeguards against expulsion; the scope of the Directive; the rules on mandatory postponement of expulsions; the rules on mandatory entry bans, the possible limits on information given to expellees; the lack of automatic suspensive effect of appeals; and the grounds for and review of detention.[600] The solution of applying 'standstill' clauses to prevent Member States from using the Directive as an excuse to worsen the standards which previously applied was unfortunately not taken up. On the whole, then, the Directive does not go far enough to ensure that minimum standards of proportionality, fairness, and humanity are satisfied.

7.7.2. Mutual recognition of expulsion measures

In order to address the issue of persons subject to expulsion who travel between Member States, the Council adopted Directive 2001/40 on the mutual recognition of expulsion orders in May 2001.[601] This Directive had to be implemented by Member States by 2 December 2002.[602] Several Member States were the subject of infringement proceedings brought by the Commission after they failed to implement the Directive on time.[603]

The Directive 'make[s] possible the enforcement of an expulsion order' issued by one Member State in another Member State, against a third-country national of any age.[604] The wording of the Directive suggests that this is only an option for the second Member State, not an obligation. While the subsequent Returns Directive now refers to an obligation for a second Member State to apply the rules in that Directive to an irregular migrant who it has taken back pursuant to a bilateral agreement with a Member State where the irregular migrant was present on an irregular basis, this obligation will probably fall outside the scope of the 2001 Directive (since, in this scenario, the first Member State need not issue a return decision at all).[605]

The expulsion decision pursuant to Directive 2001/40 shall be enforced according to the national law of the enforcing State.[606] This should in principle be understood as a reference to the enforcing State's application of the Returns

---

[600] See Acosta and the Statewatch analysis, n 508 above.

[601] [2001] OJ L 149/34. All references in this subsection are to Dir 2001/40 unless otherwise indicated.   [602] Art 8(1).

[603] Two Member States were condemned by the Court of Justice for failure to implement the Directive: Cases C-462/04 *Commission v Italy* and C-448/04 *Commission v Luxembourg*, judgments of 8 Sep 2005, unreported. Two other cases were withdrawn, presumably following late implementation of the Directive: Cases C-474/04 *Commission v Greece* and C-450/04 *Commission v France*.

[604] Art 1.

[605] Art 6(3), Dir 2008/115 ([2008] OJ L 348/98), applicable from 24 Dec 2010. See further 7.7.1 above.   [606] Art 1(2).

Directive (after the deadline to apply that Directive), because the Returns Directive does not exclude mutual recognition of expulsion decisions from its scope.[607] But the definitions in the 2001 Directive do not entirely match those in the Returns Directive;[608] to the extent that the 2001 Directive sets higher standards than the Returns Directive, it should prevail over the latter.[609] However, the 2001 Directive does not provide that national law, other EU measures, or international treaties can set higher standards.[610] Questions arise as to whether the rules in the Returns Directive on postponement of removal, entry bans, detention, forced returns, voluntary returns, safeguards pending expulsion, procedural safeguards, and exceptions from the obligation to issue a return decision are applicable within the context of Directive 2001/40.

As for its scope, the 2001 Directive does not apply to family members of an EU citizen who has exercised his or her right to free movement,[611] and is 'without prejudice' to Articles 23 and 96 of the Schengen Convention (which respectively concern return decisions and the criteria for listing persons to be denied entry into the Schengen area) and to the Dublin Convention.[612] However, there are no exclusions from the scope of the Directive as regards refusals of entry, border interceptions, or criminal law.[613]

Expulsions are enforceable under the Directive if a third-country national has received an expulsion decision on either a 'public policy and national security' ground (as further defined in the Directive) or the ground of 'failure to comply with national regulations on the entry or residence' of foreigners.[614] These criteria are taken from Article 96 of the Schengen Convention.

---

[607] See Art 2(2) of the Returns Dir (n 605 above). It is possible, however, that the decision in question will fall outside the scope of the Returns Dir because the second Member State has applied a valid exclusion from the scope of that Directive, pursuant to its Art 2(2). This raises the awkward question of what happens if the criteria for exclusion from the scope of the Returns Dir are satisfied in one or the other of the two Member States, but not both.

[608] Compare the definition of 'expulsion decision' in Art 2(b) with the definition of 'return decision' in Art 3(4) of the Returns Dir, and the definition of 'enforcement measure' in Art 2(c) with the definition of 'removal' in Art 3(5) of the Returns Dir.

[609] See Art 4(2), Returns Dir.

[610] Compare to Art 4(1)–(3), Returns Dir. As the Court of Justice has pointed out, international treaties concluded by the EU nevertheless take precedence over secondary EU law: Case C-228/06 *Soysal* [2009] ECR I-1031. However, this leaves open the question of priority as between the Directive and treaties concluded only by *Member States* with third States.

[611] Art 1(3); see 7.4.1 above.

[612] Arts 1(1) and 3(3). On Art 23 of the Convention ([2000] OJ L 239), see the introduction to 7.1 above; note that this Art will be replaced by the Returns Dir when that Directive becomes applicable (Art 21, Returns Dir). On Art 96 of the Convention, see 3.7.1 above; this Art will also be replaced when the SIS II rules become applicable (3.7.2 above). Presumably the reference to the Dublin Convention must now be taken to be a reference to the replacement Dublin Reg, and in future to the proposed new Regulation which will replace that Regulation (see 5.8 above).

[613] Compare to Art 2(2) of the Returns Dir. This raises another awkward question: what happens if a return decision is within the scope of Dir 2001/40, but is subject to the safeguards in the Returns Dir in one Member State, but not the other?   [614] Art 3(1).

The Directive must be applied with 'due respect for human rights and fundamental freedoms', but the specific implications of this are not set out.[615] Also, the expellee is entitled to a remedy against the expulsion order in the enforcing State, under that State's national law.[616] Again, it makes sense once the Returns Directive is applicable to assume that it governs these issues in the enforcing State, unless the situation falls within the scope of an exclusion from that Directive which is validly invoked by the enforcing State. The 2001 Directive also includes data protection safeguards and provisions on cooperation between the issuing and enforcing Member States.[617]

The issue of compensation of those Member States which enforce other Member States' expulsion orders pursuant to the Directive, where expulsion cannot be charged to the expellee, was left subject to the adoption of a subsequent measure, which 'shall' also apply to Article 24 of the Schengen Convention.[618] The latter provision of the Convention has now also been replaced by the Returns Directive.[619] A Council Decision on this issue was subsequently adopted in February 2004;[620] it is unclear whether this Decision should be understood to apply to the Returns Directive, once it becomes applicable. Given that this legislation does not *oblige* Member States to collect the costs of return from migrants, while other EU rules oblige Member States to collect the costs of return from employers or carriers,[621] it might be argued that there is an implied hierarchy: Member States must first attempt to collect the costs of return from employers or carriers, then (if that fails) from the migrant, and then (if that fails) from another Member State, if (in the latter case) Directive 2001/40 is applicable.

As for its substance, the 2004 Decision specifies that Member States issuing expulsion orders must compensate Member States enforcing expulsion orders for: transport costs, administrative costs, mission allowances for two escorts, and accommodation and emergency medical costs for the escorts and the expellee.[622] It also sets out the procedural requirements for submitting a valid claim for reimbursement.[623] Member States' contact points must inform the Commission of the total number of requests for reimbursement and refusals to reimburse.[624]

While there are no formal statistics or information on the use of Directive 2001/40, the Commission admitted in its 2004 report on EU policy on irregular migration that the Directive had little impact in practice.[625] The adoption of the

---

[615] Art 3(2).   [616] Arts 4.

[617] Arts 5 and 6. There are no parallel provisions in the Returns Dir.

[618] Art 7. On Art 24 of the Convention, see the introduction to 7.1 above.

[619] Art 21, Returns Dir.   [620] [2004] OJ L 60/55; in force 28 Feb 2004.

[621] Art 5(2), Dir 2009/52 ([2009] OJ L 168/24); Art 26 of the Schengen Convention ([2000] OJ L 239) and Arts 2 and 3, Dir 2001/51 ([2001] OJ L 187/45). See respectively 7.6.1 and 7.5.1 above.

[622] Art 2.   [623] Art 3.   [624] Art 4.

[625] Communication on policy regarding irregular migration (SEC (2004) 1349, 25 Oct 2004), p 10: 'So far, the impact, ie cases of formal recognition, was almost inexistent [*sic*]'. There was no

Decision on the financial aspects of the Directive might have had the intended effect of encouraging Member States to use the mechanism in the Directive more frequently. It may also have the broader importance of serving as a template for other measures which require costs to be allocated.[626] However, as the Commission has pointed out, the Directive is likely to be little used as long as there is no exchange of data on national expulsion decisions.[627] This will only be fully achieved once there are clear links between the Returns Directive and the SIS II Regulation.[628]

The ineffectiveness of Directive 2001/40 should be welcomed, because the Directive is highly problematic. It purportedly extends to persons with rights under international agreements agreed by the Community law,[629] it inappropriately extends the principles of Article 96 of the Schengen Convention to persons who are already present on the territory, and it does not sufficiently guarantee that expulsions carried out within its scope meet applicable human rights standards. Following the implementation of the Returns Directive, the question will then arise as to the relationship between that Directive and Directive 2001/40 (and the 2004 Decision on costs), due to the different wording and scope of the two measures. From a technical point of view, the 2001 Directive needs to be amended for consistency with the Returns Directive, but the broader question might then be asked of whether a second Member State needs to apply all the safeguards that have already been applied in the first Member State. The answer should be that since a Member State's expulsion of a person engages its jurisdiction and therefore its human rights obligations, a second full procedure must be necessary.[630]

7.7.3. Transit for expulsion

7.7.3.1. Expulsion via air

Following early EU soft law measures and a Schengen Executive Committee Decision on the issue of assistance in expulsion by air,[631] the Council adopted Directive 2003/110 on this issue in November 2003.[632] Member States had to

mention of the Directive in the 2006 or 2009 reports on irregular migration policy (SEC (2006) 1010, 17 July 2006 and SEC (2009) 320, 9 Mar 2009).

[626] See Conclusions on transit for expulsion via land or sea (7.7.3.2 below).

[627] See the impact assessment for the Returns Dir (SEC (2005) 1057, 1 Sep 2005), pp 6–7.

[628] See the discussion of this issue in 3.7.2 and 7.7.1 above.

[629] Although, as noted above, the EU's international agreements take priority over its secondary law, a failure to point this out expressly in the legislation concerned could lead to a failure to apply this rule by the national administrations which implement the legislation.

[630] If there were no second full procedure, the question would arise of what to do if were alleged that the first Member State had not complied with the Directive when issuing its return decision or removal order.

[631] See respectively 7.2.1 above and Sch/Com-ex (98) 10, 21 Apr 1998 ([2000] OJ L 239/193).

[632] [2003] OJ L 321/26. Art 11 of the Directive repealed the Schengen Executive Committee Decision (ibid). All references in this subsection are to Dir 2003/110 unless otherwise indicated.

implement the Directive by 6 December 2005.[633] The Commission brought an unusually high number of infringement actions against Member States for failure to apply this legislation on time.[634]

This Directive specifies that if a Member State wishes to request another to assist it with an expulsion (a 'requesting State'), it should first give priority to direct flights to the country of origin and should 'in principle' not request assistance if this involves transfer between different airports within another Member State.[635] A requested Member State may refuse to assist with expulsion if criminal charges would be brought against the person concerned in the requested State or if the person concerned 'is wanted for the carrying out of a sentence'; if transit to or admission into the State of destination is not feasible; if a change of airport in the requested State would be required; if the assistance is temporarily not available for 'practical reasons'; or if the person concerned 'will be a threat to public policy, public security, public health or to the international relations' of the requested Member State.[636] A transit authorization, once given, may also be revoked on the same grounds.[637] The requested Member State must give reasons to the requesting Member State in the event of refusal or revocation on these specified grounds 'or of any other reason why the transit is not possible';[638] this suggests strongly that the listed grounds for refusal or revocation are non-exhaustive. The preamble to the Directive states that transit by air 'should be neither requested nor granted if in the third country of destination or transit faces the threat of inhumane or humiliating treatment, torture or the death penalty' for the person concerned, 'or if his life or liberty would be at risk by reason of his race, religion, nationality, membership of a particular social group or political conviction.'

The Directive also describes the procedure for making and replying to requests and the specific obligations of requested Member States, makes clear that the requested Member State's law has responsibility for organizing such measures, sets out the status of escorts from the requesting Member States, and allocates the cost of various aspects of the expulsion between the requesting and requested Member States.[639]

There are readmission obligations for the requesting Member State in the event that: transit was refused or revoked on the grounds listed in the Directive; the expulsion was unsuccessful; or the person concerned tried to enter the requested Member State without authorization; or 'transit by air is not possible for another reason'.[640] Again this wording suggests that the grounds for refusing

---

[633] Art 10(2).

[634] Cases: C-3/07 *Commission v Belgium* (judgment largely against Belgium, 8 Nov 2007, unreported); C-4/07 *Commission v Portugal* (judgment against Portugal, 27 Sep 2007, unreported); C-29/07 *Commission v Greece* (withdrawn); C-51/07 *Commission v Luxembourg* (withdrawn); C-58/07 *Commission v Spain* (judgment against Spain, 14 Feb 2008, unreported); C-79/07 *Commission v Malta* (withdrawn); C-86/07 *Commission v Italy* (withdrawn); and C-216/07 *Commission v Germany* (withdrawn). [635] Art 3(2).

[636] Art 3(3). [637] Art 3(5). [638] Art 3(6). [639] Arts 4 and 5. [640] Art 6.

or revoking assistance listed in the Directive are not exhaustive. Escorts sent by the requesting State may act in 'self-defence' and use 'reasonable and proportionate action' to prevent risks posed by third-country nationals, but may not carry weapons, must wear civilian clothes, and must comply with the requested State's legislation.[641]

There is a 'savings clause' specifying that the Directive is 'without prejudice to' the Geneva Convention on the status of refugees, international human rights treaties or international extradition treaties.[642] An Annex sets out a standard form for use in requesting cooperation under the Directive and for replying to those requests; the Commission is empowered to amend this Annex via use of a 'comitology' procedure.[643]

The fundamental problem with this Directive, as with Directive 2001/40,[644] is the principle of mutual recognition of expulsion decisions. In the absence of a binding obligation in the Directive to refrain from requesting or to refuse to assist with transit, or to revoke the request or agreement to assist, in case of a threat of human rights breach to the person concerned in another country, or even an obligation for the requesting State's authorities to certify when they fill out the Annex that no such grounds exist, the Directive contains insufficiently clear protection for human rights. The reference to human rights treaties in the savings clause is too vague to make up for this, because there are no detailed rules on how to ensure respect for the Geneva Convention or human rights treaties. In the absence of an express provision to require a full examination of any asylum claim and effective procedural remedies in the case of any appeal before applying this Directive, the 'savings clause' is simply window-dressing.

In any event, how is the requested Member State to determine whether there is such a human rights breach? The only information available to it is the brief information included on the standard request form, and as noted above, the form does not even contain a box to tick to indicate that, in the view of the requesting Member State, there is no human rights problem with expulsion. Clearly this does not supply enough information for the requested Member State to come to its own conclusion on that subject. The requesting Member State is not obliged to limit requests to certain situations, or to consider human rights issues before deciding to expel and requesting assistance of another Member State.

Compared with Directive 2001/40, which already sets a weak standard as regards human rights protection,[645] there is no obligation in the Directive for requested Member States to ensure that there are no human rights risks before they carry out an expulsion order at another Member State's request. Also, there is no comparable requirement upon the requested Member State to permit migrants to challenge its decision to enforce expulsion decisions. Directive 2001/40 only

---

[641] Art 7.   [642] Art 8.   [643] Art 9. The Commission has not exercised this power.
[644] See 7.7.2 above.   [645] See ibid.

applies to expulsion where certain substantive criteria are met, and the family members of EU nationals are exempt from it. There are express data protection rights in the earlier Directive, and the main text of that Directive explicitly requires Member States to apply the Directive 'with due regard for human rights and fundamental freedoms'. All these essential limits and safeguards are missing from Directive 2003/110, which merely refers to human rights protection in the preamble and vaguely in the safeguard clause. So even the weak standards agreed in 2001 do not apply in the context of the 2003 Directive. Since the requested Member State will clearly be exercising jurisdiction over the person concerned if it agrees to cooperate in carrying out the expulsion, there are no grounds for a lower level of protection due to that State's more limited contact with the individual concerned.

It might be argued that following the application of the Returns Directive, these problems have been addressed sufficiently and Member States must extend mutual trust that each of them will comply with the standards in the Returns Directive. However, there is still a risk that the requesting State has failed to comply with the Returns Directive in a particular case, and moreover the Returns Directive does not itself set an adequate standard.[646] So even after the deadline to apply the Returns Directive passes, the 2003 Directive runs a risk of violating fundamental human rights when applied to particular cases.

7.7.3.2. Expulsion via land or sea

Following the agreement in principle on Directive 2003/110, Italy proposed a Directive on transit for expulsion via land (and apparently sea), which would have applied rules very similar to those governing transit for expulsion via air.[647] But due to misgivings among some Member States about this proposal, the Council adopted conclusions on the topic instead, in December 2003.[648]

These conclusions are much less specific than Directive 2003/110. First of all, the conclusions set out their scope, making it clear that they apply to transit expulsion both by land and sea. Such expulsions should only be requested when a direct or transit flight is impossible or more difficult. But such expulsions could be particularly useful where they are used to send a person to the airport or seaport of another Member State which will carry out an expulsion, if they enable avoidance of complications which would result from having to transit through a non-EU State or where the requested Member State has a bilateral readmission agreement which it could use to effect expulsion.

Next, the conclusions set out basic principles to govern expulsions by land or sea. Such expulsions should take place with the consent of the requested State, and the accompaniment of that State's escorts in all cases. The requesting State

---

[646] See the critique in 7.7.1 above.   [647] [2003] OJ C 223/5.

[648] For the text of these conclusions, see the press release of the environment Council, 22 Dec 2003.

has a duty to send the relevant information to the requested State, and is responsible for the expellee until reaching the requested State's territory. From that point, the requesting State's escorts should comply with the requested State's law. The costs of the operations should be compensated on the basis of 'appropriate financial arrangements, which may consider, in particular, the criteria defined in the Community legislation in the area of return [sic] of third-country nationals'. There is also a safeguard clause corresponding to the provision in Directive 2003/110.

These conclusions obviously share the fundamental defects of Directive 2003/110. In fact, their non-binding status exacerbates the problem, as it means that the safeguard provision is not binding either. Nor are any grounds for refusal set out. But on the other hand, it cannot be argued that a Member State is bound to accept any request to assist with such transit for expulsion, still less that there is only an exhaustive list of circumstances in which it may refuse to accept such a request.

7.7.4. Joint expulsion flights

A Decision on joint expulsion flights was adopted by the JHA Council in April 2004.[649] The Council subsequently adopted conclusions with a view to encouraging Member States to organize joint expulsion flights in practice,[650] and the EU's border agency also has a role in this area.[651] The joint flights are now supported by the EU's Return Fund.[652]

The Decision provides that Member States have to appoint national authorities responsible for organizing joint flights.[653] A Member State organizing a joint flight must first of all inform the other Member States, and has detailed obligations to make sure that the flight is organized properly.[654] If a Member State wishes to participate in the joint flight, it must inform the organizing Member State of the numbers of expellees it will be removing and provide a sufficient number of escorts.[655] The organizing and participating Member States have the common task of ensuring that the expellees and escorts have the necessary documentation and that their diplomatic and consular staff in the countries of transit and destination are informed of the expulsion flight, so that they can offer the necessary assistance.[656] When carrying out the joint expulsions, the Member States should 'take account' of detailed security guidelines set out in an Annex.[657]

---

[649] [2004] OJ L 261/28, in force 7 Aug 2004.

[650] See the press release of the General Affairs Council, 12–13 July 2004 and the JHA Council, 27–28 Apr 2006.

[651] See Art 9(1) of Reg 2007/2004 ([2004] OJ L 349/1), and the proposed amendments to this provision in COM (2010) 61, 24 Feb 2010. On the agency generally, see 3.10.1 above.

[652] See 7.8 below.   [653] Art 3.   [654] Art 4.   [655] Art 5.   [656] Art 6.

[657] Art 7 and Annex.

As with the Directive and conclusions on transit for expulsion,[658] this Decision indicates that Member States are willing to adopt EU legislation concerning operational measures on expulsion without first having ensured that EU law guarantees sufficiently high minimum standards on human rights and other matters. Although some provisions in the Annex to the Decision do provide for protection for individuals during the flights,[659] this Annex is non-binding and in any event does not address the question of whether the initial expulsion decision met minimum standards. Moreover, the organization of such joint flights could run the risk of encouraging Member States (individually or collectively) to engage in collective expulsions, which are prohibited by international human rights law.[660]

A system for public monitoring or reporting upon the joint operations might reduce this risk, but unfortunately the Decision does not provide for such a system to be established. Although a monitoring committee would have been established by the initial proposal,[661] this idea was dropped during negotiations and in any event there was no provision for public access to the committee's deliberations. Third-party recording or observation of flights would surely reduce risks of abuse of power, but any such independent scrutiny is subject to the approval of all participating Member States.[662] The Annex does make provision for mission reports to be drawn up, but '[a]ll mission reports are strictly confidential and for internal use only', even though the reports 'shall include statements on incidents, coercive and medical measures, if any have taken place'.[663] There is no reference to the requirement imposed by the ECHR to investigate the circumstances of any death or torture, or inhuman, or degrading treatment caused by the actions of public authorities. In light of the tragic deaths and injuries that have resulted during some expulsions from Europe in recent years, the Decision is wholly insufficient.

7.8. Administrative cooperation and EU funding

The EC's funding programme, 'ARGO', which ran from 2002–06, provided for spending for administrative cooperation on irregular migration.[664] Subsequently, the Commission also established a preparatory programme beginning in 2005 for

---

[658] See 7.7.3 above. In fact, Point 4 of the Annex to the Decision indicates that Dir 2003/110 will be applicable if air transit takes place through Member States.

[659] See particularly point 3 of the Annex.

[660] See 7.3.1 above, and particularly the judgment of the European Court of Human Rights in *Sultani v France,* 20 Sep 2007, which establishes the standards for such joint flights.

[661] See Art 6 of the initial proposal ([2003] OJ C 233/3).   [662] Point 3.4.1 of the Annex.

[663] Point 3.4.2 of the Annex.

[664] Decision 2002/463 ([2002] OJ L 161/11); see particularly Art 7(d)–(f). On JHA funding in general, see 2.6 above.

a 'European return fund', upon which the Council adopted conclusions in June 2004.[665] The Return Fund was formalized in 2007 by a Decision establishing it officially.[666]

Aside from EU funding measures, operational cooperation between national administrations was first established as far back as 1992 when Member States' immigration ministers established CIREFI, a system for sharing information on irregular immigration trends and methods, including legislation and statistics.[667] From July 2010, CIREFI was abolished and replaced by Frontex, the EU's border control agency.[668]

CIREFI's role was augmented by the adoption of a Council resolution establishing an 'early warning' system for information concerning irregular migration flows, adopted in 1999.[669] A later Council decision of 2005 established a web-based information and coordination network (Iconet) for Member States' migration management services.[670] This Decision conferred competence on the Commission to manage a secure system of information exchange which would include 'at least' the early warning system, the network of immigration liaison officers;[671] visas, borders, and travel documents relating to irregular immigration, and expulsion-related issues.[672] The Commission has subsequently proposed transferring the management of this system to Frontex also.[673]

As for statistics, the Council agreed in 1998 that the Commission's statistics body, Eurostat, would take over the role of compiling official statistics on immigration and asylum, while 'non-statistical confidential information' would 'continue to be processed in the context of CIREFI ... on the basis of preparatory work carried out by the General Secretariat of the Council'.[674] In 2001, the Council agreed that statistics on immigration and asylum issues would be available to the public, in the form of annual reports and (to some extent) monthly and quarterly data, subject to possible restrictions on security grounds.[675] The Commission subsequently decided that information on irregular migration (detailing the numbers refused, apprehended, and removed) should be made public on an annual basis, with delayed publication of monthly or quarterly data.[676]

---

[665] For the text of the conclusions, see JHA Council press release, 8 June 2004.

[666] [2005] OJ L 144/45.

[667] See T Bunyan, ed, *Key Texts on Justice and Home Affairs in the European Union* (1997), and also Council conclusions of 30 Nov 2004 ([1996] OJ C 274/50).

[668] Council doc 17653/09, 16 Dec 2009.   [669] Council doc 7965/99, 11 May 1999.

[670] [2005] OJ L 83/48, in force 21 Apr 2005.   [671] See 7.5.5 above.   [672] Art 2.

[673] COM (2010) 61, 24 Feb 2010 (proposed new Art 2(1)(h) in Reg 2007/2004 ([2004] OJ L 349/1)).

[674] JHA Council press release, 19 Mar 1998. For more on EU immigration statistics, see 6.11 above.

[675] JHA Council press release, 28–29 May 2001.

[676] Commission Action Plan on immigration and asylum statistics (COM (2003) 179, 15 Apr 2003).

The collection and publication of such statistics was later formalized with the adoption of EU legislation concerning asylum and migration statistics.[677] This legislation requires Member States to forward information concerning third-country nationals found to be illegally present, who are subject to return decisions, and who have in fact left, and to disaggregate this data by citizenship (which they did before), as well as by age and sex (as regards persons who are irregularly present). In principle this information should assist with assessment of the effectiveness of EU policy in this area,[678] although it would also be useful to know how many return decisions are withdrawn and why (ie decisions to regularize, or to grant international protection), how many people leave voluntarily and how many by force, how many persons are in immigration detention and for how long, and what happens to persons after expulsion (particularly in the context of readmission agreements). Also, it is important to ensure that the statistics Regulation is applied consistently with the relevant legislation, otherwise the statistics will be misleading.[679] It can only be hoped that the official publication of such statistics will make a contribution to an informed public debate on the scale of irregular migration—keeping in mind that the number of irregular residents who are not apprehended can only ever be estimated. However, the Commission has not to date taken any account of the official statistics when developing or assessing EU immigration policy.[680]

Other relevant measures in this field are a Decision on the exchange of information as regards national asylum and immigration law, the EU's Migration Network, a Joint Action on false documents, and a third pillar Decision on counterfeit documents.[681]

7.9. External relations

The EU's main mechanism for ensuring that persons its Member States wish to expel are removed from the territory is to insist that non-EU States sign readmission agreements with the EU, its Member States, or both. EU policy toward readmission agreements has evolved over time as the EU has gained new internal powers (and thus external powers) over migration law and as it has decided

---

[677] Reg 862/2007, [2007] OJ L 199/23; see particularly Arts 5(1)(b), 7, and 8(1)(d) and (f).

[678] Ie the definitions of illegal presence and return decisions in the Reg (Arts 2(1)(r) and 7(1)(a)) match the definitions in the Returns Dir (Art 3(2) and (4), Dir 2008/115 ([2008] OJ L 348/98)).

[679] Ie the data relating to irregular migration should not include any asylum seekers, in light of the Court of Justice's interpretation of the Returns Dir: Case C-357/09 PPU *Kadzoev*, judgment of 30 Nov 2009, not yet reported.   [680] See 6.11 above.

[681] Respectively: [2006] OJ L 283/40; [2008] OJ L 131/7; [1998] OJ L 333/4; and [2000] OJ L 81/1. For details and comments on the first two measures, see 6.11 above.

to place greater priority on securing readmission commitments from non-EU States, in the form of both specific stand-alone agreements and as part of association or cooperation agreements with the EU. Readmission also forms part of a broader policy integrating migration into the EU's overall external relations objectives. The EU also has external competence pursuant to its internal powers over irregular migration and related issues to ratify treaties concern the issue of visas and readmission for Chinese tourists, and the Protocols to the UN organized crime convention concerning trafficking and smuggling of persons.[682]

7.9.1. Readmission agreements[683]

Before the Treaty of Amsterdam entered into force, the EC (as it then was) lacked competence to agree readmission treaties. However, in 1995 the Council agreed a standard clause to be considered for inclusion into 'mixed' agreements (treaties which have to be ratified by the EC and the Member States).[684] Also, in order to ensure that readmission agreements signed by non-EU States with different Member States would be comparable, the Council had already agreed a Recommendation on a standard readmission agreement between a Member State and a third country in 1994,[685] along with a Recommendation in 1995 on a standard Protocol on means of proof to be attached to such agreements.[686] It had also agreed in 1994 on a Recommendation on a standard travel document to be used for expulsion proceedings.[687]

Next, with the entry into force of the Treaty of Amsterdam, the EC (as it still was) gained external powers to sign and ratify readmission treaties in its own name. Not long after the entry into force of the Treaty of Amsterdam, the Tampere European Council endorsed the Community's involvement in readmission from two perspectives, asserting that: '[t]he Amsterdam Treaty conferred powers on the Community in the field of readmission' and inviting the Council 'to conclude readmission agreements or to include standard clauses in other

---

[682] See respectively [2004] OJ L 83/12 and 7.5.3 and 7.5.4 above.

[683] See also: N Coleman, *European Readmission Policy: Third Country Interests and Refugee Rights* (Martinus Nijhoff, 2009); N Albuquerque Abell, 'The Compatibility of Readmission agreements with the 1951 Convention relating to the Status of Refugees', (1999) 11 IJRL 60; D Bouteillet-Paquet, 'Passing the Buck: A Critical Analysis of the Readmission Policy Implemented by the European Union and its Member States' (2003) 5 EJML 359; and S Peers and N Rogers, *EU Immigration and Asylum Law: Text and Commentary* (1st edn, Martinus Nijhoff, 2006), ch 31.

[684] Council doc 12509/95. See JHA Council press Releases, 23 Nov 1995 (agreement on the text) and Environment Council, 4 Apr 1996 (formal adoption of the text).

[685] [1996] OJ C 274/21. For analysis of this Recommendation, see E Guild and J Niessen, *The Developing Immigration and Asylum Policies of the European Union: Adopted Conventions, Resolutions, Recommendations, Decisions and Conclusions* (Kluwer, 1996).   [686] [1996] OJ C 274/25.

[687] [1996] OJ C 274/20. For further details, see and Coleman and Peers and Rogers (n 683 above).

agreements between the European Community and relevant third countries or groups of countries'.

To implement the first part of the conclusions, the Council decided which states should be targeted for agreements with the Community and what negotiating position the Community wished to take. It approved in September 2000 a mandate for the Commission to negotiate readmission treaties with Russia, Pakistan, Sri Lanka, and Morocco. Subsequently, in conjunction with the decision to drop visa requirements for persons with legal status granted by Hong Kong or Macao, the Council decided that these entities should in return agree readmission agreements with the Community 'as soon as possible',[688] and so it granted a negotiating mandate to the Commission for such treaties in May 2001. Next, the Commission sought a mandate to negotiate a readmission treaty with Ukraine, which the JHA Council granted in 2002. The Council then agreed criteria for which States to 'target' for future readmission agreements and applied those criteria to select four new target States (Algeria, Albania, China, and Turkey), which the Commission received a mandate to negotiate with in autumn 2002.[689] The criteria are: migration pressure upon the EU; States which have signed an association or cooperation agreement (excepting States negotiating accession); adjacent States; States where a readmission agreement would 'add value' to Member States' bilateral agreements; and 'geographical balance'. There is no explanation of how the criteria were applied to the individual cases; in fact, none of the four States which were 'targeted' meet the second criterion.[690] Also, as an implicit trade-off for the abolition of the visa requirement for their nationals to enter the EU, Romania and Bulgaria were expected to make a number of changes to national immigration law going beyond readmission obligations, but this did not take the form of a formal treaty with the Community.[691] In 2006, the EC decided that it also wished to negotiate readmission agreements with most of the remaining States in the Western Balkans (plus Moldova), in conjunction with negotiating visa facilitation treaties; such a linkage had already been made as regards Russia and Ukraine.[692] Finally, in 2008 and 2009, the Commission was granted further mandates to negotiate readmission treaties (again alongside visa facilitation treaties) with Georgia and Cape Verde.

Eleven EU readmission treaties have been concluded to date. First, a treaty with Hong Kong became the first EU readmission agreement to enter into force, on 1 March 2004.[693] Subsequently, an EU–Macao treaty entered into force on 1 June

---

[688] See JHA Council Conclusions, 30 Nov/1 Dec 2000.

[689] Council doc 7990/02, 15 Apr 2002, approved by the JHA Council, 25–26 Apr 2002.

[690] The EU association agreement with Algeria ([2005] OJ L 265) contains a readmission clause, but that agreement had not been signed in Apr 2002, when the Council adopted and applied these criteria.

[691] See COM (2001) 61, 2 Feb 2002 and COM (2001) 361, 29 June 2001; see further 4.5 above.

[692] On visa facilitation treaties, see 4.11.2 above.

[693] [2004] OJ L 64/38; see note on entry into force ([2004] OJ L 64/38).

2004;[694] an EU–Sri Lanka treaty entered into force on 1 May 2005;[695] a treaty
with Albania entered into force on 1 May 2006;[696] a treaty with Russia entered
into force on 1 June 2007, in parallel with an agreement on visa facilitation;[697]
and treaties with Ukraine, Serbia, Montenegro, Bosnia-Herzegovina, the Former
Yugoslav Republic of Macedonia, and Moldova entered into force on 1 January
2008, also in parallel with visa facilitation treaties.[698] An agreement with Pakistan
was signed in 2009, but has not yet been concluded,[699] and an agreement with
Georgia was reached in 2009, but has not yet been signed.[700] It is too early to tell
how successful negotiations will be with Cape Verde, but negotiations with the
four other States (Morocco, Algeria, China, and Turkey) have been slow. The
Commission intends to propose negotiations for readmission agreements (in parallel with visa facilitation agreements) with Belarus, Armenia, and Azerbaijan.[701]

Although there are minor differences between the agreements negotiated
and published to date, all are essentially identical. The contracting parties have
reciprocal obligations to take back their own nationals (or, in the case of Hong
Kong and Macao, permanent residents) who have entered or stayed illegally in
the other party. They must also readmit nationals of non-contracting parties or
stateless persons who have illegally entered or stayed on their territory, subject to
certain conditions.[702] Furthermore, they must also permit transit of persons back
to a non-contracting party if necessary. There are detailed rules on the procedure
for handing back persons, including the types of documents which constitute
proof or prima facie evidence that a person is a national or was on the territory.
The agreements also require use of the EU's standard travel document in certain
circumstances.[703] There are detailed provisions on data protection, although these
omit to require the non-EU parties to apply basic principles concerning the effective collective or individual enforcement of data protection rules. Each agreement
specifies that it is 'without prejudice to the rights, obligations and responsibilities'
of the parties arising from 'International Law', but there is no specific reference to
human rights or refugee law in the treaties with Hong Kong, Macao, Sri Lanka,

---

[694] [2004] OJ L 143/97; see note on entry into force ([2004] OJ L 258/17).

[695] [2005] OJ L 124/43; see note on entry into force ([2005] OJ L 138/17).

[696] [2005] OJ L 124/22; see Council Decision on conclusion by EC ([2005] OJ L 304/14) and note
on entry into force ([2006] OJ L 96/9).

[697] [2007] OJ L 129; see note on entry into force ([2007] OJ L 156/37).

[698] [2007] OJ L 332 and L 334.   [699] COM (2009) 106, 6 Mar 2009.

[700] For the proposals to sign and conclude the treaty, see COM (2010) 199 and 200, 5 May 2010.

[701] See Commission communication on the Eastern Partnership (COM (2008) 823, 3 Dec
2008).

[702] In particular, some treaties provide for delayed application of these rules (a two-year delay
for Albania and Ukraine, and a three-year delay for Russia). The treaties with the other Western
Balkan States and Moldova allow for the relevant provisions to be suspended on grounds of 'security,
protection of public order or public health'. The treaty with Pakistan limits the application of these
rules to persons who entered the territory after the treaty's entry into force.

[703] [1996] OJ C 274/20.

Ukraine, and Pakistan. A readmission committee is established by each agreement to perform specified technical tasks. Finally, each agreement provides that Member States can draw up special implementing protocols with the non-EC party, but conversely that the agreement takes precedence over any incompatible bilateral agreement between a Member State and the other contracting party. All the treaties provide for denunciation, but there is no provision for settling disputes that might arise between the parties.

The second part of the Tampere conclusions concerned the insertion of readmission clauses into broader EC external agreements. This continued the pre-Amsterdam policy discussed above, although now with the imprimatur of the backing of the European Council. However, the Council decided it should adapt the standard clauses for such agreements, because of the EC's competence over readmission treaties following the Treaty of Amsterdam. It quickly adopted a Decision adapting the standard clause in December 1999,[704] apparently hurrying to ensure that the negotiating mandate for the 'Cotonou agreement' with African, Caribbean, and Pacific (ACP) States could be amended in time before those negotiations concluded. Moreover, the new position of the Council was that such clauses should *always* be included in EC agreements, not just considered for inclusion on a case-by-case basis, because the EC had enjoyed only mixed success encouraging countries to sign up to the 'first generation' readmission clause of 1995. Agreements signed with a number of countries before 1999 contain variations on the 1995 standard clause; all agreements signed afterward include the 1999 standard clause.[705]

Shortly after the entry into force of the Treaty of Amsterdam, the Commission and the Council disputed whether the EC's competence over readmission agreements is exclusive, or rather shared with Member States. In practice, it has been assumed that the power is shared, with Member States continuing to sign readmission agreements in their own name since 1999. It is submitted that this practice is correct, since the Community has not acquired exclusive competence pursuant to full harmonization of the relevant internal law; nor can it be argued that it is absolutely essential for the Community to exercise external competence in order for it to adopt internal legislation.[706]

7.9.2. Irregular migration and external relations policy

The external aspects of migration policy has been on the EU agenda for some time. The issue was addressed in an early Commission communication on immigration,

---

[704] JHA Council press Release, 2 Dec 1999.

[705] For details of the provisions in each agreement, see Coleman (n 683 above) and S Peers, 'Irregular Immigration and EU External Relations', in Bogusz, et al, eds, *Irregular Migration and Human Rights* (Martinus Nijhoff, 2004), 193.

[706] See further the detailed analysis of the issue in Coleman and Peers and Rogers (n 683 above).

prepared in the run up to the Maastricht Treaty,[707] and the Edinburgh European Council (summit meeting) of 1992 adopted a detailed statement of principles governing external aspects of migration policy. This Declaration recognized in detail the factors that would reduce migration, referred to coordination of EU action and the effective use of development aid, and set out principles to guide EU and Member States' policies.

However, this policy was for some time only implemented in a piecemeal fashion. In late 1998, the EU Council created a 'High-Level Working Group' on asylum and immigration, in which officials from home affairs, trade, development, and foreign affairs ministries had to work together in order to develop an external immigration policy.[708] The Group was tasked with identifying a list of third States which should be subject to unilateral high-profile 'Action Plans' relating to migration policy, and then elaborating the detail of each plan. Each plan would include an analysis of 'the cause of the influx', based on the 'political and human rights situation' in the relevant country; possible 'strengthening economic cooperation' between the EU and the relevant country; 'identification of the needs for humanitarian aid', and concrete proposals for sending such aid; proposed further 'political/diplomatic consultations' with the relevant State or nearby States; an assessment of the possibility or state of play regarding a readmission agreement or readmission clauses in a mixed agreement; the possibility of temporary reception of persons in the region; and the likelihood of safe return or internal flight alternatives within a country of origin.

In 2001–02, the EU's policy on irregular migration and external relations became more operational. In addition to agreeing new criteria and targets for readmission agreements (see above), the mandate of the High-Level Working Group was expanded beyond the development and implementation of Action Plans, to examine the links between migration and other EU external policies, conduct dialogue on migration issues in certain cases with third states, intergovernmental organizations, and non-governmental organizations. Its mandate no longer referred expressly to facilitating trade with the relevant countries and the Action Plans were now to cover such new issues as joint measures on migration control policy and examination of voluntary repatriation.[709]

The Seville European Council of June 2002, which focused on immigration and asylum issues, developed a formal process and criteria regarding the external aspects of irregular migration. In its conclusions on this issue,[710] the summit first of all decided that each future EU association or cooperation agreement

---

[707] SEC (91) 1855, 23 Oct 1991, points 48 and 49.

[708] See the first edition of this book, at 102–103. The mandate of the group can be found in the General Affairs Council press release, 5–6 Dec 1998.

[709] Council doc 9433/02, 30 May 2002.

[710] For comments on all aspects of the Seville conclusions on immigration and asylum, see S Peers, 'EU Immigration and Asylum Law after Seville' (2002) 16 IANL Journal 176.

should include a clause on 'joint management of migration flows and compulsory readmission in the event of illegal immigration', having observed that trade expansion, economic cooperation, conflict prevention, and development assistance could all reduce the root causes of migration flows. Secondly, the EU declared its willingness to offer financial assistance to third States to assist with readmission of their own and other countries' nationals and broader joint migration management. Thirdly, inadequate cooperation by a third State could hamper further development of relations with the EU, following a systematic assessment of relations with that country. Finally, if a non-EU state has demonstrated 'an unjustified lack of cooperation in joint management of migration flows', according to the Council following a unanimous vote, then the Council, after 'full use of existing Community mechanisms', could take 'measures or positions' as part of the EU's foreign policy or other policies, 'while honouring the Union's contractual commitments and not jeopardising development cooperation objectives'. This is an apparent threat to *reduce* the existing level of EU relations with a third State, but there is great political and legal ambiguity in the conclusions as regards what measures might be taken, the 'legal base' for deciding on whether a State has failed to cooperate and the substantive grounds for concluding that there has been such a failure. In this area, the process and the criteria were still unclear.

EU policy then began to focus on means to ensure that the 'target' countries for readmission agreements would prove willing to agree them, given the EU's very limited willingness to lift visa requirements for most of its targets.[711] Next, the General Affairs Council on 18 November 2002 agreed to implement the Seville external relations conclusions in more detail, agreeing criteria for the application of the 'sanctions' policy and applying them.[712] The criteria for deciding which States to target were the extent of migration flows towards the EU, geography, the need to build capacity, the framework for cooperation and the attitude of that State regarding cooperation on migration issues. On this basis, the Council decided that the EU should intensify relations with Albania, China, Yugoslavia, Morocco, Russia, Tunisia, Ukraine, and Turkey, and to start cooperation with Libya as regards cooperation on migration issues, although the exact form such cooperation should take was not specified in detail. Also, the Council spelled out in detail the text of the future 'migration cooperation' clause to be included in all cooperation and association agreements with the Community (as it then was). This clause entails a dialogue on migration; a commitment to examine root causes; a joint examination of illegal immigration issues; the standard readmission clause (already, of course, part of EU policy before Seville); and 'cooperation regarding migratory flows to promote a fair treatment' of legal residents 'through an integration policy favouring non-discrimination and

---

[711] See discussion in the Green Paper on Return [expulsion] Policy (COM (2002) 175, 10 Apr 2002) and the follow-up communication (COM (2002) 564, 14 Oct 2002).
[712] Council doc 13894/02, 13 Nov 2002.

the fight against racism and xenophobia'.[713] In summer 2003, the Commission reported that this policy had been implemented in detail, comprising meetings with all the 'target' States except the former Yugoslavia.[714] As a result, Morocco agreed to negotiate the proposed readmission agreement, Turkey was aligning itself more fully with EU legislation, and there was progress in readmission talks with Ukraine.

A parallel development was a Commission paper from December 2002 covering two issues: the link between migration and development, and the EU financial resources available for implementing internal and external migration policies.[715] Despite a decade of increasing EU interest in the external relations aspect of migration policy, this was the first detailed examination of the topic as regards developing countries—or indeed any other countries. The Commission set out the push and pull factors leading to migration from developing States and surveyed some recent literature. It concluded that poverty reduction should stay the main focus of EU development policy, and surveyed other policies that might reduce migration demand: liberalized trade and market access; more liberal rules on short-term movement of people (for the first time); conflict prevention; good governance; and rural development. But as for implementing these policies, it held out little hope for quick results, again pointing to the limited leverage of the Community and now also to the limits imposed by the WTO on trade preferences for only selected developing countries, as well as the limits upon the Community budget. However, in the second part of the communication, the Commission stated an intention to expand the funds available for migration projects in non-EU countries dramatically.

The Council adopted conclusions on the Commission's paper in May 2003, stating that it did not intend to reduce current levels of funding for poverty eradication.[716] As regards dialogue to be conducted with developing countries, the EU would consider further proposals for policies on work permits; virtual returns; voluntary return programmes; management of remittances; integration of third-country nationals in the EU; problems that may arise from recruitment of highly skilled labour from developing States; and a review of the policy of placing EU expatriates in jobs that could go to skilled local staff.

The Thessaloniki European Council subsequently agreed in June 2003 to establish an 'evaluation mechanism' for third countries, taking account of the following criteria: participation in the international instruments relevant to this matter (eg Conventions on Human Rights, the Geneva Convention of 28 July 1951 relating to the status of refugees as amended by the New York Protocol of 31 January 1967); cooperation of third countries in readmission/return of their nationals and of third-country nationals; efforts in border control and interception of illegal

---

[713] These criteria took account of the criteria agreed by the JHA Council in Apr 2002 to decide which countries to negotiate Community readmission agreements with: see discussion above.

[714] SEC (2003) 815, 9 July 2003.   [715] COM (2002) 703, 3 Dec 2002.

[716] Council doc 8927/03, 5 May 2003.

immigrants; combating of trafficking in human beings, including taking legislative and other measures; cooperation on visa policy and possible adaptation of visa systems; creation of asylum systems, with specific reference to access to effective protection, and efforts in redocumentation of nationals. The policy will be assessed by an annual report from the Commission, which could make recommendations.[717] In November 2003, the Council approved more detailed guidelines for the functioning of this mechanism.[718] The guidelines concern particularly the Commission's annual report, with more detail on the application of the criteria, and a requirement of partnership 'where possible' with the relevant third countries, based on existing agreements between those countries and the EC. In a 'pilot phase', the mechanism would focus on selected countries in the Commission's first report. This first report indicated that cooperation with the EU was generally acceptable, and made recommendations for development of cooperation with the relevant States and for further development of the reporting mechanism, including the addition of more third States.[719] The Council broadly welcomed the report.[720]

In 2004, the EU established a funding programme on the external aspects of asylum and migration, since integrated into the EU's main external relations funding programmes.[721] Shortly afterward, the Commission released in 2005 a communication on the links between migration and development, addressing in detail the issues of remittances to countries of origin, the development role of diasporas, circular migration (migration back and forth to and from the EU and the country of origin), and 'brain drain', indicating its intention to address these issues through dialogue and possibly legislation.[722]

Soon afterward, in response to a call from the informal European Council (or summit meeting) held at Hampton Court in autumn 2005, the Commission suggested an action plan regarding the external aspects of migration, which the European Council largely endorsed shortly afterward, in the form of a 'Global Approach to Migration'. The plan included action by Frontex to support enhanced external border controls and further dialogue and cooperation with African and Mediterranean countries.[723]

The 'global approach' was then further developed subsequently as part of the EU's 'common immigration policy',[724] in particular being extended to develop

---

[717] Paras 19–21, Thessaloniki European Council conclusions.

[718] Council doc 15292/03, 25 Nov 2003.   [719] COM (2005) 352, 28 July 2005.

[720] See Council conclusions on external relations and migration issues (Council doc 14769/05, 21 Nov 2005), point 7.

[721] Reg 491/2004 ([2004] OJ L 80/1), integrated into Art 16 of Reg 1905/2006 ([2006] OJ L 378/41). For more detail, see the second edition of this book, at 295–296.

[722] COM (2005) 390, 1 Sep 2005. See Council conclusions on policy coherence for development, Council doc 15806/09, 12 Nov 2009.

[723] COM (2005) 621, 30 Nov 2005; Annex I to the European Council conclusions, 15/16 Dec 2005. See earlier Council conclusions on EU-Libya migration cooperation (JHA Council press release, 2–3 June 2005).

[724] See the European Council conclusions of Dec 2006 and the follow-up Commission communications: COM (2006) 735, 30 Nov 2006; COM (2007) 780 and SEC (2007) 1632, 5 Dec

the principle of 'circular migration' and to include the new concept of 'mobility partnerships'—informal agreements between the EU and certain third countries which bundle together a number of promised actions by the EU and its Member States on the one hand and the partner country on the other.[725]

The risk is ever-present that the EU's external migration policies will exacerbate human rights violations in countries of transit which will not want the burden of an increased migrant population, that insufficient attention is paid to the EU's other external objectives (relating to foreign policy, development, and trade), with the result that migration pressures actually increase, and that the root causes of migration within the EU's control (in particular the Common Agricultural Policy) are not addressed. Through harsh experience the EU learned that despite the demands of its interior ministers, few States are willing to offer it something in return for nothing. This has resulted in a more balanced policy of offering visa facilitation agreements and financial assistance in return for readmission agreements, and linking together different aspects of EU external migration policy, in particular in the form of mobility partnerships.

7.10. Conclusions

EU policy on irregular migration has, in recent years, begun to address the key aspects of this issue, in particular in the form of the Returns Directive and the Directive on the employment of irregular migrants. However, the latter measure does not address the central issue of enforcement and the former measure sets too low a standard from the point of view of human rights, in particular as regards detention. The overall legal framework in this area remains fragmented at EU level, certainly as compared to the codification of the legislation on visas and borders. Time will tell whether the EU's more intensive involvement in this area will contribute to or detract from the protection of the human rights of irregular migrants.

2007; COM (2008) 359, 17 June 2008; COM (2008) 611, 8 Oct 2008; and the Council conclusions in Council docs 9604/08, 20 May 2008 and 16041/08, 20 Nov 2008. See also COM (2007) 247, 16 May 2007, on extending the global approach to the areas to the eastern and south-eastern neighbours of the EU.

[725] See COM (2007) 248, 16 May 2007 and SEC (2009) 1240, 18 Sep 2009; the Council conclusions in Council docs 16283/07, 7 Dec 2007, and 15811/09, 12 Nov 2009; and the mobility partnerships with Moldova, Cape Verde, and Georgia (respectively Council docs: 9460/08 add 1, 21 May 2008; 9460/08 add 1, 21 May 2008; and 16396/09 add 1, 20 Nov 2009).

8

Civil Cooperation

8.1. Introduction

The substantive details of civil cooperation within the European Union are beyond the scope of this book, which focuses on matters within the scope of interior and home affairs ministries. Instead, this chapter briefly describes the place of civil cooperation within the Community (now Union) legal system. It will be seen that there are some broad similarities with the issues which arise regarding the mutual recognition principle in the area of criminal law (see Chapter 9).

8.2. Institutional framework and overview

8.2.1. Cooperation prior to the Treaty of Amsterdam

8.2.1.1 Cooperation prior to the Maastricht Treaty

It was always envisaged that Member States would wish to cooperate on civil law matters and that such cooperation would have a close relationship with economic integration to be developed within Community law. Therefore, such cooperation was provided for even in the original Treaty of Rome, in Article 220 EEC. This Article provided that:

Member States shall, so far as is necessary, enter into negotiations with each other with a view to securing for their nationals:

- the protection of persons and the enjoyment and protection of rights under the same conditions as those accorded by each State to its own nationals,
- the abolition of double taxation within the Community,
- the mutual recognition of companies or firms within the meaning of the second paragraph of Article 58,[1] the retention of legal personality in the event of transfer of their seat from one country to another, and the possibility of mergers between companies or firms governed by the laws of different countries,
- the simplification of formalities governing the reciprocal recognition and enforcement of judgments of courts or tribunals and of arbitration awards.

[1] Now Art 54 TFEU.

In 1968, agreement was reached on Conventions falling within the third and fourth indents. One Convention was agreed on the mutual recognition of companies[2] and a second was agreed on the recognition and enforcement of civil and commercial judgments, along with the rules governing jurisdiction over proceedings. The former Convention was not ratified by all Member States and has long been abandoned, but the latter, known as the Brussels Convention, was a resounding success, later extended to all of the first fifteen Member States[3] and even to non-Member States (Norway, Iceland, and Switzerland) in the form of a parallel Convention, the Lugano Convention.[4] Much later, the Member States agreed a Convention on the arbitration of double taxation disputes, falling within the scope of the second indent.[5]

Article 220, renumbered Article 293 by the Treaty of Amsterdam, and subsequently repealed by the Treaty of Lisbon, did not provide expressly for interpretation of the measures adopted pursuant to it by the EU's Court of Justice, but it was presumed that the Court's jurisdiction could be extended to such measures. Protocols on the Court's interpretation of the 1968 Conventions were agreed in 1971,[6] although no such Protocol was agreed for the Tax Arbitration Convention. The Protocol on the Court's interpretation of the Brussels Convention resulted in over a hundred rulings by the Court.

The Member States later decided that they also wished to adopt further Conventions which were closely related to the EC legal system, but which did not fall within the scope of Article 220. The solution was to agree 'purely' intergovernmental Conventions on: the creation of a Community patent;[7] the rules governing choice of law in contract (the Rome Convention);[8] the abolition of legalization of documents; and the simplification of proceedings for recovery of

---

[2] Published in *EC Bulletin* 2/69.

[3] See the consolidated version of the Convention after the accession of Austria, Sweden, and Finland ([1998] OJ C 27/1).

[4] [1988] OJ L 319/9. This Convention also applied to Sweden, Finland, and Austria before they ratified the Brussels Convention after becoming EU Member States, and to Poland before it joined the EU.

[5] [1990] OJ L 225/10. The Convention was subsequently extended to Member States joining the EU later: see [1996] OJ C 26/1, [2005] OJ C 160/1, and [2008] OJ L 174/1. It was also amended by a Protocol ([1999] OJ C 202/1).

[6] See n 3 above (Protocol to Brussels Convention); D Anderson, *References to the European Court* (Sweet and Maxwell, 1995), 377 (company recognition Convention).

[7] Convention on Community Patent ([1976] OJ L 17/18), amended by 1989 Agreement ([1989] OJ L 401/1).

[8] See the consolidated version of Convention after the accession of the first fifteen Member States ([1998] OJ C 27/34). The Member States joining in 2004 (along with the first fifteen Member States) signed an accession treaty to the Rome Convention in April 2005 ([2005] C 169/1), which entered into force on 1 May 2006 (for ratification details, see Appendix I). See the subsequent consolidated version of the Convention ([2005] OJ C 334/1). Romania and Bulgaria became parties to the Convention on 15 Jan 2008, pursuant to a Council Decision ([2007] OJ L 347/1).

maintenance payments under the Brussels Convention.[9] It was decided that the Court of Justice would have jurisdiction over the Patent Convention and the Rome Convention,[10] although the Patent Convention never came into force and the Protocols on the Court's jurisdiction to interpret the Rome Convention in the first fifteen Member States only came into force on 1 August 2004.[11] The latter Protocols have only resulted to date in two references to the Court of Justice from national courts.[12]

It should be emphasized that in civil law matters, the question of which State's courts have *jurisdiction* over a dispute is distinct from the question of which *law* applies to the dispute, as it is possible for courts to apply foreign civil law. The Brussels Convention addressed the former issue, while the Rome Convention addressed the latter.

8.2.1.2. Cooperation from Maastricht to Amsterdam

Article K.1(6) of the EU Treaty listed 'judicial cooperation in civil matters' as a common interest of the Member States falling within the scope of the third pillar, although Article K.3(2)(c) EU was expressly 'without prejudice' to Article 220 EC (later Article 293 EC, and now repealed). Member States agreed measures under both of these overlapping 'legal bases' during the Maastricht period. First, Article 220 EC was used to draw up a Convention on choice of law and jurisdiction in insolvency proceedings in 1995,[13] although the prospect of ratification of this Convention lapsed when the UK did not sign it within the six-month period allotted for the Member States' signatures. Secondly, in 1997 and in 1998 the 'third pillar' powers were used by the Council to draw up Conventions on the service of documents and on jurisdiction over and enforcement of matrimonial judgments, including decisions on parental responsibility connected to the judgment concerning dissolution of the marriage.[14] The Council also reached agreement in 1999 on amendments to the Brussels Convention.[15]

---

[9] Not published in the OJ; see respectively UK government Command Papers 626 (1989) and 1604 (1991) and Appendix I for ratification details.

[10] See Protocols to the latter ([1989] OJ L 48/1).

[11] [2004] OJ C 277/1. In fact, Ireland opted out of the Court's jurisdiction over the Rome Convention. The two Protocols also apply to the newer EU Member States pursuant to the accession treaty to the Rome Convention and the Council Decision extending that Convention to Romania and Bulgaria (n 8 above).

[12] Case C-133/08 *ICF* [2009] ECR I-9687 and C-29/10 *Koelzsch*, pending.

[13] (1996) 35 ILM 1223.

[14] [1997] OJ C 261/1 and [1998] OJ C 221/1 respectively. The latter became known as the 'Brussels II Convention'.

[15] See JHA Council press Release, 27/28 May 1999, and the Commission's earlier proposal for amendments (COM (1997) 609, 26 Nov 1997; [1998] OJ C 33/3 and 30).

8.2.2. The Treaties of Amsterdam and Nice

8.2.2.1. Institutional framework

The Treaty of Amsterdam transferred the issue of civil cooperation from the third pillar to the first with effect from 1 May 1999. Powers regarding this issue were conferred by Article 65 EC, which provided as follows:

Measures in the field of judicial cooperation in civil matters having cross-border implications, to be taken in accordance with Article 67 and insofar as necessary for the proper functioning of the internal market, shall include:

(a) improving and simplifying:
- the system for cross-border service of judicial and extra-judicial documents;
- cooperation in the taking of evidence;
- the recognition and enforcement of decisions in civil and commercial cases, including decisions in extrajudicial cases;

(b) promoting the compatibility of the rules applicable in the Member States concerning the conflict of laws and of jurisdiction;

(c) eliminating obstacles to the good functioning of civil proceedings, if necessary by promoting the compatibility of the rules on civil procedure applicable in the Member States.

These provisions were not subjected to any form of deadline, although they were covered by: the special institutional rules of Articles 67 and 68 EC, including the restrictions on the jurisdiction of the Court of Justice; the general 'opt-outs' of the UK, Ireland, and Denmark from Title IV EC; and the possibility of adopting measures on related administrative cooperation under Article 66.[16] As a result of the applicability of Article 67 EC, EC civil law measures were initially subject to unanimous voting in the Council, mere consultation of the European Parliament (EP), and (for the initial five years after entry into force of the Treaty of Amsterdam) a shared right of initiative of the Commission and the Member States.

However, the Treaty of Nice brought about an important change in the institutional framework, as from its entry into force on 1 February 2003. It inserted a new Article 67(5) into the EC Treaty, which inter alia provided that civil law measures, except for 'aspects relating to family law', would immediately be subject to the 'co-decision' procedure set out in Article 251 EC, giving equal voting powers to the EP and entailing QMV in the Council and a Commission monopoly on proposals for legislation. Family law measures remained subject to the general decision-making rules set out in Article 67 (unanimity in Council and consultation of the EP), and remained subject to unanimity and consultation even after most of Title IV of the EC Treaty became subject to QMV and

---

[16] On the institutional rules, see 2.2.2.1 above; on the opt-outs, see 8.2.5 below; on Art 66, see 8.2.4 below.

co-decision in May 2004 and January 2005.[17] However, since 1 May 2004, family law measures could only be adopted following a proposal from the Commission. It should also be recalled that a Protocol attached to the EC Treaty by the Treaty of Nice changed the decision-making rules applicable to Article 66 EC as from 1 May 2004, so that, from that date, measures on administrative cooperation were adopted by a qualified majority vote in the Council with consultation of the EP. Furthermore, in December 2005, the Commission urged that the Council adopt a decision pursuant to Article 67(2) EC, requiring a unanimous vote after consultation of the EP, in order to amend the decision-making rules to apply the co-decision procedure and QMV in Council to the issue of maintenance.[18] However, the Council did not act on this suggestion.

The Final Act of the Treaty of Amsterdam also included a Declaration (no 20) relating to Article 65 EC. This Declaration stated that measures adopted pursuant to Article 65 'shall not prevent any Member State from applying its constitutional rules relating to freedom of the press and freedom of expression in other media'. In fact, the Declaration appears to be a reaction to the *Shevill* judgment of the Court of Justice, which ruled on the application of the Brussels Convention to cross-border defamation claims.[19]

8.2.2.2. Overview of practice[20]

The EC's first priority after the entry into force of the Treaty of Amsterdam was to transpose the civil cooperation Conventions which had been agreed or adopted during the Maastricht period into EC legislation. To this end, by the end of 2000 the EC had adopted legislation concerning: the service of documents; jurisdiction over divorce matters and recognition of divorce judgments; jurisdiction, choice of law, and recognition of judgments regarding insolvency proceedings (the 'insolvency regulation'); and the general rules concerning jurisdiction over and recognition of civil and commercial judgments (the 'Brussels Regulation', replacing the Brussels Convention).

In the meantime, the Tampere European Council, meeting in autumn 1999, had set key political objectives for the development of EC law on civil judicial cooperation. According to the European Council, the 'cornerstone' of judicial cooperation, for civil law as well as criminal law, was the principle of 'mutual recognition', applying 'both to judgements and to other decisions of judicial authorities'. The development of this principle by EC law would entail the further reduction of 'intermediate measures' which apply to the recognition and enforcement of judgments issued in other EU Member States (known as 'exequatur').

---

[17] On these developments, see 2.2.2.1 above.   [18] COM (2005) 648, 15 Dec 2005.
[19] Case C-68/93 [1995] ECR I-415.
[20] For more detailed references to the legislation adopted, see 8.5 and 8.6 below. As regards EU funding measures and external relations issues, see also 8.8 and 8.9 below. On the 'common frame of reference' for contract law, see 8.7 below.

Exequatur was to be abolished entirely in particular cases (small claims and some family law judgments), possibly subject to the adoption of minimum standards in civil procedure.

The detailed application of these principles was subject to a mutual recognition programme, to be drawn up by the end of 2000.[21] This programme first called upon the EC to adopt measures concerning mutual recognition of judgments in areas where it had not already acted: property rights related to dissolution of marriage and the separation of unmarried couples; property rights related to succession; and judgments on parental responsibility where the parents are unmarried or which were taken after the dissolution of the marriage relationship. Where the EC had already acted, it should further develop the degree of mutual recognition, by gradually abolishing the barriers to the recognition of judgments from other Member States (the exequatur process and the grounds for refusing recognition). The programme also addressed the prospect of adopting measures ancillary to mutual recognition, comprising: minimum standards in civil procedure or harmonization of civil procedure (particularly regarding parental responsibility and service of documents); improved enforcement of judgments (particularly concerning information on debtors' assets); and general improvement of civil cooperation (particularly the creation of a judicial network, a system for obtaining evidence, adoption of rules on legal aid, provision of public information, and harmonization of conflict of law rules).

In order to implement this work programme, in the lead up to the entry into force of the Treaty of Nice, the EC adopted legislation concerning the cross-border taking of evidence, civil law spending programmes, the creation of a Judicial Network concerning civil matters, and legal aid. Work also began on the development of a 'common frame of reference' for European contract law.

Following the extension of QMV and co-decision to civil law matters (except for family law) in 2003, the EC adopted legislation concerning enforcement orders, small claims, payment orders, mediation, and choice of law regarding both contractual and non-contractual obligations, in particular replacing the Rome Convention on conflict of law in contracts. It also amended the legislation concerning the service of documents and the civil law judicial network, and adopted a new civil law funding programme. In the sphere of family law, the EC adopted legislation regarding maintenance claims, and amended the rules concerning jurisdiction over family law matters, inter alia extending the relevant Regulation to include certain issues relating to children. Furthermore, it adopted legislation authorizing Member States to conclude treaties within the sphere of EC exclusive external competence, subject to certain conditions. In the meantime, the Hague Programme, adopted in 2004, reiterated the basic focus on mutual recognition, set a date of 2011 for completion of the civil law mutual

---

[21] [2001] OJ C 12/1.

recognition work programme, and specified a number of further measures to be adopted to accomplish this.[22]

As for proposed legislation, the Council failed to agree before the entry into force of the Treaty of Lisbon on proposed legislation to govern the choice of law on divorce (the 'Rome III' proposal).[23] In autumn 2009, the Commission proposed a Regulation regarding jurisdiction and choice of law relating to wills and inheritance.[24] Neither was adopted before the entry into force of the Treaty of Lisbon.[25]

It is interesting to examine the practical application of the co-decision procedure and QMV to civil law. Out of ten civil law measures adopted by QMV and co-decision, three attracted opposition in the Council. More precisely: the Netherlands voted against the Common Position on the Regulation establishing the European Enforcement Order;[26] Poland abstained against the Common Position on the Regulation establishing a European payment order;[27] and Estonia and Latvia voted against the Common Position on the Regulation on conflict of law concerning non-contractual liability,[28] as well as the final Regulation.[29] However, there was unanimous support for the other seven measures: the legislation concerning small claims, EC funding, service of documents,[30] mediation,[31] choice of law in contract,[32] the European judicial network,[33] and Member States' external treaties.[34]

As for EP-Council relations, of these ten civil law measures which were subject to the co-decision process, the EP and Council reached a 'first-reading' agreement on four of them,[35] a second-reading agreement on five of them,[36] and

---

[22] [2005] OJ C 53, point 3.4. See also the work programme for implementation of the Hague programme, point 4.3 ([2005] OJ C 198/1). The common frame of reference in contract law was to be adopted by 2009; on this issue, see 8.7 below.   [23] See 8.6 below.

[24] COM (2009) 154, 14 Oct 2009.   [25] For later developments, see 8.2.3 below.

[26] See the monthly summary of Council acts for Feb 2004 (Council doc 7712/04, 24 Mar 2004, Annex III).

[27] See the monthly summary of Council acts for June 2006 (Council doc 12312/06, 28 Aug 2006, Annex III). However, all Member States voted in favour of the final Regulation at second reading: see the monthly summary of Council acts for Dec 2006 (Council doc 17121/06, 27 Feb 2007).

[28] See the monthly summary of Council acts for Sep 2006 (Council doc 14543/1/06 rev 1, 17 Apr 2008, Annex III).

[29] See the monthly summary of Council acts for June 2007 (Council doc 7311/2/08 rev 2, 17 Apr 2008).

[30] On all three measures, see the monthly summary of Council acts for June 2007 (ibid), Annexes I and III; on the final adoption of the funding decision, see the monthly summary of Council acts for Sept 2007 (Council doc 7531/2/08 rev 2, 13 Oct 2008).

[31] See the monthly summary of Council acts for Feb 2008 (Council doc 12382/1/08 rev 1, 7 Oct 2008), Annex II, Part I.

[32] See the monthly summary of Council acts for June 2008 (Council doc 12750/2/08 rev 2, 13 Mar 2009), Annex II, Part I.

[33] See the monthly summary of Council acts for June 2009 (Council doc 12639/09, 12 Aug 2009), Annex II, Part I.

[34] See the voting sheet concerning this Regulation (Council doc 11838/09, 7 July 2009).

[35] These were the Regulations on small claims, Rome I (choice of law in contract), the European judicial network, and Member States' external civil law treaties.

[36] In three cases, the EP approved the Council's common position at second reading (Regs on the European Enforcement order and the service of documents; Dir on mediation). In two cases,

a third-reading agreement on one.[37] This compares to a much higher use of first-reading deals as regards immigration and asylum law, and indeed as regards EU law more generally.

The fairly intense legislative activity in this area was matched by an increasing involvement of the Court of Justice.[38] It is notable that the restrictions on the Court's jurisdiction did not prevent a generally increasing flow of references from national courts as regards Title IV civil law legislation, although it might have been expected that the Court would have received an even greater number of cases if the restrictions on its jurisdiction had not been in place.[39] More precisely, the Court received: one reference in 2002 (which was inadmissible);[40] two references in 2003 (one was inadmissible);[41] five references in 2004 (one was withdrawn);[42] three references in 2005;[43] six references in 2006 (one was withdrawn);[44] ten references in 2007 (one was withdrawn);[45] fifteen references in 2008 (three were withdrawn);[46] and eleven references in 2009 until 1 December (one was inadmissible, because it was referred from a lower court).[47]

---

the EP adopted amendments at second reading, which were then approved by the Council (Reg on payment orders, Decision on EC funding programme).

[37] The Rome II Reg on choice of law in non-contractual liability.

[38] See Art 68 EC.

[39] Compare with the numbers of cases after the entry into force of the Treaty of Lisbon (8.2.3 below).

[40] Case C-24/02 *Marseille Fret* [2002] ECR I-3383. The case was doubly inadmissible, as it was referred from a lower court and the dispute pre-dated the date of application of the legislation concerned.

[41] Cases C-443/03 *Leffler* [2005] ECR I-9611 and C-555/03 *Ryanair* [2004] ECR I-6041. The latter case was inadmissible as it was referred from a lower court.

[42] Cases C-1/04 *Staubitz-Schreiber* [2006] ECR I-701; C-473/04 *Plumex* [2006] ECR I-1417; C-234/04 *Kapferer* [2006] ECR I-2585; C-341/04 *Eurofood* [2006] ECR I-3813; and Case C-387/04 *Donath*, which was withdrawn.

[43] Cases C-103/05 *Reisch Montage* [2006] ECR I-6827; C-283/05 *ASML* [2006] ECR I-12041; and C-386/05 *Color Drack* [2007] ECR I-3699.

[44] Cases: C-98/06 *Freeport* [2007] ECR I-8319; C-180/06 *Ilsinger* [2009] ECR I-3961; C-435/06 *C* [2007] ECR I-10141; C-462/06 *Glaxo SmithKline* [2008] ECR I-3965; and C-463/06 *FBTO Schadeverzekeringen* [2007] ECR I-11321. The withdrawn case was C-175/06 *Tedesco*, but there was an Advocate General's opinion in this case ([2007] ECR I-7929).

[45] Cases: C-14/07 *Weiss und partner* [2008] ECR I-3367; C-68/07 *Sundelind Lopez* [2007] ECR I-10403; C-185/07 *Riunione Adriatica Di Sicurta v West Tankers* [2009] ECR I-663; C-339/07 *Deko Marty Belgium* [2009] ECR I-767; C-372/07 *Hassett* [2008] ECR I-7403; C-413/07 *Haase* (withdrawn); C-420/07 *Apostolides* [2009] ECR I-3571; C-444/07 *MG Probud*, judgment of 21 Jan 2010, not yet reported; C-523/07 *A* [2009] ECR I-2805; and C-533/07 *Falco* [2009] ECR I-3327.

[46] Cases: C-14/08 *Roda Golf and Beach Resort* [2009] ECR I-5439; C-111/08 *SCT Industri* [2009] ECR I-5655; C-148/08 *Mejnersten*, withdrawn; C-167/08 *Draka-NK Cables* [2009] ECR I-3477; C-168/08 *Hadadi* [2009] ECR I-6871; C-195/08 *Rinau* [2008] ECR I-5271; C-189/08 *Zuid-Chemie* [2009] ECR I-6917; C-204/08 *Rehder* [2009] ECR I-6073; C-292/08 *German Graphics Graphische Maschinen* [2009] ECR I-8421; C-347/08 *Vorarlberger* [2009] ECR I-8661; C-381/08 *Car Trim*, judgment of 25 Feb 2010, not yet reported; C-533/08 *TNT-Express*, judgment of 4 May 2010, not yet reported; C-534/08 *KLG Europe*, withdrawn; C-584/08 *Real Madrid*, withdrawn; and C-585/08 *Pammer*, opinion of 18 May 2010, pending.

[47] Cases: C-19/09 *Wood Floor Solutions* (judgment of 11 Mar 2010, not yet reported); C-111/09 *Bilas* (judgment of 20 May 2010, not yet reported); C-144/09 *Hotel Alpenhof* (opinion of 18 May

This amounted to a total of fifty-three references, of which nearly two-thirds (thirty-three) concerned the main regulation on jurisdiction over civil and commercial judgments and the recognition of such judgments. The Regulations on family law, insolvency, and service of documents also attracted several references each,[48] while the legislation on the transmission of evidence attracted two references. There were no references on external civil law treaties concluded by the EC,[49] or on the legislation concerning simplified recognition of judgments (enforcement order, payment orders, small claims) or conflicts of law. However, the measures concerned were all quite recent at the time. Two references were subjected to the emergency ruling procedure for JHA matters which was established in 2008.[50]

As for the source of the references, the Austrian and German courts accounted for the most cases,[51] followed by the Netherlands,[52] France and Belgium,[53] Sweden and Italy,[54] Ireland, Finland, the UK, Spain, and Poland,[55] and then Lithuania, the Czech Republic, Cyprus, and Slovenia.[56] There were no references from the courts of nearly half of the Member States.[57]

EC civil law legislation did not attract other types of legal proceedings (annulment actions or infringement actions) except for one request for an opinion relating to a planned external treaty.[58] The Court did not address the issue of 'mixed jurisdiction' (where a case related to civil law measures as well as measures subject to the Court's non-JHA jurisdiction), despite the large number of cases where civil law legislation and internal market issues overlapped.[59]

8.2.3. Treaty of Lisbon

Following the entry into force of the Treaty of Lisbon on 1 December 2009, the legal basis for civil cooperation measures within the EU is now Article 81 of the

---

2010, pending); C-147/09 *Seunig* (withdrawn); C-256/09 *Purrucker I* (judgment of 15 July 2010, not yet reported); C-278/09 *Martinez* (dismissed by order of 20 Nov 2009, not yet reported); C-283/09 *Werynski* (opinion of 2 Sep 2010, pending); C-312/09 *Michalias* (order of 17 June 2010); C-396/09 *Interedil* (pending); C-403/09 PPU *Detiček* (judgment of 23 Dec 2009, not yet reported); and C-406/09 *Realchemie* (pending).

[48] Respectively eight, six, and four references. Also, several cases concerning the Brussels Reg clarified its relationship with the insolvency Reg: see 8.5.1 below.

[49] On the question of the Court of Justice's jurisdiction over such treaties, see 8.9 below.

[50] *Rinau* and *Detiček* (nn 46 and 47 above), which both concerned return of a child. On the JHA emergency ruling procedure generally, see 2.2.2.1 above.

[51] Eleven and nine references respectively.   [52] Six references.

[53] Four references each.   [54] Three references.   [55] Two references each.

[56] One reference each.

[57] Eleven Member States: Luxembourg, Denmark, Greece, Portugal, Hungary, Estonia, Latvia, Slovakia, Malta, Romania, and Bulgaria.

[58] *Opinion 1/2003* [2006] ECR I-1145; see 8.9 below.

[59] On the mixed jurisdiction issue, see generally 2.4 above; on the overlaps between civil law and internal market issues in the case law, see 8.4 below. This issue is now moot after the entry into force of the Treaty of Lisbon, except where there is a difference in territorial scope between civil law measures and other EU law measures.

Treaty on the Functioning of the European Union (TFEU), which provides as follows:

1. The Union shall develop judicial cooperation in civil matters having cross-border implications, based on the principle of mutual recognition of judgments and of decisions in extrajudicial cases. Such cooperation may include the adoption of measures for the approximation of the laws and regulations of the Member States.

2. For the purposes of paragraph 1, the European Parliament and the Council, acting in accordance with the ordinary legislative procedure, shall adopt measures, particularly when necessary for the proper functioning of the internal market, aimed at ensuring:

    (a) the mutual recognition and enforcement between Member States of judgments and of decisions in extrajudicial cases;

    (b) the cross-border service of judicial and extrajudicial documents;

    (c) the compatibility of the rules applicable in the Member States concerning conflict of laws and of jurisdiction;

    (d) cooperation in the taking of evidence;

    (e) effective access to justice;

    (f) the elimination of obstacles to the proper functioning of civil proceedings, if necessary by promoting the compatibility of the rules on civil procedure applicable in the Member States;

    (g) the development of alternative methods of dispute settlement;

    (h) support for the training of the judiciary and judicial staff.

3. Notwithstanding paragraph 2, measures concerning family law with cross-border implications shall be established by the Council, acting in accordance with a special legislative procedure. The Council shall act unanimously after consulting the European Parliament.

The Council, on a proposal from the Commission, may adopt a decision determining those aspects of family law with cross-border implications which may be the subject of acts adopted by the ordinary legislative procedure. The Council shall act unanimously after consulting the European Parliament.

The proposal referred to in the second subparagraph shall be notified to the national Parliaments. If a national Parliament makes known its opposition within six months of the date of such notification, the decision shall not be adopted. In the absence of opposition, the Council may adopt the decision.

The list of specific issues appearing within the scope of Article 81 TFEU is the same as the list in the prior Article 65 EC, with the addition of 'a high level of access to justice', 'the development of alternative methods of dispute settlement', and 'support for the training of the judiciary and judicial staff'. However, as we have seen, the EC had previously already used Article 65 EC to address such matters. There have been minor amendments to the wording as regards the items which remain in the list, for example the addition of the word 'mutual' to the item concerning recognition of judgments. Moreover, the issue of mutual recognition has been 'promoted' to the top of the list; this is consistent with the revised wording of Article 81(1) TFEU, which specifies that judicial cooperation on civil matters is 'based on' mutual recognition. This Treaty amendment entrenched the political decision taken back in 1999 in Tampere, as noted above, to prioritize the issue of mutual recognition as regards civil and criminal law cooperation in the EU.

The *chapeau* of Article 81 TFEU is wider than the *chapeau* of Article 65 EC, as the prior requirement that civil law measures must be 'necessary for the proper functioning of the internal market' is now qualified by the word 'particularly'. It seems obvious that a necessary link to the functioning of the internal market is no longer required for civil law measures.[60] On the other hand, the words 'shall include' no longer precede the list of specific measures which could be adopted; the obvious implication is that this list is now exhaustive. This interpretation is confirmed by the decision to add some additional items (reflecting the practice under the Treaty of Amsterdam) to this list. The explicit references in the Treaty to approximation of national law and the principle of mutual recognition are also changes from the prior Article 65 EC.

As for decision-making, the normal rule remains the co-decision procedure (now renamed the 'ordinary legislative procedure') with, as before, an exception for 'family law', which is still subject to unanimous voting in the Council and consultation of the EP (now referred to as a type of 'special legislative procedure'). The latter exception is now worded slightly differently, no longer referring to 'aspects' of family law (except as regards the Council's changes to decision-making rules). That possibility of changing the decision-making rules (Article 81(3) TFEU) differs from the prior Article 67(2) EC (which has been repealed by the Treaty of Lisbon) in that the proposal to change the rules must be issued by the Commission, and there is a new procedure establishing a form of control by national parliaments. In fact, the enhancement of national parliamentary powers on this point means that a decision to amend the decision-making rules relating to family law would be more difficult to adopt after the entry into force of the Treaty of Lisbon than it was previously. Also, it is arguable that Article 81(3) TFEU only allows *some* 'aspects' of family law, not all aspects, to be adopted using the co-decision procedure, whereas the use of the prior Article 67(2) EC was not subject to such limitations.

As for the civil law proposals made before the Treaty of Lisbon entered into force, the proposed Regulation on choice of law and jurisdiction in inheritance matters was not affected by the Treaty.[61] After the Treaty entered into force, the Commission proposed the use of enhanced cooperation as regards the 'Rome III' proposal on conflict of law in divorce cases;[62] the underlying proposal

---

[60] This interpretation is shared by Advocate General Sharpston: see the opinion in Case C-353/06 *Grunkin and Paul* [2008] ECR I-7639, footnote 2.   [61] COM (2009) 154, 14 Oct 2009.
[62] COM (2010) 104, 24 Mar 2010.

still remained subject to unanimous voting in the Council.[63] The Council authorized enhanced cooperation as regards this proposal.[64]

Further measures are planned. The Commission intends to present proposals in 2010 to amend the general rules relating to civil jurisdiction and mutual
recognition of judgments, on the issue of matrimonial property, and on enforcement of judgments via means of attaching bank accounts.[65] In the longer term,
the Stockholm programme refers to further measures on mutual recognition and
conflict of law, measures on recognition of civil status documents, civil procedure, legalization of documents, and the external aspects of civil law.[66] In particular, the Commission's action plan on implementing the Stockholm programme
calls for:[67] reviews and possible new proposals concerning service of documents,
evidence, and parental responsibility (2011–13); a Green Paper and legislation on
civil procedural law (2014); a Green Paper in 2010 on free circulation of documents (civil status documents, authentic acts, and the simplification of legalization), followed by legislative proposals in 2013; legislation regarding cross-border
traffic accidents in 2011; a report on the Common Frame of Reference for contract law in 2010 (issued in July 2010), followed by a legislative proposal in 2011;
legislation on transparency of debtors' assets in 2013; amendments to the insolvency Regulation in 2013; reports on the application of the legislation on payment orders, small claims, conflict of law regarding non-contractual obligations,
and enforcement orders (2011–2013); reports on assignment of claims (2010) and
insurance contracts (2013) as regards conflict of law in contracts; a Green Paper
on conflicts of law regarding companies (2014); and proposals for the negotiation
or conclusions of various international treaties.

As for other aspects of the Treaty of Lisbon rules, it should be recalled that
the restrictive provisions on the Court of Justice's jurisdiction over civil matters
were removed fully by the Treaty of Lisbon, just as they were removed almost
entirely as regards all JHA matters.[68] Following the entry into force of the Treaty
of Lisbon, there have been thirteen references from national courts concerning
EU civil law legislation.[69] The early indication is that the number of references

---

[63] COM (2010) 105, 24 Mar 2010. On the substance, see 8.6 below.

[64] [2010] OJ L 189/12.

[65] See the Commission's 2010 work programme (COM (2010) 135, 31 Mar 2010).

[66] [2010] OJ C 115, ss 3.1.2, 3.3.2, 3.4.1, 3.4.2, and 3.5.1.

[67] COM (2010) 171, 20 Apr 2010.   [68] See 2.2.3.1 above,

[69] Cases: C-509/09 eDate Advertising; C-87/10 Electrosteel; C-112/10 Zaza Retail; C-139/10 Prism
Investments; C-144/10 Berliner Verkehrsbetriebe; C-145/10 Painer; C-161/10 Martinez; C-191/10 Rastelli
Davide and C; C-213/10 F-Tex; C-211/10 PPU Povse (judgment of 1 July 2010); C-296/10 Purrucker
II; C-315/10 Companhia Siderúrgica Nacional; C-327/10 Lindner; and C-400/10 PPU, McB (all cases
except Povse pending). All the cases concern the Brussels Reg, except Zaza Retail and Rastelli Davide
and C, which both concern the insolvency Reg, and Povse, Purrucker II, and McB, which concern the
family law Reg. There have been three references from Germany, two references each from France
and Austria, and one each from Italy, Belgium, Lithuania, the Netherlands, the Czech Republic,
Portugal, and Ireland.

from national courts in this area has increased modestly as a result of the Treaty of Lisbon.

Next, the changes to the Protocols concerning the opt-outs of the UK, Ireland, and Denmark have changed the legal framework for those countries' opt-outs somewhat,[70] and the declaration concerning EU external relations powers attempts to clarify the limits of EU external competence in this field.[71] Also, as noted above, the previous Article 293 EC has been repealed by the Treaty of Lisbon; this has resolved any uncertainty about the relationship between Articles 65 and 293 EC.

In addition, the new legal basis for civil law measures is subject to the general provisions of Title V of Part Three of the TFEU, in particular the clauses setting out the objectives of Title V and providing for the adoption of measures regarding administrative cooperation. While the latter provision (Article 74 TFEU) is unchanged as compared to the prior Article 66 EC,[72] the former provision (Article 67 TFEU) now refers expressly to 'respect for fundamental rights and the different legal systems and traditions of the Member States', and refers also now to the principle of mutual recognition in civil matters, describing this as a means of fulfilling an EU obligation to 'facilitate access to justice'.[73]

The revised civil law provisions of the Treaty are also subject to the general amendments which the Treaty of Lisbon made to the rest of the Treaties, including the general *passerelle* clause[74] and the changes to the rules on enhanced cooperation. The latter changes have proven to be relevant to the adoption of civil law measures by means of enhanced cooperation.[75]

8.2.4. Competence

There are four key questions concerning EU civil law competence. Firstly, what is the definition of 'judicial cooperation in civil matters'? Secondly, to what extent is the EU prevented from regulating purely national matters, in light of the restrictions on EU competence to matters having 'cross-border implications'?[76] A parallel question arises as regards the EU's *external* powers in light of this provision; this is considered below.[77] Thirdly, what is the distinction between the

---

[70] See 2.2.5 above. [71] See 8.9 below.

[72] In particular, measures must still be adopted by QMV in Council and consultation of the EP, on the basis of a Commission proposal (as far as civil law is concerned).

[73] For more on the general provisions of Title V, see 2.2.3.2 above.

[74] Art 48(7), revised TEU.

[75] As noted above (n 64), the Council has authorized the use of enhanced cooperation as regards the 'Rome III' proposal, concerning conflict of law on divorce. On the changes made by the Treaty of Lisbon to the enhanced cooperation rules generally, see 2.2.5.5 above.

[76] On the parallel issue relating to EU criminal law competence, see 9.2.4 below.

[77] See 8.9 below.

'legal base' of Article 81 TFEU and, where relevant, Article 74 TFEU,[78] and the legal bases relating to the internal market (Articles 114 and 115 TFEU),[79] or indeed the residual powers clause of the Treaty (Article 352 TFEU[80])? Finally, how is the exercise of the EU's civil law powers to be divided between the three different decision-making procedures applicable: the normal rule (QMV and co-decision), the 'family law' exception (unanimity and consultation), and the rule for administrative cooperation (QMV and consultation)? All four of these issues arose prior to the entry into force of the Treaty of Lisbon, but are still relevant following its entry into force, while taking into account the abolition of the requirement that EC civil law measures must always be 'necessary for the proper functioning of the internal market'. A fifth issue, as to whether the EC's civil law powers under the prior Article 65 EC were exhaustive or non-exhaustive, has, as noted above,[81] been answered by the Treaty of Lisbon. However, this issue, along with the 'internal market' requirement, is still of historical relevance in case of any challenge to the validity of EC acts adopted before the entry into force of the Treaty.[82]

It is presumed that, apart from the removal of the internal market requirement and the move to an exhaustive list of powers, the EU's civil law competence after the Treaty of Lisbon remains unchanged from the EC's civil law competence as it existed beforehand, given that these were the only significant changes to the 'legal base' for civil cooperation. Therefore the case law on Article 65 EC remains largely still relevant, and is analysed below on the assumption that it applies equally to Article 81 TFEU.

Starting with the definition of 'judicial cooperation in civil matters', the Court of Justice's case law on the Brussels Convention consistently ruled that public-law actions were outside the scope of the Convention,[83] although the Convention did apply where a public authority was merely substituting itself for a private individual in private law proceedings.[84] However, in a case concerning the Brussels II Regulation, the Court of Justice determined that an action by a public authority to take a child into care was within the scope of the rules in the Regulation relating to parental responsibility.[85] The Court explained its ruling by reference to the wording of the Regulation, rather than the legal base in the EC Treaty. With respect, this begs the question, because the Regulation cannot govern a dispute which is outside the scope of the legal basis used to adopt it. However, the Advocate General's opinion in this case did address the question of the legal

---

[78] Formerly Arts 65 and 66 EC.   [79] Formerly Arts 94 and 95 EC.
[80] Formerly Art 308 EC.   [81] See 8.2.3 below.
[82] On the non-exhaustiveness of the powers conferred by the prior Art 65 EC, see the second edition of this book, at 372.
[83] See Case C-292/05 *Lechoritou* [2007] ECR I-1519, with further references. On the same point regarding the Brussels I Reg, see the judgment in *Apostolides* (Case C-420/07 [2009] ECR I-3571, paras 40–46).   [84] See, for instance, Case C-433/01 *Blijdenstein* [2004] ECR I-981.
[85] C-435/06 *C* [2007] ECR I-10141.

base, arguing that 'civil matters' had an autonomous meaning in EC law, including 'State measures which affect private law relationships such as the exercise of parental responsibility, even if corresponding measures are classified as measures of public law in some Member States'.[86] This interpretation, if correct, means that in principle the powers conferred by Article 81 TFEU are potentially quite wide, as they can be exercised as long as there is a nexus between state action and private law relationships.

As for the restriction of Article 81 TFEU to 'judicial cooperation', the scope of the EC's competence on this point was addressed in the *Roda Golf* judgment.[87] In its judgment in that case, the Court of Justice ruled that the EC legislation on service of documents did not apply only as regards legal proceedings. In the Court's view, taking account of the requirement in Article 65 EC that EC civil law legislation must be necessary for the functioning of the internal market, 'the judicial cooperation referred to by that article ... cannot be limited to legal proceedings alone. That cooperation may manifest itself both in the context of and in the absence of legal proceedings if that cooperation has cross-border implications and is necessary for the proper functioning of the internal market'.[88] Of course, with the abolition by the Treaty of Lisbon of the requirement of a link to the proper functioning of the internal market, the EU is even freer to adopt measures which do not have a link to legal proceedings. But in order to take due account of the legal base in the Treaty, it will still be necessary that there is some sort of *judicial* involvement in the relevant proceedings, such as mediation or arbitration.

On the second point, in practice, the application of the 'cross-border implications' clause has been a source of continued controversy, with the Commission usually asserting that EU legislation in this area should harmonize rules applicable not only to disputes having elements linked to more than one Member State but also rules applicable to purely national disputes.[89] Most Member States have, however, objected to this interpretation, with the result that the Council (along with the EP) has only proven willing to adopt measures limited specifically to cross-border disputes, and has consistently amended Commission proposals to this effect.[90] The Council legal service has apparently backed this view, arguing that domestic law can only be harmonized where this is purely ancillary to

---

[86] Para 52 of the opinion in *C* (ibid).

[87] Case C-14/08 *Roda Golf and Beach Resort* [2009] ECR I-5439.

[88] Para 56 of the judgment (ibid).

[89] See the explanatory memoranda to the proposals on legal aid (COM (2002) 13, 18 Jan 2002); payment orders (COM (2004) 173, 19 Mar 2004); mediation (COM (2004) 718, 22 Oct 2004); and small claims (COM (2005) 82, 15 Mar 2005). The Commission did not suggest that the EC rules on payment orders and small claims would replace national law applicable to domestic proceedings, but rather operate *as an option* alongside domestic rules.

[90] There are precise definitions of 'cross-border' limits set out in several measures: see 8.5.5–8.5.7 below.

measures concerning cross-border litigation.[91] In fact, the UK only opted in to the relevant measures on the expectation that their scope would be limited essentially to cross-border disputes.[92]

The Commission's argument in the explanatory memoranda to the proposal on payment orders was that Article 65 EC (and presumably, now Article 81 TFEU) does not expressly limit the scope of EC measures to cross-border litigation. In its view, pursuant to Article 65 (now 81), legislation can also be adopted which plays an instrumental rule in the working of the internal market; the optional nature of the EC rules should also be taken into account. In the case of mediation, the Commission argued in its explanatory memorandum that it would not be feasible to limit its proposal to cross-border cases only, since this would be arbitrary, produce discriminatory effects, reduce the practical impact of the legislation, increase legal uncertainty, allow the parties to determine the application of the Directive, and lead to the creation of parallel regimes, which would 'run counter to the principles of the internal market'. As for small claims, the Commission argued in its explanatory memorandum that Article 65 (now 81) only requires that a 'matter', rather than a 'measure', has cross-border implications, and that Article 65 should be interpreted in light of sub-paragraph (c) (now Article 81(2)(f)), which permits harmonization of national civil law. In this case, the matter had cross-border implications because 'most economic operators and consumers will sooner or later' become involved in litigation abroad. Again, dual legal regimes would create discrimination.

The Court of Justice has not yet had occasion to rule on this issue, but in a case concerning the 'external' scope of the Brussels Convention, it ruled that like the EC's internal market powers, the Convention could apply:

[T]he uniform rules of jurisdiction contained in the Brussels Convention are not intended to apply only to situations in which there is a real and sufficient link with the working of the internal market, by definition involving a number of Member States. Suffice it to observe in that regard that the consolidation as such of the rules on conflict of jurisdiction and on the recognition and enforcement of judgments, effected by the Brussels Convention in respect of cases with an international element, is without doubt intended to eliminate obstacles to the functioning of the internal market which may derive from disparities between national legislations on the subject (see, by analogy, as regards harmonisation directives based on Article 95 EC intended to improve the conditions for the establishment and working of the internal market, Joined Cases C-465/00, C-138/01 and C-139/01 *Österreichischer Rundfunk and Others* [2003] ECR I-4989, paragraphs 41 and 42).[93]

---

[91] See Council docs 11289/04, 20 July 2004 and 12283/04, 17 Sep 2004, particularly para 14.

[92] See Council docs 8560/02, 6 May 2002 (legal aid); 10965/04, 29 June 2004 (payment orders); 9622/05, 1 June 2005 (mediation); and 10775/05; 30 June 2005 (small claims). All of these opt-in letters except the last one refer to advice of the Council legal service supporting the UK position. It appears that in the case of small claims, this omission is simply because the legal service opinion had not been released by the time of the UK opt-in.

[93] Judgment in Case C-281/02 *Owusu* [2005] ECR I-1383, para 34.

In the *Rundfunk* judgment referred to, the Court of Justice found that the application of EC internal market legislation (in this case, the data protection directive) was not limited to cases with a cross-border element. Rather, the EC's powers set out in Article 95 EC (now Article 114 TFEU) allow it to harmonize national laws applicable to purely national situations, provided that the national laws in question need to be harmonized in order to ensure the functioning of the internal market.[94] In his Opinion in the *Owusu* case, the Advocate General argued that the same reasoning applied to legislation based on Article 65 EC (now Article 81 TFEU),[95] an issue not considered by the Court's judgment. If this is correct, then the EU's civil law powers clearly can serve as a basis for the adoption of harmonization of national civil law.

Which interpretation is correct? First of all, as noted above, the focus on the 'internal market' requirement is now only of historical interest following the entry into force of the Treaty of Lisbon. The remaining requirement, which also applied even before the entry into force of the Treaty of Lisbon, is that EU civil law measures must concern 'matters having cross-border implications'. While it is true that measures based on the EU's internal market powers must have some relationship to cross-border issues, because the internal market is not a purely domestic concept, the different wording of the civil law Article should not be ignored, as it was presumably inserted by the drafters of the Treaty of Amsterdam (and confirmed by the drafters of the Treaty of Lisbon) to limit the scope of the civil law powers as compared to the internal market powers.[96] Contrary to the Commission's view, the 'cross-border' requirement must be viewed as a limitation on the internal market, not the other way around, since the EU in any event would enjoy internal market powers and this interpretation would render the additional 'cross-border' restriction on the EU's powers superfluous.

As for the Commission's further arguments, it is doubtful whether the cross-border criterion is met by measures which harmonize the law applicable to purely national disputes, even on an optional basis. Although the Treaty does not require that measures be linked to cross-border litigation, in particular since there is no requirement that legislation adopted on the basis of Article 81 TFEU be limited to legal proceedings (see above), the 'implications' to be regulated explicitly require a cross-border element and must concern '*judicial* cooperation'. So the additional 'cross-border' requirement must mean that measures based on Article 81 must focus on litigation or other forms of judicial proceeding with a

---

[94] For more on this issue, see the discussion of the third competence issue, below. Since the Treaty of Lisbon has made only minor amendments to Art 95 EC (now Art 114 TFEU), it is presumed that the prior case law on the scope of this Art is still relevant.

[95] Paras 187–213 of the Opinion (n 93 above).

[96] The Court of Justice has made clear that the EC and EU Treaties should be interpreted with regard to the intentions of the drafters of the Treaty of Amsterdam: Cases C-11/00 *Commission v European Central Bank* [2003] ECR I-7147, paras 100, 103, and 130, and C-15/00 *Commission v European Investment Bank* [2003] ECR I-7281, para 131.

cross-border element. The power to regulate 'obstacles to the good functioning of civil proceedings' set out in Article 65(c) EC (now Article 81(2)(f) TFEU) cannot be divorced from the general limitations on the powers set out in the *chapeaux* of those Articles; it follows that the power conferred by Article 81(2)(f) can only be exercised where such measures would be ancillary to the object of facilitating proceedings with a cross-border element. Furthermore, the *chapeau* of Article 81 makes no distinction as to whether the measures proposed to harmonize domestic proceedings are optional or not; this point goes instead to the issue of proportionality and subsidiarity. Far from being alien to internal market law, distinct regimes for foreign and domestic cases are entrenched within it, in particular as regards free movement of persons.[97] It is rather doubtful that 'most' consumers will become involved in foreign litigation, or even domestic litigation; and in any event, this would not preclude having different rules for foreign and domestic cases. Also, it is not unfeasible to have different rules for foreign and domestic cases, as the adopted legislation in question proves; nor did it prove necessary to develop different definitions of 'foreign' cases for each EU measure, as a standard rule was developed.[98] Persons entering into legal relations across borders already have accepted that different substantive and procedural rules, including foreign courts, may well become involved if they need to enter into litigation; even the Commission's proposals on payment orders and small claims make a *renvoi* to different national laws as regards some issues. Arguments about the practical impact of legislation are irrelevant to the question of the extent of powers conferred upon the EU. A distinction based on the foreign or domestic nature of proceedings would be no more arbitrary and create no more legal uncertainty than other exclusions from the scope of EU civil legislation or the different rules applying to different categories within the scope of that legislation.

Finally, the Court's judgment in *Owusu* concerned the extent of the Member States' powers pursuant to the former Article 293 EC (now repealed), not the extent of the EC's powers pursuant to Article 65 EC (now Article 81 TFEU).

The conclusion is that the Council's and EP's practice reflects a legal requirement, which moreover continues to exist after the entry into force of the Treaty of Lisbon, because the EU lacks the power pursuant to the Treaty provisions on civil cooperation to harmonize national civil procedural law in domestic proceedings except where this is purely ancillary to measures solely concerning the regulation of litigation or comparable proceedings with a cross-border element. This interpretation is also implicit in the later opinion of a different Advocate General, which contrasts the cross-border limits of measures adopted

---

[97] See 6.4.1 above.

[98] See 8.5.5–8.5.7 below for details, although note that in one of the four measures concerned (the mediation Dir) it was necessary to elaborate on the question of the date at which the cross-border effect is to be determined.

pursuant to the civil law powers with the domestic impact of internal market legislation.[99]

This brings us to the third issue: the distinction between the civil law powers on the one hand, and the internal market powers and Article 352 TFEU (former Article 308 EC) on the other. With the abolition of the requirement that EU civil law measures be necessary to ensure the proper functioning of the internal market, there is less likely to be a conflict between the EU's civil law powers and its internal market powers,[100] but the issue is still relevant because Article 81 TFEU clearly does not preclude civil law measures from having a connection with the internal market. As for the relationship between the civil law powers and the former Article 293 EC, the issue is now irrelevant following the repeal of Article 293 by the Treaty of Lisbon, but it remains of historical importance in the event of a validity challenge to pre-Lisbon legislation.[101]

The relationship between the EU's civil law powers and its internal market powers is more complex. Article 114 TFEU (although not Article 115) applies 'save where otherwise provided in the Treaties', and so can be trumped by a *lex specialis*.[102] Also, Article 114(2) sets out express exclusions from the scope of that Article (free movement of persons, fiscal provisions, and the rights and interests of employed persons). It follows that Article 81 applies instead of Article 114 where the two provisions overlap, and that in any event Article 114 cannot be used as a basis for measures concerning civil proceedings which concern matters falling within the scope of Article 114(2). This distinction has implications for the territorial scope of the measures,[103] decision-making (as far as family law measures and administrative cooperation are concerned),[104] and the non-application to

---

[99] Case C-265/07 *Caffaro* [2008] ECR I-7085, para 32 of the opinion.

[100] On the link between the internal market and the civil law legislation under Art 65 EC, see the opinions in *Apostolides* (n 83 above), para 37, and *Roda Golf* (n 87 above), paras 53–56.

[101] See the analysis in the second edition of this book, at 369.

[102] The scope of Art 114 TFEU (formerly Art 95 EC, and prior to that Art 100a EC) has been much litigated. See Cases: C-300/89 *Commission v Council* [1991] ECR I-2867; C-70/88 *Parliament v Council* [1991] ECR I-4529; C-155/91 *Commission v Council* [1993] ECR I-939; C-187/93 *Parliament v Council* [1994] ECR I-2857; C-359/92 *Germany v Council* [1994] ECR I-3681; C-350/92 *Spain v Council* [1995] ECR I-1985; C-84/94 *UK v Council* [1996] ECR I-8755; C-233/94 *Germany v Council and EP* [1997] ECR I-2405; C-209/97 *Commission v Council* [1999] ECR I-8067; C-269/97 *Commission v Council* [2000] ECR I-2257; C-376/98 *Germany v Council and EP* [2000] ECR I-8419; C-491/01 *BAT* [2002] ECR I-11453; C-377/98 *Netherlands v Council and EP* [2001] ECR I-7079; C-338/01 *Commission v Council* [2004] ECR I-4829; C-434/02 *Arnold Andre* [2004] ECR I-11825; C-210/03 *Swedish Match* [2004] ECR I-11893; C-154/04 and C-155/04 *Alliance for Natural Health and others* [2005] ECR I-6451; C-66/04 *UK v Council and EP* [2005] ECR I-10553; C-533/03 *Commission v Council* [2006] ECR I-1025; C-436/03 *EP v Council* [2006] ECR I-3733; C-217/04 *UK v Council and EP* [2006] ECR I-3771; C-317/04 and C-318/04 *EP v Council and Commission* [2006] ECR I-4721; C-380/03 *Germany v Council and EP* [2006] ECR I-11573; C-301/06, *Ireland v Council and EP* [2009] ECR I-593; and C-58/08 *Vodafone*, judgment of 8 June 2010, not yet reported.

[103] See 8.2.5 below.

[104] For other measures, Arts 81 and 114 TFEU are subject to the same decision-making procedure, leaving aside the impact on decision-making of the limited territorial scope of Art 81.

EU civil law legislation of the national derogations and safeguards permitted by Article 114(4)–(10) TFEU.

Nevertheless, it should not be concluded that all civil law matters fall within the scope of Article 81 TFEU. There are no grounds to argue that Article 81 in any way governs *substantive* civil law, so it remains open for the EU to use the internal market power to adopt measures on that subject, if they fall within the scope of that legal base. Such legislation could include provisions on civil procedure to the extent that those provisions are purely ancillary to the substantive rules.[105] This possibility is provided for explicitly as regards rules on conflict of law.[106] The internal market power can also be used to adopt measures on administrative law or administrative procedure which fall within the scope of that legal base, so it is necessary to distinguish between administrative proceedings and 'judicial cooperation in civil matters'; the scope of the latter phrase was examined already above. The more difficult question is whether legislation on civil procedure which falls outside the scope of Article 81 (because it fails the 'cross-border' criterion) can be adopted pursuant to Article 114 (because it nevertheless meets the internal market criterion). It is arguable that such measures cannot be adopted pursuant to Article 114, because Article 81 is a *lex specialis* as regards civil law and allowing the adoption of such measures pursuant to Article 114 would circumvent the intentions of the drafters of the Treaty of Amsterdam (confirmed by the Treaty of Lisbon) to limit the scope of the EU's powers in this area, by analogy with the Court's conclusion that the EU's internal market powers could not be used to circumvent a Treaty ban on harmonization of public health law.[107] However, the contrary view has been assumed in an opinion of an Advocate General, which compares the cross-border limitation in scope of EU civil law measures with the regulation of 'execution procedures carried out within a single Member State', pursuant to a directive adopted on the basis of Article 95 EC (now Article 114 TFEU).[108] It might be argued that the issue of harmonizing civil law pursuant to the EU's internal market powers is a distinct question from harmonizing Member States' law regarding public health, because in the latter case (but not the former) the Treaty contains an express ban on harmonization of national law.[109]

---

[105] On ancillary legal bases, see particularly Case C-211/01 *Commission v Council* [2003] ECR I-8913.

[106] See discussion of the legislation in 8.4 and 8.5.3 below. See also the proposal for EC signature on the Hague Convention on the law applicable to certain rights in respect of securities held with an intermediary (COM (2003) 783, 15 Dec 2003; the proposal was later withdrawn), which was based on internal market legal bases, rather than civil law legal bases, in light of the existing internal market legislation on this topic.

[107] See the first tobacco advertising judgment: Case C-376/98 *Germany v EP and Council* (n 102 above), para 79.   [108] Opinion in *Caffaro* (n 99 above).

[109] The tobacco advertising case referred to Art 129(4), subsequently Art 152(3)(c) EC; see now Art 168(5) TFEU.

As for Article 352 TFEU, it only applies in the event that another Treaty Article (ie Articles 81, 114, or 115 TFEU) does not give the EU the necessary powers to act. Following the Treaty of Lisbon, there is no longer a requirement for a link between the use of Article 352 and the operation of the common market,[110] and it is expressly confirmed that the Article cannot be used to circumvent limits on the competence of the EU set out in other Treaty provisions.[111] It is conceivable that a civil law measure which does not satisfy either the criterion of a cross-border link set out in Article 81 or the requirements relating to internal market law set out in Articles 114 or 115 would be able nonetheless to satisfy the requirements of Article 352.[112] However, the question would again arise as to whether the ban on the use of Article 352 to circumvent restrictions on harmonization would apply where the ban on harmonization is arguably implied (as in the case of Article 81 and harmonization of purely national civil law), rather than express.

The fourth question is the division of competence *within* Title V as regards civil law matters within its scope. There are three different decision-making procedures: the ordinary legislative procedure for Article 81 measures in general; the exception in Article 81(3) TFEU for unanimity in the Council and consultation of the EP as regards 'measures concerning family law'; and QMV in Council and consultation of the EP for administrative cooperation measures (Article 74).[113] What is covered by the family law exception? That exception must surely cover legislation such as Regulation 2201/2003, which solely concerns family law proceedings;[114] conversely, it surely would not apply to Regulation 1346/2000, which solely concerns insolvency proceedings,[115] or to the Rome II and Rome I Regulations on conflict of law, which exclude family law disputes (including maintenance) from their scope.[116] The Commission has convincingly argued that its proposal relating to jurisdiction and choice of law regarding inheritance does not fall within the scope of the family law exception, because most national legal systems regard inheritance law as a property law issue, inheritance law does not regulate the family relationships between individuals, and the family law exception must be interpreted strictly.[117]

But the majority of civil law measures adopted to date could be described as 'mixed' measures, partly related to family law and partly related to other matters.

---

[110] Art 352(1) TFEU.   [111] Art 352(3) TFEU.

[112] On the previous requirement of a link to the common market for the use of the prior Art 308 EC, see Joined Cases C-402/05 P and C-415/05 P *Kadi and Al Barakaat* [2008] ECR I-6351 and Case C-166/07 *EP v Council* [2009] ECR I-7135.

[113] It is assumed in the following analysis that Arts 74 and 81(3) TFEU have the same meaning as the prior Treaty provisions which they replaced (Arts 66 and 67(5) EC), given that neither Art has been substantively amended by the Treaty of Lisbon.   [114] [2003] OJ L 338/1.

[115] [2000] OJ L 160/1.

[116] See Art 1(2)(a) and (b) of the Rome II Reg (Reg 864/2007, [2007] OJ L 199/40) and Art 1(2)(b) and (c) of the Rome I Reg (Reg 593/2008, [2008] OJ L 177/6).

[117] COM (2009) 154, 14 Oct 2009. On the requirement to interpret exceptions from the normal competence rules in the Treaty strictly, see by analogy Case C-268/06 *Impact* [2008] ECR I-2483.

The Brussels I Regulation applies to maintenance payments as well as many other types of civil and commercial proceeding,[118] until the specific Regulation on maintenance proceedings becomes applicable.[119] Similarly, the Regulation establishing a European enforcement order also applies to maintenance disputes, as it has the same scope as the Brussels I Regulation,[120] until the maintenance Regulation becomes applicable.[121] Furthermore, prima facie it appears that the EC legislation on the service of documents, requests to obtain evidence, the European judicial network, legal aid, payment orders, civil law funding programmes, and mediation also applies partly to family law issues and partly to other issues.[122] For the most part, this is confirmed by Regulation 2201/2003[123] and the maintenance Regulation.[124] So any amendments to these measures could be considered as 'mixed' legislation.

There are two possible interpretations of the family law exception. Either it applies only where the EC (now EU) adopts legislation essentially solely related to family law proceedings, or it applies to general rules which govern both family law and non-family law proceedings. In the latter case the exception would mean that such measures would have to be adopted on a dual 'legal base', which would entail adopting separate measures, since the two decision-making procedures would be incompatible.[125] The better interpretation is the former one, since an exception from the general rule should be construed strictly. Moreover, the words 'aspects relating to' support this interpretation, as they suggest that only specific rules for family law proceedings are covered by the exception. In practice, this is the interpretation applied by the EC (now EU) institutions, as evidenced by the application of the co-decision procedure to the Regulation establishing a

---

[118] Art 5(2), Reg 44/2001 ([2001] OJ L 12/1).

[119] Reg 4/2009 ([2009] L 7/1), Art 68(1). On the question of when the Regulation becomes applicable, see 8.6 below.   [120] Reg 805/2004 ([2004] L 143/15), Art 2.

[121] Art 68(2), Reg 4/2009 (n 119 above). Note though that the enforcement order Reg will continue to apply to Member States that do not apply the standard rules on conflict of law in maintenance disputes: this means the UK (see 8.2.5 below).

[122] See respectively: Reg 1348/2000 ([2000] OJ L 160/37), replaced by Reg 1393/2007 ([2007] OJ L 324/79); Reg 1206/2001 ([2001] OJ L 174/1); Decision 2001/470 ([2001] OJ L 174/25), amended in 2009 ([2009] OJ L 168/35); Dir 2003/8 ([2003] OJ L 26/41); Reg 1896/2006 ([2006] OJ L 399/1); the most recent funding programme Decision ([2007] OJ L 257/16); and Dir 2008/52 ([2008] OJ L 136/3). However, maintenance and matrimonial property disputes are excluded from the small claims Reg (Reg 861/2007, [2007] OJ L 199/1, Art 2(2)(b)).

[123] See n 114 above. See the references in Reg 2201/2003 to: Reg 1348/2000 (recital 15 of the preamble and Art 18); Reg 44/2001 (recitals 9 and 11 of the preamble); Reg 1206/2001 (recital 20 of the preamble); and Decision 2001/470 (recital 25 of the preamble and Arts 54 and 58(2)). There is no reference to Dir 2003/8, however. See also subsequently the references to Reg 2201/2003 in the preamble to Dir 2008/52 (recitals 20 and 21). The issues addressed by Reg 2201/2003 presumably fall outside the scope of Reg 1896/2006 on payment orders, because the former Regulation does not concern pecuniary claims.

[124] See n 119 above. See the references in Reg 4/2009 to Decision 2001/470 (recital 39 of the preamble and Arts 70 and 71(3)) and Dir 2003/8 (recital 36 of the preamble and Art 68(3)).

[125] For more detail on this issue, see the analysis in 3.2.4 above.

European enforcement order, which applies (until the maintenance Regulation is applicable) to proceedings concerning maintenance but does not set out special rules in that respect. Similarly, the legislation on payment orders and mediation, and the revised rules on service of documents were adopted without any apparent doubt that the general decision-making rule applied. The Commission expressly confirmed this interpretation when it invited the Council to extend co-decision and QMV to maintenance issues.[126]

More difficult questions could arise where legislation does not solely set out general rules applicable to both family and non-family civil proceedings, but contains both general rules applicable to civil law proceedings *and* specific rules relating to family law proceedings. Such legislation would be covered by a dual legal base after February 2003; this would therefore entail adoption of separate measures. But if the institutions adopted only an amendment to the general rules in the legislation or only an amendment to the specific family law rules in it, then the respectively different decision-making procedures would apply. So, for instance, the Council was correct to decide that the amendment to the Brussels I Regulation that altered the specific rules in that Regulation applicable to maintenance payments had to be adopted by unanimity in the Council, given that the issue of maintenance payments is inseparable from the substance of family law.

As for Article 74 TFEU, it should be interpreted consistently whether it applies to civil law, immigration and asylum law, or policing and criminal law.[127] This means that it cannot be used to adopt measures relating to the substance of civil proceedings as such, but solely to adopt measures concerning administrative cooperation. Also, EU funding programmes fall within the scope of Article 74 when they are intended primarily to fund cooperation between administrations (even as regards family law specifically), but will fall within the scope of Article 81 if they have other purposes within the 'field' of judicial cooperation, in particular the purposes relating to private practitioners or to judges (who, due to their independence, cannot be considered to form part of the administration).

The practice of the institutions to date is not clear, because the relevant measures adopted to date (all before the Treaty of Lisbon) did not set out whether the EC was acting on the basis of the previous Article 65 EC or of the previous Article 66 EC. But if we apply the criteria set out above, the Decision establishing the European Judicial Network fell within the scope of Article 65 EC (now Article 81 TFEU), not Article 66 EC (now Article 74 TFEU), because it addresses both administrative cooperation and cooperation between practitioners, but has the primary aim of facilitating the latter. This was confirmed when the 2009 amendment to this Decision was adopted using the co-decision procedure.[128]

---

[126] COM (2005) 648, 15 Dec 2005.

[127] On the application of Art 74 to immigration and asylum law, see 3.2.4 above; on criminal law, see 9.2.4 below. See also the discussion of the general provisions of Title V in 2.2.3.2 above.

[128] On the substance of the Decision, see 8.8.2 below.

Similarly, the civil law funding measures of 2001, 2002, and 2007 were (or are) not limited in scope to facilitating administrative cooperation, and so fell (or fall) within the scope of Article 65 EC (now Article 81 TFEU). This means that the 2007 funding Decision was correctly adopted pursuant to the co-decision procedure.[129]

8.2.5. Territorial scope

The UK and Ireland exercised the possibility to opt in to all proposed civil law measures up until 2005/06, when the UK (but not Ireland) opted out from the proposals on maintenance and conflicts of law in contract, and then both the UK and Ireland opted out from the 'Rome III' proposal on choice of law regarding divorce and the proposal on choice of law and jurisdiction over inheritance law.[130] On the other hand, the UK subsequently chose to opt in to the maintenance and conflict of law Regulations *after* their adoption, having successfully de facto negotiated changes to the proposed texts despite being formally a *non-participant* in the Council discussions. The UK opt-ins were then duly approved by the Commission.[131] However, as regards the maintenance Regulation, the UK and the other Member States agreed to separate the issue of conflict of law in maintenance matters from the main Regulation; this issue is instead addressed in a separate international treaty which the Community has concluded, but in which the UK does not participate.[132] The consequence of the UK's non-participation in these conflict rules is that UK maintenance judgments will be subject to an 'exequatur' process before they can be enforced in other Member States (although the Regulation on the European Enforcement Order could still apply to uncontested UK maintenance judgments), whereas judgments will circulate more easily within the Member States which will share common conflict of law rules on this issue. It should be recalled that after the entry into force of the Lisbon Treaty, there are special rules governing the position if the UK and Ireland opt out of measures amending acts which they are already bound by.

As for Denmark, it is fully excluded from civil law legislation as such, until and unless it exercises the option granted to it following the entry into force of the Lisbon Treaty to adopt a case-by-case opt-in system very similar to that which applies to the UK and Ireland.[133] Nevertheless, it should be recalled that during the period when civil law matters were addressed intergovernmentally, Denmark ratified the Brussels and Rome I Conventions and then later signed the Brussels II and service of documents conventions during the Maastricht era.

---

[129] On the substance of these measures, see 8.8.1 below.
[130] On the opt-outs for the UK and Ireland generally, see 2.2.5.1 above.
[131] [2009] OJ L 10/22 and [2009] OJ L 149/73.   [132] See 8.9 below.
[133] For more on the Danish Title IV position, see 2.2.5.2 above.

The Rome I Convention (but not its replacement Regulation) remains in force between Denmark and the other Member States. In order to retain Danish participation in some of the other measures following their integration into the EU legal order, Denmark and the EU (then the EC) negotiated separate treaties which affiliate Denmark to the Brussels I Regulation and the service of documents Regulation (but not to the Brussels II or Rome I Regulations).[134] The treaties provide that Denmark is not obliged to accept subsequent amendments to or measures implementing the EU legislation, but in the event that it refuses to accept such amendments or implementing measures, the main agreement(s) will be terminated, unless the parties decide otherwise.[135] In accordance with these provisions, Denmark has notified its acceptance of changes made to both the service of documents Regulation and the Brussels I Regulation.[136] The latter decision will in fact entail Denmark applying most of the EU Regulation on maintenance proceedings, except for the rules on applicable law and cooperation between central authorities, on the basis that the other provisions of this Regulation are simply amendments of provisions which were previously in the Brussels I Regulation.[137]

According to the two EU-Denmark treaties, international agreements based on the relevant EU legislation which the EU concludes are not binding on Denmark,[138] but Denmark must 'abstain' from ratifying treaties which may 'affect or alter the scope' of this EU legislation, unless it agrees this with the EU and reaches satisfactory arrangements as regards either EU–Denmark treaty and the other treaty in question.[139] There was initially no provision in the treaties or the Council decisions concluding them which sets out how the EU should adopt its position in such cases, but the Council Decisions were amended in 2009, in order to provide for such a procedure.[140] Also, the treaties provide that when negotiating international treaties in such circumstances, Denmark must coordinate its

---

[134] For the signature and text of these treaties, see [2005] OJ L 299/61 and [2005] OJ L 300/53; for ratification by the EC, see [2006] OJ L 120/22 and 23. Both treaties entered into force on 1 July 2007: see [2007] OJ L 94/70. On the parallel treaty between the EU and Denmark concerning asylum responsibility, see 5.2.5 above.

[135] Arts 3 and 4 of each agreement. Note that in accordance with the opt-out Protocols, Denmark does not have a vote within the Council on such amendments or a role regarding implementing measures.   [136] See respectively [2008] OJ L 331/21 and [2009] OJ L 149/80.

[137] On the substance of the maintenance Reg, see further 8.6 below.

[138] Art 5(1) of each agreement.

[139] Art 5(2) of each agreement. The wording 'affect or alter their scope' reflects the case law concerning the existence of exclusive EC (now EU) external competence, and now Art 3(2) TFEU (see 8.9 below).

[140] [2009] OJ L 331/24 and 26. The Decisions require the Commission to give such authorization if the ratification of the relevant agreement by Denmark 'would not render the Agreement ineffective and would not undermine the proper functioning of the system established by its rules' (new Art 1a(1)). Note that Denmark has signed and ratified the revised Lugano Convention alongside the EU (see 8.9 below). This compares in part to EU legislation which delegates competence to Member States to sign civil law treaties (Art 4(2)(b), Reg 662/2009 ([2009] OJ L 200/25): see 8.9 below).

position with the EU and must 'abstain from any actions that would jeopardise the objectives of [an EU] position within its sphere of competence in such
negotiations'.[141]

As for the Court of Justice, it has the same jurisdiction as regards the relevant
EU legislation concerning preliminary rulings, requests for interpretation, and
infringement proceedings in respect of Denmark as it does for other Member
States.[142] So far there have been no cases concerning Denmark, and a reference
from a Spanish court seeking to clarify the effect of the Danish opt-out on another
EU measure was withdrawn.[143] The treaties provide that if the Court's jurisdiction
is amended in respect of the relevant legislation, as occurred with the entry into
force of the Treaty of Lisbon, Denmark again had an option whether or not to
accept these changes. But again, if Denmark did not accept these changes within a
deadline (in this case, sixty days from the entry into force of the changes, so by 30
January 2010), the agreement(s) would have been terminated, with no possibility
for the parties to decide otherwise.[144] In the absence of any information to the contrary, Denmark has presumably accepted the changes to the Court's jurisdiction.

Finally, the treaties will also be terminated if Denmark terminates its opt-out
from Title IV of the EC Treaty (now Title V of the TFEU), or if either party
decides to denounce the treaty, following a six-month waiting period.[145]

As for the new Member States joining the EU in 2004 and 2007, the legislation in this area applied immediately to them (where that legislation was already
in force in the earlier Member States). However, because the Rome Convention
on conflict of law in contracts was still an intergovernmental measure until it was
replaced by a Regulation in 2008, it was necessary to agree an accession convention to this Convention in 2004, and for the Council to adopt a decision applying
this Convention to Romania in Bulgaria in 2007.[146] Some of the legislation was
changed automatically by the 2003 Treaty of Accession,[147] and in two cases existing measures were altered by subsequent special implementing measures pursuant
to that Accession Treaty.[148] Also, some civil law legislation was amended to add
technical references to Bulgaria and Romania when they joined the EU.[149]

A particular issue arises in the case of northern Cyprus, which is not subject to
EU law as long as the legitimate Cypriot government does not exercise de facto

---

[141] Art 5(3) of each agreement.

[142] Arts 6 and 7 of each agreement. There is no explicit provision addressing the question of
whether, and if so on what basis, Denmark could bring an annulment action against an amendment
to the relevant legislation or a measure implementing it.

[143] Case C-148/08, *Mejnersten*.   [144] Art 6(6) of each agreement.

[145] Art 11, Brussels I agreement; Art 9, service of documents agreement.

[146] [2007] OJ L 347/1.   [147] See 2.2.5.3 above.

[148] Council Reg 2116/2004 ([2004] OJ L 367/1), amending the external relations provisions of
Council Reg 44/2001 ([2001] OJ L 12/1), and Council Decision 2004/664 ([2004] OJ L 303/28),
amending Council Decision 2004/246 authorizing Member States to sign an international treaty
(see 8.9 below).   [149] Reg 1791/2006, [2006] OJ L 363/1, part 15.

control over the territory.[150] In the *Apostolides* reference to the Court of Justice,[151] the question was whether the EU rules on recognition of civil and commercial judgments applied nevertheless where a Cypriot court had issued a ruling regarding property situated in the northern part of Cyprus, and the Cypriot claimant had sought to enforce that judgment against the purported purchasers of that property in the English courts. In the Court's view, exceptions and derogations from EU law set out in accession treaties had to be interpreted narrowly (following long-established case law). Applying that rule to this case, the EU rules did apply because the issue was the recognition of a *judgment* given in the southern part of Cyprus, even though the subject matter of that judgment was *property* located in northern Cyprus. The judgment therefore had to be recognized in the UK, even though it related to an area over which the court issuing the original judgment did not exercise de facto control and even though there might therefore be practical problems enforcing the judgment.

Finally, no non-EU countries are formally associated as such with the EU's civil law measures. Civil law relationships between the EU and non-EU States are instead regulated wholly by the exercise of the EU's external relations powers in specific cases, an issue considered further below.[152]

8.3. Human rights

8.3.1. The right to a fair trial[153]

Civil law cooperation between States raises questions comparable to criminal law cooperation between States: should a State recognize another State's judgment which was issued following an unfair trial, or facilitate what appears to be an unfair trial?[154] This issue was addressed by the European Court of Human Rights in the case of *Pellegrini v Italy*,[155] which involved a woman who argued that the Italian courts had violated the right to a fair trial set out in Article 6 of the European Convention on Human Rights (ECHR) by recognizing a judgment of the Vatican courts annulling her marriage which had not observed the standards set out in Article 6.[156] The Strasbourg Court, noting that the Vatican City had not ratified the ECHR, ruled that:

The Court's task therefore consists not in examining whether the proceedings before the ecclesiastical courts complied with Article 6 of the Convention, but whether the Italian

---

[150] On other issues regarding the application of JHA law to Cyprus, see 2.2.5.3 above.
[151] Case C-420/07 *Apostolides* [2009] ECR I-3571.   [152] See 8.9 below.
[153] See generally J Fawcett, 'The Impact of Article 6(1) of the ECHR on Private International Law' (2007) 56 ICLQ 1.
[154] As regards this issue in the context of criminal law, see generally 9.3 below.
[155] Reports 2001-VIII.   [156] On the substance of Art 6, see further 9.3.1 below.

courts, before authorising enforcement of the decision annulling the marriage, duly satisfied themselves that the relevant proceedings fulfilled the guarantees of Article 6. A review of that kind is required where a decision in respect of which enforcement is requested emanates from the courts of a country which does not apply the Convention. Such a review is especially necessary where the implications of a declaration of enforceability are of capital importance for the parties.

Applying these principles to the facts, Article 6 had been violated by the Italian recognition of the foreign judgment. In subsequent judgments, the Human Rights Court clarified that as in criminal law cases, an obligation to refuse to recognize a foreign court judgment pursuant to Article 6 ECHR in civil cases would only apply where there was a 'flagrant denial of justice' in the State where the original judgment was decided.[157] This case law has so far only addressed the recognition of judgments issued by non-contracting States to the ECHR; it is not clear what standards, if any, govern recognition of judgments issued by a Contracting State.

As for the enforcement of judgments, in the case of *K v Italy*,[158] the Court ruled that Italy was responsible for the failure to guarantee a trial within a reasonable time (therefore breaching Article 6 ECHR) because it had not acted swiftly enough to enforce a judgment of the Polish courts concerning maintenance, which Italy had assumed the liability to enforce. The case law of the Strasbourg Courts also confirms that the right to access to a court applies to the process for the enforcement of judgments, including foreign judgments in particular.[159]

Finally, cases concerning child abduction obviously raise issues concerning the right to family life, as regards both parents and the child. The Human Rights Court has made clear that such cases must be decided in the best interests of the child, taking account of the 1980 Hague Convention on Child Abduction and the Convention on the Rights of the Child.[160]

8.3.2. Application to EU law

The general principles of EU law recognize the right to a fair trial as well as the right to family and private life.[161] Both rights also expressly appear in the EU

---

[157] *Eskinazi and Chelouche v Turkey*, 6 Dec 2005, and *Maumousseau and Washington v France*, 6 Dec 2007. On the test applicable to criminal law cases, see 9.3.1 below.

[158] Reports 2004-VIII.   [159] See *Vrbica v Croatia*, judgment of 1 Apr 2010.

[160] See *Eskinazi and Chelouche* and *Maumousseau and Washington* (n 157 above) and the summary of jurisprudence with references to further case law in the Grand Chamber judgment of 6 July 2010 in *Neulinger and Shuruk v Switzerland*. Both the Hague Convention and the Convention on the Rights of the Child have been ratified by all Member States (and Croatia).

[161] See respectively 9.3.5 below and 6.3.4 above.

Charter,[162] as noted by the Court of Justice, and will be enforceable against the EU as a party to the ECHR once the EU's planned accession to the ECHR is in force. The rights of the child are also recognized as part of the general principles and in the Charter.[163]

Applying these principles first of all to the recognition of judgments, the Court of Justice has ruled that the 'public policy' exception to the Brussels Convention could apply where the right to a fair trial had been breached as regards the judgment issued by another Member State's courts.[164] The same principles apply to the 'public policy' exception in the Brussels Regulation and the insolvency Regulation,[165] and presumably to the equivalent provisions in other EU legislation concerning civil jurisdiction.[166] There are also specific rules in EU legislation providing for possible non-recognition of a judgment if the defendant was not notified of the proceedings in the first Member State.[167] EU civil law legislation provides for the possible refusal to accept service of documents which have not been translated, and the Court of Justice has interpreted the relevant rules in light of the right to a fair trial, distinguishing the level of protection in civil cases from the express additional rights provided for in criminal cases.[168]

However, as regards issues of jurisdiction, the Court of Justice has ruled that there is no exception to the rules in EU civil law legislation on *lis pendens* (ie the rules which apply if the same cause of action is litigated in more than one Member State simultaneously) on the grounds that the action was brought first in a Member State which arguably systematically fails to decide cases within a reasonable time, in breach of Article 6(1) ECHR.[169] The Court reasoned that there was no express

---

[162] Arts 7 and 47 of the Charter ([2007] OJ C 303).

[163] See Case C-540/03 *EP v Council* [2006] ECR I-5769 (making express reference to the Convention on the Rights of the Child as a source of the general principles) and, as regards civil law in particular, Cases C-403/09 PPU *Detiček*, judgment of 23 Dec 2009, and C-211/10 PPU *Povse*, judgment of 1 July 2010, neither yet reported. The Court of Justice has also referred to the Hague Convention on Child Abduction: Case C-195/08 *Rinau* [2008] ECR I-5271.

[164] Case C-7/98 *Krombach* [2000] ECR I-1935. In this case, Art 6 ECHR had been breached in the underlying criminal proceedings, as confirmed by a subsequent Strasbourg judgment: see 9.3.1 below. See subsequently Case C-394/07 *Gambazzi* [2009] ECR I-2563.

[165] See Case C-420/07 *Apostolides* [2009] ECR I-3571, paras 54–62 (Brussels Reg), and Case C-341/04 *Eurofoods* [2006] ECR I-3813, paras 60–68, followed in Case C-444/07 *MG Probud*, judgment of 21 Jan 2010, not yet reported, paras 30–34 (insolvency Reg).

[166] For the relevant legislation, see 8.5.1 and 8.6 below.

[167] Art 34(2) of Reg 44/2001 ([2001] OJ L 12/1), as interpreted in Case C-283/05 *ASML* [2006] ECR I-12041 and *Apostolides* (n 165 above), paras 72–80.

[168] Case C-14/07 *Weiss* [2008] ECR I-3367, referring inter alia to the Strasbourg case law on Art 6(3)(e) ECHR, on which see 9.3.1 below. Note that in the criminal law context, the EU has agreed legislation on this issue (see 9.8.2 below).

[169] Case C-116/02 *Gasser* [2003] ECR I-14693. Since the *lis pendens* rules require the courts in all other Member States to stay their proceedings in the same cause of action until the first court seized has determined its jurisdiction, even if it is clear that the first court seized lacks jurisdiction and some other Member State's court should have jurisdiction, this strategy results in an effective denial of justice.

rule to this effect in the Brussels Convention, and that there was a requirement of 'mutual trust' between Member States' national courts. However, with great respect, the first argument fails to take account of the primary law requirement of respect for human rights in EU law, and the second argument ignores the public policy exception set out in the Convention, which shows that Member States' mutual trust was not absolute. It is submitted that this case was decided wrongly, and that there is an implied rule requiring a waiver of the jurisdiction rules in EU legislation in exceptional cases where necessary to avoid a breach of human rights.

Finally, the Court of Justice has not yet had the opportunity to rule on whether 'public policy' exception in the Rome Convention or EU legislation on conflicts of law encompasses human rights issues.[170] It seems obvious that it should, by analogy with the case law on the public policy exception to the recognition of judgments.

8.4. Impact of other EU law

The relationship between EU civil law measures and other (non-JHA) EU law measures raises general issues of competence, which are considered further elsewhere.[171] Rather, this section examines more specifically first the interaction between EU civil law legislation and non-JHA EU law, and then the more general relationship between civil law and EU law. This analysis leaves aside the general requirement of a connection between the internal market and EU civil law legislation, which applied until the entry into force of the Treaty of Lisbon, and which has already been examined above.[172] However, it should be noted that it has been argued that the very existence of a body of EU civil law legislation makes it difficult in principle to argue that a seller established in one Member State will find it more difficult to sue a consumer established in another Member State.[173]

First of all, as a general point, the EU's data protection Directive is applicable to its civil law measures, as confirmed by the preambles to several of the measures under discussion in this chapter.[174]

Moving on to specific legislation, the rules in the Brussels I Convention, now found in the Brussels I Regulation, have been integrated into Community (now

---

[170] On the relevant legislation, see 8.5.3 and 8.6 below.   [171] See 2.4 and 8.2.4 above.

[172] See the opinions in Cases C-420/07 *Apostolides* [2009] ECR I-3571 and C-14/08 *Roda Golf* [2009] ECR I-5439, and generally 8.2.2 and 8.2.4 above.

[173] See the opinion in Case C-205/07 *Gysbrechts* [2008] ECR I-9947, para 38.

[174] See Reg 1348/2000 ([2000] OJ L 160/37), Art 22(4) and recital 13 of the preamble; Reg 1206/2001 ([2001] OJ L 174/1), recital 18 of the preamble; Dir 2003/8 ([2003] OJ L 26/41), recital 27 of the preamble; Reg 1393/2007 ([2007] OJ L 324/79), Art 22(4) and recital 24 of the preamble; and Reg 4/2009 ([2009] OJ L 7/1), Art 68(4) and recital 34 of the preamble.

EU) acts on five occasions,[175] and referred to in EU legislation on a number of other occasions.[176] Also, on a number of occasions the Court of Justice has ruled on the relationship between the Brussels I Convention or Regulation and the EC Treaty (as it then was),[177] secondary EU law,[178] or the general principles of EU law.[179]

Next, as for the conflict of law rules, the Rome I Regulation (on conflict of law in contract) refers frequently to other EU legislation as regards its scope and interpretation,[180] and is also subject to a general override (as was the Rome

---

[175] Reg 40/94 on Community trade mark ([1994] OJ L 11/1); Reg 2100/94 on Community plant variety right ([1994] OJ L 227/1); Reg 2271/96 on EC response to US 'Helms-Burton' legislation ([1996] OJ L 309/1); Reg 6/2002 on Community design right ([2002] OJ L 3/1); and Dir 2005/14 on motor insurance ([2005] OJ L 149/14). References to the Brussels Convention must now be read as references to Reg 44/2001 (Art 68(2) of Reg 44/2001, [2001] OJ L 12/1).

[176] See the preambles to: Reg 392/2009 on liability for maritime accidents ([2009] OJ L 131/24), recital 11; Dir 2008/112 on timeshares ([2009] OJ L 33/11), recital 18; Dir 2002/65 on distance selling of financial services ([2002] OJ L 271/16), recital 8; Dir 2004/35 on civil liability for environmental damage ([2004] OJ L 143/56), recital 10; and the EC company statute (Reg 2157/2001, [2001] OJ L 294/1), recital 25.

[177] See particularly Case C-388/92 *Mund and Fester* [1994] ECR I-467, discussed further below; Case C-172/91 *Sontag v Waidmann* [1993] ECR I-1963, where the Court transposed the 'public employment' exception from EU free movement law to the public law exclusion from the scope of the Convention; and Case C-38/98 *Renault* [2000] ECR I-2973, on the link between the 'public policy' exception to mutual recognition under the Brussels Convention and errors in interpreting EU law. On the latter point, see also the Opinion in Case C-115/08, *CEZ II*, judgment of 27 Oct 2009, not yet reported.

[178] See: Case C-271/00 *Baten* [2002] ECR I-10489, where the Court interpreted EU law in order to define the 'social security' exclusion from the Convention; Case C-266/01 *Préservatrice Foncière Tiard* [2003] ECR I-4867, where the Court touched on interpretation of the TIR Convention, concluded on behalf of the EC (now EU) by Council Reg 2112/78 ([1978] OJ L 252/1), in order to determine the scope of the public law and customs exclusions from the Convention; Case C-347/08 *Vorarlberger* [2009] ECR I-8661, in which the Court looks at EU motor insurance Directives (Dirs 2005/14, n 175 above, and 72/166, [1972] OJ L 103/1, since consolidated by Dir 2009/103, [2009] OJ L 263/11) in order to interpret Reg 44/2001; and Case C-204/08 *Rehder* [2009] ECR I-6073, where the application of the rules on jurisdiction in Reg 44/2001 turns upon the Court's prior case law on the relationship between EU legislation on liability for, for example airline delays, (Reg 261/2004 ([2004] OJ L 46/1)) and the Montreal Convention on the same subject, which has moreover been concluded by the EC, now the EU ([2001] OJ L 194/38); see Case C-344/04 *IATA and ELFAA* [2006] ECR I-403). There was also an overlap between the Convention or Reg 44/2001 and secondary EU law in Cases C-96/00 *Gabriel* [2002] ECR I-6367; C-27/02 *Engler* [2005] ECR I-481; and C-180/06 *Ilsinger* [2009] ECR I-3961 (as regards Dir 97/7 ([1997] OJ L 144/19) on distance selling); and C-167/00 *Henkel* [2002] ECR I-3111 (as regards Dir 93/13 ([1993] OJ L 95/29) on unfair contact terms); but the overlap was not material to the Court's judgments. See similarly the Opinion and judgment in Case C-73/04 *Klein and Klein* [2005] ECR I-8667: the Opinion mentions Dir 94/47 ([1994] OJ L 280/83) on timeshare arrangements in passing, while the judgment relies upon case law concerning Dir 85/577 on doorstep sales ([1985] OJ L 372/31) to determine the scope of a jurisdictional rule in the Convention. See more generally the opinion in *Ilsinger, idem*, which examines a number of EU consumer law Directives in order to define when a contract exists for the purpose of the Brussels I rules, and the opinion of 18 May 2010 in Cases C-585/08 *Pammer* and C-144/09 *Hotel Alpenhof*, both pending, which discusses the links between myriad EU civil law measures and non-JHA EU measures. See now the questions in Case C-327/10 *Lindner*, pending.   [179] See 8.3.2 above.

[180] See recitals 18, 26, 27, 30, 31, 34, and 40 in the preamble, as well as Arts 1(2)(j), 4(1)(h), 6(4), 7(2), and 7(6) of Reg 593/2008 ([2008] OJ L 177/6).

Convention) by other EU legislation.[181] This override has been applied expressly on several occasions,[182] and implicitly on some others.[183] The Rome II Regulation (on conflict of law as regards non-contractual liability) is also subject to a potential override by other EU legislation.[184]

As for other EU civil law measures, an opinion on the Regulation on the taking of evidence in civil cases discusses the overlap with EU legislation on the enforcement of intellectual property rights,[185] and a pending case asks questions about both the latter legislation and the Brussels Regulation.[186] An opinion on the insolvency Regulation has referred to it as part of a body of EU insolvency law, along with the specific internal market legislation governing insolvency within the financial services sector.[187] Another opinion on this Regulation suggested that EU tax legislation should be interpreted in light of it.[188] The Court of Justice has also applied the insolvency Regulation by analogy to determine the issue of applicable law when the Commission brought an action against an insolvent company within the framework of EU administrative law.[189] Furthermore, the EU legislation on mediation has been referred to when interpreting non-JHA EU legislation.[190]

It should be noted, though, that the principle of integration between EU civil law and other areas of EU law has its limits. In particular, the Court of Justice has refused to transpose concepts of 'habitual residence' from other areas of EU

[181] Art 23, Reg 593/2008 (ibid).

[182] See particularly recitals 7–11 in the preamble to Dir 96/71 on the posting of workers ([1997] OJ L 18/1), and the relevant case law: paras 10–12 of the opinion in Case C-346/06 *Rüffert* [2008] ECR I-1989; para 35 of the opinion in Case C-319/06 *Commission v Luxembourg* [2008] ECR I-4323; and para 13 of the opinion in Case C-341/05 *Laval* [2007] ECR I-11767. See also Art 12 of Dir 2008/112 (n 176 above) and recital 17 in the preamble to that Directive.

[183] See Case C-70/03 *Commission v Spain* [2004] ECR I-7999, which concerns the relationship between the Rome Convention and the national application of Dir 93/13 (n 178 above). See also the proposal for EC ratification of the Hague Securities Convention (COM (2003) 783, 15 Dec 2003) and the opinions in Cases C-484/08 *Caja de Ahorros y Monte de Piedad de Madrid* (judgment of 3 June 2010, not yet reported, note 81) and C-515/08 *Palhota* (opinion of 5 May 2010, pending, note 25). On the relationship between the Convention or Regulation and other EU legislation, see: Dir 2007/64 on payment services ([2007] OJ L 319/1), recital 51 in the preamble; Dir 2002/65 (n 176 above), recital 8 in the preamble; and the proposed Dir on consumer rights (COM (2008) 614, 8 Oct 2008), recitals 10 and 59 in the preamble.

[184] Art 27 of Reg 864/2007 ([2007] OJ L 199/40). See also the links to other EU law set out in paras 22, 23, and 35 of the preamble and subsequently Dir 2009/138 on insurance ([2009] OJ L 335/1).

[185] Opinion in Case C-175/06 *Tedesco* [2007] ECR I-7929, paras 49–52, referring back to Dir 2004/48 ([2004] OJ L 157/45).   [186] Case C-406/09 *RealChemie*.

[187] Opinion in Case C-339/07 *Deko Marty Belgium* [2009] ECR I-767, para 59 and note 47, with further references. Insolvencies in the financial services sector are excluded from the scope of the insolvency Reg by Art 1(2) of the Regulation (Reg 1346/2000, [2000] OJ L 160/1).

[188] Opinion in Case C-73/06 *Planzer Luxembourg* [2007] ECR I-5655.

[189] Case C-294/02 *Commission v AMI Semiconductor Belgium* [2005] ECR I-2175.

[190] Opinion in Joined Cases C-317/08 to C-320/08 *Alassini*, judgment of 18 Mar 2010, not yet reported (note 19).

law into the family law Regulation, and also refused to transpose the definition of 'services' from other areas of EU law into the Brussels I Regulation.[191]

As regards the development of a common frame of reference for European contract law,[192] Advocates-General (but not yet the Court of Justice) have shown some willingness to interpret EU legislation in light of the draft common frame of reference (DCFR).[193]

Finally, on the question of the link between EU law and criminal law, there are sometimes civil law consequences for the criminal acts of individuals, with resulting overlaps between the EU rules applicable.[194] It is also necessary to distinguish between a civil claim and a financial penalty.[195] But in the context of liability for Europol activities, the Brussels I jurisdiction rules are applicable.[196]

The second issue to be examined is the general relationship between civil law and the rest of Community (now EU) law. On this point, first of all it should not be thought that civil cooperation issues are confined to Title V of the TFEU (formerly Title IV of the EC Treaty), and fall entirely outside the remainder of the Treaties. Civil procedural rules affecting references to the Court from national courts under Article 267 TFEU (ex-Article 234 EC) are within the scope of EU law,[197] and national rules affecting access to remedies for breach of EU law are governed by the 'equal remedies' and 'effective remedies' rules created by the Court of Justice.[198]

One judgment of the Court of Justice has required recognition of the civil status documents of other Member States, where refusal to recognize the documents would prevent EU citizens from claiming social security rights they would be due under EU law.[199] Similarly, in at least some cases, a refusal by a Member State to recognize childrens' names as registered in another Member State may

---

[191] See respectively Cases C-523/07 *A* [2009] ECR I-2805 and C-533/07 *Falco* [2009] ECR I-3327.   [192] See further 8.7 below.

[193] See the opinions in Cases: C-412/06 *Hamilton* [2007] ECR I-2383, para 24; C-445/06 *Danske Slagterier* [2009] ECR I-2119, note 57; *Ilsinger* (n 178 above), paras 49–52; C-275/07 *Commission v Italy* [2009] ECR I-2005, note 55; C-227/08 *Martin Martin*, judgment of 17 Dec 2009, not yet reported (para 51); C-215/08 *Friz*, judgment of 15 Apr 2010, not yet reported (notes 62, 65, and 72); and C-540/08 *Mediaprint Zeitungs- und Zeitschriftenverlag*, opinion of 24 Mar 2010 (pending), note 7. However, see the opinion in *Messner* (Case C-489/07 [2009] ECR I-7315), para 85, which specifically refuses to interpret EU legislation in light of the DCFR.

[194] See, for instance, Case C-7/98 *Krombach* [2000] ECR I-1935, discussed further in 8.3.2 above and 9.2.4 below.

[195] See Art 1(b)(iv) of the Framework Decision on recognition of financial penalties ([2005] OJ L 76/16), the discussion of competence in 9.2.4 below, and the case law on double jeopardy (11.8 below).   [196] See 12.8.3 below.

[197] Case C-312/93 *Peterbroek* [1995] ECR I-4599; Joined Cases C-430/93 and C-431/93 *Van Schijndel* [1995] ECR I-4705.

[198] See generally M Dougan, *National Remedies Before the Court of Justice: Issues of Harmonisation and Differentiation* (Hart, 2004).

[199] Case C-336/94 *Dafeki* [1997] ECR I-6761.

breach EU free movement law.[200] More broadly, direct or indirect discrimination in civil procedural matters has been condemned several times by the Court of Justice.[201] These cases usually involve subjecting non-citizens or non-residents to different rules on security for costs or on seizure. Initially, the Court criticized discriminatory rules for breaching the Treaty rules on free movement of services.[202] Subsequently it based its judgments on the general rule concerning non-discrimination on grounds of nationality in Article 12 EC (now Article 18 TFEU),[203] first taken in conjunction with the Brussels Convention,[204] then taken in conjunction with any rule which relates to the exercise, directly or indirectly, of the fundamental freedoms guaranteed by the Treaty.[205]

This principle is extremely broad and its outer limits are still unknown. It means that Member States are likely prohibited from procedural discrimination in a wider field than that covered by Article 81 TFEU or measures adopted under it. For example, it is arguable that Article 18 TFEU requires Member States to treat nationals or residents of other Member States equally as regards priority in insolvency claims.

Issues of inheritance, wills, and succession in cross-border cases are potentially closely linked with EU free movement law, as confirmed by the Court of Justice as regards inheritance tax.[206] It might be argued that other types of national rules (deriving for instance from property law) which restrict or complicate the movement of inheritances across borders breach the Treaty rules on free movement of capital, or alternatively Article 18 TFEU.

8.5. Overview of legislation adopted

This section provides an overview of the EC (now EU) legislation adopted or proposed within the field of civil cooperation, with the exception of family law measures and the development of a common frame of reference for European contract law.[207] Following the structure of the Treaty, this section is subdivided by topic, largely in the order set out in Article 81(2) TFEU.

---

[200] See: Case C-148/02 *Garcia Avello* [2003] ECR I-11613; *Grunkin and Paul* (n 61 above); and Case C-208/09 *Sayn-Wittgenstein*, pending.

[201] On discrimination in criminal procedure, see 9.4 below.

[202] Case C-20/92 *Hubbard v Hamburger* [1993] ECR I-3777.

[203] Previously Art 7 EEC until the TEU, and then Art 6 EC until the Treaty of Amsterdam.

[204] *Mund and Fester* (n 177 above).

[205] Cases: C-43/95 *Data Delecta* [1996] ECR I-4661; C-323/95 *Hayes* [1997] ECR I-1711; and C-122/96 *Saldanha* [1997] ECR I-5325.

[206] Cases: C-364/01 *Barbier* [2003] ECR I-15013; C-513/03 *Van Hilten-van der Heijden* [2006] ECR I-1957; C-464/05 *Geurts and Vogten* [2007] ECR I-9325; C-256/06 *Jager* [2008] ECR I-123; C-43/07 *Arens-Sikken* [2008] ECR I-6887; C-11/07 *Eckelkamp* [2008] ECR I-6845; C-67/08 *Block* [2009] ECR I-883; and C-35/08 *Busley v Cibrian* [2009] ECR I-9807.

[207] See respectively 8.6 and 8.7 below.

8.5.1. Mutual recognition, enforcement, and jurisdiction

The first topic set out in Article 81(2) TFEU is 'the mutual recognition and enforcement between Member States of judgments and of decisions in extrajudicial cases'.[208] This reflects the EU's focus on mutual recognition, originally a political principle established by the Tampere European Council in 1999, but now confirmed as a legal obligation by the Treaty of Lisbon.[209] Within the sphere of civil law (but not criminal law) the mutual recognition principle has always been directly linked to the third topic listed in Article 81(2) TFEU, namely the adoption of rules on jurisdiction.[210]

The most important measure in this field is Regulation 44/2001 (the 'Brussels I Regulation'), which fully communautarized (with amendments) the long-standing Brussels Convention, which concerns mutual recognition of civil and commercial judgments and jurisdiction regarding those judgments.[211] As noted above, the Brussels Convention has been the subject of over a hundred judgments of the Court of Justice following references from national courts, and the Brussels Regulation has now attracted over thirty references of its own.[212] It should be noted that there is a principle of continuity of interpretation of the Convention and the Regulation, to the extent that they are identical.[213]

The Brussels Regulation applies to civil and commercial cases, to the exclusion of revenue, customs, and administrative matters.[214] The Regulation also excludes from its scope: the status or legal capacity of natural persons, rights in property arising out of a matrimonial relationship, wills and succession;[215] bankruptcy and insolvency proceedings;[216] social security;[217] and arbitration.[218] A number of these issues have however been the subject of separate legislation, or plans or proposals for legislation.[219] In particular, the question of the relationship between the Brussels Regulation and the insolvency Regulation has arisen a

---

[208] Art 81(2)(a) TFEU.

[209] Art 81(1) TFEU. On mutual recognition in criminal matters, see generally ch 9.

[210] Art 81(2)(c) TFEU. On jurisdiction in criminal matters, see generally ch 11.

[211] [2001] L 12/1. The 'comitology' procedures in this Regulation were amended in 2008 by Reg 1103/2008, [2008] OJ L 304/80. On this issue, see further 2.2.2.1 above. All references in this subsection are to Reg 44/2001, unless otherwise indicated.

[212] See 8.2.2 and 8.2.3 above.

[213] See recital 19 in the preamble, and in particular Case C-533/07 *Falco Privatstiftung* [2009] ECR I-3327.

[214] Art 1(1). On the definition of 'civil and commercial', see 8.2.4 above. On the customs exclusion, see Case C-266/01 *Préservatrice Foncière Tiard* [2003] ECR I-4867.   [215] Art 1(2)(a).

[216] Art 1(2)(b).

[217] Art 1(2)(c). On this exclusion, see most recently the judgment in Case C-271/00 *Baten* [2002] ECR I-10489.

[218] Art 1(2)(d). On this exclusion, see most recently the judgment in Case C-185/07 *Riunione Adriatica Di Sicurta v West Tankers* [2009] ECR I-663, with further references.

[219] On jurisdiction over divorce, parental responsibility, and matrimonial property, see 8.6 below; on insolvency and wills and succession, see below in this section.

number of times.[220] Moreover, jurisdiction over maintenance proceedings is currently subject to the Brussels Regulation,[221] but will become subject to a separate Regulation on maintenance proceedings once the latter becomes applicable on 18 June 2011.[222]

The Regulation sets out a general rule that the court where the defendant is domiciled shall have jurisdiction.[223] But there are derogations from the general rule as regards: special jurisdiction rules (for example, concerning contract,[224] maintenance (until the separate Regulation on this issue applies),[225] or tort disputes,[226] disputes based on criminal law,[227] or cases with multiple defendants[228]); insurance contracts;[229] consumer contracts;[230] employment contracts;[231] and cases of exclusive jurisdiction (for example, relating to immovable properties,[232] companies,[233] or the validity or registration of intellectual property rights).[234] There are also related rules on issues such as *lis pendens* (related pending actions)[235] and provisional and protective measures.[236]

Next, the Regulation contains detailed rules on recognition and enforcement, in particular providing for exceptions for recognition of judgments on the grounds that they are manifestly contrary to public policy;[237] the defendant's procedural rights were breached;[238] the judgment is irreconcilable with a prior judgment; or the rules on exclusive jurisdiction or jurisdiction over consumer or insurance contracts were breached.[239]

In 2009, the Commission released a report on the implementation of the Regulation and a Green Paper on possible amendments to it.[240] The Commission in particular addressed the possible abolition of the exequatur procedure; the

---

[220] See initially Case 133/78 *Gourdain* [1979] ECR 733 and more recently the judgments in Cases: C-339/07 *Deko Marty Belgium* [2009] ECR I-767; C-111/08 *SCT Industri* [2009] ECR I-5655; and C-292/08 *German Graphics Graphische Maschinen* [2009] ECR I-8421. See also C-213/10 *F-Tex*, pending.   [221] Art 5(2).

[222] See 8.6 below.   [223] Art 2(1).

[224] Art 5(1); see the judgments in: Case C-386/05 *Color Drack* [2007] ECR I-3699; *Falco* (n 213 above); Case C-204/08 *Rehder* [2009] ECR I-6073; Case C-381/08 *Car Trim*, judgment of 25 Feb 2010, not yet reported; and Case C-19/09 *Wood Floor*, judgment of 11 Mar 2010, not yet reported.   [225] Art 5(2).

[226] Art 5(3); see the judgment in Case C-189/08 *Zuid-Chemie* [2009] ECR I-6917.

[227] Art 5(4); see Case C-7/08 *Krombach* [2000] ECR I-1935.

[228] Art 6(1); see the judgments in Cases C-103/05 *Reisch Montage* [2006] ECR I-6827, C-98/06 *Freeport* [2007] ECR I-8319, and C-462/06 *Glaxo SmithKline* [2008] ECR I-3965.

[229] Arts 8–14; see the judgments in Cases C-463/06 *FBTO Schadeverzekeringen* [2007] ECR I-11321 and C-347/08 *Vorarlberger* [2009] ECR I-8661.

[230] Arts 15–17; see the judgment in Case C-180/06 *Ilsinger* [2009] ECR I-3961.

[231] Arts 18–21; see the judgment in *Glaxo SmithKline* (n 228 above).

[232] Art 22(1); see the judgment in Case C-420/07 *Apostolides* [2009] ECR I-3571.

[233] Art 22(2); see the judgment in Case C-372/07 *Hassett* [2008] ECR I-7403.

[234] Art 22(4); see Case C-4/03 *GAT* [2006] ECR I-6509.

[235] Arts 27–30; on the same issue arising in criminal cases, see 11.6 below.   [236] Art 31.

[237] Art 34(1); see 8.3.2 above.   [238] Art 34(2); see ibid.   [239] Art 35(1).

[240] COM (2009) 174 and 175, 21 Apr 2009.

relationship between the Brussels rules and third States;[241] the issue of choice of court;[242] patent litigation; *lis pendens*;[243] provisional measures; the relationship with arbitration, the removal of maintenance from the scope of the rules; amendments to some rules on jurisdiction; and the rules on recognition and enforcement. The Commission plans to propose amendments to the Regulation in 2010.[244]

The EU has addressed jurisdiction and recognition issues in relation to some matters excluded from the scope of the Brussels I Regulation. In the area of family law, it has regulated jurisdiction and recognition as regards judgments concerning divorce and parental responsibility, and the Commission plans to issue proposals in 2010 concerning matrimonial property.[245]

In other areas, first of all, in 2000 the Council adopted a Regulation (the 'insolvency regulation') transposing the stalled Convention on insolvency proceedings into Community law.[246] There have been eight references to the Court of Justice specifically on this Regulation,[247] and furthermore several cases have concerned the relationship between the Brussels Regulation and the insolvency Regulation.[248]

As noted above, financial services are excluded from the scope of the Regulation.[249] The basic rule is that jurisdiction to open insolvency proceedings rests with the courts of the Member State where the debtor's main interests are situated,[250] although it is possible to open secondary proceedings also in other Member States where the debtor was established; the secondary proceedings can only concern the assets of the debtor in the territory of that Member State.[251] The Regulation also contains rules on applicable law.[252] It provides in detail for the recognition of insolvency judgments,[253] permitting Member States not to recognize judgments which are manifestly contrary to public policy, 'in particular [a Member State's] fundamental principles or the constitutional rights and liberties of the individual', or not to recognize or enforce 'a judgment...which

---

[241] On this point, see Case C-281/02 *Owusu* [2005] ECR I-1383.

[242] This issue is connected to possible EU ratification of the Hague Convention on choice of court. See further 8.9 below.

[243] See the judgment in Case C-116/02 *Gasser* [2003] ECR I-14693, discussed in 8.3.2 above.

[244] See 2010 work programme (COM (2010) 135, 31 Mar 2010).   [245] See 8.6 below.

[246] Council Reg 1346/2000 ([2000] OJ L 160/1), in force 31 May 2002.

[247] Decided cases: C-1/04 *Staubitz-Schreiber* [2006] ECR I-701; C-341/04 *Eurofoods* [2006] ECR I-3813; and C-444/07 *MG Probud*, judgment of 21 Jan 2010, not yet reported. Withdrawn cases: C-387/04 *Donath* and C-148/08 *Mejnersten*. Pending cases: C-396/09 *Interedil*; C-112/10 *Zaza Retail*; and C-191/10 *Rastelli Davide and C.*   [248] See n 220 above.

[249] See 8.4 above.

[250] Art 3(1). On the concept of the centre of the debtor's interest, and the application of the rules to parent companies and subsidiaries, see the *Eurofoods* judgment. If the debtor moves his or her main interests after requesting the opening of insolvency proceedings, jurisdiction does not transfer accordingly (*Staubitz-Schreiber*).

[251] Art 3(2)–(5). For the definition of 'establishment', see Art 2(h).   [252] See 8.5.3 below.

[253] Arts 16–26.

might result in a limitation of personal freedom or postal secrecy'.[254] Finally, the Regulation contains detailed rules on the opening of secondary proceedings, the position of creditors, and the relationship with other measures.[255]

Secondly, in October 2009 the Commission proposed a Regulation concerning the jurisdiction and enforcement of decisions relating to wills and succession.[256] The proposal would allocate jurisdiction, as a general rule, to the court of the Member State on whose territory the deceased was habitually resident at the time of death.[257] There are also subsidiary rules on recognition and enforcement of judgments.[258] The proposal also includes rules on the conflicts of law.[259]

As for the issue of the *enforcement* of judgments, the EC (and now the EU) has not adopted legislation dealing with this issue, although some of the measures concerning civil procedure certainly aim to contribute to the enforcement of judgments in practice.[260] More specifically, though, the Commission has released two Green Papers that examine aspects of this issue, as regards the attachment of bank accounts and the transparency of debtors' assets.[261] Legislation on both of these issues is planned.[262]

8.5.2. Service of documents

The service of documents is the subject matter of the second EU civil law power, set out in Article 81(2)(b) TFEU. First of all, the Council adopted a Regulation on the service of documents in 2000,[263] replacing a 1997 third pillar Convention that had not been ratified.[264] It should be noted that there is also a Hague Convention on the issue of service of documents, to which a large majority of Member States are parties.[265] A review of the practical operation of this Regulation in 2004 concluded that it resulted in speedier proceedings, although its operation was still limited in some respects due to ambiguities in its text and certain national divergences which it provides for.[266] The Regulation was therefore replaced by

---

[254] Arts 26 and 25(2). On the public policy exception, see the *Eurofoods* judgment (n 247 above), as well as 8.3.2 above.   [255] Respectively Arts 27–38, 39–42, and 44.

[256] COM (2009) 154, 14 Oct 2009. See earlier the Green Paper on this issue (COM (2005) 65, 1 Mar 2005). On the related competence issues, see 8.2.4 above.

[257] Art 4 of the proposal; see generally Arts 3–15 on jurisdiction rules.

[258] Arts 29–33 of the proposal.   [259] See 8.5.3 below.   [260] See 8.5.6 below.

[261] See respectively COM (2006) 618, 24 Oct 2006 and COM (2008) 128, 6 Mar 2008.

[262] See the Stockholm programme ([2010] OJ C 115) and the Commission's action plan to implement it (COM (2010) 171, 20 Apr 2010).

[263] Reg 1348/2000 ([2000] OJ L 160/37), in force 31 May 2001.

[264] [1997] OJ C 261/1.

[265] For the ratification status, see Appendix I. Both Regulations prevail over this treaty, or other international treaties, between the Member States: see Art 20(1) of both Reg 1348/2000 and Reg 1393/2007; but see also Art 21 of both Regulations, as regards legal aid provisions of prior treaties.

[266] COM (2004) 603, 1 Oct 2004.

a revised text in 2007.[267] The original version of the Regulation has been the subject of four references to the Court of Justice from national courts.[268]

Both the 2000 and the 2007 Regulation apply to civil and commercial cases; the 2007 Regulation clarified that revenue, customs, and administrative matters, as well as the liability of the State for State actions, were excluded. But there are no other exclusions from its scope.[269] The rules require documents to be served usually through designated government agencies.[270] The requested agency must try to serve the document within one month of the request, and keep trying after that period if there is still a reasonable prospect of serving the document.[271]

The addressee may refuse to accept the document if the document was not drawn up either in a language which the addressee understands[272] or in the official language of the Member State addressed (or at least (one of) the official language(s) of the place of service in that Member State).[273] The applicant can subsequently transmit a translated copy of the document.[274] The date of service of the document is usually determined by the law of Member State of service, but in some cases can be determined by the Member State of transmission.[275] There are rules on certificates to be drawn up when service is effected, and on the costs of service.[276]

There are alternative methods of service possible: consular or diplomatic channels, 'in exceptional circumstances';[277] consular or diplomatic agents;[278] by post;[279] or directly through the competent officers of the Member State addressed.[280]

---

[267] Reg 1393/2007 ([2007] OJ L 324/79), applicable from 13 Nov 2008 (Art 26).

[268] Cases: C-443/03 *Leffler* [2005] ECR I-9611; C-473/04 *Plumex* [2006] ECR I-1417; C-14/07 *Weiss* [2008] ECR I-3367; and C-14/08 *Roda Golf* [2009] ECR I-5439.

[269] Art 1(1) of both Regulations.   [270] Arts 4–6 of both Regulations.

[271] Art 7 of both Regulations; the requirement to keep trying to serve the document after the one-month period was added in the 2007 Reg (Art 7(2)(b)).

[272] Art 8(1)(b), 2007 Reg; the 2000 Reg (Art 8(1)(a)) had referred instead to a language *of the Member State of transmission* that the defendant understood. On the question of whether the defendant can be deemed to understand a language, see the *Weiss* judgment (n 268 above).

[273] Art 8(1) of both Regulations. The 2007 Reg clarified the time period and mechanism for refusal. On the definition of a 'document' to be translated, in the case of instituting proceedings, see again the *Weiss* judgment (ibid), and the discussion in 8.3.2 above.

[274] Art 8(3), added by the 2007 Reg but effectively transposing the Court of Justice ruling regarding the 2000 Reg in *Leffler* (n 268 above), also as regards the consequences for the date of service in this case.

[275] Art 9(1) and (2) of both Regulations. Art 9(3) of the 2000 Reg, which permitted a derogation from these rules, was replaced by the 2007 Reg.

[276] Arts 10 and 11 of both Regulations. The 2007 Reg now clarifies the level of fees to be charged (Art 11(2), second sub-paragraph).   [277] Art 12 of both Regulations.

[278] Art 13 of both Regulations. A Member State may refuse to permit this type of service (Art 13(2) of both Regulations).

[279] Art 14 of both Regulations. The 2007 Reg removed the possibility for Member States to insist on conditions applicable to postal service (see Art 14(2), 2000 Reg), and instead provides for standard conditions for postal service.

[280] Art 15 of both Regulations; the law of the Member State addressed may refuse to permit this method of service.

There is no hierarchy between the different methods of service: one or another or both (or presumably more than two) can validly be used. In case of multiple forms of service which are validly effected, dates start to run from the time of the first service.[281] The rules on refusal to accept service and date of service apply equally to these alternate forms of service.[282] Finally, the Regulation also applies to the transmission of extrajudicial documents.[283]

8.5.3. Conflict of laws

The conflict of laws is the subject matter in part of Article 81(2)(c) TFEU.[284] As noted above,[285] the 1980 Rome Convention on conflict of laws in contract was replaced in 2008 by an EC Regulation,[286] which applies to all contracts which were or will be concluded after 17 December 2009.[287] The Rome Convention therefore continues to be relevant to contracts concluded before that date. There have not been any references to the Court of Justice on the Regulation, although the Court has received two references concerning the Convention, and decided one of them.[288]

The Regulation applies to civil and commercial matters, excluding revenue, customs, and administrative matters,[289] and also excluding other matters outside the scope of the Brussels I Regulation (the status and legal capacity of natural persons; matrimonial property; wills and succession; arbitration).[290] It also does not apply to obligations arising from family or comparable relationships, including maintenance obligations, or to certain commercial law issues: negotiable instruments; agreements on choice of court; company law disputes (including the winding up of companies); the law of agency; the law of trusts; pre-contractual relationships; and certain insurance disputes.[291] It applies also to the designation of the law of non-Member States.[292]

---

[281] See *Plumex* (n 268 above).

[282] Arts 8(4), 8(5), and 9(3), all added by the 2007 Reg. The Regulation overturned a judgment of the Court of Justice (*Weiss*, ibid), which ruled that the rules on refusal to accept service did not apply to postal service.   [283] For interpretation of this concept, see *Roda Golf*, ibid.

[284] Art 81(2)(c) TFEU also concerns conflict of jurisdiction; this issue was examined in 8.5.1 above.   [285] See 8.2.2.2 above.

[286] Reg 593/2008 ([2008] OJ L 177/6). See the earlier Green Paper on replacing and modernizing the Convention (COM (2002) 654, 14 Jan 2003).   [287] Art 28 of the Reg (ibid).

[288] Cases C-133/08 *ICF* [2009] ECR I-9687 and C-29/10 *Koelzsch*, pending.

[289] Art 1(1) of the Regulation.

[290] Art 1(2)(a)–(c) and (e). On consistency with the Brussels I Reg, see recital 7 in the preamble. Note that the Rome I Reg does not apply to arbitration *agreements*, whereas the Brussels I Reg does not apply to arbitration; and the Rome I Reg also does not apply to property issues deriving from relationships *comparable* to marriage.

[291] Art 1(2)(d) and (f)–(j). Pre-contractual relations are covered by the Rome II Reg: see recital 10 in the preamble.   [292] Art 2.

The starting point of the Regulation is freedom of contract, leaving the parties free in principle to designate the law applicable to their contract.[293] In the absence of choice, the Regulation sets out general rules to choose the applicable law,[294] subject to special rules for particular types of contract (contracts of carriage, consumer contracts, insurance contracts, and employment contracts).[295] The Regulation permits the application of the 'overriding mandatory provisions' of the law of the forum or of the place where the contractual obligations would be performed;[296] the applicable law under the rules may also be rejected if it is 'manifestly incompatible' with the public policy of the forum.[297] Also, the Regulation contains rules on the scope of applicable law, assignment and subrogation, multiple liability, set-off, the burden of proof, the definition of 'habitual residence', the exclusion of *renvoi* (ie a reference to another state's conflict rules), the position of states with multiple legal systems, and the relationship with other legal rules.[298]

Prior to the adoption of the Rome I Regulation, the Council and EP negotiated the 'Rome II' Regulation, which governs the conflict of law in non-contractual matters.[299] There have not been any references to the Court of Justice on the Regulation.

Like the Rome I Regulation, the Rome II Regulation applies to civil and commercial matters, excluding revenue, customs, and administrative matters; the liability of the state for the exercise of public powers is also excluded.[300] The issues of matrimonial (or comparable) property and wills and succession are also excluded, as are family law matters, including maintenance.[301] Certain commercial law issues are excluded: negotiable instruments; company law disputes (including the winding up of companies); the law of trusts; nuclear damage; and violations of privacy and rights relating to personality, including defamation.[302]

---

[293] Art 3. On issues of consent, validity, and incapacity, see Arts 10, 11, and 13.

[294] Art 4.

[295] Arts 5–8. The *ICF* case (n 288 above) concerned the contracts of carriage rules in the Rome Convention, while the *Koelzsch* case (ibid) concerns employment contracts under the Convention. [296] Art 9.

[297] Art 21. On the human rights aspects of this rule, see 8.3.2 above.

[298] Arts 12, 14–20, and 22–25. On the relationship with non-JHA EU law, see further 8.4 above.

[299] Reg 864/2007 ([2007] OJ L 199/40), applicable to damages which occurred after 11 Jan 2009 (Arts 31 and 32). For the definition of non-contractual obligations, see Art 2 of the Regulation.

[300] Art 1(1) of the Regulation.

[301] Art 1(2)(a) and (b). On consistency with the Brussels I and Rome I rules, see recital 7 in the preamble. Note that issues concerning arbitration or the status and legal capacity of natural persons are not excluded from the scope of the Rome II Reg.

[302] Art 1(2)(c)–(g). The latter two issues are not excluded from the scope of the Rome I Reg. Conversely, several issues excluded from the scope of the Rome I Reg are *not* excluded from the scope of the Rome II Reg: agreements on choice of court; the law of agency; pre-contractual relationships; and certain insurance disputes. The exclusions for the law of trusts are also worded differently (compare Art 1(2)(h) of the Rome I Reg to Art 1(2)(e) of the Rome II Reg).

Like the Rome I Regulation, the Rome II Regulation applies also to the designation of the law of non-Member States.[303]

The main rule in the Regulation as regards liability for torts or delicts is that the law of the country where the damage occurred is applicable, but this rule can be set aside if the plaintiff and defendant are habitually resident in the same country, or it if appears 'that the tort/delict is manifestly more closely connected with' another country.[304] There are special rules for tort/delict as regards product liability, competition, environmental damage, intellectual property, and industrial action,[305] as well as particular rules for other forms of non-contractual liability (unjust enrichment, *negotiorum gestio* (an act performed without authority in connection with another person's affairs), and *culpa in contrahendo* (pre-contractual relations).[306] It is possible for the parties to choose the law applicable.[307] The Regulation permits the application of the 'overriding mandatory provisions' of the law of the forum;[308] the applicable law under the rules may also be rejected if it is 'manifestly incompatible' with the public policy of the forum.[309] Also, the Regulation contains rules on the scope of applicable law, rules of safety and conduct, direct actions against insurers, subrogation, multiple liability, validity, the burden of proof, the exclusion of *renvoi*, the position of states with multiple legal systems, and the relationship with other legal rules.[310]

To some extent, the exclusions from the scope of the Rome I and II Regulations are covered by other EU measures. As regards family law, the EU rules on maintenance obligations (when they become applicable) include rules on conflict of laws, EU rules on choice of law have been proposed as regards divorce, and the Commission plans to propose rules regarding matrimonial property.[311] In other areas, the Commission has proposed rules for the choice of law regarding wills and successions,[312] and there are choice of law rules in the insolvency Regulation.[313] The Stockholm programme and the related action plan include reviews of issues such as conflict of law regarding companies and assignment of claims.[314]

---

[303] Art 3.   [304] Art 4. For the definition of 'habitual residence', see Art 23.

[305] Arts 5–9.

[306] Arts 10–12. However, the rules in Art 8 cover all forms of non-contractual liability relating to intellectual property infringements (Art 13).   [307] Art 14.

[308] Art 16.   [309] Art 26. Again, for the human rights implications, see 8.3.2 above.

[310] Arts 15, 17–22, 24–25, and 27–28. On the relationship with EC law, see further 8.4 above.

[311] See 8.6 below. See the further plans set out in the Stockholm programme as regards conflicts of law (8.2.3 above).

[312] Arts 16–28 of the proposed Reg on jurisdiction and conflicts of law as regards succession (COM (2009) 154, 14 Oct 2009).

[313] Arts 4 and 28, Reg 1346/2000 ([2000] OJ L 160/1); see also Arts 5–15 of that Regulation. Presumably the exclusion of winding up of companies from the Rome I and II Regs precludes any overlap between those Regulations and the insolvency Regulation.

[314] [2010] OJ C 115 and COM (2010) 171, 20 Apr 2010.

8.5.4. Transmission of evidence

Article 81(2)(d) TFEU confers power on the EU as regards cooperation in the taking of evidence. This issue has been addressed by a Regulation adopted in 2001.[315] The Regulation has attracted two references from national courts to the Court of Justice.[316] Again there is also a Hague Convention on this issue, to which a large majority of Member States are parties.[317]

The Regulation applies to all civil and commercial matters, without any clarification of this concept, wherever one Member State's court requests another Member State's court to obtain evidence, or asks that the latter court permit the former court's officials to enter the latter Member State and collect evidence there.[318] It effectively establishes a mutual recognition regime, because the execution of requests can only be refused on limited grounds (such as incompatibility with the requested State's law, major practical difficulties, or the right of a person whose hearing is requested to refuse to testify).[319]

In 2007 the Commission issued a report on the application of the Regulation in practice,[320] which concluded that: the time to process requests for evidence had speeded up, but still often exceeded the deadlines in the Regulation; central bodies were used too often to forward requests, instead of contact directly between courts; standard forms are sometimes not filled in completely; communications technology was not widely used to take evidence yet, and nor was the direct taking of evidence by a court in another Member State; and there was confusion over the definition of 'evidence'.[321] The Commission concluded that there was no need to amend the Regulation, but rather that its application should be promoted by means, inter alia, of the European Judicial Network.

8.5.5. Access to justice

Article 81(2)(e) TFEU confers power on the EU as regards 'effective access to justice'; this power was expressly conferred for the first time by the Treaty of

---

[315] Reg 1206/2001 ([2001] OJ L 174/1), applicable from 1 Jan 2004 (Art 24(2)). All references in this subsection are to this Regulation unless otherwise indicated. The 'comitology' procedures in this Regulation were also amended in 2008 (Reg 1103/2008, [2008] OJ L 304/80).

[316] Cases C-175/06 *Tedesco* [2007] ECR I-7929 and C-283/09 *Werynski*, pending (opinion of 2 Sep 2010). The *Tedesco* case was withdrawn before judgment (but after a detailed Opinion of an Advocate General was issued).

[317] For the ratification status, see Appendix I. The Regulation prevails over the Convention, or other pre-existing treaties, in relations between the Member States: Art 21(1).

[318] Art 1(1). On the definition of this concept, see 8.2.4 above.

[319] Arts 10(2) and (3), 14, and 17. Compare with the Framework Decision establishing a European evidence warrant for use in criminal proceedings (9.6.1.2 below.) and the proposed European Investigation Order (9.6.1.3 below).   [320] COM (2007) 769, 5 Dec 2007.

[321] The withdrawn *Tedesco* case had addressed this issue (n 316 above).

Lisbon. On this topic, in 2003 the Council adopted a Directive governing legal aid in cross-border cases.[322] Because this Directive was adopted before the entry into force of the Treaty of Lisbon, the Community's competence to adopt it derived from its power to adopt legislation concerning compatibility of civil procedure rules to eliminate obstacles to the good functioning of civil proceedings.[323] Any amendments to this Directive, or other measures on the issue of access to justice, would now be adopted on the basis of Article 81(2)(e) TFEU.

The Commission has adopted measures to implement this Directive, which establish standard forms regarding legal aid applications and their transmission.[324] There have been no references to the Court of Justice concerning the Directive. There is again a Hague Convention dealing with aspects of this issue, although barely half of the Member States have ratified it.[325] However, a large majority of Member States have ratified a Council of Europe Agreement on transmission of requests for legal aid.[326]

The Directive applies to all civil and commercial matters,[327] excluding only customs, revenue, and administrative matters.[328] It applies only to cross-border matters, with the standard definition of this concept.[329] The Directive confers a right to legal aid for pre-judicial assistance with a view to a settlement and legal assistance and representation in court, including the costs of proceedings, although Member States need not ensure legal aid for specialist tribunals where the parties can make their case effectively in person, or for persons who have sufficient financial resources to pay the relevant costs.[330] Member States must grant aid without discrimination to EU citizens and legally resident third-country nationals[331]—although the obligation as regards EU citizens derives in any event from the equal treatment rule of the EC Treaty, now the TFEU.[332] Member States can reject claims which appear to be manifestly unfounded and apparently also in certain other circumstances.[333] There are also provisions concerning: cross-border costs; allocation of costs between Member States; legal aid in relation to enforcement, appeals, extrajudicial procedures, or authentic

---

[322] Dir 2003/8 ([2003] OJ L 26/41); all references in this subsection are to this Directive unless otherwise indicated. Member States had to transpose this Directive by 30 Nov 2004, except for Art 3(2)(a) on pre-judicial assistance, which they had to transpose by 30 May 2006 (Art 21). See earlier the Green Paper on the issue (COM (2000) 51, 9 Feb 2000). Compare with the planned criminal law measures on this issue (9.8.2 below).   [323] See recital 2 in the preamble.

[324] [2004] OJ L 365/27 and [2005] OJ L 225/23.

[325] For the ratification status, see Appendix I. Note that this Convention also addresses other issues relating to access to justice, such as security for costs.

[326] ETS 92 (1977); a Protocol to the Agreement, which has attracted far fewer ratifications, was agreed in 2001 (ETS 179). For ratification details, see Appendix I. The Directive takes precedence, as between Member States, over both of these measures, the Hague Convention, and any other international treaties: see Art 20.   [327] On the definition of this concept, see 8.2.4 above.

[328] Art 1(2), Dir 2003/8.   [329] Art 2.   [330] Arts 3 and 5.   [331] Art 4.

[332] See 8.4 above.   [333] Art 6.

instruments;[334] and the procedure for transmitting and processing legal aid applications.[335]

8.5.6. Civil procedure

Article 81(2)(f) TFEU, replacing the previous Article 65(c) EC, confers powers on the EU as regards 'the elimination of obstacles to the proper functioning of civil proceedings, if necessary by promoting the compatibility of the rules on civil procedure applicable in the Member States'. Before the entry into force of the Treaty of Lisbon, Article 65(c) EC was used expressly to adopt a Directive on legal aid and implicitly to adopt a Directive on mediation;[336] these two measures are considered separately, since the Treaty of Lisbon has now introduced separate legal bases on those two issues.[337]

Three other measures concerning civil procedure have been adopted, each of which aims to expedite further the recognition of judgments within the scope of the Brussels I Regulation, without amending that Regulation's rules on jurisdiction. First of all, in 2004, the Council and EP adopted a Regulation establishing a European Enforcement Order for uncontested claims.[338] This Regulation does not make clear whether its legal basis is the recognition of judgments or the harmonization of civil procedure law. It has the same scope as the Brussels I Regulation,[339] and like that Regulation it will not be applicable to maintenance claims once the EU's maintenance Regulation becomes applicable.[340]

The European Enforcement Order Regulation abolishes much of the procedural requirements to enforce a judgment in another Member State (in particular the requirement of an exequatur),[341] along with the grounds for refusal of recognition of a judgment except for the existence of a previous irreconcilable judgment,[342] provided that the claim is 'uncontested' as defined in the Regulation,[343] and that specific minimum procedural standards were complied with, in particular as regards the service of the documents concerned and the

---

[334] Arts 7–11.   [335] Arts 12–16.

[336] Dirs 2003/8 ([2003] OJ L 26/41) and 2008/52 ([2008] OJ L 136/3).

[337] See 8.5.5 above and 8.5.7 below.

[338] Reg 805/2004 ([2004] OJ L 143/15). The Regulation applied from 21 Oct 2005 (Art 33). The following six footnotes refer to this Regulation, unless otherwise indicated. The 'comitology' procedures in this Regulation were amended in 2008 (Reg 1103/2008, [2008] OJ L 304/80).

[339] Compare Art 2, Reg 805/2004 to Art 1, Reg 44/2001 ([2001] OJ L 12/1). The sole difference is the additional explicit exclusion of state liability for acts of state authority from the former Regulation, but such acts are *implicitly* excluded from the Brussels Reg: see Case C-292/05 *Lechoritou* [2007] ECR I-1519, which expressly links the scope of the Brussels Convention (now Reg 44/2001) with the wording of Reg 805/2004 and the subsequent payment orders Regulation (on which, see below).

[340] See further 8.6 below.   [341] Art 5.

[342] See Art 21; it is not specified if the grounds for refusal listed here are exhaustive.

[343] For this definition, see Art 3.

possibility of review of the judgment.[344] There have been no references to the Court of Justice concerning this Regulation yet.

Secondly, the Council and the EP adopted a Regulation establishing a European payment order in 2006.[345] It is based explicitly on Article 65(c) EC (now Article 81(2)(f) TFEU).[346] Its scope is the same as the enforcement order Regulation, except that the Regulation does not apply to claims concerning non-contractual liability, and there is no exclusion of arbitration or maintenance proceedings.[347] There is a specific definition of 'cross-border' cases.[348] So far there have been no references to the Court of Justice concerning this Regulation.

The Regulation sets out the process by which a creditor can apply to a court for a European payment order for an overdue pecuniary claim.[349] If the court issues the payment order, there are detailed rules relating to service of the payment order on the defendant,[350] which are important because the defendant has thirty days from the date of service to lodge a statement of opposition to the payment order.[351] In the absence of such a statement, the order becomes enforceable—in other words, the consent of the defendant is presumed.[352] The effect of a statement of opposition is to force the plaintiff to use normal civil proceedings in order to collect the debt.[353] If the order becomes enforceable, there is no need for an exequatur and the only express ground for refusal of recognition is irreconcilability with a prior judgment.[354] However, the Regulation grants the possibility of an exceptional review of the order for payment in the Member State of origin even after the time period for lodging a statement of opposition has expired, in specified exceptional cases.[355]

The third measure addressing the issue of simplified recognition of judgments is a Regulation establishing a European small claims procedure, adopted in 2007.[356] Like the payment order Regulation, the small claims Regulation is based explicitly on Article 65(c) EC (now Article 81(2)(f) TFEU).[357] The Regulation excludes the same matters as the Brussels I Regulation, along with the explicit exclusion of state liability for acts of state authority; also, the issues of maintenance, employment law, tenancies of immovable property (with the exception of actions

---

[344] Chapter III (Arts 12–19). The service rules apply in conjunction with the general EU legislation on service of documents (recitals 21 and 28 of the preamble).

[345] Reg 1896/2006 ([2006] OJ L 399/1). The Regulation was applicable from 12 Dec 2008 (Art 33). The following ten footnotes refer to this Regulation, unless otherwise indicated. According to a press report, the first payment order was issued on 10 June 2009 by a Czech court: see <http://www.ksb.cz/en/news-publications/649>. See earlier the Green Paper on payments orders and small claims (COM (2002) 742, 20 Dec 2002).　　　　　　　　　　　　　　[346] See recital 2 in the preamble.

[347] Art 2.　　　[348] Art 3; see 8.2.4 above.　　　[349] Arts 7–12.　　　[350] Arts 13–15.

[351] Art 16.　　　[352] Art 18.　　　[353] Art 17.

[354] Arts 19 and 22. Again it is not clear whether the grounds for refusal are exhaustive.

[355] Art 20.

[356] Reg 861/2007 ([2007] OJ L 199/1). The Regulation applied from 1 Jan 2009 (Art 29). The following nine footnotes refer to this Regulation, unless otherwise indicated. See again the earlier Green Paper on payments orders and small claims (n 345 above).　　　　[357] See recital 2 in the preamble.

on monetary claims), and violations of privacy and of rights relating to personality (including defamation) are excluded from its scope.[358] It applies to claims of €2,000 or less at the time that the claim was received by the court or tribunal with jurisdiction, excluding interest, expenses, and disbursements.[359] There is a specific definition of 'cross-border' cases, which is identical to the rule set out in the payment order Regulation.[360] So far there are no references to the Court of Justice concerning this Regulation.

The Regulation sets out the basic elements of the small claims procedure, specifying that the process is usually written, with discretion for the court to hold an oral hearing, and setting out deadlines of thirty days to respond to the claim and the counter claim.[361] Within thirty days of receiving the response, the court shall either give a judgment or move to a further procedural stage, still subject to strict deadlines; if there has been no response by the deadline, the court must give judgment.[362] Unlike the payment orders Regulation, the defendant must contest the merits of the case immediately, as there is no prospect of lodging a statement of opposition in order to require the plaintiff to commence ordinary civil proceedings instead. It is up to each Member State to decide whether an appeal of a small claims judgment is possible,[363] but at least there must be the possibility of a review of the judgment on certain limited grounds.[364] Again, there is no exequatur process as regards the recognition of the judgment, and the only express ground to refuse recognition is irreconcilability with a prior judgment.[365]

8.5.7. Alternative dispute resolution

Article 81(2)(g) TFEU confers competence on the EU as regards 'the development of alternative methods of dispute settlement'; this power was expressly conferred for the first time by the Treaty of Lisbon. Even before the entry into force of that Treaty, the issue of alternative dispute resolution was addressed by a Directive on mediation adopted in 2008.[366] Presumably the EC's competence to adopt the Directive at that time derived from its power to adopt legislation concerning compatibility of civil procedure rules to eliminate obstacles to the

---

[358] Art 2(2). In comparison with the payment orders Regulation, there is no general exclusion of claims for non-contractual liability.   [359] Art 2(1).

[360] Art 3; see 8.2.4 above.

[361] Art 5. The languages concerned are set out in Art 8, which is comparable to the languages provisions in the Regulations on service of documents; on the interpretation of the latter rules, see 8.5.2 above.   [362] Art 7; Arts 8–13 set out rules applicable to further procedural steps.

[363] Art 17.

[364] Art 18; compare to the wider possibility of review set out in Art 20 of the payment orders Reg.

[365] Arts 20 and 22. Again it is not clear whether the grounds for refusal are exhaustive.

[366] Dir 2008/52 ([2008] OJ L 136/3). Member States have to transpose this Directive by 21 May 2011 (Art 12). See earlier the Green Paper on alternative dispute settlement (COM (2002) 196, 19 Apr 2002).

good functioning of civil proceedings, although this was not made explicit in the Directive. Any amendments to the Directive, or other measures on this issue, would now be adopted on the basis of Article 81(2)(g) TFEU.

The Directive applies to all civil and commercial matters,[367] except for matters not at the parties' disposal under the applicable law, with exclusions only for customs, revenue, and administrative matters and State liability for acts of State authority.[368] It applies only to cross-border matters, with the standard definition of this concept amended to clarify the applicable date at which to determine this issue.[369] The Directive requires Member States: to encourage quality control as regards mediation and training of mediators; to permit courts to invite the parties to mediate their dispute; to make mediation agreements enforceable, subject to certain conditions (note that the Directive does not address the issue of enforceability of the agreements in other Member States); to keep mediation confidential, subject to certain exceptions; to waive limitation or prescription periods as regards access to court and arbitration while mediation is underway, unless ruled out by international treaties; and to make information on mediation available to the public.[370]

8.5.8. Judicial training

Finally, the last competence conferred upon the EU by Article 81(2) TFEU is a power to adopt measures concerning 'support for the training of the judiciary and judicial staff', a new express power added by the Treaty of Lisbon (Article 81(2)(h) TFEU). Until now, the question of judicial training in the field of civil law has been addressed alongside the issue of judicial training in the field of criminal law,[371] although training of judges as regards civil law is addressed by the EU's civil law funding decision.[372]

8.6. Family law

The most significant EC legislation in this area was Regulation 1347/2000 (the 'Brussels II' Regulation), which concerned jurisdiction over divorce proceedings and mutual recognition of divorce judgments; the Regulation also extended to parental responsibility proceedings which were linked to the

---

[367] On the definition of this concept, see 8.2.4 above.   [368] Art 1(2), Dir 2008/52.
[369] Art 2. See the discussion of the payment orders and small claims Regs (8.5.6 above).
[370] Arts 4–9.
[371] See further 9.9 below. It should be noted that the TFEU provision regarding the training of criminal law judges (Art 82(1)(c)) is identical to the provision concerning training of civil law judges.   [372] See Art 3(e) of the 2007 funding decision ([2007] OJ L 257/16).

divorce proceedings.[373] As noted above, this Regulation replaced the 'Brussels II' Convention,[374] which had been signed in 1998 but which had not yet been ratified when the Treaty of Amsterdam entered into force. In 2003 the Regulation was itself replaced by an amended text (Regulation 2201/2003), which extended the rules to apply to all proceedings concerning parental responsibility, and also provided for simplified recognition of judgments concerning access to or return of a child.[375] The 2003 Regulation has been the subject of eleven references to the Court of Justice from national courts.[376]

Subsequently, the Council adopted a Regulation on jurisdiction, mutual recognition, and cooperation as regards maintenance proceedings,[377] which furthermore refers to an international treaty (the Protocol to the Convention on maintenance proceedings) agreed within the auspices of the Hague Convention as regards applicable law on maintenance.[378] The Regulation will apply as from 18 June 2011, when this Protocol becomes applicable in the EU.[379] Currently, jurisdiction over and recognition of judgments relating to maintenance is subject to the Brussels Regulation, but that Regulation will no longer apply to maintenance claims brought after the maintenance Regulation becomes applicable.[380] Nor will the Regulation establishing the European enforcement order, except as regards UK judgments.[381] On the other hand, the maintenance Regulation is 'without prejudice' to the legal aid Directive, 'subject to' the specific rules in the maintenance Regulation on legal aid;[382] the Decision establishing the Judicial Network in civil and commercial matters is also applicable.[383] Moreover, the Lugano Convention still continues to apply for those non-Member States which do not participate in the maintenance Regulation.[384]

---

[373] [2000] OJ L 160/19, in force 1 Mar 2001.   [374] [1998] OJ C 221/1.

[375] [2003] OJ L 338/1; applicable from 1 Mar 2005 (Art 72).

[376] Cases: C-435/06 C [2007] ECR I-10141; C-68/07 Sundelind Lopez [2007] ECR I-10403; C-523/07 A [2009] ECR I-2805; C-168/08 Hadadi [2009] ECR I-6871; C-195/08 Rinau [2008] ECR I-5271; C-256/09 Purrucker I (judgment of 15 July 2010, not yet reported); C-312/09 Michalias (order of 17 June 2010); C-403/09 PPU Detiček, judgment of 23 Dec 2009, not yet reported; C-211/10 PPU Povse, judgment of 1 July 2010, not yet reported; C-296/10 Purrucker II, pending; and C-400/10 PPU McB, pending.

[377] Reg 4/2009, [2009] OJ L 7/1. See the earlier Green Paper on maintenance claims (COM (2004) 254, 15 Apr 2004).

[378] The EC (now the EU) has concluded the relevant Protocol, and the Commission has proposed that the EU also conclude the underlying Convention: see 8.9 below. The Council has not yet adopted the latter proposal. It should be recalled that the UK will not be bound by the Protocol, with consequence that the exequatur process is not abolished as regards recognition of UK judgments (see 8.2.5 above).

[379] See Art 76, Reg 4/2009. The Council's decision to conclude the Protocol (ibid) makes the Protocol provisionally applicable in the EU as of 18 June 2011, to ensure that the Regulation becomes applicable on that date as planned.   [380] See Arts 68(1) and 75, Reg 4/2009.

[381] Art 68(2), Reg 4/2009.

[382] Art 68(3), Reg 4/2009. See also recitals 36 and 37 in the preamble to the Regulation.

[383] Arts 70 and 71, Reg 4/2009.   [384] See 8.2.5 above.

Next, in 2006 the Commission proposed the 'Rome III' Regulation to set out standard rules on choice of law in divorce proceedings; the proposal would also have made some amendments to the jurisdiction rules in the Brussels II Regulation.[385] It was not possible to agree on this particular proposal by means of a unanimous vote, even without the participation of the UK, Ireland, and Denmark in the negotiations.[386] However, a number of Member States nevertheless wanted to consider the adoption of this proposal pursuant to the rules on 'enhanced cooperation',[387] and made a formal request to the Commission to this end.[388] The Commission responded to this request in March 2010, by proposing that the Council authorize enhanced cooperation to enable ten Member States to go ahead and adopt EU legislation on this issue; at the same time, it proposed a new version of the legislation on this issue.[389] In June 2010, the Council agreed in principle to authorize enhanced cooperation, and also agreed guidelines as regards the Rome III proposal itself.[390]

Finally, the Commission has released a Green Paper concerning conflict of law, jurisdiction over, and recognition of judgments concerning issues of matrimonial property, along with property issues deriving from registered partnerships and de facto unions.[391] The Commission intends to propose legislation on this issue in future.[392]

8.7. European contract law

The gradual development of a European contract law began with a detailed Commission Communication on this topic in 2001.[393] The Communication suggested consideration of four options to address contract law issues: to leave solutions to the market; to develop common principles of European contract law via research; to improve existing EU contract rules, which largely govern specified areas of consumer law; or to develop an EU instrument aimed at

---

[385] COM (2006) 499, 17 July 2006. See the earlier Green Paper on conflict of law and jurisdiction in divorce matters (COM (2005) 82, 14 Mar 2005).

[386] The text as agreed by most Member States is in Council doc 9712/08, 23 May 2008.

[387] The Council established that there was no prospect of attaining the objectives of this proposal within a reasonable period by using the provisions of the Treaties (JHA Council press release, June 2008 and Council doc 9985/08, 29 May 2008); this is a legal requirement before establishing enhanced cooperation (see Art 43a, previous TEU (now Art 20(2), revised TEU)). See also JHA Council press release, July 2008 and Council doc 11984/08, 18 July 2008.

[388] See Art 11(1) EC (now Art 329(1) TFEU).

[389] COM (2010) 104 and 105, 24 Mar 2010. On the enhanced cooperation rules generally, see 2.2.5.5 above.

[390] See the JHA Council press release, 3–4 June 2010. The Council subsequently formally adopted a Decision formally authorizing enhanced cooperation on this issue ([2010] OJ L 189/12).

[391] COM (2006) 400, 17 July 2006.

[392] 2010 work programme (COM (2010) 135, 31 Mar 2010).

[393] COM (2001) 398, 11 July 2001; [2001] OJ C 255/1.

harmonizing the general part of contract law. In February 2003, a follow-up to the Communication assessed the reaction to it and suggested an Action Plan. The Commission focused on improving the coherence of EU contract law, to research the prospect of 'common frame of reference' (CFR) for EU contract law which could be used as a non-binding model law, to gather information regarding the possible development of EU-wide general contract terms and to reflect further on a possible EU instrument setting out standard contractual rules which contracting parties could opt for.[394]

A subsequent Communication in autumn 2004 elaborated upon the Commission's plans,[395] in particular linking the development of the CFR to the simplification and standardization of EU consumer law, clarifying the Commission's intentions as regards EU-wide standard terms and conditions (the development of which is to be left to the private sector), and reflecting upon the potential usefulness of an optional instrument. The Communication then set out in detail the Commission's plans to fund research into the CFR, and suggested an outline of the CFR. Two subsequent annual reports on the implementation of this programme detailed the Commission's work, which it focused on issues of consumer law.[396]

For its part, the Council defined a view on the development of the CFR. In a first set of conclusions, it argued that: the purpose of the CFR should be to serve as a 'tool-box' for EU law-makers; the content of the CFR should consist of rules and principles drawn from a variety of sources; its scope should encompass general contract law as well as consumer contract law; and its legal effect should be as a set of non-binding guidelines.[397] The Council subsequently adopted further conclusions on the structure and scope of the CFR, respect for differing national traditions, and the role of the EU institutions,[398] as well as guidelines on the content of the CFR.[399]

The academic work funded by the Commission ultimately culminated in an interim draft CFR,[400] followed by a final draft CFR.[401] It remains to be seen whether the Commission will draw up a 'political' version of the CFR,

---

[394] COM (2003) 68, 12 Feb 2003. See further the Council resolution in response ([2003] OJ C 246/1).   [395] COM (2004) 651, 11 Oct 2004.
[396] COM (2005) 456, 23 Sep 2005 and COM (2007) 447, 25 July 2007.
[397] See Council doc 8286/08, 11 Apr 2008.   [398] See Council doc 15306/08, 7 Nov 2008.
[399] See Council conclusions (JHA Council press release, 4–5 June 2009).
[400] For the text, see: <http://webh01.ua.ac.be/storme/DCFRInterim.pdf>.
[401] For the text, see: <http://webh01.ua.ac.be/storme/2009_02_DCFR_OutlineEdition. pdf>. For detailed comments, see S Whitaker, 'The Draft "Common Frame of Reference: An Assessment"', online at: <http://www.justice.gov.uk/publications/docs/Draft_Common_ Frame_of_Reference__an_assessment.pdf>; the report prepared for the Scottish government by L MacGregor, online at: <http://www.scotland.gov.uk/Resource/Doc/262952/0078639. pdf>; and the House of Lords Select Committee on the European Union, 12th report for 2008–09.

and what influence it may have,[402] although the Commission has established an experts' group on this issue.[403] In the meantime, the Commission has taken work forward on amending EU consumer rights legislation, although its proposed Directive on this subject makes no mention of the European contract law project.[404] The Stockholm programme reaffirms that the CFR 'should be a non-binding set of fundamental principles, definitions and model rules to be used by the law-makers at Union level to ensure greater coherence and quality in the law-making process', and invites the Commission to make a proposal on the CFR.[405] In response, the Commission issued a communication on the CFR in 2010,[406] and plans to make a legislative proposal on this issue in 2011.[407]

8.8. Administrative cooperation and EU funding

The main developments in this area are the creation of a European Judicial Network in civil matters and successive EU funding programmes, which will be considered in turn.[408]

8.8.1. European Judicial Network

Following the example of the previously established judicial network relating to criminal law,[409] the Council established a European Judicial Network (EJN) in civil and commercial matters in 2001.[410] This network was initially composed of national contact points; central bodies or authorities provided for in EU or national instruments; criminal law liaison magistrates who have civil law responsibilities;[411] and other appropriate judicial or administrative authorities.[412] According to the Commission, at the beginning of 2008 the Network had 437 members falling into four categories: 102 contact points, 140 central authorities, 12 liaison magistrates, and 181 other judicial authorities active in judicial cooperation.[413] The main tasks of the EJN are to facilitate judicial cooperation

---

[402] However, as noted above the DCFR has had some influence on Advocates General of the Court of Justice (see 8.4 above).   [403] Commission Decision ([2010] OJ L 105/109).

[404] See the Green Paper on this issue (COM (2006) 744, 8 Feb 2007) and the proposed directive on consumer rights (COM (2008) 614, 8 Oct 2008).   [405] [2010] OJ C 115, point 3.4.2.

[406] COM (2010) 348, 1 July 2010.

[407] Action plan on implementing the Stockholm programme (COM (2010) 171, 20 Apr 2010).

[408] See also the Resolution establishing a network for legislative cooperation ([2008] OJ C 326/1).   [409] See 9.9 below.

[410] Decision 2001/470 ([2001] OJ L 174/25), applicable from 1 Dec 2002.

[411] On the liaison magistrates, see 9.9 below.   [412] Art 2, 2001 Decision.

[413] COM (2008) 380, 23 June 2008.

between Member States, to assist in the implementation of EC and international rules, and to furnish information to the public.[414]

The Commission released a report in 2006 on the operation of the EJN,[415] which concluded that the effectiveness of the network depended on the resources available to the contact points in each Member State, but that nevertheless the network had helped to facilitate the application of civil law instruments by speeding up the transmission and processing of requests for assistance. Its website for the public was also helpful and widely used.

In order to enhance the effectiveness of the EJN, the 2001 Decision was amended in 2009.[416] The major changes are: the participation in the network of organizations representing legal practitioners; a requirement to ensure sufficient resources for the contact points; the use of the EJN to exchange information on foreign law, given the adoption of EU measures on conflict of laws;[417] establishing time limits on the processing of requests for judicial cooperation; providing for the participation of observers (from Denmark, accession and candidate countries, and States which are party to civil law treaties concluded by the EU); and providing for relations with other networks and international organizations. Time will tell whether it is considered necessary to develop the network into an EU agency, along the lines of developments within other areas of EU JHA law.

8.8.2. EU funding

The first use of EC funds to support civil law measures was during the Maastricht period, when the Council adopted the 'Grotius' Joint Action to establish a programme of incentives and exchanges for legal practitioners.[418] This five-year programme had a budget of €8.8 million,[419] and concerned both civil and criminal law. It funded 'training, exchange and work-experience programmes, organization of meetings, studies and research, and distribution of information' as defined in the Joint Action.[420] Following the entry into force of the Treaty of Amsterdam, the civil law part of the Grotius Joint Action was extended for one year (2001) by a Council Regulation.[421]

---

[414] Art 3, 2001 Decision. For the EJN website, see: <http://ec.europa.eu/civiljustice/index_en.htm>.

[415] COM (2006) 203, 16 May 2006. See also the Council conclusions on the EJN (JHA Council press release, 19–20 Apr 2007).

[416] [2009] OJ L 168/35, applicable from 1 Jan 2011 (Art 2). The amended Decision has not been consolidated.

[417] To the same end, note also that nearly every Member State has ratified the Council of Europe Convention on information on foreign law and its additional Protocol (see Appendix I for ratification details).   [418] [1996] OJ L 287/3. On criminal law funding measures, see 9.9 below.

[419] Art 2, Joint Action.

[420] Art 1(3), Joint Action; see the definitions in Arts 2–7 of the Joint Action.

[421] Reg 290/2001 ([2001] OJ L 43/1). The budget for this year was €650,000 (Art 2(1)).

Subsequently, the Council adopted a longer-term programme, covering 2002–06.[422] This programme funded the same five types of projects,[423] but with more clearly specified objectives: promoting judicial cooperation in civil matters; ensuring mutual knowledge of national judicial systems; contributing to the application of EC legislation; and improving information to the public on relevant civil law matters.[424] An initial report on this programme indicated that it was too early to evaluate its outcome, but that the Commission had been focusing on enhancing public awareness of EC legislation and conducting research which would be useful in preparing further proposals for legislation.[425]

On the expiry of the 2002 Regulation, a new civil law funding programme was established to run from 2007–13.[426] The current programme has a budget of €109.3 million over seven years.[427]Compared to the previous programme, the new programme aims also to address issues of conflicts of jurisdiction, the evaluation of EU measures, training of legal practitioners, and to reinforce mutual confidence, as well as to facilitate the operation of the EJN in civil and commercial matters.[428]

8.9. External relations

The adoption of internal EU legislation gives rise to exclusive external powers for the EU to the extent that any treaty would affect the internal rules or alter their scope.[429] Applying these principles to civil cooperation, the Court of Justice has ruled that the main EU legislation regulating civil jurisdiction and recognition of judgments in civil and commercial matters creates an exclusive external competence for the EU as regards the revised version of the 'Lugano Convention', which extends the Brussels I Regulation rules on jurisdiction over and enforcement of civil and commercial judgments to selected non-EU countries.[430] The obvious implication of this judgment is that any rules governing jurisdiction and enforcement of judgments which are part of any international treaties fall within the exclusive external competence of the EU, to the extent that they fall within the scope of the Brussels I Regulation, and moreover that the EU equally derives exclusive external competence from its other legislation on civil jurisdiction and recognition of judgments. Furthermore, since the EU's choice of law legislation applies regardless of whether the law designated by the rules is that of a Member

---

[422] Reg 743/2002 on a general framework for EC activity on civil law ([2002] OJ L 115/1).

[423] Art 5, Reg 743/2002 (ibid).   [424] Art 2, Reg 743/2002.

[425] COM (2005) 34, 9 Feb 2005.

[426] Decision establishing the 'Civil Justice' programme ([2007] OJ L 257/16).

[427] Art 13 of Decision (ibid).   [428] Art 3 of 2007 Decision.

[429] See: Case 22/70 *Commission v Council (ERTA)* [1971] ECR 263; Art 3(2) TFEU; and generally 2.7.1 above.   [430] *Opinion 1/2003*, [2006] ECR I-1145.

State or a third state,[431] then exclusive external competence is also conferred upon the Union whenever such legislation is adopted. However, the question of whether EU legislation on service of documents, mediation, evidence, and legal aid confers exclusive or only shared external competence may be debatable.

There is no reason to doubt the continued relevance of this case law following the entry into force of the Treaty of Lisbon. Even though Declaration 36 in the Final Act of the Treaty 'confirms' that Member States have competence to 'negotiate and conclude agreements with third countries or international organisations' in this field, such competence exists only 'insofar as such agreements comply with Union law'. So the Declaration clarifies that Member States' external competence in this area is not completely extinguished, in that it still applies *where the EU has not yet acted*, but it does not restrain the existence or the intensity of the Union's competence.

In light of its exclusive powers, in recent years the Community (now the EU) has negotiated to become party to a number of international treaties which either focus largely upon the issue of jurisdiction and choice of law, or address such matters as subsidiary to regulation of substantive legal issues. In the latter case, given that the treaties concerned also address substantive matters other than civil cooperation, the Community shared external competence with its Member States for the treaty as a whole—but nevertheless its powers over the specific provisions on civil cooperation remained exclusive, so the EC had to become a party in respect of those provisions of those treaties. Also, in some cases, where negotiations on international treaties were either concluded or well underway when the Treaty of Amsterdam came into force, it was too late for the EC to become a party to the relevant treaty in its own name; therefore it authorized the Member States to sign and/or conclude the relevant treaties, as 'trustees' of the EC's competence.

The treaties which the EC (now the EU) has solely concluded, since they relate only to matters within the EU's exclusive external competence in this area, are the Lugano Convention,[432] the treaties with Denmark which extend the Brussels I Regulation and the service of documents Regulation to that Member State, despite its opt-out from EU law in this field,[433] and the Protocol to the Hague Convention on maintenance obligations concerning choice of law.[434] The EU has

---

[431] Art 3 of Reg 864/2007 ([2007] OJ L 199/40) and Art 2 of Reg 593/2008 ([2008] OJ L 177/6).

[432] For the decision on conclusion, see [2009] OJ L 147/1; for the Convention itself, see [2009] OJ L 147/5; for the explanatory memorandum on the Convention, see [2009] OJ C 319/1. The Convention, which was also signed by Denmark, Norway, Iceland, and Switzerland, entered into force for the EU, Denmark, and Norway as from 1 Jan 2010 ([2010] OJ L 140/1). For the earlier Council decision on signature of the Convention, see [2007] OJ L 339/1. For the previous version of the Convention, to which the (then) Member States and Norway, Iceland, and Switzerland were parties, see [1988] OJ C 319/9.

[433] These treaties also include obligations for Denmark as regards the exercise of its own external competence for matters within the scope of the treaties. See further 8.2.5 above.

[434] [2009] OJ L 331/17. On the implications of concluding the Protocol, see 8.6 above.

also solely signed the Hague Convention on choice-of-court agreements,[435] and
the Commission has proposed that the EU alone conclude the Hague Convention
on maintenance obligations.[436]

As for its shared competence, the EU has concluded the Unidroit Convention
on international interests in mobile equipment and its protocol relating to aircraft
equipment, as regards issues within the scope of the Brussels I Regulation, the
insolvency Regulation, and the Rome I Regulation.[437] The Union has also signed
a further Protocol to this Convention, concerning matters specific to railway
rolling stock.[438] The Commission has also proposed that the EU sign or conclude
two other treaties in its own name.[439]

For the reasons explained above, the Council has also adopted eight Decisions
authorizing Member States to sign or ratify treaties which fall partly or wholly
within the scope of the EC's (now the EU's) external competence. These decisions concern: authority to sign or ratify the Convention on civil liability for
bunker oil pollution damage (Bunkers Convention);[440] authority to ratify the
Convention on liability for damage caused by carrying hazardous and noxious
substances by sea (HNS Convention);[441] authority to sign the Hague Convention
on, for example parental responsibility for children;[442] authority to sign a Protocol
to the Paris Convention on liability in case of nuclear accident;[443] authority to sign
and ratify a 2003 Protocol to a Convention on a fund for oil pollution damage;[444]

---

[435] [2009] OJ L 133/1. The Commission has not (yet) proposed that the EU conclude the
Convention.   [436] See COM (2009) 373, 28 July 2009.

[437] [2009] OJ L 121/3.

[438] [2009] OJ L 331/1. The declaration of EU competence concerns again the Brussels I Reg, the
insolvency Reg, and the Rome I Reg, plus also some EU rail transport legislation.

[439] See proposed Decisions concerning the signature of the Council of Europe Convention on
contact concerning children (COM (2002) 520, 2 Oct 2002) and the conclusion of the Protocol
to the Athens Convention 1974 on carriage of passengers and luggage by sea (COM (2003) 375,
24 June 2003). The former proposal does not specifically set out a claim regarding EU competence,
while the latter proposal states that the EU has competence as regards the jurisdiction provisions of
the Protocol, due to the Brussels I Reg. On the latter proposal, see now Reg 392/2009 ([2009] OJ
L 131/24), recital 11 of the preamble.

[440] [2002] OJ L 256/7. The preamble to the Decision specifies that EU exclusive competence
applies to two Articles of this Convention concerning jurisdiction and enforcement of judgments,
due to the Brussels I Reg, but not to the rest of the Convention.

[441] [2002] OJ L 337/55. The preamble to the Decision specifies that EC exclusive competence
applies to three Articles of this Convention concerning jurisdiction and enforcement of judgments,
due to the Brussels I Reg, but not to the rest of the Convention.   [442] [2003] OJ L 48/1.

[443] [2003] OJ L 338/30. The Decision does not apply to Ireland, Austria, and Luxembourg,
since they are not parties to the Paris Convention. The preamble to the Decision specifies that EC
exclusive competence applies to one Article of the main Convention (as amended by the Protocol)
concerning jurisdiction, due to the Brussels I Reg, but not to the rest of the Convention.

[444] Decision 2004/246 ([2004] OJ L 78/22), amended following the 2003 Act of Accession (see
8.2.5 above). The Decision does not apply to Ireland, Austria, and Luxembourg, since they are not
parties to the Paris Convention. The preamble to the Decision specifies that EC exclusive competence applies to two Articles of the Protocol concerning jurisdiction, due to the Brussels I Reg, but
not to the rest of the Protocol. One judgment of the Court of Justice has touched on this Decision

authority to *ratify* the aforementioned Protocol to the Paris Convention on liability in case of nuclear accident;[445] authority for Slovenia, which joined the EU later, to ratify the same Protocol;[446] and authority to *ratify* the Hague Convention on, for example parental responsibility for children.[447]

Next, the EC has obtained membership in its own name of the main negotiating forum for civil law treaties—the Hague Conference on private international law.[448] However, since the EC (now EU) competence in civil law is shared with Member States, all Member States have also retained their membership in the Hague Convention.

As for the jurisdiction of the Court of Justice over the civil law treaties concluded by the Community (now the EU), and the legal effect of those treaties, so far neither issue has been addressed in the Court's case law, although the two civil law treaties with Denmark specifically give the Court jurisdiction in relation to Denmark.[449] It would be very odd, therefore, if the Court had no jurisdiction regarding those treaties in relation to the other Member States. In the case of other civil law treaties concluded by the EU, there seems no reason to doubt that the normal rules governing the Court's jurisdiction and the legal effect of international treaties in the EU legal order apply equally to civil law treaties.[450]

Finally, one key issue for Member States in light of EU exclusive external competence over many civil law issues is the power to negotiate and sign treaties in their own name.[451] Most EU legislation does permit Member States to retain in force existing treaties which they ratified before the legislation was adopted, at least as regards relations with third states,[452] but this implicitly rules out the negotiation of *future* treaties by Member States dealing with the relevant subject matter. Some Member States objected strongly to this restriction on their external competence, particularly after the Court of Justice's 2006 judgment in *Opinion 1/2003* had made clear the extent of the EC (now EU) exclusive competence over civil law matters. So Member States made clear they would only agree to the adoption of new Community (now Union) civil law legislation if they were still permitted some leeway to negotiate treaties in future.

(Case C-188/07 *Commune de Mesquer* [2008] ECR I-4501), which was not relevant on the facts of that case.

[445] [2004] OJ L 97/53.   [446] [2007] OJ L 294/23.

[447] [2008] OJ L 151/36. The preamble to this Decision asserts that the EC and Member States share competence as regards the subject matter of the Convention. As matters stand, Member States' competence principally concerns the issue of choice of law on parental responsibility (Chapter III of the Convention), which has not (yet) been the subject of EU legislation.

[448] [2006] OJ L 297.   [449] For more on these treaties, see 8.2.5 above.

[450] For more on this issue, see 2.7.1 above.

[451] It should be noted that the position regarding the capacity of Denmark to sign civil law treaties with third States is governed by the distinct rules on this issue in the two treaties with the EU by means of which Denmark has agreed to apply certain EU civil law regulations. See 8.2.5 above.

[452] See also Art 307 EC (now Art 351 TFEU), discussed further in 2.7.1 above.

The solution to this dispute was to adopt legislation in 2009 that delegates competence to the Member States to negotiate their own treaties, subject to strict substantive and procedural conditions.[453] Two separate Council Regulations authorize, on the one hand, the power to negotiate treaties relating to conflict of law matters,[454] and, on the other hand, maintenance and family law jurisdiction matters.[455] There is no EU legislation authorizing national treaty negotiations within the scope of the Brussels I Regulation or the insolvency Regulation, but of course it remains possible to adopt legislation to that effect in future,[456] or for the Council to authorize Member States to negotiate such national treaties on a case-by-case basis. It will also remain possible for the Council to authorize Member States to negotiate and conclude *multilateral* treaties within the scope of EU civil law legislation on a case-by-case basis, although in practice the Commission is unlikely to propose such authorization.

The Regulations apply either to bilateral agreements concluded between a Member State and a third country, or to a regional agreement between a 'limited' number of Member States and 'neighbouring' third States.[457] When a Member State intends to enter into negotiations for a new agreement (or to amend an existing agreement), it must inform the Commission 'at the earliest possible' time before opening negotiations, and make available to the Commission information on the planned treaties.[458] The Commission must then assess the Member State's plan to start negotiations, first of all examining whether a relevant negotiating mandate for a treaty between the EU and the country concerned is envisaged within the next two years, and then checking whether all of the following conditions are present: a 'specific interest' for the Member State to conclude the treaty 'due to economic, geographic, cultural, historical, social or political ties' with the third State concerned; the planned agreement 'appears not to render Community law ineffective and not to undermine the proper functioning of the system established by that law'; and the envisaged treaty 'would not undermine

---

[453] See similarly the legislation on border traffic treaties (3.8 above) and Art 2(1) TFEU, discussed also in 2.7.1 above.

[454] Reg 662/2009, [2009] OJ L 200/25, applicable to matters within the scope of the Rome I or Rome II Regs (Art 1(2)). The Reg entered into force on 20 Aug 2009 (Art 15).

[455] Reg 664/2009, [2009] OJ L 200/46, applicable to matters within the scope of Regs 4/2009 or 2201/2003 (Art 1(2)). The Reg also entered into force on 20 Aug 2009 (Art 15).

[456] See recitals 5 and 21 of Regs 662/2009 and 664/2009. Equally the proposals on jurisdiction and conflict of law relating to succession (COM (2009) 154, 14 Oct 2009) and on the conflict of law in divorce (COM (2010) 105, 24 Mar 2010) would not be covered by Regs 662 and 664/2009 respectively, but the point might be raised during negotiations on the proposals. In any event, both of these proposals contain a specific clause on Member States' treaties (Art 45, inheritance proposal; Art 11, Rome III proposal).

[457] Art 2, Reg 662/2009. Art 2 of Reg 664/2009 has a more specific definition of a regional agreement, by reference to the EU family law legislation concerned.

[458] Art 3, Regs 662/2009 and 664/2009.

the object and purpose of the Community's external relations policy as decided by the Community'.[459]

If the planned treaty meets these conditions, the Commission must authorize negotiations within ninety days of the Member State's request; it 'may propose negotiating guidelines and may request the inclusion of particular clauses in the envisaged agreement'. The treaty must contain a form of priority clause in case the EU subsequently negotiates a treaty with the country concerned on the same subject.[460] If the Commission believes that the planned treaty does not meet the required conditions, it shall inform the Member State concerned within ninety days. If the Member State concerned wishes to argue the point, the Regulations provide for a procedure for discussions between the Member State and the Commission—but the Commission has the final say.[461] Presumably an aggrieved Member State could then have recourse to the EU courts to bring an annulment action against the Commission's decision.

Once negotiations (if authorized) begin, the Commission may participate as an observer.[462] When negotiations conclude, the Member State concerned then needs the approval of the Commission again to conclude the agreement, and the Commission must assess it in light of most of the same substantive criteria and procedural rules which were applicable to the earlier decision to authorize the start of the negotiations.[463] Finally, there is a 'sunset' clause for the Regulations: the Commission must review their operation by 13 July 2017 at the earliest and then recommend either that they expire or that they be replaced by a new Regulation (with a proposal for legislation to that effect); the Regulations will then expire three years after the date of this report.[464]

As for future plans, the Stockholm programme refers generally to the development of the EU's international presence in the civil law field, and the Commission plans a communication on this issue in 2011 along with a number of proposals to negotiate or conclude further treaties in this area.[465]

8.10. Conclusions

Civil law measures adopted within the framework of EU law have maintained a strong focus on mutual recognition, with their basic goal of ensuring that only one court system and one set of legal rules applies to a dispute, and that a judgment issued in one Member State is recognized and enforced in another. The lack of accompanying harmonization of law has caused concern among those

---

[459] Art 4, Regs 662/2009 and 664/2009. [460] Art 5, Regs 662/2009 and 664/2009.
[461] Art 6, Regs 662/2009 and 664/2009. [462] Art 7, Regs 662/2009 and 664/2009.
[463] Arts 8 and 9, Regs 662/2009 and 664/2009.
[464] Arts 13 and 14, Regs 662/2009 and 664/2009.
[465] See [2010] OJ C 115, point 3.5.1, and COM (2010) 171, 20 Apr 2010.

who argue for greater similarity in national civil procedural laws, but the EU has shied away from any significant steps in that direction. That reticence may come under question eventually, particularly if the Common Frame of Reference for contract law is further developed.

As for human rights, while the EU's civil cooperation measures have not given rise to the same concerns over civil liberties and human rights protection as other issues discussed in this book, all such matters fall within the scope of Article 6 ECHR. The case law of the Court of Justice has largely (but not entirely) struck the right balance between developing efficient rules on civil jurisdiction and mutual recognition of judgment, on the one hand, and the protection of human rights on the other. Furthermore, effective civil cooperation measures have the desirable result of assisting the Member States to fulfil their Article 6 obligation to guarantee a trial within a reasonable time and to ensure the execution of judgments.

9

Criminal Law: Mutual Recognition and Criminal Procedure

9.1. Introduction

In order to ensure that substantive criminal law achieves its intended objectives, it is obviously necessary both to investigate alleged crimes and to prosecute the alleged offenders, and then to carry out any sentence imposed. But in democratic societies committed to human rights, ensuring effective prosecutions cannot be the sole objective. Since it is unacceptable to punish the innocent with the force of criminal sanctions such as imprisonment, the process of determining guilt or innocence needs to be fair. So the right to a fair trial carries a prominent place in any general international human rights treaty or national constitutional bill of rights, along with associated principles like the legality and non-retroactivity of criminal law.

Yet putting in practice the right to a fair trial, balancing defendants' rights with the need to ensure effective prosecutions, is a complex and often controversial process, both as regards the general rules of criminal procedure and their application to specific cases. The process is complicated when there are cross-border elements, such as the presence of a suspect, witness, or other evidence in another country. To address such issues, there is a considerable body of international treaties, mostly emanating from the Council of Europe. But since the operation of these treaties is often considered to be ineffective in light of a perceived increase in cross-border crime, the EU has been active in adopting measures in this area and planning further measures. In particular, since 1999, the EU has been implementing a principle of mutual recognition in criminal matters, according to which the decisions of the judicial authorities of one Member State should as far as possible take effect automatically in all other Member States.

There are objections to the detailed measures adopted to apply this principle, most notably from national parliaments and courts, in light of doubts in particular about the fairness of foreign criminal procedures due to the diversity of systems of criminal procedure between Member States and fears that criminal suspects facing trial in a foreign system will face de facto discrimination. These doubts could be addressed by EU-wide harmonization of domestic criminal procedural law, but there have been objections in turn to such measures due to the limited legal powers of the EU as regards domestic criminal procedure, qualms about harmonization of national law in such a sensitive and distinctive field, and doubts about the necessity of such measures in light of the fair trial provisions of the European Convention of Human Rights (ECHR) and the possibility of enforcing those rights in the European Court of Human Rights. But in the absence of harmonized procedural rights, the 'free movement of prosecutions and sentences' could arguably lead to the violation of the right to a fair trial. To address these concerns, the Treaty of Lisbon provides for a specific legal base for the adoption of measures regarding domestic criminal procedure, and the EU has committed itself to adopt legislation in this area.

This chapter surveys these issues in detail, starting with the basic issues of the institutional framework, an overview of measures adopted, legal competence, territorial scope, human rights, and overlaps with other (non-JHA) EU law. It then examines the EU's mutual recognition measures, starting with extradition and the 'flagship' European Arrest Warrant, moving to analyse pre-trial measures addressing issues such as the movement of evidence and freezing orders, and then post-trial measures such as the recognition of sentences and confiscation orders and the transfer of prisoners. It then examines EU harmonization of domestic criminal procedure, in the specific fields referred to in the Treaty of Lisbon (evidence law, suspects' rights, and victims' rights). Finally, it concludes by examining the issues of administrative cooperation and EU funding and external relations, as they apply to criminal procedure.

Issues related to jurisdiction (including cross-border double jeopardy) and prosecution, notably the development of Eurojust and the prospect of creating a European Public Prosecutor, are addressed separately in Chapter 11. The connected issue of substantive criminal law is addressed in Chapter 10, and the closely related issue of policing is examined in Chapter 12. As noted in the latter chapter, this book observes the English distinction between the prosecution and trial process before the courts (addressed in this chapter) and the *investigation* of crime by the police or similar authorities (addressed in Chapter 12), even though in continental countries, investigations are more closely linked to the judicial process.

9.2. Institutional framework and overview

9.2.1 Cooperation before the Treaty of Amsterdam

Before the entry into force of the Treaty of Amsterdam in 1999, the main source of the law on international criminal procedure was Council of Europe Conventions, which addressed in turn: extradition;[1] mutual assistance in transferring evidence;[2] the international validity of criminal judgments (or transfer of sentences);[3] the transfer of sentenced persons, with a subsequent protocol);[4] and measures concerning the proceeds of crime.[5] Most of these Conventions have been universally ratified by Member States, but the Convention on the international validity of criminal judgments attracted much less interest.[6]

At first, the EU Member States focused on agreeing European Political Cooperation (EPC) Conventions that would enhance the application of the Council of Europe Conventions among themselves, and encourage cooperation between Member States in the areas where the Council of Europe Conventions had attracted little enthusiasm.[7] To this end, they agreed on Conventions concerning the application of a Council of Europe terrorism Convention (which contains further extradition and mutual assistance rules), the faxing of extradition requests, the international validity of criminal judgments, and the transfer of sentenced persons.[8] However, none of these EPC Conventions entered into force, as they failed to attract much enthusiasm among Member States.[9]

Outside the framework of cooperation between the (then) EEC Member States, the 1990 Schengen Convention contained a number of detailed provisions on cross-border cooperation, addressing mutual assistance,[10] extradition,[11] and the transfer of sentenced persons.[12] The Schengen Executive Committee also adopted two relevant Decisions, concerning mutual assistance as regards drug trafficking and a separate agreement concerning cooperation regarding road traffic offences.[13] Furthermore, the Schengen Information System (SIS) contains data of use to prosecutions and judicial investigations, in particular as regards extradition, wanted persons, and objects which could be used as evidence.[14]

With the entry into force of the Treaty of Maastricht, the EU had a formal intergovernmental framework to address criminal procedural issues. The main development during the 'Maastricht era' was the signature of two extradition Conventions in 1995 and 1996, concerning in turn consented and disputed extradition.[15] These Conventions sought to reduce or eliminate a number of the main bars to extradition under the Council of Europe Conventions. During this period, there were also lengthy attempts, starting in 1995, to agree a Convention

---

[1] See 9.5.1 below.   [2] See 9.6.1.1 below.   [3] See 9.7 below.   [4] See ibid.
[5] See 9.6.2 and 9.7.4 below.
[6] For ratification details of all of the Conventions and Protocols, see Appendix I.
[7] On the EPC process, see 2.2.1.1 above.   [8] See 9.5.1, 9.6.1.1, and 9.7 below.
[9] For ratification details of all of the Conventions and Protocols, see Appendix I.
[10] Arts 48–53 of the Convention (Chapter 2 of Title III), [2000] OJ L 239. See 9.6.1 below.
[11] Arts 59–66 of the Convention (Chapter 4 of Title III). See 9.5.1 below.
[12] Arts 67–69 of the Convention (Chapter 5 of Title III). See 9.7.1.2 below.
[13] See respectively 9.6.1 and 9.7.1.1 below.
[14] See particularly Arts 95, 98, and 100 of the Convention. On the SIS, see 12.6.1.1 below.
[15] See 9.5.1 below.

on mutual assistance to supplement the Council of Europe measures, but these attempts did not bear fruit until after the Treaty of Amsterdam was in force. A Convention on recognition of driving disqualifications was signed in 1998, but it has attracted few ratifications.[16] There were also a handful of Joint Actions addressing criminal procedural issues. These measures concerned the exchange of liaison magistrates;[17] the 'Grotius' programme of incentives and exchanges for legal practitioners;[18] good practice in mutual legal assistance;[19] the creation of a European judicial network;[20] and money laundering and confiscation of proceeds.[21]

9.2.2. The Treaty of Amsterdam

9.2.2.1 Institutional framework

The Treaty of Amsterdam inserted an Article 31 into the EU Treaty, which provided that:

Common action on judicial cooperation in criminal matters shall include:

(a) facilitating and accelerating cooperation between competent ministries and judicial or equivalent authorities of the Member States in relation to proceedings and the enforcement of decisions;
(b) facilitating extradition between Member States;
(c) ensuring compatibility in rules applicable in the Member States, as may be necessary to improve such cooperation;
(d) preventing conflicts of jurisdiction between Member States;
(e) progressively adopting measures establishing minimum rules relating to the constituent elements of criminal acts and to penalties in the fields of organised crime, terrorism and illicit drug trafficking.

The Treaty of Nice subsequently added a second paragraph to the previous Article 31 TEU, referring to the 'Eurojust' prosecutors' agency which EU leaders had agreed to create in the meantime. This issue, along with Article 31(1)(d) regarding conflicts of jurisdiction, is addressed further in Chapter 11.

The measures adopted pursuant to Article 31 TEU were governed by the revised general third pillar rules on the jurisdiction of the Court of Justice, the role of the political institutions, and the use of specific instruments and their legal effect.[22] On the latter point, the Court's judgment in *Pupino*, finding that Framework Decisions had indirect effect,[23] was of great relevance to this area, since a number of Framework Decisions in the field of criminal procedure partly or wholly govern the legal position of individuals (particularly crime victims and

---

[16] See 9.7.3 below.   [17] See 9.9 below.   [18] See ibid.   [19] See 9.6.1 below.
[20] See 9.9 below.   [21] See 9.6.2 and 9.7.4 below.   [22] See 2.2.2.2 above.
[23] Case C-105/03 [2005] ECR I-5285; see discussion in ibid.

suspects), whose legal position may be altered significantly by the ability to invoke the indirect effect of a Framework Decision.

Also, with the entry into force of the Treaty of Amsterdam, the various Schengen rules on criminal procedural matters were allocated to the third pillar of the EU.[24]

9.2.2.2. Implementing the Treaty of Amsterdam

As with other areas of JHA cooperation, some key basic principles for development of policy and legislation in this area were set out by the Tampere European Council in the autumn of 1999.[25] The relevant conclusions focused in particular on mutual recognition of judicial decisions, described as the 'cornerstone' of criminal (and civil) judicial cooperation; the principle of mutual recognition should apply not just to judgments but also to 'other decisions of judicial authorities'. However, the conclusions also referred to the 'necessary approximation of legislation'. Approximation and mutual recognition together 'would facilitate co-operation between authorities and the judicial protection of individual rights'.

More specifically, the conclusions urged Member States to ratify the EU's two extradition Conventions, and stated that extradition as such should be abolished in the case of persons who fled after final sentencing. In other cases, there should be consideration of 'fast track' extradition procedures, 'without prejudice to the principle of fair trial'. Furthermore, there should also be mutual recognition of 'pre-trial orders, in particular' measures on seizure of assets and evidence, and 'evidence lawfully gathered by one Member State's authorities should be admissible before the courts of other Member States, taking into account the standards that apply there'. Finally, the conclusions asked the Council and Commission to adopt a programme of measures to implement the principle of mutual recognition by the end of 2000.

The conclusions also provided that 'minimum standards should be drawn up on the protection of the victims of crime, in particular on crime victims' access to justice and on their rights to compensation for damages'. Member States were called upon to provide full mutual legal assistance in the investigation and prosecution of serious economic crime (referring to taxes and duties), money laundering 'should be rooted out wherever it occurs', and the European Council was 'determined to ensure that concrete steps are taken to trace, freeze, seize and confiscate the proceeds of crime'. To that end, Member States were urged to implement various relevant EU and international measures.

To implement this agenda, the Council agreed upon the mutual recognition work programme, as requested, by the end of 2000.[26] The programme ultimately

---

[24] [1999] OJ L 176/17.   [25] Paras 32–52 of the conclusions.

[26] [2001] OJ C 12/10. See earlier Commission communication on the issue (COM (2000) 495, 26 July 2000) and discussion of the development of the principle in S Peers, 'Mutual Recognition

included a list of twenty-four measures, ranked by priority, but without dates for concluding the programme as a whole or agreeing individual measures.

According to its introduction, the mutual recognition programme was to be subject to a number of 'parameters': whether each measure should be general in scope or limited to specific crimes; whether the concept of double criminality (requiring the act in question to be a crime in both the requesting and the requested State) should be dropped; 'mechanisms for safeguarding the rights of third parties, victims and suspects'; the need to define 'common minimum standards' necessary to facilitate mutual recognition (for example, the competence of courts); whether enforcement is direct or indirect;[27] the grounds for refusing recognition (such as public policy and double jeopardy, and exclusion of military, fiscal, or political offences); and the existence of 'liability arrangements in the event of acquittal'.

Before the entry into force of the Treaty of Lisbon, this programme was implemented by Framework Decisions on: a European Arrest Warrant (EAW), which replaces extradition between Member States; freezing orders; the mutual recognition of financial penalties; execution of confiscation orders (and related domestic law on confiscation); a European Evidence Warrant (following an earlier EU Convention and Protocol on mutual assistance in criminal matters); the transfer of sentenced persons; probation and parole orders; pre-trial supervision orders; recognition of convictions; the exchange of criminal records; and *in absentia* trials (trials held without the attendance of the accused).[28] However, the Commission decided against proposing EU legislation on witness protection.[29]

The development of EU policy in this area was clearly accelerated by the terrorist attacks of 11 September 2001, which were followed almost instantly by the proposal to establish the EAW and the agreement on the text. This Framework Decision became the 'flagship' of the EU's mutual recognition policy, but it was subsequently attacked on human rights grounds in the Court of Justice and national courts.[30] The adoption of further measures in this area was also encouraged by the Hague Programme of 2004, and its related Action Plan.[31]

As for approximation of legislation, there was no real development as regards the law of evidence or suspects and defendants' rights.[32] However, victims' rights were

---

and Criminal Law in the European Union: Has the Council Got it Wrong?', (2004) 41 CML Rev 5 at 7–10.

[27] Direct enforcement means application of the foreign decision without any intervening procedure in the executing Member State. Indirect enforcement means that some form of procedure (usually quite limited) by the executing State's authorities is necessary before the decision can be executed there.   [28] See 9.5–9.7 below.

[29] See the Communication on this issue (COM (2007) 693, 13 Nov 2007).

[30] See further 9.5.2 below.

[31] [2005] OJ C 53/1 and [2005] OJ C 198/1. See also the Commission communication on mutual recognition and harmonization of criminal law (COM (2005) 195, 19 May 2005; SEC (2005) 641, 20 May 2005).   [32] See 9.8.1 and 9.8.2 below.

addressed in particular by both a third pillar measure on their position in criminal procedure and by an EC law (as it then was) measure on compensation.[33]

Other relevant measures have included the development of the Schengen Information System (SIS), in particular as regards the inclusion of further data relevant to prosecutions, access to the SIS by judicial authorities, and the creation of second-generation SIS (SIS II), which will in particular include information on EAWs.[34] Also, the Framework Decision on personal data protection, adopted in 2008, also applies to the judicial sector.[35]

There is also a link between measures on substantive criminal law and abolition of the dual criminality principle (the requirement that an (alleged) act must amount to a criminal offence in both States concerned) in the EU's mutual recognition measures, because the harmonization of substantive criminal law reduces the differences between national rules which underlie the principle of dual criminality.[36]

Finally, the Court of Justice had begun to play a significant role as regards interpretation of measures in this area even before the Treaty of Lisbon entered into force, receiving five references for interpretation of the Framework Decision on crime victims' rights,[37] a reference on the validity of the Framework Decision on the European Arrest Warrant;[38] and six references on the interpretation of the same Framework Decision.[39]

9.2.2.3. Basic principles of mutual recognition in criminal law

Although the various EU measures setting out the details of the principle of mutual recognition in criminal law differ in the detail, they have certain common features which it is useful to summarize at the outset.[40] These features remain relevant following the entry into force of the Treaty of Lisbon, as the pre-Lisbon measures will remain in force until replaced or amended, and since post-Lisbon measures appear set to follow the template established by previously adopted measures.

A frequent feature of the mutual recognition measures is that they replace or supplement the Council of Europe measures referred to above, whether those

---

[33] See 9.8.3 below.   [34] See 12.6.1.1 below.

[35] [2008] OJ L 350/60. See 12.6.4 below.   [36] See generally ch 10 below.

[37] Cases: C-105/03 *Pupino* [2005] ECR I-5285; C-467/05 *Dell'Orto* [2007] ECR I-5557; C-404/07 *Katz* [2008] ECR I-7607; C-205/09 *Eredics*, pending (opinion of 1 July 2010); and C-483/09 *Gueye*, pending. On the substance of these cases, see 9.8.3 below.

[38] Case C-303/05 *Advocaten voor de Wereld* [2007] ECR I-3633. On the substance see 9.5.2 below.

[39] Cases: C-66/08 *Koslowski* [2008] ECR I-6041; C-296/08 PPU *Santesteban Goicoechea* [2008] ECR I-6307; C-388/08 PPU *Leymann and Pustovarov* [2008] ECR I-8993; C-123/08 *Wolzenburg* [2009] ECR I-9621; C-261/09 *Mantello*, pending (opinion of 7 Sep 2010); and C-306/09 *IB*, pending (opinion of 6 July 2010). On the substance, see ibid.

[40] The Court of Justice has not yet been asked whether an identical clause must be interpreted the same way in different mutual recognition instruments, although see the opinion in *Mantello* (ibid).

measures have the full support of Member States or only limited support. It should be recalled that even those Council of Europe measures with wide support by Member States have restrictions on their scope and significant possibility for reservations, or provide only a general framework for cross-border criminal law cooperation. So there is a clear perceived 'added value' to the EU's involvement, which principle provides for a far more intensive degree of cooperation. In most cases, the EU mutual recognition measures 'replace' the 'corresponding' provisions of the relevant Council of Europe Conventions and prior EU measures as between Member States, without specifying exactly which provisions of the relevant Conventions are replaced. Most of the EU measures give a power to Member States to retain existing bilateral or multilateral treaties, or to conclude new bilateral or multilateral treaties, which expand or enlarge on the EU mutual recognition measures or simplify and facilitate the procedures for mutual recognition, subject to an obligation to inform the Council and/or Commission about such measures. This begs the question as to when such criteria are met.[41] A further underlying question is whether pursuant to such provisions, Member States can reduce protections regarding human rights in order to facilitate the movement of judgments and decisions between Member States.[42]

During the Amsterdam era, mutual recognition measures always took the form of Framework Decisions, while so far, all of the post-Lisbon proposals and agreed measures have taken the form of Directives. Their application by Member States has been reviewed by the Commission several years after the implementation date. In a few cases, there have been time-limited derogations for a small number of Member States. Usually the mutual recognition measures apply regardless of when the underlying (alleged) criminal offence was committed, but in some cases Member States must or may limit the effect of the measures in time.

As for the substance, each of the mutual recognition measures sets out an obligation to recognize another Member State's judgment or decision, with limited grounds for a refusal to recognize such decisions. The measures refer to the 'issuing' State and the 'executing' State, rather than the 'requesting' and 'requested' State pursuant to Council of Europe measures—demonstrating the more binding degree of obligation as compared to the latter measures, and the more general difference between the principle of mutual recognition in criminal matters and traditional judicial cooperation rules. Although, in the sphere of judicial cooperation, the discretion of the requested State over *whether* to assist the requesting State has been limited by successive treaties, a fundamental degree of discretion over whether to assist the requesting State remains.[43] Conversely, in the system

---

[41] See further 9.10 below.   [42] See 9.3.5 and 9.5.2 below.

[43] See A Weyembergh, 'La reconnaissance mutuelle des decisions judiciaires en matiere penale entre les Etats Membres de l'Union europeenne: mise en perspective' in G de Kerchove and A Weyembergh, eds, *La reconnaissance mutuelle des decisions judiciaires penales dans l'Union europeenne* (Institut d'Etudes Europeennes, 2001), 25–63.

of mutual recognition, the decision of the issuing State (comparable to the 'home State' in free movement law) takes effect *as such* within the legal system of the executing State (comparable to the 'host State' in free movement law), subject to the remaining grounds for refusal to execute that decision. Therefore, the effect of a mutual recognition system is that the executing State has in principle lost some of its sovereign power over the full control of the enforcement of criminal decisions on its territory.

With some mutual recognition measures, there have been issues of material scope (ie defining the concept of criminal proceedings) as well as, to some extent, personal scope (ie limitations based on nationality and/or residence). The traditional ground of refusal as regards criminal cooperation, dual criminality, has been abolished in most cases for a standard list of thirty-two crimes, as defined by the *issuing* State, subject to a three-year threshold of *possible* punishment (ie the actual sentence which was imposed, or which is subsequently imposed in the event of a conviction, is not relevant for this purpose).[44] Other traditional grounds of refusal (political offences, military offences) have also been abolished, and the traditional 'fiscal offence' ground for refusal is now limited by the standard qualification that it cannot be applied merely because the two States in question levy different taxes or duties.

As for human rights, there are standard clauses in the main text and the preambles to the mutual recognition legislation,[45] but almost all of these measures beg the fundamental question as to whether Member States may or must refuse to recognize other Member States' judgments or decisions on human rights grounds—an issue discussed further below.[46] Other remaining grounds for refusal or other forms of restriction applying to most or all Framework Decisions (sometimes subject to further exceptions or special procedural obligations) include: territoriality (ie the possibility of refusing execution because the act concerned took place partly or wholly on the territory of the executing State);[47] *de minimis* rules (ie the amount of a financial penalty, the length of the sentence which was or could be imposed, or the amount of the time of custodial sentence or supervision period still left to serve); double jeopardy or *ne bis in idem*, which raises questions as to whether the general EU double jeopardy rules, including the provisions of the EU Charter of Rights, take precedence over the specific rules in the mutual recognition legislation;[48] the age of criminal responsibility; lapse of time (also known as statute-barring, ie the expiry of a time limit to begin and/or conclude a prosecution); *lis pendens* (ie proceedings for the same offence underway in the

---

[44] For this list of crimes, see Art 2(2) of the Framework Decision establishing the European Arrest Warrant ([2002] OJ L 190/1).   [45] See 9.5–9.7 below, in particular the discussion in 9.5.2.
[46] 9.3.5 and 9.5.2.   [47] On criminal jurisdiction generally, see 11.5 below.
[48] On the general double jeopardy rules, and the case for giving priority to those rules over mutual recognition measures, see 11.8 below.

executing State);[49] immunity; amnesty or pardon—although sometimes this is a question of applicable law; *in absentia* trials, although the rules on this issue in the relevant legislation have been harmonized;[50] and the rule of specialty (ie the ban on prosecuting a person for an offence other than that which motivated the original mutual recognition decision).

The mutual recognition legislation also includes technical rules on processing applications, costs, and languages, as well as the use of standard forms. Decisions or judgments are issued through judges or prosecutors, not ministries as in Council of Europe measures. There are generally strict time limits to comply with (or refuse) the issuing State's decisions, as well as rules on applicable procedural law issues (ie determining when the power to take further decisions is transferred to the executing State, and when it is retained or transferred back to the issuing State).

Finally, an obvious distinction between the Council of Europe legal framework and the EU legal framework is the jurisdiction of the Court of Justice to interpret the relevant EU measures, and thereby to ensure a greater degree of uniform interpretation.

9.2.3. Treaty of Lisbon

The relevant provision of the Treaties following the entry into force of the Treaty of Lisbon is Article 82 of the Treaty on the Functioning of the European Union (TFEU):

1. Judicial cooperation in criminal matters in the Union shall be based on the principle of mutual recognition of judgments and judicial decisions and shall include the approximation of the laws and regulations of the Member States in the areas referred to in paragraph 2 and in Article 83.

The European Parliament and the Council, acting in accordance with the ordinary legislative procedure, shall adopt measures to:

(a) lay down rules and procedures for ensuring recognition throughout the Union of all forms of judgments and judicial decisions;

(b) prevent and settle conflicts of jurisdiction between Member States;

(c) support the training of the judiciary and judicial staff;

(d) facilitate cooperation between judicial or equivalent authorities of the Member States in relation to proceedings in criminal matters and the enforcement of decisions.

2. To the extent necessary to facilitate mutual recognition of judgments and judicial decisions and police and judicial cooperation in criminal matters having a cross-border dimension, the European Parliament and the Council may, by means of directives adopted

---

[49] On the coordination of multiple prosecutions, see 11.6 below.

[50] On the standard *in absentia* exception, see 9.3.5 and 9.5.2 below.

in accordance with the ordinary legislative procedure, establish minimum rules. Such rules shall take into account the differences between the legal traditions and systems of the Member States.

They shall concern:

(a) mutual admissibility of evidence between Member States;
(b) the rights of individuals in criminal procedure;
(c) the rights of victims of crime;
(d) any other specific aspects of criminal procedure which the Council has identified in advance by a decision; for the adoption of such a decision, the Council shall act unanimously after obtaining the consent of the European Parliament.

Adoption of the minimum rules referred to in this paragraph shall not prevent Member States from maintaining or introducing a higher level of protection for individuals.

The Treaty of Lisbon made a fundamental change to the decision-making in this area, applying the 'ordinary legislative procedure' (qualified majority voting (QMV) in Council and joint powers for the EP) in place of the prior rule of unanimity in Council with consultation of the EP. However, Article 82(3) TFEU sets out a special 'emergency brake' rule, allowing a Member State to halt discussions when a measure proposed pursuant to *Article 82(2)* (but *not* Article 82(1)) 'would affect fundamental aspects of its criminal justice system'. This special procedure, which also applies to the adoption of substantive criminal law measures,[51] is discussed in detail in Chapter 2.[52] However, the application of this rule to Article 82(2), but not to Article 82(1), makes it necessary to distinguish between these two legal bases.[53] The power to adopt measures concerning the prevention and settlement of conflicts of jurisdiction (Article 82(1)(b)) is discussed in Chapter 11.[54] Criminal procedure issues might also result from measures adopted regarding Eurojust and the European Public Prosecutor (Articles 85 and 86 TFEU); such issues are also discussed in Chapter 11.[55]

Compared to the previous Treaty provisions, Article 82 TFEU includes a reference to the principle of mutual recognition, which must include approximation of law. The Treaty retains a reference to facilitating (but not *accelerating*) cooperation between judicial or equivalent authorities (but not also ministries). However, the specific reference to facilitating extradition was dropped. There is a specific reference to ensuring mutual recognition instead, along with a further specific reference to judicial training. The previous power regarding ensuring compatibility of national law was replaced by Article 82(2) TFEU. Although the express reference to the basic principle of mutual recognition is new as compared to the previous Treaty rules, this principle had already been used as the basic principle governing the adoption of criminal law legislation within the previous

---

[51] Art 83(3) TFEU; see 10.2.3 below.   [52] See 2.2.3.4.1 above.   [53] See 9.2.4 below.
[54] See 11.6–11.8. On jurisdiction over offences as such, see 11.5.
[55] See 11.9 and 11.10. On the question of competing legal bases which might result, see 9.2.4 below.

third pillar legal framework.[56] The specific requirement that judicial cooperation 'shall include' approximation of procedural and substantive law indicates clearly that the EU cannot limit itself to adopting mutual recognition measures.

In the first nine months after the entry into force of the Treaty of Lisbon, there were five proposals or initiatives in this area: two competing proposals concerning interpretation and translation rights for criminal suspects (the first of which has been agreed between the Council and EP);[57] a proposal to establish a European protection order;[58] a proposal to establish a European Investigation Order;[59] and a proposal on the right to information for criminal suspects.[60] Two substantive criminal law proposals (one of them agreed within the Council) also include a dual legal base relating to procedural law.[61] So far, the 'emergency brake' has not been pulled. The Commission also suggested the conclusion of some treaties in this field that had been signed, but not concluded, before the entry into force of the Treaty of Lisbon.[62]

This area is subject to the enhanced jurisdiction of the Court of Justice for measures adopted after the Treaty of Lisbon; this jurisdiction will also apply to pre-existing measures after the end of a five-year transitional period (so as from 1 December 2014) and to any pre-existing measures which are amended during this transitional period.[63] In the first few months after the entry into force of the Treaty of Lisbon, there were three references to the Court of Justice in this area.[64]

The revised rules on opt-outs from JHA matters also apply to this area.[65] So do the general provisions of Title V of Part Three of the TFEU, in particular the provision that the Union JHA policy must have 'respect for fundamental rights and the different legal systems and traditions of the Member States',[66] and the power to adopt measures concerning cooperation between the administrations of Member States.[67]

For the future, the Stockholm programme and the action plan concerning its implementation provide inter alia for measures on the proceeds of crime (addressing

---

[56] See 9.2.2 above.

[57] [2010] OJ C 69/1 and COM (2010) 82, 9 Mar 2010. See 9.8.2 below.

[58] [2010] OJ C 69/5. See 9.7.6 below.   [59] [2010] OJ C 165/22. See 9.6.1.3 below.

[60] COM (2010) 392, 20 July 2010. See 9.8.2 below.

[61] COM (2010) 94 and 95, 29 Mar 2010, concerning sexual offences against children and trafficking in persons. On the legal base issues, see 9.2.4 below. For the Council's agreement on the latter proposal, see Council doc 10845/10, 10 June 2010; the Council must still agree with the EP on this proposal.   [62] See 9.10 below.

[63] On these transitional rules, see 2.2.3.3 above. The proposal for a European Investigation Order (n 59 above) would repeal one pre-existing measure and replace the corresponding provisions of several others.

[64] Cases: C-1/10 *Salmeron Sanchez*, pending, on the interpretation of the Framework Decision on standing of victims; C-105/10 PPU *Gataev*, withdrawn, concerning the interpretation of the Framework Decision on the European Arrest Warrant; and C-264/10 *Kita*, pending, on the same issue.   [65] See 9.2.5 below.

[66] Art 67(1) TFEU.   [67] Art 74 TFEU. On the general provisions, see 2.2.3.2 above.

freezing and confiscation of assets), recognition of financial penalties, mutual admissibility of evidence, the rights of criminal suspects, and victims' rights.[68]

9.2.4. Competence issues

Before the entry into force of the Treaty of Lisbon, there was a dispute as to whether the EU could harmonize domestic criminal procedural law, in particular because Article 31(1)(a)–(d) of the previous TEU referred essentially to cross-border matters, with only Article 31(1)(c) referring to powers to 'ensur[e] compatibility in rules applicable in the Member States, as may be necessary to improve such cooperation'. This issue remains relevant after the entry into force of the Treaty of Lisbon, as long as there are still pre-existing measures in force whose validity could still be called into question. On this point, the opening words of the previous Article 31(1) TEU provided that '[c]ommon action on judicial cooperation in criminal matters shall *include*' the following list of measures, indicating clearly that this list was non-exhaustive.[69] In any event, a broad interpretation of Article 31(1)(c) could be envisaged, in particular since the harmonization of law on procedural protection for suspects could in fact have facilitated national courts' willingness to cooperate with foreign courts.[70]

As for competence issues following the entry into force of the Treaty of Lisbon, the basic issues arising are the extent of the competence conferred by Article 82 TFEU as such, including the distinction between Article 82(1) and (2),[71] and the distinction between Article 82 and the rest of the JHA provisions. These issues will be examined in turn.

First of all, it is necessary to distinguish Article 82(1) and (2) TFEU, on the grounds that one paragraph is subject to the emergency brake and the other is not.[72] It would certainly be necessary to draw this distinction if a *dual* legal basis of these paragraphs would be considered incompatible due to this difference in decision-making.[73] However, since the emergency brake is not applicable every

---

[68] [2010] OJ C 115/1 and COM (2010) 171, 20 Apr 2010; see also the 'roadmap' on suspects' rights ([2009] OJ C 295/1). See further the summaries of future plans in 9.6–9.10 below.

[69] See similarly the discussion of competence in 10.2.4 below.

[70] This interpretation is confirmed by the Opinions in Cases C-105/03 *Pupino* [2005] ECR I-5285 (paras 48–52) and C-303/05 *Advocaten voor de Wereld* [2007] ECR I-3633 (note 21). See also the Opinion in Case C-467/05 *Dell'Orto* [2007] ECR I-5557, paras 36–37. For a different view, see V Mitsilegas, 'Trust-Building Measures in the European Judicial Area in Criminal Matters: Issues of Competence, Legitimacy and Institutional Balance', in T Balzacq and S Carrera, eds, *Security versus Freedom? A Challenge for Europe's Future* (Ashgate, 2006), 282, who asserts that the previous TEU conferred no competence to adopt measures on criminal procedure.

[71] The discussion here on this point is adapted from S Peers, 'EU Criminal Law and the Treaty of Lisbon' (2008) 33 ELRev (2008) 507 at 510–514.

[72] Furthermore, Art 82(2) requires the use of Directives, whereas Art 82(1) does not.

[73] On the case law on dual legal bases, see 3.2.4 above.

time that Article 82(2) TFEU is used to adopt measures, but will only apply in the exceptional cases where a Member State pulls the brake, then it should be possible to combine the two provisions. On the other hand, it is certainly necessary to distinguish between the two legal bases on the grounds that Article 82(2) is subject to a number of specific requirements ('necessary to facilitate', 'having a cross-border dimension' and 'tak[ing] into account' different national legal traditions) which do not apply to Article 82(1).[74] In the event of a dual legal base being used, an emergency brake could only be pulled as regards those aspects of a proposal that fall within the scope of Article 82(2), and so 'fast-track' enhanced cooperation could only apply to part of the relevant proposal. The remaining provisions could still be adopted separately, and would therefore apply to all Member States. But it is possible that many Member States (and/or the EP) would not want to adopt a mutual recognition measure, for example, unless all the Member States which would be bound by that measure were also bound by a parallel measure harmonizing procedural law (or substantive criminal law, where the emergency brake also applies).[75] A reasonable compromise would be to provide in the mutual recognition measure for broader grounds for refusal to execute decisions of the authorities of the Member State(s) which were not participating in to the parallel measure.[76] The same compromise could also be used to address cases where the UK or Ireland opted into a mutual recognition measure, but out of a parallel measure.

It is surprising to see that Member States were willing to accept the adoption of mutual recognition measures without a veto or at least an emergency brake, given the national constitutional disputes concerning the adoption of the EAW.[77] In light of those disputes, which reflected legitimate national concerns, it would have been preferable to allow for an emergency brake here as well. Moreover, applying an emergency brake to both paragraphs would have avoided the need to distinguish between them.

Having said that, how should Article 82(1) and (2) TFEU be distinguished? First of all, Article 82(1) concerns (inter alia) mutual recognition rules as such, whereas Article 82(2) concerns procedural harmonization in order to *facilitate* (inter alia) mutual recognition. Similarly, Article 82(2) cannot extend to rules concerning training, since Article 82(1) is a *lex specialis* for these issues. As for the power in Article 82(1)(d) to 'facilitate cooperation' as regards criminal proceedings and enforcement of decisions, it cannot extend to the *substance* of the national procedural laws which fall within the scope of Article 82(2), even though the

---

[74] The requirement to 'respect' different national legal systems (set out in Art 67(1)) also applies to Art 82(1), but this is arguably a subtly different obligation than the requirement to take those systems *into account*, as set out in Art 82(2). See the discussion of this point below.

[75] Art 83 TFEU. See 10.2.3 and 10.2.4 below.

[76] See, by analogy, the special rules regarding recognition of UK judgments in Reg 4/2009 on maintenance proceedings ([2009] OJ L 7/1), discussed in 8.2.5 above.   [77] See 9.5.2 below.

latter appears to overlap with the former (since it also concerns 'facilitation' of, inter alia, 'judicial cooperation'). Otherwise the specific safeguards in Article 82(2) could be circumvented.

Applying these principles, Article 82(1) would be a sufficient legal base for adopting measures such as the Framework Decisions on the EAW; freezing orders; the mutual recognition of financial penalties and confiscation orders; the European Evidence Warrant (EEW); the transfer of prisoners; the mutual recognition of criminal sentences; prior convictions and probation/parole and pre-trial orders; mutual assistance and the transfer of information relating to criminal records, as long as the relevant proceedings take place in a judicial context. All of the legislation adopted on these issues before the entry into force of the Treaty of Lisbon was adopted on the basis of the previous Article 31(1)(a) TEU,[78] which was interpreted to encompass mutual recognition as a form of cooperation between administrations, although several measures were additionally adopted on the basis of other provisions of Article 31(1) TEU.[79] Article 82 TFEU provides for two separate powers for mutual recognition on the one hand, and cooperation between judicial authorities on the other.

In particular, it should be observed that the prior measures on the EEW and mutual assistance rules do not concern the *admissibility* of evidence (an issue which falls within the scope of Article 82(2)(a) TFEU), but rather the *transfer* of evidence between Member States, an issue within the scope of Article 82(1). Furthermore, a measure amending the Schengen double jeopardy rules would not concern the rights of suspects as such (Article 82(2)(b)), but rather fall within the scope of Article 82(1), since such a measure would concern mutual recognition (according to the Court of Justice),[80] and possibly also conflicts of jurisdiction.

As for Article 82(2) in particular, the adoption of measures on domestic criminal procedure has to be 'necessary' to 'facilitate mutual recognition and police and [criminal law] cooperation', which has to have a 'cross-border dimension'. Only 'minimum rules' can be adopted, and these rules have to 'take into account' national legal differences. In light of Article 82(2)(d), this list of powers (unlike the list of powers in the prior Article 31(1) TEU) must necessarily be exhaustive.

First of all, the concept of 'minimum' rules is implicitly further defined in the third sub-paragraph of Article 82(2), which provides that Member States are free to introduce or maintain higher standards for individuals. This proviso must mean that Member States are free to provide for higher standards of protection for suspects and victims than the EU measures provide for, but not lower standards.

---

[78] On these measures, see 9.2.2 above.

[79] The EAW Framework Decision also had a legal base of Art 31(1)(b) TEU, while the Framework Decisions on recognition of probation and parole orders, and on recognition of pre-trial orders also had a legal base of Art 31(1)(c) TEU. Moreover, the Framework Decisions on the EEW, the recognition of convictions and criminal records were based generally on Art 31.

[80] See, for instance, Cases C-187/01 and 385/01 *Gozutok and Brugge* [2003] ECR I-1345, para 33.

Next, the requirement to take account of national legal traditions and systems is nearly identical to the general requirement set in Article 67(1) TFEU that the EU must 'respect' such systems and traditions. However, it is arguable that a requirement to 'take into account' is more of a positive obligation than an obligation to 'respect', perhaps entailing an obligation to reflect those differences in the adopted legislation, rather than merely to refrain from damaging national legal systems in that legislation.

This brings us to the most important limitation: the requirement that the measure must be necessary to facilitate mutual recognition and policing and criminal law cooperation with a cross-border dimension. It might be tempting, at first sight, to conclude that this power is be limited to matters which have a specific relationship with cross-border proceedings, like the EU's civil law powers.[81] But the wording of the criminal law power ('cross-border dimension') is broader than the wording of the civil law power ('cross-border implications'). Moreover, the phrase 'cross-border dimensions' also governs the scope of the EU's substantive criminal law powers,[82] and it is hard to believe that the Union's power to harmonize substantive criminal law was intended to be limited to cases where an alleged offence has factual links to more than one Member State. Furthermore, the EU's specific criminal procedure powers would be rendered meaningless if they could only be applied in cross-border proceedings, given that Article 82(1) already sets out a power to regulate criminal proceedings with a purely cross-border nature.

In particular, although rules on mutual admissibility of evidence must necessarily have a link to cross-border proceedings, it will be hard in practice to limit their impact to cross-border cases, given that some degree of harmonization of the laws of evidence is necessary in order to ensure mutual admissibility, and that such harmonization cannot easily be restricted to cases which have a specific cross-border element, given that the evidence might be collected before it was clear that such an element was present. The point applies equally to the EU's powers as regards victims' and suspects' rights (which might also concern evidence issues),[83] a fortiori because the Treaty does not insist upon as strong a cross-border element in these matters as it requires as regards evidence law. The better approach to the limit on the EU's criminal procedure is therefore to insist on a *degree of likelihood* that the rules in question will have a particular impact on cross-border proceedings. This will be the case in particular whenever there is (in effect) a 'free movement clause' in the legislation, which provides specifically that Member States could not refuse to recognize judgments and other decisions of judicial authorities on grounds falling within the scope of a measure adopted pursuant to Article 82(2) TFEU. This would parallel the limits which the Court

---

[81] See 8.2.4 above.   [82] See Art 83(1) TFEU, discussed in 10.2.4 below.
[83] See 9.8.3 below (as regards victims' rights) and Art 6(3)d ECHR (as regards evidence).

has set as regards the comparable general power to harmonize law for the purposes of facilitating the internal market.[84] Of course, it also assumes that Member States would otherwise have the power or even the obligation to refuse to recognize other Member States' criminal law decisions on human rights grounds, an issue examined further below.[85] More generally, it must be kept in mind that measures adopted pursuant to Article 82(2) are expressly not limited to those necessary to facilitate *mutual recognition*, but can facilitate police and criminal law cooperation more generally.

Finally, there are questions regarding the scope of the individual provisions of Article 82(2). In the absence of any specific limit, the power to regulate suspects' rights conferred by Article 82(2)(b) applies to any aspect of the right to a fair trial (other than the double jeopardy rule, as noted above), provided that the general limits on the powers conferred by Article 82(2) are complied with. As for victims' rights, Article 82(2)(c) does not apply to the harmonization of rules concerning *state compensation* of crime victims, which was the subject of a Directive adopted pursuant to the previous 'residual powers' clause of the EC Treaty,[86] because Article 82 TFEU only applies to 'judicial cooperation'. In the absence of any other specific legal base addressing this issue, it remains within the scope of the Treaty's residual powers clause.[87]

The next key issue is the distinction between Article 82 TFEU and other JHA legal bases. As compared to other criminal law powers, Article 82(1) in particular must be distinguished from the substantive criminal law powers set out in Article 83, because the latter Article is subject to the emergency brake procedure.[88] While rules concerning asserting jurisdiction can be regarded as ancillary to the definition of substantive offences, other procedural rules cannot, and the EU can only invoke such powers as the Treaty has conferred upon it. For example, it should be noted that the proposals for Directives on trafficking in persons and sexual exploitation of children include provisions on victim protection, which can be (and are) based on Article 82(2)(a) TFEU.[89]

The Treaty powers relating to Eurojust (Article 85 TFEU) must be distinguished from Article 82(2) in particular, since there is no emergency brake applicable to Article 85. It should follow that any harmonization of national

---

[84] See particularly the tobacco advertising case law: Cases C-376/98 *Germany v EP and Council* [2000] ECR I-8419 and C-380/03 *Germany v EP and Council* [2006] ECR I-11573.

[85] See 9.3.5 and 9.5.2.

[86] Dir 2004/80 ([2004] OJ L 261/15), based on the prior Art 308 EC. On the substance of this Directive, see 9.8.3 below.

[87] Art 308 EC became Art 352 TFEU after the entry into force of the Treaty of Lisbon.

[88] Furthermore, Art 83(2) will in some cases require unanimous voting. See further 10.2.4 below.

[89] For instance, the provisions on victims' rights in the proposed Directives harmonizing the *substantive* law relating to trafficking in persons and offences against children: COM (2010) 95 and 94, 29 Mar 2010.

criminal procedure directly related to the functioning of Eurojust, in particular (but not only) concerning the specific functions of Eurojust mentioned in Article 85(1)(a), (b), and (c). Similarly, the Treaty powers relating to the European Public Prosecutor (Article 86 TFEU) must be distinguished from Article 82 in that Article 86 requires unanimous voting. Again, any measure directly relating to the operation of the European Public Prosecutor, whether it concerns national procedural law or mutual recognition (ie national authorities' recognition of the Prosecutor's decisions and vice versa) must be based on Article 86.[90]

Next, there is also a need to distinguish between Article 82 and Article 87 TFEU, as regards policing powers, given that legislation on some aspects of police cooperation is not subject to an emergency brake (Article 87(2)), whereas measures on operational police cooperation are subject to unanimous voting (Article 87(3)).[91] On this point, it should be emphasized that Article 82 only extends to *judicial* proceedings, arguably as defined by Member States,[92] not to cooperation between police or other non-judicial authorities. The policing legal bases would have to be used instead (or in addition) to adopt legislation on such issues. Although by way of exception, Article 82(1)(d) extends to authorities which are *equivalent* to judicial authorities, this extension is clearly limited in scope by the *ejusdem generis* rule of interpretation, considering also that the policing provisions of the Treaty are a *lex specialis*. Although Article 82(1)(d) is not expressly limited to judicial authorities, the whole of Article 82(1) is limited in scope to '[j]udicial cooperation' and Article 82(1)(d) is expressly limited in scope to criminal proceedings. Any other interpretation could render Article 87 redundant. In any case, it is hard to see how police officers are 'equivalent' to judges. Applying this rule, it may be doubted whether some of the provisions in the proposed Directive on the European investigation order fall within the scope of Article 82.[93]

It is also necessary to distinguish between Article 82 and the civil law powers set out in Article 81 TFEU, given that civil law measures cannot be subject to an emergency brake, can only be proposed by the Commission, are subject to a stronger 'cross-border' requirement, and can potentially (and in fact usually) take the form of Regulations. The issue of distinguishing between these legal bases arose shortly after the entry into force of the Treaty of Lisbon, when the Commission queried the correct legal base for the proposed Directive on a European protection order,[94] since some Member States address such issues by means of civil or administrative law, not criminal law.

---

[90] For instance, rules on the 'admissibility of evidence' referred to in Art 86(3). For more on Arts 85 and 86, see 11.2.4 below.

[91] For further details on these provisions, including the distinction between Art 87(2) and (3), see 12.2.4 below.

[92] This follows from the requirement of respect for national legal systems, as set out in Art 67(1) TFEU.   [93] [2010] OJ C 165/22. On the substance, see 9.6.1.3 and 12.7.1 below.

[94] [2010] OJ C 69/5. On the substance, see 9.7.6 below.

It is understood that the Council legal service took the view that the proposal was correctly based on Article 82 TFEU, since the prevention of crime could fall within the scope of that Article.[95] On this point, while it is true that Article 67(3) TFEU refers to prevention of crime, more specific references to crime prevention are set out in Articles 84, 87(1), and 88(1) TFEU, not in Article 82.[96] The requirement to respect different legal systems, as set out in Article 67(1) TFEU, instead points toward the need to respect the different approaches that Member States have towards addressing this issue. So a measure based wholly on Article 82 can only address issues connected to criminal law proceedings. It would be possible to adopt a measure based jointly on Articles 81 and 82 TFEU—but it would have to be proposed by the Commission.

On the same issues, there are several criminal law measures that refer to issues which arguably fall within the scope of civil law, such as restitution of property,[97] compensation of victims by offenders, and return of property for crime victims.[98] Conversely, EU civil law measures address issues such as civil claims related to criminal proceedings and representation in criminal trials for non-intentional offences.[99]

Finally, it is necessary to distinguish the whole of Article 82, and Article 82(1)(d) in particular, from Article 74 TFEU, which is a legal base for the adoption of measures concerning cooperation between national administrations, and between national administrations and the Commission. Such measures are non-legislative acts, adopted by QMV in the Council with *consultation* of the EP. The obvious distinction between Articles 74 and 82 TFEU is that the former concerns cooperation between *civil servants*, whereas the latter concerns cooperation between *judges*.[100]

9.2.5. Territorial scope

Prior to the entry into force of the Treaty of Lisbon, there were no opt-outs for Member States in this area, except for the delayed application of the relevant Schengen *acquis* to the UK and Ireland. The *acquis* applied to the UK from

---

[95] See Council doc 6538/10, 17 Feb 2010.

[96] See also the analysis of the Commission legal service (Council doc 10005/10, 19 May 2010), which points out *inter alia* that the EU cannot harmonize national law on crime prevention pursuant to Art 84 TFEU.   [97] See the Convention on mutual assistance, discussed in 9.6.1 below.

[98] See the Framework Decision on crime victims, discussed in 9.8.3 below. Note also the exclusion of damages and restitution claims from the Framework Decision on financial penalties ([2005] OJ L 76/16, Art 1(b) of the Framework Decision).

[99] See Cases C-7/98 *Krombach* [2000] ECR I-1935 and 157/80 *Rinkau* [1981] ECR 1391. On the *Krombach* case, see further 9.3 and 11.2.4 below.

[100] On Art 74 generally, see 2.2.3.2 above.

1 January 2005,[101] and will also apply to Ireland at a date to be decided.[102] The EU rules and the Schengen *acquis* relating to criminal procedural law applied fully to the new Member States from their dates of accession (1 May 2004 and 1 January 2007),[103] and also applied fully to Denmark.[104]

The position changed with the entry into force of the Treaty of Lisbon, which extended the British and Irish opt-outs to new measures in the area of policing and criminal law, and provided for special rules if the UK and Ireland opted out of a measure which amends a measure which already applies to them.[105] In practice, the UK and Ireland have both opted into the Member States' initiative on suspects' rights to interpretation and translation, and the UK has opted in to the proposals on the European protection order and the European investigation order;[106] both have opted into the treaties in this area with Norway, Iceland, and Japan.[107] Their opt-in decisions regarding the proposal on the right to information are not yet known. On the other hand, Denmark is now excluded from measures in this area, unless those measures build upon the Schengen *acquis*.[108] If post-Lisbon measures are adopted which amend or repeal pre-Lisbon acts which already apply to the UK, Ireland, or Denmark, and those Member States do not participate in such measures, there is a possibility that their participation in the relevant pre-Lisbon acts will be terminated. In that case, the relevant Council of Europe treaties will then (re-)apply between those Member States and all other Member States.

As for non-Member States, pursuant to their association with the Schengen *acquis*, the relevant rules and measures building upon them (including aspects of the 2000 EU Convention on mutual assistance and its 2001 Protocol) also apply to Norway, Iceland, Switzerland, and (in future) Liechtenstein.[109] However, Switzerland and Liechtenstein have an exemption as regards any future measures building on the *acquis* which eliminate the 'double criminality' rule as regards search and seizure for offences relating to direct taxation.[110] It should be noted

---

[101] See the decision on UK participation in Schengen ([2000] OJ L 131/43) and on the practical application of that decision ([2004] OJ L 395/70). For more detail on UK participation, see 2.2.5.1.3 above.

[102] See the decision on Irish participation in Schengen ([2002] OJ L 64/20). For more detail on Irish participation, see 2.2.5.1.3 above.

[103] For more detail on accession and the Schengen *acquis*, see 2.2.5.3 above.

[104] On the substance of that *acquis*, see 9.2.1 above.

[105] For the detail, see 2.2.5.1.2 and 2.2.5.1.3 above.

[106] On the substance of these measures, see 9.8.2 and 9.7.6 below. However, there is a possibility that the UK will nonetheless be excluded from participation in the latter measure: see 2.2.5.1.2 above.

[107] See Council docs 9262/10, 3 May 2010, and 7670/10, 7673/10, and 7676/10, 18 Mar 2010.

[108] See 2.2.5.2 above.   [109] See 2.2.5.4 above.

[110] Art 7(5) of the Schengen association treaty with Switzerland ([2008] OJ L 53/52) and Art 5(5) of the Protocol to that treaty concerning the association of Liechtenstein (COM (2006) 752, 1 Dec 2006). It should be noted that the proposed Directive establishing the European Investigation Order (see 9.6.1.3 below) would trigger these exceptions.

that the Court of Justice has implicitly assumed that it has jurisdiction to rule on the Schengen association treaty with Norway and Iceland.[111]

The EU, Norway, and Iceland have also signed a treaty committing themselves to implement all of the provisions of the EU mutual assistance Convention and its Protocol which do *not* fall within the scope of the Schengen *acquis*,[112] as well as a treaty establishing a surrender procedure between the EU Member States and Iceland and Norway.[113] The latter agreement is very similar to the Framework Decision on the EAW, but contains variations, particularly allowing for the continuation of a 'political offence' exception and the option to refuse to extradite States' own nationals, subject to some limitations.[114] Neither of these treaties is yet in force.[115]

Finally, Switzerland and the EU (more precisely, the EC (as it was then) and the EU's Member States) have concluded a treaty which concerns the particular issue of protection of the EU's financial interests. It contains a number of provisions relevant to mutual legal assistance.[116] The Commission has proposed the signature and conclusion of a parallel treaty with Liechtenstein.[117]

9.3. Human rights

9.3.1. Right to a fair trial

As noted at the outset, the human rights principle of greatest relevance to criminal procedure is the right to a fair trial. This right is set out in national constitutions, Article 6 ECHR, and Article 14 of the International Covenant on Civil and Political Rights (ICCPR). Article 6(2) ECHR expressly sets out a right to presumption of innocence in criminal cases, and Article 6(3) sets out minimum rights to be informed promptly of an accusation (Article 6(3)(a)); to have time and facilities for a defence (Article 6(3)(b)); to have access to a defence lawyer and free legal aid if 'the interests of justice' require (Article 6(3)(c)); to examine witnesses against and call witnesses for the defence (Article 6(3)(d)); and to 'to have the free assistance of an interpreter if he [or she] cannot understand or speak the language used in court' (Article 6(3)(e)). The Seventh Protocol to the ECHR, which has been ratified by a large majority of Member States, also includes the right to an

---

[111] Case C-436/03 *Van Esbroek* [2006] ECR I-2623.   [112] [2004] OJ L 26/1.

[113] [2006] OJ L 292/1. See also the earlier Decision defining the Schengen extradition *acquis* as regards Norway and Iceland ([2003] OJ L 76/25).

[114] For details of the EAW, see 9.5.2 below.

[115] See the proposals to conclude the treaties: COM (2009) 704 and 705, 17 Dec 2009.

[116] Arts 25–38 of treaty ([2009] OJ L 46/6). The treaty entered into force as regards most Member States, the EC, and Switzerland on 8 Apr 2009 (see [2009] OJ L 177/7).

[117] COM (2009) 644, 23 Nov 2009.

appeal in criminal cases, the right to compensation for wrongful conviction, and freedom from double jeopardy; these rights also appear in the ICCPR.[118]

In light of the agreement upon EU measures in this field,[119] the case law on the right to an interpreter pursuant to Article 6(3)(e) ECHR should be examined in more detail. According to the European Court of Human Rights, the right applies 'not only to oral statements made at the trial hearing but also to documentary material and the pre-trial proceedings', and in particular to 'the translation or interpretation of all those documents or statements in the proceedings instituted against him which it is necessary for him to understand or to have rendered into the court's language in order to have the benefit of a fair trial'. However, the right 'does not go so far as to require a written translation of all items of written evidence or official documents in the procedure', but 'should be such as to enable the defendant to have knowledge of the case against him and to defend himself, notably by being able to put before the court his version of the events'. Moreover, 'the obligation of the competent authorities is not limited to the appointment of an interpreter but, if they are put on notice in the particular circumstances, may also extend to a degree of subsequent control over the adequacy of the interpretation provided'.[120] The Court has clarified that oral linguistic assistance (instead of translation) may be sufficient as regards documents; that the key issues are the 'linguistic knowledge' of the defendant, the nature of the offence with which the defendant is charged and any communications addressed to him by the domestic authorities; and that, even though the conduct of the defence is mainly a matter for the accused and his or her lawyer, the domestic courts are the 'ultimate guardians' of the right.[121] The right to 'free' assistance obviously means that the accused cannot be required to pay the relevant costs.[122] However, a waiver of the right is possible if the waiver can 'be established in an unequivocal manner and be attended by minimum safeguards commensurate with its importance' and if that waiver does 'not run counter to any important public interest'.[123]

More generally, the case law on the right to a fair trial in criminal cases is complex and voluminous,[124] but what about the particular issue of the application of Article 6 in cross-border cases?[125] In the well-known *Soering* judgment, which ruled that a State could not extradite a person to another country where there was

---

[118] Arts 2–4, Seventh Protocol. For ratification of the Protocol by Member States, see Appendix I. Double jeopardy is discussed in 11.3.1 below.

[119] See 9.8.2 below. Note also the obligations to inform a person of the reasons for any arrest or criminal charges, and of the nature and cause of any criminal accusation, 'in a language which he [or she] understands' (Arts 5(2) and 6(3)(a) ECHR).

[120] See, for instance, *Kamasinski v Austria*, (A-168), para 74, referring also to *Ludicke, Belkacem and Koç v Germany* (A-29), para 48.   [121] See paras 70–72 of *Hermi v Italy*, 18 Oct 2006.

[122] *Ozturk v Germany* (A-73).   [123] *Protopapa v Turkey*, 24 Feb 2009, para 82.

[124] For a detailed analysis, see S Trechsel and S Summers, *Human Rights in Criminal Proceedings* (OUP, 2005).   [125] On the parallel asylum issues, see 5.3 above.

a 'real risk' of treatment contrary to Article 3 ECHR,[126] the Human Rights Court also ruled that such a removal could in principle violate Article 6 ECHR:

> The right to a fair trial in criminal proceedings, as embodied in Article 6 holds a prominent place in a democratic society. The Court does not exclude that an issue might exceptionally be raised under Article 6 by an extradition decision in circumstances where the fugitive has suffered or risks suffering a flagrant denial of a fair trial in the requesting country . . . [127]

There was no violation of Article 6 on the facts in *Soering*, or in the later judgment in *Mamatkulov and Abdurasulovic v Turkey*,[128] but in the subsequent *Bader* judgment, the Court found a violation of Article 6 due to a planned execution following an unfair trial in the requesting State.[129] The Human Rights Court subsequently found that any removal to face the death penalty in another State, regardless of the fairness of the trial, is a breach of Articles 2 and 3 ECHR in light of the Thirteenth Protocol to the ECHR, which rules out the death penalty in any circumstances.[130] In a number of cases, the Human Rights Court has decided that it is unnecessary to rule on the Article 6 argument, where it had already found a breach of Article 3 if a person were to be extradited.[131]

A judgment on Article 5 ECHR (which concerns limits on detention) is relevant by analogy. In *Drozd and Janousek*,[132] the Human Rights Court considered whether France had responsibility under Article 5 for enforcing a criminal sentence which had been passed following a questionable procedure in the criminal courts of Andorra. Arguably, the detention breached Article 5(1)(a), which specifies that detention can be lawful only (inter alia) after conviction by a competent court. The argument was rejected by a narrow majority of the Court on the grounds that:[133]

> As the Convention does not require the Contracting Parties to impose its standards on third States or territories, France was not obliged to verify whether the proceedings which resulted in the conviction were compatible with all the requirements of Article 6 (art. 6) of the Convention. To require such a review of the manner in which a court not bound by the Convention had applied the principles enshrined in Article 6 (art. 6) would also thwart the current trend towards strengthening international cooperation in

---

[126] *Soering v UK* (A-161). On the question of whether life imprisonment falls within the scope of Art 3, see the admissibility decision in *Ahmad and others v UK*, 6 July 2010.

[127] Para 113 of the judgment, ibid. [128] [2005] ECHR-I.

[129] *Bader v Sweden* [2005] ECHR-XI.

[130] *Kaboulov v Ukraine*, 19 Nov 2009 and *Al-Saadoon and Mufdhi v UK*, 2 Mar 2010, para 123; note that the latter judgment expressly rejected the argument that the trial in the requesting State would be or had been a 'flagrant denial of justice'. Ultimately, the Court ruled against the merits of the Art 2 issue in the first judgment, and did not find it necessary to rule on the merits of the Art 2 point in the second judgment, as it had found a violation of Art 3.

[131] For instance, see *Kaboulov* (ibid); *Baysakov and others v Ukraine*, 18 Feb 2010; *Ismoilov and Others v Russia*, 24 Apr 2008, and by analogy, *Saadi v Italy*, 28 Feb 2008.

[132] Judgment of 26 June 1992 (A-240). [133] Para 110 of the judgment.

the administration of justice, a trend which is in principle in the interests of the persons concerned. The Contracting States are, however, obliged to refuse their co-operation if it emerges that the conviction is the result of a flagrant denial of justice [referring *'mutatis mutandis'* to *Soering*].

The Court then went on to take note of a French declaration that it would refuse to cooperate with the Andorran government if it was 'manifestly contrary to the provisions of Article 6... or the principles embodied therein', and found confirmation in French case law refusing extradition unless there were a retrial following an *in absentia* judgment or in cases where a person faced the death penalty. So in the Court's view, it had 'not been shown that in the circumstances of the case France was required to refuse its co-operation in enforcing the sentences'.[134]

So there is a '*Soering* effect' to Article 6 ECHR, applicable not just to extradition but to the enforcement of foreign custodial sentences. Logically, the principle is also applicable to enforcement of financial penalties and other forms of cross-border cooperation in the same way; but unlike the '*Soering* effect' as it applies to Article 3 ECHR, the principle does not appear to require full application of Article 6 ECHR in the other State.[135] Rather it only applies where there is a 'flagrant denial' of justice. Moreover, the standard of proof for application of the principle appears to be higher than the 'real risk' threshold applicable to Article 3 ECHR. In fact, in *Drozd and Janousek* the majority of the Court did not examine the Andorran proceedings to see if such a flagrant denial had taken place, or even the French system for potentially refusing cooperation to see whether cooperation had been wrongly refused in this case. A concurring opinion apparently suggested that the existence of the opportunity for a review in the requested State's legal system should always be sufficient to defeat any claim that the '*Soering* effect' applies to Article 6 in a particular case.[136]

Does Article 6 ECHR apply to the extradition proceedings *themselves*? The European Court of Human Rights has ruled that it does not apply to extradition of foreigners,[137] although the Court has not yet ruled in a judgment as to whether or not Article 6 covers proceedings for extradition of *nationals*. Similarly, in principle Article 6 does not apply to proceedings regarding the transfer of sentenced persons (and the transfer of sentences), because that

---

[134] Para 111 of the judgment. For a recent detailed analysis, see *Ahmad and others v UK*, n 125 above.

[135] On both points, see further the concurring opinion of Judge Matscher in the *Drozd and Janousek* judgment.

[136] See Judge Matscher's opinion (ibid), arguing expressly that 'the requested State must, to be sure, carry out a review of some kind. Such a review is provided for in all legislative systems, the thoroughness of the review and the conditions of its exercise being left to the legislation of the requested State'. The evidence for his assertion about 'all' systems carrying out a review is not offered.

[137] See, for instance, *Mamatkulov and Abdurasulovic* (n 127 above), paras 81–83.

Article does not apply to the execution of sentences.[138] However, the position is different when the transfer of persons is part of a plea bargain 'package', ie where the person concerned pleaded guilty in part in return for a promise that the sentencing State would request that the State administering the sentence would convert that sentence rather than administer it, with the result that the person concerned would spend less time in prison after the transfer. In such a case, Article 6 at least confers a right of access to court in order to challenge the sentencing State's decision to renege on its commitments.[139] It should also be noted that the right to the presumption of innocence *does* apply in the context of extradition proceedings, and so presumably applies to other cross-border criminal proceedings.[140]

What other Article 6 issues might arise as regards cross-border proceedings? As regards freezing orders, which are provisional measures pending a trial, it is arguable that since Article 6 ECHR guarantees a trial within a reasonable time, an executing State must ensure that once that reasonable time period is breached, the assets must be released.[141] As for confiscation orders following a criminal conviction, the right to a fair hearing (Article 6(1) ECHR) is applicable, but the presumption of innocence (Article 6(2)) is not, since the conviction has already been handed down.[142] Conversely, if the person concerned has been acquitted of the crime, any confiscation of assets on the basis that the person concerned can nevertheless be presumed to have committed that crime does violate Article 6(2).[143]

Since Article 6 applies throughout criminal proceedings, Article 6(1) should apply to freezing orders *mutatis mutandis* once a 'charge' is brought,[144] but in the absence of a conviction it is arguable that Article 6(2) will apply. Moreover, third parties have no standing under Article 6 ECHR when their property is seized or frozen in the context of proceedings against another person, and confiscation procedures in the absence of a criminal charge also fall outside the scope of Article 6.[145]

As for the compatibility of *in absentia* trials with the ECHR, it is clear from Strasbourg case law that the right to presence and representation at a criminal trial is breached not only where the trial goes ahead even when a defendant is

---

[138] Decisions in *Veermae v Finland* (15 Mar 2005) and *Szabo v Sweden* (27 June 2006). See also 9.3.2 and 9.3.4 below.

[139] See *Buijen v Germany* and *Smith v Germany*, judgments of 1 Apr 2010.

[140] See *Ismoilov* (n 130 above).

[141] See *Patrikova v Bulgaria*, 4 Mar 2010, where there was a breach of Art 6 due to the unreasonable time period it took to decide on a damages action following an unlawful seizure of goods.

[142] *Phillips v UK* (Reports 2001-VII).   [143] *Geerings v Netherlands*, 1 Mar 2007.

[144] See P van Dijk and G van Hoof, *Theory and Practice of the European Convention on Human Rights* (4th edn, Intersentia, 2006), 539–542.

[145] See respectively judgments of 24 Oct 1986 in *AGOSI v UK* (A 108) and of 5 May 1995 in *Air Canada v UK* (A316-A).

not informed of the proceedings,[146] but also, in some cases where a defendant *is* informed and chooses not to attend, wishes to send a legal representative in his or her place, and the representative is not allowed to appear.[147] Furthermore, the Human Rights Court has expressly stated that a breach of Article 6 which is committed due to *in absentia* proceedings should in principle be remedied by holding a retrial.[148] The *in absentia* judgments of the Human Rights Court are also relevant to detention, because detention following a national *in absentia* judgment which breached Article 6 standards, in the absence of a retrial, will breach Article 5.[149]

Another Article 6 point is the admissibility of illegally obtained evidence. The Human Rights Court has ruled that it is not a breach of Article 6 to admit evidence obtained in breach of Article 8 ECHR (which protects the right to private and family life).[150] On the other hand, the use of evidence obtained in breach of Article 3 entails a breach of Article 6,[151] except where it is clear that the conviction was not based on the evidence obtained from the torture.[152] Even where the admission of evidence obtained illegally would not violate the ECHR, it might nonetheless be in breach of national law.

It is clear that the standards of Article 6 in relation to a fair trial must be upheld even where evidence, in particular the evidence of witnesses, is submitted from a foreign country pursuant to a mutual assistance treaty.[153]

Finally, an issue related to Article 6 is the protection of the right to property, pursuant to the First Protocol to the ECHR. It is clear from the case law of the European Court of Human Rights that the seizure or confiscation of property falls within Article 1 of that Protocol, which governs the deprivation of property or control of its use or enjoyment.[154] This Article requires the use, control, or deprivation of property to be a lawful measure in pursuit of a legitimate aim, subject to the requirement of proportionality, although the extent of the Strasbourg Court's supervision of State action is less stringent than it is under Articles

---

[146] Case law beginning with *Colozza v Italy* (Series A-89); see particularly the Grand Chamber judgment of 1 Mar 2006 in *Sedjovic v Italy*.

[147] See *Poitrimol v France* (A 277-A), followed inter alia in *Lala v Netherlands* (A 297-A), *Pelladoah v Netherlands* (A 297-B), *Krombach v France* (Reports 2001-II), *Van Geyseghem v Belgium* (Reports 1999-I), and *Khalfaoui v France* (Reports 1999-IX). Compare with *Medenica v Switzerland* (Reports 2001-VI), where a trial in the absence of the accused did not violate Art 6, because his lawyers were able to attend and represent him, and *Eliazer v Netherlands* (Reports 2001-X), where the accused was not denied representation at his initial trial, but only an appeal right.   [148] See *Sedjovic* (n 145 above).

[149] *Stoichkov v Bulgaria*, 24 Mar 2005, where there was also a breach of Art 5(4) for lack of judicial review and Art 5(5) for lack of compensation for the illegal detention.

[150] See, for instance, *Khan v UK* (Reports 2000-V).

[151] See *Jalloh v Germany* (ECHR 2006-IX) and *Harutyunyan v Armenia* (ECHR 2007-XIII).

[152] *Gafgen v Germany*, Grand Chamber, 1 June 2010.

[153] See *AM v Italy* (Reports 1999-IX).

[154] See, for instance, *Phillips v UK* (n 141 above) and *Plakhteyev and Plakhteyeva v Ukraine*, 12 Mar 2009.

8–11 ECHR.[155] Applied to criminal proceedings, States can justify seizure or confiscation of property (presumably including seizure for its use as evidence) in light of the objectives underlying criminal law.[156] The rules on the right to property are also applicable to the payment of fines.[157]

9.3.2. Legality of criminal law

Article 7 ECHR provides for the legality, and particularly the non-retroactivity of criminal law. This Article is examined later as regards substantive criminal law and criminal jurisdiction,[158] but is it also relevant to criminal procedure?

Article 7 clearly applies to any judgment imposing criminal penalties, and the Strasbourg Court has ruled that it also applies to confiscation orders following a criminal conviction.[159] The 'starting point' for considering the applicability of Article 7 is whether a measure is imposed 'following conviction for a "criminal offence"',[160] which rules out its applicability to pre-trial measures. Indeed, the Human Rights Court has ruled out the applicability of Article 7 to pre-trial detention.[161]

As for applying Article 7 to criminal procedure, the Human Rights Court left the issue open in *Coeme and others v Belgium* as regards limitation periods for prosecution.[162] However, the Court did assume, without even considering the point, that the removal of an immunity fell within the scope of Article 7.[163] Article 7 also applies to retroactive applications of extended detention and confiscation,[164] and requires clarity of the law (but not non-retroactivity) as regards changes of early release policies.[165]

It is not clear whether a '*Soering* effect' requiring a refusal to assist with extradition or to execute other foreign criminal decisions applies to Article 7, with the consequence that there would be an obligation not to assist another State to enforce a criminal penalty that was retroactive or unclear, by means of extradition or the transfer of a sentence.[166] If so, the question would then arise whether the

---

[155] See A Riza Coban, *Protection of Property Rights within the European Convention on Human Rights* (Ashgate, 2004).

[156] See particularly *Phillips* (n 141 above), along with *Air Canada* (n 144 above), where criminal law considerations were relevant even though no criminal charge was laid, and *AGOSI* (ibid) where the conduct of an innocent importer was relevant to whether the confiscation of property was proportionate.   [157] See *Mamikadis v Greece*, 11 Jan 2007.

[158] See 10.3.1 and 11.3.1 below.   [159] *Welch v UK* (A 307-A), particularly para 28.

[160] Ibid.   [161] *Stephens v Malta (No 1)*, 21 Apr 2009.   [162] Reports 2000-VII.

[163] *SW v UK* and *CR v UK* (A335-B and A335-C).

[164] See respectively *M v Germany*, 17 Dec 2009 and *Nadtochiy v Ukraine*, 15 May 2008.

[165] *Kafkaris v Cyprus*, 12 Feb 2008. On recidivism and Art 7 EHCR, see *Achour v France*, 29 Mar 2006.

[166] Since Art 7 does not apply to pre-trial proceedings, any *Soering* effect could only apply as regards extradition or the transfer of a prisoner to serve a sentence already handed down in breach of Art 7. The Human Rights Court has ruled that Art 7 does not apply to the transfer of a prisoner

standard of review was the same as that applying to Article 6 (given the close links between Articles 6 and 7), or the same as that applying to Article 3 (given that Articles 3 and 7 are both non-derogable rights, pursuant to Article 15 ECHR). One such case reached the European human rights bodies, but was rejected on the merits.[167]

9.3.3. Search and seizure

Article 8(1) ECHR recognizes the right to respect for family life, private life, the home and correspondence. This right is infringed in principle by searches of private property, whether a home or (in at least some cases) a business, and by seizures of items from such private premises. However, Article 8(2) permits interferences with Article 8 rights on grounds relating to public safety and public order. Such interferences must be 'in accordance with law', which includes consideration of the quality and foreseeability of the law, as well as necessary and proportionate to the legitimate aim pursed by the interference. In a number of cases involving searches and seizure, the Human Rights Court has ruled that the 'prescribed by law' standard was not met.[168] As regards the principles of necessity and proportionality, in search and seizure cases the Human Rights Court takes into account the existence of 'adequate and effective safeguards against abuse', and 'the severity of the offence in connection with which the search and seizure was effected, the manner and circumstances in which the order had been issued, in particular further evidence available at that time, the content and scope of the order, having particular regard to the nature of the premises searched and the safeguards taken in order to confine the impact of the measure to reasonable bounds, and the extent of possible repercussions on the reputation of the person affected by the search'.[169]

9.3.4. Detention[170]

Detention for the purposes of extradition is authorized by Article 5 ECHR, provided that the detention is lawful (Article 5(1)(f)),[171] subject to the other

---

as such (*Szabo* decision, n 137 above), but that is a distinct question from the issue of whether there is an obligation to refuse assistance where the requesting State's judgment breached Art 7.

[167] *Bakhish v Germany* (Commission decision, 31 Oct 1997). On the position in EU law as regards the abolition of the dual criminality rule, see 9.3.5 below.

[168] For example, see *LM v Italy*, 8 Mar 2005 and *Sallinen and others v Finland*, 27 Sep 2005.

[169] See *Buck v Germany*, judgment of 28 Apr 2005, para 33.

[170] On the issue of detention in the context of immigration and asylum law, see 7.3.2 above.

[171] Note that detention for extradition purposes is not subject to Art 5(1)(c) ECHR, which concerns pre-trial detention, with the consequence that Art 5(3) ECHR, which sets out rules on bail in such cases, is not applicable: see *Soldatenko v Ukraine*, 23 Oct 2008.

provisions of Article 5 guaranteeing information for the detainee (Article 5(2)), judicial review (Article 5(4)), and compensation for wrongful detention (Article 5(5)).[172] As for enforcement of foreign sentences, detention to this end is not lawful without some legal basis in force, either with a basis in national law or based on the ratification by both States concerned of the relevant international treaty.[173] Neither is detention for the purpose of extradition if the person concerned is a national of the State concerned, if that State does not extradite its nationals.[174]

The ECtHR has ruled that if a person is detained for a very lengthy period purely because of a drawn-out extradition process, a State may be responsible for breaching Article 5.[175] Article 5 may also be breached if extradition is not pursued with due diligence,[176] and Article 3 may be breached if prison conditions which the detainee experiences pending extradition are sufficiently appalling.[177] But where the warrant itself is defective, the State which *issued* the warrant is liable for the wrongful detention in the executing State, until after the annulment of the warrant, when the executing State becomes liable.[178]

As we have seen, Article 5 has limited application when a person is detained following a conviction in another State;[179] this was followed as regards Article 5(4) in the *Irirbarne Perez* judgment.[180] Equally, Article 5 is not breached by the transfer of a sentenced person who will serve a greater period in prison in practice as a result of the transfer (ie because the early release policies in the State which the prisoner was transferred to are less generous), as long as the actual criminal sentence initially imposed is not increased, unless there is a 'flagrant disproportionality' as regards the time which will actually be served.[181] However, a potential '*Soering* effect', which would prevent extradition or removal to face arbitrary detention, has been recognized in principle in the case law.[182] Finally, Article 3 ECHR precludes extradition or another form of transfer of a prisoner to another country if that removal would result in the person concerned facing prison conditions in *that* State which were so appalling as to breach Article 3 standards.[183]

---

[172] For an application of all these provisions, see for instance, *Bordovskiy v Russia*, 8 Feb 2005. On the requirement of sufficiently precise rules governing detention for the purpose of extradition (ie 'lawful' detention), see, for example, *Koktysh v Ukraine*, 10 Dec 2009.

[173] See *Grori v Albania*, 7 July 2009 and more generally *Garkavyy v Ukraine*, 18 Feb 2010.

[174] See *Garabayev v Russia* (ECHR 2007-VII) and *Garkavyy*, ibid. See equally as regards refugees, if national law rules out their extradition, *Eminbeyli v Russia*, 26 Feb 2009.

[175] *Scott v Spain* (Reports 1996-VI).   [176] For example, see *Quinn v France* (A 311).

[177] See, for instance, *Koktysh v Ukraine* (n 171 above).

[178] *Stephens v Malta* (n 160 above).   [179] *Drozd* and *Janousek* (n 131 above).

[180] A325-C.   [181] *Veermae* and *Szabo* (n 137 above).

[182] See particularly decision in *Bankovic and others v UK and others*, 12 Dec 2001.

[183] See *Ryabikin v Russia*, judgment of 19 June 2008.

9.3.5. Application to EU law

This subsection will examine in turn: the sources and scope of the relevant human rights rules in EU law; the human rights implications of the principle of 'mutual trust' in other Member States, which forms a key part of the EU's mutual recognition principle in this area; and then two specific issues as regards EU mutual recognition legislation, namely the rules on *in absentia* trials in EU legislation and the application of the principle of the legality and non-retroactivity. Furthermore, the standard rules in EU mutual recognition legislation on human rights are discussed further below,[184] as is the agreed and planned EU legislation on criminal suspects' rights.[185]

On the sources and scope of the relevant EU human rights rules, it should first of all be re-emphasized that the general principles of EU law, and the EU Charter of Fundamental Rights, are only relevant where a case falls within the scope of EU law.[186] Of course, the majority of criminal proceedings are not linked to EU law. But nonetheless, any criminal proceedings with a link to non-JHA EU law, or any proceedings falling within the scope of any EU measure addressing substantive or procedural criminal law, are governed by the general principles and the Charter.[187]

As for the specific rights protected, the Court of Justice has recognized the right to a fair trial as part of the general principles on numerous occasions, in particular in the context of criminal proceedings, and has made references to ECHR jurisprudence in that context.[188] Although the Court has not yet had the occasion to rule on human rights as regards detention cases, there is little doubt that it would rule that standards at least equal to those guaranteed by the ECHR are recognized as general principles of EU law. On the other hand, the Court has affirmed on many occasions that the right, for example to private life, and the principle of non-retroactivity and legality of criminal law are recognized as general principles of EU law.[189]

The EU Charter of Rights contains a general rule on the right to a fair trial, as well as specific rules on defence rights and the non-retroactivity and legality of penal offences, as well as detention, the right to private life, and a ban on removal to face torture, etc or the death penalty.[190] The Court of Justice has made specific

---

[184] See in particular 9.5.2.

[185] See 9.8.2. See also 10.3.2 and 11.3.2 below, as regards the human rights aspects of EU law as regards substantive criminal law and criminal jurisdiction (including double jeopardy).

[186] See further 2.3 above and in the criminal law context, Case C-299/95 *Kremzov* [1997] ECR I-2629.

[187] See Cases: C-521/04 P *Tillack* [2005] ECR I-3103; C-105/03 *Pupino* [2005] ECR I-5285; C-303/05 *Advocaten voor de Wereld* [2007] ECR I-3633; and C-404/07 *Katz* [2008] ECR I-7607.

[188] See *Pupino*, ibid.

[189] On private life, etc see 6.3.4 above and 12.3.2 below; on criminal law principles as regards substantive criminal law, see further 10.3.1 below.

[190] Arts 6, 7, 19(2), 47, 48, and 49(1) and (2) of the Charter. The explanations to the Charter ([2007] OJ C 303/17) state that: Arts 6 and 7 correspond to Arts 5 and 8 ECHR, and have the same

reference to the Charter provisions on a fair trial, non-retroactivity of criminal offences, and the right to private life.[191] The EU would be bound by such rules in the context of the ECHR once it becomes a party to that Convention. However, it remains to be seen whether the EU will become a party to the Seventh Protocol to the ECHR. One of the criminal law rules in that Protocol (regarding double jeopardy) is already reflected in both the general principles and the Charter.[192] However, it is not clear whether the other criminal law rules in the Protocol (the right to an appeal and to compensation for wrongful conviction) are part of the general principles, and these rights are not explicitly mentioned in the Charter.[193] In any event, it should be noted that the EU and the Council of Europe have developed an *ad hoc* process for review of draft EU measures on suspects' rights for compatibility with the ECHR.[194]

Furthermore, given the non-application of Article 6 ECHR to extradition proceedings, it should again be reiterated that the right to a fair trial within the general principles of EU law and the EU Charter has a wider scope than Article 6 ECHR,[195] so the EU law principle and the Charter arguably govern the procedures relating to the EAW, to other extradition procedures within the scope of EU law, or to procedures governing other forms of cross-border cooperation that may fall outside the scope of Article 6 ECHR.[196] So the various rules on remedies in the EU's mutual recognition measures, as discussed below,[197] should therefore logically be interpreted consistently in line with the general principles of EU law and the Charter, not merely the ECHR.

Next, the key human rights issue underlying EU rules on mutual recognition in criminal matters is the extent of the principle that Member States must have mutual trust in each other's criminal justice systems, and in particular whether there is an exception to this principle on human rights grounds.[198] On this point, it is clear from the case law of the European Court of Human Rights that any

---

meaning, scope, and limitations (see Art 52(3) of the Charter); Art 19(2) is based on the ECtHR case law (mentioning *Soering* specifically); Art 47 has a wider scope than the ECHR (see below); Art 48 corresponds to Art 6(2) and (3) ECHR; and Art 49(1) and (2) corresponds to Art 7 ECHR. On the status of these explanations, see Art 52(7) of the Charter.

[191] See *Pupino, Katz,* and *Advocaten voor de Wereld* (n 186 above) and Case C-540/03 *EP v Council* [2006] ECR I-5769. [192] See 11.3.2 below.

[193] On this issue, see 2.3 above.

[194] See Council docs: 13759/06, 10 Oct 2006; 5431/07, 18 Jan 2007; 12926/09, 7 Sep 2009; and 5928/10, 1 Feb 2010.

[195] See in particular 6.3.4 above, and the explanations to Art 47 of the Charter (ibid).

[196] This argument is implicitly rejected in the opinion in C-296/08 PPU *Santesteban Goicoechea* [2008] ECR I-6307, para 40. But with respect, this opinion fails to take account of the wider scope of the general principles and the Charter as compared to Art 6 ECHR. Note also that EU mutual recognition legislation contains some specific rules on remedies (see 9.5–9.7 below) and that at least the first EU measure and the proposed second measure on suspects' rights will apply also to EAW proceedings (9.8.2 below). [197] See 9.5–9.7.

[198] This issue is arguably connected with the question of the extent of the EU's competence to adopt legislation pursuant to Art 82(2) TFEU: see 9.2.4 above.

potential responsibility in States that may arise from cross-border criminal cooperation cannot be wholly excluded solely because both States concerned have ratified the ECHR. The potential application of the ECHR to such cases (including cases involving two EU Member States) has been repeatedly presumed by the Court and Commission.[199] While the Commission's rulings in two cases suggested that both States' ratification of the ECHR was a factor to consider, and one case referred to a presumption of compliance with the ECHR in such 'internal' situations, the two decisions nevertheless went on to consider the merits of the human rights arguments.[200] So, to the extent that there is a presumption, it can clearly be rebutted. This is consistent with the position the European Human Rights Court has taken as regards EU asylum rules.[201]

In fact, if there were no possibility of human rights breaches in any Member State, then the ECHR and national constitutional protection for human rights would not be necessary. Although it could be argued that any human rights problem in the issuing Member State could be addressed through its national courts and ultimately the Strasbourg system, the process of waiting to use the courts of the issuing State, and then the Strasbourg system, to remedy a breach of human rights is lengthy, during which time a person could be in detention, or face paying a hefty fine, frozen assets, or confiscated property. As the Strasbourg Court has repeatedly held, 'the Convention is intended to guarantee not theoretical or illusory rights, but rights that are practical and effective'.[202]

Moreover, the possibility of applying a human rights exception in order to block the recognition of another Member State's judgment due to that judgment's breach of the right to a fair trial in criminal proceedings has been recognized by the Court of Justice, albeit in the context of civil proceedings.[203] It would hardly be justifiable to refuse to recognize the same principle in the context of criminal proceedings *per se*, given the greater consequences for accused persons.

Moving on to specific substantive points, first of all, the application of the mutual recognition principle to *in absentia* trials has been an issue as regards several EU measures. The point is relevant because a number of the ECHR judgments mentioned above[204] concern cases where a person moved from one EU Member State to another Member State (or who already resided there)[205] or a non-Member State; but this did not alter the finding of a breach of Article 6 ECHR.[206] In one

---

[199] *Koutsofotinos v Norway and Greece* (Commission decision, 10 Sep 1997); *Mills v UK and Germany* (Court decision, 5 Dec 2000). See also *Eminbeyli* and *Stephens* (nn 173 and 160 above).

[200] See *Lopez de Bergara v France*, 26 Oct 1998 and *Iruretagoyena v France*, 12 Jan 1998 (referring to a presumption).

[201] See 5.3 above, particularly the decision in *TI v UK* (Reports 2000-III). However, see the admissibility decision in *Stapleton v Ireland*, 4 May 2010.

[202] See, for example, judgment of 12 July 2001, *Prince Hans Adam II v Germany*, para 45.

[203] Case C-7/98 *Krombach* [2000] ECR I-1935. On the civil law implications, see 8.3.2 above.

[204] See 9.3.1.   [205] See *Krombach* (ibid).

[206] For example, see *Poitrimol*, *Pelladoah,* and *Krombach* (n 146 above).

of these cases (*Krombach*), the criminal conviction (which could not be enforced because the convicted person was a German national resident in Germany, which did not then extradite its own nationals) was then followed by an attempt to claim civil damages against the convicted person. Since this issue fell within the scope of an EU civil law measure, there was a reference to the Court of Justice, which held (even before the Strasbourg Court ruled on the case) that the *in absentia* ruling was a breach of the right to a fair trial, requiring the German courts to exercise the mandatory 'public policy' ground in the EU civil jurisdiction rules for non-recognition of the French judgment.[207]

The relevant EU legislation, before its amendment in 2009, provided either for a possible request for a guarantee that a person 'will have the opportunity to apply for a retrial of the case in the issuing Member State' or an option of non-execution on the grounds that if a person was convicted in an *in absentia* proceeding, if he or she had been given no summons or information about the hearing in the case.[208]

As compared to the Strasbourg case law, these provisions were problematic in that neither the scope of the definition of *in absentia* trials nor the purely optional nature of the guarantees and exceptions were sufficient. In particular, on the former point, there was no guarantee that the issuing State had to offer a retrial and that failing this, the executing State could not execute the issuing state's decision.[209] Moreover, the Strasbourg case law applies the *in absentia* guarantees not just to cases where the person concerned was unaware of the trial, but also to cases where the person knowingly avoided it, yet sought to send counsel on his or her behalf but the access by counsel was denied. To remedy this fault, the relevant legislation has to be interpreted in line with Strasbourg case law (despite its wording), perhaps by relying on the human rights exceptions which Member States may invoke. If this is not possible, the Framework Decisions must be considered invalid to the extent of their incompatibility with the ECHR. While the 2009 amendments to the EU legislation bring the rules into line with Strasbourg case law, there is an extra delay before that legislation applies to Italy and the fundamental problem remains that this ground for refusal to execute a decision remains optional.

The second specific issue as regards EU mutual recognition legislation is the application of the principle, set out in Article 7 ECHR, of non-retroactivity and legality of criminal law. First of all, the Court of Justice has taken the view that the principle does not apply to issues of criminal procedure,[210] but the Strasbourg case law has not definitively and fully settled this question.[211] Next, the Court

---

[207] *Krombach* (n 202 above).

[208] See 9.5.2., 9.7.1, 9.7.4, and 9.7.5 below. These measures were all amended by a later Framework Decision ([2009] OJ L 81/24), discussed in particular in 9.5.2 below.

[209] See also the admissibility decision in *Einhorn v France* (Reports 2001-XI), para 33.

[210] See *Pupino* (n 186 above).   [211] See the discussion in 9.3.2 above.

has also ruled that the abolition of dual criminality in EU mutual recognition legislation does *not* violate the principle of legality set out in Article 7 ECHR as regards the EAW, even in the absence of identical or very similar substantive criminal law in the relevant Member States, because the principle need only be complied with in the issuing Member State.[212]

This leaves open the question whether there may be a power or an obligation to refuse to execute another Member State's decision where the substantive criminal law in the issuing Member State breaches the principle of non-retroactivity or legality of criminal law, including cases where the dual criminality safeguard has been removed retroactively, or where extraterritorial criminal jurisdiction has been imposed retroactively (or unclearly).[213]

9.4. Impact of other EU law

EU law other than Justice and Home Affairs (JHA) law overlaps with criminal procedural rules in several respects. This section examines in turn: the impact of the free movement of persons on criminal procedure; the converse impact of criminal procedure on the free movement of persons; and the impact of criminal procedure on other non-JHA EU law.

First of all, the Court of Justice confirmed in the *Wolzenburg* case that that EU 'third pillar' measures are generally subject to the application of EU law on, inter alia, the free movement of persons: 'Member States cannot, in the context of the implementation of a framework decision, infringe Community law, in particular the provisions of the EC Treaty relating to the freedom accorded to every citizen of the Union to move and reside freely within the territory of the Member States.'[214] More specifically, while it is possible in principle to reserve the benefit of certain optional derogations set out in the Framework Decision establishing the European Arrest Warrant to nationals of the executing State,[215] EU free movement law requires that such derogations also apply to citizens of other Member States who were sufficiently integrated into that State, namely permanent residents as defined by free movement legislation.[216] The Framework Decisions on pre-trial detention and probation and parole expressly confirm

---

[212] *Advocaten voor de Wereld* (n 186 above).

[213] On the jurisdiction issue, see 11.3.2 below. The opinion in *Santesteban Goicoechea* (n 195 above), paras 42–46, states that Art 7 cannot apply to extradition proceedings, since it does not apply to procedural matters. With respect, this leaves aside the question as to whether Art 7 would apply if the issuing State's decision was based on *underlying substantive law* (or connected jurisdiction rules) which breached Art 7.   [214] Case C-123/08, [2009] ECR I-9621, para 45.

[215] See further 9.5.2 below.

[216] On the definition of permanent residents under that legislation, see 6.4.1 above. EU third pillar measures do not address the position of persons who are dual citizens of two Member States, or of a Member State and a third State. On these issues as regards immigration law, see 6.4.1 above—but it is arguable that the immigration rules might not be relevant by analogy to the issue of mutual

that they are subject to EU free movement law, without further clarification,[217] while the Framework Decision on the transfer of sentenced persons sets out a special rule (an option for Member States to waive the normal requirement of their consent) for the return to the executing Member States of non-citizens who have a permanent residence right under EU free movement law or immigration law.[218]

The latter Framework Decision also provides for the transfer of a prisoner to his or her Member State of nationality where he or she does not normally live,[219] begging the question as to whether this could only occur in the first place if the substantive and procedural free movement rules governing that person's expulsion from the other Member State which he or she has moved to were satisfied,[220] although the preamble to the Framework Decision points to such a requirement.[221] The same issue arises as regards other mutual recognition measures, most notably the issue of the EAW, where the assumption of the UK courts[222] that criminal proceedings in general are unaffected by EC law (as it was then) is obviously wrong per se,[223] but the Court of Justice has not yet been asked whether and if so, on what grounds, free movement law could be raised as a barrier to the execution of an EAW, apart from the question in *Wolzenburg* regarding equal treatment of permanent residents as regards derogations from the rules. The better view is that the execution of an EAW does not breach EU free movement law when free movement rights are not currently being exercised,[224] and that where free movement rights (or rights to reside in a Member State pursuant to EU immigration law) are being exercised, the execution of an EAW is a distinct issue from the retention or loss of the underlying right to reside in the Member State executing the EAW following the conclusion of the criminal proceedings and the completion of any custodial sentence that might be imposed in the event of conviction, or which was already imposed.[225]

---

recognition in criminal law, except where the underlying free movement or immigration rule is anyway applicable.

[217] [2008] OJ L 337/102, recital 7 in the preamble, and [2009] OJ L 294/20, recital 18 in the preamble. There was also a reference to the Court of Justice on the effect of free movement law on pre-trial detention decisions (Case C-297/09 *X*, later withdrawn).

[218] Art 4(7)(a) of that Framework Decision ([2008] OJ L 327/27), which the Court of Justice moreover referred to in the *Wolzenburg* judgment.   [219] Art 4(1)(b).

[220] On those rules, see 7.4.1 above.   [221] Points 15 and 16 in the preamble.

[222] *Healey* [1984] 3 CMLR 575 (QB); *Bullong and Kember* [1980] 2 CMLR 125 (QB); *Virdee* [1980] 1 CMLR 709 (QB).

[223] See *Wolzenburg* as regards arrest warrants; as regards substantive criminal law, see the long-standing case law discussed in 10.4.2 below.

[224] For example, where an EAW is issued for a British national *residing in the UK* relating to criminal offences which he or she allegedly committed during a *prior* visit to Spain.

[225] See paras 85 and 146 of the *Wolzenburg* opinion, which suggest such an interpretation. On the separate issue of the relationship between extradition proceedings or EAWs and asylum proceedings, see 5.7 below.

The proposed Directive establishing a European Protection Order is also linked to free movement, since it only applies where a person seeks to move between Member States.[226]

As for domestic criminal procedure, EU citizens facing criminal trials in another Member State have equal language rights as criminal defendants with citizens of the host Member State, even if the EU citizens in question are not workers but entered that country as tourists or were merely driving across it.[227] EU free movement law is also relevant to crime victims. EU citizens resident in, or even visiting, another Member State are entitled to equal treatment as regards state compensation schemes for crime victims as regards crimes committed against them in that State.[228] They are also entitled to equal treatment as regards victims' compensation for crimes committed outside the territory of the host State, at least in cases where the beneficiaries of the compensation are resident in that State on a long-term basis.[229] In fact, EC legislation (as it then was) has been adopted on State compensation of crime victims and on the immigration status of victims of trafficking in persons,[230] although the Court of Justice ruled that the EC legislation on compensation of crime victims was not relevant to the interpretation of an EU third pillar measure on the position of victims in criminal procedure.[231]

On the basis of the case law to date, it must be concluded that EU citizens involved in criminal proceedings in another Member State are generally entitled to equal treatment as regards all aspects of criminal procedure, subject only to exceptional cases where a residence (but not a nationality) requirement might be justified, due to the different position of non-residents as regards rehabilitation or as regards payments which amount to social benefits.[232] Similarly, the adoption of mutual recognition measures reduces Member States' justifications for limitations on equality rights of EU citizens in the context of imposing criminal penalties, because of the enhanced ease of enforcing national criminal law measures in other Member States.[233]

Secondly, criminal procedural law impacts on EU free movement law in several respects. As for free movement and access to employment, EU law probably

---

[226] [2010] OJ C 69/5, Art 2(1).

[227] Case C-274/06 *Bickel and Franz* [1998] ECR I-7637. See earlier, as regards workers, Case 137/84 *Mutsch* [1985] ECR 2681.   [228] Case 186/87 *Cowan* [1989] ECR 195.

[229] Case C-164/07 *Wood* [2008] ECR I-4143.   [230] See 9.8.3 below.

[231] See Case C-467/05 *Dell'Orto* [2007] ECR I-5557.

[232] See the judgment in *Wolzenburg* (n 213 above), the rules on sentenced persons discussed above, and the opinion in *Wood*, n 228 above (paras 40–60), which suggests that some form of requirement of integration (ie residence period) might be imposed as regards victim compensation benefits where the crime was committed outside the territory of the host State.

[233] See 10.4.2 below, and in particular the Opinion in Case C-224/00 *Commission v Italy* [2002] ECR I-2965, which makes a direct link between the lack of any measure (at the time) on mutual recognition of financial penalties (see now 9.7.1.1 below) and Member States' justifications for unequal treatment as regards fines.

does not give the right to apply for a job as a prison officer in another Member State, since such jobs involve powers of constraint.[234] However, private security employment and contracts must be opened to employees and businesses from other Member States.[235] Arguably, so should non-custodial jobs in prisons and work as a probation or parole officer, except perhaps where such persons control or work as officers in 'halfway houses' which can be considered similar to prisons. Although probation and parole officers often have the authority to terminate conditional release, arguably this is only an auxiliary power of constraint, comparable to powers enjoyed by private security guards, which does not bring them within the 'public employment' exception to free movement law.[236]

As for the free movement of victims, the proposal for a Directive on a European protection order aims to encourage a person to move between Member States without any loss of security.[237] But what about the free movement of *offenders*? A Member State may wish to restrict an offender on probation or parole from leaving that Member State; this might be justified, subject to EU free movement law.[238] If a Member State wishes to restrict a parolee or probationer from *entering* its territory, it may rely on the same derogations, unless of course that person is one of its nationals. After a sentence is spent, it will be increasingly hard to justify restrictions on entry or exit, because a person must represent a severe *present* threat to a Member State to do so.[239] Subsequent lawful behaviour and expressions of remorse might even oblige a Member State to allow entry to a person who had committed terrorist offences some years before.[240] An ex-offender should also be able to claim access to rehabilitation assistance in another Member State as a 'social advantage' available to workers, and to other EU citizens.[241] It will be harder to justify restrictions upon free movement of persons during probation or parole once the deadline to apply the Framework Decision on this subject has passed.[242] Similarly, it can be argued that detention of EU citizens pending trial in cases when nationals are not detained cannot be justified in light of the ease of issuing a EAW to ensure that the person concerned can be returned to the host Member State to face trial,[243] as well as (in future) the possibility of issuing a pre-trial supervision order that could be recognized in another Member State.[244] The proposal for a Directive on a European protection order provides that an

---

[234] See Case 149/79 *Commission v Belgium* [1980] ECR 3881.

[235] See the case law discussed in 12.4.3.1 below.   [236] See the cases discussed ibid.

[237] Point 5 in the preamble (n 225 above). On the substance, see 9.7.6 below.

[238] For more detail on the relevant free movement rules, see 7.4.1 above.   [239] Ibid.

[240] *Proll* [1988] 2 CMLR 387 (IAT).

[241] Art 7(2), Reg 1612/68 ([1968] OJ L 257/2); on 'social advantages' for other categories of EU citizens, see the case law beginning with Case C-85/96 *Martinez Sala* [1998] ECR I-2691, referred to in 6.4.1 above.   [242] See 9.7.5 below.

[243] See 9.5.2 below.

[244] See the Framework Decision on mutual recognition of pre-trial supervision orders (9.6.3 below).

order not to leave the territory of a Member State must be recognized by another Member State; this is problematic insofar as there is no express requirement that the original order has to be consistent with EU free movement law.[245]

The Court of Justice has not yet been asked whether the period of residence necessary for an EU citizen to obtain permanent residence in a Member State can be accrued while in detention,[246] although it has been asked whether movement between Member States due to criminal proceedings affects the possibility of loss of that permanent residence.[247] Finally, there is also a link between EU rules on social security and free movement and the transfer of sentenced persons.[248]

Thirdly, as for other areas of EU law, in the area of EU sex discrimination law, a Member State accepted during litigation that it could not discriminate between men and women in access to management, technical, and training jobs in prisons, but the Commission agreed that Member States could discriminate on grounds of sex for the job of warder and the Court agreed that they could discriminate for head warder posts.[249] A national court presumed, no doubt correctly, that women could not be banned from jobs as social workers in prisons, and they surely cannot be banned from probation and parole work.[250]

There is also a link between other non-JHA EU law and EU mutual recognition measures, for when non-JHA EU legislation prohibits something, and some or all Member States give effect to that obligation by creating a criminal offence, or alternatively when a non-JHA EU measure directly requires that Member States enforce a prohibition by criminal penalties,[251] then the double criminality rule restricting extradition, to the extent that it still exists following the application of EU mutual recognition measures,[252] is automatically weakened.

---

[245] Art 2(2)(c) of the proposal (n 225 above); the preamble only refers to free movement of the person under threat (point 5). See, less problematically, the Framework Decisions on pre-trial detention and probation and parole, which each provide for mutual recognition of such orders (Art 8(1)(d) and 4(1)(c) respectively) but refer to free movement rights in the preamble (see n 216 above).

[246] Art 16 of Dir 2004/38 on EU citizens' movement rights ([2004] OJ L 229/35) is silent on this issue. Note that in the Commission's view, 'time behind bars' should not normally count toward acquisition of permanent resident status if no links with the host Member State are built (point 3.4 of the Communication on abuse of free movement rights, COM (2009) 313, 2 July 2009). Even if this is correct in principle, the point must be clarified and is subject to the principle of proportionality: it is submitted that time 'behind bars' could only be discounted for the acquisition of permanent residence rights, if at all, if it resulted from a criminal conviction or (in the case of pre-trial detention) were regarded as 'time served' pursuant to that conviction. It is also submitted that the principle of proportionality also requires that time behind bars can only *interrupt* the process of acquiring permanent resident status, rather than *terminate* it. In other words, the time behind bars 'stops the clock' on the acquisition of that status so that, for example, a period of three years' residence before imprisonment and two years' residence afterward qualifies the person concerned for permanent residence status.

[247] Case C-145/09 *Tsakouridis*, pending (opinion of 8 June 2010).

[248] Case C-302/02 *Effing* [2005] ECR I-552.

[249] Case 318/86 *Commission v France* [1988] ECR 3359.

[250] Case 14/83 *Von Colson and Kamann* [1984] ECR 1891.

[251] See 10.4.1 below.   [252] See 9.5–9.7 below.

The protection of the EU's financial interests in a treaty with Switzerland entailed ratification of that treaty by both the Community (as it then was) and its Member States,[253] and the EU's measures on mutual assistance in criminal matters are paralleled by EU legislation which sets out rules for administrative assistance in tax matters.[254] It is striking that while mutual assistance or mutual recognition as regards the criminal law aspects of tax fraud is subject to the ordinary legislative procedure after the entry into force of the Treaty of Lisbon, administrative cooperation as regards taxation is still subject to unanimous voting.[255]

Non-JHA EU legislation also has implications for disqualifications, in particular as regards driving licences: Member States must refuse to issue a licence, or to recognize the validity of a licence, if that licence was restricted, suspended, or withdrawn in another Member State.[256] Also, it might be questioned whether measures concerning disqualifications which do not follow from a criminal conviction pronounced by a court would fall within the scope of the EU's criminal law competence.[257] A Commission proposal regarding cross-border enforcement of sanctions relating to road safety was not agreed by the Council, due to a dispute as to whether it should have a legal base in EC law (as proposed by the Commission) or the third pillar (as it then was).[258]

9.5. Extradition and the European Arrest Warrant

9.5.1. Extradition

A basic element of cooperation between States regarding criminal matters is the concept of extradition, which entails an agreement between States to send a person who is absent from a State pending a criminal trial or following the imposition of a criminal sentence there to that State, in order to serve the sentence or to appear at the criminal trial. The basic international framework for extradition for European States is the 1957 Council of Europe Convention on extradition, which

---

[253] A parallel treaty with Liechtenstein has also been proposed. See 9.2.5 above.

[254] As regards tax recovery, see Dir 76/308 ([1976] OJ L 73/18), as consolidated following later amendments by Dir 2008/55 ([2008] OJ L 150/28), replaced by Dir 2010/24 ([2010] OJ L 84/1) as from 1 Jan 2012 (Art 28(1)). As regards administrative assistance, see, as regards direct taxation, Dir 77/799 ([1977] OJ L 336/15), as amended by Dirs 2003/93 ([2003] OJ L 264/23) and 2004/56 ([2004] OJ L 157/70), and see the proposed replacement Dir in COM (2009) 29, 2 Feb 2009. As regards VAT, see Reg 218/92 ([1992] OJ L 24/1), replaced by Reg 1798/2003 ([2003] OJ L 264/1)—and see the proposed recast Reg in COM (2009) 427, 18 Aug 2009, agreed by the Council in June 2010 (Council doc 10189/10, 28 May 2010). As regards excise duties, see Reg 2073/2004 ([2004] OJ L 359/1).

[255] See Arts 113, 114(2), and 115 TFEU (former Arts 93, 95(2), and 94 EC), as interpreted in Cases C-338/01 *Commission v Council* [2004] ECR I-4829 and C-533/03 *Commission v Council* [2006] ECR I-1025.

[256] Art 11(4) of Dir 2006/126 ([2006] OJ L 403/18), applicable from 19 Jan 2009 (Art 18).

[257] See further 9.7.3 below.

[258] COM (2008) 151, 19 Mar 2008; see the progress report in Council doc 16634/08, 8 Dec 2008.

all Member States have ratified, although only some Member States have ratified the First (1975) and Second (1978) Protocols to the Convention.[259] In addition, all Member States have ratified the 1977 Council of Europe Convention on the suppression of terrorism, which affects both extradition and mutual assistance;[260] a 2003 Protocol to that Convention is not yet in force.[261]

To implement extradition, the 'requesting' State (the State of the prosecution, which wishes to assert jurisdiction over a fugitive to conduct a criminal prosecution, or to enforce a sentence or detention order) asks the 'requested' State (the 'host' State, which currently has the fugitive) to 'surrender' the fugitive to it, possibly after a provisional arrest to prevent flight. For this purpose, the requested State holds a special extradition proceeding, the details of which are left to national law.

Under the 1957 Council of Europe Convention, extradition must be granted wherever the fugitive has escaped from a custodial sentence of over four months' detention, or is accused of committing a crime which would be an offence resulting in at least one year's detention in both the requesting and requested States (the 'double criminality' rule). However, there are a number of important exceptions to this. A State may limit its extradition obligations to a selected list of crimes, or exclude a selected list from its obligations, and moreover no State has an obligation to extradite a person charged with a 'political offence' or where there would be prejudice, punishment, or prosecution 'on account of the fugitive's race, religion, nationality or political opinion'. Military offences are excluded and fiscal offences may be. Most important of all, States may choose to refuse extradition of their own nationals, and many EU Member States initially chose this option. Among other rules, lapse of time to bring criminal proceedings in the requesting or requested State prevents extradition.

A separate principle for the protection of the fugitive is the 'specialty' rule. This rule prevents the requesting State from bringing other proceedings against the fugitive for offences other than that for which he or she was extradited, except where the requested State gives its consent or the fugitive remains in or returns to the requested State. Furthermore, the fugitive cannot be sent to a *third* State ('re-extradited') by the requesting State without the requested State's consent. Requests under the Convention must be exchanged via embassies, but State parties can agree bilaterally on simpler rules for exchanges. In addition to the various options allowed in the text of the Convention, reservations to '*any* provision or provisions' are allowed.[262]

These extensive opt-outs and reservations led to the two subsequent Protocols and to the Convention on the Suppression of Terrorism, which attempted to restrict their use. The Protocols, inter alia, narrow the 'political offence' and

---

[259] ETS 24, 86, and 98 respectively. For details of ratification and signatures, see Appendix I.
[260] ETS 90.   [261] ETS 190. For details of ratification and signatures, see Appendix I.
[262] Art 26(1) (emphasis added).

fiscal offences exceptions, and the Terrorism Convention lists six 'terrorist' offences which definitely shall not be classified as 'political offences' by signatory States, and allows States to exclude other crimes from the scope of the exception. However, parties may still refuse extradition if they suspect that the requesting State is persecuting the accused, and can enter a reservation if they consider that a particular offence falling within the list of 'terrorist offences' is indeed a political offence.[263] EEC Member States agreed an EPC Convention in 1979 attempting to restrict the use of such reservations between each other, but this Convention never entered into force and ratification attempts were abandoned.[264]

Because many EU Member States had not ratified one of the Protocols to the 1957 Convention and/or had chosen à la carte from the provisions of the 1957 Convention and its Protocols, extradition between them was deemed unsatisfactory. Therefore, the Schengen Convention and two EU Conventions of 1995 and 1996 aimed to restrict Member States' use of reservations and exceptions under the Council of Europe measures,[265] although the EU Conventions are not yet in force.[266] Also a 1989 EPC Convention tried to speed up existing mechanisms by allowing authorities to fax extradition requests.[267] The Schengen provisions abolished the fiscal offences exception for VAT, customs duties, and excise duties; provided for requests to be sent to justice ministries; and allowed for speedy extradition with the fugitive's consent. Also, the inclusion of extradition requests in the Schengen Information System (SIS) facilitated the practical application of the extradition rules.[268] The first EU extradition Convention provided for detailed rules governing such speedy consented extradition, and then the second Convention attempted to address a large number of barriers to extradition, in particular: lowering the threshold for extradition to a six months' custodial sentence in the requested State; weakening the double criminality rule as regards organized crime; abolishing the 'political offence' exception, although Member States could make a renewable reservation on this point; abolishing also the 'fiscal offences' exception, although Member States could provide that the exception was only abolished to the extent that the Schengen extradition required; requiring Member States to permit extradition of their nationals to other Member States, although Member States could make a renewable reservation on this point; limiting the Council of Europe restrictions relating to lapse of time, specialty, and re-extradition (to other Member States); and integrating the EPC Convention on faxing requests into the text.

---

[263] Art 13 of the Convention.

[264] UK government Command Paper, Cm 7823 (1980).

[265] Arts 59–66 (Schengen Convention); [1995] OJ C 78/1 (consented extradition); [1996] OJ C 313/11 (disputed extradition). See also the Schengen Executive Committee Declaration on extradition ([2000] OJ L 239/435).   [266] See Appendix I for ratification details.

[267] For the text, see: <http://www.asser.nl/eurowarrant-webroot/documents/cms_eaw_12_1_Agreement1989.05.26.pdf>.   [268] On the SIS, see 12.6.1.1 below.

Furthermore, there are specific extradition rules in a number of EU criminal law measures, in particular applying an 'extradite or prosecute' principle.[269] Also, the rules on sentencing in several EU measures specifically require that in at least some cases, the penalties should be stringent enough to give rise to possible extradition proceedings.[270]

9.5.2. European Arrest Warrant

Extradition between Member States has now largely been replaced by the Framework Decision establishing the European Arrest Warrant (EAW). The Framework Decision was adopted in June 2002, and Member States were obliged to apply it by 31 December 2003.[271] It has attracted a significant amount of case law from the Court of Justice: a reference on its validity and eight references on its interpretation.[272] First of all, as to the legal form of the Framework Decision, the Court of Justice confirmed that the Council could replace Conventions by means of a Framework Decision.[273]

As for the substance of the Framework Decision, it has replaced the corresponding provisions of the prior EU, EPC, and Council of Europe measures.[274] However Member States retained the option to apply earlier extradition rules as regards acts committed before a certain date.[275] In that case, the prior measures continue to apply in part as regards requests to those Member States

---

[269] For details, see 11.5 below.   [270] See the provisions discussed in 10.6 below.

[271] Art 34(1) ([2002] OJ L 190/1). All references in this section are to this Framework Decision unless otherwise indicated. On the EAW, see N Keijzer and E van Sliedregt, eds, *The European Arrest Warrant in practice* (Asser, 2009); E Guild and L Marin, *Still not resolved? Constitutional issues of the European Arrest Warrant* (Wolf, 2009); R Blextoon, ed, *Handbook on the European Arrest Warrant* (Asser, 2005); S Alegre and M Leaf, *European Arrest Warrant: A solution ahead of its time?* (Justice, 2003); and J Wouters and F Naert, 'Of arrest warrants, terrorist offences and extradition deals: An appraisal of the EU's main criminal law measures against terrorism after "11 September"' (2004) 41 CMLRev 909.

[272] On validity, see Case C-303/05 *Advocaten voor de Wereld* [2007] ECR I-3633. On interpretation, see Cases: C-66/08 *Koslowski* [2008] ECR I-6041; C-296/08 PPU *Santesteban Goicoechea* [2008] ECR I-6307; C-388/08 PPU *Leymann and Pustovarov* [2008] ECR I-8993; C-123/08 *Wolzenburg* [2009] ECR I-9621; C-261/09 *Mantello*, pending (opinion of 7 Sep 2010); C-306/09 *I.B.*, pending (opinion of 6 July 2010); C-105/10 PPU *Gataev*, withdrawn; and C-264/10 *Kita*, pending.

[273] *Advocaten voor de Wereld*, ibid. See 2.2.2.2 above. This reasoning is presumably valid *mutatis mutandis* to a number of other mutual recognition measures which replace or repeal the corresponding provisions of Conventions: see 9.6 and 9.7 below.

[274] Art 31(1). Member States are free to retain or adopt treaties which further simplify the application of the Framework Decision (Art 31(2)). The Court of Justice has confirmed that this latter provision does not mean that Member States can keep applying the Council or Europe, EU, or EPC measures: judgment in *Santesteban Goicoechea* (n 271 above). This interpretation presumably applies *mutatis mutandis* to other mutual recognition measures with equivalent provisions.

[275] France, Italy, and Austria have applied this option (see declarations in [2002] OJ L 190/19). Also, Austria could refuse to extradite its own nationals until the end of 2008 unless dual criminality applied (Art 33(1)).

which have limited the temporal application of the Framework Decision.[276] The Council of Europe extradition Convention (and the Council of Europe's terrorism Convention, when the 2003 Protocol to that Convention enters into force) permits States to replace the application of these Conventions between themselves if they agree a uniform law of extradition.[277] So the (EU) Council adopted conclusions urging Member States to declare officially the non-applicability of the Council of Europe measures between themselves.[278] More fundamentally, the Court of Justice has ruled that the purpose of the Framework Decision is to replace the traditional extradition system with a system of surrender on the basis of an EAW.[279]

The basic rule is that EAWs must be executed 'on the basis of the principle of mutual recognition and in accordance with the provisions of [the] Framework Decision'.[280] An EAW can be issued whether a person is wanted for trial or whether a person has already been convicted and escaped application of a custodial sentence or detention order.[281] It may be issued for any act punishable in the issuing State (the Member State issuing the arrest warrant) by a period of at least twelve months or, where a sentence has already been passed, for at least four months.[282] This threshold will in principle be waived in the specific circumstances of the application of the Framework Decision on the recognition of pre-trial supervision orders, although Member States have the option of refusing to waive that threshold.[283] It should also be noted that the mere possibility of issuing an EAW in order to enforce a sentence against a person resident in another Member State does not extinguish the application of the 'enforcement condition' which applies to the Schengen double jeopardy rules.[284]

The central provision of the Framework Decision abolishes the principle of double criminality, where the warrant has been issued for one of the standard list of thirty-two offences 'as defined by the law of the issuing Member State', where such an offence could be subject to a sentence of at least three years.[285] In fact, the list contains more than thirty-two offences, since some points cover more than one offence. For acts not on the list, surrender of the person 'may' be subject to the condition of double criminality in the executing State (the State enforcing

---

[276] Art 32. The Court of Justice has confirmed that in that case, Member States are still free to ratify the EU's extradition Conventions in order to simplify extradition somewhat as regards such persons: judgment in *Santesteban Goicoechea* (n 271 above).

[277] Art 28(3) of the former Convention; Art 9 of the latter Convention (as amended by the Protocol).

[278] Council doc 12413/03, 11 Sep 2003, adopted by the JHA Council, 3 Oct 2003.

[279] Judgments in: *Advocaten voor de Wereld,* para 28; *Koslowski,* para 31; *Leymann,* para 42; and *Wolzenburg,* para 56 (all n 271 above).　　　[280] Art 1(2).

[281] Art 1(1) and clause 5 of the preamble.　　　[282] Art 2(1).

[283] Art 21 of that Framework Decision ([2009] OJ L 294/20), applicable from 1 Dec 2012 (Art 27(1)). On the substance, see 9.6.3 below.

[284] Case C-288/05 *Kretzinger* [2007] ECR I-6441. On the substance, see 11.8 below.

[285] Art 2(2).

the arrest warrant),[286] with the consequence that there will still be an obligation to establish whether the act in question would be a crime in both States.

The validity of this partial abolition of dual criminality was challenged though the national courts, on the grounds that it breached the principle of the legality of criminal proceedings and the principles of equality and non-discrimination.[287] However, according to the Court of Justice, while these principles formed part of the general principles of EU law, and were moreover reaffirmed in the EU Charter of Fundamental Rights,[288] the principle of legality was not infringed because it was for the issuing Member State to comply with it when it defined the offences which it sought to punish or prosecute by means of executing an EAW.[289] As for the principles of equality and non-discrimination, the Court held that abolishing the dual criminality rule only as regards thirty-two specific offences was not a breach of those principles, since 'the Council was able to form the view, on the basis of the principle of mutual recognition and in the light of the high degree of trust and solidarity between the Member States, that, whether by reason of their inherent nature or by reason of the punishment incurred of a maximum of at least three years, the categories of offences in question feature among those the seriousness of which in terms of adversely affecting public order and public safety justifies dispensing with the verification of double criminality', and so any distinction between persons convicted or accused of those crimes and persons convicted or accused of other crimes was justified, even if those two groups of persons were comparable.[290] Also, the lack of precision in the definition of the offences was not problematic on this ground either, since the Framework Decision did not have the purpose of harmonizing substantive criminal law and the Treaty (as it then was) did not make application of the Framework Decision conditional on such harmonization.[291] This reasoning is presumably valid *mutatis mutandis* to the abolition of the dual criminality principle in a number of other mutual recognition measures.[292]

There are three categories of grounds for which the execution of an EAW could be refused or delayed. The Court of Justice has ruled that these are the *only* grounds which could justify non-execution of an EAW.[293] Firstly, there are three

---

[286] Art 2(4).   [287] *Advocaten voor de Wereld* (n 271 above). See further 9.3.5 above.

[288] Paras 45–47 of the judgment, ibid.   [289] Paras 48–54 of the judgment, ibid.

[290] Paras 57–58 of the judgment, ibid.

[291] Para 59 of the judgment, ibid. The Court referred to its case law on the double jeopardy rule, on which see 11.8 below. Arguably the subsequent wording of the Treaty (Art 82 TFEU) entrenches the mutual recognition principle even more strongly (see 9.2.3 above).

[292] See 9.6 and 9.7 below. However, note that the Framework Decision on mutual recognition of financial penalties abolishes dual criminality for a longer list of crimes (9.7.1.1 below), and the proposed Directive establishing the European Investigation Order would abolish dual criminality entirely (9.6.1.3 below). The *Advocaten voor de Wereld* judgment cannot automatically be applied by analogy to those measures.

[293] See the judgments in: *Koslowski*, para 43; *Leymann*, para 51; and *Wolzenburg*, para 57 (all n 271 above).

grounds for *mandatory* non-execution of the warrant: an amnesty in the executing State, if that State had jurisdiction to prosecute the offence under its national
law; where the double jeopardy rule applies; and where the fugitive is below the
age of criminal responsibility in the executing State.[294] Secondly, there are seven
grounds for *optional* non-execution:[295] residual application of the double criminality rule; a pending prosecution in the executing Member State for the same
acts (*lis pendens*);[296] a decision not to prosecute, or a final sentence, in the executing State, which prevents further proceedings; time-barring of the action in the
executing Member State, if it has jurisdiction; a prior judgment for the same acts
in a third State, if that judgment has been enforced; the executing Member State's
agreement to enforce the sentence itself, against one of its nationals or residents or
a person staying there, where the EAW was issued for the purpose of enforcing a
sentence; or where the executing Member State either regards the acts as taking
place within its territory or would not exercise extraterritorial jurisdiction over
acts which took place outside the issuing State's territory.

The Court of Justice has clarified that the exception concerning time-barring
only applies where there was no final judgment; a final judgment dismissing a
prosecution due to time-barring falls instead within the scope of the mandatory
double jeopardy exception.[297] Furthermore, the exception relating to possible
execution of a sentence against nationals, residents, or persons staying in the
executing State has attracted a number of references to the Court of Justice.[298]
It will also interact with the later Framework Decision on the recognition of
custodial sentences, once the latter measure is implemented by Member States.[299]
First of all, in its *Kozlowski* judgment, the Court of Justice interpreted the part
of the exception relating to persons 'staying in' the executing State,[300] ruling
that it could not apply to all persons temporarily located in the executing State,

---

[294] Art 3. Note that this is the only mutual recognition measure which provides for mandatory
grounds for non-execution. On the interpretation of the double jeopardy exception, see Case
C-261/09 *Mantello*, pending (opinion of 7 Sep 2010). As with most other EU mutual recognition
measures, the question arises as to the relationship between this specific exception and the general
rules on double jeopardy set out in Arts 54–58 of the Schengen Convention ([2000] OJ L 239). On
this issue, see 11.8 below. The *Mantello* opinion argues that at least the interpretation of the 'same
facts' in Art 3(2) of the Framework Decision must be identical to the interpretation of the Schengen
rules.   [295] Art 4.

[296] On this point, it should be noted that the traditional 'extradite or prosecute' rule found in
many Framework Decisions on substantive criminal law (see 11.5 below) is now irrelevant where an
EAW is issued, since the EAW Framework Decision does not permit a refusal on the grounds that the
executing State is *planning* to prosecute the person concerned. On the coordination of prosecutions
in *lis pendens* cases, see 11.6 below.

[297] Case C-467/04 *Gasparini* [2006] ECR I-9199, para 31.

[298] Art 4(6). See also the discussion of Art 5(3) below.

[299] See Art 25 of that Framework Decision ([2008] OJ L 327/27), applicable from 5 Dec 2011
(Art 29(1)). On the substance, see 9.7.1.2 below. On the relationship between the EAW and the rules
on the transfer of sentenced persons in the meantime, see the pending *Kita* case (n 271 above)

[300] See n 271 above, paras 36–54.

but equally could apply to a person staying there for a period of time who had established certain connections there. Moreover, the definitions of 'resident' and 'staying in' had an EU-wide autonomous meaning not dependent on the laws of the Member States. In order to apply any of the three categories of exception, Member States 'must assess whether there is a legitimate interest which would justify the sentence imposed in the issuing Member State being executed on the territory of the executing Member State', a condition which does not in fact appear in the Framework Decision. It followed that this exception 'has in particular the objective of enabling the executing judicial authority to give particular weight to the possibility of increasing the requested person's chances of reintegrating into society when the sentence imposed on him expires', and therefore that:

...the terms 'resident' and 'staying' cover, respectively, the situations in which the person who is the subject of a European arrest warrant has either established his actual place of residence in the executing Member State or has acquired, following a stable period of presence in that State, certain connections with that State which are of a similar degree to those resulting from residence.

In order to examine whether those 'certain connections' exist:

...it is necessary to make an overall assessment of various objective factors characterising the situation of that person, which include, in particular, the length, nature and conditions of his presence and the family and economic connections which he has with the executing Member State.

Applying these principles, the Court stated that interruptions of stay and non-compliance with immigration law (ie the immigration law aspects of the person's status) could not lead automatically to the conclusion that the person concerned was not 'staying in' the Member State, but could be 'of relevance' when deciding that issue. On the other hand, the commission of crimes in that State or the detention in that State following a conviction (ie the criminal law aspects of the person's status) were not relevant at all for deciding whether that person was 'staying' there—although they could be relevant for applying the second phase of the assessment, ie deciding whether there was a 'legitimate interest' in not executing the EAW in the particular case. The Court did not offer any indication of how to interpret the concept of the 'actual state of residence' (ie the criteria to interpret the 'resident' requirement).[301] Nor did the Court address the question as to whether the person's *future* immigration status (ie whether the person had been, or could or would be, validly expelled as distinct from surrendered) was relevant to the application of the reintegration requirement.[302]

---

[301] For further suggestions as to the interpretation of these concepts, see the *Wolzenburg* opinion, paras 53–70.

[302] As the opinion in *Koslowski* convincingly argues (paras 159–172), reintegration into the executing State's society is not feasible if the person will be expelled, but also any expulsion must comply with EU free movement or immigration law. See also the *Wolzenburg* opinion, paras 84–86.

Subsequently, in the *Wolzenburg* judgment, the Court ruled that Member States retain a discretion to permit only *some* categories of nationals, residents, or persons staying on the territory to benefit from the possibility of refusing to execute a warrant,[303] on the grounds that allowing a choice for Member States to limit the scope of the exception would further the underlying objectives of the Framework Decision by bringing more people within its scope. However, this discretion was constrained by the principle of equal treatment of EU citizens who were nationals of other Member States, which meant that Member States at the very least had to treat EU citizens who had permanent residence status in that State the same as that State treated its own citizens.[304] EU citizens who had not yet obtained that status could be treated differently (ie not benefiting from the exception) because they were not in a similar position to nationals of the host State, as regards reintegration in the society of that State after serving their sentence, since they were not highly integrated into that State in the first place. The Court did not address the question of whether EU free movement or immigration law might be a potential barrier as such to execution of an arrest warrant, ie because the offence that the person is charged with or convicted of is not serious enough substantively to justify removal from the territory.[305]

Furthermore, the Court did not address the question of which third-country nationals, if any, could benefit from the same principle,[306] or the position of dual citizens.[307] Presumably the Court's ruling, by analogy, means that Member States are free to set other conditions restricting the scope of this ground for refusal of execution of an EAW, or the other optional grounds for refusal of execution in this Framework Decision or other mutual recognition measures, subject to the equality principle and also human rights obligations (on which, see the discussion further below).[308] On this point, it should be emphasized

---

[303] See n 271 above.

[304] On the broader interaction between the mutual recognition principle and EU free movement law, see 9.4 above. On the substance of the concept of permanent residence in EU free movement law, see 6.4.1 above. The Court also made a link with an optional provision of the Framework Decision on recognition of custodial penalties, which applies the same five-year rule: see 9.7.1.2 below.

[305] See 9.4 above. There is a specific provision on this point in Art 7(2) of the asylum procedures Dir (Dir 2005/85, [2005] OJ L 326/13), which was the subject of the withdrawn *Gataev* case. See now Art 8(2) of the proposed recast asylum procedures Dir (COM (2009) 551, 21 Oct 2009).

[306] Logically the Court's approach in *Wolzenburg* should apply by analogy to EU citizens' third-country national family members who have obtained permanent residence status pursuant to EU free movement law (6.4.1 above), as well as those who obtain status identical or comparable to such permanent residence pursuant to the EEA or the EU–Turkey association agreement (see 6.4.3 above). On the general question of equal treatment of third-country nationals, see 3.4.3 above. On the immigration law links, see the opinion in *Koslowski* (n 271 above).

[307] On the position of dual citizens, see 9.4 above.

[308] *Contra* the Advocate General's opinions in *Kozlowski* (para 74) and *Wolzenburg* (paras 60–63), the objective of reintegration into society is *not* the only basis for a limitation of the exception in Art 4(6), in light of the optional restrictions which the Court accepted on the scope of the Art 4(6) exception in the *Wolzenburg* judgment. So the Dutch rules limiting the Art 4(6) exception

that the equality principle applies to the entirety of this (and other) Framework Decisions, not just to the specific clauses that mention nationals and residents of the executing State.[309]

Finally on this provision, the pending *IB* case asks how to distinguish it from the separate but similar provision on possible guarantees where the EAW has been issued for the purpose of prosecution, where the trial was held *in absentia*.[310]

Next, there are three cases in which the executing judicial authority can (at its discretion) ask for certain guarantees in accordance with the executing Member State's law. Firstly, where the sentence has been passed *in absentia*, if the person concerned had not been summoned in person or otherwise informed of the details of the hearing, the executing State may request the guarantee that he or she must have 'an opportunity to apply for a retrial' and be present at the judgment.[311] This provision was amended in 2009, by means of a Framework Decision that also inserted revised (uniform) rules relating to the *in absentia* exception in four other mutual recognition measures.[312] The new rule provides that an executing State may refuse to execute an EAW unless one of four conditions applies, as specified further: the person concerned was sufficiently aware of the trial; the person concerned was defended by a lawyer which he or she had instructed; the person concerned has waived his or her right to a retrial; or the person concerned has a right to a full retrial. These new rules reflect the case law of the European Court of Human Rights more accurately.[313]

Secondly, where a life sentence could be imposed for the crime, the issuing State may be requested to guarantee that the sentence must be reviewable after twenty years at the latest.[314] Thirdly, a judicial authority may insist, where an EAW is issued for the purpose of prosecution, that a national or resident of the executing State must be returned after the trial to serve their sentence in that State.[315] This provision will also interact in future with the Framework Decision on recognition of custodial sentences,[316] and furthermore it should obviously be interpreted consistently as far as possible with the nearly identical provision

---

for non-Dutch citizens to cases where the person concerned could have been prosecuted in the Netherlands for the relevant offence and where the person concerned would not lose his or her residence right (see paras 80–86, *Wolzenburg* opinion) are only objectionable to the extent that they infringe EU free movement or immigration law.

[309] See paras 42–47 of the *Wolzenburg* judgment (n 271 above).   [310] Ibid.

[311] Art 5(1). *In absentia* trials are an issue in the pending *IB* case (ibid). Note also that *in absentia* judgments trigger the application of the Schengen double jeopardy rules: see Case C-297/07 *Bourquain* [2008] ECR I-9425, and further 11.8 below.

[312] [2009] OJ L 81/24, rescinding Art 5(1) and inserting a new Art 4a. This Framework Decision must be applied from 6 Mar 2011, except as regards Italy, which will apply it from 1 Jan 2014 (Art 8(1) and (2), 2009 Framework Decision, and declaration in [2009] OJ L 97/14). The other measures amended by the 2009 Framework Decision are the Framework Decisions on recognition of financial penalties, confiscation, custodial sentences, and probation and parole (see 9.7.1, 9.7.4, and 9.7.5 below). Note that except as regards Italy, the 2009 Framework Decision will apply even before the dates to apply the latter two Framework Decisions.   [313] See 9.3.1 and 9.3.5 above.

[314] Art 5(2).   [315] Art 5(3).   [316] See n 298 above.

permitting refusal to execute an EAW, where the EAW was issued for the purpose of enforcing a sentence, if the executing Member State will take over the sentence. An entirely identical interpretation of the two provisions is not possible, however, since only one of the two provisions can apply to persons 'staying in' the territory.[317] As noted already, the pending *IB* case concerns the difference between the two provisions when a trial was held *in absentia*.

As for other traditional restrictions on extradition obligations, Member States can no longer refuse to extradite their own nationals,[318] although there are some vestigial remnants of this principle.[319] There is no reference to a possible refusal to execute the warrant or guarantees on grounds of immunity, privilege, or pardon, although the Framework Decision provides that where a privilege or immunity exists, the time period to execute the warrant does not start until that privilege or immunity is waived.[320] Nor is there an exception for fiscal offences, military offences, or political offences as found in the Council of Europe's extradition Convention, although there is a provision in the preamble to the Framework Decision (discussed below) referring to the prohibition on execution of measures intended to persecute people on certain grounds, which corresponds to a part of the traditional 'political offence' exception. There are still possible restrictions relating to grounds of specialty (ie the principle that a person cannot be prosecuted for an 'offence other' than that named in the EAW), subsequent surrender to other Member States, and re-extradition to a non-EU State, but Member States have the option to waive the first two of these protections.[321]

The Court of Justice has clarified aspects of the specialty rule, following a reference from a national court.[322] According to the Framework Decision, the rule does not apply, leaving aside cases where Member States have waived it,

---

[317] Art 4(6), discussed above. The requirement of identical interpretation is bolstered by the reference to both provisions in the Framework Decision on custodial penalties (see ibid). The Court of Justice has also noted that the two provisions have the same objective (*Wolzenburg* judgment, para 62, n 271 above). See also the opinion in *Koslowski* (para 73), ibid.

[318] See the clearly correct interpretation on this point in the opinions in *Kozlowski*, paras 40–112 and *Wolzenburg*, paras 121–144 (both ibid), in particular as regards the German rule that nationals cannot be subject to an EAW without their consent. Of course, the German rule is understandable in light of the constitutional problems implementing the Framework Decision there as regards extradition of nationals (see further below). In any event, the point has limited relevance given the Court's interpretation of Art 4(6) (see next footnote).

[319] Arts 4(6) and 5(3), discussed above. Since the *Wolzenburg* judgment (ibid) accepted the blanket application of Art 4(6) (and probably Art 5(3), by analogy) to nationals of the executing State, Member States with qualms about surrendering their own nationals have an obvious (and legitimate) option available to address their concerns. See also the specific derogation (now expired) for Austria and the temporal limitations which some Member States apply (n 274 above).

[320] Art 20, which also refers to a request for a waiver, but does not state what happens if the waiver is not granted. On this issue, see H Fox, *The Law of State Immunity* (OUP, 2002), 503–516.

[321] Arts 27 and 28. An identical specialty provision appears in the Framework Decision on custodial penalties, except there is no possibility for Member States to waive its application (Art 18 of that measure, n 298 above; see 9.7.1.2 below). It would be logical to interpret these provisions the same way.   [322] *Leymann and Pustovarov*, n 271 above.

where: the person concerned has stayed in or returned to the State which wishes to bring the extra charges; the offence is not punishable by a custodial penalty or detention order; the criminal proceedings do not give rise to detention; the person concerned could be subject to a *restriction* on his or her liberty, as compared to a *deprivation* of it;[323] the person concerned has consented to surrender or to waiver of the specialty principle; or the executing State's authorities have consented to waiver of the principle.[324] The Court ruled that in order to determine what was an 'offence other' than that for which the person was surrendered:[325]

...it is necessary to ascertain whether the constituent elements of the offence, according to the legal description given by the issuing State, are those for which the person was surrendered and whether there is a sufficient correspondence between the information given in the arrest warrant and that contained in the later procedural document. Modifications concerning the time or place of the offence are allowed, in so far as they derive from evidence gathered in the course of the proceedings conducted in the issuing State concerning the conduct described in the arrest warrant, do not alter the nature of the offence and do not lead to grounds for non-execution under Articles 3 and 4 of the Framework Decision.

A modification of the description of the offence as regards the type of narcotics which were allegedly imported, without changing the legal description of the offence, does not amount to a charge for an 'offence other' than that for which the person concerned was surrendered, given that the offence concerned still fell within the same heading in the list of offences for which dual criminality is abolished.[326] Finally, the exception relating to cases where the criminal proceedings do not give rise to restrictions on liberty meant that such proceedings could go ahead, but that any pre-trial or post-trial detention which resulted could only be applied with the consent of the person concerned or the executing State's authorities pursuant to the rules in the Framework Decision. In the meantime, however, the person's liberty could still be restricted if that was lawful on the basis of the charges set out in the EAW.[327] It should be noted that the provisions in the Framework Decision on subsequent surrender to another Member State are to a large degree identical to the specialty provisions, and so should presumably be interpreted the same way as far as possible.[328]

---

[323] See the clarification of this point in ibid, para 70.

[324] Art 27(2) and (3). The last exception is subject to limits set out in Art 27(4): inter alia, consent must be refused where the mandatory exceptions in Art 3 apply, and otherwise may only be refused where Art 4 applies; the guarantees in Art 5 also apply.

[325] Para 57, *Leymann* judgment, n 271 above.   [326] Paras 60–63, ibid.

[327] Paras 72–76, ibid.

[328] Art 28(1)–(3). However, note the absolute requirement of the executing State's consent before the person concerned can be extradited to a non-EU State (Art 28(4)).

The Framework Decision contains provisions on human rights which have largely been repeated in subsequent Framework Decisions.[329] In particular, the preamble specifies that:

(12) This Framework Decision respects fundamental rights and observes the principles recognised by Article 6 of the Treaty on European Union and reflected in the Charter of Fundamental Rights of the European Union, in particular Chapter VI thereof. Nothing in this Framework Decision may be interpreted as prohibiting refusal to surrender a person for whom a European arrest warrant has been issued when there are reasons to believe, on the basis of objective elements, that the said arrest warrant has been issued for the purpose of prosecuting or punishing a person on the grounds of his or her sex, race, religion, ethnic origin, nationality, language, political opinions or sexual orientation, or that that person's position may be prejudiced for any of these reasons.

This Framework Decision does not prevent a Member State from applying its constitutional rules relating to due process, freedom of association, freedom of the press and freedom of expression in other media.

The main text of the Framework Decision then specifies that '[t]his Framework Decision shall not have the effect of modifying the obligation to respect fundamental rights and fundamental legal principles as enshrined in Article 6 of the Treaty on European Union'.[330] There are also provisions in the preamble, unique to this Framework Decision, concerning possible suspension of the Framework Decision if a Member State is suspended from EU membership due to human rights breaches, and protection against extradition, etc in cases of, for example torture, or the death penalty.[331] Finally, Member States are required to establish remedies for fugitives as regards a right to information about the EAW, the right to counsel and an interpreter, and the right to a hearing.[332] It should be noted that the subsequent Directive on suspects' rights to interpretation and translation and the proposed Directive on suspects' right to information expressly apply to EAW proceedings.[333]

The Commission presented an initial assessment of the national implementation of the Framework Decision in 2005,[334] and subsequently updated this analysis in 2006 to take account of the late Italian implementation (Italy being the last Member State to implement the Framework Decision) in April 2005.[335] According to the statistics available to the Commission, 2,603 warrants were issued, 653 persons were arrested, and 104 persons were surrendered up until September 2004; it estimated that the time to execute a warrant had fallen from

---

[329] However, see the different wording of the Framework Decisions on the evidence warrant, mutual recognition of financial penalties, and recognition of confiscation orders (9.6.1.2, 9.7.1.1, and 9.7.4 below), as well as the proposed Directive establishing the European Investigation Order (9.6.1.3 below). On human rights and mutual recognition in general, see 9.3.5 above.   [330] Art 1(3).

[331] Paras 10 and 13 of the preamble. On human rights protection against extradition, see 9.3.1 above.   [332] Arts 11 and 14.

[333] See 9.8.2 below.   [334] COM (2005) 63, 23 Feb 2005.

[335] COM (2006) 8, 24 Jan 2006.

nine months to forty-three days (thirteen days where the warrant was not contested). In the Commission's view, however, a number of Member States were not in full compliance with the Framework Decision, in particular by wrongly restricting its temporal scope; limiting the partial abolition of double criminality; granting decision-making powers to executive (rather than judicial) bodies; allowing their authorities to demand additional guarantees before surrender; providing for additional grounds for refusal (including an over-broad application of human rights grounds and the imposition of conditions concerning the surrender of nationals); insisting on additional procedural requirements for transmission of arrest warrants; failing to apply time limits; and setting out the procedural rights of the individual too vaguely.

This critical report on the EU's flagship mutual recognition measure resulted in an unprecedented debate in the JHA Council, which focused on the issues of the human rights ground for refusal, political grounds for refusal, the use of executive bodies instead of judicial bodies, and the limits on the temporal scope of the Framework Decision.[336] The Council did not adopt any formal conclusions on these issues, but it asked the Commission to produce a further report by June 2006 and decided to conduct a practical evaluation of the application of the EAW.[337] Member States subsequently submitted detailed responses in writing objecting to the Commission's analysis.[338]

A second Commission report in 2007 concluded that there were still problems applying the Framework Decision in some Member States, inter alia as regards transitional application of the EAW, surrender of own nationals, sentencing thresholds, double criminality checks, and incorrect or impermissible grounds for non-execution, including a large number relating to human rights.[339] Several Member States had amended national laws to bring them further into conformity with the Framework Decision. As for the Commission's previous report, half of the Member States' objections related to information which they should already have sent to the Commission, a quarter were valid corrections, and the Commission did not agree with the other quarter of the objections. In practice, according to the report, in 2005, 6,900 warrants were issued in twenty-three Member States providing statistics, resulting in 1,770 arrests and 1,532 surrenders, with half consenting to surrenders and a fifth being nationals of the executing State, guarantees of return having been agreed in half of those cases. The time to execute the warrants was still forty-three days (eleven days in the case of consent), although in 5% of cases the relevant deadlines were not met. The Commission

---

[336] See Council doc 8842/1/05, 19 May 2005.

[337] JHA Council press release, 2–3 June 2005. The questionnaire for the evaluation, which began in 2006, can be found in Council doc 14272/05, 11 Nov 2005.

[338] Council doc 11528/05, 5 Sep 2005.

[339] COM (2007) 407 and SEC (2007) 979, 11 July 2007. See the responses of two Member States (Council docs 14308/07 and add 1, 12 and 13 Nov 2007).

concluded that the Framework Decision was a 'success', and the remaining problems with its application were 'peripheral'.

The latest fairly complete statistics concerning the EAW, dating from 2008, show that in that year over 14,000 EAWs were issued by the Member States supplying statistics.[340] Over 4,500 persons were arrested, and nearly 2,900 were surrendered. Clearly the EAW is increasingly used in practice.

As for the Council's evaluation, it culminated in a series of draft recommendations, mostly concerning practical aspects of the application of the EAW but also touching on the sensitive issues of the grounds for non-recognition, including human rights grounds, and the possible abolition of the specialty rule.[341] Some recommendations were addressed to Member States, while another batch were addressed to the Council's working groups; the latter were then followed up by Council conclusions, which were adopted in June 2010.[342] The Stockholm programme invited the Commission to consider the evaluation and possibly to make proposals to 'increase efficiency and legal protection for individuals in the process of surrender'.[343] It should also be noted that Eurojust, the EU prosecutors' agency, also has a role as regards EAWs.[344]

The implementation of the EAW has been equally controversial at national level in a number of Member States,[345] and three national constitutional courts struck down the national application of the Framework Decision, at least in principle. First of all, in spring 2005, the Polish constitutional court ruled that the national law implementing the EAW Framework Decision was unconstitutional as it permitted the extradition of Polish citizens, although that court delayed the application of its judgment for eighteen months so that the constitution could be modified; the constitutional amendment duly took effect in November 2006. Next, in July 2005, the German Constitutional court ruled that the national implementing law was invalid, as regards German citizens; the Spanish and Hungarian courts responded by disapplying the EAW as regards German warrants issued for German citizens, but the national law was amended by August 2006. Finally, in November 2005, the Cypriot constitutional court ruled that the EAW conflicted with the Cypriot constitution as regards the surrender of Cypriot nationals; so the constitution was amended as from July 2006. However, the Czech constitutional court in particular upheld the Framework Decision.

How should the EAW be assessed? The initial case law of the Court of Justice is focusing on the efficient application of the EAW, overriding the sound argument that at least some EU citizens with less than five years' residence in a Member State may be sufficiently integrated there to benefit from the same protection as a

---

[340] Council doc 9734/4/09, 7 Dec 2009. [341] Council doc 8302/4/09, 28 May 2009.
[342] Council doc 8436/2/10, 28 May 2010. [343] [2010] OJ C 115, point 3.1.1.
[344] See 11.9 below.
[345] See the summary with further references in the 2007 Commission report (n 338 above), and the analysis in Guild and Marin, n 270 above.

Member States' nationals.[346] The Court's assumption in the *Wolzenburg* case that widening the application of the EAW as much as possible will necessarily assist to achieve its aims, along with the addition of a further requirement in order to apply some exceptions to the Framework Decision in the *Koslowski* case, is, with respect, misguided, as it overlooks the contrary objectives of free movement rules and fails to recognize that the enforcement of a sentence in the executing State in such cases still accomplishes the objectives of deterrence and punishment while increasing the chance of rehabilitation. The recommendation from the Council evaluation on the EAW to abolish the application of the specialty rule is profoundly unprincipled, since its abolition would allow unscrupulous prosecutors to circumvent all of the safeguards in the Framework Decision (for instance, by issuing an EAW and then proceeding with the 'real' prosecution for minor offences which fall below the punishment threshold in the Framework Decision or for offences which fall within the scope of the grounds for non-execution of an EAW). This would hardly improve the legitimacy of the EAW and could reduce the efficient application of the system by wasting executing States' time and resources chasing and processing fugitives whose alleged crime was quite trivial. This is already a problem to some extent, with some Member States issuing arrest warrants for crimes such as the 'theft of a piglet'.[347]

The most fundamental issue for the legitimacy of the EAW, other than the still-contested issue of the surrender of nationals, is the question of whether the EAW system is compatible with human rights, an issue which applies equally to all other mutual recognition measures.[348] Certainly it is problematic that the Commission keeps criticizing Member States' attempts to protect the human rights of suspects who are the subject of EAWs: the 2007 report, for instance, objected to the Danish law which provides for refusal of surrender on grounds of 'torture, degrading treatment, violation of due process as well as if the surrender appears to be unreasonable on humanitarian grounds', as well as a British law which requires *in absentia* trials to meet basic ECHR criteria.

The answer to this fundamental question depends in part on whether Member States' judicial authorities have an obligation, or at least the power, to refuse execution of other Member States' warrants on human rights grounds (in addition to the specific double jeopardy and *in absentia* provisions of the Framework Decision). The judgment in *Advocaten voor de Wereld* referred to a requirement to protect human rights within the context of the Framework Decision, but then ruled that the onus is on the issuing State to ensure the application of human rights as regards the dual criminality principle. However, this case did not address the issue of whether the executing State can examine the issuing Member State's request in order to consider non-execution on human rights grounds.

---

[346] See the opinion in *Wolzenburg* on this point.

[347] cf the inconclusive discussions on the proportionality of issuing EAWs (see the evaluation recommendations and conclusions (nn 340 and 341 above)).   [348] See generally 9.3.5 above.

While the main text of the Framework Decision is ambiguous as to whether human rights can constitute grounds for non-execution of a warrant, the express wording of the preamble is not: '[n]othing in this Framework Decision may be interpreted as prohibiting refusal to surrender a person' as regards discriminatory prosecution, and the Framework Decision 'does not prevent a Member State from applying its constitutional rules relating to due process' and other specified matters. While it would obviously have been preferable, from the point of view of legal certainty, to set out these provisions as express exclusions from the principle of mutual recognition in the main text of the legislation, it can be presumed that this was considered unnecessary because it was assumed that Member States' international human rights commitments and national constitutions, along with the primary law of the EU (Article 6 TEU) took precedence over the Framework Decision. Furthermore, for the same reasons, it must be accepted that any *further* human rights obligations stemming from international commitments or national constitutions, even if not referred to explicitly in the preamble, can also be invoked as grounds of non-execution. And given the nature of human rights obligations, non-execution on human rights grounds must be regarded as mandatory, not discretionary. The vague express reference to human rights obligations in the main text of the Framework Decision should be understood as confirming this interpretation.

Although the Court of Justice case law on the grounds for non-execution has consistently concluded that the grounds for non-recognition in the Framework Decision are exhaustive,[349] this does not answer the objection that human rights grounds for non-execution stem from the primary law of the EU (now including the EU Charter of Fundamental Rights), not secondary legislation. A series of opinions of Advocates General have concluded explicitly that Member States can refuse to recognize EAWs on human rights grounds.[350] As for the argument that Member States must have mutual trust in each others' systems, as noted above, the inability to reject mutual recognition on human rights grounds, on the assumption that the problem will be fixed months later in the issuing State or years later in the European Court of Human Rights, would mean that human rights protection in this field would be theoretical and illusory, not real and effective.[351]

There is therefore no basis for the Commission's continued arguments that Member States' legislation transposing the Framework Decision has exceeded the limits of their discretion on this point; and there is still less ground for the interpretation of the Framework Decision advocated by Eurojust or the European Parliament.[352]

---

[349] See n 271 above.

[350] See the opinions in *Wolzenburg*, *Koslowski*, and *Santesteban Goicoechea*, as well as the questions in the pending *IB* case and the withdrawn *Gataev* case (n 271 above).

[351] See 9.3.5 above. See also the balance between the mutual trust principles and human rights protection in the *Wolzenburg* and *Koslowski* opinions (ibid).

[352] See Annex II to the 2004 annual report of Eurojust and the EP recommendation to the Council of 15 Mar 2006 (P6_TA-PROV(2006)0083). See also the Commission assessments of the implementation of other Framework Decisions (9.6.2, 9.7.1.1, and 9.7.4 below).

As for specific human rights issues, the mandatory non-execution of a warrant on double jeopardy grounds is welcome, but the merely *optional* non-execution for cases of final judgments and (in some cases) termination of prosecution is objectionable, in light of the Court of Justice's interpretation of the double jeopardy rules.[353] The *in absentia* exception (which appears in most other mutual recognition measures) is not only optional, rather than mandatory, but also fails to take account of the *Poitrimol* line of jurisprudence of the European Court of Human Rights.[354] As noted above,[355] although the 2009 Framework Decision on this issue brings standards into line with ECHR case law,[356] this ground for refusal is still only optional and the long delay before the application of the 2009 measure in Italy is regrettable. It would obviously have been far better to have provided for proper protection in the first place.

Of course, if the interpretation of the relationship between this measure and human rights protection argued above is correct, then any such human rights problems can be solved by applying the national or international human rights obligations which take priority over the Framework Decision. But to ensure legal certainty on these important issues, it would of course have been better to set out this interpretation explicitly in the text of this Framework Decision, and equally in other EU mutual recognition measures.

Finally, is the basic principle of mutual recognition acceptable? And if so, is the EU's approach to mutual recognition, as embodied in particular in the Framework Decision establishing the EAW, correct? Due to the broader implications of this debate, the answer is considered fully in the conclusions to this chapter.

9.6. Pre-trial measures

Further measures in addition to (or instead of) extradition proceedings are often necessary before a trial with cross-border aspects takes place. It is obviously necessary to trace any relevant evidence or witnesses and ensure that the evidence can be used, or that the witnesses will testify, at the trial if possible. Sometimes it is necessary to issue freezing orders to ensure that property is available for evidence or for subsequent confiscation. Finally, an important issue for individuals is the length of any detention awaiting trial, which risks being longer where there are cross-border elements to a case. These three issues will be examined in turn.

9.6.1. Movement of evidence

In order to facilitate the movement of evidence in criminal cases,[357] the EU initially adopted specific and general measures on mutual judicial assistance, building on

---

[353] See 11.8 below.   [354] See further 9.3.5 above.   [355] Ibid.
[356] On that case law, see 9.3.1 above.
[357] On the movement of evidence in civil cases, see 8.5.4 above.

the existing international (Council of Europe) framework. Subsequently the EU has moved towards adopting mutual recognition measures in this area, starting with the Framework Decision on the European Evidence Warrant. Further steps are planned in this field, which are linked to plans for legislation harmonizing national evidence law, for the purpose of ensuring mutual admissibility of evidence.[358] The Commission plans to propose legislation on both issues in 2011,[359] and issued a Green Paper on both issues in 2009 to prepare these measures.[360] In the meantime, however, a group of Member States tabled an initiative in spring 2010 for a Directive establishing a 'European Investigation Order', which will would repeal or replace most (but not all) existing mutual recognition measures in this area.[361]

9.6.1.1. Mutual assistance in criminal matters

The core texts on cross-border mutual assistance between judicial authorities in criminal law cases are the 1959 Council of Europe Convention ('the 1959 Convention') on mutual assistance, which all Member States have ratified, and the first Protocol to that Convention (1978), which all but one of the Member States has ratified.[362] A Second Protocol to the Convention, which parallels the EU Convention of 2000 (see below) in several respects, was agreed in 2001, but only a minority of EU Member States have ratified it.[363]

The 1959 Convention applies to all offences except military offences, and there is no sentencing threshold or double criminality requirement for its use, as there is for extradition treaties, except for search and seizure measures.[364] A judge in the 'home State' of the prosecution, wanting to obtain evidence or other relevant material which another Member State is 'hosting', must send formal requests (called 'letters rogatory'), usually via his or her national ministry, to the relevant ministry of the host Member State, which forwards the request to a national judge. A judge in the prosecuting State can also request the attendance of a witness who is residing in another State, but any summons the prosecuting judge sends to such a witness unless the witness sets foot in the prosecuting Member State and then disobeys a second summons to appear. If a prosecuting judge would like to contact a potential witness in custody in another Member State, the would-be witness can refuse. There is an exception for political offences and fiscal offences; assistance may also be refused if a requested State considers that executing a request is 'likely to prejudice the sovereignty, security, *ordre public* or other essential interests of its country'.[365] In practice, reservations are also applied

---

[358] See further 9.8.1 below.

[359] See Commission 2010 work programme (COM (2010) 135, 31 Mar 2010, Annex II) and the Action Plan on implementing the Stockholm programme (COM (2010) 171, 20 Apr 2010).

[360] COM (2009) 624, 11 Nov 2009.   [361] On this proposal, see 9.6.1.3 below.

[362] ETS 30 and ETS 99. For ratification details, see Appendix I.

[363] ETS 182; for ratification details, see Appendix I.   [364] Art 5 of the Convention.

[365] Art 2 of the Convention.

regarding double jeopardy.[366] The First Protocol to the Convention inter alia removes the exception for fiscal offences, although a State can still retain the exemption in part.

As for EU measures, the Schengen Convention contains rules on judicial assistance, which: require Member States to abolish the fiscal offence exception for excise duties, VAT, and customs duties (if they have not yet ratified the First Protocol to the Council of Europe Convention); widen the scope of proceedings for which assistance could be requested; allow direct contact between legal authorities without ministry intervention; and provide for posting procedural documents directly to persons in other Member States.[367]

Subsequently, to supplement the Council of Europe measures in order to facilitate the movement of evidence between Member States,[368] the EU adopted a Convention on mutual assistance in 2000 and a Protocol to the EU Convention in 2001; the Convention and Protocol are in force in a large majority of Member States.[369] The most important criminal law provisions of the Convention specify that:

(a) the Schengen provisions on posting documents and contacting other judges directly have become the normal rule;[370]

(b) the State where the evidence is located must normally comply with the formalities and procedures which the home State requests;[371]

(c) the home State may request that a State with custody over a person transfer that person (possibly without his or her consent) to be a witness in the trial in the home State;[372] and

(d) the home State may request a hearing by videoconference with a witness, an expert, or the suspect in the territory of the host State; a summons to such a conference will be mandatory for a witness or expert. Member States may opt out of the provision for video hearings with the suspect.[373]

The 2001 Protocol is primarily concerned with financial crime. It provides in turn for assistance relating to requests for information on bank accounts, requests for information on bank transactions, and requests for monitoring of

---

[366] See the facts of the *Miraglia* case (C-469/03 [2005] ECR I-2009).

[367] Arts 48–53, Schengen Convention ([2000] OJ L 239).

[368] On the practice before the Convention, see the report in [2001] OJ C 216/14.

[369] [2000] OJ C 197/1 and [2001] OJ C 326/1. For ratification details, see Appendix I. On the Convention and Protocol generally, see E Denza, 'The 2000 Convention on Mutual Assistance in Criminal Matters' (2003) 40 CMLRev 1047; and D McClean, *International Cooperation in Civil and Criminal Matters* (2nd edn, OUP, 2002), 224–237. On the policing issues arising from the Convention, see 12.9 below.   [370] Arts 5 and 6.

[371] Art 4.

[372] Art 9. Consent is required by Cyprus, the Czech Republic, Denmark, Estonia, Finland, Germany, Latvia, Poland, and the UK.

[373] Art 10; Denmark, France, the Netherlands, Poland, and the UK have opted out of the provision. See also Art 11, on the hearing of witnesses and experts by telephone. On the human rights rules applicable in such cases, see *Viola v Italy*, judgment of 5 Oct 2006.

bank accounts,[374] although the first two types of assistance can be subjected to the conditions applicable to search and seizure,[375] and the first type can be limited to specific offences.[376] More generally, the Protocol contains provisions on: the obligation of requested authorities to inform the requesting authorities about their investigations; the forwarding of additional requests for mutual assistance; the waiver of banking secrecy in relation to mutual assistance; the abolition of the fiscal offence exception (copying the wording of the First Protocol to the Council of Europe Convention); abolishing the political offence exception (although Member States may limit this abolition to specific offences); and providing for dispute settlement in the Council or Eurojust in case requests are blocked on grounds of dual criminality or the remaining reservations under the mutual assistance Convention.[377]

These measures allow the prosecuting State to assert its authority de facto over persons and evidence in another Member State, albeit indirectly through the acts of the requested Member State's authorities. They also simplify the 'border controls' previously slowing down the processing of requests between Member States. However, the position of the defendant under these rules is problematic, as there is no reference to the right to cross-examine witnesses, and there are only limited minimum standards applicable to cross-border hearings (although the Council has the power to adopt a measure on this subject, which it has not yet used).[378] In fact, for suspects (as well as witnesses), there is no express right to counsel.

The EU has also adopted a number of measures on mutual assistance as regards specific crimes, in particular as regards drug trafficking,[379] and in conjunction with a number of Joint Actions harmonizing substantive criminal law.[380] More generally, a Joint Action on good practice on mutual assistance requires Member States to deposit statements with the Council Secretariat setting out in detail their intentions to respond to mutual assistance requests from other Member States swiftly and effectively,[381] and the SIS functions as a practical tool for listing persons who or objects which are connected with criminal proceedings.[382]

9.6.1.2. European Evidence Warrant

In order to apply the principle of mutual recognition to aspects of the movement of evidence between Member States, in 2008 the Council adopted a Framework

---

[374] Arts 1–3 of the Protocol; see also Art 4 (confidentiality of such requests).

[375] Arts 1(5) and 2(4).   [376] Art 1(3); but the Council can extend the scope (Art 1(6)).

[377] Arts 5–10. Denmark, France, and Latvia have invoked a permitted reservation to limit the abolition of the political offence exception.   [378] Art 10(9) of the Convention.

[379] Executive Committee Decision SCH/Com-ex (93)14 ([2000] OJ L 239/427).

[380] For details of these measures, see the first edition of this book, at 172–173. As regards identification and tracing of criminal proceeds, see also Art 4 of the Framework Decision on money laundering ([2001] OJ L 182/1).   [381] [1998] OJ L 191/1.

[382] See 12.6.1.1 below.

Decision establishing a European Evidence Warrant (EEW), which Member States must apply by 19 January 2011.[383] The Framework Decision will not apply to all movement of evidence; rather it is the first stage in a two-stage procedure replacing mutual assistance measures with mutual recognition measures.[384] So it will not apply to evidence which could only be obtained by: the holding of hearings, or similar measures; bodily examination or obtaining bodily material; gathering real-time information, for example by intercepting telecommunications or monitoring bank accounts; analysis of existing documents, objects, or data; or the furnishing of communications data by telecommunications companies.[385] The EEW can only be issued if the evidence sought is necessary and proportionate and if such evidence could be obtained according to the national law of the issuing State in similar cases; but it will be up to the issuing State alone to judge these issues.[386] Detailed procedural safeguards proposed by the Commission, such as protections relating to privacy and self-incrimination, were dropped.[387]

Dual criminality will be abolished for searches and seizures for evidence falling within the scope of the Framework Decision, for the standard list of thirty-two crimes.[388] The grounds for non-recognition (all optional) include a defective EEW, double jeopardy, immunity or privilege, territoriality, and national security.[389] As for remedies, they must be available in the executing State, at least as regards the exercise of coercive measures, although the substance of the EEW could only be challenged in the issuing State. The issuing State must grant remedies equivalent to those applicable to purely domestic proceedings, and both States have obligations as regards time limits and the facilitation of proceedings.[390] Next, the Framework Decision contains the standard human rights clauses, with the additional proviso that 'any obligations incumbent on judicial authorities in this respect shall remain unaffected'.[391] Finally, the EEW will not entirely replace traditional mutual assistance measures, but will co-exist with them for a transitional period until the second stage of the EEW is in place and mutual assistance measures are fully replaced.[392]

From a human rights perspective, it is unfortunate that the exceptions to execution of foreign decisions will be optional only, and that the Commission's

---

[383] Art 23(1) of the Framework Decision ([2008] OJ L 350/72). All further references in this section are to this Framework Decision, unless otherwise noted.

[384] On the second stage, see the proposal for a European Investigation Order (discussed below).

[385] Art 4(2).   [386] Art 7.

[387] Art 12 of the Commission's proposal (COM (2003) 688, 14 Nov 2003).

[388] Art 14. There is a special rule for Germany, allowing it to maintain dual criminality for a further six crimes: see Art 23(4) and the German declaration published in [2008] OJ L 350/92. For the definition of 'search and seizure', see Art 2(e).   [389] Art 13.

[390] Art 18.

[391] Art 1(3); similar wording appears in the Framework Decision on the execution of confiscation orders (see 9.7.4 below).   [392] Art 21 and recital 25 in the preamble.

proposed safeguards have been dropped. The safeguards proposals reflected the jurisprudence of the European Court of Human Rights.[393]

9.6.1.3. European Investigation Order

As noted above, in order to implement the objective of creating a comprehensive system governing all exchanges of criminal evidence between Member States, a group of Member States proposed a Directive to establish a European Investigation Order (EIO) in spring 2010.[394] This Directive, if adopted in the form originally proposed, would repeal the Framework Decision on the European Evidence Warrant, substitute (as regards freezing of evidence) for the Framework Decision on freezing orders,[395] and replace the 'corresponding' EU and Council of Europe Conventions and Protocols on mutual assistance (including the Schengen Convention provisions), as regards relations between participating Member States.[396] It is based on Article 82(1)(a) TFEU.[397]

The proposed Directive follows the structure of the Framework Decision establishing the EEW with certain amendments, and with the inclusion of some of the specific rules on mutual assistance set out in the 2000 EU mutual assistance Convention and its Protocol. It would apply to all 'investigative measures' (this concept is not defined) with the exception of joint investigation teams and certain measures relating to telecommunications interception.[398] It is not certain whether the proposal would apply to some issues dealt with in other EU measures, such as the criminal records legislation or the issue of covert investigations.[399] Otherwise the EIO would apply to most of the issues excluded from the EEW, ie hearings, bodily examinations, analysing data, and similar actions, along with obtaining banking data.

The proposal would amount to a 'bonfire' of the key traditional grounds for refusals of mutual assistance requests or the EEW, most notably as regards double jeopardy, dual criminality, and territoriality. This would be the first EU measure to abolish fully the possibility of refusal on any of these grounds, never mind all three together. The abolition of the double jeopardy exception takes no account of other EU rules on this issue and status of this principle in the EU Charter of Fundamental Rights,[400] while the combined abolition of the dual criminality and territoriality exceptions means that a person could be subject to home, business, and body searchers for committing an act that was not criminal under the national

---

[393] See 9.3.4 above.
[394] [2010] OJ C 165/22. All references in this subsection are to this initiative, unless otherwise noted.   [395] On this measure, see 9.6.2 below.
[396] Art 29; there is no indication of which provisions are considered to 'correspond'. On the position of non-participating Member States and associated non-EU States, see generally 9.2.5 above.
[397] On the competence issues, see 9.2.4 above.   [398] Art 3.
[399] Recital 9 in the preamble to the initiative states that it does not apply to cross-border police surveillance, which is regulated by Art 40 of the Schengen Convention (see 12.9.2 below).
[400] See 11.8 below.

law of the place where it was committed. This is fundamentally objectionable from the point of view of human rights principles or national sovereignty.[401]

Furthermore, the EIO Directive would also remove a number of sundry other restrictions or safeguards which currently apply to the EEW or mutual assistance measures: the requirements that the issue of EEWs must be proportionate, and could only be issued if such as documents, could also be obtained in the issuing State under its law (if they had been present there) would be dropped; the data protection clause in the EEW Framework Decision would be dropped;[402] the flexibility of the executing Member State not to carry out coercive measures, and the possibility of applying a validation procedure where the order was not issued by a judge, (ie was issued by a police officer) would be dropped;[403] the rules relating to remedies would be significantly weakened;[404] the possibility of videoconferences with suspects would no longer be subject to an express protection for human rights, and the requested Member State would no longer have a blanket power to refuse these requests;[405] many restrictions relating to controlled deliveries (ie 'sting' operations by police or customs officers) would be dropped;[406] and certain restrictions concerning bank information would be dropped.[407]

These changes would be counterbalanced only by the addition of a single sentence to the brief reference to the human rights safeguards in the EEW Framework Decision, referring to constitutional protection for freedom of expression.[408] For the reasons set out elsewhere in this chapter,[409] these vague provisions do not provide sufficient protection, at least in the absence of clarification from the Court of Justice.

9.6.1.4. Criminal records

One aspect of mutual assistance that has received special attention from the EU in recent years is the exchange of information concerning criminal records. This is due to a concerted attempt to increase the effectiveness of the rules concerning the exchange of this information. It should also be kept in mind that this issue is linked to other EU legislation on taking account of prior convictions, the issue

---

[401] See the comments in 11.6 below.

[402] Art 10 of the EEW Framework Decision. It is possible that Art 23 of the 2000 EU Convention on this subject (n 369 above), or the EU's 2008 Framework Decision on personal data protection (see 12.6.4 below), would apply instead, but the proposed Directive does not mention this.

[403] See Arts 11 and 12, EEW Framework Decision.

[404] Compare Art 13 of the EIO proposal to Art 18 of the EEW Framework Decision; the rule that evidence transfers could be suspended pending appeal (Art 11(5), EEW Framework Decision) would also be dropped.

[405] Compare Art 21(10) of the EIO proposal to Art 10(9), 2000 Convention.

[406] Compare Art 26 of the EIO proposal to Art 12, 2000 Convention.

[407] Compare Arts 23–25 of the EIO proposal to Arts 1(5), 2(4), and 3(3), 2001 Protocol to the EU Convention.   [408] Art 1(3).

[409] See 9.3.5 and 9.5.2 above.

of disqualifications following a criminal conviction, and to the double jeopardy principle, and can also affect a person's position in other respects as set out in national law (the increased possibility of pre-trial detention and different rules on trial procedure and enforcement of a sentence).[410]

The Council of Europe's mutual assistance Convention provides that a requested State shall send extracts from its judicial records to a requesting State, to the same extent as it complies with requests from its own authorities. Otherwise, the request shall be complied with in accordance with the requested State's law.[411] This Convention also provides that all its Contracting Parties will inform the other Contracting Parties at least once a year of all criminal convictions and subsequent measures concerning the latter's nationals which are entered into the judicial record.[412] The First Protocol to the Convention supplements the latter point by providing that further information on these convictions must be provided on request.[413]

In order to speed up the transfer of information from criminal records, the EU Council adopted, as an interim measure, a Decision in 2005 which sets out a standard form and detailed rules regarding sending requests for information on convictions and requires immediate transmission of information regarding convictions of nationals of other Member States.[414] Member States had to withdraw any reservations to the Council of Europe Convention on the first issue, but could retain them on the latter issue.

As both the mutual recognition programme and the Hague programme called for broader measures to enhance the exchange of information on criminal convictions, the Commission had released in the meantime a White Paper on the issue in early 2005.[415] This White Paper pinpointed difficulties in rapidly identifying Member States where individuals have already been convicted, obtaining information quickly and by a simple procedure, and in understanding the information provided. To address these issues, the Commission suggested a two-stage process. In the first stage, a European index of offenders would be established, in order to make it easier to identify which Member States a person had been convicted in. In a second stage, a standard format would be used to exchange detailed information about the convictions.

In response to the White Paper, the JHA Council agreed in April 2005 that information on EU citizens would instead be exchanged bilaterally between Member States, with an index of offenders used only as regards non-EU

---

[410] See respectively 9.7.2, 9.7.3, and 11.8 below. EU free movement law also contains provisions on the exchange of police records (see 7.4.1 above).

[411] Art 13 of the Convention. Five Member States have reservations on this clause.

[412] Art 22 of the Convention. Eight Member States have reservations on this clause.

[413] Art 4 of the First Protocol. The UK and Ireland have reservations on this clause.

[414] [2005] OJ L 322/33. The Decision applied from 21 May 2006 (Art 7).

[415] COM (2005) 10, 25 Jan 2005.

nationals.[416] The Commission subsequently proposed a Framework Decision concerning the exchange of information on EU citizens' criminal records, which the Council adopted in 2009, alongside an implementing Decision.[417] Member States are obliged to apply these measures by 7 and 27 April 2012;[418] on the latter date, the prior EU Decision is repealed and the Framework Decision will replace some of the relevant Council of Europe measures in relations between Member States.[419]

This Framework Decision repeats the obligation in the 2005 Decision for each Member State to send to each other Member State information on the criminal convictions of nationals of those other States as soon as possible, extending this to cases where the person concerned is a dual national of the convicting Member State.[420] This information must be stored in the system established by the Framework Decision for possible further transmission,[421] and the Framework Decision elaborates upon the process of sending and replying to requests for information on criminal convictions.[422] There are specific rules on personal data protection.[423] The criminal record information is to be exchanged using a standard format,[424] which was established by the Council in the parallel Decision establishing a European Criminal Records Information System (ECRIS).

ECRIS is not an EU-wide database; nor does it give any Member States' authorities access to the criminal records database of other Member States.[425] Instead, the 2009 Decision establishes the standard format for the supply of criminal records information which might be exchanged pursuant to the Framework Decision, by means of common codes indicating generally the type of offence and type of penalty imposed on the person concerned.[426]

A subsequent proposal from the Commission suggests further rules on criminal records, including a derogation from the 2009 Framework Decision, concerning specific sexual offences against children.[427] Regarding the criminal records of third-country nationals, the Commission has so far issued a discussion paper on the feasibility of establishing an index of their convictions.[428]

---

[416] See JHA Council press release, 14 Apr 2005.   [417] [2009] OJ L 93/23 and 33.

[418] Art 13 of the Framework Decision and Art 8 of the 2009 Decision.

[419] Art 12 of the Framework Decision. More precisely, Art 22 of the Council of Europe mutual assistance Convention and Art 4 of the First Protocol to the Convention are replaced, while Art 13 of that Convention remains in force, with a continued waiver of Member States' reservations.

[420] Art 4, Framework Decision; compare to Art 2 of the 2005 Decision. Art 4(4) of the Framework Decision incorporates Art 4 of the First Protocol to the Council of Europe Convention.

[421] Art 5, Framework Decision.

[422] Arts 6–8, Framework Decision; compare to Art 3 of the 2005 Decision.

[423] Art 9, Framework Decision; compare to Art 4 of the 2005 Decision.

[424] Art 11, Framework Decision.

[425] Art 3 of the 2009 Decision. On such forms of information exchange, see 12.6 below.

[426] Art 4 of the Decision.

[427] COM (2010) 94, 29 Mar 2010, Art 10. On the issue of disqualifications, see 9.7.3 below.

[428] COM (2006) 359, 4 July 2006.

As for the future, the Stockholm programme calls for: Member States to implement ECRIS as soon as possible; the Commission to assess whether network-
ing criminal records will prevent offences from being committed, and whether
ECRIS can be extended to include supervision measures; and the Commission
to propose legislation to establish a register of the criminal convictions of third-
country nationals in Member States' courts.[429] The action plan on implementation of the programme provides for a legislative proposal on the latter point
and proposals for measures implementing ECRIS in 2011, and an evaluation of
ECRIS and its possible extension in 2014.[430]

9.6.2. Freezing orders

The enforcement of foreign freezing orders is governed first of all by the 1990
Council of Europe Convention on the proceeds of crime, ratified by all Member
States, which requires States to enforce orders freezing the proceeds of crime
issued by other signatory States.[431] However, the obligation is subject to many
possible grounds for refusal.[432]

Initially, EU measures in this area were confined to an obligation to give freez-
ing requests from other Member States equal priority with domestic requests.[433]
But subsequently freezing orders were the subject of the EU's second Framework
Decision concerning mutual recognition in criminal matters.[434] The Framework
Decision applies to orders issued by 'judicial authorities' (as defined by the issuing
State) in the framework of criminal proceedings,[435] not only to freeze criminal
assets (the subject of the 1990 Council of Europe Convention), for the purpose
of their subsequent confiscation,[436] but also orders concerning the freezing of
evidence, for the purpose of subsequent transfer to the issuing State pursuant to
mutual assistance rules.[437]

Member States must recognize and execute the freezing order of another
Member State, subject only to the most limited list of grounds for non-recognition
appearing in any EU measure to date.[438] In particular, dual criminality is abolished for the standard list of thirty-two crimes.[439] However, where a freezing
order relates to subsequent confiscation (as distinct from securing evidence),

---

[429] [2010] OJ C 115, point 4.2.3. See also the plans for a police records index (12.6.3 below).

[430] COM (2010) 171, 20 Apr 2010.

[431] Arts 11 and 12 of the Convention (ETS 141). See now Arts 21 and 22 of the replacement 2005
Council of Europe Convention on the same issue (CETS 198), which has been ratified by only a
minority of Member States (see Appendix I for ratification details).

[432] Art 18 of the 1990 Convention and Art 28 of the 2005 Convention, both ibid.

[433] Art 4 of the 2001 Framework Decision on money laundering ([2001] OJ L 182/1); Art 3 of the
1998 Joint Action on this subject was identical ([1998] OJ L 333/1). See further 9.7.4 below.

[434] [2003] OJ L 196/45. Member States had to comply by 2 Aug 2005 (Art 14(1)).

[435] Art 2(a).   [436] On this issue, see further 9.7.4 below.

[437] Arts 3(1) and 10. On these rules, see 9.6.1 above.   [438] Art 5(1).   [439] Art 3(2).

a broader dual criminality condition can be applied, to require that an act constitute an offence *to which a freezing order could apply* in both States.[440] Other grounds
(all optional) for non-execution are a defective freezing certificate, an immunity
or privilege under the executing State's law, or where it is 'instantly clear' from
the certificate that the subsequent rendering of judicial assistance would breach
the double jeopardy principle.[441] An executing Member State may also set a time
limit for freezing the property.[442]

The Framework Decision includes the same human rights provisions as the
Framework Decision establishing the EAW,[443] so these provisions presumably
must be interpreted the same way.[444] Also, this Framework Decision provides for
remedies to be exercised in either the issuing or executing State. Although the
substantive reasons for the freezing can only be challenged in the issuing State,
both States are obliged to facilitate access to remedies and the issuing State is
obliged to set time limits that guarantee access to an effective legal remedy.[445]

According to a Commission report on the application of this Framework
Decision, eight Member States had not yet applied it by October 2008.[446] The
Commission report claims inter alia that some Member States made errors as
regards abolition of dual criminality, reimbursement, and contact between
judicial authorities, and that fourteen Member States provide for forbidden
grounds for non-execution (in particular concerning human rights). Overall,
the Commission concluded that application of the Framework Decision was 'not
satisfactory', due to the limited number of notifications and the 'numerous omissions and limitations' in the laws which had been notified.

This measure is subject to the same objections that apply to other EU mutual
recognition measures, *a fortiori* because there are so few grounds for refusing
execution (in particular, there are no grounds for refusing execution on grounds
of *in absentia* judgments and extraterritoriality), and because they are all optional.
Furthermore, the double jeopardy provision is weak, because it is highly unlikely
that it will be evident from the certificate connected to the freezing order that
the double jeopardy principle is infringed; this will only be evident following
further communication between the issuing and executing authorities, and/or
subsequent objections by the suspects. If freezing orders apply beyond the time
period for a trial to take place within a 'reasonable time', as required by Article
6 ECHR, it is arguable that they should no longer be executed; it is unfortunate that the Framework Decision does not set out this principle expressly. The

---

[440] Art 3(4).

[441] Art 7. There are also some limited grounds for postponement of execution (Art 8).

[442] Art 6(2).   [443] See clause 6 of the preamble and Art 1, second line.

[444] See 9.5.2 above.   [445] Art 11.

[446] COM (2008) 885, 22 Dec 2008. According to a later update by the Council Secretariat, four
Member States (Italy, Portugal, Greece, and Luxembourg) had not yet implemented this measure
and two (the UK and Cyprus) had only partly implemented it by spring 2009 (Council doc 9195/09,
29 Apr 2009). The UK subsequently fully implemented it (Council doc 5254/10, 12 Jan 2010).

Commission's complaints regarding non-recognition on human rights grounds should be rejected for the reasons set out above.[447]

As for the future, this Framework Decision would be replaced, as regards the freezing of evidence, by the proposed European Investigation Order, discussed above.[448] As regards freezing of assets, it would be replaced by plans to propose recast legislation on this topic in 2011.[449]

9.6.3. Recognition of pre-trial supervision orders

There is evidence that foreigners suspected of committing a crime are kept in detention while awaiting trial in cases where nationals suspected of committing the same crime would not be,[450] because of the greater difficulty in ensuring that foreigners will attend the trial and serve any criminal sentence which may be imposed. This difficulty was first of all reduced significantly with the application of the EAW,[451] and it is arguable that discriminatory detention of citizens of other Member States breaches EU free movement law.[452] The issue is now addressed by a Framework Decision adopted in 2009, which Member Sates must implement by 1 December 2012.[453] Unusually, there is no previous international measure addressing the same issues as this Framework Decision. This measure would overlap in some cases with the proposed Directive establishing a European protection order.[454]

The Framework Decision specifies that it does not confer a right to pre-trial release; this issue is left to national law.[455] Implicitly the Framework Decision does not harmonize national law as regards when a person can or must receive bail (for example in light of the seriousness of the particular offences alleged, the prior behaviour or criminal record of the person concerned, and the risk of absconding), or of any conditions that can or must be attached to bail.[456] It includes a standard human rights provision,[457] along with a novel provision specifying that it does not alter national responsibilities as regards 'the protection of victims, the general public and the safeguarding of internal security, in accordance with' Article 33 of the prior TEU (now Article 72 TFEU).[458] The Framework Decision

---

[447] See 9.5.2 above.   [448] See 9.6.1.3 above.

[449] See generally 9.7.4 below, the communication on proceeds of crime (COM (2008) 766, 20 Nov 2008), and the action plan to implement the Stockholm programme (COM (2010) 171, 20 Apr 2010).

[450] See Annex 3 to the annex to the Commission Green Paper on pre-trial supervision orders (SEC (2004) 1046, 17 Aug 2004).   [451] See 9.5.2 above.

[452] See 9.4 above and Case C-297/09 X, withdrawn.

[453] [2009] OJ L 294/20, Art 27(1). See also the earlier Commission Green Paper on this issue (COM (2004) 562, 17 Aug 2004). All subsequent references in this subsection are to this Framework Decision, unless otherwise noted.   [454] See 9.7.6 below.

[455] Art 2(2).   [456] See Art 5(3) ECHR.

[457] Art 5. See also points 16 and 17 in the preamble.   [458] Art 3.

applies to six specified types of supervision measure;[459] Member States may notify the Council of other types of supervision measure which they are willing to enforce.[460]

Member States are obliged to apply the Framework Decision where the person concerned is lawfully and ordinarily resident in their territory, subject also to that person's consent.[461] They may also, if the person concerned requests, apply the Framework Decision where that person is not lawfully and ordinarily resident, but in that case the application of the Framework Decision depends on the consent of executing state.[462] The principle of dual criminality is abolished for the standard list of thirty-two crimes with a three-year punishment threshold, but Member States may insist, at the time of adoption of the Framework Decision, on applying that principle by way of derogation for 'some or all' of the offences on the list, for 'constitutional reasons'.[463] There are optional grounds for refusal of execution: a defective certificate; absence of consent by the person concerned or the executing State in the circumstances described above; double jeopardy; residual cases of dual criminality; statute-barring (if the alleged offence fell within the jurisdiction of the executing State); immunity (in accordance with the executing State's law); the age of criminal responsibility in the executing State; and where the executing State would have to refuse to execute an EAW that might be issued in the event of a breach of the order.[464] There is no ground for refusal on grounds of territoriality, or the executing State's existing prosecution of or intention to prosecute the person concerned, but arguably this issue is covered by the link to the grounds to refuse to execute an EAW.

There are detailed provisions governing which Member State has competence to take action relating to the supervision order,[465] and providing for coordination between Member States' authorities as regards later developments after the supervision order is issued.[466] There is no provision as such which grants the person concerned a remedy against the decision to approve a supervision order, but then again the Framework Decision grants the person concerned an explicit or implicit right of consent before the supervision order can be transferred in the first place.

---

[459] Art 8(1).

[460] Art 8(2), which contains a non-exhaustive list of five other types of supervision measure.

[461] Art 9(1). The concept of consent is not further defined.

[462] Art 9(2); see also Art 9(3) and (4).

[463] Art 14. Germany, Poland, Hungary, and Lithuania made declarations to this effect ([2009] OJ L 294/40).

[464] Art 15. It is not clear if the latter point refers only to the mandatory grounds for refusal to execute an EAW, or also to the optional grounds which the Member State concerned applies. For more on the EAW, see 9.5.2 above.

[465] Arts 11, 16, and 18. See also Art 13, on the possible adaptation of the supervision measure in the executing Member State. The Framework Decision does not address the question of what happens if the executing Member State has a more severe regime relating to bail, ie if it would not have released the person concerned pending trial.   [466] Arts 17, 19, and 20.

If an EAW or similar measure is issued as regards the person concerned by the issuing Member State, the executing Member State must surrender that person in accordance with the Framework Decision establishing the EAW. In principle, the executing Member State cannot invoke the custody threshold in the latter Framework Decision (an actual sentence of more than four months, or a potential sentence of more than twelve months), except by way of derogation.[467] The preamble to this Framework Decision makes clear that otherwise the EAW Framework Decision fully applies in the event that an EAW is issued to ensure the return of the person concerned to face trial in the issuing State.

This Framework Decision may make a useful contribution to reducing unjustified pre-trial detention of EU citizens accused of crimes outside their country of nationality. If it proves insufficient to this end, it may be necessary to adopt further measures addressing this issue. On this point, it should be noted that the Commission plans to release a Green Paper on pre-trial detention.[468]

9.7. Post-trial measures

Following the conclusion of a trial, several cross-border issues may arise.[469] The most obvious possibility is the transfer of enforcement of a sentence, whether custodial or non-custodial. The next question is whether a criminal conviction in one Member State may or must be taken into account for the purpose of subsequent criminal proceedings in other Member States (in addition to the separate issue of the double jeopardy effect of the conviction).[470] There may also be a cross-border consequence to a criminal conviction as regards confiscation of criminal assets, or disqualification from carrying out a profession or activity. Finally, there are cross-border aspects to conditional release on probation or parole, as well as orders for the protection of persons.

9.7.1. Enforcement of sentences

An early Council of Europe Convention (from 1970) concerns the enforcement of both custodial and non-custodial sentences, but it has attracted few ratifications from EU Member States; a subsequent Council of Europe Convention on the transfer of sentenced persons was far more successful, attracting unanimous

---

[467] Art 21, referring to Art 2(1) of the Framework Decision establishing the EAW ([2002] OJ L 190/1). [468] See 9.8.2 below.

[469] For a detailed analysis of post-trial mutual recognition issues, particularly as regards recognition of custodial sentences, see the Commission's Green Paper on criminal sanctions (COM (2004) 334, 30 Apr 2004), particularly at 23–25, 34–46, and 57–68.

[470] On double jeopardy, see 11.8 below.

support of Member States.[471] The first EU measure concerning this issue was a Convention between the Member States in 1991, agreed in the framework of European Political Cooperation (EPC), and also addressing both types of penalties, but it failed to attract enough ratifications to enter into force.[472] The EU has subsequently adopted mutual recognition measures concerning both the enforcement of financial penalties and the transfer of custodial sentences.

9.7.1.1. Financial penalties

Initially, within the framework of Schengen cooperation, Member States negotiated an agreement on the specific issue of recognizing financial penalties imposed for road traffic offences.[473] This agreement appears not to have entered into force in practice, and the issue has been subsumed within the context of a broader Framework Decision on the mutual recognition of financial penalties, which was adopted in 2005 and had to be applied by Member States by 22 March 2007.[474] While the Stockholm programme calls on the Commission to study possible further measures relating to road traffic penalties, the Commission's action plan on implementing that programme foresees a general proposal for new legislation on recognition of financial penalties in 2011.[475] This would presumably replace the Framework Decision.

The Framework Decision follows the template established by the Framework Decision on the European Arrest Warrant, obliging Member States to recognize the judgments of other Member States except where a ground for non-recognition exists.[476] Dual criminality is abolished not only for the 'standard' list of thirty-two crimes (inevitably without any sentencing threshold, since the Framework Decision does not apply to custodial sentences) and to a further seven crimes in addition: conduct infringing 'road traffic regulations, including' breaches of law on driving hours, rest periods, and hazardous goods; 'smuggling of goods'; 'infringement of intellectual property rights'; 'threats and acts of violence against persons, including violence during sports events'; 'criminal damage'; 'theft'; and any acts constituting offences which the issuing Member State has established to implement obligations arising from first or third pillar acts.[477] Presumably these additional offences have been added because such less serious crimes are more frequently punished by fines rather than custodial sentences.

The scope of the Framework Decision includes, in certain cases, sentences imposed against legal persons and sentences not imposed by courts, although Member States had the right to opt to delay application of the Framework

---

[471] ETS 70 and 112. For ratification details, see Appendix I.

[472] For the text, see: <http://www.asser.nl/eurowarrant-webroot/documents/cms_eaw_12_1_Agreement1991.11.13.pdf>.   [473] [2000] OJ L 239/428.

[474] Art 20(1) of Framework Decision ([2005] OJ L 76/16). All references in this subsection are to this Framework Decision, except where otherwise noted.

[475] [2010] OJ C 115, point 3.1.1; COM (2010) 171, 20 Apr 2010.   [476] Art 6.

[477] Art 5.

Decision to such cases until 22 March 2010.[478] But confiscation measures and orders in *civil* proceedings fall outside its scope.[479] There are eight grounds for non-execution, comprising in particular double jeopardy (worded differently from the EAW exception), extraterritoriality, immunity, childhood, *in absentia* proceedings (as amended by the 2009 Framework Decision on this subject), and a financial threshold (penalties below the value of €70 need not be enforced).[480] In addition to the standard human rights provision, there is also an express human rights exception: a Member State *may*, 'where the certificate' describing the issuing State's judgment 'gives rise to an issue that fundamental rights or fundamental legal principles as described in Article 6 of the [EU] Treaty may have been infringed, oppose the recognition and the execution of decisions'.[481] Compared to the EU's other mutual recognition measures, this provision is unique, but if the provision is read literally, it will be impossible to apply in practice: there appears to be no way that the *certificate*, which is simply a standard form with boxes to be ticked and lines to be filled in with factual information in order to allow the prior judgment to be enforced, could *as such* give rise to concerns that human rights have been infringed by that prior judgment.[482]

According to the Commission's report on the application of the Framework Decision,[483] only a minority of Member States (eleven) had reported on their implementation of this measure by October 2008, making it impossible to draw conclusions about the implementation of the Framework Decision in practice. Of those Member States which had applied the measure, the Commission regretted that most had made the optional grounds for execution mandatory and that some had allegedly added extra grounds for refusal. However, in part the latter complaint begs the question as to whether there is an implied 'human rights' ground for refusal (broader than the express ground discussed above), since some Member States provide for a refusal to execute decisions due to a breach of due process or because of discrimination on grounds of race, political opinion, etc.

9.7.1.2. Custodial penalties

As regards the enforcement of custodial penalties, there are two parallel issues: the enforcement of the *sentence* alone (where the sentenced person is on the territory of the requested State, and, for example, cannot be extradited from that State to

---

[478] Art 20(2), read with Art 21.

[479] Art 1(b). The former are covered by the separate measure on that subject (see 9.7.4 below) while the latter are covered by Reg 44/2001 ([2001] OJ L 12/1). For instance, see Case C-7/98 *Krombach* [2000] ECR I-1935.

[480] Art 7. For details of the new *in absentia* rule, see 9.5.2 above.

[481] Art 20(3). Art 20(8) requires Member States to transmit information on the application of this provision to the Council and Commission, and Art 20(9) provides for a review of this exception by Feb 2012.

[482] See the broader points on human rights and mutual recognition in 9.3.5 and 9.5.2 above.

[483] COM (2008) 888, 22 Dec 2008.

serve the sentence in the State which imposed it), and the transfer of a *sentenced person* (who is generally already imprisoned on the territory of the requesting State) which necessarily entails the transfer of enforcement of the sentence as a corollary measure. As noted above, the first issue has been the subject of both a Council of Europe Convention which has attracted limited ratifications and an EPC measure which has not entered into force at all. In comparison, the 1983 Council of Europe Convention on the transfer of sentenced persons has attracted ratification by every EU Member State (and many other States besides).[484] There is also a Protocol to the Convention, agreed in 1997, which a large majority of Member States have ratified.[485] The main Convention requires the consent of not only the requesting and requested State, but also the sentenced person, in order for the transfer to take place; the principle of dual criminality also applies.[486] The Protocol provides first of all that if a person escapes the sentencing Member State and flees to the Member State of his or her nationality in order to escape enforcement of the penalty, the sentencing Member State may ask the State of nationality to enforce the sentence; there is no obligation in such cases to obtain the consent of the sentenced person.[487] The sentenced person's consent is also waived in cases where he or she is to be expelled pursuant to a deportation or expulsion order, although: that person may still express an opinion on the transfer; there is a specialty rule comparable to the rule applicable in extradition law; and Contracting Parties can choose not to apply this provision of the Protocol.[488]

Within the EU, the issue of the transfer of sentenced persons was first addressed by an EPC Convention of 1987, which attracted only a few ratifications.[489] Subsequently, the Schengen Convention supplemented the Council of Europe Convention by providing for the same waiver of the consent requirement for fugitives as set out in the Protocol to the latter Convention.[490]

In 2008, the Council adopted a Framework Decision on the transfer of custodial sentences, which applies the mutual recognition principle to the transfer of sentenced persons.[491] Member States must apply this Framework Decision by 5 December 2011,[492] although it will only apply to requests received after that

---

[484] ETS 112.   [485] ETS 167. For ratification details, see Appendix I.

[486] Art 3(1) of the Convention.   [487] Art 2 of the Protocol.

[488] Art 3 of the Protocol. On the specialty rule in extradition law, see 9.5.1 above. Ireland does not apply this provision, and Belgium applies it subject to a condition of habitual residence.

[489] For the text, see: <http://www.asser.nl/eurowarrant-webroot/documents/cms_eaw_12_1_Agreement1987.05.25_transf.pdf>. For ratification details, see Appendix I.

[490] Arts 67–69 of the Convention ([2000] OJ L 239). Note that the application of the Schengen Convention predated the Council of Europe Protocol for some Member States; some Member States have not ratified the Protocol yet (but conversely the Schengen Convention does not apply in Ireland yet, although the Protocol does), and the Protocol also applies to a number of non-Member States, including all of the Schengen associates. Also, the Protocol, but not the Schengen Convention, contains the additional rule waiving the consent requirement in cases of, for example deportation.

[491] [2008] OJ L 327/27.   [492] Art 29(1).

date.[493] As from that date, the Framework Decision will replace the corresponding provisions of the two Council of Europe Conventions and the Protocol to the Convention on sentenced persons, the relevant provisions of the Schengen Convention, and the EPC Convention on this issue.[494]

As for the substance of the Framework Decision, it is subject to the standard human rights provisions.[495] The Framework Decision applies either where the sentenced person lives in his or her State of nationality, or *will* live in his or her State of nationality once an expulsion or deportation order is carried out, or where another Member State consents to the transfer of the sentenced person.[496] For the latter category of cases, Member States may declare that they waive the requirement of their consent, if the person concerned has been a legal resident for at least five years and will continue to reside there as a permanent resident, as defined by reference to EU free movement and immigration law, and/or is a national of the executing State but is not either living there or due to be deported or expelled there.[497] The transfer process may be instigated by the sentenced person, although there is no obligation for the States concerned to act on his or her request.[498]

The traditional requirement for the consent of the sentenced person has also been abolished by the Framework Decision, in the two cases covered by the Protocol to the Council of Europe Convention as well as where the sentenced person lives in the Member State of his or her nationality.[499] Poland has a five-year derogation from the latter extension of the abolition of the consent requirement.[500] Where the consent requirement is waived and the sentenced person is still in the territory of the issuing State, he or she is still entitled to give an opinion on the transfer.[501]

Next, the Framework Decision abolishes the dual criminality requirement for the standard list of thirty-two offences and three-year punishability threshold, although by way of derogation, Member States can opt out of this obligation.[502]

---

[493] Art 28(1). Requests received before that date will be subject to the previous legal instruments. On the relationship between the EAW and the rules on the transfer of sentenced persons in the meantime, see Case C-264/10 *Kita*, pending. [494] Art 26(1).

[495] Art 3(4) and recitals 13 and 14 in the preamble.

[496] Art 4(1). Implicitly the requirement of consent by the executing State (required by the Council of Europe Convention on sentenced persons and its Protocol) is waived in the former two cases. In all cases, the sentenced person must be in either the issuing or the executing State (Art 3(2)). The expulsion of the person concerned is subject to EU free movement law: see recitals 15 and 16 in the preamble and 9.4 above. Note that the Framework Decision has a wider personal scope than the Council of Europe Convention on the transfer of sentenced persons, which only applies to nationals of the administering state (Art 3(1)(a) of the Convention).

[497] Art 4(7). On the links with EU free movement law, see 9.4 above. This provision is consistent with the Court's interpretation of certain exceptions to the EAW Framework Decision: see Case C-123/08 *Wolzenburg* [2009] ECR I-9621, discussed in 9.5.2 above. In fact, this judgment refers expressly to Art 4(7)(a) of the Framework Decision. [498] Art 4(5).

[499] Art 6(2). The requirement otherwise applies (Art 6(1)). [500] Art 6(5).

[501] Art 6(3). [502] Art 7.

With the abolition of the three key traditional grounds for refusing a transfer, the remaining grounds for non-execution take on greater importance. Member States may refuse to execute a request, inter alia, if: the certificate is defective; the enforcement would violate the double jeopardy rule; the judgment is statute-barred in the executing Member State; there is an immunity in the executing Member State; the person concerned would not have been liable under the executing State's law on the age of criminal responsibility; the trial took place *in absentia* (as amended by the 2009 Framework Decision on this subject); there are less than six months of the sentence remaining; or on grounds of territoriality.[503] The principle of speciality also applies, in exactly the same way as for the European Arrest Warrant, except that for this Framework Decision Member States cannot agree to waive the principle.[504]

The executing State is obliged in principle to take over enforcement of the judgment,[505] and cannot aggravate the issuing State's sentence 'in terms of its nature or duration',[506] although this begs the question as to whether a more stringent regime on early release could be applied.[507] On the other hand, the executing State may reduce the duration of sentence imposed, but only where that sentence is above the maximum that could be imposed in that State for the same offence.[508] Where the issuing State's sentence is incompatible with the executing State's sentence 'in terms of its nature', the latter State may 'adapt' the sentence, but this must 'correspond as closely as possible' to the original sentence, and cannot entail a conversion of a prison sentence into a fine.[509]

Finally, it is explicitly stated that this Framework Decision will apply where an EAW is not executed because the executing Member State has undertaken to enforce a prior sentence itself, or where the executing Member State has insisted on a guarantee that the issuing Member State return the fugitive after trial to serve his or her sentence, if imposed, in the executing State.[510]

This Framework Decision usefully clarifies the position in cases where persons are tried or serve their sentences in the Member State which had been asked to execute an EAW concerning them. But it is dubious to abolish the dual crimi-

---

[503] Art 9. On the 2009 Framework Decision on *in absentia* trials, see 9.5.2 above.

[504] Art 18; compare to Art 27 of the EAW Framework Decision ([2002] OJ L 190/1), discussed in 9.5.2 above. As noted there, it would be logical to interpret these provisions the same way; on the EAW provision, see Case C-388/08 PPU *Leymann and Pustovarov* [2008] ECR I-8993. The rule is different from the speciality rule in Art 3(4) of the Protocol to the Convention on sentenced persons, and moreover applies to all sentenced persons, not just those within the scope of Art 3 of that Protocol.   [505] Art 8(1).

[506] Art 8(4).

[507] On early release, see Art 17(3) and (4). On the human rights aspects of this issue, see the decisions of the European Court of Human Rights in *Veermae v Finland* (15 Mar 2005) and *Szabo v Sweden* (27 June 2006), discussed in 9.3 above.

[508] Art 8(2).   [509] Art 8(3).

[510] Art 25 of this Framework Decision, referring to Arts 4(6) and 5(3) of the EAW Framework Decision; see discussion of the latter provisions above (9.5.2).

nality rule where this entails serving a sentence in the territory of a State which did not criminalize the acts concerned, and for the reasons set out above, this Framework Decision goes too far in abolishing the requirement of the consent of the person concerned, considering the principles of free movement law and the objective of social rehabilitation.[511]

9.7.2. Consequences of convictions

The first adopted EU measure concerning the consequences of convictions in subsequent criminal proceedings was a Framework Decision relating to counterfeiting currency, which requires Member States to recognize final sentences for the same crime handed out in another Member State 'for the purpose of establishing habitual criminality' in the same way as they would recognize a prior domestic conviction under their national law.[512] Subsequently, the Council adopted a broader Framework Decision in 2008,[513] which requires Member States to take account of prior convictions in other Member States concerning different facts relating to the same person 'to the extent previous national convictions are taken into account'; also 'equivalent legal effects' must be attached to such prior conventions 'as to previous national convictions, in accordance with national law'.[514] This rule shall apply as regards all stages of criminal proceedings and (implicitly) for any type of offence.[515] There are no grounds for non–recognition, but the Framework Decision leaves it open to Member States to apply a dual criminality rule.[516]

It is obvious that the practical application of this Framework Decision will be dependent on developing an effective mechanism to ensure the exchange of criminal records information between Member States.[517] The problem, as noted above, is that the information supplied pursuant to the EU measures on criminal record exchange may be inaccurate or insufficient for the second Member State's courts to use fully and fairly to decide whether to classify the (alleged) offender as a recidivist for the purposes of national criminal procedure.

9.7.3. Disqualification

The first EU measure adopted in this area was a Convention on the enforcement of driving disqualifications, agreed in 1998.[518] However, this Convention has attracted few ratifications,[519] and moreover is not a mutual recognition measure,

---

[511] See 9.4. [512] [2001] OJ L 329/3.

[513] [2008] OJ L 220/32. Member States had to apply this measure by 15 Aug 2010 (Art 5(1)). The 2001 Framework Decision (ibid) has not been repealed or amended. [514] Art 3(1).

[515] Art 3(2). [516] See recital 6 in the preamble. [517] See 9.6.1.4 above.

[518] [1998] OJ C 216/1. [519] For ratification details, see Appendix I.

providing instead for *conversion* of one Member State's decision into a decision taken within the framework of the legal system of another Member State. A Belgian initiative for a Framework Decision which sought to put into practice the recognition of disqualifications for working with children following a criminal conviction for sexual offences involving them,[520] as required by the EU's Framework Decision of 2003 concerning offences against children,[521] was not successful as such, mainly because of differences in national law regarding the existence of such prohibitions, the process for deciding upon them, and the storage and transmission of relevant criminal records information.[522] However, the initiative was integrated into the Framework Decision on the exchange of criminal records, adopted in 2009.[523] The Commission subsequently proposed a more extensive rule relating to disqualification in its 2010 proposal for a Directive concerning offences against children.[524]

The difficulties encountered with the Belgian proposal explain why the Commission, in a 2006 Green Paper on recognition of disqualifications,[525] suggested a gradual piecemeal approach, applying the principle of mutual recognition to disqualifications only where a common basis between Member States existed, either on the basis of their national law (in the case of driving disqualifications) or as a result of EU measures (in the case of sexual offences or EU measures concerning procurement, for example). This view was backed by a majority of Member States.[526] Furthermore, the recast EU driving licence Directive contains some provisions on recognition of disqualification from driving, and a Commission proposal for a Directive on the cross-border enforcement of road safety sanctions was blocked due to competence disputes.[527]

For the future, the Stockholm programme invites the Commission to study 'existing legal and administrative obstacles to cross-border enforcement of penalties and administrative decisions for road traffic offences' and possibly make legislative or non-legislative proposals, and also to present a study and a draft programme relating to disqualifications, in order to exchange information with mutual recognition of disqualifications 'as a long-term goal'.[528] The action plan to implement the Stockholm programme provides for proposals for legislation on mutual recognition of financial penalties related to road traffic decisions in 2011, and of disqualifications generally in 2013.[529]

9.7.4. Confiscation orders

The starting point for any discussion of the rules on the confiscation of criminal assets is the 1990 Council of Europe Convention on the proceeds of crime,

---

[520] Council doc 14207/04, 5 Nov 2004.   [521] [2004] OJ L 13/44, Art 5(3).
[522] Council doc 7951/06, 31 Mar 2006.   [523] [2009] OJ L 93/23. See 9.6.1.4 above.
[524] COM (2010) 94, 29 Mar 2010, Art 10.   [525] COM (2006) 73, 21 Feb 2006.
[526] See Council doc 6682/05, 23 Feb 2005.   [527] See 9.4 above.
[528] [2010] OJ C 115, point 3.1.1.   [529] COM (2010) 171, 20 Apr 2010.

ratified by every EU Member State.[530] Chapter II of this Convention sets out requirements for the harmonization of domestic law on this issue, in order to facilitate the application of the Convention's rules on international cooperation. These requirements, inter alia, entail obligations to provide for the confiscation of the proceeds and instrumentalities of crime, or property which corresponds to the value of such proceeds (although States can enter a reservation limiting this obligation to specific offences), to adopt investigative measures to this end, and to set out legal remedies for interested parties.[531] Revised provisions appear in a 2005 Council of Europe Convention on the same subject, but fewer than half of Member States have ratified this Convention.[532] The 1990 and 2005 Conventions also require States to enforce confiscation orders relating to the proceeds of crime issued by other signatory States.[533] However, this obligation is subject to many possible grounds for refusal in the 1990 Convention, and most of these grounds are retained in the 2005 Convention.[534]

An initial EU Joint Action provides that Member States should not enter reservations to the 1990 Convention as regards the obligation to provide for confiscation of proceeds, as long as the offence in question can be punished by a sentence of more than one year, except as regards tax offences; Member States may also exempt 'minor crimes' from the obligation to confiscate property corresponding to the value of the proceeds of crime.[535] A later Framework Decision reiterates these two obligations in a more binding form,[536] setting a more precise threshold of €4,000 as a maximum exemption from the latter obligation.[537] Both the Joint Action and the Framework Decision specify that Member States must also give confiscation requests from other Member States equal priority with domestic requests.[538] The Commission has twice reported on the national application of this Framework Decision, concluding that several Member States appear not to have implemented the first two obligations, and complaining that it had not received enough information to assess compliance with the latter obligation.[539]

Following the judgment of the Strasbourg Court in the *Phillips* case,[540] the Council adopted two further linked Framework Decisions. The first measure,

---

[530] ETS 141.

[531] Arts 2–5 of the Convention; on the substantive criminal law obligations, see 10.5.1.2 below.

[532] Arts 3–14 of the 2005 Convention (CETS 198), in force 1 May 2008. On the extent of signature or ratification by Member States, see Appendix I.

[533] Arts 13–17 of the 1990 Convention and Arts 23–27 of the 2005 Convention.

[534] Art 18 of the 1990 Convention and Art 28 of the 2005 Convention. For instance, the 2005 Convention does not permit the fiscal and political offence exceptions to be used in cases of terrorism, qualifies the dual criminality principle, and provides for wider cooperation in relation to non-criminal sanctions.   [535] Art 1 of Joint Action ([1998] OJ L 333/1).

[536] On the legal effect of Joint actions and Framework Decisions, see 2.2.1.2 and 2.2.2.2 above.

[537] Arts 1(a) and 3 of Framework Decision ([2001] OJ L 182/1).

[538] Art 3 of Joint Action (n 535 above), and Art 4 of the 2001 Framework Decision (ibid).

[539] COM (2004) 230, 5 Apr 2004, and COM (2006) 72, 21 Feb 2006.   [540] See 9.3.1 above.

adopted in 2005, harmonizes national law on the confiscation of criminal assets,[541] while the second measure, adopted in 2006, establishes mutual recognition as regards confiscation orders.[542] This issue is also addressed by the 2003 Framework Decision on freezing orders, discussed already above.[543]

The 2005 Framework Decision, which is also linked to the EU's substantive criminal law harmonization,[544] first obliges Member States to provide for normal powers of confiscation, enabling them to prosecute criminal proceeds from offences punishable by a deprivation of liberty of more than one year, or property of the same value.[545] Secondly, Member States must revise their laws to provide for powers of 'extended confiscation' in respect of seven crimes as defined by EU Framework Decisions: counterfeiting currency, money laundering, trafficking in persons, facilitation of irregular entry or residence, sexual exploitation, drug trafficking, or terrorism, provided that the offence is punishable by a specified minimum penalty threshold and could generate financial gain.[546] For this principle to apply, a national court must be 'fully convinced', based on 'specific facts', that the assets are derived from one of three situations (at the option of each Member State): the criminal activity of the person prior to conviction; *similar* criminal activity for a period prior to conviction; or from criminal activities, without assessing the issue over a prior time period, if it is established that the assets are disproportionate to that person's lawful income.[547] Member States *may* also consider adopting legislation to confiscate the assets of the closest relatives of the person concerned, or a legal person which the person concerned controls or derives most of the income from.[548] Also, Member States are obliged to provide for legal remedies for interested persons (as set out in the 1990 Council of Europe Convention), and the Framework Decision should not have the effect of altering the obligation to respect fundamental rights, including the presumption of innocence.[549] The Commission's report on the application of this Framework Decision indicates that a significant number of Member States did not apply it by the deadline date, and that in particular a number of Member States did not communicate the measures they had taken to ensure remedies for the persons concerned.[550]

The 2006 Framework Decision applies to orders imposed by a court following criminal proceedings,[551] and obliges Member States to recognize and execute other Member State's decisions relating to confiscation, subject to reasons for

---

[541] [2005] OJ L 68/47, which Member States had to apply by 15 Mar 2007 (Art 6(1)).

[542] [2006] OJ L 328/59, which Member States had to apply by 24 Nov 2008 (Art 22(1)). See also the relevant police cooperation measures (12.7 below).   [543] See 9.6.2 above.

[544] See 10.5.1.2 below.   [545] Art 2, 2005 Framework Decision.

[546] Art 3(1), 2005 Framework Decision.

[547] Art 3(2), 2005 Framework Decision.   [548] Art 3(3), 2005 Framework Decision.

[549] Arts 4 and 5, 2005 Framework Decision. On the general issue of suspects' and defendants' rights, see 9.8.2 below.   [550] COM (2007) 805, 17 Dec 2007.

[551] Art 2(c), 2006 Framework Decision.

non-execution or for suspension of execution set out within it.[552] It should be noted that an earlier Framework Decision provides for the provisional freezing of the assets concerned before a confiscation order can be issued.[553] Dual criminality is abolished as regards the standard list of thirty-two crimes. But here, by analogy with the Framework Decision on freezing orders, dual criminality continues to exist for all other acts not on the list that do not constitute offences that *could give rise to confiscation proceedings* in the executing Member State.[554]

As for refusal to execute a confiscation order, the grounds are all optional, and consist of the same grounds applicable to freezing orders, along with several others, including a broader application of the double jeopardy principle, territoriality, *in absentia* trials (as amended by a separate Framework Decision in 2009), the rights of third parties, statute-barring under the executed State's law, and a extended confiscation order in the issuing State going beyond the provisions of the 2005 Framework Decision.[555] Even if the issuing State's order falls within the scope of the 2005 measure, an executing Member State may in effect 'convert' an issuing State's judgment if the two Member States have chosen different options for qualifying the burden and standard of proof as provided for in the 2005 measure.[556]

The 2006 Framework Decision includes the same human rights provisions as the Framework Decision establishing the EAW, with the addition of the proviso that 'any obligations incumbent on judicial authorities' in 'respect' of human rights 'shall remain unaffected'.[557] This wording confirms the interpretation of the human rights clauses in the EU's mutual recognition measures argued for above.[558]

Finally, this Framework Decision provides for remedies to be exercised in the executing State, and the substantive reasons for the confiscation order cannot be challenged there.[559] There is no reference to any procedural standards which must be applicable in the issuing State, although as noted above, the 2005 Framework Decision obliges Member State to provide for remedies to challenge any confiscation orders that are issued.[560]

The Commission issued an assessment of Member States' application of the 2006 Framework Decision in 2010.[561] In the Commission's view, the implementation of the Framework Decision was 'clearly not satisfactory' because, over a year from the deadline for implementation of the measure, only thirteen Member States had complied with their obligation to transpose it. However, the meas-

---

[552] Art 7, 2006 Framework Decision.   [553] See 9.6.2 above.

[554] Art 6, 2006 Framework Decision.

[555] Art 8, 2006 Framework Decision. On the amendments made to the *in absentia* trial exception in 2009, see 9.5.2 above.

[556] Art 8(3), 2006 Framework Decision; see Art 2(3) of the 2005 Framework Decision.

[557] See paras 13 and 14 of the preamble and Art 1(2), 2006 Framework Decision.

[558] See 9.5.2 above.   [559] Art 9, 2006 Framework Decision.

[560] Art 4 of the 2005 Framework Decision (n 541 above).

[561] COM (2010) 428, 23 Aug 2010.

ures that those thirteen Member States had taken were considered generally 'satisfactory', except for the grounds for refusal to execute another Member State's confiscation order. On this point, the Commission considered that many Member States had legislated for excessive and impermissible grounds for refusal, in particular as regards human rights. However, this analysis can be criticized for the reasons set out above (as regards the EAW Framework Decision),[562] *a fortiori* because the human rights clause in the 2006 Framework Decision on confiscation orders suggests even greater leeway for Member States on this point. Assessing the 2006 Framework Decision, it is subject to the same objections that apply to other EU mutual recognition measures, although at least a separate measure requires the issuing Member State to establish remedies against confiscation orders. It is unfortunate that all the grounds for refusing recognition are optional, including the double jeopardy ground. The human rights provision could be clearer, but human rights would appear to be a ground for resisting recognition, and at least this provision is not so circumscribed as to lose its effectiveness.[563]

For the future, the action plan for implementation of the Stockholm programme provides for a proposal for a new legal framework on asset recovery in 2011, which would presumably replace the existing legislation on this subject.[564] On this point, the Commission released in 2008 a communication on the proceeds of crime which called for recasting the existing legislation, including the possibility of adding new provisions on confiscation without a criminal conviction; creating a new criminal offence of owning 'unjustified' assets; strengthening mutual recognition obligations; extending the scope of mandatory confiscation; and enforcing the obligation to provide bank account information set out in the 2001 Protocol to the EU mutual assistance Convention.[565]

9.7.5. Probation and parole

Responsibility for rehabilitation of offenders on early release or with probation or suspended sentences can be transferred to another State under a 1964 Council of Europe Convention on supervision of conditionally released and early released offenders, if the offender has his or her residence in a State other than the State of offence. Fewer than half of the Member States have ratified this Convention.[566] In 2008, the Council adopted a Framework Decision which will replace the corresponding provisions of this Convention as from 6 December 2011, the deadline for Member States to implement the Framework Decision.[567] It should

---

[562] See 9.5.2 above.

[563] Compare with the relevant provision of the Framework Decision on mutual recognition of financial penalties (9.7.1.1 above).   [564] COM (2010) 171, 20 Apr 2010.

[565] COM (2008) 766, 20 Nov 2008. On the 2001 Protocol, see 9.6.1.1 above; and see now also the proposed European Investigation Order (9.6.1.3 above).

[566] ETS 51. For ratification details, see Appendix I.   [567] [2008] OJ L 337/102, Art 25(1).

be remembered that the detention of EU citizens from other Member States for longer periods than nationals of the host Member State is arguably a breach of EU free movement law, so this Framework Decision may facilitate full application of the principle of equal treatment.[568] This Framework Decision would be linked in some cases to the application of the proposed Directive on the European Protection Order.[569]

This Framework Decision is similar to the Framework Decision on the recognition of custodial sentences, which was adopted at the same time.[570] It applies to an exhaustive list of eleven types of probation or parole measures, or alternative sanctions, for example restrictions on leaving the territory, instructions relating to behaviour, and reporting obligations.[571] However, Member States can choose to supervise other forms of alternative sanctions and probation measures if they wish.[572] The Framework Decision is subject to the standard human rights provisions.[573]

The mutual recognition obligation only applies to the Member State in which the person concerned is lawfully and ordinarily resident, if the sentenced person 'has returned or wants to return' to that State.[574] The nationality of the person concerned is implicitly irrelevant, although of course it may have been relevant in determining whether that person obtained residence status in the State concerned in the first place. This rule also implies that the sentenced person consents to the transfer, although there is no provision in the Framework Decision which addresses the procedure for determining the intent of the person concerned. As with the Framework Decision on the recognition of custodial sentences, the sentenced person may even request the convicting State to forward a request to recognize the probation decision to a Member State *other* than the Member State where the person concerned was previously lawfully or ordinarily resident, although there is no obligation on the latter Member State to accept such requests.[575] To the extent that the person concerned could not be refused entry to that Member State pursuant to EU free movement law,[576] this power of Member States to refuse to recognize the probation order is legally questionable.

The Framework Decision abolishes the dual criminality requirement for the standard list of thirty-two crimes, with the standard three-year sentencing threshold, but for this particular Framework Decision it must particularly be emphasized that the threshold relates to *punishability*, not to the actual sentence

---

[568] See 9.4 above.   [569] See 9.7.6 below.   [570] See 9.7.1.2 above.

[571] Art 4(1). It is implicit from the requirement to observe EU free movement law, referred to in the preamble (recital 7), that restrictions on leaving the territory can only be applied in accordance with that law (see 9.4 above).   [572] Art 4(2).

[573] Art 1(4) and recital 5 in the preamble.   [574] Art 5(1).   [575] Art 5(2)–(4).

[576] For a summary of the relevant substantive and procedural law, see 7.4.1 above. Since in many cases persons covered by the Framework Decision will have been sentenced to a suspended sentence, it must follow that the crime they committed will often not be serious enough to justify refusal of entry pursuant to EU free movement law.

received—so in at least some cases suspended sentences will still satisfy this threshold. As with the Framework Decisions on pre-trial orders and the recognition of custodial sentences, it is open to Member States to maintain dual criminality requirements by way of derogation.[577] The executing Member State may refuse to execute a decision on grounds of: inadequate certification; requests exceeding the scope of the Framework Decision; double jeopardy; residual (or retained) dual criminality; statute barring (if the executing Member State had jurisdiction over the offence); immunity under the executing State's law; the age of criminal responsibility; *in absentia* trials (this provision was amended by the 2009 Framework Decision on this subject); medical treatment that cannot be provided in the executing State; a probation period of under six months; or territoriality.[578] The Framework Decision provides for competence over supervision measures to transfer to the executing Member State,[579] with the possibility of transferring competence back to the issuing State in certain cases.[580]

Compared to the Council of Europe Convention on this issue, the Framework Decision contains more grounds for refusal of recognition, but these are more specific than under the Convention, which includes grounds such as 'essential interests'; moreover, all of the grounds for refusal under the Framework Decision are optional, not mandatory.[581] Furthermore, the Framework Decision in principle waives the dual criminality rule, which is mandatory under the Convention,[582] and the underlying mutual recognition rule binds all Member States and is wider in scope.[583]

9.7.6. European Protection Order

In 2010, a group of Member States proposed a Directive to create a 'European Protection Order' (EPO), which would be issued for the purpose of protecting victims of violence who move to another Member State.[584] This proposal was agreed in principle in the Council in June 2010, but still had to be agreed with the European Parliament.

The proposed Directive defines an EPO as:[585]

...a judicial decision relating to a protection measure issued by a Member State and aiming at facilitating the taking by another Member State, where appropriate, of a protection

---

[577] Art 10.   [578] Art 11. On the revised *in absentia* trial exception, see 9.5.2 above.

[579] Art 7(1). See also Arts 13 and 14, but note the possible derogation in Art 14(3), and the consequential provisions in Arts 14(4)–(6) and 17. See also Art 19 on amnesty, pardon, and review, and Art 20, on ending jurisdiction of the executing State.   [580] Art 7(2).

[581] Compare to Art 7 of the Convention (n 566 above).   [582] Art 4 of the Convention.

[583] See Art 5 of the Convention, which gives signatory States the option to carry out supervision of the sentence only, not enforcement.

[584] [2010] OJ C 69/5. All references in this subsection are to this original proposal, except where mentioned.   [585] Art 1(1).

measure under its own national law with a view to the safeguard of the life, physical and psychological integrity, freedom or sexual integrity of a person.

A 'protection measure' would be a decision made by a Member State's competent authority which imposes an obligation on a 'person causing danger', for example, not to enter certain places, to remain in a specified place, not to leave the territory of the Member State issuing the EPO, to avoid contact with the 'protected person', or an obligation to keep a specified distance from that person, provided that the infringement of such a prohibition or obligation would constitute a criminal offence or otherwise be punishable by a deprivation of liberty.[586] It should be noted that the EPO would not necessarily have to be issued in the context of criminal proceedings, an issue which has given rise to concerns about the correct legal base for this proposal.[587]

The EPO could be issued 'at any moment when the protected person intends to leave or has left the issuing Member State for another Member State',[588] and could be revoked if 'there is evidence that the protected person has definitively left the territory of the executing State',[589] thereby drawing a strong link between this measure and the free movement rights of the victims and, implicitly, their abusers.[590] The EPO could only be issued after a request by the protected person to the authorities of the issuing State.[591]

The executing State's authority would have an obligation to recognize the EPO and to take 'all measures that would be available under its national law in a similar case to ensure the protection of the protected person', unless there were a reason for non-recognition of the EPO.[592] The issuing State would retain jurisdiction to review, withdraw, or modify the protection measure, or to issue an arrest warrant or begin new criminal proceedings in relation to that measure.[593] The authority of the executing State must also inform the person causing danger of any measure taken, take any 'urgent and provisional measure', to protect the protected person, and inform issuing Member State of any breach of the EPO.[594]

The executing State's authority could refuse to recognize an EPO if: the EPO were incomplete or delayed; the requirement of a prior relevant obligation or prohibition in the issuing State was not satisfied; there was an amnesty in the executing State for the act concerned, and the act fell within its own competence;

---

[586] Art 1(2), referring to Art 2(2). For the definitions of 'protected person' and 'person causing danger', see Art 1(3) and (4). See also the other EU measures relating to crime victims, referred to in 9.8.3 below. The measures applied to the 'person causing danger' might have been adopted pursuant to the Framework Decisions on pre-trial supervision or probation: see 9.6.3 and 9.7.5 above.

[587] See the discussion in 9.2.4 above.   [588] Art 2(1).   [589] Art 11.

[590] See generally 9.4 above.

[591] Art 5(1). The request can also be submitted via the authorities of the executing State (Art 5(2)).   [592] Art 8(1)(a).

[593] Art 10(1). The issuing State's law would apply (Art 10(2)). But where a pre-trial supervision order or a probation order had been issued, the relevant provisions of the other EU measures would apply (Art 10(3)).   [594] Art 8(1)(b)–(d).

or there was immunity in the executing State for the person causing danger.[595] There would be no grounds for refusal on grounds of dual criminality, territoriality, or double jeopardy.

There is no provision in the proposed Directive relating to remedies for the 'person causing danger', if he or she wishes to challenge the original EPO or its execution. Neither is there any provision allowing the protected person to challenge a failure to issue or execute an EPO.

In general, this is a useful initiative, but the problems with its legal base have to be addressed, there should be remedies for both persons concerned, and the grounds for refusal should include territoriality, double jeopardy, and dual criminality.

9.8. Domestic criminal procedure

As discussed above, with the entry into force of the Treaty of Lisbon, there is an express legal basis for EU measures relating to evidence law, the rights of individuals (ie suspects and accused persons), and the rights of crime victims (Article 82(2) TFEU).[596] Even before the Treaty of Lisbon, the EU had adopted legislation relating to crime victims. The planned or adopted measures in each of these areas will be examined in turn.[597]

9.8.1. Evidence law

To date, there have been no EU measures adopted or proposed harmonizing national laws on the use of evidence in criminal investigations and trials.[598] As noted above,[599] Article 82(2) TFEU limits the EU's action in this area to measures concerning the 'mutual admissibility' of evidence, so more general harmonization of evidence law is precluded, except arguably in relation to suspects' rights, although it will be hard in practice to separate rules on the admissibility of evidence from evidence law in general. This area of law is also connected to EU measures regarding mutual recognition of decisions relating to evidence and the gathering of evidence in the context of police cooperation,[600] as well as crime victims' rights.[601]

---

[595] Art 9(2).   [596] See generally 9.2.3 and (as regards competence issues) 9.2.4.

[597] There is no need to examine the purely hypothetical possibility of the adoption of EU measures in *other* areas of criminal procedure (Art 82(2)(d) TFEU), as this provision has not yet been invoked.   [598] On civil law evidence issues, see 8.5.4 above.

[599] See 9.2.4 above.

[600] Arts 82(1) and 87. On the competence issues, see ibid. On the substance of the law in these areas, see 9.6.1 above and 12.6 and 12.7 below.   [601] See 9.8.3 below.

The conceptual problem with the mutual admissibility of evidence is that the rules of evidence law are tailored closely to the specific, and widely varying, systems of criminal procedure in different Member States. Moreover, protection for the criminal suspect is built in at different stages of that procedure in different Member States. If any evidence secured in any one Member State is automatically admissible in any other, then such protection may be circumvented. As an example of the difficulties, can it be accepted that any evidence obtained illegally, in a Member State where such evidence could nonetheless be used in court, must also be admissible in Member States which do not accept the admissibility of illegally obtained evidence?[602]

The Stockholm programme invited the Commission to 'explore whether there are other means [besides mutual recognition measures] to facilitate admissibility of evidence in this area'.[603] Just before the programme was adopted, the Commission had already released a Green Paper on the mutual recognition and admissibility of evidence,[604] which inter alia raised the question of whether there should be common standards for gathering evidence in general and/or particular types of evidence. The Commission intends to make parallel proposals on mutual recognition and admissibility of evidence in 2011,[605] although it should be noted that a group of Member States have already presented an initiative on the first of these issues (a Directive to establish a European Investigation Order) in the spring of 2010.[606]

9.8.2. Suspects and defendants

Even before the entry into force of the Treaty of Lisbon, there was a sustained effort to adopt EU legislation on this issue. An initial Commission Green Paper made the case for EU action in this area, referring to the decision to address such issues as part of the mutual recognition programme and arguing that Member States' mutual trust should be based on a greater degree of protection for individual rights than secured by ratification of the ECHR.[607] The Green Paper then examined several specific issues in detail: the right to legal assistance and representation, the right to interpretation and/or translation, special protection for vulnerable groups, and consular assistance.[608] It also addressed the issues of giving a standard 'letter of rights' to criminal suspects across the EU, and of compliance with and monitoring of the rights to be examined at EU level.

---

[602] See 9.3.1 above.   [603] [2010] OJ C 115, point 3.1.1.

[604] COM (2009) 624, 11 Nov 2009.

[605] See the action plan for implementing the Stockholm programme, COM (2010) 171, 20 Apr 2010.   [606] [2010] OJ C 165/22. On the substance of this proposal, see 9.6.1.3 above.

[607] COM (2003) 75, 19 Feb 2003.

[608] Compare with the list of rights expressly set out in Art 6 ECHR (see 9.3.1 above).

Subsequently, the Commission proposed a Framework Decision addressing all of these issues.[609] Although the Hague Programme called for the adoption of this proposal by the end of 2005,[610] agreement on the substance was impossible to reach, as several Member States had legal and political objections to an EU measure on this issue.[611] There was a final attempt to agree on the text during the German Council Presidency in 2007, but agreement was still not possible, even on the basis of 'enhanced cooperation', since there was not a qualified majority of Member States in favour of authorizing it.[612]

In an attempt to revive discussions on this topic, the Commission and Council decided in 2009 to approach the issue on a case-by-case basis, instead of comprehensively. For its part, the Council adopted a Resolution just before the entry into force of the Treaty of Lisbon, setting out a 'roadmap' for strengthening the procedural rights of suspects and accused persons.[613] This Resolution sets out a political commitment to take EU action in this area, and endorses a list of specific measures to be addressed as a 'priority', although this list is expressly 'non-exhaustive'. The list comprises the following rights: interpretation and translation; information on rights and charges; legal advice and legal aid; communication with relatives, employers, and consular authorities; and special safeguards for vulnerable suspects or accused persons. These rights correspond to those listed in the Commission's 2004 proposal for a Framework Decision. The Resolution also invites the Commission to present a Green Paper on pre-trial detention.[614] Comparing this list to Article 6 ECHR, it does not expressly mention the general aspects of the right to a fair trial (Article 6(1) ECHR); the presumption of innocence (Article 6(2) ECHR); facilities to prepare a defence (Article 6(3)(b) ECHR); or the rights concerning witnesses (Article 6(3)(d) ECHR). However, the rights to interpretation and translation, legal aid and assistance, and information about charges correspond respectively to Article 6(3)(e), (c), and (a) ECHR.[615]

The Stockholm programme then incorporated the roadmap on procedural rights, and also explicitly invited the Commission to examine whether the issue of presumption of innocence, along with other (unnamed) issues not mentioned in the roadmap, needs to be addressed.[616] The action plan on the implementation of the Stockholm programme envisages proposals on interpretation and translation and information about rights in 2010 (both proposals have now been made), legal aid and assistance in 2011, communication rights in 2012, and special

---

[609] COM (2004) 328, 28 Apr 2004. For comments, see R Loof, 'Shooting from the Hip: Proposed Minimum Rights in Criminal Proceedings throughout the EU' (2006) 12 ELJ 421.

[610] [2005] OJ C 53, point 3.3.1.

[611] See the report to the Dec 2005 JHA Council (Council doc 14248/1/05, 21 Nov 2005). On the competence issues, see 9.2.4 above.

[612] See the conclusions of the June 2007 JHA Council. On enhanced cooperation generally, see 2.2.5.5 above.   [613] [2009] OJ C 295/1.

[614] On the mutual recognition aspects of this issue, see 9.6.3 above.

[615] On the substance of the various rights, see 9.3.1 above.   [616] [2010] OJ C 115, point 2.4.

safeguards for vulnerable persons in 2013. The Green Paper on pre-trial detention is scheduled for 2012, and there is to be a Green Paper in 2014 on the question of whether other rights ought to be covered.[617] It should be noted that the Commission already released a Green Paper on the presumption of innocence back in 2006.[618] This Green Paper asked questions concerning the burden of proof, the right to silence, and the right against self-incrimination, and queried whether there are particular cross-border aspects of these issues.

In the meantime, the Commission had already anticipated the new piece-meal approach and proposed, in mid-2009, a Framework Decision on the right to interpretation and translation for criminal suspects.[619] The Council reached agreement on this proposal in October 2009, but was not able to adopt it before the Treaty of Lisbon entered into force.[620] After the entry into force of the Treaty, an initiative for a Directive on this issue was tabled first by a group of Member States,[621] and subsequently by the Commission.[622] The former initiative reflected the text of the agreement which the Council had reached in October 2009, while the latter proposal was modestly more ambitious. The Council and the EP agreed on the former proposal in spring 2010, although the agreed Directive has not yet been formally adopted.[623] Member States will have to implement the Directive three years after its publication in the EU *Official Journal*.[624]

The agreed Directive will apply to 'criminal proceedings' (not defined) as well as 'proceedings for the execution of a European Arrest Warrant'.[625] The rights will apply from the moment that a person is 'made aware' by the authorities, 'by official notification or otherwise', that he or she 'is suspected or accused' of having committed a criminal offence', until the 'conclusion' of those proceedings, 'which is understood to mean the final determination of the question whether the suspected or accused person has committed the offence, including, where applicable, sentencing and the resolution of any appeal'.[626] However, where sanctions for 'minor offences' may be imposed by an authority other than a criminal court, the Directive will only apply if those sanctions are appealed to court having criminal jurisdiction.[627] The Directive will not affect national law on the presence of counsel during proceedings, or concerning the right of access to documents during criminal proceedings.[628]

---

[617] COM (2010) 171, 20 Apr 2010.   [618] COM (2006) 174, 26 Apr 2004.

[619] COM (2009) 338, 8 July 2009.

[620] For the agreed text, see Council doc 14792/09, 23 Oct 2009.   [621] [2010] OJ C 69/1.

[622] COM (2010) 82, 9 Mar 2010.

[623] For the agreed text, see Council doc 10984/10, 23 June 2010.

[624] Art 9(1), agreed text of Directive (ibid). All the following references in this subsection are to this version of the agreed text, unless otherwise mentioned.

[625] Art 1(1). Note that the Framework Decision establishing the EAW already includes some procedural rights: see 9.5.2 above.   [626] Art 1(2).

[627] Art 1(3).

[628] Art 1(4). On the first point, it should be recalled that a proposal on legal assistance and legal aid is planned for 2011.

The right to interpretation will apply 'during criminal proceedings before investigative and judicial authorities, including during police questioning, during all court hearings and during any necessary interim hearings'.[629] It will also apply to communications with legal counsel, where necessary to ensure fairness and in particular where there is a direct connection with 'any questioning or hearing during the proceedings or with the lodging of an appeal or other procedural applications'.[630] Member States will be obliged to ensure 'assistance' for a person with a hearing impediment.[631] There will also be a requirement to verify whether the person concerned understands the language of the criminal proceedings.[632] Technology such as videoconferencing, telephone, or Internet communication is permitted, unless the physical presence of an interpreter is necessary in the interests of fairness.[633]

As for the right to translation, the core of the right will be the translation into a language the person understands of 'all documents which are essential to ensure that he is able to exercise the right to defend himself and to safeguard the fairness of the proceedings'.[634] An 'essential' document includes decisions depriving the person of his or her liberty, the charge or indictment and any judgment.[635] In other cases, decisions on translation will be taken by the national competent authorities, but the agreed Directive specifies that the person concerned, or his or her counsel, will have the right to 'submit a reasoned request' for further translations.[636] However, it is not necessary to translate passages of essential documents 'which are not relevant for the suspected or accused person to have knowledge of the case against him';[637] and, as an 'exception', an 'oral translation or an oral summary of the essential documents...may be provided instead of a written translation, on condition that such oral translation or oral summary does not affect the fairness of the proceedings'.[638] Moreover, the person concerned may waive his or her translation (but not interpretation) rights at any time, if he or she 'has received prior legal advice or has otherwise obtained full knowledge of the consequences of his waiver, and...the waiver was unequivocal and given voluntarily'.[639]

For both rights, there will be an obligation for a review at 'some stage of the proceedings' of any determination that there is no need for interpretation or translation and of the quality of that interpretation or translation,[640] and both rights will apply to proceedings for the execution of a European Arrest Warrant.[641]

---

[629] Art 2(1).   [630] Art 2(2).

[631] Art 2(3). This might overlap with the planned proposal on safeguards for vulnerable persons, planned for 2013.   [632] Art 2(4).

[633] Art 2(6).   [634] Art 3(1).

[635] Art 3(2). This provision overlaps with the subsequent proposal on information about criminal proceedings (see below). Also, it should be noted that this 'essential' information must already be given to persons pursuant to Art 5(2) and 6(3)(a) ECHR.   [636] Art 3(3).

[637] Art 3(4).   [638] Art 3(7).   [639] Art 3(8).   [640] Arts 2()5 and 3(5).

[641] Arts 2(7) and 3(6).

Also, the agreed Directive will oblige Member States to cover the costs of interpretation and translation, regardless of the outcome of the proceedings,[642] and Member States will have to ensure that the interpretation and translation are of sufficient quality to safeguard the fairness of the proceedings, so that the person concerned 'has knowledge of the case against him and is able to exercise the right to defend himself' (on this point, see also the parallel proposed Resolution, discussed below).[643] Member States will have to endeavour to establish a register of qualified interpreters and translators, and ensure that interpreters and translators observe confidentiality requirements.[644] They will also have to request that training of judges and prosecutors addresses the issues faced by suspects who need interpretation, and keep a record of cases where interpretation or translation was applied, or where translation rights were waived.[645] Finally, the Directive will not derogate from ECHR rules, the EU Charter of Rights, or international law or national law which provides a higher level of protection.[646] It should be recalled in any event that the Treaties specify that the EU can only set minimum standards in this area, with Member States always free to set higher standards for the person concerned.[647]

As compared to the case law on Article 6(3)(e) ECHR,[648] the Directive is clearer as regards the definition of an 'essential' document, adds a right to interpretation as regards communication with counsel, forbids waiver of the right to interpretation, clarifies the circumstances regarding waiver of the right to translation, and confirms that the right is free and applies to documents and to pre-trial proceedings. The exceptions regarding translation of documents do not fall below the standards set by the Strasbourg case law. However, there are no provisions on the Directive dealing with courts' obligations to ensure effective translation, other than the useful (but vague) inclusion of provisions on judicial training. Also, the Directive goes beyond Article 6 ECHR in that it applies to proceedings for the execution of an EAW,[649] and moreover goes beyond the EAW Framework Decision in providing for specific interpretation and translation rights.[650]

The Council is also likely to adopt a recommendation on the practical application of the Directive, which had been agreed already shortly before the Treaty of Lisbon entered into force (in the form of a resolution of the Council and Member States' governments).[651] This Resolution would address useful issues such as representation of professionals; qualification of interpreters and translators; training;

---

[642] Art 4.   [643] Art 5(1), referring to Arts 2(8) and 3(9).   [644] Art 5(2) and (3).

[645] Arts 6 and 7.   [646] Art 8.   [647] Art 82(2), final sub-paragraph; see 9.2.4 above.

[648] See 9.3.1 above.   [649] On the scope of Art 6 ECHR, see 9.3.1 above.

[650] The EAW Framework Decision ([2002] OJ L 190/1) refers only generally to the right to be assisted by an interpreter in accordance with national law (Art 11(2)), and to a right to information about the contents of the warrant (Art 11(1)), without expressly requiring a translation of the warrant.

[651] For the original agreed version, see Council doc 14793/09, 23 Oct 2009. For the later draft recommendation, see Council doc 11471/10, 24 June 2010.

registration; remote access to interpreters; and codes of conduct and best practice guidelines. Certain parts of the Resolution have been inserted into the Directive, at the EP's behest.[652] There is a question about when and whether this Resolution can be adopted following the entry into force of the Treaty of Lisbon, because the Treaty prevents the Council and EP, while considering the adoption of a legislative act on a particular issue, from adopting other types of act on the same issue.[653] However, there seems no reason why the Resolution cannot be adopted *after* the adoption of the Directive; it would certainly be unfortunate if a pedantic approach to the interpretation of the Treaty prevented the adoption of such a useful practical measure. But in any event, unfortunately neither the Resolution nor the agreed Directive addresses sufficiently the crucial issue of monitoring of the application of the rights,[654] or of remedies for their breach.

The second suspects' rights proposal, on the right to information in criminal proceedings, was tabled in July 2010 by the Commission.[655] This proposed measure has the same scope as the agreed Directive on interpretation and translation rights, and contains the same non-derogation clause. It would require that an accused or suspected person have the rights to the following, as specified in further detail: information about the procedural rights applicable; written information about an arrest (which shall take the form of a standard 'Letter of Rights'); written information about rights in EAW proceedings; information about the charge; and access to the case-file. Member States would have to establish a procedure to verify that these rights had been observed, provide for remedies in case they were not, and also ensure appropriate training of judicial and police officials as regards these rights.

The development of EU legislation in this area is essential to ensure that suspects' rights are more effectively enforced and to guarantee a balance between the prosecution and defence interests in EU criminal law legislation. As for the first Directive agreed in this area, its application to the EAW is welcome (in light of the limited scope of Article 6 ECHR), but it is unfortunate that it does not also apply to the procedural rights which are set out in other Framework Decisions. It remains to be seen whether the second proposal and further planned proposals will be agreed and will succeed in redressing the balance within EU criminal justice policy.

9.8.3. Victims of crime

EU measures concerning victims of crime constitute a Framework Decision on the status of victims in criminal proceedings; specific rules on victims in other EU

---

[652] Compare points 10, 11, and 16 of the original draft resolution to Arts 6, 5(2) and 2(6) of the Directive.   [653] Art 296 TFEU, third paragraph.

[654] Compare Arts 15 and 16 of the Commission's 2004 proposal (n 609 above) with Art 6 of the agreed Directive.   [655] COM (2010) 392, 20 July 2010.

criminal law measures; Directives on the cross-border aspects of State compensation for victims and on the legal status of victims of human trafficking;[656] an EU funding programme regarding victims of domestic violence;[657] and Council conclusions on this issue adopted in 2009.[658] It should also be recalled that EU citizens who travel between or reside in Member States have a right to equal treatment, if they (or their family members) become crime victims.[659] The Stockholm programme calls for the improvement of legislation regarding crime victims and its implementation, as well as practical measures to support such victims, and suggests examining the possibility of merging the Framework Decision on crime victims and the Directive on crime victims' compensation.[660] However, for the reasons explained at the outset of this chapter, these measures must remain based on different legal bases even after the entry into force of the Treaty of Lisbon,[661] which could cause complications for the adoption of a merged Directive. In the meantime, the proposal for a European Protection Order would also have the effect of assisting some crime victims.[662] Measures on crime victims also affect evidence law, as we shall see.[663]

The Framework Decision on the status of victims of crime, adopted in 2001,[664] had to be applied in phases between March 2002 and March 2006.[665] It has been the subject of three judgments and three pending cases before the Court of Justice.[666] A 'victim' is defined broadly as meaning 'a natural person who has suffered harm, including physical or mental injury, emotional suffering or economic loss, directly caused by acts or omissions that are in violation of the criminal law of a Member State'.[667] The Court of Justice has confirmed that in light of this definition, the Framework Decision does not apply to legal persons.[668] The Framework Decision applies to 'criminal proceedings' defined in accordance with national law, and the Court of Justice has confirmed that it applies to private prosecutions.[669]

---

[656] On the latter Directive, see 7.6.2 above.

[657] The 'Daphne' programme: see 12.4.7 below.

[658] See: <http://www.consilium.europa.eu/uedocs/cms_data/docs/pressdata/en/jha/110726.pdf>. [659] See 9.4 above.

[660] [2010] OJ C 115, point 2.3.4. The Commission's action plan on implementing the Stockholm programme schedules this proposal for 2011 (COM (2010) 171, 20 Apr 2010). [661] See ibid.

[662] See 9.7.6 above.

[663] On EU competence to adopt measures on evidence law, see 9.8.1 above.

[664] [2001] OJ L 82/1. See earlier the Commission Communication on crime victims (COM (1999) 349, 14 July 1999). On the Council's competence to adopt the Framework Decision at the time, see 9.2.4 above. All references in this section are to the Framework Decision, unless otherwise indicated. [665] Art 17.

[666] The decided cases are: C-105/03 Pupino [2005] ECR I-5285, C-467/05 Dell'Orto [2007] ECR I-5557, and C-404/07 Katz [2008] ECR I-7607. The pending cases are Cases: C-205/09 Eredics (opinion of 1 July 2010), C-483/09 Gueye, and C-1/10 Salmeron Sanchez; the questions in the latter two cases are the same. [667] Art 1(a).

[668] Dell'Orto, n 662 above. The same issue has arisen in the pending Eredics case (ibid).

[669] Art 1(c); see Katz, ibid. The Framework Decision is not confined to acts which took place on the territory of the State where proceedings are underway.

As to the substance, the Framework Decision provides first of all generally for 'respect and recognition' for crime victims, requiring that each Member State ensure that victims have a 'real and appropriate role in its criminal legal system', that they 'are treated with due respect for the dignity of the individual during proceedings' and that it 'recognise[s] the rights and legitimate interests of victims'.[670] In the case of 'particularly vulnerable victims', there is an obligation to provide 'specific treatment best suited to their circumstances'.[671] Member States must also make provision for victims to supply evidence, but to refrain from questioning them any more than necessary.[672] Bringing these points together, the 'most vulnerable' victims must be able to testify in a manner which protects them from the effects of giving evidence in open court, by means compatible with national legal principles.[673]

In the *Pupino* judgment, which concerned very young children who were allegedly abused in a nursery by their teacher, the Court of Justice unsurprisingly ruled that such victims must be considered 'vulnerable' pursuant to the Framework Decision—leaving aside the bigger question of whether all minors must be considered 'vulnerable'.[674] So these victims were entitled to the protection of a special procedure in which they did not have to give their testimony in court, as long as this was consistent with the right to a fair trial. In the *Katz* case,[675] the Court ruled that a person bringing a private prosecution did not have the right to demand, in light of the generality of the Framework Decision, that he have the status of a witness; but nevertheless the Framework Decision required that he must be able to submit evidence in the proceedings in some form. The Court of Justice has also been asked whether these provisions of the Framework Decision preclude a national rule which does not permit the victims of domestic violence to insist on their willingness to resume family life with their violent partner.[676]

Next, victims have the right to receive information on a number of issues, inter alia on the conduct of the criminal proceedings following their complaint and on the release of the accused or convicted person, at least where there might be a danger to the victim.[677] If victims are parties or witnesses, Member States must take necessary steps to reduce any communication difficulties they face (presumably by providing for translation and interpretation).[678] Member States must also ensure legal and non-legal aid is provided to victims who are parties, and that victims who are witnesses or parties may receive reimbursement of

---

[670] Art 2(1).   [671] Art 2(2).   [672] Art 3.   [673] Art 8(4).

[674] See n 666 above. The Advocate General indeed argued that all child victims of crime must be considered to be vulnerable (paras 53–59 of the Opinion). This judgment also addressed the legal effect of Framework Decisions: see 2.2.2.2 above.   [675] Ibid.

[676] *Gueye* and *Salmeron Sanchez*, ibid.

[677] Art 4. Compare to the proposed Dir on information rights for suspects (9.8.2 above).

[678] Art 5. This right is not as fully fledged as the interpretation and translation rights agreed for suspects (see 9.8.2 above).

their expenses.[679] Victims must be protected, inter alia from reprisals from the offender.[680] Member States must ensure that it is possible for the victim to receive a decision on compensation from the offender in criminal proceedings, unless in certain cases compensation is provided in another manner; and Member States must return victims' property that is not needed for the purpose of criminal proceedings.[681] An Advocate General has argued that the former right must include compensation for pecuniary losses, and that any exception from the possibility to obtain a decision on compensation must be limited to certain cases only and take place usually within the framework of the same proceedings which resulted in a conviction of the offender. As for the return of property, the obligation to return it only applies where the ownership of the property is undisputed or has been established in criminal proceedings; otherwise the issue is a matter for civil law.[682]

The Framework Decision also requires Member States to promote penal mediation between victim and offender, and several pending cases have asked the Court of Justice to clarify this obligation.[683] There are specific provisions for victims who are resident in another Member State, and for cooperation between Member States.[684] Finally, Member States must also promote victim support organizations, train personnel in contact with victims (particularly police officers and legal practitioners), and ensure that intimidation of victims cannot occur in venues such as courts and police stations.[685]

The Commission's first report on the national transposition of most provisions of the Framework Decision was quite critical regarding the lack of reported national measures which fully met the specific requirements of the Framework Decision.[686] Its second report concluded that implementation of the Framework Decision was still 'not satisfactory', due to the continued variations and omissions in national law and the decision of some Member States to implement the Framework Decision by non-binding means.[687]

As for the Framework Decisions with specific rules on crime victims, first of all the Framework Decision on terrorism provides that investigations and prosecutions shall not be dependent upon a complaint by a victim, at least where the offence takes place on the relevant Member State's territory; also Member States must provide support for victims' families.[688] Similar provisions appear in the Framework Decisions on trafficking in persons and on sexual exploitation of persons, with the additional provisos that Member States must treat child victims of these crimes as 'particularly vulnerable' and that families of the victims must enjoy

---

[679] Arts 6 and 7. Compare to the planned measures on legal aid for suspects (ibid).
[680] Art 8(1)–(3).   [681] Art 9.   [682] Opinion in *Dell'Orto*, n 666 above, paras 73–96.
[683] Art 10; see *Eredics*, *Gueye*, and *Salmeron Sanchez*, ibid.   [684] Arts 11–12.
[685] Arts 13–15.   [686] COM (2004) 54, 3 Feb 2004.
[687] COM (2009) 166, 20 Apr 2009.
[688] Art 10 of Framework Decision ([2002] OJ L 164/3).

the right to receive information as set out in the general Framework Decision on victims' rights.[689] Subsequent proposals for Directives on the latter topics contain even more extensive provisions on victims' rights.[690] Finally, the Framework Decision on organized crime contains only the proviso that investigations and prosecutions shall not be dependent upon a complaint by a victim.[691]

The criminal law measures are supplemented by Directive 2004/80 on state compensation for victims, which Member States had to implement by 1 January 2006.[692] This Directive requires each Member State to establish a State compensation scheme for 'victims of violent intentional crimes committed in their respective territories, which guarantees fair and appropriate compensation to victims',[693] but the details of national schemes are not harmonized, due to concerns about lack of EC competence to do so. Instead, the Directive establishes a mechanism for persons who have suffered from a violent crime in a Member State other than the State of their habitual residence to claim compensation from the former State. However, a degree of harmonization has been established by a 1983 Council of Europe Convention on compensation of victims of violent crime, which the majority of Member States have ratified.[694] The Court of Justice has ruled that this Directive does not affect the interpretation of the Framework Decision on victims, and moreover only applies to violent crime, not financial crime.[695] Also, the Court has ruled on the failure by two Member States to implement the Directive.[696]

According to the Commission report on the application of this Directive,[697] most Member States were compliant with the basic rule to establish national compensation systems, as well as the rules on cross-border compensation, although the view of claimants was more critical. The Commission therefore concluded that for now it was not necessary to amend the Directive, but rather to improve its implementation at national level.

---

[689] Art 7 of the Framework Decision on trafficking in persons ([2002] OJ L 203/1); Art 9 of the Framework Decision on sexual exploitation ([2004] OJ L 13/44). A 'child' is anyone under eighteen years old (Arts 1(4) and 1(a) of the respective Framework Decisions).

[690] COM (2010) 94 and 95, 29 Mar 2010. The trafficking proposal has been agreed within the Council, but has yet to be agreed with the EP; see the victims' rights provisions in Arts 7 and 10–14 of the agreed text (Council doc 10845/10, 10 June 2010).

[691] Art 8 of the Framework Decision ([2008] OJ L 300/42).

[692] Art 18(1) of the Dir ([2004] OJ L 261/15). See the earlier Green Paper on this issue (COM (2001) 536, 28 Sep 2001). The Commission has adopted a Decision establishing standard forms relating to the implementation of the Dir ([2006] OJ L 125/25).

[693] Art 12(2) of the Directive.   [694] ETS 116. For ratification details, see Appendix I.

[695] *Dell'Orto*, n 662 above.

[696] Cases C-112/07 *Commission v Italy*, judgment of 29 Nov 2007, and C-26/07 *Commission v Greece*, judgment of 18 July 2007, neither yet reported. The Commission has begun proceedings against Greece pursuant to Art 260 TFEU (formerly Art 228 EC) for non-implementation of the latter judgment: Case C-407/09 *Commission v Greece*, pending.

[697] COM (2009) 170, 20 Apr 2009.

Compared to the international measures on the subject of protection of victims,[698] the EU's measures as regards the status of victims in criminal proceedings are less vague and are furthermore legally binding, bolstered by the principle of indirect effect. However, the EU's measures are still quite vague; for example, it would surely have been possible to agree at the outset on some groups of persons (like small children) who must be considered 'particularly vulnerable', and it should have been possible to agree that victims should have either a right to bring or attach themselves to criminal proceedings. In light of the free movement of legal persons guaranteed by EU internal market law, it would be appropriate to ensure that EU legislation applies, to the extent relevant, to crime victims who are legal persons. Furthermore, the EU has not addressed the social aspects of victimization,[699] except for State compensation, where due to legal arguments only the cross-border aspects of this issue have been addressed. It should have been possible nevertheless for Member States to agree informally that they would ratify the Council of Europe Convention on this issue.

9.9. Administrative cooperation and EU funding

EU funds have made an increasingly significant contribution to the development of judicial cooperation. First of all, the EU budget funded the 'Grotius' programme on incentives and exchanges for legal practitioners, which was established initially from 1996 until 2000,[700] and then extended for 2001–02.[701] This programme was then subsumed within a general third pillar funding programme, 'AGIS', running from 2003–07.[702] This was in turn replaced by a criminal justice programme for the period 2007–13.[703]

As for administrative cooperation, the Council has adopted a Joint Action on the exchange of liaison magistrates.[704] Like their police and customs counterparts,[705] liaison magistrates are in effect the 'ambassadors' of one legal system to another, attempting to facilitate cross-border cooperation in practice. The Council subsequently adopted a Joint Action establishing a European judicial network in criminal matters, which was replaced in 2008 by a Decision on the same subject.[706] The judicial network is a more formal structure consisting of contact points in each Member State, holding regular meetings, establishing directories of information and linked by a telecommunications network.

---

[698] See Council of Europe Committee of Ministers Recommendation (R (85) 11, 28 June 1985) and UN General Assembly Resolution 40/34 1985.

[699] See Council of Europe Committee of Ministers Recommendation (R (87) 21, 17 Sep 1987).

[700] [1996] OJ L 287/3.   [701] [2001] OJ L 186/1.   [702] [2002] OJ L 203/5.

[703] [2007] OJ L 58/13.   [704] [1996] OJ L 105/1.   [705] See 12.6.3 below.

[706] [1998] OJ L 191/4 and [2008] OJ L 348/130. See the website of the Network: <http://www.ejn-crimjust.europa.eu/>.

Finally, there are informal EU networks for legislative cooperation[707] and judicial training, the latter of which is the subject of EU funding programmes.[708] Measures to expand judicial training in the EU form part of the Stockholm programme.[709]

9.10. External relations

Apart from its special association with Norway, Iceland, Switzerland, and (in future) Liechtenstein,[710] and the particular process of evaluating States negotiating to join the EU,[711] the EU has also negotiated treaties with the US concerning extradition and mutual assistance, and a treaty with Japan regarding mutual assistance. The treaties with the US, which entered into force on 1 February 2010,[712] do not replace national bilateral treaties with the US on these matters, but rather supplement those national treaties; the EU undertook to ensure, pursuant to the EU–US treaties, that its Member States would reach separate agreements with the US as regards their bilateral treaties. These bilateral agreements were all eventually finalized.

The EU–US extradition treaty has amended Member States' bilateral extradition treaties with the US as regards widening the list of extradition offences; simplifying the transmission of documents; furnishing additional information; the temporary surrender of persons already in custody; competing requests for extradition; simplified procedures where the fugitive consents to extradition; the treatment of sensitive information; transit of fugitives; and the exclusion of the death penalty for fugitives. The mutual assistance treaty has amended bilateral treaties (where they exist) as regards the supply of banking information; joint investigation teams; videoconferencing of witnesses or experts; expedited transmission of documents; the extension of mutual assistance rules to administrative authorities; the protection of personal data; and confidentiality. However, the grounds for refusal of mutual assistance in existing treaties (or, in the absence of such treaties, in national law) are preserved.

These agreements were highly controversial, in particular for the secretive manner in which they were negotiated, but also for their content, especially as regards the prospect of joint investigation teams between officials of

---

[707] See the Resolution establishing a network for legislative cooperation ([2008] OJ C 326/1).

[708] See the Commission communication on judicial training (COM (2006) 356, 29 June 2006), the Council conclusions in the JHA Council press release, 5–6 June 2003, and the Resolution of the Council and the Member States ([2008] OJ C 299/1).

[709] [2010] OJ C 115, point 1.2.6. Commission communications on this issue are due in 2011 (COM (2010) 171, 20 Apr 2010).   [710] See 9.2.5 above.

[711] See 12.11 below.

[712] [2003] OJ L 181/25. See the decision on conclusion of the treaties ([2009] OJ L 291/40). The extradition treaty has been extended to the Netherlands Antilles: [2009] OJ L 325/4.

Member States and the US and the weakness of the provisions on personal data protection.[713]

The EU–Japan mutual assistance treaty was signed in 2009, just before the Treaty of Lisbon entered into force.[714] It must now be concluded pursuant to the revised external relations provisions of the latter Treaty.[715]

Following the entry into force of the Treaty of Lisbon, the general EU rules on external relations apply to this area,[716] raising questions about the scope of EU external competence, as regards, for instance, the question of when agreements in this area must or may take the form of 'mixed' agreements, entailing the participation of both the EU and its Member States. However, the external competence deriving from EU measures in this area adopted before the entry into force of the Treaty of Lisbon will depend, until those measures are amended or replaced, upon the rules governing the EU external competence related to the former 'third pillar'—which have not yet been clarified by the Court of Justice.[717] A fundamental question will be whether the Court will take an assertive approach to the extent of the EU's external competence as regards pre-Lisbon or post-Lisbon measures in this area, by analogy with the approach it has taken to external competence over civil jurisdiction treaties.[718] On this point, Declaration 36 in the Final Act of the Treaty of Lisbon states that Member States are still able to conclude treaties in this field 'insofar as such agreements comply with Union law'; this confirms that Member States have not lost all authority to sign treaties in this area, but does not limit the scope or intensity of the EU's competence.[719] It should be noted, however, that many EU criminal law mutual recognition measures contain detailed provisions governing Member States' obligations to disapply prior treaties (as regards relations between Member States), along with authorization to retain existing agreements or conclude new agreements that further simplify the application of the relevant mutual recognition rules.[720] It is arguable that the latter provisions refer only to agreements between Member States, not between Member States

---

[713] See <http://www.statewatch.org/news/2003/jun/01useu.htm> and V Mitsilegas, 'The New EU–USA Cooperation on Extradition, Mutual Legal Assistance and the Exchange of Police Data' (2003) 8 EFARev 515.   [714] For the text of the treaty, see [2010] OJ L 39/19.

[715] See the proposal to conclude the treaty: COM (2009) 706, 17 Dec 2009.

[716] See generally 2.7.1 above.   [717] See 2.7.2 above.

[718] See *Opinion 1/2003*, [2006] ECR I-1145, and generally 8.9 above. It should be noted, however, that *Opinion 1/2003* focused on exclusive competence regarding civil *jurisdiction*, with exclusive competence over mutual recognition as a corollary. On external competence regarding criminal jurisdiction matters, see 11.11 below.   [719] See equally 8.9 above.

[720] For instance, see Art 31 of the EAW Framework Decision ([2002] OJ L 190/1). The Court of Justice has confirmed that these clauses do not authorize the Member States to retain in force the treaties that they are explicitly obliged not to apply any longer: Case C-296/08 PPU *Santesteban Goicoechea* [2008] ECR I-6307. On the power to retain or conclude special treaties, see by analogy the civil law judgment of the Court of Justice of 4 May 2010 in C-533/08 *TNT-Express*, not yet reported.

and third States.[721] A few EU measures also directly regulate some external aspects of the relevant issue.[722]

In the field of domestic criminal procedure, the EU's power to set minimum standards only necessarily means that the external competence in this area is shared. Also in this area, as noted already, a particular procedure for consultation of the Council of Europe has been established.[723] More generally, there are Council conclusions urging continued cooperation with the Council of Europe in the criminal law field.[724]

Finally, once treaties in this area are concluded after the entry into force of the Treaty of Lisbon, the Court's normal jurisdiction will apply (ie as regards references from national courts and infringement proceedings).

As for the future, the Stockholm programme calls for a policy of encouraging ratification of international criminal law treaties by third States, and considering which third States the EU should negotiate mutual assistance and extradition treaties with.[725]

9.11. Conclusions

Mutual recognition is an attractive principle because the 'free movement of prosecutions' holds out the prospect of speedier and more effective prosecution, therefore bringing more criminals to justice and increasing public security across the EU. But as noted at the outset, effective prosecutions are not the only objective which a criminal justice system must pursue.

Should mutual recognition proceed without substantive criminal law harmonization,[726] and a degree of harmonization of procedural law? On the first point, the abolition of dual criminality without a degree of harmonization of substantive law has provoked a hostile reaction from the public and national constitutional courts as regards the protection of a State's nationals, and defensive measures have therefore been invoked, including weakening the abolition of the principle of dual criminality in more recent mutual recognition measures. The

---

[721] This is explicit as regards the Framework Decisions on financial penalties ([2005] OJ L 76/16, Art 18) and on confiscation ([2006] OJ L 328/59, Art 21). There is no such provision in the Framework Decisions on freezing orders ([2003] OJ L 196/45) or on recognition of prior convictions ([2008] OJ L 220/32).

[722] See Arts 21 and 28(4) of the EAW Framework Decision (ibid).   [723] See 9.3.5 above.

[724] [2009] OJ C 50/8.

[725] [2010] OJ C 115, point 3.5.2. A Commission report is requested in 2010.

[726] As discussed below (10.5), the EU has only harmonized the definitions of certain offences, frequently leaving options to Member States as regards these definitions. Similarly only a modest number of crimes are subjected to harmonized definitions as a result of UN or Council of Europe treaties. In EU mutual recognition measures, the principle of dual criminality has been abolished for a much longer list of crimes. See S Peers, 'Mutual Recognition and Criminal Law in the European Union: Has the Council Got it Wrong?' (2004) 41 CMLRev 5 at 26–34.

EU's model for mutual recognition in criminal law cannot be defended by reference to the internal market or civil law model, both of which require a degree of harmonization of substantive law or of conflict rules and deal with matters which are much less sensitive from the perspective of national sovereignty and the protection of civil liberties.[727]

As for the case for procedural harmonization, we should neither be so xenophobic as to assume that foreign criminal proceedings are always unjust, nor so naive as to assume that such proceedings are always above reproach. The reality lies between the extremes of paranoia on the one hand, and Polyanna on the other. So the EU needs to strike a balance between blind faith in other Member States on the one hand, and undue interference with the valuable diversity of national criminal justice systems on the other.

The principle of mutual recognition of criminal law is therefore acceptable on certain conditions, in particular as regards the abolition of dual criminality, if there is a sufficient degree of harmonization of substantive and procedural standards in parallel, and the territoriality exception to mutual recognition is fully maintained. But at present, these conditions are not being met, with the EU only beginning the process of ensuring procedural guarantees for criminal suspects, long after adopting important mutual recognition measures. In the meantime, EU measures assume too easily the fairness of each Member State's proceedings, and require (until more recently) an over-broad abolition of dual criminality, well beyond those crimes which Member States have harmonized *de jure* as a consequence of EU measures or international treaties, or de facto as a result of spontaneous harmonization. It remains to be seen whether the implementation of the roadmap on procedural rights, if successful, will redress the balance.

---

[727] See the comments in Peers, ibid, at 23–26; for an alternative view, see J Wouters and F Naert, 'Of Arrest Warrants, Terrorist Offences and Extradition Deals: an Appraisal of the EU's Main Criminal Law Measures Against Terrorism After "11 September"' (2004) 41 CMLRev 909.

10

Substantive Criminal Law

10.1. Introduction

Substantive criminal law (the definition of criminal offences) is usually a matter for States, and often for regions within those States, to decide. But there is a history of international cooperation on this issue, because States are willing to agree treaties binding themselves to harmonize their domestic law in regards to a small number of specific (but usually serious) crimes which are perceived to pose particular cross-border issues. Furthermore, the harmonization of substantive criminal law removes or weakens a traditional barrier to judicial cooperation between States: the 'double criminality' rule, which historically required an act to constitute a crime in both the State requesting assistance (such as extradition or the transfer of a prisoner) and the State which is being requested, before cooperation can go ahead.[1]

Although a number of substantive criminal law treaties have been adopted within other international frameworks, the EU has retained a distinct interest in adopting its own measures in this area, to deal with issues unique to the EU (like protection of the EU's financial interests), to address other issues not yet dealt with in other international fora (such as a harmonized definition of 'terrorism'), and to ensure a greater level of harmonization within the EU than provided for by international treaties (for example, by removing Member States' reservations to those treaties or by harmonizing their interpretation).

EU measures have now been adopted in a number of areas, and have addressed not only the definition of offences, but also aspects of the general part of criminal law (for example, attempts and complicity), the liability of legal persons, and harmonized sentencing rules.

This chapter starts with the basic issues of the institutional framework, an overview of measures adopted, legal competence, territorial scope, human rights, and overlaps with other areas of (non-JHA) EU law—a highly contested issue which the Treaty of Lisbon has attempted to resolve. It then examines offences harmonized by the EC/EU and the related general criminal law issues, followed by an analysis of EU harmonization of sentencing, and a summary of the EC/EU's

---

[1] On the partial removal of the dual criminality rule by EU legislation, see 9.5–9.7 above.

external relations powers and practice in this field. The connected issues of criminal procedure and policing are addressed in Chapters 9 and 12 respectively, and the issue of jurisdiction over criminal offences will be examined in Chapter 11,[2] because of the links between this issue, the cross-border 'double jeopardy' rule, and the coordination of prosecutions by Eurojust.

10.2. Institutional framework and overview

10.2.1. Framework prior to the Treaty of Amsterdam

For some time, the Community and Union frameworks were not used to harmonize the substantive criminal law of the Member States. This issue was left in particular to the United Nations,[3] with a limited role for the Council of Europe, although the latter organization's role has expanded in recent years.[4] There were attempts by Member States in the 1960s and 1970s to agree measures on the specific issue of fraud against the EU budget, but these efforts were unsuccessful at the time.[5]

Efforts to harmonize substantive criminal law at EU level began to develop after the entry into force of the original TEU in 1993. In fact, initially the TEU's third pillar provisions did not explicitly grant the Council competence to adopt measures harmonizing substantive criminal law. Rather, Article K.1(7) EU referred to criminal judicial cooperation. However, it was soon felt necessary to agree 'combination' acts which set out both agreed substantive law principles and rules on judicial cooperation, because the harmonization of substantive law facilitated judicial cooperation by simplifying the application of the double criminality condition for judicial cooperation.

In addition, Article K.1(4) and (5) of the original TEU referred to 'combatting drug addiction' and 'fraud on an international scale' to the extent that this fell outside the scope of judicial, police, and customs cooperation, thus implying that there was competence to harmonize substantive criminal law in these areas independently of judicial cooperation.

In practice, the EU used the third pillar powers during the Maastricht era to adopt Conventions harmonizing substantive criminal law as regards fraud against the EU budget and corruption, as well as Joint Actions harmonizing law as regards drug trafficking, racism and xenophobia, organized crime, private corruption, trafficking in persons and sexual exploitation of children, and money

---

[2] See 11.5 below.

[3] From a huge literature, see (with further references), M Bassiouni, *International Criminal Law, Vol. I: Sources, Subjects and Contents* (3rd edn, Martinus Nijhoff, 2008).

[4] In particular, there are Council of Europe Conventions in force addressing corruption (ETS 173) and cyber-crime (ETS 185). For Member States' ratification of these measures, see Appendix I.   [5] See 2.2.1.1 above.

laundering.[6] All of these Joint Actions only required Member States to present proposals to their national parliaments, without an explicit obligation upon the entire State to ensure that the national law was amended.

Also, *Community* powers were used, both before and after entry into force of the original TEU, to adopt legislation closely related to criminal law, although no EC legislation adopted before the entry into force of the Treaty of Amsterdam explicitly required Member States to impose criminal penalties.

Outside the EU framework, the Schengen Convention contained certain provisions relevant to harmonization of substantive criminal law, particularly regarding drugs and facilitation of unauthorized immigration.[7]

10.2.2. Treaty of Amsterdam

The EU's objectives in the field of policing and criminal law were set out in Article 29 TEU, as revised by the Treaty of Amsterdam, which set out an objective of, inter alia, 'preventing and combating racism and xenophobia'. This was '[w]ithout prejudice to the powers of the European Community'. The objective was to be 'achieved by preventing and combating crime, organised or otherwise, in particular terrorism, trafficking in persons and offences against children, illicit drugs trafficking and illicit arms trafficking, corruption and fraud, through... [inter alia] approximation, where necessary, of rules on criminal matters in the Member States, in accordance with the provisions of Article 31(e)'.[8] Article 31 set out a list of measures which judicial cooperation 'shall include', and point (e) concerned 'progressively adopting measures establishing minimum rules relating to the constituent elements of criminal acts and to penalties in the fields of organised crime, terrorism and illicit drug trafficking'. So the EU did not set itself the aim of harmonizing all national substantive criminal law, but rather concerned itself with certain listed crimes, although the lists in Articles 29 and 31(e) were both expressly non-exhaustive ('in particular', 'shall include'). Also, the EU was limited by the previous Article 31 TEU to setting 'minimum' rules on offences and penalties, leaving Member States free to set higher penalties or to impose criminal sanctions on a wider range of activity than required by an EU measure.

The Treaty of Amsterdam also amended the EC Treaty to provide for 'legal bases' for Community action closely related to criminal law matters. Article 280 EC, as amended by the Treaty of Amsterdam, had previously (as Article 209a EC) merely set out general principles concerning fraud against EC financial interests,

---

[6] For references to the relevant measures, see 10.5.1.2 below.

[7] See Arts 27 and 71 of the Convention ([2000] OJ L 239).

[8] The previous Art 31(e) TEU became Art 31(1)(e) after entry into force of the Treaty of Nice, which added a new Art 31(2) to the TEU, but its text was otherwise unchanged.

but now also provided a 'legal base' to adopt legislation using the co-decision procedure and qualified majority voting (QMV) in the Council on this issue, 'with a view to providing effective and equivalent protection in the Member States' for those interests. Although one would expect that such legislation would necessarily have to address criminal law issues, Article 280(4) EC specified that such measures 'shall not concern the application of national criminal law or the national administration of justice'. Also, Article 135 EC, a legal base for the adoption of measures concerning customs cooperation, was added to the EC Treaty by the Treaty of Amsterdam; it contained an identical proviso.[9]

As in other areas of JHA law and policy, the 1999 Tampere European Council (EU leaders' summit meeting) set out a political agenda concerning the exercise of the EU's powers in this area. The summit conclusions stated that 'with regard to national criminal law, efforts to agree on common definitions, incriminations and sanctions should be focused in the first instance on a limited number of sectors of particular relevance, such as financial crime (money laundering, corruption, Euro counterfeiting), drugs trafficking, trafficking in human beings, particularly exploitation of women, sexual exploitation of children, high tech crime and environmental crime', and also called for 'the approximation of criminal law and procedures on money laundering'.[10]

In practice, during the 'Amsterdam era' (1999–2009), the EU only used Framework Decisions, rather than Conventions or other measures, to harmonize substantive criminal law, except for a Decision on synthetic drugs.[11] This speeded up the harmonization process, because the Framework Decisions obliged a Member State to implement them within a relatively short period of about two years, without any form of ratification requirement in national parliaments, whereas Conventions are subject to national ratification, which usually takes over five years. Also, national courts must give 'indirect effect' to Framework Decisions (interpreting national law in light of them),[12] while it is not yet established whether EU law requires Conventions to have a particular legal effect in national legal orders. But in the area of substantive criminal law, the 'indirect effect' of Framework Decisions (and the direct and indirect effect of Directives) is apparently of limited relevance, because the Court of Justice has made clear that criminal sanctions cannot be imposed on individuals unless national law clearly provides for this.[13]

The areas covered by Framework Decisions comprise: counterfeiting of currency and of non-cash instruments (such as cheques, credit cards, and debit cards);

---

[9] Previous Arts 135 and 280 EC were renumbered Arts 33 and 325 TFEU respectively by the Treaty of Lisbon, and also amended; see 10.2.3 below.

[10] Paras 48 and 55 of the European Council conclusions.

[11] On this Decision, see 10.5.1.2 below.   [12] Case C-105/03 *Pupino* [2005] ECR I-5285.

[13] On the legal effect of third pillar measures, see further 2.2.2.2 above; on the human rights background to the implementation of substantive EU criminal law by Member States, see 10.3 below.

money laundering; private corruption; terrorism; trafficking in persons; facilitation of illegal entry and residence; environmental crime, including pollution related to shipping; child pornography and prostitution; drug trafficking; attacks on information systems; organized crime; and racism and xenophobia.[14] Most of these measures replaced the pre-Amsterdam Joint Actions on the same topics. Like the prior Joint Actions, the Framework Decisions either address subjects outside the scope of current international criminal law conventions or aim to supplement those conventions by harmonizing the law in greater detail. However, compared to the Joint Actions, the Framework Decisions usually provide for specific penalties to be imposed against offenders and define the relevant offences in further detail. Furthermore, replacing Joint Actions with Framework Decisions had the automatic effect of extending the revised institutional rules of the Treaty of Amsterdam (clearer legal effect and jurisdiction of the Court of Justice) to these measures.[15]

There are several different aspects to each Framework Decision concerning substantive criminal law. The core of each act is the definition of the offence (often several offences). This definition is usually at a level of detail comparable to international criminal law Conventions. Next, each measure usually requires criminalization of related and inchoate offences, although the details are quite different and the principles underlying inchoate offences (such as whether an 'impossible attempt' should be criminalized or the extent of planning and preparation necessary to constitute an attempt) are not expressly harmonized. In some cases (private corruption, facilitation of illegal entry and residence, child pornography and prostitution, attacks on information systems, and drug trafficking), Member States have an option *not* to criminalize aspects of the relevant activity in certain circumstances.[16]

As for the extent of obligations, almost all measures require the Member States to impose criminal or non-criminal fines or other sanctions on legal persons who breach the relevant rules. For natural persons, as noted above, most of the Framework Decisions also contain provisions on sentencing, requiring Member States to impose a maximum possible sentence of at least 'x' years for those found guilty of the specified offence. In several of these cases, there are provisions for aggravated or reduced penalties where specified conditions are met. All measures contain rules on jurisdiction; as noted above, these rules are considered in detail in Chapter 11.[17]

So far there has been no move to codify the measures which have been agreed, even in order to reduce or abolish divergences and inconsistencies on issues such as related offences, jurisdiction, and penalties.

Implementation of Framework Decisions by the Member States is overseen by the Commission, which compiles reports on implementation based on information

---

[14] For detailed references, see 10.5.1.2 below.
[15] These issues have been revisited subsequently by the Treaty of Lisbon: see 10.2.3 below.
[16] On the relevance of this for EU criminal procedural measures, see 9.11 below.
[17] See 11.5 below.

supplied by the Member States; the Council then in principle reviews national implementation based on the Commission's reports, although the Council ceased to do this towards the end of the 'Amsterdam era'.[18] However, it should be kept in mind that unlike 'first pillar' obligations, 'third pillar' obligations cannot be enforced by means of the Commission bringing infringement actions against Member States pursuant to Article 226 EC (now Article 258 TFEU), until the expiry of the five-year transitional period provided for by the Treaty of Lisbon relating to the Court's jurisdiction over third pillar acts adopted before the entry into force of that Treaty.[19] So until then (1 December 2014), or unless the Framework Decisions are amended in the meantime,[20] the Commission reports and Council reviews are the main method of checking upon implementation by Member States.[21]

As for the role of the Court of Justice, there were no references from national courts or dispute settlement cases to the Court relating to third pillar substantive criminal law measures, before the entry into force of the Treaty of Lisbon. There were, however, a large number of cases before the Court concerning Community law measures that had an impact upon criminal law.[22] Furthermore, the borderline between Community (first pillar) powers and Union (third pillar) powers over substantive criminal law was hotly disputed during the 'Amsterdam era'. As a result, the Commission brought two annulment actions against the Council, alleging that two particular Framework Decisions fell within the scope of EC law, not the third pillar.[23] Both actions were successful, with the result that the Council and European Parliament (EP) began to adopt Community law measures with provisions defining criminal offences.[24] Quite apart from these developments, there was a close relationship between a number of EC acts and third pillar measures in this area.

10.2.3. Treaty of Lisbon

Following the entry into force of the Treaty of Lisbon, the EU's competence to harmonize substantive criminal law is set out in the first two paragraphs of Article 83 TFEU:

1. The European Parliament and the Council may, by means of directives adopted in accordance with the ordinary legislative procedure, establish minimum rules concerning

---

[18] For references to the reports, see 10.5.1.2 below.   [19] See further 2.2.3.3 above.

[20] For the initial proposals for such amendments, see 10.2.3 below.

[21] For more on the issue of implementation, see 2.5 above.

[22] On this issue generally, see 10.4 below.

[23] Cases C-176/03 *Commission v Council* [2005] ECR I-7879 and C-440/05 *Commission v Council* [2007] ECR I-9097.

[24] Dir 2008/99 on environmental crime ([2008] OJ L 328/28); Dir 2009/123 on shipping pollution ([2009] OJ L 280/52); and Dir 2009/52 on employer sanctions for hiring irregular migrants ([2009] OJ L 168/24).

the definition of criminal offences and sanctions in the areas of particularly serious crime with a cross-border dimension resulting from the nature or impact of such offences or from a special need to combat them on a common basis.

These areas of crime are the following: terrorism, trafficking in human beings and sexual exploitation of women and children, illicit drug trafficking, illicit arms trafficking, money laundering, corruption, counterfeiting of means of payment, computer crime and organised crime.

On the basis of developments in crime, the Council may adopt a decision identifying other areas of crime that meet the criteria specified in this paragraph. It shall act unanimously after obtaining the consent of the European Parliament.

2. If the approximation of criminal laws and regulations of the Member States proves essential to ensure the effective implementation of a Union policy in an area which has been subject to harmonisation measures, directives may establish minimum rules with regard to the definition of criminal offences and sanctions in the area concerned. Such directives shall be adopted by the same ordinary or special legislative procedure as was followed for the adoption of the harmonisation measures in question, without prejudice to Article 76.

Article 83(3) TFEU then provides for a special 'emergency brake' procedure in the event that a Member State believes that a proposed Directive in this area 'would affect fundamental aspects of its criminal justice system', entailing a dispute settlement procedure at the level of the European Council and a fast-track authorization of the 'enhanced cooperation' procedure if the dispute is not settled there.[25]

Compared to the previous rules, the main competence to harmonize substantive criminal law has become subject to QMV and co-decision—now known as the ordinary legislative procedure—instead of unanimity in the Council and consultation of the EP. However, in the case of the 'Community criminal law' competence provided for in Article 83(2), it is possible that unanimous voting will apply in the Council in some cases, for example if the EU wanted to adopt measures on tax fraud or further measures concerning racism, because those are cases where a special legislative procedure entailing unanimous voting applies to the underlying harmonization measures.[26]

As in other areas of policing and criminal law, the Commission has influence as regards Article 83(1) TFEU because individual Member States cannot make legislative proposals anymore on the listed areas of criminal law. But since both the first and second paragraphs are subject to the possibility that a group of at least one-quarter of the Member States may table a proposal, this is a reduction in the Commission's influence as regards Article 83(2), because previously only the Commission could table proposals relevant to criminal law pursuant to the

---

[25] For detailed analysis of this process, see 2.2.3.4.1 above. The procedure also applies to harmonization of domestic criminal procedural law, pursuant to Art 82(3) TFEU (see 9.2.5 above).

[26] See respectively Arts 113 and 19(1) TFEU (ex-Arts 93 and 13(1) EC), which require unanimous voting in the Council.

relevant EC Treaty Articles. Moreover, if the Council were to adopt a decision extending the EU's criminal law competence pursuant to Article 83(1), the Council would not be required to act on the basis of a Commission proposal, because this would not be a legislative act.[27]

The Treaty of Lisbon also entailed application of the normal jurisdiction of the Court of Justice, subject to the relevant transitional rules,[28] although there were no references to the Court in this area in the first few months after the Treaty of Lisbon entered into force. Also, the instruments of 'Community' law, with their well-established legal effect, now apply to this field of law. However, it is notable that the EU is required to act by means of Directives in this area, and therefore cannot use Regulations.[29] Furthermore, the restrictions regarding criminal law that previously applied to the specific issues of fraud and customs cooperation were removed by the Treaty of Lisbon.[30]

On the eve of the entry into force of the Treaty of Lisbon, the Council adopted a resolution on model provisions in legislation relating to criminal law, intended to guide the Council's future work.[31] It broadly endorsed the Council's prior practice in this area.[32] As for actual legislation, in the first few months after the entry into force of the Treaty, the Commission tabled revised versions of the Framework Decisions on trafficking in persons and sexual offences,[33] which had previously been proposed in 2009 but had not been adopted before the entry into force of the Treaty of Lisbon.[34] In June 2010, the Council agreed in principle upon the proposed Directive on trafficking in persons.[35] The 'emergency brake' has not been used to date.

The Commission also withdrew its prior proposal on criminal law enforcement of intellectual property rights,[36] and revised the legal base of its earlier proposal for a Directive on fraud against the EU budget, referring to Article 325 TFEU alone (without the use of Article 83(2)).[37]

As for the future, the Stockholm programme generally encouraged the possible adoption of criminal law measures.[38] The action plan implementing the programme includes, in this field, proposals as regards cyber-crime and synthetic drugs (2010), intellectual property (2011), and money laundering (2012).[39] There

---

[27] See revised Art 17(2) TEU. It would also be possible for the European Council to change the voting rule applicable to extensions of competence, pursuant to Art 48(7), revised TEU.

[28] On these rules, see 2.2.3.3 below.

[29] On the legal effect of the different EU instruments, see Art 288 TFEU.

[30] Compare Arts 33 and 325 TFEU to the previous Arts 135 and 280 EC.

[31] Council doc 16542/2/09, 27 Nov 2009.   [32] See 10.5 and 10.6 below.

[33] COM (2010) 95 and 94, 29 Mar 2010.

[34] COM (2009) 135 and 136, 25 Mar 2009.

[35] See Council doc 10845/10, 10 June 2010. The Council must still agree with the EP on this proposal.

[36] See the Commission's 2010 work programme (COM (2010) 135, 31 Mar 2010).

[37] COM (2009) 665, 2 Dec 2009. For comments, see 10.2.4 below.

[38] [2010] OJ C 115, point 3.3.1.   [39] COM (2010) 171, 20 Apr 2010.

is no reference to new legislation on substantive criminal law rules regarding terrorism, drug trafficking, arms trafficking, corruption, counterfeiting means of payment, organized crime, racism, or immigration.

10.2.4. Competence issues[40]

One key question regarding substantive criminal law, as noted already, is the historic dispute regarding the division of powers between the EC and the EU (the first and third pillars) in this area, and the provisions of the Treaty of Lisbon which subsequently address this issue. This point is examined in more detail below.[41]

The remaining issues concern the scope and intensity of the EU's competence as set out in Article 83(1) TFEU, as well as the relationship between the powers conferred by Article 83(1), as well as Article 83 as a whole, and the other provisions of the Treaties. Previously, as seen above, Article 31(1)(e) TEU stated that EU powers 'shall include' the adoption of measures harmonizing the definition of offences and relevant penalties in several specific areas; Article 29 TEU stated that the EU's third pillar objectives were to be achieved, inter alia, by approximating national law regarding a different list of crimes, 'in particular' certain listed offences; and the Tampere European Council conclusions referred to a third list of areas where the EU should focus its initial efforts to harmonize substantive law, 'such as', inter alia, financial crime. These provisions appeared to be non-exhaustive, but any ambiguity on this point has been resolved by the wording of Article 83(1) TFEU, which quite clearly gives the EU powers only as regards the ten crimes listed in the second sub-paragraph. If this list were not exhaustive, there would be no point to the third sub-paragraph of Article 83(1), which provides for the possibility of extending the EU's powers to further crime. The restriction of the EU's actions to specified crimes should be understood as a *quid pro quo* for the extension of QMV in this area.

Next, both Article 83(1) and (2) TFEU expressly limit the EU to adopting 'minimum rules' only, ie full harmonization of substantive criminal law is ruled out. This limitation also appeared in the previous Article 31(1)(e) TEU, but it did not apply to the exercise of Community criminal law competence per se.[42]

---

[40] The following discussion (and the discussion in 10.4.1.2 below) is adapted from S Peers, 'EU Criminal Law and the Treaty of Lisbon' (2008) 33 ELRev 507 at 514–522.

[41] See 10.4.1 below.

[42] This point was not relevant to the EC's environmental crime Dir (Dir 2008/99, [2008] OJ L 328/28), since the EC's environmental powers limited it to setting minimum standards only (previous Art 176 EC, now Art 193 TFEU, which has not changed this rule). On the other hand it was relevant to EC Directives setting out criminal law rules as regards shipping pollution and employer sanctions for hiring irregular migrants (respectively Dirs 2009/123 and 2009/52, [2009] OJ L 280/52 and [2009] OJ L 168/24). In the latter case, the Council and EP nevertheless restrained themselves to setting minimum standards regarding offences only (see the title of Dir 2009/52), but in the first case it appears that they did not.

As for the relationship between Article 83(1) TFEU and other provisions of the Treaties, the first issue is the relationship between Article 83(1) and (2). It is necessary to distinguish between the two paragraphs because the decision-making procedure in each of them is potentially different—depending upon the other decision-making procedures in the rest of the Treaty, which, as noted above, would apply to the adoption of measures pursuant to paragraph 2. Furthermore, different substantive criteria would apply to the adoption of measures under the two paragraphs. Finally, it is arguable that the British, Danish, and Irish opt-outs from Title V do not apply to paragraph 2, whereas they undoubtedly apply to paragraph 1.[43]

So what is the relationship between the two paragraphs? In the absence of any express wording to the contrary (ie a phrase like 'without prejudice to'), each paragraph should logically be considered to be a *lex specialis* as regards the other paragraph. Therefore, the scope of paragraph 1 cannot be extended by the Council to cover offences within the scope of paragraph 2,[44] and paragraph 2 cannot be interpreted to cover items expressly listed *at the outset* as falling within the scope of paragraph 1. This is particularly relevant as regards trafficking in persons, arms trafficking, money laundering, counterfeiting means of payment, and computer crime.[45]

Next, what is the scope of Article 83 TFEU as compared to the Treaty's other policing and criminal law provisions? In particular, can Article 83 be used to adopt measures relating to jurisdiction, procedure, or investigations concerning the relevant crimes? Given that Article 83 only refers to criminal offences and penalties, and other provisions of Chapters 4 and 5 of Title V refer more specifically to conflicts of jurisdiction, procedure, and investigations,[46] it must follow, in the absence of any provisions in the Treaty regulating the relationships between the various legal bases, that the latter provisions have to be used to adopt measures concerning those aspects of criminal law and policing. This would entail the use of dual legal bases.[47] However, Article 83 TFEU must still be the correct legal base as regards rules requiring or permitting Member States to assert jurisdiction

---

[43] On this issue, see 2.2.5.1 above, where it is argued that the opt-outs do apply.

[44] Such an extension could, for instance, lead to the application of QMV and the ordinary legislative procedure to criminal law measures concerning tax fraud (see Art 113 TFEU), and therefore would circumvent to some extent national parliaments' control of the *passerelle* clause that would otherwise apply to changing decision-making in that field (see revised Art 48(7) TEU).

[45] The Commission argued that criminal law measures concerning the last three issues fell within the scope of the previous EC Treaty: see COM (2005) 583, 23 Nov 2005. As for trafficking in persons, following the entry into force of the Treaty of Lisbon there is now an express power on this subject in the immigration chapter of Title V (see 7.2.4 above); and as for arms trafficking, the Commission later proposed an amendment to the EC firearms Dir which would have required Member States to criminalize certain acts, although the Council and EP did not agree to this proposal (see 10.4.1.1 below).

[46] Moreover, these other provisions are not limited in scope to particular crimes.

[47] See the proposals for Directives on trafficking in persons and offences against children (COM (2010) 95 and 94, 29 Mar 2010), which contain the dual legal bases of Arts 83 and 82(2) (as regards

over crimes within the scope of that Article,[48] since such measures are ancillary to the definition of offences and do not fall within the scope of the power in Article 82(1) TFEU to *prevent and settle* such conflicts, except to the extent that they included rules on priority jurisdiction.[49]

On the other hand, it is surely beyond doubt that both paragraphs of Article 83 TFEU can be used to adopt rules harmonizing *penalties* for specific offences.[50] As for the first paragraph, the express reference to adopting minimum rules concerning offences and penalties is simply a continuation of the prior power set out in the previous Article 31(1)(e) TEU, as set out above. In the case of the second paragraph, the competence to define sanctions has gone beyond the EC's prior powers as defined by the Court,[51] but accepting a power to define sanctions following the entry into force of the Treaty of Lisbon respects the literal wording of this provision ('criminal offences *and* sanctions'). It should not be assumed that this provision must be subject to the same interpretation as the previous EC Treaty. After all, the drafters of the Treaty of Lisbon made the deliberate choice to amend substantially the substance of EC and EU competence as regards many aspects of JHA law. It can hardly be assumed that their only intention in doing so was merely to restate the existing law. Moreover, the interpretation of the second paragraph should be consistent with that of the first paragraph where the same wording is used; and the competence to adopt rules on sanctions to enforce other EU policies would enhance the effectiveness of those policies, which is the underlying purpose of paragraph 2.[52]

As for the relationship between Article 83 and Article 86 TFEU,[53] concerning the competence to establish the European Public Prosecutor, Article 86 is the correct legal basis for conferring specific procedural powers upon the Public Prosecutor,[54] and to that end it can be used to define the substantive crimes which the Prosecutor has jurisdiction over. However, it cannot be the source of rules harmonizing national law to this end, because Article 83 is a *lex specialis* on this issue. If the Prosecutor is ever established, presumably it will be necessary in the interests of coherence to ensure that the Prosecutor's jurisdiction matches the definition of crimes which the EU has already harmonized, or at

---

the rights of victims). Note that there is no problem per se combining legal bases with and without an emergency brake rule: see 9.2.4 above.

[48] EU measures on substantive criminal law have always contained such rules, but EC measures have not. For details see 11.5 below.

[49] A small number of third pillar measures contain such priority jurisdiction rules: see 11.5 below.

[50] The proposals tabled since the entry into force of the Treaty of Lisbon have contained such provisions (see 10.5.1.2 below).

[51] See further the more detailed discussion of para 2 in 10.4.1.2 below.

[52] See further the discussion of the effectiveness/sanctions link in 10.4.1 below.

[53] This point is particularly relevant since the Council must act unanimously pursuant to Art 86.

[54] See more precisely Art 86(3) TFEU. For more on Art 86, see 9.2.4 above and 11.2.4 and 11.10 below.

least that the EU adopts parallel harmonization measures when the Prosecutor is established.

Two awkward issues could arise in this context. First of all, the power for the European Council to expand the powers of the Public Prosecutor is prima facie wider than the EU's powers to harmonize national criminal laws, since Article 86(4) refers inter alia to 'serious crime having a cross-border dimension' while Article 83(1) refers to '*particularly* serious crime with a cross-border dimension'.[55] So in theory, the European Public Prosecutor could be awarded jurisdiction to deal with crimes that have not been harmonized and even *could* not be harmonized by the EU (assuming that such crimes do not fall within the scope of Article 83(2) either). In this case, the measure conferring powers upon the Public Prosecutor to this end would have to define its jurisdiction without thereby harmonizing national law on this subject.

Secondly, there could be complications because the EU can only harmonize national criminal law in order to establish minimum standards, whereas the Public Prosecutor would presumably have a uniform jurisdiction. This could be addressed by simply restricting the Public Prosecutor's activities to cases which fall within the scope of his or her uniform jurisdiction, while allocating competence to national authorities as regards cases falling outside the scope of that jurisdiction.

Next, what about the relationship between Article 83 TFEU and the other provisions of the Treaties, besides the other criminal law and policing provisions? Is it still possible, for instance, to adopt 'Community criminal law' on the basis of the EU's environmental law powers (Article 192 TFEU, previously Article 175 EC), rather than Article 83(2) TFEU?[56] Similarly, could 'Community criminal law' relating to money laundering, for instance, be adopted on the basis of Article 114 TFEU (previous Article 95 EC), rather than Article 83(1) TFEU?[57] The point is particularly important because there are no emergency brakes or opt-outs in most other provisions of the Treaties. To both questions, the answer is that Article 83 is a *lex specialis*, in the absence of any other provisions expressly conferring substantive criminal law competence in any other part of the Treaties. It is irrelevant that the Court of Justice has ruled that at least some provisions of the EC Treaty, before its amendment by the Treaty of Lisbon,

---

[55] This gap could not be remedied by conferring extra powers upon the EU pursuant to the third sub-paragraph of Art 83(1), since any extension of powers pursuant to that provision would be still be limited by the requirement that the other areas of crime concerned 'meet the criteria specified in this paragraph'.

[56] On the scope of such powers before the entry into force of the Treaty of Lisbon, see E Herlin-Karnell, 'Commission v Council: Some Reflections on Criminal Law in the First Pillar' (2007) 13 EPL 69; S White, 'Harmonisation of Criminal Law under the First Pillar' (2006) ELRev 81; and S Peers, 'The Community's Criminal Law Competence: The Plot Thickens' (2008) 33 ELRev 399.

[57] As noted above, the Commission argued that the previous Art 95 EC conferred criminal law competence in respect of money laundering (n 42 above).

previously conferred criminal law competence on the Community, because the prior legal framework in this area was fundamentally altered by the Treaty of Lisbon in order to introduce a specific legal base dealing precisely with this issue. So it follows that the Commission's proposed use of Article 325 TFEU alone as the legal base for the proposed measure on fraud against the EU budget is incorrect.[58]

10.2.5. Territorial scope

First of all, as for measures adopted before the entry into force of the Treaty of Lisbon, EU measures on substantive criminal law applied to all Member States, because there was no opt-out as such from the previous third pillar. For the limited number of substantive criminal law measures within the scope of the Schengen *acquis*,[59] the UK and Ireland opted in,[60] and Norway, Iceland, Switzerland, and (in future) Liechtenstein apply the relevant rules.[61] The new Member States applied these Schengen rules, and all other relevant EU third pillar rules, from the date of their accession to the EU.[62] However, in the case of one *Community* measure imposing criminal law obligations relating to immigration law, three Member States are not bound by it pursuant to their opt-out from EC immigration law.[63]

Following the entry into force of the Treaty of Lisbon, the UK and Ireland have the ability to opt out of each legislative proposal in this area, but are also now subject to special rules if they opt out of measures amending acts by which they are already bound. Although it might be questioned whether the UK and Ireland are in fact able to opt out from 'Community criminal law' measures adopted on the basis of Article 83(2) TFEU, as argued elsewhere in this book, their opt-out applies to these measures.[64] As for Denmark, it is excluded from all measures adopted after the entry into force of the Treaty of Lisbon, except those building upon the Schengen *acquis*, which are subject to special rules, until or unless it either renounces its JHA opt-out or chooses the British and Irish opt-out model.[65] So far, the UK and Ireland have both opted in to the proposed Directive on sexual offences, while Ireland has opted in to the proposal on trafficking in persons.

---

[58] COM (2009) 665, 2 Dec 2009.   [59] See 10.2.1 above.
[60] See further 2.2.5.1 above.   [61] See further 2.2.5.4 above
[62] See further 2.2.5.3 above.
[63] Dir 2009/52 on the prohibition of the employment of irregular migrants ([2009] OJ L 168/24). The three Member States not bound by this Directive are the UK, Ireland, and Denmark: see 7.2.5 above.   [64] See further 2.2.5.1 above.
[65] See further 2.2.5.2 above.

10.3. Human rights

10.3.1. International human rights law

Human rights measures do not generally impact directly upon substantive criminal law (as distinct from criminal procedure, where the right to a fair trial is a fundamental element of the law). However, in some cases the criminalization of certain acts breaches human rights obligations,[66] or the level of penalty amounts to an unlawful or disproportionate restriction on a protected right.[67] Conversely, sometimes it is necessary for States to criminalize certain acts and to carry out effective investigations and prosecutions in order to protect the human rights of the crime victims.[68]

The most significant human rights principle applicable to substantive criminal law generally is the principle of legality and non-retroactivity of criminal law, as set out in Article 7 ECHR:

1. No one shall be held guilty of any criminal offence on account of any act or omission which did not constitute a criminal offence under national or international law at the time when it was committed. Nor shall a heavier penalty be imposed than the one that was applicable at the time the criminal offence was committed.

2. This article shall not prejudice the trial and punishment of any person for any act or omission which, at the time when it was committed, was criminal according to the general principles of law recognised by civilised nations.

Article 7 ECHR requires strict interpretation of criminal offences, which must be clearly provided for, with a foreseeable application.[69] The Human Rights Court has even followed the jurisprudence of the Court of Justice (see below) in applying the non-retroactivity principle also to require that subsequent more *lenient* treatment of particular actions must apply to the benefit of those persons who committed the relevant behaviour before the law was liberalized.[70]

---

[66] For example, see the judgment of the European Court of Human Rights in *Dudgeon v UK* (A-45), where criminalization of homosexual acts violated the right to private life protected by Art 8 ECHR. Criminalization of controversial opinions (as long as they do not support violence directly) is a breach of Art 10 ECHR: see, for instance, *Jersild v Denmark* (A-298) and *Zana v Turkey* [1997] ECHR-VII, as regards racism and terrorism respectively.

[67] For example, see respectively *Sun v Russia*, 5 Feb 2009, and *Grifhorst v France*, 26 Feb 2009, as regards penalties for unauthorized declarations of cash when crossing borders.

[68] See generally A Mowbray, *The Development of Positive Obligations under the European Convention on Human Rights by the European Court of Human Rights* (Hart, 2004).

[69] For the principles, see *Kokkinakis v Greece* (A260-A); and see particularly their application in *Veeber (No 2) v Estonia* (Reports 2003-I) (altering conditions for liability retroactively) and *Baskaya and Okcuoglu v Turkey* (Reports 1999-IV) (no extension by analogy).

[70] *Scoppola v Italy*, 17 Sep 2009. On the application of this principle to procedural law and to jurisdictional issues, see respectively 9.3.2 above and 11.3.1 below.

10.3.2. Application to EU law

The principle of the legality of criminal law and non-retroactive criminal liability is recognized as one of the general principles of Community law upheld by the Court of Justice. The principle has been applied by the Court to ban Member States' imposition of criminal liability for breach of an EC Directive or Regulation before Member States implement that measure in their national law.[71] The Court has applied this principle *mutatis mutandis* to the imposition of criminal liability for breach of EU Framework Decisions, as regards substantive criminal law (but not criminal procedure).[72] Similarly, the Court has ruled that Member States cannot apply criminal sanctions for breach of Community law for events which occurred before adoption of that EC legislation.[73] Notably, the European Court of Human Rights has emphasized that the principle fully applies even where national law is implementing Community obligations.[74]

Community law did not initially recognize the principle of many national legal systems that criminal defendants were entitled to the benefit of subsequent legislation if it is more favourable for them.[75] However, where Member States did apply such a principle, the Court of Justice was willing to interpret the EC legislation or EC Treaty Article at issue in order to determine whether the accused could benefit from the later rules.[76] The principle eventually governed any administrative law sanctions which enforce EC legislation.[77] Finally, the Court declared that the principle was a general principle of EC (now EU) law,[78] which means that it must be observed within the scope of application of EC and EU law, in particular whenever Member States are implementing EU or EC measures by imposing criminal penalties. As noted above, the European Court of Human Rights has now interpreted the ECHR to the same effect.

The EU's Charter of Rights contains the principles of legality and non-retroactivity of criminal liability, along with the principle of retroactive effect of more lenient penalties, and the principle that criminal penalties should be proportionate to the offence.[79]

---

[71] Cases: 14/86 *Pretore di Salo* [1987] ECR 2545, 80/86 *Kolpinghuis Nijmegen* [1987] ECR 3969, C-168/95 *Arcaro* [1996] ECR I-4705; Joined Cases C-74/95 and C-129/95 *Criminal Proceedings v X* [1996] ECR I-6609; C-60/02 *X* [2004] ECR I-651; and C-387/02, C-391/02, and C-403/02 *Berlusconi* [2005] ECR I-3565. See also Case C-550/09 *E and F*, judgment of 29 June 2010, not yet reported.   [72] See Case C-105/03 *Pupino* [2005] ECR I-5285.

[73] Case 63/83 *Kirk* [1984] ECR 2689.   [74] *Cantoni v France* (Reports 1996-V), para 30.

[75] Case 234/83 *Duisberg* [1985] ECR 327.

[76] For example, see Joined Cases C-358/93 and C-416/93 *Bordessa* [1995] ECR I-361.

[77] Reg 2988/95 ([1995] OJ L 312/1); see Cases C-354/95 *NFU* [1997] ECR I-4559 and C-295/02 *Gerken* [2004] ECR I-6369.   [78] See the judgment in *Berlusconi* (n 71 above).

[79] Art 49 of the Charter ([2000] OJ C 364), amended in [2007] OJ C 303.

10.4. EU criminal law and other areas of EU law

There are two types of intersection between other areas of EU law (outside the scope of EU criminal law per se) and substantive national criminal law. In some cases, national criminal law is often used to give effect to EU law rules and principles, besides those of criminal law proper. The broader question has been historically whether the Community had competence to *require* Member States to set out criminal law penalties. This question has been answered by Article 83(2) TFEU, as of the entry into force of the Treaty of Lisbon. Conversely, the imposition of criminal liability by national law is in some cases precluded because it prevents the exercise of Community law rights.

10.4.1. Community criminal law competence

10.4.1.1. Before the Treaty of Lisbon

Before the entry into force of the Treaty of Lisbon, the competence of the European Community to require Member States to impose criminal sanctions was much debated. As noted already,[80] Articles 135 and 280 EC, respectively inserted and amended by the Treaty of Amsterdam, specified that EC measures concerning customs law and the protection of EC financial interests 'shall not concern the application of national criminal law or the national administration of justice'.[81] On the other hand, Article 63(3)(b) EC, which was also inserted by the Treaty of Amsterdam, conferred a power for the Community to adopt measures on 'illegal immigration and illegal residence', without any proviso similar to those in Articles 135 or 280 EC.

During this period, the Commission and EP argued that that some EC Treaty legal bases did confer the power upon the Community to require Member States to harmonize national criminal law in certain areas. However, due to the political and legal objections of Member States to the existence of EC competence over criminal law, the Council developed a practice of providing in EC legislation that the Community prohibits certain acts (in Regulations) or that the Member States must prohibit certain acts (in Directives).[82] In either case, human rights rules restrict the imposition or aggravation of criminal liability until a Member State has clearly provided for that liability in national law.[83]

But despite the Council's practice, the Court of Justice first of all developed general principles of EC law that required at least some degree of obligation

---

[80] See 10.2.2 above.

[81] Also as noted above, these provisos were repealed by the Treaty of Lisbon (see now Arts 33 and 325 TFEU).   [82] On Regulations in particular, see Case 50/76 *Amsterdam Bulb* [1977] ECR 137.

[83] See 10.3.2 above.

upon Member States to enforce Community rules by criminal law, and then later confirmed that the Community indeed had some criminal law competence. On the first point, the leading case is *Commission v Greece* (*Greek maize*), in which the Court of Justice held that a Member State had an obligation to apply its substantive and procedural criminal law to enforce EC law in the same way that it would apply its national criminal law to equivalent national offences.[84] Furthermore, such sanctions had to be 'effective, proportionate and dissuasive'. This 'equality of sanctions' principle was then inserted into the EC Treaty by the Maastricht Treaty as a principle governing fraud against the EC budget (Article 209a EC), and the Treaty of Amsterdam subsequently provided that national measures had to be 'effective' and a 'deterrent', and apply to 'other illegal activities' affecting the EC financial interests (Article 280 EC, now Article 325 TFEU). In several cases relating to EC fisheries conservation, the Court made it clear that there is an obligation to prosecute or take administrative action against individuals who breach EC law.[85]

Despite the Council's opposition, the Commission kept proposing Community measures including express obligations to criminalize certain activity. In particular, following the Treaty of Amsterdam, it proposed EC legislation, based on Article 280 EC, incorporating much of a pre-Amsterdam third pillar Convention (and Protocols) concerning fraud against the EU budget.[86] It also proposed a Directive on criminal law and the environment, and later a Directive accompanying a proposed Framework Decision on shipping pollution.[87] Within the internal market powers of the Community, the Commission proposed clauses in Directives on enforcement of intellectual property rights requiring Member States to criminalize serious infringements of such rights,[88] along with similar clauses in proposed Directives on money laundering and market abuse.[89] The Commission also argued that the Council lacked legal power under the third pillar to adopt some aspects of the Framework Decision on smuggling in persons or a Decision on counterfeit travel documents,[90] to address many 'cyber-crime'

---

[84] Case 68/88 [1989] ECR 2685. See COM (95) 162, 3 May 1995 and Council Resolution ([1995] OJ C 188/1).

[85] Cases C-333/99 *Commission v France* [2001] ECR I-1025; C-418/00 and C-419/00 *Commission v France* [2002] ECR I-3969; C-454/99 *Commission v UK* [2002] ECR I-10323; and C-140/00 *Commission v UK* [2002] ECR I-10379.

[86] COM (2001) 272, 22 May 2001; revised after EP vote: COM (2002) 577, 16 Oct 2002.

[87] See respectively COM (2001) 139, 14 Mar 2001; revised after EP vote: COM (2002) 544, 30 Sep 2002 (environmental crime); Art 6 of COM (2003) 92, 5 Mar 2003 (shipping pollution Directive); COM (2003) 227, 2 May 2003 (shipping pollution Framework Decision).

[88] Art 20 of proposed Dir (COM (2003) 46, 30 Jan 2003).

[89] Respectively Art 1(1) of COM (2004) 448, 30 Jun 2004, and Art 14 of COM (2001) 281, 30 May 2001.

[90] See respectively Statement 154/02 in the Council summary of acts adopted in Nov 2002 (Council doc 15915/02, 16 Jan 2003) and Statement 22/00 in the Council summary of acts adopted in Mar 2000 (Council doc 8080/00, 28 Apr 2000).

issues,[91] and to criminalize incitement to racism or xenophobia, on the grounds that such measures fell within the scope of the EC's anti-racism powers conferred by Article 13 EC.[92] There were also parallel disputes concerning competence related to customs issues.[93]

The Council's response was to reject any prospect of negotiating the proposed Directive on fraud against the EC budget or the Directive on environmental crime. Instead, Member States completed ratification of the Convention on the former subject and the Council adopted a Framework Decision on the latter.[94] The Council also moved the criminal law provisions of the proposed Directive on shipping pollution into the linked Framework Decision.[95] Finally, the Council removed the proposed criminal law provisions from the adopted Directives on intellectual property rights enforcement, money laundering, and market abuse.[96]

However, the Commission eventually decided to seize the Court of Justice with one of these disputes in an attempt to settle the issue. It brought a legal challenge pursuant to the previous Article 35 EU in 2003 against a Framework Decision on environmental crime, arguing that it usurped the EC's powers to adopt environmental legislation. The Court's judgment in September 2005 upheld the Commission's arguments and annulled the Framework Decision.[97] In its judgment, the Court started by referring to the previous Article 47 EU (later repealed by the Treaty of Lisbon), which provided that nothing in the TEU is to affect the EC Treaty; the rule was reiterated in the previous Article 29 EU. According to the Court's prior case law, this meant that Title VI measures could not 'encroach upon' Community powers.[98] Next, the Court set out the scope of the EC's environmental powers, beginning with the reference to the environment in the tasks and objectives of the EC, the horizontal requirement that EC policies must respect the environment, and the specific EC powers over the environment. According to consistent case law, the correct 'legal base' of a measure must be interpreted in light of its aim and its content. In this case, the Framework Decision had the aim of environmental protection and its content essentially concerned harmonization of national criminal law.

The Court reiterated the 'general rule' that 'neither criminal law nor the rules of criminal procedure fall within the Community's competence'.[99] But (as in the case of national criminal law measures restricting free movement rights)

---

[91] See the explanatory memorandum to the proposed Framework Decision on attacks on information systems (COM (2002) 173, 19 Apr 2004), p 8.

[92] See the Commission staff working paper on this point (Council doc 7880/02, 11 Apr 2002).

[93] See 12.4.1 below.   [94] For details of these measures, see 10.5.1.2 below.

[95] On the adopted measures, see ibid.

[96] See respectively Dirs 2004/48 ([2004] OJ L 157/45), 2005/60 ([2005] OJ L 309/15), and 2003/6 ([2003] OJ L 96/16).   [97] Case C-176/03 *Commission v Council* [2005] ECR I-7879.

[98] Case C-170/96 *Commission v Council* [1998] ECR I-2763. On the first/third pillar dividing line in general, see 2.4 above.   [99] Para 47 of judgment, ibid.

this rule was a presumption that could be overturned: the rule 'does not prevent the Community legislature, when the application of effective, proportionate and dissuasive criminal penalties by the competent national authorities is an essential measure for combating serious environmental offences, from taking measures which relate to the criminal law of the Member States which it considers necessary in order to ensure that the rules which it lays down on environmental protection are fully effective'.[100] The Court then added that 'in this instance, although...the framework decision determine[s] that certain conduct which is particularly detrimental to the environment is to be criminal, [it] leave[s] to the Member States the choice of the criminal penalties to apply, although...the penalties must be effective, proportionate and dissuasive'.[101] Finally, the Court rejected a contrary argument based on the prior Articles 135 and 280 EC, the legal bases concerning customs cooperation and fraud against the EC's interests, which, as noted above,[102] then precluded the use of those particular EC powers to affect 'the application of national criminal law and the administration of justice', on the grounds that it could not be inferred from those provisions that the EC lacked the power to impose criminal law sanctions in order to ensure the effectiveness of EC environmental law.[103] So the Court found that Articles 1–7 of the Framework Decision, which set out obligations for the Member States to impose criminal liability for natural persons and criminal or administrative liability for legal persons for specified offences, encroached upon EC law. Although the Commission had not challenged the remaining provisions of the Framework Decision, in particular accepting that Articles 8 and 9 concerning jurisdiction and prosecution did not fall within the scope of EC powers,[104] the Court annulled the entire measure as its provisions were indivisible.

This was a potentially far-reaching judgment, but the obvious question was its scope. Did the judgment only apply to issues within the scope of EC environmental law, or did it apply to other areas of EC law as well? Did it only apply to the definition of offences, or did it also apply to other aspects of criminal law as well? The Commission issued a communication not long after the judgment giving its interpretation of the judgment's implications.[105] In the Commission's view, the 2005 judgment applied 'to the other common policies and to the four [internal market] freedoms'.[106] Furthermore, the EC's power in such cases applied not just to the definition of offences, but also to the obligation to impose criminal penalties, and to 'the nature and level of criminal penalties applicable, or other aspects related to criminal law'.[107] It followed that a number of EU measures listed by the Commission were 'entirely or partly incorrect, since all or some of their provisions were adopted on the wrong legal basis'.[108]

---

[100] Para 48 of judgment, ibid.   [101] Para 49 of judgment, ibid.   [102] See 10.2.2 above.
[103] Para 52 of judgment, n 97 above.   [104] See para 23 of the judgment (ibid.).
[105] COM(2005)583, 23 Nov 2005.   [106] Para 8 of the communication.
[107] Para 10 of the communication (footnote omitted).   [108] Para 14 of the communication.

The Commission therefore decided to bring proceedings for annulment of one of these measures, a Framework Decision on shipping pollution, before the Court of Justice (see below), but it was out of time to challenge any other adopted measures. Pending the judgment in that case, the Commission proposed a Directive on environmental crime, following the annulment of the relevant Framework Decision,[109] and withdrew a proposed Framework Decision on counterfeiting intellectual property, instead integrating all of its criminal law provisions (except the provision on criminal jurisdiction) into a proposed Directive on this issue.[110] The Commission also subsequently proposed a Directive which defined a criminal offence as regards the employment of irregular migrants.[111] Discussion of these proposals was placed on hold pending the Court's judgment on the validity of the Framework Decision on shipping pollution.

The judgment in that case definitively answered one of the two key questions regarding Community criminal law competence, but did not clearly answer the other key question.[112] First of all, the Court ruled that the EC had no competence to define sanctions in relation to criminal offences: 'the determination of the type and level of the criminal penalties to be applied does not fall within the Community's sphere of competence'.[113] The Court did not rule, however, on Community competence to adopt measures as regards other aspects of criminal law (such as jurisdiction). More fundamentally, the Court failed to give a clear ruling on whether the EC had competence to define criminal offences in all areas of EC competence, deciding only that the definition of criminal offences with a view to protecting the environment could be integrated into a transport law measure, as in this case.[114] This meant that the provisions on criminal offences in the Framework Decision were invalid, and since the rest of the Framework Decision was indivisible from these provisions, it was annulled.[115]

The consequence of the judgment was that the Council and EP soon afterward adopted the proposed Directive on environmental crime, without the detailed provisions on offences as originally proposed by the Commission.[116] They also adopted a Directive amending the initial Directive on shipping pollution in order to add definitions of relevant criminal offences.[117] Most significantly, they agreed to exercise the EC's criminal law competence in an area *not* related to environmental protection, by adopting the proposed Directive on prohibition of employment

---

[109] COM (2007) 51, 9 Feb 2007.

[110] COM (2005) 276, 12 July 2005 (proposed Framework Decision); COM (2006) 168, 26 Apr 2006 (proposed Directive). The latter proposal was later withdrawn (see 10.2.3 above).

[111] COM (2007) 249, 15 May 2007.

[112] Case C-440/05 *Commission v Council* [2007] ECR I-9097. For further analysis of the judgment, see S Peers, 'The Community's Criminal Law Competence: The Plot Thickens' (2008) 33 ELRev 399.   [113] Para 70 of the judgment.

[114] Para 60 of the judgment.   [115] Para 73 of the judgment.

[116] Dir 2008/99 ([2008] OJ L 328/28).   [117] Dir 2009/123 ([2009] OJ L 280/52).

of irregular migrants, including criminal law offences.[118] Nevertheless, they still rejected the suggestion of introducing criminal law provisions in an EC Directive relating to firearms,[119] and the Council gave up discussions on the proposed Directive on criminal sanctions for breaches of intellectual property law.

10.4.1.2. After the Treaty of Lisbon

As from the entry into force of the Treaty of Lisbon, the existence of 'Community criminal law competence' is confirmed and clarified in Article 83(2) TFEU.[120] Nevertheless, this provision raises a number of questions.

First of all, it should be reiterated that, as argued above:[121] Article 83(1) and (2) TFEU are *lex specialis* as regards each other; the other policing and criminal law provisions of the Treaties have to be used to adopt measures concerning *conflicts* of jurisdiction, procedure, and investigations; Article 83(2) can be used to adopt measures *asserting* jurisdiction in relation to specific offences, and not only to define offences, but also to prescribe sanctions in respect of those offences; Article 83(2) applies rather than Article 86 as regards the harmonization of the national criminal law which the European Public Prosecutor, if established, would have jurisdiction to enforce; and Article 83(1) and (2) are each a *lex specialis* as compared to the rest of the Treaty as regards respectively the adoption of criminal law measures as regards specific listed crimes (Article 83(1)) and as to ensure effective harmonization (Article 83(2)).

Next, given that the previous EC criminal competence arguably only applied to issues related to environmental protection,[122] does Article 83(2) TFEU apply to other areas as well? On this point, it could not seriously be asserted that Article 83(2) applies only to environmental protection. There is no limit on its subject matter (other than the scope of the Treaties), but instead an abstract test of a requirement of a need for the effective implementation of a Union policy which has been subject to harmonization measures. Also, the wording of the second sentence of Article 83(2) refers generally to the rest of the Treaties, without any distinction. Finally, the exhaustive list of crimes in Article 83(1) TFEU suggests by *a contrario* reasoning that Article 83(2) is not limited in subject matter.

So how should the conditions for the application of Article 83(2) TFEU be interpreted? First, the criminal law measures have to be 'essential' for implementation of an EU policy. According to the Court's case law, this condition

---

[118] Dir 2009/52 ([2009] OJ L 168/24).

[119] The Commission had proposed an amendment to the EC firearms Dir (Dir 91/477, [1991] OJ L 256/51) which would have required Member States to criminalize certain acts (Art 1(3), COM (2006) 93, 2 Mar 2006). The final amendments to the firearms Dir do not include this provision (Dir 2008/51 ([2008] OJ L 179/5).

[120] This book continues to use this anachronistic phrase to describe this form of competence, in the absence of any obvious alternative.   [121] See 10.2.4 above.

[122] The validity of Dir 2009/52 on employer sanctions, which defines a criminal offence in an area not linked to environmental protection, might conceivably be questioned.

previously applied to the prior Community criminal law competence, and there is no reason to imagine that the condition should apply differently under the Treaty of Lisbon provision. However, it is not easy in practice to assess whether this condition is satisfied.[123]

The second condition is that the area concerned must have been 'subject to harmonisation measures', which was also already required pursuant to the case law on the previous competence,[124] but is more explicit pursuant to Article 83(2) TFEU. So, for example, the EU could only adopt measures on intellectual property crime to the extent that the EU has harmonized intellectual property law.[125] It could not be said that there is a 'Union policy' that needs implementing effectively in the absence of harmonization in specific areas of law. On the other hand, there is nothing in the current legal framework or the Treaty of Lisbon that requires *full* harmonization as a pre-condition. In fact, such a requirement implicitly never applied as regards the previous legal framework, given that, as noted above, the Community could not fully harmonize environmental law.[126]

While misgivings were raised about the appropriateness of harmonization of sanctions by the Community,[127] these concerns are addressed in the Treaty of Lisbon by the existence of the emergency brake, which also applies to the definition of offences, and the requirement that the EU can only establish 'minimum rules' when exercising its powers pursuant to Article 83(2) TFEU.[128] Moreover, such concerns were previously addressed in practice as regards the harmonization of sanctions related to criminal law within the scope of the previous third pillar, by means of great flexibility accorded to Member States as regards the levels of sanctions.[129]

Article 83(2) TFEU also requires that the adoption of the criminal law measures must not precede the harmonization measures in other areas of EU policy ('in an area which *has been subject* to harmonisation measures' and the use of the 'same' decision-making procedure '*as was followed* for the adoption of the harmonization measures').[130] In fact, strictly speaking, the English version of this Treaty

---

[123] See the Opinion in the 2007 *Commission v Council* judgment and the analysis in S Peers, n 112 above.

[124] See para 66 in the 2007 *Commission v Council* judgment, ibid: 'the Community legislature may require the Member States to introduce such penalties in order to ensure that *the rules which it lays down* . . . are fully effective' (emphasis added).

[125] Compare with the Commission's proposal on this issue (COM (2006) 168, 28 Apr 2006, since withdrawn), which would have provided for criminal offences and penalties regardless of whether the intellectual property right in question had been subject to harmonization by Community law or not.   [126] Art 176 EC, now Art 193 TFEU.

[127] See further the Opinion in Case C-440/05, and the discussion in Peers (n 112 above).

[128] As noted above (10.2.3), the latter rule was not expressly applicable in the previous legal framework.

[129] On the details of the penalty levels in third pillar criminal law measures, see further 10.6 below.

[130] The case law on this point as regards the previous 'Community criminal law' competence is not clear: see comments in Peers (n 112 above).

provision would seem to rule out even the *simultaneous* adoption of criminal law measures and harmonization measures.[131] This strict interpretation should be doubted in light of the wording of the rest of the new provision and the underlying purpose of that new provision, because the 'effective implementation' of a Union policy could obviously be jeopardized in the meantime if criminal law measures could only be adopted *after* the harmonization measure. However, there would be no scope to interpret the new provision in light of the effectiveness principle to permit the adoption of the criminal law measures *before* the harmonization measures—because again, there would be no Union policy to implement effectively by criminal law measures if no harmonization measures had yet been adopted. In any event, even if the strict interpretation of the temporal scope of this clause is correct, Article 83(2) does not set out any minimum waiting period before the adoption of the criminal law legislation. So the procedural requirement of a later adoption of the criminal law measure could still be satisfied if the criminal law act were adopted *immediately* after the adoption of the harmonization legislation, both measures having possibly been negotiated in parallel.

Next, do criminal law measures adopted on this basis have to form a part of the original legislation on the issue, or do they have to be adopted as separate measures? The answer is that separate measures have to be adopted. First of all, the requirement to adopt the criminal legislation after the adoption of the harmonization measures points strongly to a legal requirement to adopt separate measures, particularly the requirement to apply the 'same' decision-making procedure '*as was followed* for the adoption of the harmonisation measures'. Moreover, it should be recalled that as noted above, Article 83(2) TFEU is subject to the emergency brake procedure and possibly also the British, Irish, and Danish opt-outs. If legislation were adopted covering both the substantive and criminal law aspects of a policy, the application of the emergency brake or opt-out would mean that the same legislation would apply in part to all Member States, and in part only to some.

Admittedly, the Community has already adopted rules concerning the definition of criminal offences related to the ship-source pollution Directive in the form of an amendment to that Directive,[132] rather than a separate act. However, it must be remembered that this measure was adopted within the previous legal framework, not the post-Lisbon framework, which has changed the rules as regards the adoption of 'Community criminal law'.

Even if there is be no *legal* obligation to adopt the criminal law measures in separate acts, it is still presumably open to the EU legislator to choose to use separate acts. Although it could be argued that a single legislative act combining both the harmonization measure and the related criminal law rules would be

---

[131] So would the French version: '...dans un domaine *ayant fait* l'objet de mesures d'harmonisation...' and '... à celle *utilisée* pour l'adoption des mesures d'harmonisation...'.

[132] Dir 2009/123, n 117 above.

more transparent, on the other hand adopting a single piece of legislation which only applied in part to some Member States would hardly be transparent, and such an approach would run the risk that Member States would invoke opt-outs and emergency brakes even though their real objection was to the main subject matter of the proposed legislation, rather than the criminal law aspects of it. Having said that, there would usually likely be a link between the argument that a particular proposal would cause fundamental problems for a national criminal justice system and an objection to the substance of the underlying harmonization being proposed. This point is particularly relevant to the Protocol on the UK and Irish opt-out from JHA policies, which includes specific rules on the ability of those Member States to opt out of a measure *amending* an act by which they are already bound.[133]

Finally, it may be useful to point to some cases where Article 83(2) TFEU could apply. The prior EC legislation on criminal offences as regards environmental crime, ship-source pollution, and employers of irregular migrants all lack provisions on the specific sanctions to be applied and on jurisdiction, so Article 83(2) could be used to adopt such rules. Previous third pillar measures on the issues of protection of the EU's financial interests, racism and xenophobia, and the facilitation of irregular migration also fall within the scope of Article 83(2); most of these acts already provide for rules on penalties and jurisdiction.[134] If it were desired to adopt criminal law measures for the enforcement of EU competition law, these would have to be carefully distinguished from the competence in Article 83(1) TFEU regarding the adoption of measures concerning (private) corruption.[135] This point is relevant since the decision-making rules are different (consultation of the EP for competition law measures,[136] as distinct from the ordinary legislative procedure for measures concerning corruption).

10.4.2. Criminal law as a restriction on free movement rights

When an accused person argues that a Member State is precluded from criminalizing particular activities at all because the criminalization directly prevents the exercise of free movement rights, he or she is not really claiming a Community (now Union) law 'defence'. Rather, he or she is claiming the invalidity of the underlying national legislation, or at least its inapplicability to his or her case. Such cases most usually arise when a Member State criminalizes the sale of a good originating from another Member State or the offer of a service by another Member State's service provider, but have also arisen in cases concerning free movement of capital, free movement of workers, and freedom of establishment.

---

[133] For details, see 2.2.5.1 above.   [134] See 10.6 and 11.5 below.
[135] Previous third pillar measures apply to private corruption, as well as public corruption: see 10.2.2 above.   [136] See Art 103 TFEU (ex-Art 83 EC).

In such cases, the directly effective Articles 34, 45, 49, 56, and 63 TFEU (previously Articles 28, 39, 43, 49, and 56 EC respectively) confer a right to carry out the activity in question, and so no criminal conviction can possibly be imposed.[137] In particular, it is all but impossible for Member States to criminalize EU citizens for 'immigration offences', since their right to reside in a Member State flows directly from the Treaties.[138] Similarly, where secondary Community legislation grants free movement or other rights, Member States are precluded from imposing criminal sanctions.[139] Although the TFEU (previously the EC Treaty) and much secondary legislation allows for public policy and public security exceptions to free movement rights, the Court of Justice has consistently added that a Member State's decision to impose its criminal law to curtail free movement does not automatically mean that these exceptions are applicable. The test is whether the Member State is allowed to restrict the free movement in the first place, and while there is a presumption that criminal law is a matter for the Member States, that presumption can be overturned where its operation affects free movement.[140]

Furthermore, a criminal conviction pursuant to the law of a Member State may also infringe free movement law in two other ways. Firstly, EU free movement law or immigration and asylum law may preclude acts taken as a *consequence* of sentences, when Member States expel or refuse to allow entry to an EU citizen or third-country nationals following a criminal conviction.[141] Secondly, the Court of Justice has found that a particular sentence might violate the proportionality principle of free movement law, because the host Member State could have imposed a lesser civil penalty which would have preserved its right to combat certain behaviour with less damage to the free movement rights of EU citizens.[142] This principle also applies to the free movement of goods, where the Court has accepted that Member States can treat infringements of Value Added Tax (VAT) rules on import or export differently from internal infringements, because the latter are more easy to detect; but the difference cannot lead to a vastly more onerous penalty imposed upon importers and exporters in comparison with internal traders, because of the deterrent effect on free movement.[143]

---

[137] For examples, not all of which were successful attempts to resist the criminal conviction, see Cases 8/74 *Dassonville* [1975] ECR 837; 136/78 *Auer I* [1979] ECR 437; 222/86 *Heylens* [1987] ECR 4097; 279/80 *Webb* [1981] ECR 3305; and Joined Cases C-163/94, 165/94, and 250/94 *Sanz de Lera* [1995] ECR I-4821.

[138] Case 48/75 *Royer* [1976] ECR 497. The same applies to at least some third-country nationals who have a residence right as a result of EU law. See 7.4.2 above.

[139] For example, see Joined Cases C-358/93 and C-416/93 *Bordessa* [1995] ECR I-361; Case 148/78 *Ratti* [1979] ECR 1629.   [140] Case 203/80 *Casati* [1981] ECR 2595.

[141] See 7.4.1 above (free movement law) and the immigration and asylum measures discussed in detail in chs 5 and 6.

[142] Cases 118/75 *Watson and Bellman* [1976] ECR 1185 and C-193/94 *Skanavi* [1996] ECR I-929.

[143] Cases 299/86 *Drexl* [1988] ECR 1213 and C-276/91 *Commission v France* [1993] ECR I-4413.

A Member State prima facie breaches the principle of non-discrimination on grounds of nationality set out in Article 12 EC (now Article 18 TFEU) to apply harsher provisional penalties to non-residents, who are more likely to be nationals of other EU Member States, than it applies to residents.[144] Although such discrimination may be justified if there is no measure on the mutual recognition of criminal sentences between the relevant Member States, the difference in the provisional penalties applied to residents and non-residents must still be proportionate. Of course, it should be recalled that a number of EU measures on the mutual recognition of sentences have been adopted.[145]

10.4.3. Scope of the relationship

Not all impositions of criminal law by the Member States fall within the scope of Community (now Union) law, even where a particular case raises issues of non-JHA EU and criminal law simultaneously. For example, the Court of Justice has ruled that a person could not challenge national criminal penalties imposed upon breach of possession of illegally purchased cigarettes as a breach of Community law, because the possessor had not tried to exercise free movement rights directly.[146] An even clearer example of this distinction can be seen in the cases of *CIA Security* and *Lemmens*.[147] A Directive imposes obligations on Member States to notify their new technical standards to other Member States and to the Commission.[148] The Court of Justice ruled that while a company exercising free movement rights could use this Directive to resist application of a national technical standard which a Member State had failed to notify, a criminal defendant could not use the same Directive to object to the use of breathalyzer evidence in a drunk-driving trial, even though the Member State in question had not notified the technical standards for that breathalyzer. Similarly, a person cannot bring the validity of criminal sanctions imposed against him within the scope of free movement law merely by arguing that he might have exercised free movement rights had he not been imprisoned; there must be a more definite link to the Treaties or secondary legislation.[149]

In other cases, the Court of Justice has ruled that VAT and customs duties rules apply to illegal activities as a general rule, on the grounds that such activities (for

---

[144] Cases C-29/95 *Pastoors* [1997] ECR I-285 and C-224/00 *Commission v Italy* [2002] ECR I-2965. See also Joined Cases C-447/08 and C-448/08 *Sjoberg*, judgment of 8 July 2010, not yet reported, where a Member State breached EU law by applying criminal penalties only to cross-border infringements of national law, but not to domestic breaches of that law.

[145] See 9.7.1 above.   [146] Case C-387/93 *Banchero* [1995] ECR I-4663.

[147] Respectively Cases C-194/94 [1996] ECR I-2201 and C-226/97 [1998] ECR I-3711.

[148] Dir 83/189 as amended, consolidated in Dir 98/34 ([1998] OJ L 204/37).

[149] Case C-299/95 *Kremzov* [1997] ECR I-2629; see similarly Case C-328/04 *Vajnai* [2005] ECR I-8577.

example, the sale of counterfeit perfume and gambling services, or the export of strategic goods) compete with legitimate trade, and so there would be a distortion of the principles of competition and fiscal neutrality if the transactions, imports or exports were exempt from Community (now Union) law rules.[150] However, an exception exists for such matters as counterfeit currency and narcotic drugs (where not imported under strict controls for medical or scientific reasons), which are deemed to fall entirely outside the scope of legitimate trade. But what about cases where the sale of a product such as narcotic drugs is officially banned, but formally tolerated according to an official national policy, as is the case in the Netherlands? In the case of *Siberie*, the Court sidestepped the issue by ruling that such cases concerned the rental of a table, not the supply of drugs, and so VAT should be charged.[151] The Court of Justice has now been asked whether the Netherlands is justified in discriminating indirectly against citizens of other Member States when applying this policy, by permitting only Dutch residents to purchase narcotics in coffee shops.[152]

Finally, the Court of Justice has shown itself reluctant to give a definition of 'national criminal law', where a customs Regulation sets a common time limit for national authorities to begin administrative proceedings, but leaves time limits to bring criminal proceedings up to the Member States.[153] However, the Court defined 'criminal law' for the purposes of the former Brussels Convention, which governed jurisdiction over and enforcement of criminal law issues ancillary to civil law judgments in certain cases.[154]

10.5. Offences

10.5.1. Range of offences

The range of criminal offences relating to EC and EU law fall into three categories: the national criminal offences established pursuant to EC obligations (as they then were) to prohibit (but not necessarily criminalize) certain acts;

---

[150] See Cases C-3/97 *Goodwin* [1998] ECR I-3257 and C-283/95 *Fischer* [1998] ECR I-3369, and earlier cases cited therein, and subsequently: Case C-455/98 *Salumet* [2000] ECR I-4993; Joined Cases C-354/03, C-355/03, and C-484/03 *Optigen* [2006] ECR I-483; and Joined Cases C-439/04 and C-440/04 *Kittel* [2006] ECR I-6161. On the link between the theft of goods and VAT rules, see Case C-435/03 *BAT* [2005] ECR I-7077. Of course the imposition or exclusion of VAT or customs duties does not mean that the trader will escape criminal prosecution for such activities.

[151] Case C-158/98 [1999] ECR I-3971.

[152] Case C-137/09 *Josemans*, pending. The opinion of 15 July 2010 in this case argues that the sale of narcotic drugs falls outside the scope of the free movement of services due to the fundamentally illegal nature of the transaction, even where it is tolerated officially by the Member State concerned.

[153] Case C-273/90 *Meico-Fell* [1991] ECR I-5569; see subsequently Case C-62/06 *Zefeser* [2007] ECR I-11995 and Case C-75/09 *Agra*, judgment of 17 June 2010, not yet reported.

[154] Case 157/80 *Rinkau* [1981] ECR 3181.

EU obligations to criminalize acts pursuant to the former third pillar, and now Article 83(1) TFEU; and obligations to criminalize acts pursuant to 'Community criminal law competence' before the Treaty of Lisbon, and now Article 83(2) TFEU. These three categories will be considered separately in turn.

10.5.1.1. EC law prohibitions

The 'prohibitions' which appear in EC legislation have usually involved 'economic', or 'white-collar' crime, because these issues are most directly relevant to the functioning of the internal market. Usually, legislation has been adopted because of a fear that, without common rules governing the issue in each Member State, at least at the level of minimum standards, lawbreakers would concentrate their energies on the Member States with the weakest commitment to combating the relevant crimes: a classic 'race to the bottom' argument concerning the prospect that individuals in an internal market will locate their activities in the most favourable jurisdiction within that market, undermining the regulatory measures taken by the other jurisdictions.

The best-known EC law prohibition is that contained in the money laundering Directive, which obliges Member States to prohibit money laundering as defined in the Directive: the conversion, transfer, concealment, disguise, acquisition, possession, or use of property derived from criminal activity.[155] The scope of the Directive and its detailed provisions were amended in 2001,[156] and subsequently in 2005.[157] The Commission sued Austria for continuing to allow its nationals to open anonymous accounts, arguing that this breached the Directive, although the case was subsequently withdrawn.[158] The Court of Justice has also ruled on the validity of the 'tip-off' provisions of the Directive.[159] Furthermore, the Court has ruled that Member States cannot simply ban the export of large amounts of currency on the grounds that this currency might be used for money laundering, since that would defeat the very purpose of free movement of capital.[160] However, Member States can impose a reporting requirement on such movements.

The Community has also adopted legislation banning insider dealing,[161] later amended to ban 'market abuse' more broadly,[162] along with legislation restricting

---

[155] Dir 91/308 ([1991] OJ L 166/77), Arts 1 and 2.

[156] Dir 2001/97 ([2001] OJ L 344/76).

[157] Dir 2005/60 ([2005] OJ L 309/15). See implementing Commission Dir 2006/70 ([2006] OJ L 214/29).   [158] Case C-290/98 [2000] ECR I-7835.

[159] Case C-305/05 *Ordre des barreaux francophones et germanophone and Others* [2007] ECR I-5305.

[160] Joined Cases C-358/93 and C-416/93 *Bordessa* [1995] ECR I-361 and Joined Cases C-163/94, 165/94, and 250/94 *Sanz de Lera* [1995 ECR I-4821. See also EC legislation on cash movements across external borders (12.4.1 below).

[161] Dir 89/592, [1989] OJ L 334/30. See judgments in Cases C-28/99 *Verdonck* [2001] ECR I-3399, C-384/02 *Grøngaard and Bang* [2005] ECR I-9939, and C-391/04 *Georgakis* [2007] ECR I-3741.   [162] Dir 2003/6 ([2003] OJ L 96/16).

lorry-drivers' driving hours;[163] requiring workplace health and safety protection;[164] imposing economic and financial sanctions against third States;[165] banning unauthorized 'descrambling' of subscription-only broadcasting or Internet services;[166] restricting acquisition and possession of firearms;[167] and prohibiting various acts which affect the environment.[168]

There is another spate of Community measures which do not prohibit things, but which give effect to national, international, and EU measures which do prohibit them. The Community has competence in such areas because aspects of such trade are legal and so the operation of the common commercial policy and the internal market is inevitably affected. The most important of these regimes is the EC's drugs legislation, which comprises measures setting out procedures to monitor national production and marketing of prohibited precursor substances in the internal market and measures monitoring trade in precursors with third States.[169] Also, the Community has concluded an increasing number of treaties with third States regulating trade in precursors,[170] and has incorporated anti-drugs measures in its development policy legislation and treaties.[171]

Legislation with similar objectives exists to address the civil law aspects of both internal and external trade in cultural goods, in an attempt to prevent the illicit trade in such goods.[172] The Community has adopted legislation which both facilitates the internal free movement of strategic dual-use goods and establishes a common system for controlling exports, which is integrated with second pillar

---

[163] Initially by Reg 543/69 (OJ English Special Edition, 1969 (I) 170); subsequently by Reg 3280/85 ([1985] OJ L 370/1) and presently by Reg 561/2006 ([2006] OJ L 102/1).

[164] For example, Dir 90/270 on workplace health and safety equipment ([1990] OJ L 156/14).

[165] For example, see Reg 990/93 ([1993] OJ L 102/14) imposing sanctions against the former Yugoslavia, subsequently amended and later repealed.   [166] Dir 98/84 ([1998] OJ L 320/54).

[167] Dir 91/477 ([1991] OJ L 256/51), amended by Dir 2008/51 ([2008] OJ L 179/5). On EC firearms laws, see further 12.4.7 below. The Commission has proposed a further measure in this area (COM (2010) 273, 31 May 2010).

[168] For example, Reg 259/93 ([1993] OJ L 30/1) on waste, later replaced by Reg 1013/2006 ([2006] OJ L 190/1). See now the EC legislation on environmental crime (Dir 2008/99 [2008] OJ L 328/28), discussed further in 10.5.1.3 below.

[169] As regards internal EC trade, Reg 273/2004 ([2004] OJ L 47/1), which replaced Directive 92/109 ([1992] OJ L 370/76). As regards external trade, Reg 111/2005 ([2005] OJ L 22/1), which replaced Reg 3677/92 ([1992] OJ L 357/1). See also the substantive criminal law measures and the policing and other measures concerning drugs (respectively 10.5.1.2 and 12.7.4 below).

[170] These comprise treaties with: Bolivia, Colombia, Ecuador, Peru, and Venezuela ([1995] OJ L 324/1, 10, 18, 26, and 34); Chile ([1998] OJ L 336/46); the US ([1997] OJ L 164/22); Mexico ([1997] OJ L 77/23); Turkey ([2003] OJ L 64/28); and China ([2009] OJ L 56/6).

[171] Reg 2046/97 ([1997] OJ L 287/1), replaced by Reg 1717/2006 on stability for development ([2006] OJ L 327/1; see Art 4(1)(a)); the inclusion of drugs policy clauses in EC development treaties was approved by the Court of Justice in Case C-268/94 *Portugal v Council* [1996] ECR I-6177.

[172] On internal trade, see Dir 93/7 ([1993] OJ L 74/74); the Commission has proposed a consolidated Dir to replace it (COM (2007) 873, 11 Jan 2008). On external trade, see Reg 3911/92 ([1992] OJ L 395/1), replaced by Reg 116/2009 ([2009] OJ L 39/1).

measures.[173] Legislation also sets out the procedures governing lawful trade in explosives.[174] A customs Regulation requires Member States to prohibit the entry of goods infringing intellectual property rights onto the EC internal market from third countries,[175] and the Commission proposed a Directive (since withdrawn) which would have required Member States to criminalize infringements of intellectual property rights.[176] Finally, the Community has adopted a number of measures relating to terrorism (in particular concerning asset freezing) and counterfeiting of the euro.[177]

10.5.1.2. EU law offences

The EU has adopted third pillar measures regarding nine of the ten crimes listed in Article 83(1) TFEU:

(a) terrorism;[178]

(b) trafficking in persons;[179]

(c) child pornography and prostitution;[180]

(d) drug trafficking;[181]

(e) money laundering;[182]

(f) corruption;[183]

---

[173] Reg 3381/94 ([1994] OJ L 367/1), replaced by Reg 1334/2000 ([2000] OJ L 159/1), in turn replaced by Reg 428/2009 ([2009] OJ L 134/1).

[174] Dir 93/15 ([1993] OJ L 121/28). See further 12.4.7 below.

[175] Reg 1383/2003 ([2003] OJ L 196/7), replacing Reg 3295/94 ([1994] OJ L 341/8), as amended by Reg 241/99 ([1999] OJ L 27/1).   [176] See 10.2.3 above.

[177] See 12.4.5 and 12.7.4 below.

[178] Framework Decision ([2002] OJ L 164/3). Member States had to implement this by 31 Dec 2002. The Commission has released two reports on implementation: COM (2004) 409, 8 June 2004 and COM (2007) 681, 6 Nov 2007. The Framework Decision was amended in 2008: ([2008] OJ L 330/21); Member States have to implement the amending measure by 9 Dec 2010 (Art 3(1)).

[179] Framework Decision ([2002] L 203/1); see earlier Joint Action ([1997] OJ L 63/2). Member States had to implement the former measure by 1 Aug 2004. The Commission has released a report on implementation: COM (2006) 187, 2 May 2006, and has proposed a Directive which would amend and replace the Framework Decision (COM (2010) 95, 29 Mar 2010), agreed by the Council in June 2010 (Council doc 10845/10, 10 June 2010).

[180] Framework Decision ([2004] OJ L 13/44), which Member States had to implement by 20 Jan 2006. See the earlier Joint Action (ibid). The Commission has released a report on implementation: COM (2007) 716, 16 Nov 2007. It has also proposed a Directive which would amend and replace the Framework Decision (COM (2010) 94, 29 Mar 2010).

[181] Framework Decision ([2004] OJ L 335/8), which Member States had to implement by 12 May 2006. See also earlier the Joint Action on this subject ([1996] L 342/6); due to its broad scope, this measure was *not* repealed by the Framework Decision. The Commission has released a report on implementation (COM (2009) 669, 10 Dec 2009).

[182] Joint Action ([1998] OJ L 333/1); Framework Decision ([2001] OJ L 182/1). Member States had to implement the latter measure by 31 Dec 2002. The Commission has released two reports on implementation: COM (2004) 230, 5 Apr 2004 and COM (2006) 72, 21 Feb 2006.

[183] Convention ([1997] OJ C 195/1), in force Sep 2005; Joint Action on private corruption ([1998] OJ L 358/2); Framework Decision on private corruption ([2003] OJ L 192/54). Member States had to implement the latter by 22 July 2005 (Art 9(1)). The Commission has released a report on implementation: COM (2007) 328, 18 June 2007.

(g) counterfeiting of means of payment, which concerns both currency[184] and non-cash instruments;[185]

(h) attacks on information systems;[186] and

(i) organized crime.[187]

The fifth crime on the list, arms trafficking, was not addressed by a third pillar measure before the entry into force of the Treaty of Lisbon, and it remains to be seen whether it is addressed by an EU measure pursuant to Article 83(1) TFEU. It should be noted that although there are some EC law and foreign policy measures addressing aspects of arms trafficking,[188] Article 83(1) is a *lex specialis* as regards any substantive criminal law rules relating to arms trafficking, and it does not differentiate between internal and external aspects of the issue.

Taking these crimes in turn, first of all the EU adopted a Framework Decision on terrorism in 2002, and then amended it in 2008.[189] This measure requires Member States to criminalize terrorism as defined in a three-part test, involving the context of the acts, their aims, and the specific acts being committed.[190] The context is that the acts, 'given their nature or context, may seriously damage a country or international organization'. There must be an aim of either 'seriously intimidating a population' or 'unduly compelling a Government or international organisation' to act, or 'seriously destabilizing or destroying the fundamental political, economic, or social structures of a country or an international organization'. Thirdly, there must be a specific act from a list of eight types of specific acts, including acts such as attacks which may cause death, kidnapping or hostage-taking, hijacking, or 'causing extensive destruction' to specified public property or any private property 'likely to endanger human life or result in major economic loss'. The 2008 amendment to the Framework Decision supplements the list of 'linked offences' (aggravated theft, extortion, and drawing

---

[184] Framework Decision ([2000] OJ L 140/1). Member States had to implement part of this measure by 31 Dec 2000 and the rest by 29 May 2001. An amendment to this Framework Decision concerns procedural matters and so is considered in 9.7.2 above. The Commission has released three reports on implementation: COM (2001) 771, 13 Dec 2001; COM (2003) 532, 3 Sep 2003; and COM (2007) 524, 17 Sep 2007.

[185] Framework Decision ([2001] OJ L 149/1), which Member States had to implement by 2 June 2003. The Commission has released two reports on implementation: COM (2004) 346, 30 Apr 2004 and COM (2006) 65, 20 Feb 2006.

[186] Framework Decision ([2005] OJ L 69/67), which Member States had to implement by 16 Mar 2007. The Commission has released a report on implementation: COM (2008) 448, 14 July 2008.

[187] Joint Action ([1998] OJ L 351/1), replaced by a Framework Decision ([2008] OJ L 300/42), which Member States had to implement by 11 May 2010.

[188] See: the firearms legislation and proposals mentioned above (n 167); Dir 93/15 on explosives for civil use ([1993] OJ L 121/28); Reg 428/2009 on dual-use goods ([2009] OJ L 134/1); and the CFSP measures concerning arms exports (Common Position, [2008] OJ L 335/99), small arms and light weapons ([2002] OJ L 191/1), and arms brokering ([2003] OJ L 156/79; see Art 6 as regards criminal sanctions). On the legal base of the CFSP measures, see Case C-91/05 *Commission v Council* [2008] ECR I-3651.   [189] See n 178 above.

[190] Art 1 of 2002 Framework Decision (ibid).

up false administrative documents) with three more: provocation, recruitment, and training for terrorism, based upon a 2005 Council of Europe Convention on this issue.[191]

A particular concern regarding this Framework Decision is its human rights implications.[192] At first sight, there are no grounds for concern, since the European Court of Human Rights has consistently rejected the idea that political violence committed within the territory of signatory States to the ECHR attracts human rights protection.[193] Moreover, the preamble to the Framework Decision states expressly that the Union is 'based on the principle of democracy and on the principle of the rule of law' and that the Framework Decision 'respects fundamental rights' as guaranteed by the ECHR and national constitutions and 'observes the principles recognized by' the EU's Charter of Rights. Furthermore, the preamble states that the Framework Decision cannot be interpreted to 'reduce or restrict fundamental rights or freedoms such as the right to strike, freedom of assembly, of association and of expression, including the right of everyone to form and join trade unions...and the related right to demonstrate'. The Council also adopted a Statement connected to the Framework Decision,[194] asserting that the Framework Decision:

...covers acts which are considered by all Member States...as serious infringements of their criminal laws committed by individuals whose objectives constitute a threat to their democratic societies respecting the rule of law and the civilisation upon which the societies are founded. It has to be understood in this sense and cannot be construed so as to argue that the conduct of those who have acted in the interest of preserving or restoring those values, as was notably the case in some Member States during the Second World War, could now be considered as 'terrorist' acts. Nor can it be construed so as to incriminate on terrorist grounds persons exercising their fundamental right to manifest their opinions, even if in the course of the exercise of such right they commit criminal offences.

The main text of the Framework Decision also states that it 'shall not have the effect of altering the obligation to respect fundamental rights' as set out in Article 6 of the EU Treaty,[195] and the 2008 amendment states that it shall not require Member States 'to take measures in contradiction of fundamental principles relating to freedom of expression', as further defined therein.[196]

---

[191] CETS 196. About half of the Member States have ratified this Convention; for ratification details, see Appendix I.

[192] On these issues, see S Peers, 'EU Responses to Terrorism' (2003) 52 ICLQ 227 at 235–237.

[193] See, for instance, *Zana v Turkey* [1997] ECHR-VII.

[194] Statement 109/2002 in the summary of Council acts for June 2002 (Council doc 11532/02, 22 Aug 2002).

[195] Art 1(2) of the Framework Decision (n 178 above). Such provisions also appear in EU measures concerning criminal procedure: see 9.3.5 and 9.5.2 above.

[196] Art 2, 2008 amendments (ibid).

Firstly, given its potential application to acts committed in *non*-democratic states,[197] does the Framework Decision sufficiently distinguish between an absolute prohibition on political violence in democratic societies and a more qualified prohibition relating to non-democratic states (ideally referring instead in the latter case to international humanitarian law)? Although the statement attached to the Framework Decision accepts the legitimacy of actions taken against invading forces, the legal effect of the statement is uncertain, because it is not set out in the text.[198] Also, its scope is uncertain: is it limited to historical events, or to activities within the EU, or to invasions as distinct from activities against undemocratic regimes? It appears that the statement is not limited temporally or geographically, and due to its broad wording, applies also to actions against undemocratic regimes. Moreover, it is unfortunate that the statement does not suggest any limitation on the nature of the violence that might be justified on the basis of a 'just war' principle, for example (as already noted) by reference to international humanitarian law. The statement could therefore be misused by those who practice political violence in modern democracies to justify their behaviour.

Secondly, absent such circumstances of justified political violence, does the Framework Decision (as amended) otherwise give rise to human rights concerns, in particular as it applies to property damage and injury to police during a demonstration, or to the strong criticism of particular States or policies, in light of the broad wording of the criminalization of 'participation' in terrorist activities, and 'public provocation' to terrorism? While the express human rights protections in the preamble, the main text, and the attached statement appear to suggest that there is no cause for concern, the application of the Framework Decision in the context of subsequent EU policing measures suggests that there might be cause for concern in practice.[199]

The second crime on the list in Article 83(1) TFEU is trafficking in persons, which was addressed most recently by a Framework Decision adopted in 2002 and a proposed Directive agreed by the Council in 2010.[200] These measures are considered in more detail in Chapter 7, along with the relevant international measures on the same topic.[201]

Next, the third crime listed in Article 83(1) TFEU is child pornography and prostitution, which was originally addressed by a 1997 Joint Action, later replaced by a Framework Decision in 2003.[202] The Framework Decision requires Member States to criminalize sexual exploitation of children (defined as the coercion of a child into prostitution or pornography, or the recruitment into, profiting from, or exploitation of child prostitution or pornography, or unlawful sex with

---

[197] On jurisdiction pursuant to the Framework Decision, see 11.5 below.

[198] On this point, see Case C-292/89 *Antonissen* [1991] ECR I-745, which is applicable equally to third pillar measures: Case C-355/04 P *SEGI* [2007] ECR I-1657.

[199] See 12.6.3 and 12.7.4 below.   [200] See n 179 above.   [201] See 7.5.4 above.

[202] See n 180 above.

a child in the context of coercion, the payment or money, or abuse of trust) and child pornography (defined as the production, distribution, supply, acquisition or possession of this material, as defined in the Framework Decision). However, Member States have an option to exempt from criminal liability pornographic material involving adults who appear to be children, or comprising only computer-generated images, with a view to focusing on cases where actual children were abused.[203] This Framework Decision covers some of the offences lifted in the Council of Europe's Convention on cyber-crime, as well as the subsequent Convention on child protection.[204] The subsequent proposal for a Directive on this issue would require Member States to criminalize additional actions, with fewer possible exemptions.[205]

Drug trafficking,[206] the fourth crime listed in Article 83(1) TFEU, has been the subject of a continuing dispute between some Member States favouring a very strict enforcement on sale and possession of drugs, and others favouring instead, at least in some cases, a 'health-oriented' approach of controlled de facto criminalization. The merits of formal decriminalization, at least for 'soft' drugs, have never been considered by the Commission or Council. As a result of the difference in views, the 1990 Schengen Convention contained an awkward compromise, requiring 'prevention and punishment' of the sale and possession for sale or export and administrative and penal sanctions against illegal export and sale, possession, and handling of drugs, including cannabis; but 'illegal' was not defined except by reference to existing UN Conventions.[207] The Maastricht Treaty contained references to both approaches, with a first pillar goal of 'preventing drug dependence' in former Article 129 EC and a third pillar objective of 'combatting drug addiction' in Article K.1(4) EU.

The initial key measure implementing the latter objective was the 1996 drugs Joint Action, a framework to be implemented by more specific measures, which reiterated Member States' obligations under UN Conventions; Member States also undertook to criminalize the incitement or inducement of others to commit certain drugs offences.[208] Although Member States only had to 'take the most appropriate steps' to combat illicit drugs cultivation, that principle was implemented in more detail by a separate Resolution, inviting Member States to make the sale of cannabis seeds an offence and to ban cultivation of cannabis under glass or indoors.[209] The Council also adopted a Resolution on 'drugs tourism' in attempt to counter any 'race to the bottom' of drug users visiting the Member

---

[203] Arts 2 and 3 of the Framework Decision.

[204] Respectively ETS 185 and CETS 201. For ratification of these Conventions by the Member States, see Appendix I.   [205] Arts 3–6 of the proposal (n 180 above).

[206] For details of EC and EU anti-drug measures outside the scope of substantive criminal law, see 12.7.4 below.

[207] Art 71, 1990 Schengen Convention ([2000] OJ L 239). On the implications of this provision for the 'double jeopardy' rules in the Schengen Convention, see 11.8 below.

[208] Arts 7 and 9 (n 181 above).   [209] [1996] OJ C 389/1; see Art 8 of the 1996 Joint Action.

States with the least stringent drug laws, but the Resolution only established operational contacts, rather than harmonize national law or practice.[210]

A 1997 Joint Action on synthetic drugs established a procedure for the Council to consider adopting an EU-wide ban on 'designer drugs' after assessing their risk.[211] This procedure was implemented on six occasions, resulting in three bans.[212] In 2005, the Council replaced the Joint Action with a post-Amsterdam third pillar Decision, which revised the risk assessment process and provides for the possible adoption of control measures by a qualified majority.[213] This Decision has been applied on only one occasion to date.[214]

Finally, the Council adopted a Framework Decision on drug trafficking, which requires Member States to criminalize: the production, sale, or distribution, etc of 'drugs' as defined by the Framework Decision; the possession or purchase of such drugs to this end; the cultivation of cannabis, coca bush, and opium poppy plants; and such as the production of precursor drugs with the knowledge that they will be used for the manufacture or production of drugs. But this conduct falls outside the scope of the Framework Decision when carried out by individuals for their own personal use, as defined by national law.[215]

The sixth offence listed in Article 83(1) TFEU is money laundering. A 1998 Joint Action, amended by a 2001 Framework Decision,[216] requires Member States to criminalize money laundering related to *all* offences which are at least punishable by a maximum sentence of more than a year or a minimum sentence of six months, by withdrawing the relevant reservations to the 1990 Strasbourg Convention on the laundering, search, seizure, and confiscation of the proceeds of crime.[217]

---

[210] [1996] OJ C 375/3. On this issue, see now Case C-137/09 *Josemans*, pending (opinion of 15 July 2010).   [211] [1997] OJ L 167/1.

[212] See Decisions concerning 4-MTA ([1999] OJ L 244/1), PMMA ([2002] OJ L 63/14), and 2C-I, 2C-T-2, 2C-T-7, and TMA-2 ([2003] OJ L 321/64), and Council conclusions concerning Ketamine and GHB (JHA Council press release, 15–16 Mar 2001). The Council failed to agree on whether to subject MBDB to control measures (Council doc 6072/00, 11 Feb 2000).

[213] [2005] OJ L 127/32.

[214] [2008] OJ L 63/45, deciding to subject 1-benzylpiperazine (BZP) to control measures and criminal sanctions. See also the annual reports on the implementation of the Decision (most recently in Council doc 8009/09, 2 Apr 2009). Note also that the Commission intends to propose the replacement of this measure in 2010: see the action plan implementing the Stockholm programme (COM (2010) 171, 20 Apr 2010).

[215] Art 2 of the Framework Decision (n 181 above).   [216] See n 182 above.

[217] Art 1(1)(b) of the Joint Action and Art 1(b) of the Framework Decision (ibid), referring to Art 6 of the Convention (ETS 141), which sets out an obligation to make money laundering as defined in the Convention an offence, although States could (until the prohibition imposed by the EU measures) enter a reservation limiting this obligation to specific offences. The Convention has the same definition of 'money laundering' as the 1991, 2001, and 2005 EC money laundering Directives (nn 155–157 above). All Member States have ratified the Convention, which will ultimately be replaced by a later Convention agreed in 2005 (CETS 198), which entered into force on 1 May 2008. The latter Convention has been ratified by a minority of Member States; for ratification details, see Appendix I. It contains the same definition of money laundering as the prior Convention (Art 9(1)),

Next, still on the issue of financial crime, the seventh crime listed in Article 83(1) TFEU is corruption, which is the subject of a Convention on corruption by Community *or* national officials, which applies to any acts of corruption, whether or not it affects the EU budget.[218] This Convention defines 'active corruption' and 'passive corruption' (in lay terms, 'giving bribes' and 'taking bribes')[219] as regards a 'Community official' or 'national official'.[220] 'Corruption' is to request or receive, or promise or give, an advantage 'to act or refrain from acting in accordance with his [or her] duty or in the exercise of his [or her] functions in breach of his [or her] official duties'.

The Joint Action on private corruption, now replaced by the Framework Decision on the same issue, adjusted the definitions from the Convention to define active or passive corruption as a person acting or omitting to act 'in breach of that person's duties' for the benefit of a person acting 'in the course of business activities', which entail working for or directing a private-sector entity in any capacity.[221] A breach of duty is to be defined by national law, but covers any 'disloyal behaviour' constituting a 'breach of statutory duty' or a 'breach of professional regulations or instructions'.[222] The Framework Decision specifies that the ban also applies to non-profit entities which participate in business activities.[223] According to the Joint Action, Member States had to at least criminalize all conduct which distorted or might distort competition, at least within the common market, and which could have resulted in economic damage to others by improper awards or execution of a contract.[224] The Framework Decision replaced this provision with a similar option to limit the offence to 'conduct which involves, or could involve, a distortion of competition in relation to the purchase of goods or commercial services'.[225] In order to invoke this option, Member States must make a declaration to this effect, valid for five years from 22 July 2005 (the implementation deadline for the Framework Decision);[226] the Council was to examine the question of whether such declarations could be renewed before 22 July 2010,[227] but did not do so. Only a small number of Member States made this declaration.[228]

National law implementing the Joint Action or subsequently the Framework Decision could overlap with EU competition laws and national competition

---

and the permitted reservations to the obligation to criminalize money laundering are now in line with the EU's Framework Decision (Art 9(4), together with the Appendix to the Convention).

[218] See n 183 above.   [219] Arts 2(1) and 3(1) of the Convention.
[220] See the definitions in Art 1 of the Convention.
[221] Art 2(1) of Framework Decision (n 183 above).
[222] Art 1 of Joint Action and Art 1 of Framework Decision.
[223] Art 2(2), Framework Decision.   [224] Arts 2(2) and 3(2), Joint Action.
[225] Art 2(3), Framework Decision.   [226] Art 2(4), Framework Decision.
[227] Art 2(5), Framework Decision.
[228] According to the Commission report on the application of the Framework Decision, Poland, Germany, and Italy have made valid declarations, while Austria made an invalid declaration. On the Polish declaration, see also Council doc 12400/05, 21 Sep 2005.

laws (most of which are now similar to EU law rules). However, direct conflict between those rules may be limited, because the EU's Court of Justice has expressly ruled that Member States are free to enforce their competition laws by means of criminal sanctions in addition to EU administrative penalties.[229] It should also be noted that there are UN, OECD, and Council of Europe Conventions on corruption.[230]

Moving on to the eighth crime listed in Article 83(1) TFEU, the Framework Decision on counterfeiting currency specifies that the production and use, inter alia, of counterfeit currency (most importantly, but not only, the euro), shall constitute a criminal offence.[231] This measure aims to supplement a 1929 Geneva Convention on counterfeiting currency, and indeed it obliges Member States to ratify that Convention. Euro currency is defined by reference to EC monetary legislation, and the Framework Decision forms part of a complex package of EC measures and other third pillar measures that contribute to combating euro counterfeiting.[232]

On the same topic, a Framework Decision of 2001 requires Member States to create a number of offences concerning the counterfeiting of non-cash instruments (in practice, credit and debit cards).[233] Member States are required to criminalize the theft, counterfeiting, or falsification of such items, as well as receiving or fraudulently using such items, the use of computers to cause economic loss, or the production, sale, or use, etc of instruments or programmes designed to facilitate such offences.

As for the ninth specific EU offence, computer crime, Member States are obliged by the 2005 Framework Decision on attacks on information systems to establish offences in relation to illegal access to information systems (although Member States may opt to incriminate only cases 'where the offence is committed by infringing a security measure'), as well as illegal system interference and illegal data interference ('at least for cases which are not minor').[234] This measure concerns some of the same issues addressed by the Council of Europe's cybercrime Convention.[235]

Finally, the tenth crime on the list of specific EU powers is organized crime. This issue is addressed by a Framework Decision adopted in 2008, which replaced a Joint Action adopted in 1998.[236] The Framework Decision defines a 'criminal organisation' as 'a structured association, established over a period of time, of more than two persons acting in concert with a view to committing' crimes punishable by at least four years in prison, in order 'to obtain, directly or indirectly,

---

[229] Case 14/68 *Wilhelm* [1969] ECR 1.

[230] The EC has concluded the UN Convention (see 10.8 below), and each of the three Conventions has been ratified by a large majority of Member States: for ratification details, see Appendix I.

[231] See n 184 above.   [232] For a full summary and further references, see 12.7.4 below.

[233] See n 185 above.   [234] Arts 2–4 of the Framework Decision (n 186 above).

[235] CETS 185; for ratification details, see Appendix I.   [236] See n 187 above.

a financial or other material benefit'.[237] Member States are obliged to criminalize participation in such an organization in one (or both) of two ways: either by 'actively tak[ing] part in' an organization's criminal activities or other activities (the 'association' version) or agreeing with other persons to pursue activities that would amount to the commission of the serious offences which criminal organizations commit, 'even if that person does not take part in the actual execution of the activity' (the 'conspiracy' version).[238] Most Member States and the Community are also parties to the UN Convention on transnational organized crime, which also has a definition of organized crime.[239]

10.5.1.3. EC criminal law measures

Before the entry into force of the Treaty of Lisbon, the Community adopted three Directives pursuant to its criminal law competence, and the Union adopted a number of third pillar acts which now fall within the scope of Article 83(2) TFEU.[240] These measures concern the following:

(a) racism and xenophobia;[241]

(b) facilitation of illegal entry and residence;[242]

(c) employment of irregular migrants;[243]

(d) environmental crime, including pollution related to shipping;[244] and

(e) protection of the EU's financial interests.[245]

---

[237] Art 1(1), Framework Decision. A 'structured association' is defined in Art 1(2).

[238] Art 2, Framework Decision.

[239] As regards EC accession, see 10.8 below. As regards ratification by Member States, see Appendix I.

[240] Whether these measures (other than the environmental crime or shipping pollution directives) *should* have been adopted as EC or EU acts instead is now a moot point, unless their validity is challenged on a reference from a national court.

[241] Framework Decision ([2008] OJ L 328/55), which Member States have to implement by 28 Nov 2010 (Art 10(1)); see earlier Joint Action ([1996] OJ L 185/5).

[242] Framework Decision ([2002] OJ L 328/1). Member States had to implement this measure by 5 Dec 2004. There is a parallel Directive addressing immigration law aspects of this issue (Dir 2002/90, [2002] OJ L 328/17). The Commission has reported on national application of the Framework Decision (COM (2006) 770, 6 Dec 2006).

[243] Dir 2009/52 ([2009] OJ L 168/24), which Member States have to implement by 20 July 2011 (Art 17(1)).

[244] Dirs 2008/99 ([2009] OJ L 328/28) and 2009/123 ([2009] OJ L 280/52, amending Dir 2005/35, [2005] OJ L 255/11). Dir 2008/99 has to be implemented by 26 Dec 2010 (Art 8(1)), while Dir 2009/123 has to be implemented by 16 Nov 2010 (Art 2). These measures replaced Framework Decisions ([2003] OJ L 29/55) and [2005] OJ L 225/164), which had each been annulled by the Court of Justice: Cases C-176/03 *Commission v Council* [2005] ECR I-7879 and C-440/05 *Commission v Council* [2007] ECR I-9097, both discussed further in 10.4.1.1 above.

[245] Convention ([1995] OJ C 316/48) and First Protocol ([1996] OJ C 313/1), which entered into force on 17 Oct 2002. The Second Protocol ([1997] OJ C 221/12) entered into force on 19 May 2009. A few Member States have not yet ratified the Convention or Protocols; for ratification details, see Appendix I. On implementation by Member States, see the Commission reports (COM (2004) 709, 25 Oct 2004 and COM (2008) 77, 14 Feb 2008). The Commission has tabled a proposal for

Again, taking these measures in turn, racism and xenophobia is the subject of a Framework Decision adopted in 2008, which replaced a Joint Action adopted in 1996.[246] The Framework Decision requires Member States to criminalize: public incitement to 'violence or hatred directed against a group of persons or a member of such a group defined by reference to race, colour, religion, descent or national or ethnic origin'; the commission of such an act 'by public dissemination or distribution of tracts, pictures or other material'; and 'publicly condoning, denying or grossly trivialising crimes of genocide, crimes against humanity and war crimes' or the Holocaust, as defined in the relevant legal instruments, 'directed against a group of persons or a member of such a group defined by reference to race, colour, religion, descent or national or ethnic origin when the conduct is carried out in a manner likely to incite to violence or hatred against such a group or a member of such a group'.[247] However, these obligations are potentially limited, first of all because 'Member States may choose to punish only conduct which is either carried out in a manner likely to disturb public order or which is threatening, abusive or insulting',[248] and secondly because each Member State may make a statement that it will criminalize denial of the Holocaust and war crimes, etc, 'only if the crimes referred to in these paragraphs have been established by a final decision of a national court of this Member State and/or an international court, or by a final decision of an international court only'.[249] Also, the reference to religion is intended to cover primarily acts which serve as a 'pretext for directing acts against a group of persons or a member of such a group defined by reference to race, colour, descent, or national or ethnic origin'.[250]

Furthermore, for other offences, Member States must ensure that 'racist and xenophobic motivation is considered an aggravating circumstance, or, alternatively that such motivation may be taken into consideration by the courts in the determination of the penalties'.[251]

The entire Framework Decision is subject to the safeguard that it does not affect the obligation to ensure human rights protection in accordance with the previous Article 6 TEU, including the protection of freedom of association and expression. Also, it does not require Member States to override fundamental constitutional principles or rules relating to the liability of the press.[252] Assuming that these safeguards are properly respected, the Framework Decision should not in principle conflict with the rights of freedom of expression and association. In light of these safeguards, the limitation of the obligation to criminalize acts to

---

a Directive, which would replace the substantive criminal law provisions of the Convention and Protocols (COM (2001) 272, 22 May 2001).

[246] See n 241 above. See also the Protocol to the Council of Europe cyber-crime Convention (ETS 189), ratified by a minority of Member States (for ratification details, see Appendix I).

[247] Art 1(1), Framework Decision.   [248] Art 1(2), Framework Decision.

[249] Art 1(4), Framework Decision.   [250] Art 1(3), Framework Decision.

[251] Art 4, Framework Decision.   [252] Art 7, Framework Decision.

those which incite violence or hatred, and the possibility for Member States to place further reasonable limitations on their obligations, the Framework Decision therefore strikes the right balance between the need to combat racism and xenophobia and the right to express unpopular and even obnoxious or outrageous opinions.[253]

The second measure within the scope of Article 83(2) TFEU is the facilitation of illegal entry and residence, as set out in the Directive and Framework Decision of 2002 on this subject and previously in Article 27 of the Schengen Convention.[254] This issue concerns irregular migration, so is considered in more detail in Chapter 7, along with relevant international measures on the same topic.[255] For the same reason, the third measure, concerning the employment of irregular migrants, is also considered in detail in Chapter 7.[256]

Next, following the annulment of the Framework Decisions on environmental crime, and ship-source pollution, EC criminal law Directives were adopted on both of these issues.[257] The environmental crime Directive requires Member States to impose criminal sanctions for: pollution (as defined) of the air, soil, or water, where this results in death or serious injury to persons, or 'substantial damage' to the air, soil, or water, or to animals or plants; waste management or transport, the unlawful operation of a plant in which a dangerous activity is carried out, and the unlawful production and use, etc of such as radioactive materials, in the same circumstances; the shipment of waste; the unlawful killing, trading, or possession of protected wild flora or fauna; the deterioration of habitats; and the unlawful trade in ozone-depleting substances.[258]

The Directive on shipping pollution obviously has a narrower scope, confining itself to requiring Member States to criminalize the discharge of pollution from ships into Member States' waters (as broadly defined) and the high seas.[259]

Finally, the Convention and Protocols on protection of the EU's financial interests are intertwined with the Community law principles and the substantive Community law discussed above.[260] Despite the *Greek maize* obligation to impose equivalent, effective, dissuasive, and proportionate penalties, detailed study showed that the remaining differences between substantive and procedural national laws hindered prosecutions against fraud affecting the EU's financial interests.[261] The Protection of Financial Interests (PIF) Convention and its Protocols were the subsequent response.[262]

---

[253] On the general human rights issues, see 10.3.1 above.   [254] See n 242 above.

[255] See 7.5.3 above.   [256] See 7.6.1 above.

[257] Dirs 2008/99 and 2009/123 (n 244 above).   [258] Art 3 of Dir 2008/99, ibid.

[259] Arts 3–5 and 5a of Dir 2005/35, as amended by Dir 2009/123 (both ibid). On the validity of the underlying Dir 2005/35, see Case C-308/06 *Intertanko* [2008] ECR I-4057.

[260] See 10.4.1.1 above.

[261] SEC (93) 1172, 16 July 1993; see later COM (95) 556, 14 Nov 1995.

[262] See n 245 above.

The PIF Convention defines fraud against the EU's financial interests as 'any intentional act or omission relating to' the 'use or preparation of false, incorrect or incomplete statements or documents, which has as its effect' either the 'misappropriation or wrongful retention' of EU expenditure or the 'illegal diminution' of EU revenue.[263] The definition also includes 'non-disclosure of information in violation of a specific obligation with the same effect' and the 'misapplication of funds' for purposes other than those originally granted. Member States must criminalize such action, except where frauds are less than €4,000.[264] The First PIF Protocol, addressing corruption against the EU's financial interests, defines 'corruption' consistently with the EU's general corruption Convention.[265] EU officials must be 'assimilated' to national officials and EU Commissioners, parliamentarians, judges, and auditors must be 'assimilated' to their national equivalents for the purpose of applying the criminal law obligations.[266] The Second PIF Protocol requires Member States to criminalize money laundering 'related to' the proceeds of fraud and corruption as defined in the PIF Convention and First Protocol.[267] Member States may enter a five-year reservation from the date of ratification of the Protocol providing that they need only criminalize the laundering of money from 'serious cases' of active and passive corruption, and this reservation can be renewed once for a further period of five years.[268]

10.5.2. Scope of offences

10.5.2.1. Liability of legal persons

There are wide differences among national laws regarding the issue of corporate criminal liability. Unsurprisingly, therefore, EC legislation imposing prohibitions does not usually specify whether Member States must implement it by imposing sanctions upon legal persons or not. The Court of Justice has recognized this discretion by holding that, when enforcing EC legislation on drivers' hours, Member States are free to choose whether or not they impose criminal liability on legal persons (the usual legal form of the drivers' employers), as long as some effective, proportionate, and dissuasive penalty is applied to someone.[269] But in one case EC law does specify an approach to the issue: Member States must 'pierce the veil' and prohibit a natural person from using

---

[263] Art 1(1), PIF Convention.   [264] Arts 1(2) and 2(2), PIF Convention.

[265] See 10.5.1.2 above.   [266] Art 4, First Protocol.

[267] Art 2, Second Protocol. 'Money laundering' is defined by reference to the EC Directive, which now entails a reference to Dir 2005/60 (Art 44 of that Dir, [2005] OJ L 309/15).

[268] Art 18(1), Second Protocol. There is no definition of 'serious cases'. Of the Member States which have ratified the Protocol to date, only Spain has made a reservation. It will expire on 19 May 2014, unless it is extended until 19 May 2019.

[269] Case C-7/90 *Vandevenne* [1991] ECR I-4371.

inside information even when a legal person is the *de jure* possessor of the information.[270]

Member States were less reticent when agreeing EU third pillar measures and when exercising the Community's criminal law competence. The PIF Convention requires Member States to impose criminal liability on 'heads of businesses or any persons having power to take decisions or exercise control within a business', without further defining any of those terms.[271] This obligation was transposed to the anti-corruption obligations in the first PIF Protocol,[272] along with the Convention on national corruption law.[273]

Subsequently, Member States agreed on standard EU rules on the liability of legal persons, as first set out in the Second Protocol to the EU financial interests Convention. The Protocol defines a 'legal person' as: 'any entity having such status under the applicable national law, except for States or other public bodies in the exercise of State authority and for public international organizations'.[274] Liability must be imposed where a legal person can be held liable for specified crimes 'committed for their benefit by any person, acting either individually or as part of an organ of the legal person, who has a leading position within the legal person', based on representation of that legal person, a power to take decisions on behalf of the legal person or authority to exercise control within it. This liability extends to specified inchoate offences.[275] There is also a form of liability based on negligence, where the legal person 'can be held liable where the lack of supervision or control by' a legal person as previously defined has made commission of a specified criminal act possible 'for the benefit of that legal person by a person under its authority'.[276] It is expressly stated that corporate liability does not exclude criminal proceedings against natural persons.[277]

The Protocol then specifies the form that sanctions must take in the cases which it has set out: 'effective, proportionate and dissuasive sanctions, which shall include criminal or non-criminal fines and may include other sanctions such as': exclusion from public benefits or aid; temporary or permanent disqualification from the practice of commercial activities; judicial supervision; or a winding-up order.[278] As for negligence liability, in such cases legal persons must be punishable by 'effective, proportionate and dissuasive sanctions or measures'.[279]

The rules in this Protocol then became a template for all future EU measures (and, to a limited extent, EC measures). The subsequent substantive criminal law measures which are still in force can be divided into those which have simply set out the Second Protocol rules without amendment and those which have made

---

[270] Art 2(2), market abuse directive (Dir 2003/6, [2003] OJ L 96/16).
[271] Art 3, PIF Convention ([1995] OJ C 316/48).
[272] Art 7(1), First Protocol ([1996] OJ C 313/1).
[273] Art 6 of Convention ([1997] OJ C 195/2).   [274] Art 1(d) ([1997] OJ C 221/12).
[275] Art 3(1) (ibid).   [276] Art 3(2) (ibid).   [277] Art 3(3) (ibid).   [278] Art 4(1) (ibid).
[279] Art 4(2) (ibid).

some amendments. The first category comprises: the Framework Decision on counterfeiting currency;[280] the Framework Decision on private corruption;[281] the Framework Decision on attacks against information systems;[282] and the Framework Decision on racism and xenophobia.[283]

The second category comprises:

(a) the Framework Decision on counterfeiting payment cards, which does not oblige Member States to extend liability to legal persons as regards one of the offences defined in the Framework Decision (the theft of payment cards);[284]

(b) the Framework Decision on terrorism, which does *not* define 'legal person', although a preambular clause states that 'actions by the armed forces of a state in the exercise of their official duties are not governed by this Framework Decision'. The specified sanctions apply regardless of whether a legal person has acted deliberately or negligently, and a fifth possible sanction is listed: 'temporary or permanent closure of establishments which have been used for committing the offence';[285]

(c) the Framework Decision on facilitation of the illegal entry and residence of third-country nationals, which does not define 'legal person';[286]

(d) the Directives on environmental crimes[287] and ship-source pollution,[288] which contain the standard rule on liability for legal persons but no rules on sanctions for legal persons, besides an obligation to impose 'effective, proportionate and dissuasive penalties'; the Directive on the employment of irregular migrants is identical, except for an extra provision permitting Member States to publish a list of legal persons held liable for the relevant offence;[289]

(e) the Framework Decisions on trafficking in humans,[290] combating sexual exploitation and child pornography,[291] and organized crime,[292] which list a fifth possible sanction: 'temporary or permanent closure of establishments which have been used for committing the offence'; and

(f) the Framework Decision on combating drug trafficking, which includes two extra sanctions: 'temporary or permanent closure of establishments which have been used for committing the offence' and the confiscation of proceeds, substances, and instrumentalities connected with the offences; it also refers

---

[280] [2000] OJ L 140/1, Arts 1 (third indent), 8, and 9.

[281] [2003] OJ L 192/54, Arts 1 (first indent), 5, and 6.

[282] Arts 1(c), 8, and 9 ([2005] OJ L 69/67).   [283] Arts 5 and 6 ([2008] OJ L 328/55).

[284] Arts 1(b), 7, and 8 of the Framework Decision ([2001] OJ L 149/1).

[285] Arts 7 and 8 ([2002] OJ L 164/3). The 2008 amendment to this Framework Decision ([2008] OJ L 330/21) did not amend the rules on corporate liability.

[286] [2002] OJ L 328/1; however, the rules on liability and penalties in Arts 2 and 3 follow the template.   [287] Arts 1(d), 6, and 7 (Dir 2008/99, [2008] OJ L 328/28).

[288] Arts 8b and 8c of Dir 2005/35 ([2005] OJ L 255/11), as inserted by Dir 2009/123 ([2009] OJ L 280/52).   [289] Arts 2(g), 11, and 12 of Dir 2009/52 ([2009] OJ L 168/24).

[290] Arts 4 and 5 ([2002] OJ L 203/1).   [291] Arts 6 and 7 ([2004] OJ L 13/44).

[292] Arts 5 and 6 of the Framework Decision ([2008] OJ L 300/42).

to exclusion from 'tax benefits or other benefits' instead of exclusion from 'public benefits'.[293]

As for proposed measures, the Directives proposed or agreed since the entry into force of the Treaty of Lisbon simply copy the rules which appear in the prior Framework Decisions.[294]

10.5.2.2. Inchoate offences

The classic common law offences of attempt, conspiracy, and incitement find an echo in one form or another in other national legal systems. They are also explicitly or implicitly provided for in EC or EU legislation. The definition of money laundering includes 'participation in, association to commit, attempts to commit and...counselling' the measures prohibited by the EC Directive.[295]

The Court of Justice seems willing to find an obligation for Member States to ban attempts even when EC legislation does not expressly provide for it. In *Ebony Maritime*, the Court ruled that to ensure the '[e]ffective prevention' of breaches of EC sanctions against Yugoslavia, the legislation should apply not only to actual entries, but also to attempted entries into Yugoslav territorial waters.[296] This interpretation was bolstered by the legislation's ban on 'any activity the object or effect of which is, directly or indirectly, to promote' prohibited transactions.[297] It is clear that the primary reason for the Court's finding was not the wording of the legislation but the goal of ensuring the effectiveness of Community law, and the result of the ruling is that penalizing attempts to breach the Regulation was not an option but an obligation for Member States. If this is a general principle that applies to the interpretation of all EC legislation, its effect could be quite broad.

Inchoate offences are often explicitly provided for within EU measures. As seen above, the definition of fraud against the EU budget in the PIF Convention includes the 'presentation' of false, incorrect, or incomplete documents, as well as their 'use'. This criminalizes 'complete attempts', and the Convention also criminalizes 'incomplete attempts': Member States must criminalize the 'intentional preparation or supply' of such documents if such action is not already criminalized as a principal offence or an attempt.[298] The Convention also expressly requires Member States to criminalize 'participation in' or 'instigation of' the intentional preparation or supply of false, incorrect or incomplete documents, although there is no further definition of 'participation' or 'instigation'.[299] Furthermore, Member States have broader obligations to apply criminal penalties to attempts to commit,

---

[293] Arts 1(3), 6, and 7 of the Framework Decision ([2004] OJ L 335/8).

[294] Arts 11 and 12, proposed Dir on sexual offences (COM (2010) 94, 29 Mar 2010); Arts 11 and 12, agreed text of Dir on trafficking in persons (Council doc 10845/10, 10 June 2010).

[295] Art 1(2)(b), Dir 2005/60 (n 267 above). See also Art 3(b) of the market abuse Dir (n 270 above), on 'recommending or inducing'.   [296] Case C-177/95 [1997] ECR I-1111, para 25.

[297] Art 1(1)(d) of Reg 990/93 ([1993] OJ L 102/14).

[298] Art 1(3) of Convention (n 271 above).   [299] Ibid.

participation in, or instigation of any of the main offences in the Convention (the use or presentation of documents, non-disclosure of information or misapplication of funds).[300]

Attempts are also implicitly covered in the First PIF Protocol and in the Convention and Framework Decision on corruption, since, as seen above, these measures cover requesting and promising as well as giving and receiving advantages. The definition of the offences in the EU measures suggests that an offence of active or passive corruption is fully committed when a person agrees to act (or to omit to act) in return for an advantage. If, however, he, she, or it subsequently fails or is prevented from completing the act or omission, he, she, or it has nonetheless committed the full offence, not merely an attempt. The 'penalties' clauses of the PIF Protocol and the corruption Convention also require criminal liability for instigation or participation.[301]

According to the Second PIF Protocol, Member States must also criminalize inchoate offences related to laundering the proceeds of fraud and corruption against the EC budget.[302]

As for the EU's Framework Decisions, they establish the following:

(a) the Framework Decision on terrorism applies to attempts and incitement to commit most offences;[303]
(b) the Framework Decision on trafficking in persons applies to attempts and instigation,[304] as does the agreed replacement Directive;[305]
(c) the Framework Decision on child pornography and prostitution applies to attempts to commit most offences (not to attempts to acquire or possess child pornography), and instigation;[306] the proposed replacement Directive would apply also to advertising and organizing travel as regards the main offences, although again attempts would only have to be punishable as regards certain offences;[307]
(d) the Framework Decision on drug trafficking applies to attempts (with a possible exemption) and incitement;[308]
(e) the Framework Decision on corruption applies to instigation;[309]
(f) the Framework Decision on counterfeiting currency applies to attempts to commit most offences, and to participation and instigation;[310] the Framework

---

[300] Art 2(1) of Convention.

[301] Art 5(1) of the Protocol and Convention; Art 2 of the Framework Decision (nn 271, 273, and 281 above).   [302] Arts 1(3) and 2 of the Protocol.

[303] Art 4 of Framework Decision, as amended in 2008 (n 285 above).

[304] Art 2 of Framework Decision (n 290 above).   [305] Art 3 of agreed text (n 294 above).

[306] Art 4 of Framework Decision (n 291 above).

[307] Art 7 of proposed Directive (n 294 above).

[308] Art 3 of Framework Decision (n 293 above).

[309] Art 3 of Framework Decision (n 281 above).

[310] Art 3(2) of Framework Decision (n 280 above).

Decision on counterfeiting non-cash instruments applies to attempts to commit most offences, and to participation and instigation;[311]

(g) the Framework Decision on attacks on information systems applies to attempts to commit most offences (with a possible exception) and to instigation;[312]

(h) the Framework Decision on organized crime contains no provisions;[313] and

(i) the Framework Decision on racism and xenophobia applies to instigation to deny the Holocaust and war crimes, etc but *not* to instigation to commit the other offences referred to, or to attempts;[314] and

(j) the Directive on facilitation of irregular entry and residence applies to attempts and instigation.[315]

The EC's criminal law measures each apply to incitement, but not to attempts or conspiracy.[316]

10.5.2.3. Complicity

There are several references to complicity in EC or EU legislation. The money laundering Directive refers expressly to 'aiding, abetting [and] facilitating' the offences described in the Directive, as well as 'assisting' a person involved in converting or transferring property derived from criminal activity as defined in the Directive.[317]

The PIF Convention and its First Protocol make no reference to criminal liability for complicity per se, although the Convention does refer to complicity in its jurisdiction rules.[318] However, this does not exclude the imposition of liability, but rather leaves it up to each Member State, as the second PIF Protocol makes explicit.[319] Corporate liability for complicity must be imposed under the Second Protocol, where the legal person can be liable on a *mens rea* basis; and the Second Protocol also has the effect of requiring Member States to make legal and natural persons alike criminally liable for complicity in laundering the proceeds of fraud and corruption against the EU budget.

As for the EU's Framework Decisions, the measures on corruption, terrorism (as amended), trafficking in persons, shipping pollution, child pornography and prostitution, drug trafficking, attacks on information systems, and racism and xenophobia require Member States to criminalize aiding and abetting,[320] while

---

[311] Art 5 of Framework Decision (n 284 above).

[312] Art 5 of Framework Decision (n 282 above).   [313] See n 292 above.

[314] Art 2(1) of Framework Decision (n 283 above).

[315] Art 2(a) and (c) of Directive (n 286 above).

[316] Art 10(2), Dir 2009/52; Art 4, Dir 2008/99; and Art 5b of Dir 2005/35, as inserted by Dir 2009/123 (nn 287–289 above). In the latter two cases, the obligation to criminalize incitement only applies where the action is intentional.   [317] Definition of 'money laundering' (n 267 above).

[318] Art 4(1).   [319] Art 3(3) of Protocol.

[320] So do the proposed Dir on sexual offences and the agreed Dir on trafficking in persons.

the Framework Decision on facilitation of illegal entry and residence requires them to criminalize accomplices.

All EC criminal law Directives require Member States to establish liability for aiding and abetting the relevant offences.[321]

10.5.2.4. Possession

The money laundering Directive expressly requires Member States to prohibit the 'possession' of laundered money. The firearms Directive, as amended, also requires Member States to ban possession of some weapons altogether, and to ban possession of others without prior authorization.[322] It is rare to find such explicit bans in EC legislation, but the Court is content to allow Member States to criminalize possession of an object when enforcing that legislation, even where the legislation does not provide for it. For example, Member States are free to criminalize the possession of animals treated with hormones which the EC has prohibited, although the legislation only requires them to prohibit giving the hormones to animals and the slaughter or marketing of animals treated with the hormones and the sale of their meat.[323]

Within the former third pillar, the second PIF Protocol, by its *renvoi* to the money laundering Directive, has the effect of requiring Member States to criminalize all possession of the proceeds of fraud and corruption against the EU budget.[324] The Framework Decisions on drug trafficking, child pornography, counterfeiting currency, and counterfeiting non-cash instruments also require criminalization of possession of relevant items.[325]

10.5.2.5. Omissions

There are different views on the extent to which omissions, as distinct from acts, should be criminalized, and inevitable difficulties in determining the difference between acts and omissions. No EC or EU measures rule out the criminalization of omissions in principle, and it seems likely from the Court of Justice's 'hands-off' approach on most other criminal law issues that when interpreting Community law, the Court will leave it to the discretion of Member States to determine whether to criminalize and how to define omissions.

Obligations in the former third pillar measures are slightly more definite. Under the PIF Convention, omissions must explicitly be criminalized, while the First PIF Protocol, the corruption Convention, and the Framework Decision on private corruption criminalize omissions by implication, because they cover persons who refrain from acting in accordance with their duties or functions.

---

[321] Art 10(2), Dir 2009/52; Art 4, Dir 2008/99; and Art 5b of Dir 2005/35, as inserted by Dir 2009/123 (nn 287–289 above). In the latter two cases, the obligation to criminalize incitement only applies where the action is intentional.   [322] See n 167 above.

[323] Case C-143/91 *Van der Tas* [1992] ECR I-5045.   [324] See n 274 above.

[325] See nn 293, 291, 280, and 284 above. So does the proposed Dir on sexual offences (n 294 above).

Under the Second PIF Protocol, legal persons may be criminally liable if their omissions to supervise or control certain natural persons have made possible acts by those natural persons.

10.5.3. Conditions of criminal liability

When should persons be criminally liable for their acts and omissions? Should they be liable when their conduct was intentional, or reckless (intentional liability), when it was negligent (negligence liability), or merely when they have caused a proscribed result to occur (strict liability)? EC legislation has not usually addressed this important issue directly, in large part because Member States have developed different principles on the dividing line between criminal and administrative law and retain the option of enforcing EC legislation by either. Moreover, Member States take different views on what type of liability to apply to different offences.

Unusually, the money laundering Directive makes it clear that Member States must only prohibit the named offences 'when committed intentionally', providing further that the conversion, transfer, concealment, disguise, acquisition, possession, or use of illicit property must be done with *knowledge* that the property derives from criminal activity. However, such knowledge or intent (for the purpose of the conversion or transfer) 'may be inferred from objective factual circumstances', and since Member States may expressly adopt 'stricter provisions' than the Directive, the imposition of negligence liability or strict liability is not precluded.[326] Equally, the Directive on employment of irregular migrants requires only liability for intentional acts, but sets only a minimum standard (see further discussion below).[327]

It is more usual for EC law to remain silent on the issues of criminal liability. In its silence, can individuals claim that a Member State's decision to enforce the EC rule by imposing strict criminal liability (requiring only proof of a criminal act, not intention to commit a crime) breaches Community law? The Court has ruled that they cannot. In *Hansen*, it ruled that a Member State was free to impose strict criminal liability on employers breaching EC legislation, as long as it met the *Greek maize* principles of imposing equal, effective, proportionate, and dissuasive sanctions.[328] Denmark's imposition of strict liability to enforce EC drivers' hours legislation met that test because it applied such liability for other breaches of national law, the imposition appeared to be effective and dissuasive, and the proportionality of the fine had not been challenged. But conversely, the Court made clear in *Vandevenne* that strict liability was entirely an option; Member States

---

[326] Art 5, Dir 2005/60 (n 267 above).   [327] Art 9(1), Dir 2009/52 (n 289 above).
[328] Case C-326/88 [1990] ECR I-2611.

could certainly impose a different form of liability, or administrative penalties, if they wished, as long as the *Greek maize* principles were satisfied.[329]

Later, in *Ebony Maritime*,[330] the Court left it to the national court to find whether strict liability for breach of EC sanctions legislation was permissible in light of the *Greek maize* principles. However, it urged the national court to take account of the legislation's aim of ending massive breaches of international human rights and humanitarian law. With respect, it is inappropriate to focus solely on the impact of the offence when deciding whether criminal liability is appropriate, without considering the nature of the offence, the rights of the accused, or the severity of the penalty. In certain cases, it would conversely be appropriate to consider the overall impact of strict liability on human rights and/or on other EC objectives. For example, it is submitted that the Court should preclude Member States from implementing the EC Directive on unauthorized employment of irregular migrants by imposing strict criminal or administrative liability on employers who hire irregular migrants,[331] because of the severe effects such liability would have on employment of minorities. In fact, subsequent economic sanctions legislation states expressly that acts must be intentional to attract a prohibition.[332]

EU measures have usually expressly or by strong implication required liability for intentions. For example, the PIF Convention covers only intentional acts or omissions, although such conduct (like money laundering) 'may be inferred from objective factual circumstances', and the Convention is only a minimum standard.[333] However, the EC Directive on environmental crime applies when the relevant acts are committed 'with serious negligence',[334] and the Directive on shipping pollution requires liability to be imposed if the impugned acts are committed 'with intent, recklessly or with serious negligence'.[335]

10.5.4. Defences

Normally, EU and EC laws do not make any mention at all of the defences to the offences which they have created (although a number of measures contain exclusions from the substantive scope of criminal liability). It must be presumed that the existence and application of defences is left to national law—although it would be interesting to see what the Court of Justice would make of a 'mistake of law' defence.[336] There are two exceptions to this rule. First of all, the first PIF

---

[329] See n 269 above.   [330] See n 296 above.   [331] See n 289 above.

[332] See, for instance, Art 3(1) of Reg 2580/2001 ([2001] OJ L 344/70).

[333] Arts 1(4) and 9, PIF Convention (n 271 above).   [334] Art 4, Dir 2008/99 (n 287 above).

[335] Art 4 of Dir 2005/35, as amended by Dir 2009/123; but note the mandatory exceptions set out in Art 5, again as amended by Dir 2009/123 (n 288 above). These provisions (before amendment) were one of the grounds for the (unsuccessful) challenge to the validity of Dir 2005/35: Case C-308/06 *Intertanko* [2008] ECR I-4057.

[336] Causation issues are also presumably left to national law.

Protocol and the corruption Convention preserve the immunities enjoyed by the staff of the EC institutions, although those immunities must be waived in certain circumstances.[337] Moreover, both texts preserve special legislation that Member States may have established to govern the status of government ministers.[338] Members of the Commission may not claim entitlement to be governed by such status. Secondly the Directive on e-commerce exempts firms which host, cache, or serve as a conduit for illegal Internet material from liability (presumably including civil liability) unless they were aware of the existence of the material. In effect, this amounts to a defence of automatism.[339] The ability of Member States to retain legislation relating to the liability of the press in the context of the Framework Decision on racism and xenophobia and the amended Framework Decision on terrorism may also amount to a defence in practice.[340] Next, the agreed text of the Directive on trafficking in persons requires Member States to provide for the possibility of exempting victims from criminal liability if they have been 'compelled to commit' crimes as a 'direct consequence' of the trafficking acts (ie the defence of duress).[341] Finally, the proposal on sexual offences against children contains not only a similar provision relating to the duress of child victims, but also an exemption for consensual activities between children or persons of similar enough age (ie a 'Romeo and Juliet' exception).[342]

10.6. Penalties

As noted at the outset of this chapter,[343] most EU measures on substantive criminal law adopted after the Treaty of Amsterdam, including measures proposed or agreed after the entry into force of the Treaty of Lisbon, contain minimum sentencing rules. For the first for three years after the Treaty of Amsterdam entered into force, the length of these sentences was agreed on an ad hoc basis by the Council, without any underlying plan as to when such rules would be imposed or what standards should apply to setting such sentences. In fact, the negotiation of a number of measures was delayed by disputes as to whether penalty levels should be set at all and if so, at what level. Eventually the JHA Council of April 2002 agreed standard rules, as guidelines for sentencing rules in all later measures.[344] In the view of a Commission Green Paper, national law on criminal penalties should be approximated further,[345] but the Commission has not followed this initiative up.

---

[337] Art 4(5) of Protocol and 4(4) of Convention.
[338] Art 4(3) of Protocol and 4(2) of Convention.
[339] Arts 12–14 of Dir 2000/31, [2000] OJ L 178/1.   [340] See nn 283 and 285 above.
[341] Art 7 of the agreed text (n 294 above).   [342] Arts 8 and 13 of the proposal (ibid).
[343] See 10.2.2 and 10.2.3 above.   [344] See JHA Council press release, 25–26 Apr 2002.
[345] See the Green Paper on criminal sanctions (COM (2004) 334, 30 Apr 2004).

The measures adopted or proposed before the standard rules were agreed contain the following rules on sanctions:

(a) the Framework Decision on counterfeiting currency requires Member States to impose a maximum sentence of at least eight years for counterfeiting currency;[346]

(b) the Framework Decision on money laundering requires Member States to impose a maximum sentence of at least four years;[347]

(c) the Framework Decision on terrorism requires Member States to impose a heavier sentence than normal for those committing the offences in the Framework Decision with a terrorist intent, a maximum sentence of at least fifteen years for directing a terrorist group in most cases, and eight years for participation in a terrorist group, with possible reductions for those who assist the authorities;[348]

(d) the Framework Decision on trafficking in persons requires Member States to impose a maximum sentence of at least eight years in four special circumstances: where the crime endangered the victim's life, caused serious physical harm or involved serious violence, was committed against a vulnerable person (as defined), or was committed in the framework of the 1998 organized crime Joint Action (apart from its penalty level);[349] and

(e) the Framework Decision on facilitation of illegal entry and residence requires Member States to provide for an aggravated sentence of at least eight years, where the offence was committed for financial gain and was within the framework of the 1998 Joint Action on organized crime, or when endangering the lives of the persons subject to the offence. Member States may reduce this period to six years to retain the coherence of their national penalty system.[350]

The various references to the 1998 Joint Action on organized crime in these and other measures (see below) are now considered to be references to the Framework Decision replacing that Joint Action, now that the deadline to apply that Framework Decision has passed.[351]

All subsequent Framework Decisions agreed after April 2002 followed the template set out by the JHA Council at that time. This template sets out four levels of sanction: maximum levels of between at least one to three years, two to five years, five to ten years, and over ten years. The Council agreed that it is not

---

[346] Art 6 of Framework Decision ([2000] OJ L 140/1).

[347] Art 2 of Framework Decision ([2001] OJ L 182/1).

[348] Arts 5 and 6 of Framework Decision ([2002] OJ L 164/3). The 2008 amendment to the Framework Decision ([2008] OJ L 330/21) makes no change to these rules.

[349] Art 3 of Framework Decision ([2002] OJ L 203/1).

[350] Art 1 of Framework Decision ([2002] OJ L 328/1).

[351] The deadline to apply the Framework Decision was 11 May 2010 (Art 10 of the Framework Decision, [2008] OJ L 300/42).

necessary to set out sentencing rules in each measure or to use this sentencing template in all cases, although so far since April 2002 it has inserted sentencing provisions and used the template in every adopted or agreed measure. The template has been applied as follows:

(a) the Framework Decision on sexual exploitation requires Member States to provide for a normal maximum sentence of at least one to three years,[352] increased to five to ten years in certain circumstances, in particular (for most offences) where the child was under the age of sexual consent and the child's life was endangered, the child suffered serious violence or harm, or where the acts were committed in the framework of a criminal organization as defined by the 1998 Joint Action.[353] There is also an obligation to ban convicted persons from 'if appropriate' exercising professional activities related to the supervision of children, and an option to impose other criminal or non-criminal sanctions;[354]

(b) the Framework Decision on private corruption requires Member States to provide for a normal maximum sentence of at least one to three years, with possible prohibition from business activity;[355]

(c) the Framework Decision on attacks on information systems requires Member States to impose a maximum sentence of at least one to three years for illegal system interference or illegal data interference (but not illegal system access, which is only subject to the general obligation to criminalize), with sentences extended to two to five years for the same offences and for illegal access in breach of a security measure, when those offences are committed in the framework of the 1998 organized crime Joint Action (apart from its penalty level);[356]

(d) the Framework Decision on drug trafficking requires Member States to impose a maximum sentence of at least one to three years as a general rule, increased to five to ten years where the crime involved large quantities of drugs or the most unhealthy drugs, with at least a ten-year maximum sentence if the crime was committed in the framework of the 1998 organized crime Joint Action; lesser penalties apply to precursors. Member States may reduce penalties if persons renounce drugs and assist the authorities, and must also provide for confiscation of relevant substances, instrumentalities, and proceeds;[357]

---

[352] Art 5(1) of Framework Decision ([2004] OJ L 13/44).

[353] Art 5(2) of Framework Decision (ibid).

[354] Art 5(3) and (4) of Framework Decision (ibid). On recognition of these disqualifications in other Member States, see further 9.7.3 above.

[355] Art 4 of Framework Decision ([2003] OJ L 192/54).

[356] Arts 6 and 7 of Framework Decision ([2005] OJ L 69/67). Member States *may* also apply the aggravated penalty when the conduct has 'caused serious damages or has affected essential interests'.   [357] Arts 4 and 5 of Framework Decision ([2004] OJ L 335/8).

(e) the Framework Decision on organized crime provides for a maximum penalty of between two and five years, with a reduction in penalties (optional for Member States) for those who 'squeal' on their criminal associates;[358] and

(f) the Framework Decision on racism and xenophobia provides for a maximum penalty of between one and three years, as regards the main offences (but not as regards incitement and aiding and abetting).[359]

As for proposed new measures, the agreed text of the Directive on trafficking in persons by a Directive would require a maximum sentence of at least ten years, rather than eight years, in the same four special circumstances as before, with 'vulnerable' victims now defined to include all children, and at least five years in ordinary cases.[360] The proposed Directive on sexual offences against children would require maximum sentences of two, five, eight, or ten years for various crimes.[361] It should be noted that these measures do not follow the agreed template.

It can be seen that the agreed template is quite flexible, allowing for several years' variation between Member States at the three lowest levels. There are differences between the texts on the question of whether there are sentencing rules for all cases (there is a recent tendency to this end) or whether there are sentencing rules only in aggravated cases. It is striking that, leaving aside the annulled Framework Decision on environmental crime,[362] the Council has proved willing to agree sentencing rules in every third pillar Framework Decision except the Framework Decision on the counterfeiting of non-cash items[363] (possibly because this proposal initially pre-dated the Treaty of Amsterdam), as well as the first Directive agreed after the entry into force of the Treaty of Lisbon.

10.7. Administrative cooperation

The main type of administrative cooperation as regards substantive criminal law has been the move toward developing comparable EU-wide crime statistics. There is not yet any legislation on this issue, and the adoption of any measures would be subject to Article 343 TFEU, which now applies to the former third pillar since the entry into force of the Treaty of Lisbon. In the meantime, the Commission adopted an action plan on this issue for 2006–10,[364] which inter alia set out the objective of ultimately gathering comparable statistics on specific cross-border crimes (corruption, fraud, counterfeiting of goods, trafficking in cultural goods, and sexual offences against children), as well as money laundering and terrorist financing, trafficking in persons, juvenile crime, drug-related crime, violence

---

[358] Arts 3 and 4 of Framework Decision ([2008] OJ L 300/42).
[359] Art 3 of Framework Decision ([2008] OJ L 328/55).
[360] Art 4 of agreed text (Council doc 10845/10, 10 June 2010).
[361] COM (2010) 94, 29 Mar 2010, Arts 3–5.   [362] [2003] OJ L 29/55.
[363] [2001] OJ L 149/1.   [364] COM (2006) 437, 7 Aug 2006.

against women, domestic violence, and environmental crime. The Stockholm programme calls for these measures to be further developed after 2010.[365]

10.8. External relations

The adoption of internal EU legislation gives rise to external EU competence over international treaties. Broadly speaking, depending on the extent of the internal harmonization, the EU's external competence is either shared with the Member States or exclusive, which means that the Member States are precluded from adopting treaties on the relevant issue.[366]

In light of EC legislation (as it then was) requiring Member States to prohibit acts such as money laundering,[367] the EC concluded or signed a number of international criminal law Conventions before the entry into force of the Treaty of Lisbon, although in all cases EC competence over these treaties was shared with Member States,[368] and indeed the EC's competence related to only a handful of provisions of these treaties, ie those provisions which did *not* deal expressly with substantive criminal law. The EC's external competence in this area grew in light of the Court of Justice's confirmation of EC competence to adopt internal legislation defining substantive criminal law offences, and the subsequent adoption of EC Directives imposing criminal law obligations,[369] although before the entry into force of the Treaty of Lisbon, the EC never exercised its external competence as regards criminal law obligations as such.

In practice, the EC concluded the UN's Vienna Convention on drugs, the main UN Convention on organized crime, two of the three Protocols to the latter Convention (concerning smuggling of persons and trafficking in persons), and the UN Convention on corruption.[370] The Community also signed the firearms Protocol to the UN organized crime Convention and the 2005 Council of Europe Convention on money laundering.[371] Further negotiations are underway on an Anti-Counterfeiting Trade Agreement, which will likely include criminal sanctions.[372] The Council has also adopted conclusions encouraging cooperation with the Council of Europe as regards criminal law.[373]

---

[365] [2010] OJ C 115, point 4.3.3.

[366] On EU external competence generally, see 2.7.1 above.   [367] See 10.5.1 above.

[368] For details of ratification of all these Conventions by the Member States, see Appendix I.

[369] See 10.4.1.1 above.

[370] See respectively [1990] OJ L 326/56, [2004] OJ L 261/69, [2006] OJ L 262/34, [2006] OJ L 262/51, and [2008] OJ L 287/1.

[371] [2001] OJ L 280/5 and JHA Council press release, 27 Feb 2009. The Commission Action Plan on the implementation of the Stockholm programme plans a proposal for the EU to conclude to former treaty in 2012 (COM (2010) 171, 20 Apr 2010).

[372] For the latest draft text of this treaty, see: <http://trade.ec.europa.eu/doclib/docs/2010/april/tradoc_146029.pdf>.   [373] [2009] OJ C 50/8.

As for the previous third pillar,[374] it is not clear whether any external competence for the Union at all exists as a consequence as the adoption of internal EU measures, and the Union as such never signed or ratified any international criminal law Conventions before the entry into force of the Treaty of Lisbon. However, prior to this point, the Union's power to sign criminal law treaties was exercised to negotiate association treaties with the Schengen *acquis* for Switzerland and Liechtenstein, as well as treaties concerning extradition and mutual assistance with the US, Norway, Iceland, and Japan.[375] Moreover, the Union used its capacity to adopt Common Positions or Joint Positions on international negotiations on criminal law issues, as well as less formal means, to coordinate the negotiating position of Member States as regards as number of international criminal law treaties.[376]

The adoption of substantive criminal law measures subsequent to the entry into force of the Treaty of Lisbon falls squarely within the established legal framework regarding EC (now EU) external competence,[377] whether the measures are adopted pursuant to Article 83(1) or (2) TFEU. However, the requirement that EU measures in this area set only minimum standards means that the Union cannot in principle fully harmonize the field, and so must share competence with its Member States as regards international treaties concerning substantive criminal law. But the position may be different as regards provisions concerning criminal law jurisdiction.[378] So the declaration in the Final Act of the Treaty of Lisbon which attempts to limit the EU's external competence over (inter alia) criminal law simply confirms the obvious.[379]

10.9. Conclusions

Given the different social and cultural traditions of Member States, the close connection between criminal law and the sovereignty of States, and the democratic right of citizens within each State to decide what actions should or should not be criminalized, prima facie the idea of extensive harmonization of substantive criminal law in the EU cannot be justified. But certain crimes have long been regarded by the international community as sufficiently important to address collectively, and certain other crimes should similarly be addressed collectively by the EU.

A balance needs to be struck between the national sovereignty of States as regards deciding what actions to criminalize, and the possible impact of such

---

[374] On external competence in relation to the prior third pillar, see generally 2.7.2 above.

[375] See 9.2.5 and 9.10 above.   [376] For the details, see 2.2.2.2 and 2.7.2 above.

[377] On the specific Treaty provisions inserted by the Treaty of Lisbon regarding EU external competence generally, see 2.7.1 above.   [378] See 11.12 below.

[379] On this declaration, see also 9.10 above.

national decisions upon the interests of other Member States or the EU as a whole, given the possibility of a type of 'race to the bottom' (ie the movement of persons to commit offences in the most lenient Member States) if there are sufficiently wide divergences in criminal law as regards acts which have a significant cross-border impact. The provisions of the Treaty of Lisbon broadly strike that balance, specifying that the EU can only harmonize certain clearly specified crimes, or take action linked to harmonization in other areas,[380] and subject to the 'emergency brake' which States can invoke in order to protect their distinctive criminal law traditions and (in practice) the pre-eminence of national parliaments in this area.

In the longer term, the prospect of substantive criminal law harmonization without the emergency brake could only be justified, if at all, in exceptional cases where the EU interest heavily outweighs the national interest (only the protection of EU finances and counterfeiting of the euro qualify) or where there is an inextricable link to an area which has been very extensively harmonized by EC law, and where furthermore it is demonstrably necessary to enforce the harmonized rules by criminal law sanctions.

---

[380] It would be appropriate to limit the abolition of double criminality in principle only to the offences which the EU has thereby harmonized, or which are subject to spontaneous harmonization of national laws: see 9.11 above.

11

Criminal Law: Jurisdiction, Coordination, and Prosecution

11.1. Introduction

The adoption of legislation defining certain acts as a crime is not, of course, sufficient in itself to deter or punish many of the persons who wish to commit such crimes. It is also necessary to establish effective mechanisms to ensure that those rules are enforced. While the policing aspects of enforcement are discussed in Chapter 12, this chapter focuses on the criminal law aspects of enforcement, beginning with the preliminary issue of the allocation of criminal jurisdiction between Member States. The chapter then considers the connected issues of resolving conflicts of jurisdiction and transferring proceedings between Member States, followed by the rules, stemming from the Schengen Convention, preventing cross-border 'double jeopardy', ie a prosecution in a second Member State after a trial of the same person for the same acts has been finally disposed of in a first Member State.

The EU also plays a more operational role in the criminal law aspects of the enforcement of criminal offences, by means of Eurojust, an EU agency to facilitate and coordinate the work of prosecutors in cross-border cases, established in 2002 and given further powers in 2008. This entity could be supplemented in future by the creation of a European Public Prosecutor, which could be given the power to bring criminal proceedings directly against accused persons.

The rules discussed in this chapter obviously supplement the rules on definition of crimes (see Chapter 10) and also complement the rules on mutual recognition (Chapter 9), in particular because the latter rules contain important exceptions relating to jurisdiction and double jeopardy. The cross-border double jeopardy rules also constitute another set of EU rules for the protection of suspects.[1] Furthermore, the rules in this chapter can be compared to the EU rules on civil jurisdiction (Chapter 8) but, as will be seen, the EU's framework relating to criminal jurisdiction is far less developed than as regards civil jurisdiction, and seems likely to remain so for the foreseeable future. An essential safeguard against abuse of this flexibility is the rules preventing double jeopardy, which

---

[1] See 9.8.2 above.

have become a source of conflict between the objectives of free movement and crime prevention.[2]

11.2. Institutional framework and overview

11.2.1. Cooperation before the Treaty of Amsterdam

As noted already in Chapter 9, before the entry into force of the Treaty of Amsterdam in 1999, the main source of the law on international criminal procedure was Council of Europe Conventions. In this area, the main Convention concerned was a Convention on transfer of proceedings,[3] which included rules on cross-border double jeopardy and avoiding conflicts of jurisdiction, along with rules on the transfer of proceedings as such. An earlier convention on the international validity of criminal judgments had also contained double jeopardy rules.[4] However, these two Conventions have attracted limited interest from Member States.[5] A number of Council of Europe and UN Conventions dealing with particular crimes included provisions on criminal jurisdiction related to those crimes.[6]

These two areas were subsequently among the areas which were the subject of Conventions agreed by EU Member States, within the framework of European Political Cooperation (EPC) before the entry into force of the original TEU (known as the Maastricht Treaty). So Conventions on both the transfer of proceedings and the international validity of criminal judgments were drawn up, along with a Convention on cross-border double jeopardy, an issue not addressed separately by the prior Council of Europe Conventions.[7] However, none of these Conventions attracted sufficient ratifications from Member States to enter into force.[8]

Outside the framework of cooperation between the (then) EEC Member States, the 1990 Schengen Convention contained a number of detailed provisions on cross-border cooperation, including rules on double jeopardy (reproducing the provisions of the failed EPC Convention),[9] but not on transfer of proceedings or the international validity of judgments.

Although the entry into force of the Treaty of Maastricht gave the EU a formal intergovernmental framework to address criminal procedural issues, the EU did not use this framework to address jurisdiction issues before the entry into force of the Treaty of Amsterdam, except to adopt Conventions and Joint Actions on

---

[2] See Art 3(2) TEU.　　[3] ETS 73.　　[4] ETS 70.
[5] For ratification details, see Appendix I.
[6] On those Conventions, see further 10.5 above.　　[7] See 11.6, 11.7, and 11.8 below.
[8] For ratification details, see Appendix I.
[9] Arts 54–58 of the Convention ([2000] OJ L 239). See 11.8 below.

particular crimes which included jurisdiction rules in relation to those specific crimes, and (in two cases) rules on double jeopardy.[10]

11.2.2. Treaty of Amsterdam

EU powers concerning conflicts of jurisdiction were set out expressly in the previous Article 31(d) TEU, which provided that the EU can adopt measures concerning 'preventing conflicts of jurisdiction between Member States'.

The Treaty of Nice subsequently added a second paragraph to the previous Article 31 TEU,[11] referring to Eurojust, the prosecutors' body which EU leaders had agreed to create in the meantime (see below):

The Council shall encourage cooperation through Eurojust by:

(a) enabling Eurojust to facilitate proper coordination between Member States' national prosecuting authorities;

(b) promoting support by Eurojust for criminal investigations in cases of serious cross-border crime, particularly in the case of organised crime, taking account, in particular, of analyses carried out by Europol;

(c) facilitating close cooperation between Eurojust and the European Judicial network, particularly, in order to facilitate the execution of letters rogatory and the implementation of extradition requests.

The provisions of the revised TEU were governed by the revised general third pillar rules on the jurisdiction of the Court of Justice, the role of the political institutions, and the use of specific instruments and their legal effect.[12] On the latter point, the Court's judgment in *Pupino*, finding that Framework Decisions had indirect effect,[13] could be relevant to this area, assuming that the principle of indirect effect also applies to the Schengen Convention rules on double jeopardy.

In practice, the Tampere European Council conclusions of 1999 called for the creation of Eurojust, to be established by a measure to be adopted by the end of 2001. The Tampere conclusions also called for the adoption of a mutual recognition work programme by the end of 2000, and this work programme included the objective of adopting revised rules on double jeopardy, to replace the Schengen rules, as well as rules to facilitate the settlement of conflicts of jurisdiction.[14]

To give effect to these objectives, Eurojust was set up early in 2002, and its powers were later extended significantly in 2008.[15] A Framework Decision replacing the Schengen Convention rules on double jeopardy was proposed in 2003, but was not successful; instead, the double rules in the Schengen Convention became a major focus of the third pillar case law of the Court of Justice, following

---

[10] See 11.6 and 11.8 below.

[11] The previous Art 31(d) TEU was therefore renumbered Art 31(1)(d) TEU from that point on.

[12] See 2.2.2.2 above.　　　[13] Case C–105/03 [2005] ECR I–5285; see discussion in ibid.

[14] [2001] OJ C 12/10. See further 9.2.2.1 above.　　　[15] See 11.9 below.

references from a large number of national courts.[16] In 2009, the Council adopted a Framework Decision on the issue of conflicts of jurisdiction,[17] and also discussed a Framework Decision on transfer of proceedings,[18] but was unable to agree upon the latter measure before the Treaty of Lisbon entered into force. Finally, the EU adopted a number of measures concerning substantive criminal law which contained provisions on jurisdiction.[19]

11.2.3. Treaty of Lisbon

Following the entry into force of the Treaty of Lisbon on 1 December 2009, EU powers concerning conflicts of jurisdiction are set out in Article 82(2)(b) TFEU, which specifically provides that the EU may adopt measures to 'prevent and settle conflicts of jurisdiction between Member States'. As compared to the previous Treaty, the powers include the *settlement* of conflicts instead of merely their prevention.

The role of Eurojust is now set out in Article 85 TFEU, which reads as follows:

1. Eurojust's mission shall be to support and strengthen coordination and cooperation between national investigating and prosecuting authorities in relation to serious crime affecting two or more Member States or requiring a prosecution on common bases, on the basis of operations conducted and information supplied by the Member States' authorities and by Europol.

In this context, the European Parliament and the Council, by means of regulations adopted in accordance with the ordinary legislative procedure, shall determine Eurojust's structure, operation, field of action and tasks. These tasks may include:

    (a) the initiation of criminal investigations, as well as proposing the initiation of prosecutions conducted by competent national authorities, particularly those relating to offences against the financial interests of the Union;

    (b) the coordination of investigations and prosecutions referred to in point (a);

    (c) the strengthening of judicial cooperation, including by resolution of conflicts of jurisdiction and by close cooperation with the European Judicial Network.

These regulations shall also determine arrangements for involving the European Parliament and national Parliaments in the evaluation of Eurojust's activities.

2. In the prosecutions referred to in paragraph 1, and without prejudice to Article 86, formal acts of judicial procedure shall be carried out by the competent national officials.

As compared to the previous Article 31(2) TEU, Article 85 TFEU refers to the initiation of investigations and the proposal for initiation of prosecutions, as well as the resolution of conflicts of jurisdiction. It also refers specifically to the role of the EP and national parliaments, and provides for a reservation of national

---

[16] See 11.8 below.   [17] See 11.6 below.   [18] See 11.7 below.   [19] See 11.5 below.

competence as regards 'formal acts of judicial procedure'. Furthermore, it is clear that the three tasks for Eurojust listed in Article 85(1) are not an exhaustive list of such tasks (see the words 'shall include').

There is also a new clause concerning the possible creation of a European Public Prosecutor (Article 86 TFEU):

1. In order to combat crimes affecting the financial interests of the Union, the Council, by means of regulations adopted in accordance with a special legislative procedure, may establish a European Public Prosecutor's Office from Eurojust. The Council shall act unanimously after obtaining the consent of the European Parliament.

In the absence of unanimity in the Council, a group of at least nine Member States may request that the draft regulation be referred to the European Council. In that case, the procedure in the Council shall be suspended. After discussion, and in case of a consensus, the European Council shall, within four months of this suspension, refer the draft back to the Council for adoption.

Within the same timeframe, in case of disagreement, and if at least nine Member States wish to establish enhanced cooperation on the basis of the draft regulation concerned, they shall notify the European Parliament, the Council and the Commission accordingly. In such a case, the authorisation to proceed with enhanced cooperation referred to in Article 20(2) of the Treaty on European Union and Article 329(1) of this Treaty shall be deemed to be granted and the provisions on enhanced cooperation shall apply.

2. The European Public Prosecutor's Office shall be responsible for investigating, prosecuting and bringing to judgment, where appropriate in liaison with Europol, the perpetrators of, and accomplices in, offences against the Union's financial interests, as determined by the regulation provided for in paragraph 1. It shall exercise the functions of prosecutor in the competent courts of the Member States in relation to such offences.

3. The regulations referred to in paragraph 1 shall determine the general rules applicable to the European Public Prosecutor's Office, the conditions governing the performance of its functions, the rules of procedure applicable to its activities, as well as those governing the admissibility of evidence, and the rules applicable to the judicial review of procedural measures taken by it in the performance of its functions.

4. The European Council may, at the same time or subsequently, adopt a decision amending paragraph 1 in order to extend the powers of the European Public Prosecutor's Office to include serious crime having a cross-border dimension and amending accordingly paragraph 2 as regards the perpetrators of, and accomplices in, serious crimes affecting more than one Member State. The European Council shall act unanimously after obtaining the consent of the European Parliament and after consulting the Commission.

As for decision-making, measures concerning conflicts of jurisdiction and Eurojust are now subject to QMV and co-decision (ie the ordinary legislative procedure) as compared to unanimity in the Council and consultation of the EP previously. There is no special feature applying to decision-making here (ie an 'emergency brake'), as compared to the rules on substantive criminal law or domestic criminal procedure. It is possible that a joint proposal may be made by at least one-quarter of Member States.[20]

The rules are obviously different for the adoption of measures concerning the European Public Prosecutor (EPP). Such measures are subject to unanimous voting in Council with the consent of the EP. This is the only example of a 'special legislative procedure' as regards EU criminal law. An extension of the mandate of the Prosecutor would be subject to unanimity in the European Council (ie EU leaders) with the consent of the EP.[21] A change to the former, but not the latter, decision-making rules could be made by means of the general *passerelle* clause in the Treaties, subject to unanimity in the European Council, consent of the EP, and control by national parliaments.[22] Another particular feature of Article 86 TFEU is the possibility of a fast-track authorization of enhanced cooperation in the event of a veto; this rule also applies to measures on operational police cooperation.[23] It may also be relevant that the general provisions applying to Title V specify that JHA measures must respect 'the different legal systems and traditions' of Member States.[24]

As with other aspects of criminal law and policing, the Treaty of Lisbon also applies the normal rules applying to the jurisdiction of the EU's Court of Justice to measures adopted after the entry into force of that Treaty, as well as to measures adopted before that Treaty either after a five-year transitional period (ending on 1 December 2014) or if those measures are amended in the meantime. The standard rules on the legal effect of EU law (formerly Community law) will also apply to measures adopted after the entry into force of the Treaty of Lisbon, and to measures adopted beforehand once they are amended. These changes could be particularly relevant to the rules on double jeopardy, given that they have given rise to more references from national courts to the Court of Justice than any other EU policing and criminal law rules.

As for the practical impact of the new Treaty, so far there are no references to the Court of Justice relating to the issues addressed in this chapter. The transfer of proceedings proposal which was under discussion before the Treaty of Lisbon entered into force lapsed at that time, and has not been tabled again. However, several substantive criminal law measures with specific provisions on jurisdiction have been proposed.[25] The Stockholm programme calls for a specific measure on

---

[20] Art 76 TFEU.

[21] This compares to unanimity in the Council to extend the scope of the EU's powers over substantive criminal law or national criminal procedure (Arts 82 and 83 TFEU): see 9.2.3 and 10.2.3 above.

[22] Art 48(7), revised TEU, which only applies to Art 86(1), but not Art 86(4), because it can only be used as regards decision-making by the *Council*, not the European Council.

[23] Art 87(3) TFEU; see 12.2.3 below. For a detailed analysis of this special rule, referred to as a 'pseudo-veto' in this book, see 2.2.3.4.2 above.

[24] Art 67(1) TFEU. See further 2.2.3.2 and 9.2.4 above.   [25] See 11.5 below.

jurisdiction relating to cyber-crime,[26] and for assessment of the implementation of the legislation establishing Eurojust, with a view to amending the rules or considering the creation of a European Public Prosecutor.[27]

11.2.4. Competence issues

First of all, it is necessary to distinguish the Treaty provisions concerning conflict of jurisdiction, Eurojust, and the European Public Prosecutor (EPP) from other Treaty provisions. Then it is necessary to examine the extent of the Treaty powers as regards Eurojust and the EPP.

Starting with EU powers over criminal procedure, double jeopardy rules fall within the scope of either the power to adopt rules on mutual recognition in Article 82(1)(a) TFEU (in light of the relevant case law of the Court of Justice),[28] and/or the power to adopt rules on preventing and settling conflicts of jurisdiction (Article 82(1)(b)). This is relevant since the power to adopt rules on suspects' rights (Article 82(2)(b)) is subject to an 'emergency brake' rule, whereas Article 82(1) is not.[29] Since the Treaty provisions on Eurojust and the European Public Prosecutor are each a *lex specialis*, any rules on domestic criminal procedure linked to either entity must be adopted on the basis of the more specific legal bases. This is particularly relevant in light of the requirement for unanimous voting as regards Article 86 TFEU, and the lack of an emergency brake rule in Article 85 (as compared to Article 82(2)). A measure concerning Eurojust's role regarding conflicts of jurisdiction should have the dual legal base of Articles 82(1)(b) and 85 TFEU—keeping in mind that any measure with the latter legal base must take the form of a Regulation. However, a measure concerning conflicts of jurisdiction as regards the EPP must be based on Article 86 TFEU, given its connection to the functioning of that office.

Next, as regards EU powers over substantive criminal law, rules concerning the assertion of jurisdiction over a particular crime fall within the scope of the EU's substantive criminal law powers set out in Article 83 TFEU, because such provisions are ancillary to the substantive criminal law powers and do nothing to prevent or settle conflicts of jurisdiction.[30] In fact, those rules often exacerbate such conflicts by requiring or encouraging Member States to take extraterritorial

---

[26] [2010] OJ C 115, point 4.4.4. The action plan on implementation of the programme suggests a proposal on this issue in 2013 (COM (2010) 171, 20 Apr 2010).

[27] Point 3.1.1 of the programme; the action plan on implementation of the programme suggests legislation on Eurojust in 2012 and a communication on the EPP in 2013 (both ibid).

[28] See 11.8 below.

[29] Note that the combination of legal bases which do and do not allow for an emergency brake is not per se a problem: see 9.2.4 above.

[30] The underlying substantive rules are discussed in ch 10 above.

jurisdiction.[31] Also, rules concerning assertion of jurisdiction by the EPP must fall within the scope of Article 86, since they affect the functioning of that body.[32] However, while Article 86 is the correct legal base for defining *which* offences the EPP will have the competence to prosecute, the definition of those offences as such falls within the legal base of Article 83.[33] Certainly Article 86 is a *lex specialis* as compared to the more general provision on fraud against the EU budget (Article 325 TFEU).

As compared to the EU's policing powers, rules relating to jurisdiction over investigations must fall within the scope of Article 87 TFEU, but rules concerning the involvement of Eurojust or the EPP in investigations relate to the operations of the bodies concerned, and are therefore within the scope of Articles 85 and 86. There is nothing in the policing provisions of the Treaty that restricts the scope of the latter Articles as regards investigations.

Finally, it should be noted that where issues relating to civil jurisdiction and criminal jurisdiction overlap, the Court of Justice has ruled that Member States' courts could not refuse recognition of other Member States' courts' civil judgments purely because the latter were founded on an assertion of extraterritorial criminal jurisdiction.[34]

As for the powers of Eurojust, the restriction on giving that body the power to take 'formal acts of judicial procedure' means that it cannot itself bring prosecutions against individuals, because at the very least, that exception refers to the bringing of criminal charges against individuals, in whatever form that process takes in the national legal framework. The concept of a 'formal act of judicial procedure' should also be understood as referring to other acts of coercion and constraint, for instance a decision to search property or to freeze assets. Furthermore, it is arguable that Eurojust cannot be given the power to *require* national authorities to begin prosecutions (as distinct from 'proposing' that they do so), or to take other 'formal acts of judicial procedure', because that would render the reserve of national competence set out in Article 85(2) TFEU ineffective. On the other hand, Article 85(2) does not rule out giving Eurojust the power to require national authorities to begin *investigations*, as long as this falls short of requiring them to take formal acts of judicial procedure.

---

[31] See the rules discussed in 11.5 below. The exception would be the few cases where the legislation also sets out rules on priority jurisdiction (see *idem*), which would require the addition of Art 82(1)(b) as a legal base after the entry into force of the Treaty of Lisbon.

[32] On the limits to the territorial scope of the EPP's jurisdiction, see 11.2.5 below.

[33] For further discussion, see 10.2.4 above.

[34] Case C-7/98 *Krombach* [2000] ECR I-1935. Note that in this case, Mr Krombach was later detained in Austria because he was the subject of an alert for extradition purposes on the Schengen Information System, but that ultimately the Austrian courts released Mr Krombach due to their interpretation of the Schengen double jeopardy rules (on which see 11.8 below). See the judgment of the European Court of Human Rights in *Krombach v France* (Reports 2001-II).

As for Eurojust's power to resolve conflicts of jurisdiction, certainly Eurojust could retain the power it already has to *suggest* a resolution to conflicts of jurisdiction.[35] But could the Treaty power potentially extend further, as far as the power to require one Member State not to prosecute, in favour of another? If that power went as far as the compulsion to withdraw charges that had already been laid, it would probably (depending on the national legal framework) amount to a 'formal act of judicial procedure'. However, a power to compel a national authority to *refrain* from bringing proceedings, which would probably amount to a requirement to *omit* to take a 'formal act of judicial procedure', should be considered to fall within the scope of Eurojust's (potential) powers, since otherwise its power to 'resolve' conflicts of jurisdiction would be robbed of all effectiveness. In that case, the right to a fair trial necessarily implies that the binding decision taken by Eurojust would have to be reviewable in the courts by the authorities concerned and by the criminal suspect.

As for the EPP, the requirement to create the office 'from Eurojust' means that there would have to be a link between the two bodies, although in the absence of more precise Treaty rules there is a degree of discretion as to how close the link would have to be. It is clear from Article 86(2) TFEU that proceedings by the EPP would have to be brought in the national courts, not before the current EU courts or any other EU judicial body that might be established. The issue of whether the EPP (and thereby also the defence) would be subject to the relevant national judicial procedure, its own *sui generis* procedural rules, or some combination of the two, is left to be determined by the legislation establishing the Prosecutor. As noted above, the question of whether the EPP or national prosecutors would have jurisdiction in a particular case, and which national court the EPP would bring proceedings before in a particular case (and which would review the EPP's procedural measures, pursuant to Article 86(3)), is a matter to be decided by that legislation also. There is no restriction set out in the Treaty as regards the powers which can be given to the EPP except for the requirement to bring cases before the national courts,[36] so it would be possible to give the EPP power to issue search or arrest warrants, for instance. But it would also be possible to leave such powers with the national authorities—perhaps giving the EPP the power to require those authorities to act to support it, subject to limited exceptions.

11.2.5. Territorial scope

The measures in this chapter adopted prior to the entry into force of the Treaty of Lisbon (the jurisdictional rules in third pillar acts, the Framework Decision

---

[35] See 11.9 below.

[36] This is, moreover, necessarily implied by the reference in the Treaty to the adoption of rules on the judicial review of the EPP's procedural actions.

on conflicts of jurisdiction, and the Schengen double jeopardy rules) apply to all Member States, except that Ireland is not yet subject to the criminal law rules in the Schengen Convention.[37]

Any measures in this area which may be adopted or proposed after the entry into force of the Treaty of Lisbon are subject to possible opt-outs by the UK and Ireland, with special rules applicable if the measures amend (or, as regards the Schengen *acquis*, 'build on') measures which the UK and Ireland are already bound by. Also, measures adopted after this date shall not apply to Denmark at all, unless and until that Member State decides either to relinquish its JHA opt-out altogether or to adopt an alternative version of that opt-out, comparable to the UK and Irish opt-outs.[38] So far, Ireland has opted into both of the initial substantive criminal law proposals which contain jurisdiction provisions, while the UK has opted into one of them.[39]

Furthermore, the Schengen double jeopardy rules (but not the other measures discussed in this chapter) also apply to the Schengen associates (Norway, Iceland, Switzerland, and in future Liechtenstein).

Arguably the opt-out rules (including the possibility of enhanced cooperation as regards the EPP) imply a restriction on the territorial scope of the EPP's jurisdiction. The Council cannot confer power to bring prosecutions upon the EPP except as regards acts committed on the territory of the States participating in the legislation to establish the EPP, otherwise the rules on opt-outs and enhanced cooperation would be circumvented. Of course, it would remain possible for those participating Member States to apply their own criminal law on this point extraterritorially if they wished.

11.3. Human rights

11.3.1. International human rights law

Issues within the scope of this chapter arise as regards two issues: jurisdiction over offences and double jeopardy.

First of all, as regards jurisdiction, presumably the principle of the legality and the non-retroactivity of criminal law, as set out in Article 7 ECHR, applies.[40] So, for instance, the rules on extraterritorial jurisdiction have to be sufficiently clear and foreseeable, and extensions of extraterritorial jurisdiction cannot be

---

[37] Note, however, that Ireland provisionally applies the prior EPC treaty on this issue with several other Member States: see 11.8 below.   [38] See generally 2.2.5.1 and 2.2.5.2 above.

[39] See 10.2.5 above.

[40] On Art 7 ECHR, see also 9.3.2 and 10.3.1 above. Note that the European Court of Human Rights has ruled that 'jurisdiction is not a collateral issue since it forms the basis of any criminal proceedings', with the obvious implication that jurisdictional issues fall within the scope of Art 7 ECHR: *Stephens v Malta (No 2)*, 21 Apr 2009, para 59.

retroactive. This is true *a fortiori* to the extent that the principle of dual criminality is abolished as regards cross-border criminal cooperation, as it has been in many EU mutual recognition measures.[41] After all, the residents of foreign countries cannot generally be expected to have knowledge of an issuing State's criminal law, or even to have knowledge of its application to them.[42]

In one case, the Strasbourg Court has applied a requirement that the jurisdictional aspects of criminal law must be of sufficient quality, in the context of justifying lawful detention in a requested state pursuant to an extradition warrant. This analysis is surely applicable by analogy to Article 7 ECHR, although the Court ruled that Article 7 did not apply to pre-trial detention.[43]

Secondly, as regards double jeopardy, Article 4(1) of the Seventh Protocol to the ECHR, which several Member States have not ratified,[44] sets out a rule against double jeopardy in a single State: '[n]o one shall be liable to be tried or punished again in criminal proceedings under the jurisdiction of the same State for an offence for which he has already been finally acquitted or convicted in accordance with the law and penal procedure of that State'. Article 4(2) permits proceedings to be reopened in the event of 'if there is evidence of new or newly discovered facts, or if there has been a fundamental defect in the previous proceedings, which could affect the outcome of the case'. Derogation from the right in national emergencies is not permitted.[45] A similar provision appears in Article 14 of the ICCPR, which unlike the ECHR Protocol, has been ratified by every EU Member State. The ICCPR provision does not explicitly limit the application of the principle to one State, but the Human Rights Committee has assumed that such a territorial limitation is implicit.[46] Moreover, the ICCPR rule does not provide for a derogation, but rather can be suspended in emergency situations. It should be noted that some Member States have reservations on the Seventh Protocol provision, on the one hand, and the ICCPR, on the other.[47]

In the case law of the Strasbourg Court, the ECHR rule applies to prevent multiple criminal penalties being applied in respect of the same act, regardless of whether a person has formerly been acquitted or prosecuted; the concept of a 'criminal' offence has the same broad autonomous meaning which the Court has applied to Article 6 ECHR; and the definition of the same 'acts' includes

---

[41] See 9.5–9.7 above.

[42] The extra-territorial application of an issuing State's law to its own residents (ie who have allegedly breached that law on a visit to another State) is a different matter, as they can be expected to have knowledge of that State's law and its scope of application.

[43] *Stephens v Malta (No 1)*, 21 Apr 2009.

[44] On the ratification status of the Seventh Protocol, see Appendix I.

[45] Art 4(3) of the Seventh Protocol.

[46] Decision of 19 July 1986 in *AP v Italy* (Communication 204/1986, CCPR/C/31/D/204/1986, para 7.3).

[47] For details, see S Peers, 'Double Jeopardy and EU Law: Time for a Change?' (2006) 8 EJLR 199.

all criminal charges that are related to the same set of circumstances.[48] The case law on the latter element of the rule was confusing, and in 2009 the European Court of Human Rights revised its case law, following, inter alia, the jurisprudence of the EU's Court of Justice on this issue, and deciding that the rule applied to 'the prosecution or trial of a second "offence" in so far as it arises from identical facts or facts which are substantially the same'.[49] Moreover, '[t]he guarantee...becomes relevant on commencement of a new prosecution, where a prior acquittal or conviction has already acquired the force of *res judicata*', because it was a 'safeguard against being tried or being liable to be tried again in new proceedings rather than a prohibition on a second conviction or acquittal'.[50] The underlying test was therefore whether there was a 'set of concrete factual circumstances involving the same defendant and inextricably linked together in time and space, the existence of which must be demonstrated in order to secure a conviction or institute criminal proceedings'.[51] The rule applies as soon as there is a 'final judgment', ie it does not apply as long as an ordinary appeal is possible, but does apply even if there is still a possibility of 'extraordinary remedies such as a request for reopening of the proceedings or an application for extension of the expired time-limit'.[52]

Finally, it should be noted that the Strasbourg Court has ruled that the transfer of a sentence does not amount to a second set of proceedings.[53]

11.3.2. Application to EU law

Any obligations relating to jurisdictional issues deriving from Articles 5 or 7 ECHR must apply to EU law, given that the relevant rights are included within the EU's Charter of Fundamental Rights and the general principles of EU law.[54]

As for double jeopardy, the general principles of EU law contain a rule against it in *administrative* proceedings,[55] which does not generally extend to acts committed in third States.[56] The Court of Justice has referred to the rules as a 'fundamental

---

[48] See particularly *Gradinger v Austria*, 23 Oct 1995 (A328-C) and *Fischer v Austria*, 29 May 2001, which distinguished on the third point between *Gradinger* and the apparently contradictory judgment in *Oliveira v Switzerland* (Reports 1998-V). *Fischer* was followed in *WF v Austria*, 30 May 2002, and *Sailer v Austria*, 6 June 2002.

[49] *Zolotukhin v Russia*, 10 Feb 2009, para 82. On the EU rules, see 11.8 below. See subsequently *Tsonyo Tsonev v Bulgaria (No 2)*, 14 Jan 2010.   [50] Para 83, ibid.

[51] Para 84, ibid.   [52] Para 108, ibid; see also *Nikitin v Russia* [2004] ECHR-VIII.

[53] Decision in *Veermae v Finland* (15 Mar 2005).   [54] See 9.3.5 above.

[55] See, for example, the *PVC II* judgments (Joined Cases C-238/99 P, C-244/99 P, C-245/99 P, C-247/99 P, C-250/99 P to C-252/99 P, and C-254/99 P *LVM and others v Commission* [2002] ECR I-8375). See, however, 11.4 below, as regards overlapping EU and national administrative proceedings.

[56] For example, see Cases T-223/00 *Kyowo Hakko* [2003] ECR II-2553 and T-224/00 *Archer Daniels Midland* [2003] ECR II-2597 (the latter judgment was upheld on appeal in Case C-397/03 P [2006] ECR I-4429); and C-308/04 P *SGL Carbon* v *Commission* [2006] ECR I-5977, para 26.

principle' in the context of criminal proceedings;[57] it is not clear if this is different from a 'general principle'. But the EU's Charter of Rights contains a ban on both domestic and cross-border double jeopardy (within the EU) in Article 50, which provides that:

No one shall be liable to be tried or punished again in criminal proceedings for an offence for which he or she has already been finally acquitted or convicted within the Union in accordance with the law.

The wording of the Charter clause is based on the ECHR, with extended territorial scope. This right is subject, within a single Member State, to the same limitations as the ECHR right; the Charter's general limitations rule governs the application of the right in cross-border situations.[58] Since the Charter provision does not refer only to national proceedings, it would apply equally to the EPP, if that post were established.

Despite the provisions of the Charter, the ECHR rules, and the general principles of EU law, Court of Justice case law from 2006 emphasized the distinction between the ECHR rules and the provisions of the Schengen *acquis* which extend the double jeopardy principle to relations between Member States (and Schengen associates), on the grounds that the Schengen rules applied to the same 'acts', while the ECHR and ICCPR rules applied to the same 'offence'.[59] However, as we have seen, the interpretation of the ECHR rules by the European Court of Human Rights has subsequently been aligned to the Court of Justice's interpretation of the Schengen rules, making it unnecessary to maintain such a distinction. It remains to be seen whether the EU will accede to the Seventh Protocol to the ECHR, and thereby become bound by the ECHR definition of the rule.[60]

Finally, it should be noted that in the view of one Advocate General, a repeat extradition request does not amount to a violation of the protection against double jeopardy.[61]

11.4. Impact of other EU law

The protection of EU financial interests, or the enforcement of other EU obligations by imposing criminal penalties, can be linked to the interpretation of the EU cross-border double jeopardy rules, as seen in the *Gasparini* judgment, where the question of whether prosecutions by different Member States related to the

---

[57] Case C-436/04 *van Esbroek* [2006] ECR I-2333, para 40.
[58] Arts 52(3) and 52(1) of the Charter ([2007] OJ C 303) respectively.
[59] *Van Esbroek* (n 57 above), para 28. For detailed interpretation of these rules, see 11.8 below.
[60] On the process of EU accession to the ECHR, see 2.3 above.
[61] Opinion in Case C-296/08 PPU *Santesteban Goicoechea* [2008] ECR I-6307.

same acts required an interpretation of EU customs law.[62] Furthermore, as noted already,[63] EU law also establishes a double jeopardy principle in administrative proceedings, in particular competition proceedings. The standard test is that there must be a 'threefold condition of identity of the facts, unity of offender and unity of the legal interest protected. Under that principle, therefore, the same person cannot be sanctioned more than once for a single unlawful course of conduct designed to protect the same legal asset.'[64] As we shall see later on, the third of these criteria does not apply to the EU law rules governing double jeopardy in criminal cases.

11.5. Asserting jurisdiction

There is no standard set of agreed rules, within the UN, the Council of Europe, or the EU, to determine which State's courts have jurisdiction over a crime. This contrasts with the great willingness of EU Member States, particularly (but not only) in the EU context, to agree rules on civil jurisdiction and conflict of law in civil cases.[65] As a result, different national jurisdictional principles overlap, possibly resulting in double criminal liability,[66] or conversely a vacuum of jurisdiction. All states agree on the 'territoriality' principle: crimes committed wholly or partly within their territory fall within their jurisdiction. Although this principle may appear simple, it can be difficult to apply when only certain elements of the crime took place in one Member State, or where the full offence occurred in one Member State but inchoate offences in another.

In addition, many states, most Member States among them, apply some form of 'extra-territorial' jurisdiction for acts committed abroad, at least for certain crimes.[67] This can take the form of: the 'active personality' principle (jurisdiction over acts committed by nationals of a state outside that state); the 'passive personality' principle (jurisdiction over acts committed *against* nationals of a state outside that state); the 'protective' principle (jurisdiction over acts committed against the essential interests of a state outside that state); the 'representational' principle (where a state agrees to assume the jurisdiction which in principle belongs to another state); and the 'universal jurisdiction' principle (where a crime

---

[62] Case C-467/04, [2006] ECR I-9199.   [63] See 11.3.2 above.

[64] See, for instance, Joined Cases C-204/00 P, 205/00 P, 211/00 P, 213/00 P, 217/00 P, and 219/00 P, *Aalborg Portland and others v Commission* [2004] ECR I-123, para 338.

[65] See generally ch 8. Note that in international criminal law, unlike civil law, the choice of law automatically determines the choice of court, because few if any courts are willing to apply foreign criminal law.

[66] Some crimes, particularly if committed over the Internet, could even give rise to liability in more than two states.

[67] See G Gilbert, 'Crimes *Sans Frontières*: Jurisdictional Problems in English Law' (1992) BYIL 415.

is considered so heinous that all states have jurisdiction in principle to try a person accused of it).

EU measures have required Member States to adopt certain forms of the above principles in order to prohibit or criminalize certain acts effectively. The money laundering Directive requires Member States to prohibit laundering even if the activities which gave rise to the laundered money were perpetrated in another Member State or a third country.[68] In *Ebony Maritime*, the Court of Justice effectively treated breaches of EU economic sanctions rules as offences with universal jurisdiction, because the offence of entering Yugoslav waters imposed to implement to EC legislation could only be committed outside Member States' territory.[69] Therefore, all it took for a sanctions-breaker to fall within the criminal jurisdiction of a Member State was entry into a Member State's territory after an alleged breach of the sanctions, even when the alleged sanctions-breaker had only entered a Member State's waters after being boarded, commandeered, and then towed to a Member State's port. The nationality of the flag State, the vessel owner, the cargo owner, and presumably the crew, was irrelevant. However, the Court of Justice did not suggest that all EU legislation should receive such wide interpretation; instead, it appears that its interpretation was based upon the Security Council Resolution which the EU was implementing. Indeed, the UK Divisional Court is surely correct to conclude that, as a general principle, Community law (as it was then) does not alter national rules on criminal jurisdiction.[70]

Although there are no general EU rules on criminal jurisdiction, most EU measures concerning substantive criminal law have set out specific rules requiring or permitting Member States to assert their jurisdiction over criminal matters. The adopted measures within the scope of Article 83(1) TFEU (the current legal base concerning substantive criminal law not linked to 'Community' law, as it was previously known) which include provisions on jurisdiction comprise the following:[71]

(a) a Framework Decision on terrorism;[72]
(b) a Framework Decision on trafficking in persons;[73]
(c) a Framework Decision on child pornography and prostitution;[74]
(d) a Framework Decision on drug trafficking;[75]

---

[68] Art 1(3) of Dir 2005/60 ([2005] OJ L 309/15).   [69] Case C-177/95 [1997] ECR I-1111.

[70] *Ken Lane Transport Limited* [1995] 3 CMLR 140 (Div Ct).

[71] This list follows the order of crimes listed in Art 83(1) TFEU. On the ratification status of the Conventions and Protocols (including those listed below), see Appendix I. On the implementation deadlines for the Framework Decisions (again including those listed below), see 10.5.1.2 above. On Art 83(1) itself, see 10.2.3 and 10.2.4 above.

[72] [2002] OJ L 164/3. This Framework Decision was amended in 2008 ([2008] OJ L 330/21), but the amendment only concerns the definition of criminal offences, not the related rules on jurisdiction.   [73] [2002] OJ L 162/1.

[74] [2004] OJ L 13/44.   [75] [2004] OJ L 335/8.

(e)   a Convention and a Framework Decision on corruption;[76]
(f)   a Framework Decision on counterfeiting currency;[77]
(g)   a Framework Decision on counterfeiting non-cash instruments;[78]
(h)   a Framework Decision on attacks on information systems;[79] and
(i)   a Framework Decision on organized crime.[80]

As regards issues within the scope of Article 83(2) TFEU (which concerns criminal law within the scope of Community law, as it was previously known), the
following adopted measures include rules on jurisdiction:

(a)   a Framework Decision on racism and xenophobia;[81]
(b)   a Framework Decision on facilitation of illegal entry and residence;[82] and
(c)   a Convention on protection of the EU's financial interests (PIF Convention),
      with two Protocols.[83]

The Framework Decisions on environmental crime and on ship-source pollution
contained provisions relating to jurisdiction, but these rules are not considered
further here, since both measures were annulled by the Court of Justice and the
Directives which replaced them do not contain jurisdictional rules.[84] Also, the
Directive on the prohibition of employment of irregular migrants is not considered here either, because there are no jurisdictional rules attached to the criminal
offences set out in that Directive.[85]

As for proposed measures, the Commission has proposed Directives which
would replace the existing Framework Decisions on trafficking in persons and
sexual offences against children; the former proposal has been agreed by the
Council.[86]

The basic rule for jurisdiction in these measures is that Member States *must*
take territorial jurisdiction when a crime was committed partly or wholly in their

---

[76] Convention ([1997] OJ C 195/1); Framework Decision on private corruption ([2003] OJ L 192/54).   [77] [2000] OJ L 140/1.

[78] [2001] OJ L 149/1.   [79] [2005] OJ L 69/67.   [80] [2008] OJ L 300/42.

[81] Framework Decision ([2008] OJ L 328/55), which replaces a prior Joint Action ([1996] OJ L 185/5) as from 28 Nov 2008 (Art 10(1), Framework Decision).   [82] [2002] OJ L 328/1.

[83] Convention ([1995] OJ C 316/48); First Protocol ([1996] OJ C 313/1); and Second Protocol ([1997] OJ C 221/12).

[84] [2003] OJ L 29/55 and [2005] OJ L 255/164 (Framework Decisions); Cases C-176/03 *Commission v Council* [2005] ECR I-7879 and C-440/05 *Commission v Council* [2007] ECR I-9097 (Court judg-ments); Dirs 2008/99 ([2008] OJ L 328/28) and 2009/123 ([2009] OJ L 280/52). The Directives do however have a specific territorial scope (ie the territorial scope of the measures listed in the Annex to Dir 2008/99, and Art 3 of Dir 2005/35 ([2005] OJ L 255/11), which Dir 2009/123 amended).

[85] Dir 2009/52 ([2009] OJ L 168/24). However, the Directive has a defined territorial scope, as it applies to the employment of an irregular migrant who is 'present on the territory of a Member State, who does not fulfil, or no longer fulfils, the conditions for stay or residence in that Member State' (Art 2(b), Dir 2009/52).

[86] COM (2010) 94 and 95, 29 Mar 2010; for the agreed text of the trafficking Directive (which must still be negotiated with the EP), see Council doc 10845/10, 10 June 2010. The proposed Directive replac-ing the PIF Convention (COM (2001) 272, 23 May 2001) does not contain jurisdiction provisions.

territory, and *may* take jurisdiction where an act was committed by one of their nationals or for the benefit of a legal person established there (active personality principle).[87] Also, most EU measures set out an 'extradite or prosecute' rule, which requires a Member State which does not extradite its own nationals to prosecute them instead for the offences established by the EU measures.[88]

However, there are several variations on this approach. The 'extradite or prosecute' rule is not set out uniformly.[89] Several measures spell out in more detail what the territorial principle entails. The PIF Convention specifies that it may apply where a person on the territory assists or induces the commission of a fraud on another Member State's territory, while the Framework Decision on terrorism extends the concept to vessels flying a Member State's flag and aircraft registered there, and the Framework Decision on organized crime specifies that territorial jurisdiction applies whenever the acts take place on national territory, 'wherever the criminal organisation is based or pursues its criminal activities'. The Framework Decision on attacks on information systems requires assertion of such jurisdiction whenever a person is physically present (wherever the relevant information system is located) or against an information system on its territory (wherever the offender is physically located). Similarly, the Framework Decision (and the proposed Directive) on sexual exploitation and child pornography requires Member States to assert jurisdiction whenever an offence is committed by a system accessed from its territory, whether or not the computer system is on its territory.

---

[87] For the jurisdiction rules, see: Art 9, Framework Decision on terrorism (n 72 above); Art 6, Framework Decision on trafficking in persons (n 73 above); Art 8, Framework Decision on sexual exploitation and child pornography (n 74 above); Art 8, Framework Decision on drug trafficking (n 75 above); Art 7, Framework Decision on private corruption (n 76 above); Art 7, corruption Convention (*idem*); Art 7, Framework Decision on counterfeiting currency (n 77 above); Art 9, Framework Decision on payment card fraud (n 78 above); Art 10, Framework Decision on attacks on information systems (n 79 above); Art 7, Framework Decision on organized crime (n 80 above); Art 9, Framework Decision on racism and xenophobia (n 81 above); Art 4, Framework Decision on facilitation of illegal entry and residence (n 82 above); Art 4, PIF Convention (n 83 above); Art 16, proposed Dir on sexual offences, and Art 9, agreed Dir on trafficking in persons (both ibid). On the jurisdiction rules in pre-Amsterdam measures, see the first edition of this book, at 162–164.

[88] Art 9(3), Framework Decision on terrorism; Art 6(3), Framework Decision on trafficking in persons; Art 8(3), Framework Decision on sexual exploitation and child pornography; Art 8(3), Framework Decision on drug trafficking; Art 7(3), Framework Decision on private corruption; Art 8, corruption Convention; Art 10, Framework Decision on payment card fraud; Art 10(3), Framework Decision on attacks on information systems; Art 7(3), Framework Decision on organized crime; Art 5, Framework Decision on facilitation of illegal entry and residence; and Art 5, PIF Convention (all ibid). There is no such rule in the Framework Decisions on counterfeiting currency or on racism and xenophobia, in the proposal for a Dir on sexual offences against children, or in the agreed text of the Dir on trafficking in persons. On the nationality exception to extradition, see further 9.5.1 above.

[89] The Framework Decision on terrorism requires Member States to establish jurisdiction regardless of the nationality of the fugitive or the location of the offence; but it does not explicitly require Member States to *prosecute*. Also, the Framework Decisions on corruption, trafficking in persons, sexual offences, attacks on information systems, drug trafficking, and organized crime require prosecution (in lieu of extradition) regardless of where the offence was committed; the other measures only require it if the offence was committed in a Member State.

The corruption Convention enables (but does not require) Member States to take a form of 'passive personality' jurisdiction in certain circumstances. More importantly, several measures place additional obligations on Member States, requiring them to take extraterritorial jurisdiction. The Framework Decision on counterfeiting currency requires at least those Member States which have adopted the euro to take jurisdiction regardless of the nationality of the offender and place of commission of the offence is irrelevant where the euro is concerned. The Framework Decision on terrorism requires Member States to take jurisdiction based on a broad concept of the active personality principle (including acts committed by 'residents' and legal persons as well as citizens) and jurisdiction based on a broad concept of the protective principle, where acts are committed 'against the institutions or people' of that Member State or an EU institution or body based there. This may be intended to extend as far as the passive personality principle, depending on whether an attack on 'the people' also includes every attack on individual nationals of a Member State. Even wider jurisdiction is not precluded.[90] Finally, the agreed text of the Directive on trafficking in persons, and the proposed Directive on sexual offences against children, would require Member States to impose their jurisdiction on their nationals,[91] and to waive any requirement 'that the acts are a criminal offence at the place where they were performed' or 'that the prosecution can only be initiated following a report made by the victim in the place where the offence was committed, or a denunciation from the State of the place where the offence was committed'.

11.6. Conflicts of jurisdiction

In light of the encouragement, and in some cases the requirement, for Member States to assert extraterritorial jurisdiction, as well as the possibility that elements of a crime will fall within the territorial jurisdiction of more than one Member State,[92] there are obviously an increasing number of circumstances where multiple Member States will have criminal jurisdiction as regards a particular act. This is problematic because it is objectionable in principle for any person to be prosecuted more than once for the same acts, even by different States, and to that end the EU has banned such multiple prosecutions as a rule—although the ban only applies *after* one of those prosecutions has resulted in a final judgment.[93] But

---

[90] For a comparison of the jurisdiction rules in the Framework Decision (before its amendment in 2008) and the UN Conventions on terrorism, see S Peers, 'EU Responses to Terrorism' (2003) 52 ICLQ 227 at 233–234.

[91] The proposed Dir on sexual offences would also require Member States to impose their jurisdiction on their residents.   [92] See 11.5 above.

[93] See 11.8 below.

since only one prosecution can normally lead to a final judgment, it would be better also to avoid multiple *pending* prosecutions against the same person for the same act in different Member States (known as *lis pendens*) as well, in order to prevent wasting the time and resources of the police, prosecution, and judicial authorities and an unjustified burden on the accused. While the obvious way to do this would be to agree binding rules allocating criminal jurisdiction as between Member States, there are, as we have already seen, no such rules agreed at EU or any other level.

In particular, the Council of Europe Member States did not want to agree on a draft Convention to this end, drawn up by the Council of Europe's Parliamentary Assembly in 1965.[94] However, to take some steps towards avoiding multiple prosecutions, Council of Europe members drew up in 1972 a Convention on the transfer of proceedings in criminal matters, which included rules not only on the transfer of proceedings but also on the conflict of pending proceedings and on cross-border double jeopardy.[95]

On the conflict issue, the Council of Europe Convention provides that any State which becomes aware of any proceedings pending in another State party 'against the same person in respect of the same offence' must consider whether it can waive, suspend, or transfer its proceedings.[96] In these circumstances, the State which has discovered the existence of the parallel proceedings must inform that State where proceedings were already underway if it does not intend to waive or suspend proceedings.[97] In that case, 'the States concerned shall endeavour as far as possible to determine' which single State shall 'continue to conduct proceedings', after evaluating each of the circumstances in which the Convention provides for a possible request to transfer proceedings.[98] During this process a judgment on the merits must be suspended for up to thirty days. However, the process does not apply if the trial has already been opened in either State.[99] If agreement is reached, then the rules on the transfer of proceedings in the Convention are applicable:[100] this means that the State which has waived or suspended its proceedings may not continue with a prosecution, unless the State where the prosecution was centralized discontinues or does not institute proceedings.[101]

Within the EU, a Convention on the transfer of proceedings drawn up within the EPC context in 1990 did not address the issue of conflicts of juris-

---

[94] Rec 420 of the Parliamentary Assembly, online at: <http://assembly.coe.int/main.asp?Link=/documents/adoptedtext/ta65/erec420.htm>.

[95] ETS 73. About half of the Member States have ratified this Convention. For ratification details, see Appendix I. On the other rules in this Convention, see 11.7 and 11.8 below.

[96] Art 30(1) of the Convention. Political and military offences are excluded.

[97] Art 30(2) of the Convention.

[98] Art 31(1) of the Convention, referring to Art 8 of the Convention.

[99] Art 31(2) of the Convention.   [100] Arts 33 and 34 of the Convention.

[101] Art 21 of the Convention.

diction (other than when proceedings were transferred).[102] Subsequently, some EU measures contain rules on priority jurisdiction, to be applied in the event that more than one Member State has jurisdiction over an offence. The Framework Decisions on terrorism and organized crime require Member States to take (respectively) 'sequential account' and 'special account' of territorial jurisdiction, followed by active personality, passive personality, and the State where the person was found.[103] For its part, the Framework Decision on attacks on information systems states that Member States *may* take sequential account of territorial jurisdiction, followed by active personality, then the state where the person was found.[104] In each of these measures, the aim is to centralize proceedings in a particular Member State, and Member States should use any mechanism within the EU to attempt to coordinate jurisdiction; the Framework Decision on organized crime refers explicitly to the possibility of using Eurojust for this purpose.[105] In comparison, the Framework Decision on counterfeiting the euro and the fraud and corruption Conventions simply encourage Member States to cooperate with a view to centralizing the prosecution in a single Member State, but without setting rules for priority jurisdiction.[106]

More general provisions on the *lis pendens* issue were included in a Greek proposal for a Framework Decision that set out a list of criteria that would apply where prosecutions for the same acts were pending in multiple Member States.[107] Since Member States could not agree on this proposal (which also would have amended the Schengen double jeopardy rules), discussions were suspended pending a communication from the Commission on the issue.[108] The Commission's subsequent Green Paper, which also addressed the connected issue of the cross-border double jeopardy rules,[109] suggested that there should be rules on informing other Member States about (potentially) conflicting pending proceedings, a consultation procedure between the Member States concerned, and possibly a dispute settlement process. There would be a requirement to centralize prosecutions in a single jurisdiction, with criteria to guide the selection of that jurisdiction on a case-by-case basis. Developments in this area would be linked to a review of the double jeopardy rules, which could be reformed (for instance, to withdraw some

---

[102] For the text of this Convention, see: <http://www.asser.nl/eurowarrant-webroot/documents/cms_eaw_12_1_Agreement1990.11.06.pdf>.

[103] Respectively [2002] OJ L 164/3, Art 9(2), and [2008] OJ L 300/42, Art 7(2).

[104] Art 10(4) of the Framework Decision ([2005] OJ L 69/67).

[105] On the role of Eurojust, see 11.9 below.

[106] Art 7(3) of Framework Decision ([2000] OJ L 140/1); Art 6(2) of PIF Convention ([1995] OJ C 316/48); and Art 9(2) of corruption Convention ([1997] OJ C 195/1).

[107] [2003] OJ C 100/24, Art 3.

[108] See statement in JHA Council press release, 19 July 2004.

[109] COM (2005) 696, 23 Dec 2005; see also the staff working paper (SEC (2005) 1767, 23 Dec 2005).

exceptions to those rules) in light of the creation of an effective system to agree on centralizing the prosecution at an early stage.

Member States were not enthusiastic about these suggestions, so the Commission did not make any legislative proposal. However, ultimately the Council adopted a Framework Decision on conflicts of jurisdiction in 2009, which addresses only the information and consultation aspects of this issue.[110] Member States have to apply the Framework Decision by 15 June 2012.[111] The specific provisions on prioritizing jurisdiction that are set out in a number of earlier Framework Decisions harmonizing substantive criminal law (see above) have not been repealed by this Framework Decision, but neither is there any provision governing the relationship between this measure and those earlier acts.

The 2009 Framework Decision concerns only cases where parallel proceedings might result in the final disposal of the proceedings in multiple Member States, entailing a violation of the cross-border double jeopardy rules, also known as the *ne bis in idem* principle, as defined in the Schengen Convention rules as interpreted by the Court of Justice.[112] It should be pointed out, however, that the double jeopardy principle is violated not only by the final disposal of a case in multiple Member States, but also as soon as a second *prosecution* is begun (or continued) following the first final judgment issued in a Member State.[113] Moreover the *ne bis in idem* principle applies to Schengen associates, whereas the Framework Decision only applies to EU Member States.[114] Since the double jeopardy rules only apply where the same acts were (allegedly) committed by the same person,[115] a declaration adopted by the Council states that it will consider further measures as regards cases where there are proceedings in multiple Member States as regards different persons being tried in relation to the same or related facts, or in respect of the same criminal organization.[116]

The process established by the Framework Decision also aims to 'reach consensus on any effective solution aimed at avoiding the adverse consequences arising from such parallel proceedings'.[117] The Framework Decision does not apply to EU competition proceedings.[118]

The first obligation under the Framework Decision is for a Member State's authorities which have 'reasonable grounds to believe that parallel proceedings are being conducted in another Member State' to contact the authorities of the other

---

[110] [2009] OJ L 328/42.

[111] Art 16. All references in this section are to this Framework Decision except where otherwise indicated.

[112] Art 1(2)(a). See also the reference to the Schengen double jeopardy rules and case law (recital 3 in the preamble).   [113] See 11.8 below.

[114] See 11.2.5 above.   [115] See the definition of 'parallel proceedings' in Art 3(a).

[116] Council doc 10225/09, 20 May 2009. See also Art 32 of the Council of Europe Convention on the transfers of proceedings.   [117] Art 1(2)(b).

[118] Art 2(2). See 11.4 above.

Member State in order to 'confirm the existence' of those proceedings.[119] This authority must supply the contacted authority with basic information about the relevant criminal proceedings underway in that state.[120] The contacted authority then has an obligation to reply to the contacting authority within any deadline indicated by the latter, or otherwise 'without undue delay'. If the person concerned is in custody, the contacted authority must reply urgently.[121] This authority must indicate whether parallel proceedings are underway and if so, whether a 'final decision' has been delivered in the proceedings.[122]

If parallel proceedings are underway, the next step will be an obligation for the authorities concerned to enter into a consultation process. This consultation will have to 'aim to reach consensus on any effective solution aimed at avoiding the adverse consequences arising from such parallel proceedings'. The process 'may, where appropriate, lead to the concentration of the criminal proceedings in one Member State'.[123] The preamble to the Framework Decision refers vaguely to other possible solutions, and also indicates that the proceedings could be concentrated by means of a transfer of proceedings.[124] An indication of the criteria which may be taken into account during this consultation is set out in the preamble to the Framework Decision, which refers to guidelines on allocating jurisdiction adopted by Eurojust in 2003,[125] 'and take into account for example the place where the major part of the criminality occurred, the place where the majority of the loss was sustained, the location of the suspected or accused person and possibilities for securing its surrender or extradition to other jurisdictions, the nationality or residence of the suspected or accused person, significant interests of the suspected or accused person, significant interests of victims and witnesses, the admissibility of evidence or any delays that may occur'.[126]

Despite the consultation process established by the Framework Decision, it is clear that this process will not require authorities to waive or accept jurisdiction unless they choose to.[127] Moreover, even if the process leads to agreement on the concentration of proceedings, the Framework Decision does not specify the obvious conclusion that the other Member State(s) must waive or suspend their proceedings in favour of the Member State in which proceedings are

[119] Art 5(1). The obligation does not apply when the former authorities are already aware of the existence of such proceedings by other means (Art 5(3)). On the definition of the authorities concerned, see Art 2(d). On the concept of 'reasonable grounds', see recital 5 of the preamble to the Framework Decision.   [120] Art 8(1).

[121] Art 6(1).

[122] Art 9(1). Presumably this refers to the definitions which apply pursuant to the Schengen double jeopardy rules (see 11.8 below).   [123] Art 10(1).

[124] Recital 4 of the preamble. See 11.7 below.

[125] See Annex I to the Eurojust 2003 annual report, and more generally 11.9 below.

[126] Recital 9 of the preamble. These suggestions are similar, but not identical, to the Eurojust guidelines (ibid).   [127] Recital 11 of the preamble.

concentrated.[128] But intriguingly, the preamble to the Framework Decision does suggest that in Member States that apply the 'legality' principle (ie mandatory prosecution in principle, once information is available about an alleged offence), that principle 'should be understood and applied in a way that it is deemed to be fulfilled when *any* Member State ensures the criminal prosecution of a particular criminal offence'.[129]

If a consensus cannot be reached, then the issue 'shall where appropriate' be referred to Eurojust, which, as noted already, has a possible role in attempting to settle conflicts of jurisdiction between Member States.[130] If consensus is reached on concentrating proceedings, then the authorities in the Member State where proceedings are concentrated must inform the other Member State(s) of the outcome of the process.[131] However, there is no provision to regulate what happens if the Member State where proceedings are concentrated declines to continue prosecution (where this decision falls short of a 'final judgment' for the purpose of the double jeopardy rules) or where the Member State(s) which have waived or suspended prosecutions decide that they wish to rescind their agreement to concentrate proceedings.

The Framework Decision permits Member States to maintain in force or conclude bilateral or multilateral agreements in order to extend the Framework Decision or to simplify or facilitate the processes which it sets out.[132] Unlike the 'standard' final provisions of many Framework Decisions regulating mutual recognition, this measure does not expressly replace the corresponding provisions of the relevant Council of Europe Convention (in this case, the Convention on transfer of proceedings). The latter Convention should possibly be regarded as falling within the scope of Member States' powers to maintain or conclude treaties dealing with the same subject matter; and in any event the preamble to the Framework Decision specifies that it is 'without prejudice' to this Convention or any other arrangements between Member States.[133]

Comparing the Framework Decision with the Council of Europe Convention, the latter (unlike the former) does not establish a formal procedure for information exchange between the States concerned once there are grounds to suspect the existence of parallel proceedings. But the Convention does provide for express criteria for considering whether to centralize proceedings, and it clearly provides for the consequences of centralizing prosecution, including regulation of the important issue of when the power to prosecute would revert to the State(s) which have waived its (their) proceedings. The risk is that by

---

[128] See the vague recital 13 in the preamble. However, recital 11 in the preamble implies *a contrario* that a consensus on concentrating proceedings in one Member State will result in the discontinuation of proceedings in the other Member State(s).

[129] Recital 12 of the preamble; emphasis added.

[130] Art 12(2); see 11.9 below. The Framework Decision does not amend the Eurojust Decision on this point (see Art 12(1)).   [131] Art 13.

[132] Art 15.   [133] Recital 15 of the preamble.

creating a system for exchange of information without creating an obligation to centralize jurisdiction, the Framework Decision will lead to more *lis pendens* cases, not fewer, for instance because in some cases the informed Member State's authorities will (or must) begin a prosecution that they would not otherwise have begun (because those authorities would otherwise not have known about those facts). While the preamble to the Framework Decision states that it should not create a conflict where none existed anyway,[134] this depends on how the legality principle (ie the obligation to prosecute which exists in some national laws) is applied in practice, given that the main text of the Framework Decision does not expressly require Member States to waive that principle merely because another Member State is prosecuting an offence. Moreover, the consultation procedure could be (ab)used to 'forum-shop' the location to prosecute which is most convenient to the prosecution, or to manipulate the exceptions to the double jeopardy rules so that a second prosecution could take place even after a final judgment in one Member State.[135] The position of the individual to complain about the location of the prosecution is not enhanced by the Framework Decision.[136]

How should the Framework Decision be assessed? Ultimately this measure is disappointing, because it does not take sufficient steps to avoid multiple prosecutions, by creating an obligation to centralize prosecutions in principle, subject to objective criteria for the choice of jurisdiction which do not permit either the prosecution or the defence to forum-shop. Those criteria should in particular aim to reduce significantly the application of extraterritorial jurisdiction by Member States. Such jurisdiction is objectionable in principle, unless the suspects would otherwise benefit from impunity from their actions, because of the principle of a State's sovereignty over its territory and the reasonable expectation of a State's citizens and residents that acts they commit on the territory of that State will be subject to the criminal law of that State—over which that State's citizens exercise democratic control. Moreover, where the suspects lack knowledge of the substantive criminal law of, and/or the existence of the extraterritorial jurisdiction asserted by, the State asserting it, this is arguably a breach of Article 7 ECHR.[137] The traditional rationale for asserting extraterritorial jurisdiction was the refusal of many States to extradite their own nationals, but the abolition of this rule in the context of the European Arrest Warrant renders this traditional rationale irrelevant.[138]

Finally, the lack of harmonization of national jurisdictional rules means that Member States may refuse to apply EU mutual recognition measures on jurisdictional grounds.[139] Some degree of harmonization of these rules could mean

---

[134] Recital 12 in the preamble.
[135] See Art 55 of the Schengen Convention ([2000] OJ L 239), discussed further in 11.8 below.
[136] Recital 17 in the preamble.   [137] See 11.3.1 above.
[138] See 9.5.2 above.   [139] See 9.5–9.7 above.

that those grounds for refusal could be reconsidered.[140] But in the absence of harmonization, those grounds for refusal should certainly be fully retained and applied, otherwise the effect of the abolition of dual criminality rules, coupled with the removal of the ban on extradition of a State's nationals, risks the possible application of extraterritorial criminal jurisdiction even to acts which were not criminal on the territory where they were committed.[141]

11.7. Transfer of proceedings

One method of addressing jurisdictional issues, in particular conflicts of jurisdiction and the prevention of cross-border double jeopardy, is to establish a formal system for the transfer of criminal proceedings between States. As noted already, a Council of Europe Convention from 1972 sets out such a system, but only about half of EU Member States have ratified it.[142] Even fewer Member States have ratified an earlier Council of Europe Convention on road traffic offences, which provides for both transfer of proceedings and recognition of judgments.[143] Also as noted already, EU Member States agreed an EPC Convention on this issue among themselves, but this Convention did not attract sufficient ratifications to enter into force.[144] However, there is a brief reference to this issue in the Council of Europe Convention on mutual assistance in criminal matters, which all Member States have ratified.[145]

For some time, this issue was not on the EU's agenda, but in July 2009 a group of Member States tabled an initiative for a Framework Decision on this issue,[146] based broadly on the Council of Europe Convention of 1972. However, this proposal was not adopted or agreed before the Treaty of Lisbon entered into force, and has not been tabled since; and there is no mention of this issue in the Stockholm programme or the action plan to implement that programme.

11.8. Double jeopardy[147]

The lack of harmonization of criminal jurisdiction rules and the inadequate or partial rules on the conflict of jurisdiction and the transfer of proceedings create

---

[140] See the Commission's Green Paper (n 109 above).

[141] See the problematic proposal for a European Investigation Order (9.6.1.3 above).

[142] On the ratification details, see ibid.

[143] ETS 52. On the ratification details, see Appendix I. On the enforcement of foreign judgments concerning road traffic offences, see 9.7.1.1 below.

[144] ETS 73. See the ratification information in Appendix I.

[145] Art 21 of that Convention (ETS 30), which refers to the process for transmitting information from one Party to the courts of the other Party with a view to taking proceedings in the latter. The UK, Ireland, and Malta have reservations on this provision.   [146] [2009] OJ C 219/7.

[147] See E Sharpston and J Maria Fernandez-Martin, 'Some Reflections on Schengen Free Movement Rights and the Principle of *Ne Bis in Idem*' (2007–08) 10 CYELS 413, and S Peers, 'Double Jeopardy and EU Law: Time for a Change?' (2006) 8 EJLR 199.

a risk that a person will be tried more than once for the same act or omissions in more than one Member State. As we have seen, this would violate international human rights law if it took place within one Member State,[148] but there is no general ban on cross-border double jeopardy in international human rights instruments. However, the general principles of EU law and the EU Charter of Fundamental Rights ban cross-border double jeopardy.

There are detailed rules on this issue in specific international criminal law instruments, in particular the Council of Europe Conventions on the transfer of criminal proceedings and on the international validity of criminal judgments,[149] although as noted already, not many Member States have ratified these instruments. Nevertheless, such a ban can also be found in EU measures—a reflection of the high level of integration within the EU in the area of criminal law cooperation, and a welcome and distinctive contribution by the EU to the development of international human rights law.

11.8.1. Legal framework

Between the EU Member States, the cross-border double jeopardy principle was first set out in a pre-Maastricht 1987 EPC Convention.[150] This Convention, with wording based roughly on the prior Council of Europe Conventions that had attracted only limited support, itself attracted only limited support in turn.[151] Indeed, the EPC Convention never entered into force as such, but it is applied provisionally by those Member States which have ratified it; this is relevant because those Member States include Ireland, which does not yet apply the Schengen Convention double jeopardy rules.[152] The provisions of the EPC Convention were subsequently inserted without amendment into Articles 54–58 of the Schengen Convention, and now apply to all Member States except Ireland, plus the Schengen associates.[153]

Article 54 of the Schengen Convention sets out the basic rule:

A person whose trial has been finally disposed of in one Contracting Party may not be prosecuted in another Contracting Party for the same acts provided that, if a penalty has been imposed, it has been enforced, is actually in the process of being enforced or can no longer be enforced under the laws of the sentencing Contracting Party.

---

[148] See 11.3.1 above.

[149] Respectively ETS 73 (1972), Arts 35–37, and ETS 70 (1970) Arts 53–55. There are more limited provisions in Art 9 of the Council of Europe Convention on extradition (ETS 24), as revised by Art 2 of the First Protocol to that Convention (ETS 86). For ratification details of these measures, see Appendix I.

[150] For the text, see: <http://www.asser.nl/eurowarrant-webroot/documents/cms_eaw_12_1_conv%20double%20jeopardy.pdf>.   [151] For ratification details, see Appendix I.

[152] See 11.2.5 above.

[153] [2000] OJ L 239. All further references in this section are to the Convention, unless otherwise indicated.

Article 55 then provides for possible exceptions to the rule.

1. A Contracting Party may, when ratifying, accepting or approving this Convention, declare that it is not bound by Article 54 in one or more of the following cases:
- (a) where the acts to which the foreign judgment relates took place in whole or in part in its own territory; in the latter case, however, this exception shall not apply if the acts took place in part in the territory of the Contracting Party where the judgment was delivered;
- (b) where the acts to which the foreign judgment relates constitute an offence against national security or other equally essential interests of that Contracting Party;
- (c) where the acts to which the foreign judgment relates were committed by officials of that Contracting Party in violation of the duties of their office.

2. A Contracting Party which has made a declaration regarding the exception referred to in paragraph 1(b) shall specify the categories of offences to which this exception may apply.

3. A Contracting Party may at any time withdraw a declaration relating to one or more of the exceptions referred to in paragraph 1.

4. The exceptions which were the subject of a declaration under paragraph 1 shall not apply where the Contracting Party concerned has, in connection with the same acts, requested the other Contracting Party to bring the prosecution or has granted extradition of the person concerned.

In practice, according to the Commission, seven Member States have invoked Article 55(1)(a), four have invoked Article 55(1)(b), and none have invoked Article 55(1)(c).[154] The relevant declarations have not, however, been published. It is not clear how the timing of declarations applies as regards Member States which applied the Convention after its integration into the EU legal order.[155]

Next, the Schengen Convention provides that in the event of a second prosecution, 'any period of deprivation of liberty served in the [first] Contracting Party arising from those acts shall be deducted from any penalty imposed'. Also, the second Member State must take account of any prior non-custodial sentence, to the extent provided for by national law (the 'accounting' principle, also known as the 'set-off' rule).[156] Member States must cooperate to exchange information on the potential application of these rules, once the authorities of the second Member State have reason to believe that a charge relates to the same acts which were the subject of a final decision in another Member State.[157]

---

[154] SEC (2005) 1767, 23 Dec 2005, p 47. The Member States invoking Art 55(1)(a) are Austria, Germany, Denmark, Greece, Finland, Sweden, and the UK, while Austria, Denmark, Greece, and Finland have invoked Art 55(1)(b).

[155] The Commission's information (ibid) clearly assumes that it is possible for Member States which only applied the relevant rules after 1999 (the Nordic States and the UK) to invoke the derogations, but it is not clear whether Member States which joined the EU in 2004 or 2007 can do so.   [156] Art 56.

[157] Art 57. Compare to the exchange of information on multiple pending prosecutions (11.6 above).

Finally, Member States are authorized to apply a more generous application of double jeopardy (also known as *ne bis in idem*) rules with regard to judgments taken abroad.[158]

As compared to the Council of Europe Conventions with double jeopardy rules:[159] the definition of final judgment is less precise in the Schengen rules;[160] there is only an express restriction on further prosecution in the Schengen rules, not a restriction on further sentencing or enforcement of a sentence; the derogations are narrower in the Schengen rules; the set-off rule is more generous in the Schengen rules; and the Schengen rules provide for contacts between the national authorities concerned. The Schengen rules have obviously taken the Council of Europe rules as a model, but have on the whole strengthened the double jeopardy rule in light of the greater degree of integration between Schengen states. It is striking, though, that the Court of Justice case law on the Schengen rules makes no comparison with the Council of Europe rules.

Specific *ne bis in idem* provisions apply in the EU's fraud and corruption Conventions.[161] The basic rule and the exceptions to it are identical to the Schengen Convention rules, but neither of the more specific Conventions contains a provision on cooperation; there is no requirement to specify which provisions of national law are governed by the, for example derogation for national security; there is no provision on withdrawing derogations; relevant agreements between Member States are not affected by the provisions; and (in the fraud Convention only) there is no reference to the 'accounting' principle. It is not clear whether the fraud and corruption Conventions should be regarded as *lex specialis*, or whether the Schengen rules should be regarded as taking precedence. In any case, it should be recalled that the three instruments have different temporal and territorial scope.[162] On this point, it should be noted that the explanatory memorandum for the fraud Convention asserts that Member States which are already parties to the Schengen Convention have to renew the relevant declarations for this Convention, and those Member States cannot make any declarations besides those already applicable to the Schengen Convention.[163]

---

[158] Art 58.   [159] See n 149 above.

[160] However, as will be seen below, the case law on the definition of final judgment in the Schengen rules is consistent with the more precise definitions in the Council of Europe Conventions, as regards acquittals, amnesties (and so probably pardons), lapse of time, and suspended sentences.

[161] Art 7 of the fraud Convention and Art 10 of the corruption Convention (respectively [1995] OJ C 316/48 and respectively [1997] OJ C 195/1). The former Art is extended to the First Protocol to the fraud Convention by Art 7(2) of that Protocol, and to the Second Protocol to the fraud Convention by Art 12(2) of that Protocol ([1997] OJ C 221/12). A few Member States have not yet ratified one or both of these Conventions and the relevant Protocols. For information on ratification, see Appendix I.

[162] On the territorial scope, see 10.2.5 and 11.2.5 above; on the temporal scope, see 2.2.2.3 and 2.2.5 above (as regards the Schengen rules), compared to the ratification dates of the relevant Conventions and Protocols.   [163] [1997] OJ C 191/1.

Of the Member States which have ratified the corruption Convention, nine have made declarations concerning derogations from the *ne bis in idem* rule.[164] Equally, nine Member States have derogated from the *ne bis in idem* rule applying to the Convention on the EU's financial interests and its Protocols.[165] As regards the corruption Convention, the explanatory memorandum to the Convention points out that the derogation for public officials (which seven Member States have invoked) is particularly significant, given the subject matter of the Convention.[166]

As noted above, in 2003, Greece proposed a Framework Decision which would, inter alia, have clarified and altered the Schengen provisions, but discussions were halted in July 2004 pending a Commission communication.[167] The subsequent Green Paper suggested reconsidering the Schengen double jeopardy rules, in particular as regards the clarification of the key aspects of *ne bis in idem*, the conditions for application of the principle, and the derogations from the rule, if an agreement can be reached on a procedure for allocating criminal jurisdiction.[168] The Commission did not follow up this Green Paper with a proposal.[169] Finally, it should be noted that EU mutual recognition instruments contain provisions on *ne bis in idem* as a ground for refusal of recognition of foreign decisions, although these provisions differ greatly.[170]

11.8.2. Interpreting the rules

To date, twelve national courts have sent questions to the Court of Justice on the interpretation of the Schengen double jeopardy rules: the Court has ruled in ten of these cases,[171] and two cases were withdrawn.[172] The Court has answered a number of key questions concerning application of the double jeopardy principle,

---

[164] Austria, Denmark, Spain, Italy, and Finland have derogated on all three grounds; Austria and Denmark have moreover listed the national legislation covered by the security exception. Germany has only invoked the territoriality exception; Greece and Hungary have invoked only the security and public official exception; and Sweden has invoked only the territoriality and security exception.

[165] The position is the same as regards the corruption Convention (see ibid), except that Spain and Hungary have not derogated, while Slovenia and Slovakia have invoked the security derogation.

[166] [1998] OJ C 391/1.   [167] See 11.6 above.   [168] COM (2005) 696, 23 Dec 2005.

[169] See, however, the Framework Decision on conflicts of jurisdiction (11.6 above), which addresses other aspects of this issue.   [170] See 9.5–9.7 above.

[171] Cases: C-187/01 and C-385/01 *Gozutok and Brugge* [2003] ECR I-1345; C-469/03 *Miraglia* [2005] ECR I-2009; C-436/04 *Van Esbroek* [2006] ECR I-2333; C-467/04 *Gasparini* [2006] ECR I-9199; C-150/05 *Van Straaten* [2006] ECR I-9327; C-288/05 *Kretzinger* [2007] ECR I-6441; C-367/05 *Kraaijenbrink* [2007] ECR I-6619; C-297/07 *Bourquain* [2008] ECR I-9425; and C-491/07 *Turansky* [2008] ECR I-11039. See also the opinion of 7 Sep 2010 in the pending case of *Mantello* (Case C-261/09). In fact, the *Kretzinger* and *Gasparini* cases arguably fell within the scope of the double jeopardy rules in the PIF Convention, but this issue was not raised before the Court of Justice. See the staff working paper for the Commission's report on application of the PIF Convention (SEC (2008) 188, 14 Feb 2008).   [172] Cases C-491/03 *Hiebeler* and C-272/05 *Bowens*.

but national courts will probably need to address further questions to the Court in future.

Before examining the substantive issues, it is useful to examine the overall approach adopted by the Court of Justice. First of all, the Court has stressed that the application of double jeopardy principle is not made subject to any harmonization of substantive or procedural criminal law.[173] Moreover, underlying the double jeopardy rule, 'there is a necessary implication that the Member States have mutual trust in their criminal justice systems and that each of them recognises the criminal law in force in the other Member States even when the outcome would be different if its own national law were applied'.[174] Also, 'the integration of the Schengen *acquis* (which includes Article 54 of the [Schengen Convention] into the framework of the European Union is aimed at enhancing European integration and, in particular, at enabling the Union to become more rapidly the area of freedom, security and justice which it is its objective to maintain and develop'.[175] The objective of Article 54 'is to ensure that no one is prosecuted on the same facts in several Member States on account of his having exercised his right to freedom of movement'.[176] To that end, 'freedom of movement is effectively guaranteed only if the perpetrator of an act knows that, once he has been found guilty and served his sentence, or, where applicable, been acquitted by a final judgment in a Member State, he may travel within the Schengen territory without fear of prosecution in another Member State on the basis that the legal system of that Member State treats the act concerned as a separate offence'.[177] In particular, the double jeopardy rule 'ensures that persons who, when prosecuted, have their cases finally disposed of are left undisturbed'.[178] If the application of the rules was subject to differences between national criminal law, this 'might create as many barriers to freedom of movement within the Schengen territory as there are penal systems in the Contracting States'.[179]

On the other hand, the Court has also referred to the previous Article 2 EU, according to which 'the European Union set itself the objective of maintaining and developing the Union as an area of freedom, security and justice in which the free movement of persons is assured',[180] but this takes place 'in conjunction with appropriate measures with respect to...prevention and combating of crime'.[181] Presumably this approach remains equally valid following the entry into force of the Treaty of Lisbon, since the general definition of the EU's JHA objectives has not changed.[182]

---

[173] *Gozutok and Brugge*, para 32 and *van Esbroek*, para 29.
[174] *Gozutok and Brugge*, para 33 and *van Esbroek*, para 30.
[175] *Gozutok and Brugge*, para 37.
[176] *Gozutok and Brugge*, para 38; *Miraglia*, para 32; and *van Esbroek*, para 33.
[177] Case law beginning with *Van Esbroek*, para 34.
[178] *Gasparini*, para 27.   [179] Case law beginning with *Van Esbroek*, para 35.
[180] Case law beginning with *Gozutok and Brugge*, para 36.
[181] Case law beginning with *Miraglia*, para 34.   [182] Art 3(2), revised TEU.

Finally, the Court has ruled that the intention of the Contracting Parties to the 1990 Schengen Convention, as revealed by national parliamentary documents in the context of ratifying that Convention or the 1987 EPC Convention on double jeopardy, are not relevant following the integration of the Schengen Convention into the EU legal order.[183] This implies that the integration of the Schengen rules into the EU legal order has an impact as such on their interpretation. However, it should be noted that the Court has not, to date, expressly stated that the double jeopardy rules should be interpreted uniformly,[184] although in practice it has interpreted the rules in that manner.

As for the substantive issues raised by the double jeopardy rules, the first point to consider is the scope of the rule, which has four elements: the temporal scope, the territorial scope, the personal scope, and the material scope. On the temporal scope, the Court of Justice has ruled repeatedly, beginning with the *Van Esbroek* judgment, that in the absence of any provisions on the issue of temporal scope in the Schengen Convention double jeopardy rules, the rules prohibit a second prosecution in a State applying those rules even where the first prosecution had taken place in another State *before* that State applied those rules.[185]

Starting with the territorial scope, the Court of Justice expressly ruled in the *Bourquain* case, where the initial conviction was issued by a French court in Algeria during colonial times, that 'the application of Article 54 cannot, in special circumstances such as those of that conviction, depend on the place where the sentence was pronounced, since the decisive factor is whether the sentence was pronounced by a competent judicial authority of a State which became a Contracting Party to the' Schengen Convention.[186] Moreover, the Court stated that:

[s]ince Article 54...does not...provide that the person concerned must necessarily have been tried in the territory of the Contracting Parties, that provision, the purpose of which is to protect a person whose trial has been finally disposed of against further prosecution in respect of the same acts, cannot be interpreted as meaning that Articles 54 to 58 of the [Schengen Convention] are never applicable to persons who have been tried by a Contracting Party exercising its jurisdiction beyond the territory to which that Convention applies.[187]

---

[183] *Gozutok and Brugge*, para 46. See also the Opinion in that case, dismissing the relevance of the Council working programme on mutual recognition ([2001] OJ C 12/10) for the interpretation of the rules (paras 127–131).

[184] Compare with the Court's express assertion that the Framework Decision establishing the European Arrest Warrant should be interpreted uniformly (see 9.5.2 above), and more generally the Court's approach to the interpretation of third pillar measures (2.2.2.2 above). The opinion in *Mantello* (n 171 above) implicitly calls for an autonomous interpretation of the rules.

[185] *Van Esbroek*, paras 18–24. See subsequently *Kraaijenbrink* (para 22), *Bourquain* (para 28), and *Turansky* (para 27).   [186] *Bourquain*, para 29.

[187] *Bourquain*, para 30.

With great respect, the Court's analysis is not consistent with at least the English text of the Convention, which refers quite clearly to the disposal of a trial 'in' a Contracting Party, not 'by' or 'in the *courts* of' a Contracting Party.[188]

The Court of Justice has not ruled on whether the *location of the acts* which were the subject of the final judgment is relevant. However, it stands to reason that in the absence of any express rule on this issue in Article 54 of the Convention, or any express derogation in Article 55,[189] the rule applies regardless of where the acts were committed, even if they were committed outside the EU. This point is ever more relevant to the extent that EU measures on substantive criminal law are requiring or encouraging Member States to assert more extraterritorial jurisdiction.[190]

On the personal scope of the rules, the Court of Justice ruled in *Gasparini* that only the person who had previously been subject to a final judgment within the scope of Article 54 of the Convention could benefit from the rules; his or her co-accused could not benefit from that person's immunity from further prosecution in another Member State pursuant to the double jeopardy rules, unless of course they had previously been subject to such a final judgment themselves.[191]

It follows implicitly from the *Gozutok* judgment that the nationality of the person concerned is not relevant, given that in that case a third-country national benefited from the double jeopardy rule. This makes sense within the context of the States fully applying the free movement rules of Schengen, given the freedom to travel for resident third-country nationals,[192] but this raises further questions in turn: should the interpretation of the rules be different as regards Member States that do not (yet) apply the full Schengen rules, or (in the case of the UK) are not likely to apply them for the foreseeable future? And should the interpretation of the rules be different as regards persons living outside the EU? In either case, EU citizens and their family members should benefit from the rules, since they have the right to move to and from the Schengen area and non-Schengen States or third countries (or between non-Schengen States, or to and from non-Schengen States and third countries) on the basis of EU free movement law.[193] As for third-country nationals, they should benefit also despite their more limited

---

[188] It is possible that the other language versions suggest a different interpretation than the English-language version, but in that case the Court should have explained why some language versions were preferable to others (see, for instance, Joined Cases C-261/08 and C-348/08 *Zurita Garcia* and *Choque Cabrera*, judgment of 22 Oct 2009, not yet reported). As the Court rightly observed (para 29 of the *Bourquain* judgment), due to Art 138 of the Schengen Convention, Art 54 could not apply on the basis of the colonial link between France and Algeria at the time of the judgment, because the Convention only applies to the European territory of France.

[189] There is a possible derogation from the rule in Art 54 if the acts took place partly or wholly on the territory of the second Member State, as long as they did not take place partly in the territory of the first Member State (Art 55(1)(a)), but this exception suggests by *a contrario* reasoning that Art 54 is otherwise applicable regardless of where the acts were committed.   [190] See 11.5 above.

[191] Paras 34–37 of the judgment.   [192] See 4.9 above.   [193] See 6.4.1 above.

free movement rights, because the Schengen rules implement human rights principles that should be applicable to all persons.

Another key issue of personal scope has not yet been addressed by the Court: the application of the rules to legal persons. On this point, the Second Protocol to the PIF Convention expressly states that the cross-border double jeopardy principle extends to legal persons,[194] but the other double jeopardy rules, notably the Schengen Convention, are silent on the issue. It is submitted that in light of the corporate criminal liability encouraged by many EC and EU criminal law measures,[195] along with the mutual recognition of criminal law fines applied to legal persons,[196] and given the objective of the Schengen rules to encourage free movement rights, which of course are enjoyed by legal persons as well as natural persons as a matter of EU law, the double jeopardy rules must apply to legal persons as well.[197] This would also be consistent with the application of human rights rules to legal persons.[198] However, this raises certain questions, as regards (for instance) whether a subsidiary of a company which has been subject to final decision in the first Member State should be regarded as the same 'person' as its parent company in a second Member State. Also, the question might even be raised as to whether a final decision against natural persons (ie the managers of a company) in one Member State should preclude the prosecution of the relevant legal person in another Member State (or vice versa).[199]

This brings us to the material scope of the rules. As regards legal persons (and often natural persons as well), there is an obvious distinction between administrative and criminal liability,[200] which has been a difficult issue to agree upon in the context of mutual recognition.[201] However, the Court of Justice has not yet ruled on whether the double jeopardy rules, by analogy, apply also to administrative law proceedings; it should be noted that a form of double jeopardy principle applies to EU competition law proceedings, even though they are purportedly not criminal in nature.[202] On the other hand, in the *Gozutok and Brugge* judgments, the Court ruled that despite the ban on the further prosecution of a person in a second Member State for the same acts, the interests of victims and other persons injured by that person's acts could still be protected by civil proceedings;[203] and in the *Turansky* judgment, the Court ruled that the double jeopardy rule did not prevent multiple *investigations*, as distinct from

---

[194] Art 12(2) of the Second Protocol (n 161 above).   [195] See 10.5.2.1 above.

[196] See 9.7.1.1 above.

[197] Although the Court excluded legal persons from the protection of the Framework Decision on crime victims on the basis of a literal interpretation of the personal and material scope of that Framework Decision (Case C-467/05 *Dell'Orto* [2006] ECR I-5557), those considerations do not apply to Art 54 of the Schengen Convention.

[198] See S Trechsel and S Summers, *Human Rights in Criminal Proceedings* (OUP, 2005), 171–172.

[199] On the liability of the management of legal persons, see 10.5.2.1 above.

[200] As regards legal persons, see ibid.   [201] See 9.2.2.3 above.

[202] See 11.3.2 and 11.4 above.   [203] Para 47 of the judgment.

multiple prosecutions.[204] It follows that there must be a distinction, for the purpose of the Schengen rules, as between criminal proceedings on the one hand and investigations, civil proceedings, and (possibly) administrative proceedings on the other. This distinction could be left to national law, but in the interests of the uniform application of the rule, it would make sense to have a common EU-wide understanding of the principle, which could possibly be based on the ECHR definition of criminal proceedings, as derived from the jurisprudence of the European Court of Human Rights, in particular since the ECHR case law on double jeopardy, which has addressed this issue, has now been aligned with the Court of Justice's approach to the double jeopardy principle.[205] It is also notable that Article 57 of the Schengen Convention triggers a requirement in principle to consult with another Member State's authorities when a person is *charged*; this arguably corresponds to the concept of a 'criminal charge' for the purposes of Article 6 ECHR. In any event, it is also clear that multiple extradition or surrender proceedings are not covered by Article 54 of the Convention, since multiple requests to obtain the hand-over of a fugitive in relation to the same acts do not amount to multiple prosecutions for those acts.[206]

A final question concerning the material scope of the Schengen rules is their application to private prosecutions. The Court of Justice has not ruled on this issue yet, but it is submitted that in the absence of anything to the contrary, it must follow that private prosecutions are within the scope of the rules, in particular by analogy with the Court's ruling on the scope of the Framework Decision on victims' rights.[207] This would mean not only that a final judgment in a private prosecution in one Member State would in principle preclude further private prosecutions for the same act in another Member State, but also that *mutatis mutandis*, a final judgment in a public prosecution would preclude further private prosecutions, and a final judgment in a private prosecution would preclude further public prosecutions.[208]

Moving on to the core rules in Article 54 of the Convention, the Article contains four elements. First of all, what is meant by the phrase, 'a person whose trial has been finally disposed of'? The Court of Justice first has ruled that the double jeopardy rule applies not merely following a judgment of a court, but also where a prosecutor decides to discontinue proceedings because a person has admitted his or her guilt and made a payment to expiate it.[209] Next, the Court ruled in *Miraglia* that where a first Member State's authorities decide to terminate criminal proceedings merely because a second Member State has also opened them, the

---

[204] Para 44 of the judgment.   [205] See 11.3.1 above.

[206] See the Opinion in Case C-296/08 PPU *Santesteban Goicoechea* [2008] ECR I-6307.

[207] The Court ruled in para 41 of C-404/07 *Katz* [2008] ECR I-7607: '[t]here is no provision in the Framework Decision which aims to exclude from its scope the situation where, in criminal proceedings, the victim assumes, as in the present instance, the role of the prosecutor in place of the public authorities.'   [208] See the further discussion of the *Turansky* judgment below.

[209] See *Gozutok and Brugge*, particularly paras 25–31 of the judgment.

double jeopardy rule does not have the effect of requiring the second Member State to terminate proceedings in turn. This could be interpreted as a general rule that a trial cannot be considered 'disposed of' until there is a ruling on the merits of the case, but the Court did not unambiguously state such a general rule.

Further clarification was offered in the judgments in *Van Straaten* and *Gasparini*. In *Van Straaten*, the Court ruled that acquittals due to lack of evidence were within the scope of the rule,[210] although it expressly declined to rule on whether acquittals *not* based on the merits of the case were covered.[211] In *Gasparini*, the Court ruled that a decision to acquit due to a time-bar on further proceedings amounted to a final judgment for the purposes of the rules;[212] otherwise the free movement objective of the double jeopardy rule would be undermined.[213] In *Kretzinger*, the Court confirmed that a suspended sentence was covered by the rules,[214] while in *Bourquain*, it ruled that judgments following trials held *in absentia* were covered,[215] even though such judgments were subject to a requirement of an automatic retrial if the person concerned were arrested.[216] On the other hand, in the *Turansky* judgment, the Court ruled that a decision by a police authority which suspended proceedings but which did not definitely bar further prosecution under the law of the first Member State did not qualify as a final decision.[217]

Although the Court of Justice has now ruled on this issue no fewer than seven times, there is still some uncertainty about the exact scope of this element of the rule, in particular as regards acquittals or other forms of termination of proceedings that have not considered the merits of the case, perhaps due to amnesties or pardons during the proceedings,[218] or the termination of proceedings due to lack of jurisdiction or immunity. These circumstances must of course be distinguished from cases where a prosecution *never began at all* due to time-barring, amnesty, a pardon, lack of jurisdiction, or for any other reason, in which case it is beyond doubt that there is no final judgment for the purposes of the Schengen rules.

There is much to be said for the argument that judgments should only be considered final if they have considered the merits of a case.[219] Such a rule would not only introduce (relative) legal certainty to this issue, but also strike a reasonable balance between the objectives of ensuring free movement and fighting crime. Of course, this would require the Court of Justice to overturn its judgment in

---

[210] Paras 54–61 of the judgment. See also para 34 of the prior *Van Esbroek* judgment.

[211] Para 60 of the judgment.   [212] Paras 22–33 of the judgment.

[213] Para 28 of the judgment.   [214] Para 42 of the judgment.

[215] Paras 34–37 of the judgment. See earlier the opinion in *Kretzinger*, paras 93–100, and now the Framework Decision on *in absentia* trials ([2009] OJ L 81/24) and the pending case of *IB* (Case C-306/09, opinion of 6 July 2010).

[216] Paras 38–42 of the judgment, referring inter alia to the free movement objective of the rules (paras 41–42).   [217] Paras 30–45 of the judgment.

[218] This is a distinct issue from an amnesty or a pardon *after* a final judgment, on which see the discussion of the enforcement condition below.

[219] See the convincing arguments in favour of this approach in the *Gasparini* opinion, and also in the secondary literature: Sharpston and Fernandez-Martin, n 147 above.

Gasparini. Assuming that the Court is not willing to do this, it is hard to discern an obvious rule which would distinguish in a principled way between different categories of judgments which were not decided on the merits. Referring to the general objectives of the EU in the former Article 2 EU (or the current Article 3(2) EU) is, with great respect, unhelpful, since it would always facilitate free movement on the one hand to enlarge the scope of Article 54, but ensure more public safety on the other hand if Article 54 is interpreted restrictively.

Having said that, it is submitted that the best approach to this issue is to distinguish between cases where the national court in question terminated proceedings having had an *opportunity* to decide a case on the merits (ie the *Gasparini* case) and cases where they did not (ie the *Miraglia* case), taking into account proceedings in other Member States. While it might be objected that a better approach would be to give the national courts an *effective* opportunity to decide the case on the merits, such an approach should be rejected, as it would be difficult to apply given its inherently subjective nature, and would not take account of the many ways in which EU law facilitates effective prosecutions in cross-border cases (notably by means of the transfer of evidence or fugitives) and the possibility of national courts to deliver *in absentia* judgments if necessary.

Any test that depends to any extent on whether the merits of the case have been assessed will have to define that concept in turn. This issue has already been the subject of disagreement between Advocates General of the Court of Justice. One has argued that an acquittal on the merits covers cases where either: the issues are 'intrinsic' to the defendant, who cannot be held accountable for his or her acts due to the lack of criminal responsibility (due to age or mental disorder); or the issues are extrinsic to the defendant, such as a valid defence or excuse, the lack of a personal element of the offence, the offence is statute-barred, or the truth of the charges has not been proven.[220] The latter category comprises cases where the acts were not an offence, the defendant did not commit them, or the defendant was not proved to commit them.[221] Obviously, the *Van Straaten* judgment addresses this latter category, ruling that acquittal due to lack of evidence constitutes a ruling on the merits of the case,[222] while the *Gasparini* judgment addresses statute-barring, although the Court's judgment in the latter case does not state whether the termination of proceedings due to a time-bar should be considered as an acquittal based on the merits or not. However, a different Advocate General has disagreed that the termination of proceedings on all of these grounds will amount to acquittals on the merits of the case.[223]

---

[220] Opinion in *Van Straaten*, para 65.   [221] Ibid, para 66.

[222] Para 60 of the judgment.

[223] Opinion in *Gasparini*, note 80. The opinion particularly rejects the view that decisions on time-bars reflect the merits of the case, and also objects (at para 112) to the view that decisions to terminate proceedings due to the age of criminal responsibility should be subject to mutual recognition.

It is submitted that a judgment on the merits of a case must involve a consideration of the substantive elements of the offence, including also any applicable defences or excuses and any ruling that the facts did not constitute an offence. In principle, the personal accountability or situation of the accused should also be regarded as an element of the offence for this purpose. On the other hand, statute-barring is not an element of an offence, although as suggested above, if necessary in order to maintain its prior case law, the Court should nevertheless continue to regard the dismissal of proceedings due to statute-barring as a final judgment, on the grounds that there had been an *opportunity* to rule on the merits of the case. On any interpretation, termination of proceedings due to lack of jurisdiction, or *lis pendens* in another Member State (cf the *Miraglia* judgment), or the transfer of proceedings to another Member State is not a ruling on the merits of the case; nor was there an opportunity to try the merits of the issues in those cases, considering the proceedings underway in other Member States.

A significant issue not yet fully addressed by the Court is the definition of final judgments in the context of appeal or review procedures. While it may be assumed that a judgment is not final as long as an ordinary appeal has been lodged against it, or for as long as the possibility to bring such an appeal still exists (by the defence and/or the prosecution), this leaves open the question of whether a judgment can be regarded as final as long as some possibility of exceptional review exists. Such reviews might be possible, for instance, where later evidence suggests a miscarriage of justice,[224] or where a trial has later been condemned as unfair by the European Court of Human Rights,[225] or where national law, in accordance with the exception to the double jeopardy rule set out in the Seventh Protocol to the ECHR,[226] permits a final judgment to be reopened. On the last point in particular, one Advocate General has questioned whether a *second* Member State which has hold of relevant new evidence might be able to reopen proceedings.[227] This possibility should be rejected, for the obvious reason that it is not set out in the exhaustive list of permitted derogations from the double jeopardy rule set out in Article 55 of the Schengen Convention (on which, see below), and moreover is inconsistent with the principle that the Seventh Protocol only applies to double jeopardy within a single Member State.[228] However, the question still arises whether the *possibility* of any form of exceptional review proceedings means that

---

[224] For instance, in the UK, the Criminal Appeal Act 1995 established the Criminal Cases Review Commission to this end (except for Scotland, where there is separate legislation on the same issue).

[225] See Recommendation No R (2000) 2 of the Committee of Ministers of the Council of Europe to Member States on the re-examination or reopening of certain cases at domestic level following judgments of the European Court of Human Rights.   [226] See 11.3.1 above.

[227] Opinion in *Gasparini*, note 102.

[228] It will still remain possible for any relevant new evidence to be transmitted to the *first* Member State, pursuant to the EU and Council of Europe rules on transmission of evidence (see 9.6 above), in order for that Member State to consider whether the grounds for reopening a prior judgment exist.

a judgment cannot be considered final in the first Member State, and moreover whether, if such review proceedings are brought, *other* Member States are authorized to bring proceedings of their own in relation to the same facts, because the judgment can no longer be considered final.

The answer to the first question is implicit in the *Bourquain* judgment, in which the Court of Justice ruled that the existence of a right to an automatic retrial following an *in absentia* judgment did not mean that such judgments could not be considered final. It should follow by analogy that if the absolute right to a retrial cannot affect the finality of a judgment, the mere possibility of an exceptional review of that judgment cannot do so either. As to the second question, which could also be relevant if a retrial of a judgment delivered *in absentia* takes place (whether the retrial is mandatory or not), the answer should be that the process of reviewing or reopening judgments in criminal law cases or holding a retrial following an *in absentia* judgment is a special procedure which does not trigger a fresh opportunity for other Member States to start fresh criminal law proceedings of their own.

The same conclusion must necessarily be reached if the exceptional review proceedings quash the original judgment, in particular on the grounds that there was a breach of the suspect's fundamental rights. In any of these cases, such fresh proceedings would undermine the objectives of the double jeopardy rules, as interpreted by the Court of Justice. For example, it could hardly be acceptable for a person newly released from prison, having served five years of a custodial sentence following a wrongful conviction, to face criminal proceedings for the same acts in another Member State.[229] This interpretation is fully consistent with the ECHR case law on the double jeopardy principle, which has repeatedly confirmed that a judgment must be considered 'final' even if there is a possibility of an exceptional reopening or review.[230]

The second element of Article 54 is the definition of the 'same acts'. The Court first addressed this issue in its *van Esbroek* judgment, ruling that the term did not require identical classification of the relevant acts in national criminal law, but rather 'the only relevant criterion is the...identity of the material acts, understood in the sense of the existence of a set of concrete circumstances which are inextricably linked together'. The movement of drugs from one Member State to another (constituting the export of drugs from one Member State and import of drugs into another) 'may, in principle, constitute a set of facts which, by their very nature, are inextricably linked', but 'the definitive assessment' of the issue belongs to 'the competent national courts' to determine whether the acts 'constitute a set of facts which are inextricably linked together in time, in space and by their

---

[229] The contrary argument in the opinion in *Kretzinger* (para 101) must be rejected, with great respect; in particular the opinion does not consider the argument that a second set of criminal proceedings in these circumstances would exacerbate the injustice already suffered by the defendant.

[230] See 11.3.1 above.

subject-matter'.[231] The Court did not attach any relevance to the provisions of Article 71 of the Convention, which refers specifically to measures to be taken to combat drug trafficking.[232] Moreover, the Court specifically distinguished the Schengen rules (preventing prosecution for the same '*act*') from the international human rights rules (preventing prosecution for the same '*offence*').[233] Of course, it should be reiterated that the ECHR case law has subsequently aligned itself with the case law of the Court of Justice.[234]

These principles have been clarified further in four later judgments. In *Van Straaten*, the Court ruled that the quantities of drugs at issue or the persons who were party to the alleged offences did not have to be identical in the different Member States concerned.[235] In *Gasparini*, the Court ruled that the marketing of goods in a second Member State after the importation of the same goods into a first Member State could in principle constitute the same acts.[236] Next, in *Kretzinger* the Court confirmed that there is no need to have an identity of legal interests for the rule to apply,[237] and that the successive crossing of various Schengen borders with the same contraband goods could therefore be considered in principle to constitute the 'same acts'.[238] Finally, in *Kraajenbrink* the Court ruled that the same criminal intention behind separate actions was not sufficient in itself to constitute the 'same act' for the purpose of the double jeopardy rule; the rule required an objective link between acts, not merely a subjective link.[239]

Next, the third element of Article 54 of the Convention is the 'enforcement condition', ie the requirement that 'if a penalty has been imposed, it has been enforced, is actually in the process of being enforced or can no longer be enforced under the laws of the sentencing' Member State. The 'enforcement condition' was interpreted by the Court of Justice in the *Kretzinger* and *Bourquain* judgments. In *Kretzinger*, the Court ruled that in the case of suspended sentences, the 'penalty must be regarded as "actually in the process of being enforced" as soon as the sentence has become enforceable and during the probation period. Subsequently, once the probation period has come to an end, the penalty must be regarded as "having been enforced" within the meaning of that provision.'[240] The judgment did not comment on what would happen if the conditions of probation were

---

[231] *Van Esbroek*, paras 36–38.

[232] But see the Court's subsequent ruling on the link between Arts 58 and 71 of the Convention in the *Kraajenbrink* judgment (discussed below). On the substance of Art 71, see 12.7.4 below.

[233] Para 28 of the judgment.   [234] See 11.3.1 above.   [235] Paras 40–53 of the judgment.

[236] Paras 55–57 of the judgment.

[237] It should be noted that there is a requirement for the same legal interests to be at stake when the double jeopardy rule applies in the context of EU competition law: see the discussion in the opinion in *Gasparini* (paras 155–159) and the case law referred to in 11.4 above.

[238] Paras 28–37 of the judgment.

[239] Paras 23–36 of the judgment. See now the opinion in the pending *Mantello* case (n 171 above).   [240] Para 45–52 of the judgment.

breached during the probation period. Logically, this judgment is applicable *mutatis mutandis* to any form of parole or other early release.

The Court also ruled in the *Kretzinger* case that spending a period in detention before the first judgment (whether in police custody or detention on remand) did not satisfy the enforcement condition, even if that period would count against any subsequent custodial sentence imposed.[241] Furthermore, the Court ruled that it was irrelevant as regards the enforcement condition that a judgment *could* be enforced by the sentencing State by means of issuing a European Arrest Warrant;[242] this ruling is presumably applicable by extension to other methods of enforcing judgments pursuant to the EU rules.[243] Finally, in the *Bourquain* judgment, the Court ruled that the enforcement condition was still satisfied if it had been impossible in practice for a judgment *ever* to be enforced, due to the disappearance of the convicted person during the entire period when the judgment was in principle enforceable, because Article 54 of the Convention did not require that the judgment must have been enforceable in practice.[244]

Finally on Article 54, the fourth element of this Article is that a person 'may not be prosecuted' (the 'non-prosecution obligation') if there has been a final judgment for the same facts (subject to the enforcement condition). The question could arise as to the timing of the application of this rule. While the case law of the Court of Justice has referred to the application of the non-prosecution obligation at the point when the national court examines the possible application of the double jeopardy rules,[245] the Court has not been asked to rule explicitly on the application of this provision. However, it is obviously possible that there is no final judgment in a first Member State when proceedings start in a second Member State, or when the double jeopardy issue is assessed by the second Member State's courts, but then a judgment in a first Member State *becomes* final while proceedings in the second Member State are still underway. It is also possible that the enforcement condition was not satisfied when the second proceedings start, but becomes satisfied while they are underway. The *Bourquain* judgment refers to assessment of the enforcement condition at the time when new proceedings start,[246] but again the Court of Justice was not asked to consider the timing issue explicitly.

There is also a separate, but related, question of the scope of the non-prosecution obligation. Does it also amount to an obligation not to sentence a person or enforce a sentence? It is notable that the Schengen Convention, unlike the relevant Council of Europe rules,[247] does not contain an express rule on this point. Also, it is notable that the ECHR double jeopardy rule and the EU Charter

---

[241] Paras 56–64 of the judgment.   [242] Paras 56–64 of the judgment.

[243] cf the Framework Decisions on enforcement of financial penalties and custodial penalties: see 9.7.1 above.   [244] Paras 45–51 of the judgment.

[245] See, for instance, para 22 of the *Turansky* judgment.   [246] Para 47 of the judgment.

[247] See n 149 above.

of Fundamental Rights both refer to an obligation not to try *or punish* a person again, and this point has been emphasized in the ECHR case law.[248] This point will obviously be moot in cases where the non-prosecution obligation applies before a prosecution starts, or if the non-prosecution obligation applies during the prosecution process, since sentencing and enforcement would be impossible if the prosecution cannot begin, or has to be abandoned. But on the other hand, it would be relevant if a first judgment becomes final or the enforcement condition relating to a first judgment becomes satisfied after the prosecution phase of the second proceedings is completed.[249] It is also possible that the existence of a final first judgment only comes to light, or is confirmed, after the second judgment is delivered,[250] or even that a legal person assumes the criminal liability of another legal person by means of a merger.

On the first point (ie the timing of the application of the non-prosecution obligation), it is submitted that the obligation not to prosecute also applies if the other conditions of Article 54 only become applicable during the trial process. This gives precedence to the underlying objectives of the double jeopardy rule over an overly literal interpretation of the rule. On the second point (ie the scope of the non-prosecution rule), it is submitted that it is only appropriate to draw comparisons between the Council of Europe Conventions and the Schengen rules where that would facilitate the objectives of the Schengen rules (cf the different wording of the 'set-off' rules, discussed below), not undermine those objectives. Similarly, the differences in wording between the Schengen double jeopardy rules and the relevant human rights rules are only relevant where the Schengen rules set a higher standard (cf the different definition of the 'same acts', discussed above), not a lower standard. So, disregarding the comparisons with these other measures, it would clearly be more compatible with the underlying objectives of the double jeopardy rules to rule out not only multiple prosecutions but also multiple sentencing or enforcement of sentences, and indeed also to rule out sentencing or the enforcement of a sentence following a second judgment even if a first judgment resulted in an acquittal. Both of these points are also relevant as regards the relationship between the double jeopardy rule and other EU measures, an issue discussed further below.

---

[248] See 11.3 above.

[249] In the case of a first judgment becoming final, this assumes that the second judgment is not yet final either—otherwise the second judgment (even it was delivered later in time) would have to be considered as the first judgment.

[250] This could be relevant in particular where the first trial was held *in absentia* and the convicted person was not aware of it. It can be assumed that normally an accused person would reveal the existence of a prior final judgment concerning the same facts so as to benefit from the protection of Arts 54 and 56 of the Convention, but it is possible that an accused person in some cases would fail to reveal the prior judgment for tactical reasons (for instance, to avoid disclosing the existence of unfavourable evidence which had been used in the first trial if the second set of prosecutors were unaware of that evidence) or due to mental incapacity.

Moving on to the derogations from the double jeopardy rule set out in Article 55 of the Convention, the Court of Justice has not ruled in any detail on the interpretation of these provisions. However, the Court stated in the *Gozutok and Brugge* judgment that the derogations listed in Article 55 were exhaustive, and moreover that Article 55 referred to the same acts as Article 54.[251] Also, in the *Turansky* judgment, the Court did comment in passing that the important limit on the derogations set out in Article 55(4), which rules out the application of any of the derogations when the second Member State requested the first Member State to start a prosecution or granted extradition in respect of the same facts, was applicable.[252]

The limitation in Article 55(4) must surely now be understood as covering cases where a European Arrest Warrant (EAW) has been issued and executed by the relevant Member States, in particular in light of the particular *ne bis in idem* exception set out in the Framework Decision establishing the EAW.[253] Presumably it also applies to a transfer of proceedings, whether pursuant to the Council of Europe Convention or other arrangements,[254] for example any EU measures which might be adopted on this issue.[255] Logically, it should also apply where there has been an agreement between the States concerned on bringing a prosecution pursuant to the Framework Decision on conflicts of jurisdiction or the rules on priority jurisdiction in the EU's substantive criminal law legislation.[256]

The Convention does not make clear whether the derogations must be interpreted autonomously, or in accordance with national law, although it should be recalled that the EU's substantive criminal law measures in some cases specify more precisely when Member States must assert their territorial jurisdiction,[257] and EU measures concerning corruption to some extent define the substance of the 'public official' exception.[258]

Next, the Court of Justice has not yet interpreted Article 56 of the Convention, which sets out a 'set-off' rule as regards periods of detention in the event of a second prosecution. Presumably, as with Article 55, the concept of 'same acts' and final judgments must have the same definition as the concepts in Article 54.

---

[251] Para 44 of the judgment.   [252] Para 29 of the judgment.

[253] See further 9.5.2 above.

[254] It should be noted that the Court ruled in the *Turansky* judgment (paras 19 and 28) that Austria had requested Slovakia in the case to bring proceedings pursuant to Art 21 of the Council of Europe mutual assistance Convention (see 11.7 above), and that it was therefore necessary to examine the Schengen rules because that Council of Europe Convention (unlike the transfer of proceedings Convention) does not regulate the effect of the requested State's taking over proceedings upon the proceedings underway in the requesting State.   [255] On these rules, see 11.7 above.

[256] See 11.6 above.

[257] Note that this clarification not only impacts upon the application of the territoriality derogation pursuant to Art 55(1)(a), but also upon the *disapplication* of that derogation, since the derogation cannot apply where the final judgment followed the application of territorial jurisdiction by the first Member State.   [258] Art 55(1)(c); see 10.5.1.2 above.

An important question regarding Article 56 is the definition of the prior periods of detention which must be deducted from the second sentence. The Convention refers to prior detention 'arising from those acts', wording which differs from the double jeopardy rule in the relevant Council of Europe Conventions ('arising from the *sentence enforced*'). Given the difference in wording, the objectives of the double jeopardy rule, and the EU law principle of proportionality, it therefore seems clear that not only detention arising from a sentence, but also periods spent in police custody and remand connected to the same acts, must also be deducted from the sentence imposed.[259]

One issue raised in the opinions of Advocates General has been the scope of Article 56, in two respects. First of all, does Article 56 only apply where a second sentence is imposed pursuant to the application of the derogations in Article 55, or does it also apply where a second sentence is imposed because the enforcement condition set out in Article 54 is not satisfied? The opinion in *Van Straaten* assumes the former interpretation,[260] while the opinion in *Kraaijenbrink* argues the latter.[261] It is submitted that the second interpretation is correct, since it best reflects the objectives of the double jeopardy rule and the principle of proportionality, and moreover reflects the literal wording of Article 56, which does not suggest that the set-off rule is limited in scope to cases where the derogation applies.

The second issue is the material scope of Article 56, in particular its application to other forms of penalty besides custodial penalties. While Article 56, by itself, clearly leaves it to the national law of Member States to decide whether non-custodial penalties are deducted following a second prosecution, an opinion of an Advocate General has argued that the 'set-off' rule is a general principle of EU law, so there is an obligation to take account of non-custodial penalties also despite the express wording of Article 56.[262] Furthermore, Article 49(3) of the EU Charter of Fundamental Rights arguably also sets out this rule, as it provides that '[t]he severity of penalties must not be disproportionate to the criminal offence'.[263] The convincing argument that the set-off rule is a general principle and/or encapsulated within the EU Charter furthermore bolsters the arguments set out above in relation to the deduction of pre-trial detention from all forms of second sentences, and the application of the set-off rule in any case when a second sentence is imposed for the same acts.

---

[259] See generally paras 62–69 of the *Kretzinger* opinion. Although the judgment in *Kretzinger* rejected the argument that periods spent in pre-trial detention satisfied the enforcement condition set out in Art 54 (see above), this can clearly be distinguished from the question of whether those periods must be deducted from a second sentence pursuant to Art 56, given the different wording and context of the two provisions. It is surely also relevant in this context that, as the Court noted in *Kretzinger*, at least some national laws require periods of pre-trial detention to be deducted from any final sentence (see also para 64 of the *Kretzinger* opinion).   [260] Note 29 of the opinion.

[261] Paras 55–66 of the opinion. See also paras 71–72 of the *Kretzinger* opinion.

[262] Ibid; see also para 64 of the *Kretzinger* opinion.

[263] See note 38 of the opinion in *Kraaijenbrink*.

The consultation procedure set out in Article 57 of the Schengen Convention has also not been interpreted as such by the Court of Justice, although the Court noted that the procedure was applied in the *Bourquain* case,[264] and was not applied in the *Turansky* case, where the use of the consultation procedure could clearly have clarified the situation.[265] It might be argued that a State's failure to make a request under Article 57, or a requested State's failure to respond promptly (or at all, or accurately) could give rise to or aggravate the damages liability of the State(s) concerned (see below).

As for Article 58 of the Schengen Convention, the Court ruled in the *Kraaijenbrink* judgment that there were limits to Member States' power to apply more favourable rules; they could not refrain from prosecuting separate drugs offences pursuant to Article 71 of the Schengen Convention merely because the separate acts were motivated by the same criminal intention.[266] It should be noted that there is no provision of the Schengen Convention which expressly regulates the relationship of the double jeopardy rules with Member States' other international commitments.[267]

Next, the question might arise of the legal effect of the double jeopardy rules. This is a specific application of a general question (the legal effect of third pillar rules in general), and the answer (until the conversion of the double jeopardy rules into an EU measure after the entry into force of the Treaty of Lisbon) depends on the legal effect of third pillar rules in general.[268] At the very least, it is arguable that the rules have indirect effect so that any relevant national law should be interpreted as far as possible by national courts in order to ensure that it is consistent with the Schengen rules as interpreted by the Court of Justice. Moreover, to the extent that the established EC law rules on remedies apply to the third pillar, in particular there should be damages liability for any wrongful prosecution, conviction, or detention in breach of the Schengen rules, if those breaches are sufficiently serious as defined by the relevant EC rules. In the case of wrongful detention, the damages liability also stems from ECHR rules.[269] Furthermore, by their nature, the double jeopardy rules, in order to be effective, need to be enforced by the remedies of forestalling or terminating prosecutions, quashing convictions, and releasing from detention or otherwise ending the enforcement of criminal penalties, if possible retroactively (ie by reimbursing a fine which was already paid, with interest).

The final two points are closely connected: the relationship between the double jeopardy rule and EU mutual recognition measures on the one hand, and the EU's fundamental rights rules on the other. On the first point, as noted above, the

---

[264] Paras 23–24 of the judgment.   [265] Paras 37–38 of the judgment.
[266] Para 35 of the judgment.   [267] See further 11.11 below.
[268] See 2.2.2.2 and (as regards the transformation of prior third pillar measures) 2.2.3.3 above.
[269] See Art 5(5) ECHR. There is also a right to compensation for a wrongful conviction, following a miscarriage of justice as defined in Art 3 of Protocol 7 to the ECHR.

EU's mutual recognition measures usually include provisions concerning refusal of enforcement on grounds of double jeopardy.[270] However, this ground of refusal is not always mandatory, and it is not clear whether the double jeopardy principle in the mutual recognition measures is identical to the principle as set out in the Schengen rules. The Court of Justice has not yet addressed this issue,[271] although it has addressed other types of links between the double jeopardy rules and mutual recognition measures,[272] and links with other EU measures concerning criminal jurisdiction can be discerned.[273]

On the second point, the Court has stated explicitly that the principle of cross-border double jeopardy is, just like the purely domestic application of the principle, a 'fundamental principle of Community law';[274] the rule appears in the EU Charter of Rights; and the ECHR case law has become aligned with the Court of Justice case law.[275] It must follow that the double jeopardy principle is a rule of primary EU law, which must take precedence over conflicting secondary EU legislation.[276] The ability of the EU's political institutions to limit the double jeopardy rule is therefore restricted. In any event, in light of the requirement of lawfulness which applies to human rights law,[277] any restrictions on the application of the double jeopardy rules which might be justified pursuant to the Charter would have to specify precisely that they derogate from Article 54 of the Schengen Convention; but as we have seen, an exhaustive list of such derogations is found only in Article 55 of that Convention, which has not been amended by the EU's mutual recognition measures. Of course, even if such derogations met the 'provided for by law' requirement, they would still have to satisfy the *substantive* requirements for limiting the rights set out in the EU Charter, and the general principles of EU law.[278]

---

[270] For details, see 9.2.2.3 above.

[271] However, the opinion of 7 Sep 2010 in the pending *Mantello* case (n 171 above) argues that the double jeopardy exception in the Framework Decision on the European Arrest Warrant should be interpreted consistently with the Schengen rules, at least as regards the interpretation of the 'same acts'.

[272] The *Miraglia* judgment implicitly addressed the relationship with mutual assistance rules, and the *Turansky* case explicitly referred to Art 21 of the Council of Europe mutual assistance Convention. The *Gasparini* judgment interpreted the double jeopardy rules in the context of the Framework Decision on the European Arrest Warrant, and the *Kretzinger* judgment ruled that the possible issue of a European Arrest Warrant has no impact on the enforcement condition in Article 54 of the Convention; presumably (as noted above) other EU mutual recognition measures have no impact either.

[273] As noted above, the *Turansky* case raises implicit questions about the application of Art 55(4) when proceedings are transferred. Also, the *Miraglia* case could be relevant to the consequences of applying the Framework Decision on conflicts of jurisdiction and/or, by analogy, any future EU rules on the transfer of proceedings.   [274] Para 40 of the *Van Esbroek* judgment.

[275] See 11.3 above.

[276] On the legal effect of the general principles of EU law and the Charter, see 2.3 above.

[277] See, for instance, Art 52(1) of the Charter ('[a]ny limitation . . . must be provided for by law').

[278] According to Art 52(1) of the Charter, such limitations would have to 'respect the essence of those rights and freedoms', and would be '[s]ubject to the principle of proportionality'; moreover

11.9. Eurojust

The interim step between a purely national system of prosecution of crimes and prosecution of crimes by an EU prosecutor is Eurojust, a body intended to coordinate and support national investigations, to facilitate judicial cooperation and mutual recognition, and to assist resolving conflicts of jurisdiction. Following the mandate of the Tampere European Council, the Council adopted a Decision establishing a provisional Eurojust late in 2000.[279] Shortly after the Tampere deadline of end-2001, the Council adopted a Decision in February 2002, which established Eurojust definitively.[280] This Decision was subsequently amended as regard the financial rules governing Europol,[281] and then again more substantially in 2008, inter alia in order to strengthen Member States' support for Eurojust (in particular as regards the powers of national members), to give Eurojust a greater role settling conflicts of jurisdiction, to increase the flow of information to Eurojust, and to overhaul the external relations rules.[282] For the future, the Stockholm programme and the action plan on implementing the Stockholm programme call for a proposal on Eurojust in 2012.[283]

The JHA Council has approved Eurojust's rules of procedure,[284] and its joint supervisory body adopted its own rules of procedure.[285] According to the Court of Justice, a Member State cannot challenge Eurojust's staffing decisions before the Court pursuant to Article 230 EC (as it then was), but disappointed applicants can challenge Eurojust's decisions.[286]

Eurojust is a 'body' of the EU with legal personality,[287] with its seat in the Hague.[288] It is made up of one member seconded by each Member State, who may be a prosecutor, judge, or police officer depending on the national legal system, whose place of work must be at Eurojust. Each member must be assisted by one deputy and one assistant, and may be assisted by more people. The deputy must be able to replace the national member.[289] The Decision specifies that national members must have: a term of office of at least four years; access to the national registers on criminal records, arrested persons, investigations, and DNA; and powers to follow up mutual recognition requests, to issue such requests (in con-

---

'limitations [on rights] may be made only if they are necessary and genuinely meet objectives of general interest recognised by the Union or the need to protect the rights and freedoms of others'.

[279] [2000] OJ L 324/2.

[280] [2002] OJ L 63/1. See the Eurojust website: <http://www.eurojust.europa.eu>.

[281] [2003] OJ L 245/44.

[282] [2009] OJ L 138/14, which took effect on 4 June 2009 (Art 3). See the earlier Commission communication (COM (2007) 844, 23 Oct 2007). Member States have until 4 June 2011, if necessary, to amend their national law to comply with these amendments (Art 2). The Decision has not been consolidated. All further references in this section are to the Eurojust Decision as amended, unless otherwise indicated.   [283] [2010] OJ C 115 and COM (2010) 171, 20 Apr 2010.

[284] [2002] OJ C 286/1 and [2005] OJ C 68/1.   [285] [2004] OJ C 86/1.

[286] Case C-160/03 Spain v Eurojust [2005] ECR I-2077.   [287] Art 1.

[288] [2004] OJ L 29/15.   [289] Art 2, as amended.

junction with a national authority), to execute mutual recognition requests, and authorize controlled deliveries in urgent cases, and to participate in joint investigative teams.[290]

The activities of Eurojust are threefold: to coordinate national investigations and prosecutions; to improve cooperation between national authorities, in particular by facilitating judicial cooperation and mutual recognition; and to support in other ways the effectiveness of national investigations and prosecutions.[291] Eurojust may also become involved in assisting investigations and prosecutions involving only one Member State and a non-Member State once Eurojust has concluded an agreement with the relevant non-Member State (see below) or where there is an 'essential interest' in specific cases.[292] It may also become involved in investigations involving only one Member State and the Community.[293]

Eurojust's competence encompasses the crimes which Europol is competent to address, plus other offences committed in conjunction with any of the crimes over which it is competent.[294] Eurojust may also assist in other investigations at the request of a Member State's authorities.[295] It has established an 'on-call coordination centre' to deal with urgent requests.[296] When it acts through its individual members, it can inter alia request Member States' authorities to begin investigations or prosecutions, to accept that one of them is in a better position to undertake a prosecution, to coordinate between authorities, to set up a joint investigation team, or to take special investigative measures.[297] When acting as a college, it can do many of the same things, plus it also has a distinct role suggesting resolutions of conflicts of jurisdiction or recommending the settlement of disputes regarding the application of mutual recognition measures.[298] On the issue of conflicts of jurisdiction, several EU substantive criminal law measures also specify a role for Eurojust in advising which Member State should exercise jurisdiction over cross-border offences, and the Framework Decision on conflicts of jurisdiction requires Member States to send a dispute over jurisdiction to Eurojust, 'where appropriate', if it cannot be agreed by means of consultation.[299] Member States have to motivate 'without undue delay' any refusals to comply with a request from a national member or the college, as well as any decision not to comply with an opinion by the college in the context of dispute settlement.[300]

In order to support Eurojust's activities, Member States must appoint national correspondents and establish a national coordination system for Eurojust.[301] Also,

---

[290] Arts 9–9f, as amended. On controlled deliveries and joint investigation teams, see 12.7 and 12.9 below.   [291] Art 3(1), as amended.

[292] Art 3(2).   [293] Art 3(3).

[294] Art 4(1), as amended. On the competence of Europol, see 12.8 below.   [295] Art 4(2).

[296] Art 5a, as inserted.   [297] Art 6(1)(a), as amended.   [298] Art 7, as amended.

[299] See 11.6 above, and also the Eurojust guidelines on jurisdiction in the Annex to the 2003 annual report.

[300] Art 8, as amended. Member States may decline to give reasons for refusing to accede to requests on grounds of national security or protecting individual safety.   [301] Art 12, as amended.

Member States must exchange extensive information with Eurojust,[302] and there are detailed rules on data protection.[303]

The provisions on the status and operation of Eurojust apply EU rules to Eurojust's staff and budget and provide for annual reports to the EP and the Council.[304] As for external relations, the Eurojust Decision has specific provisions on relations with the European Judicial Network, other EU bodies (Europol, OLAF, Frontex, and the Council as regards foreign policy), and third States and bodies, including provisions on sending and receiving liaison officers and executing requests for judicial cooperation from third States.[305]

In practice, Eurojust suffered from its limited competence as a provisional unit until 2002, a delay until it could take up permanent offices in the Hague in 2003, a shortage of support staff until 2003, and Member States' tardiness in appointing data protection officers and amending national law to conform to the initial Eurojust decision.[306] Nevertheless, Eurojust has been used increasingly in practice, with the number of cases referred to Eurojust by national authorities rising from 180 in 2001 to 202 in 2002; 300 in 2003 (a 50% increase); 381 in 2004 (a 27% increase); 588 in 2005 (a 54% increase); 771 in 2006 (a 31% increase); 1,085 in 2007 (a 41% increase); 1,193 in 2008 (a 10% increase); and 1,372 in 2009 (a 15% increase). Eurojust has in particular made a number of recommendations to Member States' authorities pursuant to the Decision, including on the issue of conflicts of jurisdiction.

As for Eurojust's external relations, an agreement with Europol came into force in 2004 and was revised in 2009,[307] and a memorandum with OLAF was agreed in 2003, although the relationship with OLAF was considered unsatisfactory until a formal agreement was negotiated in 2008. Treaties with Norway, Iceland, Romania, the US, Croatia, Switzerland, and several international bodies are in force,[308] a treaty with the Former Yugoslav Republic of Macedonia has been agreed, and further treaties are planned with Russia, Ukraine, Moldova, other Western Balkan States, Liechtenstein, Cape Verde, and Israel.

Eurojust also has a role in other Council measures, in particular as regards the EAW, where it can be asked to address the issue of competing warrants and must be informed of delays in the execution of warrants.[309] In practice, Eurojust has adopted guidelines on competing warrants, and receives reports of dozens of delayed executions of EAWs every year. Furthermore, Council Decisions on the exchange of information on terrorism provide for a role for Eurojust,[310] and another Council Decision gives Eurojust access to the Schengen Information

---

[302] Art 13, as amended.   [303] Arts 14–24, as amended.   [304] Arts 28–39, as amended.

[305] Arts 25a–27b, as amended; on the judicial network and the liaison magistrates, see 9.9 above.

[306] See the annual reports for 2001–09, available on the Eurojust website, as well as the report in COM (2004) 457, 6 July 2004.   [307] See 12.8 below.

[308] For the texts, see: <http://www.eurojust.europa.eu/official_documents/eju_agreements. htm>.   [309] Arts 16 and 17 of the EAW Framework Decision ([2002] OJ L 190/1).

[310] [2003] OJ L 16/68, replaced by later Decision ([2005] OJ L 252/23).

System; this took effect in December 2007.[311] Eurojust will in future have access
to the Customs Information System (CIS).[312]

11.10. European Public Prosecutor

The Commission initially suggested during negotiation of the Treaty of Nice in
2000 that provisions on a European Public Prosecutor should be inserted into the
EC Treaty (as it then was), but the suggestion was not taken up.[313] Subsequently
in 2001, it attempted to lay the groundwork for further consideration of the idea
by releasing a Green Paper,[314] arguing that the existing and contemplated arrangements for judicial cooperation and investigation related to the EU's financial
interests were (and would be) ineffective. The Commission argued in particular
that the legal framework was inadequate as regards lack of ratification of the PIF
Convention and its Protocols, traditional judicial cooperation was 'cumbersome
and inappropriate' (without citing details), judges often did not follow up OLAF
investigations, and evidence was often inadmissible or (in the case of tax and
banking information) inaccessible. Furthermore, the Public Prosecutor would
increase the effectiveness of internal investigations within the EU institutions,
and would enhance protection of fundamental rights, by speeding up proceedings
and reducing the need for pre-trial detention.

As to the details, the Commission proposed that the Public Prosecutor would
centralize the investigation and prosecution of the crimes within his or her remit,
but that trials would subsequently take place within the criminal courts of a
Member State. The existing substantive criminal law in this area could perhaps
be supplemented, and rules on penalties for such crimes could be adopted. So
could rules on limitation periods. There would have to be agreement on whether
prosecution would be mandatory or discretionary, and on the division of competence between the Public Prosecutor and national prosecuting authorities. The
Public Prosecutor would enjoy extensive investigatory powers and would choose
in which Member State's courts a trial would take place, subject to established
criteria for making this choice. Evidence gathered lawfully in one Member State
would have to be admitted before the courts of any other Member State, and there
would have to be detailed rules on judicial review of the Public Prosecutor.

According to the Commission's communication on the follow-up to the Green
Paper,[315] the majority of those responding to the Green Paper were supportive
of the idea of a European Public Prosecutor, although most had reservations

---

[311] [2005] OJ L 68/44. On the SIS, see 12.6.1.1 below.

[312] Art 12 of the CIS Decision ([2009] OJ L 323/20), which applies from 27 May 2011 (Art 36(2)
of the Decision). On the CIS, see 12.6.1.2 below.

[313] See Annex I to the subsequent Commission Green Paper on the Public Prosecutor (COM
(2001) 715, 11 Dec 2001).   [314] Ibid.

[315] COM (2003) 128, 19 Mar 2003.

about the details. In particular, many called for an enlarged competence for the Prosecutor, a greater degree of approximation of relevant substantive criminal law, more limited investigatory powers for the Prosecutor, and further harmonization of the law of evidence and defence rights.

Article 86 TFEU, as inserted by the Treaty of Lisbon, gives the Council the power (not the obligation) to establish the Public Prosecutor, with the option to extend his or her competence to areas other than the EU's financial interests, and accepts the model of the Prosecutor bringing prosecutions in national courts.[316] As mentioned above, the Stockholm programme refers to consideration of the creation of the Public Prosecutor, and the Commission intends to issue a communication on this issue in 2013.[317]

But in any case, is a European Public Prosecutor desirable? Certainly the objective of ensuring more effective prosecutions in defence of the EU's financial interests, and potentially other serious crimes, while still securing the fundamental rights of criminal defendants, can only be supported. But with great respect to the supporters of the idea, the notion of creating the post of the Public Prosecutor as a means to this end is fundamentally flawed.

The first basic problem with the idea is that the Commission did not properly consider the effectiveness of more limited measures to achieve the same objective. Examining in turn the specific arguments made by the Commission (summarized above), the PIF Convention and both of its Protocols have now been ratified; judicial cooperation has been speeded up by adopted EU measures (the mutual assistance Convention and its Protocol, the Framework Decisions on the arrest warrant, freezing orders, evidence warrant, financial penalties, custodial penalties, probation, and pre-trial supervision) and would be further speeded up by proposed measures (the European investigation order) and further plans set out in the Stockholm programme (for example, as regards mutual admissibility of evidence);[318] the Commission has made proposals relating to OLAF powers and on cooperation on EU financial interests,[319] and further measures strengthening the relationship between OLAF and national prosecutors and/or Eurojust could be adopted; the Protocol to the Mutual Assistance and the Framework Decisions on freezing orders and the EAW have or will make tax or banking information more accessible; and the effectiveness of internal investigations could be enhanced by amending the rules applicable to OLAF. Finally, as regards individual rights, as noted already, the speed of proceedings has been increased already by the application of the EAW and the Framework Decision on pre-trial supervision should reduce detention in cross-border cases. It should be reiterated that in all mutual recognition measures adopted or agreed to date, the dual criminality principle has been dropped as regards crimes against the EU's financial interests, except for a few cases where Member States could insist on retaining the principle.

---

[316] See further 11.2.3 and 11.2.4 above.
[317] [2010] OJ C 115, point 3.1.1; COM (2010) 171, 20 Apr 2010.   [318] See generally ch 9.
[319] See 12.4.6 below.

Moving on to the detailed aspects of Public Prosecutor's role as proposed by the Commission, it would be possible to harmonize the substantive criminal law as regards the EU's financial interests further, including the adoption of harmonized rules on penalties and limitation periods, without creating a Public Prosecutor. Furthermore, a case could be made that the EU should regulate national prosecutions in this area, for example as to whether prosecutions should be mandatory, the extent of investigatory powers, and the decision on where to prosecute (going further to allocate jurisdiction than the 2009 Framework Decision on conflicts of jurisdiction).[320]

The second basic problem is that the model of centralized prosecution and decentralized trials proposed by the Commission—and now enshrined in Article 86 TFEU, following the entry into force of the Treaty of Lisbon—is half-baked. This model was notably *not* followed by the Rome Statute creating the International Criminal Court, and its defects are obvious: the rules relating to investigations and prosecutions on the one hand and trials on the other cannot be separated any more than eggs can be extracted from omelettes. In particular, this model risks lowering the protection of the rights of criminal defendants, since that protection is provided at different stages in the criminal procedure in different Member States.

11.11. External relations

The Framework Decision on conflicts of jurisdiction contains a general provision permitting Member States to sign agreements which facilitate the objectives of that Framework Decision.[321] Unlike the EU's mutual recognition measures,[322] that Framework Decision does *not* require Member States to disapply the corresponding provisions of the relevant Council of Europe Convention (on the transfer of proceedings) or any other treaties,[323] which is significant because the provisions in the transfer of proceedings Convention are, on the whole, better than those of the Framework Decision.[324] On the other hand, as noted above, the Schengen Convention does not expressly clarify the relationship of the double jeopardy provisions with any other international measures.[325] There are very specific rules governing the external relations of Eurojust.[326]

It should be kept in mind that although the Court of Justice has taken an assertive approach as regards the EU's exclusive competence over issues of civil jurisdiction,[327] the case in question concerned a fully harmonized set of

---

[320] See 11.6 above.   [321] [2009] OJ L 328/42, Art 15.   [322] See 9.10 above.

[323] See explicitly para 15 in the preamble to the Framework Decision.   [324] See 11.6 above.

[325] See 11.7 above. Compare Art 58 of the Convention with Arts 48, 59, and 67 ([2000] OJ L 239).

[326] See 11.9 above.

[327] *Opinion 1/2003* [2006] ECR I-1145. See further 8.9 above.

jurisdiction rules, including effective *lis pendens* provisions, leaving the rules on conflicting judgments (the equivalent of the criminal law double jeopardy rules) somewhat secondary.[328] As we have seen, the position as regards criminal law is rather different. There is also a declaration to the Treaty of Lisbon on the EU's external competence over civil law, but arguably it does nothing more than confirm that EU competence can only become exclusive when the relevant internal law is fully harmonized.[329] So as the law now stands, it is probably the case that the EU has exclusive competence over any international treaty provisions that could impact upon the EU's double jeopardy rules, but shares competence with the Member States as regards any other rules relating to criminal jurisdiction.[330]

11.12. Conclusions

EU action in this field is a mixture of welcome developments and disappointing shortcomings. The rules on double jeopardy, as interpreted by the Court of Justice, are generally very welcome, although a number of issues relating to these rules could usefully be clarified, in particular the definition of a 'final judgment' and the relationship with the specific double jeopardy rules in EU mutual recognition measures. In other areas, the EU's substantive criminal law measures do too much to encourage or require extraterritorial jurisdiction, in the absence of any particular need (in light of the possibility of extraditing States' nationals, and other developments in the area of mutual recognition), and without any countervailing system to ensure that individuals are not subjected to multiple prosecutions—which in any event waste the scarce time and money of prosecutors, police, and judges.

The EU should be bolder in ensuring not only that the useful rules on conflicts of jurisdiction and transfers of proceedings in the Council of Europe Convention on transfers of proceedings apply to all Member States, but also further developing those rules. There should be a prima facie obligation to centralize a prosecution in the Member State where the alleged criminal activity took place, subject to reasonable exceptions in the interests of justice, while clearly ruling out forum-shopping by the prosecution or the defence. A rule establishing that there can only be a single prosecution, determined by objective and fair criteria, would contribute significantly to the development of an EU criminal justice model. After all, why should prosecutors be treated any differently than asylum seekers?[331]

---

[328] Moreover, the double jeopardy rules apply even if the judgments in question are not conflicting.   [329] See 9.10 above.

[330] See the Council conclusions on cooperation with the Council of Europe as regards criminal law ([2009] OJ C 50/8).   [331] See the Dublin rules, discussed in 5.8 above.

12

Policing and Security

12.1. Introduction

The effective prevention and investigation of crime, particularly violent crime, is understandably a basic desire of the public in every society. But in this area there is the most acute tension between civil liberties and security objectives. Obviously, the greater the level of supervision and control of the public, the easier it is to prevent crime and to investigate it more effectively. Yet, even leaving aside their cost and practicality, such measures erode the extent of freedom in our society. There is therefore a continuing debate over the right balance to be struck between the two objectives, and this debate has been affected by the ever-greater sophistication of security technology (in particular, the development of information systems) and the perceived increase in the intensity of the threat posed by international terrorism since the terrorist attacks of September 11, 2001.

Within national legal and political systems, security-minded national executives and law enforcement authorities must justify further restrictions on civil liberties in the interests of greater security before national parliaments and courts. There are also systems of accountability for law enforcement operations. But until the entry into force of the Treaty of Lisbon, EU policing law was not subject to any effective parliamentary or judicial control, or supervision of the executive, or to a developed framework for the accountability of operations, and therefore offered an escape from these national constraints. Even the enhanced parliamentary and judicial control that will apply to measures adopted after the entry into force of the Treaty of Lisbon will not necessarily mean that operational measures in this area will be subject to effective scrutiny.

This chapter focuses on law enforcement within the European Union, beginning as always with an examination of the institutional framework as it has developed over time, an overview of measures adopted, and an examination of the relevant issues of legal competence, territorial scope, human rights, and overlaps with non-JHA EU law. It then analyses in turn EU measures concerning crime prevention, the collection and exchange of data relating to policing, other forms of cooperation between national law enforcement authorities, the operation of Europol (the EU's law enforcement agency), and cross-border police operations. Finally, it examines the issues of administrative cooperation and EU funding and EU external relations in the field of policing law.

The closely related issue of criminal procedure, including EU measures on the rights of criminal suspects (which impact upon the police) is examined in Chapter 9, and the underlying issue of substantive criminal law is addressed in Chapter 10. This book observes the English distinction between the *investigation* of crime by the police or similar authorities (addressed in this chapter) and the prosecution and trial process before the courts (addressed in Chapters 9 and 11), although of course in many continental countries investigations form part of the judicial process.[1]

This chapter examines together EU measures concerning the prevention and investigation of specific crimes, such as drug trafficking and terrorism, although it should be recalled that the EU has also harmonized the substantive law (Chapter 10) and simplified mutual recognition of criminal measures (Chapter 9) as regards specified crimes.

Finally, one particular feature of EU law in this area is the continued substantial use of soft law, which is referred to throughout as appropriate. Of course, policing and security measures cannot be fully examined without an understanding of practice, although the paucity of information made available has limited the possibility to analyse the operational aspects of the EU measures discussed in this chapter.

12.2. Institutional framework and overview

12.2.1. Cooperation prior to the Treaty of Amsterdam

Before the Maastricht Treaty entered into force, EU leaders had already agreed on the principle of establishing an EU police agency, Europol, and EU ministers had already adopted a Ministerial Agreement on the creation of that body.[2] With the entry into force of the TEU, this intergovernmental cooperation was formalized. Article K.1(8) and (9) TEU included, as matters of common interest, 'customs cooperation' and 'police cooperation for the purposes of preventing and combatting terrorism, unlawful drug trafficking and other serious forms of international crime', possibly including aspects of customs cooperation, 'in connection with a Union-wide system for exchanging information within' Europol. However, Article K.2(2) asserted that Title VI EU would not 'affect the exercise of the responsibilities incumbent upon Member States with regard to the exercise of the responsibilities incumbent upon Member States with regard to the maintenance of law and order and the safeguarding of internal security'. There was no possibility for the Commission to propose measures.

---

[1] The specific issue of search and seizure is addressed in 9.6 above, due to its link with mutual judicial assistance. [2] See 12.8 below.

During the 'Maastricht period' (November 1993 to May 1999), there were a number of important developments as regards policing and customs cooperation. The negotiations on the Europol Convention and on a Convention establishing a Customs Information System (CIS) Convention were concluded in July 1995.[3] In 1998, negotiations were concluded on the 'Naples II' Convention, which governs cross-border operations and exchanges of information by customs officers.[4] Other measures included Joint Actions establishing directories of expertise on counter-terrorism and organized crime, and concerning the exchange of liaison officers, customs and business cooperation in drug trafficking, the exchange of information on chemical profiling of drugs, security cooperation, and targeting criteria for police.[5] Three other Joint Actions established funding programmes related to law enforcement.[6] The Council also adopted a large number of soft law measures in the area of policing.[7]

Meanwhile, the Schengen States engaged in more intensive cooperation regarding policing matters. In particular, the Schengen Convention contains detailed rules specific to police cooperation, on: the exchange of information among police authorities;[8] hot pursuit or surveillance by the police of one Member State across the borders into another Member State;[9] the improvement of cross-border police communications;[10] the registration of visiting foreigners (including EU citizens) for the benefit of the police;[11] and the posting of liaison officers.[12] The Convention also includes parallel measures regarding drugs and firearms,[13] along with the creation of the Schengen Information System (SIS), which contains data relevant to the police (along with authorities responsible for immigration and criminal law).[14] Schengen cooperation also entailed the adoption of Decisions of the Schengen Executive Committee on a number of measures.[15]

12.2.2. Treaty of Amsterdam

12.2.2.1. Institutional Framework

The Treaty of Amsterdam extensively revised the 'third pillar' rules relating to police cooperation. In the revised version, according to the previous Article 29 TEU, the objectives of the third pillar were to be achieved partly through 'closer cooperation between police forces, customs authorities, and other competent authorities in the Member States, both directly and through the European Police

---

[3] See ibid and 12.6.1.2 below. See also 12.4.1 below, on the Reg paralleling the CIS Convention.   [4] See 12.6.3, 12.7.1, and 12.9 below.
    [5] See particularly 12.6.3 and 12.7.4 below.   [6] See 12.10 below.
    [7] See particularly 12.7.4 below.
    [8] See 12.6 below. The Convention is in [2000] OJ L 239/1.   [9] See 12.9 below.
[10] See 12.7.4 below.   [11] See ibid.   [12] See 12.6.3 below.   [13] See ibid.
[14] See 12.6.1.1 below.   [15] See ibid, 12.4.7, 12.6.3, and 12.7.4 below.

Office (Europol), in accordance with' the previous Articles 30 and 32 TEU.[16] The previous Article 30 TEU provided that:

1. Common action in the field of police cooperation shall include:

(a) operational cooperation between the competent authorities, including the police, customs and other specialised law enforcement services of the Member States in relation to the prevention, detection and investigation of criminal offences;

(b) the collection, storage, processing, analysis and exchange of relevant information, including information held by law enforcement services on reports on suspicious financial transactions, in particular through Europol, subject to appropriate provisions on the protection of personal data;

(c) cooperation and joint initiatives in training, the exchange of liaison officers, secondments, the use of equipment, and forensic research;

(d) the common evaluation of particular investigative techniques in relation to the detection of serious forms of organised crime.

2. The Council shall promote cooperation through Europol and shall in particular, within a period of five years after the date of entry into force of the Treaty of Amsterdam:

(a) enable Europol to facilitate and support the preparation, and to encourage the coordination and carrying out, of specific investigative actions by the competent authorities of the Member States, including operational actions of joint teams comprising representatives of Europol in a support capacity;

(b) adopt measures allowing Europol to ask the competent authorities of the Member States to conduct and coordinate their investigations in specific cases and to develop specific expertise which may be put at the disposal of Member States to assist them in investigating cases of organised crime;

(c) promote liaison arrangements between prosecuting/investigating officials specialising in the fight against organised crime in close cooperation with Europol;

(d) establish a research, documentation and statistical network on cross-border crime.

The previous Article 32 TEU provided that:

The Council shall lay down the conditions and limitations under which the competent authorities referred to in Articles 30 and 31 may operate in the territory of another Member State in liaison and in agreement with the authorities of that State.

The previous Article 33 TEU copied the guarantee of national competence over law and order and security found in the original Article K.2(2) TEU. The policing provisions of the TEU were not amended at all by the subsequent Treaty of Nice.

Customs cooperation continued to fall within the scope of the third pillar, as customs was expressly referred to in the previous Articles 29 and 30(1)(a) TEU.

---

[16] For the objectives, see 10.2.2 above.

The Treaty of Amsterdam did, however, create a new legal base for customs cooperation falling within the scope of the first pillar.[17]

Many of the measures foreseen in the previous Article 30(1) TEU had already been agreed in some form, noted above. Similarly, liaison officers (Article 30(2)(c)) were already connected to Europol and its precursor organization.[18] But Article 30(2)(a) and (b) were new.

As for the relevant Schengen *acquis*, the Council easily agreed on the allocation of most of the policing provisions of the Schengen Convention and the related Executive Committee Decisions to the previous Articles 30 and 32 EU,[19] although certain drugs and firearms provisions were allocated to the 'first pillar' (or not allocated at all). However, it could not originally agree on how to allocate the *acquis* relating to the SIS, so it allocated it by default to the third pillar.[20]

12.2.2.2. Implementing the Treaty of Amsterdam

As with other fields of JHA cooperation, the objectives of the EU in this area were set out in the 1999 Tampere European Council conclusions, which referred in particular to: the development of a crime prevention network; the establishment of joint investigation teams, including the participation of Europol representatives; the creation of a 'European Police Chiefs operational Task Force' which would exchange 'experience, best practices and information on current trends in cross-border crime and contribute to the planning of operative actions'; the strengthening of Europol by 'receiving operational data from Member States and authorising it to ask Member States to initiate, conduct or coordinate investigations or to create joint investigative teams in certain areas of crime'; the creation of a 'European Police College for the training of senior law enforcement officials', starting as a 'network of existing national training institutes'; the adoption of a 2000–04 Drugs Strategy; the improvement of the exchange of information between financial intelligence units (FIUs) as regards money laundering; and the extension of Europol's competence to money laundering in general.

In order to implement this agenda, as regards crime prevention, the Council adopted an initial Decision establishing a crime prevention network, and later amended that decision in 2009.[21] Joint investigative teams were to be established in accordance with a Framework Decision.[22] A Police Chiefs task force was established.[23] Europol's competence was expanded, and three Protocols to the Europol Convention provided for a number of changes to its operations; subsequently the Europol Convention and its Protocols were replaced by a third pillar Decision, which made further changes to the legal framework governing Europol.[24] The

---

[17] The previous Art 135 EC; see 12.4.1 below.   [18] See 12.6.3 below.
[19] [1999] OJ L 176/17.
[20] On the issue of allocation of the SIS, see further 2.2.2.3 and 2.4 above.
[21] See 12.5 below.   [22] See 12.9.4 below.   [23] See 12.7.3 below.
[24] See 12.8 below.

Police College was promptly established in 2000, and its status was subsequently transformed in 2004 and 2005.[25] An anti-drugs strategy was adopted, and implemented *inter alia* by several law enforcement measures.[26] Finally, a Decision establishing financial intelligence units was quickly adopted.[27]

Since the adoption of the Tampere programme, the European Council returned to policing and security issues several times, in particular following the terrorist offences of September 2001 in the US, March 2004 in Madrid, and July 2005 in London, by holding emergency summits and/or adopting declarations with detailed agendas for further anti-terrorist measures—most of which have an impact well beyond terrorist crimes.[28] In another priority area, the Council adopted an organized crime action plan.[29] The 2004 Hague programme set out objectives for this field, concerning in particular implementation of the anti-terrorist plan and measures on data retention, passenger name records, and the enhanced mutual access to national police databases.[30] Moreover, a number of measures in this area were taken from the text of a Convention initially agreed among a group of Member States (the Prum Convention).[31]

More specifically, in the area of customs, a Protocol to the CIS Convention concerning customs files was signed in May 2003, and ultimately the CIS Convention and its Protocols were, like the Europol Convention, replaced by a third pillar Council Decision.[32] A detailed strategy for EU customs cooperation was also agreed in 2003, and updated in 2009.[33] There were also many amendments to the Schengen rules on policing, as regards: the extension of the rules on cross-border surveillance;[34] amendment of the rules on the exchange of information among police;[35] changes to the rules establishing the SIS; the adoption of legislation to establish a second generation Schengen Information System (SIS II);[36] and amendments to the Schengen and EU rules on liaison officers.[37]

Investigations were facilitated by Decisions concerning, inter alia, Internet child pornography, currency counterfeiting, and vehicle crime, as well as soft law concerning other types of crime, while control of persons was the subject of a Decision on football match security and soft law on summit meetings. The Council was keen to establish networks dealing with particular forms of crime, for example for the protection of VIPs, as regards corruption, and for the investigation and prosecution of war crimes.[38] Furthermore, the Council adopted

---

[25] See 12.7.2 below.   [26] See particularly 12.7.4 below.   [27] See ibid.
[28] See the Statewatch analysis, online at: <http://www.statewatch.org/news/2004/mar/swscoreboard.pdf>.   [29] [2000] OJ C 124/1.
[30] [2005] OJ C 53/1.
[31] For the text of the Prum Convention, see Council doc 10900/05, 7 July 2005.
[32] See 12.6.1.2 below.   [33] [2003] OJ C 247 and [2009] OJ C 260/1.
[34] See 12.9.2.below.   [35] See 12.6.3 below.   [36] See 12.6.1.1 below.
[37] See 12.6.3 below.   [38] On all these measures, see 12.7.4 below.

fresh funding measures related to law enforcement, when the pre-Amsterdam measures expired.[39]

A particular focus of EU activity was the exchange of information regarding investigations, not just by developing the rules governing Europol, the SIS, and the Schengen rules on police information exchange (as mentioned above), but by further controversial measures, in particular concerning the adoption of rules on telecoms data retention (requiring the private sector to keep information on telephone and Internet use in case law enforcement services request it), the exchange of information on passengers, the enhancement of national police services' access to each others' databases, and the access by law enforcement services to the Visa Information System (VIS).[40] The Council also adopted a Framework Decision which harmonized aspects of national law regarding data protection in the criminal law and policing sector.[41]

There was particular attention paid to the evaluation of Member States' compliance with EU measures in this field. Evaluation of compliance was carried out in accordance with a 1997 Joint Action, a Schengen Executive Committee decision, and a 2002 Decision regarding evaluation of compliance with anti-terrorism measures.[42]

Finally, it should be noted that there were no references to the Court of Justice from national courts on any EU police cooperation measures before the entry into force of the Treaty of Lisbon. However, annulment actions were brought against EC measures which arguably should have been adopted as third pillar acts,[43] and against a third pillar measure which arguably should have permitted greater participation for the UK.[44]

12.2.3. Treaty of Lisbon

Following the entry into force of the Treaty of Lisbon on 1 December 2009, police cooperation within the EU is primarily governed by Article 84 of the Treaty on the Functioning of the European Union (TFEU), which concerns crime prevention, along with Articles 87–89 TFEU (Chapter 5 of Title V of Part Three of the Treaty).

---

[39] See 12.10 below.   [40] See 12.6 below.

[41] [2008] OJ L 350/60; see 12.6.1 below. On the legal effect of Framework Decisions, see Case C-105/03 *Pupino* [2005] ECR I-5285 and further 2.2.2.2 above.

[42] See respectively [1997] OJ L 344/7; [2000] OJ L 239/138; and [2002] OJ L 349/1. See also the Joint Action evaluating candidate Member States (12.11 below).

[43] Joined Cases C-317/04 and C-318/04 *EP v Council and Commission* [2006] ECR I-4721 and Case C-301/06 *Ireland v Council and EP* [2009] ECR I-593. See 12.4.3.2 below.

[44] Case C-482/08, *UK v Council*, pending (opinion of 24 June 2010), concerning the validity of the Decision on police access to the VIS ([2008] OJ L 218/129). See 12.2.5 below.

Article 84 TFEU provides as follows:

The European Parliament and the Council, acting in accordance with the ordinary legislative procedure, may establish measures to promote and support the action of Member States in the field of crime prevention, excluding any harmonisation of the laws and regulations of the Member States.

Articles 87 TFEU sets out the general provisions on police cooperation, replacing the prior Article 30(1) TEU:

1. The Union shall establish police cooperation involving all the Member States' competent authorities, including police, customs and other specialised law enforcement services in relation to the prevention, detection and investigation of criminal offences.

2. For the purposes of paragraph 1, the European Parliament and the Council, acting in accordance with the ordinary legislative procedure, may establish measures concerning:

   (a) the collection, storage, processing, analysis and exchange of relevant information;
   (b) support for the training of staff, and cooperation on the exchange of staff, on equipment and on research into crime-detection;
   (c) common investigative techniques in relation to the detection of serious forms of organised crime.

3. The Council, acting in accordance with a special legislative procedure, may establish measures concerning operational cooperation between the authorities referred to in this Article. The Council shall act unanimously after consulting the European Parliament.

   In case of the absence of unanimity in the Council, a group of at least nine Member States may request that the draft measures be referred to the European Council. In that case, the procedure in the Council shall be suspended. After discussion, and in case of a consensus, the European Council shall, within four months of this suspension, refer the draft back to the Council for adoption.

   Within the same timeframe, in case of disagreement, and if at least nine Member States wish to establish enhanced cooperation on the basis of the draft measures concerned, they shall notify the European Parliament, the Council and the Commission accordingly. In such a case, the authorisation to proceed with enhanced cooperation referred to in Article 20(2) of the Treaty on European Union and Article 329(1) of this Treaty shall be deemed to be granted and the provisions on enhanced cooperation shall apply.

   The specific procedure provided for in the second and third subparagraphs shall not apply to acts which constitute a development of the Schengen *acquis*.

Article 88 TFEU concerns Europol, and replaced the previous Article 30(2) TEU:

1. Europol's mission shall be to support and strengthen action by the Member States' police authorities and other law enforcement services and their mutual cooperation in preventing and combating serious crime affecting two or more Member States, terrorism and forms of crime which affect a common interest covered by a Union policy.

2. The European Parliament and the Council, by means of regulations adopted in accordance with the ordinary legislative procedure, shall determine Europol's structure, operation, field of action and tasks. These tasks may include:

(a) the collection, storage, processing, analysis and exchange of information, in particular that forwarded by the authorities of the Member States or third countries or bodies;

(b) the coordination, organisation and implementation of investigative and operational action carried out jointly with the Member States' competent authorities or in the context of joint investigative teams, where appropriate in liaison with Eurojust.

These regulations shall also lay down the procedures for scrutiny of Europol's activities by the European Parliament, together with national Parliaments.

3. Any operational action by Europol must be carried out in liaison and in agreement with the authorities of the Member State or States whose territory is concerned. The application of coercive measures shall be the exclusive responsibility of the competent national authorities.

Finally, Article 89 TFEU, in place of the prior Article 32 TEU, now governs cross-border operation measures:

The Council, acting in accordance with a special legislative procedure, shall lay down the conditions and limitations under which the competent authorities of the Member States referred to in Articles 82 and 87 may operate in the territory of another Member State in liaison and in agreement with the authorities of that State. The Council shall act unanimously after consulting the European Parliament.

Taking these provisions in turn, Article 84 TFEU essentially provides for the affirmation of the prior status quo,[45] providing, as before, for EU support for national measures concerning crime prevention without any harmonization of national law. But the decision-making procedure changed to qualified majority voting (QMV) in the Council and co-decision with the European Parliament (known as the 'ordinary legislative procedure' since the Treaty of Lisbon entered into force).[46] Another change is the use of 'Community' instruments in place of third pillar acts previously. On that point, it is now possible to adopt Directives on the subject of crime prevention, whereas Framework Decisions were never used in this area.

As for the general rules on police cooperation (Article 87 TFEU), compared to the prior rules, the decision-making procedure has changed as regards non-operational police cooperation (Article 87(2) TFEU) from the previous unanimity in Council and consultation of the EP to QMV and co-decision (now the 'ordinary legislative procedure'). However, the previous decision-making rules have been retained as regards operational cooperation (Article 87(3) TFEU); these are now described as a type of 'special legislative procedure',[47] but in some

---

[45] On which, see 12.5 below.   [46] On this procedure, see Art 294 TFEU.

[47] See Art 289(2) TFEU.

cases there is now a possible fast-track to enhanced cooperation in the event of a national veto.[48] The EU's competence has been amended slightly.[49]

Comparing Article 87(2) TFEU to the prior Article 30(1)(b)–(d) TEU, Article 87(2)(a) is nearly identical to the prior Article 30(1)(b), except that a specific example of the content of these powers has been dropped (suspicious financial transactions), along with references to Europol and to data protection rules. The first change is immaterial, since reports on suspicious financial transactions fall within the scope of this provision anyway. Secondly, the change concerning Europol simply takes account of Article 88(2)(a) TFEU. The third change takes account of the inclusion of a general legal base for data protection in the TFEU (Article 16), which clearly confers power on the EU to adopt data protection rules covering both the previous first pillar and the previous third pillar,[50] subject to a declaration attached to the Final Act of the Treaty indicating that specific provisions will be adopted to address national security concerns.[51]

Next, Article 87(2)(b) is very similar to the previous Article 30(1)(c) TEU, with minor changes to the wording regarding training, staff exchange, and research, and a more significant change as regards dropping any reference to liaison officers.[52] Article 87(2)(c), compared to the previous Article 30(1)(d) TEU, confers power to adopt common investigative techniques, rather than just a common *evaluation* of such techniques, suggesting a possible greater degree of harmonization in this area. Finally, the power over police operations set out in Article 87(3) is prima facie identical to the competence set out in the previous Article 30(1)(a) TEU.

Moving on to Europol (Article 88 TFEU), the decision-making procedure has changed fully to QMV in Council and co-decision with the EP (the ordinary legislative procedure) with no exceptions provided for. However, it should be noted that only Regulations, not any other form of EU act, have to be used as regards Europol. Compared to the previous Article 30(2) TEU, there is an express exclusion from exercising 'coercive measures' and a requirement to act in liaison and agreement with each Member State as regards 'operational action'. More specifically, 'investigative and operational action' has to be carried out either 'jointly' with Member States or 'in the context of joint investigative teams'. The reference to specific rules concerning EP and national parliamentary scrutiny of Europol is new.

Overall, Europol is no longer assigned a role *supporting, facilitating*, and *requesting* action by national police forces, but rather (implicitly) a role in *partnership* with

---

[48] This process could also be invoked as regards Art 86 TFEU, concerning the possible creation of a European Public Prosecutor (see 11.2.3 above). On this procedure, referred to as a 'pseudo-veto' in this book, see 2.2.3.4.2 above.   [49] See 12.2.4 below.

[50] On the competence issues which arise, see 12.2.4 below.

[51] Declaration 20 to the Final Act of the Treaty of Lisbon.

[52] On the competence issues which arise regarding liaison officers, see 12.2.4 below.

national forces. But the partnership is not fully equal since Europol cannot have the capacity to apply coercive measures. Moreover, the Treaty does not refer to any *independent* role for Europol to act fully by itself, although since the listed powers are non-exhaustive ('may include') it would be possible to adopt rules to that effect—as long as Europol would not thereby carry out operational action independently, or exercise coercive powers, in light of the limits on its powers set out in Article 88(3).

Finally, Article 89 TFEU (as regards cross-border operations) essentially copied the prior Article 32 TEU with no substantive amendments, either to decision-making rules (again now described as a 'special legislative procedure') or competence.

As regards all aspects of police cooperation, the extended jurisdiction of the Court of Justice applies, subject to the transitional period applying to pre-existing third pillar measures and to the special derogation applying to law enforcement measures, which could be particularly relevant to police coopera-tion measures.[53]

All of the police cooperation provisions are also affected by the general pro-visions in Title V of the TFEU,[54] particularly the provisions relating to: the evaluation of national implementing measures;[55] the establishment of the stand-ing committee on security;[56] national competence for law and order measures (which is identical to the prior Article 33 TEU);[57] security cooperation between Member States;[58] administrative cooperation between Member States;[59] and the adoption of anti-terrorist sanctions measures.[60] It also remains possible for a group of Member States to make proposals for measures in this field.[61]

The remaining provisions permitting unanimous voting in this area (as regards cross-border police action and operational police cooperation) are subject to the possibility of simplified treaty amendment to introduce QMV in Council and co-decision by the EP.[62] Furthermore, a group of Member States can request to apply enhanced cooperation in this area, with the possibility that they can change the relevant decision-making procedures between themselves.[63] The revised and extended rules on JHA opt-outs also apply to policing issues.[64]

As regards the rest of the Treaty of Lisbon, the revised rules on human rights (accession of the EU to the ECHR and the enhanced status of the Charter) could impact upon the area of police cooperation. The previous Article 135 EC on customs cooperation was amended to drop the prior limitation concerning the

---

[53] Art 275 TFEU. See further 2.2.3.3 (transitional rules) and 2.2.3.2 above (derogation).
[54] See 2.2.3.2 above.   [55] Art 70 TFEU.   [56] Art 71 TFEU.   [57] Art 72 TFEU.
[58] Art 73 TFEU. See also Art 4(2), revised TEU.   [59] Art 74 TFEU.
[60] Art 75 TFEU. On the substantive measures concerned, see 12.4.5 below.
[61] Art 76 TFEU.   [62] See Art 48(7), revised TEU.
[63] For a discussion of the enhanced cooperation rules, see 2.2.5.5 above.   [64] 12.2.5 below.

application of criminal law or criminal justice.[65] Finally, the specific power to adopt measures on civil protection and the 'solidarity' clause introduced by the Treaty of Lisbon will also impact upon the issues discussed in this chapter.[66]

In practice, no binding police cooperation measures were proposed or adopted in the first few months after the Treaty of Lisbon entered into force, apart from measures concerning the migration of data between the SIS and SIS II, the proposed conclusion of treaties in this field (most of which were signed—but not concluded—before that Treaty entered into force), and the adoption of a decision establishing a committee on operational security (known as 'COSI', based on the French acronym).[67] Equally, there were no references to the Court of Justice on policing measures during the first few months after the Treaty entered into force.

As for the future, the Stockholm programme and the plans for its implementation refer to:[68] increasing the training of police and customs officers; revising the legal framework for data protection (to be proposed in 2010), including negotiation of an EU–US data protection agreement as regards exchange of law enforcement data;[69] defining an internal security strategy, including a possible Internal Security Fund;[70] implementing a strategy for law enforcement information management,[71] including a review of existing measures on exchange of personal data; the development of a European Police Records Index System (EPRIS, planned for 2012); the adoption of legislation on a passenger name record system (proposals planned for 2010); the further use of databases for law enforcement purposes, and information exchange on 'travelling violent offenders including those attending sporting events or large public gatherings'; the further development of Europol (proposal in 2013), operational cooperation, and forensic quality standards; the creation of an 'Observatory for the Prevention of Crime' (proposal by 2013); and the possible development of a Police Cooperation Code (proposal in 2014).

12.2.4. Competence issues

Before the entry into force of the Treaty of Lisbon, the most difficult competence issues regarding EU policing and security were the extent of the crossover with

---

[65] Art 33 TFEU. See further 12.4.1 below.

[66] Arts 196 and 222 TFEU. See further 12.4.7 below.

[67] See respectively 12.6.1.1 below, 12.11 below, and [2010] OJ L 52/50 (discussed further in 2.2.3.2 above).

[68] [2010] OJ C 115 (ss 1.2.6, 2.5, and 4.1–4.3.3) and COM (2010) 171, 20 Apr 2010.

[69] The Commission has already proposed negotiations to this end. See 12.11 below.

[70] The strategy has already been adopted: see Council doc 5842/2/10, 23 Feb 2010.

[71] The strategy has also already been adopted: see Council doc 16637/09, 25 Nov 2009.

EC legislation (as it then was), in particular as regards the use of private-sector data by law enforcement agencies. These issues are examined further below.[72]

As for the competence issues arising after the entry into force of the Treaty of Lisbon, first of all a number of the general provisions of Title V of the TFEU raise questions, given that they are subject to different decision-making procedures than all of the specific policing provisions of the Treaty. The scope of the legal bases for measures concerning evaluations (Article 70 TFEU), the creation of the standing committee on internal security (Article 71 TFEU), and anti-terrorist sanctions (Article 75 TFEU) has been examined already in Chapter 2.[73] So has the specific rule in Article 72 TFEU (previous Article 33 EU), which refers to Member States' responsibilities as regards law, order, and security; this provision simply confirms that the implementation of EU policing measures is left to the Member States' authorities, particularly as regards coercive measures.[74] It should also be noted that the Treaty provides for a specific restriction of competence as regards intelligence cooperation.[75] Finally, as regards the power to adopt measures on administrative cooperation (Article 74), this is distinct from the powers to adopt measures concerning law enforcement *practitioners*, and so has limited scope as compared to the policing powers set out in Articles 84 and 87–89 TFEU.

Next, as noted already,[76] Article 16 TFEU, the legal base for measures concerning data protection, applies not only to the former first pillar but also to the former third pillar, and provides for the use of the ordinary legislative procedure (and therefore, the power of consent for the EP as regards the conclusion of treaties). The measures to be adopted on this issue will often cross over with the substantive rules on the exchange of information as such between law enforcement authorities, but there is no problem having a joint legal base of Articles 16 and 87(2) TFEU, because the decision-making procedure is the same and the possible conflict of rules regarding territorial scope has been resolved by specific provisions in the opt-out Protocols relating to the UK, Ireland, and Denmark.[77]

The other competence issues relevant to EU policing law fall into three main categories: the distinction between policing law and the non-JHA provisions of the Treaties; the distinction between policing law and criminal law; and the distinction between the different powers relating to policing law. The first category of issues is discussed below,[78] while the second and third are discussed in turn in this section.

The distinction between the policing and criminal law provisions is significant to the extent that several policing provisions (Articles 87(3) and 89 TFEU) are subject to a special legislative procedure, whereas most criminal law provisions are subject to the ordinary legislative procedure. However, Article 86 TFEU

---

[72] See 12.4.3.2 below.   [73] See 2.2.3.2 above.
[74] See the interpretation of Art 72 TFEU in 2.2.3.2 above.
[75] See Art 73 TFEU and Art 4(2), revised TEU, discussed in ibid.   [76] See 12.2.3 above.
[77] See 12.2.5 below.   [78] See 12.4 below.

is subject to a special legislative procedure; and certain criminal law provisions (Articles 82(2) and 83 TFEU)—but no policing law provisions—are subject to an 'emergency brake' procedure.[79] As discussed in other chapters, any criminal procedure or substantive criminal law measures which also address investigations by police need a dual legal base from the policing provisions of the Treaty.[80] Any involvement by Eurojust or the European Public Prosecutor in investigations requires the *lex specialis* of Articles 85 or 86 TFEU, and any rule concerning jurisdiction over investigations (as distinct from prosecutions) falls within the scope of the policing provisions.[81]

As for the distinctions between the different legal bases relating to EU policing law, there are four different issues. Firstly, and most obviously, it is necessary to distinguish between the non-operational police cooperation within the scope of Article 87(2) TFEU, and the operational police cooperation within the scope of Article 87(3) TFEU, because the former provisions are subject to the ordinary legislative procedure, while the latter provisions are subject to a special legislative procedure, in particular involving unanimity.[82] Secondly, it is necessary to distinguish within Article 87(3) the issues that can be the subject of fast-track enhanced cooperation in the event of a veto (because they do not build upon the Schengen *acquis*) and those which cannot (because they build upon that *acquis*). Thirdly, it is necessary to distinguish the legal base concerning Europol from the legal bases concerning operational powers (ie Articles 87(3) and 89), again because of the different decision-making process; this includes the definition of the limits on Europol's powers. Fourthly, it is necessary to distinguish Articles 87(3) and 89, again because of the fast-track route to enhanced cooperation that applies to the former (in part), but not the latter.[83]

First of all, there is extensive prior practice of the Council adopting policing measures on various legal bases before the Treaty of Lisbon, but it should be kept in mind that the mere practice of the institutions does not establish a legally binding precedent.[84] Moreover, many of the Council's decisions regarding legal bases could be questioned: for instance, the Decision establishing SIS II was in part adopted on the legal base of the previous Article 30(1)(a) TEU, addressed operational police cooperation marginally, to the extent that it set out rules for action following policing alerts;[85] but essentially it concerned only such as the collection, of information, and should have had only Article 30(1)(b) TEU (now Article 87(2)(a) TFEU) as a legal base. Also, the specific legal base for measures concerning liaison officers (previous Article 30(1)(c) TEU) was repealed by the

---

[79] On this procedure, see 2.2.3.4.1 above. Note that the combination of a legal base subject to the emergency brake with a legal base which is not per se a problem: see 9.2.4 above.

[80] See 9.2.4 and 10.2.4 above.   [81] See 11.2.4 above.

[82] It is assumed that this analysis applies *mutatis mutandis* to distinguish Arts 87(2) and 89 TFEU.

[83] As with the emergency brake, however, a dual legal base should not be impossible per se (see the discussion in 9.2.4 by analogy).   [84] *Opinion 1/94* [1994] ECR I-5273.

[85] Arts 33, 37, and 39 of the Decision ([2007] OJ L 205/63).

Treaty of Lisbon, so any further measures on this issue will need a legal base which reflects the specific tasks of the liaison officers.[86]

The starting point for deciding on the correct legal base, according to the case law of the Court of Justice,[87] is to look at the aim and content of each measure. It must be kept in mind in particular that the legal base for operational cooperation concerns cooperation *between* the services of *different* Member States, ie there must be a specific cross-border element. Of course, the distinction between operational and non-operational policing measures is difficult to define precisely, as there is an obvious link between the exchange of data in particular on the one hand and police cooperation on the other—since the operational activity of law enforcement bodies will often be based on information received, and will also often result in the collection of information which can then be exchanged. However, the concept of operational cooperation must be distinct from the exchange and analysis of information, since Article 87 TFEU requires a distinction to be made between these issues. In the absence of any positive definition of 'operational measures' in the Treaty, the concept should be defined *a contrario* as compared to the specific powers set out in Article 87(2), and should in particular include coercive measures (on which, see the discussion of Article 88 below). By analogy with case law on competence in other areas of EU law, it is arguable that Article 87(3) is an exception which has to be interpreted narrowly.[88]

Secondly, there is case law of the Court of Justice defining the concept of a measure building upon the Schengen *acquis*, ruling that the concept must be defined by analogy with the 'legal base' case law.[89] The case law does not set out any abstract test for defining when a measure builds upon the Schengen *acquis*, although it should be noted that it is implicitly possible that a measure could be considered as building upon the Schengen *acquis* even if it does not amend an existing measure which forms part of that *acquis*. It might be argued that the concept of 'building upon' the *acquis* has a wider scope as regards external borders and visas issues than policing matters, given that the former issues are more directly connected to the core Schengen principle of abolishing internal border controls.

Moving on to the third issue, what is the distinction between Europol's powers pursuant to Article 88 on the one hand, and the provisions of Article 87(3) and 89 on the other? The obvious dividing line is that the latter provisions refer to *Member States'* authorities as distinct from Europol, and so a measure solely dealing with Europol (including the relationship of national law enforcement bodies *with*

---

[86] Since the pre-Lisbon measures on this issue concern the exchange of information by liaison officers (see 12.6.3 below), the correct legal base for further measures would be Art 87(2)(a), unless the officers are given other tasks.　　　　　[87] See the summary of the case law in 3.2.4 above.

[88] See Case C-268/06 *Impact* [2008] ECR I-2483.

[89] See Cases C-77/05 *UK v Council* [2007] ECR I-11459, C-137/05 *UK v Council* [2007] ECR I-11593, and C-482/08 *UK v Council*, pending (opinion of 24 June 2010).

Europol) falls within the scope of Article 88, while measures which only govern operational actions by national authorities fall within the scope of the other provisions. Any measure governing both issues will need joint legal bases (if this is legally feasible). The prospect of legislation on Europol circumventing the unanimity requirement of Articles 87(3) and 89 (ie by adopting legislation permitting Europol to have powers that national bodies cannot) is ruled out by the limits on Europol's power set out in Article 88(3) TFEU (ie the ban on exercising 'coercive powers' and operational action without Member States' approval); and those limits cannot in turn be circumvented by the use of Articles 87(3) or 89, because, as noted already, the latter provisions only confer power to regulate Member States' authorities.

This brings us to the interpretation of the 'coercive powers' exception set out in Article 88(3) TFEU. At the very least, 'coercive measures' must refer to authorized violence (ie the use of physical force) against individuals or other forms of constraint, including detention. It has also been argued convincingly that the concept also extends to arrest, search and seizure, the power to examine books and records, and the interception of telecommunications.[90]

Fourthly, as for the distinction between Articles 87(3) and 89, the former Article is the legal base for measures concerning 'operational cooperation between' the national law enforcement officers of different Member States, while the latter Article concerns the 'conditions and limitations' which apply when law enforcement officers from one Member State wish to 'operate' in another Member State. There is little to distinguish the two provisions, considering that measures adopted on the basis of Article 87(3) will often involve some movement of law enforcement officers between Member States (since this is obviously a form of 'operational' activity), while the latter provision requires close links between the law enforcement officers who move and the host Member State's authorities ('in liaison and in agreement'). The best view is that Article 89 alone applies where the 'guest' law enforcement officials play an essentially *independent* role in the host State's territory (leaving aside the liaison with and agreement of the host State's authorities), while Article 87(3) alone applies where the guest officers and the home State's officers work together *jointly*, or where law enforcement authorities coordinate their operational actions in different Member States. Arguably, where EU measures regulate the issue of the operational powers of guest officers in a host State in the context of a joint operation, then a *dual* legal base of both Articles 87(3) and 89 will be required.

12.2.5. Territorial scope

The policing rules in the Schengen *acquis* (except for the SIS provisions) applied to the UK from 1 January 2005 and will apply to Ireland, as soon as the latter's

---

[90] N Grief, 'EU Law and Security' (2007) 32 ELRev 752 at 759 and 761.

opt-ins to the Schengen *acquis* fully enter into force.[91] The SIS provisions will apply to those Member States at a later date. However, due to their geographical position and political reservations, both States have opted out of the Schengen rules on hot pursuit by police officers, and Ireland has also opted out of the rules on cross-border surveillance. The Schengen and EU policing rules fully apply to Denmark.[92] One particular dispute in this area is the question of whether the UK and Ireland can fully participate in the third pillar Decision which gave law enforcement bodies access to the Visa Information System.[93]

Since the entry into force of the Treaty of Lisbon, the UK and Ireland have the capacity to opt out of new measures in this area, subject to special rules if they opt out of measures amending acts which already apply to those States. Denmark is not subject to any measures in this area adopted after the Treaty of Lisbon, except those building upon the Schengen *acquis*. There are specific provisions on data protection, which provide that those Member States are not bound by measures adopted on the basis of Article 16 TFEU, to the extent that they are not bound by the underlying policing measure in question.[94] So far these revised opt-out rules have not been relevant in practice.

As for the new Member States, the EU's policing rules all applied immediately, except for the rules on cross-border surveillance and hot pursuit and on the SIS, which only applied once the Schengen *acquis* was fully extended to the new Member States (entailing abolition of border controls between old and new Schengen States).[95] It follows that those rules do not yet apply to Cyprus, Romania, and Bulgaria, since the Schengen *acquis* does not yet fully extend to those States.

Norway and Iceland have applied all the Schengen policing rules (and subsequent measures building upon them) since 2001, when their Schengen accession treaty entered into force.[96] Switzerland has done the same since its Schengen accession treaty came into force in 2008, and Liechtenstein will follow once its own accession treaty applies.[97]

Norway and Iceland (but not Switzerland and Liechtenstein) have also agreed a separate treaty with the EU as regards their participation in most of the provisions

---

[91] See further 2.2.5.1.3 above. On the content of the Schengen *acquis* as regards policing, see 12.2.1 above.   [92] See further 2.2.5.2 above.

[93] [2008] OJ L 218/129, subject to a pending legal challenge on this point: Case C-482/08 *UK v Council*, pending (opinion of 24 June 2010). On the substance of this Decision, see 12.6.1.3 below; on the VIS generally, see 4.8 above.   [94] See 2.2.5.1.2 and 2.2.5.2 above.

[95] See further 2.2.5.3 above.   [96] [1999] OJ L 176/35. See further 2.2.5.4 above.

[97] [2008] OJ L 53/52 (treaty with Switzerland) and COM (2006) 752, 1 Dec 2006 (proposed treaty with Liechtenstein). See further ibid. Also see the EU–Swiss treaty on judicial cooperation against fraud ([2009] OJ L 46/6, in force as regards most Member States, the EC, and Switzerland on 8 Apr 2009 (see [2009] OJ L 177/7)), contains some policing provisions. So does the proposed treaty on the same topic with Liechtenstein (COM (2009) 644, 23 Nov 2009).

of the 'Prum Decision',[98] which puts into force within EU law many of the provisions of the Prum Convention, which had earlier been agreed between a group of Member States in 2005.[99] This treaty also applies to the relevant provisions of a Decision which implements the Prum Decision, but does not apply to a separate Decision on special intervention units, which was also carved out of the Prum Convention.[100]

12.3. Human rights

12.3.1. International human rights law

Police operations and investigations raise questions in particular about the right to life, freedom from torture etc, rights regarding detention, and the gathering of evidence. The latter two points are best addressed as aspects of criminal procedure,[101] and the other points have limited relevance to EU law given the limitations upon both EU policing bodies and national police forces operating across borders pursuant to EU law. The focus in this chapter is therefore on the issues most affected by EU policing measures, particularly data protection and privacy rights in the context of police surveillance, monitoring, and exchange and storing of information, the impact of EU policing measures on freedom of expression and assembly, and the impact of EU anti-terrorist sanctions.[102]

The starting point on the issue of privacy and data protection is Article 8(1) of the European Convention on Human Rights (ECHR), which recognizes the 'right to respect for...private and family life...home...and correspondence'. However, Article 8(2) ECHR provides that public authorities may interfere with the exercise of this right if the interference 'is in accordance with the law and is necessary in a democratic society in the interests of national security, public safety,' and, inter alia, 'the prevention of disorder or crime'.

There is an obvious tension between the right to privacy and the interests of law enforcement and state security, in particular because of the nearly 'zero-sum' relationship between the two objectives: any increase in State surveillance and control could in principle potentially lead to an increase in the effectiveness of crime prevention and police investigations. Of course, this assumes that the competence and integrity of law enforcement and security service officials and the accuracy and efficiency of the technology they are using is beyond doubt; but unfortunately such assumptions are sometimes misplaced. Furthermore, it may

---

[98] [2008] OJ L 210/1. Norway and Iceland will participate in all of the provisions of the Decisions except the institutional clauses (see Art 1 of the treaty). On the substance of the Prum Decision, see 12.6.2, 12.6.3, and 12.9.4 below.

[99] [2009] OJ L 353/1. The treaty has been signed, but is not yet in force.

[100] See respectively [2008] OJ L 210/12 and 73. On the latter Decision, see 12.9.5 below.

[101] See ch 9.   [102] The last of these issues is discussed in 12.4.5 below.

be a more efficient use of resources for law enforcement and security services to concentrate their surveillance efforts upon a small number of criminal suspects and their associates, rather than the entire society. Finally, it is often argued that only people with something to hide should be concerned about maintaining their privacy from law enforcement or security service officials, but quite apart from the risks posed by technical and human failings, there is surely something intrinsically so valuable about our privacy that a degree of it must be protected, even if this comes at the cost of a greater risk to public safety. Quite simply, there has to be a balance between privacy on the one hand and combating crime and security risks on the other; but the precise place to draw the line is more and more contested as technology allows for ever wider interference with privacy, in particular the mass surveillance of most of all of the population, and the perceived risk from serious crime and terrorism increases.

Some indication of where to draw the line can be gleaned from the jurisprudence of the Strasbourg organs, which have addressed the application of Article 8 to policing activities on a number of occasions. A leading judgment of the European Court of Human Rights is *Klass*,[103] which ruled that telephone tapping (interception) was an interference with Article 8 rights, but that the German measures attacked in that case did not breach Article 8 because the interference had a legitimate aim and the safeguards on interception were sufficient. As in many subsequent cases in this field, the judgment turned on whether the national measures were 'in accordance with the law', meaning that there must be a basis for interferences with Article 8 rights in domestic law, such domestic laws have to be accessible, and the circumstances of their application to individuals has to foreseeable. The following principles were established:

The Court has... to accept that the existence of some legislation granting powers of secret surveillance over the mail, post and telecommunications is, under exceptional conditions, necessary in a democratic society in the interests of national security and/or for the prevention of disorder or crime... Nevertheless, the Court stresses that this does not mean that the Contracting States enjoy an unlimited discretion to subject persons within their jurisdiction to secret surveillance. The Court, being aware of the danger such a law poses of undermining or even destroying democracy on the ground of defending it, affirms that the Contracting States may not, in the name of the struggle against espionage and terrorism, adopt whatever measures they deem appropriate. The Court must be satisfied that, whatever system of surveillance is adopted, there exist adequate and effective guarantees against abuse. This assessment has only a relative character: it depends on all the circumstances of the case, such as the nature, scope and duration of the possible measures, the grounds required for ordering such measures, the authorities competent to permit, carry out and supervise such measures, and the kind of remedy provided by the national law.[104]

---

[103] *Klass v Germany* (A-28).   [104] Paras 48–50 of the judgment (ibid).

It is clear that while some interference with the right to privacy must be permitted in the interests of security and combating crime, the discretion granted to States cannot be absolute, or the very principle of a free society underlying the Convention would be threatened. Later case law elaborated on these principles, condemning Member States for interfering with privacy without a clear legal basis.[105]

A series of intertwined cases have addressed the particular privacy issues arising from data protection. In *Leander*,[106] the Human Rights Court found, by analogy with *Klass*, that it was a legitimate interference with the right to privacy for States to establish a security file on citizens and to vet applicants for public service, provided that sufficient safeguards were put in place. Subsequently, the Court referred to the Council of Europe's data protection Convention (see below) when ruling on the application of Article 8 to data files kept by security services.[107] Further cases condemned actions by law enforcement authorities in obtaining and/or storing or further transferring data such as recorded video footage, or taped conversations even as regards footage taken from security cameras in a public street or in police stations or prison cells.[108] Member States have also violated Article 8 ECHR when they kept personal data for longer than necessary.[109] Furthermore, the Human Rights Court has confirmed that storing cell samples, DNA information, and fingerprints falls within the scope of Article 8, and that the indefinite retention of such information from all persons who are charged, but not convicted, of any offence violates Article 8.[110] But on the other hand, establishing a database on offenders does not violate Article 8 if access to information is limited and subject to a duty of confidentiality,[111] and States have an obligation to waive the anonymity of Internet users if necessary in order to ensure that serious criminal offences which amount to a violation of privacy are prosecuted.[112]

Further detailed rules on data protection are set out in the 1981 Council of Europe data protection Convention, which has been ratified by all EU Member States.[113] The Convention applies to personal data processed by automatic means,[114] and its key provision requires States to apply key 'data quality' principles: data must be 'obtained and processed fairly and lawfully'; 'stored for specified and legitimate purposes and not used in a way incompatible with those purposes'; 'adequate, relevant

---

[105] See *Malone v UK* (A-82); *Kruslin v France* (A-176-A); *Huvig v France* (A-176-B); *Halford v UK* (Reports 1997-III); *Kopp v Switzerland* (Reports 1998-II); *Valenzeula Contreras v Spain* (Reports 1998-III); *Lambert v France* (Reports 1998-V); *Khan v UK* (Reports 2000-V); *Doerga v Netherlands* (27 Apr 2004); *Vetter v France* (31 May 2005); and *Wisse v France* (20 Dec 2005).

[106] *Leander v Sweden* (A-116).

[107] For instance, *Amann v Switzerland* (Reports 2000-II); *Rotaru v Romania* (Reports 2000-V); Art 13 ECHR was also violated in both cases due to the lack of a remedy in relation to the data.

[108] See *PG and JH v UK* (Reports 2001-IX); *Peck v UK* (Reports 2003-I), and *Perry v UK* (Reports 2003-IX).   [109] *Segerstedt-Wiberg v Sweden* (6 June 2006).

[110] *S and Marper v UK*, 5 Dec 2008.   [111] *Bouchacourt and others v France*, 17 Dec 2009.

[112] *KU v Finland*, 2 Dec 2008.   [113] ETS 108.

[114] For the definitions of these concepts, see Art 2 of the Convention.

and not excessive in relation to the purposes for which they are stored'; 'accurate and, where necessary, kept up to date'; and 'preserved in a form which permits identification of the data subjects for no longer than is required for the purpose for which those data are stored'.[115] Certain data (known in practice as 'sensitive data') cannot be processed unless there are 'appropriate safeguards' (data revealing racial origin, political opinion, or religious beliefs, concerning health and sexual life, or relating to criminal convictions).[116] Individuals have the right: to establish the existence of a file on them, its purpose, and details about the controller of the file; to obtain confirmation of whether their personal data is being stored, as well as obtaining access to the data; to obtain rectification or erasure of the data if it has been kept in violation of national law; and to have a remedy in relation to any of these rights.[117] However, derogations from these rights and the rules on data quality and sensitive data are permitted if they are 'provided for by the law' of the relevant State and constitute 'a necessary measure in a democratic society in the interests of' inter alia, 'protecting State security, public safety...or the suppression of criminal offences'.[118]

A Protocol of 2001, in force in 2004 and ratified by a majority of EU Member States,[119] supplements the Convention with two provisions, requiring States to establish a supervisory authority to facilitate the application of the Convention and prohibiting transmission of data to States or organizations which have not ratified the Convention unless they provide an 'adequate level of protection' for the data, or inter alia, 'legitimate prevailing interests, especially important public interests' justify the transfer. A further agreement, not yet in force, permits the EC (now the EU) as such to become party to the Convention.

As for the freedoms of expression and assembly, those rights are protected by Articles 10 and 11 ECHR, but again those rights may be limited on grounds similar to those permitting interference with Article 8 rights, provided that the interference is 'prescribed by law' and is 'necessary in a democratic society'. Although there is limited case law of the Strasbourg Court concerning demonstrations as such, it is clear that national authorities should not in principle restrict the movement of persons, even across *de jure* or de facto borders, who wish to participate in meetings or demonstrations.[120]

12.3.2. Application to EU law

The protection of privacy is recognized as a general principle of EU law,[121] as are data protection rights;[122] both rights are also recognized by the EU Charter

---

[115] Art 5 of the Convention.   [116] Art 6 of the Convention.
[117] Art 8 of the Convention.   [118] Art 9 of the Convention.
[119] ETS 181; for ratification details, see Appendix I.
[120] *Chorherr v Austria* (A-226-B); *Piermont v France* (A-314); and *Djavit An v Turkey* (Reports 2003-III). See also 3.3.1 above.   [121] See the case law referred to in 6.3.1 above.
[122] Case C-369/98 *Fisher* [2000] ECR I-6751.

of Fundamental Rights.[123] There is also detailed EU legislation on the specifics of data protection: within the scope of Community law (as it was before the Treaty of Lisbon), there is a Directive (applicable to Member States) and a Regulation (applicable to the EU institutions and bodies),[124] while within the scope of the third pillar (as it was before the Treaty of Lisbon) there is both a general Framework Decision and separate rules in specific third pillar acts. The third pillar measures are discussed further below.[125] As noted above, following the entry into force of the Treaty of Lisbon, there is a single legal base for measures governing data protection issues (Article 16 TFEU) and the Commission intends to propose legislation which will amend (and perhaps consolidate) the EU rules in future.[126]

The EC data protection measures are similar and essentially set out the principles of the Council of Europe Convention (and also the Protocol to that Convention, even though it was opened for signature later) in greater detail. In particular, the EC measures guarantee the free flow of data between Member States, but establish an elaborate regime regarding the transfer of data outside the EU. In particular, a detailed procedure is established to determine whether a third State has an 'adequate level of protection'; there may be a Commission decision or negotiation of a treaty to be concluded by the Council to this end.[127] The EU measures, unlike the Council of Europe Convention, set out detailed rules on when personal data may be processed; this includes cases where the controller is subject to a legal obligation, or where necessary to carry out a task in the public interest or the exercise of official authority.[128] There are also more detailed provisions on individual remedies and the powers of supervisory authorities;[129] the Regulation creates a European Data Protection Supervisor to exercise those powers as regards EC bodies.[130] However, the EC measures have limited scope, as they expressly do not apply to the processing of data 'by a natural person within the course of a purely personal or household activity', or to 'an activity which falls outside the scope of Community law, such as those provided for by Titles V and VI of the Treaty on European Union [the second and third pillars] and in any case to processing operations concerning public security, defence, State security (including the economic well-being of the State when the processing operation relates to State security matters) and the activities of the State in areas of criminal law'.[131] Even though the Treaty of Lisbon has repealed the former

---

[123] Arts 7 and 8 ([2007] OJ C 303).

[124] Respectively Dir 95/46 ([1995] OJ L 281/31) and Reg 45/2001 ([2001] OJ L 8/1). On the implementation of the Directive, see the Commission's report (COM (2003) 265, 15 May 2003).

[125] See 12.6.4 below.

[126] See 12.2.3 above. On the scope of this legal base, see 12.2.4 above.

[127] Arts 25 and 26 of the Directive.   [128] Art 7 of the Directive.

[129] Arts 22 and 28 of the Directive.   [130] Arts 41–48, Reg 45/2001 (n 68 above).

[131] Art 3(2) of the Directive.

Title VI of the TEU, the data protection rules adopted within the framework of the former third pillar will remain valid until they are amended as planned, due to the continuing exclusion of matters relating to criminal law and public security from the Directive.

The Court of Justice has ruled several times on the application of the Directive, defining its scope broadly to include data processing within a single Member State, interpreting the 'household' exception from its scope narrowly, aligning the interpretation of the data protection rights and possible exceptions with the jurisprudence of the Human Rights Court on Article 8 ECHR, ruling that the regime on external transfers of data does not apply to material posted on websites, limiting the information on EU citizens who have moved to another Member State which it is necessary to store in the public interest, addressing the balance between data protection rights and the freedom of expression, specifying the extent of the obligation to keep information on data processing, and clarifying the extent of the required independence of supervisory authorities.[132] The Court also ruled that the Directive does not apply to the transfer of data from EU airlines to American law enforcement authorities, given the public security context of the issue.[133]

As for the Regulation on data protection as regards the EU institutions, the Court of Justice has ruled that it takes priority over the EU's legislation on access to documents, meaning that anyone who wishes to know the names of persons who have lobbied the Commission on particular issues must show a legitimate interest in obtaining access to that data, unless the lobbyists have consented to the release of their names.[134] There is also a separate Directive providing for additional specific rules relating to data protection in the field of electronic communications (known generally as the 'e-privacy Directive').[135] The Court of Justice has ruled that the e-privacy Directive does not preclude Member States from requiring Internet service providers to make available to copyright holders information on illegal downloads of their music, subject to the principle of proportionality.[136] Finally, there is also a separate Directive establishing a requirement

---

[132] Cases: C-465/00, C-138/01, and C-139/01, *Osterreichischer Rundfunk* [2003] ECR I-4989; Case C-101/01 *Lindqvist* [2003] ECR I-12971; C-524/06 *Huber* [2008] ECR I-9705; C-73/07 *Satamedia* [2008] ECR I-9831; C-553/07 *Rijkeboer* [2009] ECR I-3889; and C-518/07 *Commission v Germany*, judgment of 9 Mar 2010, not yet reported.

[133] Joined Cases C-317/04 and C-318/04 *EP v Council and Commission* [2006] ECR I-4721. See the discussion of the legal base issue in 12.4.3.2 below, the human rights issues in 12.6.3 below, and the external relations context in 12.11 below.

[134] Case C-28/08 P *Bavarian Lager II*, judgment of 29 June 2010, not yet reported. For a similarly strict approach as regards the release of information on the beneficiaries of EU agricultural spending, see Joined Cases C-92 and 93/07 *Eifert and Volcker*, opinion of 17 June 2010, pending.

[135] Dir 2002/58, [2002] OJ L 201/37, amended in 2009 (Dir 2009/136, [2009] OJ L 337/11).

[136] C-275/06 *Promusicae* [2008] ECR I-271 (see also the order in Case C-557/07 *LSG* [2009] ECR I-1227 and the pending case of C-70/10 *Scarlet Extended*).

for telecommunications service providers to retain data on their customers, for use by the law enforcement authorities.[137]

The Court of Justice has addressed the interface between the freedom of expression and assembly and police action to enforce EU law rules on free movement of goods, in a case in which national police permitted demonstrators to block the movement of goods between Member States for a period.[138] In the Court's view, Member States in principle must use police action to enforce EU free movement rights, which are a public interest which can in principle justify limitations on the rights set out in Articles 10 and 11 ECHR. On the other hand, the protection of human rights is a legitimate ground justifying a restriction by Member States upon free movement rights. To reconcile the conflicting rules, the Court stated that 'the interests involved must be weighed having regard to all the circumstances of the case in order to determine whether a fair balance was struck between those interests'.[139] In all the circumstances of this case, a correct balance was struck.

12.4. Impact of other EU law

JHA customs cooperation is obviously closely linked with non-JHA EU law, given the EU's powers to regulate customs issues both as regards trade between Member States and the external trade between the EU and the rest of the world. Moreover, there are a number of links between police cooperation and non-JHA EU law, particularly as regards free movement law and private sector links with law enforcement activities. There are also important non-JHA EU measures on, inter alia, transport security, infrastructure protection, anti-terrorist sanctions, anti-fraud measures, and civil protection.[140] It is still necessary to draw distinctions between these areas of law and policing measures even after the entry into force of the Treaty of Lisbon, at least due to the differences in territorial scope of the measures concerned.

12.4.1. Customs cooperation

As regards customs cooperation, the EU has both a third pillar Convention (replaced by a Decision in 2009) establishing a Customs Information System as

[137] Dir 2006/24 ([2006] OJ L 105/1), discussed further in 12.4.3.2 and 12.6.3 below. The Court of Justice has upheld the internal market legal basis of this Directive: C-301/06 *Ireland v Council and EP* [2009] ECR I-593.

[138] C-112/00 *Schmidberger* [2003] ECR I-5659. See further 12.4.2 below.

[139] Para 81 of the judgment.

[140] Note also the application of Art 16 TFEU to data protection issues in both the former first pillar and the former third pillar (see 12.2.4 above).

regards criminal offences, and a 'first-pillar' Regulation (adopted pursuant to Community law, as it then was) establishing that system as regards administrative offences.[141] The Regulation was amended in 2008, inter alia in order to match the 2003 Protocol to the third pillar Convention.[142]

When adopted in 1997, this Regulation had to have the 'legal base' of Article 308 EC (the 'residual powers' clause),[143] but the Treaty of Amsterdam subsequently inserted a new Article 135 into the EC Treaty, allowing the adoption of measures using the co-decision procedure (as it then was) 'in order to strengthen customs cooperation between the Member States and between the latter and the Commission'. Until the entry into force of the Treaty of Lisbon, this Article expressly provided that '[t]hese measures shall not concern the application of national criminal law or national administration of justice' and that measures could only be taken '[w]ithin the scope of application of' the EC Treaty. The Treaty of Lisbon has since removed these restrictions.[144]

In practice, Article 135 EC was used to adopt several measures with an impact on security. Following the events of September 11, 2001, the US tightened its control of foreign goods shipped to the US on security grounds, and ultimately the EC (as it then was) agreed a treaty with the US on container security.[145] More broadly, the Commission issued a communication on the role of customs in ensuring security at the external borders,[146] and security-related amendments to the EU customs code were adopted in 2005.[147] EU customs powers are also relevant to combating breaches of intellectual property law.[148]

Furthermore, a Regulation requiring Member States to control the movement of large volumes of cash at external borders was also adopted in 2005.[149] This Regulation is complementary to EU legislation on money laundering, and requires persons to make a declaration if they are carrying more than €10,000 across the external border of a Member State.[150] The EU also adopted a new customs code in 2008.[151]

---

[141] Reg 515/97 ([1997] OJ L 82/1). On the Convention (now Decision), and on the application of both measures, see 12.6.1.2 below.

[142] Reg 766/2008, [2008] OJ L 218/48. The legislation has not been codified.

[143] The Commission's argument for use of the EU's 'internal market' powers to adopt the Reg instead was rejected by the Court of Justice: Case C-209/97 Commission v Council [1999] ECR I-8067. The Treaty of Lisbon replaced Art 308 EC (following amendment) with Art 352 TFEU.

[144] See Art 33 TFEU.   [145] [2004] OJ L 304/32.

[146] COM (2003) 452, 24 July 2003. See the parallel issues concerning external border controls on persons (3.6 above).   [147] Reg 648/2005 ([2005] OJ L 117/13).

[148] See further 10.4.1 and 10.5.1.1 above, and also the Commission communication and Council resolution on this issue (COM (2005) 479, 11 Oct 2005 and [2006] OJ C 67/1).

[149] Reg 1889/2005 ([2005] OJ L 309/9), applicable from 15 June 2007 (Art 11). The Commission has positively assessed the implementation of the Regulation in practice (COM (2010) 429, 12 Aug 2010).

[150] On EU money laundering legislation, see 10.5.1 above.

[151] Reg 450/2008 ([2008] OJ L 145/1).

The cash checks Regulation and the revised Customs Code raised issues about the scope of EC powers (as they then were) as regards criminal law, and in particular the interpretation of the limitation on the scope of the former Article 135 EC—although it should be noted that both measures entailed the use of other legal bases as well. Since both measures were stripped of detailed proposed criminal provisions,[152] they fell within the scope of EC powers at the time.[153]

12.4.2. Police cooperation

As for police cooperation, it is clear that Member States can deny access to employment as a police officer to nationals of other Member States,[154] but policing employment falls within the scope of EU discrimination law. The result is that Member States' decisions to ban women from policing jobs are justiciable, and while certain police duties can be barred to women, it might be disproportionate to ban women from serving as reserve police officers and separate recruitment systems for male and female police officers might also breach EU law.[155] Furthermore, Member States are precluded from arguing that policing difficulties justify state action which restricts free movement rights. If they wish to argue that free movement rights must be suspended, or that their illegal state aid cannot be reclaimed, because of public unrest, they must show that such unrest will occur and that they are unable to meet the anticipated unrest from the police resources available to them.[156]

Moreover, the Court of Justice has ruled that Member States' discretion over police operations may be curtailed in cases of omissions, if Member States refrain from taking the necessary steps to ensure free movement of goods in spite of action by private parties.[157] According to the Court, Member States 'retain exclusive competence as regards the maintenance of public order and the safeguarding

---

[152] Compare the final cash checks Reg with the original proposal (COM (2002) 328, 25 June 2002) and the final customs Code with Art 22 of the original proposal (COM (2005) 608, 30 Nov 2005).

[153] On this issue, see further 10.4.1.1 above, which also discusses further the similar limitations on EC power set out in the former Art 280(4) EC (now Art 325 TFEU after the Treaty of Lisbon). On the 'legal base' of the cash checks legislation, see the 1st Report of the House of Commons Select Committee on European Scrutiny (2004–05), with further references.

[154] See Case 149/79 *Commission v Belgium* [1979] ECR 1845 (night watchmen working for the State excluded from free movement rights); Commission Communication on Art 39(4) EC ([1988] OJ C 72/2).

[155] Cases 222/84 *Johnston* [1986] ECR 1651 and 318/86 *Commission v France* [1988] ECR 3659.

[156] Case 231/83 *Cullet* [1985] ECR 305; Case C-280/95 *Commission v Italy* (tax breaks for truckers) [1998] ECR I-259. See also *R v Coventry City Council, ex parte Phoenix Aviation and Others* [1995] All ER 37 (QB) and subsequently Case C-175/97 *Commission v France* [1998] ECR I-963.

[157] Case C-265/95 *Commission v France* (revolting farmers) [1997] ECR I-6959.

of internal security',[158] and thus have a 'margin of discretion' when deciding how best to combat threats to free movement, a 'fundamental principle' of the Treaty. But although the EU institutions cannot prescribe what policing operations the Member States must undertake to ensure free movement, the Court of Justice has asserted power to review whether a Member State has 'adopted appropriate measures' to that end. In *Commission v France*, ongoing attacks by farmers' groups on foreign produce had been met by relative inaction by the French police, and while the Court accepted in principle that police forces might appropriately refrain from interfering in a dispute for fear of sparking broader unrest, this could only apply to a specific incident and the Member State (as in *Cullet* and *Commission v Italy*) bears the burden of proof in showing that it would not be able to respond effectively. Therefore, France had breached Article 28 EC taken with Article 10 EC (the 'solidarity' clause).[159]

This principle raises two important questions. First, what limits exist upon Member States' obligation to spend their police resources in order to ensure the free movement of goods? The UK courts wrestled with this question when one county police force decided that it would only offer policing on certain days to protect the legal export of veal crates from a nearby port, because of the huge cost of preventing the exports from being blocked by animal rights protesters. The exporters sued to quash this decision and claim damages. Ultimately, the House of Lords, hearing the appeal after the Court of Justice's *Commission v France* ruling, dismissed the case.[160] Lord Slynn declined to rule on whether the police force had violated Articles 29 and 10 EC (now Article 35 TFEU and Article 4(3), revised TEU), because even if it had, it could defend its relative inaction under the 'public policy' defence of Article 30 EC (now Article 36 TFEU), because it had done as much as it reasonably and proportionately could in light of other legitimate claims upon it. Lord Cooke ruled that the police force had breached Article 29 EC taken alone, but could defend its inaction under Article 30 EC, even after embarking upon a slightly more stringent review than Lord Slynn had undertaken. However, Lord Hoffman ruled that the force's inaction was not a measure which could be challenged under Articles 29 and 10 EC, because under the circumstances, the exporters' rights were not directly effective. With great respect, this does not dispose of the issue (even if it is correct), because damages can still be claimed under EU law even if a Member State breaches an EU law

---

[158] The Court's wording is almost identical to the initial Art K.2(2) EU and the previous Art 100c(5) EC, which were in force at the time of the judgment, although it made no reference to those provisions. As noted above (12.2.2.1 and 12.2.3), these provisions are identical to the subsequent Art 33 EU, and now Art 72 TFEU.

[159] These provisions are now Art 34 TFEU and Art 4(3), revised TEU, respectively.

[160] *R v Chief Constable for Sussex, ex parte International Traders' Ferry* [1995] 3 CMLR 485 (QB); [1997] 2 CMLR 164 (CA); [1998] 3 WLR 1260 (HL).

right which is not directly effective.[161] Lord Hoffman further took the view that when relying on the exception in Article 30, Member States could not invoke local police force discretion but only national-level discretion—a caveat that would make it difficult for locally based police forces (like most English forces) to rely on Article 30. The multiplicity of reasoning in this case did not clarify matters much for lower British courts that might be faced with similar disputes in future.[162]

In comparison with the *Commission v France* ruling, the later judgment in *Schmidberger* sets out circumstances in which police inaction is justified, in particular due to the human rights context of that case.[163] In this case, the demonstration had been authorized by the authorities, the restriction on free movement was limited in time and space, the demonstration was not aiming to restrict trade in foreign goods per se (or indeed to destroy foreign goods), the authorities took steps to limit the disruption to free movement, there was no creation of a 'general climate of insecurity', and the alternatives to permitting the demonstration might have resulted in more serious disruption to free movement and would have impinged more upon the freedoms of expression and assembly.

In the meantime, there was legislative action by the EU, in the form of a Council Regulation and a Resolution of the Council and the Member States adopted in 1998.[164] The former requires Member States to inform other Member States and the Commission of obstacles to trade, which may include a Member State's inaction in response to acts of private parties, to take 'all necessary and proportionate steps' to assure free movement, and to reply very quickly to possible urgent requests from the Commission to take action. Fundamental rights, such as the right or freedom to strike, are expressly protected. The accompanying Resolution makes clear that the Commission requests under the Regulation will be part of the infringement procedure under Article 226 EC (now Article 258 TFEU), thus speeding up that procedure considerably. Member States also undertook to inform injured parties of effective remedies for their damages; furthermore, the Resolution allows for possible emergency Council meetings and raises the possibility of amending the Court of Justice's Rules of Procedure to expedite the hearing of relevant infringement actions which reach the Court. However, the Commission is not required to apply the procedure in the Regulation before using Article 258 TFEU.[165] A Commission report on the application of the Regulation expressed some disappointment at the lack of clarity in the Regulation and the lack of full implementation by Member

---

[161] Joined Cases C-6/90 and 9/90 *Francovich and Bonifaci* [1991] ECR I-5357.

[162] Lord Nolan agreed with Lord Slynn, while Lord Hope problematically agreed with *both* Lord Slynn and Lord Hoffman.

[163] Case C-112/00 [2003] ECR I-5659, paras 82–93 of the judgment.

[164] Reg 2679/98 ([1998] OJ L 337/8); [1998] OJ L 337/10 (Resolution).

[165] Case C-320/03 *Commission v Austria* [2005] ECR I-9871.

States, but the further actions suggested by the Commission (clarification and/or amendment of the Regulation) have not materialized.[166]

EU free movement law thus has an important impact upon the interests which national policing must protect and upon the operational decisions of police forces. It requires the interests of free trade to be protected in principle and in practice. Although national police forces have historically represented the inner core of state sovereignty, they can no longer be deployed purely in pursuit of national goals, with purely national decisions about operations and without any accountability to 'foreign' citizens, governments, or courts. As we shall see, EU policing law measures have affected national policing law even more substantially.

12.4.3. The private sector and security

12.4.3.1. Private security industry

Despite its links with law enforcement authorities, the sizable and significant private security industry essentially falls outside the scope of JHA law, due to its nature as an economic activity. The Court of Justice has delivered a series of seven judgments against various national restrictions which infringe, in the field of private security, the free movement of workers, freedom of establishment, and the freedom to provide services set out in the previous Articles 39, 43, and 49 EC (now Articles 45, 49, and 56 TFEU).[167] In these cases, the Court has consistently ruled that private security activities do not fall within the exceptions for 'public employment' or 'official authority' in the relevant Treaty Articles, because private security staff are not state employees and merely contributing to public security does not constitute an exercise of official authority. Nor do the Treaty exceptions for 'public policy, public security or public health' apply, because those exceptions do not remove entire sectors of economic activity from the scope of the free movement rules.

More precisely, Member States cannot justify directly discriminatory rules which require managers or staff, including self-employed persons, to have the nationality of the host State, or which ban foreign companies altogether from providing security services.[168] Residence requirements for managers or staff are not justified, since checks on non-residents could be carried out and guarantee requirements could be imposed on non-residents.[169] Similarly, host Member States cannot require security companies to have a place of business in the host State (or parts of it),[170] or demand

---

[166] COM (2001) 160, 22 Mar 2001.

[167] Cases: C-114/97 *Commission v Spain (I)* [1998] ECR I-6717; C-355/98 *Commission v Belgium* [2000] ECR I-1221; C-283/99 *Commission v Italy (I)* [2001] ECR I-4363; C-171/02 *Commission v Portugal* [2004] ECR I-5645; C-189/03 *Commission v Netherlands* [2004] ECR I-9289; C-514/03 *Commission v Spain (II)* [2006] ECR I-963; and C-465/05 *Commission v Italy (II)* [2007] ECR I-11091.   [168] *Commission v Spain (I)* and *Commission v Italy (I)*, ibid.

[169] *Commission v Spain (I)* and *Commission v Belgium*, ibid.

[170] *Commission v Belgium*, *Commission v Portugal*, and *Commission v Italy (II)*, ibid.

prior authorization or a licence for the company, managers, or staff from the host State government,[171] to insist on a bank guarantee or to control the prices of private security services.[172] Nor can a host State: require staff to carry a special national identity card;[173] ban natural persons from providing security services or to require persons providing security services to have a minimum share capital;[174] regulate the numbers of staff providing a private security service (except as regards the transport of explosives);[175] insist that security staff make an oath of allegiance to the host State;[176] or make security staff hold a professional certificate issued by the host State, although the Commission has generally failed to establish that Member States have infringed EU rules on mutual recognition of qualifications in this sector.[177]

Also, the private security sector is subject to EU rules on posted workers, which must be applied more flexibly in this sector as compared to construction.[178] However, private security has been excluded from general EU legislation on the provision of services.[179]

Finally, the private security sector is subject to a Council recommendation adopted in 2002,[180] which encourages Member States to exchange experience and best practices regarding the handling of information supplied by the private security sector. The Recommendation was adopted in place of a proposed Decision,[181] which was rightly criticized for infringing EC competence (as it then was), since it concerned the regulation and activities of the private security sector; it is clearly implicit in the Court's case law that only first pillar measures could address such issues.

An appropriate degree of regulation of private security activities is in the public interest in order to guarantee appropriate ethical standards, and in particular to ensure that no convicted criminals or persons disqualified in disgrace from the police or military take up private security activities. In the absence of at least an EU framework for exchanging information on national legislation or the qualifications of individuals, there is a risk that justified national regulation of private security could be undercut. There may even be a case for establishing common minimum EU standards for regulation of private security activities. It is unfortunate that the Commission has concentrated on infringement actions without also examining these broader issues.

---

[171] *Commission v Belgium, Commission v Portugal, Commission v Netherlands, Commission v Spain (II)*, and *Commission v Italy (II)*, ibid.　　　　　　　　　　　　[172] *Commission v Italy (II)*, ibid.

[173] *Commission v Belgium* and *Commission v Netherlands*, ibid.

[174] *Commission v Portugal* and *Commission v Spain (II)*, ibid.

[175] *Commission v Spain (II)* and *Commission v Italy (II)*, ibid.

[176] *Commission v Italy (II)*, ibid.

[177] *Commission v Portugal* and *Commission v Spain (II)*, ibid. However, in the latter case, Spain infringed EU law as regards recognition of the qualifications of private detectives.

[178] Case C-165/98 *Mazzoleni* [2001] ECR I-2189.

[179] See Dir 2006/123 ([2006] OJ L 376/36), Art 2(2)(k).　　　　[180] [2002] OJ C 153/1.

[181] [2002] OJ C 42/15.

12.4.3.2. Private sector security cooperation

In several areas, controversial EU legislation requires the private security to take extensive—and expensive—measures in pursuit of security objectives.[182] In particular, EU law requires: the telecommunications industry to retain substantial amounts of data on its customers, because that data may be of later use to law enforcement agencies; the passenger transport industry to transmit information on passengers to Member States' immigration authorities (and US law enforcement bodies); and the financial services industry to transmit information on its customers to US law enforcement bodies.[183]

First of all, as for the legal bases applicable to these measures, the Court of Justice ruled that the transfer of passenger name records (PNR) to the US was outside the scope of the data protection Directive adopted by the EC (as it then was), because the basic purpose of the measures concerned was to regulate their use by the US law enforcement bodies concerned.[184] On the other hand, the Court ruled that the EC Directive (as it then was) on data retention by the telecom industry fell within the EC's internal market powers, because this legislation essentially concerned the regulation of private sector activity, not the use of the data by the law enforcement authorities.[185]

It might be argued that these judgments are inconsistent, although in principle the distinction between the regulation of the use of the data concerned and the regulation of its initial collection is defensible. But with respect, the better approach would have been to uphold the Community's powers to regulate both issues, given the impact of both measures on the competition between private sector actors (an argument which was decisive in the data retention judgment, but dismissed in the PNR judgment), and (by analogy) the Court's ruling in another case that if a measure fell partly within the scope of EC law and partly within the scope of the second pillar (as they then were), the Community's powers always took priority.[186] This reasoning is comparable to Court judgments regarding the EU's common commercial policy, where a measure regulating foreign trade has a foreign or defence policy impact.[187]

12.4.4. Transport security and infrastructure protection

Following the terrorist offences of September 11, 2001, the EU institutions were quick to adopt a Regulation on the security of civil aviation, addressing the safety

---

[182] The details and merits of these measures are considered in 12.6.3 and 12.6.5 below.

[183] On the external relations context of the latter two measures, see 12.11 below.

[184] Joined Cases C-317/04 and C-318/04 *EP v Council and Commission* [2006] ECR I-4721.

[185] Case C-301/06 *Ireland v Council and EP* [2009] ECR I-593, concerning Dir 2006/24 ([2006] OJ L 105/54).   [186] Case C-91/05 *Commission v Council* [2008] ECR I-3651.

[187] See Cases C-70/94 *Werner* [1995] ECR I-3189, C-83/94 *Liefer* [1995] ECR I-3231, and C-124/95 *Centro-com* [1997] ECR I-81.

of airports and aircraft, including a requirement for Commission monitoring and the development of national aviation safety plans.[188] In light of experience with the application of the Regulation, a revised Regulation was adopted in 2008.[189] A series of Commission implementing measures address in more detail issues such as screening of staff, searching of passengers, the performance standards of X-ray machines, and items prohibited on board aircraft.[190] Initially most of these measures were not public, including the rules setting out which items passengers were prohibited from carrying on board aircraft. Following prosecution of a man who carried on board a tennis racket in breach of these unpublished rules, the Court of Justice ruled that those rules were unenforceable,[191] and they were mostly duly published.[192]

Subsequently, the EU institutions adopted a Regulation on maritime security and a Directive on port security;[193] there is also extensive legislation governing the transport of dangerous goods.[194] A Commission proposal for a Regulation on freight security was withdrawn, however.[195]

Furthermore, due to the risk that terrorist attacks would affect energy, food, or water supplies, the Council adopted a Directive establishing a European critical infrastructure protection programme in 2008.[196] A further Commission proposal for a critical infrastructure warning information network was not adopted before the entry into force of the Treaty of Lisbon,[197] but since the entry into force of that Treaty, it (and any further measures in this field) could be adopted on the basis of the ordinary legislative procedure, as a civil protection measure.[198]

---

[188] Reg 2320/2002 ([2002] OJ L 355/1).   [189] Reg 300/2008 ([2008] OJ L 97/72).

[190] See most recently Reg 573/2010 ([2010] OJ L 166.1). For an overview of these measures and of the application of the Regulation in practice, see the most recent report on application of the Reg (COM (2009) 518, 8 Oct 2009). See also the Commission communication on body scanners (COM (2010) 311, 15 June 2010).   [191] Case C-345/06 *Heinrich* [2009] ECR I-1659.

[192] Commission Reg 820/2008 ([2008] OJ L 221/8).

[193] Respectively Reg 725/2004 ([2004] OJ L 129/6) and Dir 2005/65 ([2005] OJ L 310/28); Member States had to implement the Dir by 15 June 2007 (Art 18). See also the earlier communication on maritime security (COM (2003) 229, 2 May 2003); the report on financing transport security (COM (2006) 431, 1 Aug 2008); and the report on the application of the Dir (COM (2009) 2, 20 Jan 2009). On the external competence resulting from the Reg, see Case C-45/07 *Commission v Greece* [2009] ECR I-701.

[194] Dir 2008/68 ([2008] OJ L 260/13); and see further: <http://ec.europa.eu/transport/security/dangerous_goods_en.htm>.

[195] COM (2006) 79, 27 Feb 2006, withdrawn with the 2010 work programme (COM (2010) 135, 31 Mar 2010).

[196] Dir 2008/114, [2008] OJ L 345/75. Member States must implement this Directive by 12 Jan 2011 (Art 12). Also on this subject, see the earlier Commission communication (COM (2004) 702, 20 Oct 2004) and Green Paper (COM (2005) 576, 17 Nov 2005), and the Commission communications on critical infrastructure protection (COM (2006) 786, 12 Dec 2006) and protection of critical infrastructure from cyber-attacks (COM (2009) 149, 30 Mar 2009).

[197] COM (2008) 676, 27 Oct 2008.

[198] See the discussion of Art 196 TFEU and of other civil protection measures, in 12.4.7 below.

The Stockholm programme calls for the review of the 2008 Directive to add additional sectors.[199]

12.4.5. Anti-terrorist sanctions[200]

The EU's well-known and controversial anti-terrorist sanctions measures address three categories of persons and groups. First of all, there are measures establishing sanctions against persons or groups deemed by the UN Security Council to be connected with Al-Qaeda and the Taliban. For this first category, before the entry into force of the Treaty of Lisbon, the EU adopted a foreign policy measure which is implemented by an EC (now EU) measure establishing a list of the persons concerned.[201] The measures (as amended) list the persons and groups considered to be terrorists; to this end, the EU has simply listed those persons and groups which a committee of the Security Council considers to be terrorists, apparently on the basis of allegations from Western intelligence agencies. It appears that the names of any non-EU citizens on the UN list are also added to the SIS, in order to list them as persons to be denied entry into the EU.[202]

It was assumed in practice that, before the entry into force of the Treaty of Lisbon this EC legislation had to be adopted on the basis of the prior Article 308 EC, which gave the EC (as it then was) the residual power to adopt measures which impacted upon the common market. The more specific power for the EC to adopt measures relating to economic and financial sanctions against third States (Article 301 EC) was rejected as unsuitable, since the persons and groups concerned did not control States. This approach was approved by the Court of Justice.[203] After the entry into force of the Treaty of Lisbon, there are two possible competing 'legal bases' for the legislation concerned: Article 215 TFEU, which now provides for the adoption of economic and financial sanctions against third States *or* non-State entities, and Article 75 TFEU, which provides for the adoption of financial sanctions against terrorists. The latter legal base, which is within the JHA provisions of the TFEU, gives more power to the EP. Unsurprisingly, the Council has favoured the use of Article 215 TFEU instead, and the EP has challenged the Council's view.[204]

---

[199] [2010] OJ C 115, point 4.6. A report and review of the Directive are scheduled for 2011 and 2012 respectively: see the Action plan to implement the Stockholm programme (COM (2010) 171, 20 Apr 2010).

[200] From a huge literature, see C Eckes, *EU Counter-Terrorist Policies and Fundamental Rights: The Case of Individual Sanctions* (OUP, 2009) and the contributions in (2009) 29 YEL, with further references.

[201] Reg 881/2002 ([2002] OJ L 139/9), replacing Reg 337/2000 ([2000] OJ L 43/1).

[202] Council doc 9358/02, 28 May 2002. The legislation establishing SIS II provides expressly for this practice (see 3.7.2 above).

[203] Joined Cases C-402/05 P and C-415/05 P *Kadi and Al Barakaat* [2008] ECR I-6351.

[204] Case C-130/10 *EP v Council*, pending. See the more detailed discussion of the 'legal base' issue in 2.2.3.2 above.

The other categories of sanctions concern those persons or groups which the EU has *autonomously* decided are terrorists, and who are either based outside the EU (the second category, ie 'international terrorists') or inside the EU (the third category, ie 'domestic terrorists'). This policy began following the terrorist attacks of September 11, 2001, and comprises a package of four acts which were originally adopted in December 2001,[205] and have subsequently been amended.[206] The package includes two Common Positions adopted jointly on the basis of the prior Articles 15 and 34 EU (therefore addressing both foreign police and police/ criminal law issues), an EC (now EU) Regulation implementing the second Common Position, and an EC (now EU) Decision further implementing that Regulation.

As to the substance, the first Common Position essentially transposes UN Security Council Resolution 1373/2001 on the suppression of terrorism, although the Common Position makes several provisions of the Resolution mandatory,[207] and alters the obligation for States to refrain from active or passive support for terrorism into an obligation for *individuals* to refrain from such support.[208] Since the Resolution does not define 'terrorism', it is equally unclear how the Common Position defines the term.

The second Common Position does define terrorism, by copying the definition that had been agreed by the Council in the context of the (then) proposed Framework Decision on terrorism, since adopted in June 2002.[209] However, the Common Position does not include the human rights provisions set out in the preamble and main text of the Framework Decision or in the statements attached to it. Nor is it limited (as is the Framework Decision) to acts committed on the territory of the EU or against EU citizens, institutions, or Member States. This distinction is crucial since there is no legal or ethical case for using political violence in a democracy, but the position may arguably be different in a non-democratic State.[210]

The impact of this second Common Position is that (by means of the Regulation and Decision), sanctions consisting of a freezing of all assets and a ban on the transfer of any sort of funds (including wages and social benefits) must be applied to all *international* terrorists, while *domestic* terrorist persons and groups are not covered by such sanctions. Both the international and domestic terrorists are subject to intensified police and judicial cooperation, an issue considered later in this chapter.[211]

---

[205] Common Positions 2001/930 and 931 ([2001] OJ L 344/90 and 93); Reg 2580/2001 ([2001] OJ L 344/70) and Decision 2001/927 ([2001] OJ L 344/83).

[206] The latest text of the second Common Position (now a Decision, after the entry into force of the Treaty of Lisbon) is in [2010] OJ L 178/28.

[207] Compare Arts 13–17 of the Common Position to para 3 of the Resolution.

[208] Compare Art 4 of the Common Position to para 2(a) of the Resolution.

[209] On this definition, see 10.5.1.2 above.   [210] See ibid.

[211] See 12.6.3 and 12.7.4 below.

The obvious problem with these measures is that persons and groups are listed as terrorists without any criminal trial or any alternative form of hearing at which they could dispute the categorization. As the result of the listing, for the first and second categories of persons and groups, is the freezing of all assets and income in the EU, except for a derogation to meet basic needs, the impact is substantial and indefinite. The sanctions were inevitably challenged in the EU courts directly by some of the persons and groups subjected to them, and through the national courts by other persons and groups indirectly affected by them. Moreover, the EU sanctions regime was questioned in the context of the broader public debate about the proportionality and legality of the international community's response to the September 11, 2001 terrorist attacks.

First of all, as for the first category of alleged terrorists (persons or groups with supposed links to Al-Qaeda or the Taliban, in the view of the Security Council), the Court of First Instance (as it then was) would not, in effect, rule on the legality of the listing of such persons or groups, on the grounds that the EC/EU was bound by the decisions of the Security Council, which took priority over all other legal obligations as a matter of international law. In the view of the Court, it would be possible for *jus cogens* principles to take priority over Security Council decisions, but the actions of the Security Council did not constitute a breach of those principles.[212]

However, on appeal to the Court of Justice, these rulings were overturned, in one of the most important judgments of the Court in recent years.[213] In the view of the Court, the EU could not avoid a full review of the legality of its decisions, even where its actions were based on resolutions of the Security Council, due to the fundamental rule that EU measures had to be accountable from a human rights perspective. As to the merits of the case, the procedure for listing the persons and groups concerned had 'patently' not respected the rights of the defence and did not provide for effective judicial review, since the persons and groups concerned had a right to know the reasons for the listing either at the time they were listed or as soon as possible thereafter. There was, however, no right to be told the reasons for the listing in advance, since the listing needed to have a 'surprise effect' in order to achieve the purpose of the rules. While considerations of safety and international relations meant that some information could legitimately be withheld from the persons concerned, this did 'not mean, with regard to the principle of effective judicial protection, that [sanctions] measures...escape all review by the Community judicature once it has been claimed that the act laying them down concerns national security and terrorism'. The failure to communicate any evidence to the persons or groups concerned

---

[212] Cases T-306/01 *Yusuf* [2005] ECR II-3633 and T-315/01 *Kadi* [2005] ECR II-3649, followed in Cases T-49/04 *Hassan* [2006] ECR II-52* and T-253/02 *Ayadi* [2006] ECR II-2139.

[213] *Kadi and Al Barakaat* (n 203 above), followed in Joined Cases C-399/06 P and C-403/06 P *Hassan* and *Ayadi*, judgment of 3 Dec 2009, not yet reported, and in Case T-318/01 *Othman* [2009] ECR II-1627. See also Joined Cases T-135-138/06, *Al-Faqih* and others, pending.

meant that their rights to be heard, and to effective judicial protection, had been breached. For similar reasons, their right to property had also been breached on procedural grounds, although substantively the restriction on their right to property was justified in the public interest.

Given that this judgment was decided on essentially procedural grounds, the Council and Commission took the view that the persons and groups concerned could simply be re-listed as terrorists, following the communication to them of the reasons for the listings. This re-listing has in turn been challenged.[214] Moreover, the basic framework for adopting sanctions measures against persons or groups allegedly linked to Al-Qaeda has been amended to take account of the *Kadi* judgment, in order to provide for a statement of reasons for persons or groups added to the list in the future, as well as those already on the list who request one. In the latter case the Commission will review the sanctions decision if the persons or groups concerned make observations, and forward such observations to the UN Sanctions Committee; it does not have the power to remove the person or group from the list (or to refuse to accept a new listing made by the Security Council).[215]

Furthermore, there have been references from national courts concerning the extent of the financial sanctions as regards third parties. The Court of Justice has confirmed that the sanctions extend to a ban on completing the process of selling a property to the persons or groups concerned,[216] and to raising money for a listed organization, although a prosecution to this end is tainted by the illegality of the listings decision.[217] On the other hand, the EU rules do not require Member States to refuse to pay social benefits to the family members of the persons concerned.[218]

As for the second category of alleged terrorists (ie the 'international terrorists' designated by the EU), right from the outset the Court of First Instance (as it then was) accepted to rule on the merits of challenges to the EU listings, given that the names of the persons and groups concerned had been decided on by the EU institutions, not designated by the UN Security Council. The leading case is *OMPI I*, in which the Court decided from the outset that the right to a hearing, to reasons, and to effective judicial protection apply to the second category of sanctions measures.[219] The basic rules in the relevant legislation require the

---

[214] Cases T-85/09 *Kadi II* and T-4/10 *Al-Saadi (ie Hassan)*, both pending.

[215] Reg 1286/2009, [2009] OJ L 346/42, particularly new Arts 7a and 7c. This raises the question as to whether the Commission's review of the listing can at least be challenged in the EU courts; the basic right of judicial review surely suggests that it can. This Regulation has been challenged by the EP on 'legal base' grounds (n 204 above).

[216] Case C-117/06 *Möllendorf and Möllendorf-Niehuus* [2007] ECR I-8361.

[217] Case C-550/07 *E and F*, judgment of 29 June 2010, not yet reported, by analogy (the case concerned a group covered by the second category of sanctions measures).

[218] Case C-340/08 *M and Others*, judgment of 29 Apr 2010, not yet reported.

[219] Case T-228/02 [2006] ECR II-4665.

listing to take place on the basis of 'precise information or material in the relevant file which indicates that a decision has been taken by a competent authority' as regards the persons or groups concerned, 'irrespective of whether it concerns the instigation of investigations or prosecution for a terrorist act, an attempt to perpetrate, participate in or facilitate such an act based on serious and credible evidence or clues, or condemnation for such deeds'; a 'competent authority' is a judicial authority or its equivalent, and the list has to be reviewed every six months.[220] There is therefore a two-step procedure, with a right to a fair hearing at both the national and EU level. At EU level, the person concerned has the right to a hearing as regards whether there is information in the file indicating that a relevant decision has been taken by a national competent authority (in the case of an initial listing), or the reasons for maintaining the listing (following a review). This does not entail a review of the merits of the national decision, which is in principle a matter for national law and procedure. As with the first category of sanctions, the initial decision to freeze funds can be taken in advance of a hearing; but the decisions to maintain the persons or groups on the sanctions list cannot. The statement of reasons must set out precisely how the criteria for imposing the sanctions are satisfied. Applying these rules to the case, there had been no com-munication of evidence or reasons at all—it was not even clear which national decision was the basis of the Council's listing decision—and so judicial review was impossible; the decision was therefore invalid on procedural grounds.

This case was followed by a number of other annulments of decisions to list various groups and persons as terrorists, because of the same procedural flaws.[221] However, from 2007, the Council improved its procedural standards in light of the Court's case law, and gave a statement of reasons to each group or person on its list. A series of new challenges have followed,[222] in which the Court of First Instance (as it then was) has ruled that there are good reasons for a listing if a person or group has been convicted of terrorist offences,[223] but that conversely the Council had to take account of subsequent developments, in particular the termination of the national decision which gave rise to the original listing.[224] The Court also clarified that national court judgments relating to immigration law issues did not constitute

---

[220] Art 1(4)–(6) of Common Position 2001/931 (n 205 above).

[221] Cases: T-47/03 *Sison* v *Council* [2007] ECR II-2047; Case T-327/03 *Al-Aqsa* v *Council* [2007] ECR II-79★; T-229/02 *PKK* v *Council* [2008] ECR II-45★; and T-253/04 *Kongra-Gel and Others* v *Council* [2008] ECR II-46★. Note that the *PKK* case had initially been dismissed as inadmissible by the CFI (Case T-229/02 *PKK and KNK* v *Council* [2005] ECR II-539), on the grounds of the lack of legal form of the group concerned, but the Court of Justice overturned that decision on appeal, on the highly convincing grounds that if the group concerned has sufficient legal existence to be subject to sanctions, it must have sufficient legal existence to challenge them (Case C-229/05 P *PKK and KNK* [2007] ECR I-439).

[222] There are also several cases pending: Cases T-76/07, T-362/07, and T-409/08 *El-Fatmi*, and Case T-49/07 *Fahas*.

[223] Joined Cases T-37/07 and T-323/07 *El-Morabit*, judgment of 3 Sep 2009, not yet reported.

[224] Case T-256/07 *PMOI II* [2008] ECR II-3019. See similarly Case T-348/07 *Al-Aqsa II*, judgment of 9 Sep 2010, not yet reported.

a decision which could justify a listing at EU level.[225] Certainly a national decision cannot be a valid reason for an EU listing if the Member State concerned refused to supply any of the reasons for that decision.[226]

As for references from national courts, as noted above, the Court of Justice has confirmed that raising money for a listed organization falls within the scope of the sanctions, although a prosecution to this end is tainted by the illegality of the listings decisions taken before the Council's procedures were improved in 2007.[227] The references relating to the first category of sanctions (as regards property sanctions and family members) are also relevant by analogy.[228]

Finally, as for the third category of alleged terrorist groups and persons (the 'domestic terrorists' subjected only to police and judicial cooperation by the EU, but not to economic sanctions), the European Court of Human Rights dismissed their arguments because they were not sufficiently affected by EU measures to claim 'victim' status,[229] and the Court of First Instance dismissed their claim for damages as regards the EU measures due to its lack of jurisdiction.[230] On appeal, the Court of Justice confirmed that the EU courts had no jurisdiction to hear damages actions against the EU institutions as regards third pillar Common Positions, but referred to the prospect of bringing such claims before national courts. The Court of Justice also stated that Common Positions could not in themselves have any binding impact on individuals, and the validity of any Common Position which nevertheless appeared to have such an effect could be referred to the Court of Justice by national courts.[231]

The EU Courts' case law on these issues is transformed from the original position of effectively refusing to review the EU's sanctions decisions. As regards listings made by the UN Security Council, the *Kadi* judgment of the Court of Justice is highly welcome, but it remains to be seen how robust the review of the original listings decision is in practice. Arguably, in the absence of sufficient procedural rights for individuals at UN level, it must be possible in principle for the EU to withdraw or to refuse to apply a UN decision in some cases, where the evidence available is insufficient. As for the second category of sanctions, the case law of the EU courts broadly sets the right balance, but it might be desirable to review the underlying rules relating to national decisions, in order to ensure that basic procedural standards are being applied before a listing is made,[232] for instance

---

[225] Case T-341/07 *Sison II*, judgment of 30 Sep 2009, not yet reported.

[226] Case T-284/08 *PMOI III* [2008] ECR II-3487, on appeal by France (Case C-27/09 P, pending)   [227] *E and F*, n 217 above.

[228] *Mollendorf* and *M*, nn 216 and 218 above.

[229] Decision in *Segi and others v 15 Member States* (Reports 2002-V).

[230] Order of the Court of First Instance in Case T-338/02 *SEGI and others* [2004] ECR II-1647. See by analogy also the order in Case T-299/04 *Selmani* [2005] ECR II-20*.

[231] Cases C-354/04 P *Gestoras pro Amnistia* [2007] ECR I-1579 and C-355/04 P *SEGI* [2007] ECR I-1657. See the discussion of the legal effect and jurisdiction issues in 2.2.2.2 above.

[232] cf the legislation being adopted in order to underpin mutual recognition in criminal matters: see 9.8.2 above.

to set reasonable time limits to begin or conclude prosecutions in order to justify continued listings. Finally, as for the third category, the allegation of terrorism is serious enough that it must be judicially reviewable, even in the absence of parallel financial sanctions against the alleged terrorists. Decisions in this category made before the Treaty of Lisbon arguably already met the criteria in the *SEGI* judgment for judicial review of the listings, and certainly any decision made or confirmed made after that Treaty entered into force is indisputably reviewable.

12.4.6. OLAF

Following extensive criticism of the Commission's anti-fraud unit, UCLAF, created in 1987, the EU institutions decided to create a replacement body, OLAF, pursuant to legislation adopted in 1999.[233] OLAF, an independent body but situated within the Commission, has both an 'internal affairs' function within the EU, examining allegations of fraud, and an 'external' function examining allegations within the Member States within the context of EU law. However, it does not have police or prosecution powers, and must hand over information to national authorities for prosecution and/or EU bodies to take disciplinary action. It also has a role in drafting relevant EU legislation and in EU operations, for example operating the Customs Information System (CIS) and contributing to combating euro counterfeiting.[234] OLAF's powers extend to all EU bodies; attempts by the EU's Central Bank and Investment Bank to avoid OLAF's remit were illegal.[235] An attempt by MEPs to challenge the principle that OLAF could search their offices was dismissed as inadmissible.[236] OLAF's powers to conduct investigations in Member States are set out in an earlier Regulation.[237]

In practice, OLAF has been controversial, in particular in regards to allegations of corruption at Eurostat, the EU's statistics body, where it allegedly withheld information from the Commission, and in regards to the case of a journalist whom OLAF allegedly libelled. Following an assessment of the functioning of OLAF,[238] the Commission proposed amendments to the legislation establishing the Office, inter alia suggesting the codification of defence rights, further powers for OLAF, and enhanced control of OLAF's operations by its Supervisory Committee.[239]

---

[233] Reg 1073/1999, Inter-Institutional Agreement, and Commission Decision ([1999] OJ L 136). For the background, see the first edition of this book, at 204–205.

[234] On the CIS, see 12.6.1.2 below. For an overview of OLAF, see House of Lords, Committee on European Union, *Strengthening OLAF, the European Anti-Fraud Office*, 24th Report, 2003–04.

[235] Cases C-15/00 *Commission v ECB* [2003] ECR I-7147 and C-15/00 *Commission v EIB* [2003] ECR I-7281.

[236] Case T-17/00 *Rothley* [2002] ECR I-579 (see interim measures ruling, [2000] ECR II-2085), upheld on appeal (Case C-167/02 P *Rothley* [2004] ECR I-3149).

[237] Reg 1285/96 ([1996] OJ L 292/2).

[238] COM (2003) 154, 2 Apr 2003. See the Council conclusions on the report (press release of Environment Council, 22 Dec 2003).   [239] COM (2004) 103, 10 Feb 2004.

A subsequent relevant proposal suggested a system of administrative cooperation between Member States and the Commission as regards fraud against the EU budget.[240] Neither proposal has attracted interest in the Council, in particular in light of a critical audit of OLAF issued in the meantime by the EU's Court of Auditors,[241] but the Commission has proposed a fresh text of the OLAF proposal and a revised text of the proposal on administrative cooperation.[242]

For their part, the EU courts have begun to exercise effective judicial control over OLAF in the context of staff cases,[243] but their review of OLAF's actions towards journalists has been less searching.[244]

OLAF (and its predecessor) have faced difficulties accomplishing their objectives in practice due to complaints about their ineffectiveness, as well as concerns about the procedural rights of those under investigation, including the (in)adequacy of judicial control by the EU courts. In part, these difficulties are connected to the underlying dispute between Member States as to the division of power in this area, and in particular whether the EU should develop a public prosecutor and/or develop the role of Europol and Eurojust instead.[245]

12.4.7. Other measures

A broad array of non-JHA EU law issues overlap with law enforcement issues in general, and anti-terrorism policy in particular. Coordinated reactions to the effects of terrorist attacks fall within the scope of EU civil protection rules, most particularly the general EU civil protection coordination mechanism and the EU civil protection funding programme.[246] Moreover, the Commission has specifically taken account of anti-terrorism issues within the scope of civil protection policy, drawing up an action plan on nuclear, radiological, biological, and chemical threats,[247] and addressing in detail the issue of preparedness and consequence

---

[240] COM (2004) 509, 20 July 2004.   [241] [2005] OJ C 202/1.

[242] COM (2006) 244, 24 May 2006 and COM (2006) 473, 14 Sep 2006.

[243] See Cases: T-215/02 *Gómez-Reino* [2003] ECR II-1685; C-471/02 P (R) *Gómez-Reino* [2003] ECR I-3207; T-96/03 *Camos Grau* [2004] ECR II-707; and particularly T-309/03 *Camos Grau* [2006] ECR II-1173, T-48/05 *Franchet and Byk* [2008] ECR II-1585. However, see the appeal judgment in T-261/09 P *Violetti*, judgment of 20 May 2010, not yet reported, overturning the Civil Service Tribunal judgment in F-5/05 and 7/05 *Violetti*, judgment of 28 Apr 2009, not yet reported.

[244] Case T-193/04 *Tillack* [2006] ECR I-3995.

[245] On the idea of the prosecutor, see 11.10 above. On the issues arising from OLAF, see W Hetzer, 'Fight Against Fraud and Protection of Fundamental Rights in the European Union', (2006) 14 IJCCLCJ 1: 20.

[246] For the mechanism, see [2001] OJ L 297/7, recast in 2007 ([2007] OJ L 314/7); for the funding programme, see originally [1999] OJ L 327/53, extended to end-2006 ([2005] OJ L 6/7), and now established for 2007–13 ([2007] OJ L 71/9). See generally Council conclusions on civil protection ([2005] OJ C 304/1).

[247] See: COM (2001) 707, 28 Nov 2001 (communication on state of alert against emergencies); COM (2002) 302, 11 June 2002 (report on implementation); COM (2004) 200, 25 Mar 2004

management in the fight against terrorism, calling especially for a centralized Commission alert system and a third pillar law enforcement network to be managed by Europol.[248] The latter communication was endorsed by the Council, and resulted in the creation of a Commission alert system at the end of 2005.[249] Furthermore, the Council has established a specific civil protection funding programme concerning terrorism-related issues.[250]

Before the entry into force of the Treaty of Lisbon, the EU's civil protection measures were adopted on the basis of the former Article 308 EC, which provided for a residual power for the EC to adopt measures to achieve its objectives, in the absence of any more specific legal basis, by means of a unanimous vote in Council and consultation of the EP. The Treaty of Lisbon introduced a specific legal base for civil protection measures, entailing the use of the ordinary legislative procedure,[251] as well as a 'solidarity clause',[252] which provides for joint action 'in a spirit of solidarity if a Member State is the object of a terrorist attack or the victim of a natural or man-made disaster'. The Council can adopt measures to this end following a joint proposal of the Commission and High Representative, by QMV in most cases, but must vote unanimously where defence matters are concerned. The EP is only informed of the adopted measures. Due to the different decision-making procedures, there is a possible conflict between the civil protection legal base and the solidarity clause.

Measures against the financing of terrorism involve, as well as the sanctions and customs legislation discussed above, the application of EU legislation concerning money laundering and (indirectly) the regulation of wire transfers and of payments more generally.[253] A number of further measures are under consideration,[254] in particular as regards regulation of the non-profit sector.[255]

(reinforcing civil protection capacity); Council doc 15480/04, 1 Dec 2004 (revised programme on the consequences of terrorist attacks); and COM (2009) 273, 24 June 2009 (action plan on chemical, biological, radiological, and nuclear security).

[248] See COM (2004) 701, 20 Oct 2004.

[249] See respectively Council conclusions (Council doc 15232/04, 25 Nov 2004) and amendment to Commission Rules of Procedure ([2006] OJ L 19/20). The Council also adopted crisis coordination arrangements in Dec 2005: see <http://ue.eu.int/uedocs/cmsUpload/WEB15106.pdf>.

[250] [2007] OJ L 58/1; see further 12.10 below.

[251] Art 196 TFEU. No measures have been adopted on the basis of this provision yet. However, see the proposal to establish a critical infrastructure warning information network (COM (2008) 676, 27 Oct 2008; see generally 12.4.4 above): the Commission communication on the effect of the Treaty of Lisbon on pending proposals amended the legal base of this proposal from the prior Art 308 EC to Art 196 TFEU (COM (2009) 665, 2 Dec 2009, Annex 1).

[252] Art 222 TFEU. No measures have been adopted on the basis of this provision yet.

[253] On EU money laundering legislation, see 10.5 above; see also Reg 1781/2006 on wire transfers ([2006] OJ L 345/1) and Dir 2007/64 on payment services ([2007] OJ L 319/1).

[254] See generally, as regards terrorism finance, COM (2004) 700, 20 Oct 2004); the subsequent EU strategy (Council doc 16089/04, 14 Dec 2004), and regular Council reports on the implementation of the strategy (see most recently Council doc 14744/05, 21 Nov 2005).

[255] See Conclusions of the JHA Council (JHA Council press release, 1–2 Dec 2005) and Commission communication and Recommendation (COM (2005) 620, 29 Nov 2005).

Of course, it should be recalled that financial regulation measures are relevant to other forms of organized crime as well.[256]

The EU has also developed a policy on the radicalization of potential terrorists, which focuses upon disrupting recruitment by terrorist networks, ensuring that moderate voices are more successful than extremists, and promoting equality and integration within the EU and supporting good governance and conflict resolution outside it.[257] However, the concrete implementation of the strategy is left entirely to Member States.

A final area of EU law of particular relevance to terrorism is the regulation of explosives, which is affected by EU internal market legislation dating from 1993 as well as legislation on other issues (for example, fertilizers).[258] The Commission has established an action plan to enhance the security of explosives,[259] and intends to propose legislation controlling explosives precursors in 2010.[260]

The related issue of firearms regulation is addressed both by a Directive dating from 1991, as amended in 2008, and by provisions of the Schengen Convention.[261] Due to the overlap between these measures, only some of the provisions of the Schengen *acquis* were allocated to the EC/EU legal order.[262] Furthermore, the Commission proposed EU legislation establishing an import/export regime for firearms in 2010.[263] There is an obvious need for consolidation of these disparate measures. The EC (as it then was) has signed a Protocol to the UN Convention on Organized Crime concerning firearms,[264] and the Commission intends to propose the conclusion of this Protocol by the EU in 2012.[265]

---

[256] See Commission communication concerning organized crime in the financial sector (COM (2004) 262, 14 Apr 2004).

[257] Council doc 14781/1/05, 24 Nov 2005; see earlier Commission communication (COM (2005) 313, 21 Sep 2005). The most recent version of the plan in this area is secret (Council doc 15374/09, 5 Nov 2009).

[258] Dir 93/15 ([1993] OJ L 121/20), implemented by Commission Decisions setting out a standard form for intra-EU transfers ([2004] OJ L 120/43, amended in [2010] OJ L 155/54) and establishing rules on the traceability of explosives ([2008] OJ L 94/8). On implementation of the Directive, see Case C-327/98 *Commission v France* [2000] ECR I-1851 and Council conclusions (JHA Council press release, 2 Oct 2003).

[259] COM (2007) 651, 6 Nov 2007; see earlier COM (2005) 329, 18 July 2005.

[260] See the action plan on implementing the Stockholm programme (COM (2010) 171, 20 Apr 2010).

[261] Dir 91/477 ([1991] OJ L 256/51), amended by Dir 2008/51 ([2008] OJ L 179/5) and Arts 77–91 of the Convention ([2000] OJ L 239). There is also a Schengen Executive Committee Decision on illegal trade in firearms: [2000] OJ L 239/469. Member States had to implement Dir 2008/51 by 28 July 2010 (Art 2(1), Dir 2008/51).

[262] Arts 82 and 91 of the Convention (concerning derogations from the rules and exchanges of information respectively). These provisions, and the Executive Committee Decision, were allocated to Art 95 EC, now Art 114 TFEU (see Decision allocating the *acquis*, [1999] OJ L 176/17).

[263] COM (2010) 273, 31 May 2010.

[264] [2001] OJ L 280/5. The Protocol entered into force on 3 July 2005. For ratification details, see Appendix I.

[265] See the Stockholm programme action plan (COM (2010) 171, 21 Apr 2010).

There are links between the EU's policing measures and the EU's powers over immigration, etc particularly as regards the SIS, which is addressed both by EU policing legislation and EU immigration legislation, as well as non-JHA EU legislation concerning access to the SIS by vehicle registration authorities.[266] EU immigration legislation has also established a Visa Information System (VIS), which law enforcement authorities will have access to once the System is operational.[267] There are also EU immigration law measures concerning trafficking and smuggling in persons,[268] and links between the EU's border control agency and EU policing law.[269] Finally, EU immigration law measures relating to passenger data are connected with third pillar measures.[270]

Offences against children are addressed by a Recommendation on the protection of minors and human dignity in the audiovisual field,[271] and by a Decision establishing a 'safer Internet action plan' funding programme.[272] There is also an EU funding programme addressing the health aspects of violence against women and children.[273] The development of EU policy on crime statistics also has a non-JHA legal base, after the entry into force of the Treaty of Lisbon.[274]

Another area of non-JHA EU law with security implications is the field of research, where the Commission first of all managed a preparatory action on security research funding from 2004,[275] and security research subsequently formed part of the EU's overall research programme for 2007–13.[276]

EU external policies concerning development and association also provide a framework for encouraging alignment with the EU's policing and security

---

[266] For details, see 12.6.1.1 below. On the 'legal base' issues relevant to the SIS, see 2.4.2 above.

[267] See 12.6.1.3 below.   [268] See 7.5.3, 7.5.4, and 7.6.2 above.   [269] See 3.10.1 above.

[270] See 12.4.3.2 above.   [271] [1998] OJ L 270/48, amended in 2006 ([2006] OJ L 378/72).

[272] The 1999–2004 programme was set out in Decision 276/1999 ([1999] OJ L 33/1, extended and amended in [2003] OJ L 162/1); the 2004–2008 programme was set out in Decision 854/2005 ([2005] OJ L 149/1); and the 2009–2013 programme was set out in Decision 1351/2008 ([2008] OJ L 348/118). On the policing law aspects of this issue, see 12.7.4 below; see also the criminal law legislation (10.5.2.1 below).

[273] Daphne I programme ([2000] OJ L 34/1); Daphne II programme ([2004] OJ L 143/1); and Daphne III programme ([2007] OJ L 173/19).

[274] See COM (2006) 437, 7 Aug 2006 and Art 335 TFEU (the legal base for statistics measures), which applies to policing and criminal law issues after the entry into force of the Treaty of Lisbon.

[275] See Commission Communication (COM (2004) 72, 3 Mar 2004); Commission Decision on implementation ([2004] OJ L 67/18); a report on Security Research by a 'Group of Personalities', online at: <http://www.src09.se/upload/External%20Documents/gop_en.pdf>; and a further Communication in response to this report (COM (2004) 590, 7 Sep 2004).

[276] See Art 2(1)(i)(j) of Decision 1982/2006 ([2006] OJ L 412/1), establishing the 7th Research Framework Programme. For critiques, see B Hayes, *NeoConOpticon: The EU's Security-Industrial Complex* (Transnational Institute and Statewatch, 2009), online at: <http://www.statewatch.org/analyses/neoconopticon-report.pdf>, and B Hayes, *Arming Big Brother: The EU's Security Research Programme* (Transnational Institute and Statewatch, 2006), online at: <http://www.statewatch.org/news/2006/apr/bigbrother.pdf>. See also the Commission Communication on a public/private dialogue in the field of European security research and innovation (COM (2007) 511, 11 Sep 2007).

objectives, although the use of development funds explicitly for anti-terrorist measures was successfully challenged in the absence of a specific legal base.[277]

Finally, various non-JHA EU law measures have an impact on the fight against counterfeiting the euro, and on anti-drug policy, in conjunction with EU policing measures.[278]

12.5. Crime prevention

Before the Treaty of Amsterdam entered into force, the Council adopted a broad-ranging Resolution on crime prevention.[279] Subsequently, in 2001 the Council adopted a Decision establishing a crime prevention network,[280] and a specific Decision on funding measures for crime prevention, later incorporated into broader law enforcement funding programmes.[281] The Network originally consisted of contact points designated by Member States, supported by a Secretariat provided by the Commission, and its objectives included: facilitating cooperation and the exchange of information and experience; the collection, analysis, and evaluation of information on crime prevention activities; helping to identify and develop the main areas for research, training, and evaluation as regards crime prevention; and organizing conferences, seminars, and similar meetings on crime prevention and disseminating the results. It had to submit annual reports on its activities, and the Council had to evaluate the application of the Decision in 2004.

The initial annual reports of the Network established a focus on juvenile, urban, and drug-related crime, as well as issues of crime statistics, crime proofing, fear of crime, and crime-prevention partnerships. The Network was hindered in practice by funding issues, since only its secretariat was funded from the EU budget, although it was able to achieve some of its objectives as regards holding conferences and producing reports.[282]

In 2004, the Commission released a communication on crime prevention,[283] which suggested that: a solution must be found for the Network's funding and support problems; the Network should focus further on particular types of crime; the Network should draw up a list of good practices; there should be a system of monitoring and evaluation of national crime prevention policies; and the EU

---

[277] Case C-403/05 *EP v Commission* [2007] ECR I-9045; see now the EU development policy legislation that explicitly addresses such issues: Reg 1717/2006, [2006] OJ L 317/1.

[278] For details of both topics, see 12.7.4 below.

[279] [1998] OJ C 408/1. For more on crime prevention prior to the Treaty of Amsterdam, see the first edition of this book, at 192–193.

[280] [2001] OJ L 153/1. See website: <http://www.eucpn.org/>. See also the Commission communication (COM (2000) 786, 29 Nov 2000).   [281] See 12.10 below.

[282] Council docs: 7632/03, 26 Mar 2003 (2002 report); 13421/04, 13 Oct 2004 (2003 report); and 11140/05, 15 July 2005 (2004 report).

[283] COM (2004) 165, 12 Mar 2004; [2004] OJ C 92/2.

should harmonize rules on crime statistics. The 2004 evaluation of the Network also addressed funding issues and called for further prioritization on specific forms of crime, and this approach was also supported by the Hague programme and by Council conclusions on the evaluation of the Network.[284]

The later annual reports on the operation of the Network detailed the amendment of its structure to include an operational board, the development of an independent website, and the greater focus of its work.[285] Eventually, the original Council Decision was replaced by a revised Decision just before the Treaty of Lisbon entered into force in 2009,[286] which, inter alia, establishes an Executive Committee charged with developing a long-term strategy for the Network, gives more clearly defined roles and objectives to national representatives, and allows the Network's Board more flexibility as regards the organization of its Secretariat.

As for the future, the Stockholm programme calls upon the Commission to make a proposal to establish an Observatory for the Prevention of Crime by 2013 at the latest. This Observatory will 'build on' the work of the Crime Prevention Network and 'include or replace' that network, 'with a secretariat located within an existing Union agency and functioning as a separate unit'. Its tasks 'will be to collect, analyse and disseminate knowledge on crime, including organised crime (including statistics) and crime prevention, to support and promote Member States and Union institutions when they take preventive measures and to exchange best practice'.[287]

12.6. Exchange of information

The main focus of EU measures concerning policing has been the facilitation of the 'free movement of investigations' by facilitating the gathering, transfer, and/or analysis of information—although of course there is a close connection and overlap between gathering and analysing information and operational activities.[288] In fact, EU measures concerning operational activities frequently contain specific ancillary provisions on exchange of information.[289]

This section examines in turn: the development of EU-wide databases; access to national databases; the ad hoc exchange of information between national

---

[284] Council doc 13419/04, 13 Oct 2004. See point III.2.6 of the Hague Programme ([2005] OJ C 53/1) and Council doc 14649/04, 17 Nov 2004. See subsequent progress report (Council doc 13945/1/05, 29 Nov 2005).

[285] Council docs: 11131/06, 4 July 2006 (2005 report); 6683/07, 5 Mar 2007 (2006 report); 8815/08, 28 Apr 2008 (2007 report); 9397/09, 4 May 2009 (2008 report); and 7025/10, 3 Mar 2010 (2009 report). [286] [2009] OJ L 321/44.

[287] [2010] OJ C 115, point 4.3.2. [288] On the operational measures, see 12.7 below.

[289] See, for example, Art 4 of the Decision on protection of the euro against counterfeiting ([2001] OJ L 329/1) and Art 2 of the 2003 Decision on war crimes, et al ([2003] OJ L 118/12). On the distinction between the legal bases for data exchange on the one hand, and operational cooperation on the other, see 12.2.4 above.

authorities; and the rules on personal data protection as regards policing and criminal law. Further measures in this area, including a reform of EU data protection law and the creation of a police records index system, are planned.[290] The specific rules relating to Europol, which is also primarily concerned with information exchange and analysis, are discussed further below.[291]

12.6.1. EU databases

The EU has established two major information systems relating, inter alia, to policing and customs: the Schengen Information System (SIS), for the use of national immigration, border control, police, and customs authorities; and the Customs Information System (CIS), for the use of the customs authorities. Also, law enforcement authorities will have access to the EU's database of information on visa applicants, the Visa Information System (VIS), and possibly also to Eurodac, the database containing asylum-seekers' fingerprints.[292] Furthermore, the Commission has suggested the interoperability and further development of EU databases.[293] Most of these databases (SIS, VIS, and Eurodac) will be managed by an agency, once the proposed legislation establishing this body has been adopted.[294]

12.6.1.1. Schengen Information System

The SIS went into operation with the entry into effect of the Schengen Convention in March 1995.[295] In addition to the relevant provisions of the Convention, the SIS was also the subject of a number of implementing measures adopted by the Schengen Executive Committee.[296] The power of the Executive Committee and its working groups was transferred by the Treaty of Amsterdam to the Council

---

[290] See the discussion of the Stockholm programme agenda in 12.2.3 above.

[291] See 12.8 below.   [292] See 12.6.1.3 and 12.6.1.4 below.

[293] COM (2005) 597, 24 Nov 2005.

[294] For the original proposals, see COM (2009) 293, 24 June 2009 (first pillar) and COM (2009) 294, 24 June 2009 (third pillar). These proposals were merged after the entry into force of the Treaty of Lisbon: COM (2010) 93, 19 Mar 2010.

[295] Arts 92–119 of Schengen Convention ([2000] OJ L 239). On the overall framework of Schengen integration, see 2.2.2.3 above.

[296] These Decisions concerned: a financial regulation; a contract for a preliminary study on SIS II; contributions from Norway and Iceland; the development of the SIS; the number of national connections; a help desk budget; installation expenses; the adoption of the 'Sirene manual' (explained below); and a catch-all decision authorizing the SIS technical *acquis* ([2000] OJ L 239, respectively 439 and 444, 440, 441, 442, 452, 453, 454, 457, and 144). There were also declarations on the definition of 'alien' and the structure of the SIS ([2000] OJ L 239/458 and 459). The Sirene manual was published later: [2003] OJ C 38/1. See also the Decisions on declassification of parts of the manual: [2003] OJ L 8/34; [2007] OJ L 179/52; and [2008] OJ L 149/78.

and its working groups.[297] The Council has also adopted a catalogue of best practices and recommendations regarding the SIS.[298]

The SIS exists firstly for the use of national police, customs, and border control authorities when making checks on persons at external borders or within Schengen states; and secondly, for the use of immigration officers when administering third-country nationals, in particular when deciding whether to issue visas or residence permits.[299] To that end, Member States can enter certain types of information about or relating to persons (certain personal details and an indication of whether they are armed or dangerous) as well as specified information on vehicles and objects.[300] There are six broadly defined reasons for which information can be included on the SIS (types of SIS 'alerts'):

(a) when a person is 'wanted for arrest for extradition purposes' (now including the European Arrest Warrant);[301]

(b) when a person has been listed to be refused entry to all the Schengen States;[302]

(c) when a person has disappeared or needs to be placed in a secure location to protect his or her safety;[303]

(d) when a judicial authority in one Member State wants to know the whereabouts of a person (such as a witness or a person being prosecuted) in another Member State during the course of a prosecution;[304]

(e) when one Member State wants others to subject a vehicle or person to discreet surveillance or checks, because of 'clear evidence' that the person 'intends to commit, or is committing numerous and extremely serious offences' or 'where an overall evaluation of the person', particularly his or her prior offences, 'gives reasons to suppose' that he or she 'will also commit extremely serious criminal offences in the future', or because the security services believe that the person is a 'serious threat';[305] and

(f) where objects are sought 'for the purposes of seizure or for evidence in criminal proceedings'.[306]

SIS data can be accessed by relevant national policing, border control, immigration, or customs authorities, but officials may only search the data necessary for

---

[297] In addition to the measures discussed below, the Council adopted several measures concerning SIS contracts and Decisions on the Joint Supervisory Body secretariat (see 2.2.2.3 above and [2000] OJ L 271/1).   [298] The latest version is in Council doc 16613/3/08, 8 May 2009.
[299] Art 92(1), Schengen Convention (n 295 above). On the operation of SIS in practice, see Cases: C-503/03 *Commission v Spain* [2006] ECR I-1097; C-150/05 *Van Straaten* [2006] ECR I-9327; and C-123/08 *Wolzenburg* [2009] ECR I-9621.   [300] Arts 94(3), 99(4), and 100(3).
[301] Art 95; see 9.5 above.   [302] Art 96; see 3.7, 4.7, and 4.9 above.
[303] Art 97; see the Schengen Executive Committee declaration on the abduction of minors ([2000] OJ L 239/436).   [304] Art 98; see 9.6.1 above.
[305] Art 99.   [306] Art 100; see 9.6.1 above.

the performance of their tasks.[307] The existing SIS rules were amended in 2004 and 2005 in order to make certain changes which the Member States desired that could be implemented within the current technical framework.[308] Inter alia, these amendments: insert express references for the first time to the 'Sirene' system (a supplementary system for the exchange of information between Member States following a 'hit' in the SIS); give access to SIS data for judicial authorities, Europol, and Eurojust; permit national security services to place the names of persons into the SIS without prior consultation of other Member States; and expand the list of objects that could be placed under surveillance or listed as wanted in the SIS. A further Regulation was adopted in 2005, giving access to SIS data by vehicle registration authorities.[309] Finally, a Regulation and a parallel third pillar Decision adopted in 2004 conferred power upon the Commission to amend the 'Sirene manual', which regulates the use of the Sirene system.[310]

In order, inter alia, to add additional categories of data to the SIS (notably fingerprints and photographs), the EU has for some time been trying to develop a second-generation SIS (SIS II) that will take the place of the current SIS. Parallel EC and third pillar measures adopted in 2001 (under the legal framework which applied before the entry into force of the Treaty of Lisbon) conferred power upon the Commission until the end of 2006 to manage the development of SIS II, which is being funded from the EU budget.[311] Since SIS II was not operational by the end of 2006, these measures were amended at that time to extend their application to the end of 2008 and to designate Strasbourg, France as the main location of SIS II and an Austrian location as the main location of the back-up system.[312] When it became obvious that SIS II would not be operational by the end of 2008, the EU adopted fresh parallel measures which regulate in detail the process of migration from SIS to SIS II.[313] These measures were amended in

---

[307] Art 101.

[308] Reg 871/2004 ([2004] OJ L 162/29) and third pillar Decision ([2005] OJ L 68/44). These measures amended Arts 92, 94, 99–101, 103, and 113 of the Schengen Convention, and inserted Arts 101A, 101B, 112A, and 113A into the Convention. Different provisions of these measures applied from different dates: see Art 2(2) of the Reg; Art 2(3) of the Decision, and Decisions in [2005] OJ L 158/26; [2005] L 271/54; [2005] L 273/25 and 26; and [2006] OJ L 81/45 and 46; and [2006] OJ L 256/15 and 18.   [309] Reg 1160/2005 ([2005] OJ L 191/18), applicable from 11 Jan 2006.

[310] Reg 378/2004 ([2004] OJ L 64/5); Decision ([2004] OJ L 64/45). The Commission used these powers to adopt new versions of the Sirene manual in 2006: [2006] OJ L 317.

[311] Reg 2424/2001 and Decision 2001/886/JHA ([2001] OJ L 328/1 and 4).

[312] Reg 1988/2006 and Decision 2006/1007/JHA ([2006] OJ L 411/1 and 78). Measures implementing these acts were subsequently adopted: Commission Decisions on the network requirements for SIS II development ([2007] OJ L 79/20 and 29); Council Reg 189/2008 and Decision 2008/173 ([2008] OJ L 57/1 and 14) on tests of SIS II.

[313] Reg 1104/2008 and Decision 2008/839 ([2008] OJ L 299/1 and 43). These measures inter alia inserted an Art 92A into the Schengen Convention and amended Art 119 of that Convention. The Commission adopted Decisions implementing these measures, in order to change the date of migration to SIS II from Sep 2009 to June 2010: [2009] OJ L 257/26 and 41.

2010, inter alia extending their validity to the end of 2013.[314] Pursuant to these measures, the Commission has released a number of reports on its management of the SIS II project.[315] SIS II is now projected to begin operations by the first quarter of 2013.[316]

As for the legislative framework, in order to establish SIS II, the Council adopted three measures (a Regulation concerning immigration aspects, a Decision concerning criminal law and policing aspects, and a Regulation on access by vehicle registration authorities) in 2006 and 2007.[317] Once SIS II is operational, these rules will fully replace the existing Schengen Convention rules (as already amended) and Executive Committee Decisions.[318] Compared to the current SIS rules, the types of alert will be the same, although the grounds for issuing immigration alerts will be altered, the extradition alerts will include more data relating to the European Arrest Warrant, and there will be minor changes to other policing and criminal law alerts.[319] Categories of data will be expanded to include photographs and fingerprints, and links between alerts will be established.

The operation of SIS II will be funded from the EU budget, and operational management of the SIS will ultimately, as noted above, be handed over to an agency to be established. There will also be changes to the rules governing data protection.[320] The Commission has used the power to implement these measures in order to adopt a new version of the Sirene manual as well as rules on security of SIS II.[321]

12.6.1.2. Customs Information System

The CIS Convention was opened for signature in 1995,[322] but only entered into force on Christmas Day 2005, following ratification by all of the first fifteen Member States.[323] Previously the Convention had applied provisionally in those Member States which had ratified an Agreement of provisional application, which had entered into force on 1 November 2000, following its ratification by a majority of the first fifteen Member States.[324] The CIS began operations on 24 March 2003, once the technical requirements for operation of the system were satisfied. As noted above, the CIS Convention is closely intertwined with a Regulation setting up a nearly identical system of information exchange (also called the CIS)

---

[314] [2010] OJ L 155/19 and 23.

[315] The reports available online are: SEC (2008) 35, 17 Jan 2008 (Jan–June 2007); COM (2008) 239 and SEC (2008) 552, 7 May 2008 (July–Dec 2007); COM (2008) 710, 10 Nov 2008 (Jan–June 2008); COM (2009) 133, 24 Mar 2009 (July–Dec 2008); COM (2009) 555, 22 Oct 2009 (Jan–June 2009); and COM (2010) 221, 6 May 2010 (July–Dec 2009).

[316] JHA Council press release, 3–4 June 2010.

[317] See respectively Reg 1987/2006 ([2006] OJ L 381/4), Decision 2007/533 ([2007] OJ L 205/63, and Reg 1986/2006 ([2006] OJ L 381/1).   [318] Arts 68 and 69 of the Decision (ibid).

[319] Arts 26–39 of the Decision (ibid).   [320] Arts 56–63 of the Decision (ibid).

[321] Respectively [2008] OJ L 123/1 and 39 and [2010] OJ L 112/31.

[322] [1995] OJ C 316/33.

[323] All of the new Member States have also ratified the Convention.

[324] [1995] OJ C 316/58.

to detect breaches of legislation outside the JHA context (ie in relation to inter-national trade regulations).[325]

There were also three Protocols to the CIS Convention. First of all, a Protocol on the jurisdiction of the Court of Justice to interpret the Convention on refer-ences from national courts was agreed in 1996, and entered into force at the same time as the Convention.[326] Secondly, a Protocol signed in 1999 aligned the defi-nition of 'money laundering' in the CIS Convention with that in the Naples II Convention on customs operations,[327] and allowed the third pillar CIS system to keep data on licence plates, in line with the parallel CIS Regulation;[328] this Protocol entered into force on 14 April 2008.[329] Finally, a Protocol signed in 2003 established a Customs Files Information System as part of the CIS; this Protocol entered into force on 15 October 2007.[330]

In November 2009, the Council adopted a third pillar Decision which will replace the CIS Convention and its substantive Protocols as from 27 May 2011.[331] According to this Decision, the CIS is implemented and applied by a committee made up of Member States' representatives, which oversees the functioning of the CIS, reporting annually to the Council, with the Commission taking part.[332] The CIS is confined to assisting in 'preventing, investigating and prosecuting serious contraventions of national [customs] laws', namely the movement of goods which Member States can ban or restrict in accordance with EU law, cash checks, the property or proceeds of international drug trafficking, and EU rules on indirect tax, agriculture, and trade.[333] The CIS cannot store the very sensitive data referred to in the Framework Decision on data protection.[334] The reasons for storage of data in the CIS are limited to the purposes of 'sighting and reporting, discreet surveillance, specific checks and strategic or operational analysis'.[335] Direct access to the CIS system is limited to national customs authorities and other national law enforcement authorities, along with Europol and Eurojust.[336] Member States may use CIS information 'for administrative or other purposes', or pass it on to non-Member States and international or regional organizations, if the Member State supplying the information agrees.[337]

---

[325] See 12.4.1 above.   [326] [1997] OJ C 151/15. Malta has not ratified this Protocol.

[327] [1998] OJ C 24/1. On this Convention, see 12.7.4 and 12.9 below.

[328] [1999] OJ C 91/1.   [329] All Member States have ratified this Protocol.

[330] [2003] OJ C 139/1. Several Member States have not yet ratified this Protocol. For ratification details, see Appendix I.

[331] [2009] OJ L 323/20. On the background to the Decision, see Council doc 14600/1/08, 3 Nov 2008.   [332] Art 27, CIS Decision (ibid).

[333] Arts 1(2) and 2(1), CIS Decision.

[334] Art 4(5), CIS Decision, referring to Art 6 of the Framework Decision, on which see 12.6.4.1 below.

[335] Art 5(1), CIS Decision. For the definitions of 'strategic analysis' and 'operational analysis', see Art 2(4) and (5) of the Decision.   [336] Arts 7(1), 11, and 12, CIS Decision.

[337] Art 8, CIS Decision. The Council can also decide to give access to national or international organizations: Art 7(3) of the Decision.

The 2004 annual report on the operation of the CIS indicated that it initially suffered from a 'very low level of use', due to training shortfalls, technical problems, and delayed ratification of the CIS Convention.[338] A team of experts produced an assessment with an action plan of recommendations to improve the situation,[339] but the 2005 report still reported a 'very low level of use'.[340] The 2006 report indicated that there was a 'significant increase in the use of CIS' since the start, but that 95 per cent of the data in the CIS was inputted by only five Member States.[341] According to the 2007 report, there was a further increase in the use of the CIS, but a drop in the number of active cases; most data was still inputted by only a small number of Member States.[342] The 2008 report indicated that there were fewer active third pillar CIS files, but increasing consultation of those files; only a few files were at first included in the new customs files database.[343]

12.6.1.3. Access to the Visa Information System

In 2008, the Council adopted a Regulation establishing the VIS, on the basis of the EU's powers over visas.[344] Simultaneously, it adopted a third pillar Decision giving law enforcement authorities and Europol access to the data to be held in the VIS, when it begins operations.[345] The UK has challenged the validity of this measure, on the grounds that it was not allowed to participate fully due to its non-participation in the VIS itself.[346] The Decision requires Member States to designate the law enforcement authorities which will have access to the VIS, for the purpose of preventing, detecting, or investigating terrorism or the other thirty-two 'serious crimes' referred to in the list set out in the Framework Decision establishing the European Arrest Warrant (EAW).[347] There is a special process for law enforcement authorities to request access to the data, subject to

---

[338] Council doc 7361/1/04, 26 Apr 2004. In particular, only forty-five first pillar and twenty-seven third pillar cases had been inputted.   [339] See Council doc 9085/1/04, 2 June 2004.

[340] See Council doc 12701/1/05, 13 Oct 2005. By Sep 2005, 164 third pillar cases had been inputted.

[341] Council doc 14694/2/06, 12 Jan 2007. By Oct 2006, over 600 third pillar cases had been inputted.

[342] Council doc 16245/07, 7 Dec 2007. By Nov 2007, over 1,000 third pillar cases had been inputted. Eight Member States had inputted 93% of the data.

[343] Council doc 15651/08, 13 Nov 2008, referring to 287 active third pillar cases (the total number of cases was no longer listed). There were thirteen third pillar files in the customs files database, which was operational from 15 Sep 2008 following the entry into force of the 2003 Protocol to the Convention (n 330 above) and the 2008 amendments to the CIS Regulation (12.4.1 above). This report contains a number of criticisms of the operation of the system.

[344] Reg 767/2008 ([2008] OJ L 218/60). The VIS is intended to start operations by the end of 2010. For details, see 4.8 above.

[345] [2008] OJ L 218/129. See also Art 3 of Reg 767/2008, ibid.

[346] Case C-482/08, *UK v Council*, pending (opinion of 24 June 2010). The special rule concerned is set out in Art 6 of the Decision.

[347] Arts 3(1) and 2(1)(d) and (e) of the Decision. For the EAW Framework Decision ([2002] OJ L 190/1), see 9.5.2 above.

the conditions that the access is 'necessary for the purpose of the prevention, detection or investigation' of the relevant offences; that access is 'necessary in a specific case', and there are 'reasonable grounds to consider' that access to the data will 'substantially contribute to the prevention, detection or investigation of any of the criminal offences' in question.[348] Law enforcement authorities will only have access to certain data,[349] and Europol will have access to the data for very specific purposes.[350]

As for the merits of police access to the VIS, it might be doubted that the VIS data will be of much use to police except possibly identifying fingerprints left a crime scene or providing further information about a suspect for the purpose of tracing him or her. The VIS Regulation and the parallel third pillar Decision leave lots of discretion to give extensive access to the police services, but at least a prior check will apply in principle before access is granted. But it might be doubted whether this procedure will be independent or critical of police requests. At least it is certainly welcome that access for the police is limited to specific cases, with no general power to search the entire database to produce 'risk assessments'.

12.6.1.4. Access to Eurodac

Eurodac, the EU system for the comparison of asylum seekers' fingerprints for the purpose of applying the EU rules on asylum applications, was established by legislation adopted in 2000 and became operational in 2003.[351] A proposal for a third pillar Decision to give law enforcement authorities and Europol access to the Eurodac database was presented by the Commission in 2009 and lapsed when the Treaty of Lisbon entered into force,[352] although a new proposal on this issue is planned for 2010.[353]

12.6.2. Access to national databases

In 2008, the Council adopted a Decision (known informally as the 'Prum Decision'),[354] which incorporates a large number of provisions from the Prum Convention, a separate treaty agreed originally in 2005 between a small group of Member States.[355] This Decision includes, inter alia, rules on access by one Member States' authorities to another Member States' databases as regards fingerprint data,

---

[348] Arts 4 and 5(1) of the Decision.   [349] Art 5(2) of the Decision.

[350] Art 7 of the Decision.

[351] See Reg 2725/2000 ([2000] L 316/1); see generally 5.8.3 above.

[352] COM (2009) 342, 10 Sep 2009. See also the parallel proposal to amend the Eurodac Reg: COM (2009) 344, 10 Sep 2009.

[353] See the Commission's forward programming for 2010: <http://ec.europa.eu/atwork/programmes/docs/forward_programming_2010.pdf>.   [354] [2008] OJ L 210/1.

[355] On the background to the Prum Convention, see 12.2.3 above.

DNA data, and vehicle registration information.[356] This Decision also includes a number of other provisions discussed elsewhere in this chapter,[357] and there is also another Decision, adopted at the same time and similarly carved out of the Prum Convention, concerning cross-border movement of special intervention units in crisis situations.[358] A parallel Decision sets out rules which implement the details of the Prum Decision.[359] It should be noted that these provisions of the Prum Decision and the relevant provisions of the implementing Decision will be extended to Norway and Iceland by means of a separate treaty, which does not apply to the separate Decision on special intervention units.[360]

First of all, as regards DNA data,[361] the Prum Decision requires Member States to establish files of such data in order to assist with criminal investigations. Reference data from these files (which cannot as such be used to identify individuals) must be available for searching automatically by other Member States' authorities. In the event of a match, further data shall be supplied to the requesting Member State. If there is no DNA profile available for a particular individual, the requested State shall obtain DNA samples from that person if requested by another Member State, if the national law of both States permits it.

As regards fingerprint data, similarly Member States must make anonymized reference data from their national files available for automatic searches to other Member States, and supply further data in the event of a match.[362] Finally, as regards vehicle registration data, Member States must open up their national registers to searches by other Member States' authorities, as regards searches for information on owners or vehicles.[363]

12.6.3. Ad hoc exchange of information

Many EU measures have been adopted dealing with the exchange of information on a case-by-case basis and/or in specific areas. First of all, general rules on the exchange of information on a case-by-case basis between national law enforcement authorities are set out in a Framework Decision adopted in 2006, which replaced prior rules in the Schengen Convention.[364] This Framework Decision, inter alia, specifies that Member States shall not apply different rules for providing

---

[356] Arts 2–12 of the Decision. These provisions must be applied by Member States by 26 Aug 2011: see Arts 36(1) and 37.　　　　　　　　　　　　[357] See 12.6.3 and 12.9 below.

[358] [2010] OJ L 218/73. See 12.9.5 below.　　　[359] [2008] OJ L 210/12.

[360] [2009] OJ L 353/1. The treaty has been signed, but is not yet in force. See further 12.2.5 above.　　　　　　　　　　　　　　　　　　　　　[361] Arts 2–7, Prum Decision.

[362] Arts 8–11, Prum Decision.　　　[363] Art 12, Prum Decision.

[364] [2006] OJ L 386/89, known in practice as the 'Swedish Framework Decision'. It had to be implemented by 19 Dec 2008 (Art 11(2)) and replaced Art 39(1)–(3) and 46 of the Schengen Convention ([2000] OJ L 239), as well as two Schengen Executive Committee Decisions (Art 12). See the guidelines on the implementation of the Framework Decision (Council doc 9512/10, 26 May 2010).

information and intelligence to other Member States than the rules which apply to such provision within the same Member State, including rules on judicial authorization of information transfer.[365] If judicial authorization is required for the requested authority to access the information or intelligence, it must ask for that authorization in the event of a request for that intelligence or information from another Member State's authority.[366]

The Framework Decision sets a time limit of eight hours for responding to 'urgent' requests for information and intelligence as regard offences to which dual criminality no longer applies pursuant to the Framework Decision establishing the European Arrest Warrant (EAW).[367] In non-urgent cases relating to the same offences, Member States should respond within one week, if the information is in a database which the requested law enforcement authority can directly access.[368] In all other cases, the requested authority must respond to requests for information within fourteen days.[369] Furthermore, there is a requirement to exchange information spontaneously, ie without a request from other Member States' authorities.[370] Member States can refuse to reply to a request 'only' if there are reasons to assume that supply of the information would 'harm essential national security interests of the requested Member State', or 'jeopardise the success of a current investigation or a criminal intelligence operation or the safety of individuals', or would 'clearly be disproportionate or irrelevant with regard to the purposes for which it has been requested'.[371] A request *may* also be refused if the offence in question is punishable by imprisonment of one year or less in the requested Member State, and *shall* be refused if any required judicial authorization has not been obtained.[372]

Furthermore, the cross-border exchange of information is greatly facilitated by the exchange of liaison officers between Member States.[373] Another general measure is an EU Decision of 2005 which facilitates the exchange of information between Member States on criminal records, followed up by further measures adopted in 2009.[374]

As regards customs, the Naples II Convention also sets out rules on the exchange of information upon request, as well as spontaneous assistance.[375] Also, an early Joint Action vaguely encourages the exchange of information and intel-

---

[365] Art 3(3).   [366] Art 3(4).

[367] Art 4(1), referring to Art 2(2) of the EAW Framework Decision: [2002] OJ L 190/1. For exceptions to this rule, see Art 4(2).   [368] Art 4(3).

[369] Art 4(4).   [370] Art 7.   [371] Art 10(1).

[372] Art 10(2) and (3), referring to Art 3(4).

[373] Arts 47(2)(b) and 125, Schengen Convention (n 364 above); Schengen Executive Committee Decision on liaison officers ([2000] OJ L 239/411); Art 6(3)(b) and (d), Naples II Convention ([1998] OJ C 24/1); and Decision on liaison officers ([2003] OJ L 67/27), as amended ([2006] OJ L 219/31). See also the Resolution on posting of drugs liaison officers to Albania (12.11 below). On the past and present 'legal base' for measures concerning liaison officers, see 12.2.4 above.

[374] [2005] OJ L 322/33 and [2009] OJ L 93/23 and 33. See further 9.6.1.4 above.

[375] Arts 8–10 and 13–18 (1998] OJ C 24/1).

ligence between and the development of risk analysis techniques by customs authorities.[376]

Measures concerning terrorism comprise Decisions implementing the EU's Common Position on terrorism as regards police and judicial cooperation,[377] which require the transmission of information concerning terrorist groups or individuals on the EU list to Europol and Eurojust, and a number of soft law measures;[378] one of the latter is questionable on human rights grounds due to the link between terrorists and non-violent protesters which it initially alleged.[379] The Prum Decision also provides for the exchange of information, even without request, 'as is necessary because particular circumstances give reason to believe that the data subjects will commit criminal offences as' provided for in the EU legislation defining terrorism.[380]

The Council has also adopted a number of measures on football security in particular and cooperation on public order more generally.[381] One of these relates particularly to security at summits, and concerns the exchange of information on persons where there are 'substantial grounds for believing that they intend to enter the Member State with the aim of disrupting public order and security at the event or committing offences relating to the event'.[382] The Prum Decision also provides for the exchange of non-personal or personal data relating to such meetings, in the latter case 'if any final convictions or other circumstances give reason to believe that the data subjects will commit criminal offences at the events or pose a threat to public order and security'.[383]

In the sphere of drugs, the Council has adopted a Joint Action on the exchange of chemical profiling information, in order to assist 'strategic' analysis of the sources and routes of drug traffickers and the trends in drug production.[384] A later Decision regulates the transmission of samples of controlled substances between Member States.[385] The related field of money laundering is addressed by a Decision requiring Member States to establish financial intelligence units.[386]

---

[376] [1997] OJ L 159/1.

[377] [2003] OJ L 16/68, replaced by later Decision ([2005] OJ L 252/23).

[378] Recommendation on cooperation on terrorist financing ([1999] OJ C 373/1); Recommendation on assessing the risk of terrorism against visiting persons ([2001] OJ C 356/1); and Recommendation on exchange of information on terrorists (unpublished; on file with the author).

[379] The Recommendation on exchange of information on terrorists (ibid); for criticism, see S Peers, 'EU Responses to Terrorism' (2003) 52 ICLQ 227 at 241–243.

[380] [2008] OJ L 210/1, Art 16. For the legislation referred to, see 10.5.2.1 above.

[381] Resolution on football hooliganism ([1996] OJ C 131/1); Recommendation on football hooliganism ([1996] OJ C 193/1); Joint Action on cooperation on law, order, and security ([1997] OJ L 147/1); Decision concerning security in connection with football matches with an international dimension ([2002] OJ L 121/1); Council conclusions on implementation of the Decision (JHA Council press release, 29 Apr 2004); and a Resolution on security at summits ([2004] OJ C 116/18).   [382] Point 1 of the 2004 Resolution (ibid).

[383] Arts 14–15 of the Decision (n 354 above).   [384] [1996] OJ L 322/5.

[385] [2001] OJ L 150/1.

[386] [2000] OJ L 271/4. See the Commission review of implementation (COM (2007) 827, 20 Dec 2007).

As regards immigration offences, the Council has adopted a Decision concerning the exchange of information on counterfeit travel documents,[387] and a Common Position requiring the transfer of data on lost, stolen, or misappropriated passports to Interpol.[388] The Commission has reported that most Member States are implementing this Common Position, resulting in a significant increase in the data transmitted and accessed by Member States.[389]

But the most controversial measures in this area both concern the exchange of data from the private sector to law enforcement authorities. First of all, the EU has a treaty with the US requiring the exchange of passenger data with the US;[390] there are also treaties to the same effect with Canada and Australia.[391] There is also a Directive regulating the transfer of passenger data to immigration authorities of EU Member States, which leaves open to Member States the possibility of further requiring transfer of this data for law enforcement purposes.[392] In 2007, the Commission proposed a Framework Decision on the transfer of such data to law enforcement authorities, but this measure was not agreed before the entry into force of the Treaty of Lisbon.[393] The Commission intends to propose a new measure on this issue.

The second particularly controversial issue is the requirement that telecommunications companies collect data and then share it with law enforcement authorities. On this point, the Council has adopted a number of non-binding measures, in particular a Resolution on the interception of telecommunications.[394] The mutual assistance Convention also contains provisions on interception,[395] which concern requests from one Member State to another to intercept telecommunications and the facility, subject to certain conditions, to intercept the telecommunications of a person who is on the territory of another Member State.

But the most hotly disputed issue has been the adoption of a Directive in 2006 requiring Member States to compel telecommunications companies to retain traffic and location data not just as regards suspected criminal suspects or their associates, but the entire population (the 'data retention Directive').[396] The

---

[387] [2000] L 81/1.   [388] [2005] OJ L 27/61.   [389] COM (2006) 167, 21 Apr 2006.

[390] See [2004] OJ L 183/83 and L 235/11 (US agreement) and the subsequent agreements in [2006] OJ L 298/27 and [2007] OJ L 204/16 (not yet ratified, but applied provisionally). For more information on the EU–US agreement, see the Statewatch observatory on this issue, online at: <http://www.statewatch.org/pnrobservatory.htm>. See also the Commission Communication on a global EU policy on this issue (COM (2003) 826, 16 Dec 2003).

[391] Respectively [2006] OJ L 82/14 and [2008] OJ L 213/47 (the latter is only applied provisionally). The Commission has proposed the conclusion of the latter treaty: COM (2009) 701, 17 Dec 2009.   [392] Dir 2004/82, [2004] OJ L 261/24. For details, see 7.5.2 above.

[393] COM (2007) 654, 6 Nov 2007.

[394] [1996] OJ C 329/1, discussed further in the first edition of this book, at 199–200. See also the Council conclusions on information technology and the investigation and prosecution of organized crime (JHA Council press release, 19 Dec 2002) and on mobile phone cards (JHA Council press release, 8 May 2003).   [395] Arts 17–22 of the Convention ([2000] OJ C 197/1).

[396] Dir 2006/24 ([2006] OJ L 105/54), which Member States had to implement by 15 Sep 2007 (Art 15(1)). The 'legal base' of this measure in the first pillar (rather than the third) was disputed

background to the Directive dates to 2002, when the EP and Council adopted a Directive on the specific issue of telecommunications privacy, which states that Member States *may* adopt measures derogating from the Directive's rules on privacy of communications, traffic data, and location data:[397]

> ...when such restriction constitutes a necessary, appropriate and proportionate measure within a democratic society to safeguard national security (i.e. State security), defence, public security, and the prevention, investigation, detection and prosecution of criminal offences...To this end, Member States may, inter alia, adopt legislative measures providing for the retention of data for a limited period justified on the grounds laid down in this paragraph. All the measures referred to in this paragraph shall be in accordance with the general principles of Community law, including those referred to in Article 6(1) and (2) of the Treaty on European Union.

The 2006 Directive takes this further by *requiring* Member States to compel telecommunications providers to retain traffic and location data on customers (although the Directive does not apply to the content of communications). Member States were allowed to postpone application of the Directive to Internet connections (including e-mails) for eighteen months; no fewer than sixteen Member States did so.[398]

The retention obligation also applies to unsuccessful calls (calls where the phone rang, but no one answered, or where the phone was engaged), although not to unconnected calls (calls which were never connected to a line at the other end). The purpose of retaining the data is to assist 'the investigation, prosecution and detection of serious crime, as defined by each Member State in its national law';[399] the 2002 Directive will still apply to the retention of other types of data (in particular as regards the content of communications, or unconnected calls), or data retained for other purposes (for security services, and arguably for crime prevention and to assist investigation, etc of *less* serious crime).[400] As for access to the data, the conditions of access are defined by reference to national law, although this is subject to the necessity and proportionality principles and observance of, inter alia, the ECHR.[401] The data must be kept for at least six months and no more than two years; but the 'legal base' of the Directive permits Member States to retain pre-existing national law which requires retention for more than two years on public security grounds, and the Directive furthermore permits Member States to

---

unsuccessfully: see 12.4.3.2 above. On the detailed background to the Directive, see <http://www.statewatch.org/soseurope.htm>, 'surveillance of telecommunications' section. On the issues, see P Breyer, 'Telecommunications Data Retention and Human Rights: The Compatibility of Blanket Traffic Data Retention with the ECHR' (2005) 11 ELJ 373.

[397] Art 15(1), Dir 2002/58 ([2002] OJ L 201/37), amended in 2009 (Dir 2009/136, [2009] OJ L 337/11).

[398] Art 15(3) of the Directive (permitting a delay until 15 Mar 2009) and attached declarations.

[399] Art 1(1) of the Directive.

[400] See Art 11 of the Directive, inserting an Art 15(1a) into Dir 2002/58.

[401] Art 4 of the Directive.

introduce new laws which have the same effect. In both cases, there is a procedure for Commission approval of the national law, but the Commission can apparently take into account only internal market issues, not human rights principles.[402]

This Directive was challenged in the constitutional courts of Germany and Romania on human rights grounds,[403] and a reference from the Irish courts challenging its validity on the same grounds is pending.[404]

Finally, the EU and the US decided in 2007 to regulate the informal arrangements by which US anti-terrorist investigators had access to all data concerning financial transfers within the EU.[405] These arrangements subsequently took the form of a treaty, originally rejected by the EP but then approved after renegotiation.[406]

12.6.4. Data protection

The key question from a civil liberties perspective regarding all of the EU measures relating to exchange of information is the rules on data protection. These rules can be found either in a general measure adopted in 2008 or in specific policing measures—or sometimes in both. This section examines the general and the specific data protection rules in turn.

12.6.4.1. General rules on data protection

In 2008, after difficult negotiations, the Council adopted a Framework Decision regulating data protection within the context of policing and criminal law.[407] The purpose of the Framework Decision is:[408]

... to ensure a high level of protection of the fundamental rights and freedoms of natural persons, and in particular their right to privacy, with respect to the processing of personal data in the framework of police and judicial cooperation in criminal matters, provided for by Title VI of the Treaty on European Union, while guaranteeing a high level of public safety.

---

[402] See Arts 95(4)–(10) EC and Art 12 of the Directive.

[403] Both judgments criticized the national implementing law, but did not impugn the validity of the Directive directly: see <http://www.bundesverfassungsgericht.de/pressemitteilungen/bvg10-011> and <http://www.legi-internet.ro/english/jurisprudenta-it-romania/decizii-it/romanian-constitutional-court-decision-regarding-data-retention.html>.

[404] For the national decision, see: <http://www.scribd.com/doc/30950035/Data-Retention-Challenge-Judgment-re-Preliminary-Reference-Standing-Security-for-Costs>. An earlier reference to the Court of Justice also challenged its validity on the same grounds, but the Opinion in that case argues that this point is irrelevant: Cases C-92 and 93/07 *Eifert and Volcker*, opinion of 17 June 2010, pending.				[405] [2007] OJ C 166/18 and 27.

[406] For the rejected treaty, see [2010] OJ L 8; for the approved treaty, see [2010] OJ L 195.

[407] [2008] OJ L 350/60. Member States must implement this measure by 27 Nov 2010: Art 29(1). All references in this subsection are to this Framework Decision, unless otherwise indicated.

[408] Art 1(1).

As for its scope, the Framework Decision applies to the transmission of personal data 'for the purpose of [the prevention, investigation, detection or prosecution of criminal offences or the execution of criminal penalties]', if those data 'are or have been transmitted or made available' either 'between Member States', or 'by Member States to authorities or to information systems established on the basis of Title VI of the [former TEU]', or 'to the competent authorities of the Member States by authorities or information systems established on the basis of the [TEU or the former EC Treaty]'.[409] However, unlike the EC data protection Directive,[410] the Framework Decision does not apply to the processing of data within a Member State, and it permits Member States to apply higher standards regarding the processing of data at national level.[411] It is also 'without prejudice to essential national security interests and specific intelligence activities in the field of national security'.[412] Like the data protection Directive, the Framework Decision applies to the processing of personal data 'wholly or partly by automatic means, and to the processing otherwise than by automatic means, of personal data which form part of a filing system or are intended to form part of a filing system'.[413]

The main substantive provisions of the Framework Decision on data protection provide for the application of the basic data protection principles of lawfulness, proportionality, and purpose limitation, although in a vaguer form than in the data protection Directive.[414] There are also obligations as regards rectification, erasure, and blocking, which differ in some respects from those in the data protection Directive.[415] The obligations to establish time limits for erasure and review and the qualified ban on the processing of 'sensitive' data are broadly similar to the rules in the Directive,[416] as is the ban on taking automated individual decisions, except where this is authorized by a law which lays down necessary safeguards.[417] Member States are required to verify data quality,[418] and there are general rules relating to time limits for keeping data.[419]

The Framework Decision contains specific rules on logging and documentation and exceptions from the purpose limitation rule, as regards data received from other Member States.[420] Member States may set rules on the receipt of data by other Member States or EU agencies, provided that they do not apply restrictions above those applicable in similar domestic cases.[421] There are specific rules on the transfer of data to third states or international bodies, which

---

[409] Art 1(2).   [410] Dir 95/46 ([1995] OJ L 281/31); see 12.3.2 above.
[411] See respectively recital 7 in the preamble, and Art 1(5).
[412] Art 1(4). See the discussion of Art 72 TFEU, in 2.2.3.2 above.   [413] Art 1(3).
[414] Art 3.   [415] Compare Art 4 of the Framework Decision to Art 12 of the Directive.
[416] Compare Arts 5 and 6 of the Framework Decision to Arts 6(1)(e) and 8 of the Directive.
[417] Compare Art 7 of the Framework Decision to Art 15 of the Directive.
[418] Art 8; compare to Art 6(1)(d) of the Directive.
[419] Art 9; compare to Art 6(1)(e) of the Directive.   [420] Arts 10 and 11.   [421] Art 12.

differ significantly from the rules in the Directive (Article 13);[422] the Framework Decision also confers protection for pre-existing treaties of the EU or its Member States with third states.[423] Furthermore, there are special rules on the transmission of data to private parties in Member States, and a requirement for the recipient of the data to inform the sending authority about the use made of the data, on its request.[424]

As for the rights of data subjects, the right to information for the data subject differs significantly from the rules in the Directive;[425] the right of access to data is weaker than the Directive;[426] there are similar rights to rectification, erasure, or blocking, and to compensation;[427] and the right to a judicial remedy is essentially identical.[428] There are also broad similarities with the Directive as regards the rules on confidentiality, data security, the creation of and relations with national supervisory authorities, and penalties for breach of the Framework Decision.[429]

Overall, as compared to the data protection Directive, the Framework Decision on data protection is generally similar, with a number of differences of detail, which mostly (but not entirely) set lower standards than the Directive. The most significant differences are the territorial scope of the measures, ie the limitation of the Framework Decision to data exchanged between Member States, and the quite different standards as regards data transferred to third States. Furthermore, of course, the Framework Decision is not directly effective and there are more limited possibilities to interpret it and enforce it in the EU's Court of Justice, due to the transitional restrictions on the Court's jurisdiction.

However, it should be recalled that the Commission is planning to propose amendments to the Directive and Framework Decision which could well amend or even merge both of these measures. It remains to be seen whether negotiations on this proposal will be successful and raise the standards applicable in this field.

12.6.4.2. Specific rules on data protection

The Framework Decision expressly specifies that where third pillar acts adopted beforehand which concern personal data exchange between Member States or Member States' law enforcement authorities' access to data held in information systems established pursuant to EC legislation (as it was then) set out 'specific conditions' regarding the use of such data by the receiving Member State, those

---

[422] Compare Art 13 of the Framework Decision to Arts 25 and 26 of the Directive. Also, the Framework Decision only applies to external movements of personal data where that data was *first transferred between Member States*; the Directive contains no such limitation.

[423] Art 26; there is no equivalent in the Directive.   [424] Arts 14 and 15.

[425] Compare Art 16 of the Framework Decision to Arts 10 and 11 of the Directive.

[426] Compare Art 17 of the Framework Decision to Art 12(a) of the Directive.

[427] Compare Arts 18 and 19 of the Framework Decision to Arts 12(b) and 23 of the Directive.

[428] Compare Art 20 of the Framework Decision to Art 22 of the Directive.

[429] Compare Arts 21–24 of the Framework Decision to Arts 16, 22, 18, 24, and 28 of the Directive.

rules have priority over the rules in the Framework Decision.[430] Two clauses in the preamble to the Framework Decision address this issue further, setting out two categories of prior measures. First of all, the preamble refers to those acts which establish a 'complete and coherent set of rules covering all relevant aspects of data protection (principles of data quality, rules on data security, regulation of the rights and safeguards of data subjects, organisation of supervision and liability)', in more detail than the Framework Decision, 'in particular' the rules on Europol, Eurojust, the SIS, the CIS, and access to other Member States' databases in the Prum Decision.[431] Presumably the specific rules in these measures apply entirely instead of the rules in the Framework Decision.

Secondly, the preamble refers to prior third pillar acts which have data protection rules which are 'more limited in scope', including rules governing the purpose for which a receiving Member State can use data, but otherwise referring to the Council of Europe data protection Convention or to national law. In this case, those specific rules in these measures (no such measures are named) apply instead of the Framework Decision if they are 'more restrictive' than the Framework Decision, but otherwise the Framework Decision applies.[432] Arguably this applies in particular to: the 'Swedish' Framework Decision on the exchange of police information and intelligence;[433] the data protection rules in the Schengen Convention generally;[434] the Decision on police access to the VIS;[435] the other aspects of data exchange under the Prum Decision;[436] the exchange of information among customs authorities pursuant to the Naples II Convention;[437] and exchanges between judicial authorities under the mutual assistance Convention and pursuant to the Framework Decision establishing the European Evidence Warrant.[438]

As for the measures adopted after the entry into force of the Framework Decision, the Decision establishing the CIS,[439] which replaces the CIS Convention and its Protocols as from 27 May 2011,[440] contains a number of specific references to the data protection Framework Decision, which applies to the CIS unless otherwise provided for in the Decision;[441] the Decision establishing Europol, and the amendment to the Decision establishing Eurojust, each specify that the Framework Decision applies to the processing by Member States of the data transmitted

---

[430] Art 28.

[431] Para 39 of the preamble. Presumably the reference to the SIS encompasses also the immigration provisions of the current SIS, which are still allocated in principle to the third pillar, as well as the policing and criminal law aspects of SIS II, when this new system becomes operational.

[432] Para 40 of the preamble.   [433] [2006] OJ L 386/89; see Art 8.

[434] [2000] OJ L 239, Arts 126–130.   [435] [2008] OJ L 218/129, Arts 8–16,

[436] [2008] OJ L 210/1, Arts 13–16; and see the data protection rules in Arts 24–32.

[437] Art 25 of the Convention ([1998] OJ C 24).

[438] Art 23 of the Convention ([2000] OJ C 197/1), and Art 10 of the Framework Decision ([2008] OJ L 350/72).   [439] [2009] OJ L 323/20.

[440] Art 34.   [441] Art 20.

between the Member States and Eurojust or Europol, but that the data protection rules applying to Eurojust and Europol as such are not affected by the Framework Decision, because of the 'particular nature, functions and competences of' those bodies;[442] several measures simply state that the Framework Decision applies to any personal data exchanged pursuant to that measure;[443] and the Decision on criminal records states that the Framework Decision 'should' apply in the context of computerized exchange of data between Member States, while allowing Member States to set higher levels of protection,[444] but the Framework Decision on criminal records exchange, which the Decision on this issue implements, states that the specific data protection rules in this Framework Decision complement the general data protection rules in force, with no reference to the Framework Decision on data protection.[445] Finally, although the data protection Framework Decision states that treaties agreed after its adoption should be subject to its rules, the EU–US treaty on the transfer of terrorist financial data does not refer to the Framework Decision, and arguably does not comply with its rules in any event.[446]

12.6.5. Assessment

Are the EU rules on information exchange and data protection adequate? First of all, as for the three most controversial measures, each provides for mass exchange of information on a large proportion of the population, not just criminal suspects, and thus is particularly difficult to justify in light of the jurisprudence of the European Court of Human Rights.[447] The treaty on transfers of financial information to the US at first sight limits itself to requests in specific cases only, but as the European Data Protection Supervisor has pointed out, in practice the information concerned will still be transferred in bulk, and Europol is an unsuitable body to carry out a supervisory function.[448]

As for passenger name data exchange, the EP had rightly argued before the Court of Justice that the treaty with the US does not guarantee an 'adequate level of protection' for personal data, as required by EU data protection law, in particular because the measures are not sufficiently prescribed by law, the amount of data to be transferred and the period of storage are disproportionate, judicial review is not adequate, and there are insufficient controls on the further exchange

---

[442] [2009] OJ L 138/14, recital 13 in the preamble (Eurojust) and [2009] OJ L 121/37, recital 12 in the preamble (Europol),

[443] See the Framework Decisions on conflicts of jurisdiction ([2009] OJ L 328/42), recital 18 in the preamble and on the recognition of pre-trial supervision orders ([2009] OJ L 294/20), recital 19 in the preamble.   [444] [2009] OJ L 93/33, recital 18 in the preamble.

[445] [2009] OJ L 93/23, recital 13 in the preamble.

[446] [2010] OJ L 195/1. In particular, there is no consent by Member States before transfer of the data (see Art 13(1)(c) of the Framework Decision).   [447] See 12.3.1 above.

[448] See: <http://www.edps.europa.eu/EDPSWEB/webdav/site/mySite/shared/Documents/Consultation/Opinions/2010/10-06-22_Opinion_TFTP_EN.pdf>.

of data with other authorities.[449] However, the Court of Justice did not rule on this part of the complaint.

Finally, as for the data retention Directive, although this Directive was (controversially) subject to co-decision with the EP, it is clear that the EP essentially 'sold out' the civil liberties principles that it professed to be concerned about.[450] On the key issues—the purposes for which data must be retained, the types of data that must be kept, and the length of the retention period—there is nothing to show from a human rights point of view following the application of the co-decision process to this legislation. Specifically, more data will be included than the EP had wished, access to it will be essentially unregulated by EU law, data will be retained for up to double the period that the EP wanted, and indeed Member States will be unconstrained in requesting (and probably getting authorization for) longer periods of retention. While the purposes for which data can be retained falling within the scope of the Directive are relatively constrained, the Directive gives carte blanche to Member States to retain other data, or data for less serious crime or crime prevention purposes, as they wish. In fact, in light of Member States' power to retain existing requirements, or adopt new requirements, to retain data for over two years, the Directive has placed no absolute constraints concerning data retention upon Member States at all. Put simply, Member States can insist on (or at least request) the retention of any type of data for any type of security or law enforcement purpose for any period at all. This Directive is therefore a significant contribution to establishing a 'surveillance society', entailing a degree of State supervision or control of the *entire* population, across the EU.

Moving on to the EU's data protection rules, the Framework Decision is problematic due to its limited scope of application and relatively low standards overall, as compared to the EU's data protection Directive. The EU's more specific data protection rules create a fragmented system and neither these measures nor the Framework Decision explain their relationship to each other sufficiently clearly. As for the substance, the grounds to refuse access to information about their data to data subjects are so broad that any effective scrutiny of the processes depends upon the supervisory authorities, but it is doubtful that they have the money or resources to perform this function effectively.

12.7. Other forms of police cooperation

As explained at the outset of this chapter,[451] while the Treaty of Amsterdam made a distinction between policing operations and issues such as training, research, and

---

[449] See Joined Cases C-317/04 and C-318/04 *EP v Council and Commission* [2006] ECR I-4721.

[450] For more detailed criticism, see S Peers, 'The European Parliament and data retention: Chronicle of a "sell-out" foretold?', online at: <http://www.statewatch.org/news/2005/dec/sp_dataret_dec05.pdf>.   [451] See 12.2.3 above.

investigative techniques, this distinction did not have any relevance until the entry into force of the Treaty of Lisbon, which set out different decision-making procedures in Article 87 TFEU for operational police cooperation on the one hand and non-operational police cooperation on the other. While it is therefore necessary to distinguish between these two types of cooperation as regards future measures,[452] no clear distinction between them was made in the past. So the discussion in this section of the measures which were adopted previously does not seek to draw that distinction retroactively. Rather it first examines certain specific measures which have been adopted, as regards controlled deliveries, the European Police College, and the Police Chiefs' Task Force, and then examines other forms of cooperation generally, bringing together the various instruments affecting different forms of crime.

12.7.1. Controlled deliveries

In order to increase the effectiveness of investigations into the criminal organizations behind the import or export of drugs or other illegal products, EU measures facilitate 'controlled deliveries', under which national law enforcement officers do not intercept shipments at the border, but rather allow the products to cross the territory under surveillance, in the hope of finding out more information about the criminal networks involved.

Controlled deliveries were first mentioned in the Schengen Convention, when Member States undertook to permit them as regards drug trafficking, subject to prior authorization and the guarantee that Member States would retain responsibility and control over and the right to intervene as regards deliveries carried out on their territory.[453] A similar provision, applicable 'in the framework of criminal investigations into extraditable offences', appears in the EU's mutual judicial assistance Convention.[454] This provision would be amended by the proposed Directive establishing a European Investigation Order.[455] As for customs, the Naples II Convention requires Member States to permit controlled deliveries for customs supervision of other types of goods, again as regards all extraditable offences.[456]

12.7.2. European Police College

As called for by the Tampere European Council, the European Police College was established by a Decision in December 2000.[457] The College was established

---

[452] For analysis of this issue, see 12.2.4 above. The measures adopted concerning the cross-border movement of police officers are considered separately in 12.9 below.

[453] Art 73 of the Convention ([2000] OJ L 239).

[454] Art 12 of the Convention ([2000] OJ C 197).

[455] [2010] OJ C 165/22; see 9.6.1.3 above.

[456] Art 22, Naples II Convention ([1998] OJ C 24).

[457] [2000] OJ L 336/1. See the College website: <http://www.cepol.net>.

as a network of national training institutes, and its governing board is made up
of the directors of the national institutes for training senior police officers. Its
main task is to provide training for senior police officers, along with training of
trainers and development of training programmes; it is also obliged to develop
links with third countries.

A report on the first three years of operation of the College indicated that there
were practical difficulties with the framework established by the initial Decision,
in particular the lack of legal personality for the College, an under-funded permanent Secretariat, and the lack of a permanent seat.[458] Due to an ongoing dispute
about the seat of various EU bodies, the College had been located provisionally
in Denmark in facilities offered by the Danish government. The secretariat comprised only three staff, and the College finances were precarious in the absence
of regular funding from the EU budget.

Subsequent to this report, and to a European Council summit agreement in
December 2003 on the location of various EU institutions,[459] the Council adopted
further decisions respectively conferring legal personality upon the College and
officially setting the seat of the College in Bramshill in the UK.[460] Subsequently,
the Decision establishing the College was overhauled, with effect from the start
of 2006, to integrate it into the EU institutional framework, in particular funding the College from the EU budget, and applying EU rules on privileges and
immunities, budgeting, and staff.[461] The 2005 Decision also elaborates on the
functions of the College's Governing Board and Director.

According to its most recent annual report, the College has offered steadily
more courses (87 in 2008, for over 2,000 trainees), has drafted curricula for a
number of courses, and is active in disseminating police research.[462]

12.7.3. Police Chiefs' Task Force

Following the decision, as set out in the Tampere conclusions, to create a task
force of EU police chiefs, the task force was established in the spring of 2000 and
has met regularly since then. However, the task force has never been placed on a
formal footing by any formal EU measure—even by an EU soft law measure—or
by its establishment as a Council working group. After much discussion, it decided
to focus inter alia upon planning joint operations and making policy recommendations to the Council.[463] In the Commission's view, '[t]here is general agreement,

---

[458] Council doc 15722/03, 9 Dec 2003.   [459] [2004] OJ C 20/18.

[460] [2004] OJ L 251/19 and 20. See also the JHA Council conclusions on the College report (JHA
Council press release, 19 Feb 2004).   [461] [2005] OJ L 256/63.

[462] See the 2008 annual report, online at: <http://www.cepol.europa.eu/fileadmin/website/
newsroom/publications/Annual_Report_2008.pdf>.

[463] For a summary of developments, see the Statewatch analysis by T Bunyan, *The EU's Police Chief
Task Force (PCTF) and Police Chiefs Committee*, online at: <http://www.statewatch.org/news/2006/

however, that so far, these efforts have not led to an operational added value at EU level'.[464] Subsequently, it was decided that the Task Force would meet within the framework of Europol as regards its operational tasks, and within Council structures as regards its strategic tasks.[465] The Task Force has been criticized for its unclear legal status and the lack of transparency of its proceedings (since the Council claims that the EU access to documents rules do not apply to it), in light of its apparently significant role in operations and policy development.[466]

12.7.4. Other measures

There are a number of general EU measures in this area. First of all, the Schengen Convention contains provisions on enhancing communications between border police forces and requiring Member States to ensure that, such as hotel staff, register foreigners staying in commercial accommodation.[467] The Schengen Executive Committee also adopted Decisions, now integrated into EU law, concerning crime prevention and detection in the context of cross-border police cooperation, a Handbook on cross-border police cooperation, police telecommunications, and principles governing the payment of informers.[468] The Council, in the Maastricht period, adopted a parallel Resolution regarding use of informers.[469] Subsequently, the Council adopted a catalogue of best practices and recommendations regarding Schengen police cooperation.[470] The Council has adopted conclusions concerning police professional standards applicable to international police operations, with a view towards developing such standards, but has not addressed this issue further.[471] Finally, the Council has adopted a Framework Decision governing forensic standards.[472]

As for specific issues, first of all, the Schengen Convention contains a number of provisions on drugs.[473] Member States 'undertake' to adopt 'all necessary measures to prevent and punish the illicit trafficking' in drugs, and 'to prevent and

---

mar/pctf.pdf>, and the Commission's Communication on police cooperation (COM (2004) 376, 19 May 2004), 19–21.

[464] Ibid, 21.   [465] See JHA Council press release, 19 Nov 2004.

[466] See Bunyan (n 463 above).   [467] Arts 44 and 45 of the Convention ([2000] OJ L 239).

[468] Respectively [2000] OJ L 239/407, 408, 409, and 417. The first of these measures has been repealed by the 2006 Framework Decision on police cooperation ([2006] OJ L 386/89, Art 12(2)), on which see 12.6.3 above.   [469] [1997] OJ C 10/1.

[470] The latest version is in Council doc 10842/09, 16 June 2009.

[471] Council doc 14633/04, 15 Nov 2004, adopted by the Dec 2004 JHA Council.

[472] [2009] OJ L 322/14, applicable from 20 Nov 2013 (DNA data) and 30 Nov 2015 (fingerprints) (Art 7).

[473] Arts 70–76 of the Convention and an Executive Committee Decision ([2000] OJ L 239/463). Arts 70 and 74 were not integrated into the EU legal order (see Council Decision, [1999] OJ L 176/1). Arts 71–73 were allocated to the third pillar; Art 75 and the Executive Committee Decision were allocated to Art 95 EC; and Art 76 was allocated jointly to the third pillar and to Arts 95 and 152 EC (see Council Decision, [1999] OJ L 176/17). Arts 95 and 152 are now Arts 114 and 168 TFEU.

punish by administrative and penal measures the illegal export...as well as the sale, supply and handing over' of drugs. To 'combat the illegal import' of drugs, checks on external borders must be increased.[474] Member States must also provide for seizure and confiscation of the proceeds of drug trafficking, and undertake to permit 'controlled deliveries' regarding drug trafficking.[475] Individuals who move between Member States can carry drugs necessary for their treatment, as long as they carry a certificate.[476] Finally, Member States shall, 'where necessary', adopt measures to control drugs which are subject to greater restriction in other Member States.[477]

EU measures against narcotic drugs have been developed in the framework of successive multi-annual Action Plans.[478] Over the years, EU action has included further measures concerning substantive criminal law, particularly harmonizing the law concerning drug precursors, drug trafficking, and synthetic drugs.[479] Specific anti-drugs measures concerning the harmonizing of policing have comprised Resolutions or Recommendations on: coordination between police and customs regarding combating drugs;[480] drugs statistics;[481] drugs indicators;[482] generic classification of new synthetic drugs;[483] drug abuse in prisons;[484] investigation methods (in particular suggesting simultaneous investigation into criminal assets),[485] cooperation between national authorities;[486] training of drugs law enforcement officers,[487] and guidelines for taking samples of seized drugs.[488] A Joint Action addresses customs/business cooperation against drug trafficking.[489]

Non-policing measures have included Resolutions and Recommendations on the recreational use of drugs;[490] prevention and reduction of health-related harm associated with drug dependence;[491] the incorporation of drug prevention in the school curriculum;[492] inclusion of substance abuse in the university curriculum;[493] drug dependencies and national health care;[494] the role of families;[495] and road accidents.[496] The EU also has established an agency

---

[474] Art 71. See the opinion of 15 July 2010 in Case C-137/09 *Josemans*, pending.

[475] Arts 72 and 73; on 'controlled deliveries', see further 12.7.1 above.

[476] Art 75 and Executive Committee Decision (n 473 above). Furthermore, restrictions on cross-border purchases of prescription drugs will, to an extent, violate EU free movement rules: see Cases C-62/90 *Commission v Germany* [1992] ECR I-2575 and C-322/01 *Doc Morris* [2003] ECR I-14887.   [477] Art 76.

[478] The most recent Plan is set out in [2008] OJ C 326/7.   [479] See 10.5.1.2 above.

[480] [1996] OJ C 375/1, replaced by [2006] OJ L 124/1.

[481] Council doc 12411/01, 10 Oct 2001.   [482] Council doc 13932/01, 15 Nov 2001

[483] See JHA council press release, 28 Nov 2002.

[484] See JHA council press release, 27–28 Feb 2003.   [485] [2002] OJ C 114/1.

[486] [2002] OJ C 114/3.   [487] [2004] OJ C 38/1.   [488] [2004] OJ C 86/10.

[489] [1996] OJ L 322/3.   [490] Council doc 5095/3/02, 15 Apr 2002.

[491] [2003] OJ L 165/31. See earlier Conclusions on the health aspects of drugs ([1997] OJ C 241/7).   [492] See JHA Council press release, 13 June 2002.

[493] See Agriculture Council press release, June 2003.   [494] See ibid.

[495] [2004] OJ C 97/4.   [496] [2004] OJ C 97/1.

monitoring the use of narcotic drugs,[497] and its health funding programmes address drug-related issues.[498]

EU measures combating terrorism usually address the exchange of information,[499] but the EU has also adopted a Joint Action establishing an inventory of expertise on this issue,[500] as well as a 2002 Recommendation on the drawing up of terrorist profiles.[501]

Another issue to which the EU has devoted considerable effort is the fight against organized crime. In this field,[502] measures comprise a Joint Action establishing an inventory of competences concerning organized crime;[503] a Resolution on policing international crime routes;[504] a Resolution establishing a model protocol on public/private partnerships against organized crime;[505] and Council conclusions on an administrative approach to tackling organized crime.[506]

Measures concerning trafficking in persons comprise a number of soft law measures, in particular a Recommendation of November 2003 concerning the law enforcement response to trafficking.[507] As regards missing children, a Council Resolution addresses the role of civil society in assisting police investigations.[508] Also, a Decision concerning child pornography sets out a number of measures in order to combat this crime.[509]

As for public order, the Council has adopted a Resolution on a Handbook containing detailed suggestions regarding public order at football matches.[510] Following conflicts between police and protestors at EU summits ('European Council' meetings), the Council adopted detailed conclusions in July 2001; a manual concerning security at summits in November 2002;[511] and a Resolution on security at summits in April 2004.[512]

---

[497] Reg 302/93 ([1993] OJ L 36/1), recast by Reg 1920/2006 ([2006] OJ L 376/1).

[498] Initially there was a specific measure on drug-related matters (Decision 102/97, [1997] OJ L 19/25, extended by Decision 521/2001, [2001] OJ L 79/1). Drug-related health measures then formed part of the EU's general health funding programme (Decision 1786/2002, [2002] OJ L 271/1), and now again form a separate programme (still with the legal base of health policy): Decision 1750/2007, [2007] OJ L 257/23.

[499] See 12.6.3 above, and also 12.4.5 above (sanctions), and 12.9.4 below (joint investigations).

[500] [1996] OJ L 273/1.

[501] See text at: <http://ue.eu.int/ueDocs/cms_Data/docs/polju/EN/EJN280.pdf>.

[502] See also the Commission communication on a strategy against organized crime (COM (2005) 232, 2 June 2005).   [503] [1996] OJ L 342/2.

[504] [1999] OJ C 162/1.   [505] [2004] OJ C 116/20.

[506] Council doc 14125/2/04, 24 Nov 2004, adopted by the Dec 2004 JHA Council.

[507] Council doc 15028/03, 19 Nov 2003. See also Council conclusions on trafficking in persons ([2003] OJ C 137/1); a Council resolution on the law enforcement response ([2003] OJ C 260/4); a Commission decision establishing an expert group of advisers ([2003] OJ L 79/25); and an Action Plan against human trafficking ([2005] OJ C 311/1). See further 7.5.4 above.

[508] [2001] OJ C 283/1.

[509] [2000] OJ L 138. See also the measures referred to in 12.4.7 above.

[510] [1999] OJ C 196/1, replaced by subsequent Resolutions ([2002] OJ C 22/1, [2006] OJ C 322/1, and [2010] OJ C 165/1).   [511] Council doc 12637/3/02, 12 Nov 2002.

[512] See also 12.6.3 above.

High-technology crime has been addressed by a Council Recommendation on Member States' creation of twenty-four-hour specialized contact points,[513] and a number of aspects of vehicle crime have been addressed by a Council Decision of 2004.[514] The EU has created formal networks of national officials to encourage operational cooperation as regards: the protection of public figures;[515] the exchange of information and contact points concerning genocide, crimes against humanity, and war crimes;[516] asset recovery;[517] and anti-corruption.[518]

Finally, the EU and EC have adopted a number of related instruments concerning the protection of the euro from counterfeiting.[519] Framework Decisions have harmonized the substantive law and extended mutual recognition to sentences in this field.[520] Other early measures comprised a Regulation which laid down detailed obligations regarding counterfeit notes and coins,[521] a parallel third pillar Decision concerning criminal investigations,[522] and an EU funding programme, 'Pericles'.[523] Subsequently the Council adopted a further Recommendation on the issue,[524] and the Commission established a scientific centre to assist cooperation against euro counterfeiting.[525] The European Central Bank has also adopted measures.[526] Most recently, the Commission has proposed legislation concerning the transport of euro cash by road.[527]

12.8. Europol

The EU's law enforcement body, Europol is now so well-known that a Hollywood film (*Ocean's Twelve*) has featured a Europol officer, portrayed by the delectable Catherine Zeta-Jones! Sadly, the reality of Europol is rather less exciting.

---

[513] [2001] OJ C 187/5.   [514] [2004] OJ L 389/28.

[515] Council Decision ([2002] OJ L 333/1), amended in 2009 ([2009] OJ L 283/62); see implementation in [2003] OJ C 260/6.

[516] Council Decisions ([2002] L 167/1 and [2003] OJ L 118/12).

[517] [2007] OJ L 332/103. For analysis of the role of asset recovery offices, see the Commission communication on crime proceeds (COM (2008) 766, 20 Nov 2008).

[518] [2008] OJ L 301/38.

[519] For further information, see: <http://ec.europa.eu/anti_fraud/pages_euro/index_en.html>.

[520] See 10.5.1.2 and 9.7.2 above.   [521] Reg 1338/2001 ([2001] OJ L 181/6).

[522] [2001] OJ L 329/1.

[523] [2001] OJ L 339/50; the programme has since been extended ([2006] OJ L 26/40 and [2006] OJ L 330/28).

[524] Council doc 6927/5/03, 22 Sep 2003, adopted by the JHA Council, 2–3 Oct 2003.

[525] See Council Decision conferring power on Commission ([2003] OJ L 325/44) and Commission Decision establishing the Centre ([2005] OJ L 19/73).

[526] See ECB Recommendation on euro counterfeiting ([1999] OJ C 11/13), Decision on access to counterfeit monitoring system ([2001] OJ C 337/49), and treaties with Interpol ([2004] OJ C 134/6) and Europol (12.11 below).   [527] COM (2010) 377, 14 July 2010.

Europol had an embryonic existence for over five years in the form of the Europol Drugs Unit (EDU). The EDU was created before the TEU entered into force, by a Ministerial agreement in June 2003, and initially focused solely on combating drug trafficking and associated criminal organizations and money laundering.[528] Its legal status was subsequently based on a 1995 Council Joint Action, which also expanded its role to cover trafficking in nuclear and radioactive substances, 'crimes involving clandestine immigration networks', and 'illicit vehicle trafficking'.[529] Its role was expanded again by a 1996 Joint Action, which gave it the mandate to cover 'traffic in human beings'.[530] The EDU's role was to exchange information (including personal information) about investigations and to prepare 'general situation reports and analyses of criminal activities', but it lacked a central database and so information could only be exchanged between Member States' liaison officers on the basis of each officer's national data protection law.[531]

The EDU was finally replaced by Europol as from 1 July 1999, when Europol began operations because the Europol Convention, signed in 1995,[532] had entered into force on 1 October 1998, and the last of various required supplementary measures had entered into force.[533] This institutional framework was supplemented by five Protocols to the Convention:

(a) a Protocol signed in 1996, which conferred jurisdiction upon national courts to refer questions on the Europol Convention to the Court of Justice;[534]

(b) a Protocol signed in 1997, which provided for privileges and immunities for Europol staff;[535]

(c) a Protocol signed in 2000, which extended Europol's competence to cover all forms of money laundering;[536]

(d) a Protocol signed in 2002, which expressly permitted Europol to participate in joint investigative teams and to ask the competent authorities of Member States to begin investigations;[537] and

(e) a Protocol signed in 2003, which made a number of amendments to the Convention,[538] inter alia as regards extensions of Europol's competence, further communication of data to third States and bodies, an enhanced role for the EP, and rules on a right of access to Europol documents.

---

[528] T Bunyan, ed, *Key Texts on Justice and Home Affairs in the European Union* (1997), 47.

[529] [1995] OJ L 62/1.   [530] [1996] OJ L 342/4.

[531] On the EDU in practice, see the first edition of this book, at 211.

[532] [1995] OJ C 316/1.   [533] [1999] OJ C 185/1.

[534] [1996] OJ C 299/1, in force 29 Dec 1998. Some Member States opted out of the Court's jurisdiction. No cases have yet been referred to the Court.

[535] [1997] OJ C 221/1, in force 1 July 1999.

[536] [2000] OJ C 358/1, in force 29 Mar 2007.

[537] [2002] OJ C 312/1, in force 3 Apr 2007. See also two earlier Council Recommendations on these issues: [2000] OJ C 289/8 and C 357/7.

[538] [2003] OJ C 358/1, in force 18 Apr 2007.

There were also a large number of secondary measures adopted by the Council or Europol's Management Board.[539]

However, as from 1 January 2010, the basic legal acts governing Europol (the Convention and Protocols) were replaced by a third pillar Council Decision (the 'Europol Decision') adopted in 2009.[540] From that point on, EU rules on staff and budgets (including finance from the EU budget) have applied to Europol.[541] A parallel Regulation specifies that Europol staff do not have immunity when they participate in joint investigation teams.[542] The Europol Decision is supplemented by a number of implementing measures,[543] and the Council has also adopted a Decision establishing a joint secretariat for the data protection authority for Europol, the SIS, and the CIS.[544]

Europol is an international organization with legal personality,[545] headquartered in the Hague.[546] Its chief organ is a Management Board, made up of one representative from each Member State with one from the Commission and taking most decisions by a two-thirds vote,[547] although day-to-day management is in the hands of a Director and Deputy Directors.[548] The Board must report annually to the Council on both the previous year's activities and plans for the previous year, and the Council forwards these reports to the European Parliament.[549]

Europol's main tasks are to: 'collect, store, process, analyse and exchange information and intelligence'; inform national authorities of information about criminal activities; aid national investigations; ask national authorities to begin or coordinate investigations; provide intelligence and support as regards major events; and draw up threat assessments and strategic analyses.[550] These tasks include analysis of Internet information, and it has the additional tasks of developing knowledge of investigative procedures, advising on investigations, and providing strategic intelligence.[551] It may also assist with 'support, advice and research' as regards training national staff, technical support, crime prevention methods, and technical and forensic police methods and investigative procedures,[552] and acts as the central office for coordinating action against

---

[539] For more details of the legal framework governing Europol before 2010, see the second edition of this book, at 536–538.

[540] [2009] OJ L 121/27. All further references in this section are to this Decision, unless otherwise noted.   [541] Arts 39 and 42–44.

[542] Reg 371/2009, [2009] OJ L 121/1.

[543] Rules of procedure of the Joint Supervisory Board [2010] OJ C 45/2; Management Board decision on appointment of the Director and Deputy Directors ([2009] OJ L 348/3); Management Board decision on conditions for data processing ([2009] OJ L 348/1); Council decision on confidentiality rules ([2009] OJ L 332/17); Management Board decision on the rules for analysis work files ([2009] OJ L 325/14); Council decision on the States which Europol can sign treaties with ([2009] OJ L 325/12); and Council decision on Europol's relations with external partners ([2009] OJ L 325/6).

[544] [2000] OJ L 271/1.   [545] Art 2(1).   [546] Protocol 6 to the consolidated Treaties.

[547] Art 37.   [548] Art 38.   [549] Art 37(10).   [550] Art 5(1).   [551] Art 5(2) and (3).

[552] Art 5(4).

euro counterfeiting.[553] Europol's external relations are considered later in this chapter.[554]

Europol has competence over 'organised crime, terrorism and other forms of serious crime' listed in the Annex to the Europol Decision, as long as those crimes '[affect] two or more Member States in such a way as to require a common approach by the Member States owing to the scale, significance and consequences of the offences'.[555] It has competence also over specified 'related criminal offences'.[556] Europol has also been given further tasks in various legislative measures adopted by the Council,[557] as well as the role of supervisory body as regards transfers of financial data to the US.[558] It has also been given access to the data in the SIS, and will be given access to data in SIS II, the VIS, the CIS, and possibly Eurodac.[559]

In concrete terms, Europol can participate in joint investigation teams, request national authorities to begin investigations, establish information systems (in particular the Europol Information System), and open analysis work files.[560] Member States must establish national units for relations with Europol, which shall send liaison officers to it.[561] For the future, the legal base for measures concerning Europol, Article 88 TFEU, allows the Council to confer further powers on Europol, falling short of 'coercive powers';[562] the Commission plans to propose further legislation on Europol in 2013.[563] Only at this point would the provisions on scrutiny by national parliaments and the EP referred to in Article 88 be invoked.

Is Europol sufficiently accountable? It must be admitted that Europol does not have powers as extensive as those of national police authorities; in particular, it lacks the power to arrest, question, and detain suspects. Nevertheless, there is still insufficient national or European parliamentary accountability as regards the powers Europol does exercise, and the position regarding judicial control is not clear. While Europol's annual reports are somewhat informative, they inevitably reflect the position of the agency; there is an obvious need for

---

[553] Art 5(5), referring to the earlier Decision on this issue ([2005] OJ L 185/35).

[554] See 12.11 below.

[555] Art 4(1). The Annex lists a further twenty-four crimes, with definitions of four of them.

[556] Art 4(3).

[557] See particularly: the Council Resolution concerning international crime routes ([1999] OJ C 162/1); Art 2 of the Decision concerning child pornography ([2000] OJ L 138); Arts 3 and 4(1) of the Decision on counterfeiting the euro ([2001] OJ L 329/1); Art 8 of the Decision on liaison officers ([2003] OJ L 67/27), as amended ([2006] OJ L 219/31); Art 7 of the Decision on vehicle crime ([2004] OJ L 389/28); the Recommendation on use of joint investigation teams ([2003] OJ C 121/1, subsequently amended in [2010] OJ C 70/1); the Decisions on exchange of information on terrorism ([2003] OJ L 16/68 and [2005] OJ L 253/22); and the Decision on procedure for banning designer drugs ([2005] OJ L 127/32).   [558] Art 4 of the 'Swift' treaty ([2010] OJ L 195/1).

[559] See Art 21 and further 12.6.1 above.   [560] Arts 6–7 and 10–16.   [561] Arts 8–9.

[562] For interpretation of the scope of this legal base, see 12.2.4 above.

[563] COM (2010) 171, 20 Apr 2010.

a continuing independent and objective scrutiny and evaluation of Europol in practice.[564]

12.9. Cross-border operations

There are no specific principles to determine which State has jurisdiction over an investigation when there are several possible 'home' States. Investigating authorities presume jurisdiction to investigate a crime based on the jurisdiction rules which apply in their home State,[565] and the Court of Justice has confirmed that multiple investigations do not breach the rule on cross-border double jeopardy.[566]

While the basic rules concerning operations by police officers are set out in the Schengen Convention, the basic rules concerning customs operations are set out in the Naples II Convention,[567] which entered into force in all Member States in 2009. The latter Convention sets out basic rules regarding all types of operations, as well as special rules for each type.[568] As well as the measures discussed below, the Convention allows one Member State's customs investigators to request another's to carry out surveillance or inquiries on their own territory.[569] Certain relevant provisions also appear in the EU's mutual judicial assistance Convention,[570] which is in force in a large majority of Member States.[571] The Convention contains general rules on the civil and criminal liability of national officials involved in operations.[572]

12.9.1. Hot pursuit

The Schengen Convention and Naples II Convention provide for hot pursuit by police and customs officers respectively.[573] Schengen rules permit the police officers from specified forces from the 'home State' of an investigation to chase persons across a land border without authorization of the 'host State' if there is not enough time to inform the host State authorities or for the latter to reach the

---

[564] For more detailed criticism and analysis, see S Peers, 'Governance and the Third Pillar: The Accountability of Europol' in D Curtin and R Wessel, eds, *Good Governance and the European Union* (Intersentia, 2005), 253.   [565] See 11.5 above.

[566] Case C-491/07 *Turansky* [2008] ECR I-11039. Nevertheless, overlapping investigations, unless coordinated effectively, may lead to wasted resources (due to the EU ban on prosecuting a person after a prior final judgment relating to the same acts in another Member State: see 11.8 above) or an uncooperative 'turf battle'.   [567] Ibid; explanatory report at [1998] OJ C 189/1.

[568] The basic rules, including rules on liability of officers, are in Art 19; the specific rules are in Arts 20–24.   [569] Arts 11 and 12 ([1998] OJ C 24).

[570] [2000] OJ C 197/1.   [571] See ratification details in Appendix I.

[572] Arts 15 and 16 of the Convention.

[573] Arts 41 and 20 of each Convention respectively.

scene.[574] In view of the sensitivity of this power, the pursuit is essentially governed by the host State's law. The pursuing officers must inform host State authorities of their pursuit as soon as possible and the latter can order a stop to the pursuit. A number of additional conditions are attached:

(a) police can only chase persons who have escaped a custodial sentence or provisional custody, or who were apprehended committing or participating in certain crimes;[575]

(b) a host State may limit home State police to acting within a specified area or for a specified time;

(c) a host State may prohibit home State officers from apprehending a suspect; if it does not, then the pursuing officers may 'detain' the person being pursued until the host State officers can make an arrest or establish the person's identity;

(d) home State officers are subject to host State laws and to the instructions of host State authorities;

(e) home State officers must be identifiable from their vehicle, uniform, or armband, and cannot enter private homes or places not accessible to the public;

(f) home State officers may carry service weapons, but can only use them in 'legitimate self-defence';

(g) a person who is 'apprehended' by home State officers (see the rule in (c), above) may be handcuffed during the transfer and subjected only to a security search by those officers; items he or she is carrying may be seized by those officers;[576]

(h) the home State officers must always account for each operation before the host State's authorities and must assist in any subsequent inquiries if requested by the host State.

It is implicit that if the pursuing police catch the person they are chasing, they cannot simply take him or her back across the border, but must hand the person they have caught over to the host State authorities and arrange to issue an extradition request (or presumably now issue a European Arrest Warrant, in most cases).[577] The pursued person may be questioned by the host State authorities after

---

[574] Art 44 of the Convention provides that the technical means to ensure quick communication, particularly in hot pursuit cases, should be established.

[575] The specified crimes are (at each host State's discretion) either all extraditable offences or the following serious crimes: murder; manslaughter; rape; arson; forgery; aggravated burglary and robbery and receiving stolen goods; extortion; kidnapping and hostage taking; trafficking in human beings; drug trafficking; breach of the laws on arms and explosives; wilful damage through use of explosives; illicit transportation of toxic and hazardous waste; and hit-and-run driving. Note that 'escaping arrest' is not included.

[576] It might be questioned whether the search and seizure powers cover only the person, and items on the person, of the person who was caught, or whether they would also cover a search of the *vehicle* and objects within it.

[577] On the scope of application of the European Arrest Warrant, see 9.5.2 above.

arrest, whatever his or her nationality; this is subject to the host State's national law. But if the apprehended person is not a national of the host State, he or she must be released by those authorities within six hours (discounting midnight to 9.00am) unless an extradition request has been made. It is not specified who the extradition request may be made by. This appears to mean that the host State authorities cannot lay charges against the person even if he or she is wanted in that State, or has been convicted of an offence and escaped a custodial sentence, unless they send an extradition request to the *home* State.

Home State officers are treated as host State officers if they commit, or are victims of, offences,[578] and are liable for any damages under the host State's law.[579] The host State must repair any damage under its own law and can claim reimbursement of such costs from the home State, but is discouraged from doing so. Member States may make bilateral arrangements providing for more extensive hot pursuit.

There is no limitation regarding the particular methods used to flee across a land border, so in theory the rules could cover persons fleeing by foot or on a bicycle, although in practice the rules are obviously largely relevant to persons fleeing by car (or perhaps motorcycle); they are also applicable in principle to railways.

The Schengen provisions have been amended by a Council Decision adopted in 2000, which allows Member States to change the name of the police forces which have the power to conduct cross-border operations.[580]

The Naples II Convention obviously took the Schengen rules as a model. Hot pursuit, along with other 'special forms of cooperation', can be allowed for the 'prevention, investigation and prosecution' of illicit trafficking in drugs (including precursors), weapons, arms, explosives, cultural goods, dangerous and toxic waste, nuclear material and items for use in manufacturing atomic, biological, or chemical weapons, as well as trade in goods prohibited by national or EU law or illegal trade in goods to evade tax or to obtain authorized payments which would have 'considerable' cost to the national or EU budget.[581] The differences from the Schengen rules are that hot pursuit can be granted for any extraditable offence falling among the offences listed above, but not for persons escaping a custodial sentence or provisional custody; pursuit is allowed by sea as well as land; pursuit on the high seas is governed by relevant international law; a host State can ban home State officers from carrying service weapons generally, or in a specific case; and Member States can opt out of all or part of the hot pursuit rules altogether.[582]

---

[578] Art 42 of the Convention.   [579] Art 43 of the Convention.

[580] [2000] OJ L 248/1.   [581] Art 19(2).

[582] The UK, Greece, Ireland, Slovenia, Latvia, and Poland have declared that they are not bound by Art 20; Lithuania has declared that it is not bound in the absence of any reciprocity from neighbouring States.

12.9.2. Surveillance

Again, the chief provisions derive from the Schengen Convention.[583] Unlike hot pursuit, advance approval of the host State is necessary before observation can be carried out as a general rule, but cross-border observation is allowed without prior approval on similar grounds to those justifying hot pursuit. In particular, according to the initial version of the rules, police officers from a specified force in the home State of the investigation may enter another Member State with prior approval to 'continue their observation' of a person who is 'presumed to have participated in' an extraditable criminal offence, or without prior approval 'where prior authorisation cannot be requested . . . for particularly urgent reasons' to observe a person 'presumed to have committed' one or more of thirteen serious crimes.[584] The conditions for observation are similar to those governing hot pursuit, except that observing officers need not be publicly identifiable (for obvious reasons);[585] a host State may ban carrying of service weapons in particular cases; the home State officers can never challenge or arrest the observed person (so there need be no rules on arrests or detention); there is no possibility to limit the surveillance to a certain period or area, or to following a person across land borders only (a point of particular relevance to the UK);[586] and the observing officers need only give a report of their activities, usually written, to the host State. The offences and damages rules are the same as for hot pursuit.[587]

The Council adopted a Decision making a technical amendment to Article 40 of the Schengen Convention in 2000,[588] followed by a more substantive amendment in 2003.[589] This entailed two changes to the rules. Firstly, police officers can keep under surveillance not only suspects, but also persons 'who can assist in identifying or tracing' a suspect, subject always to prior authorization. Secondly, the list of crimes for which previously unauthorized surveillance of suspects could take place was enlarged to add six further crimes and to amend the definition of two others.[590] It should be noted that the proposed Directive establishing a European Investigation Order will not affect these rules.[591]

---

[583] Art 40, Schengen Convention.

[584] These are the same crimes as the crimes to which Schengen States can limit hot pursuit under the Schengen hot pursuit rules (see 12.9.1 above), with the exception of hit-and-run driving.

[585] However, they must carry proof of their authority and (usually) their approval to observe.

[586] Indeed, unlike hot pursuit, surveillance will likely sometimes be carried out in a distant Member State, not an adjoining one. However, the host State may attach conditions to its authorization of surveillance, which might include conditions concerning the time and place of the surveillance.

[587] Arts 42 and 43, Schengen Convention.   [588] [2000] OJ L 248/1.

[589] [2003] OJ L 260/37. This Decision applied from 11 Oct 2003 (Art 3).

[590] The additional crimes are serious fraud, smuggling of 'aliens', money laundering, illicit trafficking in nuclear and radioactive substances, organized crime, and terrorism (the last two crimes as defined by EU measures: see further 10.5 above). The amended definitions concern the replacement of 'rape' by serious sexual offences and the broadening of 'forgery of money' to include counterfeiting and forgery of all means of payment.

[591] See recital 9 in the preamble to the proposal ([2010] OJ C 165/22).

The Naples II provisions[592] allow surveillance where 'there are serious grounds for believing [a person is] involved in one of the infringements' referred to in the special cooperation rules.[593] Otherwise the Naples II rules are the same as the original Schengen rules, except that a Member State can opt out of the provisions entirely and host Member States can impose a general ban on home State officers carrying firearms.[594]

12.9.3. Covert operations

'Covert operations' going beyond the scope of surveillance were not mentioned in the Schengen Convention. However, as regards customs officers, the Naples II Convention provides for such actions, although Member States may opt out of this provision in its entirety.[595] If a Member State wishes to 'make contact with subjects and other persons associated with them' in another Member State, it may ask another Member State to allow its customs officers or 'officers acting on behalf' of its administration to enter 'under cover of a false identity'. Presumably this means that private detectives authorized by a State might be sent.[596]

There is no rule restricting covert investigations to certain types of offences, and no list of general conditions attaching to the authorization of the investigations. Instead, the host State's rules on such investigations apply, and the host State is given great latitude to restrict or lay conditions upon the scope of the home State agents' undercover work.

As for cross-border covert operations by the police, the EU's Convention on mutual assistance in criminal matters applies.[597] The rules in this Convention are even vaguer than those in the Naples II Convention, leaving the 'duration', 'the detailed conditions' and 'the legal status of the officers concerned' to be agreed between the relevant Member States. In general, the investigations must take place under the host State's rules, with much latitude to that State to set conditions. It is not clear whether the proposed Directive establishing a European Investigation Order would apply to this issue.[598]

The accountability problems arising from undercover police operations would be magnified if there is extensive use of cross-border undercover

---

[592] Art 21, Naples II Convention. Greece, Slovenia, Latvia, and Ireland have declared that Art 21 is inapplicable to them.

[593] See Art 19 of the Convention. The infringements need *not* necessarily be extraditable offences.

[594] There is also a Danish declaration, limiting surveillance without approval to extraditable offences.

[595] Art 23 of the Convention (ibid). Greece, Denmark, Slovenia, Latvia, and Ireland have opted out.   [596] For the implications of EU law on this, see 12.4.3.1 above.

[597] Art 12 of the Convention ([2000] OJ C 197/1).   [598] See n 591 above.

investigations—although it is likely that there was already some de facto cross-border undercover work which the two Conventions have simply legitimized.

12.9.4. Joint operations and investigations

The issue of joint operations and joint investigation teams was first explicitly addressed by the EU's Convention on mutual criminal assistance, which provides for two or more Member States to set up a joint investigation team 'for a specific purpose and a limited period', which may be extended.[599] Teams may be set up 'in particular' where one Member State is conducting a 'difficult and demanding' investigation with links to other Member States, or where Member States are conducting overlapping investigations which should be coordinated. The leader of the team shall be a representative of the Member State in which the team operates; the team is also subject to the laws of that State. Those team members 'seconded' by other Member States may normally participate in investigations and may be given tasks by the team leader.

While the team does not have power to operate as such in multiple Member States, it may request the assistance of authorities in Member States other than the Member State where the team operates. Information gathered by the team which would not be otherwise available to a Member States' authorities can be used, subject to limited safeguards. Subject to national law and international rules, persons other than national officials can form part of the team, in particular staff members of EU bodies (a reference to Europol, Eurojust, and OLAF).[600]

In order to apply the provisions of the Convention as early as possible, a Framework Decision comprising the text of the relevant Convention Articles was adopted in 2002;[601] it will cease to apply once all Member States have ratified the Convention.[602] The early adoption of these provisions had the particular objective of facilitating investigations into terrorism, but the Framework Decision is in no way limited to such investigations. Member States had to apply the Framework Decision by 1 January 2003,[603] and its use was encouraged by a Council Recommendation which set out a model agreement establishing a team which Member States could use.[604]

According to a Commission report, only fourteen Member States had applied the Framework Decision in their national law by August 2004, and there were some deficiencies in their application of the measure.[605] The Commission did not report whether any teams had been established or whether they were effective,

---

[599] Art 13 of the Convention (n 597 above).
[600] On Europol participation, see 12.8 above.   [601] [2002] OJ L 162/1.
[602] Art 5, Framework Decision.   [603] Art 4(1), Framework Decision.
[604] [2003] OJ C 121/1, subsequently amended ([2010] OJ C 70/1).
[605] COM (2004) 858, 7 Jan 2005.

although it appears that only one team was formed by spring 2005.[606] Nor has the Council assessed the application of the Framework Decision, as required.[607] It should be noted that the Framework Decision would not be amended or repealed by the proposed Directive establishing a European Investigation Order.[608]

In addition to this measure, the Council adopted in April 2002 a Recommendation establishing multinational police anti-terrorist teams.[609] It is unclear, given the background to this measure, whether it is intended to deal with criminal investigations, non-criminal investigations, or both.[610] There is no clear definition of 'terrorism', and previous scandals involving similar investigations in Member States law give rise to doubts that there will be sufficient accountability and control of these teams.[611]

Next, in 2008 the Council adopted the 'Prum Decision', which includes much of the text of the Prum Convention, which was originally agreed between a group of Member States.[612] This Decision includes rules on joint patrols and other joint operations, as well as on assistance in connection with mass gatherings, disasters, and serious accidents, which can include notification of such situations, coordination of joint responses, as well as dispatching personnel and equipment onto the territory of another Member State.[613] There are related provisions governing the use of arms and ammunition, protection of guest officers, civil and criminal liability, and the applicable employment relationship.[614]

Finally, for many years, EU customs administrations have been carrying out several joint operations each year, without any formal binding legal framework. A Council Resolution of 1997 established a Handbook, which sets out a standard procedure for deciding upon operations and evaluating them,[615] and a subsequent Guide sets out even more detailed procedures to be followed.[616] Due to the difficulties of planning and carrying out joint operations, the idea of a permanent operational coordination unit has been considered,[617] but the idea has not yet been implemented. Regular reports on the joint customs operations indicate that

---

[606] See the outcome of proceedings of the Police Chiefs' Task Force meeting on 12 May 2005 (Council doc 9494/05, 30 May 2005, 9).

[607] Art 4(2), Framework Decision. However, on the application in practice, see the report of the first meeting of experts (Council doc 15227/05, 2 Dec 2005) and the guidelines agreed (Council doc 8160/2/04, 25 May 2004).   [608] [2010] OJ C 165/22, Art 3(2)(a).

[609] See text at: <http://ue.eu.int/ueDocs/cms_Data/docs/polju/EN/EJN278.pdf>.

[610] For details, see S Peers, 'EU Responses to Terrorism' (2003) 52 ICLQ 227 at 239–240.

[611] For instance, on the 'Gladio' network, see Statewatch Briefing, July 1991, and the annexed EP Resolution of 22 Nov 1990, which stated that 'security services (or uncontrolled branches thereof) were involved in serious cases of terrorism and crime as evidenced by various judicial enquiries'.

[612] [2008] OJ L 210/1. On the background to the Prum Decision, see 12.2.3 above. On the substance of the rest of the Decision, see 12.6.2 and 12.6.3 above.

[613] Arts 17–18 of the Prum Decision, ibid.   [614] Arts 19–23 of the Prum Decision, ibid.

[615] [1997] OJ C 193/5.   [616] Council doc 8249/2/05, 12 Sep 2005.

[617] Council doc 9335/1/04, 16 July 2004.

they are generally considered successful, resulting in the seizure in particular of significant quantities of drugs and smuggled cigarettes.[618]

12.9.5. Special intervention units

In 2008, the Council adopted a Decision governing the movement of 'special intervention units' from one Member State to another.[619] Like the Prum Decision, this measure is also taken from the text of the Prum Convention.[620] According to the Decision, a 'special intervention unit' is 'any law enforcement unit of a Member State which is specialised in the control of a crisis situation',[621] and a 'crisis situation' is defined as 'any situation in which the competent authorities of a Member State have reasonable grounds to believe that there is a criminal offence presenting a serious direct physical threat to persons, property, infrastructure or institutions in that Member State, in particular those situations referred to in' the Framework Decision defining terrorism.[622]

The Decision provides that one Member State can request another for the assistance of a special intervention team to deal with a crisis situation. The requested Member State is entirely free to refuse.[623] According to the agreement between the two Member States, assistance may entail 'providing the requesting Member State with equipment and/or expertise and/or of carrying out actions on the territory of that Member State, using weapons if so required'.[624] If actions are authorized by officers of the requested State on the requesting State's territory, those officers would be operating under the 'responsibility, authority and direction' of the requesting State and in accordance with its law; at the same time, such officers would also have to act within the limits of the powers of their own law.[625] The rules on civil and criminal liability in the 'Prum Decision' apply.[626] There are also provisions on meetings and joint training, costs, and the maintenance in force or conclusion of treaties on the same subject.[627]

12.10. EU funding

During the Maastricht period, the EU Treaty provided that operational spending on JHA should normally be funded by Member States, with the EU budget to be used if the Council obtained the unanimous approval of the Member States.

---

[618] See most recently the report on operations in 2003 (Council doc 10036/1/04, 6 July 2004), and previously the first edition of this book, at 203–204.

[619] [2008] OJ L 210/73. This Decision applied from 23 Dec 2009 (Art 9).

[620] See n 612 above.   [621] Art 2(a).

[622] Art 2(b). On the Framework Decision, see 10.5.2.1 above.   [623] Art 3(1).

[624] Art 3(2).   [625] Art 3(3).   [626] Art 4.   [627] Arts 5–7.

The position was reversed by the Treaty of Amsterdam, with the EU budget to be used unless the Council decides otherwise, with a unanimous vote.[628]

Under the Maastricht rules, the Council adopted Joint Actions on the 'STOP' programme on combating sexual exploitation,[629] the 'Oisin' programme on support for law enforcement,[630] and the 'Falcone' programme on combating international organized crime.[631] Following the entry into force of the Treaty of Amsterdam, the Oisin and STOP programmes were extended for 2001–02, joined by a programme concerning crime prevention (Hippocrates).[632] All the third pillar programmes were then replaced by a general third pillar funding programme, 'AGIS', running from 2003–07,[633] and subsequently by programmes on law enforcement and terrorism-related civil protection, which run from 2007–13.[634]

As for EU databases and agencies, the costs of the third pillar aspects of SIS II development had to be charged to the EU budget, as there was not unanimous support for charging the costs to Member States' budgets.[635] SIS II operations will be funded from the EU budget once SIS II is operational.[636] Although the European Police College and Europol were initially funded by Member States, they have been funded from the EU budget since the start of 2006 and 2010 respectively.[637] The costs of the Customs Information System will largely be charged to the EU budget from 2011.[638]

12.11. External relations

Before the entry into force of the Treaty of Lisbon, the EU agreed treaties with the US and Australia as regards passenger name data,[639] with Norway and Iceland as regards the extension of the Prum Decision to those States,[640] and with the US as regards access to financial information for anti-terrorist purposes. However, these treaties did not enter into force before the entry into force of the Treaty of Lisbon. After the entry into force of the latter Treaty, the EP gained the power of consent over these measures, and voted down the original version of the treaty on exchange of financial information, which was then renegotiated (with the EP's approval).[641] The Commission has also requested a mandate to negotiate a general treaty with the US on sharing of information in this area.

---

[628] See 2.7 above.   [629] [1996] OJ L 322/7, applicable initially from 1996–2000.

[630] [1997] OJ L 7/5, applicable initially from 1997–2000.

[631] [1998] OJ L 99/8, applicable initially from 1998–2002.

[632] [2001] OJ L 186/4, 7, and 11.   [633] [2002] OJ L 203/5.

[634] [2007] OJ L 58/7 and 1. The latter measure was adopted on the basis of the former Art 308 EC; see now Art 196 and 222 TFEU.   [635] See JHA Council conclusions, 28/29 May 2001.

[636] See 12.6.1.1 above.   [637] See respectively 12.7.2 and 12.8 above.

[638] [2009] OJ L 323/20, Art 31.   [639] [2007] OJ L 204 and [2008] OJ L 213/47.

[640] [2009] OJ L 353/1; see 12.2.5 above.

[641] [2010] OJ L 8 (first treaty); [2010] OJ L 195/1 (second treaty); the latter treaty entered into force on 1 Aug 2010. The other treaties have not yet entered into force, although the EU has concluded the treaty extending the Prum Decision to Norway and Iceland ([2010] OJ L 238/1).

There have been several other external measures in this area,[642] in particular the treaties between Europol and third States or bodies, pursuant to rules adopted to implement the Europol Convention, and later the Europol Decision.[643]

12.12. Conclusions

EU law on policing and security has not gone so far as to create EU-wide police forces, or to give national police forces the jurisdiction to exercise their full powers on the territory of another State. Rather there are a large number of specific measures concerning the facilitation of operational cooperation and allowing for limited cross-border operations, EU bodies with limited (but significant) powers, and a number of measures with significant impact on data protection, in particular the creation and development of substantial databases. The underlying problems, which can be linked to the lack of adequate parliamentary and judicial control of EU measures, are the insufficiencies of the rules (where they exist at all) on accountability of operations or the protection of personal data, and in particular the lack of public accountability through the means of regular reporting on or objective evaluation of the application of most EU measures in practice. Overall, EU measures have failed to strike the right balance between the objective of ensuring public security and the protection of civil liberties, and some EU measures moreover will contribute significantly towards the creation of a 'surveillance society' across Europe.

[642] See the Action Plan with Russia concerning organized crime ([2000] OJ C 106/5); the JHA Action Plan with Ukraine ([2003] OJ C 77/1); the pre-accession pact on organized crime ([1998] OJ C 220/1); the Joint Action on evaluation of candidates' compliance with the JHA *acquis* ([1998] OJ L 191/8); and the Resolution on the posting of drugs liaison officers to Albania ([2003] OJ C 97/6).

[643] See 12.8 above. For an overview of the framework for Europol external relations, see C Rijken, 'Legal and Technical Aspects of Cooperation Between Europol, Third States and Interpol', in V Kronenberger, ed, *The European Union and the International Legal Order: Discord or Harmony?* (Asser, 2001), 577. For a detailed analysis and critique of the practice, see S Peers, 'Governance and the Third Pillar: The Accountability of Europol' in D Curtin and R Wessel, eds, *Good Governance and the European Union* (Intersentia, 2005), 253. The texts of most of the agreements in force can be found online at: <http://www.europol.europa.eu/index.asp?page=agreements>.

Appendix I

Ratification of Treaties

(as of 10 Sep 2010)

★ An asterisk indicates that the treaty is not yet in force.

Information is also given as regards Croatia (except as regards treaties only between EU Member States), due to the advanced stage of its accession negotiations.

EU/Member States' Treaties

Extradition (1995)★

Ratified by: 20 Member States: all the 'old' Member States except Italy, plus Cyprus, Poland, Estonia, Lithuania, Latvia, and Slovenia

Applied by: 14 Member States: the ratifying States except Greece, Ireland, Netherlands, Portugal, Cyprus, and Estonia

Report: [1996] OJ C 375/4

Court of Justice Protocol to the Customs Information System Convention (1996)

Ratified by: 26 Member States: all except Malta

Convention on Protection of EC Financial Interests (PIF) (1995)

Ratified by: 25 Member States: all except Malta and the Czech Republic

Report: [1997] OJ C 191/1

Extradition (1996)★

Ratified by: 20 Member States: all the 'old' Member States except Italy, plus Cyprus, Poland, Estonia, Lithuania, Latvia, and Slovenia

Applied by: 14 Member States: the ratifying States except Greece, Ireland, Netherlands, Cyprus, Estonia, and Latvia

Report: [1997] OJ C 191/13

First Protocol to PIF Convention (1996)

Ratified by: 25 Member States: all except Malta and Czech Republic

Report: [1998] OJ C 11/5

Court of Justice Protocol to PIF Convention (1996)

Ratified by: 24 Member States: all except Estonia, Malta, and Czech Republic

Second Protocol to PIF Convention (1997)

Ratified by: 25 Member States: all except Malta and Czech Republic

Report: [1999] OJ C 91/8

Convention on corruption (1997)

Ratified by: 25 Member States: all except Malta and Czech Republic
Report: [1998] OJ C 391/1

Naples II Convention (1998)

Ratified by: all Member States
Report: [1998] OJ C 189/1

Driving Disqualification Convention (1998)★

Ratified by: 7 Member States: Bulgaria, Cyprus, Spain, United Kingdom, Ireland, Romania, and Slovakia
Applied by: Ireland and UK
Report: [1999] OJ C 211/1

Protocol to Convention on customs information system (1999)

Ratified by: all Member States

Convention on mutual assistance (2000)

Ratified by: 23 Member States: all except Greece, Italy, Ireland, and Luxembourg
Report: [2000] OJ C 379/7

Protocol to Convention on mutual assistance (2001)

Ratified by: 22 Member States: all except Estonia, Greece, Italy, Ireland, and Luxembourg
Report: [2002] OJ C 257/1

Protocol to Convention on customs information system (2003)

Ratified by: 23 Member States: all except Belgium, Greece, Italy, and Ireland

Rome Convention accession treaty (2005)

Ratified by: 24 Member States: all except UK, Denmark, and Ireland

European Political Cooperation

Abolition of legalization of documents (1987)★

Ratified by: 7 Member States: Belgium, Denmark, France, Italy, Ireland, Cyprus, and Latvia

Double jeopardy (1987)★

Ratified by: 9 Member States: Austria, Belgium, Germany, Denmark, France, Italy, Ireland, Netherlands, and Portugal
Signed by: 3 Member States: Luxembourg, Spain and United Kingdom

Transfer of sentenced persons (1987)★

Ratified by: 6 Member States: Belgium, Denmark, Spain, Italy, Ireland, and Luxembourg

Faxing of extradition requests (1989)★

Ratified by: 9 Member States: Austria, Belgium, Germany, Spain, United Kingdom, Italy, Luxembourg, Netherlands, and Sweden

Transfer of criminal proceedings (1990)★

Ratified by: 2 Member States: France and Portugal
Signed by: 1 Member State: Luxembourg

Maintenance payments (1990)★

Ratified by: 5 Member States: Spain, United Kingdom, Greece, Italy, and Ireland
Signed by: 1 Member State: France

Enforcement of criminal sentences (1991)★

Ratified by: 5 Member States: Cyprus, Germany, Spain, Latvia, and Netherlands
Signed by: 1 Member State: Portugal
Applied
provisionally by: Germany, Latvia, and Netherlands

Council of Europe

ETS 24 *Extradition Convention (1957)*
Ratified by: all Member States and Croatia

ETS 25 *European Agreement on Regulations governing the Movement of Persons between Member States of the Council of Europe (1957)*
Ratified by: 12 Member States: Austria, Belgium, France, Germany, Greece, Italy, Luxembourg, the Netherlands, Portugal, Spain, Malta, and Slovenia.
Signed by: 1 Member State: Cyprus

ETS 30 *Convention on mutual assistance (1959)*
Ratified by: all Member States and Croatia

ETS 31 *European Agreement on the Abolition of Visas for Refugees (1959)*
Ratified by: 17 Member States: Belgium, Czech Republic, Denmark, Finland, Germany, Ireland, Italy, Luxembourg, Malta, Netherlands, Portugal, Spain, Sweden, Poland, Slovakia, Hungary, and Romania; not ratified by Croatia
Signed by: 1 Member State: Cyprus
Denounced by: 2 Member States: France, UK

ETS 46 *Fourth Protocol to the ECHR (1963)*
Ratified by: 25 Member States: all except Greece and United Kingdom; also ratified by Croatia
Signed by: 1 Member State: United Kingdom

ETS 51 *Convention on the supervision of conditionally released or conditionally sentenced offenders (1964)*
Ratified by: 12 Member States: Austria, Belgium, Czech Republic, Estonia, France, Italy, Luxembourg, Netherlands, Portugal, Slovakia, Slovenia, and Sweden; Croatia has also ratified
Signed by: 4 Member States: Denmark, Germany, Greece, Malta

ETS 52   *Convention on road traffic offences (1964)*
Ratified by: 4 Member States: Cyprus, Denmark, France, and Sweden; not ratified
                by Croatia
Signed by: 8 Member States: Austria, Belgium, Germany, Greece, Italy, Luxembourg,
                Netherlands, and Portugal

ETS 62   *Convention on information on foreign law (1968)*
Ratified by: 26 Member States: all except Ireland; not ratified by Croatia

ETS 70   *Convention on the international validity of criminal judgments (1970)*
Ratified by: 12 Member States: Austria, Belgium, Bulgaria, Cyprus, Denmark,
                Estonia, Latvia, Lithuania, Netherlands, Romania, Spain, and Sweden;
                Croatia has not ratified
Signed by: 6 Member States: Germany, Greece, Italy, Luxembourg, Portugal, and
                Slovenia

ETS 73   *Convention on transfer of criminal proceedings (1972)*
Ratified by: 13 Member States: Austria, Bulgaria, Czech Republic, Cyprus, Denmark,
                Estonia, Latvia, Lithuania, Netherlands, Romania, Slovakia, Spain, and
                Sweden
Signed by: 7 Member States: Belgium, Greece, Hungary, Italy, Luxembourg,
                Portugal, and Slovenia; also signed by Croatia

ETS 86   *First Protocol, Extradition Convention (1975)*
Ratified by: 19 Member States: all except Austria, Finland, France, Germany, Greece,
                Ireland, Italy, United Kingdom; also ratified by Croatia
Signed by: 1 Member State: Greece

ETS 90   *Convention on the suppression of terrorism (1977)*
Ratified by: all Member States

ETS 92   *European Agreement on the transmission of applications for legal aid (1977)*
Ratified by: 21 Member States: all except Cyprus, Germany, Hungary, Malta,
                Slovenia, and Slovakia; not ratified by Croatia
Signed by: Cyprus and Germany

ETS 97   *Additional Protocol to the Convention on information on foreign law (1978)*
Ratified by: 25 Member States: all except Ireland and Slovenia; not ratified by
                Croatia

ETS 98   *Second Protocol, Extradition Convention (1978)*
Ratified by: 25 Member States: all except France, Greece, Ireland, and Luxembourg;
                also ratified by Croatia
Signed by: 1 Member State: Greece

ETS 99   *First Protocol to Convention on mutual assistance (1978)*
Ratified by: 26 Member States: all except Malta; also ratified by Croatia
Signed by: Malta

ETS 108   *Data protection Convention (1981)*
Ratified by: all Member States; also ratified by Croatia

ETS 112   *Convention on the transfer of sentenced persons (1983)*
Ratified by: all Member States; also ratified by Croatia

ETS 116   *Compensation for crime victims (1983)*
Ratified by: 17 Member States: Austria, Belgium, Cyprus, Czech Republic, Denmark, Estonia, Finland, France, Germany, Luxembourg, Netherlands, Portugal, Romania, Slovakia, Spain, Sweden, and United Kingdom; also ratified by Croatia
Signed by: 3 Member States: Greece, Hungary, and Lithuania

ETS 117   *Seventh Protocol to the ECHR (1984)*
Ratified by: 23 Member States: all *except* Belgium, Germany, Netherlands, and United Kingdom; Croatia has also ratified
Signed by: 4 Member States: Belgium, Germany, and Netherlands

ETS 141   *Convention on the proceeds of crime, et al (1990)*
Ratified by: all EU Member States; Croatia has also ratified

ETS 167   *Protocol to the Convention on the transfer of sentenced persons (1997)*
Ratified by: 22 Member States: all except Italy, Portugal, Spain, Slovenia, and Slovakia; also in force in Croatia
Signed by: 2 Member States: Italy and Portugal

ETS 173   *Criminal law Convention on corruption (1999)*
Ratified by: 24 Member States: all except Austria, Germany, and Italy; also in force in Croatia
Signed by: 3 Member States: Austria, Germany, and Italy

ETS 179   *Protocol to Agreement on the transmission of applications for legal aid (2000)*
Ratified by: 7 Member States: Czech Republic, Denmark, Estonia, Finland, Latvia, Lithuania, Sweden; not ratified by Croatia
Signed by: 10 Member States: Belgium, Cyprus, France, Ireland, Italy, Luxembourg, Poland, Portugal, Romania, and UK

ETS 181   *Protocol to the data protection Convention (2001)*
Ratified by: 19 Member States: all except Belgium, Denmark, Finland, Greece, Italy, Malta, Slovenia, and United Kingdom; also ratified by Croatia
Signed by: 6 Member States: Belgium, Denmark, Finland, Greece, Italy, and United Kingdom

ETS 182   *Second Protocol to Convention on mutual assistance (2001)*
Ratified by: 12 Member States: Belgium, Bulgaria, Czech Republic, Denmark, Estonia, Latvia, Lithuania, Poland, Portugal, Romania, Slovakia, and United Kingdom; Croatia has also ratified
Signed by: 10 Member States: Finland, France, Hungary, Greece, Germany, Ireland, Malta, Netherlands, Slovenia, and Sweden

ETS 185   *Cyber-crime (2001)*
Ratified by: 16 Member States: Bulgaria, Cyprus, Denmark, Estonia, Finland, France, Germany, Hungary, Italy, Latvia, Lithuania, Netherlands, Portugal, Romania, Slovakia, and Slovenia; Croatia has also ratified
Signed by: 11 Member States: all other Member States

ETS 189	*Protocol to Cyber-crime Convention (2003)*
Ratified by:	9 Member States: Cyprus, Denmark, France, Latvia, Lithuania, Netherlands, Portugal, Romania, and Slovenia; Croatia has also ratified
Signed by:	10 Member States: Austria, Belgium, Estonia, Finland, Germany, Greece, Luxembourg, Malta, Poland, and Sweden
ETS 187	*Protocol 13 to the ECHR (2002)*
Ratified by:	25 Member States: all except Latvia and Poland; Croatia has also ratified
ETS 190	*Protocol to Convention on the suppression of terrorism (2003)★*
Ratified by:	15 Member States: Belgium, Bulgaria, Cyprus, Denmark, Estonia, Finland, France, Latvia, Lithuania, Luxembourg, Netherlands, Poland, Romania, Slovakia, and Slovenia; Croatia has also ratified
Signed by:	12 Member States: all other Member States
CETS 196	*Convention on the prevention of terrorism (2005)*
Ratified by:	15 Member States: Austria, Bulgaria, Cyprus, Denmark, Estonia, Finland, France, Latvia, Netherlands, Poland, Slovenia, Slovakia, Sweden, and Spain; Croatia has also ratified
Signed by:	11 Member States: all others except Czech Republic
CETS 197	*Convention on trafficking in persons (2005)*
Ratified by:	19 Member States: Austria, Belgium, Bulgaria, Cyprus, Denmark, France, Ireland, Latvia, Luxembourg, Malta, Netherlands, Poland, Portugal, Romania, Slovakia, Slovenia, Spain, Sweden, United Kingdom; also ratified by Croatia
Signed by:	7 Member States: all others except Czech Republic
CETS 198	*Convention on the proceeds of crime, et al (2005)*
Ratified by:	12 Member States: Belgium, Cyprus, Hungary, Latvia, Malta, Netherlands, Poland, Portugal, Romania, Slovakia, Slovenia, and Spain; Croatia has also ratified
Signed by:	7 Member States: Austria, Bulgaria, Finland, Greece, Italy, Luxembourg, and Sweden
CETS 201	*Convention on the Protection of Children against Sexual Exploitation and Sexual Abuse (2007)*
Ratified by:	5 Member States: Denmark, Greece, Malta, Spain, and Netherlands
Signed by:	19 Member States: all other Member States except Czech Republic, Hungary, and Latvia; Croatia has also signed

United Nations

	Convention on transnational organized crime
Ratified by:	25 Member States: all except Czech Republic and Greece; also ratified by Croatia
Signed by:	2 Member States: Czech Republic and Greece

Protocol on smuggling, Convention on transnational organized crime

Ratified by: 23 Member States: all except the Czech Republic, Greece, Ireland, and Luxembourg; Croatia has also ratified

Signed by: 4 Member States: Czech Republic, Greece, Ireland, and Luxembourg

Protocol on trafficking in persons, Convention on transnational organized crime

Ratified by: 25 Member States: all except Czech Republic and Greece; Croatia has also ratified

Signed by: 2 Member States: Czech Republic and Greece

Protocol on firearms, Convention on transnational organized crime

Ratified by: 13 Member States: all except Austria, Denmark, Finland, France, Germany, Greece, Luxembourg, Portugal, Sweden, UK, Czech Republic, Hungary, Ireland, Malta; also ratified by Croatia

Signed by: 9 Member States: Austria, Denmark, Finland, Germany, Greece, Luxembourg, Portugal, Sweden, and the United Kingdom

Convention on corruption

Ratified by: 24 Member States: all except Czech Republic, Germany, and Ireland; also ratified by Croatia

Signed by: 3 Member States: Czech Republic, Germany, and Ireland

Hague Conference

14.   *Service of documents (1969)*

Ratified by: 25 Member States: all except Austria and Malta; also ratified by Croatia

20.   *Evidence convention (1970)*

Ratified by: 23 Member States: all except Austria, Belgium, Ireland, and Malta; also ratified by Croatia

29.   *International access to justice (1980)*

Ratified by: 16 Member States: all except Austria, Belgium, Denmark, Germany, Greece, Hungary, Ireland, Italy, Malta, Portugal, and United Kingdom; also ratified by Croatia

Signed by: 3 Member States: Germany, Greece, and Italy

OECD

Anti-bribery (corruption) convention (1997)

Ratified by: 26 Member States: all except Romania; not ratified by Croatia

Appendix II

The JHA 'acquis' after the entry into force of the Treaty of Lisbon

Part A

'Third pillar' measures still in force

The following 'third pillar' measures adopted before the entry into force of the Treaty of Lisbon were still in force (or could come into force in future) as of 10 September 2010. These measures are subject to the old rules on the jurisdiction of the Court of Justice, and on the legal effect of third pillar acts, until they are amended or repealed, or (as regards Court of Justice jurisdiction) until 1 December 2014.

*The provisions of the 'Schengen acquis' which were **not** allocated to the 'third pillar' are discussed in Part B below.*

(1) Schengen acquis (integrated into EU legal order 1.5.1999)— [2000] OJ L 239

(a) Schengen Convention:

Arts 39–45, 47–49, 51, 54–58, 71–72, 75–76, 92–119, 126–30; also some provisions of Schengen accession treaties

Notes: Arts 92–119 have been amended by Decisions concerning the SIS in 2005 and 2008 (see below); they will be repealed with effect from when the decision setting up SIS II (adopted in 2007, see below) becomes operational (2013 at the earliest)

Arts 39(1), (2), and (3) and 46 were repealed by the Framework Decision on exchange of data between law enforcement services ([2006] OJ L 386/89), Art 12(1); Art 47(4) was repealed by a 2003 Decision ([2003] OJ L 67/27); Art 40(1) and (7) were amended by a 2003 Decision ([2003] OJ L 260/47)

Arts 49(a), 52, 53, and 73 were repealed by the 2000 EU mutual assistance Convention, Art 2(2); Art 50 was repealed by Art 8(3) of the 2001 protocol to that Convention (see below); but note that a few Member States have not ratified the Convention or the Protocol (see Appendix I)

Arts 59–60, 62–66 (extradition) were repealed by the Framework Decision on the European Arrest Warrant ([2002] OJ L 190/1), Art 31(1)(e), but might still apply in a few cases where the effect of the EAW is restricted, and to Schengen associates

Articles 67–69 were repealed by the Framework Decision on transfer of prisoners (OJ 2008 L 327/27), Art 26(1), but this is not applicable yet (see below); they will still apply to Schengen associates

(a) Schengen Executive Committee Decisions/Declarations/Central Group acts:

(i) repealed with effect from when SIS II Decision is operational:

SCH/Com-ex (93) 16—14.12.1993—Financial Regulations on the installation and operating costs for the Schengen C.SIS

SCH/Com-ex (97) 18—7.10.1997—Contributions from Norway and Iceland to the C.SIS operating costs

SCH/Com-ex (97) 24—7.10.1997—Future of the SIS

SCH/Com-ex (97) 35—15.12.1997—Amendment to the C.SIS Financial Regulations

SCH/Com-ex (98) 11—21.4.1998—C.SIS with 15/18 connections

SCH/Com-ex (99) Decl 2 Rev—28.4.1999—SIS-structure

SCH/Com-ex (99) 4—28.4.1999—C.SIS installation costs

SCH/Com-ex (99) 5—28.4.1999—SIRENE Manual

SCH/Com-ex (96) Decl 5—18.4.1996—Determination of the concept of third-country alien

(ii) other (within scope of third pillar)

SCH/Com-ex (93) 10—14.12.1993—Confirmation of the declarations by the Ministers and Secretaries of State of 19 June 1992 and 30 June 1993 on bringing into force

SCH/Com-ex (93) 14—14.12.1993—Improving practical cooperation between the judicial authorities to combat drug trafficking

SCH/Com-ex (97) 2 Rev 2—25.4.1997—Awarding the tender for the SIS II preliminary study

SCH/Com-ex (97) 6 Rev 2—24.6.1997—Schengen Manual on police cooperation in the field of public order and security

SCH/Com-ex (97) 29 Rev 2—7.10.1997—Bringing into force the Convention implementing the Schengen Agreement in Greece

SCH/Com-ex (98) 26 def—16.9.1998—Setting up of the Schengen implementing Convention Standing Committee

SCH/Com-ex (98) 29 Rev—23.6.1998—Catch-all clause to cover the whole technical Schengen acquis

SCH/Com-ex (98) 37 def 2—16.9.1998—Action plan to combat illegal immigration

SCH/Com-ex (98) 43 Rev—16.12.1998—Ad hoc Committee for Greece

SCH/Com-ex (98) 49 Rev 3—16.12.1998—Bringing the Convention implementing the Schengen Agreement into force in Greece

SCH/Com-ex (98) 52—16.12.1998—Handbook on cross-border police cooperation

SCH/Com-ex (99) 3—28.4.1999—Help Desk budget for 1999

SCH/Com-ex (99) 6—28.4.1999—Telecomms situation

SCH/Com-ex (99) 7 Rev 2—28.4.1999—Liaison officers

SCH/Com-ex (99) 8 Rev 2—28.4.1999—Payments to informers

SCH/Com-ex (99) 11 Rev 2—28.4.1999—Agreement on cooperation in proceedings for road traffic offences

SCH/Com-ex (96) Decl 6—Rev 2—26.6.1996—Declaration on extradition

SCH/Com-ex (97) Decl 13—Rev 2—21.4.1998—Abduction of minors

SCH/C (98) 117—27.10.1998—Action plan to combat illegal immigration

SCH/C (99) 25—22.3.1999—General principles for the remuneration of informants and infiltrators

(2) Maastricht era (1 Nov 2003 to 1 May 1999)

(a) Joint Actions

1. Council Joint Action 94/795/JHA on crossing internal borders by organised school groups ([1994] OJ L 327/1)
2. Joint Action 98/700/JHA on European Imaging Archive System ([1998] OJ L 333/4)
3. Joint Action 96/277/JHA on exchange of liaison magistrates ([1996] OJ L 105/1)
4. Joint Action 96/443/JHA on racism and xenophobia ([1996] OJ L 185/5)

Note: replaced by Framework Decision on subject (see below), as from 2010

5. Joint Action 96/750/JHA on drug trafficking ([1996] OJ L 342/6)
6. Joint Action 98/427/JHA on good practice in mutual legal assistance ([1998] OJ L 191/1)
7. Joint Action 98/699/JHA on money laundering and confiscation of proceeds ([1998] OJ L 333/1)

Note: Framework Decision of 2001 amended and supplemented this Joint Action in part (see below)

8. Joint Action 96/610/JHA on directory of specialist counter-terrorist expertise ([1996] OJ L 273/1)
9. Joint Action 96/698/JHA on customs and business cooperation in drug trafficking ([1996] OJ L 322/3)
10. Joint Action 96/699/JHA on exchange of information on chemical profiling of drugs ([1996] OJ L 322/5)
11. Joint Action 96/747/JHA on directory of expertise on international organised crime ([1996] OJ L 342/2)
12. Joint Action 97/339/JHA on cooperation in law and order ([1997] OJ L 147/1)
13. Joint Action 97/372/JHA on targeting criteria for police ([1997] OJ L 159/1)
14. Joint Action 97/827/JHA on evaluation ([1997] OJ L 344/7)
15. Joint Action 98/429/JHA on collective evaluation of application of acquis by applicant states ([1998] OJ L 191/8)
16. Joint Action 96/658/JHA on US Helms-Burton legislation ([1996] OJ L 309/7)

(b) Conventions

1. Convention on simplified extradition ([1995] OJ C 78/1)

Note: not in force; provisionally applied by some Member States (see Appendix I)

2. Convention on fraud against EC budget ([1995] OJ C 316/48)
2a. First Protocol to Convention on fraud against EC budget ([1996] OJ C 313/1)
2b. ECJ Protocol to Convention on fraud against EC budget ([1997] OJ C 151/1)
2c. Second Protocol to Convention on fraud against EC budget ([1997] OJ C 221/12)
3. Convention on extradition ([1996] OJ C 313/11)

Note: not in force; provisionally applied by some Member States (see Appendix I)

4. Convention on corruption ([1997] OJ C 195/1)
5. Driving Disqualification Convention ([1998] OJ C 216/1)

Note: not in force; provisionally applied by some Member States (see Appendix I)

6. Convention on Customs Information System (CIS) ([1995] OJ C 316/33)

6a. ECJ Protocol to CIS Convention ([1997] OJ C 151/15)

6b. Protocol to CIS Convention ([1999] OJ C 91/1)

Note: the CIS measures will all be replaced by a third pillar Decision with effect from 27 May 2011 (see below)

7. Naples II Convention ([1998] OJ C 24/1)

(3) Treaty of Amsterdam period—Title VI EU Police and Criminal Law

(a) *Common Positions*

1. Combatting terrorism ([2001] OJ L 344/90)

Note: also a CFSP measure

2. Application of specific measures to combat terrorism ([2001] OJ L 344/93)

Note: amended since the entry into force of the Treaty of Lisbon ([2009] OJ L 346/58)

3. Common Position on transfer of data to Interpol ([2005] OJ L 27/61)

(b) *Decisions*

1. Exchange of information on counterfeit travel documents ([2000] OJ L 81/1)
2. Combatting child pornography on the Internet ([2000] OJ L 138/1)
3. Decision 2000/586/JHA: Procedure for amending Articles 40(4) and (5), 41(7) and 65(2) of Schengen Convention ([2000] OJ L 248/1)
4. Decision 2000/641/JHA: Joint Secretariat for third pillar data protection authorities ([2000] OJ L 271/1)
5. Decision 2000/642 concerning Member States' Financial intelligence units (FIUs) ([2000] OJ L 271/4)
6. Decision 2001/419/JHA on the transmission of samples of controlled substances ([2001] OJ L 150/1)
7. Decision 2001/887/JHA on protection of the euro against counterfeiting ([2001] OJ L 329/1)
8. Decision establishing Eurojust ([2002] OJ L 63/1)
9. Decision 2002/348/JHA concerning security in connection with football matches with an international dimension ([2002] OJ L 121/1)
10. Decision 2002/494 on exchange of information and contact points concerning genocide, crimes against humanity, and war crimes ([2002] OJ L 167/1)
11. Decision on network for protection of public figures ([2002] OJ L 333/1)
12. Decision on evaluating Member States' implementation of international commitments regarding terrorism ([2002] OJ L 349/1)
13. Decision 2003/169 designating which provisions of the 1995 and 1996 EU extradition Conventions are related to the Schengen acquis ([2003] OJ L 76/25)
14. Decision 2003/170 on joint use of liaison officers ([2003] OJ L 67/27)
15. Decision 2003/335 on investigation and prosecution of genocide, crimes against humanity, and war crimes ([2003] OJ L 118/12)
16. Decision extending Convention on corruption to Gibraltar ([2003] OJ L 226/27)

Note: this was not a legislative act, but a *sui generis* decision

17. Decision amending Eurojust decision ([2003] OJL 245/44)
18. Decision amending Article 40, Schengen Convention to permit extended cross-border police surveillance ([2003] OJL 260/37)
19. Decision on amending Sirene manual ([2004] OJ L 64/45)

Note: this will be repealed when once SIS II Decision applies

20. Decision on vehicle crime ([2004] OJ L 389/28)
21. Decision on future functionalities for SIS ([2005] OJ L 68/44)

Note: this will be repealed when once SIS II Decision applies

22. Decision on synthetic drugs ([2005] OJ L 127/32)
23. Decision designating Europol as the central office for counterfeiting the euro ([2005] OJ L 185/35)
24. Decision on exchange of information on terrorism ([2005] OJ L 253/22)
25. Decision on European police college ([2005] OJ L 256/63)
26. Decision on criminal record information exchange ([2005] OJ L 322/33)

Note: this is repealed by 2009 Framework Decision on criminal records exchange (see below), Art 12(4) – as from 2012

27. Decision amending 2003 Decision on police liaison officers ([2006] OJ L 219/31)
28. Decision establishing 'criminal justice' programme ([2007] OJ L 58/13)
29. Decision establishing 'Crime prevention/fight against crime' programme ([2007] OJ L 58/7)
30. Decision establishing SIS II (Criminal law/policing aspects) ([2007] OJ L 205/63)

Note: this Decision is not yet applied

31. Decision amending Decision on football hooligans ([2007] OJ L 155/76)
32. Decision establishing an asset recovery network ([2007] OJ L 332/103)
33. Decision on cross-border intervention teams ([2008] OJ L 210/73)
34. Decision on cross-border police cooperation (Prum Treaty Decision) ([2008] OJ L 210/1)

Note: Application date is 26 Aug 2011 (for Chapter 2)

35. Decision on cross-border police cooperation (Prum Treaty Decision) ([2008] OJ L 210/12)

Note: application date is the same as Prum treaty decision

36. Decision on law enforcement access to VIS ([2008] OJ L 218/129)

Note: application date to be set by Council; latest planned date for start of VIS operations is Dec 2010; legality challenged by UK (Case C-482/08 *UK v Council*, pending)

37. Decision establishing an anti-corruption network ([2008] OJ L 301/38)
38. Decision on migration from SIS to SIS II ([2008] OJ L 299/43)

Note: amended by Reg 542/2010 ([2010] OJ L 155/23) after the entry into force of the Treaty of Lisbon

39. Decision amending Decision establishing Eurojust ([2009] OJ L 138/14)

Application date (for Member States): 4 June 2011

40. Decision on the European Judicial Network ([2008] OJ L 348/130)
41. Decision implementing the Framework Decision on the exchange of criminal records ([2009] OJ L 93/33)

Application date: 7 April 2012

42. Decision establishing Europol ([2009] OJ L 121/37)
43. Decision amending the Decision establishing a network for the protection of public figures ([2009] OJ L 283/62)
44. Decision on a crime prevention network ([2009] OJ L 321/44)
45. Decision on Customs Information System ([2009] OJ L 323/20)

Application date: 27 May 2011

46. Decision extending US/EU extradition treaty to such as Aruba ([2009] OJ L 325/4)

Note: this is not a legislative act, but a *sui generis* decision

(c) Framework Decisions

1. Criminal sanctions for counterfeiting the euro ([2000] OJ L 140/1)
2. Framework Decision 2001/220/JHA on the status of victims ([2001] OJ L 82/1)
3. Framework Decision 2001/413/JHA on payment card fraud and counterfeiting ([2001] OJ L 149/1)
4. Framework Decision 2001/500 on money laundering, the identification, tracing, freezing, seizing and confiscation of instrumentalities and the proceeds from crime ([2001] OJ L 182/1)
5. Framework Decision 2001/888/JHA on criminal records for counterfeiting the euro
6. Framework Decision on terrorism ([2002] OJ L 164/3)
7. Framework Decision on European arrest warrant ([2002] OJ L 190/1)
8. Framework Decision on joint investigation teams ([2002] OJ L 162/1)
9. Framework Decision on trafficking in humans ([2002] OJ L 203/1)

Note: there is a proposal to repeal this measure: COM (2010) 95

10. Framework Decision on the penal framework to prevent the facilitation of illegal entry and residence ([2002] OJ L 328/1)
11. Framework Decision on the execution of orders freezing assets and evidence ([2003] OJ L 196/45)
12. Framework Decision on corruption in private sector ([2003] OJ L 192/54)
13. Framework Decision on the sexual exploitation of children and child pornography ([2004] OJ L 13/44)

Note: there is a proposal to repeal this measure: COM (2010) 94

14. Framework Decision on illicit drug trafficking ([2004] OJ L 335/8)
15. Framework Decision on mutual recognition of financial penalties ([2005] OJ L 76/16)
16. Framework Decision concerning attacks on information systems ([2005] OJ L 69/67)

17. Framework Decision on confiscation ([2005] OJ L 68/49)
18. Framework Decision on the execution of confiscation orders ([2006] OJ L 328/59)
19. Framework decision on exchange of data between law enforcement services ([2006] OJ L 386/89)
20. Framework decision on taking account of prior convictions in another Member State ([2008] OJ L 220/32)
21. Framework Decision on organised crime ([2008] OJ L 300/42)
22. Framework Decision on the transfer of custodial sentences ([2008] OJ L 327/27)

Deadline to apply: 5 Dec 2011

23. Framework Decision on data protection in the sphere of criminal law and policing ([2008] OJ L 350/60)

Deadline to apply: 27 Nov 2010

24. Framework Decision on mutual recognition of alternative sanctions and suspended sentences ([2008] OJ L 337/102)

Deadline to apply: 6 Dec 2011

25. Framework Decision on racism and xenophobia ([2008] OJ L 328/55)

Deadline to apply: 28 Nov 2010

26. Framework Decision amending the framework decision on terrorism ([2008] OJ L 330/21)

Deadline to apply: 9 Dec 2010

27. Framework Decision on European evidence warrant ([2008] OJ L 350/72)

Deadline to apply: 19 Jan 2011

28. Framework decision on criminal record exchange ([2009] OJ L 93/23)

Deadline to apply: 27 Apr 2012

29. Framework Decision on 'in absentia' trials ([2009] OJ L 81/24)

Deadline to apply: 28 Mar 2011; 1 Jan 2014 for Italy Art 8(3))

30. Framework decision on mutual recognition of pre-trial supervision orders ([2009] OJ L 294/20)

Deadline to apply: 1 Dec 2012

31. Framework decision on conflicts of jurisdiction ([2009] OJ L 328/42)

Deadline to apply: 15 June 2012

32. Framework decision on accreditation of forensic laboratory activities ([2009] OJ L 322/14)

Deadline to apply: 30 Nov 2013 (DNA); 30 Nov 2015 (fingerprints)

Conventions

1. Mutual assistance on criminal matters ([2000] OJ C 197/1)
2. Protocol to May 2000 Mutual Assistance Convention ([2001] OJ C 326/1)

3. Protocol to Customs Information System Convention, regarding customs files ([2003] OJC 139/1)

Note: replaced by Decision as from 27 May 2011 (see above)

(5) International treaties

in force:

1. Schengen association agreement with Norway and Iceland ([1999] OJ L 176)
2. Schengen association agreement with Switzerland ([2008] OJ L 53)
3. Treaties with US on mutual assistance and extradition ([2003] OJ L 181/25)

provisionally in force:

1. Treaty with USA on passenger name data ([2006] OJ L 298)
2. Treaty with Australia on passenger name data ([2008] OJ L 218)

Part B

Other provisions of Schengen acquis

Article 1
  – *still in force*
Articles 2–8
  – *repealed by Schengen Borders Code ([2006] OJ L 105/1)*
Articles 9–17
  – *repealed by Schengen visas code ([2009] OJ L 243/1)*
Article 18
  – *amended by Reg 1091/2001 ([2001] OJ L 150/4), then again by Reg 265/2010 ([2010] OJ L 85/1)*
Articles 19–22
  – *Reg 265/2010 ([2010] OJ L 85/1) amended Art 21*
Articles 23–24
  – *repealed by Returns Directive 2008/115 ([2008] OJ L 348/98), as from 24 Dec 2010*
Article 25
  – *amended by Reg 265/2010 ([2010] OJ L 85/1)*
Article 26
  – *supplemented by carrier sanctions Directive 2001/51, ([2001] OJ L 187/45)*
Article 27
  – *repealed by Directive 2002/90 and Framework Decision on facilitation ([2002] OJ L 190/1)*
Articles 82, 91
  – *still in force*
Article 136
  – *Art 136(3) amended by Reg 1931/2006 on border traffic rules ([2006] OJ L 405)*

Executive Committee Decisions

SCH/Com-ex (93) 21—14.12.1993—Extending the uniform visa Article 62(2)(b) TEC
- *repealed by Schengen Visas Code*

SCH/Com-ex (93) 22 Rev—14.12.1993—Confidential nature of certain documents
- *repealed by 2003 Council Decision ([2003] OJ L 5/78)*

SCH/Com-ex (93) 24—14.12.1993—Common procedures for cancelling, recinding, or shortening the length of validity of the uniform visa
- *repealed by Schengen Visas Code*

SCH/Com-ex (94) 1 Rev 2—26.4.1994—Adjustment measures aiming to remove the obstacles and restrictions on traffic flows at road border crossing points at internal borders
- *repealed by Schengen Borders Code*

SCH/Com-ex (94) 2—26.4.1994—Issuing uniform visas at the borders
- *repealed by Reg 415/2003*

SCH/Com-ex (94) 15 Rev—21.11.1994—Introducing a computerised procedure for consulting the central authorities provided for in Article 17(2) of the implementing Convention
- *still in force*

SCH/Com-ex (94) 16 Rev—21.11.1994—Acquisition of common entry and exit stamps
- *still in force*

SCH/Com-ex (94) 17 Rev 4—22.12.1994—Introducing and applying the Schengen system in airports and aerodromes
- *repealed by Schengen Borders Code*

SCH/Com-ex (94) 25—22.12.1994—Exchanges of statistical information on the issue of visas
- *repealed by Schengen Visas Code*

SCH/Com-ex (94) 28 Rev—22.12.1994—Certificate provided for in Article 75 for the transportation of drugs and/or psychotropic substances
- *still in force*

SCH/Com-ex (94) 29 Rev 2—22.12.1994—Bringing into force the Convention implementing the Schengen Agreement of 19 June 1990
- *still in force*

SCH/Com-ex (95) PV 1 Rev (Point No 8)—Common visa policy
- *still in force*

SCH/Com-ex (95) 20 Rev 2—20.12.1995—Approval of document SCH/I (95) 40 Rev 6 on the procedure for applying Article 2(2) of the Convention implementing the Schengen Agreement
- *repealed by Schengen Borders Code*

SCH/Com-ex (95) 21—20.12.1995—Swift exchange between the Schengen States of statistical and tangible data on possible malfunctions at the external borders
- *still in force*

SCH/Com-ex (96) 13 Rev—27.6.1996—Principles for issuing Schengen visas in accordance with Article 30(1)(a) of the Convention implementing the Schengen Agreement
- *still in force*

SCH/Com-ex (96) 27—19.12.1996—Issuing visas at borders to seamen in transit
- *repealed by Reg 415/2003*

SCH/Com-ex (97) 29 Rev 2—7.10.1997—Bringing into force the Convention implementing the Schengen Agreement in Greece
  − *still in force*

SCH/Com-ex (97) 32—15.12.1997—Harmonization of visa policy
  − *repealed by Reg 539/2001, Art. 7(3)*

SCH/Com-ex (97) 34 Rev—15.12.1997—Implementation of the Joint Action on a uniform format for residence permits
  − *still in force*

SCH/Com-ex (97) 39 Rev—15.12.1997—Guiding Principles for means of proof and indicative evidence within the framework of readmission agreements between Schengen States
  − *still in force*

SCH/Com-ex (98) 1, 2 Rev—21.4.1998—Report on the activities of the task force
  − *still in force*

SCH/Com-ex (98) 10—21.4.1998—Cooperation between the Contracting Parties in returning aliens by air
  − *repealed by Directive 2003/110*

SCH/Com-ex (98) 12—21.4.1998—Exchange at local level of statistics on visas
  − *repealed by Schengen Visas Code*

SCH/Com-ex (98) 17—23.6.1998—Confidential nature of certain documents
  − *repealed by 2003 Council Decision ([2003] OJ L 5/78)*

SCH/Com-ex (98) 18 Rev—23.6.1998—Measures to be taken in respect of countries posing problems with regard to the issue of documents required to remove their nationals from Schengen territory
  − *still in force*

SCH/Com-ex (98) 19—23.6.1998—Monaco
  − *still in force*

SCH/Com-ex (98) 21—23.6.1998—Stamping of passports of visa applicants
  − *still in force*

SCH/Com-ex (98) 26 def—16.9.1998—Setting up of the Schengen implementing Convention Standing Committee
  − *still in force*

SCH/Com-ex (98) 35 Rev 2—16.9.1998—Forwarding the Common Manual to EU applicant States
  − *still in force*

SCH/Com-ex (98) 37 def 2—16.9.1998—Action plan to combat illegal immigration
  − *still in force*

SCH/Com-ex (98) 43 Rev—16.12.1998—Ad hoc Committee for Greece Article 2 in conjunction with Annex to Schengen Protocol
  − *still in force*

SCH/Com-ex (98) 49 Rev 3—16.12.1998—Bringing the Convention implementing the Schengen Agreement into force in Greece
  − *still in force*

SCH/Com-ex (98) 53 Rev 2—16.12.1998—Harmonization of visa policy
  − *repealed by Reg 539/2001*

SCH/Com-ex (98) 56—16.12.1998—Manual of documents to which a visa may be affixed
  – *still in force*
SCH/Com-ex (98) 57—16.12.1998—Introduction of a harmonized form for invitations, proof of accommodation, and the acceptance of obligations of maintenance support
  – *repealed by Schengen Visas Code*
SCH/Com-ex (98) 59 Rev—16.12.1998—Coordinated deployment of document advisers
  – *still in force*
SCH/Com-ex (99) 10—28.4.1999—Illegal trade in weapons
  – *still in force*
SCH/Com-ex (99) 13—28.4.1999—Withdrawal of old versions of the Common Manual and the Common Consular Instructions and Adoption of new versions
  – *Common Manual repealed by Schengen Borders Code; CCI repealed by Visas Code*
SCH/Com-ex (99) 14—28.4.1999—Manual of documents on which a visa may be affixed
  – *still in force*

Decisions of the Central Group

SCH/C (98) 117—27.10.1998—Action plan to combat illegal immigration
  – *still in force*

Bibliography

Books

Alegre, S and Leaf, M, *European Arrest Warrant: A Solution Ahead of its Time?* (Justice, 2003)

Anderson, D, *References to the European Court* (Sweet and Maxwell, 1995)

Andenas, M and Türk, A, eds, *Delegated Legislation and the Role of Committees in the EU* (Kluwer, 2000)

Askola, H, *Legal Responses to Trafficking in Women for Sexual Exploitation in the European Union* (Hart, 2007)

Baldaccini, A, *Asylum Support: A Practitioners' Guide to the EU Reception Directive* (Justice, 2005)

Bassiouni, M, *International Criminal Law, Vol. I: Sources, Subjects and Contents* (3rd edn, Martinus Nijhoff, 2008)

Battjes, H, *European Asylum Law and International Law* (Martinus Nijhoff, 2006)

Blextoon, R, ed, *Handbook on the European Arrest Warrant* (Asser, 2005)

Boeles, P, et al, *A New Immigration Law for Europe: the 1992 London and 1993 Copenhagen Rules on Immigration* (Standing Committee of Experts on Immigration, 1994).

Bunyan, T, ed, *Key Texts on Justice and Home Affairs in the European Union* (1997)

Cholewinski, R, *Migrant Workers in International Human Rights Law* (OUP, 1997)

Coleman, N, *European Readmission Policy: Third Country Interests and Refugee Rights* (Martinus Nijhoff, 2009)

Da Lomba, S, *The Right to Seek Refugee Status in the European Union* (Intersentia, 2004)

Denza, E, *The Intergovernmental Pillars of the European Union* (OUP, 2002)

Dougan, M, *National Remedies Before the Court of Justice: Issues of Harmonisation and Differentiation* (Hart, 2004)

Eckes, C, *EU Counter-Terrorist Policies and Fundamental Rights: The Case of Individual Sanctions* (OUP, 2009)

Eeckhout, P, *External Relations of the European Union: Legal and Constitutional Foundations* (OUP, 2004)

Feller, E, Turk, V and Nicholson, F, eds, *Refugee Protection in International Law: UNHCR's Global Consultations on Refugee Protection* (CUP, 2003)

Fox, H, *The Law of State Immunity* (OUP, 2002)

Goodwin-Gill, G and McAdam, J, *The Refugee in International Law* (3rd edn, OUP, 2007)

Guild, E, *European Community Law from a Migrant's Perspective* (Kluwer, 2001)

Guild, E and Marin, L, *Still not resolved? Constitutional Issues of the European Arrest Warrant* (Wolf, 2009)

Guild, E and Niessen, J, *The Developing Immigration and Asylum Policies of the European Union: Adopted Conventions, Resolutions, Recommendations, Decisions and Conclusions* (Kluwer, 1996)

Hathaway, J, *The Rights of Refugees under International Law* (CUP, 2005)

Hughes, J and Liebaut, F, eds, *Detention of Asylum-Seekers in Europe: Analysis and Perspectives* (Martinus Nijhoff, 1998)

Ingelse, C, *The UN Committee Against Torture: An Assessment* (Kluwer, 2001)

Joerges, C and Vos, E, eds, *EU Committees: Social Regulation, Law and Politics* (Hart, 1999)

Joseph, S, Schultz, J and Castan, M, *The International Covenant on Civil and Political Rights: Cases, Materials and Commentary* (2nd edn, OUP, 2004)

Justice report, *The Schengen Information System: A Human Rights Audit* (Justice, 2000)

Keijzer, N and van Sliedregt, E, eds, *The European Arrest Warrant in practice* (Asser, 2009)

Klabbers, J, *Treaty Conflict and the European Union* (CUP, 2009)

Lenaerts, K, Arts, D and Maselis, I, *Procedural Law of the European Union* (2nd edn, Thomson, 2006).

Marinho, C, ed, *The Dublin Convention on Asylum* (EIPA, 2000)

Martenczuk, B and van Thiel, S, eds, *Justice, Liberty, Security: New Challenges for EU External Relations* (VUBPress, 2008)

McClean, D, *International Cooperation in Civil and Criminal Matters* (2nd edn, OUP, 2002)

Mowbray, A, *The Development of Positive Obligations under the European Convention on Human Rights by the European Court of Human Rights* (Hart, 2004)

Papagianni, G, *Institutional and Policy Dynamics of EU Migration Law* (Martinus Nijhoff, 2006)

Peers, S and Rogers, N, eds, *EU Immigration and Asylum Law: Text and Commentary* (1st edn, Martinus Nijhoff, 2006)

Riza Coban, A, *Protection of Property Rights within the European Convention on Human Rights* (Ashgate, 2004)

Trechsel, S and Summers, S, *Human Rights in Criminal Proceedings* (OUP, 2005)

Tridimas, T, *The General Principles of EU Law* (2nd edn, OUP, 2006)

UNHCR, *Asylum in the European Union, A Study on the Implementation of the Qualification Directive*, Nov 2007 <http://www.unhcr.org/cgi-bin/texis/vtx/refworld/rwmain?doc id=473050632&page=search>.

UNHCR, *Improving Asylum Procedures: Comparative Analysis and Recommendations for Law and Practice* (2010)

van Dijk, P and van Hoof, G, *Theory and Practice of the European Convention on Human Rights* (4th edn, Intersentia, 2006)

Zwaan, K, ed, *The Qualification Directive: Central Themes, Problem Issues, and Implementation in Selected Member States* (Wolf Legal Publishers, 2007)

Zwaan, K, ed, *The Asylum Procedures Directive: Central themes, Problem issues, and Implementation in selected Member States*, (Wolf Legal Publishers, 2008)

Articles

Abell, N Albuquerque 'The Compatibility of Readmission agreements with the 1951 Convention relating to the Status of Refugees' (1999) 11 IJRL 60

Acosta, D, 'The Good, the Bad, and the Ugly in EU Migration Law' (2009) 11 EJML 19

Allain, J, 'The *jus cogens* nature of *non-refoulement*' (2002) 4 IJRL 533

Baldaccini, A, 'The Return and Removal of Irregular Migrants under EU Law: An Analysis of the Returns Directive' (2009) 11 EJML 1

Barnard, C, 'The PPU: Is it Worth the Candle? An Early Assessment' (2009) 34 ELRev 281

Barrett, G, 'Creation's Final Laws: The Impact of the Treaty of Lisbon on the "Final Provisions" of Earlier Treaties' (2008) 27 YEL 3

Boeles, P, 'Schengen and the Rule of Law' in H Meijers, et al, *Schengen: Internationalisation of Central Chapters of the Law on Aliens, Refugees, Privacy, Security and the Police* (2nd edn, Stichting NJCM-Boekerij, 1992)

Bouteillet-Paquet, D, 'Passing the Buck: A Critical Analysis of the Readmission Policy Implemented by the European Union and its Member States' (2003) 5 EJML 359

Breyer, P, 'Telecommunications Data Retention and Human Rights: The Compatibility of Blanket Traffic Data Retention with the ECHR' (2005) 11 ELJ 373

Brinkmann, G, 'Family Reunion, Third-Country Nationals and the Community's New Powers', in E Guild and C Harlow, *Implementing Amsterdam: Immigration and Asylum Rights in EC Law* (Hart, 2001), 241

Brouwer, E, 'Eurodac: Its Temptations and Limitations' (2002) 4 EJML 231

Bunyan, T, *The EU's Police Chief Task Force (PCTF) and Police Chiefs Committee*, online at: <http://www.statewatch.org/news/2006/mar/pctf.pdf>.

Byrne, R, 'Remedies of Limited Effect: Appeals under the forthcoming Directive on EU Minimum Standards on Procedures' (2005) 7 EJML 71

Carrera, S and Geyer, F, *The Reform Treaty and Justice and Home Affairs: Implications for the Common Area of Freedom, Security and Justice* (CEPS Policy Brief No 141, Aug 2007)

Cholewinski, R, 'The Protection of the Right of Economic Migrants to Family Reunion in Europe' (1994) 43 ICLQ 568

Cholewinski, R, *Borders and Discrimination in the European Union* (ILPA/MPG, 2002)

Cholewinski, R, 'Family Reunification and Conditions Placed on Family Members: Dismantling a Fundamental Human Right' (2002) 4 EJML 271

Cholewinski, R, 'No Right of Entry: The Legal Regime on Crossing the EU External Border' in E Guild, P Minderhoud, and K Groenendijk, eds, *In Search of Europe's Borders* (Kluwer, 2003), 105

Cholewinski, R, 'European Union Policy on Irregular Migration: Human Rights Lost?' in B Bogusz, et al, eds, *Irregular Migration and Human Rights* (Martinus Nijhoff, 2004), 159

Coleman, N, '*Non-Refoulement* Revised. Renewed Review of the Status of *Non-refoulement* as customary international law' (2003) 5 EJML 23

Corthaut, T and Lenaerts, K, 'Of Birds and Hedges: The Role of Primacy in Invoking Norms of EU Law' (2006) 31 ELRev 287

Costello, C, 'The Asylum Procedures Directive and the Proliferation of Safe Third Countries Practices: Deterrence, Deflection and the Dismantling of International Protection?' (2005) 7 EJML 35

Costello, C, 'The Asylum Procedures Directive in Legal Context: Equivocal Standards Meet General Principles', in A Baldaccini, E Guild, and H Toner, eds, *Whose Freedom, Security and Justice? EU Immigration and Asylum Law and Policy* (Hart, 2007), 151

Curtin, D, 'The Constitutional Structure of the Union: A Europe of Bits and Pieces' (1993) 30 CMLRev 17

Denza, E, 'The 2000 Convention on Mutual Assistance in Criminal Matters' (2003) 40 CMLRev 1047

Doerfel, J, 'The Convention Against Torture and the Protection of Refugees' (2005) 24 RSQ 24:2 83

Donner, J, 'Abolition of Border Controls', in H Schermers, et al, eds, *Free Movement of Persons in Europe: Legal Problems and Experiences* (Martinus Nijhoff, 1993), 5

de Witte, B, 'Past and Future Role of the European Court of Justice in the Protection of Human Rights', in P Alston, ed, *The EU and Human Rights* (OUP, 1999), 859

de Witte, B and Toggenburg, G, 'Human Rights and Membership of the European Union', in S Peers and A Ward, eds, *The EU Charter of Rights: Politics, Law and Policy* (Hart, 2004), 141

ECRE, 'The EC Directive on the Reception of Asylum Seekers: Are Asylum Seekers in Europe Receiving Material Support and Access to Employment in Accordance with European Legislation?' November 2005

ECRE, *Comments from the European Council on Refugees and Exiles on the European Commission proposal to recast the Qualification directive*, Mar 2010, online at: <http://www.ecre.org/files/ECRE_Position_Recast_Qualification_Directive.pdf>.

Eicke, T, 'Paradise Lost? Exclusion and Expulsion from the EU' in E Guild, P Minderhoud, and K Groenendijk, eds, *In Search of Europe's Borders* (Kluwer, 2003), 147

ELENA/ECRE, *The Impact of the EU Qualification Directive on International Protection*, Oct 2008, online at: <http://www.ecre.org/files/ECRE_QD_study_full.pdf>.

Fawcett, J, 'The Impact of Article 6(1) of the ECHR on Private International Law' (2007) 56 ICLQ 1

Gil-Bazo, MT, 'Refugee Status and Subsidiary Protection under EC Law: The Qualification Directive and the Right to Be Granted Asylum', in A Baldaccini, E Guild, and H Toner, eds, *Whose Freedom, Security and Justice? EU Immigration and Asylum Law and Policy* (Hart, 2007), 229

Gilbert, G, 'Crimes *Sans Frontières*: Jurisdictional Problems in English Law' (1992) BYIL 415

Goodwin-Gill, G, 'Article 31 of the 1951 Convention Relating to the Status of Refugees: non-penalization, detention and protection', in E Feller, V Turk, and F Nicholson, eds, *Refugee Protection in International Law: UNHCR's Global Consultations on Refugee Protection* (CUP, 2003), 185

Gortazar, C, 'Abolishing Border Controls: Individual Rights and Common Control of EU External Borders', in E Guild and C Harlow, eds, *Implementing Amsterdam* (Hart, 2001), 121

Groenendijk, K, 'New Borders Behind Old Ones: Post Schengen Controls Behind the Internal Borders—Inside the Netherlands and Germany' in E Guild, P Minderhoud, and K Groenendijk, eds, *In Search of Europe's Borders* (Kluwer, 2003), 131

Grief, N, 'EU Law and Security' (2007) 32 ELRev 752

Guild, E, 'The Border Abroad—Visas and Border Controls', in E Guild, P Minderhoud, and K Groenendijk, eds., *In Search of Europe's Borders* (Kluwer, 2003), 87

Guild, E, 'Who is an Irregular Migrant?' in B Bogusz, R Cholewinski, A Cygan, and E Szyszczak, eds, *Irregular Migration and Human Rights* (Martinus Nijhoff, 2004), 3

Hailbronner, K, 'Visa Regulations and Third-Country Nationals in EC Law' (1994) 31 CMLRev 969

Hailbronner, K, 'Migration Law and Policy Within the Third Pillar of the European Union' in R Bieber and J Monar, eds, *Justice and Home Affairs in the European Union* (European University Press, 1995)

Hailbronner, K, 'European Immigration and Asylum Law after the Amsterdam Treaty' (1998) 35 CMLRev 1047

Hailbronner, K and Thiery, C, 'Schengen II and Dublin: Responsibility for Asylum Applications in Europe' (1997) 34 CMLRev 957

Handoll, J, 'Directive 2003/9 on Reception Conditions of Asylum Seekers: Ensuring "Mere Subsistence" or a "Dignified Standard of Living"?', in A Baldaccini, E Guild, and H Toner, eds, *Whose Freedom, Security and Justice? EU Immigration and Asylum Law and Policy* (Hart, 2007), 195

Harvey, C, 'Promoting Insecurity: Public Order, Expulsion and the European Convention on Human Rights', in E Guild and P Minderhoud, eds, *Security of Residence and Expulsion: Protection of Aliens in Europe* (Kluwer, 2001), 41

Hayes, B, *Arming Big Brother: The EU's Security Research Programme* (Transnational Institute and Statewatch, 2006), online at: <http://www.statewatch.org/news/2006/apr/bigbrother.pdf>.

Hayes, B, *NeoConOpticon: The EU's Security-Industrial Complex* (Transnational Institute and Statewatch, 2009), online at: <http://www.statewatch.org/analyses/neoconopticon-report.pdf>.

Haynes, D, 'Used, Abused, Arrested and Deported: Extending Immigration Benefits to Protect the Victims of Trafficking and to Secure the Prosecution of Traffickers' (2004) 26 HRQ 221

Hedemann-Robinson, M, 'Third-Country Nationals, European Union citizenship and free movement of persons: A time for bridges rather than divisions?' (1996) 16 YEL 321

Hedemann-Robinson, M, 'From Object to Subject? Non-EC Nationals and the Draft Proposal of the Commission for a Council Act Establishing the Rules for Admission of Third-Country Nationals to the Member States' (1998) 18 YEL 289

Herlin-Karnell, E, 'Commission v Council: Some Reflections on Criminal Law in the First Pillar' (2007) 13 EPL 69

Hetzer, W, 'Fight Against Fraud and Protection of Fundamental Rights in the European Union' (2006) 14 IJCCLCJ 1:20

Hurwitz, A, 'The 1990 Dublin Convention: A Comprehensive Assessment' (1999) IJRL 646

Jileva, E, 'Insiders and Outsiders in Central and Eastern Europe: the Case of Bulgaria' in E Guild, P Minderhoud, and K Groenendijk, eds, *In Search of Europe's Borders* (Kluwer, 2003), 273.

Kerber, K, 'The Temporary Protection Directive' (2002) 4 EJML 193

Lambert, H, 'Protection Against Refoulement from Europe: Human Rights Law comes to the Rescue' (1999) 48 ICLQ 515

Lambert, H, 'The European Court of Human Rights and the Right of Refugees and Other Persons in Need of Protection to Family Reunion' (1999) 11 IJRL 427

Lambert, H, 'The European Convention on Human Rights and the Protection of Refugees: Limits and Opportunities' (2005) 24:2 RSQ 39

Lauterpacht, E and Bethlehem, D, 'The scope and content of the principle of *non-refoulement*: an Opinion', in E Feller, V Turk, and F Nicholson, eds, *Refugee Protection in International Law: UNHCR's Global Consultations on Refugee Protection* (CUP, 2003)

Legomsky, S, 'Secondary Refugee Movements and the Return of Asylum Seekers to Third Countries: the Meaning of Effective Protection' (2003) 15 IJRL 567

Lenaerts, K and Verhoeven, A, 'Towards a Legal Framework for Executive Rule-Making in the EU? The Contribution of the new Comitology Decision' (2000) 37 CMLRev 645

Loof, R, 'Shooting from the Hip: Proposed Minimum Rights in Criminal Proceedings throughout the EU' (2006) 12 ELJ 421

MacGregor, L, Report on the Common Frame of Reference, online at: <http://www.scotland.gov.uk/Resource/Doc/262952/0078639.pdf>.

Marin, J and O'Connell, J 'The European Convention and the Relative Rights of Resident Aliens' (1999) 5 ELJ 4

Martenczuk, B, 'Visa Policy and EU External Relations,' in B Martenczuk and S van Thiel, eds, *Justice, Liberty, Security: New Challenges for EU External Relations* (VUB Press, 2008), 21

McAdam, J, 'The European Union Qualification Directive: The Creation of a Subsidiary Protection Regime' (2005) 17 IJRL 461

McMahon, R, 'Maastricht's Third Pillar: load-bearing or purely decorative?' (1995) LIEI 1:51

Mitsilegas, V, 'The New EU–USA Cooperation on Extradition, Mutual Legal Assistance and the Exchange of Police Data' (2003) 8 EFARev 515

Mitsilegas, V, 'Trust-Building Measures in the European Judicial Area in Criminal Matters: Issues of Competence, Legitimacy and Institutional Balance', in T Balzacq and S Carrera, eds, *Security versus Freedom? A Challenge for Europe's Future* (Ashgate, 2006), 282

Monar, J, 'Justice and Home Affairs in the Treaty of Amsterdam: Reform at the Price of Fragmentation' (1998) 23 ELRev 320

Muller-Graff, P, 'The legal bases of the Third Pillar and its position in the framework of the Union Treaty' (1994) 29 CMLRev 493

Nicol, A, 'From Dublin Convention to Dublin Regulation: A Progressive Move?', in A Baldaccini, E Guild, and H Toner, eds, *Whose Freedom, Security and Justice? EU Immigration and Asylum Law and Policy* (Hart, 2007), 265

Noll, G, 'Visions of the Exceptional: Legal and Theoretical Issues Raised by Transit Processing Centers and Reception Zones' (2003) 5 EJML 303

O'Keeffe, D, 'The Schengen Convention: A Suitable Model for European Integration?' (1991) 11 YEL 185

Peers, S, 'Equality, Free Movement and Social Security' (1997) 22 ELRev 342

Peers, S, 'Border in Channel: Continent cut off' (1998) 19 JSWFL 108

Peers, S, 'Building Fortress Europe: The Development of EU Migration Law' (1998) 35 CMLRev 1235

Peers, S, 'Raising Minimum Standards or Racing to the Bottom? The Commission's Proposed Migration Convention', in E Guild, ed, *The Legal Framework and Social Consequences of Free Movement of Persons in the European Union* (Kluwer, 1999), 149

Peers, S, 'Social Security Equality for Turkish Nationals' (1999) 24 EL Rev 627

Peers, S, '*Caveat Emptor*? Integrating the Schengen *Acquis* into the European Union Legal Order' (2000) 2 CYELS 87

Peers, S, 'The EC–Switzerland Agreement on Free Movement of Persons: Overview and Analysis' (2000) 2 EJML 127

Peers, S, 'Who's Judging the Watchmen?' The Judicial System of the Area of Freedom, Security and Justice' (2000) 18 YEL 337

Peers, S, 'The New Regulation on Access to Documents: A Critical Analysis' (2001–2002) 21 YEL 385

Peers, S, Case note on *Khalil and Addou* (2002) 39 CMLRev 1395

Peers, S, 'EU Immigration and Asylum Law after Seville' (2002) 16 IANL Journal 176

Peers, S, 'EU Borders and Globalisation' in Groenendijk, Guild, and Minderhoud, eds, *In Search of Europe's Borders* (Kluwer, 2003), 45

Peers, S, 'EU Responses to Terrorism' (2003) 52 ICLQ 227

Peers, S, 'The European Court of Justice and the European Court of Human Rights: Comparative Approaches', in E Orucu, ed, *Judicial Comparativism in Human Rights Cases* (UKNCCL, 2003), 107

Peers, S, 'EU Immigration and Asylum Law: Internal Market Model or Human Rights Model?', in Tridimas and Nebbia, eds, *EU Law for the Twenty-First Century: Rethinking the New Legal Order, Vol. 1* (Hart, 2004), 345

Peers, S, 'Family Reunion and Community Law', in N Walker, ed, *Towards an Area of Freedom, Security and Justice* (OUP, 2004), 143

Peers, S, 'Mutual Recognition and Criminal Law in the European Union: Has the Council Got it Wrong?' (2004) 41 CMLRev 5

Peers, S, 'Taking Rights Away? Derogations and Limitations' in S Peers and A Ward, eds, *The EU Charter of Rights: Politics, Law and Policy* (Hart, 2004), 141

Peers, S, 'Civil and Political Rights: the Role of an EU Human Rights Agency', in P Alston and O De Schutter, eds, *Monitoring Fundamental Rights in the EU: The Contribution of the Fundamental Rights Agency* (Hart, 2005)

Peers, S, 'EC law on family members of persons seeking or receiving international protection' in P Shah, ed, *The Challenge of Asylum to Legal Systems* (Cavendish, 2005)

Peers, S, 'Governance and the Third Pillar: The Accountability of Europol' in D Curtin and R Wessel, eds, *Good Governance and the European Union* (Intersentia, 2005), 253

Peers, S, 'Human Rights, Asylum and European Community Law' (2005) 24 RSQ 2:24

Peers, S, 'The future of the EU judicial system and EC immigration and asylum law' (2005) 7 EJML 263

Peers, S, 'Transforming Decision-Making on EC Immigration and Asylum Law' (2005) 30 ELRev 283

Peers, S, 'Double Jeopardy and EU Law: Time for a Change?' (2006) 8 EJLR 199

Peers, S, 'Salvation outside the Church: Judicial Protection in the Third Pillar after the *Pupino* and *SEGI* judgments' (2007) 44 CMLRev 883

Peers, S, 'EU Criminal Law and the Treaty of Lisbon' (2008) 33 ELRev 507

Peers, S, 'EU Immigration and Asylum Competence and Decision-Making in the Treaty of Lisbon' (2008) 10 EJML 219

Peers, S, 'EU Migration Law and Association Agreements', in B Martenczuk and S van Thiel, eds, *Justice, Liberty, Security: New Challenges for EU External Relations* (VUB Press, 2008), 53

Peers, S, 'Finally "Fit for Purpose?" The Treaty of Lisbon and the end of the Third Pillar legal order' (2008) 27 YEL 47

Peers, S, 'The Community's Criminal Law Competence: The Plot Thickens' (2008) 33 ELRev 399

Peers, S, 'In a world of their own? Justice and Home Affairs opt-outs and the Treaty of Lisbon' (2008–09) 10 CYELS 383

Peers, S, 'EC immigration law and EC association agreements: fragmentation or integration?' (2009) 34 ELRev 628

Piotrowicz, R and van Eck, C, 'Subsidiary Protection and Primary Rights' (2004) 53 ICLQ 107

Rijken, C, 'Legal and Technical Aspects of Cooperation Between Europol, Third States and Interpol', in V Kronenberger, ed, *The European Union and the International Legal Order: Discord or Harmony?* (Asser, 2001), 577

Rosas, A, 'The European Union and International Human Rights Instruments', in V Kronenberger, ed, *The EU and the International Legal Order: Discord or Harmony?* (Asser Press, 2001)

Schutte, J, 'Schengen: Its Meaning for the Free Movement of Persons in Europe' (1991) 28 CMLRev 549

Sharpston, E and Maria Fernandez-Martin, J, 'Some Reflections on Schengen Free Movement Rights and the Principle of *Ne Bis in Idem*' (2007–08) 10 CYELS 413

Steenbergen, J, 'Schengen and the Movement of Persons' in H Meijers, et al, *Schengen: Internationalisation of Central Chapters of the law on aliens, refugees, privacy, security and the police* (2nd edn, Stichting NJCM-Boekerij, 1992)

Storey, H, 'The Right to Family Life and Immigration Case Law at Strasbourg' (1990) 39 ICLQ 329

Szyszczak, E, 'Regularising Migration in the European Union' in Bogusz, et al, *Irregular Migration and Human Rights* (Martinus Nijhoff, 2004), 407

Thym, D, 'Schengen Law: A Challenge for Legal Accountability in the European Union' (2002) 8 ELJ 218

Timmermans, C, 'Free movement of persons and the division of powers between the Community and its Member States: Why do it the intergovernmental way?', in H Schermers, et al, eds, *Free Movement of Persons in Europe: Legal Problems and Experiences* (Martinus Nijhoff, 1993), 352

van Dijk, J, 'Protection of 'Integrated' Aliens against Expulsion under the European Convention on Human Rights', in E Guild and P Minderhoud, eds, *Security of Residence and Expulsion: Protection of Aliens in Europe* (Kluwer, 2001), 23

Verschueren, H, 'EC Social Security Coordination Excluding Third-Country Nationals: Still in Line with Fundamental rights After the *Gaygusuz* judgment?' (1997) 24 CMLRev 991

Weyembergh, A, 'La reconnaissance mutuelle des decisions judiciaires en matiere penale entre les Etats Membres de l'Union europeenne: mise en perspective' in G de Kerchove and A Weyembergh, eds, *La reconnaissance mutuelle des decisions judiciaires penales dans l'Union europeenne* (Institut d'Etudes Europeennes, 2001), 25

Whitaker, S, 'The Draft "Common Frame of Reference": An Assessment', online at: <http://www.justice.gov.uk/publications/docs/Draft_Common_Frame_of_Reference__an_assessment.pdf>.

White, S, 'Harmonisation of Criminal Law under the First Pillar' (2006) ELRev 81

Wilsher, D, 'Detention of Asylum-Seekers and Refugees and International Human Rights Law' in P Shah, ed, *The Challenge of Asylum to Legal Systems* (Cavendish, 2005), 145

Wouters, J and Naert, F, 'Of arrest warrants, terrorist offences and extradition deals: An appraisal of the EU's main criminal law measures against terrorism after "11 September"', (2004) 41 CMLRev 909

Index